HANDBOOK OF
U.S. LABOR
STATISTICS

HANDBOOK OF U.S. LABOR STATISTICS

Employment, Earnings, Prices, Productivity, and Other Labor Data

15th Edition
2012

Edited by Mary Meghan Ryan

Bernan Press

Lanham, MD

Published in the United States of America
by Bernan Press, a wholly owned subsidiary of
The Rowman & Littlefield Publishing Group, Inc.
4501 Forbes Boulevard, Suite 200
Lanham, Maryland 20706

Bernan Press
800-865-3457
customercare@bernan.com
www.bernan.com

ISBN-13: 978-1-59888-519-4
eISBN-13: 978-1-59888-520-0

ISSN: 1526-2553

™ The paper used in this publication meets the minimum requirements of
American National Standard for Information Sciences—Permanence of
Paper for Printed Library Materials, ANSI/NISO Z39.48-1992.
Manufactured in the United States of America.

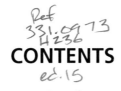

Ref
331.0973
H236
ed.15
2012

CONTENTS

LIST OF TABLES

Persons with a Disability: Labor Force Characteristics

CHAPTER 2: EMPLOYMENT AND HOURS

Employment and Hours

Earnings

CHAPTER 7: RECENT TRENDS IN THE LABOR MARKET

CHAPTER 10: INTERNATIONAL LABOR COMPARISONS

CHAPTER 11: CONSUMER EXPENDITURES

LIST OF FIGURES

PREFACE

Bernan Press is pleased to present a compilation of Bureau of Labor Statistics (BLS) data in this 15th edition of its award-winning *Handbook of U.S Labor Statistics: Employment, Earnings, Prices, Productivity, and Other Labor Data.* BLS provides a treasure trove of historical information about all aspects of labor and employment in the United States. The current edition maintains the content of previous editions and updates the text with additional data and new features. The data in this *Handbook* are excellent sources of information for analysts in both government and the private sector.

The *Handbook* addresses many of the issues that are being discussed across the United States, such as high unemployment, the decline in real median household income, the rapidly increasing costs of health care services and prescription drugs, employment projections for the future, and the dramatic aging of the labor force. In addition, this publication provides an abundance of data on topics such as prices, productivity, consumer expenditures, occupational safety and health, international labor comparisons, and much more.

The comprehensive and historical data presented in the *Handbook* allow the user to understand the background of current events and compare today's economy with previous years. Select data in this publication go back to 1913 and several tables have data going back to the 1940s.

FEATURES OF THIS PUBLICATION

Over 200 tables that present authoritative data on labor market statistics, including employment and unemployment, mass layoffs, prices, productivity, and data from the American Time Use Survey (ATUS).

Each section is preceded by a figure that calls attention to noteworthy trends in the data.

In addition to the figures, the introductory material for to each chapter also contains highlights of other salient data. For example, the highlights in Chapter 1 showcase the increase in the unemployment and in Chapter 13, the highlights call attention to the continual decline in real median income.

The tables in each section are also preceded by notes and definitions, which contain concise descriptions of the data sources, concepts, definitions, and methodology from which the data are derived.

The introductory notes also include references to more comprehensive reports. These reports provide additional data and more extensive descriptions of estimation methods, sampling, and reliability measures.

NEW IN THIS EDITION

Several changes have taken place in this edition. Most notably, Chapter 4 includes newly released labor force and employment projections up until the year 2020. In addition, new tables have been added to Chapter 6 "Compensation of Employees" and Chapter 10 "International Labor Comparisons." There are also several new figures throughout the book on a variety of topics including the labor force, mean annual wages, employee compensation, and the average annual rate of change in employment in 10 countries.

SOURCES OF ADDITIONAL INFORMATION

BLS data are primarily derived from surveys conducted by the federal government or through federal-state cooperative arrangements. The comparability of data over time can be affected by changes in the surveys, which are essential for keeping pace with the current structure of economic institutions and for taking advantage of improved survey techniques. Revisions of current data are also periodically made as a result of the availability of new information. In addition, some tables in this *Handbook* were dropped due to the data being from a one-time survey that is now outdated or due to the survey being entirely restructured. Introductory notes to each chapter summarize specific factors that may affect the data. In the tables, the ellipsis character ("...") indicates that data are not available.

More extensive methodological information, including further discussion of the sampling and estimation procedures used for each BLS program, is contained in the *BLS Handbook of Methods.* This publication is in the process of being updated, and completed chapters are available on the BLS Web site at <http://www.bls.gov>. Other sources of current data and analytical include the *Monthly Labor Review* and a daily Internet publication, *The Editor's Desk* (TED). All of these publications can be found on the BLS Web site as well. Other relevant publications, including those from the Census Bureau, are noted in the notes and definitions in each chapter.

OTHER PUBLICATIONS BY BERNAN PRESS

The *Handbook of U.S. Labor Statistics Handbook of U.S Labor Statistics: Employment, Earnings, Prices, Productivity, and Other Labor Data* is just one of a number of publications in Bernan Press's award-winning U.S. Data-Book Series. Other titles include *The Almanac of American Education*; *Business Statistics of the United States: Patterns of Economic Change*; *Crime in the United States*; *States Profiles: The Population and Economy of Each U.S. State*; *United States Foreign Trade Highlights: Trends in the Global Market*; and *Vital Statistics of the United States: Births, Life Expectancy, Deaths, and Selected Health Data.* In addition, Bernan Press publishes *Employment, Hours, and Earnings: States and Areas* as a special edition of this *Handbook.* Each of these titles provides the public with statistical information from official government sources.

Chapter One

POPULATION, LABOR FORCE, AND EMPLOYMENT STATUS

POPULATION, LABOR FORCE, AND EMPLOYMENT STATUS

HIGHLIGHTS

This chapter presents the detailed historical information collected in the Current Population Survey (CPS), a monthly survey of households that gathers data on the employment status of the population. Basic data on labor force, employment, and unemployment are shown for various characteristics of the population, including age, sex, race, Hispanic origin, and marital status.

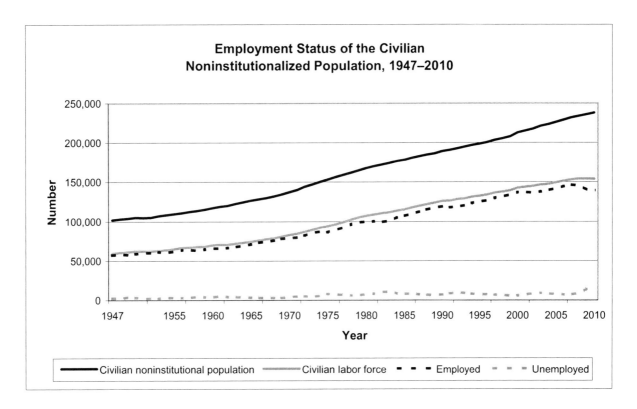

In 2010, the number of people in the labor force continued to decline after increasing every year from 1951 through 2008. Meanwhile, the percent of the population employed declined to its lowest level since 1983 as employment fell for the third consecutive year. (See Table 1-1.)

OTHER HIGHLIGHTS

- Although employment declined again in 2010, it did so at a slower rate. From 2008 to 2009, employment fell 3.8 percent but it only dropped 0.6 percent between 2009 and 2010. Employment increased 4.9 percent in agricultural industries, however, it declined 0.7 percent in nonagricultural industries. (See Table 1-1.)

- The civilian labor force participation dropped to 64.7 percent—the lowest it has been since 1984. It fell or remained steady for all age groups except for those 65 years and over. (See Table 1-8.)

- While the number of men continued to outnumber the number of women in the labor force, the gap is narrowing. In 1948, men made up 71. 4 percent of the labor force and in 1975 they comprised 60.0 percent of the labor force. By 2010, men only made up 53.3 percent of the labor force. (See Table 1-7.)

NOTES AND DEFINITIONS

CURRENT POPULATION SURVEY OF HOUSEHOLDS

Collection and Coverage

The Current Population Survey (CPS) is a monthly survey that analyzes and publishes statistics on the labor force, employment, and unemployment, classified by a variety of demographic, social, and economic characteristics. This survey is conducted by the Census Bureau for the Bureau of Labor Statistics (BLS). The information is collected from a probability sample of approximately 60,000 households. Respondents are interviewed to obtain information about the employment status of each household member age 16 years and over. Persons under 16 years of age are excluded from the official estimates because child labor laws, compulsory school attendance, and general social custom in the United States severely limit the types and amount of work that these children can do.

The inquiry relates to the household member's employment status during the calendar week, Sunday through Saturday that includes the 12th day of the month. This is known as the "reference week." Actual field interviewing is conducted during the following week (the week that contains the 19th day of the month).

Concepts and Definitions

The concepts and definitions underlying the labor force data have been modified—but not substantially altered—since the inception of the survey in 1940 when it began as a Work Projects Administration program. Current definitions of some of the major concepts used in the CPS are described below.

The civilian noninstitutional population includes persons 16 years of age and over who reside in the 50 states and the District of Columbia who are not inmates of institutions (such as penal and mental facilities and homes for the aged) and who are not on active duty in the armed forces.

An *employed person* is any person who, during the reference week: (1) did any work at all (at least one hour) as a paid employee in their own business, profession, or on their own farm, or who worked 15 hours or more as an unpaid worker in an enterprise operated by a member of the family; and (2) any person who was not working but who had a job or business from which he or she was temporarily absent due to vacation, illness, bad weather, childcare problems, maternity or paternity leave, labor-management disputes, job training, or other family or personal reasons, despite whether the employee was being paid for the time off or was seeking other jobs.

Each employed person is counted only once, even if he or she holds more than one job. For purposes of occupation and industry classification, multiple jobholders are counted as being in the job at which they worked the greatest number of hours during the reference week.

Included in the total are employed citizens of foreign countries who were temporarily in the United States but not living on the premises of an embassy. Excluded are persons whose only activity during the reference week consisted of work around their own house (painting, repairing, or own home housework) or volunteer work for religious, charitable, and similar organizations.

Unemployed persons are all persons who had no employment during the reference week, but who were available for work (except for temporary illness) and had made specific efforts to find employment some time during the four-week period ending with the reference week. Persons who were waiting to be recalled to a job from which they had been laid off need not have been looking for work to be classified as unemployed.

Reasons for unemployment are divided into four major groups: (1) job losers, defined as (a) persons on temporary layoff, who have been given a date to return to work or who expect to return to work within six months; (b) permanent job losers, whose employment ended involuntarily and who began looking for work; and (c) persons who completed a temporary job and began looking for work after the job ended; (2) job leavers, defined as persons who quit or otherwise terminated their employment voluntarily and immediately began looking for work; (3) reentrants, defined as persons who previously worked but were out of the labor force prior to beginning their job search; and (4) new entrants, defined as persons who had never worked but were currently searching for work.

Duration of unemployment represents the length of time (through the current reference week) that persons classified as unemployed had been looking for work. For persons on layoff, duration of unemployment represents the number of full weeks they had been on layoff. Mean duration of unemployment is the arithmetic average computed from single weeks of unemployment; median duration of unemployment is the midpoint of a distribution of weeks of unemployment.

A *spell of unemployment* is a continuous period of unemployment of at least one week's duration and is terminated by either employment or withdrawal from the labor force.

Extent of unemployment refers to the number of workers and proportion of the labor force that were unemployed at some time during the year. The number of weeks unemployed is the total number of weeks accumulated during the entire calendar year.

The *unemployment rate* is the number of unemployed persons as a percentage of the civilian labor force.

The *civilian labor force* comprises all civilians classified as employed or unemployed.

The *participation rate* represents the proportion of the civilian noninstitutional population currently in the labor force.

The *employment-population ratio* represents the proportion of the population that is currently employed.

Persons not in the labor force are all persons in the civilian noninstitutional population who are neither employed nor unemployed. Information is collected about their desire for and availability to take a job at the time of the CPS interview, job search activity during the prior year, and reason for not looking for work during the four-week period ending with the reference week. Persons not in the labor force who want and are available for a job and who have looked for work within the past 12 months (or since the end of their last job, if they had held one within the past 12 months), but who are not currently looking, are designated as *marginally attached to the labor force.* The marginally attached are divided into those not currently looking because they believe their search would be futile—so-called *discouraged workers*—and those not currently looking for other reasons, such as family responsibilities, ill health, or lack of transportation.

Discouraged workers are defined as persons not in the labor force who want and are available for a job and who have looked for work sometime in the past 12 months (or since the end of their last job, if they held one within the past 12 months), but who are not currently looking because they believe that there are no jobs available or there are none for which they would qualify. The reasons for not currently looking for work include a person's belief that no work is available in his or her line of work or area; he or she could not find any work; he or she lacks necessary schooling, training, skills, or experience; employers would think he or she is too young or too old; or he or she would encounter hiring discrimination.

Usual full- or part-time status refers to hours usually worked per week. Full-time workers are those who usually work 35 hours or more (at all jobs). This group includes some individuals who worked less than 35 hours during the reference week for economic or noneconomic reasons. Part-time workers are those who usually work less than 35 hours per week (at all jobs), regardless of the number of hours worked during the reference week. These concepts are used to differentiate a person's normal schedule from his or her specific activity during the reference week. Unemployed persons who are looking for full-time work or who are on layoff from full-time jobs are counted as part of the full-time labor force; unemployed persons who are seeking part-time work or who are on layoff from part-time jobs are counted as part of the part-time labor force.

Year-round, full-time workers are workers who primarily worked at full-time jobs for 50 weeks or more during the preceding calendar year. Part-year workers worked either full- or part-time for 1 to 49 weeks.

At work part-time for economic reasons, sometimes called involuntary part-time, refers to individuals who gave an economic reason for working 1 to 34 hours during the reference week. Economic reasons include slack work or unfavorable business conditions, inability to find full-time work, and seasonal declines in demand. Those who usually work part-time must also indicate that they want and are available to work full-time to be classified as working part-time for economic reasons.

At work part-time for noneconomic reasons refers to persons who usually work part-time and were at work 1 to 34 hours during the reference week for a noneconomic reason. Noneconomic reasons include illness or other medical limitations, childcare problems or other family or personal obligations, school or training, retirement or Social Security limits on earnings, and being in a job where full-time work is less than 35 hours. This also includes workers who gave an economic reason for usually working 1 to 34 hours but said they do not want to work full-time or were unavailable for full-time work.

Absences are defined as instances in which persons who usually work 35 or more hours a week worked less than that during the reference period for reasons of illness or family obligations. Excluded are situations in which work was missed for vacation, holidays, or other reasons. The estimates are based on one-fourth of the sample only.

Earnings are all money income of $1 or more from wages and salaries and all net money income of $1 or more from farm and nonfarm self-employment.

Usual weekly earnings for wage and salary workers include any overtime pay, commissions, or tips usually received (at the main job in the case of multiple jobholders). Earnings reported on a basis other than weekly (such as annual, monthly, or hourly) are converted to weekly. The term "usual" is as perceived by the respondent. If the respondent asks for a definition of usual, interviewers are instructed to define the term as more than half the weeks worked during the past 4 or 5 months.

Minimum wage refers to the prevailing federal minimum wage which was $7.25 in 2010. It increased from $6.55 per hour to $7.25 per hour on July 24, 2009. Data are for wage and salary workers who were paid hourly rates and refer to a person's earnings at the sole or principal job.

A *multiple jobholder* is an employed person who, during the reference week, had two or more jobs as a wage and salary worker, was self-employed and also held a wage and salary job, or worked as an unpaid family worker and also held a wage and salary job. Self-employed persons with multiple businesses and persons with multiple jobs as unpaid family workers are excluded.

Occupation, industry, and class of worker for members of the employed population are determined by the job held during the reference week. Persons with two or more jobs are classified as being in the job at which they worked the greatest number of hours. The unemployed are classified according to their last job. Beginning with data published in 2003, the systems used to classify occupational and industry data changed. They are currently based on the Standard Occupational Classification (SOC) system and the North American Industry Classification System (NAICS). (See the following section on historical comparability for a discussion of previous classification systems used in the CPS.) The class-of-worker breakdown assigns workers to one of the following categories: private and government wage and salary workers, self-employed workers, and unpaid family workers. Wage and salary workers receive wages, salaries, commissions, tips, or pay in kind from a private employer or from a government unit. Self-employed workers are those who work for profit or fees in their own businesses, professions, trades, or on their own farms. Only the unincorporated self-employed are included in the self-employed category in the class-of-worker typology. Self-employed workers who respond that their businesses are incorporated are included among wage and salary workers, because they are technically paid employees of a corporation. An unpaid family worker is a person working without pay for 15 hours or more per week on a farm or in a business operated by a member of the household to whom he or she is related by birth or marriage.

Educational attainment refers to years of school completed in regular schools, which include graded public, private, and parochial elementary, and high schools, whether day or night school. Colleges, universities, and professional schools are also included.

Tenure refers to length of time a worker has been continuously employed by his or her current employer. These data are collected through a supplement to the CPS. All employed persons were asked how long they had been working continuously for their present employer and, if the length of time was one or two years, a follow-up question was asked about the exact number of months. The follow-up question was included for the first time in the February 1996 supplement to the CPS. CPS supplements that obtained information on tenure in January of 1983, 1987, and 1991 did not include the follow-up question. Prior to 1983, the question on tenure was asked differently. Data prior to 1983 are thus not strictly comparable to data for subsequent years.

White, Black, and Asian are terms used to describe the race of persons. Persons in these categories are those who selected that race only. Persons in the remaining race categories— American Indian or Alaskan Native, Native Hawaiian or Other Pacific Islander, and persons who selected more than one race category—are included in the estimates of total employment and unemployment but are not shown separately because the number of survey respondents is too small to develop estimates of sufficient quality for monthly publication.

Hispanic origin refers to persons who identified themselves in the enumeration process as being Spanish, Hispanic, or Latino. Persons of Hispanic or Latino origin may be of any race.

Single, never married; married, spouse present; and other marital status are the terms used to define the marital status of individuals at the time of the CPS interview. Married, spouse present, applies to a husband and wife if both were living in the same household, even though one may be temporarily absent on business, vacation, in a hospital, etc. Other marital status applies to persons who are married, spouse absent; widowed; or divorced. Married, spouse absent relates to persons who are separated due to marital problems, as well as husbands and wives living apart because one was employed elsewhere, on duty with the armed forces, or any other reason.

A *household* consists of all persons—related family members and all unrelated persons—who occupy a housing unit and have no other usual address. A house, an apartment, a group of rooms, or a single room is regarded as a housing unit when occupied or intended for occupancy as separate living quarters.

A *householder* is the person (or one of the persons) in whose name the housing unit is owned or rented. The term is not applied to either husbands or wives in married-couple families; it refers only to persons in families maintained by either men or women without a spouse.

A *family* is defined as a group of two or more persons residing together who are related by birth, marriage, or adoption. All such persons are considered as members of one family. Families are classified as either married-couple families or families maintained by women or men without spouses.

Children refer to "own" children of the husband, wife, or person maintaining the family, including sons and daughters, stepchildren, and adopted children. Excluded are other related children, such as grandchildren, nieces, nephews, cousins, and unrelated children.

Persons are referred to as *disabled* if they answer yes to the following questions: (1) Are you deaf or do you have serious difficulty hearing? (2) Are you blind or do you have serious difficulty seeing even when wearing glasses? (3) Because of a physical, mental, or emotional condition, do you have serious difficulty concentrating, remembering, or making decisions? (4) Do you have serious difficulty walking or climbing stairs? (5) Do you have difficulty dressing or bathing? (6) Because of a physical, mental, or emotional condition, do you have difficulty doing errands alone such as visiting a doctor's office or shopping? Labor force measures are only tabulated for persons 16 years and over.

Historical Comparability

While the concepts and methods are very similar to those used for the inaugural survey in 1940, a number of changes have been made over the years to improve the accuracy and usefulness of the data. Only recent major changes are described here.

Major changes to the CPS, such as the complete redesign of the questionnaire and the use of computer-assisted interviewing for the entire survey, were introduced in 1994. In addition, there were revisions to some of the labor force concepts and definitions, including the implementation of changes recommended in 1979 by the National Commission on Employment and Unemployment Statistics (NCEUS, also known as the Levitan Commission). Some of the major changes to the survey at this time were:

1) The introduction of a redesigned and automated questionnaire. The CPS questionnaire was totally redesigned in order to obtain more accurate, comprehensive, and relevant information, and to take advantage of state-of-the-art computer interviewing techniques. Computer-assisted interviewing has important benefits most notably that it facilitates the use of a relatively complex questionnaire that incorporates complicated skip patterns and standardized follow-up questions. Additionally, certain questions are automatically tailored to the individual's situation to make them more understandable.

2) Official labor force measures were defined more precisely. While the labor force status of most people is straightforward, some persons are more difficult to classify correctly, especially if they are engaged in activities that are relatively informal or intermittent. Many of the changes to the questionnaire were made to deal with such cases. This was accomplished by rewording and adding questions to conform more precisely to the official definitions, making the questions easier to understand and answer, minimizing reliance on volunteered responses, revising response categories, and taking advantage of the benefits of an automated interview.

3) The amount of data available was expanded. The questionnaire redesign also made it possible to collect several types of data on topics such as multiple job holding and usual hours regularly for the first time.

4) Several labor definitions were modified. The most important definitional changes concerned discouraged workers. The Levitan Commission had criticized the former definition because it was based on a subjective desire for work and on somewhat arbitrary assumptions about an individual's availability to take a job. As a result of the redesign, two requirements were added: For persons to qualify as discouraged they must have engaged in some job search within the past year (or since they last worked, if they worked within the past year), and they must be currently available to take a job. (Formerly, availability was inferred from responses to other questions; now, there is a direct question.) Also, beginning in January 1994, questions on this subject are asked of the full CPS sample, permitting estimates of the number of discouraged workers to be published monthly (rather than quarterly).

Beginning in January 2003, several other changes were introduced into the CPS. These changes included the following:

1) Population controls that reflected the results of the 2000 census were introduced into the monthly CPS estimation process. The new controls increased the size of the civilian noninstitutional population by about 3.5 million in May 2002. As a result, they also increased the estimated numbers of people unemployed and employed. Because the increases were roughly proportional, however, the overall unemployment rate did not change significantly. Data from January 2000 through December 2002 were revised to reflect these new controls. Over and above these revisions, the U.S. Census Bureau introduced another large upward adjustment to the controls as part of its annual update of population estimates for 2003. These updated population estimates were not available in time to incorporate them into the revised population controls for January 2000 to December 2002. Thus, the data on employment and unemployment levels for January 2003 (and beyond) are not strictly comparable with those for earlier months. The unemployment rate and other ratios, however, were not substantially affected by the 2003 population control revisions.

2) Questions on race and Hispanic origin were modified to comply with the new standards for maintaining, collecting, and presenting federal data on race and ethnicity for federal statistical agencies. The questions were reworded to indicate that individuals could select more than once race category and to convey more clearly that individuals should report their own perception of what race is. These changes had no impact on the overall civilian noninstitutional population and civilian labor force. However, they did reduce the population and labor force levels of Whites, Blacks, and Asians beginning in January 2003.

3) Improvements were introduced to both the second stage and composite weighting procedures. These changes adapted the weighting procedures to the new race/ethnic classification system and enhanced the stability over time for demographic groups. The second-stage weighting procedure substantially reduced the variability of estimates and corrected, to some extent, for CPS underreporting.

Changes in the Occupational and Industrial Classification System

In January 2003, the CPS adopted the 2002 census industry and occupational classification systems, which were derived, respectively, from the 2002 North American Industry Classification System (NAICS) and the 2000 Standard Occupational Classification (SOC) system. The 1990 Census occupational and industry classifications were replaced. The introduction of the new industry and occupational classification systems in 2003 created a complete break in comparability at all levels of industry and occupation aggregation. The composition of detailed occupations and industries changed substantially in the 2002 systems compared with the 1990 systems, as did the structure for aggregating them into major groups. Therefore, any comparisons of data on the different classifications are not possible without major adjustments.

Historical employment series on the 2002 Census classifications are available at broad levels of occupational and industry aggregation back to 1983. However, historical employment series at the detailed occupational and industry levels on the 2002 classifications are available back to 2000 only.

Starting with industry data in 2009, BLS began using the 2007 Census industry classification system, which was derived from the 2007 NAICS series. Several industry titles were revised with no change to the industry definitions. The differences between the 2002 and 2007 classifications are relatively insignificant. BLS did not make any revisions to historical data with the introduction of 2007 NAICS series.

Sources of Additional Information

A complete description of sampling and estimation procedures and further information on the impact of historical changes in the surveys can be found in the updated version of Chapter 1 of the *BLS Handbook of Methods*. This can be found on the BLS Web site at <http://www.bls.gov/opub/hom/>.

Table 1-1. Employment Status of the Civilian Noninstitutional Population, 1947–2010

(Thousands of people, percent.)

Year	Civilian noninstitutional population	Civilian labor force									Not in labor force
		Total	Participation rate	Employed				Unemployed			
				Total	Percent of population	Agriculture	Nonagricultural industries	Number	Unemploy-ment rate		
1947	101 827	59 350	58.3	57 038	56.0	7 890	49 148	2 311	3.9		42 477
1948	103 068	60 621	58.8	58 343	56.6	7 629	50 714	2 276	3.8		42 447
1949	103 994	61 286	58.9	57 651	55.4	7 658	49 993	3 637	5.9		42 708
1950	104 995	62 208	59.2	58 918	56.1	7 160	51 758	3 288	5.3		42 787
1951	104 621	62 017	59.2	59 961	57.3	6 726	53 235	2 055	3.3		42 604
1952	105 231	62 138	59.0	60 250	57.3	6 500	53 749	1 883	3.0		43 093
1953[1]	107 056	63 015	58.9	61 179	57.1	6 260	54 919	1 834	2.9		44 041
1954	108 321	63 643	58.8	60 109	55.5	6 205	53 904	3 532	5.5		44 678
1955	109 683	65 023	59.3	62 170	56.7	6 450	55 722	2 852	4.4		44 660
1956	110 954	66 552	60.0	63 799	57.5	6 283	57 514	2 750	4.1		44 402
1957	112 265	66 929	59.6	64 071	57.1	5 947	58 123	2 859	4.3		45 336
1958	113 727	67 639	59.5	63 036	55.4	5 586	57 450	4 602	6.8		46 088
1959	115 329	68 369	59.3	64 630	56.0	5 565	59 065	3 740	5.5		46 960
1960[1]	117 245	69 628	59.4	65 778	56.1	5 458	60 318	3 852	5.5		47 617
1961	118 771	70 459	59.3	65 746	55.4	5 200	60 546	4 714	6.7		48 312
1962[1]	120 153	70 614	58.8	66 702	55.5	4 944	61 759	3 911	5.5		49 539
1963	122 416	71 833	58.7	67 762	55.4	4 687	63 076	4 070	5.7		50 583
1964	124 485	73 091	58.7	69 305	55.7	4 523	64 782	3 786	5.2		51 394
1965	126 513	74 455	58.9	71 088	56.2	4 361	66 726	3 366	4.5		52 058
1966	128 058	75 770	59.2	72 895	56.9	3 979	68 915	2 875	3.8		52 288
1967	129 874	77 347	59.6	74 372	57.3	3 844	70 527	2 975	3.8		52 527
1968	132 028	78 737	59.6	75 920	57.5	3 817	72 103	2 817	3.6		53 291
1969	134 335	80 734	60.1	77 902	58.0	3 606	74 296	2 832	3.5		53 602
1970	137 085	82 771	60.4	78 678	57.4	3 463	75 215	4 093	4.9		54 315
1971	140 216	84 382	60.2	79 367	56.6	3 394	75 972	5 016	5.9		55 834
1972[1]	144 126	87 034	60.4	82 153	57.0	3 484	78 669	4 882	5.6		57 091
1973[1]	147 096	89 429	60.8	85 064	57.8	3 470	81 594	4 365	4.9		57 667
1974	150 120	91 949	61.3	86 794	57.8	3 515	83 279	5 156	5.6		58 171
1975	153 153	93 774	61.2	85 846	56.1	3 408	82 438	7 929	8.5		59 377
1976	156 150	96 158	61.6	88 752	56.8	3 331	85 421	7 406	7.7		59 991
1977	159 033	99 008	62.3	92 017	57.9	3 283	88 734	6 991	7.1		60 025
1978[1]	161 910	102 250	63.2	96 048	59.3	3 387	92 661	6 202	6.1		59 659
1979	164 863	104 962	63.7	98 824	59.9	3 347	95 477	6 137	5.8		59 900
1980	167 745	106 940	63.8	99 302	59.2	3 364	95 938	7 637	7.1		60 806
1981	170 130	108 670	63.9	100 397	59.0	3 368	97 030	8 273	7.6		61 460
1982	172 271	110 204	64.0	99 526	57.8	3 401	96 125	10 678	9.7		62 067
1983	174 215	111 550	64.0	100 834	57.9	3 383	97 450	10 717	9.6		62 665
1984	176 383	113 544	64.4	105 005	59.5	3 321	101 685	8 539	7.5		62 839
1985	178 206	115 461	64.8	107 150	60.1	3 179	103 971	8 312	7.2		62 744
1986[1]	180 587	117 834	65.3	109 597	60.7	3 163	106 434	8 237	7.0		62 752
1987	182 753	119 865	65.6	112 440	61.5	3 208	109 232	7 425	6.2		62 888
1988	184 613	121 669	65.9	114 968	62.3	3 169	111 800	6 701	5.5		62 944
1989	186 393	123 869	66.5	117 342	63.0	3 199	114 142	6 528	5.3		62 523
1990[1]	189 164	125 840	66.5	118 793	62.8	3 223	115 570	7 047	5.6		63 324
1991	190 925	126 346	66.2	117 718	61.7	3 269	114 449	8 628	6.8		64 578
1992	192 805	128 105	66.4	118 492	61.5	3 247	115 245	9 613	7.5		64 700
1993	194 838	129 200	66.3	120 259	61.7	3 115	117 144	8 940	6.9		65 638
1994[1]	196 814	131 056	66.6	123 060	62.5	3 409	119 651	7 996	6.1		65 758
1995	198 584	132 304	66.6	124 900	62.9	3 440	121 460	7 404	5.6		66 280
1996	200 591	133 943	66.8	126 708	63.2	3 443	123 264	7 236	5.4		66 647
1997[1]	203 133	136 297	67.1	129 558	63.8	3 399	126 159	6 739	4.9		66 836
1998[1]	205 220	137 673	67.1	131 463	64.1	3 378	128 085	6 210	4.5		67 547
1999[1]	207 753	139 368	67.1	133 488	64.3	3 281	130 207	5 880	4.2		68 385
2000[1]	212 577	142 583	67.1	136 891	64.4	2 464	134 427	5 692	4.0		69 994
2001	215 092	143 734	66.8	136 933	63.7	2 299	134 635	6 801	4.7		71 359
2002	217 570	144 863	66.6	136 485	62.7	2 311	134 174	8 378	5.8		72 707
2003[1]	221 168	146 510	66.2	137 736	62.3	2 275	135 461	8 774	6.0		74 658
2004[1]	223 357	147 401	66.0	139 252	62.3	2 232	137 020	8 149	5.5		75 956
2005[1]	226 082	149 320	66.0	141 730	62.7	2 197	139 532	7 591	5.1		76 762
2006[1]	228 815	151 428	66.2	144 427	63.1	2 206	142 221	7 001	4.6		77 387
2007[1]	231 867	153 124	66.0	146 047	63.0	2 095	143 952	7 078	4.6		78 743
2008[1]	233 788	154 287	66.0	145 362	62.2	2 168	143 194	8 924	5.8		79 501
2009[1]	235 801	154 142	65.4	139 877	59.3	2 103	137 775	14 265	9.3		81 659
2010[1]	237 830	153 889	64.7	139 064	58.5	2 206	136 858	14 825	9.6		83 941

[1]Not strictly comparable with data for prior years. See notes and definitions for information on historical comparability.

Table 1-2. Employment Status of the Civilian Noninstitutional Population, by Sex, 1975–2010

(Thousands of people, percent.)

| Sex and year | Civilian noninstitutional population | Civilian labor force | | Employed | | | | Unemployed | | Not in labor force |
		Total	Participation rate	Total	Percent of population	Agriculture	Non-agricultural industries	Number	Unemploy-ment rate	
Men										
1975	72 291	56 299	77.9	51 857	71.7	2 824	49 032	4 442	7.9	15 993
1976	73 759	57 174	77.5	53 138	72.0	2 744	50 394	4 036	7.1	16 585
1977	75 193	58 396	77.7	54 728	72.8	2 671	52 057	3 667	6.3	16 797
1978¹	76 576	59 620	77.9	56 479	73.8	2 718	53 761	3 142	5.3	16 956
1979	78 020	60 726	77.8	57 607	73.8	2 686	54 921	3 120	5.1	17 293
1980	79 398	61 453	77.4	57 186	72.0	2 709	54 477	4 267	6.9	17 945
1981	80 511	61 974	77.0	57 397	71.3	2 700	54 697	4 577	7.4	18 537
1982	81 523	62 450	76.6	56 271	69.0	2 736	53 534	6 179	9.9	19 073
1983	82 531	63 047	76.4	56 787	68.8	2 704	54 083	6 260	9.9	19 484
1984	83 605	63 835	76.4	59 091	70.7	2 668	56 423	4 744	7.4	19 771
1985	84 469	64 411	76.3	59 891	70.9	2 535	57 356	4 521	7.0	20 058
1986¹	85 798	65 422	76.3	60 892	71.0	2 511	58 381	4 530	6.9	20 376
1987	86 899	66 207	76.2	62 107	71.5	2 543	59 564	4 101	6.2	20 692
1988	87 857	66 927	76.2	63 273	72.0	2 493	60 780	3 655	5.5	20 930
1989	88 762	67 840	76.4	64 315	72.5	2 513	61 802	3 525	5.2	20 923
1990¹	90 377	69 011	76.4	65 104	72.0	2 546	62 559	3 906	5.7	21 367
1991	91 278	69 168	75.8	64 223	70.4	2 589	61 634	4 946	7.2	22 110
1992	92 270	69 964	75.8	64 440	69.8	2 575	61 866	5 523	7.9	22 306
1993	93 332	70 404	75.4	65 349	70.0	2 478	62 871	5 055	7.2	22 927
1994¹	94 354	70 817	75.1	66 450	70.4	2 554	63 896	4 367	6.2	23 538
1995	95 178	71 360	75.0	67 377	70.8	2 559	64 818	3 983	5.6	23 818
1996¹	96 206	72 086	74.9	68 207	70.9	2 573	65 634	3 880	5.4	24 119
1997¹	97 715	73 261	75.0	69 685	71.3	2 552	67 133	3 577	4.9	24 454
1998¹	98 758	73 959	74.9	70 693	71.6	2 553	68 140	3 266	4.4	24 799
1999¹	99 722	74 512	74.7	71 446	71.6	2 432	69 014	3 066	4.1	25 210
2000¹	101 964	76 280	74.8	73 305	71.9	1 861	71 444	2 975	3.9	25 684
2001	103 282	76 886	74.4	73 196	70.9	1 708	71 488	3 690	4.8	26 396
2002	104 585	77 500	74.1	72 903	69.7	1 724	71 179	4 597	5.9	27 085
2003¹	106 435	78 238	73.5	73 332	68.9	1 695	71 636	4 906	6.3	28 197
2004¹	107 710	78 980	73.3	74 524	69.2	1 687	72 838	4 456	5.6	28 730
2005¹	109 151	80 033	73.0	75 973	69.6	1 654	74 319	4 059	5.0	29 119
2006¹	110 605	81 255	73.5	77 502	70.1	1 663	75 838	3 753	4.6	29 350
2007¹	112 173	82 136	73.2	78 254	69.8	1 604	76 650	3 882	4.7	30 036
2008¹	113 113	82 520	73.0	77 486	68.5	1 650	75 836	5 033	6.1	30 593
2009¹	114 136	82 123	72.0	73 670	64.5	1 607	72 062	8 453	10.3	32 013
2010¹	115 174	81 985	71.2	73 359	63.7	1 665	71 694	8 626	10.5	33 189
Women										
1975	80 860	37 475	46.3	33 989	42.0	584	33 404	3 486	9.3	43 386
1976	82 390	38 983	47.3	35 615	43.2	588	35 027	3 369	8.6	43 406
1977	83 840	40 613	48.4	37 289	44.5	612	36 677	3 324	8.2	43 227
1978¹	85 334	42 631	50.0	39 569	46.4	669	38 900	3 061	7.2	42 703
1979	86 843	44 235	50.9	41 217	47.5	661	40 556	3 018	6.8	42 608
1980	88 348	45 487	51.5	42 117	47.7	656	41 461	3 370	7.4	42 861
1981	89 618	46 696	52.1	43 000	48.0	667	42 333	3 696	7.9	42 922
1982	90 748	47 755	52.6	43 256	47.7	665	42 591	4 499	9.4	42 993
1983	91 684	48 503	52.9	44 047	48.0	680	43 367	4 457	9.2	43 181
1984	92 778	49 709	53.6	45 915	49.5	653	45 262	3 794	7.6	43 068
1985	93 736	51 050	54.5	47 259	50.4	644	46 615	3 791	7.4	42 686
1986¹	94 789	52 413	55.3	48 706	51.4	652	48 054	3 707	7.1	42 376
1987	95 853	53 658	56.0	50 334	52.5	666	49 668	3 324	6.2	42 195
1988	96 756	54 742	56.6	51 696	53.4	676	51 020	3 046	5.6	42 014
1989	97 630	56 030	57.4	53 027	54.3	687	52 341	3 003	5.4	41 601
1990¹	98 787	56 829	57.5	53 689	54.3	678	53 011	3 140	5.5	41 957
1991	99 646	57 178	57.4	53 496	53.7	680	52 815	3 683	6.4	42 468
1992	100 535	58 141	57.8	54 052	53.8	672	53 380	4 090	7.0	42 394
1993	101 506	58 795	57.9	54 910	54.1	637	54 273	3 885	6.6	42 711
1994¹	102 460	60 239	58.8	56 610	55.3	855	55 755	3 629	6.0	42 221
1995	103 406	60 944	58.9	57 523	55.6	881	56 642	3 421	5.6	42 462
1996	104 385	61 857	59.3	58 501	56.0	871	57 630	3 356	5.4	42 528
1997¹	105 418	63 036	59.8	59 873	56.8	847	59 026	3 162	5.0	42 382
1998¹	106 462	63 714	59.8	60 771	57.1	825	59 945	2 944	4.6	42 748
1999¹	108 031	64 855	60.0	62 042	57.4	849	61 193	2 814	4.3	43 175
2000¹	110 613	66 303	59.9	63 586	57.5	602	62 983	2 717	4.1	44 310
2001	111 811	66 848	59.8	63 737	57.0	591	63 147	3 111	4.7	44 962
2002	112 985	67 363	59.6	63 582	56.3	587	62 995	3 781	5.6	45 621
2003¹	114 733	68 272	59.5	64 404	56.1	580	63 824	3 868	5.7	46 461
2004¹	115 647	68 421	59.2	64 728	56.0	546	64 182	3 694	5.4	47 225
2005¹	116 931	69 288	59.3	65 757	56.2	544	65 213	3 531	5.1	47 643
2006¹	118 210	70 173	59.4	66 925	56.6	543	66 382	3 247	4.6	48 037
2007¹	119 694	70 988	59.3	67 792	56.6	490	67 302	3 196	4.5	48 707
2008¹	120 675	71 767	59.5	67 876	56.2	518	67 358	3 891	5.4	48 908
2009¹	121 665	72 019	59.2	66 208	54.4	496	65 712	5 811	8.1	49 646
2010¹	122 656	71 904	58.6	65 705	53.6	541	65 164	6 199	8.6	50 752

¹Not strictly comparable with data for prior years. See notes and definitions for information on historical comparability.

Table 1-3. Employment Status of the Civilian Noninstitutional Population, by Sex, Age, Race, and Hispanic Origin, 1990–2010

(Thousands of people.)

Characteristic	1990	1991	1992	1993	1994	1995	1996	1997	1998	1999	2000
ALL RACES											
Both Sexes											
Civilian noninstitutional population	189 164	190 925	192 805	194 838	196 814	198 584	200 591	203 133	205 220	207 753	212 577
Civilian labor force	125 840	126 346	128 105	129 200	131 056	132 304	133 943	136 297	137 673	139 368	142 583
Employed	118 793	117 718	118 492	120 259	123 060	124 900	126 708	129 558	131 463	133 488	136 891
Agriculture	3 223	3 269	3 247	3 115	3 409	3 440	3 443	3 399	3 378	3 281	2 464
Nonagricultural industries	115 570	114 449	115 245	117 144	119 651	121 460	123 264	126 159	128 085	130 207	134 427
Unemployed	7 047	8 628	9 613	8 940	7 996	7 404	7 236	6 739	6 210	5 880	5 692
Not in labor force	63 324	64 578	64 700	65 638	65 758	66 280	66 647	66 837	67 547	68 385	69 994
Men, 16 Years and Over											
Civilian noninstitutional population	90 377	91 278	92 270	93 332	94 355	95 178	96 206	97 715	98 758	99 722	101 964
Civilian labor force	69 011	69 168	69 964	70 404	70 817	71 360	72 087	73 261	73 959	74 512	76 280
Employed	65 104	64 223	64 440	65 349	66 450	67 377	68 207	69 685	70 693	71 446	73 305
Agriculture	2 546	2 589	2 575	2 478	2 554	2 559	2 573	2 552	2 553	2 432	1 861
Nonagricultural industries	62 559	61 634	61 866	62 871	63 896	64 818	65 634	67 133	68 140	69 014	71 444
Unemployed	3 906	4 946	5 523	5 055	4 367	3 983	3 880	3 577	3 266	3 066	2 975
Not in labor force	21 367	22 110	22 306	22 927	23 538	23 818	24 119	24 454	24 799	25 210	25 684
Men, 20 Years and Over											
Civilian noninstitutional population	83 030	84 144	85 247	86 256	87 151	87 811	88 606	89 879	90 790	91 555	93 875
Civilian labor force	64 916	65 374	66 213	66 642	66 921	67 324	68 044	69 166	69 715	70 194	72 010
Employed	61 678	61 178	61 496	62 355	63 294	64 085	64 897	66 284	67 135	67 761	69 634
Agriculture	2 329	2 383	2 385	2 293	2 351	2 335	2 356	2 356	2 350	2 244	1 756
Nonagricultural industries	59 349	58 795	59 111	60 063	60 943	61 750	62 541	63 927	64 785	65 517	67 878
Unemployed	3 239	4 195	4 717	4 287	3 627	3 239	3 146	2 882	2 580	2 433	2 376
Not in labor force	18 114	18 770	19 034	19 613	20 230	20 487	20 563	20 713	21 075	21 362	21 864
Women, 16 Years and Over											
Civilian noninstitutional population	98 787	99 646	100 535	101 506	102 460	103 406	104 385	105 418	106 462	108 031	110 613
Civilian labor force	56 829	57 178	58 141	58 795	60 239	60 944	61 857	63 036	63 714	64 855	66 303
Employed	53 689	53 496	54 052	54 910	56 610	57 523	58 501	59 873	60 771	62 042	63 586
Agriculture	678	680	672	637	855	881	871	847	825	849	602
Nonagricultural industries	53 011	52 815	53 380	54 273	55 755	56 642	57 630	59 026	59 945	61 193	62 983
Unemployed	3 140	3 683	4 090	3 885	3 629	3 421	3 356	3 162	2 944	2 814	2 717
Not in labor force	41 957	42 468	42 394	42 711	42 221	42 462	42 528	42 382	42 748	43 175	44 310
Women, 20 Years and Over											
Civilian noninstitutional population	91 614	92 708	93 718	94 647	95 467	96 262	97 050	97 889	98 786	100 158	102 790
Civilian labor force	53 131	53 708	54 796	55 388	56 655	57 215	58 094	59 198	59 702	60 840	62 301
Employed	50 535	50 634	51 328	52 099	53 606	54 396	55 311	56 613	57 278	58 555	60 067
Agriculture	631	639	625	598	809	830	827	798	768	803	567
Nonagricultural industries	49 904	49 995	50 702	51 501	52 796	53 566	54 484	55 815	56 510	57 752	59 500
Unemployed	2 596	3 074	3 469	3 288	3 049	2 819	2 783	2 585	2 424	2 285	2 235
Not in labor force	38 483	39 000	38 922	39 260	38 813	39 047	38 956	38 691	39 084	39 318	40 488
Both Sexes, 16 to 19 Years											
Civilian noninstitutional population	14 520	14 073	13 840	13 935	14 196	14 511	14 934	15 365	15 644	16 040	15 912
Civilian labor force	7 792	7 265	7 096	7 170	7 481	7 765	7 806	7 932	8 256	8 333	8 271
Employed	6 581	5 906	5 669	5 805	6 161	6 419	6 500	6 661	7 051	7 172	7 189
Agriculture	264	247	237	224	249	275	261	244	261	234	141
Nonagricultural industries	6 317	5 659	5 432	5 580	5 912	6 144	6 239	6 417	6 790	6 938	7 049
Unemployed	1 212	1 359	1 427	1 365	1 320	1 346	1 306	1 271	1 205	1 162	1 081
Not in labor force	6 727	6 808	6 745	6 765	6 715	6 746	7 128	7 433	7 388	7 706	7 642
WHITE[1]											
Both Sexes											
Civilian noninstitutional population	160 625	161 759	162 972	164 289	165 555	166 914	168 317	169 993	171 478	173 085	176 220
Civilian labor force	107 447	107 743	108 837	109 700	111 082	111 950	113 108	114 693	115 415	116 509	118 545
Employed	102 261	101 182	101 669	103 045	105 190	106 490	107 808	109 856	110 931	112 235	114 424
Agriculture	2 998	3 026	3 018	2 895	3 162	3 194	3 276	3 208	3 160	3 083	2 320
Nonagricultural industries	99 263	98 157	98 650	100 150	102 027	103 296	104 532	106 648	107 770	109 152	112 104
Unemployed	5 186	6 560	7 169	6 655	5 892	5 459	5 300	4 836	4 484	4 273	4 121
Not in labor force	53 178	54 061	54 135	54 589	54 473	54 965	55 209	55 301	56 064	56 577	57 675
Men, 16 Years and Over											
Civilian noninstitutional population	77 369	77 977	78 651	79 371	80 059	80 733	81 489	82 577	83 352	83 930	85 370
Civilian labor force	59 638	59 656	60 168	60 484	60 727	61 146	61 783	62 639	63 034	63 413	64 466
Employed	56 703	55 797	55 959	56 656	57 452	58 146	58 888	59 998	60 604	61 139	62 289
Agriculture	2 353	2 384	2 378	2 286	2 347	2 347	2 436	2 389	2 376	2 273	1 743
Nonagricultural industries	54 350	53 413	53 580	54 370	55 104	55 800	56 452	57 608	58 228	58 866	60 546
Unemployed	2 935	3 859	4 209	3 828	3 275	2 999	2 896	2 641	2 431	2 274	2 177
Not in labor force	17 731	18 321	18 484	18 887	19 332	19 587	19 706	19 938	20 317	20 517	20 905
Men, 20 Years and Over											
Civilian noninstitutional population	71 457	72 274	73 040	73 721	74 311	74 879	75 454	76 320	76 966	77 432	78 966
Civilian labor force	56 116	56 387	56 976	57 284	57 411	57 719	58 340	59 126	59 421	59 747	60 850
Employed	53 685	53 103	53 357	54 021	54 676	55 254	55 977	56 986	57 500	57 934	59 119
Agriculture	2 148	2 192	2 197	2 114	2 151	2 132	2 224	2 201	2 182	2 094	1 640
Nonagricultural industries	51 537	50 912	51 160	51 907	52 525	53 122	53 753	54 785	55 319	55 839	57 479
Unemployed	2 431	3 284	3 620	3 263	2 735	2 465	2 363	2 140	1 920	1 813	1 731
Not in labor force	15 340	15 887	16 064	16 436	16 900	17 161	17 114	17 194	17 545	17 685	18 116

[1]Beginning in 2003, persons who selected this race group only; persons who selected more than one race group are not included. Prior to 2003, persons who reported more than one race group were included in the group they identified as the main race.

Table 1-3. Employment Status of the Civilian Noninstitutional Population, by Sex, Age, Race, and Hispanic Origin, 1990–2010—*Continued*

(Thousands of people.)

Characteristic	2001	2002	2003	2004	2005	2006	2007	2008	2009	2010
ALL RACES										
Both Sexes										
Civilian noninstitutional population	215 092	217 570	221 168	223 357	226 082	228 815	231 867	233 788	235 801	237 830
Civilian labor force	143 734	144 863	146 510	147 401	149 320	151 428	153 124	154 287	154 142	153 889
Employed	136 933	136 485	137 736	139 252	141 730	144 427	146 047	145 362	139 877	139 064
Agriculture	2 299	2 311	2 275	2 232	2 197	2 206	2 095	2 168	2 103	2 206
Nonagricultural industries	134 635	134 174	135 461	137 020	139 532	142 221	143 952	143 194	137 775	136 858
Unemployed	6 801	8 378	8 774	8 149	7 591	7 001	7 078	8 924	14 265	14 825
Not in labor force	71 359	72 707	74 658	75 956	76 762	77 387	78 743	79 501	81 659	83 941
Men, 16 Years and Over										
Civilian noninstitutional population	103 282	104 585	106 435	107 710	109 151	110 605	112 173	113 113	114 136	115 174
Civilian labor force	76 886	77 500	78 238	78 980	80 033	81 255	82 136	82 520	82 123	81 985
Employed	73 196	72 903	73 332	74 524	75 973	77 502	78 254	77 486	73 670	73 359
Agriculture	1 708	1 724	1 695	1 688	1 654	1 663	1 604	1 650	1 607	1 665
Nonagricultural industries	71 488	71 179	71 636	72 836	74 319	75 838	76 650	75 836	72 062	71 694
Unemployed	3 690	4 597	4 906	4 456	4 059	3 753	3 882	5 033	8 453	8 626
Not in labor force	26 396	27 085	28 197	28 730	29 119	29 350	30 036	30 593	32 013	33 189
Men, 20 Years and Over										
Civilian noninstitutional population	95 181	96 439	98 272	99 476	100 835	102 145	103 555	104 453	105 493	106 596
Civilian labor force	72 816	73 630	74 623	75 364	76 443	77 562	78 596	79 047	78 897	78 994
Employed	69 776	69 734	70 415	71 572	73 050	74 431	75 337	74 750	71 341	71 230
Agriculture	1 613	1 629	1 614	1 596	1 577	1 579	1 514	1 552	1 514	1 589
Nonagricultural industries	68 163	68 104	68 801	69 976	71 473	72 852	73 823	73 198	69 828	69 641
Unemployed	3 040	3 896	4 209	3 791	3 392	3 131	3 259	4 297	7 555	7 763
Not in labor force	22 365	22 809	23 649	24 113	24 392	24 584	24 959	25 406	26 596	27 603
Women, 16 Years and Over										
Civilian noninstitutional population	111 811	112 985	114 733	115 647	116 931	118 210	119 694	120 675	121 665	122 656
Civilian labor force	66 848	67 363	68 272	68 421	69 288	70 173	70 988	71 767	72 019	71 904
Employed	63 737	63 582	64 404	64 728	65 757	66 925	67 792	67 876	66 208	65 705
Agriculture	591	587	580	547	544	543	490	518	496	541
Nonagricultural industries	63 147	62 995	63 824	64 181	65 213	66 382	67 302	67 358	65 712	65 164
Unemployed	3 111	3 781	3 868	3 694	3 531	3 247	3 196	3 891	5 811	6 199
Not in labor force	44 962	45 621	46 461	47 225	47 643	48 037	48 707	48 908	49 646	50 752
Women, 20 Years and Over										
Civilian noninstitutional population	103 983	105 136	106 800	107 658	108 850	109 992	111 330	112 260	113 265	114 333
Civilian labor force	63 016	63 648	64 716	64 923	65 714	66 585	67 516	68 382	68 856	68 990
Employed	60 417	60 420	61 402	61 773	62 702	63 834	64 799	65 039	63 699	63 456
Agriculture	558	557	550	515	519	520	460	491	471	519
Nonagricultural industries	59 860	59 863	60 852	61 258	62 182	63 315	64 339	64 548	63 228	62 936
Unemployed	2 599	3 228	3 314	3 150	3 013	2 751	2 718	3 342	5 157	5 534
Not in labor force	40 967	41 488	42 083	42 735	43 136	43 407	43 814	43 878	44 409	45 343
Both Sexes, 16 to 19 Years										
Civilian noninstitutional population	15 929	15 994	16 096	16 222	16 398	16 678	16 982	17 075	17 043	16 901
Civilian labor force	7 902	7 585	7 170	7 114	7 164	7 281	7 012	6 858	6 390	5 906
Employed	6 740	6 332	5 919	5 907	5 978	6 162	5 911	5 573	4 837	4 378
Agriculture	128	124	111	121	100	108	121	125	119	98
Nonagricultural industries	6 611	6 207	5 808	5 786	5 877	6 054	5 790	5 448	4 719	4 281
Unemployed	1 162	1 253	1 251	1 208	1 186	1 119	1 101	1 285	1 552	1 528
Not in labor force	8 027	8 409	8 926	9 108	9 234	9 397	9 970	10 218	10 654	10 995
WHITE[1]										
Both Sexes										
Civilian noninstitutional population	178 111	179 783	181 292	182 643	184 446	186 264	188 253	189 540	190 902	192 075
Civilian labor force	119 399	120 150	120 546	121 086	122 299	123 834	124 935	125 635	125 644	125 084
Employed	114 430	114 013	114 235	115 239	116 949	118 833	119 792	119 126	114 996	114 168
Agriculture	2 174	2 171	2 148	2 103	2 077	2 063	1 953	2 021	1 968	2 071
Nonagricultural industries	112 256	111 841	112 087	113 136	114 872	116 769	117 839	117 104	113 028	112 098
Unemployed	4 969	6 137	6 311	5 847	5 350	5 002	5 143	6 509	10 648	10 916
Not in labor force	58 713	59 633	60 746	61 558	62 148	62 429	63 319	63 905	65 258	66 991
Men, 16 Years and Over										
Civilian noninstitutional population	86 452	87 361	88 249	89 044	90 027	91 021	92 073	92 725	93 433	94 082
Civilian labor force	64 966	65 308	65 509	65 994	66 694	67 613	68 158	68 351	68 051	67 728
Employed	62 212	61 849	61 866	62 712	63 763	64 883	65 289	64 624	61 630	61 252
Agriculture	1 606	1 611	1 597	1 583	1 562	1 554	1 501	1 539	1 499	1 557
Nonagricultural industries	60 606	60 238	60 269	61 129	62 201	63 330	63 788	63 085	60 131	59 695
Unemployed	2 754	3 459	3 643	3 282	2 931	2 730	2 869	3 727	6 421	6 476
Not in labor force	21 486	22 053	22 740	23 050	23 334	23 408	23 915	24 374	25 382	26 353
Men, 20 Years and Over										
Civilian noninstitutional population	80 029	80 922	81 860	82 615	83 556	84 466	85 420	86 056	86 789	87 502
Civilian labor force	61 519	62 067	62 473	62 944	63 705	64 540	65 214	65 483	65 372	65 265
Employed	59 245	59 124	59 348	60 159	61 255	62 259	62 806	62 304	59 626	59 438
Agriculture	1 512	1 519	1 517	1 495	1 488	1 473	1 417	1 447	1 410	1 483
Nonagricultural industries	57 733	57 605	57 831	58 664	59 767	60 785	61 389	60 857	58 216	57 955
Unemployed	2 275	2 943	3 125	2 785	2 450	2 281	2 408	3 179	5 746	5 828
Not in labor force	18 510	18 855	19 386	19 671	19 851	19 927	20 206	20 573	21 417	22 236

[1]Beginning in 2003, persons who selected this race group only; persons who selected more than one race group are not included. Prior to 2003, persons who reported more than one race group were included in the group they identified as the main race.

Table 1-3. Employment Status of the Civilian Noninstitutional Population, by Sex, Age, Race, and Hispanic Origin, 1990–2010—*Continued*

(Thousands of people.)

Characteristic	1990	1991	1992	1993	1994	1995	1996	1997	1998	1999	2000
WHITE[1]											
Women, 16 Years and Over											
Civilian noninstitutional population	83 256	83 781	84 321	84 918	85 496	86 181	86 828	87 417	88 126	89 156	90 850
Civilian labor force	47 809	48 087	48 669	49 216	50 356	50 804	51 325	52 054	52 380	53 096	54 079
Employed	45 558	45 385	45 710	46 390	47 738	48 344	48 920	49 859	50 327	51 096	52 136
Agriculture	645	641	640	609	815	847	840	819	784	810	578
Nonagricultural industries	44 913	44 744	45 070	45 780	46 923	47 497	48 080	49 040	49 543	50 286	51 558
Unemployed	2 251	2 701	2 959	2 827	2 617	2 460	2 404	2 195	2 053	1 999	1 944
Not in labor force	35 447	35 695	35 651	35 702	35 141	35 377	35 503	35 363	35 746	36 060	36 770
Women, 20 Years and Over											
Civilian noninstitutional population	77 539	78 285	78 928	79 490	79 980	80 567	81 041	81 492	82 073	82 953	84 718
Civilian labor force	44 648	45 111	45 839	46 311	47 314	47 686	48 162	48 847	49 029	49 714	50 740
Employed	42 796	42 862	43 327	43 910	45 116	45 643	46 164	47 063	47 342	48 098	49 145
Agriculture	598	601	594	572	772	799	798	771	729	765	546
Nonagricultural industries	42 198	42 261	42 733	43 339	44 344	44 844	45 366	46 292	46 612	47 333	48 599
Unemployed	1 852	2 248	2 512	2 400	2 197	2 042	1 998	1 784	1 688	1 616	1 595
Not in labor force	32 891	33 174	33 089	33 179	32 666	32 881	32 879	32 645	33 044	33 239	33 978
Both Sexes, 16 to 19 Years											
Civilian noninstitutional population	11 630	11 200	11 004	11 078	11 264	11 468	11 822	12 181	12 439	12 700	12 535
Civilian labor force	6 683	6 245	6 022	6 105	6 357	6 545	6 607	6 720	6 965	7 048	6 955
Employed	5 779	5 216	4 985	5 113	5 398	5 593	5 667	5 807	6 089	6 204	6 160
Agriculture	252	233	228	209	239	262	254	236	250	224	135
Nonagricultural industries	5 528	4 984	4 757	4 904	5 158	5 331	5 413	5 571	5 839	5 980	6 025
Unemployed	903	1 029	1 037	992	960	952	939	912	876	844	795
Not in labor force	4 947	4 955	4 982	4 973	4 907	4 923	5 215	5 462	5 475	5 652	5 581
BLACK[1]											
Both Sexes											
Civilian noninstitutional population	21 477	21 799	22 147	22 521	22 879	23 246	23 604	24 003	24 373	24 855	24 902
Civilian labor force	13 740	13 797	14 162	14 225	14 502	14 817	15 134	15 529	15 982	16 365	16 397
Employed	12 175	12 074	12 151	12 382	12 835	13 279	13 542	13 969	14 556	15 056	15 156
Agriculture	142	160	153	143	136	101	98	117	138	117	77
Nonagricultural industries	12 034	11 914	11 997	12 239	12 699	13 178	13 444	13 852	14 417	14 939	15 079
Unemployed	1 565	1 723	2 011	1 844	1 666	1 538	1 592	1 560	1 426	1 309	1 241
Not in labor force	7 737	8 002	7 985	8 296	8 377	8 429	8 470	8 474	8 391	8 490	8 505
Men, 16 Years and Over											
Civilian noninstitutional population	9 573	9 725	9 896	10 083	10 258	10 411	10 575	10 763	10 927	11 143	11 129
Civilian labor force	6 802	6 851	6 997	7 019	7 089	7 183	7 264	7 354	7 542	7 652	7 702
Employed	5 995	5 961	5 930	6 047	6 241	6 422	6 456	6 607	6 871	7 027	7 082
Agriculture	124	139	138	128	118	93	86	103	118	99	67
Nonagricultural industries	5 872	5 822	5 791	5 919	6 122	6 329	6 371	6 504	6 752	6 952	7 015
Unemployed	806	890	1 067	971	848	762	808	747	671	671	620
Not in labor force	2 772	2 874	2 899	3 064	3 169	3 228	3 311	3 409	3 386	3 386	3 427
Men, 20 Years and Over											
Civilian noninstitutional population	8 364	8 479	8 652	8 840	9 171	9 280	9 414	9 575	9 727	9 926	9 952
Civilian labor force	6 221	6 357	6 451	6 568	6 646	6 730	6 806	6 910	7 053	7 182	7 240
Employed	5 602	5 692	5 706	5 681	5 964	6 137	6 167	6 325	6 530	6 702	6 741
Agriculture	119	117	131	131	115	89	83	101	112	96	67
Nonagricultural industries	5 483	5 576	5 575	5 550	5 849	6 048	6 084	6 224	6 418	6 606	6 675
Unemployed	619	664	745	886	682	593	639	585	524	480	499
Not in labor force	2 143	2 122	2 202	801	2 525	2 550	2 608	2 665	2 673	2 743	2 711
Women, 16 Years and Over											
Civilian noninstitutional population	11 904	12 074	12 251	12 438	12 621	12 835	13 029	13 241	13 446	13 711	13 772
Civilian labor force	6 938	6 946	7 166	7 206	7 413	7 634	7 869	8 175	8 441	8 713	8 695
Employed	6 180	6 113	6 221	6 334	6 595	6 857	7 086	7 362	7 685	8 029	8 073
Agriculture	18	21	15	15	18	8	13	14	20	18	10
Nonagricultural industries	6 162	6 092	6 206	6 320	6 577	6 849	7 073	7 348	7 665	8 011	8 064
Unemployed	758	833	944	872	818	777	784	813	756	684	621
Not in labor force	4 965	5 129	5 086	5 231	5 208	5 201	5 159	5 066	5 005	4 999	5 078
Women, 20 Years and Over											
Civilian noninstitutional population	10 760	10 959	11 152	11 332	11 496	11 682	11 833	12 016	12 023	12 451	12 561
Civilian labor force	6 517	6 572	6 778	6 824	7 004	7 175	7 405	7 686	7 912	8 224	8 215
Employed	5 884	5 874	5 978	6 095	6 320	6 556	6 762	7 013	7 290	7 663	7 703
Agriculture	18	20	15	14	17	7	12	13	19	17	9
Nonagricultural industries	5 867	5 853	5 963	6 081	6 303	6 548	6 749	7 000	7 272	7 646	7 694
Unemployed	633	698	800	729	685	620	643	673	622	561	512
Not in labor force	4 243	4 388	4 374	4 508	4 492	4 507	4 428	4 330	4 291	4 226	4 346
Both Sexes, 16 to 19 Years											
Civilian noninstitutional population	2 238	2 187	2 155	2 181	2 211	2 284	2 356	2 412	2 443	2 479	2 389
Civilian labor force	866	774	816	807	852	911	923	933	1 017	959	941
Employed	598	494	492	494	552	586	613	631	736	691	711
Agriculture	7	8	7	9	1	5	3	3	8	4	1
Nonagricultural industries	591	486	485	485	547	581	611	611	728	687	710
Unemployed	268	280	324	313	300	325	310	310	281	268	230
Not in labor force	1 372	1 413	1 339	1 374	1 360	1 372	1 434	1 434	1 427	1 520	1 448

[1]Beginning in 2003, persons who selected this race group only; persons who selected more than one race group are not included. Prior to 2003, persons who reported more than one race group were included in the group they identified as the main race.

Table 1-3. Employment Status of the Civilian Noninstitutional Population, by Sex, Age, Race, and Hispanic Origin, 1990–2010—*Continued*

(Thousands of people.)

Characteristic	2001	2002	2003	2004	2005	2006	2007	2008	2009	2010
WHITE[1]										
Women, 16 Years and Over										
Civilian noninstitutional population	91 660	92 422	93 043	93 599	94 419	95 242	96 180	96 814	97 469	97 993
Civilian labor force	54 433	54 842	55 037	55 092	55 605	56 221	56 777	57 284	57 593	57 356
Employed	52 218	52 164	52 369	52 527	53 186	53 950	54 503	54 501	53 366	52 916
Agriculture	568	560	551	520	515	510	452	482	469	513
Nonagricultural industries	51 650	51 604	51 818	52 007	52 672	53 440	54 050	54 019	52 897	52 402
Unemployed	2 215	2 678	2 668	2 565	2 419	2 271	2 274	2 782	4 227	4 440
Not in labor force	37 227	37 581	38 006	38 508	38 814	39 021	39 403	39 531	39 876	40 638
Women, 20 Years and Over										
Civilian noninstitutional population	85 526	86 266	86 905	87 430	88 200	88 942	89 790	90 400	91 078	91 683
Civilian labor force	51 218	51 717	52 099	52 212	52 643	53 286	53 925	54 508	54 976	54 957
Employed	49 369	49 448	49 823	50 040	50 589	51 359	51 996	52 124	51 231	50 997
Agriculture	537	532	522	488	492	488	423	457	444	492
Nonagricultural industries	48 831	48 916	49 301	49 552	50 097	50 871	51 572	51 667	50 787	50 505
Unemployed	1 849	2 269	2 276	2 172	2 054	1 927	1 930	2 384	3 745	3 960
Not in labor force	34 308	34 548	34 806	35 218	35 557	35 656	35 864	35 892	36 101	36 725
Both Sexes, 16 to 19 Years										
Civilian noninstitutional population	12 556	12 596	12 527	12 599	12 690	12 856	13 043	13 084	13 035	12 891
Civilian labor force	6 661	6 366	5 973	5 929	5 950	6 009	5 795	5 644	5 295	4 861
Employed	5 817	5 441	5 064	5 039	5 105	5 215	4 990	4 697	4 138	3 733
Agriculture	125	121	109	116	97	102	113	118	114	96
Nonagricultural industries	5 692	5 320	4 955	4 923	5 008	5 113	4 877	4 580	4 025	3 637
Unemployed	845	925	909	890	845	794	805	947	1 157	1 128
Not in labor force	5 894	6 230	6 554	6 669	6 739	6 847	7 248	7 440	7 740	8 030
BLACK[1]										
Both Sexes										
Civilian noninstitutional population	25 138	25 578	25 686	26 065	26 517	27 007	27 485	27 843	28 241	28 708
Civilian labor force	16 421	16 565	16 526	16 638	17 013	17 314	17 496	17 740	17 632	17 862
Employed	15 006	14 872	14 739	14 909	15 313	15 765	16 051	15 953	15 025	15 010
Agriculture	62	69	63	50	51	60	53	55	66	59
Nonagricultural industries	14 944	14 804	14 676	14 859	15 261	15 705	15 998	15 898	14 959	14 951
Unemployed	1 416	1 693	1 787	1 729	1 700	1 549	1 445	1 788	2 606	2 852
Not in labor force	8 717	9 013	9 161	9 428	9 504	9 693	9 989	10 103	10 609	10 846
Men, 16 Years and Over										
Civilian noninstitutional population	11 172	11 391	11 454	11 656	11 882	12 130	12 361	12 516	12 705	12 939
Civilian labor force	7 647	7 794	7 711	7 773	7 998	8 128	8 252	8 347	8 265	8 415
Employed	6 938	6 959	6 820	6 912	7 155	7 354	7 500	7 398	6 817	6 865
Agriculture	56	63	52	43	43	51	46	49	56	53
Nonagricultural industries	6 882	6 896	6 768	6 869	7 111	7 303	7 454	7 350	6 761	6 812
Unemployed	709	835	891	860	844	774	752	949	1 448	1 550
Not in labor force	3 525	3 597	3 743	3 884	3 884	4 002	4 110	4 169	4 441	4 524
Men, 20 Years and Over										
Civilian noninstitutional population	9 993	10 196	10 278	11 656	10 659	10 864	11 057	11 194	11 379	11 626
Civilian labor force	7 200	7 347	7 346	7 773	7 600	7 720	7 867	7 962	7 914	8 076
Employed	6 627	6 652	6 586	6 912	6 901	7 079	7 245	7 151	6 628	6 680
Agriculture	55	62	51	274	43	49	45	47	55	52
Nonagricultural industries	55	6 591	6 535	6 638	6 858	7 030	7 201	7 104	6 573	6 628
Unemployed	573	695	760	860	699	640	622	811	1 286	1 396
Not in labor force	2 792	2 848	2 932	3 884	3 060	3 144	3 189	3 232	3 465	3 550
Women, 16 Years and Over										
Civilian noninstitutional population	13 966	14 187	14 232	14 409	14 635	14 877	15 124	15 328	15 536	15 769
Civilian labor force	8 774	8 772	8 815	8 865	9 014	9 186	9 244	9 393	9 367	9 447
Employed	8 068	7 914	7 919	7 997	8 158	8 410	8 551	8 554	8 208	8 145
Agriculture	6	6	11	7	8	9	7	6	10	6
Nonagricultural industries	8 062	7 907	7 908	7 990	8 150	8 402	8 544	8 548	8 198	8 139
Unemployed	706	858	895	868	856	775	693	839	1 159	1 302
Not in labor force	5 192	5 415	5 418	5 544	5 621	5 691	5 879	5 934	6 169	6 322
Women, 20 Years and Over										
Civilian noninstitutional population	12 758	12 966	13 026	14 409	13 377	13 578	13 788	13 974	14 178	14 425
Civilian labor force	8 323	8 348	8 409	8 865	8 610	8 723	8 828	8 991	8 988	9 110
Employed	7 741	7 610	7 636	7 997	7 876	8 068	8 240	8 260	7 956	7 944
Agriculture	6	5	10	7	7	7	7	6	10	6
Nonagricultural industries	7 735	7 604	7 626	7 701	7 868	8 060	8 233	8 254	7 946	7 938
Unemployed	582	738	772	868	734	656	588	732	1 032	1 165
Not in labor force	4 434	4 618	4 618	5 544	4 768	4 854	4 960	4 982	5 190	5 315
Both Sexes, 16 to 19 Years										
Civilian noninstitutional population	2 388	2 416	2 382	2 423	2 481	2 565	2 640	2 676	28 241	28 708
Civilian labor force	898	870	771	762	803	871	801	787	17 632	17 862
Employed	637	611	516	520	536	618	566	541	15 025	15 010
Agriculture	1	2	1	0	1	3	1	1	66	59
Nonagricultural industries	637	609	515	520	535	614	564	540	14 959	14 951
Unemployed	260	260	255	241	267	253	235	246	2 606	2 852
Not in labor force	1 490	1 546	1 611	1 661	1 677	1 694	1 839	1 889	10 609	10 846

[1]Beginning in 2003, persons who selected this race group only; persons who selected more than one race group are not included. Prior to 2003, persons who reported more than one race group were included in the group they identified as the main race.

Table 1-3. Employment Status of the Civilian Noninstitutional Population, by Sex, Age, Race, and Hispanic Origin, 1990–2010—*Continued*

(Thousands of people.)

Characteristic	1990	1991	1992	1993	1994	1995	1996	1997	1998	1999	2000
HISPANIC[2]											
Both Sexes											
Civilian noninstitutional population	15 904	16 425	16 961	17 532	18 117	18 629	19 213	20 321	21 070	21 650	23 938
Civilian labor force	10 720	10 920	11 338	11 610	11 975	12 267	12 774	13 796	14 317	14 665	16 689
Employed	9 845	9 828	10 027	10 361	10 788	11 127	11 642	12 726	13 291	13 720	15 735
Agriculture	517	512	524	523	560	604	609	660	742	734	536
Nonagricultural industries	9 328	9 315	9 503	9 838	10 227	10 524	11 033	12 067	12 549	12 986	15 199
Unemployed	876	1 092	1 311	1 248	1 187	1 140	1 132	1 069	1 026	945	954
Not in labor force	5 184	5 506	5 623	5 922	6 142	6 362	6 439	6 526	6 753	6 985	7 249
Men, 16 Years and Over											
Civilian noninstitutional population	8 041	8 296	8 553	8 824	9 104	9 329	9 604	10 368	10 734	10 713	12 174
Civilian labor force	6 546	6 664	6 900	7 076	7 210	7 376	7 646	8 309	8 571	8 546	9 923
Employed	6 021	5 979	6 093	6 328	6 530	6 725	7 039	7 728	8 018	8 067	9 428
Agriculture	449	453	468	469	494	527	537	571	651	642	449
Nonagricultural industries	5 572	5 526	5 625	5 860	6 036	6 198	6 502	7 157	7 367	7 425	8 979
Unemployed	524	685	807	747	680	651	607	582	552	480	494
Not in labor force	1 495	1 632	1 654	1 749	1 894	1 952	1 957	2 059	2 164	2 167	2 252
Men, 20 Years and Over											
Civilian noninstitutional population	7 126	7 392	7 655	7 930	8 178	8 375	8 611	9 250	9 573	9 523	10 841
Civilian labor force	6 034	6 198	6 432	6 621	6 747	6 898	7 150	7 779	8 005	7 950	9 247
Employed	5 609	5 623	5 757	5 992	6 189	6 367	6 655	7 307	7 570	7 576	8 859
Agriculture	415	419	437	441	466	501	510	544	621	602	423
Nonagricultural industries	5 195	5 204	5 320	5 551	5 722	5 866	6 145	6 763	6 949	6 974	8 435
Unemployed	425	575	675	629	558	530	495	471	436	374	388
Not in labor force	1 092	1 194	1 223	1 309	1 431	1 477	1 461	1 471	1 568	1 573	1 595
Women, 16 Years and Over											
Civilian noninstitutional population	7 863	8 130	8 408	8 708	9 014	9 300	9 610	9 953	10 335	10 937	11 764
Civilian labor force	4 174	4 256	4 439	4 534	4 765	4 891	5 128	5 486	5 746	6 119	6 767
Employed	3 823	3 848	3 934	4 033	4 258	4 403	4 602	4 999	5 273	5 653	6 307
Agriculture	68	59	57	55	66	76	72	89	91	92	87
Nonagricultural industries	3 755	3 789	3 877	3 978	4 191	4 326	4 531	4 910	5 182	5 561	6 220
Unemployed	351	407	504	501	508	488	525	488	473	466	460
Not in labor force	3 689	3 874	3 969	4 174	4 248	4 409	4 482	4 466	4 589	4 819	4 997
Women, 20 Years and Over											
Civilian noninstitutional population	7 041	7 301	7 569	7 846	8 122	8 382	8 654	8 950	9 292	9 821	10 574
Civilian labor force	3 941	4 110	4 218	4 421	4 520	4 779	5 106	5 304	5 666	6 275	6 557
Employed	3 567	3 603	3 693	3 800	3 989	4 116	4 341	4 705	4 928	5 290	5 903
Agriculture	62	53	51	49	61	72	69	83	85	88	81
Nonagricultural industries	3 505	3 549	3 642	3 751	3 928	4 044	4 272	4 622	4 843	5 202	5 822
Unemployed	289	339	418	418	431	404	438	401	376	376	371
Not in labor force	3 184	3 360	3 459	3 628	3 701	3 863	3 875	3 845	3 988	4 155	4 299
Both Sexes, 16 to 19 Years											
Civilian noninstitutional population	1 737	1 732	1 737	1 756	1 818	1 872	1 948	2 121	2 204	2 307	2 523
Civilian labor force	829	781	796	771	807	850	845	911	1 007	1 049	1 168
Employed	668	602	577	570	609	645	646	714	793	854	973
Agriculture	40	41	36	33	32	31	29	33	36	45	31
Nonagricultural industries	628	562	541	537	577	614	617	682	757	809	942
Unemployed	161	179	219	201	198	205	199	197	214	196	194
Not in labor force	907	951	941	985	1 010	1 022	1 103	1 210	1 197	1 257	1 355

[2]May be of any race.

Table 1-3. Employment Status of the Civilian Noninstitutional Population, by Sex, Age, Race, and Hispanic Origin, 1990–2010—*Continued*

(Thousands of people.)

Characteristic	2001	2002	2003	2004	2005	2006	2007	2008	2009	2010
HISPANIC[2]										
Both Sexes										
Civilian noninstitutional population	24 942	25 963	27 551	28 109	29 133	30 103	31 383	32 141	32 891	33 713
Civilian labor force	17 328	17 943	18 813	19 272	19 824	20 694	21 602	22 024	22 352	22 748
Employed	16 190	16 590	17 372	17 930	18 632	19 613	20 382	20 346	19 647	19 906
Agriculture	423	448	446	441	423	428	426	441	426	480
Nonagricultural industries	15 767	16 141	16 927	17 489	18 209	19 185	19 956	19 904	19 221	19 426
Unemployed	1 138	1 353	1 441	1 342	1 191	1 081	1 220	1 678	2 706	2 843
Not in labor force	7 614	8 020	8 738	8 837	9 310	9 409	9 781	10 116	10 539	10 964
Men, 16 Years and Over										
Civilian noninstitutional population	12 695	13 221	14 098	14 417	14 962	15 473	16 154	16 524	16 897	17 359
Civilian labor force	10 279	10 609	11 288	11 587	11 985	12 488	13 005	13 255	13 310	13 511
Employed	9 668	9 845	10 479	10 832	11 337	11 887	12 310	12 248	11 640	11 800
Agriculture	345	361	350	356	350	347	352	364	344	377
Nonagricultural industries	9 323	9 484	10 129	10 476	10 987	11 540	11 958	11 884	11 296	11 423
Unemployed	611	764	809	755	647	601	695	1 007	1 670	1 711
Not in labor force	2 416	2 613	2 810	2 831	2 977	2 985	3 149	3 270	3 588	3 849
Men, 20 Years and Over										
Civilian noninstitutional population	11 386	11 928	12 797	13 082	13 586	14 046	14 649	14 971	15 305	15 693
Civilian labor force	9 595	9 977	10 756	11 020	11 408	11 888	12 403	12 629	12 730	12 958
Employed	9 100	9 341	10 063	10 385	10 872	11 391	11 827	11 769	11 256	11 438
Agriculture	328	345	336	335	341	337	337	351	332	367
Nonagricultural industries	8 773	8 996	9 727	10 050	10 532	11 054	11 490	11 418	10 924	11 071
Unemployed	495	636	693	635	536	497	576	860	1 474	1 519
Not in labor force	1 791	1 951	2 041	2 061	2 177	2 157	2 246	2 342	2 575	2 735
Women, 16 Years and Over										
Civilian noninstitutional population	12 247	12 742	13 452	13 692	14 172	14 630	15 229	15 616	15 993	16 353
Civilian labor force	7 049	7 334	7 525	7 685	7 839	8 206	8 597	8 769	9 043	9 238
Employed	6 522	6 744	6 894	7 098	7 295	7 725	8 072	8 098	8 007	8 106
Agriculture	77	87	96	85	73	80	74	77	82	103
Nonagricultural industries	6 445	6 657	6 798	7 013	7 222	7 645	7 999	8 021	7 925	8 003
Unemployed	527	590	631	587	544	480	525	672	1 036	1 132
Not in labor force	5 198	5 408	5 928	6 007	6 333	6 424	6 632	6 847	6 951	7 116
Women, 20 Years and Over										
Civilian noninstitutional population	11 049	11 528	12 211	12 420	12 858	13 262	13 791	14 127	14 463	14 776
Civilian labor force	6 863	7 096	7 096	7 257	7 377	7 735	8 108	8 274	8 560	8 789
Employed	6 121	6 367	6 541	6 752	6 913	7 321	7 662	7 707	59	7 788
Agriculture	73	84	91	78	70	77	69	75	78	101
Nonagricultural industries	6 048	6 283	6 450	6 674	6 843	7 244	7 593	7 632	7 570	7 687
Unemployed	436	496	555	504	464	414	446	567	911	1 001
Not in labor force	4 492	4 666	5 114	5 163	5 481	5 527	5 682	5 853	5 903	5 987
Both Sexes, 16 to 19 Years										
Civilian noninstitutional population	2 508	2 507	2 543	2 608	2 689	2 796	2 944	3 042	3 123	3 243
Civilian labor force	1 176	1 103	960	995	1 038	1 071	1 091	1 121	1 063	1 002
Employed	969	882	768	792	847	900	894	870	742	680
Agriculture	22	19	19	25	13	14	20	15	16	12
Nonagricultural industries	947	863	749	767	834	887	874	855	726	668
Unemployed	208	221	192	203	191	170	197	251	321	322
Not in labor force	1 331	1 404	1 583	1 612	1 651	1 725	1 853	1 921	2 061	2 242

[2]May be of any race.

Table 1-4. Employment Status of the Civilian Noninstitutional Population, by Sex, Race, and Marital Status, 1990–2010

(Thousands of people.)

Race, marital status, and year	Men				Women			
	Civilian noninstitutional population	Civilian labor force			Civilian noninstitutional population	Civilian labor force		
		Total	Employed	Unemployed		Total	Employed	Unemployed
ALL RACES								
Single								
1990	25 870	19 357	17 405	1 952	21 901	14 612	13 336	1 276
1991	26 197	19 411	17 011	2 400	22 173	14 681	13 198	1 482
1992	26 436	19 709	17 098	2 611	22 475	14 872	13 263	1 609
1993	26 570	19 706	17 261	2 445	22 713	15 031	13 484	1 547
1994	26 786	19 786	17 604	2 181	23 000	15 333	13 847	1 486
1995	26 918	19 841	17 833	2 007	23 151	15 467	14 053	1 413
1996	27 387	20 071	18 055	2 016	23 623	15 842	14 403	1 439
1997	28 311	20 689	18 783	1 906	24 285	16 492	15 037	1 455
1998	28 693	21 037	19 240	1 798	24 941	17 087	15 755	1 332
1999	29 104	21 351	19 686	1 665	25 576	17 575	16 267	1 308
2000	29 887	22 002	20 339	1 663	25 920	17 849	16 628	1 221
2001	30 646	22 285	20 298	1 988	26 462	18 021	16 635	1 386
2002	31 072	22 289	19 983	2 306	26 999	18 203	16 583	1 621
2003	31 691	22 297	19 841	2 457	27 802	18 397	16 723	1 674
2004	32 422	22 776	20 395	2 381	28 228	18 616	16 995	1 621
2005	33 125	23 214	21 006	2 209	29 046	19 183	17 588	1 595
2006	33 931	23 974	21 907	2 067	29 624	19 474	17 978	1 496
2007	34 650	24 276	22 143	2 132	30 219	19 745	18 322	1 422
2008	35 274	24 643	21 938	2 705	30 980	20 231	18 513	1 717
2009	36 087	24 640	20 628	4 011	31 500	20 224	17 800	2 424
2010	37 137	24 985	20 850	4 135	32 548	20 592	17 950	2 642
Married, Spouse Present								
1990	53 793	42 275	40 829	1 446	52 917	30 901	29 714	1 188
1991	54 158	42 303	40 429	1 875	53 169	31 112	29 698	1 415
1992	54 509	42 491	40 341	2 150	53 501	31 700	30 100	1 600
1993	55 178	42 834	40 935	1 899	53 838	31 980	30 499	1 482
1994	55 560	43 005	41 414	1 592	54 155	32 888	31 536	1 352
1995	56 100	43 472	42 048	1 424	54 716	33 359	32 063	1 296
1996	56 363	43 739	42 417	1 322	54 970	33 618	32 406	1 211
1997	56 396	43 808	42 642	1 167	54 915	33 802	32 755	1 047
1998	56 670	43 957	42 923	1 034	55 331	33 857	32 872	985
1999	57 089	44 244	43 254	990	56 178	34 372	33 450	921
2000	58 167	44 987	44 078	908	57 557	35 146	34 209	937
2001	58 448	45 233	44 007	1 226	57 610	35 236	34 153	1 083
2002	59 102	45 766	44 116	1 650	58 165	35 477	34 153	1 323
2003	60 063	46 404	44 653	1 751	59 069	36 046	34 695	1 352
2004	60 412	46 550	45 084	1 466	59 278	35 845	34 600	1 244
2005	60 545	46 771	45 483	1 287	59 205	35 941	34 773	1 168
2006	60 751	46 842	45 700	1 142	59 576	36 314	35 272	1 042
2007	61 760	47 520	46 314	1 206	60 474	36 881	35 832	1 049
2008	61 794	47 450	45 860	1 590	60 554	37 194	35 869	1 325
2009	61 773	47 114	43 998	3 115	60 675	37 264	35 207	2 057
2010	61 254	46 430	43 292	3 138	60 257	36 742	34 582	2 160
Divorced, Widowed, or Separated								
1990	10 714	7 378	6 871	508	23 968	11 315	10 639	676
1991	10 924	7 454	6 783	671	24 304	11 385	10 600	786
1992	11 325	7 763	7 001	762	24 559	11 570	10 689	881
1993	11 584	7 864	7 153	711	24 955	11 784	10 927	856
1994	12 008	8 026	7 432	594	25 304	12 018	11 227	791
1995	12 160	8 048	7 496	551	25 539	12 118	11 407	712
1996	12 456	8 276	7 735	541	25 791	12 397	11 691	706
1997	13 009	8 764	8 260	504	26 218	12 742	12 082	660
1998	13 394	8 965	8 530	435	26 190	12 771	12 143	628
1999	13 528	8 918	8 507	411	26 276	12 909	12 324	585
2000	13 910	9 291	8 888	403	27 135	13 308	12 748	559
2001	14 188	9 367	8 892	476	27 738	13 592	12 949	642
2002	14 411	9 445	8 804	641	27 821	13 683	12 846	837
2003	14 680	9 537	8 838	699	27 862	13 828	12 986	842
2004	14 875	9 654	9 045	608	28 141	13 961	13 133	828
2005	15 481	10 048	9 484	563	28 680	14 163	13 396	768
2006	15 923	10 440	9 895	545	29 010	14 385	13 675	709
2007	15 763	10 341	9 797	544	29 001	14 362	13 638	724
2008	16 044	10 427	9 688	739	29 141	14 342	13 494	849
2009	16 275	10 370	9 043	1 326	29 490	14 531	13 201	1 330
2010	16 783	10 570	9 217	1 352	29 851	14 570	13 173	1 397

Note: See notes and definitions for information on historical comparability.

Table 1-4. Employment Status of the Civilian Noninstitutional Population, by Sex, Race, and Marital Status, 1990–2010—*Continued*

(Thousands of people.)

Race, marital status, and year	Men				Women			
	Civilian noninstitutional population	Civilian labor force			Civilian noninstitutional population	Civilian labor force		
		Total	Employed	Unemployed		Total	Employed	Unemployed
WHITE[1]								
Single								
1990	20 746	15 993	14 617	1 376	16 555	11 522	10 729	794
1991	20 899	15 989	14 233	1 756	16 569	11 497	10 557	939
1992	21 025	16 129	14 285	1 844	16 684	11 502	10 526	976
1993	20 974	16 033	14 303	1 730	16 768	11 613	10 633	980
1994	21 071	16 074	14 539	1 535	16 936	11 805	10 885	920
1995	21 132	16 080	14 674	1 406	17 046	11 830	10 967	864
1996	21 454	16 285	14 891	1 394	17 282	11 977	11 099	878
1997	22 236	16 810	15 507	1 303	17 728	12 322	11 443	879
1998	22 513	17 007	15 746	1 261	18 247	12 742	11 945	797
1999	22 788	17 272	16 116	1 157	18 635	13 029	12 206	823
2000	23 266	17 659	16 504	1 154	18 808	13 215	12 449	766
2001	23 979	17 970	16 561	1 409	19 253	13 368	12 491	877
2002	24 289	17 924	16 289	1 635	19 625	13 556	12 550	1 006
2003	24 419	17 755	16 031	1 723	19 924	13 462	12 461	1 001
2004	24 929	18 090	16 435	1 655	20 210	13 597	12 628	969
2005	25 436	18 338	16 833	1 505	20 702	13 906	12 957	949
2006	26 012	18 928	17 500	1 428	21 085	14 109	13 199	909
2007	26 431	19 063	17 580	1 483	21 408	14 255	13 357	897
2008	27 023	19 395	17 474	1 920	22 064	14 648	13 578	1 070
2009	27 559	19 392	16 528	2 864	22 371	14 733	13 193	1 540
2010	28 250	19 582	16 653	2 929	23 000	14 803	13 171	1 632
Married, Spouse Present								
1990	47 841	37 515	36 338	1 177	47 240	27 271	26 285	986
1991	48 137	37 507	35 923	1 585	47 456	27 479	26 290	1 189
1992	48 416	37 671	35 886	1 785	47 705	27 951	26 623	1 329
1993	48 937	37 953	36 396	1 557	47 944	28 221	26 993	1 228
1994	49 169	38 008	36 719	1 288	48 120	29 017	27 888	1 129
1995	49 597	38 376	37 211	1 165	48 497	29 360	28 290	1 070
1996	49 800	38 616	37 522	1 094	48 684	29 517	28 496	1 020
1997	49 719	38 593	37 636	957	48 542	29 664	28 809	855
1998	49 901	38 629	37 793	836	48 722	29 534	28 727	808
1999	50 091	38 765	37 968	797	49 296	29 806	29 056	749
2000	50 775	39 169	38 451	717	50 194	30 344	29 582	762
2001	50 850	39 246	38 265	981	50 077	30 336	29 472	864
2002	51 284	39 580	38 261	1 319	50 489	30 511	29 463	1 048
2003	51 859	39 908	38 529	1 379	50 957	30 805	29 740	1 065
2004	51 992	39 935	38 774	1 161	50 939	30 544	29 549	996
2005	52 034	40 141	39 130	1 011	50 865	30 599	29 676	922
2006	52 035	40 103	39 207	896	51 200	30 950	30 111	839
2007	52 775	40 559	39 594	965	51 868	31 363	30 533	830
2008	52 708	40 404	39 157	1 247	51 637	31 456	30 367	1 089
2009	52 693	40 142	37 644	2 498	51 786	31 584	29 891	1 694
2010	52 211	39 489	36 999	2 490	51 364	31 161	29 412	1 748
Divorced, Widowed, or Separated								
1990	8 782	6 131	5 748	382	19 461	9 016	8 544	471
1991	8 941	6 159	5 641	518	19 757	9 111	8 538	573
1992	9 210	6 368	5 788	580	19 931	9 216	8 561	654
1993	9 459	6 498	5 957	541	20 206	9 382	8 764	618
1994	9 819	6 644	6 193	451	20 439	9 533	8 965	569
1995	10 005	6 689	6 261	428	20 638	9 613	9 087	526
1996	10 234	6 883	6 474	408	20 862	9 831	9 325	506
1997	10 622	7 236	6 855	382	21 147	10 068	9 607	461
1998	10 937	7 398	7 064	334	21 157	10 104	9 656	449
1999	11 050	7 375	7 056	320	21 225	10 261	9 834	427
2000	11 329	7 638	7 333	305	21 847	10 521	10 105	416
2001	11 623	7 750	7 386	364	22 330	10 729	10 255	474
2002	11 789	7 804	7 299	505	22 308	10 775	10 151	624
2003	11 971	7 846	7 305	541	22 162	10 769	10 168	602
2004	12 124	7 969	7 503	466	22 450	10 950	10 350	600
2005	12 558	8 215	7 800	415	22 853	11 101	10 552	548
2006	12 974	8 583	8 176	407	22 957	11 162	10 640	523
2007	12 867	8 536	8 115	421	22 904	11 159	10 613	547
2008	12 995	8 552	7 992	560	23 112	11 180	10 556	624
2009	13 181	8 517	7 459	1 058	23 312	11 275	10 282	993
2010	13 620	8 657	7 601	1 056	23 630	11 392	10 333	1 059

Note: See notes and definitions for information on historical comparability.

[1]Beginning in 2003, persons who selected this race group only; persons who selected more than one race group are not included. Prior to 2003, persons who reported more than one race group were included in the group they identified as their main race.

Table 1-4. Employment Status of the Civilian Noninstitutional Population, by Sex, Race, and Marital Status, 1990–2010—*Continued*

(Thousands of people.)

Race, marital status, and year	Men				Women			
	Civilian noninstitutional population	Civilian labor force			Civilian noninstitutional population	Civilian labor force		
		Total	Employed	Unemployed		Total	Employed	Unemployed
ALL OTHER RACES								
Single								
1990	5 124	3 364	2 788	576	5 346	3 090	2 607	482
1991	5 298	3 422	2 778	644	5 604	3 184	2 641	543
1992	5 411	3 580	2 813	767	5 791	3 370	2 737	633
1993	5 596	3 673	2 958	715	5 945	3 418	2 851	567
1994	5 715	3 712	3 065	646	6 064	3 528	2 962	566
1995	5 786	3 761	3 159	601	6 105	3 637	3 086	549
1996	5 933	3 786	3 164	622	6 341	3 865	3 304	561
1997	6 075	3 879	3 276	603	6 557	4 170	3 594	576
1998	6 180	4 030	3 494	537	6 694	4 345	3 810	535
1999	6 316	4 079	3 570	508	6 941	4 546	4 061	485
2000	6 621	4 343	3 835	509	7 112	4 634	4 179	455
2001	6 667	4 315	3 737	579	7 209	4 653	4 144	509
2002	6 783	4 365	3 694	671	7 374	4 647	4 033	615
2003	7 272	4 542	3 810	734	7 878	4 935	4 262	673
2004	7 493	4 686	3 960	726	8 018	5 019	4 367	652
2005	7 689	4 876	4 173	704	8 344	5 277	4 631	646
2006	7 919	5 046	4 407	639	8 539	5 365	4 779	587
2007	8 219	5 213	4 563	649	8 811	5 490	4 965	525
2008	8 251	5 248	4 464	785	8 916	5 583	4 935	647
2009	8 528	5 248	4 100	1 147	9 129	5 491	4 607	884
2010	8 887	5 403	4 197	1 206	9 548	5 789	4 779	1 010
Married, Spouse Present								
1990	5 952	4 760	4 491	269	5 677	3 630	3 429	202
1991	6 021	4 796	4 506	290	5 713	3 633	3 408	226
1992	6 093	4 820	4 455	365	5 796	3 749	3 477	271
1993	6 241	4 881	4 539	342	5 894	3 759	3 506	254
1994	6 391	4 997	4 695	304	6 035	3 871	3 648	223
1995	6 503	5 096	4 837	259	6 219	3 999	3 773	226
1996	6 563	5 123	4 895	228	6 286	4 101	3 910	191
1997	6 677	5 215	5 006	210	6 373	4 138	3 946	192
1998	6 769	5 328	5 130	198	6 609	4 323	4 145	177
1999	6 998	5 479	5 286	193	6 882	4 566	4 394	172
2000	7 392	5 818	5 627	191	7 363	4 802	4 627	175
2001	7 598	5 987	5 742	245	7 533	4 900	4 681	219
2002	7 818	6 186	5 855	331	7 676	4 966	4 690	275
2003	8 204	6 496	6 124	372	8 112	5 241	4 955	287
2004	8 420	6 615	6 310	305	8 339	5 301	5 051	248
2005	8 511	6 630	6 353	276	8 340	5 342	5 097	246
2006	8 716	6 739	6 493	246	8 376	5 364	5 161	203
2007	8 985	6 961	6 720	241	8 606	5 518	5 299	219
2008	9 086	7 046	6 703	343	8 917	5 738	5 502	236
2009	9 080	6 972	6 354	617	8 889	5 680	5 316	363
2010	9 043	6 941	6 293	648	8 893	5 581	5 170	412
Divorced, Widowed, or Separated								
1990	1 932	1 247	1 123	126	4 507	2 299	2 095	205
1991	1 983	1 295	1 142	153	4 547	2 274	2 062	213
1992	2 115	1 395	1 213	182	4 628	2 354	2 128	227
1993	2 125	1 366	1 196	170	4 749	2 402	2 163	238
1994	2 189	1 382	1 239	143	4 865	2 485	2 262	222
1995	2 155	1 359	1 235	123	4 901	2 505	2 320	186
1996	2 222	1 393	1 261	133	4 929	2 566	2 366	200
1997	2 387	1 528	1 405	122	5 071	2 674	2 475	199
1998	2 457	1 567	1 466	101	5 033	2 667	2 487	179
1999	2 478	1 543	1 451	91	5 051	2 648	2 490	158
2000	2 581	1 653	1 555	98	5 288	2 787	2 643	143
2001	2 565	1 617	1 506	112	5 408	2 863	2 694	168
2002	2 622	1 641	1 505	136	5 513	2 908	2 695	213
2003	2 709	1 691	1 533	158	5 700	3 059	2 818	240
2004	2 751	1 685	1 542	142	5 691	3 011	2 783	228
2005	2 923	1 833	1 684	148	5 827	3 062	2 844	220
2006	2 949	1 857	1 719	138	6 053	3 223	3 035	186
2007	2 896	1 805	1 682	123	6 097	3 203	3 025	177
2008	3 049	1 875	1 696	179	6 029	3 162	2 938	225
2009	3 094	1 853	1 584	268	6 178	3 256	2 919	337
2010	3 163	1 913	1 616	296	6 221	3 178	2 840	338

Note: See notes and definitions for information on historical comparability.

Table 1-5. Employment Status of the Civilian Noninstitutional Population, by Region, Division, State, and Selected Territory, 2009–2010

(Thousands of people, percent.)

Region, division, and state	2009						2010					
	Civilian noninstitutional population	Civilian labor force					Civilian noninstitutional population	Civilian labor force				
		Total	Participation rate	Employed	Unemployed	Unemploy-ment rate		Total	Participation rate	Employed	Unemployed	Unemploy-ment rate
UNITED STATES[1]	235 801	154 142	65.4	139 877	14 265	9.3	237 830	153 889	64.7	139 064	14 825	9.6
Northeast	43 515	28 321	65.1	25 950	2 370	8.4	43 762	28 243	64.5	25 784	2 459	8.7
New England	11 455	7 733	67.5	7 100	633	8.2	11 532	7 770	67.4	7 109	660	8.5
Connecticut	2 747	1 887	68.7	1 730	157	8.3	2 765	1 897	68.6	1 724	173	9.1
Maine	1 065	698	65.5	641	57	8.2	1 066	697	65.4	642	55	7.9
Massachusetts	5 237	3 477	66.4	3 190	286	8.2	5 282	3 494	66.1	3 197	297	8.5
New Hampshire	1 057	745	70.5	698	47	6.3	1 063	744	70.0	699	45	6.1
Rhode Island	842	566	67.2	505	61	10.8	845	576	68.2	509	67	11.6
Vermont	507	360	71.0	335	25	6.9	510	361	70.8	338	22	6.2
Middle Atlantic	32 060	20 587	64.2	18 850	1 737	8.4	32 230	20 473	63.5	18 675	1 799	8.8
New Jersey	6 766	4 527	66.9	4 116	410	9.1	6 812	4 502	66.1	4 077	426	9.5
New York	15 354	9 678	63.0	8 864	813	8.4	15 431	9 631	62.4	8 807	824	8.6
Pennsylvania	9 939	6 383	64.2	5 870	514	8.0	9 987	6 340	63.5	5 791	549	8.7
Midwest	51 568	34 637	67.2	31 317	3 319	9.6	51 830	34 480	66.5	31 237	3 243	9.4
East North Central	35 927	23 667	65.9	21 155	2 513	10.6	36 072	23 538	65.3	21 091	2 448	10.4
Illinois	9 877	6 588	66.7	5 928	660	10.0	9 936	6 646	66.9	5 965	681	10.3
Indiana	4 907	3 184	64.9	2 852	332	10.4	4 939	3 142	63.6	2 823	320	10.2
Michigan	7 772	4 859	62.5	4 211	648	13.3	7 780	4 790	61.6	4 193	597	12.5
Ohio	8 954	5 936	66.3	5 335	601	10.1	8 976	5 898	65.7	5 303	595	10.1
Wisconsin	4 417	3 101	70.2	2 829	271	8.7	4 440	3 063	69.0	2 807	255	8.3
West North Central	15 640	10 969	70.1	10 163	806	7.4	15 759	10 942	69.4	10 146	796	7.3
Iowa	2 334	1 665	71.3	1 572	94	5.6	2 348	1 671	71.2	1 568	103	6.1
Kansas	2 129	1 508	70.8	1 402	107	7.1	2 146	1 502	70.0	1 397	106	7.0
Minnesota	4 083	2 951	72.3	2 712	238	8.1	4 112	2 963	72.1	2 746	217	7.3
Missouri	4 610	3 051	66.2	2 768	283	9.3	4 642	3 014	64.9	2 726	289	9.6
Nebraska	1 363	981	72.0	934	47	4.8	1 375	977	71.1	931	45	4.7
North Dakota	504	369	73.2	353	16	4.3	510	370	72.5	356	15	3.9
South Dakota	618	444	71.8	422	22	5.0	625	444	71.0	423	21	4.8
South	85 998	55 051	64.0	50 166	4 885	8.9	87 017	55 210	63.4	50 060	5 150	9.3
South Atlantic	45 522	29 378	64.5	26 621	2 758	9.4	46 029	29 303	63.7	26 388	2 915	9.9
Delaware	686	435	63.4	400	35	8.0	693	426	61.5	390	36	8.5
District of Columbia	486	332	68.3	300	32	9.6	496	334	67.3	301	33	9.9
Florida	14 589	9 139	62.6	8 209	930	10.2	14 736	9 224	62.6	8 159	1 065	11.5
Georgia	7 301	4 766	65.3	4 302	464	9.7	7 396	4 694	63.5	4 214	480	10.2
Maryland	4 397	3 001	68.3	2 786	215	7.1	4 443	2 981	67.1	2 758	223	7.5
North Carolina	7 118	4 555	64.0	4 065	490	10.8	7 200	4 513	62.7	4 036	476	10.6
South Carolina	3 490	2 175	62.3	1 928	247	11.3	3 530	2 165	61.3	1 923	242	11.2
Virginia	6 001	4 180	69.7	3 895	284	6.8	6 077	4 185	68.9	3 896	289	6.9
West Virginia	1 453	797	54.9	735	62	7.7	1 458	782	53.6	711	71	9.1
East South Central	14 019	8 597	61.3	7 722	875	10.2	14 125	8 581	60.8	7 727	855	10.0
Alabama	3 621	2 171	60.0	1 960	211	9.7	3 646	2 127	58.3	1 925	202	9.5
Kentucky	3 329	2 079	62.5	1 858	222	10.7	3 354	2 084	62.1	1 866	218	10.5
Mississippi	2 200	1 296	58.9	1 171	125	9.6	2 211	1 313	59.4	1 176	137	10.4
Tennessee	4 868	3 052	62.7	2 734	317	10.4	4 913	3 057	62.2	2 759	297	9.7
West South Central	26 458	17 076	64.5	15 823	1 253	7.3	26 863	17 326	64.5	15 946	1 380	8.0
Arkansas	2 204	1 356	61.5	1 256	100	7.4	2 221	1 353	60.9	1 247	107	7.9
Louisiana	3 389	2 060	60.8	1 924	136	6.6	3 420	2 082	60.9	1 926	155	7.5
Oklahoma	2 774	1 753	63.2	1 637	116	6.6	2 802	1 755	62.6	1 631	124	7.1
Texas	18 091	11 907	65.8	11 006	900	7.6	18 419	12 136	65.9	11 142	994	8.2
West	54 236	35 817	66.0	32 161	3 656	10.2	54 927	35 767	65.1	31 812	3 955	11.1
Mountain	16 613	11 108	66.9	10 135	973	8.8	16 841	11 084	65.8	10 014	1 070	9.7
Arizona	4 951	3 157	63.8	2 851	306	9.7	5 027	3 176	63.2	2 860	316	10.0
Colorado	3 838	2 728	71.1	2 502	226	8.3	3 899	2 687	68.9	2 448	240	8.9
Idaho	1 150	751	65.3	693	58	7.7	1 163	758	65.2	687	71	9.3
Montana	767	496	64.7	465	31	6.3	773	497	64.3	461	36	7.2
Nevada	2 000	1 354	67.7	1 184	170	12.5	2 015	1 350	67.0	1 150	201	14.9
New Mexico	1 516	942	62.1	876	66	7.0	1 535	953	62.1	873	80	8.4
Utah	1 972	1 383	70.1	1 285	98	7.1	2 007	1 368	68.2	1 262	106	7.7
Wyoming	418	297	71.1	278	19	6.5	422	294	69.7	273	20	7.0
Pacific	37 622	24 709	65.7	22 026	2 683	10.9	38 086	24 683	64.8	21 798	2 885	11.7
Alaska	512	359	70.1	331	28	7.8	518	361	69.7	332	29	8.0
California	27 947	18 204	65.1	16 142	2 063	11.3	28 293	18 176	64.2	15 916	2 260	12.4
Hawaii	982	632	64.4	589	43	6.8	989	629	63.6	587	42	6.6
Oregon	3 008	1 980	65.8	1 760	221	11.1	3 039	1 985	65.3	1 770	215	10.8
Washington	5 174	3 534	68.3	3 206	329	9.3	5 247	3 532	67.3	3 192	340	9.6

Note: Data refer to place of residence. Region and division data are derived from summing the component states. Sub-national data reflect revised population controls and model reestimation.

[1]Due to separate processing and weighing procedures, totals for the United States differ from the results obtained by aggregating data for regions, divisions, or states.

Table 1-6. Civilian Noninstitutional Population, by Age, Race, Sex, and Hispanic Origin, 1948–2010

(Thousands of people.)

Race, Hispanic origin, sex, and year	16 years and over	16 to 19 years			20 years and over						
		Total	16 to 17 years	18 to 19 years	Total	20 to 24 years	25 to 34 years	35 to 44 years	45 to 54 years	55 to 64 years	65 years and over
ALL RACES											
Both Sexes											
1948	103 068	8 449	4 265	4 185	94 618	11 530	22 610	20 097	16 771	12 885	10 720
1949	103 994	8 215	4 139	4 079	95 778	11 312	22 822	20 401	17 002	13 201	11 035
1950	104 995	8 143	4 076	4 068	96 851	11 080	23 013	20 681	17 240	13 469	11 363
1951	104 621	7 865	4 096	3 771	96 755	10 167	22 843	20 863	17 464	13 692	11 724
1952	105 231	7 922	4 234	3 689	97 305	9 389	23 044	21 137	17 716	13 889	12 126
1953	107 056	8 014	4 241	3 773	99 041	8 960	23 266	21 922	17 991	13 830	13 075
1954	108 321	8 224	4 336	3 889	100 095	8 885	23 304	22 135	18 305	14 085	13 375
1955	109 683	8 364	4 440	3 925	101 318	9 036	23 249	22 348	18 643	14 309	13 728
1956	110 954	8 434	4 482	3 953	102 518	9 271	23 072	22 567	19 012	14 516	14 075
1957	112 265	8 612	4 587	4 026	103 653	9 486	22 849	22 786	19 424	14 727	14 376
1958	113 727	8 986	4 872	4 114	104 737	9 733	22 563	23 025	19 832	14 923	14 657
1959	115 329	9 618	5 337	4 282	105 711	9 975	22 201	23 207	20 203	15 134	14 985
1960	117 245	10 187	5 573	4 615	107 056	10 273	21 998	23 437	20 601	15 409	15 336
1961	118 771	10 513	5 462	5 052	108 255	10 583	21 829	23 585	20 893	15 675	15 685
1962	120 153	10 652	5 503	5 150	109 500	10 852	21 503	23 797	20 916	15 874	16 554
1963	122 416	11 370	6 301	5 070	111 045	11 464	21 400	23 948	21 144	16 138	16 945
1964	124 485	12 111	6 974	5 139	112 372	12 017	21 367	23 940	21 452	16 442	17 150
1965	126 513	12 930	6 936	5 995	113 582	12 442	21 417	23 832	21 728	16 727	17 432
1966	128 058	13 592	6 914	6 679	114 463	12 638	21 543	23 579	21 977	17 007	17 715
1967	129 874	13 480	7 003	6 480	116 391	13 421	22 057	23 313	22 256	17 310	18 029
1968	132 028	13 698	7 200	6 499	118 328	13 891	22 912	23 036	22 534	17 614	18 338
1969	134 335	14 095	7 422	6 673	120 238	14 488	23 645	22 709	22 806	17 930	18 657
1970	137 085	14 519	7 643	6 876	122 566	15 323	24 435	22 489	23 059	18 250	19 007
1971	140 216	15 022	7 849	7 173	125 193	16 345	25 337	22 274	23 244	18 581	19 406
1972	144 126	15 510	8 076	7 435	128 614	17 143	26 740	22 258	23 338	19 007	20 023
1973	147 096	15 840	8 227	7 613	131 253	17 692	28 172	22 287	23 431	19 281	20 389
1974	150 120	16 180	8 373	7 809	133 938	17 994	29 439	22 461	23 578	19 517	20 945
1975	153 153	16 418	8 419	7 999	136 733	18 595	30 710	22 526	23 535	19 844	21 525
1976	156 150	16 614	8 442	8 171	139 536	19 109	31 953	22 796	23 409	20 185	22 083
1977	159 033	16 688	8 482	8 206	142 345	19 582	33 117	23 296	23 197	20 557	22 597
1978	161 910	16 695	8 484	8 211	145 216	20 007	34 091	24 099	22 977	20 875	23 166
1979	164 863	16 657	8 389	8 268	148 205	20 353	35 261	24 861	22 752	21 210	23 767
1980	167 745	16 543	8 279	8 264	151 202	20 635	36 558	25 578	22 563	21 520	24 350
1981	170 130	16 214	8 068	8 145	153 916	20 820	37 777	26 291	22 422	21 756	24 850
1982	172 271	15 763	7 714	8 049	156 508	20 845	38 492	27 611	22 264	21 909	25 387
1983	174 215	15 274	7 385	7 889	158 941	20 799	39 147	28 932	22 167	22 003	25 892
1984	176 383	14 735	7 196	7 538	161 648	20 688	39 999	30 251	22 226	22 052	26 433
1985	178 206	14 506	7 232	7 274	163 700	20 097	40 670	31 379	22 418	22 140	26 997
1986	180 587	14 496	7 386	7 110	166 091	19 569	41 731	32 550	22 732	22 011	27 497
1987	182 753	14 606	7 501	7 104	168 147	18 970	42 297	33 755	23 183	21 835	28 108
1988	184 613	14 527	7 284	7 243	170 085	18 434	42 611	34 784	24 004	21 641	28 612
1989	186 393	14 223	6 886	7 338	172 169	18 025	42 845	35 977	24 744	21 406	29 173
1990	189 164	14 520	6 893	7 626	174 644	18 902	42 976	37 719	25 081	20 719	29 247
1991	190 925	14 073	6 901	7 173	176 852	18 963	42 688	39 116	25 709	20 675	29 700
1992	192 805	13 840	6 907	6 933	178 965	18 846	42 278	39 852	27 206	20 604	30 179
1993	194 838	13 935	7 010	6 925	180 903	18 642	41 771	40 733	28 549	20 574	30 634
1994	196 814	14 196	7 245	6 951	182 619	18 353	41 306	41 534	29 778	20 635	31 012
1995	198 584	14 511	7 407	7 104	184 073	17 864	40 798	42 254	30 974	20 735	31 448
1996	200 591	14 934	7 678	7 256	185 656	17 409	40 252	43 086	32 167	20 990	31 751
1997	203 133	15 365	7 861	7 504	187 769	17 442	39 559	43 883	33 391	21 505	31 989
1998	205 220	15 644	7 895	7 749	189 576	17 593	38 778	44 299	34 373	22 296	32 237
1999	207 753	16 040	8 060	7 979	191 713	17 968	37 976	44 635	35 587	23 064	32 484
2000	212 577	15 912	7 978	7 934	196 664	18 311	38 703	44 312	37 642	24 230	33 466
2001	215 092	15 929	8 020	7 909	199 164	18 877	38 505	44 195	38 904	25 011	33 672
2002	217 570	15 994	8 099	7 895	201 576	19 348	38 472	43 894	39 711	26 343	33 808
2003	221 168	16 096	8 561	7 535	205 072	19 801	39 021	43 746	40 522	27 728	34 253
2004	223 357	16 222	8 574	7 648	207 134	20 197	38 939	43 226	41 245	28 919	34 609
2005	226 082	16 398	8 778	7 619	209 685	20 276	39 064	43 005	42 107	30 165	35 068
2006	228 815	16 678	9 089	7 589	212 137	20 265	39 230	42 753	42 901	31 375	35 613
2007	231 867	16 982	9 222	7 760	214 885	20 427	39 751	42 401	43 544	32 533	36 228
2008	233 788	17 075	9 133	7 942	216 713	20 409	39 993	41 699	43 960	33 491	37 161
2009	235 801	17 043	8 944	8 100	218 757	20 524	40 280	40 919	44 365	34 671	37 998
2010	237 830	16 901	8 943	7 957	220 929	21 047	40 903	40 090	44 297	35 885	38 706

Table 1-6. Civilian Noninstitutional Population, by Age, Race, Sex, and Hispanic Origin, 1948–2010
—Continued

(Thousands of people.)

Race, Hispanic origin, sex, and year	16 years and over	16 to 19 years			20 years and over						
		Total	16 to 17 years	18 to 19 years	Total	20 to 24 years	25 to 34 years	35 to 44 years	45 to 54 years	55 to 64 years	65 years and over
ALL RACES											
Men											
1948	49 996	4 078	2 128	1 951	45 918	5 527	10 767	9 798	8 290	6 441	5 093
1949	50 321	3 946	2 062	1 884	46 378	5 405	10 871	9 926	8 379	6 568	5 226
1950	50 725	3 962	2 043	1 920	46 763	5 270	10 963	10 034	8 472	6 664	5 357
1951	49 727	3 725	2 039	1 687	46 001	4 451	10 709	10 049	8 551	6 737	5 503
1952	49 700	3 767	2 121	1 647	45 932	3 788	10 855	10 164	8 655	6 798	5 670
1953	50 750	3 823	2 122	1 701	46 927	3 482	11 020	10 632	8 878	6 798	6 119
1954	51 395	3 953	2 174	1 780	47 441	3 509	11 067	10 718	9 018	6 885	6 241
1955	52 109	4 022	2 225	1 798	48 086	3 708	11 068	10 804	9 164	6 960	6 380
1956	52 723	4 020	2 238	1 783	48 704	3 970	10 983	10 889	9 322	7 032	6 505
1957	53 315	4 083	2 284	1 800	49 231	4 166	10 889	10 965	9 499	7 109	6 602
1958	54 033	4 293	2 435	1 858	49 740	4 339	10 787	11 076	9 675	7 179	6 683
1959	54 793	4 652	2 681	1 971	50 140	4 488	10 625	11 149	9 832	7 259	6 785
1960	55 662	4 963	2 805	2 159	50 698	4 679	10 514	11 230	10 000	7 373	6 901
1961	56 286	5 112	2 742	2 371	51 173	4 844	10 440	11 286	10 112	7 483	7 006
1962	56 831	5 150	2 764	2 386	51 681	4 925	10 207	11 389	10 162	7 610	7 386
1963	57 921	5 496	3 162	2 334	52 425	5 240	10 165	11 476	10 274	7 740	7 526
1964	58 847	5 866	3 503	2 364	52 981	5 520	10 144	11 466	10 402	7 873	7 574
1965	59 782	6 318	3 488	2 831	53 463	5 701	10 182	11 427	10 512	7 990	7 649
1966	60 262	6 658	3 478	3 180	53 603	5 663	10 224	11 294	10 598	8 099	7 723
1967	60 905	6 537	3 528	3 010	54 367	5 977	10 495	11 161	10 705	8 218	7 809
1968	61 847	6 683	3 634	3 049	55 165	6 127	10 944	11 040	10 819	8 336	7 897
1969	62 898	6 928	3 741	3 187	55 969	6 379	11 309	10 890	10 935	8 464	7 990
1970	64 304	7 145	3 848	3 299	57 157	6 861	11 750	10 810	11 052	8 590	8 093
1971	65 942	7 430	3 954	3 477	58 511	7 511	12 227	10 721	11 129	8 711	8 208
1972	67 835	7 705	4 081	3 624	60 130	8 061	12 911	10 762	11 167	8 895	8 330
1973	69 292	7 855	4 152	3 703	61 436	8 429	13 641	10 746	11 202	8 990	8 426
1974	70 808	8 012	4 231	3 781	62 796	8 600	14 262	10 834	11 315	9 140	8 641
1975	72 291	8 134	4 252	3 882	64 158	8 950	14 899	10 874	11 298	9 286	8 852
1976	73 759	8 244	4 266	3 978	65 515	9 237	15 528	11 010	11 243	9 444	9 053
1977	75 193	8 288	4 290	4 000	66 904	9 477	16 108	11 260	11 144	9 616	9 297
1978	76 576	8 309	4 295	4 014	68 268	9 693	16 598	11 665	11 045	9 758	9 509
1979	78 020	8 310	4 251	4 060	69 709	9 873	17 193	12 046	10 944	9 907	9 746
1980	79 398	8 260	4 195	4 064	71 138	10 023	17 833	12 400	10 861	10 042	9 979
1981	80 511	8 092	4 087	4 005	72 419	10 116	18 427	12 758	10 797	10 151	10 170
1982	81 523	7 879	3 911	3 968	73 644	10 136	18 787	13 410	10 726	10 215	10 371
1983	82 531	7 659	3 750	3 908	74 872	10 140	19 143	14 067	10 689	10 261	10 573
1984	83 605	7 386	3 655	3 731	76 219	10 108	19 596	14 719	10 724	10 285	10 788
1985	84 469	7 275	3 689	3 586	77 195	9 746	19 864	15 265	10 844	10 392	11 084
1986	85 798	7 275	3 768	3 507	78 523	9 498	20 498	15 858	10 986	10 336	11 347
1987	86 899	7 335	3 824	3 510	79 565	9 195	20 781	16 475	11 215	10 267	11 632
1988	87 857	7 304	3 715	3 588	80 553	8 931	20 937	17 008	11 625	10 193	11 859
1989	88 762	7 143	3 524	3 619	81 619	8 743	21 080	17 590	11 981	10 092	12 134
1990	90 377	7 347	3 534	3 813	83 030	9 320	21 117	18 529	12 238	9 778	12 049
1991	91 278	7 134	3 548	3 586	84 144	9 367	20 977	19 213	12 554	9 780	12 254
1992	92 270	7 023	3 542	3 481	85 247	9 326	20 792	19 585	13 271	9 776	12 496
1993	93 332	7 076	3 595	3 481	86 256	9 216	20 569	20 037	13 944	9 773	12 717
1994	94 355	7 203	3 718	3 486	87 151	9 074	20 361	20 443	14 545	9 810	12 918
1995	95 178	7 367	3 794	3 573	87 811	8 835	20 079	20 800	15 111	9 856	13 130
1996	96 206	7 600	3 955	3 645	88 606	8 611	19 775	21 222	15 674	9 997	13 327
1997	97 715	7 836	4 053	3 783	89 879	8 706	19 478	21 669	16 276	10 282	13 469
1998	98 758	7 968	4 059	3 909	90 790	8 804	19 094	21 857	16 773	10 649	13 613
1999	99 722	8 167	4 143	4 024	91 555	8 899	18 565	21 969	17 335	11 008	13 779
2000	101 964	8 089	4 096	3 993	93 875	9 101	19 106	21 683	18 365	11 583	14 037
2001	103 282	8 101	4 102	3 999	95 181	9 368	19 056	21 643	18 987	11 972	14 155
2002	104 585	8 146	4 140	4 006	96 439	9 627	19 037	21 523	19 379	12 641	14 233
2003	106 435	8 163	4 365	3 797	98 272	9 878	19 347	21 463	19 784	13 305	14 496
2004	107 710	8 234	4 318	3 916	99 476	10 125	19 358	21 255	20 160	13 894	14 684
2005	109 151	8 317	4 481	3 836	100 835	10 181	19 446	21 177	20 585	14 502	14 944
2006	110 605	8 459	4 613	3 846	102 145	10 191	19 568	21 082	20 991	15 095	15 219
2007	112 173	8 618	4 658	3 960	103 555	10 291	19 858	20 910	21 313	15 658	15 525
2008	113 113	8 660	4 625	4 035	104 453	10 249	19 999	20 567	21 512	16 123	16 002
2009	114 136	8 643	4 548	4 095	105 493	10 284	20 167	20 199	21 731	16 698	16 414
2010	115 174	8 578	4 540	4 038	106 596	10 550	20 465	19 807	21 713	17 291	16 769

Table 1-6. Civilian Noninstitutional Population, by Age, Race, Sex, and Hispanic Origin, 1948–2010
—*Continued*

(Thousands of people.)

Race, Hispanic origin, sex, and year	16 years and over	16 to 19 years			20 years and over						
		Total	16 to 17 years	18 to 19 years	Total	20 to 24 years	25 to 34 years	35 to 44 years	45 to 54 years	55 to 64 years	65 years and over
ALL RACES											
Women											
1948	53 071	4 371	2 137	2 234	48 700	6 003	11 843	10 299	8 481	6 444	5 627
1949	53 670	4 269	2 077	2 195	49 400	5 907	11 951	10 475	8 623	6 633	5 809
1950	54 270	4 181	2 033	2 148	50 088	5 810	12 050	10 647	8 768	6 805	6 006
1951	54 895	4 140	2 057	2 084	50 754	5 716	12 134	10 814	8 913	6 955	6 221
1952	55 529	4 155	2 113	2 042	51 373	5 601	12 189	10 973	9 061	7 091	6 456
1953	56 305	4 191	2 119	2 072	52 114	5 478	12 246	11 290	9 113	7 032	6 956
1954	56 925	4 271	2 162	2 109	52 654	5 376	12 237	11 417	9 287	7 200	7 134
1955	57 574	4 342	2 215	2 127	53 232	5 328	12 181	11 544	9 479	7 349	7 348
1956	58 228	4 414	2 244	2 170	53 814	5 301	12 089	11 678	9 690	7 484	7 570
1957	58 951	4 529	2 303	2 226	54 421	5 320	11 960	11 821	9 925	7 618	7 774
1958	59 690	4 693	2 437	2 256	54 997	5 394	11 776	11 949	10 157	7 744	7 974
1959	60 534	4 966	2 656	2 311	55 570	5 487	11 576	12 058	10 371	7 875	8 200
1960	61 582	5 224	2 768	2 456	56 358	5 594	11 484	12 207	10 601	8 036	8 435
1961	62 484	5 401	2 720	2 681	57 082	5 739	11 389	12 299	10 781	8 192	8 679
1962	63 321	5 502	2 739	2 764	57 819	5 927	11 296	12 408	10 754	8 264	9 168
1963	64 494	5 874	3 139	2 736	58 620	6 224	11 235	12 472	10 870	8 398	9 419
1964	65 637	6 245	3 471	2 775	59 391	6 497	11 223	12 474	11 050	8 569	9 576
1965	66 731	6 612	3 448	3 164	60 119	6 741	11 235	12 405	11 216	8 737	9 783
1966	67 795	6 934	3 436	3 499	60 860	6 975	11 319	12 285	11 379	8 908	9 992
1967	68 968	6 943	3 475	3 470	62 026	7 445	11 562	12 152	11 551	9 092	10 220
1968	70 179	7 015	3 566	3 450	63 164	7 764	11 968	11 996	11 715	9 278	10 441
1969	71 436	7 167	3 681	3 486	64 269	8 109	12 336	11 819	11 871	9 466	10 667
1970	72 782	7 373	3 796	3 578	65 408	8 462	12 684	11 679	12 008	9 659	10 914
1971	74 274	7 591	3 895	3 697	66 682	8 834	13 110	11 553	12 115	9 870	11 198
1972	76 290	7 805	3 994	3 811	68 484	9 082	13 829	11 597	12 171	10 113	11 693
1973	77 804	7 985	4 076	3 909	69 819	9 263	14 531	11 541	12 229	10 290	11 963
1974	79 312	8 168	4 142	4 028	71 144	9 393	15 177	11 627	12 263	10 377	12 304
1975	80 860	8 285	4 168	4 117	72 576	9 645	15 811	11 652	12 237	10 558	12 673
1976	82 390	8 370	4 176	4 194	74 020	9 872	16 425	11 786	12 166	10 742	13 030
1977	83 840	8 400	4 193	4 206	75 441	10 103	17 008	12 036	12 053	10 940	13 300
1978	85 334	8 386	4 189	4 197	76 948	10 315	17 493	12 435	11 932	11 118	13 658
1979	86 843	8 347	4 139	4 208	78 496	10 480	18 070	12 815	11 808	11 303	14 021
1980	88 348	8 283	4 083	4 200	80 065	10 612	18 725	13 177	11 701	11 478	14 372
1981	89 618	8 121	3 981	4 140	81 497	10 705	19 350	13 533	11 625	11 605	14 680
1982	90 748	7 884	3 804	4 081	82 864	10 709	19 705	14 201	11 538	11 694	15 017
1983	91 684	7 616	3 635	3 981	84 069	10 660	20 004	14 865	11 478	11 742	15 319
1984	92 778	7 349	3 542	3 807	85 429	10 580	20 403	15 532	11 501	11 768	15 645
1985	93 736	7 231	3 543	3 688	86 506	10 351	20 805	16 114	11 574	11 748	15 913
1986	94 789	7 221	3 618	3 603	87 567	10 072	21 233	16 692	11 746	11 675	16 150
1987	95 853	7 271	3 677	3 594	88 583	9 776	21 516	17 279	11 968	11 567	16 476
1988	96 756	7 224	3 569	3 655	89 532	9 503	21 674	17 776	12 378	11 448	16 753
1989	97 630	7 080	3 361	3 719	90 550	9 282	21 765	18 387	12 763	11 314	17 039
1990	98 787	7 173	3 359	3 813	91 614	9 582	21 859	19 190	12 843	10 941	17 198
1991	99 646	6 939	3 353	3 586	92 708	9 597	21 711	19 903	13 155	10 895	17 446
1992	100 535	6 818	3 366	3 452	93 718	9 520	21 486	20 267	13 935	10 828	17 682
1993	101 506	6 859	3 415	3 444	94 647	9 426	21 202	20 696	14 605	10 801	17 917
1994	102 460	6 993	3 528	3 465	95 467	9 279	20 945	21 091	15 233	10 825	18 094
1995	103 406	7 144	3 613	3 531	96 262	9 029	20 719	21 454	15 862	10 879	18 318
1996	104 385	7 335	3 723	3 612	97 050	8 798	20 477	21 865	16 493	10 993	18 424
1997	105 418	7 528	3 808	3 721	97 889	8 736	20 081	22 214	17 115	11 224	18 520
1998	106 462	7 676	3 835	3 840	98 786	8 790	19 683	22 442	17 600	11 646	18 625
1999	108 031	7 873	3 917	3 955	100 158	9 069	19 411	22 666	18 251	12 056	18 705
2000	110 613	7 823	3 882	3 941	102 790	9 211	19 597	22 628	19 276	12 647	19 430
2001	111 811	7 828	3 917	3 910	103 983	9 509	19 449	22 552	19 917	13 039	19 517
2002	112 985	7 848	3 959	3 889	105 136	9 721	19 435	22 371	20 332	13 703	19 575
2003	114 733	7 934	4 195	3 738	106 800	9 924	19 674	22 283	20 738	14 423	19 758
2004	115 647	7 989	4 257	3 732	107 658	10 072	19 581	21 970	21 085	15 025	19 925
2005	116 931	8 081	4 297	3 784	108 850	10 095	19 618	21 828	21 521	15 663	20 125
2006	118 210	8 218	4 476	3 742	109 992	10 074	19 662	21 671	21 910	16 280	20 394
2007	119 694	8 364	4 564	3 800	111 330	10 137	19 893	21 491	22 231	16 876	20 703
2008	120 675	8 415	4 508	3 907	112 260	10 160	19 994	21 132	22 448	17 367	21 160
2009	121 665	8 401	4 396	4 004	113 265	10 240	20 113	20 721	22 633	17 973	21 584
2010	122 656	8 323	4 403	3 919	114 333	10 497	20 438	20 283	22 584	18 594	21 937

Table 1-6. Civilian Noninstitutional Population, by Age, Race, Sex, and Hispanic Origin, 1948–2010
—Continued

(Thousands of people.)

Race, Hispanic origin, sex, and year	16 years and over	16 to 19 years			20 years and over						
		Total	16 to 17 years	18 to 19 years	Total	20 to 24 years	25 to 34 years	35 to 44 years	45 to 54 years	55 to 64 years	65 years and over
WHITE											
Both Sexes											
1954	97 705	7 180	3 786	3 394	90 524	7 794	20 818	19 915	16 569	12 993	12 438
1955	98 880	7 292	3 874	3 419	91 586	7 912	20 742	20 110	16 869	13 169	12 785
1956	99 976	7 346	3 908	3 438	92 629	8 106	20 564	20 314	17 198	13 341	13 105
1957	101 119	7 505	4 007	3 498	93 612	8 293	20 342	20 514	17 562	13 518	13 383
1958	102 392	7 843	4 271	3 573	94 547	8 498	20 063	20 734	17 924	13 681	13 645
1959	103 803	8 430	4 707	3 725	95 370	8 697	19 715	20 893	18 257	13 858	13 951
1960	105 282	8 924	4 909	4 016	96 355	8 927	19 470	21 049	18 578	14 070	14 260
1961	106 604	9 211	4 785	4 427	97 390	9 203	19 289	21 169	18 845	14 304	14 581
1962	107 715	9 343	4 818	4 526	98 371	9 484	18 974	21 293	18 872	14 450	15 297
1963	109 705	9 978	5 549	4 430	99 725	10 069	18 867	21 398	19 082	14 681	15 629
1964	111 534	10 616	6 137	4 481	100 916	10 568	18 838	21 375	19 360	14 957	15 816
1965	113 284	11 319	6 049	5 271	101 963	10 935	18 882	21 258	19 604	15 215	16 070
1966	114 566	11 862	5 993	5 870	102 702	11 094	18 989	21 005	19 822	15 469	16 322
1967	116 100	11 682	6 051	5 632	104 417	11 797	19 464	20 745	20 067	15 745	16 602
1968	117 948	11 840	6 225	5 616	106 107	12 184	20 245	20 474	20 310	16 018	16 875
1969	119 913	12 179	6 418	5 761	107 733	12 677	20 892	20 156	20 546	16 305	17 156
1970	122 174	12 521	6 591	5 931	109 652	13 359	21 546	19 929	20 760	16 591	17 469
1971	124 758	12 937	6 750	6 189	111 821	14 208	22 295	19 694	20 907	16 884	17 833
1972	127 906	13 301	6 910	6 392	114 603	14 897	23 555	19 673	20 950	17 250	18 278
1973	130 097	13 533	7 021	6 512	116 563	15 264	24 685	19 532	20 991	17 484	18 607
1974	132 417	13 784	7 114	6 671	118 632	15 502	25 711	19 628	21 061	17 645	19 085
1975	134 790	13 941	7 132	6 808	120 849	15 980	26 746	19 641	20 981	17 918	19 587
1976	137 106	14 055	7 125	6 930	123 050	16 368	27 757	19 827	20 816	18 220	20 064
1977	139 380	14 095	7 150	6 944	125 285	16 728	28 703	20 231	20 575	18 540	20 508
1978	141 612	14 060	7 132	6 928	127 552	17 038	29 453	20 932	20 322	18 799	21 007
1979	143 894	13 994	7 029	6 964	129 900	17 284	30 371	21 579	20 058	19 071	21 538
1980	146 122	13 854	6 912	6 943	132 268	17 484	31 407	22 174	19 837	19 316	22 050
1981	147 908	13 516	6 704	6 813	134 392	17 609	32 367	22 778	19 666	19 485	22 487
1982	149 441	13 076	6 383	6 693	136 366	17 579	32 863	23 910	19 478	19 591	22 945
1983	150 805	12 623	6 089	6 534	138 183	17 492	33 286	25 027	19 349	19 625	23 403
1984	152 347	12 147	5 918	6 228	140 200	17 304	33 889	26 124	19 348	19 629	23 906
1985	153 679	11 900	5 922	5 978	141 780	16 853	34 450	27 100	19 405	19 620	24 352
1986	155 432	11 879	6 036	5 843	143 553	16 353	35 293	28 062	19 587	19 477	24 780
1987	156 958	11 939	6 110	5 829	145 020	15 808	35 667	29 036	19 965	19 242	25 301
1988	158 194	11 838	5 893	5 945	146 357	15 276	35 876	29 818	20 652	18 996	25 739
1989	159 338	11 530	5 506	6 023	147 809	14 879	35 951	30 774	21 287	18 743	26 175
1990	160 625	11 630	5 464	6 166	148 996	15 538	35 661	31 739	21 535	18 204	26 319
1991	161 759	11 200	5 451	5 749	150 558	15 516	35 342	32 854	22 052	18 074	26 721
1992	162 972	11 004	5 478	5 526	151 968	15 354	34 885	33 305	23 364	17 951	27 108
1993	164 289	11 078	5 562	5 516	153 210	15 087	34 365	33 919	24 456	17 892	27 493
1994	165 555	11 264	5 710	5 554	154 291	14 708	33 865	34 582	25 435	17 924	27 776
1995	166 914	11 468	5 822	5 646	155 446	14 313	33 355	35 222	26 418	17 986	28 153
1996	168 317	11 822	6 026	5 796	156 495	13 907	32 852	35 810	27 403	18 136	28 387
1997	169 993	12 181	6 213	5 968	157 812	13 983	32 091	36 325	28 388	18 511	28 514
1998	171 478	12 439	6 264	6 176	159 039	14 138	31 286	36 610	29 132	19 231	28 642
1999	173 085	12 700	6 342	6 358	160 385	14 394	30 516	36 755	30 048	19 855	28 818
2000	176 220	12 535	6 264	6 271	163 685	14 552	30 948	36 261	31 550	20 757	29 617
2001	178 111	12 556	6 291	6 265	165 556	15 001	30 770	36 113	32 475	21 434	29 762
2002	179 783	12 596	6 346	6 250	167 187	15 360	30 676	35 750	33 012	22 540	29 849
2003	181 292	12 527	6 629	5 898	168 765	15 536	30 789	35 352	33 466	23 589	30 033
2004	182 643	12 599	6 561	6 038	170 045	15 817	30 585	34 845	34 005	24 549	30 245
2005	184 446	12 690	6 768	5 921	171 757	15 871	30 592	34 554	34 649	25 534	30 556
2006	186 264	12 856	6 981	5 875	173 408	15 848	30 661	34 217	35 228	26 486	30 968
2007	188 253	13 043	7 026	6 018	175 210	15 945	31 011	33 770	35 665	27 392	31 426
2008	189 540	13 084	6 962	6 122	176 456	15 914	31 234	33 093	35 941	28 109	32 165
2009	190 902	13 035	6 775	6 261	177 867	15 963	31 471	32 378	36 166	29 022	32 867
2010	192 075	12 891	6 799	6 091	179 184	16 280	31 813	31 647	36 064	29 983	33 396

Table 1-6. Civilian Noninstitutional Population, by Age, Race, Sex, and Hispanic Origin, 1948–2010
—Continued

(Thousands of people.)

Race, Hispanic origin, sex, and year	16 years and over	16 to 19 years			20 years and over						
		Total	16 to 17 years	18 to 19 years	Total	20 to 24 years	25 to 34 years	35 to 44 years	45 to 54 years	55 to 64 years	65 years and over
WHITE											
Men											
1954	46 462	3 455	1 902	1 553	43 007	3 074	9 948	9 688	8 172	6 341	5 787
1955	47 076	3 507	1 945	1 563	43 569	3 241	9 936	9 768	8 303	6 398	5 923
1956	47 602	3 500	1 955	1 546	44 102	3 464	9 851	9 848	8 446	6 455	6 038
1957	48 119	3 556	2 000	1 557	44 563	3 638	9 758	9 917	8 605	6 518	6 127
1958	48 745	3 747	2 140	1 607	44 998	3 783	9 656	10 018	8 765	6 574	6 203
1959	49 408	4 079	2 370	1 710	45 329	3 903	9 499	10 081	8 909	6 639	6 298
1960	50 065	4 349	2 476	1 874	45 716	4 054	9 373	10 131	9 042	6 721	6 395
1961	50 608	4 479	2 407	2 073	46 129	4 204	9 290	10 178	9 148	6 819	6 490
1962	51 054	4 520	2 426	2 094	46 534	4 306	9 080	10 239	9 191	6 917	6 801
1963	52 031	4 827	2 792	2 036	47 204	4 610	9 039	10 309	9 297	7 031	6 919
1964	52 869	5 148	3 090	2 059	47 721	4 862	9 024	10 301	9 417	7 153	6 963
1965	53 681	5 541	3 050	2 492	48 140	5 017	9 056	10 262	9 516	7 261	7 028
1966	54 061	5 820	3 023	2 798	48 241	4 974	9 085	10 136	9 592	7 362	7 092
1967	54 608	5 671	3 058	2 613	48 937	5 257	9 339	10 013	9 688	7 474	7 167
1968	55 434	5 787	3 153	2 635	49 647	5 376	9 752	9 902	9 790	7 585	7 242
1969	56 348	6 005	3 246	2 759	50 343	5 589	10 074	9 760	9 895	7 705	7 320
1970	57 516	6 179	3 329	2 851	51 336	5 988	10 441	9 678	9 999	7 822	7 409
1971	58 900	6 420	3 412	3 008	52 481	6 546	10 841	9 578	10 066	7 933	7 517
1972	60 473	6 627	3 503	3 125	53 845	7 042	11 495	9 568	10 078	8 089	7 573
1973	61 577	6 737	3 555	3 182	54 842	7 312	12 075	9 514	10 099	8 178	7 664
1974	62 791	6 851	3 604	3 247	55 942	7 476	12 599	9 564	10 165	8 288	7 849
1975	63 981	6 929	3 609	3 320	57 052	7 766	13 131	9 578	10 134	8 413	8 031
1976	65 132	6 993	3 609	3 384	58 138	7 987	13 655	9 674	10 063	8 556	8 203
1977	66 301	7 024	3 625	3 399	59 278	8 175	14 139	9 880	9 957	8 708	8 420
1978	67 401	7 022	3 619	3 404	60 378	8 335	14 528	10 236	9 845	8 826	8 608
1979	68 547	7 007	3 568	3 439	61 540	8 470	15 008	10 563	9 730	8 949	8 820
1980	69 634	6 941	3 508	3 433	62 694	8 581	15 529	10 863	9 636	9 059	9 027
1981	70 480	6 764	3 401	3 363	63 715	8 644	16 005	11 171	9 560	9 139	9 195
1982	71 211	6 556	3 249	3 307	64 655	8 621	16 260	11 756	9 463	9 188	9 367
1983	71 922	6 340	3 098	3 242	65 581	8 597	16 499	12 314	9 408	9 208	9 556
1984	72 723	6 113	3 019	3 094	66 610	8 522	16 816	12 853	9 434	9 217	9 768
1985	73 373	5 987	3 026	2 961	67 386	8 246	17 042	13 337	9 488	9 262	10 010
1986	74 390	5 977	3 084	2 894	68 413	8 002	17 564	13 840	9 578	9 201	10 229
1987	75 189	6 015	3 125	2 890	69 175	7 729	17 754	14 338	9 771	9 101	10 481
1988	75 855	5 968	3 015	2 953	69 887	7 473	17 867	14 743	10 114	9 001	10 688
1989	76 468	5 813	2 817	2 996	70 654	7 279	17 908	15 237	10 434	8 900	10 897
1990	77 369	5 913	2 809	3 103	71 457	7 764	17 766	15 770	10 598	8 680	10 879
1991	77 977	5 704	2 805	2 899	72 274	7 748	17 615	16 340	10 856	8 640	11 074
1992	78 651	5 611	2 819	2 792	73 040	7 676	17 403	16 579	11 513	8 602	11 268
1993	79 371	5 650	2 862	2 788	73 721	7 545	17 158	16 900	12 058	8 590	11 470
1994	80 059	5 748	2 938	2 810	74 311	7 357	16 915	17 247	12 545	8 618	11 629
1995	80 733	5 854	2 995	2 859	74 879	7 163	16 653	17 567	13 028	8 653	11 815
1996	81 489	6 035	3 099	2 936	75 454	6 971	16 395	17 868	13 518	8 734	11 968
1997	82 577	6 257	3 209	3 048	76 320	7 087	16 043	18 163	14 030	8 929	12 067
1998	83 352	6 386	3 233	3 153	76 966	7 170	15 644	18 310	14 400	9 286	12 155
1999	83 930	6 498	3 266	3 232	77 432	7 244	15 150	18 340	14 834	9 581	12 283
2000	85 370	6 404	3 224	3 181	78 966	7 329	15 528	18 003	15 578	10 028	12 501
2001	86 452	6 422	3 229	3 194	80 029	7 564	15 486	17 960	16 047	10 369	12 604
2002	87 361	6 439	3 251	3 189	80 922	7 750	15 470	17 792	16 317	10 918	12 676
2003	88 249	6 390	3 378	3 012	81 860	7 856	15 569	17 620	16 555	11 442	12 818
2004	89 044	6 429	3 301	3 129	82 615	8 024	15 486	17 404	16 834	11 922	12 946
2005	90 027	6 471	3 464	3 006	83 556	8 057	15 507	17 286	17 169	12 415	13 123
2006	91 021	6 555	3 551	3 004	84 466	8 052	15 567	17 467	17 467	12 891	13 346
2007	92 073	6 653	3 567	3 086	85 420	8 113	15 762	16 927	17 686	13 341	13 591
2008	92 725	6 669	3 550	3 120	86 056	8 072	15 884	16 599	17 830	13 698	13 972
2009	93 433	6 644	3 469	3 175	86 789	8 076	16 011	16 260	17 956	14 154	14 332
2010	94 082	6 580	3 473	3 107	87 502	8 240	16 174	15 920	17 919	14 634	14 615

Table 1-6. Civilian Noninstitutional Population, by Age, Race, Sex, and Hispanic Origin, 1948–2010
—Continued

(Thousands of people.)

Race, Hispanic origin, sex, and year	16 years and over	16 to 19 years			20 years and over						
		Total	16 to 17 years	18 to 19 years	Total	20 to 24 years	25 to 34 years	35 to 44 years	45 to 54 years	55 to 64 years	65 years and over
WHITE											
Women											
1954	51 242	3 725	1 884	1 841	47 517	4 720	10 870	10 227	8 397	6 652	6 651
1955	51 802	3 785	1 929	1 856	48 017	4 671	10 806	10 342	8 566	6 771	6 862
1956	52 373	3 846	1 953	1 892	48 527	4 642	10 713	10 466	8 752	6 886	7 067
1957	52 998	3 949	2 007	1 941	49 049	4 655	10 584	10 597	8 957	7 000	7 256
1958	53 645	4 096	2 131	1 966	49 549	4 715	10 407	10 716	9 159	7 107	7 442
1959	54 392	4 351	2 337	2 015	50 041	4 794	10 216	10 812	9 348	7 219	7 653
1960	55 214	4 575	2 433	2 142	50 639	4 873	10 097	10 918	9 536	7 349	7 865
1961	55 993	4 732	2 378	2 354	51 261	4 999	9 999	10 991	9 697	7 485	8 091
1962	56 660	4 823	2 392	2 432	51 837	5 178	9 894	11 054	9 681	7 533	8 496
1963	57 672	5 151	2 757	2 394	52 521	5 459	9 828	11 089	9 785	7 650	8 710
1964	58 663	5 468	3 047	2 422	53 195	5 706	9 814	11 074	9 943	7 804	8 853
1965	59 601	5 778	2 999	2 779	53 823	5 918	9 826	10 996	10 088	7 954	9 042
1966	60 503	6 042	2 970	3 072	54 461	6 120	9 904	10 869	10 230	8 107	9 230
1967	61 491	6 011	2 993	3 019	55 480	6 540	10 125	10 732	10 379	8 271	9 435
1968	62 512	6 053	3 072	2 981	56 460	6 809	10 493	10 572	10 520	8 433	9 633
1969	63 563	6 174	3 172	3 002	57 390	7 089	10 818	10 396	10 651	8 600	9 836
1970	64 656	6 342	3 262	3 080	58 315	7 370	11 105	10 251	10 761	8 769	10 060
1971	65 857	6 518	3 338	3 180	59 340	7 662	11 454	10 117	10 841	8 951	10 315
1972	67 431	6 673	3 407	3 267	60 758	7 855	12 060	10 105	10 872	9 161	10 705
1973	68 517	6 796	3 466	3 331	61 721	7 951	12 610	10 018	10 891	9 306	10 943
1974	69 623	6 933	3 510	3 424	62 690	8 026	13 112	10 064	10 896	9 356	11 236
1975	70 810	7 011	3 523	3 488	63 798	8 214	13 615	10 063	10 847	9 505	11 556
1976	71 974	7 062	3 516	3 546	64 912	8 381	14 102	10 153	10 752	9 664	11 860
1977	73 077	7 071	3 525	3 545	66 007	8 553	14 564	10 351	10 618	9 832	12 088
1978	74 213	7 038	3 513	3 524	67 174	8 704	14 926	10 696	10 476	9 974	12 399
1979	75 347	6 987	3 460	3 527	68 360	8 815	15 363	11 017	10 327	10 122	12 717
1980	76 489	6 914	3 403	3 511	69 575	8 904	15 878	11 313	10 201	10 256	13 022
1981	77 428	6 752	3 303	3 449	70 677	8 965	16 362	11 606	10 106	10 346	13 292
1982	78 230	6 519	3 134	3 385	71 711	8 959	16 603	12 154	10 015	10 402	13 579
1983	78 884	6 282	2 991	3 292	72 601	8 895	16 788	12 714	9 941	10 418	13 847
1984	79 624	6 034	2 899	3 135	73 590	8 782	17 073	13 271	9 914	10 412	14 138
1985	80 306	5 912	2 895	3 017	74 394	8 607	17 409	13 762	9 917	10 358	14 342
1986	81 042	5 902	2 953	2 949	75 140	8 351	17 728	14 223	10 009	10 277	14 551
1987	81 769	5 924	2 985	2 939	75 845	8 079	17 913	14 698	10 194	10 141	14 820
1988	82 340	5 869	2 878	2 991	76 470	7 804	18 009	15 074	10 537	9 994	15 052
1989	82 871	5 716	2 690	3 027	77 154	7 600	18 043	15 537	10 853	9 843	15 278
1990	83 256	5 717	2 654	3 063	77 539	7 774	17 895	15 969	10 937	9 524	15 440
1991	83 781	5 497	2 646	2 850	78 285	7 768	17 726	16 514	11 196	9 435	15 647
1992	84 321	5 393	2 659	2 734	78 928	7 678	17 482	16 727	11 851	9 350	15 841
1993	84 918	5 428	2 700	2 728	79 490	7 542	17 206	17 019	12 398	9 302	16 023
1994	85 496	5 516	2 772	2 744	79 980	7 351	16 950	17 335	12 890	9 306	16 148
1995	86 181	5 614	2 827	2 787	80 567	7 150	16 702	17 654	13 390	9 333	16 337
1996	86 828	5 787	2 927	2 860	81 041	6 936	16 457	17 943	13 884	9 402	16 419
1997	87 417	5 924	3 004	2 920	81 492	6 896	16 047	18 162	14 357	9 582	16 447
1998	88 126	6 053	3 031	3 023	82 073	6 969	15 642	18 300	14 732	9 944	16 486
1999	89 156	6 202	3 076	3 127	82 953	7 150	15 366	18 415	15 214	10 274	16 536
2000	90 850	6 131	3 041	3 090	84 718	7 223	15 420	18 258	15 972	10 729	17 116
2001	91 660	6 134	3 062	3 071	85 526	7 438	15 284	18 153	16 428	11 065	17 158
2002	92 422	6 157	3 096	3 061	86 266	7 611	15 207	17 958	16 695	11 622	17 173
2003	93 043	6 137	3 251	2 886	86 905	7 680	15 220	17 731	16 911	12 147	17 216
2004	93 599	6 169	3 260	2 909	87 430	7 794	15 099	17 441	17 170	12 627	17 299
2005	94 419	6 219	3 304	2 915	88 200	7 814	15 086	17 268	17 480	13 119	17 433
2006	95 242	6 301	3 429	2 871	88 942	7 796	15 094	17 074	17 760	13 596	17 623
2007	96 180	6 390	3 458	2 932	89 790	7 832	15 249	16 843	17 979	14 051	17 835
2008	96 814	6 414	3 412	3 003	90 400	7 842	15 349	16 493	18 111	14 411	18 193
2009	97 469	6 391	3 306	3 086	91 078	7 887	15 460	16 118	18 210	14 868	18 535
2010	97 993	6 311	3 327	2 984	91 683	8 040	15 640	15 727	18 146	15 349	18 781

Table 1-6. Civilian Noninstitutional Population, by Age, Race, Sex, and Hispanic Origin, 1948–2010
—*Continued*

(Thousands of people.)

Race, Hispanic origin, sex, and year	16 years and over	16 to 19 years			20 years and over						
		Total	16 to 17 years	18 to 19 years	Total	20 to 24 years	25 to 34 years	35 to 44 years	45 to 54 years	55 to 64 years	65 years and over
BLACK											
Both Sexes											
1973	14 917	2 095	1 095	1 000	12 823	2 132	2 957	2 333	2 156	1 616	1 628
1974	15 329	2 137	1 122	1 014	13 192	2 137	3 103	2 382	2 202	1 679	1 689
1975	15 751	2 191	1 146	1 046	13 560	2 228	3 258	2 395	2 211	1 717	1 755
1976	16 196	2 264	1 165	1 098	13 932	2 303	3 412	2 435	2 220	1 736	1 826
1977	16 605	2 273	1 175	1 097	14 332	2 400	3 566	2 493	2 225	1 765	1 883
1978	16 970	2 270	1 169	1 101	14 701	2 483	3 717	2 547	2 226	1 794	1 932
1979	17 397	2 276	1 167	1 109	15 121	2 556	3 899	2 615	2 240	1 831	1 980
1980	17 824	2 289	1 171	1 119	15 535	2 606	4 095	2 687	2 249	1 870	2 030
1981	18 219	2 288	1 161	1 127	15 931	2 642	4 290	2 758	2 260	1 913	2 069
1982	18 584	2 252	1 119	1 134	16 332	2 697	4 438	2 887	2 263	1 935	2 113
1983	18 925	2 225	1 092	1 133	16 700	2 734	4 607	2 999	2 260	1 964	2 135
1984	19 348	2 161	1 056	1 105	17 187	2 783	4 789	3 167	2 288	1 977	2 183
1985	19 664	2 160	1 083	1 077	17 504	2 649	4 873	3 290	2 372	2 060	2 259
1986	19 989	2 137	1 090	1 048	17 852	2 625	5 026	3 410	2 413	2 079	2 298
1987	20 352	2 163	1 123	1 040	18 189	2 578	5 139	3 563	2 460	2 097	2 352
1988	20 692	2 179	1 130	1 049	18 513	2 527	5 234	3 716	2 524	2 110	2 402
1989	21 021	2 176	1 116	1 060	18 846	2 479	5 308	3 900	2 587	2 118	2 454
1990	21 477	2 238	1 101	1 138	19 239	2 554	5 407	4 328	2 618	1 970	2 362
1991	21 799	2 187	1 085	1 102	19 612	2 585	5 419	4 538	2 682	1 985	2 403
1992	22 147	2 155	1 086	1 069	19 992	2 615	5 404	4 722	2 809	1 996	2 446
1993	22 521	2 181	1 113	1 069	20 339	2 600	5 409	4 886	2 941	2 016	2 487
1994	22 879	2 211	1 168	1 044	20 668	2 616	5 362	5 038	3 084	2 045	2 524
1995	23 246	2 284	1 198	1 086	20 962	2 554	5 337	5 178	3 244	2 079	2 571
1996	23 604	2 356	1 238	1 118	21 248	2 519	5 311	5 290	3 408	2 110	2 609
1997	24 003	2 412	1 255	1 158	21 591	2 515	5 279	5 410	3 571	2 164	2 653
1998	24 373	2 443	1 241	1 202	21 930	2 546	5 221	5 510	3 735	2 224	2 695
1999	24 855	2 479	1 250	1 229	22 376	2 615	5 197	5 609	3 919	2 295	2 741
2000	24 902	2 389	1 205	1 183	22 513	2 611	5 089	5 488	4 168	2 407	2 750
2001	25 138	2 388	1 212	1 176	22 750	2 686	5 003	5 467	4 343	2 478	2 775
2002	25 578	2 416	1 235	1 181	23 162	2 779	5 015	5 460	4 513	2 571	2 823
2003	25 686	2 382	1 309	1 074	23 304	2 773	4 978	5 387	4 628	2 692	2 846
2004	26 065	2 423	1 350	1 072	23 643	2 821	5 020	5 335	4 739	2 827	2 899
2005	26 517	2 481	1 341	1 140	24 036	2 835	5 075	5 311	4 869	2 980	2 967
2006	27 007	2 565	1 408	1 157	24 442	2 851	5 133	5 302	4 992	3 137	3 027
2007	27 485	2 640	1 497	1 143	24 845	2 891	5 210	5 271	5 110	3 284	3 080
2008	27 843	2 676	1 459	1 217	25 168	2 914	5 262	5 198	5 183	3 429	3 182
2009	28 241	2 684	1 462	1 221	25 557	2 973	5 349	5 109	5 290	3 596	3 239
2010	28 708	2 657	1 438	1 219	26 051	3 097	5 491	5 031	5 322	3 773	3 337
BLACK											
Men											
1973	6 704	1 007	539	468	5 697	979	1 327	1 027	962	718	684
1974	6 875	1 027	554	471	5 848	956	1 381	1 055	997	753	707
1975	7 060	1 051	565	486	6 009	1 002	1 452	1 060	997	769	730
1976	7 265	1 099	579	518	6 167	1 036	1 521	1 077	999	774	756
1977	7 431	1 102	586	516	6 329	1 080	1 589	1 102	998	786	774
1978	7 577	1 093	579	514	6 484	1 120	1 657	1 128	995	794	789
1979	7 761	1 100	581	519	6 661	1 151	1 738	1 159	998	809	804
1980	7 944	1 110	583	526	6 834	1 171	1 828	1 191	999	825	822
1981	8 117	1 110	577	534	7 007	1 189	1 914	1 224	1 003	844	835
1982	8 283	1 097	556	542	7 186	1 225	1 983	1 282	1 003	848	846
1983	8 447	1 087	542	545	7 360	1 254	2 068	1 333	1 000	857	847
1984	8 654	1 055	524	531	7 599	1 292	2 164	1 411	1 012	858	861
1985	8 790	1 059	543	517	7 731	1 202	2 180	1 462	1 060	924	902
1986	8 956	1 049	548	503	7 907	1 195	2 264	1 517	1 072	934	924
1987	9 128	1 065	566	499	8 063	1 173	2 320	1 587	1 092	944	947
1988	9 289	1 074	569	505	8 215	1 151	2 367	1 656	1 121	951	970
1989	9 439	1 075	575	501	8 364	1 128	2 403	1 741	1 145	956	989
1990	9 573	1 094	555	540	8 479	1 144	2 412	1 968	1 183	855	917
1991	9 725	1 072	546	526	8 652	1 168	2 417	2 060	1 211	864	933
1992	9 896	1 056	544	512	8 840	1 194	2 409	2 150	1 268	868	951
1993	10 083	1 075	559	516	9 008	1 181	2 425	2 228	1 330	874	969
1994	10 258	1 087	586	501	9 171	1 207	2 399	2 300	1 392	889	985
1995	10 411	1 131	601	530	9 280	1 161	2 388	2 362	1 462	901	1 006
1996	10 575	1 161	623	538	9 414	1 154	2 373	2 413	1 534	914	1 025
1997	10 763	1 188	634	553	9 575	1 153	2 363	2 471	1 607	936	1 045
1998	10 927	1 201	623	578	9 727	1 166	2 335	2 520	1 682	956	1 068
1999	11 143	1 218	628	589	9 926	1 197	2 321	2 566	1 765	986	1 091
2000	11 129	1 178	605	572	9 952	1 195	2 277	2 471	1 889	1 067	1 053
2001	11 172	1 179	606	573	9 993	1 224	2 212	2 440	1 960	1 096	1 060
2002	11 391	1 195	615	580	10 196	1 281	2 223	2 437	2 042	1 137	1 075
2003	11 454	1 176	661	515	10 278	1 291	2 210	2 401	2 094	1 189	1 093
2004	11 656	1 195	680	516	10 461	1 326	2 242	2 382	2 150	1 250	1 111
2005	11 882	1 223	682	541	10 659	1 341	2 277	2 372	2 202	1 319	1 148
2006	12 130	1 266	713	552	10 864	1 355	2 318	2 369	2 261	1 390	1 170
2007	12 361	1 305	742	563	11 057	1 380	2 366	2 352	2 318	1 454	1 186
2008	12 516	1 322	718	604	11 194	1 384	2 398	2 313	2 335	1 519	1 245
2009	12 705	1 326	736	590	11 379	1 410	2 454	2 271	2 392	1 592	1 260
2010	12 939	1 313	715	598	11 626	1 474	2 540	2 234	2 406	1 673	1 299

Table 1-6. Civilian Noninstitutional Population, by Age, Race, Sex, and Hispanic Origin, 1948–2010
—Continued

(Thousands of people.)

Race, Hispanic origin, sex, and year	16 years and over	16 to 19 years			20 years and over						
		Total	16 to 17 years	18 to 19 years	Total	20 to 24 years	25 to 34 years	35 to 44 years	45 to 54 years	55 to 64 years	65 years and over
BLACK											
Women											
1973	8 214	1 088	556	532	7 126	1 153	1 631	1 306	1 194	898	944
1974	8 454	1 110	567	542	7 344	1 181	1 723	1 327	1 206	926	981
1975	8 691	1 141	581	560	7 550	1 226	1 806	1 334	1 213	948	1 025
1976	8 931	1 165	585	580	7 765	1 266	1 890	1 357	1 220	962	1 070
1977	9 174	1 171	590	581	8 003	1 320	1 978	1 390	1 228	979	1 108
1978	9 394	1 177	589	588	8 217	1 363	2 061	1 419	1 231	999	1 143
1979	9 636	1 176	586	589	8 460	1 405	2 160	1 455	1 242	1 022	1 176
1980	9 880	1 180	587	593	8 700	1 435	2 267	1 496	1 250	1 045	1 208
1981	10 102	1 178	584	593	8 924	1 453	2 376	1 534	1 257	1 069	1 234
1982	10 300	1 155	563	592	9 146	1 472	2 455	1 605	1 260	1 087	1 267
1983	10 477	1 138	550	588	9 340	1 480	2 539	1 666	1 260	1 107	1 288
1984	10 694	1 106	532	574	9 588	1 491	2 625	1 756	1 276	1 119	1 322
1985	10 873	1 101	540	560	9 773	1 447	2 693	1 828	1 312	1 136	1 357
1986	11 033	1 088	542	545	9 945	1 430	2 762	1 893	1 341	1 145	1 374
1987	11 224	1 098	557	541	10 126	1 405	2 819	1 976	1 368	1 153	1 405
1988	11 402	1 105	561	544	10 298	1 376	2 867	2 060	1 403	1 159	1 432
1989	11 582	1 100	541	559	10 482	1 351	2 905	2 159	1 441	1 162	1 464
1990	11 904	1 144	546	598	10 760	1 410	2 995	2 360	1 435	1 114	1 446
1991	12 074	1 115	539	576	10 959	1 417	3 003	2 478	1 471	1 121	1 470
1992	12 251	1 099	542	557	11 152	1 421	2 995	2 573	1 542	1 127	1 495
1993	12 438	1 106	554	552	11 332	1 419	2 983	2 659	1 611	1 142	1 518
1994	12 621	1 125	582	543	11 496	1 410	2 963	2 738	1 692	1 156	1 538
1995	12 835	1 153	597	556	11 682	1 392	2 948	2 816	1 782	1 178	1 565
1996	13 029	1 195	615	580	11 833	1 364	2 938	2 877	1 874	1 196	1 584
1997	13 241	1 225	620	604	12 016	1 362	2 916	2 939	1 964	1 228	1 608
1998	13 446	1 243	618	624	12 203	1 380	2 886	2 991	2 053	1 268	1 626
1999	13 711	1 261	621	640	12 451	1 418	2 876	3 043	2 153	1 310	1 650
2000	13 772	1 211	600	611	12 561	1 416	2 812	3 017	2 279	1 340	1 697
2001	13 966	1 209	606	603	12 758	1 462	2 790	3 026	2 383	1 382	1 714
2002	14 187	1 221	620	601	12 966	1 498	2 792	3 023	2 471	1 434	1 747
2003	14 232	1 206	648	558	13 026	1 482	2 768	2 986	2 534	1 504	1 753
2004	14 409	1 227	670	557	13 182	1 495	2 778	2 954	2 590	1 577	1 789
2005	14 635	1 258	659	598	13 377	1 494	2 797	2 939	2 666	1 661	1 819
2006	14 877	1 299	694	605	13 578	1 495	2 815	2 933	2 731	1 747	1 857
2007	15 124	1 336	755	581	13 788	1 511	2 844	2 918	2 792	1 830	1 893
2008	15 328	1 354	741	613	13 974	1 530	2 864	2 885	2 848	1 910	1 937
2009	15 536	1 357	726	631	14 178	1 563	2 895	2 839	2 898	2 004	1 979
2010	15 769	1 344	723	621	14 425	1 623	2 951	2 796	2 916	2 101	2 038
HISPANIC[1]											
Both Sexes											
1974	6 564	926	...	...	5 645	...	...	...	...	...	...
1975	6 862	962	...	...	5 900	...	...	...	...	...	...
1976	6 910	953	494	480	6 075	1 053	1 775	1 261	936	570	479
1977	7 362	1 024	513	508	6 376	1 163	1 869	1 283	989	587	485
1978	7 912	1 076	561	515	6 836	1 265	2 004	1 378	1 033	627	529
1979	8 207	1 095	544	551	7 113	1 296	2 117	1 458	1 015	659	566
1980	9 598	1 281	638	643	8 317	1 564	2 508	1 575	1 190	782	698
1981	10 120	1 301	641	660	8 819	1 650	2 698	1 680	1 231	832	728
1982	10 580	1 307	639	668	9 273	1 724	2 871	1 779	1 264	880	755
1983	11 029	1 304	635	670	9 725	1 790	3 045	1 883	1 298	928	781
1984	11 478	1 300	633	667	10 178	1 839	3 224	1 996	1 336	973	810
1985	11 915	1 298	638	661	10 617	1 864	3 401	2 117	1 377	1 015	843
1986	12 344	1 302	658	644	11 042	1 899	3 510	2 239	1 496	1 023	875
1987	12 867	1 332	651	681	11 536	1 910	3 714	2 464	1 492	1 061	895
1988	13 325	1 354	662	692	11 970	1 948	3 807	2 565	1 571	1 159	920
1989	13 791	1 399	672	727	12 392	1 950	3 953	2 658	1 649	1 182	1 001
1990	15 904	1 737	821	915	14 167	2 428	4 589	3 001	1 817	1 247	1 084
1991	16 425	1 732	819	913	14 693	2 481	4 674	3 243	1 879	1 283	1 134
1992	16 961	1 737	836	901	15 224	2 444	4 806	3 458	1 980	1 321	1 216
1993	17 532	1 756	855	901	15 776	2 487	4 887	3 632	2 094	1 324	1 353
1994	18 117	1 818	902	916	16 300	2 518	5 000	3 756	2 223	1 401	1 401
1995	18 629	1 872	903	969	16 757	2 528	5 050	3 965	2 294	1 483	1 437
1996	19 213	1 948	962	986	17 265	2 524	5 181	4 227	2 275	1 546	1 512
1997	20 321	2 121	1 088	1 033	18 200	2 623	5 405	4 453	2 581	1 580	1 558
1998	21 070	2 204	1 070	1 135	18 865	2 731	5 447	4 636	2 775	1 615	1 662
1999	21 650	2 307	1 113	1 194	19 344	2 700	5 512	4 833	2 868	1 713	1 718
2000	23 938	2 523	1 214	1 309	21 415	3 255	6 466	5 189	3 061	1 736	1 708
2001	24 942	2 508	1 173	1 334	22 435	3 417	6 726	5 346	3 339	1 816	1 792
2002	25 963	2 507	1 216	1 291	23 456	3 508	7 010	5 606	3 494	1 953	1 885
2003	27 551	2 543	1 346	1 197	25 008	3 533	7 506	6 003	3 845	2 093	2 027
2004	28 109	2 608	1 337	1 270	25 502	3 666	7 470	6 055	3 987	2 208	2 115
2005	29 133	2 689	1 415	1 274	26 444	3 647	7 684	6 293	4 217	2 361	2 242
2006	30 103	2 796	1 518	1 277	27 307	3 603	7 856	6 519	4 466	2 516	2 347
2007	31 383	2 944	1 559	1 385	28 440	3 648	8 129	6 785	4 720	2 685	2 473
2008	32 141	3 042	1 620	1 422	29 098	3 620	8 147	6 946	4 937	2 840	2 609
2009	32 891	3 123	1 602	1 522	29 768	3 623	8 099	7 078	5 192	3 017	2 759
2010	33 713	3 243	1 673	1 570	30 469	3 880	8 084	7 123	5 351	3 167	2 864

[1]May be of any race.
. . . = Not available.

Table 1-6. Civilian Noninstitutional Population, by Age, Race, Sex, and Hispanic Origin, 1948–2010
—Continued

(Thousands of people.)

Race, Hispanic origin, sex, and year	16 years and over	16 to 19 years			20 years and over						
		Total	16 to 17 years	18 to 19 years	Total	20 to 24 years	25 to 34 years	35 to 44 years	45 to 54 years	55 to 64 years	65 years and over
HISPANIC[1]											
Men											
1974	3 130	...	...	...	2 680	...	...	...	...	...	...
1975	3 219	...	...	...	2 741	...	...	...	...	...	...
1976	3 241	...	...	...	2 764	...	...	...	...	...	...
1977	3 483	...	...	...	2 982	...	...	...	...	...	...
1978	3 750	...	...	...	3 228	...	...	...	...	...	...
1979	3 917	...	...	...	3 362	...	...	...	...	...	...
1980	4 689	...	...	...	4 036	...	...	...	...	...	...
1981	4 968	...	...	...	4 306	...	...	...	...	...	...
1982	5 203	...	...	...	4 539	...	...	...	...	...	...
1983	5 432	...	...	...	4 771	...	...	...	...	...	...
1984	5 661	...	...	...	5 005	...	...	...	...	...	...
1985	5 885	...	...	...	5 232	...	...	...	...	...	...
1986	6 106	...	...	...	5 451	...	...	...	...	...	...
1987	6 371	...	...	...	5 700	...	...	...	...	...	...
1988	6 604	...	...	...	5 921	...	...	...	...	...	...
1989	6 825	...	...	...	6 114	...	...	...	...	...	...
1990	8 041	...	...	...	7 126	...	...	...	...	...	...
1991	8 296	...	...	...	7 392	...	...	...	...	...	...
1992	8 553	...	...	...	7 655	...	...	...	...	...	...
1993	8 824	...	...	...	7 930	...	...	...	...	...	...
1994	9 104	926	472	454	8 178	1 346	2 627	1 871	1 076	644	614
1995	9 329	954	481	473	8 375	1 337	2 657	1 966	1 127	668	619
1996	9 604	992	485	507	8 611	1 321	2 692	2 144	1 111	712	630
1997	10 368	1 119	585	534	9 250	1 439	2 872	2 275	1 266	747	651
1998	10 734	1 161	586	575	9 573	1 462	2 907	2 377	1 342	771	714
1999	10 713	1 190	571	619	9 523	1 398	2 805	2 407	1 397	767	749
2000	12 174	1 333	640	693	10 841	1 784	3 380	2 626	1 527	799	725
2001	12 695	1 310	619	690	11 386	1 846	3 529	2 765	1 650	848	749
2002	13 221	1 293	615	678	11 928	1 890	3 727	2 875	1 716	902	817
2003	14 098	1 301	674	627	12 797	1 905	4 033	3 098	1 910	989	862
2004	14 417	1 336	664	672	13 082	1 981	4 024	3 147	1 990	1 046	894
2005	14 962	1 376	730	646	13 586	1 956	4 155	3 284	2 114	1 123	953
2006	15 473	1 428	763	664	14 046	1 916	4 266	3 414	2 251	1 204	996
2007	16 154	1 505	790	714	14 649	1 928	4 430	3 563	2 384	1 287	1 058
2008	16 524	1 553	838	716	14 971	1 890	4 438	3 655	2 502	1 365	1 121
2009	16 897	1 593	818	774	15 305	1 875	4 405	3 735	2 647	1 459	1 184
2010	17 359	1 666	847	819	15 693	2 016	4 381	3 783	2 741	1 538	1 234
HISPANIC[1]											
Women											
1974	3 434	...	...	...	2 959	...	...	...	...	...	...
1975	3 644	...	...	...	3 161	...	...	...	...	...	...
1976	3 669	...	...	...	3 263	...	...	...	...	...	...
1977	3 879	...	...	...	3 377	...	...	...	...	...	...
1978	4 159	...	...	...	3 608	...	...	...	...	...	...
1979	4 291	...	...	...	3 751	...	...	...	...	...	...
1980	4 909	...	...	...	4 281	...	...	...	...	...	...
1981	5 151	...	...	...	4 513	...	...	...	...	...	...
1982	5 377	...	...	...	4 734	...	...	...	...	...	...
1983	5 597	...	...	...	4 954	...	...	...	...	...	...
1984	5 816	...	...	...	5 173	...	...	...	...	...	...
1985	6 029	...	...	...	5 385	...	...	...	...	...	...
1986	6 238	...	...	...	5 591	...	...	...	...	...	...
1987	6 496	...	...	...	5 835	...	...	...	...	...	...
1988	6 721	...	...	...	6 050	...	...	...	...	...	...
1989	6 965	...	...	...	6 278	...	...	...	...	...	...
1990	7 863	...	...	...	7 041	...	...	...	...	...	...
1991	8 130	...	...	...	7 301	...	...	...	...	...	...
1992	8 408	...	...	...	7 569	...	...	...	...	...	...
1993	8 708	...	...	...	7 846	...	...	...	...	...	...
1994	9 014	892	430	462	8 122	1 173	2 373	1 885	1 147	757	787
1995	9 300	918	422	496	8 382	1 191	2 393	1 999	1 167	815	818
1996	9 610	956	477	479	8 654	1 203	2 489	2 082	1 164	834	882
1997	9 953	1 003	503	500	8 950	1 184	2 533	2 178	1 315	833	907
1998	10 335	1 044	483	560	9 292	1 269	2 539	2 259	1 433	844	948
1999	10 937	1 116	542	575	9 821	1 302	2 707	2 425	1 470	947	969
2000	11 764	1 190	574	616	10 574	1 471	3 086	2 564	1 534	937	982
2001	12 247	1 198	554	644	11 049	1 571	3 198	2 581	1 689	968	1 043
2002	12 742	1 214	601	613	11 528	1 617	3 283	2 732	1 777	1 051	1 068
2003	13 452	1 242	672	570	12 211	1 628	3 473	2 905	1 935	1 105	1 166
2004	13 692	1 272	674	598	12 420	1 685	3 447	2 908	1 997	1 162	1 221
2005	14 172	1 313	685	628	12 858	1 692	3 529	3 009	2 103	1 237	1 289
2006	14 630	1 368	755	613	13 262	1 688	3 590	3 105	2 215	1 313	1 351
2007	15 229	1 439	769	670	13 791	1 720	3 698	3 222	2 336	1 398	1 416
2008	15 616	1 489	782	706	14 127	1 730	3 710	3 291	2 435	1 475	1 488
2009	15 993	1 531	783	748	14 463	1 748	3 694	3 343	2 545	1 558	1 576
2010	16 354	1 578	826	752	14 776	1 864	3 703	3 340	2 610	1 628	1 630

[1] May be of any race.
... = Not available.

Table 1-7. Civilian Labor Force, by Age, Sex, Race, and Hispanic Origin, 1948–2010

(Thousands of people.)

Race, Hispanic origin, sex, and year	16 years and over	16 to 19 years			20 years and over						
		Total	16 to 17 years	18 to 19 years	Total	20 to 24 years	25 to 34 years	35 to 44 years	45 to 54 years	55 to 64 years	65 years and over
ALL RACES											
Both Sexes											
1948	60 621	4 435	1 780	2 654	56 187	7 392	14 258	13 397	10 914	7 329	2 897
1949	61 286	4 288	1 704	2 583	57 000	7 340	14 415	13 711	11 107	7 426	3 010
1950	62 208	4 216	1 659	2 557	57 994	7 307	14 619	13 954	11 444	7 633	3 036
1951	62 017	4 103	1 743	2 360	57 914	6 594	14 668	14 100	11 739	7 796	3 020
1952	62 138	4 064	1 806	2 257	58 075	5 840	14 904	14 383	11 961	7 980	3 005
1953	63 015	4 027	1 727	2 299	58 989	5 481	14 898	15 099	12 249	8 024	3 236
1954	63 643	3 976	1 643	2 300	59 666	5 475	14 983	15 221	12 524	8 269	3 192
1955	65 023	4 092	1 711	2 382	60 931	5 666	15 058	15 400	12 992	8 513	3 305
1956	66 552	4 296	1 878	2 418	62 257	5 940	14 961	15 694	13 407	8 830	3 423
1957	66 929	4 275	1 843	2 433	62 653	6 071	14 826	15 847	13 768	8 853	3 290
1958	67 639	4 260	1 818	2 442	63 377	6 272	14 668	16 028	14 179	9 031	3 199
1959	68 369	4 492	1 971	2 522	63 876	6 413	14 435	16 127	14 518	9 227	3 158
1960	69 628	4 841	2 095	2 747	64 788	6 702	14 382	16 269	14 852	9 385	3 195
1961	70 459	4 936	1 984	2 951	65 524	6 950	14 319	16 402	15 071	9 636	3 146
1962	70 614	4 916	1 919	2 997	65 699	7 082	14 023	16 589	15 096	9 757	3 154
1963	71 833	5 139	2 171	2 966	66 695	7 473	14 050	16 788	15 338	10 006	3 041
1964	73 091	5 388	2 449	2 940	67 702	7 963	14 056	16 771	15 637	10 182	3 090
1965	74 455	5 910	2 486	3 425	68 543	8 259	14 233	16 840	15 756	10 350	3 108
1966	75 770	6 558	2 664	3 893	69 219	8 410	14 458	16 738	15 984	10 575	3 053
1967	77 347	6 521	2 734	3 786	70 825	9 010	15 055	16 703	16 172	10 792	3 097
1968	78 737	6 619	2 817	3 803	72 118	9 305	15 708	16 591	16 397	10 964	3 153
1969	80 734	6 970	3 009	3 959	73 763	9 879	16 336	16 458	16 730	11 135	3 227
1970	82 771	7 249	3 135	4 115	75 521	10 597	17 036	16 437	16 949	11 283	3 222
1971	84 382	7 470	3 192	4 278	76 913	11 331	17 714	16 305	17 024	11 390	3 149
1972	87 034	8 054	3 420	4 636	78 980	12 130	18 960	16 398	16 967	11 412	3 114
1973	89 429	8 507	3 665	4 839	80 924	12 846	20 376	16 492	16 983	11 256	2 974
1974	91 949	8 871	3 810	5 059	83 080	13 314	21 654	16 763	17 131	11 284	2 934
1975	93 775	8 870	3 740	5 131	84 904	13 750	22 864	16 903	17 084	11 346	2 956
1976	96 158	9 056	3 767	5 288	87 103	14 284	24 203	17 317	16 982	11 422	2 895
1977	99 009	9 351	3 919	5 431	89 658	14 825	25 500	17 943	16 878	11 577	2 934
1978	102 251	9 652	4 127	5 526	92 598	15 370	26 703	18 821	16 891	11 744	3 070
1979	104 962	9 638	4 079	5 559	95 325	15 769	27 938	19 685	16 897	11 931	3 104
1980	106 940	9 378	3 883	5 496	97 561	15 922	29 227	20 463	16 910	11 985	3 054
1981	108 670	8 988	3 647	5 340	99 682	16 099	30 392	21 211	16 970	11 969	3 042
1982	110 204	8 526	3 336	5 189	101 679	16 082	31 186	22 431	16 889	12 062	3 030
1983	111 550	8 171	3 073	5 098	103 379	16 052	31 834	23 611	16 851	11 992	3 040
1984	113 544	7 943	3 050	4 894	105 601	16 046	32 723	24 933	17 006	11 961	2 933
1985	115 461	7 901	3 154	4 747	107 560	15 718	33 550	26 073	17 322	11 991	2 907
1986	117 834	7 926	3 287	4 639	109 908	15 441	34 591	27 232	17 739	11 894	3 010
1987	119 865	7 988	3 384	4 604	111 878	14 977	35 233	28 460	18 210	11 877	3 119
1988	121 669	8 031	3 286	4 745	113 638	14 505	35 503	29 435	19 104	11 808	3 284
1989	123 869	7 954	3 125	4 828	115 916	14 180	35 896	30 601	19 916	11 877	3 446
1990	125 840	7 792	2 937	4 856	118 047	14 700	35 929	32 145	20 248	11 575	3 451
1991	126 346	7 265	2 789	4 476	119 082	14 548	35 507	33 312	20 828	11 473	3 413
1992	128 105	7 096	2 769	4 327	121 009	14 521	35 369	33 899	22 160	11 587	3 473
1993	129 200	7 170	2 831	4 338	122 030	14 354	34 780	34 562	23 296	11 599	3 439
1994	131 056	7 481	3 134	4 347	123 576	14 131	34 353	35 226	24 318	11 713	3 834
1995	132 304	7 765	3 225	4 540	124 539	13 688	34 198	35 751	25 223	11 860	3 819
1996	133 943	7 806	3 263	4 543	126 137	13 377	33 833	36 556	26 397	12 146	3 828
1997	136 297	7 932	3 237	4 695	128 365	13 532	33 380	37 326	27 574	12 665	3 887
1998	137 673	8 256	3 335	4 921	129 417	13 638	32 813	37 536	28 368	13 215	3 847
1999	139 368	8 333	3 337	4 996	131 034	13 933	32 143	37 882	29 388	13 682	4 005
2000	142 583	8 271	3 261	5 010	134 312	14 250	32 755	37 567	31 071	14 356	4 312
2001	143 734	7 902	3 088	4 814	135 832	14 557	32 361	37 404	32 025	15 104	4 382
2002	144 863	7 585	2 870	4 715	137 278	14 781	32 196	36 926	32 597	16 309	4 469
2003	146 510	7 170	2 857	4 313	139 340	14 928	32 343	36 695	33 270	17 312	4 792
2004	147 401	7 114	2 747	4 367	140 287	15 154	32 207	36 158	33 758	18 013	4 998
2005	149 320	7 164	2 825	4 339	142 157	15 127	32 341	36 030	34 402	18 979	5 278
2006	151 428	7 281	2 952	4 329	144 147	15 113	32 573	35 848	35 146	19 984	5 484
2007	153 124	7 012	2 771	4 242	146 112	15 205	33 130	35 527	35 697	20 750	5 804
2008	154 287	6 858	2 552	4 306	147 429	15 174	33 332	35 061	36 003	21 615	6 243
2009	154 142	6 390	2 227	4 163	147 752	14 971	33 298	34 239	36 205	22 505	6 534
2010	153 889	5 906	2 000	3 905	147 983	15 028	33 614	33 366	35 960	23 297	6 718

Table 1-7. Civilian Labor Force, by Age, Sex, Race, and Hispanic Origin, 1948–2010—*Continued*

(Thousands of people.)

Race, Hispanic origin, sex, and year	16 years and over	16 to 19 years			20 years and over						
		Total	16 to 17 years	18 to 19 years	Total	20 to 24 years	25 to 34 years	35 to 44 years	45 to 54 years	55 to 64 years	65 years and over
ALL RACES											
Men											
1948	43 286	2 600	1 109	1 490	40 687	4 673	10 327	9 596	7 943	5 764	2 384
1949	43 498	2 477	1 056	1 420	41 022	4 682	10 418	9 722	8 008	5 748	2 454
1950	43 819	2 504	1 048	1 456	41 316	4 632	10 527	9 793	8 117	5 794	2 453
1951	43 001	2 347	1 081	1 266	40 655	3 935	10 375	9 799	8 205	5 873	2 469
1952	42 869	2 312	1 101	1 210	40 558	3 338	10 585	9 945	8 326	5 949	2 416
1953	43 633	2 320	1 070	1 249	41 315	3 053	10 736	10 437	8 570	5 975	2 543
1954	43 965	2 295	1 023	1 272	41 669	3 051	10 771	10 513	8 702	6 105	2 526
1955	44 475	2 369	1 070	1 299	42 106	3 221	10 806	10 595	8 838	6 122	2 526
1956	45 091	2 433	1 142	1 291	42 658	3 485	10 685	10 663	9 002	6 220	2 602
1957	45 197	2 415	1 127	1 289	42 780	3 629	10 571	10 731	9 153	6 222	2 477
1958	45 521	2 428	1 133	1 295	43 092	3 771	10 475	10 843	9 320	6 304	2 378
1959	45 886	2 596	1 206	1 390	43 289	3 940	10 346	10 899	9 438	6 345	2 322
1960	46 388	2 787	1 290	1 496	43 603	4 123	10 251	10 967	9 574	6 399	2 287
1961	46 653	2 794	1 210	1 583	43 860	4 253	10 176	11 012	9 668	6 530	2 220
1962	46 600	2 770	1 178	1 592	43 831	4 279	9 920	11 115	9 715	6 560	2 241
1963	47 129	2 907	1 321	1 586	44 222	4 514	9 876	11 187	9 836	6 675	2 135
1964	47 679	3 074	1 499	1 575	44 604	4 754	9 876	11 156	9 956	6 741	2 124
1965	48 255	3 397	1 532	1 866	44 857	4 894	9 903	11 120	10 045	6 763	2 132
1966	48 471	3 685	1 609	2 075	44 788	4 820	9 948	10 983	10 100	6 847	2 089
1967	48 987	3 634	1 658	1 976	45 354	5 043	10 207	10 859	10 189	6 937	2 118
1968	49 533	3 681	1 687	1 995	45 852	5 070	10 610	10 725	10 267	7 025	2 154
1969	50 221	3 870	1 770	2 100	46 351	5 282	10 941	10 556	10 344	7 058	2 170
1970	51 228	4 008	1 810	2 199	47 220	5 717	11 327	10 469	10 417	7 126	2 165
1971	52 180	4 172	1 856	2 315	48 009	6 233	11 731	10 347	10 451	7 155	2 090
1972	53 555	4 476	1 955	2 522	49 079	6 766	12 350	10 372	10 412	7 155	2 026
1973	54 624	4 693	2 073	2 618	49 932	7 183	13 056	10 338	10 416	7 028	1 913
1974	55 739	4 861	2 138	2 721	50 879	7 387	13 665	10 401	10 431	7 063	1 932
1975	56 299	4 805	2 065	2 740	51 494	7 565	14 192	10 398	10 401	7 023	1 914
1976	57 174	4 886	2 069	2 817	52 288	7 866	14 784	10 500	10 293	7 020	1 826
1977	58 396	5 048	2 155	2 893	53 348	8 109	15 353	10 771	10 158	7 100	1 857
1978	59 620	5 149	2 227	2 923	54 471	8 327	15 814	11 159	10 083	7 151	1 936
1979	60 726	5 111	2 192	2 919	55 615	8 535	16 387	11 531	10 008	7 212	1 943
1980	61 453	4 999	2 102	2 897	56 455	8 607	16 971	11 836	9 905	7 242	1 893
1981	61 974	4 777	1 957	2 820	57 197	8 648	17 479	12 166	9 868	7 170	1 866
1982	62 450	4 470	1 776	2 694	57 980	8 604	17 793	12 781	9 784	7 174	1 845
1983	63 047	4 303	1 621	2 682	58 744	8 601	18 038	13 398	9 746	7 119	1 842
1984	63 835	4 134	1 591	2 542	59 701	8 594	18 488	14 037	9 776	7 050	1 755
1985	64 411	4 134	1 663	2 471	60 277	8 283	18 808	14 506	9 870	7 060	1 750
1986	65 422	4 102	1 707	2 395	61 320	8 148	19 383	15 029	9 994	6 954	1 811
1987	66 207	4 112	1 745	2 367	62 095	7 837	19 656	15 587	10 176	6 940	1 899
1988	66 927	4 159	1 714	2 445	62 768	7 594	19 742	16 074	10 566	6 831	1 960
1989	67 840	4 136	1 630	2 505	63 704	7 458	19 905	16 622	10 919	6 783	2 017
1990	69 011	4 094	1 537	2 557	64 916	7 866	19 872	17 481	11 103	6 627	1 967
1991	69 168	3 795	1 452	2 343	65 374	7 820	19 641	18 077	11 362	6 550	1 924
1992	69 964	3 751	1 453	2 297	66 213	7 770	19 495	18 347	12 040	6 551	2 010
1993	70 404	3 762	1 497	2 265	66 642	7 671	19 214	18 713	12 562	6 502	1 980
1994	70 817	3 896	1 630	2 266	66 921	7 540	18 854	18 966	12 962	6 423	2 176
1995	71 360	4 036	1 668	2 368	67 324	7 338	18 670	19 189	13 421	6 504	2 201
1996	72 087	4 043	1 665	2 378	68 044	7 104	18 430	19 602	13 967	6 693	2 247
1997	73 261	4 095	1 676	2 419	69 166	7 184	18 110	20 058	14 564	6 952	2 298
1998	73 959	4 244	1 728	2 516	69 715	7 221	17 796	20 242	14 963	7 253	2 240
1999	74 512	4 318	1 732	2 587	70 194	7 291	17 318	20 382	15 394	7 477	2 333
2000	76 280	4 269	1 676	2 594	72 010	7 521	17 844	20 093	16 269	7 795	2 488
2001	76 886	4 070	1 568	2 501	72 816	7 640	17 671	20 018	16 804	8 171	2 511
2002	77 500	3 870	1 431	2 439	73 630	7 769	17 596	19 828	17 143	8 751	2 542
2003	78 238	3 614	1 405	2 209	74 623	7 906	17 767	19 762	17 352	9 144	2 692
2004	78 980	3 616	1 329	2 288	75 364	8 057	17 798	19 539	17 635	9 547	2 787
2005	80 033	3 590	1 368	2 222	76 443	8 054	17 837	19 495	18 053	10 045	2 959
2006	81 255	3 693	1 453	2 240	77 562	8 116	17 944	19 407	18 489	10 509	3 096
2007	82 136	3 541	1 354	2 187	78 596	8 095	18 308	19 299	18 801	10 904	3 188
2008	82 520	3 472	1 238	2 235	79 047	8 065	18 302	18 972	18 928	11 345	3 436
2009	82 123	3 226	1 103	2 123	78 897	7 839	18 211	18 518	19 001	11 730	3 598
2010	81 985	2 991	990	2 002	78 994	7 864	18 352	18 119	18 856	12 103	3 701

Table 1-7. Civilian Labor Force, by Age, Sex, Race, and Hispanic Origin, 1948–2010—*Continued*

(Thousands of people.)

Race, Hispanic origin, sex, and year	16 years and over	16 to 19 years			20 years and over						
		Total	16 to 17 years	18 to 19 years	Total	20 to 24 years	25 to 34 years	35 to 44 years	45 to 54 years	55 to 64 years	65 years and over
ALL RACES											
Women											
1948	17 335	1 835	671	1 164	15 500	2 719	3 931	3 801	2 971	1 565	513
1949	17 788	1 811	648	1 163	15 978	2 658	3 997	3 989	3 099	1 678	556
1950	18 389	1 712	611	1 101	16 678	2 675	4 092	4 161	3 327	1 839	583
1951	19 016	1 756	662	1 094	17 259	2 659	4 293	4 301	3 534	1 923	551
1952	19 269	1 752	705	1 047	17 517	2 502	4 319	4 438	3 635	2 031	589
1953	19 382	1 707	657	1 050	17 674	2 428	4 162	4 662	3 679	2 049	693
1954	19 678	1 681	620	1 028	17 997	2 424	4 212	4 708	3 822	2 164	666
1955	20 548	1 723	641	1 083	18 825	2 445	4 252	4 805	4 154	2 391	779
1956	21 461	1 863	736	1 127	19 599	2 455	4 276	5 031	4 405	2 610	821
1957	21 732	1 860	716	1 144	19 873	2 442	4 255	5 116	4 615	2 631	813
1958	22 118	1 832	685	1 147	20 285	2 501	4 193	5 185	4 859	2 727	821
1959	22 483	1 896	765	1 132	20 587	2 473	4 089	5 228	5 080	2 882	836
1960	23 240	2 054	805	1 251	21 185	2 579	4 131	5 302	5 278	2 986	908
1961	23 806	2 142	774	1 368	21 664	2 697	4 143	5 390	5 403	3 106	926
1962	24 014	2 146	741	1 405	21 868	2 803	4 103	5 474	5 381	3 197	913
1963	24 704	2 232	850	1 380	22 473	2 959	4 174	5 601	5 502	3 331	906
1964	25 412	2 314	950	1 365	23 098	3 209	4 180	5 615	5 681	3 441	966
1965	26 200	2 513	954	1 559	23 686	3 365	4 330	5 720	5 711	3 587	976
1966	27 299	2 873	1 055	1 818	24 431	3 590	4 510	5 755	5 884	3 728	964
1967	28 360	2 887	1 076	1 810	25 475	3 966	4 848	5 844	5 983	3 855	979
1968	29 204	2 938	1 130	1 808	26 266	4 235	5 098	5 866	6 130	3 939	999
1969	30 513	3 100	1 239	1 859	27 413	4 597	5 395	5 902	6 386	4 077	1 057
1970	31 543	3 241	1 325	1 916	28 301	4 880	5 708	5 968	6 532	4 157	1 056
1971	32 202	3 298	1 336	1 963	28 904	5 098	5 983	5 957	6 573	4 234	1 059
1972	33 479	3 578	1 464	2 114	29 901	5 364	6 610	6 027	6 555	4 257	1 089
1973	34 804	3 814	1 592	2 221	30 991	5 663	7 320	6 154	6 567	4 228	1 061
1974	36 211	4 010	1 672	2 338	32 201	5 926	7 989	6 362	6 699	4 221	1 002
1975	37 475	4 065	1 674	2 391	33 410	6 185	8 673	6 505	6 683	4 323	1 042
1976	38 983	4 170	1 698	2 470	34 814	6 418	9 419	6 817	6 689	4 402	1 069
1977	40 613	4 303	1 765	2 538	36 310	6 717	10 149	7 171	6 720	4 477	1 078
1978	42 631	4 503	1 900	2 603	38 128	7 043	10 888	7 662	6 807	4 593	1 134
1979	44 235	4 527	1 887	2 639	39 708	7 234	11 551	8 154	6 889	4 719	1 161
1980	45 487	4 381	1 781	2 599	41 106	7 315	12 257	8 627	7 004	4 742	1 161
1981	46 696	4 211	1 691	2 520	42 485	7 451	12 912	9 045	7 101	4 799	1 176
1982	47 755	4 056	1 561	2 495	43 699	7 477	13 393	9 651	7 105	4 888	1 185
1983	48 503	3 868	1 452	2 416	44 636	7 451	13 796	10 213	7 105	4 873	1 198
1984	49 709	3 810	1 458	2 351	45 900	7 451	14 234	10 896	7 230	4 911	1 177
1985	51 050	3 767	1 491	2 276	47 283	7 434	14 742	11 567	7 452	4 932	1 156
1986	52 413	3 824	1 580	2 244	48 589	7 293	15 208	12 204	7 746	4 940	1 199
1987	53 658	3 875	1 638	2 237	49 783	7 140	15 577	12 873	8 034	4 937	1 221
1988	54 742	3 872	1 572	2 300	50 870	6 910	15 761	13 361	8 537	4 977	1 324
1989	56 030	3 818	1 495	2 323	52 212	6 721	15 990	13 980	8 997	5 095	1 429
1990	56 829	3 698	1 400	2 298	53 131	6 834	16 058	14 663	9 145	4 948	1 483
1991	57 199	3 470	1 337	2 133	53 708	6 728	15 867	15 235	9 465	4 924	1 489
1992	58 141	3 345	1 316	2 030	54 796	6 750	15 875	15 552	10 120	5 035	1 464
1993	58 795	3 408	1 335	2 073	55 388	6 683	15 566	15 849	10 733	5 097	1 459
1994	60 239	3 585	1 504	2 081	56 655	6 592	15 499	16 259	11 357	5 289	1 658
1995	60 944	3 729	1 557	2 172	57 215	6 349	15 528	16 562	11 801	5 356	1 618
1996	61 857	3 763	1 599	2 164	58 094	6 273	15 403	16 954	12 430	5 452	1 581
1997	63 036	3 837	1 561	2 277	59 198	6 348	15 271	17 268	13 010	5 713	1 590
1998	63 714	4 012	1 607	2 405	59 702	6 418	15 017	17 294	13 405	5 962	1 607
1999	64 855	4 015	1 606	2 410	60 840	6 643	14 826	17 501	13 994	6 204	1 673
2000	66 303	4 002	1 585	2 416	62 301	6 730	14 912	17 473	14 802	6 561	1 823
2001	66 848	3 832	1 520	2 313	63 016	6 917	14 690	17 386	15 221	6 932	1 870
2002	67 363	3 715	1 439	2 277	63 648	7 012	14 600	17 098	15 454	7 559	1 926
2003	68 272	3 556	1 452	2 104	64 716	7 021	14 576	16 933	15 919	8 168	2 099
2004	68 421	3 498	1 418	2 080	64 923	7 097	14 409	16 619	16 123	8 466	2 211
2005	69 288	3 574	1 457	2 117	65 714	7 073	14 503	16 535	16 349	8 934	2 319
2006	70 173	3 588	1 499	2 089	66 585	6 997	14 628	16 441	16 656	9 475	2 388
2007	70 988	3 471	1 417	2 055	67 516	7 110	14 822	16 227	16 896	9 846	2 615
2008	71 767	3 385	1 314	2 071	68 382	7 109	15 030	16 089	17 075	10 270	2 808
2009	72 019	3 163	1 124	2 039	68 856	7 132	15 087	15 720	17 204	10 776	2 937
2010	71 904	2 914	1 011	1 904	68 990	7 164	15 263	15 247	17 104	11 194	3 017

Table 1-7. Civilian Labor Force, by Age, Sex, Race, and Hispanic Origin, 1948–2010—*Continued*

(Thousands of people.)

Race, Hispanic origin, sex, and year	16 years and over	16 to 19 years			20 years and over						
		Total	16 to 17 years	18 to 19 years	Total	20 to 24 years	25 to 34 years	35 to 44 years	45 to 54 years	55 to 64 years	65 years and over
WHITE											
Both Sexes											
1954	56 816	3 501	1 448	2 054	53 315	4 752	13 226	13 540	11 258	7 591	2 946
1955	58 085	3 598	1 511	2 087	54 487	4 941	13 267	13 729	11 680	7 810	3 062
1956	59 428	3 771	1 656	2 113	55 657	5 194	13 154	14 000	12 061	8 080	3 166
1957	59 754	3 775	1 637	2 135	55 979	5 283	13 044	14 117	12 382	8 091	3 049
1958	60 293	3 757	1 615	2 144	56 536	5 449	12 884	14 257	12 727	8 254	2 964
1959	60 952	4 000	1 775	2 225	56 952	5 544	12 670	14 355	13 048	8 411	2 925
1960	61 915	4 275	1 871	2 405	57 640	5 787	12 594	14 450	13 322	8 522	2 964
1961	62 656	4 362	1 767	2 594	58 294	6 026	12 503	14 557	13 517	8 773	2 917
1962	62 750	4 354	1 709	2 645	58 396	6 164	12 218	14 695	13 551	8 856	2 912
1963	63 830	4 559	1 950	2 608	59 271	6 537	12 229	14 859	13 789	9 067	2 790
1964	64 921	4 784	2 211	2 572	60 137	6 952	12 235	14 852	14 043	9 239	2 817
1965	66 137	5 267	2 221	3 044	60 870	7 189	12 391	14 900	14 162	9 392	2 839
1966	67 276	5 827	2 367	3 460	61 449	7 324	12 591	14 785	14 370	9 583	2 793
1967	68 699	5 749	2 432	3 318	62 950	7 886	13 123	14 765	14 545	9 817	2 821
1968	69 976	5 839	2 519	3 320	64 137	8 109	13 740	14 683	14 756	9 968	2 884
1969	71 778	6 168	2 698	3 470	65 611	8 614	14 289	14 564	15 057	10 132	2 954
1970	73 556	6 442	2 824	3 617	67 113	9 238	14 896	14 525	15 269	10 255	2 930
1971	74 963	6 681	2 894	3 787	68 282	9 889	15 445	14 374	15 343	10 351	2 880
1972	77 275	7 193	3 096	4 098	70 082	10 605	16 584	14 399	15 283	10 402	2 809
1973	79 151	7 579	3 320	4 260	71 572	11 182	17 764	14 440	15 256	10 240	2 687
1974	81 281	7 899	3 441	4 459	73 381	11 600	18 862	14 644	15 375	10 241	2 656
1975	82 831	7 899	3 375	4 525	74 932	12 019	19 897	14 753	15 308	10 287	2 668
1976	84 767	8 088	3 410	4 679	76 678	12 444	20 990	15 088	15 187	10 371	2 599
1977	87 141	8 352	3 562	4 790	78 789	12 892	22 099	15 604	15 053	10 495	2 647
1978	89 634	8 555	3 715	4 839	81 079	13 309	23 067	16 353	15 004	10 602	2 745
1979	91 923	8 548	3 668	4 881	83 375	13 632	24 101	17 123	14 965	10 767	2 787
1980	93 600	8 312	3 485	4 827	85 286	13 769	25 181	17 811	14 956	10 812	2 759
1981	95 052	7 962	3 274	4 688	87 089	13 926	26 208	18 445	14 993	10 764	2 753
1982	96 143	7 518	3 001	4 518	88 625	13 866	26 814	19 491	14 879	10 832	2 742
1983	97 021	7 186	2 765	4 421	89 835	13 816	27 237	20 488	14 798	10 732	2 766
1984	98 492	6 952	2 720	4 232	91 540	13 733	27 958	21 588	14 899	10 701	2 660
1985	99 926	6 841	2 777	4 065	93 085	13 469	28 640	22 591	15 101	10 679	2 605
1986	101 801	6 862	2 895	3 967	94 939	13 176	29 497	23 571	15 379	10 583	2 732
1987	103 290	6 893	2 963	3 931	96 396	12 764	29 956	24 581	15 792	10 497	2 806
1988	104 756	6 940	2 861	4 079	97 815	12 311	30 167	25 358	16 573	10 462	2 943
1989	106 355	6 809	2 685	4 124	99 546	11 940	30 388	26 312	17 278	10 533	3 094
1990	107 447	6 683	2 543	4 140	100 764	12 397	30 174	27 265	17 515	10 290	3 123
1991	107 743	6 245	2 432	3 813	101 498	12 248	29 794	28 213	18 028	10 129	3 086
1992	108 837	6 022	2 388	3 633	102 815	12 187	29 518	28 580	19 200	10 196	3 135
1993	109 700	6 105	2 458	3 647	103 595	11 987	29 027	29 056	20 181	10 215	3 129
1994	111 082	6 357	2 681	3 677	104 725	11 688	28 580	29 626	21 026	10 319	3 486
1995	111 950	6 545	2 749	3 796	105 404	11 266	28 325	30 112	21 804	10 432	3 466
1996	113 108	6 607	2 780	3 826	106 502	11 003	27 901	30 683	22 781	10 648	3 485
1997	114 693	6 720	2 779	3 941	107 973	11 127	27 362	31 171	23 709	11 086	3 517
1998	115 415	6 965	2 860	4 105	108 450	11 244	26 707	31 221	24 282	11 548	3 448
1999	116 509	7 048	2 849	4 199	109 461	11 436	25 978	31 391	25 102	11 960	3 595
2000	118 545	6 955	2 768	4 186	111 590	11 626	26 336	30 968	26 353	12 463	3 846
2001	119 399	6 661	2 626	4 035	112 737	11 883	26 010	30 778	27 062	13 121	3 883
2002	120 150	6 366	2 445	3 921	113 784	12 073	25 908	30 286	27 405	14 148	3 965
2003	120 546	5 973	2 414	3 560	114 572	12 064	25 752	29 788	27 786	14 944	4 238
2004	121 086	5 929	2 309	3 620	115 156	12 192	25 548	29 305	28 181	15 522	4 408
2005	122 299	5 950	2 390	3 560	116 349	12 109	25 548	29 107	28 685	16 275	4 624
2006	123 834	6 009	2 473	3 536	117 825	12 128	25 681	28 849	29 231	17 132	4 805
2007	124 935	5 795	2 326	3 470	119 139	12 176	26 076	28 394	29 627	17 782	5 085
2008	125 635	5 644	2 126	3 518	119 990	12 142	26 210	27 932	29 780	18 464	5 463
2009	125 644	5 295	1 883	3 413	120 349	11 995	26 277	27 263	29 903	19 199	5 711
2010	125 084	4 861	1 693	3 168	120 223	11 948	26 455	26 510	29 632	19 808	5 869

Table 1-7. Civilian Labor Force, by Age, Sex, Race, and Hispanic Origin, 1948–2010—*Continued*

(Thousands of people.)

Race, Hispanic origin, sex, and year	16 years and over	16 to 19 years			20 years and over						
		Total	16 to 17 years	18 to 19 years	Total	20 to 24 years	25 to 34 years	35 to 44 years	45 to 54 years	55 to 64 years	65 years and over
WHITE											
Men											
1954	39 759	1 989	896	1 095	37 770	2 654	9 695	9 516	7 913	5 653	2 339
1955	40 197	2 056	935	1 121	38 141	2 803	9 721	9 597	8 025	5 654	2 343
1956	40 734	2 114	1 002	1 110	38 620	3 036	9 595	9 661	8 175	5 736	2 417
1957	40 826	2 108	992	1 114	38 718	3 152	9 483	9 719	8 317	5 735	2 307
1958	41 080	2 116	1 001	1 116	38 964	3 278	9 386	9 822	8 465	5 800	2 213
1959	41 397	2 279	1 077	1 202	39 118	3 409	9 261	9 876	8 581	5 833	2 158
1960	41 743	2 433	1 140	1 293	39 310	3 559	9 153	9 919	8 689	5 861	2 129
1961	41 986	2 439	1 067	1 372	39 547	3 681	9 072	9 961	8 776	5 988	2 068
1962	41 931	2 432	1 041	1 391	39 499	3 726	8 846	10 029	8 820	5 995	2 082
1963	42 404	2 563	1 183	1 380	39 841	3 955	8 805	10 079	8 944	6 090	1 967
1964	42 894	2 716	1 345	1 371	40 178	4 166	8 800	10 055	9 053	6 161	1 942
1965	43 400	2 999	1 359	1 639	40 401	4 279	8 824	10 023	9 130	6 188	1 959
1966	43 572	3 253	1 423	1 830	40 319	4 200	8 859	9 892	9 189	6 250	1 928
1967	44 041	3 191	1 464	1 727	40 851	4 416	9 102	9 785	9 260	6 348	1 944
1968	44 553	3 236	1 504	1 732	41 318	4 432	9 477	9 662	9 340	6 427	1 981
1969	45 185	3 413	1 583	1 830	41 772	4 615	9 773	9 509	9 413	6 467	1 996
1970	46 035	3 551	1 629	1 922	42 483	4 988	10 099	9 414	9 487	6 517	1 978
1971	46 904	3 719	1 681	2 039	43 185	5 448	10 444	9 294	9 528	6 550	1 922
1972	48 118	3 980	1 758	2 223	44 138	5 937	11 039	9 278	9 473	6 562	1 846
1973	48 920	4 174	1 875	2 300	44 747	6 274	11 621	9 212	9 445	6 452	1 740
1974	49 843	4 312	1 922	2 391	45 532	6 470	12 135	9 246	9 455	6 464	1 759
1975	50 324	4 290	1 871	2 418	46 034	6 642	12 579	9 231	9 415	6 425	1 742
1976	51 033	4 357	1 869	2 489	46 675	6 890	13 092	9 289	9 310	6 437	1 657
1977	52 033	4 496	1 949	2 548	47 537	7 097	13 575	9 509	9 175	6 492	1 688
1978	52 955	4 565	2 002	2 563	48 390	7 274	13 939	9 858	9 068	6 508	1 744
1979	53 856	4 537	1 974	2 563	49 320	7 421	14 415	10 183	8 968	6 571	1 761
1980	54 473	4 424	1 881	2 543	50 049	7 479	14 893	10 455	8 877	6 618	1 727
1981	54 895	4 224	1 751	2 473	50 671	7 521	15 340	10 740	8 836	6 530	1 704
1982	55 133	3 933	1 602	2 331	51 200	7 438	15 549	11 289	8 727	6 520	1 677
1983	55 480	3 764	1 452	2 312	51 716	7 406	15 707	11 817	8 649	6 446	1 691
1984	56 062	3 609	1 420	2 189	52 453	7 370	16 037	12 348	8 683	6 410	1 606
1985	56 472	3 576	1 467	2 109	52 895	7 122	16 306	12 767	8 730	6 370	1 595
1986	57 217	3 542	1 502	2 040	53 675	6 986	16 769	13 207	8 791	6 260	1 663
1987	57 779	3 547	1 524	2 023	54 232	6 717	16 963	13 674	8 945	6 200	1 733
1988	58 317	3 583	1 487	2 095	54 734	6 468	17 018	14 068	9 285	6 108	1 787
1989	58 988	3 546	1 401	2 146	55 441	6 316	17 077	14 516	9 615	6 082	1 835
1990	59 638	3 522	1 333	2 189	56 116	6 688	16 920	15 026	9 713	5 957	1 811
1991	59 656	3 269	1 266	2 003	56 387	6 619	16 709	15 523	9 926	5 847	1 763
1992	60 168	3 192	1 260	1 932	56 976	6 542	16 512	15 701	10 570	5 821	1 830
1993	60 484	3 200	1 292	1 908	57 284	6 449	16 244	15 971	11 010	5 784	1 825
1994	60 727	3 315	1 403	1 912	57 411	6 294	15 879	16 188	11 327	5 726	1 998
1995	61 146	3 427	1 429	1 998	57 719	6 096	15 669	16 414	11 730	5 809	2 000
1996	61 783	3 444	1 421	2 023	58 340	5 922	15 475	16 728	12 217	5 943	2 054
1997	62 639	3 513	1 440	2 073	59 126	6 029	15 120	17 019	12 710	6 154	2 094
1998	63 034	3 614	1 487	2 127	59 421	6 063	14 770	17 157	13 003	6 415	2 013
1999	63 413	3 666	1 478	2 188	59 747	6 151	14 292	17 201	13 368	6 618	2 117
2000	64 466	3 615	1 422	2 193	60 850	6 244	14 666	16 880	13 977	6 840	2 243
2001	64 966	3 446	1 334	2 112	61 519	6 363	14 536	16 809	14 400	7 169	2 241
2002	65 308	3 241	1 215	2 026	62 067	6 444	14 499	16 583	14 615	7 665	2 261
2003	65 509	3 036	1 193	1 843	62 473	6 479	14 529	16 398	14 708	7 973	2 386
2004	65 994	3 050	1 127	1 923	62 944	6 586	14 429	16 192	14 934	8 326	2 478
2005	66 694	2 988	1 162	1 826	63 705	6 562	14 426	16 080	15 273	8 734	2 631
2006	67 613	3 074	1 222	1 852	64 540	6 597	14 469	15 962	15 606	9 152	2 753
2007	68 158	2 944	1 147	1 798	65 214	6 567	14 715	15 765	15 846	9 500	2 821
2008	68 351	2 868	1 040	1 829	65 483	6 526	14 715	15 436	15 905	9 855	3 046
2009	68 051	2 679	933	1 746	65 372	6 348	14 669	15 066	15 943	10 160	3 186
2010	67 728	2 463	844	1 619	65 265	6 342	14 734	14 713	15 791	10 422	3 263

Table 1-7. Civilian Labor Force, by Age, Sex, Race, and Hispanic Origin, 1948–2010—*Continued*

(Thousands of people.)

Race, Hispanic origin, sex, and year	16 years and over	16 to 19 years			20 years and over						
		Total	16 to 17 years	18 to 19 years	Total	20 to 24 years	25 to 34 years	35 to 44 years	45 to 54 years	55 to 64 years	65 years and over
WHITE											
Women											
1954	17 057	1 512	552	959	15 545	2 098	3 531	4 024	3 345	1 938	607
1955	17 888	1 542	576	966	16 346	2 138	3 546	4 132	3 655	2 156	719
1956	18 694	1 657	654	1 003	17 037	2 158	3 559	4 339	3 886	2 344	749
1957	18 928	1 667	645	1 021	17 261	2 131	3 561	4 398	4 065	2 356	742
1958	19 213	1 641	614	1 028	17 572	2 171	3 498	4 435	4 262	2 454	751
1959	19 555	1 721	698	1 023	17 834	2 135	3 409	4 479	4 467	2 578	767
1960	20 172	1 842	731	1 112	18 330	2 228	3 441	4 531	4 633	2 661	835
1961	20 670	1 923	700	1 222	18 747	2 345	3 431	4 596	4 741	2 785	849
1962	20 819	1 922	668	1 254	18 897	2 438	3 372	4 666	4 731	2 861	830
1963	21 426	1 996	767	1 228	19 430	2 582	3 424	4 780	4 845	2 977	823
1964	22 027	2 068	866	1 201	19 959	2 786	3 435	4 797	4 990	3 078	875
1965	22 737	2 268	862	1 405	20 469	2 910	3 567	4 877	5 032	3 204	880
1966	23 704	2 574	944	1 630	21 130	3 124	3 732	4 893	5 181	3 333	865
1967	24 658	2 558	968	1 591	22 100	3 471	4 021	4 980	5 285	3 469	877
1968	25 423	2 603	1 015	1 588	22 821	3 677	4 263	5 021	5 416	3 541	903
1969	26 593	2 755	1 115	1 640	23 839	3 999	4 516	5 055	5 644	3 665	958
1970	27 521	2 891	1 195	1 695	24 630	4 250	4 797	5 111	5 781	3 738	952
1971	28 060	2 962	1 213	1 748	25 097	4 441	5 001	5 080	5 816	3 801	958
1972	29 157	3 213	1 338	1 875	25 945	4 668	5 544	5 121	5 810	3 839	963
1973	30 231	3 405	1 445	1 960	26 825	4 908	6 143	5 228	5 811	3 788	947
1974	31 437	3 588	1 520	2 068	27 850	5 131	6 727	5 399	5 920	3 777	897
1975	32 508	3 610	1 504	2 107	28 898	5 378	7 318	5 522	5 892	3 862	926
1976	33 735	3 731	1 541	2 189	30 004	5 554	7 898	5 799	5 877	3 935	940
1977	35 108	3 856	1 614	2 243	31 253	5 795	8 523	6 095	5 877	4 003	959
1978	36 679	3 990	1 713	2 276	32 689	6 035	9 128	6 495	5 936	4 094	1 001
1979	38 067	4 011	1 694	2 318	34 056	6 211	9 687	6 940	5 997	4 196	1 024
1980	39 127	3 888	1 605	2 284	35 239	6 290	10 289	7 356	6 079	4 194	1 032
1981	40 157	3 739	1 523	2 216	36 418	6 406	10 868	7 704	6 157	4 235	1 049
1982	41 010	3 585	1 399	2 186	37 425	6 428	11 264	8 202	6 152	4 313	1 065
1983	41 541	3 422	1 314	2 109	38 119	6 410	11 530	8 670	6 149	4 285	1 074
1984	42 431	3 343	1 300	2 043	39 087	6 363	11 922	9 240	6 217	4 292	1 054
1985	43 455	3 265	1 310	1 955	40 190	6 348	12 334	9 824	6 371	4 303	1 010
1986	44 584	3 320	1 393	1 927	41 264	6 191	12 729	10 364	6 588	4 323	1 069
1987	45 510	3 347	1 439	1 908	42 164	6 047	12 993	10 907	6 847	4 297	1 073
1988	46 439	3 358	1 374	1 984	43 081	5 844	13 149	11 291	7 288	4 354	1 156
1989	47 367	3 262	1 284	1 978	44 105	5 625	13 311	11 796	7 663	4 451	1 259
1990	47 809	3 161	1 210	1 951	44 648	5 709	13 254	12 239	7 802	4 333	1 312
1991	48 087	2 976	1 166	1 810	45 111	5 629	13 085	12 689	8 101	4 282	1 324
1992	48 669	2 830	1 128	1 702	45 839	5 645	13 006	12 879	8 630	4 375	1 305
1993	49 216	2 905	1 167	1 739	46 311	5 539	12 783	13 085	9 171	4 430	1 304
1994	50 356	3 042	1 278	1 764	47 314	5 394	12 702	13 439	9 699	4 593	1 487
1995	50 804	3 118	1 320	1 798	47 686	5 170	12 656	13 697	10 074	4 622	1 466
1996	51 325	3 163	1 360	1 803	48 162	5 081	12 426	13 955	10 563	4 706	1 431
1997	52 054	3 207	1 339	1 867	48 847	5 099	12 242	14 153	10 999	4 932	1 422
1998	52 380	3 351	1 373	1 977	49 029	5 180	11 937	14 064	11 279	5 133	1 435
1999	53 096	3 382	1 371	2 010	49 714	5 285	11 685	14 190	11 734	5 342	1 478
2000	54 079	3 339	1 346	1 993	50 740	5 381	11 669	14 088	12 376	5 623	1 602
2001	54 433	3 215	1 292	1 923	51 218	5 519	11 474	13 969	12 662	5 952	1 642
2002	54 842	3 125	1 229	1 895	51 717	5 628	11 409	13 703	12 790	6 482	1 704
2003	55 037	2 937	1 221	1 716	52 099	5 584	11 223	13 390	13 078	6 970	1 852
2004	55 092	2 879	1 182	1 697	52 212	5 606	11 119	13 114	13 247	7 197	1 930
2005	55 605	2 962	1 228	1 733	52 643	5 546	11 123	13 027	13 413	7 542	1 993
2006	56 221	2 935	1 251	1 684	53 286	5 530	11 212	12 886	13 625	7 980	2 052
2007	56 777	2 851	1 179	1 672	53 925	5 609	11 360	12 629	13 781	8 282	2 264
2008	57 284	2 776	1 086	1 690	54 508	5 616	11 495	12 495	13 875	8 609	2 417
2009	57 593	2 616	950	1 667	54 976	5 647	11 608	12 197	13 960	9 039	2 525
2010	57 356	2 398	849	1 549	54 957	5 607	11 721	11 796	13 841	9 386	2 607

Table 1-7. Civilian Labor Force, by Age, Sex, Race, and Hispanic Origin, 1948–2010—*Continued*

(Thousands of people.)

Race, Hispanic origin, sex, and year	16 years and over	16 to 19 years			20 years and over						
		Total	16 to 17 years	18 to 19 years	Total	20 to 24 years	25 to 34 years	35 to 44 years	45 to 54 years	55 to 64 years	65 years and over
BLACK											
Both Sexes											
1972	8 707	788	293	496	7 919	1 393	2 107	1 735	1 496	909	281
1973	8 976	833	307	525	8 143	1 489	2 242	1 741	1 513	901	258
1974	9 167	851	317	534	8 317	1 492	2 358	1 777	1 517	917	253
1975	9 263	838	312	524	8 426	1 477	2 466	1 775	1 519	929	258
1976	9 561	837	304	532	8 724	1 544	2 646	1 824	1 518	925	268
1977	9 932	861	304	557	9 072	1 641	2 798	1 894	1 530	943	267
1978	10 432	930	341	589	9 501	1 739	2 961	1 975	1 560	978	289
1979	10 678	912	340	572	9 766	1 793	3 094	2 039	1 584	974	281
1980	10 865	891	326	565	9 975	1 802	3 259	2 081	1 596	978	257
1981	11 086	862	308	554	10 224	1 828	3 365	2 164	1 608	1 009	249
1982	11 331	824	268	556	10 507	1 849	3 492	2 303	1 610	1 012	243
1983	11 647	809	248	561	10 838	1 871	3 675	2 406	1 630	1 032	224
1984	12 033	827	268	558	11 206	1 926	3 800	2 565	1 671	1 020	224
1985	12 364	889	311	578	11 476	1 854	3 888	2 681	1 742	1 059	252
1986	12 654	883	322	562	11 770	1 881	4 028	2 793	1 793	1 051	224
1987	12 993	899	336	563	12 094	1 818	4 147	2 942	1 838	1 098	251
1988	13 205	889	344	545	12 316	1 782	4 226	3 069	1 894	1 069	276
1989	13 497	925	353	572	12 573	1 789	4 295	3 227	1 954	1 023	285
1990	13 740	866	306	560	12 874	1 758	4 307	3 566	2 003	977	262
1991	13 797	774	266	508	13 023	1 750	4 254	3 719	2 042	1 001	256
1992	14 162	816	285	532	13 346	1 763	4 309	3 843	2 142	1 029	259
1993	14 225	807	283	524	13 418	1 764	4 232	3 960	2 212	1 013	237
1994	14 502	852	351	501	13 650	1 800	4 199	4 068	2 308	1 007	267
1995	14 817	911	366	545	13 906	1 754	4 267	4 165	2 404	1 046	271
1996	15 134	923	366	556	14 211	1 738	4 305	4 287	2 553	1 073	255
1997	15 529	933	352	580	14 596	1 783	4 329	4 401	2 724	1 093	265
1998	15 982	1 017	370	646	14 966	1 797	4 332	4 531	2 863	1 163	278
1999	16 365	959	352	607	15 406	1 866	4 430	4 653	2 992	1 180	285
2000	16 397	941	356	585	15 456	1 873	4 281	4 515	3 203	1 264	320
2001	16 421	898	332	565	15 524	1 878	4 180	4 483	3 298	1 335	350
2002	16 565	870	297	574	15 695	1 908	4 134	4 458	3 435	1 407	353
2003	16 526	771	289	482	15 755	1 892	4 060	4 465	3 506	1 466	366
2004	16 638	762	272	489	15 876	1 926	4 076	4 380	3 578	1 538	380
2005	17 013	803	279	525	16 209	1 957	4 145	4 370	3 686	1 647	403
2006	17 314	871	318	553	16 443	1 960	4 197	4 348	3 785	1 739	414
2007	17 496	801	300	501	16 695	1 974	4 254	4 357	3 866	1 811	432
2008	17 740	787	270	517	16 953	1 981	4 328	4 316	3 945	1 908	476
2009	17 632	729	231	499	16 902	1 961	4 300	4 175	3 976	1 995	495
2010	17 862	677	203	473	17 186	2 072	4 418	4 095	3 991	2 104	506
BLACK											
Men											
1972	4 816	453	180	272	4 364	761	1 158	935	824	522	165
1973	4 924	460	175	286	4 464	819	1 217	935	842	499	153
1974	5 020	480	189	291	4 540	798	1 279	953	838	519	152
1975	5 016	447	168	279	4 569	790	1 328	948	833	520	150
1976	5 101	454	168	285	4 648	820	1 383	969	824	504	149
1977	5 263	476	178	299	4 787	856	1 441	1 003	818	515	154
1978	5 435	491	186	306	4 943	883	1 504	1 022	829	540	166
1979	5 559	480	179	301	5 079	928	1 577	1 049	844	524	156
1980	5 612	479	181	298	5 134	935	1 659	1 061	830	509	138
1981	5 685	462	169	293	5 223	940	1 702	1 093	829	524	134
1982	5 804	436	137	300	5 368	964	1 769	1 152	824	525	135
1983	5 966	433	134	300	5 533	997	1 840	1 196	845	536	119
1984	6 126	440	141	299	5 686	1 022	1 924	1 270	847	505	118
1985	6 220	471	162	310	5 749	950	1 937	1 313	879	544	125
1986	6 373	458	164	294	5 915	957	2 029	1 359	901	552	116
1987	6 486	463	179	284	6 023	914	2 074	1 406	915	586	130
1988	6 596	469	186	283	6 127	913	2 114	1 459	936	565	139
1989	6 701	480	190	291	6 221	904	2 157	1 544	945	530	141
1990	6 802	445	161	284	6 357	879	2 142	1 733	988	496	119
1991	6 851	400	140	260	6 451	896	2 111	1 806	1 010	507	122
1992	6 997	429	149	280	6 568	900	2 121	1 859	1 037	521	130
1993	7 019	425	154	270	6 594	875	2 118	1 918	1 065	506	112
1994	7 089	443	176	266	6 646	891	2 068	1 975	1 102	484	125
1995	7 183	453	184	269	6 730	866	2 089	1 987	1 148	490	150
1996	7 264	458	182	276	6 806	848	2 077	2 036	1 204	509	132
1997	7 354	444	178	266	6 910	832	2 052	2 096	1 287	508	134
1998	7 542	488	181	307	7 053	837	2 034	2 142	1 343	548	150
1999	7 652	470	180	291	7 182	835	2 069	2 206	1 387	547	138
2000	7 702	462	181	281	7 240	875	1 999	2 105	1 497	612	151
2001	7 647	447	166	281	7 200	853	1 915	2 073	1 537	645	177
2002	7 794	446	149	297	7 347	906	1 909	2 064	1 623	664	181
2003	7 711	365	138	228	7 346	918	1 872	2 058	1 627	685	186
2004	7 773	359	128	231	7 414	927	1 931	2 000	1 654	714	188
2005	7 998	399	139	260	7 600	940	1 948	2 028	1 732	756	196
2006	8 128	409	152	256	7 720	971	1 986	1 999	1 792	777	195
2007	8 252	384	137	247	7 867	981	2 037	2 030	1 822	791	206
2008	8 347	385	124	261	7 962	984	2 047	2 008	1 846	852	225
2009	8 265	350	111	239	7 914	954	2 041	1 932	1 852	904	231
2010	8 415	339	96	244	8 076	986	2 118	1 924	1 862	950	236

Table 1-7. Civilian Labor Force, by Age, Sex, Race, and Hispanic Origin, 1948–2010—*Continued*

(Thousands of people.)

Race, Hispanic origin, sex, and year	16 years and over	16 to 19 years			20 years and over						
		Total	16 to 17 years	18 to 19 years	Total	20 to 24 years	25 to 34 years	35 to 44 years	45 to 54 years	55 to 64 years	65 years and over
BLACK											
Women											
1972	3 890	335	113	224	3 555	632	949	800	672	387	116
1973	4 052	373	133	240	3 678	670	1 026	806	670	402	105
1974	4 148	371	128	243	3 777	694	1 079	824	679	398	100
1975	4 247	391	144	245	3 857	687	1 138	827	686	409	108
1976	4 460	384	136	247	4 076	723	1 264	855	694	421	119
1977	4 670	385	127	258	4 286	785	1 357	891	712	429	113
1978	4 997	439	155	283	4 558	856	1 456	953	731	439	124
1979	5 119	432	161	271	4 687	865	1 517	990	740	451	124
1980	5 253	412	144	267	4 841	867	1 600	1 020	767	469	119
1981	5 401	400	139	261	5 001	888	1 663	1 071	779	485	115
1982	5 527	387	131	256	5 140	885	1 723	1 151	786	487	108
1983	5 681	375	114	261	5 306	874	1 835	1 210	785	496	105
1984	5 907	387	127	260	5 520	904	1 876	1 294	823	515	106
1985	6 144	417	149	268	5 727	904	1 951	1 368	862	515	127
1986	6 281	425	157	268	5 855	924	1 999	1 434	892	499	107
1987	6 507	435	157	278	6 071	904	2 073	1 537	924	512	121
1988	6 609	419	158	262	6 190	869	2 112	1 610	958	504	137
1989	6 796	445	163	281	6 352	885	2 138	1 683	1 009	493	144
1990	6 938	421	145	276	6 517	879	2 165	1 833	1 015	481	143
1991	6 946	374	126	248	6 572	854	2 143	1 913	1 032	494	135
1992	7 166	387	135	252	6 778	863	2 188	1 985	1 105	508	129
1993	7 206	383	129	254	6 824	889	2 115	2 042	1 147	506	125
1994	7 413	409	174	235	7 004	909	2 131	2 093	1 206	523	142
1995	7 634	458	182	276	7 175	887	2 177	2 178	1 256	556	121
1996	7 869	464	184	280	7 405	890	2 228	2 251	1 349	565	122
1997	8 175	489	175	314	7 686	951	2 277	2 305	1 437	585	131
1998	8 441	528	189	339	7 912	960	2 298	2 390	1 520	615	128
1999	8 713	489	172	316	8 224	1 031	2 360	2 447	1 606	633	147
2000	8 695	479	175	305	8 215	998	2 282	2 409	1 706	652	168
2001	8 774	451	166	284	8 323	1 025	2 265	2 410	1 762	690	173
2002	8 772	424	148	276	8 348	1 002	2 225	2 394	1 812	743	171
2003	8 815	406	151	255	8 409	973	2 188	2 407	1 879	781	180
2004	8 865	403	144	259	8 462	999	2 144	2 380	1 924	824	192
2005	9 014	405	140	265	8 610	1 017	2 197	2 342	1 954	891	207
2006	9 186	462	166	297	8 723	989	2 211	2 349	1 993	963	218
2007	9 244	417	163	254	8 828	993	2 218	2 328	2 044	1 019	227
2008	9 393	402	146	256	8 991	997	2 281	2 308	2 099	1 056	251
2009	9 367	379	119	260	8 988	1 008	2 258	2 243	2 124	1 091	264
2010	9 447	337	108	230	9 110	1 086	2 299	2 171	2 129	1 153	270
HISPANIC[1]											
Both Sexes											
1974	4 012	442	. . .	. . .	. . .	. . .	. . .	. . .	. . .	. . .	. . .
1975	4 171	444	. . .	. . .	. . .	. . .	. . .	. . .	. . .	. . .	. . .
1976	4 205	447	176	285	3 820	729	1 248	875	625	294	48
1977	4 536	493	184	305	4 059	813	1 325	916	656	293	55
1978	4 979	533	221	312	4 446	901	1 446	1 008	701	323	67
1979	5 219	551	207	343	4 668	960	1 532	1 062	704	339	72
1980	6 146	645	241	404	5 502	1 136	1 843	1 163	860	414	85
1981	6 492	603	215	388	5 888	1 231	2 015	1 239	886	430	87
1982	6 734	585	192	393	6 148	1 251	2 163	1 313	891	444	85
1983	7 033	590	189	401	6 442	1 282	2 267	1 380	931	495	86
1984	7 451	618	209	409	6 833	1 325	2 436	1 509	954	524	84
1985	7 698	579	199	379	7 119	1 358	2 571	1 595	985	527	82
1986	8 076	571	203	368	7 505	1 414	2 685	1 713	1 097	511	84
1987	8 541	610	206	404	7 931	1 425	2 890	1 904	1 086	545	81
1988	8 982	671	234	437	8 311	1 486	2 957	1 996	1 147	621	103
1989	9 323	680	224	456	8 643	1 483	3 118	2 092	1 205	625	120
1990	10 720	829	276	554	9 891	1 839	3 590	2 386	1 320	647	110
1991	10 920	781	249	532	10 139	1 835	3 596	2 539	1 376	681	111
1992	11 338	796	263	533	10 542	1 815	3 740	2 735	1 442	687	122
1993	11 610	771	246	525	10 839	1 811	3 800	2 865	1 534	684	145
1994	11 975	807	285	522	11 168	1 863	3 865	2 965	1 626	698	151
1995	12 267	850	291	559	11 417	1 818	3 943	3 113	1 671	720	152
1996	12 774	845	284	561	11 929	1 845	4 054	3 361	1 697	806	166
1997	13 796	911	315	596	12 884	2 004	4 298	3 601	1 945	850	186
1998	14 317	1 007	320	688	13 310	2 077	4 372	3 707	2 090	894	169
1999	14 665	1 049	333	717	13 616	2 052	4 330	3 929	2 178	927	199
2000	16 689	1 168	368	800	15 521	2 546	5 197	4 241	2 387	940	209
2001	17 328	1 176	352	824	16 152	2 616	5 380	4 377	2 583	1 000	195
2002	17 943	1 103	335	769	16 840	2 678	5 645	4 545	2 657	1 091	224
2003	18 813	960	322	638	17 853	2 672	5 960	4 867	2 894	1 201	259
2004	19 272	995	297	698	18 277	2 732	5 931	4 931	3 093	1 284	306
2005	19 824	1 038	331	708	18 785	2 651	6 080	5 110	3 256	1 378	311
2006	20 694	1 071	360	710	19 623	2 681	6 295	5 337	3 452	1 490	369
2007	21 602	1 091	347	744	20 511	2 728	6 559	5 552	3 707	1 569	395
2008	22 024	1 121	353	768	20 903	2 668	6 557	5 698	3 862	1 701	417
2009	22 352	1 063	301	762	21 290	2 647	6 435	5 752	4 116	1 866	472
2010	22 748	1 002	264	738	21 747	2 760	6 517	5 783	4 238	1 936	513

[1]May be of any race.
. . . = Not available.

Table 1-7. Civilian Labor Force, by Age, Sex, Race, and Hispanic Origin, 1948–2010—*Continued*

(Thousands of people.)

Race, Hispanic origin, sex, and year	16 years and over	16 to 19 years			20 years and over						
		Total	16 to 17 years	18 to 19 years	Total	20 to 24 years	25 to 34 years	35 to 44 years	45 to 54 years	55 to 64 years	65 years and over
HISPANIC[1]											
Men											
1974	2 556	...	...	...	2 306	...	...	...	...	...	...
1975	2 597	...	...	...	2 343	...	...	...	...	...	...
1976	2 580	260	104	155	2 326	433	771	541	398	189	34
1977	2 817	285	105	179	2 530	485	828	567	416	197	42
1978	3 041	299	129	171	2 742	546	882	620	425	217	52
1979	3 184	315	121	194	2 869	562	941	648	445	216	56
1980	3 818	392	147	245	3 426	697	1 161	713	522	270	62
1981	4 005	359	130	229	3 647	747	1 269	756	535	278	61
1982	4 148	333	111	221	3 815	759	1 361	808	539	290	58
1983	4 362	348	109	239	4 014	789	1 447	852	557	311	58
1984	4 563	345	113	232	4 218	822	1 540	910	570	325	51
1985	4 729	334	116	218	4 395	835	1 629	957	591	331	53
1986	4 948	336	114	222	4 612	888	1 669	1 015	661	323	56
1987	5 163	345	112	233	4 818	865	1 801	1 121	652	325	55
1988	5 409	378	123	255	5 031	897	1 834	1 189	686	355	69
1989	5 595	400	129	271	5 195	909	1 899	1 221	719	375	71
1990	6 546	512	165	346	6 034	1 182	2 230	1 403	775	380	65
1991	6 664	466	141	325	6 198	1 202	2 260	1 487	780	401	67
1992	6 900	468	154	314	6 432	1 141	2 366	1 593	844	414	74
1993	7 076	455	145	310	6 621	1 147	2 417	1 675	900	394	88
1994	7 210	463	163	300	6 747	1 184	2 430	1 713	922	410	89
1995	7 376	479	168	311	6 898	1 153	2 469	1 795	965	417	98
1996	7 646	496	156	340	7 150	1 132	2 510	1 966	967	469	105
1997	8 309	531	177	354	7 779	1 267	2 684	2 091	1 112	511	113
1998	8 571	565	188	377	8 005	1 288	2 733	2 173	1 164	541	106
1999	8 546	596	181	415	7 950	1 231	2 633	2 219	1 205	526	136
2000	9 923	676	204	471	9 247	1 590	3 181	2 451	1 337	555	134
2001	10 279	684	200	484	9 595	1 602	3 294	2 562	1 430	582	125
2002	10 609	632	183	449	9 977	1 627	3 484	2 647	1 478	607	134
2003	11 288	532	164	368	10 756	1 642	3 776	2 877	1 630	680	150
2004	11 587	567	156	410	11 020	1 671	3 765	2 934	1 736	728	186
2005	11 985	577	179	398	11 408	1 645	3 879	3 058	1 855	779	192
2006	12 488	600	189	411	11 888	1 646	4 014	3 203	1 960	838	228
2007	13 005	602	189	412	12 403	1 645	4 170	3 346	2 104	904	233
2008	13 255	626	202	424	12 629	1 594	4 172	3 425	2 216	979	243
2009	13 310	580	160	420	12 730	1 542	4 046	3 472	2 350	1 046	273
2010	13 511	553	132	420	12 958	1 612	4 061	3 515	2 407	1 061	302
HISPANIC[1]											
Women											
1974	1 456	...	...	...	1 264	...	...	...	...	...	...
1975	1 574	...	...	...	1 384	...	...	...	...	...	...
1976	1 625	201	71	130	1 454	295	479	334	227	105	13
1977	1 720	204	80	125	1 523	327	497	349	240	96	13
1978	1 938	233	93	142	1 704	354	564	388	275	106	16
1979	2 035	235	86	149	1 800	397	590	413	258	124	15
1980	2 328	252	93	159	2 076	439	682	450	337	144	22
1981	2 486	244	85	159	2 242	484	745	483	351	152	27
1982	2 586	252	81	172	2 333	492	802	504	352	155	28
1983	2 671	242	80	162	2 429	493	820	529	374	184	29
1984	2 888	273	96	177	2 615	503	896	599	384	199	34
1985	2 970	245	84	161	2 725	524	943	639	394	196	29
1986	3 128	236	89	147	2 893	526	1 016	698	436	189	28
1987	3 377	265	94	171	3 112	559	1 090	783	434	220	27
1988	3 573	293	111	182	3 281	589	1 123	806	461	267	34
1989	3 728	280	95	185	3 448	574	1 219	871	486	251	49
1990	4 174	318	110	207	3 857	657	1 360	983	545	268	45
1991	4 256	315	107	207	3 941	633	1 336	1 052	596	279	44
1992	4 439	328	110	219	4 110	674	1 374	1 142	599	273	48
1993	4 534	316	101	215	4 218	664	1 383	1 190	633	290	57
1994	4 765	345	122	222	4 421	679	1 435	1 252	704	288	62
1995	4 891	371	123	249	4 520	666	1 473	1 318	706	303	54
1996	5 128	349	128	221	4 779	713	1 544	1 395	729	338	61
1997	5 486	381	138	242	5 106	737	1 614	1 510	833	338	73
1998	5 746	442	132	310	5 304	789	1 639	1 533	927	353	62
1999	6 119	453	151	302	5 666	821	1 698	1 710	973	401	63
2000	6 767	492	164	328	6 275	956	2 016	1 791	1 051	386	75
2001	7 049	492	152	340	6 557	1 014	2 086	1 815	1 153	418	70
2002	7 334	471	152	320	6 863	1 051	2 161	1 897	1 179	484	90
2003	7 525	428	158	271	7 096	1 030	2 183	1 990	1 264	520	109
2004	7 685	429	141	288	7 257	1 060	2 166	1 998	1 357	556	119
2005	7 839	462	152	310	7 377	1 005	2 201	2 052	1 401	599	119
2006	8 206	471	171	300	7 735	1 035	2 280	2 134	1 492	652	141
2007	8 597	489	158	332	8 108	1 083	2 389	2 205	1 604	665	162
2008	8 769	495	151	344	8 274	1 074	2 384	2 274	1 646	722	174
2009	9 043	483	141	342	8 560	1 105	2 388	2 280	1 767	820	200
2010	9 238	449	132	317	8 789	1 147	2 456	2 268	1 831	875	211

[1]May be of any race.
. . . = Not available.

Table 1-8. Civilian Labor Force Participation Rates, by Age, Sex, Race, and Hispanic Origin, 1948–2010

(Percent.)

Race, Hispanic origin, sex, and year	16 years and over	16 to 19 years	20 years and over						
			Total	20 to 24 years	25 to 34 years	35 to 44 years	45 to 54 years	55 to 64 years	65 years and over
ALL RACES									
Both Sexes									
1948	58.8	52.5	59.4	64.1	63.1	66.7	65.1	56.9	27.0
1949	58.9	52.2	59.5	64.9	63.2	67.2	65.3	56.2	27.3
1950	59.2	51.8	59.9	65.9	63.5	67.5	66.4	56.7	26.7
1951	59.2	52.2	59.8	64.8	64.2	67.6	67.2	56.9	25.8
1952	59.0	51.3	59.7	62.2	64.7	68.0	67.5	57.5	24.8
1953	58.9	50.2	59.6	61.2	64.0	68.9	68.1	58.0	24.8
1954	58.8	48.3	59.6	61.6	64.3	68.8	68.4	58.7	23.9
1955	59.3	48.9	60.1	62.7	64.8	68.9	69.7	59.5	24.1
1956	60.0	50.9	60.7	64.1	64.8	69.5	70.5	60.8	24.3
1957	59.6	49.6	60.4	64.0	64.9	69.5	70.9	60.1	22.9
1958	59.5	47.4	60.5	64.4	65.0	69.6	71.5	60.5	21.8
1959	59.3	46.7	60.4	64.3	65.0	69.5	71.9	61.0	21.1
1960	59.4	47.5	60.5	65.2	65.4	69.4	72.2	60.9	20.8
1961	59.3	46.9	60.5	65.7	65.6	69.5	72.1	61.5	20.1
1962	58.8	46.1	60.0	65.3	65.2	69.7	72.2	61.5	19.1
1963	58.7	45.2	60.1	65.1	65.6	70.1	72.5	62.0	17.9
1964	58.7	44.5	60.2	66.3	65.8	70.0	72.9	61.9	18.0
1965	58.9	45.7	60.3	66.4	66.4	70.7	72.5	61.9	17.8
1966	59.2	48.2	60.5	66.5	67.1	71.0	72.7	62.2	17.2
1967	59.6	48.4	60.9	67.1	68.2	71.6	72.7	62.3	17.2
1968	59.6	48.3	60.9	67.0	68.6	72.0	72.8	62.2	17.2
1969	60.1	49.4	61.3	68.2	69.1	72.5	73.4	62.1	17.3
1970	60.4	49.9	61.6	69.2	69.7	73.1	73.5	61.8	17.0
1971	60.2	49.7	61.4	69.3	69.9	73.2	73.2	61.3	16.2
1972	60.4	51.9	61.4	70.8	70.9	73.3	72.7	60.0	15.6
1973	60.8	53.7	61.7	72.6	72.3	74.0	72.5	58.4	14.6
1974	61.3	54.8	62.0	74.0	73.6	74.6	72.7	57.8	14.0
1975	61.2	54.0	62.1	73.9	74.4	75.0	72.6	57.2	13.7
1976	61.6	54.5	62.4	74.7	75.7	76.0	72.5	56.6	13.1
1977	62.3	56.0	63.0	75.7	77.0	77.0	72.8	56.3	13.0
1978	63.2	57.8	63.8	76.8	78.3	78.1	73.5	56.3	13.3
1979	63.7	57.9	64.3	77.5	79.2	79.2	74.3	56.2	13.1
1980	63.8	56.7	64.5	77.2	79.9	80.0	74.9	55.7	12.5
1981	63.9	55.4	64.8	77.3	80.5	80.7	75.7	55.0	12.2
1982	64.0	54.1	65.0	77.1	81.0	81.2	75.9	55.1	11.9
1983	64.0	53.5	65.0	77.2	81.3	81.6	76.0	54.5	11.7
1984	64.4	53.9	65.3	77.6	81.8	82.4	76.5	54.2	11.1
1985	64.8	54.5	65.7	78.2	82.5	83.1	77.3	54.2	10.8
1986	65.3	54.7	66.2	78.9	82.9	83.7	78.0	54.0	10.9
1987	65.6	54.7	66.5	78.9	83.3	84.3	78.6	54.4	11.1
1988	65.9	55.3	66.8	78.7	83.3	84.6	79.6	54.6	11.5
1989	66.5	55.9	67.3	78.7	83.8	85.1	80.5	55.5	11.8
1990	66.5	53.7	67.6	77.8	83.6	85.2	80.7	55.9	11.8
1991	66.2	51.6	67.3	76.7	83.2	85.2	81.0	55.5	11.5
1992	66.4	51.3	67.6	77.0	83.7	85.1	81.5	56.2	11.5
1993	66.3	51.5	67.5	77.0	83.3	84.9	81.6	56.4	11.2
1994	66.6	52.7	67.7	77.0	83.2	84.8	81.7	56.8	12.4
1995	66.6	53.5	67.7	76.6	83.8	84.6	81.4	57.2	12.1
1996	66.8	52.3	67.9	76.8	84.1	84.8	82.1	57.9	12.1
1997	67.1	51.6	68.4	77.6	84.4	85.1	82.6	58.9	12.2
1998	67.1	52.8	68.3	77.5	84.6	84.7	82.5	59.3	11.9
1999	67.1	52.0	68.3	77.5	84.6	84.9	82.6	59.3	12.3
2000	67.1	52.0	68.3	77.8	84.6	84.8	82.5	59.2	12.9
2001	66.8	49.6	68.2	77.1	84.0	84.6	82.3	60.4	13.0
2002	66.6	47.4	68.1	76.4	83.7	84.1	82.1	61.9	13.2
2003	66.2	44.5	67.9	75.4	82.9	83.9	82.1	62.4	14.0
2004	66.0	43.9	67.7	75.0	82.7	83.6	81.8	62.3	14.4
2005	66.0	43.7	67.8	74.6	82.8	83.8	81.7	62.9	15.1
2006	66.2	43.7	67.9	74.6	83.0	83.8	81.9	63.7	15.4
2007	66.0	41.3	68.0	74.4	83.3	83.8	82.0	63.8	16.0
2008	66.0	40.2	68.0	74.4	83.3	84.1	81.9	64.5	16.8
2009	65.4	37.5	67.5	72.9	82.7	83.7	81.6	64.9	17.2
2010	64.7	34.9	67.0	71.4	82.2	83.2	81.2	64.9	17.4

Table 1-8. Civilian Labor Force Participation Rates, by Age, Sex, Race, and Hispanic Origin, 1948–2010
—*Continued*

(Percent.)

Race, Hispanic origin, sex, and year	16 years and over	16 to 19 years	20 years and over						
			Total	20 to 24 years	25 to 34 years	35 to 44 years	45 to 54 years	55 to 64 years	65 years and over
ALL RACES									
Men									
1948	86.6	63.7	88.6	84.6	95.9	97.9	95.8	89.5	46.8
1949	86.4	62.8	88.5	86.6	95.8	97.9	95.6	87.5	47.0
1950	86.4	63.2	88.4	87.9	96.0	97.6	95.8	86.9	45.8
1951	86.3	63.0	88.2	88.4	96.9	97.5	95.9	87.2	44.9
1952	86.3	61.3	88.3	88.1	97.5	97.8	96.2	87.5	42.6
1953	86.0	60.7	88.0	87.7	97.4	98.2	96.5	87.9	41.6
1954	85.5	58.0	87.8	86.9	97.3	98.1	96.5	88.7	40.5
1955	85.4	58.9	87.6	86.9	97.6	98.1	96.4	87.9	39.6
1956	85.5	60.5	87.6	87.8	97.3	97.9	96.6	88.5	40.0
1957	84.8	59.1	86.9	87.1	97.1	97.9	96.3	87.5	37.5
1958	84.2	56.6	86.6	86.9	97.1	97.9	96.3	87.8	35.6
1959	83.7	55.8	86.3	87.8	97.4	97.8	96.0	87.4	34.2
1960	83.3	56.1	86.0	88.1	97.5	97.7	95.7	86.8	33.1
1961	82.9	54.6	85.7	87.8	97.5	97.6	95.6	87.3	31.7
1962	82.0	53.8	84.8	86.9	97.2	97.6	95.6	86.2	30.3
1963	81.4	52.9	84.4	86.1	97.1	97.5	95.7	86.2	28.4
1964	81.0	52.4	84.2	86.1	97.3	97.3	95.7	85.6	28.0
1965	80.7	53.8	83.9	85.8	97.2	97.3	95.6	84.6	27.9
1966	80.4	55.3	83.6	85.1	97.3	97.2	95.3	84.5	27.1
1967	80.4	55.6	83.4	84.4	97.2	97.3	95.2	84.4	27.1
1968	80.1	55.1	83.1	82.8	96.9	97.1	94.9	84.3	27.3
1969	79.8	55.9	82.8	82.8	96.7	96.9	94.6	83.4	27.2
1970	79.7	56.1	82.6	83.3	96.4	96.9	94.3	83.0	26.8
1971	79.1	56.1	82.1	83.0	95.9	96.5	93.9	82.1	25.5
1972	78.9	58.1	81.6	83.9	95.7	96.4	93.2	80.4	24.3
1973	78.8	59.7	81.3	85.2	95.7	96.2	93.0	78.2	22.7
1974	78.7	60.7	81.0	85.9	95.8	96.0	92.2	77.3	22.4
1975	77.9	59.1	80.3	84.5	95.2	95.6	92.1	75.6	21.6
1976	77.5	59.3	79.8	85.2	95.2	95.4	91.6	74.3	20.2
1977	77.7	60.9	79.7	85.6	95.3	95.7	91.1	73.8	20.0
1978	77.9	62.0	79.8	85.9	95.3	95.7	91.3	73.3	20.4
1079	77.8	61.6	70.8	86.4	05.3	05.7	01.4	72.8	19.9
1980	77.4	60.5	79.4	85.9	95.2	95.5	91.2	72.1	19.0
1981	77.0	59.0	79.0	85.5	94.9	95.4	91.4	70.6	18.4
1982	76.6	56.7	78.7	84.9	94.7	95.3	91.2	70.2	17.8
1983	76.4	56.2	78.5	84.8	94.2	95.2	91.2	69.4	17.4
1984	76.4	56.0	78.3	85.0	94.4	95.4	91.2	68.5	16.3
1985	76.3	56.8	78.1	85.0	94.7	95.0	91.0	67.9	15.8
1986	76.3	56.4	78.1	85.8	94.6	94.8	91.0	67.3	16.0
1987	76.2	56.1	78.0	85.2	94.6	94.6	90.7	67.6	16.3
1988	76.2	56.9	77.9	85.0	94.3	94.5	90.9	67.0	16.5
1989	76.4	57.9	78.1	85.3	94.4	94.5	91.1	67.2	16.6
1990	76.4	55.7	78.2	84.4	94.1	94.3	90.7	67.8	16.3
1991	75.8	53.2	77.7	83.5	93.6	94.1	90.5	67.0	15.7
1992	75.8	53.4	77.7	83.3	93.8	93.7	90.7	67.0	16.1
1993	75.4	53.2	77.3	83.2	93.4	93.4	90.1	66.5	15.6
1994	75.1	54.1	76.8	83.1	92.6	92.8	89.1	65.5	16.8
1995	75.0	54.8	76.7	83.1	93.0	92.3	88.8	66.0	16.8
1996	74.9	53.2	76.8	82.5	93.2	92.4	89.1	67.0	16.9
1997	75.0	52.3	77.0	82.5	93.0	92.6	89.5	67.6	17.1
1998	74.9	53.3	76.8	82.0	93.2	92.6	89.2	68.1	16.5
1999	74.7	52.9	76.7	81.9	93.3	92.8	88.8	67.9	16.9
2000	74.8	52.8	76.7	82.6	93.4	92.7	88.6	67.3	17.7
2001	74.4	50.2	76.5	81.6	92.7	92.5	88.5	68.3	17.7
2002	74.1	47.5	76.3	80.7	92.4	92.1	88.5	69.2	17.9
2003	73.5	44.3	75.9	80.0	91.8	92.1	87.7	68.7	18.6
2004	73.3	43.9	75.8	79.6	91.9	91.9	87.5	68.7	19.0
2005	73.3	43.2	75.8	79.1	91.7	92.1	87.7	69.3	19.8
2006	73.5	43.7	75.9	79.6	91.7	92.1	88.1	69.6	20.3
2007	73.2	41.1	75.9	78.7	92.2	92.3	88.2	69.6	20.5
2008	73.0	40.1	75.7	78.7	91.5	92.2	88.0	70.4	21.5
2009	72.0	37.3	74.8	76.2	90.3	91.7	87.4	70.2	21.9
2010	71.2	34.9	74.1	74.5	89.7	91.5	86.8	70.0	22.1

Table 1-8. Civilian Labor Force Participation Rates, by Age, Sex, Race, and Hispanic Origin, 1948–2010
—*Continued*

(Percent.)

Race, Hispanic origin, sex, and year	16 years and over	16 to 19 years	20 years and over						
			Total	20 to 24 years	25 to 34 years	35 to 44 years	45 to 54 years	55 to 64 years	65 years and over
ALL RACES									
Women									
1948	32.7	42.0	31.8	45.3	33.2	36.9	35.0	24.3	9.1
1949	33.1	42.4	32.3	45.0	33.4	38.1	35.9	25.3	9.6
1950	33.9	41.0	33.3	46.0	34.0	39.1	37.9	27.0	9.7
1951	34.6	42.4	34.0	46.5	35.4	39.8	39.7	27.6	8.9
1952	34.7	42.2	34.1	44.7	35.4	40.4	40.1	28.7	9.1
1953	34.4	40.7	33.9	44.3	34.0	41.3	40.4	29.1	10.0
1954	34.6	39.4	34.2	45.1	34.4	41.2	41.2	30.0	9.3
1955	35.7	39.7	35.4	45.9	34.9	41.6	43.8	32.5	10.6
1956	36.9	42.2	36.4	46.3	35.4	43.1	45.5	34.9	10.8
1957	36.9	41.1	36.5	45.9	35.6	43.3	46.5	34.5	10.5
1958	37.1	39.0	36.9	46.3	35.6	43.4	47.8	35.2	10.3
1959	37.1	38.2	37.1	45.1	35.3	43.4	49.0	36.6	10.2
1960	37.7	39.3	37.6	46.1	36.0	43.4	49.9	37.2	10.8
1961	38.1	39.7	38.0	47.0	36.4	43.8	50.1	37.9	10.7
1962	37.9	39.0	37.8	47.3	36.3	44.1	50.0	38.7	10.0
1963	38.3	38.0	38.3	47.5	37.2	44.9	50.6	39.7	9.6
1964	38.7	37.0	38.9	49.4	37.2	45.0	51.4	40.2	10.1
1965	39.3	38.0	39.4	49.9	38.5	46.1	50.9	41.1	10.0
1966	40.3	41.4	40.1	51.5	39.8	46.8	51.7	41.8	9.6
1967	41.1	41.6	41.1	53.3	41.9	48.1	51.8	42.4	9.6
1968	41.6	41.9	41.6	54.5	42.6	48.9	52.3	42.4	9.6
1969	42.7	43.2	42.7	56.7	43.7	49.9	53.8	43.1	9.9
1970	43.3	44.0	43.3	57.7	45.0	51.1	54.4	43.0	9.7
1971	43.4	43.4	43.3	57.7	45.6	51.6	54.3	42.9	9.5
1972	43.9	45.8	43.7	59.1	47.8	52.0	53.9	42.1	9.3
1973	44.7	47.8	44.4	61.1	50.4	53.3	53.7	41.1	8.9
1974	45.7	49.1	45.3	63.1	52.6	54.7	54.6	40.7	8.1
1975	46.3	49.1	46.0	64.1	54.9	55.8	54.6	40.9	8.2
1976	47.3	49.8	47.0	65.0	57.3	57.8	55.0	41.0	8.2
1977	48.4	51.2	48.1	66.5	59.7	59.6	55.8	40.9	8.1
1978	50.0	53.7	49.6	68.3	62.2	61.6	57.1	41.3	8.3
1979	50.9	54.2	50.6	69.0	63.9	63.6	58.3	41.7	8.3
1980	51.5	52.9	51.3	68.9	65.5	65.5	59.9	41.3	8.1
1981	52.1	51.8	52.1	69.6	66.7	66.8	61.1	41.4	8.0
1982	52.6	51.4	52.7	69.8	68.0	68.0	61.6	41.8	7.9
1983	52.9	50.8	53.1	69.9	69.0	68.7	61.9	41.5	7.8
1984	53.6	51.8	53.7	70.4	69.8	70.1	62.9	41.7	7.5
1985	54.5	52.1	54.7	71.8	70.9	71.8	64.4	42.0	7.3
1986	55.3	53.0	55.5	72.4	71.6	73.1	65.9	42.3	7.4
1987	56.0	53.3	56.2	73.0	72.4	74.5	67.1	42.7	7.4
1988	56.6	53.6	56.8	72.7	72.7	75.2	69.0	43.5	7.9
1989	57.4	53.9	57.7	72.4	73.5	76.0	70.5	45.0	8.4
1990	57.5	51.6	58.0	71.3	73.5	76.4	71.2	45.2	8.6
1991	57.4	50.0	57.9	70.1	73.1	76.5	72.0	45.2	8.5
1992	57.8	49.1	58.5	70.9	73.9	76.7	72.6	46.5	8.3
1993	57.9	49.7	58.5	70.9	73.4	76.6	73.5	47.2	8.1
1994	58.8	51.3	59.3	71.0	74.0	77.1	74.6	48.9	9.2
1995	58.9	52.2	59.4	70.3	74.9	77.2	74.4	49.2	8.8
1996	59.3	51.3	59.9	71.3	75.2	77.5	75.4	49.6	8.6
1997	59.8	51.0	60.5	72.7	76.0	77.7	76.0	50.9	8.6
1998	59.8	52.3	60.4	73.0	76.3	77.1	76.2	51.2	8.6
1999	60.0	51.0	60.7	73.2	76.4	77.2	76.7	51.5	8.9
2000	59.9	51.2	60.6	73.1	76.1	77.2	76.8	51.9	9.4
2001	59.8	49.0	60.6	72.7	75.5	77.1	76.4	53.2	9.6
2002	59.6	47.3	60.5	72.1	75.1	76.4	76.0	55.2	9.8
2003	59.5	44.8	60.6	70.8	74.1	76.0	76.8	56.6	10.6
2004	59.2	43.8	60.3	70.5	73.6	75.6	76.5	56.3	11.1
2005	59.3	44.2	60.4	70.1	73.9	75.8	76.0	57.0	11.5
2006	59.4	43.7	60.5	69.5	74.4	75.9	76.0	58.2	11.7
2007	59.3	41.5	60.6	70.1	74.5	75.5	76.0	58.3	12.6
2008	59.5	40.2	60.9	70.0	75.2	76.1	76.1	59.1	13.3
2009	59.2	37.7	60.8	69.6	75.0	75.9	76.0	60.0	13.6
2010	58.6	35.0	60.3	68.3	74.7	75.2	75.7	60.2	13.8

Table 1-8. Civilian Labor Force Participation Rates, by Age, Sex, Race, and Hispanic Origin, 1948–2010
—*Continued*

(Percent.)

Race, Hispanic origin, sex, and year	16 years and over	16 to 19 years	20 years and over						
			Total	20 to 24 years	25 to 34 years	35 to 44 years	45 to 54 years	55 to 64 years	65 years and over
WHITE									
Both Sexes									
1954	58.2	48.8	58.9	61.0	63.5	68.0	67.9	58.4	23.7
1955	58.7	49.3	59.5	62.4	64.0	68.3	69.2	59.3	23.9
1956	59.4	51.3	60.1	64.1	64.0	68.9	70.1	60.6	24.2
1957	59.1	50.3	59.8	63.7	64.1	68.8	70.5	59.9	22.8
1958	58.9	47.9	59.8	64.1	64.2	68.8	71.0	60.3	21.7
1959	58.7	47.4	59.7	63.7	64.3	68.7	71.5	60.7	21.0
1960	58.8	47.9	59.8	64.8	64.7	68.6	71.7	60.6	20.8
1961	58.8	47.4	59.9	65.5	64.8	68.8	71.7	61.3	20.0
1962	58.3	46.6	59.4	65.0	64.4	69.0	71.8	61.3	19.0
1963	58.2	45.7	59.4	64.9	64.8	69.4	72.3	61.8	17.9
1964	58.2	45.1	59.6	65.8	64.9	69.5	72.5	61.8	17.8
1965	58.4	46.5	59.7	65.7	65.6	70.1	72.2	61.7	17.7
1966	58.7	49.1	59.8	66.0	66.3	70.4	72.5	61.9	17.1
1967	59.2	49.2	60.3	66.8	67.4	71.2	72.5	62.3	17.0
1968	59.3	49.3	60.4	66.6	67.9	71.7	72.7	62.2	17.1
1969	59.9	50.6	60.9	67.9	68.4	72.3	73.3	62.1	17.2
1970	60.2	51.4	61.2	69.2	69.1	72.9	73.5	61.8	16.8
1971	60.1	51.6	61.1	69.6	69.3	73.0	73.4	61.3	16.1
1972	60.4	54.1	61.2	71.2	70.4	73.2	72.9	60.3	15.4
1973	60.8	56.0	61.4	73.3	72.0	73.9	72.7	58.6	14.4
1974	61.4	57.3	61.9	74.8	73.4	74.6	73.0	58.0	13.9
1975	61.5	56.7	62.0	75.2	74.4	75.1	73.0	57.4	13.6
1976	61.8	57.5	62.3	76.0	75.6	76.1	73.0	56.9	13.0
1977	62.5	59.3	62.9	77.1	77.0	77.1	73.2	56.6	12.9
1978	63.3	60.8	63.6	78.1	78.3	78.1	73.8	56.4	13.1
1979	63.9	61.1	64.2	78.9	79.4	79.3	74.6	56.5	12.9
1980	64.1	60.0	64.5	78.7	80.2	80.3	75.4	56.0	12.5
1981	64.3	58.9	64.8	79.1	81.0	81.0	76.2	55.2	12.2
1982	64.3	57.5	65.0	78.9	81.6	81.5	76.4	55.3	12.0
1983	64.3	56.9	65.0	79.0	81.8	81.9	76.5	54.7	11.8
1984	64.6	57.2	65.3	79.4	82.5	82.6	77.0	54.5	11.1
1985	65.0	57.5	65.7	79.9	83.1	83.4	77.8	54.4	10.7
1986	65.5	57.8	66.1	80.6	83.6	84.0	78.5	54.3	11.0
1987	65.8	57.7	66.5	80.7	84.0	84.7	79.1	54.6	11.1
1988	66.2	58.6	66.8	80.6	84.1	85.0	80.3	55.1	11.4
1989	66.7	59.1	67.3	80.2	84.5	85.5	81.2	56.2	11.8
1990	66.9	57.5	67.6	79.8	84.6	85.9	81.3	56.5	11.9
1991	66.6	55.8	67.4	78.9	84.3	85.9	81.8	56.0	11.6
1992	66.8	54.7	67.7	79.4	84.6	85.8	82.2	56.8	11.6
1993	66.8	55.1	67.6	79.5	84.5	85.7	82.5	57.1	11.4
1994	67.1	56.4	67.9	79.5	84.4	85.7	82.7	57.6	12.5
1995	67.1	57.1	67.8	78.7	84.9	85.5	82.5	58.0	12.3
1996	67.2	55.9	68.1	79.1	84.9	85.7	83.1	58.7	12.3
1997	67.5	55.2	68.4	79.6	85.3	85.8	83.5	59.9	12.3
1998	67.3	56.0	68.2	79.5	85.4	85.3	83.4	60.1	12.0
1999	67.3	55.5	68.2	79.5	85.1	85.4	83.5	60.2	12.5
2000	67.3	55.5	68.2	79.9	85.1	85.4	83.5	60.0	13.0
2001	67.0	53.1	68.1	79.2	84.5	85.2	83.3	61.2	13.0
2002	66.8	50.5	68.1	78.6	84.5	84.7	83.0	62.8	13.3
2003	66.5	47.7	67.9	77.7	83.6	84.3	83.0	63.3	14.1
2004	66.3	47.1	67.7	77.1	83.5	84.1	82.9	63.2	14.6
2005	66.3	46.9	67.7	76.3	83.5	84.2	82.8	63.7	15.1
2006	66.5	46.7	67.9	76.5	83.8	84.3	83.0	64.7	15.5
2007	66.4	44.4	68.0	76.4	84.1	84.1	83.1	64.9	16.2
2008	66.3	43.1	68.0	76.3	83.9	84.4	82.9	65.7	17.0
2009	65.8	40.6	67.7	75.1	83.5	84.2	82.7	66.2	17.4
2010	65.1	37.7	67.1	73.4	83.2	83.8	82.2	66.1	17.6

Table 1-8. Civilian Labor Force Participation Rates, by Age, Sex, Race, and Hispanic Origin, 1948–2010
—Continued

(Percent.)

Race, Hispanic origin, sex, and year	16 years and over	16 to 19 years	20 years and over						
			Total	20 to 24 years	25 to 34 years	35 to 44 years	45 to 54 years	55 to 64 years	65 years and over
WHITE									
Men									
1954	85.6	57.6	87.8	86.3	97.5	98.2	96.8	89.1	40.4
1955	85.4	58.6	87.5	86.5	97.8	98.2	96.7	88.4	39.6
1956	85.6	60.4	87.6	87.6	97.4	98.1	96.8	88.9	40.0
1957	84.8	59.2	86.9	86.6	97.2	98.0	96.7	88.0	37.7
1958	84.3	56.5	86.6	86.7	97.2	98.0	96.6	88.2	35.7
1959	83.8	55.9	86.3	87.3	97.5	98.0	96.3	87.9	34.3
1960	83.4	55.9	86.0	87.8	97.7	97.9	96.1	87.2	33.3
1961	83.0	54.5	85.7	87.6	97.7	97.9	95.9	87.8	31.9
1962	82.1	53.8	84.9	86.5	97.4	97.9	96.0	86.7	30.6
1963	81.5	53.1	84.4	85.8	97.4	97.8	96.2	86.6	28.4
1964	81.1	52.7	84.2	85.7	97.5	97.6	96.1	86.1	27.9
1965	80.8	54.1	83.9	85.3	97.4	97.7	95.9	85.2	27.9
1966	80.6	55.9	83.6	84.4	97.5	97.6	95.8	84.9	27.2
1967	80.6	56.3	83.5	84.0	97.5	97.7	95.6	84.9	27.1
1968	80.4	55.9	83.2	82.4	97.2	97.6	95.4	84.7	27.4
1969	80.2	56.8	83.0	82.6	97.0	97.4	95.1	83.9	27.3
1970	80.0	57.5	82.8	83.3	96.7	97.3	94.9	83.3	26.7
1971	79.6	57.9	82.3	83.2	96.3	97.0	94.7	82.6	25.6
1972	79.6	60.1	82.0	84.3	96.0	97.0	94.0	81.1	24.4
1973	79.4	62.0	81.6	85.8	96.2	96.8	93.5	78.9	22.7
1974	79.4	62.9	81.4	86.6	96.3	96.7	93.0	78.0	22.4
1975	78.7	61.9	80.7	85.5	95.8	96.4	92.9	76.4	21.7
1976	78.4	62.3	80.3	86.3	95.9	96.0	92.5	75.2	20.2
1977	78.5	64.0	80.2	86.8	96.0	96.2	92.1	74.6	20.0
1978	78.6	65.0	80.1	87.3	95.9	96.3	92.1	73.7	20.3
1979	78.6	64.8	80.1	87.6	96.0	96.4	92.2	73.4	20.0
1980	78.2	63.7	79.8	87.2	95.9	96.2	92.1	73.1	19.1
1981	77.9	62.4	79.5	87.0	95.8	96.1	92.4	71.5	18.5
1982	77.4	60.0	79.2	86.3	95.6	96.0	92.2	71.0	17.9
1983	77.1	59.4	78.9	86.1	95.2	96.0	91.9	70.0	17.7
1984	77.1	59.0	78.7	86.5	95.4	96.1	92.0	69.5	16.4
1985	77.0	59.7	78.5	86.4	95.7	95.7	92.0	68.8	15.9
1986	76.9	59.3	78.5	87.3	95.5	95.4	91.8	68.0	16.3
1987	76.8	59.0	78.4	86.9	95.5	95.4	91.6	68.1	16.5
1988	76.9	60.0	78.3	86.6	95.2	95.4	91.8	67.9	16.7
1989	77.1	61.0	78.5	86.8	95.4	95.3	92.2	68.3	16.8
1990	77.1	59.6	78.5	86.2	95.2	95.3	91.7	68.6	16.6
1991	76.5	57.3	78.0	85.4	94.9	95.0	91.4	67.7	15.9
1992	76.5	56.9	78.0	85.2	94.9	94.7	91.8	67.7	16.2
1993	76.2	56.6	77.7	85.5	94.7	94.5	91.3	67.3	15.9
1994	75.9	57.7	77.3	85.5	93.9	93.9	90.3	66.4	17.2
1995	75.7	58.5	77.1	85.1	94.1	93.4	90.0	67.1	16.9
1996	75.8	57.1	77.3	85.0	94.4	93.6	90.4	68.0	17.2
1997	75.9	56.1	77.5	85.1	94.2	93.7	90.6	68.9	17.4
1998	75.6	56.6	77.2	84.6	94.4	93.7	90.3	69.1	16.6
1999	75.6	56.4	77.2	84.9	94.3	93.8	90.1	69.1	17.2
2000	75.5	56.5	77.1	85.2	94.5	93.8	89.7	68.2	17.9
2001	75.1	53.7	76.9	84.1	93.9	93.6	89.7	69.1	17.8
2002	74.8	50.3	76.7	83.2	93.7	93.2	89.6	70.2	17.8
2003	74.2	47.5	76.3	82.5	93.3	93.1	88.8	69.7	18.6
2004	74.1	47.4	76.2	82.1	93.2	93.0	88.7	69.8	19.1
2005	74.1	46.2	76.2	81.4	93.0	93.0	89.0	70.4	20.0
2006	74.3	46.9	76.4	81.9	92.9	93.1	89.3	71.0	20.6
2007	74.0	44.3	76.3	80.9	93.4	93.1	89.6	71.2	20.8
2008	73.7	43.0	76.1	80.8	92.6	93.0	89.2	71.9	21.8
2009	72.8	40.3	75.3	78.6	91.6	92.7	88.8	71.8	22.2
2010	72.0	37.4	74.6	77.0	91.1	92.4	88.1	71.2	22.3

Table 1-8. Civilian Labor Force Participation Rates, by Age, Sex, Race, and Hispanic Origin, 1948–2010
—Continued

(Percent.)

Race, Hispanic origin, sex, and year	16 years and over	16 to 19 years	20 years and over						
			Total	20 to 24 years	25 to 34 years	35 to 44 years	45 to 54 years	55 to 64 years	65 years and over
WHITE									
Women									
1954	33.3	40.6	32.7	44.4	32.5	39.3	39.8	29.1	9.1
1955	34.5	40.7	34.0	45.8	32.8	40.0	42.7	31.8	10.5
1956	35.7	43.1	35.1	46.5	33.2	41.5	44.4	34.0	10.6
1957	35.7	42.2	35.2	45.8	33.6	41.5	45.4	33.7	10.2
1958	35.8	40.1	35.5	46.0	33.6	41.4	46.5	34.5	10.1
1959	36.0	39.6	35.6	44.5	33.4	41.4	47.8	35.7	10.0
1960	36.5	40.3	36.2	45.7	34.1	41.5	48.6	36.2	10.6
1961	36.9	40.6	36.6	46.9	34.3	41.8	48.9	37.2	10.5
1962	36.7	39.8	36.5	47.1	34.1	42.2	48.9	38.0	9.8
1963	37.2	38.7	37.0	47.3	34.8	43.1	49.5	38.9	9.4
1964	37.5	37.8	37.5	48.8	35.0	43.3	50.2	39.4	9.9
1965	38.1	39.2	38.0	49.2	36.3	44.4	49.9	40.3	9.7
1966	39.2	42.6	38.8	51.0	37.7	45.0	50.6	41.1	9.4
1967	40.1	42.5	39.8	53.1	39.7	46.4	50.9	41.9	9.3
1968	40.7	43.0	40.4	54.0	40.6	47.5	51.5	42.0	9.4
1969	41.8	44.6	41.5	56.4	41.7	48.6	53.0	42.6	9.7
1970	42.6	45.6	42.2	57.7	43.2	49.9	53.7	42.6	9.5
1971	42.6	45.4	42.3	58.0	43.7	50.2	53.6	42.5	9.3
1972	43.2	48.1	42.7	59.4	46.0	50.7	53.4	41.9	9.0
1973	44.1	50.1	43.5	61.7	48.7	52.2	53.4	40.7	8.7
1974	45.2	51.7	44.4	63.9	51.3	53.6	54.3	40.4	8.0
1975	45.9	51.5	45.3	65.5	53.8	54.9	54.3	40.6	8.0
1976	46.9	52.8	46.2	66.3	56.0	57.1	54.7	40.7	7.9
1977	48.0	54.5	47.3	67.8	58.5	58.9	55.3	40.7	7.9
1978	49.4	56.7	48.7	69.3	61.2	60.7	56.7	41.1	8.1
1979	50.5	57.4	49.8	70.5	63.1	63.0	58.1	41.5	8.1
1980	51.2	56.2	50.6	70.6	64.8	65.0	59.6	40.9	7.9
1981	51.9	55.4	51.5	71.5	66.4	66.4	60.9	40.9	7.9
1982	52.4	55.0	52.2	71.8	67.8	67.5	61.4	41.5	7.8
1983	52.7	54.5	52.5	72.1	68.7	68.2	61.9	41.1	7.8
1984	53.3	55.4	53.1	72.5	69.8	69.6	62.7	41.2	7.5
1985	54.1	55.2	54.0	73.8	70.9	71.4	64.2	41.5	7.0
1986	55.0	56.3	54.9	74.1	71.8	72.9	65.8	42.1	7.3
1987	55.7	56.5	55.6	74.8	72.5	74.2	67.2	42.4	7.2
1988	56.4	57.2	56.3	74.9	73.0	74.9	69.2	43.6	7.7
1989	57.2	57.1	57.2	74.0	73.8	75.9	70.6	45.2	8.2
1990	57.4	55.3	57.6	73.4	74.1	76.6	71.3	45.5	8.5
1991	57.4	54.1	57.6	72.5	73.8	76.8	72.4	45.4	8.5
1992	57.7	52.5	58.1	73.5	74.4	77.0	72.8	46.8	8.2
1993	58.0	53.5	58.3	73.4	74.3	76.9	74.0	47.6	8.1
1994	58.9	55.1	59.2	73.4	74.9	77.5	75.2	49.4	9.2
1995	59.0	55.5	59.2	72.3	75.8	77.6	75.2	49.5	9.0
1996	59.1	54.7	59.4	73.3	75.5	77.8	76.1	50.1	8.7
1997	59.5	54.1	59.9	73.9	76.3	77.9	76.6	51.5	8.6
1998	59.4	55.4	59.7	74.3	76.3	76.9	76.6	51.6	8.7
1999	59.6	54.5	59.9	73.9	76.0	77.1	77.1	52.0	8.9
2000	59.5	54.5	59.9	74.5	75.7	77.2	77.5	52.4	9.4
2001	59.4	52.4	59.9	74.2	75.1	77.0	77.1	53.8	9.6
2002	59.3	50.8	60.0	74.0	75.0	76.3	76.6	55.8	9.9
2003	59.2	47.9	59.9	72.7	73.7	75.5	77.3	57.4	10.8
2004	58.9	46.7	59.7	71.9	73.6	75.2	77.1	57.0	11.2
2005	58.9	47.6	59.7	71.0	73.7	75.4	76.7	57.5	11.4
2006	59.0	46.6	59.9	70.9	74.3	75.5	76.7	58.7	11.6
2007	59.0	44.6	60.1	71.6	74.5	75.0	76.6	58.9	12.7
2008	59.2	43.3	60.3	71.6	74.9	75.8	76.6	59.7	13.3
2009	59.1	40.9	60.4	71.6	75.1	75.7	76.7	60.8	13.6
2010	58.5	38.0	59.9	69.7	74.9	75.0	76.3	61.1	13.9

Table 1-8. Civilian Labor Force Participation Rates, by Age, Sex, Race, and Hispanic Origin, 1948–2010
—*Continued*

(Percent.)

Race, Hispanic origin, sex, and year	16 years and over	16 to 19 years	20 years and over						
			Total	20 to 24 years	25 to 34 years	35 to 44 years	45 to 54 years	55 to 64 years	65 years and over
BLACK									
Both Sexes									
1973	60.2	39.8	63.4	69.7	75.7	74.5	70.3	55.9	16.0
1974	59.8	39.8	63.0	69.8	75.8	74.6	69.1	54.7	15.1
1975	58.8	38.2	62.0	66.1	75.6	74.1	69.0	54.3	14.9
1976	59.0	37.0	62.5	66.8	77.4	74.9	68.6	53.4	14.9
1977	59.8	37.9	63.2	68.2	78.3	75.9	69.0	53.7	14.5
1978	61.5	41.0	64.5	69.9	79.6	77.4	70.4	54.8	15.3
1979	61.4	40.1	64.5	70.0	79.2	77.9	71.1	53.5	14.5
1980	61.0	38.9	64.1	69.0	79.5	77.4	71.4	52.6	13.0
1981	60.8	37.7	64.2	69.2	78.5	78.4	71.2	52.8	12.0
1982	61.0	36.6	64.3	68.6	78.7	79.8	71.1	52.3	11.5
1983	61.5	36.4	64.9	68.4	79.8	80.2	72.1	52.5	10.5
1984	62.2	38.3	65.2	69.2	79.3	81.0	73.0	51.6	10.3
1985	62.9	41.2	65.6	70.0	79.8	81.5	73.4	51.4	11.2
1986	63.3	41.3	65.9	71.7	80.1	81.9	74.3	50.6	9.7
1987	63.8	41.6	66.5	70.5	80.7	82.6	74.7	52.4	10.7
1988	63.8	40.8	66.5	70.5	80.8	82.6	75.0	50.6	11.5
1989	64.2	42.5	66.7	72.2	80.9	82.7	75.5	48.3	11.6
1990	64.0	38.7	66.9	68.8	79.7	82.4	76.5	49.6	11.1
1991	63.3	35.4	66.4	67.7	78.5	82.0	76.2	50.4	10.7
1992	63.9	37.9	66.8	67.4	79.7	81.4	76.2	51.6	10.6
1993	63.2	37.0	66.0	67.8	78.3	81.0	75.2	50.2	9.5
1994	63.4	38.5	66.0	68.8	78.3	80.8	74.8	49.3	10.6
1995	63.7	39.9	66.3	68.7	80.0	80.4	74.1	50.3	10.5
1996	64.1	39.2	66.9	69.0	81.1	81.0	74.9	50.9	9.8
1997	64.7	38.7	67.6	70.9	82.0	81.4	76.3	50.5	10.0
1998	65.6	41.6	68.2	70.6	83.0	82.2	76.7	52.3	10.3
1999	65.8	38.7	68.9	71.4	85.2	83.0	76.4	51.4	10.4
2000	65.8	39.4	68.7	71.8	84.1	82.3	76.9	52.5	11.6
2001	65.3	37.6	68.2	69.9	83.6	82.0	75.9	53.9	12.6
2002	64.8	36.0	67.8	68.6	82.4	81.6	76.1	54.7	12.5
2003	64.3	32.4	67.6	68.2	81.6	82.9	75.8	54.4	12.9
2004	63.8	31.4	67.2	68.3	81.2	82.1	75.5	54.4	13.1
2005	64.2	32.4	67.4	69.0	81.7	82.3	75.7	55.3	13.6
2006	64.1	34.0	67.3	68.8	81.8	82.0	75.8	55.4	13.7
2007	63.7	30.3	67.2	68.3	81.7	82.7	75.7	55.1	14.0
2008	63.7	29.4	67.4	68.0	82.2	83.0	76.1	55.6	15.0
2009	62.4	27.2	66.1	66.0	80.4	81.7	75.2	55.5	15.3
2010	62.2	25.5	66.0	66.9	80.5	81.4	75.0	55.7	15.2
BLACK									
Men									
1973	73.4	45.7	78.4	83.7	91.8	91.0	87.4	69.5	22.3
1974	72.9	46.7	77.6	83.6	92.8	90.4	84.0	68.9	21.6
1975	70.9	42.6	76.0	78.7	91.6	89.4	83.5	67.7	20.7
1976	70.0	41.3	75.4	79.0	90.9	89.9	82.4	65.1	19.8
1977	70.6	43.2	75.6	79.2	90.7	91.0	82.0	65.5	20.0
1978	71.5	44.9	76.2	78.8	90.9	90.5	83.2	67.9	21.1
1979	71.3	43.6	76.3	80.7	90.8	90.4	84.5	64.8	19.5
1980	70.3	43.2	75.1	79.9	90.9	89.1	83.0	61.9	16.9
1981	70.0	41.6	74.5	79.2	88.9	89.3	82.7	62.1	16.0
1982	70.1	39.8	74.7	78.7	89.2	89.8	82.2	61.9	15.9
1983	70.6	39.9	75.2	79.4	89.0	89.7	84.5	62.6	14.0
1984	70.8	41.7	74.8	79.1	88.9	90.0	83.7	58.9	13.7
1985	70.8	44.6	74.4	79.0	88.8	89.8	83.0	58.9	13.9
1986	71.2	43.7	74.8	80.1	89.6	89.6	84.1	59.1	12.6
1987	71.1	43.6	74.7	77.8	89.4	88.6	83.7	62.1	13.7
1988	71.0	43.8	74.6	79.3	89.3	88.2	83.5	59.4	14.3
1989	71.0	44.6	74.4	80.2	89.7	88.7	82.5	55.5	14.3
1990	71.0	40.7	75.0	76.8	88.8	88.1	83.5	58.0	13.0
1991	70.4	37.3	74.6	76.7	87.3	87.7	83.4	58.7	13.0
1992	70.7	40.6	74.3	75.4	88.0	86.5	81.8	60.0	13.7
1993	69.6	39.5	73.2	74.1	87.3	86.1	80.0	57.9	11.6
1994	69.1	40.8	72.5	73.9	86.2	85.9	79.1	54.5	12.7
1995	69.0	40.1	72.5	74.6	87.5	84.1	78.5	54.4	14.9
1996	68.7	39.5	72.3	73.4	87.5	84.4	78.5	55.6	12.9
1997	68.3	37.4	72.2	72.1	86.8	84.8	80.1	54.3	12.9
1998	69.0	40.7	72.5	71.8	87.1	85.0	79.9	57.3	14.0
1999	68.7	38.6	72.4	69.8	89.2	86.0	78.5	55.5	12.7
2000	69.2	39.2	72.8	73.3	87.8	85.2	79.2	57.4	14.4
2001	68.4	37.9	72.1	69.7	86.6	84.9	78.4	58.9	16.7
2002	68.4	37.3	72.1	70.7	85.9	84.7	79.5	58.4	16.9
2003	67.3	31.1	71.5	71.1	84.7	85.7	77.7	57.6	17.0
2004	66.7	30.0	70.9	69.9	86.1	84.0	76.9	57.1	17.0
2005	67.3	32.6	71.3	70.1	85.5	85.5	78.6	57.3	17.1
2006	67.0	32.3	71.1	71.6	85.7	84.4	79.2	55.9	16.7
2007	66.8	29.4	71.2	71.1	86.1	86.3	78.6	54.4	17.3
2008	66.7	29.1	71.1	71.1	85.3	86.8	79.1	56.1	18.1
2009	65.0	26.4	69.6	67.6	83.2	85.1	77.4	56.8	18.3
2010	65.0	25.8	69.5	66.9	83.4	86.1	77.4	56.8	18.1

Table 1-8. Civilian Labor Force Participation Rates, by Age, Sex, Race, and Hispanic Origin, 1948–2010 —*Continued*

(Percent.)

Race, Hispanic origin, sex, and year	16 years and over	16 to 19 years	20 years and over						
			Total	20 to 24 years	25 to 34 years	35 to 44 years	45 to 54 years	55 to 64 years	65 years and over
BLACK									
Women									
1973	49.3	34.2	51.6	58.0	62.7	61.7	56.1	44.7	11.4
1974	49.0	33.4	51.4	58.8	62.4	62.2	56.4	42.8	10.4
1975	48.8	34.2	51.1	55.9	62.8	62.0	56.6	43.1	10.7
1976	49.8	32.9	52.5	56.9	66.7	63.0	56.8	43.7	11.3
1977	50.8	32.9	53.6	59.3	68.5	64.1	57.9	43.7	10.5
1978	53.1	37.3	55.5	62.7	70.6	67.2	59.4	43.8	11.1
1979	53.1	36.8	55.4	61.5	70.1	68.0	59.6	44.0	10.9
1980	53.1	34.9	55.6	60.2	70.5	68.1	61.4	44.8	10.2
1981	53.5	34.0	56.0	61.1	70.0	69.8	62.0	45.4	9.3
1982	53.7	33.5	56.2	60.1	70.2	71.7	62.4	44.8	8.5
1983	54.2	33.0	56.8	59.1	72.3	72.6	62.3	44.8	8.2
1984	55.2	35.0	57.6	60.7	71.5	73.7	64.5	46.1	8.0
1985	56.5	37.9	58.6	62.5	72.4	74.8	65.7	45.3	9.4
1986	56.9	39.1	58.9	64.6	72.4	75.8	66.5	43.6	7.8
1987	58.0	39.6	60.0	64.4	73.5	77.8	67.5	44.4	8.6
1988	58.0	37.9	60.1	63.2	73.7	78.1	68.3	43.4	9.6
1989	58.7	40.4	60.6	65.5	73.6	78.0	70.0	42.4	9.8
1990	58.3	36.8	60.6	62.4	72.3	77.7	70.7	43.2	9.9
1991	57.5	33.5	60.0	60.3	71.4	77.2	70.2	44.1	9.2
1992	58.5	35.2	60.8	60.8	73.1	77.1	71.7	45.1	8.6
1993	57.9	34.6	60.2	62.6	70.9	76.8	71.2	44.4	8.3
1994	58.7	36.3	60.9	64.5	71.9	76.4	71.3	45.3	9.2
1995	59.5	39.8	61.4	63.7	73.9	77.3	70.5	47.2	7.7
1996	60.4	38.9	62.6	65.2	75.9	78.2	72.0	47.2	7.7
1997	61.7	39.9	64.0	69.9	78.1	78.4	73.2	47.6	8.2
1998	62.8	42.5	64.8	69.6	79.6	79.9	74.0	48.5	7.9
1999	63.5	38.8	66.1	72.7	82.1	80.4	74.6	48.4	8.9
2000	63.1	39.6	65.4	70.5	81.1	79.9	74.9	48.6	9.9
2001	62.8	37.3	65.2	70.1	81.2	79.6	73.9	49.9	10.1
2002	61.8	34.7	64.4	66.9	79.7	79.2	73.3	51.8	9.8
2003	61.9	33.7	64.6	65.7	79.1	80.6	74.2	51.9	10.3
2004	61.5	32.8	64.2	66.8	77.2	80.6	74.3	52.3	10.7
2005	61.6	32.2	64.4	68.1	78.5	79.7	73.3	53.7	11.4
2006	61.7	35.6	64.2	66.2	78.6	80.1	73.0	55.1	11.8
2007	61.1	31.2	64.0	65.7	78.0	79.8	73.2	55.7	12.0
2008	61.3	29.7	64.3	65.2	79.6	80.0	73.7	55.3	13.0
2009	60.3	27.9	63.4	64.5	78.0	79.0	73.3	54.4	13.3
2010	59.9	25.1	63.2	66.9	77.9	77.7	73.0	54.9	13.3
HISPANIC[1]									
Both Sexes									
1973	60.2	46.9	. . .	. . .	. . .	. . .	. . .	. . .	. . .
1974	61.1	47.7	. . .	. . .	. . .	. . .	. . .	. . .	. . .
1975	60.8	46.2	. . .	. . .	. . .	. . .	. . .	. . .	. . .
1976	60.8	46.9	62.9	. . .	. . .	. . .	. . .	. . .	. . .
1977	61.6	48.2	63.7	. . .	. . .	. . .	. . .	. . .	. . .
1978	62.9	49.6	65.0	. . .	. . .	. . .	. . .	. . .	. . .
1979	63.6	50.3	65.6	. . .	. . .	. . .	. . .	. . .	. . .
1980	64.0	50.3	66.2	. . .	. . .	. . .	. . .	. . .	. . .
1981	64.1	46.4	66.8	. . .	. . .	. . .	. . .	. . .	. . .
1982	63.6	44.8	66.3	. . .	. . .	. . .	. . .	. . .	. . .
1983	63.8	45.3	66.2	. . .	. . .	. . .	. . .	. . .	. . .
1984	64.9	47.5	67.1	. . .	. . .	. . .	. . .	. . .	. . .
1985	64.6	44.6	67.1	. . .	. . .	. . .	. . .	. . .	. . .
1986	65.4	43.9	68.0	. . .	. . .	. . .	. . .	. . .	. . .
1987	66.4	45.8	68.8	. . .	. . .	. . .	. . .	. . .	. . .
1988	67.4	49.6	69.4	. . .	. . .	. . .	. . .	. . .	. . .
1989	67.6	48.6	69.7	. . .	. . .	. . .	. . .	. . .	. . .
1990	67.4	47.8	69.8	. . .	. . .	. . .	. . .	. . .	. . .
1991	66.5	45.1	69.0	. . .	. . .	. . .	. . .	. . .	. . .
1992	66.8	45.8	69.2	. . .	. . .	. . .	. . .	. . .	. . .
1993	66.2	43.9	68.7	. . .	. . .	. . .	. . .	. . .	. . .
1994	66.1	44.4	68.5	74.0	77.3	78.9	73.1	49.8	10.7
1995	65.8	45.4	68.1	71.9	78.1	78.5	72.8	48.6	10.5
1996	66.5	43.4	69.1	73.1	78.2	79.5	74.6	52.2	11.0
1997	67.9	43.0	70.8	76.4	79.5	80.9	75.4	53.8	11.9
1998	67.9	45.7	70.6	76.1	80.3	80.0	75.3	55.4	10.1
1999	67.7	45.5	70.4	76.0	78.6	81.3	75.9	54.1	11.6
2000	69.7	46.3	72.5	78.2	80.4	81.7	78.0	54.2	12.3
2001	69.5	46.9	72.0	76.6	80.0	81.9	77.4	55.1	10.9
2002	69.1	44.0	71.8	76.3	80.5	81.1	76.1	55.8	11.9
2003	68.3	37.7	71.4	75.6	79.4	81.1	75.3	57.4	12.8
2004	68.6	38.2	71.7	74.5	79.4	81.4	77.6	58.1	14.5
2005	68.0	38.6	71.0	72.7	79.1	81.2	77.2	58.4	13.9
2006	68.7	38.3	71.9	74.4	80.1	81.9	77.3	59.2	15.7
2007	68.8	37.1	72.1	74.8	80.7	81.8	78.6	58.5	16.0
2008	68.5	36.9	71.8	73.7	80.5	82.0	78.2	59.9	16.0
2009	68.0	34.0	71.5	73.1	79.5	81.3	79.3	61.9	17.1
2010	67.5	30.9	71.4	71.1	80.6	81.2	79.2	61.1	17.9

[1] May be of any race.
. . . = Not available.

Table 1-8. Civilian Labor Force Participation Rates, by Age, Sex, Race, and Hispanic Origin, 1948–2010
—Continued

(Percent.)

Race, Hispanic origin, sex, and year	16 years and over	16 to 19 years	20 years and over						
			Total	20 to 24 years	25 to 34 years	35 to 44 years	45 to 54 years	55 to 64 years	65 years and over
HISPANIC[1]									
Men									
1973	81.5	. . .	85.9	. . .	. . .	. . .	. . .	. . .	. . .
1974	81.7	. . .	86.0	. . .	. . .	. . .	. . .	. . .	. . .
1975	80.7	. . .	85.5	. . .	. . .	. . .	. . .	. . .	. . .
1976	79.6	. . .	84.2	. . .	. . .	. . .	. . .	. . .	. . .
1977	80.9	. . .	84.8	. . .	. . .	. . .	. . .	. . .	. . .
1978	81.1	. . .	84.9	. . .	. . .	. . .	. . .	. . .	. . .
1979	81.3	. . .	85.3	. . .	. . .	. . .	. . .	. . .	. . .
1980	81.4	. . .	84.9	. . .	. . .	. . .	. . .	. . .	. . .
1981	80.6	. . .	84.7	. . .	. . .	. . .	. . .	. . .	. . .
1982	79.7	. . .	84.0	. . .	. . .	. . .	. . .	. . .	. . .
1983	80.3	. . .	84.1	. . .	. . .	. . .	. . .	. . .	. . .
1984	80.6	. . .	84.3	. . .	. . .	. . .	. . .	. . .	. . .
1985	80.3	. . .	84.0	. . .	. . .	. . .	. . .	. . .	. . .
1986	81.0	. . .	84.6	. . .	. . .	. . .	. . .	. . .	. . .
1987	81.0	. . .	84.5	. . .	. . .	. . .	. . .	. . .	. . .
1988	81.9	. . .	85.0	. . .	. . .	. . .	. . .	. . .	. . .
1989	82.0	. . .	85.0	. . .	. . .	. . .	. . .	. . .	. . .
1990	81.4	. . .	84.7	. . .	. . .	. . .	. . .	. . .	. . .
1991	80.3	. . .	83.8	. . .	. . .	. . .	. . .	. . .	. . .
1992	80.7	. . .	84.0	. . .	. . .	. . .	. . .	. . .	. . .
1993	80.2	. . .	83.5	. . .	. . .	. . .	. . .	. . .	. . .
1994	79.2	50.0	82.5	88.0	92.5	91.5	85.7	63.6	14.4
1995	79.1	50.2	82.4	86.2	92.9	91.3	85.6	62.4	15.8
1996	79.6	50.0	83.0	85.7	93.2	91.7	87.0	65.9	16.7
1997	80.1	47.4	84.1	88.1	93.5	91.9	87.8	68.4	17.3
1998	79.8	48.7	83.6	88.1	94.0	91.4	86.7	70.2	14.9
1999	79.8	50.1	83.5	88.1	93.9	92.2	86.2	68.6	18.2
2000	81.5	50.7	85.3	89.1	94.1	93.3	87.6	69.4	18.5
2001	81.0	52.2	84.3	86.8	93.4	92.7	86.7	68.6	16.8
2002	80.2	48.8	83.6	86.1	93.5	92.1	86.1	67.3	16.3
2003	80.1	40.9	84.1	86.2	93.6	92.9	85.4	68.8	17.4
2004	80.4	42.4	84.2	84.4	93.6	93.2	87.2	69.6	20.8
2005	80.1	41.9	84.0	84.1	93.3	93.1	87.7	69.3	20.1
2006	80.7	42.0	84.6	85.9	94.1	93.8	87.1	69.6	22.9
2007	80.5	40.0	84.7	85.3	94.1	93.9	88.3	70.3	22.0
2008	80.2	40.3	84.4	84.3	94.0	93.7	88.6	71.7	21.7
2009	78.8	36.4	83.2	82.3	91.9	93.0	88.8	71.7	23.0
2010	77.8	33.2	82.6	80.0	92.7	92.9	87.8	69.0	24.5
HISPANIC[1]									
Women									
1973	41.0	. . .	41.3	. . .	. . .	. . .	. . .	. . .	. . .
1974	42.4	. . .	42.7	. . .	. . .	. . .	. . .	. . .	. . .
1975	43.2	. . .	43.8	. . .	. . .	. . .	. . .	. . .	. . .
1976	44.3	. . .	44.6	. . .	. . .	. . .	. . .	. . .	. . .
1977	44.3	. . .	45.1	. . .	. . .	. . .	. . .	. . .	. . .
1978	46.6	. . .	47.2	. . .	. . .	. . .	. . .	. . .	. . .
1979	47.4	. . .	48.0	. . .	. . .	. . .	. . .	. . .	. . .
1980	47.4	. . .	48.5	. . .	. . .	. . .	. . .	. . .	. . .
1981	48.3	. . .	49.7	. . .	. . .	. . .	. . .	. . .	. . .
1982	48.1	. . .	49.3	. . .	. . .	. . .	. . .	. . .	. . .
1983	47.7	. . .	49.0	. . .	. . .	. . .	. . .	. . .	. . .
1984	49.6	. . .	50.5	. . .	. . .	. . .	. . .	. . .	. . .
1985	49.3	. . .	50.6	. . .	. . .	. . .	. . .	. . .	. . .
1986	50.1	. . .	51.7	. . .	. . .	. . .	. . .	. . .	. . .
1987	52.0	. . .	53.3	. . .	. . .	. . .	. . .	. . .	. . .
1988	53.2	. . .	54.2	. . .	. . .	. . .	. . .	. . .	. . .
1989	53.5	. . .	54.9	. . .	. . .	. . .	. . .	. . .	. . .
1990	53.1	. . .	54.8	. . .	. . .	. . .	. . .	. . .	. . .
1991	52.4	. . .	54.0	. . .	. . .	. . .	. . .	. . .	. . .
1992	52.8	. . .	54.3	. . .	. . .	. . .	. . .	. . .	. . .
1993	52.1	. . .	53.8	. . .	. . .	. . .	. . .	. . .	. . .
1994	52.9	38.7	54.4	57.9	60.5	66.4	61.4	38.1	7.9
1995	52.6	40.4	53.9	55.9	61.6	65.9	60.5	37.2	6.6
1996	53.4	36.5	55.2	59.2	62.0	67.0	62.7	40.5	6.9
1997	55.1	38.0	57.0	62.3	63.7	69.3	63.3	40.6	8.1
1998	55.6	42.4	57.1	62.2	64.5	67.9	64.7	41.9	6.6
1999	55.9	40.6	57.7	63.0	62.7	70.5	66.2	42.4	6.5
2000	57.5	41.4	59.3	65.0	65.3	69.9	68.5	41.2	7.7
2001	57.6	41.1	59.3	64.6	65.2	70.3	68.3	43.2	6.7
2002	57.6	38.8	59.5	65.0	65.8	69.5	66.3	46.1	8.5
2003	55.9	34.5	58.1	63.3	62.9	68.5	65.3	47.1	9.4
2004	56.1	33.7	58.4	62.9	62.9	68.7	67.9	47.8	9.8
2005	55.3	35.2	57.4	59.4	62.4	68.2	66.6	48.4	9.3
2006	56.1	34.4	58.3	61.3	63.5	68.7	67.4	49.7	10.4
2007	56.5	34.0	58.8	62.9	64.6	68.4	68.7	47.6	11.4
2008	56.2	33.3	58.6	62.1	64.3	69.1	67.6	48.9	11.7
2009	56.5	31.6	59.2	63.2	64.7	68.2	69.4	52.6	12.7
2010	56.5	28.5	59.5	61.6	66.3	67.9	70.2	53.7	13.0

[1]May be of any race.
. . . = Not available.

Table 1-9. Employed and Unemployed Full- and Part-Time Workers, by Age, Sex, and Race, 2000–2010

(Thousands of people.)

Race, sex, age, and year	Employed[1]								Unemployed	
	Full-time workers				Part-time workers					
		At work				At work[2]				
	Total	35 hours or more	1 to 34 hours for economic or noneconomic reasons	Not at work	Total	For economic reasons	For noneconomic reasons	Not at work	Looking for full-time work	Looking for part-time work
ALL RACES										
Both Sexes, 16 Years and Over										
2000	113 846	100 533	9 125	4 188	23 044	2 003	19 548	1 493	4 538	1 154
2001	113 573	99 047	10 464	4 061	23 361	2 297	19 494	1 570	5 546	1 254
2002	112 700	99 042	9 746	3 912	23 785	2 755	19 549	1 481	7 063	1 314
2003	113 324	99 539	9 841	3 944	24 412	3 184	19 702	1 525	7 361	1 413
2004	114 518	100 496	10 053	3 969	24 734	3 113	20 109	1 513	6 762	1 388
2005	117 016	103 044	9 983	3 990	24 714	2 963	20 229	1 522	6 175	1 415
2006	119 688	105 328	10 223	4 137	24 739	2 774	20 356	1 609	5 675	1 326
2007	121 091	106 990	9 976	4 125	24 956	2 851	20 511	1 594	5 789	1 289
2008	120 030	105 575	10 426	4 030	25 332	3 814	20 009	1 509	7 446	1 478
2009	112 634	95 911	12 853	3 870	27 244	6 353	19 327	1 563	12 523	1 741
2010	111 714	97 946	10 217	3 551	27 350	6 965	18 876	1 509	12 970	1 854
Both Sexes, 20 Years and Over										
2000	111 353	98 439	8 787	4 127	18 348	1 747	15 297	1 304	3 978	632
2001	111 323	97 161	10 156	4 006	18 870	2 013	15 486	1 371	4 956	682
2002	110 679	97 342	9 474	3 862	19 475	2 448	15 704	1 322	6 395	730
2003	111 578	98 087	9 587	3 904	20 239	2 875	16 001	1 363	6 705	818
2004	112 747	99 034	9 789	3 924	20 598	2 817	16 436	1 345	6 178	764
2005	115 206	101 534	9 729	3 942	20 546	2 698	16 489	1 359	5 619	786
2006	117 844	103 779	9 974	4 090	20 421	2 510	16 478	1 433	5 117	765
2007	119 317	105 499	9 738	4 080	20 819	2 587	16 819	1 413	5 234	742
2008	118 404	104 212	10 204	3 989	21 385	3 492	16 543	1 350	6 790	849
2009	111 414	94 928	12 647	3 839	23 626	5 934	16 286	1 406	11 651	1 061
2010	110 622	97 037	10 057	3 528	24 064	6 552	16 138	1 373	12 155	1 142
Men, 16 Years and Over										
2000	65 930	59 345	4 555	2 030	7 375	856	6 105	414	2 486	488
2001	65 623	58 386	5 241	1 996	7 573	1 021	6 129	424	3 144	546
2002	65 205	58 318	4 971	1 916	7 697	1 246	6 050	401	4 029	568
2003	65 379	58 428	5 023	1 927	7 953	1 473	6 056	423	4 291	615
2004	66 444	59 363	5 148	1 933	8 080	1 405	6 258	417	3 843	613
2005	67 858	60 825	5 096	1 937	8 115	1 316	6 370	429	3 444	616
2006	69 307	62 087	5 237	1 984	8 194	1 232	6 510	452	3 192	561
2007	70 035	62 965	5 095	1 975	8 220	1 319	6 424	477	3 326	556
2008	68 853	61 436	5 443	1 974	8 634	1 842	6 349	442	4 396	637
2009	63 951	55 317	6 772	1 862	9 719	3 035	6 170	514	7 696	757
2010	63 501	56 425	5 352	1 723	9 858	3 316	6 066	476	7 827	799
Men, 20 Years and Over										
2000	64 464	58 095	4 370	2 000	5 170	733	4 109	328	2 162	214
2001	64 311	57 273	5 072	1 966	5 465	881	4 253	331	2 801	239
2002	64 006	57 302	4 815	1 889	5 728	1 093	4 299	336	3 642	254
2003	64 364	57 580	4 879	1 905	6 051	1 314	4 388	348	3 906	302
2004	65 377	58 471	5 000	1 906	6 196	1 251	4 600	345	3 511	281
2005	66 803	59 934	4 955	1 914	6 247	1 182	4 705	360	3 118	274
2006	68 193	61 140	5 095	1 958	6 238	1 100	4 762	376	2 861	270
2007	68 968	62 057	4 959	1 952	6 369	1 190	4 782	397	2 990	268
2008	67 895	60 625	5 315	1 955	6 855	1 675	4 802	378	3 994	303
2009	63 242	54 738	6 659	1 845	8 099	2 827	4 828	445	7 151	404
2010	62 854	55 887	5 258	1 710	8 376	3 102	4 857	417	7 336	427
Women, 16 Years and Over										
2000	47 916	41 188	4 570	2 158	15 670	1 147	13 443	1 080	2 052	666
2001	47 950	40 661	5 223	2 065	15 788	1 276	13 365	1 146	2 402	709
2002	47 494	40 723	4 775	1 996	16 088	1 509	13 498	1 080	3 034	747
2003	47 946	41 111	4 818	2 017	16 459	1 711	13 646	1 102	3 070	798
2004	48 073	41 133	4 905	2 036	16 654	1 708	13 851	1 096	2 919	775
2005	49 158	42 219	4 887	2 052	16 598	1 647	13 859	1 092	2 732	799
2006	50 380	43 241	4 986	2 153	16 545	1 542	13 846	1 157	2 483	764
2007	51 056	44 025	4 881	2 150	16 736	1 532	14 087	1 117	2 463	732
2008	51 178	44 139	4 983	2 056	16 698	1 972	13 660	1 067	3 050	841
2009	48 683	40 594	6 080	2 009	17 525	3 318	13 157	1 050	4 827	984
2010	48 214	41 521	4 865	1 828	17 491	3 648	12 810	1 033	5 144	1 055

Note: Beginning in January 2004, data reflect revised population controls used in the household survey. See notes and definitions for information on historical comparability.

[1]Employed persons are classified as full- or part-time workers based on their usual weekly hours at all jobs, regardless of the number of hours they were at work during the reference week. Persons absent from work are also classified according to their usual status.

[2]Includes some persons at work 35 hours or more classified by their reason for working part time.

Table 1-9. Employed and Unemployed Full- and Part-Time Workers, by Age, Sex, and Race, 2000–2010
—Continued

(Thousands of people.)

Race, sex, age, and year	Employed[1]								Unemployed	
	Full-time workers				Part-time workers					
		At work				At work[2]				
	Total	35 hours or more	1 to 34 hours for economic or noneconomic reasons	Not at work	Total	For economic reasons	For noneconomic reasons	Not at work	Looking for full-time work	Looking for part-time work

ALL RACES

Women, 20 Years and Over
2000	46 889	40 344	4 417	2 128	13 178	1 013	11 188	976	1 816	419
2001	47 012	39 889	5 083	2 040	13 405	1 132	11 233	1 040	2 155	444
2002	46 673	40 040	4 660	1 973	13 747	1 355	11 406	986	2 752	476
2003	47 215	40 507	4 708	2 000	14 188	1 560	11 613	1 015	2 799	515
2004	47 371	40 563	4 790	2 017	14 402	1 567	11 836	1 000	2 667	483
2005	48 403	41 600	4 774	2 028	14 299	1 516	11 784	999	2 501	512
2006	49 651	42 639	4 880	2 132	14 183	1 410	11 716	1 057	2 256	495
2007	50 349	43 442	4 779	2 128	14 450	1 397	12 037	1 016	2 244	474
2008	50 509	43 587	4 888	2 034	14 530	1 817	11 740	973	2 796	546
2009	48 171	40 190	5 988	1 994	15 527	3 107	11 459	961	4 500	657
2010	47 767	41 150	4 799	1 818	15 688	3 450	11 282	956	4 819	715

WHITE[3]

Men, 16 Years and Over
2000	56 068	50 434	3 896	1 738	6 221	656	5 213	351	1 798	379
2001	55 830	49 625	4 504	1 701	6 381	793	5 225	364	2 323	431
2002	55 369	49 459	4 267	1 644	6 480	980	5 150	350	3 017	443
2003	55 216	49 323	4 266	1 628	6 650	1 146	5 148	357	3 164	479
2004	55 926	49 891	4 396	1 638	6 786	1 092	5 331	363	2 805	477
2005	56 955	50 965	4 334	1 656	6 808	1 014	5 424	370	2 459	471
2006	58 063	51 894	4 484	1 685	6 820	947	5 481	393	2 299	432
2007	58 494	52 460	4 359	1 676	6 795	1 022	5 368	406	2 444	425
2008	57 432	51 104	4 653	1 675	7 192	1 433	5 379	379	3 235	492
2009	53 506	46 153	5 770	1 583	8 124	2 438	5 240	446	5 819	602
2010	53 086	47 055	4 554	1 477	8 166	2 662	5 102	402	5 832	644

Men, 20 Years and Over
2000	54 778	49 335	3 733	1 710	4 341	558	3 505	278	1 566	165
2001	54 666	48 636	4 354	1 676	4 579	677	3 616	285	2 080	195
2002	54 333	48 581	4 133	1 619	4 790	857	3 640	293	2 743	200
2003	54 339	48 585	4 145	1 609	5 010	1 016	3 703	291	2 893	231
2004	55 005	49 124	4 267	1 614	5 154	961	3 895	299	2 567	217
2005	56 050	50 203	4 213	1 634	5 205	905	3 990	310	2 242	209
2006	57 108	51 081	4 365	1 662	5 150	840	3 987	324	2 074	208
2007	57 591	51 691	4 243	1 656	5 216	915	3 967	334	2 204	204
2008	56 623	50 421	4 542	1 660	5 681	1 302	4 055	324	2 944	235
2009	52 899	45 654	5 676	1 569	6 728	2 269	4 075	384	5 421	325
2010	52 530	46 592	4 472	1 466	6 907	2 484	4 071	352	5 481	347

Women, 16 Years and Over
2000	38 438	32 942	3 729	1 767	13 698	867	11 870	961	1 422	521
2001	38 445	32 491	4 252	1 702	13 773	971	11 787	1 015	1 664	551
2002	38 152	32 623	3 896	1 633	14 011	1 152	11 903	956	2 084	595
2003	38 249	32 659	3 939	1 652	14 120	1 304	11 860	956	2 038	629
2004	38 240	32 555	4 018	1 667	14 287	1 280	12 038	969	1 968	597
2005	38 973	33 325	3 976	1 672	14 213	1 207	12 043	963	1 807	612
2006	39 813	33 980	4 082	1 751	14 137	1 157	11 967	1 013	1 670	601
2007	40 238	34 486	4 014	1 738	14 265	1 143	12 148	973	1 694	579
2008	40 292	34 569	4 076	1 647	14 209	1 518	11 761	931	2 119	664
2009	38 456	31 885	4 946	1 626	14 910	2 579	11 418	913	3 442	785
2010	38 158	32 710	3 958	1 490	14 758	2 846	11 029	883	3 612	828

Women, 20 Years and Over
2000	37 585	32 242	3 600	1 743	11 560	754	9 935	872	1 256	339
2001	37 658	31 839	4 139	1 680	11 711	853	9 933	924	1 492	357
2002	37 467	32 049	3 803	1 615	11 981	1 029	10 079	873	1 888	381
2003	37 640	32 158	3 845	1 637	12 183	1 180	10 124	879	1 866	411
2004	37 663	32 085	3 927	1 652	12 377	1 166	10 326	885	1 795	377
2005	38 354	32 820	3 882	1 652	12 235	1 108	10 248	879	1 653	401
2006	39 232	33 500	3 998	1 733	12 128	1 050	10 151	927	1 524	402
2007	39 670	34 015	3 932	1 722	12 326	1 037	10 402	887	1 547	383
2008	39 765	34 128	4 005	1 632	12 359	1 392	10 116	851	1 949	435
2009	38 033	31 547	4 872	1 614	13 198	2 411	9 952	835	3 216	529
2010	37 789	32 404	3 904	1 481	13 208	2 684	9 705	818	3 389	571

Note: Beginning in January 2004, data reflect revised population controls used in the household survey. See notes and definitions for information on historical comparability.

[1] Employed persons are classified as full- or part-time workers based on their usual weekly hours at all jobs, regardless of the number of hours they were at work during the reference week. Persons absent from work are also classified according to their usual status.
[2] Includes some persons at work 35 hours or more classified by their reason for working part time.
[3] Beginning in 2003, persons who selected this race group only; persons who selected more than one race group are not included. Prior to 2003, persons who reported more than one race group were included in the group they identified as their main race.

Table 1-9. Employed and Unemployed Full- and Part-Time Workers, by Age, Sex, and Race, 2000–2010
—Continued

(Thousands of people.)

Race, sex, age, and year	Employed[1]								Unemployed	
	Full-time workers				Part-time workers					
		At work				At work[2]				
	Total	35 hours or more	1 to 34 hours for economic or noneconomic reasons	Not at work	Total	For economic reasons	For noneconomic reasons	Not at work	Looking for full-time work	Looking for part-time work
BLACK[3]										
Men, 16 Years and Over										
2000	6 350	5 704	445	202	732	144	548	41	542	78
2001	6 178	5 509	468	200	761	165	557	39	626	83
2002	6 194	5 541	480	173	765	188	546	30	749	86
2003	6 055	5 414	453	188	765	221	505	39	804	87
2004	6 177	5 538	460	179	736	205	499	32	763	98
2005	6 381	5 745	463	174	773	207	533	33	742	102
2006	6 529	5 907	446	176	825	201	590	34	681	93
2007	6 673	6 068	429	176	826	195	589	42	660	92
2008	6 548	5 935	440	173	850	276	542	32	849	100
2009	5 871	5 166	556	150	946	379	530	36	1 348	100
2010	5 856	5 279	446	130	1 009	419	550	41	1 448	102
Men, 20 Years and Over										
2000	6 222	5 594	429	199	520	125	363	32	468	31
2001	6 069	5 417	455	197	558	145	382	31	542	31
2002	6 073	5 437	465	171	579	166	387	26	660	35
2003	5 980	5 355	439	185	607	201	372	34	717	43
2004	6 089	5 463	449	177	592	189	376	27	689	44
2005	6 287	5 662	452	174	614	189	397	28	655	44
2006	6 424	5 816	433	175	655	185	441	30	596	44
2007	6 574	5 983	417	174	671	181	452	37	580	43
2008	6 461	5 860	430	171	690	252	409	29	764	46
2009	5 811	5 119	544	148	817	355	428	34	1 238	49
2010	5 803	5 235	439	129	877	392	447	37	1 344	52
Women, 16 Years and Over										
2000	6 780	5 862	632	287	1 293	211	1 005	77	515	106
2001	6 761	5 777	715	270	1 307	223	998	85	584	122
2002	6 588	5 685	640	263	1 326	259	991	76	744	114
2003	6 552	5 709	595	247	1 367	274	1 017	76	774	121
2004	6 597	5 740	611	246	1 399	306	1 022	71	744	124
2005	6 750	5 871	619	260	1 407	320	1 018	70	723	133
2006	7 001	6 131	605	265	1 410	274	1 054	82	655	120
2007	7 119	6 272	584	263	1 432	273	1 085	75	589	104
2008	7 105	6 238	596	272	1 449	302	1 070	77	717	122
2009	6 666	5 696	718	252	1 542	480	984	78	1 027	132
2010	6 525	5 727	582	215	1 621	528	1 010	82	1 142	160
Women, 20 Years and Over										
2000	6 651	5 753	615	283	1 052	197	788	67	456	56
2001	6 647	5 684	695	268	1 094	203	816	75	521	61
2002	6 492	5 605	626	261	1 117	234	816	68	671	67
2003	6 468	5 639	583	246	1 168	257	842	69	698	75
2004	6 512	5 674	595	243	1 195	287	844	64	679	76
2005	6 653	5 789	606	258	1 222	298	861	63	660	74
2006	6 893	6 042	588	263	1 175	255	848	72	588	67
2007	7 024	6 194	570	260	1 216	254	897	65	527	61
2008	7 006	6 160	580	267	1 254	283	902	68	654	78
2009	6 600	5 644	705	250	1 356	449	837	71	951	82
2010	6 471	5 681	575	215	1 473	504	894	75	1 063	103

Note: Beginning in January 2004, data reflect revised population controls used in the household survey. See notes and definitions for information on historical comparability.

[1]Employed persons are classified as full- or part-time workers based on their usual weekly hours at all jobs, regardless of the number of hours they were at work during the reference week. Persons absent from work are also classified according to their usual status.
[2]Includes some persons at work 35 hours or more classified by their reason for working part time.
[3]Beginning in 2003, persons who selected this race group only; persons who selected more than one race group are not included. Prior to 2003, persons who reported more than one race group were included in the group they identified as their main race.

Table 1-10. Persons Not in the Labor Force, by Age, Sex, and Desire and Availability for Work, 2005–2010

(Thousands of people.)

Category	Total		Age 16 to 24 years		Age 25 to 54 years		Age 55 years and over		Men		Women	
	2005	2006	2005	2006	2005	2006	2005	2006	2005	2006	2005	2006
TOTAL, NOT IN THE LABOR FORCE	76 762	77 387	14 383	14 549	21 403	21 318	40 976	41 520	29 119	30 036	47 643	48 037
Do Not Want a Job Now[1]	71 777	72 602	12 585	12 867	19 238	19 221	39 954	40 514	26 926	27 914	44 851	45 354
Want a Job[1]	4 985	4 786	1 798	1 682	2 165	2 097	1 022	1 006	2 193	2 122	2 792	2 684
Did not search for work in the previous year	2 841	2 758	963	883	1 163	1 155	715	720	1 173	1 173	1 668	1 612
Searched for work in the previous year[2]	2 144	2 028	836	800	1 002	942	307	286	1 020	950	1 124	1 071
Not available to work now	599	580	285	282	260	252	54	46	231	223	368	354
Available to work now	1 545	1 448	551	518	742	690	252	240	789	726	756	717
Reason not currently looking:												
Discouragement over job prospects[3]	436	381	141	118	217	195	78	68	260	226	176	152
Reasons other than discouragement	1 109	1 067	410	399	525	495	175	172	529	500	580	565
Family responsibilities	159	152	32	31	105	97	22	24	36	37	123	117
In school or training	217	207	179	177	35	28	2	2	118	102	99	96
Ill health or disability	119	130	16	18	69	76	34	36	64	57	55	68
Other[4]	614	578	182	174	316	294	116	110	311	305	302	285

Category	Total		Age 16 to 24 years		Age 25 to 54 years		Age 55 years and over		Men		Women	
	2007	2008	2007	2008	2007	2008	2007	2008	2007	2008	2007	2008
TOTAL, NOT IN THE LABOR FORCE	78 743	79 501	15 192	15 452	21 343	21 255	42 207	42 794	30 036	30 593	48 707	48 908
Do Not Want a Job Now[1]	74 040	74 519	13 510	13 719	19 256	19 087	41 275	41 712	27 914	28 365	46 126	46 154
Want a Job[1]	4 703	4 983	1 683	1 733	2 088	2 168	933	1 082	2 122	2 228	2 581	2 755
Did not search for work in the previous year	2 748	2 826	931	913	1 148	1 145	668	768	1 173	1 187	1 575	1 639
Searched for work in the previous year[2]	1 955	2 157	751	819	939	1 023	264	314	950	1 041	1 005	1 115
Not available to work now	560	543	272	252	234	244	53	48	223	214	336	329
Available to work now	1 395	1 614	479	568	705	780	211	266	726	827	669	787
Reason not currently looking:												
Discouragement over job prospects[3]	369	462	110	145	199	226	61	90	226	282	143	180
Reasons other than discouragement	1 026	1 152	370	422	506	554	150	176	500	545	526	607
Family responsibilities	160	171	31	35	109	111	21	25	37	45	123	126
In school or training	180	218	149	173	27	42	3	3	102	108	78	109
Ill health or disability	114	124	11	16	66	68	37	40	57	55	58	69
Other[4]	572	640	178	199	304	332	90	108	305	337	267	303

Category	Total		Age 16 to 24 years		Age 25 to 54 years		Age 55 years and over		Men		Women	
	2009	2010	2009	2010	2009	2010	2009	2010	2009	2010	2009	2010
TOTAL, NOT IN THE LABOR FORCE	81 659	83 941	16 207	17 014	21 823	22 350	43 629	44 577	32 013	33 189	49 646	50 752
Do Not Want a Job Now[1]	75 765	77 882	14 263	14 990	19 199	19 659	42 303	43 233	29 234	30 309	46 531	47 573
Want a Job[1]	5 894	6 059	1 944	2 024	2 624	2 691	1 325	1 344	2 779	2 880	3 115	3 179
Did not search for work in the previous year	3 075	2 948	960	968	1 241	1 189	874	791	1 344	1 279	1 731	1 669
Searched for work in the previous year[2]	2 818	3 111	983	1 056	1 383	1 502	452	553	1 435	1 601	1 384	1 510
Not available to work now	592	623	275	274	256	284	61	65	251	264	341	359
Available to work now	2 226	2 487	708	782	1 127	1 218	391	487	1 184	1 337	1 043	1 151
Reason not currently looking:												
Discouragement over job prospects[3]	778	1 173	200	291	427	595	151	287	485	731	293	442
Reasons other than discouragement	1 449	1 315	509	491	699	623	240	200	699	606	749	709
Family responsibilities	209	286	38	49	131	171	41	66	50	83	159	203
In school or training	306	350	234	262	65	81	7	7	163	191	144	158
Ill health or disability	136	50	19	4	68	21	49	25	70	21	66	29
Other[4]	798	629	219	176	435	350	144	102	417	311	381	318

[1]Includes some persons who were not asked if they wanted a job.
[2]Persons who had a job during the prior 12 months must have searched since the end of that job.
[3]Includes believes no work available, could not find work, lacks necessary schooling or training, employer thinks too young or old, and other types of discrimination.
[4]Includes those who did not actively look for work in the prior four weeks for reasons such as childcare and transportation problems, as well as a small number for whom reason for nonparticipation was not ascertained.

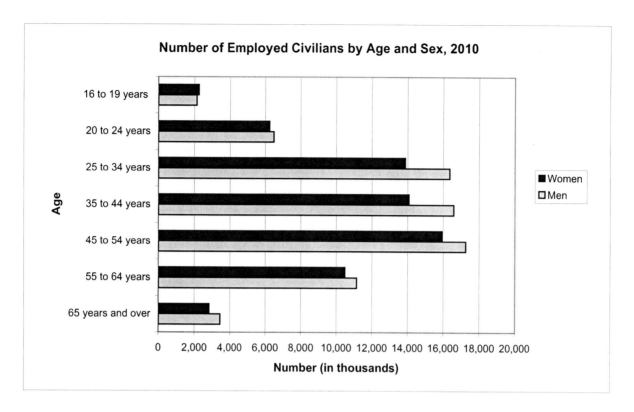

There were over 139 million employed civilians in the labor force in 2010—the lowest number since 2003. Men outnumbered women in every age group except among the 16–19 year olds. In 2010, 47.2 percent of employed civilians were women. (See Table 1-11.)

OTHER HIGHLIGHTS

- While men made up 52.8 percent of employed civilians, they only made up 26.2 percent of employees in education, training, and library occupations; 26.2 percent of employees in office and administrative support occupations; and 11.1 percent of employees in healthcare support occupations. (See Table 1-13.)

- Among those 25 years of age and over, employment increased 0.7 percent for those with a bachelor's degree or more and 0.3 percent for those with an associate's degree in 2010. However, for those with lower levels of education, employment declined. Employment fell 2.5 percent for those with less than a high school diploma and 0.6 percent for high school graduates who never attended college. (See Table 1-16.)

- The multiple jobholding rate declined slightly in 2010 after remaining steady at 5.2 percent the previous three years. It was significantly higher for women (5.5 percent) than for men (4.7 percent). (See Table 1-17.)

- In 2010, 12.4 percent of families had an unemployed member compared to 12.0 percent in 2009 and 7.8 percent in 2008. (See Table 1-20.)

Table 1-11. Employed Civilians, by Age, Sex, Race, and Hispanic Origin, 1948–2010

(Thousands of people.)

Race, Hispanic origin, sex, and year	16 years and over	16 to 19 years			20 years and over						
		Total	16 to 17 years	18 to 19 years	Total	20 to 24 years	25 to 34 years	35 to 44 years	45 to 54 years	55 to 64 years	65 years and over

ALL RACES

Both Sexes

1948	58 343	4 026	1 600	2 426	54 318	6 937	13 801	13 050	10 624	7 103	2 804
1949	57 651	3 712	1 466	2 246	53 940	6 660	13 639	13 108	10 636	7 042	2 864
1950	58 918	3 703	1 433	2 270	55 218	6 746	13 917	13 424	10 966	7 265	2 899
1951	59 961	3 767	1 575	2 192	56 196	6 321	14 233	13 746	11 421	7 558	2 917
1952	60 250	3 719	1 626	2 092	56 536	5 572	14 515	14 058	11 687	7 785	2 919
1953	61 179	3 720	1 577	2 142	57 460	5 225	14 519	14 774	11 969	7 806	3 166
1954	60 109	3 475	1 422	2 053	56 634	4 971	14 190	14 541	11 976	7 895	3 060
1955	62 170	3 642	1 500	2 143	58 528	5 270	14 481	14 879	12 556	8 158	3 185
1956	63 799	3 818	1 647	2 171	59 983	5 545	14 407	15 218	12 978	8 519	3 314
1957	64 071	3 778	1 613	2 167	60 291	5 641	14 253	15 348	13 320	8 553	3 179
1958	63 036	3 582	1 519	2 063	59 454	5 571	13 675	15 157	13 448	8 559	3 045
1959	64 630	3 838	1 670	2 168	60 791	5 870	13 709	15 454	13 915	8 822	3 023
1960	65 778	4 129	1 770	2 360	61 648	6 119	13 630	15 598	14 238	8 989	3 073
1961	65 746	4 108	1 621	2 486	61 638	6 227	13 429	15 552	14 320	9 120	2 987
1962	66 702	4 195	1 607	2 588	62 508	6 446	13 311	15 901	14 491	9 346	3 013
1963	67 762	4 255	1 751	2 504	63 508	6 815	13 318	16 114	14 749	9 596	2 915
1964	69 305	4 516	2 013	2 503	64 789	7 303	13 449	16 166	15 094	9 804	2 973
1965	71 088	5 036	2 075	2 962	66 052	7 702	13 704	16 294	15 320	10 028	3 005
1966	72 895	5 721	2 269	3 452	67 178	7 964	14 017	16 312	15 615	10 310	2 961
1967	74 372	5 682	2 334	3 348	68 690	8 499	14 575	16 281	15 789	10 536	3 011
1968	75 920	5 781	2 403	3 377	70 141	8 762	15 265	16 220	16 083	10 745	3 065
1969	77 902	6 117	2 573	3 543	71 785	9 319	15 883	16 100	16 410	10 919	3 155
1970	78 678	6 144	2 598	3 546	72 534	9 731	16 318	15 922	16 473	10 974	3 118
1971	79 367	6 208	2 596	3 613	73 158	10 201	16 781	15 675	16 451	11 009	3 040
1972	82 153	6 746	2 787	3 959	75 407	10 999	18 082	15 822	16 457	11 044	3 003
1973	85 064	7 271	3 032	4 239	77 793	11 839	19 509	16 041	16 553	10 966	2 886
1974	86 794	7 448	3 111	4 338	79 347	12 101	20 610	16 203	16 633	10 964	2 835
1975	85 846	7 104	2 941	4 162	78 744	11 885	21 087	15 953	16 190	10 827	2 801
1976	88 752	7 336	2 972	4 363	81 416	12 570	22 493	16 468	16 224	10 912	2 747
1977	92 017	7 688	3 138	4 550	84 329	13 196	23 850	17 157	16 212	11 126	2 787
1978	96 048	8 070	3 330	4 739	87 979	13 887	25 281	18 128	16 338	11 400	2 946
1979	98 824	8 083	3 340	4 743	90 741	14 327	26 492	18 981	16 357	11 585	2 999
1980	99 303	7 710	3 106	4 605	91 593	14 087	27 204	19 523	16 234	11 586	2 960
1981	100 397	7 225	2 866	4 359	93 172	14 122	28 180	20 145	16 255	11 525	2 945
1982	99 526	6 549	2 505	4 044	92 978	13 690	28 149	20 879	15 923	11 414	2 923
1983	100 834	6 342	2 320	4 022	94 491	13 722	28 756	21 960	15 812	11 315	2 927
1984	105 005	6 444	2 404	4 040	98 562	14 207	30 348	23 598	16 178	11 395	2 835
1985	107 150	6 434	2 492	3 941	100 716	13 980	31 208	24 732	16 509	11 474	2 813
1986	109 597	6 472	2 622	3 850	103 125	13 790	32 201	25 861	16 949	11 405	2 919
1987	112 440	6 640	2 736	3 905	105 800	13 524	33 105	27 179	17 487	11 465	3 041
1988	114 968	6 805	2 713	4 092	108 164	13 244	33 574	28 269	18 447	11 433	3 197
1989	117 342	6 759	2 588	4 172	110 582	12 962	34 045	29 443	19 279	11 499	3 355
1990	118 793	6 581	2 410	4 171	112 213	13 401	33 935	30 817	19 525	11 189	3 346
1991	117 718	5 906	2 202	3 704	111 812	12 975	33 061	31 593	19 882	11 001	3 300
1992	118 492	5 669	2 128	3 540	112 824	12 872	32 667	31 923	21 022	10 998	3 341
1993	120 259	5 805	2 226	3 579	114 455	12 840	32 385	32 666	22 175	11 058	3 331
1994	123 060	6 161	2 510	3 651	116 899	12 758	32 286	33 599	23 348	11 228	3 681
1995	124 900	6 419	2 573	3 846	118 481	12 443	32 356	34 202	24 378	11 435	3 666
1996	126 708	6 500	2 646	3 853	120 208	12 138	32 077	35 051	25 514	11 739	3 690
1997	129 558	6 661	2 648	4 012	122 897	12 380	31 809	35 908	26 744	12 296	3 761
1998	131 463	7 051	2 762	4 289	124 413	12 557	31 394	36 278	27 587	12 872	3 725
1999	133 488	7 172	2 793	4 379	126 316	12 891	30 865	36 728	28 635	13 315	3 882
2000	136 891	7 189	2 759	4 431	129 701	13 229	31 549	36 433	30 310	14 002	4 179
2001	136 933	6 740	2 558	4 182	130 194	13 348	30 863	36 049	31 036	14 645	4 253
2002	136 485	6 332	2 330	4 002	130 154	13 351	30 306	35 235	31 281	15 674	4 306
2003	137 736	5 919	2 312	3 607	131 817	13 433	30 383	34 881	31 914	16 598	4 608
2004	139 252	5 907	2 193	3 714	133 345	13 723	30 423	34 580	32 469	17 331	4 819
2005	141 730	5 978	2 284	3 694	135 752	13 792	30 680	34 630	33 207	18 349	5 094
2006	144 427	6 162	2 444	3 719	138 265	13 878	31 051	34 569	34 052	19 389	5 325
2007	146 047	5 911	2 286	3 625	140 136	13 964	31 586	34 302	34 563	20 108	5 614
2008	145 362	5 573	1 989	3 584	139 790	13 629	31 383	33 457	34 529	20 812	5 979
2009	139 877	4 837	1 651	3 187	135 040	12 764	30 014	31 517	33 613	21 019	6 114
2010	139 064	4 378	1 418	2 960	134 686	12 699	30 229	30 663	33 191	21 636	6 268

Table 1-11. Employed Civilians, by Age, Sex, Race, and Hispanic Origin, 1948–2010—*Continued*

(Thousands of people.)

Race, Hispanic origin, sex, and year	16 years and over	16 to 19 years			20 years and over						
		Total	16 to 17 years	18 to 19 years	Total	20 to 24 years	25 to 34 years	35 to 44 years	45 to 54 years	55 to 64 years	65 years and over
ALL RACES											
Men											
1948	41 725	2 344	996	1 348	39 382	4 349	10 038	9 363	7 742	5 587	2 303
1949	40 925	2 124	911	1 213	38 803	4 197	9 879	9 308	7 661	5 438	2 329
1950	41 578	2 186	909	1 277	39 394	4 255	10 060	9 445	7 790	5 508	2 336
1951	41 780	2 156	979	1 177	39 626	3 780	10 134	9 607	8 012	5 711	2 382
1952	41 682	2 107	985	1 121	39 578	3 183	10 352	9 753	8 144	5 804	2 343
1953	42 430	2 136	976	1 159	40 296	2 901	10 500	10 229	8 374	5 808	2 483
1954	41 619	1 985	881	1 104	39 634	2 724	10 254	10 082	8 330	5 830	2 414
1955	42 621	2 095	936	1 159	40 526	2 973	10 453	10 267	8 553	5 857	2 424
1956	43 379	2 164	1 008	1 156	41 216	3 245	10 337	10 385	8 732	6 004	2 512
1957	43 357	2 115	987	1 130	41 239	3 346	10 222	10 427	8 851	6 002	2 394
1958	42 423	2 012	948	1 064	40 411	3 293	9 790	10 291	8 828	5 955	2 254
1959	43 466	2 198	1 015	1 183	41 267	3 597	9 862	10 492	9 048	6 058	2 210
1960	43 904	2 361	1 090	1 271	41 543	3 754	9 759	10 552	9 182	6 105	2 191
1961	43 656	2 315	989	1 325	41 342	3 795	9 591	10 505	9 195	6 155	2 098
1962	44 177	2 362	990	1 372	41 815	3 898	9 475	10 711	9 333	6 260	2 138
1963	44 657	2 406	1 073	1 334	42 251	4 118	9 431	10 801	9 478	6 385	2 038
1964	45 474	2 587	1 242	1 345	42 886	4 370	9 531	10 832	9 637	6 478	2 039
1965	46 340	2 918	1 285	1 634	43 422	4 583	9 611	10 837	9 792	6 542	2 057
1966	46 919	3 253	1 389	1 863	43 668	4 599	9 709	10 764	9 904	6 668	2 024
1967	47 479	3 186	1 417	1 769	44 294	4 809	9 988	10 674	9 990	6 774	2 058
1968	48 114	3 255	1 453	1 802	44 859	4 812	10 405	10 554	10 102	6 893	2 093
1969	48 818	3 430	1 526	1 904	45 388	5 012	10 736	10 401	10 187	6 931	2 122
1970	48 990	3 409	1 504	1 905	45 581	5 237	10 936	10 216	10 170	6 928	2 094
1971	49 390	3 478	1 510	1 968	45 912	5 593	11 218	10 028	10 139	6 916	2 019
1972	50 896	3 765	1 598	2 167	47 130	6 138	11 884	10 088	10 139	6 929	1 953
1973	52 349	4 039	1 721	2 318	48 310	6 655	12 617	10 126	10 197	6 857	1 856
1974	53 024	4 103	1 744	2 359	48 922	6 739	13 119	10 135	10 181	6 880	1 869
1975	51 857	3 839	1 621	2 219	48 018	6 484	13 205	9 891	9 902	6 722	1 811
1976	53 138	3 947	1 626	2 321	49 190	6 915	13 869	10 069	9 881	6 724	1 732
1977	54 728	4 174	1 733	2 441	50 555	7 232	14 483	10 399	9 832	6 848	1 761
1978	56 479	4 336	1 800	2 535	52 143	7 559	15 124	10 845	9 806	6 954	1 855
1979	57 607	4 300	1 799	2 501	53 308	7 791	15 688	11 202	9 735	7 015	1 876
1980	57 186	4 085	1 672	2 412	53 101	7 532	15 832	11 355	9 548	6 999	1 835
1981	57 397	3 815	1 526	2 289	53 582	7 504	16 266	11 613	9 478	6 909	1 812
1982	56 271	3 379	1 307	2 072	52 891	7 197	16 002	11 902	9 234	6 781	1 776
1983	56 787	3 300	1 213	2 087	53 487	7 232	16 216	12 450	9 133	6 686	1 770
1984	59 091	3 322	1 244	2 078	55 769	7 571	17 166	13 309	9 326	6 694	1 703
1985	59 891	3 328	1 300	2 029	56 562	7 339	17 564	13 800	9 411	6 753	1 695
1986	60 892	3 323	1 352	1 971	57 569	7 250	18 092	14 266	9 554	6 654	1 753
1987	62 107	3 381	1 393	1 988	58 726	7 058	18 487	14 898	9 750	6 682	1 850
1988	63 273	3 492	1 403	2 089	59 781	6 918	18 702	15 457	10 201	6 591	1 911
1989	64 315	3 477	1 327	2 150	60 837	6 799	18 952	16 002	10 569	6 548	1 968
1990	65 104	3 427	1 254	2 173	61 678	7 151	18 779	16 771	10 690	6 378	1 909
1991	64 223	3 044	1 135	1 909	61 178	6 909	18 265	17 086	10 813	6 245	1 860
1992	64 440	2 944	1 096	1 848	61 496	6 819	17 966	17 230	11 365	6 173	1 943
1993	65 349	2 994	1 155	1 839	62 355	6 805	17 877	17 665	11 927	6 166	1 916
1994	66 450	3 156	1 288	1 868	63 294	6 771	17 741	18 111	12 439	6 142	2 089
1995	67 377	3 292	1 316	1 977	64 085	6 665	17 709	18 374	12 958	6 272	2 108
1996	68 207	3 310	1 318	1 992	64 897	6 429	17 527	18 816	13 483	6 470	2 172
1997	69 685	3 401	1 355	2 045	66 284	6 548	17 338	19 327	14 107	6 735	2 229
1998	70 693	3 558	1 398	2 161	67 135	6 638	17 097	19 634	14 544	7 052	2 171
1999	71 446	3 685	1 437	2 249	67 761	6 729	16 694	19 811	14 991	7 274	2 263
2000	73 305	3 671	1 394	2 276	69 634	6 974	17 241	19 537	15 871	7 606	2 406
2001	73 196	3 420	1 268	2 151	69 776	6 952	16 915	19 305	16 268	7 900	2 437
2002	72 903	3 169	1 130	2 040	69 734	6 978	16 573	18 932	16 419	8 378	2 455
2003	73 332	2 917	1 115	1 802	70 415	7 065	16 670	18 774	16 588	8 733	2 585
2004	74 524	2 952	1 037	1 915	71 572	7 246	16 818	18 700	16 951	9 174	2 683
2005	75 973	2 923	1 067	1 855	73 050	7 279	16 993	18 780	17 429	9 714	2 857
2006	77 502	3 071	1 182	1 888	74 431	7 412	17 134	18 765	17 920	10 192	3 008
2007	78 254	2 917	1 091	1 827	75 337	7 374	17 452	18 666	18 210	10 556	3 080
2008	77 486	2 736	926	1 810	74 750	7 145	17 183	18 097	18 124	10 919	3 282
2009	73 670	2 328	786	1 543	71 341	6 510	16 223	16 918	17 443	10 890	3 357
2010	73 359	2 129	675	1 454	71 230	6 466	16 358	16 585	17 242	11 140	3 439

Table 1-11. Employed Civilians, by Age, Sex, Race, and Hispanic Origin, 1948–2010—*Continued*

(Thousands of people.)

Race, Hispanic origin, sex, and year	16 years and over	16 to 19 years			20 years and over						
		Total	16 to 17 years	18 to 19 years	Total	20 to 24 years	25 to 34 years	35 to 44 years	45 to 54 years	55 to 64 years	65 years and over
ALL RACES											
Women											
1948	16 617	1 682	604	1 078	14 936	2 588	3 763	3 687	2 882	1 516	501
1949	16 723	1 588	555	1 033	15 137	2 463	3 760	3 800	2 975	1 604	535
1950	17 340	1 517	524	993	15 824	2 491	3 857	3 979	3 176	1 757	563
1951	18 181	1 611	596	1 015	16 570	2 541	4 099	4 139	3 409	1 847	535
1952	18 568	1 612	641	971	16 958	2 389	4 163	4 305	3 543	1 981	576
1953	18 749	1 584	601	983	17 164	2 324	4 019	4 545	3 595	1 998	683
1954	18 490	1 490	541	949	17 000	2 247	3 936	4 459	3 646	2 065	646
1955	19 551	1 547	564	984	18 002	2 297	4 028	4 612	4 003	2 301	761
1956	20 419	1 654	639	1 015	18 767	2 300	4 070	4 833	4 246	2 515	802
1957	20 714	1 663	626	1 037	19 052	2 295	4 031	4 921	4 469	2 551	785
1958	20 613	1 570	571	999	19 043	2 278	3 885	4 866	4 620	2 604	791
1959	21 164	1 640	655	985	19 524	2 273	3 847	4 962	4 867	2 764	813
1960	21 874	1 768	680	1 089	20 105	2 365	3 871	5 046	5 056	2 884	882
1961	22 090	1 793	632	1 161	20 296	2 432	3 838	5 047	5 125	2 965	889
1962	22 525	1 833	617	1 216	20 693	2 548	3 836	5 190	5 158	3 086	875
1963	23 105	1 849	678	1 170	21 257	2 697	3 887	5 313	5 271	3 211	877
1964	23 831	1 929	771	1 158	21 903	2 933	3 918	5 334	5 457	3 326	934
1965	24 748	2 118	790	1 328	22 630	3 119	4 093	5 457	5 528	3 486	948
1966	25 976	2 468	880	1 589	23 510	3 365	4 308	5 548	5 711	3 642	937
1967	26 893	2 496	917	1 579	24 397	3 690	4 587	5 607	5 799	3 762	953
1968	27 807	2 526	950	1 575	25 281	3 950	4 860	5 666	5 981	3 852	972
1969	29 084	2 687	1 047	1 639	26 397	4 307	5 147	5 699	6 223	3 988	1 033
1970	29 688	2 735	1 094	1 641	26 952	4 494	5 382	5 706	6 303	4 046	1 023
1971	29 976	2 730	1 086	1 645	27 246	4 609	5 563	5 647	6 313	4 093	1 021
1972	31 257	2 980	1 188	1 792	28 276	4 861	6 197	5 734	6 318	4 115	1 051
1973	32 715	3 231	1 310	1 920	29 484	5 184	6 893	5 915	6 356	4 109	1 029
1974	33 769	3 345	1 367	1 978	30 424	5 363	7 492	6 068	6 451	4 084	966
1975	33 989	3 263	1 320	1 943	30 726	5 401	7 882	6 061	6 288	4 105	989
1976	35 615	3 389	1 346	2 043	32 226	5 655	8 624	6 400	6 343	4 188	1 017
1977	37 289	3 514	1 403	2 110	33 775	5 965	9 367	6 758	6 380	4 279	1 027
1978	39 569	3 734	1 530	2 204	35 836	6 328	10 157	7 282	6 532	4 446	1 091
1979	41 217	3 783	1 541	2 242	37 434	6 538	10 802	7 779	6 622	4 569	1 124
1980	42 117	3 625	1 433	2 192	38 492	6 555	11 370	8 168	6 686	4 587	1 125
1981	43 000	3 411	1 340	2 070	39 590	6 618	11 914	8 532	6 777	4 616	1 133
1982	43 256	3 170	1 198	1 972	40 086	6 492	12 147	8 977	6 689	4 634	1 147
1983	44 047	3 043	1 107	1 935	41 004	6 490	12 540	9 510	6 678	4 629	1 157
1984	45 915	3 122	1 161	1 962	42 793	6 636	13 182	10 289	6 852	4 700	1 133
1985	47 259	3 105	1 193	1 913	44 154	6 640	13 644	10 933	7 097	4 721	1 118
1986	48 706	3 149	1 270	1 879	45 556	6 540	14 109	11 595	7 395	4 751	1 165
1987	50 334	3 260	1 343	1 917	47 074	6 466	14 617	12 281	7 737	4 783	1 191
1988	51 696	3 313	1 310	2 003	48 383	6 326	14 872	12 811	8 246	4 841	1 286
1989	53 027	3 282	1 261	2 021	49 745	6 163	15 093	13 440	8 711	4 950	1 388
1990	53 689	3 154	1 156	1 998	50 535	6 250	15 155	14 046	8 835	4 811	1 437
1991	53 496	2 862	1 067	1 794	50 634	6 066	14 796	14 507	9 069	4 756	1 440
1992	54 052	2 724	1 032	1 692	51 328	6 053	14 701	14 693	9 657	4 825	1 398
1993	54 910	2 811	1 071	1 740	52 099	6 035	14 508	15 002	10 248	4 892	1 414
1994	56 610	3 005	1 222	1 783	53 606	5 987	14 545	15 488	10 908	5 085	1 592
1995	57 523	3 127	1 258	1 869	54 396	5 779	14 647	15 828	11 421	5 163	1 558
1996	58 501	3 190	1 328	1 862	55 311	5 709	14 549	16 235	12 031	5 269	1 518
1997	59 873	3 260	1 293	1 967	56 613	5 831	14 471	16 581	12 637	5 561	1 532
1998	60 771	3 493	1 364	2 128	57 278	5 919	14 298	16 644	13 043	5 820	1 554
1999	62 042	3 487	1 357	2 130	58 555	6 163	14 171	16 917	13 644	6 041	1 619
2000	63 586	3 519	1 364	2 154	60 067	6 255	14 308	16 897	14 438	6 396	1 773
2001	63 737	3 320	1 289	2 031	60 417	6 396	13 948	16 744	14 768	6 745	1 815
2002	63 582	3 162	1 200	1 962	60 420	6 374	13 733	16 303	14 863	7 296	1 851
2003	64 404	3 002	1 197	1 805	61 402	6 367	13 714	16 106	15 326	7 866	2 023
2004	64 728	2 955	1 156	1 799	61 773	6 477	13 605	15 880	15 518	8 157	2 135
2005	65 757	3 055	1 217	1 838	62 702	6 513	13 687	15 850	15 779	8 635	2 238
2006	66 925	3 091	1 261	1 830	63 834	6 467	13 917	15 804	16 132	9 198	2 316
2007	67 792	2 994	1 195	1 798	64 799	6 590	14 133	15 636	16 353	9 553	2 534
2008	67 876	2 837	1 063	1 774	65 039	6 484	14 200	15 360	16 406	9 893	2 697
2009	66 208	2 509	865	1 644	63 699	6 254	13 791	14 599	16 170	10 128	2 757
2010	65 705	2 249	743	1 506	63 456	6 233	13 870	14 078	15 949	10 496	2 830

Table 1-11. Employed Civilians, by Age, Sex, Race, and Hispanic Origin, 1948–2010—*Continued*

(Thousands of people.)

Race, Hispanic origin, sex, and year	16 years and over	16 to 19 years			20 years and over						
		Total	16 to 17 years	18 to 19 years	Total	20 to 24 years	25 to 34 years	35 to 44 years	45 to 54 years	55 to 64 years	65 years and over
WHITE											
Both Sexes											
1954	53 957	3 078	1 257	1 822	50 879	4 358	12 616	13 000	10 811	7 262	2 831
1955	55 833	3 225	1 330	1 896	52 608	4 637	12 855	13 327	11 322	7 510	2 957
1956	57 269	3 389	1 465	1 922	53 880	4 897	12 748	13 637	11 706	7 822	3 068
1957	57 465	3 374	1 442	1 931	54 091	4 952	12 619	13 716	12 009	7 829	2 951
1958	56 613	3 216	1 370	1 847	53 397	4 908	12 128	13 571	12 113	7 849	2 828
1959	58 006	3 475	1 520	1 955	54 531	5 138	12 144	13 830	12 552	8 063	2 805
1960	58 850	3 700	1 598	2 103	55 150	5 331	12 021	13 930	12 820	8 192	2 855
1961	58 913	3 693	1 472	2 220	55 220	5 460	11 835	13 905	12 906	8 335	2 778
1962	59 698	3 774	1 447	2 327	55 924	5 676	11 703	14 173	13 066	8 511	2 795
1963	60 622	3 851	1 600	2 250	56 771	6 036	11 689	14 341	13 304	8 718	2 683
1964	61 922	4 076	1 846	2 230	57 846	6 444	11 794	14 380	13 596	8 916	2 717
1965	63 446	4 562	1 892	2 670	58 884	6 752	11 992	14 473	13 804	9 116	2 748
1966	65 021	5 176	2 052	3 124	59 845	6 986	12 268	14 449	14 072	9 356	2 713
1967	66 361	5 114	2 121	2 993	61 247	7 493	12 763	14 429	14 224	9 596	2 746
1968	67 750	5 195	2 193	3 002	62 555	7 687	13 410	14 386	14 487	9 781	2 804
1969	69 518	5 508	2 347	3 161	64 010	8 182	13 935	14 270	14 788	9 947	2 888
1970	70 217	5 571	2 386	3 185	64 645	8 559	14 326	14 092	14 854	9 979	2 835
1971	70 878	5 670	2 404	3 266	65 208	9 000	14 713	13 858	14 843	10 014	2 780
1972	73 370	6 173	2 581	3 592	67 197	9 718	15 904	13 940	14 845	10 077	2 714
1973	75 708	6 623	2 806	3 816	69 086	10 424	17 099	14 083	14 886	9 983	2 610
1974	77 184	6 796	2 881	3 916	70 388	10 676	18 040	14 196	14 948	9 958	2 568
1975	76 411	6 487	2 721	3 770	69 924	10 546	18 485	13 979	14 555	9 827	2 533
1976	78 853	6 724	2 762	3 962	72 129	11 119	19 662	14 407	14 549	9 923	2 470
1977	81 700	7 068	2 926	4 142	74 632	11 696	20 844	14 984	14 483	10 107	2 518
1978	84 936	7 367	3 085	4 282	77 569	12 251	22 008	15 809	14 550	10 311	2 642
1979	87 259	7 356	3 079	4 278	79 904	12 594	23 033	16 578	14 522	10 477	2 699
1980	87 715	7 021	2 861	4 161	80 694	12 405	23 653	17 071	14 405	10 475	2 684
1981	88 709	6 588	2 645	3 943	82 121	12 477	24 551	17 617	14 414	10 386	2 676
1982	87 903	5 984	2 317	3 667	81 918	12 097	24 531	18 268	14 083	10 283	2 656
1983	88 893	5 799	2 156	3 643	83 094	12 138	24 955	19 194	13 961	10 169	2 678
1984	92 120	5 836	2 209	3 627	86 284	12 451	26 235	20 552	14 239	10 227	2 580
1985	93 736	5 768	2 270	3 498	87 968	12 235	26 945	21 552	14 459	10 247	2 530
1986	95 660	5 792	2 386	3 406	89 869	12 027	27 746	22 515	14 750	10 176	2 654
1987	97 789	5 898	2 468	3 431	91 890	11 748	28 429	23 596	15 216	10 164	2 738
1988	99 812	6 030	2 424	3 606	93 782	11 438	28 796	24 468	16 054	10 153	2 874
1989	101 584	5 946	2 278	3 668	95 638	11 084	29 091	25 442	16 775	10 223	3 024
1990	102 261	5 779	2 141	3 638	96 481	11 498	28 773	26 282	16 933	9 960	3 035
1991	101 182	5 216	1 971	3 246	95 966	11 116	27 989	26 883	17 269	9 719	2 990
1992	101 669	4 985	1 904	3 081	96 684	11 031	27 552	27 097	18 285	9 701	3 019
1993	103 045	5 113	1 990	3 123	97 932	10 931	27 274	27 645	19 273	9 772	3 037
1994	105 190	5 398	2 210	3 188	99 792	10 736	27 101	28 442	20 247	9 912	3 354
1995	106 490	5 593	2 273	3 320	100 897	10 400	27 014	28 951	21 127	10 070	3 335
1996	107 808	5 667	2 325	3 343	102 141	10 149	26 678	29 566	22 071	10 313	3 364
1997	109 856	5 807	2 341	3 466	104 049	10 362	26 294	30 137	23 061	10 785	3 411
1998	110 931	6 089	2 436	3 653	104 842	10 512	25 729	30 320	23 662	11 272	3 347
1999	112 235	6 204	2 435	3 769	106 032	10 716	25 113	30 548	24 507	11 657	3 491
2000	114 424	6 160	2 383	3 777	108 264	10 944	25 500	30 151	25 762	12 169	3 738
2001	114 430	5 817	2 224	3 593	108 613	11 054	24 948	29 793	26 301	12 743	3 774
2002	114 013	5 441	2 037	3 404	108 572	11 096	24 568	29 049	26 401	13 630	3 828
2003	114 235	5 064	1 999	3 065	109 171	11 052	24 399	28 501	26 762	14 375	4 083
2004	115 239	5 039	1 895	3 145	110 199	11 233	24 337	28 176	27 228	14 965	4 260
2005	116 949	5 105	1 999	3 106	111 844	11 231	24 443	28 102	27 801	15 788	4 480
2006	118 833	5 215	2 099	3 117	113 618	11 296	24 652	27 929	28 419	16 652	4 670
2007	119 792	4 990	1 965	3 026	114 802	11 325	25 024	27 492	28 779	17 262	4 921
2008	119 126	4 697	1 703	2 994	114 428	11 055	24 875	26 736	28 686	17 829	5 247
2009	114 996	4 138	1 443	2 696	110 858	10 438	23 957	25 237	27 891	17 978	5 357
2010	114 168	3 733	1 248	2 485	110 435	10 334	24 097	24 540	27 502	18 464	5 496

Table 1-11. Employed Civilians, by Age, Sex, Race, and Hispanic Origin, 1948–2010—*Continued*

(Thousands of people.)

Race, Hispanic origin, sex, and year	16 years and over	16 to 19 years			20 years and over						
		Total	16 to 17 years	18 to 19 years	Total	20 to 24 years	25 to 34 years	35 to 44 years	45 to 54 years	55 to 64 years	65 years and over
WHITE											
Men											
1954	37 846	1 723	771	953	36 123	2 394	9 287	9 175	7 614	5 412	2 241
1955	38 719	1 824	821	1 004	36 895	2 607	9 461	9 351	7 792	5 431	2 254
1956	39 368	1 893	890	1 002	37 475	2 850	9 330	9 449	7 950	5 559	2 336
1957	39 349	1 865	874	990	37 484	2 930	9 226	9 480	8 067	5 542	2 234
1958	38 591	1 783	852	932	36 808	2 896	8 861	9 386	8 061	5 501	2 103
1959	39 494	1 961	915	1 046	37 533	3 153	8 911	9 560	8 261	5 588	2 060
1960	39 755	2 092	973	1 119	37 663	3 264	8 777	9 589	8 372	5 618	2 043
1961	39 588	2 055	891	1 164	37 533	3 311	8 630	9 566	8 394	5 670	1 961
1962	40 016	2 098	883	1 215	37 918	3 426	8 514	9 718	8 512	5 749	1 998
1963	40 428	2 156	972	1 184	38 272	3 646	8 463	9 782	8 650	5 844	1 887
1964	41 115	2 316	1 128	1 188	38 799	3 856	8 538	9 800	8 787	5 945	1 872
1965	41 844	2 612	1 159	1 453	39 232	4 025	8 598	9 795	8 924	5 998	1 892
1966	42 331	2 913	1 245	1 668	39 418	4 028	8 674	9 719	9 029	6 096	1 871
1967	42 833	2 849	1 278	1 571	39 985	4 231	8 931	9 632	9 093	6 208	1 892
1968	43 411	2 908	1 319	1 589	40 503	4 226	9 315	9 522	9 198	6 316	1 926
1969	44 048	3 070	1 385	1 685	40 978	4 401	9 608	9 379	9 279	6 359	1 953
1970	44 178	3 066	1 374	1 692	41 112	4 601	9 784	9 202	9 271	6 340	1 914
1971	44 595	3 157	1 393	1 764	41 438	4 935	10 026	9 026	9 256	6 339	1 856
1972	45 944	3 416	1 470	1 947	42 528	5 431	10 664	9 047	9 236	6 363	1 786
1973	47 085	3 660	1 590	2 071	43 424	5 863	11 268	9 046	9 257	6 299	1 689
1974	47 674	3 728	1 611	2 117	43 946	5 965	11 701	9 027	9 242	6 304	1 706
1975	46 697	3 505	1 502	2 002	43 192	5 770	11 783	8 818	9 005	6 160	1 656
1976	47 775	3 604	1 501	2 103	44 171	6 140	12 362	8 944	8 968	6 176	1 579
1977	49 150	3 824	1 607	2 217	45 326	6 437	12 893	9 212	8 898	6 279	1 605
1978	50 544	3 950	1 664	2 286	46 594	6 717	13 413	9 608	8 840	6 339	1 677
1979	51 452	3 904	1 654	2 250	47 546	6 868	13 888	9 930	8 748	6 406	1 707
1980	51 127	3 708	1 534	2 174	47 419	6 652	14 009	10 077	8 586	6 412	1 684
1981	51 315	3 469	1 402	2 066	47 846	6 652	14 398	10 307	8 518	6 309	1 662
1982	50 287	3 079	1 214	1 865	47 209	6 372	14 164	10 593	8 267	6 188	1 624
1983	50 621	3 003	1 124	1 879	47 618	6 386	14 297	11 062	8 152	6 084	1 637
1984	52 462	3 001	1 140	1 861	49 461	6 647	15 045	11 776	8 320	6 108	1 564
1985	53 046	2 985	1 185	1 800	50 061	6 428	15 374	12 214	8 374	6 118	1 552
1986	53 785	2 966	1 225	1 741	50 818	6 340	15 790	12 620	8 442	6 012	1 612
1987	54 647	2 999	1 252	1 747	51 649	6 150	16 084	13 138	8 596	5 991	1 690
1988	55 550	3 084	1 248	1 836	52 466	5 987	16 241	13 590	8 992	5 909	1 748
1989	56 352	3 060	1 171	1 889	53 292	5 839	16 383	14 046	9 335	5 891	1 797
1990	56 703	3 018	1 119	1 899	53 685	6 179	16 124	14 496	9 383	5 744	1 760
1991	55 797	2 694	1 017	1 677	53 103	5 942	15 644	14 743	9 488	5 578	1 707
1992	55 959	2 602	990	1 612	53 357	5 855	15 357	14 842	10 027	5 503	1 772
1993	56 656	2 634	1 031	1 603	54 021	5 830	15 230	15 178	10 497	5 514	1 772
1994	57 452	2 776	1 144	1 632	54 676	5 738	15 052	15 562	10 910	5 490	1 925
1995	58 146	2 892	1 169	1 723	55 254	5 613	14 958	15 793	11 359	5 609	1 921
1996	58 888	2 911	1 161	1 750	55 977	5 444	14 820	16 136	11 834	5 755	1 987
1997	59 998	3 011	1 206	1 806	56 986	5 590	14 567	16 470	12 352	5 972	2 037
1998	60 604	3 103	1 233	1 870	57 500	5 659	14 259	16 715	12 661	6 251	1 955
1999	61 139	3 205	1 254	1 951	57 934	5 753	13 851	16 781	13 046	6 447	2 056
2000	62 289	3 169	1 205	1 965	59 119	5 876	14 238	16 477	13 675	6 678	2 175
2001	62 212	2 967	1 102	1 865	59 245	5 870	13 989	16 280	13 987	6 941	2 178
2002	61 849	2 725	987	1 738	59 124	5 882	13 727	15 910	14 060	7 360	2 184
2003	61 866	2 518	972	1 546	59 348	5 890	13 731	15 675	14 117	7 640	2 295
2004	62 712	2 553	903	1 650	60 159	6 026	13 735	15 572	14 418	8 018	2 390
2005	63 763	2 508	942	1 566	61 255	6 041	13 840	15 544	14 810	8 471	2 550
2006	64 883	2 625	1 020	1 605	62 259	6 114	13 903	15 480	15 189	8 893	2 680
2007	65 289	2 483	951	1 531	62 806	6 066	14 112	15 287	15 399	9 215	2 727
2008	64 624	2 320	808	1 512	62 304	5 858	13 931	14 775	15 300	9 518	2 922
2009	61 630	2 004	692	1 312	59 626	5 379	13 230	13 858	14 710	9 465	2 984
2010	61 252	1 815	598	1 217	59 438	5 347	13 282	13 583	14 542	9 637	3 047

Table 1-11. Employed Civilians, by Age, Sex, Race, and Hispanic Origin, 1948–2010—*Continued*

(Thousands of people.)

Race, Hispanic origin, sex, and year	16 years and over	16 to 19 years			20 years and over						
		Total	16 to 17 years	18 to 19 years	Total	20 to 24 years	25 to 34 years	35 to 44 years	45 to 54 years	55 to 64 years	65 years and over
WHITE											
Women											
1954	16 111	1 355	486	869	14 756	1 964	3 329	3 825	3 197	1 850	590
1955	17 114	1 401	509	892	15 713	2 030	3 394	3 976	3 530	2 079	703
1956	17 901	1 496	575	920	16 405	2 047	3 418	4 188	3 756	2 263	732
1957	18 116	1 509	568	941	16 607	2 022	3 393	4 236	3 942	2 287	717
1958	18 022	1 433	518	915	16 589	2 012	3 267	4 185	4 052	2 348	725
1959	18 512	1 514	605	909	16 998	1 985	3 233	4 270	4 291	2 475	745
1960	19 095	1 608	625	984	17 487	2 067	3 244	4 341	4 448	2 574	812
1961	19 325	1 638	581	1 056	17 687	2 149	3 205	4 339	4 512	2 665	817
1962	19 682	1 676	564	1 112	18 006	2 250	3 189	4 455	4 554	2 762	797
1963	20 194	1 695	628	1 066	18 499	2 390	3 226	4 559	4 654	2 874	796
1964	20 807	1 760	718	1 042	19 047	2 588	3 256	4 580	4 809	2 971	845
1965	21 602	1 950	733	1 217	19 652	2 727	3 394	4 678	4 880	3 118	856
1966	22 690	2 263	807	1 456	20 427	2 958	3 594	4 730	5 043	3 260	842
1967	23 528	2 265	843	1 422	21 263	3 262	3 832	4 797	5 131	3 388	854
1968	24 339	2 287	874	1 413	22 052	3 461	4 095	4 864	5 289	3 465	878
1969	25 470	2 438	962	1 476	23 032	3 781	4 327	4 891	5 509	3 588	935
1970	26 039	2 505	1 012	1 493	23 534	3 959	4 542	4 890	5 582	3 640	921
1971	26 283	2 513	1 011	1 502	23 770	4 065	4 687	4 831	5 588	3 675	924
1972	27 426	2 755	1 111	1 645	24 669	4 286	5 240	4 893	5 608	3 714	928
1973	28 623	2 962	1 217	1 746	25 661	4 562	5 831	5 036	5 628	3 684	920
1974	29 511	3 069	1 269	1 799	26 442	4 711	6 340	5 169	5 706	3 654	862
1975	29 714	2 983	1 215	1 767	26 731	4 775	6 701	5 161	5 550	3 667	877
1976	31 078	3 120	1 260	1 860	27 958	4 978	7 300	5 462	5 580	3 746	891
1977	32 550	3 244	1 319	1 923	29 306	5 259	7 950	5 772	5 585	3 829	912
1978	34 392	3 416	1 420	1 996	30 975	5 535	8 595	6 201	5 710	3 972	964
1979	35 807	3 451	1 423	2 027	32 357	5 726	9 145	6 648	5 773	4 071	993
1980	36 587	3 314	1 327	1 986	33 275	5 753	9 644	6 994	5 818	4 064	1 001
1981	37 394	3 119	1 242	1 877	34 275	5 826	10 153	7 311	5 896	4 077	1 013
1982	37 615	2 905	1 103	1 802	34 710	5 724	10 367	7 675	5 816	4 095	1 032
1983	38 272	2 796	1 032	1 764	35 476	5 751	10 659	8 132	5 809	4 084	1 041
1984	39 659	2 835	1 069	1 766	36 823	5 804	11 190	8 776	5 920	4 118	1 015
1985	40 690	2 783	1 085	1 698	37 907	5 807	11 671	9 338	6 084	4 128	978
1986	41 876	2 825	1 160	1 665	39 050	5 687	11 956	9 895	6 307	4 164	1 042
1987	43 142	2 900	1 216	1 684	40 242	5 598	12 345	10 459	6 620	4 172	1 047
1988	44 262	2 946	1 176	1 770	41 316	5 450	12 555	10 878	7 062	4 244	1 126
1989	45 232	2 886	1 107	1 779	42 346	5 245	12 708	11 395	7 440	4 332	1 227
1990	45 558	2 762	1 023	1 739	42 796	5 319	12 649	11 785	7 551	4 217	1 275
1991	45 385	2 523	954	1 569	42 862	5 174	12 344	12 139	7 781	4 141	1 283
1992	45 710	2 383	915	1 468	43 327	5 176	12 195	12 254	8 258	4 198	1 246
1993	46 390	2 479	959	1 520	43 910	5 101	12 044	12 467	8 776	4 258	1 265
1994	47 738	2 622	1 066	1 556	45 116	4 997	12 049	12 880	9 338	4 423	1 429
1995	48 344	2 701	1 104	1 597	45 643	4 787	12 056	13 157	9 768	4 461	1 415
1996	48 920	2 756	1 164	1 592	46 164	4 705	11 858	13 430	10 237	4 558	1 376
1997	49 859	2 796	1 136	1 660	47 063	4 773	11 727	13 667	10 709	4 813	1 374
1998	50 327	2 986	1 203	1 783	47 342	4 853	11 470	13 604	11 001	5 021	1 392
1999	51 096	2 999	1 181	1 817	48 098	4 963	11 262	13 767	11 461	5 211	1 435
2000	52 136	2 991	1 178	1 813	49 145	5 068	11 262	13 674	12 087	5 490	1 564
2001	52 218	2 850	1 122	1 727	49 369	5 184	10 959	13 513	12 314	5 802	1 597
2002	52 164	2 716	1 050	1 665	49 448	5 214	10 842	13 138	12 341	6 269	1 644
2003	52 369	2 546	1 027	1 519	49 823	5 161	10 668	12 826	12 645	6 735	1 788
2004	52 527	2 486	991	1 495	50 040	5 207	10 602	12 604	12 810	6 947	1 870
2005	53 186	2 597	1 057	1 540	50 589	5 190	10 603	12 558	12 991	7 317	1 930
2006	53 950	2 590	1 079	1 512	51 359	5 182	10 750	12 449	13 230	7 758	1 991
2007	54 503	2 507	1 013	1 494	51 996	5 259	10 912	12 205	13 380	8 047	2 193
2008	54 501	2 377	895	1 482	52 124	5 197	10 943	11 961	13 386	8 312	2 325
2009	53 366	2 134	751	1 383	51 231	5 060	10 727	11 379	13 181	8 513	2 373
2010	52 916	1 918	650	1 268	50 997	4 988	10 815	10 958	12 960	8 827	2 450

Table 1-11. Employed Civilians, by Age, Sex, Race, and Hispanic Origin, 1948–2010—*Continued*

(Thousands of people.)

Race, Hispanic origin, sex, and year	16 years and over	16 to 19 years			20 years and over						
		Total	16 to 17 years	18 to 19 years	Total	20 to 24 years	25 to 34 years	35 to 44 years	45 to 54 years	55 to 64 years	65 years and over
BLACK											
Both Sexes											
1973	8 128	570	194	378	7 559	1 258	2 062	1 659	1 460	872	249
1974	8 203	554	190	364	7 649	1 231	2 157	1 682	1 452	884	243
1975	7 894	507	183	325	7 386	1 115	2 145	1 617	1 393	874	241
1976	8 227	508	170	338	7 719	1 193	2 309	1 679	1 416	870	252
1977	8 540	508	169	339	8 031	1 244	2 443	1 754	1 448	892	251
1978	9 102	571	191	380	8 531	1 359	2 641	1 848	1 479	932	273
1979	9 359	579	204	376	8 780	1 424	2 759	1 902	1 502	927	266
1980	9 313	547	192	356	8 765	1 376	2 827	1 910	1 487	925	239
1981	9 355	505	170	335	8 849	1 346	2 872	1 957	1 489	954	231
1982	9 189	428	138	290	8 761	1 283	2 830	2 025	1 469	928	225
1983	9 375	416	123	294	8 959	1 280	2 976	2 107	1 456	937	204
1984	10 119	474	146	328	9 645	1 423	3 223	2 311	1 533	945	209
1985	10 501	532	175	356	9 969	1 399	3 325	2 427	1 598	985	235
1986	10 814	536	183	353	10 278	1 429	3 464	2 524	1 666	982	214
1987	11 309	587	203	385	10 722	1 421	3 614	2 695	1 714	1 036	241
1988	11 658	601	223	378	11 057	1 433	3 725	2 839	1 783	1 018	261
1989	11 953	625	237	388	11 328	1 467	3 801	2 981	1 844	970	265
1990	12 175	598	194	404	11 577	1 409	3 803	3 287	1 897	933	248
1991	12 074	494	161	334	11 580	1 373	3 714	3 401	1 892	957	243
1992	12 151	492	157	335	11 659	1 343	3 699	3 441	1 964	965	246
1993	12 382	494	171	323	11 888	1 377	3 700	3 584	2 059	941	226
1994	12 835	552	224	328	12 284	1 449	3 732	3 722	2 178	953	251
1995	13 279	586	223	363	12 693	1 443	3 844	3 861	2 288	1 004	253
1996	13 542	613	233	380	12 929	1 411	3 851	3 974	2 426	1 025	241
1997	13 969	631	229	401	13 339	1 456	3 903	4 094	2 588	1 048	249
1998	14 556	736	246	490	13 820	1 496	3 967	4 238	2 739	1 118	262
1999	15 056	691	243	448	14 365	1 594	4 091	4 404	2 872	1 134	271
2000	15 156	711	260	451	14 444	1 593	3 993	4 261	3 073	1 226	300
2001	15 006	637	230	408	14 368	1 571	3 840	4 200	3 139	1 283	335
2002	14 872	611	193	417	14 262	1 543	3 726	4 109	3 220	1 332	332
2003	14 739	516	196	320	14 222	1 516	3 618	4 080	3 289	1 373	346
2004	14 909	520	169	351	14 389	1 572	3 635	4 039	3 332	1 452	359
2005	15 313	536	164	372	14 776	1 599	3 722	4 060	3 464	1 555	375
2006	15 765	618	215	402	15 147	1 643	3 809	4 072	3 570	1 659	394
2007	16 051	566	202	364	15 485	1 674	3 888	4 120	3 658	1 732	413
2008	15 953	541	172	369	15 411	1 625	3 870	4 015	3 670	1 791	440
2009	15 025	442	131	310	14 584	1 474	3 582	3 686	3 562	1 827	453
2010	15 010	386	106	280	14 624	1 532	3 641	3 561	3 531	1 899	460
BLACK											
Men											
1973	4 527	330	112	220	4 197	711	1 142	898	816	483	148
1974	4 527	322	114	209	4 204	668	1 176	912	803	500	145
1975	4 275	276	98	179	3 998	595	1 159	865	755	487	137
1976	4 404	283	100	184	4 120	635	1 217	897	763	472	137
1977	4 565	291	105	186	4 273	659	1 271	940	777	484	143
1978	4 796	312	106	206	4 483	697	1 357	969	788	516	155
1979	4 923	316	111	205	4 606	754	1 425	983	801	498	147
1980	4 798	299	109	191	4 498	713	1 438	975	770	478	126
1981	4 794	273	95	178	4 520	693	1 457	991	764	492	123
1982	4 637	223	65	158	4 414	660	1 414	997	750	471	122
1983	4 753	222	64	158	4 531	684	1 483	1 034	749	477	105
1984	5 124	252	79	173	4 871	750	1 635	1 138	780	460	108
1985	5 270	278	92	186	4 992	726	1 669	1 187	795	501	114
1986	5 428	278	96	182	5 150	732	1 756	1 211	831	507	112
1987	5 661	304	109	195	5 357	728	1 821	1 283	853	547	124
1988	5 824	316	122	193	5 509	736	1 881	1 348	878	536	131
1989	5 928	327	124	202	5 602	742	1 931	1 415	886	498	131
1990	5 995	303	99	204	5 692	702	1 895	1 586	926	469	114
1991	5 961	255	85	170	5 706	695	1 859	1 634	923	481	114
1992	5 930	249	78	170	5 681	679	1 819	1 650	930	478	124
1993	6 047	254	88	166	5 793	674	1 858	1 717	978	461	106
1994	6 241	276	107	169	5 964	718	1 850	1 795	1 030	455	115
1995	6 422	285	111	174	6 137	714	1 895	1 836	1 085	468	138
1996	6 456	289	109	180	6 167	685	1 867	1 878	1 129	482	126
1997	6 607	282	108	174	6 325	668	1 874	1 955	1 215	487	127
1998	6 871	341	120	221	6 530	686	1 886	2 008	1 284	524	142
1999	7 027	325	120	205	6 702	700	1 926	2 092	1 327	525	131
2000	7 082	341	129	211	6 741	730	1 865	1 984	1 425	596	142
2001	6 938	311	115	196	6 627	703	1 757	1 931	1 452	614	170
2002	6 959	306	95	212	6 652	725	1 729	1 899	1 503	624	172
2003	6 820	234	89	145	6 586	726	1 660	1 868	1 518	638	176
2004	6 912	231	76	155	6 681	739	1 720	1 840	1 534	668	180
2005	7 155	254	76	178	6 901	748	1 759	1 886	1 616	711	182
2006	7 354	275	99	175	7 079	804	1 797	1 882	1 680	734	184
2007	7 500	254	82	172	7 245	816	1 851	1 916	1 717	750	195
2008	7 398	247	70	177	7 151	794	1 805	1 854	1 703	792	204
2009	6 817	189	56	133	6 628	689	1 635	1 662	1 622	813	206
2010	6 865	185	48	137	6 680	692	1 710	1 638	1 594	834	211

Table 1-11. Employed Civilians, by Age, Sex, Race, and Hispanic Origin, 1948–2010—*Continued*

(Thousands of people.)

Race, Hispanic origin, sex, and year	16 years and over	16 to 19 years			20 years and over						
		Total	16 to 17 years	18 to 19 years	Total	20 to 24 years	25 to 34 years	35 to 44 years	45 to 54 years	55 to 64 years	65 years and over
BLACK											
Women											
1973	3 601	239	81	158	3 362	546	920	761	644	389	101
1974	3 677	232	77	155	3 445	562	981	770	649	383	98
1975	3 618	231	85	146	3 388	520	985	752	638	387	104
1976	3 823	224	70	154	3 599	558	1 092	782	653	398	115
1977	3 975	217	64	153	3 758	585	1 172	814	671	408	109
1978	4 307	260	85	175	4 047	662	1 283	879	691	416	118
1979	4 436	263	92	171	4 174	670	1 333	919	702	428	119
1980	4 515	248	82	165	4 267	663	1 389	936	717	448	113
1981	4 561	232	75	157	4 329	653	1 415	966	725	462	108
1982	4 552	205	73	132	4 347	623	1 416	1 028	719	457	103
1983	4 622	194	59	136	4 428	596	1 493	1 073	707	460	99
1984	4 995	222	67	155	4 773	673	1 588	1 173	753	485	101
1985	5 231	254	83	171	4 977	673	1 656	1 240	804	484	121
1986	5 386	259	87	171	5 128	696	1 708	1 313	835	475	102
1987	5 648	283	93	190	5 365	693	1 793	1 412	860	489	117
1988	5 834	285	101	184	5 548	697	1 844	1 491	905	482	129
1989	6 025	298	113	185	5 727	725	1 870	1 566	959	472	134
1990	6 180	296	96	200	5 884	707	1 907	1 701	971	464	135
1991	6 113	239	76	164	5 874	677	1 855	1 768	969	476	129
1992	6 221	243	79	164	5 978	664	1 880	1 791	1 034	487	123
1993	6 334	239	82	157	6 095	703	1 842	1 867	1 081	480	121
1994	6 595	275	117	158	6 320	731	1 882	1 926	1 147	497	136
1995	6 857	301	112	189	6 556	729	1 949	2 025	1 202	536	114
1996	7 086	324	124	200	6 762	726	1 984	2 096	1 297	543	115
1997	7 362	349	122	227	7 013	789	2 029	2 139	1 373	561	122
1998	7 685	395	126	268	7 290	810	2 081	2 230	1 455	594	120
1999	8 029	366	123	243	7 663	893	2 165	2 312	1 545	609	139
2000	8 073	370	131	240	7 703	862	2 128	2 277	1 647	630	158
2001	8 068	327	115	212	7 741	868	2 084	2 269	1 686	668	165
2002	7 914	304	99	205	7 610	819	1 997	2 209	1 717	708	160
2003	7 919	283	107	175	7 636	790	1 959	2 211	1 770	735	171
2004	7 997	289	93	196	7 707	833	1 914	2 199	1 798	784	179
2005	8 158	282	88	194	7 876	852	1 964	2 175	1 848	844	193
2006	8 410	343	116	227	8 068	839	2 012	2 191	1 890	925	210
2007	8 551	311	120	191	8 240	858	2 037	2 205	1 941	982	218
2008	8 554	294	102	192	8 260	831	2 065	2 161	1 967	1 000	236
2009	8 208	252	75	178	7 956	784	1 947	2 024	1 939	1 014	246
2010	8 145	201	58	143	7 944	841	1 931	1 923	1 936	1 065	248
HISPANIC[1]											
Both Sexes											
1973	3 396	325	. . .	. . .	. . .	. . .	. . .	. . .	. . .	. . .	. . .
1974	3 687	355	. . .	. . .	. . .	. . .	. . .	. . .	. . .	. . .	. . .
1975	3 663	322	. . .	. . .	. . .	. . .	. . .	. . .	. . .	. . .	. . .
1976	3 720	341	124	230	3 436	614	1 135	803	573	269	42
1977	4 079	381	135	245	3 715	715	1 212	860	608	269	50
1978	4 527	423	159	264	4 104	803	1 330	942	661	307	62
1979	4 785	445	152	292	4 340	860	1 430	996	666	319	69
1980	5 527	500	174	325	5 028	998	1 675	1 074	811	389	80
1981	5 813	459	155	304	5 354	1 060	1 837	1 147	829	399	82
1982	5 805	410	119	291	5 394	1 030	1 896	1 173	816	399	80
1983	6 072	423	125	297	5 649	1 068	1 997	1 224	837	441	81
1984	6 651	468	148	320	6 182	1 160	2 201	1 385	883	474	79
1985	6 888	438	144	294	6 449	1 187	2 316	1 473	913	486	75
1986	7 219	430	146	284	6 789	1 231	2 427	1 570	1 011	474	76
1987	7 790	474	149	325	7 316	1 273	2 668	1 775	1 010	512	76
1988	8 250	523	171	353	7 727	1 341	2 749	1 876	1 078	585	97
1989	8 573	548	165	383	8 025	1 325	2 900	1 968	1 129	589	114
1990	9 845	668	208	460	9 177	1 672	3 327	2 229	1 235	611	103
1991	9 828	602	169	433	9 225	1 622	3 264	2 333	1 266	637	103
1992	10 027	577	169	408	9 450	1 575	3 350	2 468	1 316	628	112
1993	10 361	570	160	410	9 792	1 574	3 446	2 605	1 402	630	135
1994	10 788	609	195	415	10 178	1 643	3 517	2 737	1 495	647	139
1995	11 127	645	194	450	10 483	1 609	3 618	2 889	1 565	666	135
1996	11 642	646	199	447	10 996	1 628	3 758	3 115	1 595	748	152
1997	12 726	714	228	487	12 012	1 798	4 029	3 371	1 846	794	173
1998	13 291	793	230	563	12 498	1 883	4 113	3 504	1 994	846	158
1999	13 720	854	254	600	12 866	1 881	4 097	3 738	2 074	886	190
2000	15 735	973	285	688	14 762	2 356	4 950	4 052	2 308	898	197
2001	16 190	969	268	701	15 221	2 404	5 065	4 149	2 472	944	187
2002	16 590	882	254	628	15 708	2 413	5 272	4 273	2 511	1 029	209
2003	17 372	768	242	525	16 604	2 399	5 541	4 573	2 711	1 132	249
2004	17 930	792	211	581	17 138	2 477	5 560	4 671	2 932	1 210	288
2005	18 632	847	253	595	17 785	2 423	5 756	4 879	3 114	1 317	296
2006	19 613	900	287	614	18 712	2 487	6 001	5 106	3 324	1 441	354
2007	20 382	894	269	625	19 488	2 516	6 237	5 314	3 547	1 499	376
2008	20 346	870	248	622	19 476	2 361	6 119	5 371	3 620	1 619	385
2009	19 647	742	192	550	18 905	2 218	5 704	5 168	3 700	1 680	435
2010	19 906	680	165	515	19 226	2 281	5 781	5 185	3 779	1 737	464

[1] May be of any race.
. . . = Not available.

Table 1-11. Employed Civilians, by Age, Sex, Race, and Hispanic Origin, 1948–2010—*Continued*

(Thousands of people.)

Race, Hispanic origin, sex, and year	16 years and over	16 to 19 years			20 years and over						
		Total	16 to 17 years	18 to 19 years	Total	20 to 24 years	25 to 34 years	35 to 44 years	45 to 54 years	55 to 64 years	65 years and over
HISPANIC[1]											
Men											
1973	2 198	...	...	...	2 010	...	...	...	...	...	...
1974	2 369	...	...	...	2 165	...	...	...	...	...	...
1975	2 301	...	...	...	2 117	...	...	...	...	...	...
1976	2 303	199	74	125	2 109	364	708	504	369	173	...
1977	2 564	225	78	147	2 335	427	763	540	394	184	...
1978	2 808	241	93	147	2 568	494	824	590	405	207	...
1979	2 962	260	93	168	2 701	511	891	615	427	205	...
1980	3 448	306	109	198	3 142	611	1 065	662	491	254	...
1981	3 597	272	90	182	3 325	642	1 157	707	504	259	...
1982	3 583	229	66	162	3 354	621	1 192	729	498	261	...
1983	3 771	248	71	177	3 523	655	1 280	760	499	275	...
1984	4 083	258	78	180	3 825	718	1 398	841	530	292	...
1985	4 245	251	82	169	3 994	727	1 473	888	550	308	...
1986	4 428	254	82	172	4 174	773	1 510	929	614	297	...
1987	4 713	268	81	188	4 444	777	1 664	1 044	606	303	...
1988	4 972	292	87	205	4 680	815	1 706	1 120	645	331	...
1989	5 172	319	94	225	4 853	821	1 787	1 152	676	350	...
1990	6 021	412	126	286	5 609	1 083	2 076	1 312	722	355	...
1991	5 979	356	94	263	5 623	1 063	2 050	1 360	719	369	...
1992	6 093	336	97	238	5 757	985	2 127	1 437	768	372	...
1993	6 328	337	95	242	5 992	1 003	2 200	1 527	822	360	...
1994	6 530	341	109	233	6 189	1 056	2 227	1 600	847	379	79
1995	6 725	358	110	248	6 367	1 030	2 284	1 675	908	384	85
1996	7 039	384	107	277	6 655	1 015	2 345	1 842	918	438	96
1997	7 728	420	130	290	7 307	1 142	2 547	1 978	1 059	477	105
1998	8 018	449	133	315	7 570	1 173	2 592	2 077	1 115	512	101
1999	8 067	491	139	352	7 576	1 135	2 524	2 135	1 151	502	130
2000	9 428	570	159	411	8 859	1 486	3 063	2 358	1 295	532	126
2001	9 668	568	149	419	9 100	1 473	3 142	2 446	1 375	545	119
2002	9 845	504	141	363	9 341	1 476	3 271	2 503	1 396	569	125
2003	10 479	415	121	294	10 063	1 485	3 537	2 724	1 533	639	144
2004	10 832	446	108	338	10 385	1 514	3 557	2 801	1 654	687	174
2005	11 337	465	137	328	10 872	1 511	3 711	2 939	1 781	748	183
2006	11 887	496	146	350	11 391	1 535	3 845	3 088	1 894	809	220
2007	12 310	483	145	338	11 827	1 524	3 982	3 220	2 012	869	220
2008	12 248	479	140	340	11 769	1 406	3 897	3 233	2 080	929	224
2009	11 640	383	94	289	11 256	1 287	3 576	3 108	2 104	930	251
2010	11 800	361	78	283	11 438	1 319	3 591	3 169	2 137	949	273
HISPANIC[1]											
Women											
1973	1 198	...	...	...	1 060	...	...	...	...	...	...
1974	1 319	...	...	...	1 166	...	...	...	...	...	...
1975	1 362	...	...	...	1 224	...	...	...	...	...	...
1976	1 417	155	50	106	1 288	249	427	300	204	96	...
1977	1 516	155	57	98	1 370	288	449	320	214	86	...
1978	1 719	182	65	117	1 537	308	506	352	256	99	...
1979	1 824	185	60	125	1 638	349	539	381	241	115	...
1980	2 079	193	65	128	1 886	387	610	412	320	136	...
1981	2 216	187	65	122	2 029	418	680	440	326	139	...
1982	2 222	181	52	129	2 040	409	704	444	318	139	...
1983	2 301	175	54	120	2 127	413	717	464	338	166	...
1984	2 568	211	71	140	2 357	442	804	544	354	181	...
1985	2 642	187	62	125	2 456	460	843	585	362	178	...
1986	2 791	176	64	112	2 615	458	917	641	397	177	...
1987	3 077	206	69	137	2 872	496	1 004	732	405	209	...
1988	3 278	231	84	147	3 047	526	1 042	756	434	254	...
1989	3 401	229	71	158	3 172	504	1 114	816	453	239	...
1990	3 823	256	82	174	3 567	588	1 251	917	513	256	...
1991	3 848	246	76	170	3 603	559	1 214	972	548	268	...
1992	3 934	242	72	170	3 693	591	1 223	1 031	548	256	...
1993	4 033	233	65	168	3 800	571	1 246	1 077	581	269	...
1994	4 258	268	86	182	3 989	587	1 290	1 137	648	268	59
1995	4 403	287	85	202	4 116	579	1 334	1 213	657	282	50
1996	4 602	261	92	169	4 341	612	1 412	1 273	677	310	56
1997	4 999	294	98	196	4 705	656	1 482	1 393	787	318	69
1998	5 273	345	97	247	4 928	710	1 521	1 428	879	334	57
1999	5 653	363	115	248	5 290	746	1 574	1 603	923	384	60
2000	6 307	404	127	277	5 903	870	1 887	1 695	1 013	366	72
2001	6 522	401	119	282	6 121	931	1 923	1 703	1 097	398	67
2002	6 744	378	113	265	6 367	937	2 001	1 770	1 114	460	84
2003	6 894	353	121	231	6 541	914	2 004	1 849	1 178	493	105
2004	7 098	346	103	243	6 752	964	2 003	1 870	1 279	523	114
2005	7 295	382	116	266	6 913	912	2 045	1 940	1 333	569	113
2006	7 725	404	140	264	7 321	951	2 155	2 018	1 430	632	135
2007	8 072	410	124	287	7 662	991	2 255	2 094	1 535	631	155
2008	8 098	391	108	282	7 707	955	2 222	2 138	1 541	690	161
2009	8 007	358	98	261	7 649	931	2 128	2 060	1 596	751	183
2010	8 106	318	87	231	7 788	962	2 189	2 016	1 642	788	191

[1]May be of any race.
... = Not available.

Table 1-12. Civilian Employment-Population Ratios, by Sex, Age, Race, and Hispanic Origin, 1948–2010

(Percent.)

Race, Hispanic origin, and year	Both sexes			Men			Women		
	16 years and over	16 to 19 years	20 years and over	16 years and over	16 to 19 years	20 years and over	16 years and over	16 to 19 years	20 years and over
ALL RACES									
1948	56.6	47.7	57.4	83.5	57.5	85.8	31.3	38.5	30.7
1949	55.4	45.2	56.3	81.3	53.8	83.7	31.2	37.2	30.6
1950	56.1	45.5	57.0	82.0	55.2	84.2	32.0	36.3	31.6
1951	57.3	47.9	58.1	84.0	57.9	86.1	33.1	38.9	32.6
1952	57.3	46.9	58.1	83.9	55.9	86.2	33.4	38.8	33.0
1953	57.1	46.4	58.0	83.6	55.9	85.9	33.3	37.8	32.9
1954	55.5	42.3	56.6	81.0	50.2	83.5	32.5	34.9	32.3
1955	56.7	43.5	57.8	81.8	52.1	84.3	34.0	35.6	33.8
1956	57.5	45.3	58.5	82.3	53.8	84.6	35.1	37.5	34.9
1957	57.1	43.9	58.2	81.3	51.8	83.8	35.1	36.7	35.0
1958	55.4	39.9	56.8	78.5	46.9	81.2	34.5	33.5	34.6
1959	56.0	39.9	57.5	79.3	47.2	82.3	35.0	33.0	35.1
1960	56.1	40.5	57.6	78.9	47.6	81.9	35.5	33.8	35.7
1961	55.4	39.1	56.9	77.6	45.3	80.8	35.4	33.2	35.6
1962	55.5	39.4	57.1	77.7	45.9	80.9	35.6	33.3	35.8
1963	55.4	37.4	57.2	77.1	43.8	80.6	35.8	31.5	36.3
1964	55.7	37.3	57.7	77.3	44.1	80.9	36.3	30.9	36.9
1965	56.2	38.9	58.2	77.5	46.2	81.2	37.1	32.0	37.6
1966	56.9	42.1	58.7	77.9	48.9	81.5	38.3	35.6	38.6
1967	57.3	42.2	59.0	78.0	48.7	81.5	39.0	35.9	39.3
1968	57.5	42.2	59.3	77.8	48.7	81.3	39.6	36.0	40.0
1969	58.0	43.4	59.7	77.6	49.5	81.1	40.7	37.5	41.1
1970	57.4	42.3	59.2	76.2	47.7	79.7	40.8	37.1	41.2
1971	56.6	41.3	58.4	74.9	46.8	78.5	40.4	36.0	40.9
1972	57.0	43.5	58.6	75.0	48.9	78.4	41.0	38.2	41.3
1973	57.8	45.9	59.3	75.5	51.4	78.6	42.0	40.5	42.2
1974	57.8	46.0	59.2	74.9	51.2	77.9	42.6	41.0	42.8
1975	56.1	43.3	57.6	71.7	47.2	74.8	42.0	39.4	42.3
1976	56.8	44.2	58.3	72.0	47.9	75.1	43.2	40.5	43.5
1977	57.9	46.1	59.2	72.8	50.4	75.6	44.5	41.8	44.8
1978	59.3	48.3	60.6	73.8	52.2	76.4	46.4	44.5	46.6
1979	59.9	48.5	61.2	73.8	51.7	76.5	47.5	45.3	47.7
1980	59.2	46.6	60.8	72.0	49.5	74.6	47.7	43.8	48.1
1981	59.0	44.6	60.5	71.3	47.1	74.0	48.0	42.0	48.6
1982	57.8	41.5	59.4	69.0	42.9	71.8	47.7	40.2	48.4
1983	57.9	41.5	59.5	68.8	43.1	71.4	48.0	40.0	48.8
1984	59.5	43.7	61.0	70.7	45.0	73.2	49.5	42.5	50.1
1985	60.1	44.4	61.5	70.9	45.7	73.3	50.4	42.9	51.0
1986	60.7	44.6	62.1	71.0	45.7	73.3	51.4	43.6	52.0
1987	61.5	45.5	62.9	71.5	46.1	73.8	52.5	44.8	53.1
1988	62.3	46.8	63.6	72.0	47.8	74.2	53.4	45.9	54.0
1989	63.0	47.5	64.2	72.5	48.7	74.5	54.3	46.4	54.9
1990	62.8	45.3	64.3	72.0	46.6	74.3	54.3	44.0	55.2
1991	61.7	42.0	63.2	70.4	42.7	72.7	53.7	41.2	54.6
1992	61.5	41.0	63.0	69.8	41.9	72.1	53.8	40.0	54.8
1993	61.7	41.7	63.3	70.0	42.3	72.3	54.1	41.0	55.0
1994	62.5	43.4	64.0	70.4	43.8	72.6	55.3	43.0	56.2
1995	62.9	44.2	64.4	70.8	44.7	73.0	55.6	43.8	56.5
1996	63.2	43.5	64.7	70.9	43.6	73.2	56.0	43.5	57.0
1997	63.8	43.4	65.5	71.3	43.4	73.7	56.8	43.3	57.8
1998	64.1	45.1	65.6	71.6	44.7	73.9	57.1	45.5	58.0
1999	64.3	44.7	65.9	71.6	45.1	74.0	57.4	44.3	58.5
2000	64.4	45.2	66.0	71.9	45.4	74.2	57.5	45.0	58.4
2001	63.7	42.3	65.4	70.9	42.2	73.3	57.0	42.4	58.1
2002	62.7	39.6	64.6	69.7	38.9	72.3	56.3	40.3	57.5
2003	62.3	36.8	64.3	68.9	35.7	71.7	56.1	37.8	57.5
2004	62.3	36.4	64.4	69.2	35.9	71.9	56.0	37.0	57.4
2005	62.7	36.5	64.7	69.6	35.1	72.4	56.2	37.8	57.6
2006	63.1	36.9	65.2	70.1	36.3	72.9	56.6	37.6	58.0
2007	63.0	34.8	65.2	69.8	33.9	72.8	56.6	35.8	58.2
2008	62.2	32.6	64.5	68.5	31.6	71.6	56.2	33.7	57.9
2009	59.3	28.4	61.7	64.5	26.9	67.6	54.4	29.9	56.2
2010	58.5	25.9	61.0	63.7	24.8	66.8	53.6	27.0	55.5

Table 1-12. Civilian Employment-Population Ratios, by Sex, Age, Race, and Hispanic Origin, 1948–2010
—*Continued*

(Percent.)

Race, Hispanic origin, and year	Both sexes			Men			Women		
	16 years and over	16 to 19 years	20 years and over	16 years and over	16 to 19 years	20 years and over	16 years and over	16 to 19 years	20 years and over
WHITE[1]									
1954	55.2	42.9	56.2	81.5	49.9	84.0	31.4	36.4	31.1
1955	56.5	44.2	57.4	82.2	52.0	84.7	33.0	37.0	32.7
1956	57.3	46.1	58.2	82.7	54.1	85.0	34.2	38.9	33.8
1957	56.8	45.0	57.8	81.8	52.4	84.1	34.2	38.2	33.9
1958	55.3	41.0	56.5	79.2	47.6	81.8	33.6	35.0	33.5
1959	55.9	41.2	57.2	79.9	48.1	82.8	34.0	34.8	34.0
1960	55.9	41.5	57.2	79.4	48.1	82.4	34.6	35.1	34.5
1961	55.3	40.1	56.7	78.2	45.9	81.4	34.5	34.6	34.5
1962	55.4	40.4	56.9	78.4	46.4	81.5	34.7	34.8	34.7
1963	55.3	38.6	56.9	77.7	44.7	81.1	35.0	32.9	35.2
1964	55.5	38.4	57.3	77.8	45.0	81.3	35.5	32.2	35.8
1965	56.0	40.3	57.8	77.9	47.1	81.5	36.2	33.7	36.5
1966	56.8	43.6	58.3	78.3	50.1	81.7	37.5	37.5	37.5
1967	57.2	43.8	58.7	78.4	50.2	81.7	38.3	37.7	38.3
1968	57.4	43.9	59.0	78.3	50.3	81.6	38.9	37.8	39.1
1969	58.0	45.2	59.4	78.2	51.1	81.4	40.1	39.5	40.1
1970	57.5	44.5	59.0	76.8	49.6	80.1	40.3	39.5	40.4
1971	56.8	43.8	58.3	75.7	49.2	79.0	39.9	38.6	40.1
1972	57.4	46.4	58.6	76.0	51.5	79.0	40.7	41.3	40.6
1973	58.2	48.9	59.3	76.5	54.3	79.2	41.8	43.6	41.6
1974	58.3	49.3	59.3	75.9	54.4	78.6	42.4	44.3	42.2
1975	56.7	46.5	57.9	73.0	50.6	75.7	42.0	42.5	41.9
1976	57.5	47.8	58.6	73.4	51.5	76.0	43.2	44.2	43.1
1977	58.6	50.1	59.6	74.1	54.4	76.5	44.5	45.9	44.4
1978	60.0	52.4	60.8	75.0	56.3	77.2	46.3	48.5	46.1
1979	60.6	52.6	61.5	75.1	55.7	77.3	47.5	49.4	47.3
1980	60.0	50.7	61.0	73.4	53.4	75.6	47.8	47.9	47.8
1981	60.0	48.7	61.1	72.8	51.3	75.1	48.3	46.2	48.5
1982	58.8	45.8	60.1	70.6	47.0	73.0	48.1	44.6	48.4
1983	58.9	45.9	60.1	70.4	47.4	72.6	48.5	44.5	48.9
1984	60.5	48.0	61.5	72.1	49.1	74.3	49.8	47.0	50.0
1985	61.0	48.5	62.0	72.3	49.9	74.3	50.7	47.1	51.0
1986	61.5	48.8	62.6	72.3	49.6	74.3	51.7	47.9	52.0
1987	62.3	49.4	63.4	72.7	49.9	74.7	52.8	49.0	53.1
1988	63.1	50.9	64.1	73.2	51.7	75.1	53.8	50.2	54.0
1989	63.8	51.6	64.7	73.7	52.6	75.4	54.6	50.5	54.9
1990	63.7	49.7	64.8	73.3	51.0	75.1	54.7	48.3	55.2
1991	62.6	46.6	63.7	71.6	47.2	73.5	54.2	45.9	54.8
1992	62.4	45.3	63.6	71.1	46.4	73.1	54.2	44.2	54.9
1993	62.7	46.2	63.9	71.4	46.6	73.3	54.6	45.7	55.2
1994	63.5	47.9	64.7	71.8	48.3	73.6	55.8	47.5	56.4
1995	63.8	48.8	64.9	72.0	49.4	73.8	56.1	48.1	56.7
1996	64.1	47.9	65.3	72.3	48.2	74.2	56.3	47.6	57.0
1997	64.6	47.7	65.9	72.7	48.1	74.7	57.0	47.2	57.8
1998	64.7	48.9	65.9	72.7	48.6	74.7	57.1	49.3	57.7
1999	64.8	48.8	66.1	72.8	49.3	74.8	57.3	48.3	58.0
2000	64.9	49.1	66.1	73.0	49.5	74.9	57.4	48.8	58.0
2001	64.2	46.3	65.6	72.0	46.2	74.0	57.0	46.5	57.7
2002	63.4	43.2	64.9	70.8	42.3	73.1	56.4	44.1	57.3
2003	63.0	40.4	64.7	70.1	39.4	72.5	56.3	41.5	57.3
2004	63.1	40.0	64.8	70.4	39.7	72.8	56.1	40.3	57.2
2005	63.4	40.2	65.1	70.8	38.8	73.3	56.3	41.8	57.4
2006	63.8	40.6	65.5	71.3	40.0	73.7	56.6	41.1	57.7
2007	63.6	38.3	65.5	70.9	37.3	73.5	56.7	39.2	57.9
2008	62.8	35.9	64.8	69.7	34.8	72.4	56.3	37.1	57.7
2009	60.2	31.7	62.3	66.0	30.2	68.7	54.8	33.4	56.3
2010	59.4	29.0	61.6	65.1	27.6	67.9	54.0	30.4	55.6

[1]Beginning in 2003, persons who selected this race group only; persons who selected more than one race group are not included. Prior to 2003, persons who reported more than one race group were included in the group they identified as their main race.

Table 1-12. Civilian Employment-Population Ratios, by Sex, Age, Race, and Hispanic Origin, 1948–2010
—*Continued*

(Percent.)

Race, Hispanic origin, and year	Both sexes			Men			Women		
	16 years and over	16 to 19 years	20 years and over	16 years and over	16 to 19 years	20 years and over	16 years and over	16 to 19 years	20 years and over
BLACK[1]									
1975	50.1	23.1	54.5	60.6	26.3	66.5	41.6	20.2	44.9
1976	50.8	22.4	55.4	60.6	25.8	66.8	42.8	19.2	46.4
1977	51.4	22.3	56.0	61.4	26.4	67.5	43.3	18.5	47.0
1978	53.6	25.2	58.0	63.3	28.5	69.1	45.8	22.1	49.3
1979	53.8	25.4	58.1	63.4	28.7	69.1	46.0	22.4	49.3
1980	52.3	23.9	56.4	60.4	27.0	65.8	45.7	21.0	49.1
1981	51.3	22.1	55.5	59.1	24.6	64.5	45.1	19.7	48.5
1982	49.4	19.0	53.6	56.0	20.3	61.4	44.2	17.7	47.5
1983	49.5	18.7	53.6	56.3	20.4	61.6	44.1	17.0	47.4
1984	52.3	21.9	56.1	59.2	23.9	64.1	46.7	20.1	49.8
1985	53.4	24.6	57.0	60.0	26.3	64.6	48.1	23.1	50.9
1986	54.1	25.1	57.6	60.6	26.5	65.1	48.8	23.8	51.6
1987	55.6	27.1	58.9	62.0	28.5	66.4	50.3	25.8	53.0
1988	56.3	27.6	59.7	62.7	29.4	67.1	51.2	25.8	53.9
1989	56.9	28.7	60.1	62.8	30.4	67.0	52.0	27.1	54.6
1990	56.7	26.7	60.2	62.6	27.7	67.1	51.9	25.8	54.7
1991	55.4	22.6	59.0	61.3	23.8	65.9	50.6	21.5	53.6
1992	54.9	22.8	58.3	59.9	23.6	64.3	50.8	22.1	53.6
1993	55.0	22.6	58.4	60.0	23.6	64.3	50.9	21.6	53.8
1994	56.1	24.9	59.4	60.8	25.4	65.0	52.3	24.5	55.0
1995	57.1	25.7	60.5	61.7	25.2	66.1	53.4	26.1	56.1
1996	57.4	26.0	60.8	61.1	24.9	65.5	54.4	27.1	57.1
1997	58.2	26.1	61.8	61.4	23.7	66.1	55.6	28.5	58.4
1998	59.7	30.1	63.0	62.9	28.4	67.1	57.2	31.8	59.7
1999	60.6	27.9	64.2	63.1	26.7	67.5	58.6	29.0	61.5
2000	60.9	29.8	64.2	63.6	28.9	67.7	58.6	30.6	61.3
2001	59.7	26.7	63.2	62.1	26.4	66.3	57.8	27.0	60.7
2002	58.1	25.3	61.6	61.1	25.6	65.2	55.8	24.9	58.7
2003	57.4	21.7	61.0	59.5	19.9	64.1	55.6	23.4	58.6
2004	57.2	21.5	60.9	59.3	19.3	63.9	55.5	23.6	58.5
2005	57.7	21.6	61.5	60.2	20.8	64.7	55.7	22.4	58.9
2006	58.4	24.1	62.0	60.6	21.7	65.2	56.5	26.4	59.4
2007	58.4	21.4	62.3	60.7	19.5	65.5	56.5	23.3	59.8
2008	57.3	20.2	61.2	59.1	18.7	63.9	55.8	21.7	59.1
2009	53.2	16.5	57.1	53.7	14.3	58.2	52.8	18.6	56.1
2010	52.3	14.5	56.1	53.1	14.1	57.5	51.7	14.9	55.1
HISPANIC[2]									
1975	53.4	...	...	...	...	...	...	...	...
1976	53.8	...	56.6	...	...	...	...	...	...
1977	55.4	...	58.3	...	...	...	...	...	...
1978	57.2	...	60.0	...	...	...	...	...	...
1979	58.3	...	61.0	...	...	...	...	...	...
1980	57.6	...	60.5	...	...	...	...	...	...
1981	57.4	...	60.7	...	...	...	...	...	...
1982	54.9	...	58.2	...	...	...	...	...	...
1983	55.1	...	58.1	...	...	...	...	...	...
1984	57.9	...	60.7	...	...	...	...	...	...
1985	57.8	...	60.7	...	...	...	...	...	...
1986	58.5	...	61.5	...	...	...	...	...	...
1987	60.5	...	63.4	...	...	...	...	...	...
1988	61.9	...	64.6	...	...	...	...	...	...
1989	62.2	...	64.8	...	...	...	...	...	...
1990	61.9	...	64.8	...	...	...	...	...	...
1991	59.8	...	62.8	...	...	...	...	...	...
1992	59.1	...	62.1	...	...	...	...	...	...
1993	59.1	...	62.1	...	...	...	...	...	...
1994	59.5	33.5	62.4	71.7	36.8	...	47.2	30.1	...
1995	59.7	34.4	62.6	72.1	37.5	...	47.3	31.3	...
1996	60.6	33.1	63.7	73.3	38.8	...	47.9	27.3	...
1997	62.6	33.7	66.0	74.5	37.6	...	50.2	29.3	...
1998	63.1	36.0	66.2	74.7	38.6	...	51.0	33.0	...
1999	63.4	37.0	66.5	75.3	41.2	...	51.7	32.5	...
2000	65.7	38.6	68.9	77.4	42.8	81.7	53.6	33.9	55.8
2001	64.9	38.6	67.8	76.2	43.3	79.9	53.3	33.5	55.4
2002	63.9	35.2	67.0	74.5	39.0	78.3	52.9	31.1	55.2
2003	63.1	30.2	66.4	74.3	31.9	78.6	51.2	28.4	53.6
2004	63.8	30.4	67.2	75.1	33.4	79.4	51.8	27.2	54.4
2005	64.0	31.5	67.3	75.8	33.8	80.0	51.5	29.1	53.8
2006	65.2	32.2	68.5	76.8	34.8	81.1	52.8	29.5	55.2
2007	64.9	30.4	68.5	76.2	32.1	80.7	53.0	28.5	55.6
2008	63.3	28.6	66.9	74.1	30.9	78.6	51.9	26.2	54.6
2009	59.7	23.7	63.5	68.9	24.1	73.5	50.1	23.4	52.9
2010	59.0	21.0	63.1	68.0	21.7	72.9	49.6	20.2	52.7

[1]Beginning in 2003, persons who selected this race group only; persons who selected more than one race group are not included. Prior to 2003, persons who reported more than one race group were included in the group they identified as their main race.
[2]May be of any race.
. . . = Not available.

Table 1-13. Employed Civilians, by Sex, Race, Hispanic Origin, and Occupation, 2008–2010

(Thousands of people.)

Year and occupation	Total	Men	Women	White[1]	Black[1]	Hispanic[2]
2008						
All Occupations	145 362	77 486	67 876	119 126	15 953	20 346
Management, professional, and related occupations	52 761	25 948	26 813	44 090	4 374	3 723
Management, business, and financial operations	22 059	12 647	9 412	18 938	1 599	1 652
Computer and mathematical occupations	3 676	2 765	911	2 730	267	188
Architecture and engineering occupations	2 931	2 536	395	2 446	148	196
Life, physical and social science occupations	1 307	704	603	1 030	93	62
Community and social service occupations	2 293	909	1 383	1 741	436	205
Legal occupations	1 671	803	867	1 481	116	110
Education, training, and library occupations	8 605	2 234	6 371	7 337	792	641
Arts, design, entertainment, sports, and media occupations	2 820	1 471	1 349	2 466	172	234
Healthcare practitioner and technical occupations	7 399	1 878	5 521	5 920	751	434
Healthcare support occupations	3 212	359	2 853	2 156	827	436
Protective service occupations	3 047	2 352	695	2 330	582	332
Food preparation and serving related occupations	7 824	3 443	4 381	6 199	946	1 645
Building and grounds cleaning and maintenance occupations	5 445	3 254	2 192	4 295	818	1 821
Personal care and service occupations	4 923	1 064	3 859	3 701	722	699
Sales and related occupations	35 544	13 067	22 477	29 160	4 075	4 361
Office and administrative support occupations	19 249	4 845	14 404	15 563	2 499	2 459
Farming, fishing, and forestry occupations	988	780	208	878	45	389
Construction and extraction occupations	8 667	8 448	219	7 747	545	2 564
Installation, maintenance, and repair occupations	5 152	4 953	199	4 451	437	749
Production occupations	8 973	6 313	2 661	7 210	1 093	1 892
Transportation and material moving occupations	8 827	7 507	1 319	6 909	1 487	1 736
2009						
All Occupations	139 877	73 670	66 208	114 996	15 025	19 647
Management, professional, and related occupations	52 219	25 385	26 833	43 649	4 388	3 817
Management, business, and financial operations	21 529	12 330	9 199	18 582	1 516	1 642
Computer and mathematical occupations	3 481	2 618	863	2 633	233	189
Architecture and engineering occupations	2 740	2 363	377	2 276	151	196
Life, physical and social science occupations	1 328	707	621	1 052	80	1 328
Community and social service occupations	2 341	868	1 474	1 764	463	2 341
Legal occupations	1 710	859	851	1 510	110	85
Education, training, and library occupations	8 627	2 221	6 407	7 343	797	671
Arts, design, entertainment, sports, and media occupations	2 724	1 453	1 271	2 387	183	239
Healthcare practitioner and technical occupations	7 738	1 968	5 770	6 101	855	488
Healthcare support occupations	3 309	350	2 959	2 258	836	456
Protective service occupations	3 164	2 457	707	2 411	594	389
Food preparation and serving related occupations	7 733	3 422	4 310	6 184	884	1 672
Building and grounds cleaning and maintenance occupations	5 349	3 186	2 163	4 304	737	1 823
Personal care and service occupations	5 043	1 106	3 937	3 804	733	721
Sales and related occupations	33 787	12 498	21 289	27 777	3 793	1 864
Office and administrative support occupations	18 146	4 618	13 527	14 715	2 298	2 313
Farming, fishing, and forestry occupations	926	736	190	834	46	377
Construction and extraction occupations	7 439	7 248	191	6 682	447	2 123
Installation, maintenance, and repair occupations	4 957	4 751	206	4 286	418	726
Production occupations	15 951	12 530	3 421	12 808	2 149	1 675
Transportation and material moving occupations	8 297	7 028	1 269	6 587	1 270	1 689
2010						
All Occupations	139 064	73 359	65 705	114 168	15 010	19 906
Management, professional, and related occupations	51 743	25 070	26 673	43 268	4 363	3 755
Management, business, and financial operations	20 938	11 945	8 993	18 043	1 537	1 562
Computer and mathematical occupations	3 531	2 620	911	2 663	237	194
Architecture and engineering occupations	2 619	2 282	337	2 205	135	177
Life, physical and social science occupations	1 409	755	655	1 139	88	85
Community and social service occupations	2 337	836	1 500	1 750	451	229
Legal occupations	1 716	878	838	1 510	111	94
Education, training, and library occupations	8 628	2 261	6 367	7 325	810	686
Arts, design, entertainment, sports, and media occupations	2 759	1 484	1 276	2 430	152	244
Healthcare practitioner and technical occupations	7 805	2 009	5 796	6 204	842	484
Healthcare support occupations	3 332	370	2 962	2 252	849	506
Protective service occupations	3 289	2 587	703	2 530	585	437
Food preparation and serving related occupations	7 660	3 439	4 221	6 110	866	1 703
Building and grounds cleaning and maintenance occupations	5 328	3 164	2 164	4 290	722	1 877
Personal care and service occupations	5 024	1 092	3 932	3 756	741	734
Sales and related occupations	33 433	12 419	21 015	27 470	1 503	1 814
Office and administrative support occupations	18 047	4 716	13 331	14 685	2 259	2 413
Farming, fishing, and forestry occupations	987	755	231	889	51	412
Construction and extraction occupations	7 175	6 990	185	6 449	441	2 090
Installation, maintenance, and repair occupations	4 911	4 721	190	4 281	384	769
Production occupations	16 180	12 751	3 429	12 873	2 247	1 755
Transportation and material moving occupations	8 182	6 959	1 224	6 405	1 339	1 640

[1]Beginning in 2003, persons who selected this race group only; persons who selected more than one race group are not included. Prior to 2003, persons who reported more than one race group were included in the group they identified as the main race.
[2]May be of any race.

Table 1-14. Employed Civilians, by Selected Occupation and Industry, 2008–2010

(Thousands of people.)

Year and industry	Total employed	Agriculture, forestry, fishing, and hunting	Mining	Construction	Manufacturing Total	Durable goods	Nondurable goods	Wholesale trade
2008								
All Occupations	145 362	2 168	819	10 974	15 904	10 273	5 631	4 052
Management, professional, and related occupations	52 761	1 041	199	2 018	4 688	3 243	1 445	693
Management, business, and financial operations	22 059	996	117	1 804	2 523	1 639	884	553
Computer and mathematical occupations	3 676	4	8	18	513	425	88	56
Architecture and engineering occupations	2 931	4	45	159	1 107	955	152	24
Life, physical and social science occupations	1 307	24	20	7	242	47	194	12
Community and social service occupations	2 293	X	X	1	3	3	X	1
Legal occupations	1 671	1	4	2	24	13	11	7
Education, training, and library occupations	8 605	4	1	1	27	14	13	3
Arts, design, entertainment, sports, and media occupations	2 820	7	4	24	212	127	85	29
Healthcare practitioner and technical occupations	7 399	2	0	2	37	19	17	9
Healthcare support occupations	3 212	0	X	0	5	3	2	3
Protective service occupations	3 047	25	5	14	32	20	11	7
Food preparation and serving related occupations	7 824	2	1	2	38	11	27	14
Building and grounds cleaning and maintenance occupations	5 445	29	4	46	144	74	70	25
Personal care and service occupations	4 923	36	X	4	12	6	7	2
Sales and related occupations	16 295	11	11	81	625	334	291	1 468
Office and administrative support occupations	19 249	82	57	610	1 507	924	583	697
Farming, fishing, and forestry occupations	988	836	2	3	48	7	41	41
Construction and extraction occupations	8 667	6	285	7 241	322	254	68	38
Installation, maintenance, and repair occupations	5 152	19	74	527	798	538	260	151
Production occupations	8 973	14	63	169	6 434	4 158	2 275	123
Transportation and material moving occupations	8 827	66	120	260	1 250	700	551	788
2009								
All Occupations	139 877	2 103	707	9 702	14 202	8 927	5 275	3 808
Management, professional, and related occupations	52 219	1 008	187	1 987	4 406	3 044	1 362	677
Management, business, and financial operations	21 529	977	108	1 746	2 433	1 604	829	528
Computer and mathematical occupations	3 481	3	11	21	455	368	87	149
Architecture and engineering occupations	2 740	3	38	171	1 017	866	151	33
Life, physical and social science occupations	1 328	20	23	8	216	42	174	11
Community and social service occupations	2 341	0	X	3	1	0	1	1
Legal occupations	1 710	0	4	6	24	16	8	5
Education, training, and library occupations	8 627	1	1	1	23	14	8	8
Arts, design, entertainment, sports, and media occupations	2 724	2	1	28	194	117	77	23
Healthcare practitioner and technical occupations	7 738	2	2	2	42	17	26	8
Healthcare support occupations	3 309	1	X	1	8	4	4	2
Protective service occupations	3 164	17	7	12	31	21	10	4
Food preparation and serving related occupations	7 733	6	2	5	47	11	36	9
Building and grounds cleaning and maintenance occupations	5 349	24	4	46	156	78	79	36
Personal care and service occupations	5 043	46	X	3	9	3	6	1
Sales and related occupations	15 641	15	7	101	643	358	285	1 424
Office and administrative support occupations	18 146	76	58	560	1 337	831	506	616
Farming, fishing, and forestry occupations	926	779	2	5	43	5	38	40
Construction and extraction occupations	7 439	8	236	6 114	299	230	69	30
Installation, maintenance, and repair occupations	4 957	25	64	499	760	495	265	131
Production occupations	15 951	98	142	368	6 463	3 847	2 616	838
Transportation and material moving occupations	8 297	77	93	240	1 108	556	552	701
2010								
All Occupations	139 064	2 206	731	9 077	14 081	8 789	5 293	3 805
Management, professional, and related occupations	51 743	1 022	195	1 825	4 274	2 942	1 332	698
Management, business, and financial operations	20 938	982	121	1 610	2 317	1 515	802	538
Computer and mathematical occupations	3 531	6	6	18	434	349	85	61
Architecture and engineering occupations	2 619	3	44	140	995	850	144	27
Life, physical and social science occupations	1 409	24	21	6	215	41	175	21
Community and social service occupations	2 337	1	0	0	1	0	1	X
Legal occupations	1 716	1	0	6	29	16	13	5
Education, training, and library occupations	8 628	3	2	3	26	21	5	4
Arts, design, entertainment, sports, and media occupations	2 759	1	2	39	214	124	90	25
Healthcare practitioner and technical occupations	7 805	3	1	2	43	25	18	17
Healthcare support occupations	3 332	1	X	0	5	4	1	1
Protective service occupations	3 289	19	3	8	31	23	8	4
Food preparation and serving related occupations	7 660	6	1	6	38	8	29	11
Building and grounds cleaning and maintenance occupations	5 328	21	2	37	124	61	63	29
Personal care and service occupations	5 024	54	0	3	9	4	4	2
Sales and related occupations	15 386	20	7	86	630	320	311	1 368
Office and administrative support occupations	18 047	90	57	462	1 323	833	490	639
Farming, fishing, and forestry occupations	987	813	1	1	59	5	54	53
Construction and extraction occupations	7 175	14	269	5 786	296	232	64	31
Installation, maintenance, and repair occupations	4 911	29	61	510	662	431	231	136
Production occupations	7 998	24	40	131	5 539	3 410	2 130	133
Transportation and material moving occupations	8 182	94	93	222	1 092	516	575	700

X = Not applicable.

Table 1-14. Employed Civilians, by Selected Occupation and Industry, 2008–2010—*Continued*

(Thousands of people.)

Year and industry	Retail trade	Transportation and warehousing	Utilities	Information	Finance and insurance	Real estate and rental and leasing	Professional and technical services
2008							
All Occupations	16 533	6 501	1 225	3 481	7 279	2 949	9 362
Management, professional, and related occupations	1 746	726	380	1 815	3 679	878	7 367
Management, business, and financial operations	913	591	194	711	3 076	806	2 718
Computer and mathematical occupations	128	60	42	297	403	28	1 371
Architecture and engineering occupations	24	44	98	107	13	6	1
Life, physical and social science occupations	12	6	19	12	18	2	317
Community and social service occupations	4	1	X	X	18	5	7
Legal occupations	8	3	6	9	65	14	1 133
Education, training, and library occupations	24	12	5	109	24	3	39
Arts, design, entertainment, sports, and media occupations	209	8	10	565	29	8	641
Healthcare practitioner and technical occupations	425	2	6	4	33	5	156
Healthcare support occupations	46	3	X	2	3	5	51
Protective service occupations	60	40	11	4	30	15	30
Food preparation and serving related occupations	336	14	0	29	5	21	4
Building and grounds cleaning and maintenance occupations	153	53	20	21	22	215	30
Personal care and service occupations	51	183	1	36	6	19	22
Sales and related occupations	9 127	116	18	377	1 278	1 150	257
Office and administrative support occupations	2 481	1 610	217	657	2 198	329	1 321
Farming, fishing, and forestry occupations	13	4	X	0	1	0	0
Construction and extraction occupations	100	63	127	14	6	50	41
Installation, maintenance, and repair occupations	663	362	187	384	24	141	82
Production occupations	481	101	210	77	15	30	156
Transportation and material moving occupations	1 277	3 225	54	65	12	97	31
2009							
All Occupations	15 877	6 012	1 233	3 239	6 826	2 796	9 159
Management, professional, and related occupations	1 677	690	388	1 659	3 473	888	7 197
Management, business, and financial operations	860	562	186	639	2 914	819	2 615
Computer and mathematical occupations	817	128	202	1 020	559	69	4 583
Architecture and engineering occupations	24	49	122	87	8	5	884
Life, physical and social science occupations	13	4	21	17	21	3	335
Community and social service occupations	2	0	0	1	19	5	10
Legal occupations	11	6	6	7	66	18	1 175
Education, training, and library occupations	23	12	5	109	24	3	10
Arts, design, entertainment, sports, and media occupations	181	4	7	540	24	9	629
Healthcare practitioner and technical occupations	444	2	5	2	28	7	189
Healthcare support occupations	30	2	X	1	3	6	41
Protective service occupations	66	31	7	11	36	25	24
Food preparation and serving related occupations	299	5	1	26	4	24	6
Building and grounds cleaning and maintenance occupations	149	54	18	19	22	183	23
Personal care and service occupations	46	171	0	32	6	24	33
Sales and related occupations	8 762	98	24	405	1 188	1 011	234
Office and administrative support occupations	2 417	1 478	200	604	2 037	330	1 291
Farming, fishing, and forestry occupations	13	7	1	X	0	X	1
Construction and extraction occupations	89	73	120	18	9	52	49
Installation, maintenance, and repair occupations	628	320	229	326	22	130	94
Production occupations	1 699	3 084	244	138	27	123	165
Transportation and material moving occupations	1 211	2 997	51	64	7	99	47
2010							
All Occupations	15 934	5 880	1 253	3 149	6 605	2 745	9 115
Management, professional, and related occupations	1 722	643	396	1 647	3 384	894	7 073
Management, business, and financial operations	904	525	195	613	2 853	823	2 534
Computer and mathematical occupations	117	41	37	270	328	11	1 349
Architecture and engineering occupations	21	53	112	88	13	10	814
Life, physical and social science occupations	14	5	25	15	21	7	373
Community and social service occupations	2	X	0	1	11	2	9
Legal occupations	20	5	3	11	80	21	1 147
Education, training, and library occupations	22	7	2	122	22	6	50
Arts, design, entertainment, sports, and media occupations	186	5	12	526	28	12	620
Healthcare practitioner and technical occupations	436	2	8	1	28	3	178
Healthcare support occupations	36	1	0	1	7	4	53
Protective service occupations	66	43	15	5	39	22	29
Food preparation and serving related occupations	362	4	0	32	6	21	7
Building and grounds cleaning and maintenance occupations	177	51	16	18	21	201	30
Personal care and service occupations	42	157	0	44	7	28	24
Sales and related occupations	8 704	94	24	403	1 066	1 011	275
Office and administrative support occupations	2 430	1 418	217	562	2 003	298	1 282
Farming, fishing, and forestry occupations	14	8	0	1	0	0	2
Construction and extraction occupations	78	75	119	15	5	42	70
Installation, maintenance, and repair occupations	605	322	216	304	24	115	96
Production occupations	504	89	205	65	35	20	126
Transportation and material moving occupations	1 195	2 974	44	53	7	88	47

X = Not applicable.

Table 1-14. Employed Civilians, by Selected Occupation and Industry, 2008–2010—*Continued*

(Thousands of people.)

Year and industry	Management, administrative, and waste services	Educational services	Health care and social assistance	Arts, entertainment, and recreation	Accommodation and food services	Other services (except public administration)	Public administration
2008							
All Occupations	6 178	13 169	18 233	2 972	9 795	7 005	6 763
Management, professional, and related occupations	1 114	9 895	9 655	1 017	1 511	1 539	2 799
Management, business, and financial operations	795	1 164	1 540	305	1 439	641	1 174
Computer and mathematical occupations	67	195	163	15	14	33	260
Architecture and engineering occupations	X	X	0	X	X	X	0
Life, physical and social science occupations	24	184	202	12	2	12	181
Community and social service occupations	9	309	897	4	5	645	384
Legal occupations	34	14	25	2	1	18	300
Education, training, and library occupations	15	7 531	608	64	15	51	68
Arts, design, entertainment, sports, and media occupations	35	190	69	600	20	96	63
Healthcare practitioner and technical occupations	93	273	6 130	5	7	30	182
Healthcare support occupations	78	35	2 791	20	12	118	39
Protective service occupations	526	110	60	142	46	21	1 868
Food preparation and serving related occupations	19	452	382	252	6 168	48	37
Building and grounds cleaning and maintenance occupations	2 151	599	485	274	467	581	128
Personal care and service occupations	26	239	1 678	689	101	1 741	75
Sales and related occupations	307	75	64	184	711	401	36
Office and administrative support occupations	988	1 189	2 664	226	415	657	1 343
Farming, fishing, and forestry occupations	5	5	1	3	1	3	22
Construction and extraction occupations	103	63	38	14	18	38	99
Installation, maintenance, and repair occupations	185	137	101	59	52	1 053	154
Production occupations	678	369	314	92	292	805	164
Transportation and material moving occupations	463	314	137	72	189	310	96
2009							
All Occupations	5 849	13 188	18 632	3 018	9 717	6 935	6 875
Management, professional, and related occupations	1 125	10 011	9 980	994	1 464	1 558	2 850
Management, business, and financial operations	796	1 203	1 547	276	1 387	689	1 244
Computer and mathematical occupations	329	8 808	8 433	718	77	869	1 606
Architecture and engineering occupations	32	42	24	11	7	10	175
Life, physical and social science occupations	17	203	191	10	2	11	202
Community and social service occupations	12	339	960	7	2	618	362
Legal occupations	33	11	37	3	0	14	285
Education, training, and library ooouupations	12	339	960	7	2	618	362
Arts, design, entertainment, sports, and media occupations	48	195	56	602	24	93	64
Healthcare practitioner and technical occupations	93	287	6 402	4	6	23	189
Healthcare support occupations	62	37	2 912	18	5	131	48
Protective service occupations	517	124	77	186	42	22	1 925
Food preparation and serving related occupations	21	419	376	278	6 121	52	32
Building and grounds cleaning and maintenance occupations	2 067	603	474	274	500	562	135
Personal care and service occupations	24	234	1 755	721	104	1 756	79
Sales and related occupations	285	65	81	143	721	403	30
Office and administrative support occupations	861	1 124	2 568	234	403	621	1 331
Farming, fishing, and forestry occupations	8	2	1	4	1	1	18
Construction and extraction occupations	91	49	38	19	12	29	106
Installation, maintenance, and repair occupations	195	139	101	71	49	1 023	151
Production occupations	593	381	268	76	297	777	170
Transportation and material moving occupations	415	340	131	61	211	349	94
2010							
All Occupations	6 138	13 155	18 907	2 966	9 564	6 769	6 983
Management, professional, and related occupations	1 086	10 049	10 150	1 007	1 384	1 502	2 790
Management, business, and financial operations	765	1 283	1 522	289	1 305	606	1 153
Computer and mathematical occupations	86	204	192	20	8	45	299
Architecture and engineering occupations	34	36	24	9	2	16	179
Life, physical and social science occupations	22	189	230	13	2	17	188
Community and social service occupations	10	356	980	9	4	608	342
Legal occupations	26	16	30	2	1	20	293
Education, training, and library occupations	13	7 450	656	80	24	50	86
Arts, design, entertainment, sports, and media occupations	36	218	50	577	33	108	68
Healthcare practitioner and technical occupations	93	297	6 467	8	5	31	183
Healthcare support occupations	57	33	2 926	21	11	135	41
Protective service occupations	563	130	73	176	53	18	1 992
Food preparation and serving related occupations	17	402	374	246	6 045	44	39
Building and grounds cleaning and maintenance occupations	2 166	575	493	237	486	530	115
Personal care and service occupations	25	243	1 771	734	89	1 707	85
Sales and related occupations	280	75	69	146	745	351	32
Office and administrative support occupations	939	1 085	2 597	225	392	604	1 424
Farming, fishing, and forestry occupations	7	1	0	2	0	2	20
Construction and extraction occupations	93	61	43	20	13	27	117
Installation, maintenance, and repair occupations	186	149	113	80	49	1 100	152
Production occupations	237	52	158	16	94	445	82
Transportation and material moving occupations	480	300	140	56	201	303	95

X = Not applicable.

Table 1-15. Employed Civilians in Agriculture and Nonagricultural Industries, by Class of Worker and Sex, 1990–2010

(Thousands of people.)

Sex and year	Total employed	Agriculture				Nonagricultural industries						
		Total	Wage and salary workers	Self-employed workers	Unpaid family workers	Total employed	Wage and salary workers				Self-employed workers	Unpaid family workers
							Total	Government	Private household	Other industries except private households		
Both Sexes												
1990	118 793	3 223	1 740	1 378	105	115 570	106 598	17 769	1 027	87 802	8 719	253
1991	117 718	3 269	1 729	1 423	118	114 449	105 373	17 934	1 010	86 429	8 851	226
1992	118 492	3 247	1 750	1 385	112	115 245	106 437	18 136	1 135	87 166	8 575	233
1993	120 259	3 115	1 689	1 320	106	117 144	107 966	18 579	1 126	88 261	8 959	218
1994	123 060	3 409	1 715	1 645	49	119 651	110 517	18 293	966	91 258	9 003	131
1995	124 900	3 440	1 814	1 580	45	121 460	112 448	18 362	963	93 123	8 902	110
1996	126 707	3 443	1 869	1 518	56	123 264	114 171	18 217	928	95 026	8 971	122
1997	129 558	3 399	1 890	1 457	51	126 159	116 983	18 131	915	97 937	9 056	120
1998	131 463	3 378	2 000	1 341	38	128 085	119 019	18 383	962	99 674	8 962	103
1999	133 488	3 281	1 944	1 297	40	130 207	121 323	18 903	933	101 487	8 790	95
2000	136 891	2 464	1 421	1 010	33	134 427	125 114	19 248	718	105 148	9 205	108
2001	136 933	2 299	1 283	988	28	134 635	125 407	19 335	694	105 378	9 121	107
2002	136 485	2 311	1 282	1 003	26	134 174	125 156	19 636	757	104 764	8 923	95
2003	137 736	2 275	1 299	951	25	135 461	126 015	19 634	764	105 616	9 344	101
2004	139 252	2 232	1 242	964	27	137 020	127 463	19 983	779	106 701	9 467	90
2005	141 730	2 197	1 212	955	30	139 532	129 931	20 357	812	108 761	9 509	93
2006	144 427	2 206	1 287	901	18	142 221	132 449	20 337	803	111 309	9 685	87
2007	146 047	2 095	1 220	856	19	143 952	134 283	21 003	813	112 467	9 557	112
2008	145 362	2 168	1 279	860	28	143 194	133 882	21 258	805	111 819	9 219	93
2009	139 877	2 103	1 242	836	25	137 775	128 713	21 178	783	106 752	836	25
2010	139 064	2 206	1 353	821	33	136 858	127 914	21 003	667	106 244	8 860	84
Men												
1990	65 105	2 546	1 355	1 151	39	62 559	56 913	8 245	149	48 519	5 597	48
1991	64 223	2 589	1 359	1 185	45	61 634	55 899	8 300	143	47 456	5 700	35
1992	64 441	2 575	1 371	1 164	40	61 866	56 212	8 348	156	47 708	5 613	41
1993	65 349	2 478	1 323	1 117	39	62 871	56 926	8 435	146	48 345	5 894	50
1994	66 450	2 554	1 330	1 197	27	63 896	58 300	8 327	99	49 874	5 560	37
1995	67 377	2 559	1 395	1 138	26	64 818	59 332	8 267	96	50 969	5 461	25
1996	68 207	2 573	1 418	1 124	31	65 634	60 133	8 110	99	51 924	5 465	36
1997	69 685	2 552	1 439	1 084	29	67 133	61 595	8 015	81	53 499	5 506	31
1998	70 693	2 553	1 526	1 005	23	68 140	62 630	8 178	86	54 366	5 480	29
1999	71 446	2 432	1 450	962	20	69 014	63 624	8 278	74	55 272	5 366	25
2000	73 305	1 861	1 116	725	20	71 444	65 838	8 309	71	57 458	5 573	33
2001	73 196	1 708	990	703	15	71 488	65 930	8 342	63	57 524	5 527	31
2002	72 903	1 724	979	731	14	71 179	65 726	8 437	76	57 212	5 425	29
2003	73 332	1 695	991	694	11	71 636	65 871	8 368	59	57 444	5 736	30
2004	74 525	1 687	970	702	15	72 838	66 951	8 616	60	58 275	5 860	27
2005	75 973	1 654	949	688	17	74 319	68 345	8 760	67	59 518	5 944	30
2006	77 502	1 663	989	664	10	75 838	69 811	8 696	60	61 055	6 004	23
2007	78 254	1 604	973	623	8	76 650	70 697	9 022	76	61 599	5 920	32
2008	77 486	1 650	997	637	16	75 836	70 072	9 089	70	60 912	5 736	29
2009	73 670	1 607	977	613	17	72 062	66 517	9 013	74	57 430	5 527	19
2010	73 359	1 665	1 051	598	17	71 694	66 189	9 059	60	57 070	5 472	33
Women												
1990	53 689	678	385	227	66	53 011	49 685	9 524	879	39 282	3 122	205
1991	53 495	680	369	237	73	52 815	49 474	9 635	867	38 972	3 150	191
1992	54 052	672	379	221	73	53 380	50 225	9 788	979	39 458	2 963	192
1993	54 910	637	367	204	67	54 273	51 040	10 144	980	39 916	3 065	168
1994	56 610	855	384	448	23	55 755	52 217	9 965	867	41 385	3 443	95
1995	57 523	881	419	442	20	56 642	53 115	10 095	867	42 153	3 440	86
1996	58 501	871	452	394	25	57 630	54 037	10 107	830	43 100	3 506	87
1997	59 873	847	451	373	23	59 026	55 388	10 116	834	44 438	3 550	89
1998	60 770	825	474	336	15	59 945	56 389	10 205	876	45 308	3 482	74
1999	62 042	849	494	335	20	61 193	57 699	10 625	859	46 215	3 424	70
2000	63 586	602	305	285	12	62 983	59 277	10 939	647	47 690	3 631	76
2001	63 737	591	293	284	13	63 147	59 477	10 993	630	47 853	3 594	75
2002	63 582	587	303	272	12	62 995	59 431	11 199	680	47 552	3 499	66
2003	64 404	580	309	257	14	63 824	60 144	11 267	705	48 172	3 609	72
2004	64 728	546	271	262	12	64 182	60 512	11 367	719	48 426	3 607	63
2005	65 757	544	263	267	13	65 213	61 586	11 598	745	49 243	3 565	63
2006	66 925	543	298	237	8	66 382	62 638	11 641	742	50 254	3 681	64
2007	67 792	490	247	233	11	67 302	63 586	11 981	737	50 868	3 637	80
2008	67 876	518	282	224	12	67 358	63 810	12 169	735	50 907	3 483	65
2009	66 208	496	265	223	8	65 712	62 197	12 165	709	49 322	3 468	47
2010	65 705	541	302	223	16	65 164	61 725	11 944	607	49 174	3 388	51

Note: See notes and definitions for information on historical comparabilty.

Table 1-16. Number of Employed Persons Age 25 Years and Over, by Educational Attainment, Sex, Race, and Hispanic Origin, 2000–2010

(Thousands of people.)

Race, Hispanic origin, sex, and year	Total	Less than a high school diploma	High school graduate, no college	Some college, no degree	Associate's degree	College graduate or higher	
						Total	Bachelor's degree only
All Races							
2000	116 473	11 692	36 452	21 601	10 707	36 020	23 706
2001	116 846	11 669	36 078	21 459	11 127	36 514	23 907
2002	116 802	11 535	35 779	20 928	11 166	37 395	24 570
2003	118 385	11 537	35 857	21 107	11 313	38 570	25 188
2004	119 622	11 408	35 944	21 284	11 693	39 293	25 484
2005	121 960	11 712	36 398	21 380	12 245	40 225	26 027
2006	124 386	11 892	36 702	21 630	12 514	41 649	26 960
2007	126 172	11 521	36 857	22 076	12 535	43 182	28 055
2008	126 161	11 073	36 097	22 092	12 948	43 951	28 460
2009	122 277	10 371	34 487	21 016	12 872	43 531	27 964
2010	121 987	10 115	34 293	20 838	12 910	43 832	27 977
Men							
2000	62 661	7 199	19 388	11 260	5 013	19 800	12 742
2001	62 824	7 188	19 274	11 076	5 226	20 060	12 872
2002	62 756	7 220	19 154	10 811	5 221	20 350	13 076
2003	63 349	7 290	19 200	10 858	5 231	20 770	13 354
2004	64 326	7 276	19 535	10 896	5 426	21 192	13 575
2005	65 772	7 487	20 127	10 993	5 739	21 427	13 687
2006	67 019	7 614	20 345	11 110	5 835	22 114	14 138
2007	67 963	7 450	20 434	11 382	5 862	22 835	14 680
2008	67 605	7 108	20 093	11 356	6 021	23 027	14 845
2009	64 831	6 569	19 085	10 772	5 864	22 541	14 368
2010	64 765	6 434	19 159	10 737	5 829	22 606	14 359
Women							
2000	53 812	4 493	17 064	10 341	5 694	16 220	10 964
2001	54 021	4 480	16 804	10 383	5 901	16 453	11 035
2002	54 046	4 315	16 624	10 117	5 945	17 045	11 493
2003	55 035	4 248	16 657	10 249	6 081	17 800	11 834
2004	55 296	4 132	16 409	10 387	6 267	18 101	11 908
2005	56 188	4 226	16 271	10 388	6 506	18 798	12 340
2006	57 367	4 278	16 357	10 520	6 678	19 535	12 822
2007	58 209	4 071	16 423	10 695	6 674	20 346	13 375
2008	58 555	3 965	16 004	10 737	6 926	20 924	13 614
2009	57 445	3 802	15 402	10 244	7 008	20 990	13 597
2010	57 222	3 681	15 134	10 101	7 080	21 226	13 618
White[1]							
2000	97 320	9 544	30 438	17 770	9 075	30 493	20 078
2001	97 560	9 550	30 126	17 671	9 393	30 821	20 136
2002	97 476	9 394	29 836	17 209	9 440	31 597	20 670
2003	98 120	9 437	29 645	17 227	9 476	32 335	21 103
2004	98 967	9 335	29 571	17 445	9 817	32 799	21 299
2005	100 613	9 579	29 911	17 515	10 256	33 352	21 550
2006	102 322	9 720	30 188	17 632	10 424	34 357	22 272
2007	103 477	9 446	30 140	17 936	10 419	35 535	23 138
2008	103 373	9 036	29 495	17 873	10 742	36 228	23 511
2009	100 419	8 497	28 372	16 983	10 714	35 854	23 109
2010	100 100	8 290	28 128	16 800	10 707	36 176	23 179
Black[1]							
2000	12 852	1 499	4 571	2 910	1 160	2 713	1 866
2001	12 797	1 492	4 492	2 871	1 216	2 727	1 921
2002	12 719	1 498	4 453	2 843	1 210	2 715	1 955
2003	12 706	1 376	4 465	2 780	1 199	2 887	2 056
2004	12 817	1 326	4 606	2 717	1 195	2 973	2 097
2005	13 177	1 369	4 742	2 720	1 288	3 057	2 106
2006	13 504	1 389	4 697	2 816	1 338	3 263	2 243
2007	13 811	1 293	4 783	2 912	1 389	3 435	2 362
2008	13 786	1 234	4 719	2 972	1 439	3 423	2 354
2009	13 110	1 096	4 375	2 855	1 422	3 363	2 253
2010	13 092	1 103	4 234	2 864	1 482	3 409	2 260
Hispanic[2]							
2000	12 406	4 468	3 658	1 828	756	1 696	1 198
2001	12 817	4 601	3 796	1 916	781	1 723	1 223
2002	13 294	4 744	3 921	1 900	823	1 906	1 370
2003	14 205	5 073	4 169	2 037	889	2 039	1 468
2004	14 661	5 135	4 330	2 137	931	2 127	1 538
2005	15 362	5 367	4 535	2 230	997	2 232	1 595
2006	16 225	5 620	4 801	2 282	1 095	2 428	1 698
2007	16 973	5 677	5 110	2 382	1 160	2 644	1 898
2008	17 115	5 426	5 232	2 484	1 236	2 736	1 930
2009	18 642	6 064	5 658	2 670	1 357	2 894	2 063
2010	16 946	5 183	5 175	2 474	1 252	2 862	2 025

[1]Beginning in 2003, persons who selected this race group only; persons who selected more than one race group are not included. Prior to 2003, persons who reported more than one race group were included in the group they identified as their main race.
[2]May be of any race.

Table 1-16. Number of Employed Persons Age 25 Years and Over, by Educational Attainment, Sex, Race, and Hispanic Origin, 2000–2010—Continued

(Thousands of people.)

Race, Hispanic origin, sex, and year	Total	Less than a high school diploma	High school graduate, no college	Some college, no degree	Associate's degree	College graduate or higher	
						Total	Bachelor's degree only
White Men[1]							
2000	53 243	6 085	16 373	9 435	4 320	17 030	11 029
2001	53 375	6 080	16 292	9 344	4 501	17 158	11 060
2002	53 242	6 072	16 148	9 102	4 497	17 423	11 217
2003	53 458	6 192	16 068	9 042	4 431	17 725	11 461
2004	54 133	6 188	16 297	9 125	4 613	17 910	11 555
2005	55 214	6 368	16 750	9 225	4 851	18 021	11 551
2006	56 145	6 448	17 018	9 244	4 952	18 483	11 881
2007	56 740	6 364	17 039	9 409	4 964	18 964	12 260
2008	56 446	6 066	16 741	9 397	5 070	19 171	12 482
2009	54 248	5 583	15 966	8 937	4 948	18 813	12 112
2010	54 091	5 461	15 952	8 846	4 922	18 910	12 128
White Women[1]							
2000	44 077	3 459	14 065	8 335	4 755	13 463	9 049
2001	44 184	3 469	13 834	8 327	4 891	13 663	9 075
2002	44 234	3 322	13 688	8 107	4 944	14 173	9 453
2003	44 662	3 245	13 576	8 185	5 045	14 610	9 643
2004	44 834	3 146	13 275	8 320	5 203	14 888	9 744
2005	45 399	3 211	13 162	8 290	5 405	15 331	9 999
2006	46 177	3 272	13 171	8 388	5 473	15 874	10 391
2007	46 737	3 082	13 102	8 527	5 455	16 571	10 878
2008	46 928	2 970	12 753	8 477	5 672	17 056	11 029
2009	46 172	2 913	12 406	8 046	5 766	17 040	10 997
2010	46 010	2 829	12 176	7 953	5 785	17 266	11 051
Black Men[1]							
2000	6 011	755	2 253	1 326	466	1 210	828
2001	5 924	762	2 232	1 258	486	1 186	834
2002	5 928	785	2 212	1 264	482	1 185	855
2003	5 860	693	2 190	1 256	492	1 230	890
2004	5 942	676	2 287	1 172	503	1 305	931
2005	6 153	697	2 417	1 171	558	1 310	938
2006	6 276	720	2 338	1 249	535	1 433	1 002
2007	6 429	653	2 340	1 320	570	1 547	1 076
2008	6 357	616	2 358	1 296	579	1 508	1 036
2009	5 939	551	2 199	1 225	544	1 419	958
2010	5 988	561	2 164	1 270	567	1 426	960
Black Women[1]							
2000	6 841	743	2 318	1 583	694	1 503	1 038
2001	6 873	730	2 260	1 612	729	1 541	1 087
2002	6 791	713	2 241	1 579	729	1 530	1 101
2003	6 846	683	2 275	1 524	707	1 657	1 166
2004	6 874	650	2 319	1 545	691	1 668	1 166
2005	7 024	672	2 325	1 549	730	1 748	1 169
2006	7 228	669	2 359	1 567	803	1 830	1 241
2007	7 382	641	2 443	1 592	819	1 888	1 286
2008	7 429	617	2 361	1 676	859	1 915	1 318
2009	7 171	544	2 176	1 631	877	1 943	1 295
2010	7 104	542	2 070	1 594	915	1 983	1 300
Hispanic Men[2]							
2000	7 373	2 937	2 128	995	397	916	634
2001	7 628	3 041	2 174	1 082	386	945	669
2002	7 865	3 141	2 244	1 029	415	1 035	732
2003	8 578	3 424	2 461	1 105	451	1 137	806
2004	8 872	3 508	2 583	1 158	468	1 155	837
2005	9 361	3 639	2 775	1 251	503	1 193	847
2006	9 856	3 823	2 932	1 260	547	1 293	891
2007	10 303	3 947	3 100	1 285	567	1 403	1 000
2008	10 363	3 714	3 231	1 371	607	1 439	1 008
2009	9 969	3 508	3 114	1 321	595	1 431	992
2010	10 120	3 517	3 176	1 341	595	1 491	1 045
Hispanic Women[2]							
2000	5 033	1 531	1 529	833	359	780	564
2001	5 190	1 560	1 622	834	395	778	553
2002	5 429	1 604	1 676	871	408	871	638
2003	5 627	1 649	1 708	932	438	901	661
2004	5 789	1 628	1 746	980	463	972	701
2005	6 000	1 728	1 759	979	495	1 039	748
2006	6 370	1 797	1 868	1 021	548	1 135	807
2007	6 670	1 730	2 010	1 097	593	1 241	898
2008	6 752	1 712	2 001	1 113	629	1 297	922
2009	6 718	1 724	1 955	1 093	647	1 298	941
2010	6 826	1 666	1 999	1 133	656	1 371	979

[1]Beginning in 2003, persons who selected this race group only; persons who selected more than one race group are not included. Prior to 2003, persons who reported more than one race group were included in the group they identified as their main race.
[2]May be of any race.

Table 1-17. Multiple Jobholders and Multiple Jobholding Rates, by Selected Characteristics, May of Selected Years, 1970–2011

(Thousands of people, percent, not seasonally adjusted.)

Year	Total employed	Multiple jobholders				Multiple jobholding rate[1]						
		Total	Men	Women		Total	Men	Women	White	Black[2]	Asian	Hispanic[3]
				Number	Percent of all multiple jobholders							
1970	78 358	4 048	3 412	636	15.7	5.2	7.0	2.2	5.3	4.4	. . .	. . .
1971	78 708	4 035	3 270	765	19.0	5.1	6.7	2.6	5.3	3.8	. . .	. . .
1972	81 224	3 770	3 035	735	19.5	4.6	6.0	2.4	4.8	3.7	. . .	. . .
1973	83 758	4 262	3 393	869	20.4	5.1	6.6	2.7	5.1	4.7	. . .	. . .
1974	85 786	3 889	3 022	867	22.3	4.5	5.8	2.6	4.6	3.8	. . .	. . .
1975	84 146	3 918	2 962	956	24.4	4.7	5.8	2.9	4.8	3.7	. . .	. . .
1976	87 278	3 948	3 037	911	23.1	4.5	5.8	2.6	4.7	2.8	. . .	. . .
1977	90 482	4 558	3 317	1 241	27.2	5.0	6.2	3.4	5.3	2.6	. . .	. . .
1978	93 904	4 493	3 212	1 281	28.5	4.8	5.8	3.3	5.0	3.1	. . .	. . .
1979	96 327	4 724	3 317	1 407	29.8	4.9	5.9	3.5	5.1	3.0	. . .	. . .
1980	96 809	4 759	3 210	1 549	32.5	4.9	5.8	3.8	5.1	3.2	. . .	. . .
1985	106 878	5 730	3 537	2 192	38.3	5.4	5.9	4.7	5.7	3.2	. . .	. . .
1989	117 084	7 225	4 115	3 109	43.0	6.2	6.4	5.9	6.5	4.3	. . .	. . .
1991	116 626	7 183	4 054	3 129	43.6	6.2	6.4	5.9	6.4	4.9	. . .	. . .
1994	122 946	7 316	3 973	3 343	45.7	6.0	6.0	5.9	6.1	4.9	. . .	3.8
1995	124 554	7 952	4 225	3 727	46.9	6.4	6.3	6.5	6.6	5.2	. . .	3.6
1996	126 391	7 846	4 352	3 494	44.5	6.2	6.4	6.0	6.4	5.1	. . .	4.0
1997	129 565	8 197	4 398	3 800	46.4	6.3	6.3	6.4	6.5	5.7	. . .	4.1
1998	131 476	8 126	4 438	3 688	45.4	6.2	6.3	6.1	6.3	5.5	. . .	4.4
1999	133 411	7 895	4 117	3 778	47.9	5.9	5.8	6.1	6.0	5.5	. . .	3.6
2000	136 685	7 751	4 084	3 667	47.3	5.7	5.6	5.8	5.9	4.9	3.4	3.2
2001	137 121	7 540	3 914	3 626	48.1	5.5	5.3	5.7	5.6	5.3	3.7	3.4
2002	130 559	7 247	3 736	3 511	48.4	5.3	5.1	5.5	5.5	4.7	4.0	3.8
2003	137 567	7 338	3 841	3 498	47.7	5.3	5.3	5.4	5.5	4.3	4.2	3.4
2004	138 867	7 258	3 653	3 605	49.7	5.2	4.9	5.6	5.3	5.1	3.7	3.4
2005	141 591	7 348	3 741	3 607	49.1	5.2	4.9	5.5	5.4	4.4	3.5	2.8
2006	144 041	7 641	3 863	3 778	49.4	5.3	5.0	5.7	5.3	5.4	3.7	3.1
2007	145 864	7 693	3 835	3 858	50.1	5.3	4.9	5.7	5.5	4.4	3.7	3.0
2008	145 927	7 653	3 842	3 812	49.8	5.2	4.9	5.6	5.4	4.9	3.8	2.9
2009	140 363	7 265	3 540	3 725	51.3	5.2	4.8	5.6	5.3	4.8	3.9	3.0
2010	139 497	7 261	3 559	3 702	51.0	5.2	4.8	5.6	5.4	4.6	3.1	3.1
2011	140 028	7 084	3 491	3 593	50.7	5.1	4.7	5.5	5.3	4.5	3.1	3.3

Note: Data prior to 1985 reflect 1970 census–based population controls; years 1985–1991 reflect 1980 census–based controls; years 1994–1999 reflect 1990 census–based controls adjusted for the estimated undercount; and data for years 2000–2002 have been revised to incorporate population controls from the 2000 census. Prior to 1994, data on multiple jobholders were collected only through special periodic supplements to the Current Population Survey (CPS) in May of various years; these supplemental surveys were not conducted in 1981–1984, 1986–1988, 1990, or 1992–1993. Beginning in 1994, data reflect the introduction of a major redesign of the CPS, including the collection of monthly data on multiple jobholders.

[1] Multiple jobholders as a percent of all employed persons in specified group.
[2] Data for years prior to 1977 refer to the Black-and-Other population group.
[3] May be of any race.
. . . = Not available.

Table 1-18. Multiple Jobholders, by Sex, Age, Marital Status, Race, Hispanic Origin, and Job Status, 2007–2010

(Thousands of people, percent.)

Characteristic	Both sexes				Men				Women			
	Number		Rate[1]		Number		Rate[1]		Number		Rate[1]	
	2007	2008	2007	2008	2007	2008	2007	2008	2007	2008	2007	2008
Age												
Total, 16 years and over[2]	7 655	7 620	5.2	5.2	3 833	3 837	4.9	5.0	3 822	3 783	5.6	5.6
16 to 19 years	249	225	4.2	4.0	96	94	3.3	3.4	153	131	5.1	4.6
20 to 24 years	738	752	5.3	5.5	309	329	4.2	4.6	429	423	6.5	6.5
25 to 34 years	1 662	1 555	5.3	5.0	876	846	5.0	4.9	786	710	5.6	5.0
35 to 44 years	1 844	1 841	5.4	5.5	948	941	5.1	5.2	896	900	5.7	5.9
45 to 54 years	1 926	1 958	5.6	5.7	959	959	5.3	5.3	967	999	5.9	6.1
55 to 64 years	1 022	1 067	5.1	5.1	522	539	4.9	4.9	501	528	5.2	5.3
65 years and over	214	223	3.8	3.7	123	129	4.0	3.9	91	94	3.6	3.5
Marital Status												
Single	2 101	2 089	5.2	5.2	952	989	4.3	4.5	1 149	1 100	6.3	5.9
Married, spouse present	4 215	4 166	5.1	5.1	2 435	2 386	5.3	5.2	1 780	1 780	5.0	5.0
Widowed, divorced, or separated	1 339	1 365	5.7	5.9	446	462	4.6	4.8	893	903	6.5	6.7
Race and Hispanic Origin												
White[3]	6 467	6 405	5.4	5.4	3 250	1 923	5.0	5.0	3 217	3 151	5.9	5.8
Black[3]	753	756	4.7	4.7	375	240	5.0	5.0	379	385	4.4	4.5
Hispanic[4]	638	671	3.1	3.3	353	235	2.9	3.1	284	294	3.5	3.6
Full- or Part-Time Status												
Primary job full time, secondary job part time	4 174	4 165	. . .	. . .	2 320	2 289	. . .	. . .	1 854	1 876	. . .	. . .
Primary and secondary jobs, both part time	1 764	1 791	. . .	. . .	531	588	. . .	. . .	1 233	1 203	. . .	. . .
Primary and secondary jobs, both full time	288	284	. . .	. . .	193	192	. . .	. . .	95	92	. . .	. . .
Hours vary on primary or secondary job	1 383	1 338	. . .	. . .	765	747	. . .	. . .	618	591	. . .	. . .

Characteristic	Both sexes				Men				Women			
	Number		Rate[1]		Number		Rate[1]		Number		Rate[1]	
	2009	2010	2009	2010	2009	2010	2009	2010	2009	2010	2009	2010
Age												
Total, 16 years and over[2]	7 271	6 878	5.2	4.9	3 530	3 326	4.8	4.5	3 741	3 552	5.6	5.4
16 to 19 years	186	167	3.8	3.8	71	61	3.1	2.9	115	106	4.6	4.7
20 to 24 years	710	695	5.6	5.5	307	289	4.7	4.5	403	406	6.4	6.5
25 to 34 years	1 546	1 519	5.1	5.0	795	768	4.9	4.7	750	751	5.4	5.4
35 to 44 years	1 675	1 554	5.3	5.1	822	798	4.9	4.8	853	756	5.8	5.4
45 to 54 years	1 903	1 724	5.7	5.2	907	809	5.2	4.7	996	916	6.2	5.7
55 to 64 years	1 039	1 021	4.9	4.7	507	490	4.7	4.4	532	531	5.2	5.1
65 years and over	212	197	3.5	3.1	120	112	3.6	3.2	92	86	3.3	3.0
Marital Status												
Single	1 989	2 000	5.2	5.2	890	895	4.3	4.3	1 099	1 105	6.2	6.2
Married, spouse present	3 993	3 644	5.0	4.7	2 212	2 015	5.0	4.7	1 781	1 629	5.1	4.7
Widowed, divorced, or separated	1 289	1 233	5.8	5.2	429	416	4.7	4.5	861	817	6.5	6.2
Race and Hispanic Origin												
White[3]	6 166	5 857	5.4	5.1	3 016	2 861	4.9	4.7	3 150	2 996	5.9	5.7
Black[3]	714	653	4.8	4.3	319	298	4.7	4.3	395	653	4.8	4.3
Hispanic[4]	643	638	3.3	3.2	354	360	3.0	3.1	289	638	3.6	3.4
Full- or Part-Time Status												
Primary job full time, secondary job part time	3 868	3 591	. . .	. . .	2 042	211	. . .	. . .	1 825	352	. . .	. . .
Primary and secondary jobs, both part time	1 821	1 805	. . .	. . .	599	67	. . .	. . .	1 222	152	. . .	. . .
Primary and secondary jobs, both full time	249	263	. . .	. . .	157	33	. . .	. . .	92	47	. . .	. . .
Hours vary on primary or secondary job	1 287	1 182	. . .	. . .	704	48	. . .	. . .	583	83	. . .	. . .

Note: Estimates for the above race groups (White or Black) do not sum to totals because data are not presented for all races. Beginning in January 2003, data reflect the revised population controls used in the household survey.

[1] Multiple jobholders as a percent of all employed persons in specified group.
[2] Includes a small number of persons who work part time at their primary job and full time at their secondary job(s), not shown separately.
[3] Beginning in 2003, persons who selected this race group only; persons who selected more than one race group are not included. Prior to 2003, persons who reported more than one race group were included in the group they identified as their main race.
[4] May be of any race.
. . . = Not available.

Table 1-19. Multiple Jobholders, by Sex and Industry of Principal Secondary Job, Annual Averages, 2008–2010

(Thousands of people.)

Year and industry of secondary job	Both sexes	Men	Women
2008			
All Nonagricultural Industries, Wage and Salary Workers	5 322	2 480	2 842
Mining	6	5	1
Construction	242	202	40
Manufacturing	173	108	65
Durable goods	101	72	29
Nondurable goods	72	36	36
Wholesale and retail trade	1 142	461	681
Wholesale trade	78	46	31
Retail trade	1 065	415	650
Transportation and utilities	188	145	43
Transportation and warehousing	171	133	39
Utilities	17	13	4
Information	135	89	46
Financial activities	354	215	139
Professional and business services	863	521	342
Education and health services	1 527	544	983
Leisure and hospitality	1 146	519	626
Other services	622	287	335
Other services, except private households	535	279	256
Other services, private households	87	8	79
Public administration	190	123	67
2009			
All Nonagricultural Industries, Wage and Salary Workers	5 245	2 325	2 920
Mining	2	2	0
Construction	206	165	40
Manufacturing	159	98	60
Durable goods	96	63	33
Nondurable goods	63	35	28
Wholesale and retail trade	1 060	435	626
Wholesale trade	77	47	30
Retail trade	984	388	596
Transportation and utilities	173	124	50
Transportation and warehousing	151	107	44
Utilities	22	17	5
Information	148	97	51
Financial activities	340	208	132
Professional and business services	784	446	338
Education and health services	1 635	510	1 125
Leisure and hospitality	1 173	549	623
Other services	582	266	316
Other services, except private households	498	259	239
Other services, private households	84	7	77
Public administration	186	119	67
2010			
All Nonagricultural Industries, Wage and Salary Workers	4 885	2 210	2 675
Mining	8	8	0
Construction	188	158	30
Manufacturing	160	95	65
Durable goods	89	60	29
Nondurable goods	71	35	36
Wholesale and retail trade	902	392	511
Wholesale trade	58	37	21
Retail trade	844	354	490
Transportation and utilities	178	129	50
Transportation and warehousing	156	115	41
Utilities	22	14	8
Information	129	80	49
Financial activities	287	163	125
Professional and business services	713	399	314
Education and health services	1 640	542	1 097
Leisure and hospitality	1 040	489	551
Other services	499	208	291
Other services, except private households	449	204	245
Other services, private households	50	4	46
Public administration	196	128	68

Table 1-20. Employment and Unemployment in Families, by Race and Hispanic Origin, Annual Averages, 2000–2010

(Thousands of people, percent.)

Characteristic	2000	2001	2002	2003	2004	2005	2006	2007	2008	2009	2010
ALL RACES											
Total Families	71 680	73 306	74 169	75 301	75 872	76 443	77 017	77 894	77 943	78 361	78 246
With employed member(s)	59 626	60 707	61 121	61 761	62 424	62 933	63 492	64 330	64 058	63 010	62 560
As percent of total families	83.2	82.8	82.4	82.0	82.3	82.3	82.4	82.6	82.2	80.4	80.0
Some usually work full time[1]	55 683	56 519	56 742	57 229	57 813	58 276	58 918	59 616	59 116	57 037	56 471
With no employed member	12 054	12 600	13 048	13 540	13 447	13 509	13 525	13 564	13 884	15 351	15 686
As percent of total families	16.8	17.2	17.6	18.0	17.7	17.7	17.6	17.4	17.8	19.6	20.0
With unemployed member(s)	4 110	4 847	5 809	6 079	5 593	5 318	4 913	4 914	6 104	9 381	9 695
As percent of total families	5.7	6.6	7.8	8.1	7.4	7.0	6.4	6.3	7.8	12.0	12.4
Some member(s) employed	2 973	3 494	4 126	4 285	3 915	3 717	3 419	3 497	4 319	6 438	6 566
As percent of families with unemployed member(s)	72.3	72.1	71.0	70.5	70.0	69.9	69.6	71.2	70.8	68.6	67.7
Some usually work full time[1]	2 675	3 122	3 668	3 790	3 494	3 310	3 049	3 096	3 830	5 460	5 572
As percent of families with unemployed member(s)	65.1	64.4	63.1	62.3	62.5	62.2	62.1	63.0	62.7	58.2	57.5
WHITE[2]											
Total Families	59 918	60 921	61 494	61 995	62 250	62 567	62 977	63 667	63 490	63 774	63 551
With employed member(s)	49 877	50 505	50 785	51 002	51 350	51 645	52 054	52 669	52 273	51 494	51 048
As percent of total families	83.2	83.0	82.6	82.3	82.5	82.5	82.7	82.7	82.3	80.7	80.3
Some usually work full time[1]	46 639	47 060	47 193	47 356	47 620	47 883	48 395	48 879	48 271	46 629	46 150
With no employed member	10 042	10 416	10 709	10 993	10 900	10 922	10 923	10 997	11 217	12 280	12 502
As percent of total families	16.8	17.0	17.4	17.7	17.5	17.5	17.3	17.3	17.7	19.3	19.7
With unemployed member(s)	3 010	3 553	4 275	4 411	4 078	3 801	3 556	3 587	4 506	7 089	7 202
As percent of total families	5.0	5.8	7.0	7.1	6.6	6.1	5.6	5.6	7.1	11.1	11.3
Some member(s) employed	2 276	2 661	3 164	3 245	3 000	2 782	2 582	2 653	3 332	5 072	5 069
As percent of families with unemployed member(s)	75.6	74.9	74.0	73.6	73.6	73.2	72.6	73.9	74.0	71.5	70.4
Some usually work full time[1]	2 052	2 379	2 808	2 873	2 677	2 477	2 306	2 350	2 955	4 294	4 289
As percent of families with unemployed member(s)	68.2	67.0	65.7	65.1	65.7	65.2	64.8	65.5	65.6	60.6	59.6
BLACK[2]											
Total Families	8 600	8 674	8 845	8 869	8 860	8 952	9 058	9 184	9 297	9 318	9 404
With employed member(s)	6 964	6 933	6 987	6 906	6 920	6 986	7 078	7 249	7 290	7 022	7 030
As percent of total families	81.0	80.0	79.0	77.9	78.1	78.0	78.1	78.9	78.4	75.4	74.8
Some usually work full time[1]	6 401	6 373	6 390	6 270	6 292	6 353	6 437	6 608	6 622	6 265	6 222
With no employed member	1 636	1 742	1 858	1 963	1 940	1 966	1 980	1 935	2 006	2 296	2 374
As percent of total families	19.0	20.1	21.0	22.1	21.9	22.0	21.9	21.1	21.6	24.6	25.2
With unemployed member(s)	881	990	1 162	1 213	1 127	1 140	1 036	990	1 188	1 624	1 807
As percent of total families	10.2	11.4	13.1	13.7	12.7	12.7	11.4	10.8	12.8	17.4	19.2
Some member(s) employed	535	596	689	695	625	657	596	591	686	886	1 009
As percent of families with unemployed member(s)	60.8	60.2	59.3	57.3	55.5	57.7	57.6	59.7	57.8	54.5	55.8
Some usually work full time[1]	476	533	611	612	556	583	526	519	605	748	862
As percent of families with unemployed member(s)	54.1	53.8	52.6	50.5	49.3	51.1	50.8	52.4	50.9	46.0	47.7
HISPANIC[3]											
Total Families	7 581	8 140	8 650	9 185	9 305	9 603	9 905	10 332	10 500	10 489	10 561
With employed member(s)	6 633	7 100	7 485	7 907	8 071	8 312	8 641	9 048	9 135	8 852	8 897
As percent of total families	87.5	87.2	86.5	86.1	86.7	86.6	87.2	87.6	87.0	84.4	84.2
Some usually work full time[1]	6 255	6 692	6 989	7 383	7 566	7 786	8 129	8 492	8 466	7 923	7 934
With no employed member	947	1 040	1 165	1 277	1 235	1 291	1 264	1 285	1 365	1 637	1 664
As percent of total families	12.5	12.8	13.5	13.9	13.3	13.4	12.8	12.4	13.0	15.6	15.8
With unemployed member(s)	679	809	965	1 020	950	860	793	876	1 159	1 770	1 841
As percent of total families	9.0	9.9	11.2	11.1	10.2	9.0	8.0	8.5	11.0	16.9	17.4
Some member(s) employed	493	592	686	715	664	606	544	619	846	1 228	1 262
As percent of families with unemployed member(s)	72.7	73.2	71.1	70.1	69.9	70.5	68.6	70.6	73.0	69.3	68.6
Some usually work full time[1]	446	537	615	640	594	544	491	554	743	1 021	1 060
As percent of families with unemployed member(s)	65.8	66.4	63.7	62.7	62.5	63.2	61.9	63.2	64.1	57.7	57.6

Note: The race or ethnicity of the family is determined by the race of the householder. Estimates for the above race groups (White or Black) do not sum to totals because data are not presented for all races. Detail may not sum to total due to rounding. Data for 2003 reflect the revised population controls used in the Current Population Survey (CPS). Estimates for 2000 are not strictly comparable with data for later years due to population controls reflecting Census 2000 results.

[1]Usually work 35 hours or more a week at all jobs.
[2]Beginning in 2003, families where the householder selected this race group only; families where the householder selected more than one race group are excluded. Prior to 2003, families where the householder selected more than one race group were included in the group that the householder identified as the main race.
[3]May be of any race.

Table 1-21. Families, by Presence and Relationship of Employed Members and Family Type, Annual Averages, 2000–2010

(Thousands of people, percent.)

Characteristic	Number of families										
	2000	2001	2002	2003	2004	2005	2006	2007	2008	2009	2010
MARRIED-COUPLE FAMILIES											
Total	54 704	55 749	56 280	57 074	57 188	57 167	57 509	58 145	58 125	58 124	57 524
Member(s) employed, total	45 967	46 680	46 976	47 535	47 767	47 895	48 196	48 676	48 541	47 876	47 238
Husband only	10 500	10 833	11 174	11 403	11 712	11 562	11 399	11 509	11 351	11 371	11 311
Wife only	2 946	3 257	3 613	3 863	3 843	3 715	3 754	3 858	4 036	4 909	4 937
Husband and wife	29 128	29 241	28 873	29 077	28 991	29 330	29 799	30 055	29 854	28 211	27 501
Other employment combinations	3 394	3 350	3 317	3 193	3 222	3 288	3 244	3 254	3 300	3 384	3 489
No member(s) employed	8 737	9 068	9 303	9 539	9 420	9 272	9 313	9 469	9 585	10 248	10 286
FAMILIES MAINTAINED BY WOMEN[1]											
Total	12 775	13 037	13 215	13 450	13 614	14 035	14 208	14 423	14 383	14 610	14 913
Member(s) employed, total	10 026	10 131	10 169	10 187	10 358	10 609	10 796	11 087	10 929	10 642	10 715
Householder only	5 581	5 667	5 944	5 987	6 021	6 052	6 103	6 307	6 250	6 135	6 189
Householder and other member(s)	2 806	2 778	2 559	2 539	2 701	2 830	2 955	2 994	2 870	2 642	2 603
Other member(s), not householder	1 639	1 686	1 666	1 660	1 636	1 727	1 738	1 785	1 809	1 866	1 923
No member(s) employed	2 749	2 906	3 047	3 263	3 255	3 426	3 412	3 336	3 454	3 968	4 198
FAMILIES MAINTAINED BY MEN[1]											
Total	4 200	4 521	4 674	4 777	5 071	5 242	5 300	5 327	5 435	5 627	5 809
Member(s) employed, total	3 632	3 895	3 976	4 039	4 299	4 430	4 500	4 568	4 589	4 492	4 607
Householder only	1 761	1 875	1 939	1 954	2 060	2 093	2 089	2 170	2 178	2 104	2 215
Householder and other member(s)	1 358	1 450	1 440	1 427	1 557	1 639	1 715	1 696	1 659	1 557	1 525
Other member(s), not householder	514	570	598	658	682	698	696	701	752	831	867
No member(s) employed	567	625	698	739	772	812	800	759	845	1 135	1 202

Characteristic	Percent distribution										
	2000	2001	2002	2003	2004	2005	2006	2007	2008	2009	2010
MARRIED-COUPLE FAMILIES											
Total	100.0	100.0	100.0	100.0	100.0	100.0	100.0	100.0	100.0	100.0	100.0
Member(s) employed, total	84.0	83.7	83.5	83.3	83.5	83.8	83.8	83.7	83.5	82.4	82.1
Husband only	19.2	19.4	19.9	20.0	20.5	20.2	19.8	19.8	19.5	19.6	19.7
Wife only	5.4	5.8	6.4	6.8	6.7	6.5	6.5	6.6	6.9	8.4	8.6
Husband and wife	53.2	52.5	51.3	50.9	50.7	51.3	51.8	51.7	51.4	48.5	47.8
Other employment combinations	6.2	6.0	5.9	5.6	5.6	5.8	5.6	5.6	5.7	5.8	6.1
No member(s) employed	16.0	16.3	16.5	16.7	16.5	16.2	16.2	16.3	16.5	17.6	17.9
FAMILIES MAINTAINED BY WOMEN[1]											
Total	100.0	100.0	100.0	100.0	100.0	100.0	100.0	100.0	100.0	100.0	100.0
Member(s) employed, total	78.5	77.7	77.0	75.7	76.1	75.6	76.0	76.9	76.0	72.8	71.9
Householder only	43.7	43.5	45.0	44.5	44.2	43.1	43.0	43.7	43.5	42.0	41.5
Householder and other member(s)	22.0	21.3	19.4	18.9	19.8	20.2	20.8	20.8	20.0	18.1	17.5
Other member(s), not householder	12.8	12.9	12.6	12.3	12.0	12.3	12.2	12.4	12.6	12.8	12.9
No member(s) employed	21.5	22.3	23.1	24.3	23.9	24.4	24.0	23.1	24.0	27.2	28.1
FAMILIES MAINTAINED BY MEN[1]											
Total	100.0	100.0	100.0	100.0	100.0	100.0	100.0	100.0	100.0	100.0	100.0
Member(s) employed, total	86.5	86.2	85.1	84.6	84.8	84.5	84.9	85.7	84.4	79.8	79.3
Householder only	41.9	41.5	41.5	40.9	40.6	39.9	39.4	40.7	40.1	37.4	38.1
Householder and other member(s)	32.3	32.1	30.8	29.9	30.7	31.3	32.4	31.8	30.5	27.7	26.2
Other member(s), not householder	12.2	12.6	12.8	13.8	13.5	13.3	13.1	13.2	13.8	14.8	14.9
No member(s) employed	13.5	13.8	14.9	15.5	15.2	15.5	15.1	14.3	15.6	20.2	20.7

Note: Detail may not sum to total due to rounding. Estimates for 2000 are not strictly comparable with data for later years due to population controls reflecting Census 2000 results.

[1]No spouse present.

Table 1-22. Unemployment in Families, by Presence and Relationship of Employed Members and Family Type, Annual Averages, 2000–2010

(Thousands of people, percent.)

Characteristic	Number										
	2000	2001	2002	2003	2004	2005	2006	2007	2008	2009	2010
MARRIED-COUPLE FAMILIES											
With Unemployed Member(s), Total	2 584	3 081	3 772	3 857	3 521	3 243	2 968	2 978	3 796	6 056	6 147
No member employed	411	531	676	713	615	580	526	512	663	1 218	1 263
Some member(s) employed	2 174	2 550	3 096	3 144	2 906	2 664	2 442	2 467	3 133	4 838	4 884
Husband unemployed	836	1 160	1 523	1 600	1 333	1 190	1 061	1 110	1 439	2 808	2 813
Wife employed	531	736	993	1 023	850	753	679	725	927	1 799	1 783
Wife unemployed	789	918	1 117	1 129	1 041	1 004	898	902	1 114	1 630	1 697
Husband employed	694	809	969	991	913	873	772	783	975	1 397	1 455
Other family member unemployed	959	1 003	1 133	1 129	1 147	1 049	1 010	966	1 243	1 618	1 637
FAMILIES MAINTAINED BY WOMEN[1]											
With Unemployed Member(s), Total	1 194	1 324	1 504	1 612	1 521	1 539	1 429	1 416	1 666	2 309	2 446
No member employed	587	643	787	842	829	797	753	701	849	1 244	1 351
Some member(s) employed	607	681	717	770	692	743	675	714	817	1 065	1 094
Householder unemployed	522	593	737	791	758	746	688	650	796	1 141	1 227
Other member(s) employed	102	129	147	162	146	161	132	144	181	225	254
Other member(s) unemployed	672	731	767	821	764	793	740	766	870	1 168	1 218
FAMILIES MAINTAINED BY MEN[1]											
With Unemployed Member(s), Total	331	442	533	610	551	536	516	520	642	1 016	1 102
No member employed	139	178	220	239	234	225	215	205	274	482	515
Some member(s) employed	192	264	313	371	316	310	301	316	368	535	587
Householder unemployed	173	234	303	340	296	301	284	294	385	626	680
Other member(s) employed	67	96	129	158	117	122	118	137	164	239	259
Other member(s) unemployed	158	208	230	270	255	235	232	226	257	391	422

Characteristic	Percent distribution										
	2000	2001	2002	2003	2004	2005	2006	2007	2008	2009	2010
MARRIED-COUPLE FAMILIES											
With Unemployed Member(s), Total	100.0	100.0	100.0	100.0	100.0	100.0	100.0	100.0	100.0	100.0	100.0
No member employed	15.9	17.2	17.9	18.5	17.5	17.9	17.7	17.2	17.5	20.1	20.6
Some member(s) employed	84.0	82.8	82.1	81.5	82.5	82.1	82.3	82.8	82.5	79.9	79.4
Husband unemployed	32.0	37.7	40.4	41.5	37.9	36.7	35.7	37.3	37.9	46.4	45.8
Wife employed	20.5	23.9	26.3	26.5	24.2	23.2	22.9	24.3	24.4	29.7	29.0
Wife unemployed	31.0	29.8	29.6	29.3	29.6	31.0	30.3	30.3	29.3	26.9	27.6
Husband employed	26.8	26.3	25.7	25.7	25.9	26.9	26.0	26.3	25.7	23.1	23.7
Other family member unemployed	37.0	32.6	30.0	29.3	32.6	32.4	34.0	32.4	32.7	26.7	26.6
FAMILIES MAINTAINED BY WOMEN[1]											
With Unemployed Member(s), Total	100.0	100.0	100.0	100.0	100.0	100.0	100.0	100.0	100.0	100.0	100.0
No member employed	49.1	48.6	52.3	52.3	54.5	51.8	52.7	49.5	50.9	53.9	55.3
Some member(s) employed	50.9	51.4	47.7	47.8	45.5	48.2	47.3	50.5	49.1	46.1	44.7
Householder unemployed	43.7	44.8	49.0	49.1	49.8	48.5	48.2	45.9	47.8	49.4	50.2
Other member(s) employed	8.5	9.7	9.8	10.0	9.6	10.5	9.3	10.2	10.9	9.7	10.4
Other member(s) unemployed	56.3	55.2	51.0	50.9	50.2	51.5	51.8	54.1	52.2	50.6	49.8
FAMILIES MAINTAINED BY MEN[1]											
With Unemployed Member(s), Total	100.0	100.0	100.0	100.0	100.0	100.0	100.0	100.0	100.0	100.0	100.0
No member employed	42.0	40.3	41.3	39.2	42.5	42.1	41.7	39.3	42.7	47.4	46.7
Some member(s) employed	58.0	59.7	58.7	60.8	57.5	57.9	58.3	60.7	57.3	52.6	53.3
Householder unemployed	52.2	52.9	56.8	55.7	53.7	56.1	55.0	56.6	60.0	61.6	61.7
Other member(s) employed	20.4	21.7	24.2	25.9	21.3	22.8	22.8	26.3	25.6	23.5	23.5
Other member(s) unemployed	47.8	47.1	43.2	44.3	46.3	43.9	45.0	43.4	40.0	38.4	38.3

Note: Detail may not sum to total due to rounding. Estimates for 2000 are not strictly comparable with data for later years due to population controls reflecting Census 2000 results.

[1]No spouse present.

Table 1-23. Employment Status of the Population, by Sex, Marital Status, and Presence and Age of Own Children Under 18 Years, Annual Averages, 2001–2010

(Thousands of people, percent.)

Characteristic	2001			2002			2003			2004			2005		
	Both sexes	Men	Women	Both sexes	Men	Women	Both sexes	Men	Women	Both sexes	Men	Women	Both sexes	Men	Women
With Own Children Under 18 Years, Total															
Civilian noninstitutional population	64 100	28 076	36 024	64 399	28 137	36 263	64 932	28 402	36 530	64 758	28 272	36 486	64 482	28 065	36 417
Civilian labor force	52 489	26 551	25 938	52 566	26 529	26 036	52 727	26 739	25 988	52 288	26 607	25 681	52 056	26 399	25 657
Participation rate	81.9	94.6	72.0	81.6	94.3	71.8	81.2	94.1	71.1	80.7	94.1	70.4	80.7	94.1	70.5
Employed	50 455	25 750	24 704	50 022	25 474	24 549	50 103	25 638	24 466	49 957	25 696	24 261	49 882	25 587	24 294
Employment-population ratio	78.7	91.7	68.6	77.7	90.5	67.7	77.2	90.3	67.0	77.1	90.9	66.5	77.4	91.2	66.7
Full-time workers[1]	43 424	24 964	18 460	42 884	24 644	18 240	42 880	24 762	18 118	42 758	24 794	17 964	42 852	24 713	18 139
Part-time workers[2]	7 031	787	6 244	7 138	829	6 308	7 223	876	6 347	7 200	902	6 298	7 029	875	6 155
Unemployed	2 034	801	1 233	2 543	1 056	1 488	2 624	1 101	1 523	2 331	911	1 420	2 174	811	1 363
Unemployment rate	3.9	3.0	4.8	4.8	4.0	5.7	5.0	4.1	5.9	4.5	3.4	5.5	4.2	3.1	5.3
Married, Spouse Present															
Civilian noninstitutional population	51 981	25 796	26 185	51 947	25 781	26 166	52 476	26 049	26 427	52 109	25 852	26 258	51 519	25 578	25 942
Civilian labor force	42 712	24 512	18 201	42 492	24 425	18 067	42 776	24 638	18 138	42 247	24 449	17 798	41 905	24 215	17 690
Participation rate	82.2	95.0	69.5	81.8	94.7	69.0	81.5	94.6	68.6	81.1	94.6	67.8	81.3	94.7	68.2
Employed	41 431	23 849	17 581	40 867	23 533	17 334	41 128	23 712	17 416	40 847	23 703	17 144	40 614	23 556	17 058
Employment-population ratio	79.7	92.5	67.1	78.7	91.3	66.2	78.4	91.0	65.9	78.4	91.7	65.3	78.8	92.1	65.8
Full-time workers[1]	35 772	23 169	12 603	35 180	22 825	12 356	35 315	22 954	12 360	35 141	22 935	12 206	35 086	22 808	12 278
Part-time workers[2]	5 659	680	4 979	5 687	708	4 979	5 813	757	5 056	5 706	768	4 938	5 528	748	4 780
Unemployed	1 282	662	619	1 625	893	733	1 648	926	722	1 400	747	653	1 291	659	632
Unemployment rate	3.0	2.7	3.4	3.8	3.7	4.1	3.9	3.8	4.0	3.3	3.1	3.7	3.1	2.7	3.6
Other Marital Status[3]															
Civilian noninstitutional population	12 119	2 280	9 839	12 452	2 355	10 096	12 455	2 354	10 102	12 649	2 420	10 229	12 963	2 487	10 475
Civilian labor force	9 777	2 039	7 737	10 073	2 103	7 970	9 950	2 100	7 850	10 042	2 158	7 883	10 151	2 184	7 967
Participation rate	80.7	89.4	78.6	80.9	89.3	78.9	79.9	89.2	77.7	79.4	89.2	77.1	78.3	87.8	76.1
Employed	9 024	1 902	7 123	9 155	1 941	7 215	8 975	1 926	7 050	9 110	1 993	7 117	9 268	2 032	7 236
Employment-population ratio	74.5	83.4	72.4	73.5	82.4	71.5	72.1	81.8	69.8	72.0	82.4	69.6	71.5	81.7	69.1
Full-time workers[1]	7 652	1 795	5 857	7 704	1 820	5 885	7 566	1 807	5 759	7 617	1 859	5 757	7 766	1 905	5 861
Part-time workers[2]	1 372	107	1 265	1 451	122	1 329	1 411	118	1 291	1 494	134	1 360	1 502	127	1 375
Unemployed	752	138	614	918	163	755	976	175	800	931	165	766	883	152	731
Unemployment rate	7.7	6.8	7.9	9.1	7.8	9.5	9.8	8.3	10.2	9.3	7.6	9.7	8.7	7.0	9.2
With Own Children 6 to 17 Years, None Younger															
Civilian noninstitutional population	35 523	15 486	20 038	35 829	15 580	20 250	35 943	15 653	20 290	35 874	15 597	20 277	35 937	15 590	20 348
Civilian labor force	30 182	14 489	15 693	30 371	14 541	15 830	30 362	14 572	15 790	30 182	14 516	15 666	30 068	14 496	15 572
Participation rate	85.0	93.6	78.3	84.8	93.3	78.2	84.5	93.1	77.8	84.1	93.1	77.3	83.7	93.0	76.5
Employed	29 174	14 096	15 078	29 122	14 023	15 099	29 040	14 008	15 032	29 013	14 056	14 957	28 953	14 066	14 887
Employment-population ratio	82.1	91.0	75.2	81.3	90.0	74.6	80.8	89.5	74.1	80.9	90.1	73.8	80.6	90.2	73.2
Full-time workers[1]	25 382	13 689	11 693	25 225	13 586	11 638	25 116	13 558	11 557	25 069	13 597	11 473	25 074	13 606	11 468
Part-time workers[2]	3 792	407	3 385	3 898	437	3 461	3 925	450	3 475	3 944	459	3 485	3 880	460	3 419
Unemployed	1 008	393	615	1 249	518	731	1 322	564	758	1 170	460	709	1 115	430	684
Unemployment rate	3.3	2.7	3.9	4.1	3.6	4.6	4.4	3.9	4.8	3.9	3.2	4.5	3.7	3.0	4.4
With Own Children Under 6 Years															
Civilian noninstitutional population	28 577	12 590	15 986	28 570	12 557	16 013	28 988	12 749	16 240	28 884	12 675	16 210	28 545	12 475	16 070
Civilian labor force	22 307	12 062	10 245	22 194	11 988	10 206	22 365	12 167	10 198	22 106	12 091	10 014	21 988	11 903	10 085
Participation rate	78.1	95.8	64.1	77.7	95.5	63.7	77.2	95.4	62.8	76.5	95.4	61.8	77.0	95.4	62.8
Employed	21 280	11 654	9 626	20 900	11 450	9 450	21 063	11 630	9 433	20 944	11 640	9 304	20 928	11 521	9 407
Employment-population ratio	74.5	92.6	60.2	73.2	91.2	59.0	72.7	91.2	58.1	72.5	91.8	57.4	73.3	92.4	58.5
Full-time workers[1]	18 041	11 274	6 767	17 660	11 058	6 602	17 764	11 203	6 561	17 689	11 197	6 491	17 778	11 107	6 671
Part-time workers[2]	3 239	380	2 859	3 240	392	2 848	3 299	426	2 872	3 256	443	2 813	3 150	414	2 736
Unemployed	1 026	408	619	1 294	538	757	1 302	538	765	1 162	451	710	1 060	381	678
Unemployment rate	4.6	3.4	6.0	5.8	4.5	7.4	5.8	4.4	7.5	5.3	3.7	7.1	4.8	3.2	6.7
With No Own Children Under 18 Years															
Civilian noninstitutional population	149 643	73 857	75 786	151715	74 993	76 722	154714	76 510	78 204	156900	77 739	79 160	159751	79 237	80 514
Civilian labor force	90 171	49 249	40 922	90 971	49 644	41 327	92 319	50 036	42 284	93 511	50 771	42 740	95 545	51 914	43 631
Participation rate	60.3	66.7	54.0	60.0	66.2	53.9	59.7	65.4	54.1	59.6	65.3	54.0	59.8	65.5	54.2
Employed	85 421	46 371	39 050	85 187	46 154	39 034	86 233	46 294	39 939	87 748	47 282	40 467	90 171	48 709	41 462
Employment-population ratio	57.1	62.8	51.5	56.1	61.5	50.9	55.7	60.5	51.1	55.9	60.8	51.1	56.4	61.5	51.5
Full-time workers[1]	69 074	39 596	29 478	68 574	39 319	29 254	69 073	39 245	29 827	70 244	40 134	30 110	72 515	41 496	31 019
Part-time workers[2]	16 347	6 776	9 572	16 614	6 834	9 779	17 160	7 049	10 111	17 505	7 148	10 357	17 657	7 213	10 444
Unemployed	4 750	2 878	1 872	5 784	3 491	2 293	6 087	3 741	2 345	5 763	3 489	2 274	5 374	3 205	2 169
Unemployment rate	5.3	5.8	4.6	6.4	7.0	5.5	6.6	7.5	5.5	6.2	6.9	5.3	5.6	6.2	5.0

Note: Own children include sons, daughters, stepchildren, and adopted children. Not included are nieces, nephews, grandchildren, and other related and unrelated children. Detail may not sum to total due to rounding. Estimates for 2000 are not strictly comparable with data for later years due to population controls reflecting Census 2000 results.

[1] Usually work 35 hours or more a week at all jobs.
[2] Usually work less than 35 hours a week at all jobs.
[3] Includes never-married, divorced, separated, and widowed persons.

Table 1-23. Employment Status of the Population, by Sex, Marital Status, and Presence and Age of Own Children Under 18 Years, Annual Averages, 2001–2010—*Continued*

(Thousands of people, percent.)

Characteristic	2006			2007			2008			2009			2010		
	Both sexes	Men	Women	Both sexes	Men	Women	Both sexes	Men	Women	Both sexes	Men	Women	Both sexes	Men	Women
With Own Children Under 18 Years, Total															
Civilian noninstitutional population	65 941	29 449	36 492	66 801	29 684	37 117	65 655	29 142	36 513	64 854	28 778	36 076	64 488	28 463	36 025
Civilian labor force	53 590	27 730	25 861	54 370	28 002	26 368	53 506	27 422	26 085	52 748	26 985	25 763	52 159	26 661	25 499
Participation rate	81.3	94.2	70.9	81.4	94.3	71.0	81.5	94.1	71.4	81.3	93.8	71.4	80.9	93.7	70.8
Employed	51 561	26 948	24 614	52 373	27 216	25 157	51 017	26 380	24 637	48 621	24 989	23 632	47 863	24 653	23 210
Employment-population ratio	78.2	91.5	67.4	78.4	91.7	67.8	77.7	90.5	67.5	75.0	86.8	65.5	74.2	86.6	64.4
Full-time workers[1]	44 634	26 033	18 601	45 336	26 282	19 053	43 967	25 338	18 629	41 003	23 583	17 419	40 282	23 176	17 106
Part-time workers[2]	6 927	914	6 013	7 037	933	6 104	7 050	1 042	6 008	7 618	1 406	6 212	7 581	1 477	6 104
Unemployed	2 029	782	1 247	1 998	786	1 211	2 490	1 041	1 448	4 128	1 996	2 132	4 296	2 008	2 289
Unemployment rate	3.8	2.8	4.8	3.7	2.8	4.6	4.7	3.8	5.6	7.8	7.4	8.3	8.2	7.5	9.0
Married, Spouse Present															
Civilian noninstitutional population	52 930	26 908	26 022	53 432	27 205	26 227	52 433	26 647	25 786	51 634	26 249	25 385	50 868	25 820	25 049
Civilian labor force	43 336	25 494	17 842	43 824	25 784	18 041	43 137	25 205	17 933	42 424	24 763	17 661	41 600	24 332	17 268
Participation rate	81.9	94.7	68.6	82.0	94.8	68.8	82.3	94.6	69.5	82.2	94.3	69.6	81.8	94.2	68.9
Employed	42 134	24 854	17 280	42 625	25 134	17 492	41 611	24 353	17 258	39 732	23 100	16 632	38 870	22 689	16 181
Employment-population ratio	79.6	92.4	66.4	79.8	92.4	66.7	79.4	91.4	66.9	76.9	88.0	65.5	76.4	87.9	64.6
Full-time workers[1]	36 649	24 074	12 575	37 120	24 332	12 788	36 128	23 444	12 685	33 846	21 871	11 975	33 142	21 444	11 698
Part-time workers[2]	5 485	780	4 705	5 505	802	4 704	5 482	909	4 573	5 886	1 229	4 657	5 728	1 245	4 482
Unemployed	1 202	640	562	1 199	650	549	1 527	852	675	2 692	1 663	1 029	2 730	1 643	1 087
Unemployment rate	2.8	2.5	3.1	2.7	2.5	3.0	3.5	3.4	3.8	6.3	6.7	5.8	6.6	6.8	6.3
Other Marital Status[3]															
Civilian noninstitutional population	13 010	2 541	10 470	13 369	2 479	10 890	13 222	2 495	10 727	13 221	2 529	10 691	13 620	2 643	10 977
Civilian labor force	10 255	2 236	8 019	10 546	2 219	8 328	10 369	2 217	8 152	10 325	2 223	8 102	10 559	2 329	8 230
Participation rate	78.8	88.0	76.6	78.9	89.5	76.5	78.4	88.9	76.0	78.1	87.9	75.8	77.5	88.1	75.0
Employed	9 427	2 094	7 333	9 747	2 082	7 665	9 406	2 027	7 379	8 889	1 889	7 000	8 994	1 964	7 029
Employment-population ratio	72.5	82.4	70.0	72.9	84.0	70.4	71.1	81.3	68.8	67.2	74.7	65.5	66.0	74.3	64.0
Full-time workers[1]	7 985	1 960	6 026	8 216	1 950	6 266	7 838	1 894	5 944	7 157	1 712	5 445	7 140	1 732	5 408
Part-time workers[2]	1 442	134	1 308	1 531	132	1 400	1 568	133	1 435	1 732	177	1 555	1 853	232	1 621
Unemployed	827	142	686	799	137	662	963	190	773	1 436	334	1 103	1 566	365	1 201
Unemployment rate	8.1	6.3	8.5	7.6	6.2	8.0	9.3	8.6	9.5	13.9	15.0	13.6	14.8	15.7	14.6
With Own Children 6 to 17 Years, None Younger															
Civilian noninstitutional population	36 530	16 212	20 318	36 983	16 384	20 599	36 581	16 256	20 325	35 885	15 982	19 903	35 402	15 639	19 763
Civilian labor force	30 675	15 091	15 585	31 179	15 269	15 910	30 846	15 128	15 718	30 200	14 821	15 379	29 625	14 515	15 110
Participation rate	84.0	93.1	76.7	84.3	93.2	77.2	84.3	93.1	77.3	84.2	92.7	77.3	83.7	92.8	76.5
Employed	29 643	14 690	14 952	30 176	14 866	15 310	29 590	14 588	15 003	28 059	13 775	14 284	27 421	13 482	13 939
Employment-population ratio	81.1	90.6	73.6	81.6	90.7	74.3	80.9	89.7	73.8	78.2	86.2	71.8	77.5	86.2	70.5
Full-time workers[1]	25 835	14 206	11 629	26 288	14 378	11 910	25 733	14 054	11 679	23 864	13 067	10 798	23 239	12 725	10 514
Part-time workers[2]	3 808	485	3 323	3 888	488	3 400	3 858	534	3 324	4 194	708	3 486	4 182	757	3 425
Unemployed	1 032	400	632	1 003	403	600	1 255	541	715	2 141	1 046	1 095	2 204	1 032	1 172
Unemployment rate	3.4	2.7	4.1	3.2	2.6	3.8	4.1	3.6	4.5	7.1	7.1	7.1	7.4	7.1	7.8
With Own Children Under 6 Years															
Civilian noninstitutional population	29 411	13 237	16 174	29 818	13 299	16 518	29 074	12 886	16 188	28 969	12 796	16 173	29 086	12 824	16 262
Civilian labor force	22 915	12 639	10 276	23 192	12 733	10 458	22 661	12 293	10 367	22 549	12 164	10 384	22 534	12 146	10 388
Participation rate	77.9	95.5	63.5	77.8	95.7	63.3	77.9	95.4	64.0	77.8	95.1	64.2	77.5	94.7	63.9
Employed	21 919	12 257	9 661	22 197	12 350	9 847	21 426	11 792	9 634	20 562	11 214	9 348	20 442	11 171	9 271
Employment-population ratio	74.5	92.6	59.7	74.4	92.9	59.6	73.7	91.5	59.5	71.0	87.6	57.8	70.3	87.1	57.0
Full-time workers[1]	18 800	11 828	6 972	19 048	11 904	7 143	18 234	11 284	6 950	17 138	10 517	6 622	17 043	10 451	6 592
Part-time workers[2]	3 119	430	2 689	3 149	446	2 704	3 193	508	2 684	3 424	697	2 726	3 399	720	2 679
Unemployed	997	382	615	995	383	611	1 234	501	733	1 987	950	1 036	2 092	975	1 117
Unemployment rate	4.3	3.0	6.0	4.3	3.0	5.8	5.4	4.1	7.1	8.8	7.8	10.0	9.3	8.0	10.8
With No Own Children Under 18 Years															
Civilian noninstitutional population	162874	81 156	81 718	165066	82 489	82 577	168133	83 971	84 162	170947	85 358	85 589	173342	86 711	86 631
Civilian labor force	97 837	53 525	44 312	98 754	54 134	44 620	100780	55 098	45 682	101394	55 138	46 256	101729	55 324	46 405
Participation rate	60.1	66.0	54.2	59.8	65.6	54.0	59.9	65.6	54.3	59.3	64.6	54.0	58.7	63.8	53.6
Employed	92 866	50 554	42 312	93 674	51 039	42 635	94 346	51 106	43 239	91 257	48 681	42 576	91 201	48 706	42 495
Employment-population ratio	57.0	62.3	51.8	56.7	61.9	51.6	56.1	60.9	51.4	53.4	57.0	49.7	52.6	56.2	49.1
Full-time workers[1]	75 054	43 274	31 780	75 755	43 752	32 003	76 064	43 515	32 549	71 631	40 368	31 263	71 432	40 325	31 108
Part-time workers[2]	17 812	7 280	10 532	17 919	7 286	10 632	18 282	7 592	10 690	19 626	8 313	11 313	19 769	8 381	11 387
Unemployed	4 971	2 971	2 000	5 080	3 095	1 984	6 435	3 992	2 443	10 137	6 457	3 680	10 528	6 618	3 910
Unemployment rate	5.1	5.6	4.5	5.1	5.7	4.4	6.4	7.2	5.3	10.0	11.7	8.0	10.3	12.0	8.4

Note: Own children include sons, daughters, stepchildren, and adopted children. Not included are nieces, nephews, grandchildren, and other related and unrelated children. Detail may not sum to total due to rounding. Estimates for 2000 are not strictly comparable with data for later years due to population controls reflecting Census 2000 results.

[1]Usually work 35 hours or more a week at all jobs.
[2]Usually work less than 35 hours a week at all jobs.
[3]Includes never-married, divorced, separated, and widowed persons.

Table 1-24. Employment Status of Mothers with Own Children Under 3 Years of Age, by Age of Youngest Child and Marital Status, Annual Averages, 2001–2010

(Thousands of people, percent.)

Year and characteristic	Civilian noninsti-tutional population	Civilian labor force						Unemployed	
		Total	Percent of population	Employed				Number	Percent of labor force
				Total	Percent of population	Full-time workers[1]	Part-time workers[2]		
2001									
Total Mothers with Own Children Under 3 Years	9 352	5 613	60.0	5 227	55.9	3 591	1 636	387	6.9
2 years	2 844	1 868	65.7	1 751	61.6	1 218	533	117	6.3
1 year	3 405	2 050	60.2	1 911	56.1	1 308	603	140	6.8
Under 1 year	3 103	1 695	54.6	1 565	50.4	1 065	500	130	7.7
Married, Spouse Present with Own Children Under 3 Years	7 079	4 058	57.3	3 884	54.9	2 601	1 282	175	4.3
2 years	2 120	1 310	61.8	1 258	59.3	839	419	53	4.0
1 year	2 589	1 479	57.1	1 416	54.7	940	475	63	4.3
Under 1 year	2 370	1 269	53.5	1 210	51.1	822	388	59	4.6
Other Marital Status with Own Children Under 3 Years[3]	2 269	1 555	68.5	1 343	59.2	989	352	212	13.6
2 years	723	558	77.2	493	68.2	379	114	65	11.6
1 year	814	571	70.1	495	60.8	367	127	76	13.3
Under 1 year	732	426	58.2	355	48.5	243	111	71	16.7
2002									
Total Mothers with Own Children Under 3 Years	9 350	5 632	60.2	5 181	55.4	3 513	1 667	451	8.0
2 years	2 949	1 895	64.3	1 758	59.6	1 234	524	137	7.2
1 year	3 310	2 003	60.5	1 852	56.0	1 241	610	151	7.5
Under 1 year	3 091	1 734	56.1	1 571	50.8	1 038	533	163	9.4
Married, Spouse Present with Own Children Under 3 Years	7 073	4 071	57.6	3 869	54.7	2 572	1 297	203	5.0
2 years	2 201	1 333	60.6	1 274	57.9	870	404	59	4.4
1 year	2 509	1 446	57.6	1 379	55.0	902	477	67	4.6
Under 1 year	2 363	1 292	54.7	1 216	51.5	800	416	77	6.0
Other Marital Status with Own Children Under 3 Years[3]	2 278	1 562	68.6	1 313	57.6	941	372	248	15.9
2 years	748	562	75.1	484	64.7	364	120	77	13.7
1 year	802	557	69.5	473	59.0	340	134	84	15.1
Under 1 year	728	443	60.9	356	48.9	237	118	87	19.6
2003									
Total Mothers with Own Children Under 3 Years	9 450	5 563	58.9	5 115	54.1	3 430	1 685	446	8.0
2 years	2 987	1 896	63.5	1 752	58.7	1 205	547	143	7.5
1 year	3 353	1 997	59.6	1 842	54.9	1 223	619	154	7.7
Under 1 year	3 110	1 670	53.7	1 521	48.9	1 002	519	149	8.9
Married, Spouse Present with Own Children Under 3 Years	7 165	4 068	56.8	3 872	54.0	2 529	1 342	197	4.8
2 years	2 243	1 350	60.2	1 281	57.1	853	428	69	5.1
1 year	2 541	1 458	57.4	1 395	54.9	906	488	64	4.4
Under 1 year	2 381	1 260	52.9	1 196	50.2	770	426	64	5.1
Other Marital Status with Own Children Under 3 Years[3]	2 287	1 495	65.4	1 244	54.4	902	341	250	16.7
2 years	744	546	73.4	471	63.3	352	118	75	13.7
1 year	813	539	66.3	448	55.1	317	131	91	16.9
Under 1 year	730	410	56.2	325	44.5	233	92	84	20.5
2004									
Total Mothers with Own Children Under 3 Years	9 345	5 377	57.5	4 964	53.1	3 360	1 604	414	7.7
2 years	2 813	1 746	62.1	1 630	57.9	1 152	477	116	6.6
1 year	3 273	1 906	58.2	1 759	53.7	1 172	587	147	7.7
Under 1 year	3 259	1 725	52.9	1 575	48.3	1 035	540	151	8.7
Married, Spouse Present with Own Children Under 3 Years	7 071	3 910	55.3	3 740	52.9	2 513	1 227	170	4.4
2 years	2 111	1 246	59.0	1 200	56.8	839	361	46	3.7
1 year	2 519	1 401	55.6	1 337	53.1	877	459	65	4.6
Under 1 year	2 441	1 262	51.7	1 203	49.3	797	406	59	4.7
Other Marital Status with Own Children Under 3 Years[3]	2 274	1 467	64.5	1 224	53.8	847	377	243	16.6
2 years	702	499	71.1	430	61.2	314	116	70	13.9
1 year	754	505	66.9	422	56.0	295	127	82	16.3
Under 1 year	818	463	56.6	372	45.4	238	134	91	19.7
2005									
Total Mothers with Own Children Under 3 Years	9 365	5 470	58.4	5 077	54.2	3 501	1 576	393	7.2
2 years	2 845	1 773	62.3	1 654	58.1	1 162	492	119	6.7
1 year	3 287	1 958	59.6	1 823	55.5	1 247	576	135	6.9
Under 1 year	3 233	1 740	53.8	1 600	49.5	1 092	508	140	8.0
Married, Spouse Present with Own Children Under 3 Years	6 951	3 939	56.7	3 776	54.3	2 588	1 188	164	4.2
2 years	2 118	1 268	59.9	1 214	57.3	840	374	55	4.3
1 year	2 435	1 389	57.0	1 337	54.9	901	436	52	3.7
Under 1 year	2 398	1 282	53.5	1 225	51.1	847	378	58	4.5
Other Marital Status with Own Children Under 3 Years[3]	2 414	1 531	63.4	1 301	53.9	913	388	230	15.0
2 years	726	504	69.5	440	60.6	322	118	64	12.7
1 year	852	569	66.8	486	57.0	346	139	83	14.6
Under 1 year	836	457	54.7	375	44.9	245	130	82	18.0

Note: Own children include sons, daughters, stepchildren, and adopted children. Not included are nieces, nephews, grandchildren, and other related and unrelated children. Detail may not sum to total due to rounding. Updated population controls are introduced annually with the release of January data.

[1]Usually work 35 hours or more a week at all jobs.
[2]Usually work less than 35 hours a week at all jobs.
[3]Includes never-married, divorced, separated, and widowed persons.

Table 1-24. Employment Status of Mothers with Own Children Under 3 Years of Age, by Age of Youngest Child and Marital Status, Annual Averages, 2001–2010—*Continued*

(Thousands of people, percent.)

Year and characteristic	Civilian noninstitutional population	Civilian labor force						Unemployed	
		Total	Percent of population	Employed				Number	Percent of labor force
				Total	Percent of population	Full-time workers[1]	Part-time workers[2]		
2006									
Total Mothers with Own Children Under 3 Years	9 431	5 675	60.2	5 315	56.4	3 751	1 564	360	6.3
2 years	2 864	1 847	64.5	1 746	61.0	1 280	466	101	5.5
1 year	3 318	2 006	60.5	1 883	56.7	1 305	577	123	6.1
Under 1 year	3 248	1 822	56.1	1 686	51.9	1 166	520	136	7.4
Married, Spouse Present with Own Children Under 3 Years	6 998	4 076	58.2	3 933	56.2	2 756	1 177	143	3.5
2 years	2 114	1 305	61.7	1 265	59.8	910	354	40	3.1
1 year	2 494	1 456	58.4	1 404	56.3	962	442	52	3.6
Under 1 year	2 390	1 315	55.0	1 264	52.9	883	381	51	3.9
Other Marital Status with Own Children Under 3 Years[3]	2 433	1 600	65.7	1 382	56.8	996	386	217	13.6
2 years	750	543	72.3	481	64.2	369	112	61	11.3
1 year	824	550	66.7	479	58.1	344	135	71	13.0
Under 1 year	859	507	59.0	422	49.2	283	139	85	16.7
2007									
Total Mothers with Own Children Under 3 Years	9 659	5 721	59.2	5 354	55.4	3 783	1 571	367	6.4
2 years	2 812	1 808	64.3	1 694	60.2	1 225	469	114	6.3
1 year	3 501	2 068	59.1	1 938	55.4	1 350	589	130	6.3
Under 1 year	3 346	1 845	55.1	1 721	51.4	1 208	513	123	6.7
Married, Spouse Present with Own Children Under 3 Years	7 018	4 027	57.4	3 888	55.4	2 730	1 157	140	3.5
2 years	2 076	1 281	61.7	1 230	59.2	881	349	51	4.0
1 year	2 536	1 433	56.5	1 388	54.7	954	434	46	3.2
Under 1 year	2 406	1 313	54.6	1 270	52.8	896	374	43	3.3
Other Marital Status with Own Children Under 3 Years[3]	2 641	1 694	64.1	1 466	55.5	1 052	414	227	13.4
2 years	736	528	71.6	464	63.1	344	120	63	12.0
1 year	965	635	65.8	551	57.1	396	155	84	13.2
Under 1 year	940	531	56.5	451	48.0	312	139	80	15.1
2008									
Total Mothers with Own Children Under 3 Years	9 595	5 792	60.4	5 354	55.8	3 782	1 573	438	7.6
2 years	2 934	1 852	63.1	1 734	59.1	1 264	470	118	6.4
1 year	3 342	2 069	61.9	1 905	57.0	1 337	568	164	7.9
Under 1 year	3 319	1 871	56.4	1 715	51.7	1 180	535	156	8.4
Married, Spouse Present with Own Children Under 3 Years	6 868	4 035	58.7	3 848	56.0	2 717	1 132	186	4.6
2 years	2 088	1 255	60.1	1 206	57.8	871	335	49	3.9
1 year	2 414	1 450	60.1	1 380	57.2	970	410	70	4.8
Under 1 year	2 366	1 330	56.2	1 263	53.4	875	388	67	5.0
Other Marital Status with Own Children Under 3 Years[3]	2 727	1 758	64.4	1 506	55.2	1 065	441	252	14.3
2 years	847	597	70.5	528	62.4	393	135	69	11.5
1 year	928	619	66.7	525	56.6	367	159	94	15.1
Under 1 year	953	542	56.8	452	47.5	305	147	89	16.5
2009									
Total Mothers with Own Children Under 3 Years	9 476	5 787	61.1	5 191	54.8	3 626	1 565	595	10.3
2 years	2 848	1 855	65.1	1 693	59.4	1 195	498	162	8.7
1 year	3 398	2 104	61.9	1 880	55.3	1 314	566	224	10.6
Under 1 year	3 231	1 828	56.6	1 619	50.1	1 117	502	209	11.4
Married, Spouse Present with Own Children Under 3 Years	6 784	4 047	59.7	3 780	55.7	2 657	1 123	267	6.6
2 years	2 053	1 288	62.7	1 208	58.8	858	350	80	6.2
1 year	2 425	1 465	60.4	1 369	56.4	963	406	96	6.6
Under 1 year	2 306	1 293	56.1	1 204	52.2	836	368	90	7.0
Other Marital Status with Own Children Under 3 Years[3]	2 693	1 740	64.6	1 411	52.4	969	442	328	18.9
2 years	795	567	71.3	485	61.0	337	148	82	14.4
1 year	973	639	65.6	511	52.5	351	160	127	20.0
Under 1 year	925	534	57.8	415	44.9	281	134	119	22.3
2010									
Total Mothers with Own Children Under 3 Years	9 503	5 770	60.7	5 114	53.8	3 570	1 543	656	11.4
2 years	2 968	1 908	64.3	1 708	57.6	1 200	509	199	10.5
1 year	3 351	2 062	61.5	1 815	54.2	1 243	572	246	12.0
Under 1 year	3 184	1 800	56.5	1 590	49.9	1 128	462	210	11.7
Married, Spouse Present with Own Children Under 3 Years	6 642	3 941	59.3	3 670	55.3	2 596	1 074	271	6.9
2 years	2 055	1 275	62.1	1 195	58.2	841	354	80	6.3
1 year	2 344	1 403	59.8	1 301	55.5	896	405	101	7.2
Under 1 year	2 243	1 263	56.3	1 174	52.3	859	315	89	7.1
Other Marital Status with Own Children Under 3 Years[3]	2 862	1 828	63.9	1 444	50.4	974	470	385	21.0
2 years	914	633	69.2	514	56.2	359	155	119	18.8
1 year	1 007	659	65.5	514	51.1	346	168	145	22.0
Under 1 year	941	537	57.0	416	44.2	269	147	121	22.5

Note: Own children include sons, daughters, stepchildren, and adopted children. Not included are nieces, nephews, grandchildren, and other related and unrelated children. Detail may not sum to total due to rounding. Updated population controls are introduced annually with the release of January data.

[1]Usually work 35 hours or more a week at all jobs.
[2]Usually work less than 35 hours a week at all jobs.
[3]Includes never-married, divorced, separated, and widowed persons.

UNEMPLOYMENT

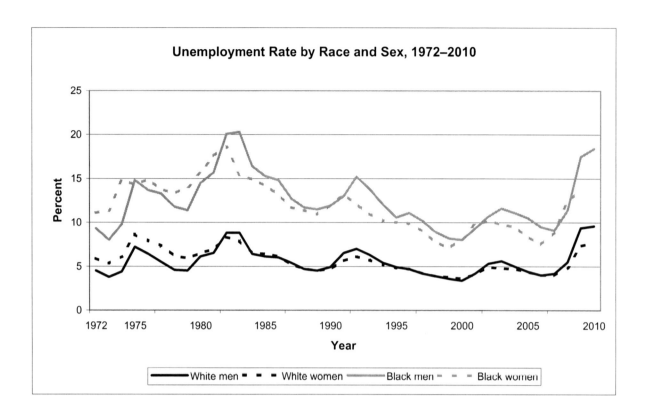

Unemployment Rate by Race and Sex, 1972–2010

Legend: White men — White women — Black men — Black women

The unemployment rate rose to 9.6 percent in 2010—the highest it has been since 1983. The unemployment rate was substantially higher for men (10.5 percent) than for women (8.6 percent). All racial and ethnic groups experienced an increase in unemployment in 2010. Black men had the highest unemployment rate at 18.4 percent followed by Black women with an unemployment rate of 13.8 percent. From 2009 to 2010, the unemployment rate increased by 1.2 percent for Blacks and 0.2 percent for Whites. (See Table 1-27.)

OTHER HIGHLIGHTS

- Although unemployment rates increased for every age group, the disparity in unemployment rates among age groups continued to be substantial as younger workers experienced much higher levels of unemployment. In 2010, the unemployment rate for those age 16 to 19 years was 25.9 percent, while it was only 7.1 percent for those age 55 to 64 years. (See Table 1-27.)

- Among the major industries, construction had the highest unemployment rate at 20.6 percent, followed by agriculture and private wage salary workers (13.9 percent) and leisure and hospitality workers (12.2 percent). Government had the lowest unemployment rate at 4.4 percent. (See Table 1-29.)

- The median duration of unemployment in 2010 was 21.4 weeks, significantly longer than the median duration of 15.1 weeks in 2009 and 9.4 weeks in 2008. (See Table 1-30.)

- In 2010, unemployment rates ranged from a low of 3.9 percent in North Dakota to a high of 14.9 percent in Nevada. (See Table 1-5.)

Table 1-25. Unemployment Rate, by Selected Characteristics, 1948–2010

(Unemployment as a percent of civilian labor force.)

Year	All civilian workers	Both sexes, 16 to 19 years	Men, 20 years and over	Women, 20 years and over	White[1]	Black[1]	Asian[1]	Hispanic[2]	Marital status and sex					
									Men			Women		
									Single, never married	Married, spouse present	Widowed, divorced, or separated	Single, never married	Married, spouse present	Widowed, divorced, or separated
1948	3.8	9.2	3.2	3.6	. . .	. . .	. . .	. . .	. . .	. . .	. . .	. . .	. . .	. . .
1949	5.9	13.4	5.4	5.3	. . .	. . .	. . .	. . .	. . .	. . .	. . .	. . .	. . .	. . .
1950	5.3	12.2	4.7	5.1	. . .	. . .	. . .	. . .	. . .	. . .	. . .	. . .	. . .	. . .
1951	3.3	8.2	2.5	4.0	. . .	. . .	. . .	. . .	. . .	. . .	. . .	. . .	. . .	. . .
1952	3.0	8.5	2.4	3.2	. . .	. . .	. . .	. . .	. . .	. . .	. . .	. . .	. . .	. . .
1953	2.9	7.6	2.5	2.9	. . .	. . .	. . .	. . .	. . .	. . .	. . .	. . .	. . .	. . .
1954	5.5	12.6	4.9	5.5	5.0	. . .	. . .	. . .	. . .	. . .	. . .	. . .	. . .	. . .
1955	4.4	11.0	3.8	4.4	3.9	. . .	. . .	. . .	8.6	2.6	7.1	5.0	3.7	5.0
1956	4.1	11.1	3.4	4.2	3.6	. . .	. . .	. . .	7.7	2.3	6.2	5.3	3.6	5.0
1957	4.3	11.6	3.6	4.1	3.8	. . .	. . .	. . .	9.2	2.8	6.8	5.6	4.3	4.7
1958	6.8	15.9	6.2	6.1	6.1	. . .	. . .	. . .	13.3	5.1	11.2	7.4	6.5	6.7
1959	5.5	14.6	4.7	5.2	4.8	. . .	. . .	. . .	11.6	3.6	8.6	7.1	5.2	6.2
1960	5.5	14.7	4.7	5.1	5.0	. . .	. . .	. . .	11.7	3.7	8.4	7.5	5.2	5.9
1961	6.7	16.8	5.7	6.3	6.0	. . .	. . .	. . .	13.1	4.6	10.3	8.7	6.4	7.4
1962	5.5	14.7	4.6	5.4	4.9	. . .	. . .	. . .	11.2	3.6	9.9	7.9	5.4	6.4
1963	5.7	17.2	4.5	5.4	5.0	. . .	. . .	. . .	12.4	3.4	9.6	8.9	5.4	6.7
1964	5.2	16.2	3.9	5.2	4.6	. . .	. . .	. . .	11.5	2.8	8.9	8.7	5.1	6.4
1965	4.5	14.8	3.2	4.5	4.1	. . .	. . .	. . .	10.1	2.4	7.2	8.2	4.5	5.4
1966	3.8	12.8	2.5	3.8	3.4	. . .	. . .	. . .	8.6	1.9	5.5	7.9	3.7	4.7
1967	3.8	12.9	2.3	4.2	3.4	. . .	. . .	. . .	8.3	1.8	4.9	7.5	4.5	4.6
1968	3.6	12.7	2.2	3.8	3.2	. . .	. . .	. . .	8.0	1.6	4.2	7.6	3.9	4.2
1969	3.5	12.2	2.1	3.7	3.1	. . .	. . .	. . .	8.0	1.5	4.0	7.3	3.9	4.0
1970	4.9	15.3	3.5	4.8	4.5	. . .	. . .	. . .	11.2	2.6	6.4	9.0	4.9	5.2
1971	5.9	16.9	4.4	5.7	5.4	. . .	. . .	. . .	13.2	3.2	7.4	10.5	5.7	6.3
1972	5.6	16.2	4.0	5.4	5.1	10.4	. . .	. . .	12.4	2.8	7.0	10.1	5.4	6.1
1973	4.9	14.5	3.3	4.9	4.3	9.4	. . .	7.5	10.4	2.3	5.4	9.4	4.7	5.8
1974	5.6	16.0	3.8	5.5	5.0	10.5	. . .	8.1	11.8	2.7	6.2	10.5	5.3	6.3
1975	8.5	19.9	6.8	8.0	7.8	14.8	. . .	12.2	16.1	5.1	11.0	13.0	7.9	8.9
1976	7.7	19.0	5.9	7.4	7.0	14.0	. . .	11.5	14.9	4.2	9.8	12.1	7.1	8.7
1977	7.1	17.8	5.2	7.0	6.2	14.0	. . .	10.1	13.5	3.6	8.2	12.1	6.5	7.9
1978	6.1	16.4	4.3	6.0	5.2	12.8	. . .	9.1	11.7	2.8	6.6	10.9	5.5	6.9
1979	5.8	16.1	4.2	5.7	5.1	12.3	. . .	8.3	11.1	2.8	6.5	10.4	5.1	6.7
1980	7.1	17.8	5.9	6.4	6.3	14.3	. . .	10.1	13.6	4.2	8.6	10.9	5.8	7.2
1981	7.6	19.6	6.3	6.8	6.7	15.6	. . .	10.4	14.6	4.3	9.1	11.9	6.0	8.1
1982	9.7	23.2	8.8	8.3	8.6	18.9	. . .	13.8	17.7	6.5	12.4	13.6	7.4	9.5
1983	9.6	22.4	8.9	8.1	8.4	19.5	. . .	13.7	17.3	6.5	13.0	13.1	7.0	9.9
1984	7.5	18.9	6.6	6.8	6.5	15.9	. . .	10.7	13.5	4.6	9.4	11.1	5.7	8.4
1985	7.2	18.6	6.2	6.6	6.2	15.1	. . .	10.5	12.7	4.3	9.2	10.7	5.6	8.3
1986	7.0	18.3	6.1	6.2	6.0	14.5	. . .	10.6	12.2	4.4	8.8	10.7	5.2	7.7
1987	6.2	16.9	5.4	5.4	5.3	13.0	. . .	8.8	11.1	3.9	7.6	9.5	4.3	7.0
1988	5.5	15.3	4.8	4.9	4.7	11.7	. . .	8.2	9.9	3.3	7.0	8.6	3.9	6.3
1989	5.3	15.0	4.5	4.7	4.5	11.4	. . .	8.0	9.6	3.0	6.3	8.4	3.7	5.9
1990	5.6	15.5	5.0	4.9	4.8	11.4	. . .	8.2	10.1	3.4	6.9	8.7	3.8	6.0
1991	6.8	18.7	6.4	5.7	6.1	12.5	. . .	10.0	12.4	4.4	9.0	10.1	4.5	6.9
1992	7.5	20.1	7.1	6.3	6.6	14.2	. . .	11.6	13.2	5.1	9.8	10.8	5.0	7.6
1993	6.9	19.0	6.4	5.9	6.1	13.0	. . .	10.8	12.4	4.4	9.0	10.3	4.6	7.3
1994	6.1	17.6	5.4	5.4	5.3	11.5	. . .	9.9	11.0	3.7	7.4	9.7	4.1	6.6
1995	5.6	17.3	4.8	4.9	4.9	10.4	. . .	9.3	10.1	3.3	6.9	9.1	3.9	5.9
1996	5.4	16.7	4.6	4.8	4.7	10.5	. . .	8.9	10.0	3.0	6.5	9.1	3.6	5.7
1997	4.9	16.0	4.2	4.4	4.2	10.0	. . .	7.7	9.2	2.7	5.8	8.8	3.1	5.2
1998	4.5	14.6	3.7	4.1	3.9	8.9	. . .	7.2	8.5	2.4	4.8	7.8	2.9	4.9
1999	4.2	13.9	3.5	3.8	3.7	8.0	. . .	6.4	7.8	2.2	4.6	7.4	2.7	4.5
2000	4.0	13.1	3.3	3.6	3.5	7.6	3.6	5.7	7.6	2.0	4.3	6.8	2.7	4.2
2001	4.7	14.7	4.2	4.1	4.2	8.6	4.5	6.6	8.9	2.7	5.1	7.7	3.1	4.7
2002	5.8	16.5	5.3	5.1	5.1	10.2	5.9	7.5	10.3	3.6	6.8	8.9	3.7	6.1
2003	6.0	17.5	5.6	5.1	5.2	10.8	6.0	7.7	11.0	3.8	7.3	9.1	3.7	6.1
2004	5.5	17.0	5.0	4.9	4.8	10.4	4.4	7.0	10.5	3.1	6.3	8.7	3.5	5.9
2005	5.1	16.6	4.4	4.6	4.4	10.0	4.0	6.0	9.5	2.8	5.6	8.3	3.3	5.4
2006	4.6	15.4	4.0	4.1	4.0	8.9	3.0	5.2	8.6	2.4	5.2	7.7	2.9	4.9
2007	4.6	15.7	4.1	4.0	4.1	8.3	3.2	5.6	8.8	2.5	5.3	7.2	2.8	5.0
2008	5.8	18.7	5.4	4.9	5.2	10.1	4.0	7.6	11.0	3.4	7.1	8.5	3.6	5.9
2009	9.3	24.3	9.6	7.5	8.5	14.8	7.3	12.1	16.3	6.6	12.8	12.0	5.5	9.2
2010	9.6	25.9	9.8	8.0	8.7	16.0	7.5	12.5	16.5	6.8	12.8	12.8	5.9	9.6

Note: See notes and definitions for information on historical comparability.

[1]Beginning in 2003, persons who selected this race group only; persons who selected more than one race group are not included. Prior to 2003, persons who reported more than one race group were included in the group they identified as their main race.
[2]May be of any race.
. . . = Not available.

Table 1-26. Unemployed Persons, by Age, Sex, Race, and Hispanic Origin, 1948–2010

(Thousands of people.)

Race, Hispanic origin, sex, and year	16 years and over	16 to 19 years			20 years and over						
		Total	16 to 17 years	18 to 19 years	Total	20 to 24 years	25 to 34 years	35 to 44 years	45 to 54 years	55 to 64 years	65 years and over
ALL RACES											
Both Sexes											
1948	2 276	409	180	228	1 869	455	457	347	290	226	93
1949	3 637	576	238	337	3 060	680	776	603	471	384	146
1950	3 288	513	226	287	2 776	561	702	530	478	368	137
1951	2 055	336	168	168	1 718	273	435	354	318	238	103
1952	1 883	345	180	165	1 539	268	389	325	274	195	86
1953	1 834	307	150	157	1 529	256	379	325	280	218	70
1954	3 532	501	221	247	3 032	504	793	680	548	374	132
1955	2 852	450	211	239	2 403	396	577	521	436	355	120
1956	2 750	478	231	247	2 274	395	554	476	429	311	109
1957	2 859	497	230	266	2 362	430	573	499	448	300	111
1958	4 602	678	299	379	3 923	701	993	871	731	472	154
1959	3 740	654	301	354	3 085	543	726	673	603	405	135
1960	3 852	712	325	387	3 140	583	752	671	614	396	122
1961	4 714	828	363	465	3 886	723	890	850	751	516	159
1962	3 911	721	312	409	3 191	636	712	688	605	411	141
1963	4 070	884	420	462	3 187	658	732	674	589	410	126
1964	3 786	872	436	437	2 913	660	607	605	543	378	117
1965	3 366	874	411	463	2 491	557	529	546	436	322	103
1966	2 875	837	395	441	2 041	446	441	426	369	265	92
1967	2 975	839	400	438	2 140	511	480	422	383	256	86
1968	2 817	838	414	426	1 978	543	443	371	314	219	88
1969	2 832	853	436	416	1 978	560	453	358	320	216	72
1970	4 093	1 106	537	569	2 987	866	718	515	476	309	104
1971	5 016	1 262	596	665	3 755	1 130	933	630	573	381	109
1972	4 882	1 308	633	676	3 573	1 132	878	576	510	368	111
1973	4 365	1 235	634	600	3 130	1 008	866	451	430	290	88
1974	5 156	1 422	699	722	3 733	1 212	1 044	559	498	321	99
1975	7 929	1 767	799	968	6 161	1 865	1 776	951	893	520	155
1976	7 406	1 719	796	924	5 687	1 714	1 710	849	758	510	147
1977	6 991	1 663	781	881	5 330	1 629	1 650	785	666	450	147
1978	6 202	1 583	796	787	4 620	1 483	1 422	694	552	345	123
1979	6 137	1 555	739	816	4 583	1 442	1 446	705	540	346	104
1980	7 637	1 669	778	890	5 969	1 835	2 024	940	676	399	94
1981	8 273	1 763	781	981	6 510	1 976	2 211	1 065	715	444	98
1982	10 678	1 977	831	1 145	8 701	2 392	3 037	1 552	966	647	107
1983	10 717	1 829	753	1 076	8 888	2 330	3 078	1 650	1 039	677	114
1984	8 539	1 499	646	854	7 039	1 838	2 374	1 335	828	566	97
1985	8 312	1 468	662	806	6 844	1 738	2 341	1 340	813	518	93
1986	8 237	1 454	665	789	6 783	1 651	2 390	1 371	790	489	91
1987	7 425	1 347	648	700	6 077	1 453	2 129	1 281	723	412	78
1988	6 701	1 226	573	653	5 475	1 261	1 929	1 166	657	375	87
1989	6 528	1 194	537	657	5 333	1 218	1 851	1 159	637	379	91
1990	7 047	1 212	527	685	5 835	1 299	1 995	1 328	723	386	105
1991	8 628	1 359	587	772	7 269	1 573	2 447	1 719	946	473	113
1992	9 613	1 427	641	787	8 186	1 649	2 702	1 976	1 138	589	132
1993	8 940	1 365	606	759	7 575	1 514	2 395	1 896	1 121	541	108
1994	7 996	1 320	624	696	6 676	1 373	2 067	1 627	971	485	153
1995	7 404	1 346	652	695	6 058	1 244	1 841	1 549	844	425	153
1996	7 236	1 306	617	689	5 929	1 239	1 757	1 505	883	406	139
1997	6 739	1 271	589	683	5 467	1 152	1 571	1 418	830	369	127
1998	6 210	1 205	573	632	5 005	1 081	1 419	1 258	782	343	122
1999	5 880	1 162	544	618	4 718	1 042	1 278	1 154	753	367	124
2000	5 692	1 081	502	579	4 611	1 022	1 207	1 133	762	355	132
2001	6 801	1 162	531	632	5 638	1 209	1 498	1 355	989	458	129
2002	8 378	1 253	540	714	7 124	1 430	1 890	1 691	1 315	635	163
2003	8 774	1 251	545	706	7 523	1 495	1 960	1 815	1 356	713	183
2004	8 149	1 208	554	653	6 942	1 431	1 784	1 578	1 288	682	179
2005	7 591	1 186	541	645	6 405	1 335	1 661	1 400	1 195	630	184
2006	7 001	1 119	509	610	5 882	1 234	1 521	1 279	1 094	595	159
2007	7 078	1 101	485	616	5 976	1 241	1 544	1 225	1 135	642	190
2008	8 924	1 285	563	722	7 639	1 545	1 949	1 604	1 473	803	264
2009	14 265	1 552	576	976	12 712	2 207	3 284	2 722	2 592	1 487	421
2010	14 825	1 528	582	945	13 297	2 329	3 386	2 703	2 769	1 660	449

Table 1-26. Unemployed Persons, by Age, Sex, Race, and Hispanic Origin, 1948–2010—*Continued*

(Thousands of people.)

Race, Hispanic origin, sex, and year	16 years and over	16 to 19 years			20 years and over						
		Total	16 to 17 years	18 to 19 years	Total	20 to 24 years	25 to 34 years	35 to 44 years	45 to 54 years	55 to 64 years	65 years and over
ALL RACES											
Men											
1948	1 559	256	113	142	1 305	324	289	233	201	177	81
1949	2 572	353	145	207	2 219	485	539	414	347	310	125
1950	2 239	318	139	179	1 922	377	467	348	327	286	117
1951	1 221	191	102	89	1 029	155	241	192	193	162	87
1952	1 185	205	116	89	980	155	233	192	182	145	73
1953	1 202	184	94	90	1 019	152	236	208	196	167	60
1954	2 344	310	142	168	2 035	327	517	431	372	275	112
1955	1 854	274	134	140	1 580	248	353	328	285	265	102
1956	1 711	269	134	135	1 442	240	348	278	270	216	90
1957	1 841	300	140	159	1 541	283	349	304	302	220	83
1958	3 098	416	185	231	2 681	478	685	552	492	349	124
1959	2 420	398	191	207	2 022	343	484	407	390	287	112
1960	2 486	426	200	225	2 060	369	492	415	392	294	96
1961	2 997	479	221	258	2 518	458	585	507	473	375	122
1962	2 423	408	188	220	2 016	381	445	404	382	300	103
1963	2 472	501	248	252	1 971	396	445	386	358	290	97
1964	2 205	487	257	230	1 718	384	345	324	319	263	85
1965	1 914	479	247	232	1 435	311	292	283	253	221	75
1966	1 551	432	220	212	1 120	221	239	219	196	179	65
1967	1 508	448	241	207	1 060	235	219	185	199	163	60
1968	1 419	426	234	193	993	258	205	171	165	132	61
1969	1 403	440	244	196	963	270	205	155	157	127	48
1970	2 238	599	306	294	1 638	479	391	253	247	198	71
1971	2 789	693	346	347	2 097	640	513	320	313	239	71
1972	2 659	711	357	355	1 948	628	466	284	272	227	73
1973	2 275	653	352	300	1 624	528	439	211	219	171	57
1974	2 714	757	394	362	1 957	649	546	266	250	183	63
1975	4 442	966	445	521	3 476	1 081	986	507	499	302	103
1976	4 036	939	443	496	3 098	951	914	431	411	296	94
1977	3 667	874	421	453	2 794	877	869	373	326	252	97
1978	3 142	813	426	388	2 328	768	691	314	277	198	81
1979	3 120	811	393	418	2 308	744	699	329	272	196	67
1980	4 267	913	429	485	3 353	1 076	1 137	482	357	243	58
1981	4 577	962	431	531	3 615	1 144	1 213	552	390	261	55
1982	6 179	1 090	469	621	5 089	1 407	1 791	879	550	393	69
1983	6 260	1 003	408	595	5 257	1 369	1 822	947	613	433	73
1984	4 744	812	348	464	3 932	1 023	1 322	728	450	356	53
1985	4 521	806	363	443	3 715	944	1 244	706	459	307	55
1986	4 530	779	355	424	3 751	899	1 291	763	440	301	58
1987	4 101	732	353	379	3 369	779	1 169	689	426	258	49
1988	3 655	667	311	356	2 987	676	1 040	617	366	240	49
1989	3 525	658	303	355	2 867	660	953	619	351	234	49
1990	3 906	667	283	384	3 239	715	1 092	711	413	249	59
1991	4 946	751	317	433	4 195	911	1 375	990	550	305	64
1992	5 523	806	357	449	4 717	951	1 529	1 118	675	378	67
1993	5 055	768	342	426	4 287	865	1 338	1 049	636	336	64
1994	4 367	740	342	398	3 627	768	1 113	855	522	281	88
1995	3 983	744	352	391	3 239	673	961	815	464	233	94
1996	3 880	733	347	387	3 146	675	903	786	484	223	76
1997	3 577	694	321	373	2 882	636	772	732	457	217	69
1998	3 266	686	330	355	2 580	583	699	609	420	201	69
1999	3 066	633	295	338	2 433	562	624	571	403	203	70
2000	2 975	599	281	317	2 376	547	602	557	398	189	83
2001	3 690	650	300	350	3 040	688	756	714	536	272	74
2002	4 597	700	301	399	3 896	792	1 023	897	725	373	87
2003	4 906	697	291	407	4 209	841	1 097	988	764	412	107
2004	4 456	664	292	372	3 791	811	980	839	684	373	104
2005	4 059	667	300	367	3 392	775	844	715	624	331	102
2006	3 753	622	271	352	3 131	705	810	642	569	318	88
2007	3 882	623	263	360	3 259	721	856	634	591	349	108
2008	5 033	736	312	425	4 297	920	1 119	875	804	425	153
2009	8 453	898	317	581	7 555	1 329	1 988	1 600	1 558	840	241
2010	8 626	863	315	548	7 763	1 398	1 993	1 534	1 614	962	262

Table 1-26. Unemployed Persons, by Age, Sex, Race, and Hispanic Origin, 1948–2010—*Continued*

(Thousands of people.)

Race, Hispanic origin, sex, and year	16 years and over	16 to 19 years			20 years and over						
		Total	16 to 17 years	18 to 19 years	Total	20 to 24 years	25 to 34 years	35 to 44 years	45 to 54 years	55 to 64 years	65 years and over
ALL RACES											
Women											
1948	717	153	67	86	564	131	168	114	89	49	12
1949	1 065	223	93	130	841	195	237	189	124	74	21
1950	1 049	195	87	108	854	184	235	182	151	82	20
1951	834	145	66	79	689	118	194	162	125	76	16
1952	698	140	64	76	559	113	156	133	92	50	13
1953	632	123	56	67	510	104	143	117	84	51	10
1954	1 188	191	79	79	997	177	276	249	176	99	20
1955	998	176	77	99	823	148	224	193	151	90	18
1956	1 039	209	97	112	832	155	206	198	159	95	19
1957	1 018	197	90	107	821	147	224	195	146	80	28
1958	1 504	262	114	148	1 242	223	308	319	239	123	30
1959	1 320	256	110	147	1 063	200	242	266	213	118	23
1960	1 366	286	125	162	1 080	214	260	256	222	102	26
1961	1 717	349	142	207	1 368	265	305	343	278	141	37
1962	1 488	313	124	189	1 175	255	267	284	223	111	38
1963	1 598	383	172	210	1 216	262	287	288	231	120	29
1964	1 581	385	179	207	1 195	276	262	281	224	115	32
1965	1 452	395	164	231	1 056	246	237	263	183	101	28
1966	1 324	405	175	229	921	225	202	207	173	86	27
1967	1 468	391	159	231	1 078	277	261	237	184	93	26
1968	1 397	412	180	233	985	285	238	200	149	87	27
1969	1 429	413	192	220	1 015	290	248	203	163	89	24
1970	1 855	506	231	275	1 349	387	327	262	229	111	33
1971	2 227	568	250	318	1 658	489	420	310	260	142	38
1972	2 222	598	276	322	1 625	503	413	293	237	141	38
1973	2 089	583	282	301	1 507	480	427	240	212	119	31
1974	2 441	665	305	360	1 777	564	497	294	248	137	36
1975	3 486	802	355	447	2 684	783	791	444	395	219	52
1976	3 369	780	352	429	2 588	763	795	417	346	214	53
1977	3 324	789	361	428	2 535	752	782	412	340	198	50
1978	3 061	769	370	399	2 292	714	731	381	275	148	43
1979	3 018	743	346	396	2 276	697	748	375	268	150	38
1980	3 370	755	349	407	2 615	760	886	459	318	155	36
1981	3 696	800	350	450	2 895	833	998	513	325	184	43
1982	4 499	886	362	524	3 613	985	1 246	673	416	254	38
1983	4 457	825	344	481	3 632	961	1 255	703	427	244	41
1984	3 794	687	298	390	3 107	815	1 052	607	378	211	45
1985	3 791	661	298	363	3 129	794	1 098	634	355	211	39
1986	3 707	675	310	365	3 032	752	1 099	609	350	189	33
1987	3 324	616	295	321	2 709	674	960	592	298	155	30
1988	3 046	558	262	297	2 487	585	889	550	291	136	38
1989	3 003	536	234	302	2 467	558	897	540	286	144	41
1990	3 140	544	243	301	2 596	584	902	617	310	137	46
1991	3 683	608	270	338	3 074	662	1 071	728	396	168	49
1992	4 090	621	283	338	3 469	698	1 173	858	463	210	66
1993	3 885	597	264	333	3 288	648	1 058	847	485	205	45
1994	3 629	580	282	298	3 049	605	954	772	449	204	66
1995	3 421	602	299	303	2 819	571	880	735	381	193	60
1996	3 356	573	270	303	2 783	564	854	720	399	183	63
1997	3 162	577	268	310	2 585	516	800	686	373	152	58
1998	2 944	519	242	277	2 424	498	720	650	362	141	53
1999	2 814	529	249	280	2 285	480	654	584	350	163	54
2000	2 717	483	221	262	2 235	475	604	577	364	165	50
2001	3 111	512	230	282	2 599	521	742	641	453	187	55
2002	3 781	553	238	315	3 228	638	866	795	591	263	76
2003	3 868	554	255	299	3 314	654	863	827	592	302	76
2004	3 694	543	262	281	3 150	619	804	739	605	309	75
2005	3 531	519	240	278	3 013	560	817	685	571	299	82
2006	3 247	496	238	258	2 751	530	711	637	524	277	71
2007	3 196	478	222	256	2 718	520	688	591	544	293	81
2008	3 891	549	251	297	3 342	625	830	730	669	377	111
2009	5 811	654	259	395	5 157	878	1 296	1 121	1 034	647	180
2010	6 199	665	268	397	5 534	931	1 392	1 169	1 156	698	187

Table 1-26. Unemployed Persons, by Age, Sex, Race, and Hispanic Origin, 1948–2010—*Continued*

(Thousands of people.)

Race, Hispanic origin, sex, and year	16 years and over	16 to 19 years			20 years and over						
		Total	16 to 17 years	18 to 19 years	Total	20 to 24 years	25 to 34 years	35 to 44 years	45 to 54 years	55 to 64 years	65 years and over
WHITE											
Both Sexes											
1954	2 859	423	191	232	2 436	394	610	540	447	329	115
1955	2 252	373	181	191	1 879	304	412	402	358	300	105
1956	2 159	382	191	191	1 777	297	406	363	355	258	98
1957	2 289	401	195	204	1 888	331	425	401	373	262	98
1958	3 680	541	245	297	3 139	541	756	686	614	405	136
1959	2 946	525	255	270	2 421	406	526	525	496	348	120
1960	3 065	575	273	302	2 490	456	573	520	502	330	109
1961	3 743	669	295	374	3 074	566	668	652	611	438	139
1962	3 052	580	262	318	2 472	488	515	522	485	345	117
1963	3 208	708	350	358	2 500	501	540	518	485	349	107
1964	2 999	708	365	342	2 291	508	441	472	447	323	100
1965	2 691	705	329	374	1 986	437	399	427	358	276	91
1966	2 255	651	315	336	1 604	338	323	336	298	227	80
1967	2 338	635	311	325	1 703	393	360	336	321	221	75
1968	2 226	644	326	318	1 582	422	330	297	269	187	80
1969	2 260	660	351	309	1 601	432	354	294	269	185	66
1970	3 339	871	438	432	2 468	679	570	433	415	275	95
1971	4 085	1 011	491	521	3 074	887	732	517	500	338	100
1972	3 906	1 021	515	506	2 885	887	679	459	439	324	95
1973	3 442	955	513	443	2 486	758	664	358	371	257	77
1974	4 097	1 104	561	544	2 993	925	821	448	427	283	88
1975	6 421	1 413	657	755	5 007	1 474	1 413	774	753	460	136
1976	5 914	1 364	649	715	4 550	1 326	1 329	682	637	448	128
1977	5 441	1 284	636	648	4 157	1 195	1 255	621	569	388	129
1978	4 698	1 189	631	558	3 509	1 059	1 059	543	453	290	104
1979	4 664	1 193	589	603	3 472	1 038	1 068	545	443	290	87
1980	5 884	1 291	625	666	4 593	1 364	1 528	740	550	335	74
1981	6 343	1 374	629	745	4 968	1 449	1 658	827	578	379	77
1982	8 241	1 534	683	851	6 707	1 770	2 283	1 223	796	549	86
1983	8 128	1 387	609	778	6 741	1 678	2 282	1 294	837	563	88
1984	6 372	1 116	510	605	5 256	1 282	1 723	1 036	660	475	81
1985	6 191	1 074	507	567	5 117	1 235	1 695	1 039	642	432	75
1986	6 140	1 070	509	561	5 070	1 149	1 751	1 056	629	407	78
1987	5 501	995	495	500	4 506	1 017	1 527	984	576	333	68
1988	4 944	910	437	473	4 033	874	1 371	890	520	309	69
1989	4 770	863	407	456	3 908	856	1 297	871	503	311	70
1990	5 186	903	401	502	4 283	899	1 401	983	582	330	88
1991	6 560	1 029	461	568	5 532	1 132	1 805	1 330	759	410	96
1992	7 169	1 037	484	553	6 132	1 156	1 967	1 483	915	495	116
1993	6 655	992	468	523	5 663	1 057	1 754	1 411	907	442	92
1994	5 892	960	471	489	4 933	952	1 479	1 184	779	407	132
1995	5 459	952	476	476	4 507	866	1 311	1 161	676	362	131
1996	5 300	939	456	484	4 361	854	1 223	1 117	709	336	122
1997	4 836	912	438	475	3 924	765	1 068	1 035	648	302	106
1998	4 484	876	424	451	3 608	731	978	901	620	276	101
1999	4 273	844	414	430	3 429	720	865	843	595	303	104
2000	4 121	795	386	409	3 326	682	835	817	591	294	107
2001	4 969	845	402	443	4 124	829	1 062	985	761	378	109
2002	6 137	925	407	518	5 212	977	1 340	1 237	1 004	518	137
2003	6 311	909	414	495	5 401	1 012	1 354	1 287	1 025	569	155
2004	5 847	890	414	476	4 957	959	1 211	1 130	953	557	148
2005	5 350	845	391	454	4 505	878	1 106	1 006	884	488	144
2006	5 002	794	375	419	4 208	832	1 029	920	813	480	135
2007	5 143	805	361	444	4 338	851	1 052	902	848	520	164
2008	6 509	947	422	524	5 562	1 087	1 336	1 196	1 094	634	216
2009	10 648	1 157	440	717	9 491	1 556	2 320	2 026	2 012	1 221	355
2010	10 916	1 128	445	683	9 788	1 614	2 358	1 969	2 130	1 344	373

Table 1-26. Unemployed Persons, by Age, Sex, Race, and Hispanic Origin, 1948–2010—*Continued*

(Thousands of people.)

Race, Hispanic origin, sex, and year	16 years and over	16 to 19 years			20 years and over						
		Total	16 to 17 years	18 to 19 years	Total	20 to 24 years	25 to 34 years	35 to 44 years	45 to 54 years	55 to 64 years	65 years and over
WHITE											
Men											
1954	1 913	266	125	142	1 647	260	408	341	299	241	98
1955	1 478	232	114	117	1 246	196	260	246	233	223	89
1956	1 366	221	112	108	1 145	186	265	212	225	177	81
1957	1 477	243	118	124	1 234	222	257	239	250	193	73
1958	2 489	333	149	184	2 156	382	525	436	404	299	110
1959	1 903	318	162	156	1 585	256	350	316	320	245	98
1960	1 988	341	167	174	1 647	295	376	330	317	243	86
1961	2 398	384	176	208	2 014	370	442	395	382	318	107
1962	1 915	334	158	176	1 581	300	332	311	308	246	84
1963	1 976	407	211	196	1 569	309	342	297	294	246	80
1964	1 779	400	217	183	1 379	310	262	255	266	216	70
1965	1 556	387	200	186	1 169	254	226	228	206	190	67
1966	1 241	340	178	162	901	172	185	173	160	154	57
1967	1 208	342	186	156	866	185	171	153	167	140	52
1968	1 142	328	185	143	814	206	162	140	142	111	55
1969	1 137	343	198	145	794	214	165	130	134	108	43
1970	1 857	485	255	230	1 372	388	316	212	216	177	64
1971	2 309	562	288	275	1 747	513	418	268	272	211	66
1972	2 173	564	288	276	1 610	506	375	231	237	199	60
1973	1 836	513	284	229	1 323	411	353	166	188	153	51
1974	2 169	584	311	274	1 585	505	434	218	213	161	53
1975	3 627	785	369	416	2 841	871	796	412	411	265	86
1976	3 258	754	368	385	2 504	750	730	346	341	259	78
1977	2 883	672	342	330	2 211	660	682	297	276	213	82
1978	2 411	615	338	277	1 797	558	525	250	227	169	68
1979	2 405	633	319	313	1 773	553	526	253	220	165	56
1980	3 345	716	347	369	2 629	827	884	378	291	206	44
1981	3 580	755	349	406	2 825	869	943	433	317	221	42
1982	4 846	854	387	467	3 991	1 066	1 385	696	460	331	53
1983	4 859	761	328	433	4 098	1 019	1 410	755	497	362	54
1984	3 600	608	280	328	2 992	722	991	572	363	302	42
1085	3 426	592	282	310	2 834	694	931	553	356	257	43
1986	3 433	576	276	299	2 857	645	978	586	349	248	51
1987	3 132	548	272	276	2 584	568	879	536	350	209	43
1988	2 766	499	239	260	2 268	480	777	477	293	200	40
1989	2 636	487	230	257	2 149	476	694	470	280	191	38
1990	2 935	504	214	290	2 431	510	796	530	330	214	51
1991	3 859	575	249	327	3 284	677	1 064	780	438	269	55
1992	4 209	590	270	319	3 620	686	1 155	858	543	318	58
1993	3 828	565	261	305	3 263	619	1 015	793	512	270	53
1994	3 275	540	259	280	2 735	555	827	626	417	236	74
1995	2 999	535	260	275	2 465	483	711	621	371	200	79
1996	2 896	532	260	273	2 363	478	655	592	383	188	67
1997	2 641	502	234	268	2 140	439	553	549	358	182	58
1998	2 431	510	254	257	1 920	405	512	441	342	164	58
1999	2 274	461	223	237	1 813	398	441	419	322	172	61
2000	2 177	446	217	229	1 731	368	428	403	302	162	68
2001	2 754	479	232	247	2 275	494	547	529	413	229	64
2002	3 459	516	228	288	2 943	562	772	672	554	305	77
2003	3 643	518	221	298	3 125	589	798	723	591	333	91
2004	3 282	497	224	274	2 785	560	694	620	516	307	88
2005	2 931	480	220	260	2 450	522	586	536	463	263	81
2006	2 730	449	202	247	2 281	483	567	482	417	259	73
2007	2 869	461	195	266	2 408	501	604	478	447	285	93
2008	3 727	548	231	317	3 179	668	784	662	604	337	124
2009	6 421	675	241	434	5 746	969	1 439	1 208	1 233	695	202
2010	6 476	648	246	402	5 828	995	1 452	1 131	1 249	785	216

Table 1-26. Unemployed Persons, by Age, Sex, Race, and Hispanic Origin, 1948–2010—*Continued*

(Thousands of people.)

Race, Hispanic origin, sex, and year	16 years and over	16 to 19 years			20 years and over						
		Total	16 to 17 years	18 to 19 years	Total	20 to 24 years	25 to 34 years	35 to 44 years	45 to 54 years	55 to 64 years	65 years and over
WHITE											
Women											
1954	946	157	66	90	789	134	202	199	148	88	17
1955	774	141	67	74	633	108	152	156	125	77	16
1956	793	161	79	83	632	111	141	151	130	81	17
1957	812	158	77	80	654	109	168	162	123	69	25
1958	1 191	208	96	113	983	159	231	250	210	106	26
1959	1 043	207	93	114	836	150	176	209	176	103	22
1960	1 077	234	106	128	843	161	197	190	185	87	23
1961	1 345	285	119	166	1 060	196	226	257	229	120	32
1962	1 137	246	104	142	891	188	183	211	177	99	33
1963	1 232	301	139	162	931	192	198	221	191	103	27
1964	1 220	308	148	159	912	198	179	217	181	107	30
1965	1 135	318	129	188	817	183	173	199	152	86	24
1966	1 014	311	137	174	703	166	138	163	138	73	23
1967	1 130	293	125	169	837	209	189	183	154	81	23
1968	1 084	316	141	175	768	216	168	157	127	76	25
1969	1 123	317	153	164	806	218	189	164	135	77	23
1970	1 482	386	183	202	1 096	291	254	221	199	98	31
1971	1 777	449	203	246	1 328	376	314	249	228	126	34
1972	1 733	457	227	230	1 275	381	304	227	202	125	35
1973	1 606	442	228	214	1 164	347	311	192	183	104	26
1974	1 927	519	250	270	1 408	420	387	230	214	122	35
1975	2 794	628	288	340	2 166	602	617	362	342	195	49
1976	2 656	611	280	330	2 045	577	598	336	296	188	49
1977	2 558	612	294	318	1 946	536	573	323	293	175	47
1978	2 287	574	292	281	1 713	500	533	294	226	122	37
1979	2 260	560	270	290	1 699	485	542	293	223	125	32
1980	2 540	576	278	298	1 964	537	645	362	259	129	31
1981	2 762	620	281	339	2 143	580	715	394	261	158	36
1982	3 395	680	296	384	2 715	704	898	527	337	217	33
1983	3 270	626	282	345	2 643	659	872	539	340	201	33
1984	2 772	508	231	277	2 264	559	731	464	297	173	39
1985	2 765	482	225	257	2 283	541	763	486	286	175	32
1986	2 708	495	233	262	2 213	504	773	470	281	159	27
1987	2 369	447	223	224	1 922	449	648	448	227	124	25
1988	2 177	412	198	214	1 766	393	594	413	227	110	30
1989	2 135	376	177	199	1 758	380	603	401	223	120	32
1990	2 251	399	187	212	1 852	389	605	453	251	116	37
1991	2 701	453	212	241	2 248	455	741	550	320	141	41
1992	2 959	447	214	233	2 512	469	811	625	372	177	58
1993	2 827	426	208	219	2 400	438	739	618	395	172	39
1994	2 617	420	211	208	2 197	397	652	558	361	170	58
1995	2 460	418	216	201	2 042	384	600	540	306	162	52
1996	2 404	407	196	211	1 998	376	568	525	326	148	55
1997	2 195	411	204	207	1 784	326	515	486	290	119	49
1998	2 053	365	171	195	1 688	327	467	460	279	112	43
1999	1 999	383	190	193	1 616	322	423	423	273	131	43
2000	1 944	349	168	180	1 595	314	407	414	289	133	39
2001	2 215	366	170	196	1 849	335	515	456	348	150	45
2002	2 678	409	179	230	2 269	415	567	565	449	213	60
2003	2 668	391	194	197	2 276	423	555	564	434	235	64
2004	2 565	393	191	202	2 172	399	516	510	437	250	60
2005	2 419	365	172	193	2 054	356	520	469	421	225	63
2006	2 271	345	173	172	1 927	349	462	437	395	222	62
2007	2 274	344	166	178	1 930	350	448	425	401	235	71
2008	2 782	399	191	207	2 384	419	552	534	489	298	92
2009	4 227	482	199	283	3 745	587	881	818	780	526	153
2010	4 440	480	199	281	3 960	619	906	839	881	559	157

Table 1-26. Unemployed Persons, by Age, Sex, Race, and Hispanic Origin, 1948–2010—*Continued*

(Thousands of people.)

Race, Hispanic origin, sex, and year	16 years and over	16 to 19 years			20 years and over						
		Total	16 to 17 years	18 to 19 years	Total	20 to 24 years	25 to 34 years	35 to 44 years	45 to 54 years	55 to 64 years	65 years and over
BLACK											
Both Sexes											
1972	906	279	113	167	627	226	183	106	62	37	12
1973	846	262	114	148	584	231	181	82	53	29	9
1974	965	297	127	170	666	261	201	95	65	33	10
1975	1 369	330	130	200	1 040	362	321	157	126	54	17
1976	1 334	330	134	195	1 005	350	338	145	101	54	16
1977	1 393	354	135	218	1 040	397	355	140	81	51	16
1978	1 330	360	150	210	972	379	320	127	82	47	17
1979	1 319	333	137	197	986	369	335	137	82	48	15
1980	1 553	343	134	210	1 209	426	433	171	109	53	18
1981	1 731	357	138	219	1 374	483	493	207	119	55	17
1982	2 142	396	130	266	1 747	565	662	278	141	84	17
1983	2 272	392	125	267	1 879	591	700	299	174	95	21
1984	1 914	353	122	230	1 561	504	577	253	138	75	15
1985	1 864	357	135	221	1 507	455	562	254	143	74	18
1986	1 840	347	138	209	1 493	453	564	269	127	69	10
1987	1 684	312	134	178	1 373	397	533	247	124	62	10
1988	1 547	288	121	167	1 259	349	502	230	111	51	15
1989	1 544	300	116	184	1 245	322	494	246	109	53	20
1990	1 565	268	112	156	1 297	349	505	278	106	44	14
1991	1 723	280	105	175	1 443	378	539	318	151	44	13
1992	2 011	324	127	197	1 687	421	610	402	178	64	13
1993	1 844	313	112	201	1 530	387	532	376	153	72	11
1994	1 666	300	127	173	1 366	351	468	346	130	55	16
1995	1 538	325	143	182	1 213	311	423	303	116	42	18
1996	1 592	310	133	177	1 282	327	454	313	127	48	13
1997	1 560	302	123	179	1 258	327	426	307	136	45	16
1998	1 426	281	124	156	1 146	301	366	294	125	45	16
1999	1 309	268	109	159	1 041	273	339	249	121	46	14
2000	1 241	230	96	134	1 011	281	289	254	131	38	20
2001	1 416	260	102	158	1 155	307	340	283	159	52	15
2002	1 693	260	103	156	1 433	365	407	349	215	76	21
2003	1 787	255	93	162	1 532	375	442	385	217	93	20
2004	1 729	241	103	138	1 487	353	441	341	245	86	21
2005	1 700	267	115	152	1 433	358	423	310	222	92	28
2006	1 549	253	102	151	1 296	318	388	276	214	81	19
2007	1 445	235	98	138	1 210	300	367	237	208	79	19
2008	1 788	246	98	148	1 542	355	458	301	275	117	36
2009	2 606	288	99	189	2 319	488	717	489	415	168	42
2010	2 852	291	97	194	2 562	539	776	534	461	204	47
BLACK											
Men											
1972	448	143	66	77	305	113	84	45	31	23	9
1973	395	128	62	66	267	108	75	37	27	16	5
1974	494	159	75	82	336	129	103	41	35	19	8
1975	741	170	71	100	571	195	169	83	78	33	13
1976	698	170	69	103	528	185	166	73	60	32	13
1977	698	187	73	114	512	197	170	63	40	31	12
1978	641	180	80	101	462	185	148	53	40	24	11
1979	636	164	68	97	473	174	152	66	44	27	10
1980	815	179	72	108	636	222	222	88	60	32	12
1981	891	188	73	115	703	248	245	102	65	32	10
1982	1 167	213	72	141	954	304	355	154	74	54	12
1983	1 213	211	70	142	1 002	313	358	162	96	59	14
1984	1 003	188	62	126	815	272	289	132	67	45	9
1985	951	193	69	124	757	224	268	127	85	43	11
1986	946	180	68	112	765	225	273	148	70	44	5
1987	826	160	70	90	666	186	253	122	61	39	6
1988	771	154	64	90	617	177	233	111	58	30	8
1989	773	153	65	88	619	162	226	129	59	33	10
1990	806	142	62	80	664	177	247	146	62	27	6
1991	890	145	54	91	745	201	252	172	87	25	7
1992	1 067	180	71	109	886	221	301	208	107	42	6
1993	971	170	66	104	801	201	260	201	87	46	7
1994	848	167	69	97	682	173	218	180	72	29	10
1995	762	168	73	95	593	153	195	150	63	21	11
1996	808	169	73	96	639	163	210	158	75	26	7
1997	747	162	70	92	585	165	178	141	72	22	7
1998	671	147	61	86	524	151	148	133	60	24	8
1999	626	145	60	85	480	135	143	114	60	22	7
2000	620	121	52	70	499	145	134	121	72	17	9
2001	709	136	51	85	573	150	159	142	84	31	7
2002	835	140	54	85	695	181	180	165	120	40	9
2003	891	132	49	83	760	192	212	189	109	47	10
2004	860	128	52	75	733	188	211	160	120	46	8
2005	844	145	63	82	699	192	189	143	116	45	14
2006	774	134	53	81	640	167	189	118	112	43	11
2007	752	130	55	75	622	166	186	114	106	41	10
2008	949	138	54	84	811	190	242	154	143	61	21
2009	1 448	161	55	106	1 286	264	406	270	230	91	24
2010	1 550	154	47	107	1 396	294	408	286	268	116	24

Table 1-26. Unemployed Persons, by Age, Sex, Race, and Hispanic Origin, 1948–2010—*Continued*

(Thousands of people.)

Race, Hispanic origin, sex, and year	16 years and over	16 to 19 years			20 years and over						
		Total	16 to 17 years	18 to 19 years	Total	20 to 24 years	25 to 34 years	35 to 44 years	45 to 54 years	55 to 64 years	65 years and over
BLACK											
Women											
1972	458	136	47	90	322	113	99	61	31	14	3
1973	451	134	51	82	317	123	105	45	26	13	4
1974	470	139	51	87	331	132	98	55	30	14	2
1975	629	160	60	100	469	167	153	75	48	22	4
1976	637	160	66	93	477	165	172	73	41	23	3
1977	695	167	63	104	528	200	185	77	41	21	4
1978	690	179	70	110	510	194	173	74	41	23	6
1979	683	169	69	100	513	195	183	71	38	21	5
1980	738	164	62	102	574	204	211	83	49	21	6
1981	840	169	65	104	671	235	248	105	54	23	7
1982	975	182	58	124	793	261	307	123	67	29	5
1983	1 059	181	56	125	878	278	342	137	77	36	7
1984	911	165	60	104	747	231	288	121	71	30	5
1985	913	164	66	98	750	231	295	127	58	31	7
1986	894	167	70	97	728	228	291	121	57	25	5
1987	858	152	64	88	706	211	280	125	63	23	4
1988	776	134	57	78	642	172	269	118	53	22	7
1989	772	147	51	96	625	160	267	118	50	21	9
1990	758	126	49	76	633	172	258	132	44	17	8
1991	833	135	51	84	698	177	288	145	64	19	6
1992	944	144	56	88	800	200	308	194	71	22	6
1993	872	143	46	97	729	186	272	175	66	26	5
1994	818	133	57	76	685	178	249	166	59	26	6
1995	777	157	. . .	87	620	158	228	153	53	20	7
1996	784	141	60	80	643	164	244	155	52	21	7
1997	813	140	53	87	673	163	248	166	64	24	9
1998	756	134	63	71	622	150	218	160	65	21	8
1999	684	123	49	74	561	138	196	135	61	25	7
2000	621	109	44	65	512	136	154	132	59	22	10
2001	706	124	52	72	582	157	181	141	75	21	8
2002	858	120	49	71	738	183	228	185	95	35	12
2003	895	123	44	79	772	183	230	195	109	46	10
2004	868	114	51	63	755	166	230	180	126	40	13
2005	856	123	52	70	734	166	233	168	106	47	14
2006	775	120	50	70	656	150	199	158	102	38	8
2007	693	106	43	63	588	135	181	123	103	38	9
2008	839	108	44	64	732	166	216	147	132	56	15
2009	1 159	127	44	82	1 032	223	311	219	185	77	17
2010	1 302	137	50	87	1 165	245	369	248	193	88	22
HISPANIC[1]											
Both Sexes											
1974	325	88	. . .	. . .	. . .	. . .	. . .	. . .	. . .	. . .	. . .
1975	508	123	. . .	. . .	. . .	. . .	. . .	. . .	. . .	. . .	. . .
1976	485	106	51	55	385	116	113	72	53	26	6
1977	456	113	50	60	344	98	114	56	48	24	5
1978	452	110	63	47	342	98	116	65	41	16	5
1979	434	106	54	51	329	100	102	65	37	20	4
1980	620	145	66	79	474	138	168	90	49	24	5
1981	678	144	60	84	533	171	178	92	57	31	5
1982	929	175	73	102	754	221	267	140	75	45	6
1983	961	167	64	104	793	214	270	156	93	54	5
1984	800	149	60	88	651	164	235	124	71	51	5
1985	811	141	55	85	670	171	256	123	73	41	7
1986	857	141	57	84	716	183	258	143	85	38	9
1987	751	136	57	79	615	152	222	128	75	33	5
1988	732	148	63	84	585	145	209	120	69	36	6
1989	750	132	59	73	618	158	218	124	76	36	6
1990	876	161	68	94	714	167	263	156	85	36	7
1991	1 092	179	79	99	913	214	332	206	110	44	8
1992	1 311	219	94	124	1 093	240	390	267	126	59	10
1993	1 248	201	86	115	1 047	237	354	261	132	54	10
1994	1 187	198	90	108	989	220	348	227	132	51	12
1995	1 140	205	96	109	934	209	325	224	106	54	16
1996	1 132	199	85	114	933	217	296	246	101	59	14
1997	1 069	197	87	110	872	206	269	229	99	56	13
1998	1 026	214	89	125	812	194	260	203	96	48	11
1999	945	196	79	117	750	171	233	190	104	42	10
2000	954	194	83	112	759	190	247	189	79	42	12
2001	1 138	208	84	123	931	212	315	228	111	56	9
2002	1 353	221	81	140	1 132	265	373	271	146	62	15
2003	1 441	192	79	113	1 249	273	419	294	183	69	10
2004	1 342	203	86	117	1 139	255	371	261	161	74	18
2005	1 191	191	78	113	1 000	227	324	231	142	61	15
2006	1 081	170	74	97	911	194	294	231	128	49	14
2007	1 220	197	78	119	1 023	213	322	238	161	70	19
2008	1 678	251	105	146	1 427	307	437	328	242	81	32
2009	2 706	321	109	212	2 385	429	731	584	416	186	38
2010	2 843	322	99	223	2 520	479	736	598	459	199	49

[1]May be of any race.
. . . = Not available.

Table 1-26. Unemployed Persons, by Age, Sex, Race, and Hispanic Origin, 1948–2010—*Continued*

(Thousands of people.)

Race, Hispanic origin, sex, and year	16 years and over	16 to 19 years			20 years and over						
		Total	16 to 17 years	18 to 19 years	Total	20 to 24 years	25 to 34 years	35 to 44 years	45 to 54 years	55 to 64 years	65 years and over
HISPANIC[1]											
Men											
1974	187	...	...	...	139	...	...	...	...	...	...
1975	296	...	...	...	225	...	...	...	...	...	...
1976	278	60	30	31	217	69	63	38	29	16	...
1977	253	60	27	33	195	57	65	28	22	15	...
1978	234	59	35	24	175	51	59	30	20	10	...
1979	223	55	29	27	168	52	50	33	19	11	...
1980	370	86	39	47	284	85	96	51	31	16	...
1981	408	87	40	47	321	105	113	49	31	19	...
1982	565	104	45	59	461	138	169	80	40	29	...
1983	591	100	38	62	491	134	168	92	57	36	...
1984	480	87	36	51	393	103	142	69	41	33	...
1985	483	82	34	49	401	108	156	69	40	23	...
1986	520	82	33	50	438	115	159	86	46	26	...
1987	451	77	32	45	374	88	137	77	46	22	...
1988	437	86	36	50	351	83	128	70	42	24	...
1989	423	81	36	45	342	88	113	69	43	25	...
1990	524	100	40	60	425	99	154	91	53	25	...
1991	685	110	47	62	575	139	210	126	62	33	...
1992	807	132	56	75	675	156	239	156	75	42	...
1993	747	118	50	68	629	144	217	148	79	33	...
1994	680	121	54	67	558	128	203	113	75	30	9
1995	651	121	59	63	530	123	185	120	57	33	13
1996	607	112	49	63	495	117	165	124	49	31	9
1997	582	110	47	63	471	125	137	113	54	35	8
1998	552	117	54	62	436	115	142	97	49	29	5
1999	480	106	42	63	374	96	109	83	54	24	7
2000	494	106	46	60	388	105	118	93	42	23	8
2001	611	117	52	65	495	129	152	116	55	36	6
2002	764	127	42	86	636	151	213	144	82	38	8
2003	809	116	42	74	693	157	239	153	98	41	5
2004	755	120	48	72	635	158	207	133	82	41	13
2005	647	112	42	70	536	134	168	119	74	31	9
2006	601	104	43	61	497	110	169	114	66	29	8
2007	695	119	44	74	576	121	189	126	92	35	13
2008	1 007	147	63	84	860	188	275	192	136	50	19
2009	1 670	196	66	131	1 474	255	470	364	246	117	21
2010	1 711	191	54	137	1 519	294	470	346	269	112	28
HISPANIC[1]											
Women											
1974	137	...	...	...	98	...	...	...	...	...	...
1975	212	...	...	...	160	...	...	...	...	...	...
1976	207	45	22	24	166	47	52	33	22	10	...
1977	204	50	23	27	153	40	49	28	25	11	...
1978	219	51	28	23	168	46	58	36	20	8	...
1979	211	50	26	24	160	48	52	32	18	10	...
1980	249	59	28	31	190	53	72	39	18	8	...
1981	269	57	20	37	212	65	65	43	25	13	...
1982	364	71	28	43	293	83	98	60	35	16	...
1983	369	68	26	42	302	80	102	65	36	18	...
1984	320	62	25	37	258	61	93	55	30	17	...
1985	327	58	22	37	269	63	100	54	32	18	...
1986	337	59	25	35	278	68	99	57	39	12	...
1987	300	59	25	34	241	64	85	51	29	11	...
1988	296	62	27	34	234	63	81	50	27	12	...
1989	327	51	23	28	276	70	105	55	33	11	...
1990	351	62	28	34	289	68	109	65	32	11	...
1991	407	69	32	37	339	74	122	80	48	12	...
1992	504	87	38	49	418	84	151	111	51	17	...
1993	501	83	36	47	418	93	136	113	53	21	...
1994	508	77	36	40	431	92	145	115	57	21	2
1995	488	84	38	46	404	86	140	104	50	21	3
1996	525	88	36	52	438	100	131	122	52	27	5
1997	488	87	40	46	401	81	132	117	46	21	4
1998	473	98	35	63	376	80	118	106	48	19	5
1999	466	90	36	54	376	75	124	107	50	17	3
2000	460	88	37	51	371	86	129	96	38	19	4
2001	527	91	33	58	436	83	163	112	56	20	3
2002	590	94	39	54	496	113	160	127	65	24	7
2003	631	76	37	39	555	116	180	141	86	28	5
2004	587	83	38	45	504	97	164	128	78	32	5
2005	544	80	36	43	464	93	156	112	68	30	6
2006	480	67	31	36	414	84	125	116	62	20	6
2007	525	79	34	45	446	92	134	111	69	35	6
2008	672	104	42	62	567	119	162	136	105	32	13
2009	1 036	125	44	81	911	174	260	220	170	70	17
2010	1 132	131	45	86	1 001	186	267	252	190	87	20

[1]May be of any race.
... = Not available.

Table 1-27. Unemployment Rates of Civilian Workers, by Age, Sex, Race, and Hispanic Origin, 1948–2010

(Percent of labor force.)

Race, Hispanic origin, sex, and year	16 years and over	16 to 19 years			20 years and over						
		Total	16 to 17 years	18 to 19 years	Total	20 to 24 years	25 to 34 years	35 to 44 years	45 to 54 years	55 to 64 years	65 years and over
ALL RACES											
Both Sexes											
1948	3.8	9.2	10.1	8.6	3.3	6.2	3.2	2.6	2.7	3.1	3.2
1949	5.9	13.4	14.0	13.0	5.4	9.3	5.4	4.4	4.2	5.2	4.9
1950	5.3	12.2	13.6	11.2	4.8	7.7	4.8	3.8	4.2	4.8	4.5
1951	3.3	8.2	9.6	7.1	3.0	4.1	3.0	2.5	2.7	3.1	3.4
1952	3.0	8.5	10.0	7.3	2.7	4.6	2.6	2.3	2.3	2.4	2.9
1953	2.9	7.6	8.7	6.8	2.6	4.7	2.5	2.2	2.3	2.7	2.2
1954	5.5	12.6	13.5	10.7	5.1	9.2	5.3	4.5	4.4	4.5	4.1
1955	4.4	11.0	12.3	10.0	3.9	7.0	3.8	3.4	3.4	4.2	3.6
1956	4.1	11.1	12.3	10.2	3.7	6.6	3.7	3.0	3.2	3.5	3.2
1957	4.3	11.6	12.5	10.9	3.8	7.1	3.9	3.1	3.3	3.4	3.4
1958	6.8	15.9	16.4	15.5	6.2	11.2	6.8	5.4	5.2	5.2	4.8
1959	5.5	14.6	15.3	14.0	4.8	8.5	5.0	4.2	4.2	4.4	4.3
1960	5.5	14.7	15.5	14.1	4.8	8.7	5.2	4.1	4.1	4.2	3.8
1961	6.7	16.8	18.3	15.8	5.9	10.4	6.2	5.2	5.0	5.4	5.1
1962	5.5	14.7	16.3	13.6	4.9	9.0	5.1	4.1	4.0	4.2	4.5
1963	5.7	17.2	19.3	15.6	4.8	8.8	5.2	4.0	3.8	4.1	4.1
1964	5.2	16.2	17.8	14.9	4.3	8.3	4.3	3.6	3.5	3.7	3.8
1965	4.5	14.8	16.5	13.5	3.6	6.7	3.7	3.2	2.8	3.1	3.3
1966	3.8	12.8	14.8	11.3	2.9	5.3	3.1	2.5	2.3	2.5	3.0
1967	3.8	12.9	14.6	11.6	3.0	5.7	3.2	2.5	2.4	2.4	2.8
1968	3.6	12.7	14.7	11.2	2.7	5.8	2.8	2.2	1.9	2.0	2.8
1969	3.5	12.2	14.5	10.5	2.7	5.7	2.8	2.2	1.9	1.9	2.2
1970	4.9	15.3	17.1	13.8	4.0	8.2	4.2	3.1	2.8	2.7	3.2
1971	5.9	16.9	18.7	15.5	4.9	10.0	5.3	3.9	3.4	3.3	3.5
1972	5.6	16.2	18.5	14.6	4.5	9.3	4.6	3.5	3.0	3.2	3.6
1973	4.9	14.5	17.3	12.4	3.9	7.8	4.2	2.7	2.5	2.6	3.0
1974	5.6	16.0	18.3	14.3	4.5	9.1	4.8	3.3	2.9	2.8	3.4
1975	8.5	19.9	21.4	18.9	7.3	13.6	7.8	5.6	5.2	4.6	5.2
1976	7.7	19.0	21.1	17.5	6.5	12.0	7.1	4.9	4.5	4.5	5.1
1977	7.1	17.8	19.9	16.2	5.9	11.0	6.5	4.4	3.9	3.9	5.0
1978	6.1	16.4	19.3	14.2	5.0	9.6	5.3	3.7	3.3	2.9	4.0
1979	5.8	16.1	18.1	14.7	4.8	9.1	5.2	3.6	3.2	2.9	3.4
1980	7.1	17.8	20.0	16.2	6.1	11.5	6.9	4.6	4.0	3.3	3.1
1981	7.6	19.6	21.4	18.4	6.5	12.3	7.3	5.0	4.2	3.7	3.2
1982	9.7	23.2	24.9	22.1	8.6	14.9	9.7	6.9	5.7	5.4	3.5
1983	9.6	22.4	24.5	21.1	8.6	14.5	9.7	7.0	6.2	5.6	3.7
1984	7.5	18.9	21.2	17.4	6.7	11.5	7.3	5.4	4.9	4.7	3.3
1985	7.2	18.6	21.0	17.0	6.4	11.1	7.0	5.1	4.7	4.3	3.2
1986	7.0	18.3	20.2	17.0	6.2	10.7	6.9	5.0	4.5	4.1	3.0
1987	6.2	16.9	19.1	15.2	5.4	9.7	6.0	4.5	4.0	3.5	2.5
1988	5.5	15.3	17.4	13.8	4.8	8.7	5.4	4.0	3.4	3.2	2.7
1989	5.3	15.0	17.2	13.6	4.6	8.6	5.2	3.8	3.2	3.2	2.6
1990	5.6	15.5	17.9	14.1	4.9	8.8	5.6	4.1	3.6	3.3	3.0
1991	6.8	18.7	21.0	17.2	6.1	10.8	6.9	5.2	4.5	4.1	3.3
1992	7.5	20.1	23.1	18.2	6.8	11.4	7.6	5.8	5.1	5.1	3.8
1993	6.9	19.0	21.4	17.5	6.2	10.5	6.9	5.5	4.8	4.7	3.2
1994	6.1	17.6	19.9	16.0	5.4	9.7	6.0	4.6	4.0	4.1	4.0
1995	5.6	17.3	20.2	15.3	4.9	9.1	5.4	4.3	3.3	3.6	4.0
1996	5.4	16.7	18.9	15.2	4.7	9.3	5.2	4.1	3.3	3.3	3.6
1997	4.9	16.0	18.2	14.5	4.3	8.5	4.7	3.8	3.0	2.9	3.3
1998	4.5	14.6	17.2	12.8	3.9	7.9	4.3	3.4	2.8	2.6	3.2
1999	4.2	13.9	16.3	12.4	3.6	7.5	4.0	3.0	2.6	2.7	3.1
2000	4.0	13.1	15.4	11.6	3.4	7.2	3.7	3.0	2.5	2.5	3.1
2001	4.7	14.7	17.2	13.1	4.2	8.3	4.6	3.6	3.1	3.0	2.9
2002	5.8	16.5	18.8	15.1	5.2	9.7	5.9	4.6	4.0	3.9	3.6
2003	6.0	17.5	19.1	16.4	5.4	10.0	6.1	4.9	4.1	4.1	3.8
2004	5.5	17.0	20.2	15.0	4.9	9.4	5.5	4.4	3.8	3.8	3.6
2005	5.1	16.6	19.1	14.9	4.5	8.8	5.1	3.9	3.5	3.3	3.5
2006	4.6	15.4	17.2	14.1	4.1	8.2	4.7	3.6	3.1	3.0	2.9
2007	4.6	15.7	17.5	14.5	4.1	8.2	4.7	3.4	3.2	3.1	3.3
2008	5.8	18.7	22.1	16.8	5.2	10.2	5.8	4.6	4.1	3.7	4.2
2009	9.3	24.3	25.9	23.4	8.6	14.7	9.9	7.9	7.2	6.6	6.4
2010	9.6	25.9	29.1	24.2	9.0	15.5	10.1	8.1	7.7	7.1	6.7

Table 1-27. Unemployment Rates of Civilian Workers, by Age, Sex, Race, and Hispanic Origin, 1948–2010
—*Continued*

(Percent of labor force.)

Race, Hispanic origin, sex, and year	16 years and over	16 to 19 years			20 years and over						
		Total	16 to 17 years	18 to 19 years	Total	20 to 24 years	25 to 34 years	35 to 44 years	45 to 54 years	55 to 64 years	65 years and over
ALL RACES											
Men											
1948	3.6	9.8	10.2	9.5	3.2	6.9	2.8	2.4	2.5	3.1	3.4
1949	5.9	14.3	13.7	14.6	5.4	10.4	5.2	4.3	4.3	5.4	5.1
1950	5.1	12.7	13.3	12.3	4.7	8.1	4.4	3.6	4.0	4.9	4.8
1951	2.8	8.1	9.4	7.0	2.5	3.9	2.3	2.0	2.4	2.8	3.5
1952	2.8	8.9	10.5	7.4	2.4	4.6	2.2	1.9	2.2	2.4	3.0
1953	2.8	7.9	8.8	7.2	2.5	5.0	2.2	2.0	2.3	2.8	2.4
1954	5.3	13.5	13.9	13.2	4.9	10.7	4.8	4.1	4.3	4.5	4.4
1955	4.2	11.6	12.5	10.8	3.8	7.7	3.3	3.1	3.2	4.3	4.0
1956	3.8	11.1	11.7	10.5	3.4	6.9	3.3	2.6	3.0	3.5	3.5
1957	4.1	12.4	12.4	12.3	3.6	7.8	3.3	2.8	3.3	3.5	3.4
1958	6.8	17.1	16.3	17.8	6.2	12.7	6.5	5.1	5.3	5.5	5.2
1959	5.2	15.3	15.8	14.9	4.7	8.7	4.7	3.7	4.1	4.5	4.8
1960	5.4	15.3	15.5	15.0	4.7	8.9	4.8	3.8	4.1	4.6	4.2
1961	6.4	17.1	18.3	16.3	5.7	10.8	5.7	4.6	4.9	5.7	5.5
1962	5.2	14.7	16.0	13.8	4.6	8.9	4.5	3.6	3.9	4.6	4.6
1963	5.2	17.2	18.8	15.9	4.5	8.8	4.5	3.5	3.6	4.3	4.5
1964	4.6	15.8	17.1	14.6	3.9	8.1	3.5	2.9	3.2	3.9	4.0
1965	4.0	14.1	16.1	12.4	3.2	6.4	2.9	2.5	2.5	3.3	3.5
1966	3.2	11.7	13.7	10.2	2.5	4.6	2.4	2.0	1.9	2.6	3.1
1967	3.1	12.3	14.5	10.5	2.3	4.7	2.1	1.7	2.0	2.3	2.8
1968	2.9	11.6	13.9	9.7	2.2	5.1	1.9	1.6	1.6	1.9	2.8
1969	2.8	11.4	13.8	9.3	2.1	5.1	1.9	1.5	1.5	1.8	2.2
1970	4.4	15.0	16.9	13.4	3.5	8.4	3.5	2.4	2.4	2.8	3.3
1971	5.3	16.6	18.7	15.0	4.4	10.3	4.4	3.1	3.0	3.3	3.4
1972	5.0	15.9	18.3	14.1	4.0	9.3	3.8	2.7	2.6	3.2	3.6
1973	4.2	13.9	17.0	11.4	3.3	7.3	3.4	2.0	2.1	2.4	3.0
1974	4.9	15.6	18.4	13.3	3.8	8.8	4.0	2.6	2.4	2.6	3.3
1975	7.9	20.1	21.6	19.0	6.8	14.3	6.9	4.9	4.8	4.3	5.4
1976	7.1	19.2	21.4	17.6	5.9	12.1	6.2	4.1	4.0	4.2	5.1
1977	6.3	17.3	19.5	15.6	5.2	10.8	5.7	3.5	3.2	3.6	5.2
1978	5.3	15.8	19.1	13.3	4.3	9.2	4.4	2.8	2.7	2.8	4.2
1979	5.1	15.9	17.9	14.3	4.2	8.7	4.3	2.9	2.7	2.7	3.4
1980	6.9	18.3	20.4	16.7	5.9	12.5	6.7	4.1	3.6	3.4	3.1
1981	7.4	20.1	22.0	18.8	6.3	13.2	6.9	4.5	4.0	3.6	2.9
1982	9.9	24.4	26.4	23.1	8.8	16.4	10.1	6.9	5.6	5.5	3.7
1983	9.9	23.3	25.2	22.2	8.9	15.9	10.1	7.1	6.3	6.1	3.9
1984	7.4	19.6	21.9	18.3	6.6	11.9	7.2	5.2	4.6	5.0	3.0
1985	7.0	19.5	21.9	17.9	6.2	11.4	6.6	4.9	4.6	4.3	3.1
1986	6.9	19.0	20.8	17.7	6.1	11.0	6.7	5.1	4.4	4.3	3.2
1987	6.2	17.8	20.2	16.0	5.4	9.9	5.9	4.4	4.2	3.7	2.6
1988	5.5	16.0	18.2	14.6	4.8	8.9	5.3	3.8	3.5	3.5	2.5
1989	5.2	15.9	18.6	14.2	4.5	8.8	4.8	3.7	3.2	3.5	2.4
1990	5.7	16.3	18.4	15.0	5.0	9.1	5.5	4.1	3.7	3.8	3.0
1991	7.2	19.8	21.8	18.5	6.4	11.6	7.0	5.5	4.8	4.6	3.3
1992	7.9	21.5	24.6	19.5	7.1	12.2	7.8	6.1	5.6	5.8	3.3
1993	7.2	20.4	22.9	18.8	6.4	11.3	7.0	5.6	5.1	5.2	3.2
1994	6.2	19.0	21.0	17.6	5.4	10.2	5.9	4.5	4.0	4.4	4.0
1995	5.6	18.4	21.1	16.5	4.8	9.2	5.1	4.2	3.5	3.6	4.3
1996	5.4	18.1	20.8	16.3	4.6	9.5	4.9	4.0	3.5	3.3	3.4
1997	4.9	16.9	19.1	15.4	4.2	8.9	4.3	3.6	3.1	3.1	3.0
1998	4.4	16.2	19.1	14.1	3.7	8.1	3.9	3.0	2.8	2.8	3.1
1999	4.1	14.7	17.0	13.1	3.5	7.7	3.6	2.8	2.6	2.7	3.0
2000	3.9	14.0	16.8	12.2	3.3	7.3	3.4	2.8	2.4	2.4	3.3
2001	4.8	16.0	19.1	14.0	4.2	9.0	4.3	3.6	3.2	3.3	3.0
2002	5.9	18.1	21.1	16.4	5.3	10.2	5.8	4.5	4.2	4.3	3.4
2003	6.3	19.3	20.7	18.4	5.6	10.6	6.2	5.0	4.4	4.5	4.0
2004	5.6	18.4	22.0	16.3	5.0	10.1	5.5	4.3	3.9	3.9	3.7
2005	5.1	18.6	22.0	16.5	4.4	9.6	4.7	3.7	3.5	3.3	3.4
2006	4.6	16.9	18.6	15.7	4.0	8.7	4.5	3.3	3.1	3.0	2.8
2007	4.7	17.6	19.4	16.5	4.1	8.9	4.7	3.3	3.1	3.2	3.4
2008	6.1	21.2	25.2	19.0	5.4	11.4	6.1	4.6	4.2	3.8	4.5
2009	10.3	27.8	28.7	27.4	9.6	17.0	10.9	8.6	8.2	7.2	6.7
2010	10.5	28.8	31.8	27.4	9.8	17.8	10.9	8.5	8.6	8.0	7.1

Table 1-27. Unemployment Rates of Civilian Workers, by Age, Sex, Race, and Hispanic Origin, 1948–2010
—Continued

(Percent of labor force.)

Race, Hispanic origin, sex, and year	16 years and over	16 to 19 years			20 years and over						
		Total	16 to 17 years	18 to 19 years	Total	20 to 24 years	25 to 34 years	35 to 44 years	45 to 54 years	55 to 64 years	65 years and over
ALL RACES											
Women											
1948	4.1	8.3	10.0	7.4	3.6	4.8	4.3	3.0	3.0	3.1	2.3
1949	6.0	12.3	14.4	11.2	5.3	7.3	5.9	4.7	4.0	4.4	3.8
1950	5.7	11.4	14.2	9.8	5.1	6.9	5.7	4.4	4.5	4.5	3.4
1951	4.4	8.3	10.0	7.2	4.0	4.4	4.5	3.8	3.5	4.0	2.9
1952	3.6	8.0	9.1	7.3	3.2	4.5	3.6	3.0	2.5	2.5	2.2
1953	3.3	7.2	8.5	6.4	2.9	4.3	3.4	2.5	2.3	2.5	1.4
1954	6.0	11.4	12.7	7.7	5.5	7.3	6.6	5.3	4.6	4.6	3.0
1955	4.9	10.2	12.0	9.1	4.4	6.1	5.3	4.0	3.6	3.8	2.3
1956	4.8	11.2	13.2	9.9	4.2	6.3	4.8	3.9	3.6	3.6	2.3
1957	4.7	10.6	12.6	9.4	4.1	6.0	5.3	3.8	3.2	3.0	3.4
1958	6.8	14.3	16.6	12.9	6.1	8.9	7.3	6.2	4.9	4.5	3.7
1959	5.9	13.5	14.4	13.0	5.2	8.1	5.9	5.1	4.2	4.1	2.8
1960	5.9	13.9	15.5	12.9	5.1	8.3	6.3	4.8	4.2	3.4	2.9
1961	7.2	16.3	18.3	15.1	6.3	9.8	7.4	6.4	5.1	4.5	4.0
1962	6.2	14.6	16.7	13.5	5.4	9.1	6.5	5.2	4.1	3.5	4.2
1963	6.5	17.2	20.2	15.2	5.4	8.9	6.9	5.1	4.2	3.6	3.2
1964	6.2	16.6	18.8	15.2	5.2	8.6	6.3	5.0	3.9	3.3	3.3
1965	5.5	15.7	17.2	14.8	4.5	7.3	5.5	4.6	3.2	2.8	2.9
1966	4.8	14.1	16.6	12.6	3.8	6.3	4.5	3.6	2.9	2.3	2.8
1967	5.2	13.5	14.8	12.8	4.2	7.0	5.4	4.1	3.1	2.4	2.7
1968	4.8	14.0	15.9	12.9	3.8	6.7	4.7	3.4	2.4	2.2	2.7
1969	4.7	13.3	15.5	11.8	3.7	6.3	4.6	3.4	2.6	2.2	2.3
1970	5.9	15.6	17.4	14.4	4.8	7.9	5.7	4.4	3.5	2.7	3.1
1971	6.9	17.2	18.7	16.2	5.7	9.6	7.0	5.2	4.0	3.3	3.6
1972	6.6	16.7	18.8	15.2	5.4	9.4	6.2	4.9	3.6	3.3	3.5
1973	6.0	15.3	17.7	13.5	4.9	8.5	5.8	3.9	3.2	2.8	2.9
1974	6.7	16.6	18.2	15.4	5.5	9.5	6.2	4.6	3.7	3.2	3.6
1975	9.3	19.7	21.2	18.7	8.0	12.7	9.1	6.8	5.9	5.1	5.0
1976	8.6	18.7	20.8	17.4	7.4	11.9	8.4	6.1	5.2	4.9	5.0
1977	8.2	18.3	20.5	16.9	7.0	11.2	7.7	5.7	5.1	4.4	4.7
1978	7.2	17.1	19.5	15.3	6.0	10.1	6.7	5.0	4.0	3.2	3.8
1979	6.8	16.4	18.3	15.0	5.7	9.6	6.5	4.6	3.9	3.2	3.3
1980	7.4	17.2	19.6	15.6	6.4	10.4	7.2	5.3	4.5	3.3	3.1
1981	7.9	19.0	20.7	17.9	6.8	11.2	7.7	5.7	4.6	3.8	3.6
1982	9.4	21.9	23.2	21.0	8.3	13.2	9.3	7.0	5.9	5.2	3.2
1983	9.2	21.3	23.7	19.9	8.1	12.9	9.1	6.9	6.0	5.0	3.4
1984	7.6	18.0	20.4	16.6	6.8	10.9	7.4	5.6	5.2	4.3	3.8
1985	7.4	17.6	20.0	16.0	6.6	10.7	7.4	5.5	4.8	4.3	3.3
1986	7.1	17.6	19.6	16.3	6.2	10.3	7.2	5.0	4.5	3.8	2.8
1987	6.2	15.9	18.0	14.3	5.4	9.4	6.2	4.6	3.7	3.1	2.4
1988	5.6	14.4	16.6	12.9	4.9	8.5	5.6	4.1	3.4	2.7	2.9
1989	5.4	14.0	15.7	13.0	4.7	8.3	5.6	3.9	3.2	2.8	2.9
1990	5.5	14.7	17.4	13.1	4.9	8.5	5.6	4.2	3.4	2.8	3.1
1991	6.4	17.5	20.2	15.9	5.7	9.8	6.8	4.8	4.2	3.4	3.3
1992	7.0	18.6	21.5	16.6	6.3	10.3	7.4	5.5	4.6	4.2	4.5
1993	6.6	17.5	19.8	16.1	5.9	9.7	6.8	5.3	4.5	4.0	3.1
1994	6.0	16.2	18.7	14.3	5.4	9.2	6.2	4.7	4.0	3.9	4.0
1995	5.6	16.1	19.2	14.0	4.9	9.0	5.7	4.4	3.2	3.6	3.7
1996	5.4	15.2	16.9	14.0	4.8	9.0	5.5	4.2	3.2	3.4	4.0
1997	5.0	15.0	17.2	13.6	4.4	8.1	5.2	4.0	2.9	2.7	3.6
1998	4.6	12.9	15.1	11.5	4.1	7.8	4.8	3.8	2.7	2.4	3.3
1999	4.3	13.2	15.5	11.6	3.8	7.2	4.4	3.3	2.5	2.6	3.2
2000	4.1	12.1	13.9	10.8	3.6	7.1	4.1	3.3	2.5	2.5	2.7
2001	4.7	13.4	15.2	12.2	4.1	7.5	5.1	3.7	3.0	2.7	2.9
2002	5.6	14.9	16.6	13.8	5.1	9.1	5.9	4.6	3.8	3.5	3.9
2003	5.7	15.6	17.5	14.2	5.1	9.3	5.9	4.9	3.7	3.7	3.6
2004	5.4	15.5	18.5	13.5	4.9	8.7	5.6	4.4	3.7	3.6	3.4
2005	5.1	14.5	16.5	13.1	4.6	7.9	5.6	4.1	3.5	3.3	3.5
2006	4.6	13.8	15.9	12.4	4.1	7.6	4.9	3.9	3.1	2.9	3.0
2007	4.5	13.8	15.7	12.5	4.0	7.3	4.6	3.6	3.2	3.0	3.1
2008	5.4	16.2	19.1	14.3	4.9	8.8	5.5	4.5	3.9	3.7	3.9
2009	8.1	20.7	23.1	19.4	7.5	12.3	8.6	7.1	6.0	6.0	6.1
2010	8.6	22.8	26.5	20.9	8.0	13.0	9.1	7.7	6.8	6.2	6.2

Table 1-27. Unemployment Rates of Civilian Workers, by Age, Sex, Race, and Hispanic Origin, 1948–2010 —Continued

(Percent of labor force.)

Race, Hispanic origin, sex, and year	16 years and over	16 to 19 years			20 years and over						
		Total	16 to 17 years	18 to 19 years	Total	20 to 24 years	25 to 34 years	35 to 44 years	45 to 54 years	55 to 64 years	65 years and over
WHITE											
Both Sexes											
1954	5.0	12.1	13.2	11.3	4.6	8.3	4.6	4.0	4.0	4.3	3.9
1955	3.9	10.4	12.0	9.2	3.4	6.2	3.1	2.9	3.1	3.8	3.4
1956	3.6	10.1	11.5	9.0	3.2	5.7	3.1	2.6	2.9	3.2	3.1
1957	3.8	10.6	11.9	9.6	3.4	6.3	3.3	2.8	3.0	3.2	3.2
1958	6.1	14.4	15.2	13.9	5.6	9.9	5.9	4.8	4.8	4.9	4.6
1959	4.8	13.1	14.4	12.1	4.3	7.3	4.2	3.7	3.8	4.1	4.1
1960	5.0	13.5	14.6	12.6	4.3	7.9	4.5	3.6	3.8	3.9	3.7
1961	6.0	15.3	16.7	14.4	5.3	9.4	5.3	4.5	4.5	5.0	4.8
1962	4.9	13.3	15.3	12.0	4.2	7.9	4.2	3.6	3.6	3.9	4.0
1963	5.0	15.5	17.9	13.7	4.2	7.7	4.4	3.5	3.5	3.8	3.8
1964	4.6	14.8	16.5	13.3	3.8	7.3	3.6	3.2	3.2	3.5	3.5
1965	4.1	13.4	14.8	12.3	3.3	6.1	3.2	2.9	2.5	2.9	3.2
1966	3.4	11.2	13.3	9.7	2.6	4.6	2.6	2.3	2.1	2.4	2.9
1967	3.4	11.0	12.8	9.8	2.7	5.0	2.7	2.3	2.2	2.3	2.7
1968	3.2	11.0	12.9	9.6	2.5	5.2	2.4	2.0	1.8	1.9	2.8
1969	3.1	10.7	13.0	8.9	2.4	5.0	2.5	2.0	1.8	1.8	2.2
1970	4.5	13.5	15.5	11.9	3.7	7.3	3.8	3.0	2.7	2.7	3.2
1971	5.4	15.1	17.0	13.8	4.5	9.0	4.7	3.6	3.3	3.3	3.5
1972	5.1	14.2	16.6	12.3	4.1	8.4	4.1	3.2	2.9	3.1	3.4
1973	4.3	12.6	15.4	10.4	3.5	6.8	3.7	2.5	2.4	2.5	2.9
1974	5.0	14.0	16.3	12.2	4.1	8.0	4.4	3.1	2.8	2.8	3.3
1975	7.8	17.9	19.5	16.7	6.7	12.3	7.1	5.2	4.9	4.5	5.1
1976	7.0	16.9	19.0	15.3	5.9	10.7	6.3	4.5	4.2	4.3	4.9
1977	6.2	15.4	17.9	13.5	5.3	9.3	5.7	4.0	3.8	3.7	4.9
1978	5.2	13.9	17.0	11.5	4.3	8.0	4.6	3.3	3.0	2.7	3.8
1979	5.1	14.0	16.1	12.4	4.2	7.6	4.4	3.2	3.0	2.7	3.1
1980	6.3	15.5	17.9	13.8	5.4	9.9	6.1	4.2	3.7	3.1	2.7
1981	6.7	17.3	19.2	15.9	5.7	10.4	6.3	4.5	3.9	3.5	2.8
1982	8.6	20.4	22.8	18.8	7.6	12.8	8.5	6.3	5.4	5.1	3.1
1983	8.4	19.3	22.0	17.6	7.5	12.1	8.4	6.3	5.7	5.2	3.2
1984	6.5	16.0	18.8	14.3	5.7	9.3	6.2	4.8	4.4	4.4	3.0
1985	6.2	15.7	18.3	13.9	5.5	9.2	5.9	4.6	4.3	4.0	2.9
1986	6.0	15.6	17.6	14.1	5.3	8.7	5.9	4.5	4.1	3.8	2.9
1987	5.3	14.4	16.7	12.7	4.7	8.0	5.1	4.0	3.7	3.2	2.4
1988	4.7	13.1	15.3	11.6	4.1	7.1	4.5	3.5	3.1	3.0	2.4
1989	4.5	12.7	15.2	11.1	3.9	7.2	4.3	3.3	2.9	3.0	2.3
1990	4.8	13.5	15.8	12.1	4.3	7.3	4.6	3.6	3.3	3.2	2.8
1991	6.1	16.5	19.0	14.9	5.5	9.2	6.1	4.7	4.2	4.0	3.1
1992	6.6	17.2	20.3	15.2	6.0	9.5	6.7	5.2	4.8	4.9	3.7
1993	6.1	16.2	19.0	14.4	5.5	8.8	6.0	4.9	4.5	4.3	3.0
1994	5.3	15.1	17.6	13.3	4.7	8.1	5.2	4.0	3.7	3.9	3.8
1995	4.9	14.5	17.3	12.5	4.3	7.7	4.6	3.9	3.1	3.5	3.8
1996	4.7	14.2	16.4	12.6	4.1	7.8	4.4	3.6	3.1	3.2	3.5
1997	4.2	13.6	15.8	12.0	3.6	6.9	3.9	3.3	2.7	2.7	3.0
1998	3.9	12.6	14.8	11.0	3.3	6.5	3.7	2.9	2.6	2.4	2.9
1999	3.7	12.0	14.5	10.2	3.1	6.3	3.3	2.7	2.4	2.5	2.9
2000	3.5	11.4	13.9	9.8	3.0	5.9	3.2	2.6	2.2	2.4	2.8
2001	4.2	12.7	15.3	11.0	3.7	7.0	4.1	3.2	2.8	2.9	2.8
2002	5.1	14.5	16.7	13.2	4.6	8.1	5.2	4.1	3.7	3.7	3.5
2003	5.2	15.2	17.2	13.9	4.7	8.4	5.3	4.3	3.7	3.8	3.7
2004	4.8	15.0	17.9	13.1	4.3	7.9	4.7	3.9	3.4	3.6	3.3
2005	4.4	14.2	16.4	12.7	3.9	7.2	4.3	3.5	3.1	3.0	3.1
2006	4.0	13.2	15.1	11.9	3.6	6.9	4.0	3.2	2.8	2.8	2.8
2007	4.1	13.9	15.5	12.8	3.6	7.0	4.0	3.2	2.9	2.9	3.2
2008	5.2	16.8	19.9	14.9	4.6	9.0	5.1	4.3	3.7	3.4	4.0
2009	8.5	21.8	23.4	21.0	7.9	13.0	8.8	7.4	6.7	6.4	6.2
2010	8.7	23.2	26.3	21.6	8.1	13.5	8.9	7.4	7.2	6.8	6.4

Table 1-27. Unemployment Rates of Civilian Workers, by Age, Sex, Race, and Hispanic Origin, 1948–2010
—Continued

(Percent of labor force.)

Race, Hispanic origin, sex, and year	16 years and over	16 to 19 years			20 years and over						
		Total	16 to 17 years	18 to 19 years	Total	20 to 24 years	25 to 34 years	35 to 44 years	45 to 54 years	55 to 64 years	65 years and over
WHITE											
Men											
1954	4.8	13.4	14.0	13.0	4.4	9.8	4.2	3.6	3.8	4.3	4.2
1955	3.7	11.3	12.2	10.4	3.3	7.0	2.7	2.6	2.9	3.9	3.8
1956	3.4	10.5	11.2	9.7	3.0	6.1	2.8	2.2	2.8	3.1	3.4
1957	3.6	11.5	11.9	11.1	3.2	7.0	2.7	2.5	3.0	3.4	3.2
1958	6.1	15.7	14.9	16.5	5.5	11.7	5.6	4.4	4.8	5.2	5.0
1959	4.6	14.0	15.0	13.0	4.1	7.5	3.8	3.2	3.7	4.2	4.5
1960	4.8	14.0	14.6	13.5	4.2	8.3	4.1	3.3	3.6	4.1	4.0
1961	5.7	15.7	16.5	15.2	5.1	10.1	4.9	4.0	4.4	5.3	5.2
1962	4.6	13.7	15.2	12.7	4.0	8.1	3.8	3.1	3.5	4.1	4.0
1963	4.7	15.9	17.8	14.2	3.9	7.8	3.9	2.9	3.3	4.0	4.1
1964	4.1	14.7	16.1	13.3	3.4	7.4	3.0	2.5	2.9	3.5	3.6
1965	3.6	12.9	14.7	11.3	2.9	5.9	2.6	2.3	2.3	3.1	3.4
1966	2.8	10.5	12.5	8.9	2.2	4.1	2.1	1.7	1.7	2.5	3.0
1967	2.7	10.7	12.7	9.0	2.1	4.2	1.9	1.6	1.8	2.2	2.7
1968	2.6	10.1	12.3	8.3	2.0	4.6	1.7	1.4	1.5	1.7	2.8
1969	2.5	10.0	12.5	7.9	1.9	4.6	1.7	1.4	1.4	1.7	2.2
1970	4.0	13.7	15.7	12.0	3.2	7.8	3.1	2.3	2.3	2.7	3.2
1971	4.9	15.1	17.1	13.5	4.0	9.4	4.0	2.9	2.9	3.2	3.4
1972	4.5	14.2	16.4	12.4	3.6	8.5	3.4	2.5	2.5	3.0	3.3
1973	3.8	12.3	15.2	10.0	3.0	6.6	3.0	1.8	2.0	2.4	2.9
1974	4.4	13.5	16.2	11.5	3.5	7.8	3.6	2.4	2.2	2.5	3.0
1975	7.2	18.3	19.7	17.2	6.2	13.1	6.3	4.5	4.4	4.1	5.0
1976	6.4	17.3	19.7	15.5	5.4	10.9	5.6	3.7	3.7	4.0	4.7
1977	5.5	15.0	17.6	13.0	4.7	9.3	5.0	3.1	3.0	3.3	4.9
1978	4.6	13.5	16.9	10.8	3.7	7.7	3.8	2.5	2.5	2.6	3.9
1979	4.5	13.9	16.1	12.2	3.6	7.5	3.7	2.5	2.5	2.5	3.2
1980	6.1	16.2	18.5	14.5	5.3	11.1	5.9	3.6	3.3	3.1	2.5
1981	6.5	17.9	19.9	16.4	5.6	11.6	6.1	4.0	3.6	3.4	2.4
1982	8.8	21.7	24.2	20.0	7.8	14.3	8.9	6.2	5.3	5.1	3.2
1983	8.8	20.2	22.6	18.7	7.9	13.8	9.0	6.4	5.7	5.6	3.2
1984	6.4	16.8	19.7	15.0	5.7	9.8	6.2	4.6	4.2	4.7	2.6
1985	6.1	16.5	19.2	14.7	5.4	9.7	5.7	4.3	4.1	4.0	2.7
1986	6.0	16.3	18.4	14.7	5.3	9.2	5.8	4.4	4.0	4.0	3.0
1987	5.4	15.5	17.9	13.7	4.8	8.4	5.2	3.9	3.9	3.4	2.5
1988	4.7	13.9	16.1	12.4	4.1	7.4	4.6	3.4	3.2	3.3	2.2
1989	4.5	13.7	16.4	12.0	3.9	7.5	4.1	3.2	2.9	3.1	2.1
1990	4.9	14.3	16.1	13.2	4.3	7.6	4.7	3.5	3.4	3.6	2.8
1991	6.5	17.6	19.7	16.3	5.8	10.2	6.4	5.0	4.4	4.6	3.1
1992	7.0	18.5	21.5	16.5	6.4	10.5	7.0	5.5	5.1	5.5	3.2
1993	6.3	17.7	20.2	16.0	5.7	9.6	6.2	5.0	4.7	4.7	2.9
1994	5.4	16.3	18.5	14.7	4.8	8.8	5.2	3.9	3.7	4.1	3.7
1995	4.9	15.6	18.2	13.8	4.3	7.9	4.5	3.8	3.2	3.4	4.0
1996	4.7	15.5	18.3	13.5	4.1	8.1	4.2	3.5	3.1	3.2	3.2
1997	4.2	14.3	16.3	12.9	3.6	7.3	3.7	3.2	2.8	3.0	2.7
1998	3.9	14.1	17.1	12.1	3.2	6.7	3.5	2.6	2.6	2.6	2.9
1999	3.6	12.6	15.1	10.8	3.0	6.5	3.1	2.4	2.4	2.6	2.9
2000	3.4	12.3	15.3	10.4	2.8	5.9	2.9	2.4	2.2	2.4	3.0
2001	4.2	13.9	17.4	11.7	3.7	7.8	3.8	3.1	2.9	3.2	2.8
2002	5.3	15.9	18.8	14.2	4.7	8.7	5.3	4.1	3.8	4.0	3.4
2003	5.6	17.1	18.5	16.1	5.0	9.1	5.5	4.4	4.0	4.2	3.8
2004	5.0	16.3	19.8	14.2	4.4	8.5	4.8	3.8	3.5	3.7	3.5
2005	4.4	16.1	18.9	14.3	3.8	7.9	4.1	3.3	3.0	3.0	3.1
2006	4.0	14.6	16.5	13.4	3.5	7.3	3.9	3.0	2.7	2.8	2.7
2007	4.2	15.7	17.0	14.8	3.7	7.6	4.1	3.0	2.8	3.0	3.3
2008	5.5	19.1	22.2	17.3	4.9	10.2	5.3	4.3	3.8	3.4	4.1
2009	9.4	25.2	25.9	24.8	8.8	15.3	9.8	8.0	7.7	6.8	6.3
2010	9.6	26.3	29.2	24.8	8.9	15.7	9.9	7.7	7.9	7.5	6.6

Table 1-27. Unemployment Rates of Civilian Workers, by Age, Sex, Race, and Hispanic Origin, 1948–2010
—*Continued*

(Percent of labor force.)

Race, Hispanic origin, sex, and year	16 years and over	16 to 19 years			20 years and over						
		Total	16 to 17 years	18 to 19 years	Total	20 to 24 years	25 to 34 years	35 to 44 years	45 to 54 years	55 to 64 years	65 years and over
WHITE											
Women											
1954	5.5	10.4	12.0	9.4	5.1	6.4	5.7	4.9	4.4	4.5	2.8
1955	4.3	9.1	11.6	7.7	3.9	5.1	4.3	3.8	3.4	3.6	2.2
1956	4.2	9.7	12.1	8.3	3.7	5.1	4.0	3.5	3.3	3.5	2.3
1957	4.3	9.5	11.9	7.8	3.8	5.1	4.7	3.7	3.0	2.9	3.4
1958	6.2	12.7	15.6	11.0	5.6	7.3	6.6	5.6	4.9	4.3	3.5
1959	5.3	12.0	13.3	11.1	4.7	7.0	5.2	4.7	3.9	4.0	2.9
1960	5.3	12.7	14.5	11.5	4.6	7.2	5.7	4.2	4.0	3.3	2.8
1961	6.5	14.8	17.0	13.6	5.7	8.4	6.6	5.6	4.8	4.3	3.8
1962	5.5	12.8	15.6	11.3	4.7	7.7	5.4	4.5	3.7	3.5	4.0
1963	5.8	15.1	18.1	13.2	4.8	7.4	5.8	4.6	3.9	3.5	3.3
1964	5.5	14.9	17.1	13.2	4.6	7.1	5.2	4.5	3.6	3.5	3.4
1965	5.0	14.0	15.0	13.4	4.0	6.3	4.9	4.1	3.0	2.7	2.7
1966	4.3	12.1	14.5	10.7	3.3	5.3	3.7	3.3	2.7	2.2	2.7
1967	4.6	11.5	12.9	10.6	3.8	6.0	4.7	3.7	2.9	2.3	2.6
1968	4.3	12.1	13.9	11.0	3.4	5.9	3.9	3.1	2.3	2.1	2.8
1969	4.2	11.5	13.7	10.0	3.4	5.5	4.2	3.2	2.4	2.1	2.4
1970	5.4	13.4	15.3	11.9	4.4	6.9	5.3	4.3	3.4	2.6	3.3
1971	6.3	15.1	16.7	14.1	5.3	8.5	6.3	4.9	3.9	3.3	3.6
1972	5.9	14.2	17.0	12.3	4.9	8.2	5.5	4.4	3.5	3.3	3.7
1973	5.3	13.0	15.8	10.9	4.3	7.1	5.1	3.7	3.2	2.7	2.8
1974	6.1	14.5	16.4	13.0	5.1	8.2	5.8	4.3	3.6	3.2	3.9
1975	8.6	17.4	19.2	16.1	7.5	11.2	8.4	6.5	5.8	5.0	5.3
1976	7.9	16.4	18.2	15.1	6.8	10.4	7.6	5.8	5.0	4.8	5.3
1977	7.3	15.9	18.2	14.2	6.2	9.3	6.7	5.3	5.0	4.4	4.9
1978	6.2	14.4	17.1	12.4	5.2	8.3	5.8	4.5	3.8	3.0	3.7
1979	5.9	14.0	15.9	12.5	5.0	7.8	5.6	4.2	3.7	3.0	3.1
1980	6.5	14.8	17.3	13.1	5.6	8.5	6.3	4.9	4.3	3.1	3.0
1981	6.9	16.6	18.4	15.3	5.9	9.1	6.6	5.1	4.2	3.7	3.4
1982	8.3	19.0	21.2	17.6	7.3	10.9	8.0	6.4	5.5	5.0	3.1
1983	7.9	18.3	21.4	16.4	6.9	10.3	7.6	6.2	5.5	4.7	3.1
1984	6.5	15.2	17.8	13.6	5.8	8.8	6.1	5.0	4.8	4.0	3.7
1985	6.4	14.8	17.2	13.1	5.7	8.5	6.2	4.9	4.5	4.1	3.1
1986	6.1	14.9	16.7	13.6	5.4	8.1	6.1	4.5	4.3	3.7	2.6
1987	5.2	13.4	15.5	11.7	4.6	7.4	5.0	4.1	3.3	2.9	2.4
1988	4.7	12.3	14.4	10.8	4.1	6.7	4.5	3.7	3.1	2.5	2.6
1989	4.5	11.5	13.8	10.1	4.0	6.8	4.5	3.4	2.9	2.7	2.5
1990	4.7	12.6	15.5	10.9	4.1	6.8	4.6	3.7	3.2	2.7	2.8
1991	5.6	15.2	18.2	13.3	5.0	8.1	5.7	4.3	4.0	3.3	3.1
1992	6.1	15.8	18.9	13.7	5.5	8.3	6.2	4.9	4.3	4.0	4.5
1993	5.7	14.7	17.8	12.6	5.2	7.9	5.8	4.7	4.3	3.9	3.0
1994	5.2	13.8	16.6	11.8	4.6	7.4	5.1	4.2	3.7	3.7	3.9
1995	4.8	13.4	16.4	11.2	4.3	7.4	4.7	3.9	3.0	3.5	3.5
1996	4.7	12.9	14.4	11.7	4.1	7.4	4.6	3.8	3.1	3.1	3.8
1997	4.2	12.8	15.2	11.1	3.7	6.4	4.2	3.4	2.6	2.4	3.4
1998	3.9	10.9	12.4	9.8	3.4	6.3	3.9	3.3	2.5	2.2	3.0
1999	3.8	11.3	13.9	9.6	3.3	6.1	3.6	3.0	2.3	2.5	2.9
2000	3.6	10.4	12.5	9.0	3.1	5.8	3.5	2.9	2.3	2.4	2.4
2001	4.1	11.4	13.1	10.2	3.6	6.1	4.5	3.3	2.7	2.5	2.7
2002	4.9	13.1	14.6	12.1	4.4	7.4	5.0	4.1	3.5	3.3	3.5
2003	4.8	13.3	15.9	11.5	4.4	7.6	4.9	4.2	3.3	3.4	3.5
2004	4.7	13.6	16.1	11.9	4.2	7.1	4.6	3.9	3.3	3.5	3.1
2005	4.4	12.3	14.0	11.1	3.9	6.4	4.7	3.6	3.1	3.0	3.2
2006	4.0	11.7	13.8	10.2	3.6	6.3	4.1	3.4	2.9	2.8	3.0
2007	4.0	12.1	14.1	10.6	3.6	6.2	3.9	3.4	2.9	2.8	3.1
2008	4.9	14.4	17.6	12.3	4.4	7.5	4.8	4.3	3.5	3.5	3.8
2009	7.3	18.4	20.9	17.0	6.8	10.4	7.6	6.7	5.6	5.8	6.0
2010	7.7	20.0	23.4	18.1	7.2	11.0	7.7	7.1	6.4	6.0	6.0

Table 1-27. Unemployment Rates of Civilian Workers, by Age, Sex, Race, and Hispanic Origin, 1948–2010
—Continued

(Percent of labor force.)

Race, Hispanic origin, sex, and year	16 years and over	16 to 19 years			20 years and over						
		Total	16 to 17 years	18 to 19 years	Total	20 to 24 years	25 to 34 years	35 to 44 years	45 to 54 years	55 to 64 years	65 years and over
BLACK											
Both Sexes											
1973	9.4	31.5	37.0	28.1	7.2	15.5	8.1	4.7	3.5	3.2	3.5
1974	10.5	35.0	40.0	31.8	8.0	17.5	8.5	5.4	4.3	3.6	3.9
1975	14.8	39.5	41.6	38.1	12.3	24.5	13.0	8.9	8.3	5.9	6.6
1976	14.0	39.3	44.2	36.7	11.5	22.7	12.8	8.0	6.7	5.9	5.9
1977	14.0	41.1	44.5	39.2	11.5	24.2	12.7	7.4	5.3	5.5	5.9
1978	12.8	38.7	43.9	35.7	10.2	21.8	10.8	6.4	5.2	4.8	5.8
1979	12.3	36.5	40.2	34.4	10.1	20.6	10.8	6.7	5.2	4.9	5.3
1980	14.3	38.5	41.1	37.1	12.1	23.6	13.3	8.2	6.8	5.4	6.9
1981	15.6	41.4	44.8	39.5	13.4	26.4	14.7	9.5	7.4	5.5	7.0
1982	18.9	48.0	48.6	47.8	16.6	30.6	19.0	12.1	8.7	8.3	7.1
1983	19.5	48.5	50.5	47.6	17.3	31.6	19.0	12.4	10.7	9.2	9.2
1984	15.9	42.7	45.7	41.2	13.9	26.1	15.2	9.9	8.2	7.4	6.5
1985	15.1	40.2	43.6	38.3	13.1	24.5	14.5	9.5	8.2	7.0	7.0
1986	14.5	39.3	43.0	37.2	12.7	24.1	14.0	9.6	7.1	6.6	4.5
1987	13.0	34.7	39.7	31.6	11.3	21.8	12.8	8.4	6.8	5.6	3.9
1988	11.7	32.4	35.1	30.7	10.2	19.6	11.9	7.5	5.9	4.8	5.5
1989	11.4	32.4	32.9	32.2	9.9	18.0	11.5	7.6	5.6	5.2	6.9
1990	11.4	30.9	36.5	27.8	10.1	19.9	11.7	7.8	5.3	4.6	5.3
1991	12.5	36.1	39.5	34.4	11.1	21.6	12.7	8.5	7.4	4.4	5.2
1992	14.2	39.7	44.7	37.1	12.6	23.8	14.2	10.5	8.3	6.2	4.9
1993	13.0	38.8	39.7	38.4	11.4	21.9	12.6	9.5	6.9	7.1	4.7
1994	11.5	35.2	36.1	34.6	10.0	19.5	11.1	8.5	5.6	5.4	6.2
1995	10.4	35.7	39.1	33.4	8.7	17.7	9.9	7.3	4.8	4.0	6.7
1996	10.5	33.6	36.3	31.7	9.0	18.8	10.5	7.3	5.0	4.4	5.3
1997	10.0	32.4	35.0	30.8	8.6	18.3	9.9	7.0	5.0	4.2	6.1
1998	8.9	27.6	33.6	24.2	7.7	16.8	8.4	6.5	4.4	3.9	5.6
1999	8.0	27.9	31.0	26.2	6.8	14.6	7.6	5.3	4.0	3.9	5.0
2000	7.6	24.5	26.9	22.9	6.5	15.0	6.7	5.6	4.1	3.0	6.1
2001	8.6	29.0	30.8	27.9	7.4	16.3	8.1	6.3	4.8	3.9	4.3
2002	10.2	29.8	34.9	27.2	9.1	19.1	9.9	7.8	6.3	5.4	5.9
2003	10.8	33.0	32.2	33.5	9.7	19.8	10.9	8.6	6.2	6.3	5.4
2004	10.4	31.7	37.8	28.3	9.4	18.4	10.8	7.8	6.9	5.6	5.5
2005	10.0	33.3	41.2	29.0	8.8	18.3	10.2	7.1	6.0	5.6	6.9
2006	8.9	29.1	32.2	27.3	7.9	16.2	9.3	6.3	5.7	4.6	4.7
2007	8.3	29.4	32.6	27.4	7.2	15.2	8.6	5.4	5.4	4.3	4.5
2008	10.1	31.2	36.3	28.5	9.1	17.9	10.6	7.0	7.0	6.1	7.5
2009	14.8	39.5	43.1	37.8	13.7	24.9	16.7	11.7	10.4	8.4	8.5
2010	16.0	43.0	47.8	40.9	14.9	26.0	17.6	13.0	11.5	9.7	9.2
BLACK											
Men											
1973	8.0	27.8	35.7	23.0	6.0	13.2	6.2	3.9	3.2	3.2	3.3
1974	9.8	33.1	39.9	28.3	7.4	16.2	8.1	4.3	4.2	3.6	5.3
1975	14.8	38.1	41.9	35.9	12.5	24.7	12.7	8.7	9.3	6.3	8.7
1976	13.7	37.5	40.8	36.0	11.4	22.6	12.0	7.5	7.3	6.3	8.7
1977	13.3	39.2	41.0	38.2	10.7	23.0	11.8	6.2	4.9	6.0	7.8
1978	11.8	36.7	43.0	32.9	9.3	21.0	9.8	5.1	4.9	4.4	6.6
1979	11.4	34.2	37.9	32.2	9.3	18.7	9.6	6.3	5.2	5.1	6.4
1980	14.5	37.5	39.7	36.2	12.4	23.7	13.4	8.2	7.2	6.2	8.7
1981	15.7	40.7	43.2	39.2	13.5	26.4	14.4	9.3	7.8	6.1	7.5
1982	20.1	48.9	52.7	47.1	17.8	31.5	20.1	13.4	9.0	10.3	9.3
1983	20.3	48.8	52.2	47.3	18.1	31.4	19.4	13.5	11.4	11.0	11.8
1984	16.4	42.7	44.0	42.2	14.3	26.6	15.0	10.4	7.9	8.9	7.9
1985	15.3	41.0	42.9	40.0	13.2	23.5	13.8	9.6	9.7	7.9	8.9
1986	14.8	39.3	41.4	38.2	12.9	23.5	13.5	10.9	7.8	8.0	4.3
1987	12.7	34.4	39.0	31.6	11.1	20.3	12.2	8.7	6.7	6.6	4.3
1988	11.7	32.7	34.4	31.7	10.1	19.4	11.0	7.6	6.2	5.2	5.6
1989	11.5	31.9	34.4	30.3	10.0	17.9	10.5	8.4	6.2	6.2	7.4
1990	11.9	31.9	38.8	28.0	10.4	20.1	11.5	8.4	6.3	5.4	4.6
1991	13.0	36.3	39.0	34.8	11.5	22.4	11.9	9.5	8.6	5.0	6.1
1992	15.2	42.0	47.5	39.1	13.5	24.6	14.2	11.2	10.3	8.1	4.9
1993	13.8	40.1	42.7	38.6	12.1	23.0	12.3	10.5	8.1	9.0	5.8
1994	12.0	37.6	39.3	36.5	10.3	19.4	10.6	9.1	6.5	6.0	8.2
1995	10.6	37.1	39.7	35.4	8.8	17.6	9.3	7.6	5.5	4.4	7.6
1996	11.1	36.9	39.9	34.9	9.4	19.2	10.1	7.8	6.3	5.2	5.0
1997	10.2	36.5	39.5	34.4	8.5	19.8	8.7	6.7	5.6	4.2	5.5
1998	8.9	30.1	33.9	27.9	7.4	18.0	7.3	6.2	4.4	4.5	5.2
1999	8.2	30.9	33.3	29.4	6.7	16.2	6.9	5.2	4.3	3.9	5.0
2000	8.0	26.2	28.5	24.7	6.9	16.6	6.7	5.8	4.8	2.7	6.3
2001	9.3	30.4	30.5	30.4	8.0	17.6	8.3	6.9	5.5	4.8	4.0
2002	10.7	31.3	36.6	28.7	9.5	20.0	9.4	8.0	7.4	6.1	5.0
2003	11.6	36.0	35.6	36.3	10.3	20.9	11.3	9.2	6.7	6.8	5.6
2004	11.1	35.6	40.8	32.7	9.9	20.3	10.9	8.0	7.2	6.4	4.2
2005	10.5	36.3	45.1	31.5	9.2	20.5	9.7	7.0	6.7	5.9	7.1
2006	9.5	32.7	34.8	31.5	8.3	17.2	9.5	5.9	6.3	5.5	5.8
2007	9.1	33.8	40.1	30.2	7.9	16.9	9.1	5.6	5.8	5.2	5.0
2008	11.4	35.9	43.9	32.0	10.2	19.3	11.8	7.7	7.7	7.1	9.5
2009	17.5	46.0	49.3	44.5	16.3	27.7	19.9	14.0	12.4	10.1	10.6
2010	18.4	45.4	49.4	43.9	17.3	29.8	19.3	14.9	14.4	12.2	10.4

Table 1-27. Unemployment Rates of Civilian Workers, by Age, Sex, Race, and Hispanic Origin, 1948–2010
—Continued

(Percent of labor force.)

Race, Hispanic origin, sex, and year	16 years and over	16 to 19 years			20 years and over						
		Total	16 to 17 years	18 to 19 years	Total	20 to 24 years	25 to 34 years	35 to 44 years	45 to 54 years	55 to 64 years	65 years and over
BLACK											
Women											
1973	11.1	36.1	38.6	34.2	8.6	18.4	10.3	5.6	3.9	3.3	3.7
1974	11.3	37.4	40.2	36.0	8.8	19.0	9.0	6.6	4.4	3.6	1.9
1975	14.8	41.0	41.2	40.6	12.2	24.3	13.4	9.0	7.0	5.3	3.6
1976	14.3	41.6	48.4	37.6	11.7	22.8	13.6	8.5	5.9	5.4	2.4
1977	14.9	43.4	49.5	40.4	12.3	25.5	13.6	8.7	5.8	4.8	3.4
1978	13.8	40.8	45.0	38.7	11.2	22.7	11.9	7.8	5.6	5.2	4.7
1979	13.3	39.1	42.7	36.9	10.9	22.6	12.1	7.2	5.2	4.7	3.9
1980	14.0	39.8	42.9	38.2	11.9	23.5	13.2	8.2	6.4	4.5	4.9
1981	15.6	42.2	46.5	39.8	13.4	26.4	14.9	9.8	6.9	4.7	6.0
1982	17.6	47.1	44.2	48.6	15.4	29.6	17.8	10.7	8.5	6.1	4.5
1983	18.6	48.2	48.6	48.0	16.5	31.8	18.6	11.4	9.9	7.3	6.3
1984	15.4	42.6	47.5	40.2	13.5	25.6	15.4	9.4	8.6	5.9	4.9
1985	14.9	39.2	44.3	36.4	13.1	25.6	15.1	9.3	6.8	6.0	5.2
1986	14.2	39.2	44.6	36.1	12.4	24.7	14.6	8.5	6.4	5.0	4.9
1987	13.2	34.9	40.5	31.7	11.6	23.3	13.5	8.1	6.9	4.5	3.4
1988	11.7	32.0	35.9	29.6	10.4	19.8	12.7	7.4	5.6	4.3	5.4
1989	11.4	33.0	31.1	34.0	9.8	18.1	12.5	7.0	5.0	4.2	6.4
1990	10.9	29.9	34.1	27.6	9.7	19.6	11.9	7.2	4.3	3.6	5.9
1991	12.0	36.0	40.1	33.9	10.6	20.7	13.4	7.6	6.2	3.8	4.4
1992	13.2	37.2	41.7	34.8	11.8	23.1	14.1	9.8	6.4	4.2	5.0
1993	12.1	37.4	36.1	38.1	10.7	20.9	12.9	8.6	5.8	5.1	3.6
1994	11.0	32.6	32.9	32.5	9.8	19.6	11.7	8.0	4.9	4.9	4.4
1995	10.2	34.3	38.5	31.5	8.6	17.8	10.5	7.0	4.2	3.6	. . .
1996	10.0	30.3	32.8	28.6	8.7	18.4	11.0	6.9	3.8	3.8	5.6
1997	9.9	28.7	30.3	27.8	8.8	17.1	10.9	7.2	4.4	4.1	6.6
1998	9.0	25.3	33.2	20.9	7.9	15.7	9.5	6.7	4.3	3.4	6.1
1999	7.8	25.1	28.5	23.3	6.8	13.4	8.3	5.5	3.8	3.9	5.0
2000	7.1	22.8	25.3	21.3	6.2	13.6	6.8	5.5	3.4	3.3	6.0
2001	8.1	27.5	31.2	25.4	7.0	15.3	8.0	5.8	4.3	3.1	4.6
2002	9.8	28.3	33.2	25.6	8.8	18.3	10.2	7.7	5.3	4.7	6.9
2003	10.2	30.3	29.1	31.1	9.2	18.8	10.5	8.1	5.8	5.9	5.3
2004	9.8	28.2	35.2	24.3	8.9	16.6	10.7	7.6	6.5	4.8	6.8
2005	9.5	30.3	37.3	26.6	8.5	16.3	10.6	7.2	5.4	5.3	6.6
2006	8.4	25.9	29.9	23.6	7.5	15.2	9.0	6.7	5.1	3.9	3.7
2007	7.5	25.3	26.4	24.7	6.7	13.6	8.1	5.3	5.0	3.7	4.0
2008	8.9	26.8	29.9	25.0	8.1	16.6	9.5	6.4	6.3	5.3	5.8
2009	12.4	33.4	37.2	31.7	11.5	22.2	13.8	9.7	8.7	7.1	6.6
2010	13.8	40.5	46.4	37.7	12.8	22.6	16.0	11.4	9.1	7.6	8.2
HISPANIC[1]											
Both Sexes											
1974	8.1	19.8	23.5	17.2	6.6	9.8	6.3	5.9	4.6	6.1	6.3
1975	12.2	27.7	30.0	26.5	10.3	16.7	9.9	8.6	8.1	7.7	9.9
1976	11.5	23.8	29.2	19.2	10.1	15.9	9.1	8.2	8.4	8.8	12.6
1977	10.1	22.9	27.0	19.6	8.5	12.0	8.6	6.1	7.3	8.2	9.2
1978	9.1	20.7	28.3	15.1	7.7	10.9	8.0	6.5	5.8	5.0	7.5
1979	8.3	19.2	26.0	14.9	7.0	10.4	6.7	6.2	5.2	6.0	5.7
1980	10.1	22.5	27.6	19.5	8.6	12.1	9.1	7.7	5.7	5.9	6.0
1981	10.4	23.9	28.0	21.7	9.1	13.9	8.8	7.4	6.4	7.3	5.4
1982	13.8	29.9	38.1	25.9	12.3	17.7	12.3	10.7	8.4	10.1	6.5
1983	13.7	28.4	33.8	25.8	12.3	16.7	11.9	11.3	10.0	10.9	5.8
1984	10.7	24.1	28.9	21.6	9.5	12.4	9.7	8.2	7.5	9.7	6.1
1985	10.5	24.3	27.8	22.5	9.4	12.6	9.9	7.7	7.4	7.8	8.1
1986	10.6	24.7	28.1	22.9	9.5	12.9	9.6	8.4	7.8	7.3	10.1
1987	8.8	22.3	27.7	19.5	7.8	10.6	7.7	6.7	6.9	6.0	6.5
1988	8.2	22.0	27.1	19.3	7.0	9.8	7.1	6.0	6.0	5.8	5.6
1989	8.0	19.4	26.4	16.0	7.2	10.7	7.0	5.9	6.3	5.8	5.3
1990	8.2	19.5	24.5	16.9	7.2	9.1	7.3	6.6	6.4	5.6	6.0
1991	10.0	22.9	31.9	18.7	9.0	11.6	9.2	8.1	8.0	6.5	7.0
1992	11.6	27.5	35.7	23.4	10.4	13.2	10.4	9.8	8.8	8.6	8.1
1993	10.8	26.1	35.1	21.8	9.7	13.1	9.3	9.1	8.6	8.0	6.6
1994	9.9	24.5	31.7	20.6	8.9	11.8	9.0	7.7	8.1	7.3	7.9
1995	9.3	24.1	33.1	19.5	8.2	11.5	8.2	7.2	6.4	7.5	10.6
1996	8.9	23.6	30.0	20.3	7.8	11.8	7.3	7.3	6.0	7.3	8.2
1997	7.7	21.6	27.7	18.4	6.8	10.3	6.3	6.4	5.1	6.5	6.8
1998	7.2	21.3	28.0	18.1	6.1	9.4	5.9	5.5	4.6	5.3	6.4
1999	6.4	18.6	23.7	16.3	5.5	8.3	5.4	4.8	4.8	4.5	5.0
2000	5.7	16.6	22.5	13.9	4.9	7.5	4.8	4.5	3.3	4.5	5.7
2001	6.6	17.7	24.0	15.0	5.8	8.1	5.9	5.2	4.3	5.6	4.5
2002	7.5	20.1	24.2	18.2	6.7	9.9	6.6	6.0	5.5	5.7	6.8
2003	7.7	20.0	24.6	17.7	7.0	10.2	7.0	6.0	6.3	5.7	3.9
2004	7.0	20.4	29.0	16.8	6.2	9.3	6.3	5.3	5.2	5.8	6.0
2005	6.0	18.4	23.6	16.0	5.3	8.6	5.3	4.5	4.4	4.4	4.9
2006	5.2	15.9	20.4	13.6	4.6	7.2	4.7	4.3	3.7	3.3	3.9
2007	5.6	18.1	22.5	16.0	5.0	7.8	4.9	4.3	4.3	4.5	4.9
2008	7.6	22.4	29.8	19.0	6.8	11.5	6.7	5.8	6.3	4.8	7.8
2009	12.1	30.2	36.3	27.8	11.2	16.2	11.4	10.2	10.1	10.0	8.0
2010	12.5	32.2	37.6	30.2	11.6	17.4	11.3	10.3	10.8	10.3	9.5

[1] May be of any race.
. . . = Not available.

Table 1-27. Unemployment Rates of Civilian Workers, by Age, Sex, Race, and Hispanic Origin, 1948–2010
—Continued

(Percent of labor force.)

Race, Hispanic origin, sex, and year	16 years and over	16 to 19 years			20 years and over						
		Total	16 to 17 years	18 to 19 years	Total	20 to 24 years	25 to 34 years	35 to 44 years	45 to 54 years	55 to 64 years	65 years and over
HISPANIC[1]											
Men											
1974	7.3	19.0	22.0	17.1	6.0	9.9	5.5	5.0	4.3	5.4	...
1975	11.4	27.6	29.3	26.5	9.6	16.3	9.6	7.9	7.0	6.8	...
1976	10.8	23.3	28.7	19.7	9.4	16.0	8.1	7.0	7.4	8.7	...
1977	9.0	20.9	25.9	18.2	7.7	11.7	7.9	4.9	5.4	7.4	...
1978	7.7	19.7	27.5	13.9	6.4	9.4	6.6	4.8	4.8	4.4	...
1979	7.0	17.5	23.5	13.8	5.8	9.2	5.3	5.1	4.4	5.0	...
1980	9.7	21.9	26.2	19.3	8.3	12.2	8.3	7.1	6.0	5.9	...
1981	10.2	24.3	30.9	20.3	8.8	14.1	8.9	6.5	5.9	6.7	...
1982	13.6	31.3	40.2	26.8	12.1	18.2	12.4	9.9	7.5	10.0	...
1983	13.6	28.7	34.7	25.9	12.2	17.0	11.6	10.8	10.3	11.7	...
1984	10.5	25.2	31.5	22.2	9.3	12.5	9.2	7.6	7.2	10.2	...
1985	10.2	24.7	29.1	22.4	9.1	12.9	9.6	7.2	6.8	7.0	...
1986	10.5	24.5	28.5	22.4	9.5	13.0	9.5	8.5	7.0	8.0	...
1987	8.7	22.2	28.2	19.3	7.8	10.2	7.6	6.9	7.1	6.7	...
1988	8.1	22.7	29.5	19.5	7.0	9.2	7.0	5.9	6.1	6.7	...
1989	7.6	20.2	27.6	16.8	6.6	9.7	5.9	5.7	6.0	6.6	...
1990	8.0	19.5	24.0	17.4	7.0	8.4	6.9	6.5	6.8	6.5	...
1991	10.3	23.5	33.6	19.2	9.3	11.6	9.3	8.5	7.9	8.1	...
1992	11.7	28.2	36.6	24.0	10.5	13.7	10.1	9.8	8.9	10.2	...
1993	10.6	25.9	34.5	21.9	9.5	12.6	9.0	8.8	8.8	8.5	...
1994	9.4	26.3	33.3	22.5	8.3	10.8	8.4	6.6	8.1	7.4	10.5
1995	8.8	25.3	34.8	20.2	7.7	10.6	7.5	6.7	5.9	7.9	12.9
1996	7.9	22.5	31.5	18.4	6.9	10.3	6.6	6.3	5.1	6.7	8.3
1997	7.0	20.8	26.5	17.9	6.1	9.8	5.1	5.4	4.8	6.8	7.2
1998	6.4	20.6	29.0	16.4	5.4	8.9	5.2	4.5	4.2	5.3	5.0
1999	5.6	17.8	23.4	15.3	4.7	7.8	4.1	3.8	4.5	4.6	5.0
2000	5.0	15.7	22.3	12.8	4.2	6.6	3.7	3.8	3.1	4.1	6.2
2001	5.9	17.1	25.8	13.4	5.2	8.1	4.6	4.5	3.8	6.3	4.8
2002	7.2	20.2	22.9	19.1	6.4	9.3	6.1	5.4	5.5	6.2	6.3
2003	7.2	21.9	25.9	20.1	6.4	9.6	6.3	5.3	6.0	6.0	3.6
2004	6.5	21.2	30.7	17.6	5.8	9.4	5.5	4.5	4.7	5.7	6.9
2005	5.4	19.3	23.4	17.5	4.7	8.2	4.3	3.9	4.0	4.0	4.8
2006	4.8	17.3	22.6	14.8	4.2	6.7	4.2	3.6	3.4	3.5	3.7
2007	5.3	19.7	23.4	18.0	4.6	7.4	4.5	3.8	4.4	3.9	5.5
2008	7.6	23.4	30.9	19.9	6.8	11.8	6.6	5.6	6.2	5.1	7.8
2009	12.5	33.8	41.1	31.1	11.6	16.6	11.6	10.5	10.5	11.2	7.8
2010	12.7	34.6	41.0	32.6	11.7	18.2	11.6	9.8	11.2	10.6	9.4
HISPANIC[1]											
Women											
1973	9.0	20.7	26.8	16.7	7.3	9.0	6.9	8.3	5.1	5.6	...
1974	9.4	20.8	25.3	17.4	7.7	9.7	7.7	7.5	5.3	7.5	...
1975	13.5	27.9	31.0	26.4	11.5	17.2	10.5	9.9	10.0	9.3	...
1976	12.7	22.2	30.3	18.7	11.4	15.8	10.8	10.0	9.8	9.0	...
1977	11.9	24.4	28.5	21.9	10.1	12.1	9.8	8.2	10.6	11.0	...
1978	11.3	21.8	29.9	16.6	9.8	13.0	10.3	9.2	7.4	7.2	...
1979	10.3	21.2	30.0	15.8	8.9	12.1	8.9	7.7	7.1	7.9	...
1980	10.7	23.4	29.7	19.8	9.2	12.0	10.6	8.6	5.3	5.8	...
1981	10.8	23.4	23.5	23.4	9.5	13.5	8.7	8.9	7.2	8.4	...
1982	14.1	28.2	35.1	25.0	12.5	16.8	12.2	11.9	9.9	10.4	...
1983	13.8	28.0	32.5	25.7	12.4	16.2	12.5	12.2	9.7	9.6	...
1984	11.1	22.8	26.1	21.0	9.9	12.2	10.3	9.1	7.9	8.8	...
1985	11.0	23.8	26.2	22.6	9.9	12.1	10.6	8.5	8.1	9.2	...
1986	10.8	25.1	27.6	23.6	9.6	12.9	9.8	8.2	8.9	6.2	...
1987	8.9	22.4	27.1	19.9	7.7	11.4	7.8	6.5	6.7	5.0	...
1988	8.3	21.0	24.5	18.9	7.1	10.7	7.2	6.2	5.9	4.6	...
1989	8.8	18.2	24.7	14.9	8.0	12.2	8.6	6.3	6.7	4.5	...
1990	8.4	19.4	25.4	16.2	7.5	10.4	8.0	6.7	6.0	4.3	...
1991	9.6	21.9	29.6	17.9	8.6	11.7	9.1	7.6	8.1	4.1	...
1992	11.4	26.4	34.5	22.4	10.2	12.4	11.0	9.7	8.5	6.2	...
1993	11.0	26.3	36.0	21.7	9.9	14.0	9.9	9.5	8.3	7.2	...
1994	10.7	22.2	29.7	18.1	9.8	13.5	10.1	9.2	8.0	7.1	3.6
1995	10.0	22.6	30.7	18.7	8.9	13.0	9.5	7.9	7.0	6.8	6.4
1996	10.2	25.1	28.2	23.3	9.2	14.1	8.5	8.7	7.2	8.1	8.0
1997	8.9	22.7	29.2	19.1	7.9	11.0	8.2	7.7	5.5	6.1	6.0
1998	8.2	22.1	26.4	20.2	7.1	10.1	7.2	6.9	5.1	5.4	8.8
1999	7.6	19.8	24.0	17.7	6.6	9.1	7.3	6.3	5.1	4.3	4.8
2000	6.8	18.0	22.7	15.6	5.9	9.0	6.4	5.4	3.6	5.0	4.8
2001	7.5	18.5	21.6	17.1	6.6	8.2	7.8	6.2	4.8	4.8	4.0
2002	8.0	19.9	25.8	17.0	7.2	10.8	7.4	6.7	5.5	5.0	7.5
2003	8.4	17.7	23.2	14.4	7.8	11.3	8.2	7.1	6.8	5.3	4.4
2004	7.6	19.3	27.0	15.5	7.0	9.1	7.6	6.4	5.8	5.8	4.6
2005	6.9	17.2	23.8	14.0	6.3	9.2	7.1	5.5	4.8	5.0	5.1
2006	5.9	14.1	18.1	11.9	5.3	8.1	5.5	5.5	4.2	3.1	4.2
2007	6.1	16.1	21.3	13.6	5.5	8.5	5.6	5.1	4.3	5.2	4.0
2008	7.7	21.1	28.1	18.0	6.9	11.1	6.8	6.0	6.4	4.4	7.7
2009	11.5	25.8	30.8	23.8	10.6	15.7	10.9	9.7	9.6	8.5	8.3
2010	12.3	29.1	34.2	27.0	11.4	16.2	10.9	11.1	10.4	9.9	9.6

[1]May be of any race.
. . . = Not available.

Table 1-28. Unemployed Persons and Unemployment Rates, by Selected Occupation, 2000–2010

(Thousands of people, percent of civilian labor force.)

Occupation	2000	2001	2002	2003	2004	2005	2006	2007	2008	2009	2010
Total Unemployed Persons, 16 Years and Over[1] ...	5 692	6 801	8 378	8 774	8 149	7 591	7 001	7 078	8 924	14 265	14 825
Management, professional, and related	827	1 102	1 482	1 556	1 346	1 172	1 065	1 090	1 463	2 531	2 566
Management, business, and financial operations ...	320	455	622	627	544	464	427	429	619	1 105	1 117
Professional and related	507	647	859	929	801	708	638	662	844	1 427	1 449
Services	1 132	1 311	1 544	1 681	1 617	1 587	1 485	1 521	1 769	2 605	2 819
Sales and office	1 446	1 652	2 110	2 070	1 937	1 820	1 667	1 638	2 006	3 143	3 315
Sales and related	673	779	998	995	912	874	812	835	980	1 501	1 596
Office and administrative support	773	873	1 112	1 076	1 025	946	856	804	1 026	1 642	1 719
Natural resources, construction, and maintenance	758	943	1 155	1 244	1 140	1 069	1 007	1 052	1 421	2 464	2 504
Farming, fishing, and forestry	133	163	142	136	132	103	101	89	112	179	193
Construction and extraction	507	626	788	814	786	751	699	781	1 067	1 825	1 809
Installation, maintenance, and repair	119	154	225	295	222	214	207	182	243	459	503
Production, transportation, and material moving	1 081	1 318	1 530	1 555	1 393	1 245	1 127	1 128	1 474	2 453	2 365
Production	575	759	848	807	714	677	544	564	746	1 322	1 206
Transportation and material moving	505	559	682	748	679	568	583	564	727	1 131	1 159
Total Unemployment Rate, 16 Years and Over[1]	4.0	4.7	5.8	6.0	5.5	5.1	4.6	4.6	5.8	9.3	9.6
Management, professional, and related	1.8	2.3	3.0	3.1	2.7	2.3	2.1	2.1	2.7	4.6	4.7
Management, business, and financial operations ...	1.6	2.2	3.0	3.1	2.6	2.2	2.0	1.9	2.7	4.9	5.1
Professional and related	1.9	2.3	3.0	3.2	2.8	2.4	2.1	2.1	2.7	4.4	4.5
Services	5.2	5.8	6.6	7.1	6.6	6.4	5.9	5.9	6.7	9.6	10.3
Sales and office	3.8	4.4	5.6	5.5	5.2	4.8	4.4	4.3	5.3	8.5	9.0
Sales and related	4.1	4.7	5.9	5.9	5.4	5.0	4.7	4.8	5.7	8.8	9.4
Office and administrative support	3.6	4.2	5.4	5.2	5.0	4.6	4.2	4.0	5.1	8.3	8.7
Natural resources, construction, and maintenance	5.3	6.4	7.8	8.1	7.3	6.5	6.0	6.3	8.8	15.6	16.1
Farming, fishing, and forestry	10.2	13.4	12.0	11.4	11.8	9.6	9.5	8.5	10.2	16.2	16.3
Construction and extraction	6.2	7.3	9.1	9.1	8.4	7.6	6.8	7.6	11.0	19.7	20.1
Installation, maintenance, and repair	2.4	3.2	4.6	5.5	4.2	3.9	3.7	3.4	4.5	8.5	9.3
Production, transportation, and material moving	5.1	6.4	7.6	7.9	7.2	6.5	5.8	5.8	7.6	13.3	12.8
Production	4.8	6.6	7.8	7.7	7.0	6.7	5.5	5.7	7.7	14.7	13.1
Transportation and material moving	5.6	6.2	7.4	8.2	7.4	6.2	6.2	6.0	7.6	12.0	12.4

[1]Includes persons with no work experience and persons whose last job was in the armed forces.

Table 1-29. Unemployed Persons and Unemployment Rates, by Class of Worker and Industry, 2000–2010

(Thousands of people, percent.)

Class of worker and industry	2000	2001	2002	2003	2004	2005	2006	2007	2008	2009	2010
Total Unemployed Persons, 16 Years and Over	5 692	6 801	8 378	8 774	8 149	7 591	7 001	7 078	8 924	14 265	14 825
Nonagricultural private wage and salary workers ...	4 483	5 540	6 926	7 131	6 484	5 989	5 523	5 559	7 118	11 654	11 808
Mining	21	23	33	37	21	20	22	25	25	90	73
Construction	513	609	800	810	769	712	671	757	1 030	1 770	1 801
Manufacturing	691	992	1 205	1 166	966	812	699	706	945	1 890	1 622
Durable goods	400	630	789	762	590	485	410	436	597	1 279	1 074
Nondurable goods	290	362	416	404	375	326	289	270	348	611	548
Wholesale trade and retail trade	837	945	1 202	1 237	1 197	1 137	1 039	975	1 205	1 844	1 963
Transportation and utilities	193	236	274	283	236	232	229	233	312	525	492
Information	124	190	253	246	189	163	126	120	167	294	303
Financial activities	208	252	320	319	332	272	264	289	380	598	626
Professional and business services	573	768	1 009	1 042	861	792	746	740	921	1 522	1 561
Education and health services	383	463	570	640	617	627	568	575	698	1 100	1 243
Leisure and hospitality	720	833	961	1 006	972	921	865	896	1 102	1 543	1 592
Other services	219	229	301	347	324	301	293	241	332	477	533
Agriculture and related private wage and salary workers	134	153	139	140	129	104	95	78	123	200	211
Government workers	422	430	512	568	548	534	473	505	534	799	969
Self-employed and unpaid family workers	219	218	265	294	303	298	293	309	383	577	617
Total Unemployment Rate, 16 Years and Over[1]	4.0	4.7	5.8	6.0	5.5	5.1	4.6	4.6	5.8	9.3	9.6
Nonagricultural private wage and salary workers ...	4.1	5.0	6.2	6.3	5.7	5.2	4.7	4.7	5.9	9.8	9.9
Mining	4.4	4.2	6.3	6.7	3.9	3.1	3.2	3.4	3.1	11.6	9.4
Construction	6.2	7.1	9.2	9.3	8.4	7.4	6.7	7.4	10.6	19.0	20.6
Manufacturing	3.5	5.2	6.7	6.6	5.7	4.9	4.2	4.3	5.8	12.1	10.6
Durable goods	3.2	5.2	6.9	6.9	5.5	4.6	3.9	4.2	5.6	12.9	11.2
Nondurable goods	4.0	5.2	6.2	6.1	5.9	5.3	4.8	4.5	6.0	10.6	9.6
Wholesale trade and retail trade	4.3	4.9	6.1	6.0	5.8	5.4	4.9	4.7	5.9	9.0	9.5
Transportation and utilities	3.4	4.3	4.9	5.3	4.4	4.1	4.0	3.9	5.1	8.9	8.4
Information	3.2	4.9	6.9	6.8	5.7	5.0	3.7	3.6	5.0	9.2	9.7
Financial activities	2.4	2.9	3.5	3.5	3.6	2.9	2.7	3.0	3.9	6.4	6.9
Professional and business services	4.8	6.1	7.9	8.2	6.8	6.2	5.6	5.3	6.5	10.8	10.8
Education and health services	2.5	2.8	3.4	3.6	3.4	3.4	3.0	3.0	3.5	5.3	5.8
Leisure and hospitality	6.6	7.5	8.4	8.7	8.3	7.8	7.3	7.4	8.6	11.7	12.2
Other services	3.9	4.0	5.1	5.7	5.3	4.8	4.7	3.9	5.3	7.5	8.5
Agriculture and related private wage and salary workers	9.0	11.2	10.1	10.2	9.9	8.3	7.2	6.3	9.2	14.3	13.9
Government workers	2.1	2.2	2.5	2.8	2.7	2.6	2.3	2.3	2.4	3.6	4.4
Self-employed and unpaid family workers	2.1	2.1	2.6	2.7	2.8	2.7	2.7	2.8	3.6	5.5	5.9

Note: See notes and definitions for information on historical comparability.

[1] Includes persons with no work experience and persons whose last job was in the armed forces.

Table 1-30. Unemployed Persons, by Duration of Unemployment, 1948–2010

(Thousands of people, number of weeks.)

Year	Total unemployed	Less than 5 weeks		5 to 14 weeks		15 weeks and over						Average duration, in weeks	Median duration, in weeks
								15 to 26 weeks		27 weeks and over			
		Number	Percent	Number	Percent	Number	Percent	Number	Percent	Number	Percent		
1948	2 276	1 300	57.1	669	29.4	309	13.6	193	8.5	116	5.1	8.6	. . .
1949	3 637	1 756	48.3	1 194	32.8	684	18.8	428	11.8	256	7.0	10.0	. . .
1950	3 288	1 450	44.1	1 055	32.1	782	23.8	425	12.9	357	10.9	12.1	. . .
1951	2 055	1 177	57.3	574	27.9	303	14.7	166	8.1	137	6.7	9.7	. . .
1952	1 883	1 135	60.3	516	27.4	232	12.3	148	7.9	84	4.5	8.4	. . .
1953	1 834	1 142	62.3	482	26.3	210	11.5	132	7.2	78	4.3	8.0	. . .
1954	3 532	1 605	45.4	1 116	31.6	812	23.0	495	14.0	317	9.0	11.8	. . .
1955	2 852	1 335	46.8	815	28.6	702	24.6	366	12.8	336	11.8	13.0	. . .
1956	2 750	1 412	51.3	805	29.3	533	19.4	301	10.9	232	8.4	11.3	. . .
1957	2 859	1 408	49.2	891	31.2	560	19.6	321	11.2	239	8.4	10.5	. . .
1958	4 602	1 753	38.1	1 396	30.3	1 452	31.6	785	17.1	667	14.5	13.9	. . .
1959	3 740	1 585	42.4	1 114	29.8	1 040	27.8	469	12.5	571	15.3	14.4	. . .
1960	3 852	1 719	44.6	1 176	30.5	957	24.8	503	13.1	454	11.8	12.8	. . .
1961	4 714	1 806	38.3	1 376	29.2	1 532	32.5	728	15.4	804	17.1	15.6	. . .
1962	3 911	1 663	42.5	1 134	29.0	1 119	28.6	534	13.7	585	15.0	14.7	. . .
1963	4 070	1 751	43.0	1 231	30.2	1 088	26.7	535	13.1	553	13.6	14.0	. . .
1964	3 786	1 697	44.8	1 117	29.5	973	25.7	491	13.0	482	12.7	13.3	. . .
1965	3 366	1 628	48.4	983	29.2	755	22.4	404	12.0	351	10.4	11.8	. . .
1966	2 875	1 573	54.7	779	27.1	526	18.3	287	10.0	239	8.3	10.4	. . .
1967	2 975	1 634	54.9	893	30.0	448	15.1	271	9.1	177	5.9	8.7	2.3
1968	2 817	1 594	56.6	810	28.8	412	14.6	256	9.1	156	5.5	8.4	4.5
1969	2 832	1 629	57.5	827	29.2	375	13.2	242	8.5	133	4.7	7.8	4.4
1970	4 093	2 139	52.3	1 290	31.5	663	16.2	428	10.4	235	5.8	8.6	4.9
1971	5 016	2 245	44.8	1 585	31.6	1 187	23.7	668	13.3	519	10.4	11.3	6.3
1972	4 882	2 242	45.9	1 472	30.2	1 167	23.9	601	12.3	566	11.6	12.0	6.2
1973	4 365	2 224	51.0	1 314	30.1	826	18.9	483	11.1	343	7.9	10.0	5.2
1974	5 156	2 604	50.5	1 597	31.0	955	18.5	574	11.1	381	7.4	9.8	5.2
1975	7 929	2 940	37.1	2 484	31.3	2 505	31.6	1 303	16.4	1 203	15.2	14.2	8.4
1976	7 406	2 844	38.4	2 196	29.6	2 366	32.0	1 018	13.8	1 348	18.2	15.8	8.2
1977	6 991	2 919	41.8	2 132	30.5	1 942	27.8	913	13.1	1 028	14.7	14.3	7.0
1978	6 202	2 865	46.2	1 923	31.0	1 414	22.8	766	12.3	648	10.5	11.9	5.9
1979	6 137	2 950	48.1	1 946	31.7	1 241	20.2	706	11.5	535	8.7	10.8	5.4
1980	7 637	3 295	43.2	2 470	32.3	1 871	24.5	1 052	13.8	820	10.7	11.9	6.5
1981	8 273	3 449	41.7	2 539	30.7	2 285	27.6	1 122	13.6	1 162	14.0	13.7	6.9
1982	10 678	3 883	36.4	3 311	31.0	3 485	32.6	1 708	16.0	1 776	16.6	15.6	8.7
1983	10 717	3 570	33.3	2 937	27.4	4 210	39.3	1 652	15.4	2 559	23.9	20.0	10.1
1984	8 539	3 350	39.2	2 451	28.7	2 737	32.1	1 104	12.9	1 634	19.1	18.2	7.9
1985	8 312	3 498	42.1	2 509	30.2	2 305	27.7	1 025	12.3	1 280	15.4	15.6	6.8
1986	8 237	3 448	41.9	2 557	31.0	2 232	27.1	1 045	12.7	1 187	14.4	15.0	6.9
1987	7 425	3 246	43.7	2 196	29.6	1 983	26.7	943	12.7	1 040	14.0	14.5	6.5
1988	6 701	3 084	46.0	2 007	30.0	1 610	24.0	801	12.0	809	12.1	13.5	5.9
1989	6 528	3 174	48.6	1 978	30.3	1 375	21.1	730	11.2	646	9.9	11.9	4.8
1990	7 047	3 265	46.3	2 257	32.0	1 525	21.6	822	11.7	703	10.0	12.0	5.3
1991	8 628	3 480	40.3	2 791	32.4	2 357	27.3	1 246	14.4	1 111	12.9	13.7	6.8
1992	9 613	3 376	35.1	2 830	29.4	3 408	35.4	1 453	15.1	1 954	20.3	17.7	8.7
1993	8 940	3 262	36.5	2 584	28.9	3 094	34.6	1 297	14.5	1 798	20.1	18.0	8.3
1994	7 996	2 728	34.1	2 408	30.1	2 860	35.8	1 237	15.5	1 623	20.3	18.8	9.2
1995	7 404	2 700	36.5	2 342	31.6	2 363	31.9	1 085	14.6	1 278	17.3	16.6	8.3
1996	7 236	2 633	36.4	2 287	31.6	2 316	32.0	1 053	14.6	1 262	17.4	16.7	8.3
1997	6 739	2 538	37.7	2 138	31.7	2 062	30.6	995	14.8	1 067	15.8	15.8	8.0
1998	6 210	2 622	42.2	1 950	31.4	1 637	26.4	763	12.3	875	14.1	14.5	6.7
1999	5 880	2 568	43.7	1 832	31.2	1 480	25.2	755	12.8	725	12.3	13.4	6.4
2000	5 692	2 558	44.9	1 815	31.9	1 318	23.2	669	11.8	649	11.4	12.6	5.9
2001	6 801	2 853	42.0	2 196	32.3	1 752	25.8	951	14.0	801	11.8	13.1	6.8
2002	8 378	2 893	34.5	2 580	30.8	2 904	34.7	1 369	16.3	1 535	18.3	16.6	9.1
2003	8 774	2 785	31.7	2 612	29.8	3 378	38.5	1 442	16.4	1 936	22.1	19.2	10.1
2004	8 149	2 696	33.1	2 382	29.2	3 072	37.7	1 293	15.9	1 779	21.8	19.6	9.8
2005	7 591	2 667	35.1	2 304	30.4	2 619	34.5	1 130	14.9	1 490	19.6	18.4	8.9
2006	7 001	2 614	37.3	2 121	30.3	2 266	32.4	1 031	14.7	1 235	17.6	16.8	8.3
2007	7 078	2 542	35.9	2 232	31.5	2 303	32.5	1 061	15.0	1 243	17.6	16.8	8.5
2008	8 924	2 932	32.8	2 804	31.4	3 188	35.7	1 427	16.0	1 761	19.7	17.9	9.4
2009	14 265	3 165	22.2	3 828	26.8	7 272	51.0	2 775	19.5	4 496	31.5	24.4	15.1
2010	14 825	2 771	18.7	3 267	22.0	8 786	59.3	2 371	16.0	6 415	43.3	33.0	21.4

. . . = Not available.

Table 1-31. Long-Term Unemployment, by Industry and Selected Occupation, 2000–2010

(Thousands of people.)

Length of unemployment, industry, and occupation	2000	2001	2002	2003	2004	2005	2006	2007	2008	2009	2010
UNEMPLOYED 15 WEEKS AND OVER											
Total	1 318	1 752	2 904	3 378	3 072	2 619	2 266	2 303	3 188	7 272	8 786
Wage and Salary Workers, by Industry											
Agriculture and related	32	44	39	44	38	29	30	28	42	96	100
Mining [1]	7	7	11	17	8	8	5	6	7	44	46
Construction	107	130	236	262	248	216	177	215	339	907	1 083
Manufacturing	184	303	528	575	467	326	257	259	385	1 059	1 122
Durable goods	99	183	348	389	293	199	140	162	246	702	773
Nondurable goods	86	120	180	186	174	127	116	97	139	357	350
Wholesale and retail trade	186	241	423	472	455	415	337	334	440	962	1 215
Transportation and utilities	57	71	124	132	114	91	87	95	142	290	343
Information	33	52	119	128	87	76	55	49	66	170	204
Financial activities	58	75	131	144	139	91	103	100	168	357	446
Professional and business services	143	217	377	440	345	299	266	247	346	810	985
Education and health services	124	149	232	300	304	271	263	253	320	691	898
Leisure and hospitality	146	196	279	328	321	277	259	274	356	755	898
Other services	54	58	95	132	126	117	97	80	132	245	310
Public administration	41	36	51	59	72	62	34	51	55	107	164
Experienced Workers, by Occupation											
Management, professional, and related	213	313	603	692	571	436	373	368	569	1 331	1 600
Services	246	323	447	564	565	511	464	482	595	1 243	1 557
Sales and office	331	419	759	810	750	641	561	560	741	1 675	2 048
Natural resources, construction, and maintenance ..	161	212	346	424	386	341	294	299	463	1 224	1 445
Production, transportation, and material moving	273	360	575	654	561	461	380	384	570	1 302	1 498
UNEMPLOYED 27 WEEKS AND OVER											
Total	649	801	1 535	1 936	1 779	1 490	1 235	1 243	1 761	4 496	6 415
Wage and Salary Workers, by Industry											
Agriculture and related	13	16	18	21	18	16	13	14	17	51	57
Mining [1]	4	3	5	10	6	4	3	3	4	23	37
Construction	44	60	111	132	133	108	92	107	168	530	773
Manufacturing	100	132	291	366	302	195	140	152	230	657	888
Durable goods	50	75	191	255	196	124	75	93	150	428	619
Nondurable goods	50	57	100	111	106	71	64	58	80	229	269
Wholesale and retail trade	80	114	226	261	261	230	183	171	237	607	904
Transportation and utilities	27	33	67	74	63	50	42	58	77	180	263
Information	18	21	62	80	58	41	30	29	38	115	159
Financial activities	32	34	131	88	79	56	56	50	97	232	332
Professional and business services	67	90	377	262	193	172	144	130	184	510	722
Education and health services	63	71	232	167	168	156	144	132	182	432	644
Leisure and hospitality	69	90	279	166	169	148	135	142	196	445	624
Other services	26	31	95	71	76	74	51	43	73	161	223
Public administration	23	18	51	33	44	38	21	29	29	66	121
Experienced Workers, by Occupation											
Management, professional, and related	101	135	340	429	356	269	206	207	569	840	6 415
Services	128	156	225	295	307	284	249	251	595	750	1 094
Sales and office	151	185	397	459	419	354	299	285	741	1 067	1 513
Natural resources, construction, and maintenance ..	74	96	164	229	221	186	158	157	463	724	1 042
Production, transportation, and material moving	140	162	313	388	336	261	206	219	570	814	1 142

Note: Beginning in January 2004, data reflect revised population controls used in the household survey. See notes and definitions for information on historical comparability.

[1]For 2009 and 2010, mining includes quarrying, and oil and gas extraction.

Table 1-32. Unemployed Persons and Unemployment Rates, by Reason for Unemployment, Sex, and Age, 1975–2010

(Thousands of people, percent.)

Sex, age, and year	Number of unemployed					Unemployed as a percent of the total civilian labor force			
	Total	Job losers and persons who completed temporary jobs	Job leavers	Entrants		Job losers and persons who completed temporary jobs	Job leavers	Entrants	
				Reentrants	New entrants			Reentrants	New entrants
Both Sexes, 16 Years and Over									
1975	7 929	4 386	827	1 892	823	4.7	0.9	2.0	0.9
1976	7 406	3 679	903	1 928	895	3.8	0.9	2.0	0.9
1977	6 991	3 166	909	1 963	953	3.2	0.9	2.0	1.0
1978	6 202	2 585	874	1 857	885	2.5	0.9	1.8	0.9
1979	6 137	2 635	880	1 806	817	2.5	0.8	1.7	0.8
1980	7 637	3 947	891	1 927	872	3.7	0.8	1.8	0.8
1981	8 273	4 267	923	2 102	981	3.9	0.8	1.9	0.9
1982	10 678	6 268	840	2 384	1 185	5.7	0.8	2.2	1.1
1983	10 717	6 258	830	2 412	1 216	5.6	0.7	2.2	1.1
1984	8 539	4 421	823	2 184	1 110	3.9	0.7	1.9	1.0
1985	8 312	4 139	877	2 256	1 039	3.6	0.8	2.0	0.9
1986	8 237	4 033	1 015	2 160	1 029	3.4	0.9	1.8	0.9
1987	7 425	3 566	965	1 974	920	3.0	0.8	1.6	0.8
1988	6 701	3 092	983	1 809	816	2.5	0.8	1.5	0.7
1989	6 528	2 983	1 024	1 843	677	2.4	0.8	1.5	0.5
1990	7 047	3 387	1 041	1 930	688	2.7	0.8	1.5	0.5
1991	8 628	4 694	1 004	2 139	792	3.7	0.8	1.7	0.6
1992	9 613	5 389	1 002	2 285	937	4.2	0.8	1.8	0.7
1993	8 940	4 848	976	2 198	919	3.8	0.8	1.7	0.7
1994	7 996	3 815	791	2 786	604	2.9	0.6	2.1	0.5
1995	7 404	3 476	824	2 525	579	2.6	0.6	1.9	0.4
1996	7 236	3 370	774	2 512	580	2.5	0.6	1.9	0.4
1997	6 739	3 037	795	2 338	569	2.2	0.6	1.7	0.4
1998	6 210	2 822	734	2 132	520	2.1	0.5	1.5	0.4
1999	5 880	2 622	783	2 005	469	1.9	0.6	1.4	0.3
2000	5 692	2 517	780	1 961	434	1.8	0.5	1.4	0.3
2001	6 801	3 476	835	2 031	459	2.4	0.6	1.4	0.3
2002	8 378	4 607	866	2 368	536	3.2	0.6	1.6	0.4
2003	8 774	4 838	818	2 477	641	3.3	0.6	1.7	0.4
2004	8 149	4 197	858	2 408	686	2.8	0.6	1.6	0.5
2005	7 591	3 667	872	2 386	666	2.5	0.6	1.6	0.4
2006	7 001	3 321	827	2 237	616	2.2	0.5	1.5	0.4
2007	7 078	3 515	793	2 142	627	2.3	0.5	1.4	0.4
2008	8 924	4 789	896	2 472	766	3.1	0.6	1.6	0.5
2009	14 265	9 160	882	3 187	1 035	5.9	0.6	2.1	0.7
2010	14 825	9 250	889	3 466	1 220	6.0	0.6	2.3	0.8
Both Sexes, 16 to 19 Years									
1975	1 767	450	155	529	634	5.1	1.7	6.0	7.1
1976	1 719	387	153	496	683	4.3	1.7	5.5	7.5
1977	1 663	318	156	477	711	3.4	1.7	5.1	7.6
1978	1 583	300	167	455	660	3.1	1.7	4.7	6.8
1979	1 555	319	184	452	599	3.3	1.9	4.7	6.2
1980	1 669	388	156	481	643	4.1	1.7	5.1	6.9
1981	1 763	385	162	487	728	4.3	1.8	5.4	8.1
1982	1 977	460	134	509	874	5.4	1.6	6.0	10.2
1983	1 829	370	110	482	867	4.6	1.3	5.9	10.6
1984	1 499	271	114	370	745	3.4	1.4	4.7	9.4
1985	1 468	275	113	390	689	3.5	1.4	4.9	8.7
1986	1 454	240	145	374	695	3.0	1.8	4.7	8.8
1987	1 347	210	146	375	617	2.7	1.8	4.7	7.7
1988	1 226	207	159	310	550	2.6	2.0	3.9	6.8
1989	1 194	198	200	345	452	2.5	2.5	4.3	5.7
1990	1 212	233	181	338	460	3.0	2.3	4.3	5.9
1991	1 359	289	180	365	524	4.0	2.5	5.0	7.2
1992	1 427	259	149	377	643	3.6	2.1	5.3	9.1
1993	1 365	233	151	353	628	3.3	2.1	4.9	8.8
1994	1 320	185	84	634	416	2.5	1.1	8.5	5.6
1995	1 346	214	102	615	415	2.8	1.3	7.9	5.3
1996	1 306	182	91	625	409	2.3	1.2	8.0	5.2
1997	1 271	174	104	606	388	2.2	1.3	7.6	4.9
1998	1 205	181	86	577	361	2.2	1.0	7.0	4.4
1999	1 162	173	114	547	328	2.1	1.4	6.6	3.9
2000	1 081	157	109	516	299	1.9	1.3	6.2	3.6
2001	1 162	185	98	568	311	2.3	1.2	7.2	3.9
2002	1 253	197	91	597	368	2.6	1.2	7.9	4.9
2003	1 251	188	85	554	424	2.6	1.2	7.7	5.9
2004	1 208	165	76	510	456	2.3	1.1	7.2	6.4
2005	1 186	155	76	489	466	2.2	1.1	6.8	6.5
2006	1 119	145	78	461	435	2.0	1.1	6.3	6.0
2007	1 101	176	71	435	419	2.5	1.0	6.2	6.0
2008	1 285	203	80	490	511	3.0	1.2	7.1	7.5
2009	1 552	271	56	548	677	4.2	0.9	8.6	10.6
2010	1 528	220	42	487	778	3.7	0.7	8.2	13.2

Note: See notes and definitions for information on historical comparability.

Table 1-32. Unemployed Persons and Unemployment Rates, by Reason for Unemployment, Sex, and Age, 1975–2010—*Continued*

(Thousands of people, percent.)

Sex, age, and year	Number of unemployed					Unemployed as a percent of the total civilian labor force			
	Total	Job losers and persons who completed temporary jobs	Job leavers	Entrants		Job losers and persons who completed temporary jobs	Job leavers	Entrants	
				Reentrants	New entrants			Reentrants	New entrants
Men, 20 Years and Over									
1975	3 476	2 598	298	506	76	5.0	0.6	1.0	0.1
1976	3 098	2 167	323	521	86	4.1	0.6	1.0	0.2
1977	2 794	1 816	335	540	103	3.4	0.6	1.0	0.2
1978	2 328	1 433	337	471	86	2.6	0.6	0.9	0.2
1979	2 308	1 464	325	446	73	2.6	0.6	0.8	0.1
1980	3 353	2 389	359	516	90	4.2	0.6	0.9	0.2
1981	3 615	2 565	356	592	102	4.5	0.6	1.0	0.2
1982	5 089	3 965	327	678	119	6.8	0.6	1.2	0.2
1983	5 257	4 088	336	695	138	6.9	0.6	1.2	0.2
1984	3 932	2 800	324	663	146	4.7	0.5	1.1	0.2
1985	3 715	2 568	352	671	124	4.3	0.6	1.1	0.2
1986	3 751	2 568	444	611	128	4.1	0.7	1.0	0.2
1987	3 369	2 289	413	558	108	3.7	0.7	0.9	0.2
1988	2 987	1 939	416	534	98	3.1	0.7	0.9	0.2
1989	2 867	1 843	394	541	88	2.9	0.6	0.8	0.1
1990	3 239	2 100	431	626	82	3.2	0.7	1.0	0.1
1991	4 195	2 982	411	698	105	4.6	0.6	1.1	0.2
1992	4 717	3 420	421	765	111	5.2	0.6	1.2	0.2
1993	4 287	2 996	429	747	114	4.5	0.6	1.1	0.2
1994	3 627	2 296	367	898	65	3.4	0.5	1.3	0.1
1995	3 239	2 051	356	775	57	3.0	0.5	1.2	0.1
1996	3 146	2 043	322	731	51	3.0	0.5	1.1	0.1
1997	2 882	1 795	358	675	55	2.6	0.5	1.0	0.1
1998	2 580	1 588	318	611	63	2.3	0.5	0.9	0.1
1999	2 433	1 459	336	592	46	2.1	0.5	0.8	0.1
2000	2 376	1 416	328	577	55	2.0	0.5	0.8	0.1
2001	3 040	1 999	372	612	56	2.7	0.5	0.8	0.1
2002	3 896	2 702	386	743	65	3.7	0.5	1.0	0.1
2003	4 209	2 899	376	846	88	3.9	0.5	1.1	0.1
2004	3 791	2 503	398	791	99	3.3	0.5	1.0	0.1
2005	4 059	2 188	445	1 067	359	2.7	0.5	1.0	0.1
2006	3 131	1 927	368	757	78	2.5	0.5	1.0	0.1
2007	3 259	2 064	371	723	101	2.6	0.5	0.9	0.1
2008	4 297	2 918	410	969	856	3.7	0.5	1.1	0.1
2009	7 555	5 796	407	1 190	162	7.3	0.5	1.5	0.2
2010	7 763	5 773	433	1 346	211	7.3	0.5	1.7	0.3
Women, 20 Years and Over									
1975	2 684	1 339	375	858	114	4.0	1.1	2.6	0.3
1976	2 588	1 124	427	912	126	3.2	1.2	2.6	0.4
1977	2 535	1 031	419	945	140	2.8	1.2	2.6	0.4
1978	2 292	852	371	930	138	2.2	1.0	2.4	0.4
1979	2 276	851	370	908	145	2.1	0.9	2.3	0.4
1980	2 615	1 170	376	930	139	2.8	0.9	2.3	0.3
1981	2 895	1 317	404	1 023	151	3.1	1.0	2.4	0.4
1982	3 613	1 844	379	1 197	192	4.2	0.9	2.7	0.4
1983	3 632	1 801	384	1 235	212	4.0	0.9	2.8	0.5
1984	3 107	1 350	386	1 151	220	2.9	0.8	2.5	0.5
1985	3 129	1 296	412	1 195	227	2.7	0.9	2.5	0.5
1986	3 032	1 225	426	1 175	206	2.5	0.9	2.4	0.4
1987	2 709	1 067	406	1 041	194	2.2	0.8	2.1	0.4
1988	2 487	946	408	965	168	1.9	0.8	1.9	0.3
1989	2 467	942	430	958	137	1.8	0.8	1.8	0.3
1990	2 596	1 054	429	966	146	2.0	0.8	1.8	0.3
1991	3 074	1 423	413	1 075	163	2.6	0.8	2.0	0.3
1992	3 469	1 710	433	1 142	183	3.1	0.8	2.1	0.3
1993	3 288	1 619	395	1 098	176	2.9	0.7	2.0	0.3
1994	3 049	1 334	339	1 253	122	2.4	0.6	2.2	0.2
1995	2 819	1 211	366	1 135	107	2.1	0.6	2.0	0.2
1996	2 783	1 145	361	1 156	120	2.0	0.6	2.0	0.2
1997	2 585	1 069	333	1 057	126	1.8	0.6	1.8	0.2
1998	2 424	1 053	330	944	97	1.8	0.6	1.6	0.2
1999	2 285	990	333	866	96	1.6	0.5	1.4	0.2
2000	2 235	943	343	868	80	1.5	0.6	1.4	0.1
2001	2 599	1 291	365	850	92	2.0	0.6	1.3	0.1
2002	3 228	1 708	389	1 028	102	2.7	0.6	1.6	0.2
2003	3 314	1 751	357	1 076	130	2.7	0.6	1.7	0.2
2004	3 150	1 529	384	1 107	131	2.4	0.6	1.7	0.2
2005	3 013	1 417	391	1 103	101	2.2	0.6	1.7	0.2
2006	2 751	1 249	380	1 019	103	1.9	0.6	1.5	0.2
2007	2 718	1 276	351	984	107	1.9	0.5	1.7	0.4
2008	3 342	1 668	406	1 126	143	2.4	0.6	1.6	0.2
2009	5 157	3 093	419	1 449	196	4.5	0.6	2.1	0.3
2010	5 534	3 257	413	1 633	231	4.7	0.6	2.4	0.3

Note: See notes and definitions for information on historical comparability.

Table 1-33. Percent of the Population with Work Experience During the Year, by Age and Sex, 1987–2010

(Percent.)

Sex and year	Total	16 to 17 years	18 to 19 years	20 to 24 years	25 to 34 years	35 to 44 years	45 to 54 years	55 to 59 years	60 to 64 years	65 to 69 years	70 years and over
Both Sexes											
1987	69.7	51.8	76.6	85.5	85.7	86.1	81.6	69.4	51.3	26.2	10.2
1988	70.2	50.6	75.5	85.7	86.0	86.8	82.2	70.5	52.2	27.9	10.3
1989	70.5	51.9	75.4	84.9	86.6	86.9	82.8	70.4	52.5	28.4	10.0
1990	70.2	48.6	74.2	84.1	86.2	87.0	82.8	70.9	53.4	28.3	10.2
1991	69.5	43.4	70.8	83.4	85.9	86.6	83.0	70.3	52.9	27.2	9.8
1992	69.1	43.8	69.9	82.7	85.2	85.9	82.8	70.8	53.5	25.5	9.8
1993	69.2	42.1	70.4	82.0	85.0	85.3	82.8	71.6	51.6	27.5	10.7
1994	69.6	44.1	71.5	82.5	85.5	85.6	83.8	72.2	52.8	27.5	10.0
1995	69.6	44.4	71.2	82.0	85.6	85.9	83.4	72.2	53.3	28.0	10.2
1996	69.9	43.3	70.5	83.1	86.1	85.7	84.3	73.3	54.3	27.8	10.4
1997	70.1	43.6	70.5	83.0	87.1	85.9	84.4	73.8	53.8	28.5	10.0
1998	70.1	42.1	69.9	82.9	86.7	86.3	84.2	73.7	54.5	29.2	10.6
1999	70.7	43.7	71.2	82.7	87.3	86.9	85.0	72.3	55.8	30.5	11.6
2000	70.5	42.2	69.6	82.6	87.1	87.0	84.6	72.9	55.1	30.8	11.4
2001	69.4	37.7	66.7	80.8	86.1	85.8	83.7	73.5	56.7	30.6	10.5
2002	68.5	34.5	62.8	78.5	84.4	85.0	83.7	74.7	56.8	33.1	10.4
2003	67.8	32.0	61.7	77.5	83.7	84.0	82.9	73.9	56.5	33.2	11.4
2004	67.7	32.6	59.8	76.9	83.3	84.2	82.6	73.9	57.0	32.7	12.2
2005	67.8	31.1	60.1	77.3	83.7	84.1	82.8	74.4	58.2	32.0	12.1
2006	67.9	30.9	58.3	76.9	84.4	84.3	82.8	74.5	58.2	33.6	12.6
2007	67.8	28.5	57.3	76.6	84.2	84.4	82.4	75.6	59.7	35.2	13.0
2008	67.1	24.6	55.3	76.0	84.1	83.9	81.8	74.6	60.3	34.9	13.5
2009	65.0	21.9	48.7	71.0	81.6	82.0	80.5	73.8	59.3	35.3	12.8
2010	63.8	17.8	43.9	69.1	80.2	81.3	79.2	73.8	58.4	37.1	13.0
Men											
1987	78.9	52.4	77.4	90.4	94.3	94.1	91.9	83.3	63.2	34.2	15.4
1988	79.1	51.8	78.9	90.7	94.3	94.6	91.6	82.1	63.1	35.6	15.6
1989	79.4	53.2	77.7	89.9	94.7	94.7	91.9	82.0	64.2	35.4	15.1
1990	78.9	50.3	76.7	88.7	94.4	94.7	91.3	82.0	65.8	35.8	14.0
1991	77.9	45.4	72.2	87.9	93.5	93.6	91.3	81.5	63.6	35.0	14.4
1992	77.4	46.6	73.7	87.1	93.3	92.8	89.9	80.9	63.2	32.4	14.3
1993	76.8	43.9	71.4	86.6	92.5	92.0	89.3	79.8	59.1	34.3	15.3
1994	77.2	44.4	74.7	87.2	92.9	92.0	90.0	81.3	61.4	33.9	14.8
1995	77.0	43.7	73.6	86.4	92.6	92.2	89.7	81.5	62.1	34.5	14.9
1996	77.2	44.1	71.8	86.7	93.4	92.1	90.4	81.8	62.5	33.6	15.2
1997	77.1	43.4	70.3	86.6	94.1	92.3	90.7	81.4	62.9	33.8	13.9
1998	76.9	40.4	71.6	86.4	93.5	92.7	90.1	81.7	63.5	35.5	14.7
1999	77.3	44.7	72.3	85.5	93.9	93.2	89.9	79.2	65.1	37.4	16.5
2000	77.1	42.1	70.2	85.1	93.4	93.6	89.8	80.6	64.4	38.4	16.0
2001	76.3	37.4	67.7	84.8	93.2	92.2	89.1	80.4	64.3	37.8	14.5
2002	75.2	34.7	62.8	82.1	91.6	91.8	88.9	80.7	64.3	39.3	14.6
2003	74.3	32.8	61.7	80.2	90.8	90.9	87.7	80.9	63.1	37.3	15.8
2004	74.2	32.1	58.9	80.2	91.0	91.1	87.9	80.1	64.5	37.1	16.7
2005	74.6	31.1	60.7	80.8	91.3	91.6	88.2	80.1	64.3	37.6	17.0
2006	74.5	30.9	57.9	80.1	91.9	91.8	88.0	80.6	64.1	38.3	17.3
2007	74.3	28.5	59.0	80.5	90.5	91.5	88.2	80.3	66.2	39.3	17.9
2008	73.2	24.4	55.1	78.7	90.7	91.1	86.4	79.3	66.0	40.3	17.9
2009	70.8	22.2	48.0	73.3	87.7	89.1	85.0	78.3	64.8	39.8	17.2
2010	69.4	16.9	43.2	71.3	86.0	88.0	84.1	78.9	62.8	43.4	17.5
Women											
1987	61.3	51.1	75.8	81.0	77.3	78.5	71.9	56.7	41.0	19.6	6.8
1988	62.1	49.3	72.2	81.0	78.1	79.4	73.5	60.0	42.5	21.4	6.8
1989	62.3	50.6	73.1	80.2	78.6	79.3	74.2	59.9	42.4	22.5	6.7
1990	62.2	46.8	71.7	79.6	78.0	79.6	74.9	60.4	42.5	22.1	7.7
1991	61.8	41.4	69.4	79.0	78.3	79.9	75.3	59.9	43.6	20.6	6.7
1992	61.5	40.9	66.1	78.4	77.2	79.1	76.1	61.5	44.4	20.0	6.7
1993	62.1	40.3	69.4	77.5	77.6	78.7	76.5	63.9	44.7	22.1	7.7
1994	62.5	43.7	68.4	77.8	78.1	79.4	78.0	63.9	45.0	22.2	6.8
1995	62.8	45.2	68.7	77.7	78.8	79.8	77.6	63.2	45.6	22.4	7.1
1996	63.2	42.5	69.2	79.5	78.9	79.5	78.4	65.4	46.9	23.0	7.1
1997	63.6	43.9	70.7	79.5	80.1	79.6	78.4	66.7	45.6	24.0	7.3
1998	63.7	44.1	68.2	79.4	80.1	80.0	78.6	66.3	46.2	23.8	7.8
1999	64.5	42.6	70.1	79.9	80.9	80.7	80.3	66.2	47.3	24.4	8.2
2000	64.3	42.3	69.0	80.2	80.9	80.5	79.5	65.7	47.0	23.9	8.2
2001	63.1	38.1	65.7	76.9	79.2	79.5	78.6	67.1	49.8	24.2	7.9
2002	62.3	34.3	62.8	74.9	77.2	78.4	78.7	69.1	50.0	27.8	7.4
2003	61.7	31.2	61.6	74.6	76.6	77.2	78.4	67.3	50.7	29.6	8.3
2004	61.5	33.1	60.7	73.7	75.6	77.4	77.5	68.2	50.3	28.7	9.0
2005	61.4	31.2	59.6	73.7	76.1	76.8	77.6	68.9	52.7	27.1	8.7
2006	61.6	30.9	58.7	73.7	76.9	76.9	77.9	68.8	53.0	29.5	9.3
2007	61.6	28.5	55.6	72.6	77.8	77.4	76.9	71.2	53.7	31.5	9.5
2008	61.3	24.8	55.4	73.2	77.3	76.7	77.3	70.1	55.0	30.1	10.3
2009	59.6	21.6	49.5	68.6	75.4	75.0	76.1	69.5	54.4	31.1	9.7
2010	58.5	18.7	44.5	66.9	74.3	74.7	74.4	69.1	54.2	31.6	9.6

Note: See notes and definitions for information on historical comparability.

Table 1-34. Persons with Work Experience During the Year, by Industry and Class of Worker of Job Held the Longest, 2002–2010

(Thousands of people.)

Industry and class of worker	2002	2003	2004	2005	2006	2007	2008	2009	2010
TOTAL	151 546	151 553	153 024	155 127	157 352	158 468	158 317	154 772	153 141
Agriculture	2 490	2 521	2 492	2 344	2 332	2 407	2 382	2 581	2 383
Wage and salary workers	1 583	1 605	1 549	1 501	1 495	1 525	1 522	1 733	1 578
Self-employed workers	875	894	918	829	812	846	824	813	788
Unpaid family workers	33	22	25	14	25	36	37	35	17
Nonagricultural Industries	149 055	149 032	150 532	152 783	155 021	156 061	155 934	152 191	150 759
Wage and salary workers	139 909	139 747	140 885	143 002	145 152	146 485	146 521	142 946	141 686
Mining	594	576	630	696	758	746	840	778	771
Construction	9 488	9 423	10 076	10 423	10 989	10 547	10 234	9 443	8 633
Manufacturing	17 660	17 349	17 196	17 243	17 112	16 641	16 332	14 956	14 865
Durable goods	11 013	10 622	10 814	10 930	10 995	10 687	10 477	9 342	9 288
Nondurable goods	6 647	6 727	6 382	6 313	6 116	5 954	5 855	5 613	5 577
Wholesale and retail trade	21 615	21 650	22 091	22 479	21 822	21 837	21 838	21 210	20 854
Wholesale trade	4 402	4 691	4 470	4 517	4 395	4 017	4 016	3 849	3 921
Retail trade	17 213	16 959	17 621	17 962	17 427	17 820	17 822	17 361	16 933
Transportation and utilities	7 039	6 934	7 040	7 248	7 413	8 023	7 675	7 309	6 993
Transportation and warehousing	5 745	5 736	5 827	6 095	6 197	6 750	6 365	6 025	5 701
Utilities	1 294	1 198	1 213	1 153	1 216	1 273	1 310	1 284	1 292
Information	3 989	3 755	3 359	3 495	3 710	3 687	3 455	3 375	3 380
Financial activities	9 591	9 822	9 956	9 748	10 101	10 013	9 671	9 409	9 239
Finance and insurance	6 986	7 135	7 192	7 011	7 190	7 347	6 994	6 792	6 726
Real estate and rental and leasing	2 605	2 687	2 764	2 737	2 912	2 666	2 677	2 617	2 512
Professional and business services	13 883	13 485	13 277	13 537	14 412	14 659	14 868	14 633	15 094
Professional, scientific, and technical services	7 989	7 855	7 793	7 768	8 294	8 676	8 742	8 475	8 841
Management, administration, and waste management services	5 894	5 629	5 484	5 769	6 118	5 982	6 127	6 159	6 253
Education and health services	29 343	29 571	29 814	30 552	31 314	31 921	32 828	33 465	33 596
Education services	12 765	13 026	13 169	13 282	13 659	13 989	14 396	14 457	14 157
Health care and social assistance services	16 578	16 544	16 645	17 270	17 655	17 932	18 432	19 008	19 439
Leisure and hospitality	13 260	13 110	13 345	13 405	13 455	13 959	14 242	13 917	13 718
Arts, entertainment, and recreation	2 852	2 789	2 888	2 877	2 797	3 124	3 047	3 284	2 993
Accommodation and food services	10 408	10 321	10 457	10 528	10 658	10 835	11 195	10 633	10 725
Other services and private household	6 416	6 529	6 473	6 490	6 341	6 603	6 590	6 233	6 111
Private households	873	897	907	866	912	888	912	757	816
Public administration	6 290	6 734	6 897	6 917	7 076	7 095	7 121	7 332	7 597
Self-employed workers	9 023	9 169	9 520	9 658	9 733	9 451	9 332	9 121	8 962
Unpaid family workers	124	116	128	123	135	126	82	124	111

Note: See notes and definitions for information on historical comparability.

Table 1-35. Number of Persons with Work Experience During the Year, by Extent of Employment and Sex, 1987–2010

(Thousands of people.)

Sex and year	Total	Full-time workers				Part-time workers			
		Total	50 to 52 weeks	27 to 49 weeks	1 to 26 weeks	Total	50 to 52 weeks	27 to 49 weeks	1 to 26 weeks
Both Sexes									
1987	128 315	100 288	77 015	13 361	9 912	28 027	10 973	6 594	10 460
1988	130 451	102 131	79 627	12 875	9 629	28 320	11 384	6 624	10 312
1989	132 817	104 876	81 117	14 271	9 488	27 941	11 275	6 987	9 679
1990	133 535	105 323	80 932	14 758	9 633	28 212	11 507	7 012	9 693
1991	133 410	104 472	80 385	14 491	9 596	28 938	11 946	7 003	9 989
1992	133 912	104 813	81 523	13 587	9 703	29 099	12 326	6 841	9 932
1993	136 354	106 299	83 384	13 054	9 861	30 055	12 818	6 777	10 460
1994	138 468	108 141	85 764	13 051	9 326	30 327	12 936	6 956	10 435
1995	139 724	110 063	88 173	12 970	8 920	29 661	12 725	6 831	10 105
1996	142 201	112 313	90 252	12 997	9 064	29 888	13 382	6 643	9 863
1997	143 968	113 879	92 631	12 508	8 740	30 089	13 810	6 565	9 714
1998	145 566	116 412	95 772	12 156	8 484	29 155	13 538	6 480	9 137
1999	148 295	119 096	97 941	12 294	8 861	29 199	13 680	6 317	9 202
2000	149 361	120 591	100 349	12 071	8 171	28 770	13 865	6 161	8 744
2001	151 042	121 921	100 357	13 172	8 392	29 121	14 038	6 139	8 944
2002	151 546	121 726	100 659	12 544	8 523	29 819	14 635	6 184	9 000
2003	151 553	121 158	100 700	11 972	8 486	30 395	15 333	6 027	9 035
2004	153 024	122 404	102 427	11 862	8 115	30 621	15 552	6 077	8 992
2005	155 127	124 683	104 876	11 816	7 991	30 444	15 374	6 161	8 909
2006	157 352	127 340	107 734	11 736	7 870	30 012	15 131	6 223	8 657
2007	158 468	128 332	108 617	11 901	7 814	30 136	15 477	6 194	8 466
2008	158 317	125 937	104 023	13 421	8 493	32 380	16 562	6 630	9 188
2009	154 772	121 355	99 306	12 350	9 698	33 418	17 417	6 674	9 327
2010	153 141	119 940	99 250	11 705	8 985	33 201	17 122	6 582	9 497
Men									
1987	69 144	59 736	47 040	7 503	5 193	9 408	3 260	2 191	3 957
1988	70 021	60 504	48 299	7 329	4 876	9 517	3 468	2 199	3 850
1989	71 640	62 108	49 693	7 642	4 773	9 532	3 619	2 254	3 659
1990	71 953	62 319	49 175	8 188	4 956	9 634	3 650	2 322	3 662
1991	71 700	61 636	47 895	8 324	5 417	10 064	3 820	2 342	3 902
1992	72 007	61 722	48 300	7 965	5 457	10 285	3 864	2 354	4 067
1993	72 872	62 513	49 832	7 317	5 364	10 359	4 005	2 144	4 210
1994	73 958	63 634	51 582	7 094	4 958	10 324	3 948	2 358	4 018
1995	74 381	64 145	52 671	6 973	4 501	10 236	4 034	2 257	3 945
1996	75 760	65 356	53 795	6 891	4 670	10 404	4 321	2 136	3 947
1997	76 408	66 089	54 918	6 638	4 533	10 319	4 246	2 274	3 799
1998	76 918	67 250	56 953	6 208	4 089	9 669	4 197	2 090	3 382
1999	78 145	68 347	57 520	6 401	4 426	9 797	4 297	2 062	3 438
2000	78 804	68 925	58 756	6 094	4 075	9 879	4 485	1 957	3 437
2001	79 971	70 074	58 715	7 087	4 272	9 897	4 306	1 989	3 602
2002	80 282	70 132	58 765	6 804	4 563	10 151	4 519	2 042	3 590
2003	80 317	69 766	58 778	6 479	4 509	10 551	5 042	1 872	3 637
2004	81 261	70 780	60 096	6 428	4 256	10 482	4 987	1 992	3 503
2005	82 735	72 056	61 510	6 299	4 247	10 679	5 153	2 074	3 452
2006	83 767	73 578	63 058	6 373	4 147	10 189	4 747	2 046	3 396
2007	84 292	73 734	62 994	6 583	4 157	10 558	4 933	2 165	3 460
2008	83 889	72 204	59 869	7 645	4 690	11 685	5 425	2 457	3 803
2009	81 835	69 178	56 058	7 339	5 780	12 658	5 911	2 526	4 221
2010	81 076	68 402	56 416	6 760	5 225	12 674	5 883	2 523	4 267
Women									
1987	59 171	40 552	29 975	5 858	4 719	18 619	7 713	4 403	6 503
1988	60 430	41 627	31 328	5 546	4 753	18 803	7 916	4 425	6 462
1989	61 178	42 768	31 424	6 629	4 715	18 410	7 656	4 733	6 021
1990	61 582	43 004	31 757	6 570	4 677	18 578	7 857	4 690	6 031
1991	61 712	42 837	32 491	6 167	4 179	18 875	8 126	4 662	6 087
1992	61 904	43 090	33 223	5 621	4 246	18 814	8 462	4 487	5 865
1993	63 481	43 785	33 552	5 736	4 497	19 696	8 813	4 633	6 250
1994	64 511	44 508	34 182	5 957	4 369	20 003	8 988	4 598	6 417
1995	65 342	45 917	35 502	5 997	4 418	19 425	8 691	4 574	6 160
1996	66 439	46 955	36 457	6 105	4 393	19 484	9 061	4 507	5 916
1997	67 559	47 790	37 713	5 870	4 207	19 769	9 564	4 291	5 914
1998	68 648	49 162	38 819	5 948	4 395	19 486	9 341	4 390	5 755
1999	70 150	50 748	40 421	5 892	4 435	19 402	9 383	4 255	5 764
2000	70 556	51 665	41 593	5 977	4 095	18 891	9 380	4 204	5 307
2001	71 071	51 848	41 642	6 085	4 120	19 223	9 731	4 150	5 342
2002	71 263	51 593	41 893	5 741	3 959	19 671	10 117	4 143	5 411
2003	71 236	51 391	41 921	5 493	3 977	19 844	10 291	4 155	5 398
2004	71 763	51 624	42 331	5 434	3 859	20 139	10 565	4 085	5 489
2005	72 392	52 627	43 366	5 517	3 744	19 765	10 222	4 087	5 456
2006	73 585	53 762	44 676	5 364	3 723	19 823	10 384	4 178	5 261
2007	74 176	54 598	45 622	5 318	3 657	19 579	10 543	4 029	5 006
2008	74 428	53 733	44 154	5 776	3 803	20 695	11 137	4 172	5 385
2009	72 937	52 177	43 248	5 012	3 918	20 760	11 506	4 147	5 107
2010	72 066	51 538	42 834	4 944	3 760	20 528	11 239	4 058	5 230

Note: See notes and definitions for information on historical comparability.

Table 1-36. Percent Distribution of the Population with Work Experience During the Year, by Extent of Employment and Sex, 1987–2010

(Percent of total people with work experience.)

Sex and year	Total	Full-time workers				Part-time workers			
		Total	50 to 52 weeks	27 to 49 weeks	1 to 26 weeks	Total	50 to 52 weeks	27 to 49 weeks	1 to 26 weeks
Both Sexes									
1987	100.0	78.1	60.0	10.4	7.7	21.9	8.6	5.1	8.2
1988	100.0	78.3	61.0	9.9	7.4	21.7	8.7	5.1	7.9
1989	100.0	78.9	61.1	10.7	7.1	21.1	8.5	5.3	7.3
1990	100.0	78.9	60.6	11.1	7.2	21.2	8.6	5.3	7.3
1991	100.0	78.4	60.3	10.9	7.2	21.7	9.0	5.2	7.5
1992	100.0	78.2	60.9	10.1	7.2	21.7	9.2	5.1	7.4
1993	100.0	78.0	61.2	9.6	7.2	22.1	9.4	5.0	7.7
1994	100.0	78.0	61.9	9.4	6.7	21.8	9.3	5.0	7.5
1995	100.0	78.8	63.1	9.3	6.4	21.2	9.1	4.9	7.2
1996	100.0	79.0	63.5	9.1	6.4	21.0	9.4	4.7	6.9
1997	100.0	79.1	64.3	8.7	6.1	20.9	9.6	4.6	6.7
1998	100.0	80.0	65.8	8.4	5.8	20.1	9.3	4.5	6.3
1999	100.0	80.3	66.0	8.3	6.0	19.7	9.2	4.3	6.2
2000	100.0	80.8	67.2	8.1	5.5	19.3	9.3	4.1	5.9
2001	100.0	80.7	66.4	8.7	5.6	19.3	9.3	4.1	5.9
2002	100.0	80.3	66.4	8.3	5.6	19.7	9.7	4.1	5.9
2003	100.0	79.9	66.4	7.9	5.6	20.1	10.1	4.0	6.0
2004	100.0	80.0	66.9	7.8	5.3	20.1	10.2	4.0	5.9
2005	100.0	80.4	67.6	7.6	5.2	19.6	9.9	4.0	5.7
2006	100.0	80.9	68.5	7.5	5.0	19.1	9.6	4.0	5.5
2007	100.0	81.0	68.5	7.5	4.9	19.0	9.8	3.9	5.3
2008	100.0	79.5	65.7	8.5	5.4	20.5	10.5	4.2	5.8
2009	100.0	78.4	64.2	8.0	6.3	21.6	11.3	4.3	6.0
2010	100.0	78.3	64.8	7.6	5.9	21.7	11.2	4.3	6.2
Men									
1987	100.0	86.4	68.0	10.9	7.5	13.6	4.7	3.2	5.7
1988	100.0	86.5	69.0	10.5	7.0	13.6	5.0	3.1	5.5
1989	100.0	86.8	69.4	10.7	6.7	13.3	5.1	3.1	5.1
1990	100.0	86.6	68.3	11.4	6.9	13.4	5.1	3.2	5.1
1991	100.0	86.0	66.8	11.6	7.6	14.0	5.3	3.3	5.4
1992	100.0	85.8	67.1	11.1	7.6	14.3	5.4	3.3	5.6
1993	100.0	85.8	68.4	10.0	7.4	14.2	5.5	2.9	5.8
1994	100.0	86.0	69.7	9.6	6.7	13.9	5.3	3.2	5.4
1995	100.0	86.3	70.8	9.4	6.1	13.7	5.4	3.0	5.3
1996	100.0	86.3	71.0	9.1	6.2	13.7	5.7	2.8	5.2
1997	100.0	86.5	71.9	8.7	5.9	13.6	5.6	3.0	5.0
1998	100.0	87.4	74.0	8.1	5.3	12.6	5.5	2.7	4.4
1999	100.0	87.5	73.6	8.2	5.7	12.5	5.5	2.6	4.4
2000	100.0	87.5	74.6	7.7	5.2	12.6	5.7	2.5	4.4
2001	100.0	87.6	73.4	8.9	5.3	12.4	5.4	2.5	4.5
2002	100.0	87.4	73.2	8.5	5.7	12.6	5.6	2.5	4.5
2003	100.0	86.9	73.2	8.1	5.6	13.1	6.3	2.3	4.5
2004	100.0	87.1	74.0	7.9	5.2	12.9	6.1	2.5	4.3
2005	100.0	87.0	74.3	7.6	5.1	12.9	6.2	2.5	4.2
2006	100.0	87.8	75.3	7.6	5.0	12.2	5.7	2.4	4.1
2007	100.0	87.5	74.7	7.8	4.9	12.5	5.9	2.6	4.1
2008	100.0	86.1	71.4	9.1	5.6	13.9	6.5	2.9	4.5
2009	100.0	84.5	68.5	9.0	7.1	15.5	7.2	3.1	5.2
2010	100.0	84.4	69.6	8.3	6.4	15.6	7.3	3.1	5.3
Women									
1987	100.0	68.6	50.7	9.9	8.0	31.4	13.0	7.4	11.0
1988	100.0	68.9	51.8	9.2	7.9	31.1	13.1	7.3	10.7
1989	100.0	69.9	51.4	10.8	7.7	30.0	12.5	7.7	9.8
1990	100.0	69.9	51.6	10.7	7.6	30.2	12.8	7.6	9.8
1991	100.0	69.4	52.6	10.0	6.8	30.7	13.2	7.6	9.9
1992	100.0	69.7	53.7	9.1	6.9	30.4	13.7	7.2	9.5
1993	100.0	69.0	52.9	9.0	7.1	31.0	13.9	7.3	9.8
1994	100.0	69.0	53.0	9.2	6.8	30.9	13.9	7.1	9.9
1995	100.0	70.3	54.3	9.2	6.8	29.7	13.3	7.0	9.4
1996	100.0	70.7	54.9	9.2	6.6	29.3	13.6	6.8	8.9
1997	100.0	70.7	55.8	8.7	6.2	29.4	14.2	6.4	8.8
1998	100.0	71.6	56.5	8.7	6.4	28.4	13.6	6.4	8.4
1999	100.0	72.3	57.6	8.4	6.3	27.7	13.4	6.1	8.2
2000	100.0	73.2	58.9	8.5	5.8	26.8	13.3	6.0	7.5
2001	100.0	73.0	58.6	8.6	5.8	27.0	13.7	5.8	7.5
2002	100.0	72.5	58.8	8.1	5.6	27.6	14.2	5.8	7.6
2003	100.0	72.1	58.8	7.7	5.6	27.8	14.4	5.8	7.6
2004	100.0	72.0	59.0	7.6	5.4	28.0	14.7	5.7	7.6
2005	100.0	72.7	59.9	7.6	5.2	27.2	14.1	5.6	7.5
2006	100.0	73.1	60.7	7.3	5.1	26.9	14.1	5.7	7.1
2007	100.0	73.6	61.5	7.2	4.9	26.4	14.2	5.4	6.7
2008	100.0	72.2	59.3	7.8	5.1	27.8	15.0	5.6	7.2
2009	100.0	71.5	59.3	6.9	5.4	28.5	15.8	5.7	7.0
2010	100.0	71.5	59.4	6.9	5.2	28.5	15.6	5.6	7.3

Note: See notes and definitions for information on historical comparability.

Table 1-37. Extent of Unemployment During the Year, by Sex, 1987–2010

(Thousands of people, percent.)

Sex and extent of unemployment	1987	1988	1989	1990	1991	1992	1993	1994	1995	1996	1997	1998
BOTH SEXES												
Total Who Worked or Looked for Work	130 353	132 185	134 394	135 408	135 826	136 654	139 786	141 325	142 413	144 528	146 096	147 295
Percent with unemployment	14.1	12.9	12.9	14.6	15.7	15.7	14.7	13.4	12.7	11.6	10.7	9.5
Total with Unemployment	18 399	17 096	17 273	19 809	21 276	21 455	20 527	18 966	18 067	16 789	15 637	14 044
Did not work but looked for work	2 037	1 735	1 577	1 874	2 415	2 742	3 432	2 857	2 690	2 329	2 129	1 729
Worked during the year	16 362	15 362	15 697	17 936	18 861	18 714	17 094	16 109	15 377	14 460	13 508	12 316
Year-round workers with 1 or 2 weeks of unemployment	792	830	833	1 056	966	871	688	746	715	589	611	630
Part-year workers with unemployment	15 570	14 532	14 864	16 880	17 895	17 843	16 406	15 363	14 662	13 871	12 897	11 686
1 to 4 weeks	3 363	3 256	3 489	3 645	3 224	2 944	2 626	2 788	2 812	2 550	2 582	2 323
5 to 10 weeks	3 191	3 148	3 359	3 669	3 655	3 496	2 898	2 983	2 725	2 671	2 601	2 495
11 to 14 weeks	2 258	2 128	2 235	2 501	2 587	2 574	2 300	2 265	2 147	2 020	1 822	1 701
15 to 26 weeks	3 904	3 479	3 600	4 316	4 927	4 877	4 549	4 158	4 013	3 662	3 378	3 019
27 weeks or more	2 854	2 521	2 181	2 749	3 502	3 952	4 033	3 169	2 965	2 968	2 514	2 148
With 2 or more spells of unemployment	5 149	5 136	5 073	5 811	5 864	5 734	5 338	4 783	4 468	4 237	4 044	3 628
2 spells	2 442	2 460	2 460	2 855	2 738	2 698	2 572	2 207	1 963	1 982	1 853	1 650
3 or more spells	2 707	2 676	2 613	2 956	3 126	3 036	2 766	2 576	2 505	2 255	2 191	1 978
MEN												
Total Who Worked or Looked for Work	69 995	70 738	72 362	72 844	72 909	73 387	74 516	75 244	75 698	76 786	77 385	77 704
Percent with unemployment	15.0	13.7	13.5	15.5	17.3	17.5	15.7	14.1	13.2	11.9	11.1	9.4
Total with Unemployment	10 504	9 696	9 792	11 307	12 642	12 844	11 723	10 582	9 996	9 157	8 604	7 284
Did not work but looked for work	852	717	723	891	1 210	1 379	1 641	1 286	1 317	1 026	978	787
Worked during the year	9 653	8 978	9 071	10 415	11 432	11 466	10 082	9 296	8 679	8 130	7 626	6 497
Year-round workers with 1 or 2 weeks of unemployment	536	585	568	711	612	567	449	527	462	395	382	386
Part-year workers with unemployment	9 117	8 393	8 503	9 704	10 820	10 899	9 633	8 769	8 217	7 735	7 244	6 111
1 to 4 weeks	1 561	1 633	1 742	1 819	1 591	1 563	1 343	1 365	1 398	1 272	1 275	1 085
5 to 10 weeks	1 824	1 808	1 890	2 041	2 111	2 039	1 647	1 666	1 434	1 478	1 474	1 363
11 to 14 weeks	1 415	1 279	1 365	1 462	1 659	1 615	1 354	1 370	1 253	1 258	1 068	980
15 to 26 weeks	2 514	2 124	2 188	2 645	3 206	3 165	2 862	2 449	2 439	2 076	1 949	1 585
27 weeks or more	1 803	1 549	1 318	1 737	2 253	2 517	2 427	1 919	1 693	1 651	1 478	1 098
With 2 or more spells of unemployment	3 300	3 366	3 178	3 689	3 886	3 889	3 451	2 940	2 793	2 554	2 437	2 014
2 spells	1 488	1 560	1 517	1 676	1 742	1 781	1 580	1 266	1 110	1 109	1 078	880
3 or more spells	1 812	1 806	1 661	2 013	2 144	2 108	1 871	1 674	1 683	1 445	1 359	1 134
WOMEN												
Total Who Worked or Looked for Work	60 357	61 447	62 032	62 564	62 917	63 267	65 270	66 081	66 716	67 742	68 710	69 591
Percent with unemployment	13.1	12.0	12.1	13.6	13.7	13.6	13.5	12.7	12.1	11.3	10.2	9.7
Total with Unemployment	7 895	7 400	7 481	8 502	8 634	8 611	8 804	8 383	8 070	7 632	7 033	6 760
Did not work but looked for work	1 185	1 017	854	982	1 205	1 363	1 791	1 570	1 373	1 303	1 151	942
Worked during the year	6 710	6 382	6 628	7 520	7 427	7 247	7 014	6 813	6 696	6 330	5 882	5 816
Year-round workers with 1 or 2 weeks of unemployment	255	244	265	344	354	304	239	219	253	194	229	243
Part-year workers with unemployment	6 455	6 138	6 363	7 176	7 073	6 943	6 775	6 594	6 443	6 136	5 653	5 573
1 to 4 weeks	1 802	1 623	1 747	1 827	1 633	1 380	1 284	1 422	1 413	1 279	1 307	1 237
5 to 10 weeks	1 368	1 340	1 469	1 627	1 544	1 457	1 252	1 317	1 291	1 192	1 127	1 131
11 to 14 weeks	844	849	870	1 038	927	959	946	896	893	762	754	721
15 to 26 weeks	1 391	1 354	1 413	1 671	1 720	1 712	1 687	1 708	1 574	1 586	1 429	1 434
27 weeks or more	1 050	972	864	1 013	1 249	1 435	1 606	1 251	1 272	1 317	1 036	1 050
With 2 or more spells of unemployment	1 849	1 769	1 895	2 122	1 979	1 844	1 887	1 843	1 675	1 682	1 607	1 614
2 spells	954	899	943	1 179	997	916	992	941	853	872	775	770
3 or more spells	895	870	952	943	982	928	895	902	822	810	832	844

Table 1-37. Extent of Unemployment During the Year, by Sex, 1987–2010—*Continued*

(Thousands of people, percent.)

Sex and extent of unemployment	1999	2000	2001	2002	2003	2004	2005	2006	2007	2008	2009	2010
BOTH SEXES												
Total Who Worked or Looked for Work	149 798	150 786	153 056	154 205	154 315	155 576	157 549	159 259	160 565	161 506	160 624	159 706
Percent with unemployment	8.7	8.1	10.4	10.9	10.7	9.7	9.2	9.1	9.4	13.1	16.3	15.8
Total with Unemployment	13 068	12 269	15 843	16 824	16 462	15 074	14 558	14 447	15 130	21 231	26 151	25 262
Did not work but looked for work	1 503	1 425	2 014	2 660	2 762	2 551	2 422	1 907	2 097	3 189	5 851	6 564
Worked during the year	11 566	10 845	13 829	14 164	13 699	12 522	12 136	12 540	13 033	18 042	20 300	18 698
Year-round workers with 1 or 2 weeks of unemployment	562	573	602	584	534	465	431	450	500	763	693	591
Part-year workers with unemployment	11 004	10 272	13 227	13 580	13 165	12 057	11 705	12 090	12 533	17 279	19 607	18 107
1 to 4 weeks	2 361	2 233	2 368	2 002	1 839	1 985	1 941	2 601	2 593	2 794	2 528	2 267
5 to 10 weeks	2 218	2 014	2 557	2 373	2 264	2 100	2 170	2 107	2 090	2 944	2 562	2 397
11 to 14 weeks	1 594	1 505	2 038	1 970	1 749	1 773	1 698	1 615	1 888	2 438	2 414	2 302
15 to 26 weeks	2 803	2 641	3 683	3 848	3 778	3 448	3 349	3 176	3 373	4 859	5 698	5 116
27 weeks or more	2 028	1 879	2 582	3 387	3 535	2 751	2 547	2 592	2 589	4 244	6 405	6 025
With 2 or more spells of unemployment	3 225	3 079	3 421	3 226	3 093	2 896	3 095	3 076	3 108	3 991	4 152	3 875
2 spells	1 449	1 397	1 643	1 556	1 585	1 344	1 477	1 564	1 427	1 987	1 918	1 789
3 or more spells	1 776	1 682	1 779	1 670	1 508	1 552	1 618	1 513	1 681	2 004	2 234	2 086
MEN												
Total Who Worked or Looked for Work	78 905	79 546	80 975	81 651	81 804	82 478	83 951	84 736	85 368	85 563	85 161	84 738
Percent with unemployment	9.0	8.6	11.0	11.8	11.4	10.0	9.7	9.6	10.2	14.4	18.6	17.6
Total with Unemployment	7 091	6 806	8 928	9 621	9 339	8 256	8 116	8 115	8 698	12 331	15 877	14 900
Did not work but looked for work	760	742	1 004	1 369	1 487	1 217	1 216	969	1 076	1 674	3 325	3 662
Worked during the year	6 332	6 064	7 924	8 252	7 854	7 039	6 899	7 146	7 622	10 656	12 552	11 238
Year-round workers with 1 or 2 weeks of unemployment	373	379	421	365	359	289	296	295	365	484	458	379
Part-year workers with unemployment	5 959	5 685	7 502	7 887	7 495	6 750	6 603	6 850	7 257	10 172	12 093	10 859
1 to 4 weeks	1 166	1 070	1 247	1 075	958	1 028	1 052	1 283	1 367	1 523	1 466	1 186
5 to 10 weeks	1 168	1 135	1 446	1 342	1 314	1 170	1 209	1 267	1 214	1 701	1 594	1 423
11 to 14 weeks	937	880	1 207	1 186	1 039	1 021	1 024	961	1 163	1 467	1 558	1 441
15 to 26 weeks	1 655	1 595	2 191	2 282	2 178	2 065	1 923	1 868	2 058	3 035	3 564	3 233
27 weeks or more	1 033	1 005	1 412	2 002	2 006	1 466	1 395	1 472	1 455	2 445	3 911	3 577
With 2 or more spells of unemployment	1 845	1 809	2 100	1 920	1 882	1 828	1 975	1 936	1 992	2 623	2 865	2 623
2 spells	787	804	1 002	914	946	808	940	945	847	1 234	1 299	1 133
3 or more spells	1 058	1 005	1 099	1 006	936	1 020	1 035	991	1 145	1 389	1 566	1 491
WOMEN												
Total Who Worked or Looked for Work	70 893	71 240	72 081	72 554	72 511	73 097	73 598	74 523	75 197	75 943	75 463	74 968
Percent with unemployment	8.4	7.7	9.6	9.9	9.8	9.3	8.8	8.5	8.6	11.7	13.6	13.8
Total with Unemployment	5 976	5 463	6 915	7 203	7 123	6 818	6 442	6 332	6 432	8 900	10 274	10 362
Did not work but looked for work	743	683	1 010	1 291	1 275	1 334	1 206	938	1 021	1 514	2 526	2 903
Worked during the year	5 234	4 779	5 905	5 913	5 848	5 484	5 236	5 394	5 411	7 385	7 748	7 459
Year-round workers with 1 or 2 weeks of unemployment	189	193	180	220	176	177	136	154	135	279	235	211
Part-year workers with unemployment	5 045	4 586	5 725	5 693	5 672	5 307	5 100	5 240	5 276	7 106	7 513	7 248
1 to 4 weeks	1 194	1 164	1 121	927	882	957	888	1 317	1 226	1 270	1 061	1 081
5 to 10 weeks	1 050	878	1 111	1 031	950	929	961	840	876	1 243	968	974
11 to 14 weeks	657	625	831	784	710	752	674	655	725	971	857	861
15 to 26 weeks	1 148	1 045	1 492	1 566	1 600	1 384	1 426	1 307	1 316	1 823	2 134	1 883
27 weeks or more	996	874	1 170	1 385	1 530	1 285	1 151	1 120	1 134	1 800	2 494	2 448
With 2 or more spells of unemployment	1 379	1 270	1 321	1 306	1 211	1 069	1 120	1 140	1 116	1 368	1 287	1 252
2 spells	662	593	641	642	639	537	537	619	580	753	619	657
3 or more spells	717	677	680	664	572	532	583	521	536	616	668	595

Table 1-38. Percent Distribution of Persons with Unemployment During the Year, by Sex and Extent of Unemployment, 1987–2010

(Percent.)

Sex and extent of unemployment	1987	1988	1989	1990	1991	1992	1993	1994	1995	1996	1997	1998
BOTH SEXES												
Total with Unemployment Who Worked During the Year	100.0	100.0	100.0	100.0	100.0	100.0	100.0	100.0	100.0	100.0	100.0	100.0
Year-round workers with 1 or 2 weeks of unemployment	4.8	5.4	5.3	5.9	5.1	4.7	4.0	4.6	4.6	4.1	4.5	5.1
Part-year workers with unemployment	95.2	94.5	94.6	94.1	94.8	95.4	96.1	95.4	95.4	96.0	95.5	95.0
1 to 4 weeks	20.6	21.2	22.2	20.3	17.1	15.7	15.4	17.3	18.3	17.6	19.1	18.9
5 to 10 weeks	19.5	20.5	21.4	20.5	19.4	18.7	17.0	18.5	17.7	18.5	19.3	20.3
11 to 14 weeks	13.8	13.8	14.2	13.9	13.7	13.8	13.5	14.1	14.0	14.0	13.5	13.8
15 to 26 weeks	23.9	22.6	22.9	24.1	26.1	26.1	26.6	25.8	26.1	25.3	25.0	24.5
27 weeks or more	17.4	16.4	13.9	15.3	18.5	21.1	23.6	19.7	19.3	20.6	18.6	17.5
With 2 or more spells of unemployment	31.4	33.4	32.3	32.4	31.1	30.6	31.2	29.7	29.1	29.3	29.9	29.5
2 spells	14.9	16.0	15.7	15.9	14.5	14.4	15.0	13.7	12.8	13.7	13.7	13.4
3 or more spells	16.5	17.4	16.6	16.5	16.6	16.2	16.2	16.0	16.3	15.6	16.2	16.1
MEN												
Total with Unemployment Who Worked During the Year	100.0	100.0	100.0	100.0	100.0	100.0	100.0	100.0	100.0	100.0	100.0	100.0
Year-round workers with 1 or 2 weeks of unemployment	5.6	6.5	6.3	6.8	5.4	4.9	4.4	5.7	5.3	4.9	5.0	5.9
Part-year workers with unemployment	94.5	93.4	93.7	93.2	94.6	95.0	95.5	94.3	94.7	95.1	95.1	94.1
1 to 4 weeks	16.2	18.2	19.2	17.5	13.9	13.6	13.3	14.7	16.1	15.6	16.7	16.7
5 to 10 weeks	18.9	20.1	20.8	19.6	18.5	17.8	16.3	17.9	16.5	18.2	19.3	21.0
11 to 14 weeks	14.7	14.2	15.1	14.0	14.5	14.1	13.4	14.7	14.4	15.5	14.0	15.1
15 to 26 weeks	26.0	23.7	24.1	25.4	28.0	27.6	28.4	26.4	28.1	25.5	25.6	24.4
27 weeks or more	18.7	17.2	14.5	16.7	19.7	21.9	24.1	20.6	19.5	20.3	19.4	16.9
With 2 or more spells of unemployment	34.2	37.5	35.0	35.4	34.0	33.9	34.3	31.6	32.2	31.4	31.9	31.0
2 spells	15.4	17.4	16.7	16.1	15.2	15.5	15.7	13.6	12.8	13.6	14.1	13.5
3 or more spells	18.8	20.1	18.3	19.3	18.8	18.4	18.6	18.0	19.4	17.8	17.8	17.5
WOMEN												
Total With Unemployment Who Worked During the Year	100.0	100.0	100.0	100.0	100.0	100.0	100.0	100.0	100.0	100.0	100.0	100.0
Year-round workers with 1 or 2 weeks of unemployment	3.8	3.8	4.0	4.6	4.8	4.2	3.4	3.2	3.8	3.1	3.9	4.2
Part-year workers with unemployment	96.3	96.1	96.0	95.3	95.3	95.7	96.6	96.7	96.2	96.9	96.1	95.8
1 to 4 weeks	26.9	25.4	26.4	24.3	22.0	19.0	18.3	20.9	21.1	20.2	22.2	21.3
5 to 10 weeks	20.4	21.0	22.2	21.6	20.8	20.1	17.8	19.3	19.3	18.8	19.2	19.4
11 to 14 weeks	12.6	13.3	13.1	13.8	12.5	13.2	13.5	13.1	13.3	12.0	12.8	12.4
15 to 26 weeks	20.7	21.2	21.3	22.2	23.2	23.6	24.1	25.1	23.5	25.1	24.3	24.7
27 weeks or more	15.7	15.2	13.0	13.4	16.8	19.8	22.9	18.3	19.0	20.8	17.6	18.0
With 2 or more spells of unemployment	27.5	27.7	28.6	28.2	26.6	25.4	26.9	27.0	25.0	26.6	27.3	27.7
2 spells	14.2	14.1	14.2	15.7	13.4	12.6	14.1	13.8	12.7	13.8	13.2	13.2
3 or more spells	13.3	13.6	14.4	12.5	13.2	12.8	12.8	13.2	12.3	12.8	14.1	14.5

Table 1-38. Percent Distribution of Persons with Unemployment During the Year, by Sex and Extent of Unemployment, 1987–2010—*Continued*

(Percent.)

Sex and extent of unemployment	1999	2000	2001	2002	2003	2004	2005	2006	2007	2008	2009	2010
BOTH SEXES												
Total with Unemployment Who Worked During the Year	100.0	100.0	100.0	100.0	100.0	100.0	100.0	100.0	100.0	100.0	100.0	100.0
Year-round workers with 1 or 2 weeks of unemployment	4.9	5.3	4.4	4.1	3.9	3.7	3.6	3.6	3.8	4.2	3.4	3.2
Part-year workers with unemployment	95.1	94.8	95.6	95.9	96.1	96.3	96.4	96.4	96.1	95.8	96.5	96.8
1 to 4 weeks	20.4	20.6	17.1	14.1	13.4	15.9	16.0	20.7	19.9	15.5	12.5	12.1
5 to 10 weeks	19.2	18.6	18.5	16.8	16.5	16.8	17.9	16.8	16.0	16.3	12.6	12.8
11 to 14 weeks	13.8	13.9	14.7	13.9	12.8	14.2	14.0	12.9	14.5	13.5	11.9	12.3
15 to 26 weeks	24.2	24.4	26.6	27.2	27.6	27.5	27.6	25.3	25.9	26.9	28.1	27.4
27 weeks or more	17.5	17.3	18.7	23.9	25.8	22.0	20.9	20.7	19.8	23.5	31.5	32.2
With 2 or more spells of unemployment	27.9	28.4	24.8	22.8	22.6	23.1	25.5	24.5	23.8	22.1	20.5	20.7
2 spells	12.5	12.9	11.9	11.0	11.6	10.7	12.2	12.5	10.9	11.0	9.4	9.6
3 or more spells	15.4	15.5	12.9	11.8	11.0	12.4	13.3	12.1	12.9	11.1	11.0	11.2
MEN												
Total with Unemployment Who Worked During the Year	100.0	100.0	100.0	100.0	100.0	100.0	100.0	100.0	100.0	100.0	100.0	100.0
Year-round workers with 1 or 2 weeks of unemployment	5.9	6.3	5.3	4.4	4.6	4.1	4.3	4.1	4.8	4.5	3.7	3.4
Part-year workers with unemployment	94.0	93.6	94.7	95.6	95.4	95.9	95.7	95.9	95.2	95.5	96.4	96.6
1 to 4 weeks	18.4	17.6	15.7	13.0	12.2	14.6	15.3	18.0	17.9	14.3	11.7	10.5
5 to 10 weeks	18.4	18.7	18.2	16.3	16.7	16.6	17.5	17.7	15.9	16.0	12.7	12.7
11 to 14 weeks	14.8	14.5	15.2	14.4	13.2	14.5	14.8	13.4	15.3	13.8	12.4	12.8
15 to 26 weeks	26.1	26.3	27.6	27.7	27.7	29.3	27.9	26.1	27.0	28.5	28.4	28.8
27 weeks or more	16.3	16.5	17.8	24.3	25.5	20.8	20.2	20.6	19.1	22.9	31.2	31.8
With 2 or more spells of unemployment	29.1	29.9	26.5	23.3	24.0	26.0	28.6	27.1	26.1	24.6	22.8	23.3
2 spells	12.4	13.3	12.6	11.1	12.1	11.5	13.6	13.2	11.1	11.6	10.3	10.1
3 or more spells	16.7	16.6	13.9	12.2	11.9	14.5	15.0	13.9	15.0	13.0	12.5	13.3
WOMEN												
Total With Unemployment Who Worked During the Year	100.0	100.0	100.0	100.0	100.0	100.0	100.0	100.0	100.0	100.0	100.0	100.0
Year-round workers with 1 or 2 weeks of unemployment	3.6	4.0	3.1	3.7	3.0	3.2	2.6	2.9	2.5	3.8	3.0	2.8
Part-year workers with unemployment	96.4	96.0	96.9	96.3	97.0	96.8	97.4	97.1	97.4	96.2	96.9	97.2
1 to 4 weeks	22.8	24.3	19.0	15.7	15.1	17.4	17.0	24.4	22.6	17.2	13.7	14.5
5 to 10 weeks	20.1	18.4	18.8	17.4	16.2	16.9	18.4	15.6	16.2	16.8	12.5	13.1
11 to 14 weeks	12.6	13.1	14.1	13.3	12.1	13.7	12.9	12.1	13.4	13.1	11.1	11.5
15 to 26 weeks	21.9	21.9	25.3	26.5	27.4	25.2	27.2	24.2	24.3	24.7	27.5	25.2
27 weeks or more	19.0	18.3	19.8	23.4	26.2	23.5	22.0	20.8	20.9	24.4	32.1	32.8
With 2 or more spells of unemployment	26.3	26.6	22.4	22.1	20.7	19.5	21.4	21.1	20.6	18.5	16.6	16.8
2 spells	12.6	12.4	10.9	10.9	10.9	9.8	10.3	11.5	10.7	10.2	8.0	8.8
3 or more spells	13.7	14.2	11.5	11.2	9.8	9.7	11.1	9.7	9.9	8.3	8.6	8.0

Table 1-39. Number and Median Annual Earnings of Year-Round, Full-Time Wage and Salary Workers, by Age, Sex, and Race, 1987–2010

(Thousands of people, dollars.)

Sex, age, and race	1987	1988	1989	1990	1991	1992	1993	1994	1995	1996	1997	1998
NUMBER												
Both Sexes, 16 Years and Over	71 069	73 598	74 898	74 728	74 449	75 517	77 427	79 875	83 407	85 611	86 905	89 748
16 to 24 years	7 563	7 400	7 471	6 978	6 571	6 224	6 685	6 684	6 892	6 809	7 063	7 618
25 to 44 years	42 211	44 036	45 082	45 086	44 811	45 022	45 951	47 150	48 695	49 225	49 513	50 264
25 to 34 years	22 884	23 727	23 721	23 201	22 541	22 469	22 637	23 193	23 310	23 071	23 186	23 048
35 to 44 years	19 327	20 309	21 361	21 885	22 270	22 553	23 314	23 957	25 385	26 154	26 327	27 216
45 to 54 years	12 764	13 506	13 848	14 070	14 718	15 652	16 424	17 366	18 436	19 714	20 109	21 274
55 to 64 years	7 406	7 529	7 321	7 458	7 219	7 590	7 208	7 500	8 122	8 455	8 901	9 273
65 years and over	1 125	1 127	1 177	1 137	1 130	1 029	1 159	1 174	1 263	1 408	1 318	1 318
Men, 16 Years and Over	42 490	43 785	45 107	44 574	43 523	43 894	45 494	47 255	49 334	50 407	50 772	52 509
16 to 24 years	4 145	4 165	4 223	3 982	3 596	3 457	3 853	3 918	4 094	3 942	4 021	4 479
25 to 44 years	25 293	26 246	27 321	27 069	26 353	26 335	27 161	28 000	28 940	29 282	29 453	29 763
25 to 34 years	13 659	14 163	14 439	13 941	13 303	13 146	13 400	13 749	13 844	13 817	13 735	13 612
35 to 44 years	11 634	12 083	12 882	13 128	13 050	13 189	13 761	14 251	15 096	15 465	15 718	16 151
45 to 54 years	7 726	8 086	8 276	8 168	8 479	8 908	9 522	10 120	10 589	11 372	11 388	12 030
55 to 64 years	4 654	4 616	4 562	4 650	4 403	4 588	4 238	4 460	4 884	4 908	5 133	5 438
65 years and over	672	672	725	705	694	606	719	757	827	903	775	801
Women, 16 Years and Over	28 579	29 812	29 791	30 155	30 925	31 622	31 933	32 619	34 073	35 203	36 133	37 239
16 to 24 years	3 418	3 235	3 249	2 995	2 976	2 767	2 832	2 767	2 798	2 867	3 041	3 140
25 to 44 years	16 918	17 790	17 760	18 017	18 458	18 688	18 790	19 150	19 755	19 942	20 060	20 503
25 to 34 years	9 225	9 564	9 282	9 260	9 238	9 323	9 237	9 444	9 467	9 254	9 451	9 437
35 to 44 years	7 693	8 226	8 478	8 757	9 220	9 365	9 553	9 706	10 288	10 688	10 609	11 066
45 to 54 years	5 037	5 420	5 572	5 902	6 239	6 744	6 902	7 246	7 847	8 343	8 721	9 244
55 to 64 years	2 752	2 913	2 758	2 808	2 816	3 002	2 970	3 040	3 238	3 547	3 767	3 836
65 years and over	453	455	451	433	436	423	439	417	436	505	543	517
White, 16 Years and Over	61 546	63 357	64 246	64 128	63 926	64 706	65 656	67 370	70 430	72 068	72 650	75 046
Men	37 461	38 449	39 430	38 915	38 018	38 267	39 347	40 589	42 608	43 554	43 429	44 901
Women	24 085	24 908	24 815	25 213	25 908	26 439	26 309	26 782	27 822	28 514	29 221	30 145
Black, 16 Years and Over	7 440	7 907	8 140	8 027	7 941	7 995	8 478	9 074	9 446	9 706	10 248	10 532
Men	3 838	3 976	4 219	4 162	4 001	4 011	4 259	4 598	4 686	4 682	5 026	5 202
Women	3 602	3 931	3 920	3 865	3 940	3 984	4 219	4 476	4 759	5 024	5 222	5 329
MEDIAN ANNUAL EARNINGS												
Both Sexes, 16 Years and Over	21 000	22 000	23 000	24 000	25 000	25 871	26 000	26 620	27 000	28 000	30 000	30 000
16 to 24 years	13 000	13 500	14 000	14 400	14 100	15 000	15 000	15 000	15 500	15 600	16 000	18 000
25 to 34 years	20 000	21 000	22 000	22 000	23 000	24 000	24 000	24 480	25 000	25 300	27 000	28 500
35 to 44 years	25 000	26 000	27 000	27 970	28 000	29 483	30 000	30 000	30 000	31 000	32 000	33 000
45 to 54 years	25 000	26 000	27 000	28 000	29 000	30 000	30 500	32 343	32 000	33 000	35 000	35 000
55 to 64 years	23 000	24 000	26 000	26 000	27 000	27 430	28 000	30 000	30 000	30 000	32 000	34 000
65 years and over	18 000	19 500	23 000	23 841	22 000	24 000	24 000	24 377	29 600	26 496	28 200	26 000
Men, 16 Years and Over	25 900	26 570	27 300	28 000	29 120	30 000	30 000	30 000	31 000	32 000	34 000	35 000
16 to 24 years	14 000	14 200	15 000	15 000	15 000	15 000	15 000	15 000	16 000	17 000	17 000	18 720
25 to 34 years	23 000	24 000	24 000	25 000	25 000	26 000	25 000	26 000	27 000	28 000	29 852	30 000
35 to 44 years	30 000	31 000	32 000	32 000	33 000	34 000	35 000	35 000	35 000	36 000	37 000	38 000
45 to 54 years	31 200	32 000	34 000	35 000	36 000	37 000	38 000	40 000	40 000	40 000	41 000	42 000
55 to 64 years	29 181	30 000	32 000	31 875	33 000	33 000	34 000	36 000	36 000	36 000	39 000	40 000
65 years and over	24 000	25 000	30 000	29 000	28 000	30 000	28 000	30 000	36 000	33 000	36 400	35 000
Women, 16 Years and Over	17 000	18 000	18 574	20 000	20 000	21 500	22 000	22 150	23 000	24 000	25 000	25 000
16 to 24 years	12 000	13 000	13 167	13 392	13 800	14 000	14 872	14 560	15 000	15 000	15 000	17 000
25 to 34 years	17 000	18 000	19 000	19 500	20 000	21 000	21 000	22 000	22 000	23 000	24 000	25 000
35 to 44 years	19 000	20 000	20 200	22 000	22 510	23 397	24 000	25 000	25 000	25 000	26 000	27 200
45 to 54 years	18 148	19 000	20 000	21 000	22 000	24 000	24 000	25 000	25 000	26 000	27 040	28 132
55 to 64 years	17 000	17 000	18 000	19 000	20 000	22 000	21 500	22 000	22 500	24 000	24 800	25 775
65 years and over	16 000	15 600	17 566	18 586	17 000	18 500	20 000	19 000	23 290	20 800	24 000	22 000
White, 16 Years and Over	22 000	23 000	24 000	25 000	25 000	26 200	27 000	28 000	28 000	29 000	30 000	31 000
Men	26 500	27 489	28 500	29 000	30 000	31 000	30 700	32 000	32 000	33 000	35 000	36 000
Women	17 000	18 000	19 000	20 000	20 500	22 000	22 000	23 000	23 000	24 000	25 000	26 000
Black, 16 Years and Over	17 000	18 000	19 000	19 350	20 000	21 000	20 800	21 000	22 000	23 784	24 000	25 000
Men	18 850	20 000	20 000	20 800	22 000	22 312	23 000	23 500	24 500	26 000	26 000	27 000
Women	15 500	16 200	17 115	18 000	18 500	20 000	19 843	20 000	20 000	21 000	22 000	23 000

Table 1-39. Number and Median Annual Earnings of Year-Round, Full-Time Wage and Salary Workers, by Age, Sex, and Race, 1987–2010—*Continued*

(Thousands of people, dollars.)

Sex, age, and race	1999	2000	2001	2002	2003	2004	2005	2006	2007	2008	2009	2010
NUMBER												
Both Sexes, 16 Years and Over	91 722	94 359	94 531	94 526	94 731	96 098	98 632	101 353	102 441	98 493	94 012	94 110
16 to 24 years	7 631	8 384	7 989	7 903	7 631	7 702	7 956	8 113	8 064	7 242	6 302	6 073
25 to 44 years	50 532	51 159	49 939	49 120	48 343	48 421	49 149	50 056	49 725	47 364	44 579	44 441
25 to 34 years	22 952	23 044	22 744	22 657	22 512	22 405	22 808	23 613	23 646	22 786	21 572	21 894
35 to 44 years	27 580	28 115	27 195	26 463	25 831	26 016	26 341	26 443	26 080	24 578	23 007	22 546
45 to 54 years	22 375	23 307	23 855	23 999	24 507	25 074	25 661	26 338	26 566	25 722	24 877	24 388
55 to 64 years	9 594	9 870	10 948	11 584	12 207	12 812	13 605	14 340	15 248	15 286	15 274	16 073
65 years and over	1 590	1 639	1 800	1 921	2 042	2 090	2 262	2 507	2 837	2 879	2 980	3 135
Men, 16 Years and Over	53 132	54 477	54 630	54 420	54 575	55 610	57 020	58 533	58 673	55 973	52 362	52 793
16 to 24 years	4 347	4 602	4 605	4 570	4 421	4 493	4 663	4 812	4 719	4 112	3 494	3 462
25 to 44 years	29 738	30 080	29 271	28 855	28 499	28 763	29 151	29 589	29 004	27 546	25 324	25 449
25 to 34 years	13 471	13 497	13 386	13 400	13 288	13 430	13 629	13 933	13 706	13 208	12 085	12 475
35 to 44 years	16 267	16 583	15 885	15 455	15 211	15 333	15 522	15 655	15 298	14 337	13 239	12 974
45 to 54 years	12 546	13 045	13 363	13 330	13 616	13 975	14 382	14 758	14 810	14 199	13 521	13 373
55 to 64 years	5 498	5 693	6 253	6 502	6 872	7 165	7 489	7 905	8 449	8 397	8 289	8 727
65 years and over	1 003	1 057	1 138	1 163	1 165	1 213	1 334	1 469	1 692	1 720	1 733	1 782
Women, 16 Years and Over	38 591	39 887	39 901	40 106	40 156	40 488	41 613	42 820	43 768	42 520	41 650	41 318
16 to 24 years	3 285	3 782	3 384	3 333	3 210	3 209	3 293	3 301	3 345	3 130	2 808	2 611
25 to 44 years	20 794	21 081	20 668	20 264	19 844	19 656	19 997	20 467	20 721	19 819	19 255	18 992
25 to 34 years	9 481	9 548	9 358	9 257	9 224	8 974	9 179	9 679	9 940	9 578	9 487	9 420
35 to 44 years	11 313	11 533	11 310	11 007	10 620	10 682	10 818	10 788	10 782	10 240	9 768	9 572
45 to 54 years	9 829	10 263	10 493	10 669	10 891	11 099	11 279	11 580	11 757	11 524	11 356	11 016
55 to 64 years	4 096	4 178	4 695	5 082	5 335	5 647	6 116	6 434	6 799	6 889	6 984	7 346
65 years and over	586	583	662	758	877	877	927	1 038	1 146	1 158	1 247	1 354
White, 16 Years and Over	76 203	77 790	78 306	77 632	77 545	78 236	80 546	82 411	83 139	79 980	76 470	76 557
Men	45 211	46 105	46 373	45 823	45 816	46 317	47 790	48 897	48 825	46 608	43 622	44 018
Women	30 992	31 685	31 933	31 809	31 729	31 919	32 756	33 513	34 314	33 372	32 848	32 540
Black, 16 Years and Over	11 145	11 899	11 001	10 966	10 979	11 301	11 417	11 988	11 987	11 424	10 716	10 676
Men	5 411	5 636	5 281	5 150	5 196	5 470	5 402	5 679	5 689	5 377	4 952	4 957
Women	5 734	6 264	5 720	5 816	5 783	5 832	6 015	6 309	6 299	6 046	5 764	5 719
MEDIAN ANNUAL EARNINGS												
Both Sexes, 16 Years and Over	31 000	32 000	34 000	35 000	35 000	35 672	36 400	38 000	40 000	40 000	41 000	42 000
16 to 24 years	18 000	19 000	20 000	20 000	20 000	20 000	20 000	21 000	22 421	24 000	23 532	23 000
25 to 34 years	30 000	30 000	31 000	31 800	32 000	33 000	33 000	35 000	35 000	36 500	38 000	37 815
35 to 44 years	34 992	35 000	36 000	37 000	39 000	40 000	40 000	41 000	43 000	45 000	45 000	45 000
45 to 54 years	36 000	38 000	39 500	40 000	40 000	40 000	42 000	44 000	45 000	45 000	46 000	48 000
55 to 64 years	35 000	35 000	36 400	39 145	40 000	40 000	41 000	43 000	45 000	46 000	48 000	49 000
65 years and over	30 000	32 000	32 000	33 000	32 000	35 000	35 000	35 001	40 000	42 000	42 000	45 000
Men, 16 Years and Over	36 000	37 600	38 500	40 000	40 000	40 000	40 051	42 000	45 000	46 000	48 000	48 000
16 to 24 years	19 000	20 000	20 000	20 000	20 800	20 800	20 800	22 000	23 000	25 000	25 000	24 000
25 to 34 years	32 000	33 500	34 000	34 740	35 000	35 000	35 000	36 000	38 000	40 000	40 000	40 000
35 to 44 years	40 000	40 000	42 000	43 000	43 900	45 000	45 000	48 000	50 000	50 000	50 000	50 000
45 to 54 years	44 616	45 000	45 000	47 000	48 000	48 000	50 000	50 000	50 000	50 000	52 000	55 000
55 to 64 years	40 853	44 000	45 000	47 000	50 000	50 000	50 000	50 000	52 000	54 000	55 000	55 000
65 years and over	36 000	35 999	35 000	37 861	42 000	40 000	41 000	44 000	44 000	50 000	49 000	50 002
Women, 16 Years and Over	26 000	27 500	29 000	30 000	30 000	30 001	32 000	33 000	35 000	35 000	36 000	37 000
16 to 24 years	17 000	18 000	19 000	19 000	20 000	20 000	20 000	20 000	22 000	22 000	22 000	20 816
25 to 34 years	26 000	27 000	28 080	29 500	30 000	30 000	30 000	31 000	33 000	34 000	35 000	35 000
35 to 44 years	28 000	29 000	30 000	30 400	32 000	32 800	35 000	35 000	36 000	38 000	38 000	40 000
45 to 54 years	30 000	30 000	32 000	32 000	33 466	34 771	35 000	36 000	37 163	38 000	40 000	40 000
55 to 64 years	27 000	28 000	30 000	31 410	32 000	33 000	33 000	35 000	37 100	39 000	40 000	40 000
65 years and over	20 800	24 000	25 000	28 000	26 000	27 000	28 768	27 878	31 000	34 193	36 000	40 000
White, 16 Years and Over	32 000	34 000	35 000	35 000	36 000	37 000	38 000	40 000	40 000	41 600	42 000	43 502
Men	37 200	39 000	40 000	40 000	40 000	42 000	42 000	44 707	45 000	48 000	49 000	50 000
Women	27 000	28 000	30 000	30 000	31 000	31 800	32 000	34 000	35 000	35 500	36 002	38 000
Black, 16 Years and Over	25 760	26 000	28 500	29 000	30 000	30 000	30 000	31 000	33 000	34 000	35 000	35 000
Men	30 000	30 000	30 000	30 000	32 000	30 000	33 000	34 000	35 000	37 500	38 000	36 000
Women	24 000	25 000	26 000	26 000	27 000	28 000	29 141	30 000	30 000	30 002	32 000	32 000

Table 1-40. Number and Median Annual Earnings of Year-Round, Full-Time Wage and Salary Workers, by Sex and Occupation of Job Held the Longest, 2002–2010

(Thousands of people, dollars.)

Sex and occupation	2002	2003	2004	2005	2006	2007	2008	2009	2010
Both Sexes, Number of Workers									
Management, business, and financial operations	15 707	15 552	15 575	16 299	16 806	17 115	17 259	16 491	16 889
Management	11 350	11 102	11 125	11 685	11 866	12 191	12 256	11 733	11 804
Business and financial operations	4 357	4 450	4 451	4 613	4 941	4 924	5 003	4 758	5 085
Professional and related	19 149	19 607	19 592	20 093	21 268	21 939	21 748	21 831	21 966
Computer and mathematical	2 644	2 598	2 680	2 779	2 888	3 180	3 089	3 100	2 993
Architecture and engineering	2 257	2 273	2 349	2 361	2 491	2 467	2 360	2 133	2 409
Life, physical, and social sciences	1 094	1 010	999	1 096	1 142	1 026	1 044	1 054	993
Community and social services	1 694	1 698	1 632	1 728	1 835	1 791	1 754	1 827	1 905
Legal	1 006	1 149	1 087	1 093	1 168	1 159	1 228	1 230	1 255
Education, training, and library	4 606	4 918	4 742	4 894	5 195	5 482	5 478	5 500	5 510
Arts, design, entertainment, sports, and media	1 453	1 374	1 416	1 362	1 633	1 554	1 415	1 404	1 380
Health care practitioner and technical	4 395	4 586	4 688	4 780	4 916	5 278	5 380	5 583	5 521
Services	12 011	11 990	12 457	13 117	13 236	13 553	13 034	12 944	12 855
Health care support	1 767	1 703	1 781	2 027	2 081	2 027	2 019	2 135	2 008
Protective services	2 042	2 385	2 406	2 429	2 506	2 511	2 472	2 593	2 589
Food preparation and serving related	3 592	3 223	3 383	3 586	3 646	3 769	3 504	3 307	3 408
Building and grounds cleaning and maintenance	2 843	2 942	3 116	3 285	3 120	3 198	3 027	2 870	2 942
Personal care and services	1 767	1 735	1 771	1 790	1 883	2 048	2 012	2 038	1 908
Sales and office	23 791	23 766	23 619	24 010	24 467	24 472	23 058	22 320	21 859
Sales and related	9 929	9 804	9 951	10 251	10 497	10 301	9 763	9 275	9 187
Office and administrative support	13 862	13 962	13 668	13 758	13 970	14 171	13 294	13 045	12 671
Natural resources, construction, and maintenance	9 823	9 709	10 574	10 864	11 295	10 745	10 002	8 599	8 298
Farming, fishing, and forestry	573	562	629	556	585	607	581	555	532
Construction and extraction	5 256	5 070	5 711	6 145	6 484	5 885	5 158	4 172	4 029
Installation, maintenance, and repair	3 994	4 077	4 234	4 163	4 226	4 252	4 264	3 872	3 737
Production, transportation, and material moving	13 386	13 391	13 648	13 586	13 704	13 907	12 649	11 062	11 518
Production	7 736	7 670	7 787	7 623	7 762	7 589	6 652	5 834	6 226
Transportation and material moving	5 650	5 721	5 861	5 963	5 942	6 318	5 997	5 228	5 292
Armed forces	658	717	632	664	576	709	744	765	727
Both Sexes, Median Annual Earnings									
Management, business, and financial operations	50 000	52 000	55 000	57 000	60 000	60 000	60 800	60 000	64 000
Management	55 000	58 000	60 000	60 000	62 500	65 000	65 000	65 000	68 000
Business and financial operations	44 000	45 000	45 000	49 000	50 000	50 000	52 000	55 000	56 000
Professional and related	46 000	46 000	48 000	50 000	50 000	51 000	54 000	55 000	55 000
Computer and mathematical	60 000	60 000	62 000	62 400	68 000	70 000	70 000	72 000	70 000
Architecture and engineering	59 400	62 000	60 000	65 000	69 000	70 000	70 000	70 000	75 000
Life, physical, and social sciences	50 000	50 000	50 000	53 500	57 000	60 000	57 532	60 000	60 000
Community and social services	34 000	34 349	36 000	36 000	36 780	39 000	40 000	40 000	40 000
Legal	61 860	75 000	70 000	72 000	70 000	70 000	75 000	80 000	75 000
Education, training, and library	38 000	39 000	40 000	40 000	40 282	44 984	45 000	46 000	45 000
Arts, design, entertainment, sports, and media	43 500	40 000	40 000	42 000	45 000	44 297	47 000	49 000	48 000
Health care practitioner and technical	46 000	48 000	50 000	50 000	52 000	52 800	55 000	55 000	57 638
Services	22 000	22 000	22 000	23 000	24 000	25 000	25 000	26 000	26 000
Health care support	22 100	22 000	22 000	22 000	23 000	24 500	26 000	26 000	26 270
Protective services	38 000	42 000	42 000	42 000	45 000	45 000	45 000	46 000	48 000
Food preparation and serving related	18 000	18 000	18 000	19 656	19 000	20 000	20 800	20 000	20 800
Building and grounds cleaning and maintenance	20 000	20 000	20 000	21 000	23 000	23 000	24 000	24 024	25 000
Personal care and services	21 840	20 678	22 537	23 000	23 000	25 000	25 000	25 000	25 000
Sales and office	30 000	30 000	30 000	31 200	32 002	34 000	35 000	35 000	35 000
Sales and related	35 000	35 000	35 000	35 000	37 000	38 000	38 500	38 000	40 000
Office and administrative support	28 000	29 000	30 000	30 000	30 000	32 000	32 500	34 000	34 000
Natural resources, construction, and maintenance	33 000	34 000	35 000	35 000	35 000	36 000	40 000	40 000	40 000
Farming, fishing, and forestry	20 000	20 000	20 000	21 000	20 000	24 000	24 000	24 000	23 000
Construction and extraction	31 200	32 000	33 000	32 000	35 000	35 000	39 000	40 000	40 000
Installation, maintenance, and repair	36 000	38 000	38 300	40 000	40 000	40 000	42 000	44 192	43 981
Production, transportation, and material moving	28 704	30 000	30 000	30 200	30 000	33 000	34 000	34 000	34 000
Production	28 000	30 000	30 000	30 000	30 000	33 000	34 000	32 006	34 000
Transportation and material moving	29 000	30 000	30 000	30 800	30 000	33 800	34 000	35 000	33 000
Armed forces	36 000	36 000	40 000	39 000	40 000	42 000	45 000	47 000	47 000

Table 1-40. Number and Median Annual Earnings of Year-Round, Full-Time Wage and Salary Workers, by Sex and Occupation of Job Held the Longest, 2002–2010—*Continued*

(Thousands of people, dollars.)

Sex and occupation	2002	2003	2004	2005	2006	2007	2008	2009	2010
Men, Number of Workers									
Management, business, and financial operations	9 178	8 961	8 849	9 496	9 519	9 784	9 836	9 418	9 569
Management	7 145	6 991	6 911	7 477	7 361	7 619	7 714	7 300	7 249
Business and financial operations	2 033	1 970	1 938	2 019	2 157	2 165	2 122	2 117	2 320
Professional and related	9 299	9 535	9 497	9 561	10 387	10 274	10 074	10 036	10 126
Computer and mathematical	1 953	1 913	1 972	2 060	2 159	2 378	2 348	2 227	2 244
Architecture and engineering	1 984	2 004	2 049	2 041	2 174	2 172	2 068	1 859	2 110
Life, physical, and social sciences	667	668	626	668	748	611	581	575	562
Community and social services	726	730	705	713	756	744	675	707	701
Legal	490	610	537	490	546	515	595	645	605
Education, training, and library	1 407	1 476	1 386	1 421	1 587	1 651	1 535	1 650	1 601
Arts, design, entertainment, sports, and media	847	811	848	789	953	790	782	829	839
Health care practitioner and technical	1 225	1 323	1 374	1 378	1 464	1 413	1 490	1 544	1 464
Services	5 988	6 204	6 314	6 658	6 715	6 871	6 389	6 379	6 426
Health care support	181	178	208	240	252	261	204	247	242
Protective services	1 689	1 967	1 906	1 919	1 998	2 000	1 930	2 026	2 070
Food preparation and serving related	1 836	1 638	1 716	1 873	1 991	1 985	1 816	1 744	1 743
Building and grounds cleaning and maintenance	1 788	1 914	2 002	2 153	1 939	2 048	1 911	1 832	1 862
Personal care and services	494	508	482	473	535	576	527	530	508
Sales and office	9 453	9 398	9 380	9 464	9 747	9 694	9 128	8 680	8 872
Sales and related	5 933	5 891	5 892	5 896	6 125	6 019	5 690	5 231	5 363
Office and administrative support	3 520	3 507	3 488	3 568	3 622	3 675	3 438	3 449	3 509
Natural resources, construction, and maintenance	9 434	9 348	10 178	10 503	10 904	10 343	9 627	8 225	7 936
Farming, fishing, and forestry	463	470	536	469	482	516	489	425	430
Construction and extraction	5 156	4 972	5 576	6 026	6 344	5 753	5 056	4 068	3 909
Installation, maintenance, and repair	3 815	3 905	4 065	4 008	4 078	4 074	4 081	3 732	3 597
Production, transportation, and material moving	10 472	10 492	10 812	10 747	10 733	11 047	10 226	8 921	9 214
Production	5 517	5 513	5 637	5 503	5 525	5 461	4 983	4 370	4 612
Transportation and material moving	4 955	4 979	5 176	5 244	5 208	5 585	5 242	4 552	4 602
Armed forces	600	636	580	591	528	660	696	703	649
Men, Median Annual Earnings									
Management, business, and financial operations	60 000	60 200	65 000	69 000	68 000	70 000	72 000	72 000	75 000
Management	65 000	65 000	70 000	70 000	70 000	75 000	75 000	75 000	78 000
Business and financial operations	52 000	51 000	55 000	60 000	60 000	60 000	65 000	65 000	67 000
Professional and related	55 000	58 000	58 000	60 000	61 000	62 000	67 000	65 000	67 000
Computer and mathematical	60 000	65 000	65 000	65 000	70 000	70 000	74 000	75 000	75 000
Architecture and engineering	60 000	64 558	61 785	66 921	70 000	72 000	74 000	72 000	77 000
Life, physical, and social sciences	52 000	50 801	55 000	62 000	61 000	65 000	65 000	65 000	64 000
Community and social services	35 000	35 000	38 000	40 000	39 000	40 000	44 085	45 000	42 002
Legal	100 000	100 000	101 000	108 000	100 000	104 146	130 000	120 000	120 000
Education, training, and library	45 600	48 000	47 000	50 000	50 000	50 000	54 000	52 000	53 000
Arts, design, entertainment, sports, and media	46 000	45 000	45 000	50 000	50 000	50 000	52 000	50 000	50 000
Health care practitioner and technical	72 000	65 500	70 000	70 000	72 000	75 000	75 000	74 000	75 000
Services	25 000	26 000	25 000	26 000	29 000	29 000	30 000	30 000	30 002
Health care support	24 000	22 537	20 400	22 880	25 000	25 000	28 000	30 000	34 000
Protective services	40 000	44 000	44 000	45 000	46 886	49 000	49 000	49 500	50 000
Food preparation and serving related	20 000	18 720	18 720	20 000	20 000	21 000	21 500	21 000	23 000
Building and grounds cleaning and maintenance	24 500	22 156	24 000	24 000	25 000	25 000	27 012	26 000	28 600
Personal care and services	30 000	28 559	26 000	30 000	30 000	30 000	30 500	30 000	30 000
Sales and office	38 000	39 000	40 000	40 000	40 000	42 000	40 000	42 002	42 000
Sales and related	41 600	41 000	44 000	42 000	45 000	45 000	48 000	48 002	48 000
Office and administrative support	32 000	32 000	34 000	34 000	35 000	36 000	35 000	37 400	37 000
Natural resources, construction, and maintenance	33 592	34 283	35 000	35 000	35 674	36 000	40 000	40 000	40 000
Farming, fishing, and forestry	22 000	22 000	22 000	22 500	20 000	24 000	24 000	25 000	23 400
Construction and extraction	31 304	32 000	33 000	32 000	35 000	35 000	40 000	40 000	40 000
Installation, maintenance, and repair	36 000	38 000	38 870	40 000	40 000	40 000	42 685	45 000	44 000
Production, transportation, and material moving	30 000	32 000	33 000	34 000	33 358	35 000	35 360	35 198	36 000
Production	30 360	32 000	34 000	35 000	35 000	36 000	36 000	36 000	36 944
Transportation and material moving	30 000	30 000	32 000	32 760	32 000	35 000	35 000	35 000	35 000
Armed forces	36 000	36 000	40 000	40 000	40 000	42 000	45 000	47 000	47 000

Table 1-40. Number and Median Annual Earnings of Year-Round, Full-Time Wage and Salary Workers, by Sex and Occupation of Job Held the Longest, 2002–2010—Continued

(Thousands of people, dollars.)

Sex and occupation	2002	2003	2004	2005	2006	2007	2008	2009	2010
Women, Number of Workers									
Management, business, and financial operations	6 529	6 591	6 726	6 803	7 287	7 332	7 423	7 073	7 320
Management	4 205	4 111	4 214	4 209	4 504	4 573	4 542	4 432	4 555
Business and financial operations	2 324	2 479	2 512	2 594	2 783	2 759	2 881	2 641	2 765
Professional and related	9 851	10 071	10 095	10 532	10 881	11 664	11 675	11 795	11 840
Computer and mathematical	691	685	708	718	729	802	741	873	748
Architecture and engineering	273	269	300	320	317	295	293	274	299
Life, physical, and social sciences	428	342	373	428	394	415	462	479	431
Community and social services	968	968	927	1 015	1 079	1 047	1 079	1 119	1 204
Legal	516	539	550	603	622	645	633	585	650
Education, training, and library	3 199	3 441	3 356	3 473	3 608	3 831	3 944	3 850	3 909
Arts, design, entertainment, sports, and media	606	563	568	573	681	764	633	575	541
Health care practitioner and technical	3 170	3 263	3 314	3 403	3 452	3 865	3 890	4 039	4 057
Services	6 026	5 786	6 144	6 459	6 522	6 682	6 645	6 565	6 429
Health care support	1 586	1 525	1 573	1 787	1 829	1 766	1 815	1 888	1 766
Protective services	354	419	500	510	509	511	541	567	519
Food preparation and serving related	1 757	1 585	1 668	1 713	1 655	1 784	1 688	1 563	1 665
Building and grounds cleaning and maintenance	1 055	1 029	1 115	1 132	1 181	1 150	1 116	1 038	1 079
Personal care and services	1 274	1 228	1 289	1 317	1 349	1 471	1 485	1 508	1 400
Sales and office	14 338	14 368	14 239	14 546	14 720	14 778	13 930	13 640	12 986
Sales and related	3 996	3 913	4 060	4 355	4 372	4 282	4 073	4 044	3 824
Office and administrative support	10 342	10 455	10 180	10 191	10 348	10 496	9 856	9 596	9 162
Natural resources, construction, and maintenance	391	361	396	360	391	402	376	374	361
Farming, fishing, and forestry	111	92	93	87	104	92	91	130	102
Construction and extraction	100	97	135	119	140	132	101	104	120
Installation, maintenance, and repair	180	172	169	155	148	178	183	140	140
Production, transportation, and material moving	2 914	2 899	2 835	2 839	2 971	2 861	2 423	2 141	2 304
Production	2 219	2 157	2 150	2 120	2 237	2 128	1 668	1 464	1 614
Transportation and material moving	695	742	685	719	734	733	755	676	690
Armed forces	58	81	52	73	48	49	49	62	78
Women, Median Annual Earnings									
Management, business, and financial operations	41 000	43 000	43 000	46 000	50 000	50 000	50 000	50 000	52 779
Management	44 000	47 000	46 000	50 000	52 000	52 000	55 000	52 999	55 000
Business and financial operations	38 500	40 000	40 000	41 000	46 000	45 000	48 000	48 000	50 000
Professional and related	40 000	40 000	40 000	42 000	43 000	45 000	46 000	48 002	49 000
Computer and mathematical	51 627	52 000	57 000	57 000	60 000	60 000	62 000	65 000	65 000
Architecture and engineering	50 000	48 000	47 500	55 000	52 000	55 000	50 000	61 000	60 000
Life, physical, and social sciences	44 000	45 000	45 995	50 000	48 000	48 000	49 000	54 651	56 000
Community and social services	33 000	33 000	35 000	35 000	36 000	37 000	37 700	39 000	39 000
Legal	45 000	45 000	46 000	47 500	50 000	47 500	52 001	60 000	57 257
Education, training, and library	35 000	35 000	37 000	38 000	38 632	41 000	42 000	43 000	42 000
Arts, design, entertainment, sports, and media	40 000	35 000	36 000	35 000	38 000	40 000	40 000	45 000	42 000
Health care practitioner and technical	41 000	43 000	45 000	46 000	48 000	50 000	50 000	52 000	53 000
Services	20 000	20 000	20 000	20 000	20 500	22 000	23 516	24 000	23 000
Health care support	22 000	22 000	22 000	21 000	23 000	24 500	26 000	25 000	25 000
Protective services	30 900	32 000	32 000	34 344	37 896	35 000	35 000	38 000	38 500
Food preparation and serving related	16 160	17 000	16 000	18 000	18 000	19 000	20 000	19 000	19 000
Building and grounds cleaning and maintenance	16 491	16 000	16 866	18 000	19 000	19 500	20 000	20 000	20 000
Personal care and services	20 000	20 000	21 000	20 800	20 000	24 000	24 000	24 700	23 000
Sales and office	26 989	28 000	28 000	29 000	30 000	30 000	30 600	31 400	32 000
Sales and related	25 000	26 000	26 000	26 000	26 000	28 000	29 000	30 000	30 000
Office and administrative support	27 000	28 000	28 000	29 800	30 000	30 002	32 000	32 100	33 000
Natural resources, construction, and maintenance	26 000	28 000	30 000	30 200	27 000	37 025	30 000	30 000	30 000
Farming, fishing, and forestry	17 000	16 000	15 700	18 000	18 808	24 117	24 685	21 000	20 000
Construction and extraction	26 000	29 500	40 000	31 200	24 980	40 000	34 500	31 000	33 670
Installation, maintenance, and repair	34 000	37 000	33 000	36 000	40 000	42 000	33 913	38 139	41 888
Production, transportation, and material moving	22 000	22 100	23 000	23 000	23 000	25 000	25 000	25 000	25 000
Production	21 632	22 000	23 000	23 400	23 000	25 000	25 000	25 000	25 000
Transportation and material moving	22 000	22 710	23 000	21 000	24 000	27 000	24 000	25 000	25 000
Armed forces	40 000	32 000	35 100	32 652	32 000	41 000	32 000	43 600	50 000

Table 1-41. Wage and Salary Workers Paid Hourly Rates with Earnings at or Below the Prevailing Federal Minimum Wage, by Selected Characteristics, 2009–2010

(Thousands of people, percent.)

Characteristic	Workers paid hourly rates				
	Total	Below prevailing federal minimum wage	At prevailing federal minimum wage	Total at or below prevailing federal minimum wage	
				Number	Percent of hourly-paid workers
2009					
Age and Sex					
Both sexes, 16 years and over	72 611	2 592	980	3 572	4.9
16 to 24 years	14 389	1 229	508	1 737	12.1
25 years and over	58 222	1 363	472	1 835	3.2
Men, 16 years and over	35 185	990	368	1 358	3.9
16 to 24 years	7 045	460	214	674	9.6
25 years and over	28 140	530	154	684	2.4
Women, 16 years and over	37 426	1 603	612	2 215	5.9
16 to 24 years	7 344	769	295	1 064	14.5
25 years and over	30 082	833	318	1 151	3.8
Race, Sex, and Hispanic Origin					
White, 16 years and over	58 633	2 094	763	2 857	4.9
Men	28 873	774	300	1 074	3.7
Women	29 760	1 320	463	1 783	6.0
Black, 16 years and over	9 269	327	168	495	5.3
Men	4 038	142	50	192	4.8
Women	5 231	185	117	303	5.8
Asian, 16 years and over	2 718	96	21	117	4.3
Men	1 258	41	6	47	3.8
Women	1 460	55	15	70	4.8
Hispanic,[1] 16 years and over	12 740	439	183	622	4.9
Men	7 291	210	80	291	4.0
Women	5 449	229	102	331	6.1
Full- and Part-Time Status[2] and Sex					
Full-time workers	52 454	952	320	1 273	2.4
Men	28 388	442	137	579	2.0
Women	24 066	511	183	694	2.9
Part-time workers	20 027	1 625	656	2 281	11.4
Men	6 721	540	229	768	11.4
Women	13 307	1 085	428	1 513	11.4
2010					
Age and Sex					
Both sexes, 16 years and over	72 902	2 541	1 820	4 360	6.0
16 to 24 years	14 061	1 180	955	2 135	15.2
25 years and over	58 842	1 360	865	2 225	3.8
Men, 16 years and over	35 498	943	669	1 612	4.5
16 to 24 years	6 913	438	413	850	12.3
25 years and over	28 585	505	257	762	2.7
Women, 16 years and over	37 404	1 598	1 151	2 748	7.3
16 to 24 years	7 148	743	543	1 285	18.0
25 years and over	30 256	855	608	1 463	4.8
Race, Sex, and Hispanic Origin					
White, 16 years and over	58 529	2 015	1 414	3 429	5.9
Men	28 949	716	538	1 254	4.3
Women	29 580	1 299	875	2 174	7.4
Black, 16 years and over	9 436	349	301	650	6.9
Men	4 137	152	92	244	5.9
Women	5 299	197	209	406	7.7
Asian, 16 years and over	2 920	104	36	140	4.8
Men	1 406	47	12	60	4.2
Women	1 513	57	24	80	5.3
Hispanic,[1] 16 years and over	12 977	462	360	822	6.3
Men	7 474	201	154	355	4.7
Women	5 503	261	207	468	8.5
Full- and Part-Time Status[2] and Sex					
Full-time workers	52 803	1 039	595	1 634	3.1
Men	28 574	444	255	699	2.4
Women	24 229	595	340	934	3.9
Part-time workers	19 994	1 496	1 220	2 716	13.6
Men	6 871	498	413	911	13.3
Women	13 123	998	807	1 806	13.8

Note: In 2009, the prevailing federal minimum wage was $6.55 until July 23, 2009. Beginning July 24, 2009, it increased to $7.25 per hour and remained $7.25 in 2010. Data are for wage and salary workers, excluding the incorporated self-employed. The data refer to a person's earnings on the sole or principal job, and pertain only to workers who are paid hourly rates. Salaried workers and other nonhourly workers are not included. The presence of workers with hourly earnings below the minimum wage does not necessarily indicate violation of the Fair Labor Standards Act, as there are exceptions to the minimum wage provisions of the law. In addition, some survey respondents reported hourly earnings below the minimum wage even though they earned the minimum wage or higher. Updated population controls are introduced annually with the release of January data.

[1]May be of any race.
[2]The distinction between full- and part-time workers is based on the hours usually worked. These data will not sum to totals because full- or part-time status on the principal job is not identifiable for a small number of multiple jobholders.
. . . = Not available.

Table 1-42. Absences from Work of Employed Full-Time Wage and Salary Workers, by Age and Sex, 2008–2010

(Thousands of people, percent.)

Year, sex, and age	Total employed	Absence rate[1]			Lost worktime rate[2]		
		Total	Illness or injury	Other reasons	Total	Illness or injury	Other reasons
2008							
Both Sexes, 16 Years and Over	102 307	3.1	2.2	0.9	1.7	1.2	0.5
16 to 19 years	1 345	2.4	1.5	0.9	1.3	0.7	0.5
20 to 24 years	8 528	2.9	2.0	0.9	1.4	0.9	0.6
25 years and over	92 433	3.2	2.2	0.9	1.7	1.2	0.5
25 to 54 years	75 837	3.1	2.1	1.0	1.7	1.1	0.6
55 years and over	16 597	3.6	2.9	0.7	2.0	1.7	0.3
Men, 16 Years and Over	57 019	2.3	1.8	0.5	1.2	1.0	0.3
16 to 19 years	799	1.5	1.0	0.5	0.6	0.5	0.2
20 to 24 years	4 797	2.0	1.5	0.4	0.9	0.7	0.2
25 years and over	51 424	2.3	1.8	0.5	1.3	1.0	0.3
25 to 54 years	42 477	2.2	1.7	0.5	1.2	0.9	0.3
55 years and over	8 946	3.0	2.5	0.5	1.8	1.5	0.3
Women, 16 Years and Over	45 288	4.1	2.7	1.4	2.3	1.4	0.9
16 to 19 years	546	3.6	2.2	1.4	2.2	1.1	1.1
20 to 24 years	3 732	4.0	2.5	1.5	2.2	1.1	1.0
25 years and over	41 010	4.2	2.8	1.4	2.3	1.4	0.8
25 to 54 years	33 359	4.2	2.6	1.5	2.3	1.3	0.9
55 years and over	7 650	4.2	3.4	0.8	2.3	1.9	0.4
2009							
Both Sexes, 16 Years and Over	99 838	3.3	2.3	1.0	1.7	1.2	0.5
16 to 19 years	1 135	4.0	2.8	1.2	1.3	0.8	0.4
20 to 24 years	7 804	3.2	2.2	1.0	1.4	0.9	0.5
25 years and over	90 898	3.3	2.3	1.0	1.7	1.2	0.5
25 to 54 years	73 626	3.2	2.2	1.0	1.7	1.1	0.6
55 years and over	17 272	3.5	2.9	0.7	1.9	1.6	0.3
Men, 16 Years and Over	55 047	2.4	1.8	0.6	1.2	1.0	0.2
16 to 19 years	662	2.8	2.1	0.7	0.9	0.8	0.1
20 to 24 years	4 305	2.2	1.7	0.6	0.8	0.6	0.2
25 years and over	50 080	2.4	1.9	0.5	1.3	1.0	0.2
25 to 54 years	40 870	2.3	1.7	0.5	1.2	0.9	0.3
55 years and over	9 210	3.0	2.4	0.5	1.7	1.5	0.2
Women, 16 Years and Over	44 791	4.4	2.9	1.5	2.3	1.4	0.9
16 to 19 years	473	5.7	3.9	1.8	1.8	0.9	0.9
20 to 24 years	3 499	4.4	2.9	1.5	2.0	1.1	0.9
25 years and over	40 818	4.4	2.9	1.5	2.3	1.5	0.9
25 to 54 years	32 756	4.4	2.8	1.6	2.4	1.4	1.0
55 years and over	8 062	4.2	3.4	0.8	2.2	1.9	0.4
2010							
Both Sexes, 16 Years and Over	99 390	3.1	2.2	0.9	1.6	1.1	0.5
16 to 19 years	1 017	3.5	2.6	0.9	1.1	0.7	0.4
20 to 24 years	7 518	3.0	2.1	0.9	1.3	0.8	0.5
25 years and over	90 855	3.1	2.2	0.9	1.6	1.1	0.5
25 to 54 years	73 026	3.1	2.1	1.0	1.6	1.0	0.5
55 years and over	17 830	3.4	2.8	0.6	1.8	1.6	0.3
Men, 16 Years and Over	54 991	2.3	1.8	0.5	1.2	0.9	0.2
16 to 19 years	606	2.8	2.2	0.6	1.1	0.8	0.3
20 to 24 years	4 125	2.0	1.5	0.5	0.7	0.6	0.2
25 years and over	50 260	2.3	1.8	0.5	1.2	1.0	0.2
25 to 54 years	40 763	2.2	1.6	0.5	1.1	0.9	0.2
55 years and over	9 497	2.9	2.4	0.5	1.6	1.4	0.2
Women, 16 Years and Over	44 399	4.2	2.8	1.4	2.2	1.3	0.8
16 to 19 years	411	4.5	3.2	1.3	1.2	0.6	0.5
20 to 24 years	3 393	4.3	2.9	1.4	2.1	1.2	0.9
25 years and over	40 596	4.2	2.8	1.4	2.2	1.4	0.8
25 to 54 years	32 263	4.2	2.7	1.5	2.2	1.3	1.0
55 years and over	8 333	4.0	3.3	0.8	2.1	1.7	0.3

Note: Since 2009, data reflect a modification in the estimation of the absence universe and are not strictly comparable with absence measures for prior years.

[1]Absences are defined as instances when persons who usually work 35 or more hours a week worked less than 35 hours during the reference week for reasons including own illness, injury, or medical problems; childcare problems; other family or personal obligations; civic or military duty; and maternity or paternity leave. Excluded are situations in which work was missed due to vacation or personal days, holidays, labor disputes, and other reasons. For multiple jobholders, absence data refer only to work missed at their main jobs. The absence rate is the ratio of workers with absences to total full-time wage and salary employment. The estimates of full-time wage and salary employment shown in this table do not match those in other tables because the estimates in this table are based on the full Current Population Survey (CPS) sample. Those in the other tables are based on a quarter of the sample only.
[2]Hours absent as a percentage of hours usually worked.

Table 1-43. Median Years of Tenure with Current Employer for Employed Wage and Salary Workers, by Age and Sex, Selected Years, February 1996–January 2010

(Number of years.)

Sex and age	February 1996	February 1998	February 2000	January 2002	January 2004	January 2006	January 2008	January 2010
Both Sexes								
16 years and over	3.8	3.6	3.5	3.7	4.0	4.0	4.1	4.4
16 to 17 years	0.7	0.6	0.6	0.7	0.7	0.6	0.7	0.7
18 to 19 years	0.7	0.7	0.7	0.8	0.8	0.7	0.8	1.0
20 to 24 years	1.2	1.1	1.1	1.2	1.3	1.3	1.3	1.5
25 years and over	5.0	4.7	4.7	4.7	4.9	4.9	5.1	5.2
25 to 34 years	2.8	2.7	2.6	2.7	2.9	2.9	2.7	3.1
35 to 44 years	5.3	5.0	4.8	4.6	4.9	4.9	4.9	5.1
45 to 54 years	8.3	8.1	8.2	7.6	7.7	7.3	7.6	7.8
55 to 64 years	10.2	10.1	10.0	9.9	9.6	9.3	9.9	10.0
65 years and over	8.4	7.8	9.4	8.6	9.0	8.8	10.2	9.9
Men								
16 years and over	4.0	3.8	3.8	3.9	4.1	4.1	4.2	4.6
16 to 17 years	0.6	0.6	0.6	0.8	0.7	0.7	0.7	0.7
18 to 19 years	0.7	0.7	0.7	0.8	0.8	0.7	0.8	1.0
20 to 24 years	1.2	1.2	1.2	1.4	1.3	1.4	1.4	1.6
25 years and over	5.3	4.9	4.9	4.9	5.1	5.0	5.2	5.3
25 to 34 years	3.0	2.8	2.7	2.8	3.0	2.9	2.8	3.2
35 to 44 years	6.1	5.5	5.3	5.0	5.2	5.1	5.2	5.3
45 to 54 years	10.1	9.4	9.5	9.1	9.6	8.1	8.2	8.5
55 to 64 years	10.5	11.2	10.2	10.2	9.8	9.5	10.1	10.4
65 years and over	8.3	7.1	9.0	8.1	8.2	8.3	10.4	9.7
Women								
16 years and over	3.5	3.4	3.3	3.4	3.8	3.9	3.9	4.2
16 to 17 years	0.7	0.6	0.6	0.7	0.6	0.6	0.6	0.7
18 to 19 years	0.7	0.7	0.7	0.8	0.8	0.7	0.8	1.0
20 to 24 years	1.2	1.1	1.0	1.1	1.3	1.2	1.3	1.5
25 years and over	4.7	4.4	4.4	4.4	4.7	4.8	4.9	5.1
25 to 34 years	2.7	2.5	2.5	2.5	2.8	2.8	2.6	3.0
35 to 44 years	4.8	4.5	4.3	4.2	4.5	4.6	4.7	4.9
45 to 54 years	7.0	7.2	7.3	6.5	6.4	6.7	7.0	7.1
55 to 64 years	10.0	9.6	9.9	9.6	9.2	9.2	9.8	9.7
65 years and over	8.4	8.7	9.7	9.4	9.6	9.5	9.9	10.1

Table 1-44. Median Years of Tenure with Current Employer for Employed Wage and Salary Workers, by Industry, Selected Years, February 2000–January 2010

(Number of years.)

Industry	February 2000	January 2002	January 2004	January 2006	January 2008	January 2010
TOTAL, 16 YEARS AND OVER	3.5	3.7	4.0	4.0	4.1	4.4
Private Sector	3.2	3.3	3.5	3.6	3.6	4.0
Agriculture and related industries	3.7	4.2	3.7	3.8	4.3	4.8
Nonagricultural industries	3.2	3.3	3.5	3.6	3.6	4.0
Mining	4.8	4.5	5.2	3.8	4.1	4.8
Construction	2.7	3.0	3.0	3.0	3.5	4.2
Manufacturing	4.9	5.4	5.8	5.5	5.9	6.1
Durable goods manufacturing	4.8	5.5	6.0	5.6	6.1	6.6
Nonmetallic mineral product	5.5	5.3	4.8	5.0	4.8	7.7
Primary metals and fabricated metal product	5.0	6.3	6.4	6.2	5.2	7.2
Machinery manufacturing	5.3	6.8	6.4	6.6	6.0	8.3
Computers and electronic product	3.9	4.7	5.2	5.9	6.7	5.9
Electrical equipment and appliances	5.0	5.5	9.8	6.2	6.2	5.0
Transportation equipment	6.4	7.0	7.7	7.2	7.8	8.3
Wood product	3.7	4.3	5.0	4.7	6.2	4.7
Furniture and fixtures	4.4	4.7	4.7	4.2	5.2	5.0
Miscellaneous manufacturing	3.7	4.5	4.6	3.9	4.7	5.4
Nondurable goods manufacturing	5.0	5.3	5.5	5.4	5.4	5.5
Food manufacturing	4.6	5.0	4.9	5.2	4.3	4.7
Beverage and tobacco product	5.5	4.6	8.0	5.4	6.9	8.1
Textiles, apparel, and leather	4.7	5.0	5.0	4.4	4.6	4.7
Paper and printing	5.1	6.2	6.9	6.3	5.5	6.8
Petroleum and coal product	9.5	9.8	11.4	5.0	4.3	5.1
Chemicals	6.0	5.7	5.3	6.1	7.6	7.3
Plastics and rubber product	4.6	5.3	5.7	5.0	5.3	7.4
Wholesale and retail trade	2.7	2.8	3.1	3.1	3.2	3.6
Wholesale trade	3.9	3.9	4.3	4.6	5.0	5.2
Retail trade	2.5	2.6	2.8	2.8	2.9	3.3
Transportation and utilities	4.7	4.9	5.3	4.9	5.1	5.3
Transportation and warehousing	4.0	4.3	4.7	4.3	4.6	5.0
Utilities	11.5	13.4	13.3	10.4	10.1	9.1
Information[1]	3.4	3.3	4.3	4.8	4.7	5.0
Publishing, except Internet	4.2	4.8	4.7	5.3	4.7	5.6
Motion picture and sound recording industries	1.6	2.3	2.2	1.9	1.9	3.8
Broadcasting, except Internet	3.6	3.1	4.0	4.6	3.4	4.3
Telecommunications	4.3	3.4	4.6	5.3	6.9	6.6
Financial activities	3.5	3.6	3.9	4.0	4.5	4.6
Finance and insurance	3.6	3.9	4.1	4.1	4.7	4.8
Finance	3.3	3.6	4.0	3.9	4.4	4.5
Insurance	4.4	4.5	4.4	4.7	5.2	5.5
Real estate and rental and leasing	3.1	3.0	3.3	3.4	3.7	3.9
Real estate	3.1	3.2	3.5	3.5	3.9	4.1
Rental and leasing services	3.0	2.2	2.9	3.1	3.0	3.3
Professional and business services	2.4	2.7	3.2	3.2	3.1	3.4
Professional and technical services	2.6	3.1	3.6	3.8	3.3	4.0
Management, administrative, and waste services[1]	2.0	2.1	2.6	2.5	2.5	2.9
Administrative and support services	1.8	1.9	2.4	2.4	2.4	2.8
Waste management and remediation services	3.6	4.3	3.4	4.1	4.1	2.9
Education and health services	3.4	3.5	3.6	4.0	4.1	4.1
Education services	3.2	3.6	3.8	4.0	4.3	4.4
Health care and social assistance	3.5	3.5	3.6	4.1	4.1	4.1
Hospitals	5.1	4.9	4.7	5.2	5.4	5.3
Health services, except hospitals	3.2	3.1	3.3	3.6	3.6	3.6
Social assistance	2.4	2.5	2.8	3.1	3.0	3.1
Leisure and hospitality	1.7	1.8	2.0	1.9	2.1	2.5
Arts, entertainment, and recreation	2.6	2.3	2.8	3.1	2.8	3.3
Accommodation and food services	1.5	1.6	1.9	1.6	1.9	2.3
Accommodation	2.8	2.7	3.1	2.5	3.1	3.3
Food services and drinking places	1.4	1.4	1.6	1.4	1.6	2.2
Other services	3.1	3.3	3.3	3.2	3.3	4.0
Other services, except private households	3.2	3.3	3.5	3.3	3.4	4.1
Repair and maintenance	3.0	3.0	3.2	2.9	3.0	4.0
Personal and laundry services	2.7	2.8	3.4	2.8	3.2	3.5
Membership associations and organizations	4.0	4.1	3.9	4.2	4.4	4.5
Other services, private households	3.0	2.7	2.3	2.8	2.8	3.4
Public Sector	7.1	6.7	6.9	6.9	7.2	7.2
Federal government	11.5	11.3	10.4	9.9	9.9	7.9
State government	5.5	5.4	6.4	6.3	6.5	6.4
Local government	6.7	6.2	6.4	6.6	7.1	7.5

Note: Data beginning in 2000 reflect the introduction of Census 2000 population controls. Data for 2004 forward reflect updated population controls introduced annually with the release of January data.

[1]Includes other industries not shown separately.

Table 1-45. Employment Status of the Population, by Sex and Marital Status, March 1990–March 2011

(Thousands of people, percent.)

Marital status and year	Men Population	Men Labor force Total Number	Men Labor force Total Percent of population	Men Employed	Men Unemployed Number	Men Unemployed Percent of labor force	Women Population	Women Labor force Total Number	Women Labor force Total Percent of population	Women Employed	Women Unemployed Number	Women Unemployed Percent of labor force
Single												
1990	25 757	18 829	73.1	16 893	1 936	10.3	21 088	14 003	66.4	12 856	1 147	8.2
1991	26 220	19 014	72.5	16 418	2 596	13.7	21 688	14 125	65.1	12 887	1 238	8.8
1992	26 529	19 229	72.5	16 401	2 828	14.7	21 738	14 072	64.7	12 793	1 279	9.1
1993	26 951	19 625	72.8	16 858	2 767	14.1	21 848	14 091	64.5	12 711	1 380	9.8
1994	28 350	20 365	71.8	17 826	2 539	12.5	22 885	14 903	65.1	13 419	1 484	10.0
1995	28 318	20 449	72.2	18 286	2 163	10.6	22 853	14 974	65.5	13 673	1 301	8.7
1996	28 695	20 561	71.7	18 097	2 464	12.0	23 632	15 417	65.2	14 084	1 333	8.6
1997	29 294	20 942	71.5	18 683	2 259	10.8	24 215	16 178	66.8	14 747	1 431	8.8
1998	29 558	21 255	71.9	19 124	2 131	10.0	24 808	16 885	68.1	15 626	1 259	7.5
1999	29 883	21 329	71.4	19 465	1 864	8.7	25 674	17 486	68.1	16 185	1 301	7.4
2000	30 232	21 641	71.6	19 823	1 818	8.4	25 863	17 749	68.6	16 446	1 303	7.3
2001	30 968	22 232	71.8	20 239	1 993	9.0	26 180	17 900	68.4	16 631	1 269	7.1
2002	32 220	22 761	70.6	20 066	2 695	11.8	26 942	18 079	67.1	16 499	1 580	8.7
2003	32 852	22 821	69.5	20 194	2 627	11.5	27 527	17 901	65.0	16 219	1 682	9.4
2004	33 786	23 212	68.7	20 434	2 778	12.0	28 033	18 089	64.5	16 506	1 583	8.8
2005	34 069	23 335	68.5	20 831	2 504	10.7	28 508	18 554	65.1	16 902	1 652	8.9
2006	34 906	24 369	69.8	21 961	2 408	9.9	29 357	18 989	64.7	17 444	1 545	8.1
2007	35 359	24 506	69.3	22 224	2 281	9.3	29 695	19 218	64.7	17 935	1 284	6.7
2008	36 522	25 229	69.1	22 695	2 534	10.0	30 772	19 889	64.6	18 369	1 520	7.6
2009	36 907	24 930	67.5	20 645	4 284	17.2	31 038	19 785	63.7	17 714	2 071	10.5
2010	38 110	25 663	67.3	21 038	4 626	18.0	32 085	19 973	62.3	17 517	2 457	12.3
2011	38 766	25 646	66.2	21 389	4 256	16.6	33 041	20 581	62.3	18 117	2 463	12.0
Married, Spouse Present												
1990	52 464	41 020	78.2	39 562	1 458	3.6	53 207	30 967	58.2	29 870	1 097	3.5
1991	52 460	40 883	77.9	38 843	2 040	5.0	53 176	31 103	58.5	29 668	1 435	4.6
1992	52 780	40 930	77.5	38 650	2 280	5.6	53 464	31 686	59.3	30 130	1 556	4.9
1993	53 488	41 255	77.1	39 069	2 186	5.3	54 146	32 158	59.4	30 757	1 401	4.4
1994	53 436	40 993	76.7	39 085	1 908	4.7	54 198	32 863	60.6	31 397	1 466	4.5
1995	54 166	41 806	77.2	40 262	1 544	3.7	54 902	33 563	61.1	32 267	1 296	3.9
1996	53 996	41 837	77.5	40 356	1 481	3.5	54 640	33 382	61.1	32 258	1 124	3.4
1997	53 981	41 967	77.7	40 628	1 339	3.2	54 611	33 907	62.1	32 836	1 071	3.2
1998	54 685	42 288	77.3	41 039	1 249	3.0	55 241	34 136	61.8	33 028	1 108	3.2
1999	55 256	42 557	77.0	41 476	1 081	2.5	55 801	34 349	61.6	33 403	946	2.8
2000	55 897	43 254	77.4	42 261	993	2.3	56 432	34 959	61.9	33 998	961	2.7
2001	56 152	43 463	77.4	42 245	1 218	2.8	56 740	35 234	62.1	34 273	961	2.7
2002	57 325	44 271	77.2	42 508	1 763	4.0	57 883	35 624	61.5	34 295	1 329	3.7
2003	57 940	44 700	77.1	42 797	1 903	4.3	58 545	36 185	61.8	34 806	1 379	3.8
2004	58 395	44 860	76.8	43 247	1 613	3.6	59 008	35 918	60.9	34 582	1 336	3.7
2005	58 854	45 263	76.9	43 763	1 500	3.3	59 449	35 809	60.2	34 738	1 071	3.0
2006	58 850	45 082	76.6	43 877	1 205	2.7	59 476	36 192	60.9	35 185	1 007	2.8
2007	60 126	46 129	76.7	44 813	1 317	2.9	60 656	37 335	61.6	36 370	965	2.6
2008	59 455	45 451	76.4	43 958	1 493	3.3	60 108	37 074	61.7	35 919	1 155	3.1
2009	60 132	45 741	76.1	42 667	3 074	6.7	60 818	37 536	61.7	35 540	1 996	5.3
2010	59 694	45 110	75.6	41 762	3 348	7.4	60 339	37 201	61.7	34 964	2 237	6.0
2011	59 477	44 553	74.9	41 667	2 886	6.5	60 095	36 383	60.5	34 340	2 043	5.6
Widowed, Divorced, or Separated												
1990	11 152	7 513	67.4	6 959	554	7.4	23 857	11 168	46.8	10 530	638	5.7
1991	11 588	7 804	67.3	6 985	819	10.5	24 105	11 145	46.2	10 386	759	6.8
1992	11 927	8 049	67.5	7 140	909	11.3	24 582	11 486	46.7	10 610	876	7.6
1993	11 861	7 956	67.1	7 055	901	11.3	24 661	11 308	45.9	10 528	780	6.9
1994	12 239	8 156	66.6	7 382	774	9.5	25 098	11 879	47.3	10 995	884	7.4
1995	12 410	8 315	67.0	7 632	683	8.2	25 373	12 001	47.3	11 308	693	5.8
1996	13 176	8 697	66.0	7 976	721	8.3	25 786	12 430	48.2	11 742	688	5.5
1997	14 113	9 420	66.7	8 715	705	7.5	26 301	12 814	48.7	12 071	743	5.8
1998	14 166	9 482	66.9	8 954	528	5.6	26 092	12 880	49.4	12 235	645	5.0
1999	14 225	9 449	66.4	8 971	478	5.1	26 199	12 951	49.4	12 307	644	5.0
2000	14 289	9 623	67.3	9 152	471	4.9	26 354	13 228	50.2	12 657	571	4.3
2001	14 392	9 421	65.5	8 927	494	5.2	26 747	13 454	50.3	12 887	567	4.2
2002	14 617	9 650	66.0	8 931	719	7.5	27 802	13 716	49.3	12 855	861	6.3
2003	15 180	9 855	64.9	9 020	835	8.5	28 240	14 154	50.1	13 240	914	6.5
2004	15 059	9 789	65.0	9 059	730	7.5	28 228	14 194	50.3	13 324	870	6.1
2005	15 779	10 256	65.0	9 569	687	6.7	28 576	14 233	49.8	13 472	761	5.3
2006	16 405	10 815	65.9	10 141	674	6.2	28 981	14 220	49.1	13 539	681	4.8
2007	16 247	10 799	66.5	10 150	650	6.0	28 950	14 320	49.5	13 620	700	4.9
2008	16 718	10 896	65.2	10 083	812	7.5	29 419	14 553	49.5	13 765	787	5.4
2009	16 719	10 687	63.9	9 224	1 463	13.7	29 471	14 449	49.0	13 169	1 281	8.9
2010	17 016	10 863	63.8	9 188	1 675	15.4	29 915	14 707	49.2	13 285	1 422	9.7
2011	17 744	11 095	62.5	9 676	1 420	12.8	29 876	14 610	48.9	13 221	1 389	9.5

Note: See notes and definitions for information on historical comparability.

Table 1-45. Employment Status of the Population, by Sex and Marital Status, March 1990–March 2011 —Continued

(Thousands of people, percent.)

Marital status and year	Men						Women					
	Population	Labor force					Population	Labor force				
		Total		Employed	Unemployed			Total		Employed	Unemployed	
		Number	Percent of population		Number	Percent of labor force		Number	Percent of population		Number	Percent of labor force
Widowed												
1990	2 331	519	22.3	490	29	5.6	11 477	2 243	19.5	2 149	94	4.2
1991	2 385	486	20.4	448	38	7.8	11 288	2 150	19.0	2 044	106	4.9
1992	2 529	566	22.4	501	65	11.5	11 325	2 131	18.8	2 029	102	4.8
1993	2 468	596	24.1	535	61	10.2	11 214	1 961	17.5	1 856	105	5.4
1994	2 220	474	21.4	440	34	7.2	11 073	1 945	17.6	1 825	120	6.2
1995	2 282	496	21.7	469	27	5.4	11 080	1 941	17.5	1 844	97	5.0
1996	2 476	487	19.7	466	21	4.3	11 070	1 916	17.3	1 820	96	5.0
1997	2 686	559	20.8	529	30	5.4	11 058	2 018	18.2	1 926	92	4.6
1998	2 567	563	21.9	551	12	2.1	11 027	2 157	19.6	2 071	86	4.0
1999	2 540	562	22.1	532	30	5.3	10 943	2 039	18.6	1 942	97	4.8
2000	2 601	583	22.4	547	36	6.2	11 061	2 011	18.2	1 911	100	5.0
2001	2 638	568	21.5	546	22	3.9	11 182	2 137	19.1	2 045	92	4.3
2002	2 635	629	23.9	581	48	7.6	11 411	2 001	17.5	1 887	114	5.7
2003	2 694	628	23.3	588	40	6.4	11 295	2 087	18.5	1 991	96	4.6
2004	2 651	581	21.9	558	23	4.0	11 159	2 157	19.3	2 048	109	5.1
2005	2 729	618	22.6	590	28	4.5	11 125	2 111	19.0	2 005	106	5.0
2006	2 626	610	23.2	563	47	7.7	11 305	2 164	19.1	2 094	70	3.2
2007	2 697	631	23.4	588	43	6.8	11 220	2 058	18.3	1 971	87	4.2
2008	2 911	656	22.5	611	44	6.8	11 399	2 218	19.5	2 101	117	5.3
2009	2 813	632	22.5	543	90	14.2	11 446	2 174	19.0	2 032	143	6.6
2010	2 969	776	26.1	684	92	11.8	11 379	2 214	19.5	2 036	178	8.0
2011	2 931	698	23.8	648	50	7.1	11 310	2 291	20.3	2 118	173	7.6
Divorced												
1990	6 256	5 004	80.0	4 639	365	7.3	8 845	6 678	75.5	6 333	345	5.2
1991	6 586	5 262	79.9	4 722	540	10.3	9 152	6 779	74.1	6 365	414	6.1
1992	6 743	5 418	80.3	4 823	595	11.0	9 569	7 076	73.9	6 578	498	7.0
1993	6 770	5 330	78.7	4 736	594	11.1	9 879	7 183	72.7	6 736	447	6.2
1994	7 222	5 548	76.8	5 028	520	9.4	10 113	7 473	73.9	6 962	511	6.8
1995	7 343	5 739	78.2	5 266	473	8.2	10 262	7 559	73.7	7 206	353	4.7
1996	7 734	5 954	77.0	5 468	486	8.2	10 508	7 829	74.5	7 468	361	4.6
1997	8 191	6 298	76.9	5 851	447	7.1	11 102	8 092	72.9	7 666	426	5.3
1998	8 307	6 378	76.8	6 045	333	5.2	11 065	8 038	72.6	7 687	351	4.4
1999	8 529	6 481	76.0	6 151	330	5.1	11 130	8 171	73.4	7 841	330	4.0
2000	8 532	6 583	77.2	6 279	304	4.6	11 061	8 505	76.9	8 217	288	3.4
2001	8 580	6 403	74.6	6 074	329	5.1	11 719	8 662	73.9	8 335	327	3.8
2002	8 643	6 519	75.4	6 053	466	7.1	12 227	8 902	72.8	8 416	486	5.5
2003	8 938	6 621	74.1	6 052	569	8.6	12 653	9 191	72.6	8 673	518	5.6
2004	8 942	6 622	74.1	6 104	518	7.8	12 817	9 246	72.1	8 706	540	5.8
2005	9 196	6 754	73.4	6 281	473	7.0	12 950	9 253	71.5	8 836	417	4.5
2006	9 646	7 065	73.2	6 631	434	6.1	13 107	9 188	70.1	8 799	389	4.2
2007	9 608	7 110	74.0	6 679	431	6.1	13 214	9 334	70.6	8 896	439	4.7
2008	9 767	7 106	72.8	6 607	499	7.0	13 551	9 387	69.3	8 938	449	4.8
2009	9 938	7 052	71.0	6 064	988	14.0	13 301	9 176	69.0	8 402	774	8.4
2010	9 944	7 018	70.6	5 888	1 131	16.1	13 758	9 394	68.3	8 510	885	9.4
2011	10 635	7 394	69.5	6 430	965	13.0	13 757	9 230	67.1	8 407	823	8.9
Separated												
1990	2 565	1 990	77.6	1 830	160	8.0	3 535	2 247	63.6	2 048	199	8.9
1991	2 616	2 057	78.6	1 816	241	11.7	3 665	2 216	60.5	1 977	239	10.8
1992	2 655	2 065	77.8	1 816	249	12.1	3 688	2 279	61.8	2 003	276	12.1
1993	2 623	2 030	77.4	1 784	246	12.1	3 568	2 165	60.7	1 937	228	10.5
1994	2 797	2 134	76.3	1 914	220	10.3	3 911	2 461	62.9	2 208	253	10.3
1995	2 784	2 081	74.7	1 898	183	8.8	4 031	2 501	62.0	2 258	243	9.7
1996	2 966	2 255	76.0	2 041	214	9.5	4 209	2 684	63.8	2 453	231	8.6
1997	3 236	2 563	79.2	2 335	228	8.9	4 141	2 705	65.3	2 480	225	8.3
1998	3 293	2 542	77.2	2 358	184	7.2	4 000	2 683	67.1	2 476	207	7.7
1999	3 156	2 405	76.2	2 287	118	4.9	4 126	2 740	66.4	2 523	217	7.9
2000	3 157	2 456	77.8	2 326	130	5.3	4 012	2 711	67.6	2 528	183	6.8
2001	3 174	2 450	77.2	2 307	143	5.8	3 846	2 654	69.0	2 507	147	5.5
2002	3 339	2 502	74.9	2 297	205	8.2	4 164	2 812	67.5	2 551	261	9.3
2003	3 548	2 606	73.4	2 380	226	8.7	4 293	2 877	67.0	2 576	301	10.5
2004	3 466	2 586	74.6	2 397	189	7.3	4 251	2 791	65.7	2 569	222	8.0
2005	3 855	2 884	74.8	2 698	186	6.4	4 501	2 870	63.8	2 632	238	8.3
2006	4 132	3 141	76.0	2 947	194	6.2	4 569	2 869	62.8	2 647	222	7.7
2007	3 943	3 058	77.6	2 883	176	5.7	4 516	2 927	64.8	2 753	174	6.0
2008	4 040	3 134	77.6	2 865	269	8.6	4 469	2 947	65.9	2 726	221	7.5
2009	3 968	3 002	75.7	2 617	386	12.8	4 725	3 099	65.6	2 734	364	11.8
2010	4 103	3 069	74.8	2 616	452	14.7	4 778	3 099	64.8	2 739	359	11.6
2011	4 178	3 004	71.9	2 598	406	13.5	4 809	3 089	64.2	2 696	393	12.7

Note: See notes and definitions for information on historical comparability.

Table 1-46. Employment Status of All Women and Single Women, by Presence and Age of Children, March 1990–March 2011

(Thousands of women, percent.)

Presence and age of children and year	All women							Single women					
	Civilian labor force	Civilian labor force as percent of population	Employed			Unemployed		Civilian labor force	Civilian labor force as percent of population	Employed			Unemployed	
			Number	Percent full time	Percent part time	Number	Percent of labor force			Number	Percent full time	Percent part time	Number	Percent of labor force
Women with No Children Under 18 Years														
1990	33 942	52.3	32 391	74.4	25.6	1 551	4.6	12 478	68.1	11 611	65.9	34.1	866	6.9
1991	34 047	52.0	32 167	74.0	26.0	1 880	5.5	12 472	67.0	11 529	66.2	33.8	943	7.6
1992	34 487	52.3	32 481	74.3	25.7	2 006	5.8	12 355	66.9	11 374	66.6	33.4	982	7.9
1993	34 495	52.1	32 476	74.6	25.4	2 020	5.9	12 223	66.4	11 201	66.1	33.9	1 022	8.4
1994	35 454	53.1	33 343	72.7	27.3	2 110	6.0	12 737	66.8	11 674	64.5	35.5	1 063	8.3
1995	35 843	52.9	34 054	72.9	27.1	1 789	5.0	12 870	67.1	11 919	64.5	35.5	951	7.4
1996	36 509	53.0	34 698	73.3	26.7	1 811	5.0	13 172	66.1	12 255	64.6	35.4	918	7.0
1997	37 295	53.6	35 572	73.7	26.3	1 723	4.6	13 405	66.5	12 442	64.0	36.0	964	7.2
1998	38 253	54.1	36 680	74.1	25.9	1 573	4.1	13 888	67.2	13 082	64.8	35.2	806	5.8
1999	39 316	54.3	37 589	74.6	25.4	1 727	4.4	14 435	67.1	13 491	65.6	34.4	944	6.5
2000	40 142	54.8	38 408	75.4	24.6	1 733	4.3	14 677	67.6	13 713	66.6	33.4	964	6.6
2001	40 836	54.9	39 219	75.7	24.3	1 617	4.0	14 877	67.4	13 993	67.3	32.7	884	5.9
2002	41 278	54.0	39 038	75.1	24.9	2 241	5.4	14 855	65.6	13 682	65.9	34.1	1 173	7.9
2003	42 039	54.1	39 667	74.8	25.2	2 372	5.6	14 678	63.5	13 430	65.1	34.9	1 249	8.5
2004	42 289	53.8	40 000	74.6	25.4	2 289	5.4	14 828	63.0	13 670	65.5	34.5	1 157	7.8
2005	42 039	54.1	39 667	74.8	25.2	2 372	5.6	14 678	63.5	13 430	65.1	34.9	1 249	8.5
2006	43 392	53.6	41 440	75.3	24.7	1 952	4.5	15 673	63.4	14 547	66.5	33.5	1 125	7.2
2007	44 039	53.9	42 279	75.3	24.7	1 760	4.0	15 704	63.4	14 801	66.4	33.6	903	5.7
2008	45 585	54.3	43 417	75.7	24.3	2 168	4.8	16 378	63.4	15 261	67.4	32.6	1 116	6.8
2009	45 649	53.8	42 343	73.3	26.7	3 306	7.2	16 112	62.1	14 607	64.9	35.1	1 506	9.3
2010	46 098	53.5	42 256	73.5	26.5	3 842	8.3	16 331	60.7	14 533	65.6	34.4	1 798	11.0
2011	46 198	53.0	42 569	73.3	26.7	3 629	7.9	16 758	60.8	15 016	65.2	34.8	1 743	10.4
Women with Children Under 18 Years														
1990	22 196	66.7	20 865	73.0	27.0	1 331	6.0	1 525	55.2	1 244	79.1	20.9	280	18.4
1991	22 327	66.6	20 774	73.0	27.0	1 552	7.0	1 654	53.6	1 358	76.4	23.6	296	17.9
1992	22 756	67.2	21 052	73.8	26.2	1 704	7.5	1 716	52.5	1 420	75.9	24.1	297	17.3
1993	23 063	66.9	21 521	73.9	26.1	1 541	6.7	1 869	54.4	1 510	74.8	25.2	359	19.2
1994	24 191	68.4	22 467	70.8	29.2	1 724	7.1	2 166	56.9	1 745	73.9	26.1	421	19.4
1995	24 695	69.7	23 195	71.7	28.3	1 500	6.1	2 104	57.5	1 754	73.6	26.4	350	16.6
1996	24 720	70.2	23 386	72.6	27.4	1 334	5.4	2 245	60.5	1 829	73.5	26.5	416	18.5
1997	25 604	72.1	24 082	74.1	25.9	1 522	5.9	2 772	68.1	2 305	76.6	23.4	467	16.8
1998	25 647	72.3	24 209	74.0	26.0	1 438	5.6	2 997	72.5	2 544	75.6	24.4	453	15.1
1999	25 469	72.1	24 305	74.1	25.9	1 165	4.6	3 051	73.4	2 694	75.8	24.2	357	11.7
2000	25 795	72.9	24 693	74.6	25.4	1 102	4.3	3 073	73.9	2 734	79.7	20.3	339	11.0
2001	25 751	73.1	24 572	75.6	24.4	1 179	4.6	3 022	73.8	2 638	81.8	18.2	385	12.7
2002	26 140	72.2	24 612	74.8	25.2	1 529	5.8	3 224	75.3	2 818	79.1	20.9	406	12.6
2003	26 202	71.7	24 598	74.3	25.7	1 603	6.1	3 222	73.1	2 789	79.5	20.5	433	13.4
2004	25 913	70.7	24 413	74.2	25.8	1 501	5.8	3 262	72.6	2 836	76.8	23.2	426	13.1
2005	26 202	71.7	24 598	74.3	25.7	1 603	6.1	3 222	73.1	2 789	79.5	20.5	433	13.4
2006	26 009	70.6	24 728	75.6	24.4	1 281	4.9	3 317	71.5	2 896	77.8	22.2	420	12.7
2007	26 834	71.3	25 646	75.2	24.8	1 188	4.4	3 514	71.4	3 133	76.4	23.6	381	10.8
2008	25 930	71.2	24 637	75.7	24.3	1 294	5.0	3 511	71.0	3 108	78.0	22.0	403	11.5
2009	26 122	71.6	24 079	74.6	25.4	2 043	7.8	3 673	72.0	3 108	75.8	24.2	566	18.2
2010	25 783	71.3	23 510	73.7	26.3	2 273	8.8	3 642	70.1	2 984	71.9	28.1	659	18.1
2011	25 376	70.9	23 109	74.2	25.8	2 266	8.9	3 822	70.0	3 102	71.9	28.1	721	18.9
Women with Children Under 6 Years														
1990	9 397	58.2	8 732	69.6	30.4	664	7.1	929	48.7	736	75.0	25.0	194	20.9
1991	9 636	58.4	8 758	69.5	30.5	878	9.1	1 050	48.8	819	72.2	27.8	231	22.0
1992	9 573	58.0	8 662	70.2	29.8	911	9.5	1 029	45.8	829	73.2	26.8	200	19.4
1993	9 621	57.9	8 764	70.1	29.9	857	8.9	1 125	47.4	869	70.0	30.0	257	22.8
1994	10 328	60.3	9 394	67.1	32.9	935	9.1	1 379	52.2	1 062	70.0	30.0	317	23.0
1995	10 395	62.3	9 587	67.5	32.5	809	7.8	1 328	53.0	1 069	68.6	31.4	259	19.5
1996	10 293	62.3	9 592	68.4	31.6	701	6.8	1 378	55.1	1 099	67.3	32.7	279	20.2
1997	10 610	65.0	9 800	70.5	29.5	810	7.6	1 755	65.1	1 424	71.6	28.4	330	18.8
1998	10 619	65.2	9 839	69.8	30.2	780	7.3	1 755	67.3	1 448	71.7	28.3	307	17.5
1999	10 322	64.4	9 674	69.0	31.0	648	6.3	1 811	68.1	1 565	71.0	29.0	246	13.6
2000	10 316	65.3	9 763	70.5	29.5	553	5.4	1 835	70.5	1 603	75.3	24.7	232	12.6
2001	10 200	64.9	9 618	71.2	28.8	582	5.7	1 783	69.7	1 542	79.1	20.9	242	13.6
2002	10 193	64.1	9 441	70.4	29.6	752	7.4	1 819	71.0	1 568	74.5	25.5	251	13.8
2003	10 209	62.9	9 433	70.0	30.0	776	7.6	1 893	70.2	1 614	75.2	24.8	279	14.7
2004	10 131	62.2	9 407	69.4	30.6	724	7.1	1 885	68.4	1 605	70.1	29.9	279	14.8
2005	10 209	62.9	9 433	70.0	30.0	776	7.6	1 893	70.2	1 614	75.2	24.8	279	14.7
2006	10 430	63.0	9 779	72.0	28.0	651	6.2	1 934	68.6	1 659	72.8	27.2	276	14.3
2007	10 894	63.5	10 305	71.9	28.1	589	5.4	2 066	67.4	1 827	72.7	27.3	239	11.6
2008	10 452	63.6	9 794	72.1	27.9	657	6.3	1 982	66.0	1 705	72.2	27.8	277	14.0
2009	10 497	63.6	9 517	71.8	28.2	980	9.3	2 137	67.8	1 754	70.3	29.7	383	17.9
2010	10 536	64.2	9 452	70.9	29.1	1 085	10.3	2 076	65.6	1 643	67.0	33.0	433	20.9
2011	10 403	64.2	9 268	71.3	28.7	1 135	10.9	2 177	65.8	1 678	65.5	34.5	499	22.9

Note: See notes and definitions for information on historical comparability.

Table 1-47. Employment Status of Ever-Married Women and Married Women, Spouse Present, by Presence and Age of Children, March 1990–March 2011

(Thousands of women, percent.)

Presence and age of children and year	Ever-married women[1]						Married women, spouse present					
	Civilian labor force	Civilian labor force as percent of population	Employed			Unemployed		Civilian labor force	Civilian labor force as percent of population	Employed			Unemployed
			Number	Percent full time	Percent part time	Number	Percent of labor force			Number	Percent full time	Percent part time	Number	Percent of labor force
Women with No Children Under 18														
1990	21 464	46.1	20 779	79.1	20.9	685	3.2	14 467	51.1	14 068	77.3	22.7	399	2.8
1991	21 575	46.1	20 637	78.4	21.6	937	4.3	14 529	51.2	13 976	77.6	22.4	552	3.8
1992	22 132	46.6	21 108	78.5	21.5	1 024	4.6	14 851	51.9	14 247	77.8	22.2	604	4.1
1993	22 273	46.6	21 275	79.0	21.0	998	4.5	15 211	52.4	14 630	77.6	22.4	581	3.8
1994	22 716	47.6	21 669	77.1	22.9	1 047	4.6	15 234	53.2	14 641	75.6	24.4	593	3.9
1995	22 973	47.3	22 134	77.4	22.6	839	3.7	15 594	53.2	15 072	76.3	23.7	522	3.3
1996	23 337	47.7	22 444	78.1	21.9	893	3.8	15 628	53.4	15 123	76.8	23.2	506	3.2
1997	23 890	48.3	23 130	78.9	21.1	760	3.2	15 750	54.2	15 315	77.7	22.3	435	2.8
1998	24 366	48.7	23 598	79.3	20.7	767	3.1	16 007	54.1	15 581	78.3	21.7	426	2.7
1999	24 881	48.9	24 098	79.7	20.3	783	3.1	16 484	54.4	16 061	78.2	21.8	423	2.6
2000	25 465	49.4	24 695	80.3	19.7	769	3.0	16 786	54.7	16 357	79.1	20.9	429	2.6
2001	25 959	49.6	25 226	80.4	19.6	733	2.8	16 909	54.8	16 528	78.7	21.3	381	2.3
2002	26 423	49.1	25 356	80.0	20.0	1 068	4.0	17 353	54.8	16 780	78.4	21.6	573	3.3
2003	27 361	50.1	26 238	79.7	20.3	1 123	4.1	17 901	55.7	17 273	78.6	21.4	628	3.5
2004	27 461	49.8	26 329	79.3	20.7	1 131	4.1	17 965	55.0	17 367	78.6	21.4	598	3.3
2005	27 361	50.1	26 238	79.7	20.3	1 123	4.1	17 901	55.7	17 273	78.6	21.4	628	3.5
2006	27 719	49.3	26 893	80.1	19.9	827	3.0	18 124	54.8	17 691	79.3	20.7	434	2.4
2007	28 335	49.8	27 477	80.1	19.9	858	3.0	18 766	55.4	18 326	79.6	20.4	441	2.3
2008	29 207	50.3	28 156	80.2	19.8	1 052	3.6	19 188	55.9	18 650	79.8	20.2	539	2.8
2009	29 536	50.2	27 737	77.8	22.2	1 800	6.1	19 541	55.8	18 521	77.3	22.7	1 019	5.2
2010	29 767	50.2	27 723	77.7	22.3	2 044	6.9	19 579	55.8	18 454	77.3	22.7	1 125	5.7
2011	29 440	49.4	27 553	77.7	22.3	1 886	6.4	19 316	54.6	18 285	77.4	22.6	1 031	5.3
Women with Children Under 18 Years														
1990	20 671	67.8	19 621	72.6	27.4	1 051	5.1	16 500	66.3	15 803	69.8	30.2	698	4.2
1991	20 673	67.9	19 416	72.8	27.2	1 257	6.1	16 575	66.8	15 692	70.1	29.9	883	5.3
1992	21 040	68.8	19 633	73.6	26.4	1 407	6.7	16 835	67.8	15 884	71.3	28.7	952	5.7
1993	21 194	68.3	20 011	73.9	26.1	1 183	5.6	16 947	67.5	16 127	71.4	28.6	820	4.8
1994	22 025	69.8	20 722	70.5	29.5	1 303	5.9	17 628	69.0	16 755	68.0	32.0	873	5.0
1995	22 591	71.1	21 441	71.5	28.5	1 150	5.1	17 969	70.2	17 195	68.8	31.2	774	4.3
1996	22 475	71.4	21 556	72.5	27.5	919	4.1	17 754	70.0	17 136	69.6	30.4	618	3.5
1997	22 831	72.6	21 777	73.9	26.1	1 054	4.6	18 157	71.1	17 521	71.6	28.4	636	3.5
1998	22 650	72.3	21 665	73.8	26.2	985	4.3	18 129	70.6	17 447	71.5	28.5	682	3.8
1999	22 419	71.9	21 611	73.9	26.1	808	3.6	17 865	70.1	17 342	71.5	28.5	523	2.9
2000	22 722	72.7	21 960	74.0	26.0	763	3.4	18 174	70.6	17 641	71.7	28.3	533	2.9
2001	22 729	73.0	21 934	74.9	25.1	795	3.5	18 325	70.8	17 745	72.6	27.4	580	3.2
2002	22 917	71.8	21 794	74.3	25.7	1 122	4.9	18 271	69.6	17 515	71.7	28.3	756	4.1
2003	22 979	71.5	21 809	73.7	26.3	1 170	5.1	18 284	69.2	17 533	71.0	29.0	751	4.1
2004	22 651	70.5	21 576	73.8	26.2	1 075	4.7	17 953	68.2	17 215	71.3	28.7	738	4.1
2005	22 979	71.5	21 809	73.7	26.3	1 170	5.1	18 284	69.2	17 533	71.0	29.0	751	4.1
2006	22 692	70.5	21 831	75.3	24.7	861	3.8	18 067	68.4	17 494	73.0	27.0	574	3.2
2007	23 320	71.3	22 513	75.0	25.0	807	3.5	18 569	69.3	18 045	72.6	27.4	524	2.8
2008	22 419	71.2	21 529	75.4	24.6	890	4.0	17 886	69.4	17 269	73.6	26.4	616	3.4
2009	22 449	71.5	20 972	74.5	25.5	1 477	6.6	17 995	69.8	17 018	73.1	26.9	977	5.4
2010	22 141	71.5	20 526	74.0	26.0	1 615	7.3	17 622	69.7	16 510	72.6	27.4	1 112	6.3
2011	21 553	71.1	20 008	74.6	25.4	1 546	7.2	17 067	69.1	16 055	73.1	26.9	1 012	5.9
Women with Children Under 6 Years														
1990	8 467	59.5	7 996	69.1	30.9	471	5.6	7 247	58.9	6 901	67.4	32.6	346	4.8
1991	8 585	59.9	7 938	69.2	30.8	647	7.5	7 434	59.9	6 933	67.5	32.5	501	6.7
1992	8 544	60.0	7 832	69.9	30.1	711	8.3	7 333	59.9	6 819	68.5	31.5	514	7.0
1993	8 496	59.6	7 895	70.2	29.8	600	7.1	7 289	59.6	6 840	68.8	31.2	450	6.2
1994	8 949	61.8	8 332	66.7	33.3	617	6.9	7 723	61.7	7 291	65.4	34.6	432	5.6
1995	9 067	63.9	8 517	67.4	32.6	550	6.1	7 759	63.5	7 349	66.1	33.9	409	5.3
1996	8 915	63.6	8 493	68.6	31.4	422	4.7	7 590	62.7	7 297	66.5	33.5	293	3.9
1997	8 856	64.9	8 376	70.3	29.7	480	5.4	7 582	63.6	7 252	69.1	30.9	330	4.4
1998	8 864	64.8	8 391	69.5	30.5	473	5.3	7 655	63.7	7 309	68.1	31.9	346	4.5
1999	8 511	63.7	8 109	68.6	31.4	402	4.7	7 246	61.8	6 979	67.1	32.9	267	3.7
2000	8 481	64.3	8 159	69.5	30.5	321	3.8	7 341	62.8	7 087	68.1	31.9	254	3.5
2001	8 417	64.0	8 077	69.7	30.3	340	4.0	7 319	62.5	7 062	68.5	31.5	257	3.5
2002	8 373	62.8	7 873	69.6	30.4	501	6.0	7 166	60.8	6 804	67.7	32.3	363	5.1
2003	8 315	61.4	7 818	68.9	31.1	497	6.0	7 175	59.8	6 826	67.1	32.9	349	4.9
2004	8 246	61.0	7 801	69.3	30.7	445	5.4	7 107	59.3	6 774	68.1	31.9	332	4.7
2005	8 315	61.4	7 818	68.9	31.1	497	6.0	7 175	59.8	6 826	67.1	32.9	349	4.9
2006	8 496	61.9	8 121	71.8	28.2	375	4.4	7 366	60.3	7 092	70.6	29.4	274	3.7
2007	8 829	62.7	8 479	71.7	28.3	350	4.0	7 664	61.5	7 407	70.8	29.2	257	3.4
2008	8 470	63.0	8 089	72.1	27.9	381	4.5	7 285	61.6	6 999	70.9	29.1	285	3.9
2009	8 360	62.6	7 763	72.1	27.9	597	7.1	7 231	61.6	6 805	71.4	28.6	426	5.9
2010	8 460	63.8	7 809	71.7	28.3	651	7.7	7 227	62.5	6 741	71.5	28.5	486	6.7
2011	8 226	63.7	7 590	72.5	27.5	636	7.7	7 061	62.3	6 608	71.9	28.1	453	6.4

[1]Ever-married women are women who are, or have ever been, married.

Table 1-48. Employment Status of Women Who Maintain Families, by Marital Status and Presence and Age of Children, March 1995–March 2011

(Thousands of women, percent.)

Marital status, age of children, and year	Civilian noninstitutional population	Civilian labor force					Not in the labor force
		Number	Percent of the population	Employed	Unemployed		
					Number	Percent of the labor force	
Total, Women Who Maintain Families							
1995	12 762	8 192	64.2	7 527	665	8.1	4 570
1996	12 993	8 460	65.1	7 832	628	7.4	4 532
1997	13 258	8 998	67.9	8 192	806	9.0	4 260
1998	13 102	8 976	68.5	8 309	667	7.4	4 127
1999	13 191	9 213	69.8	8 596	617	6.7	3 978
2000	13 145	9 226	70.2	8 592	634	6.9	3 918
2001	12 930	9 034	69.9	8 453	581	6.4	3 897
2002	13 489	9 523	70.6	8 755	768	8.1	3 966
2003	14 000	9 759	69.7	8 898	861	8.8	4 241
2004	14 165	9 869	69.7	9 054	815	8.3	4 297
2005	14 391	9 941	69.1	9 140	801	8.1	4 450
2006	14 485	9 966	68.8	9 227	739	7.4	4 520
2007	14 833	10 172	68.6	9 510	661	6.5	4 662
2008	14 820	10 166	68.6	9 447	719	7.1	4 654
2009	14 813	10 140	68.5	9 034	1 106	10.9	4 673
2010	15 214	10 206	67.1	9 027	1 179	11.6	5 008
2011	15 461	10 462	67.7	9 141	1 321	12.6	5 000
Women with No Children Under 18 Years							
1995	4 610	2 471	53.6	2 394	77	3.1	2 139
1996	4 847	2 552	52.7	2 462	90	3.5	2 295
1997	4 909	2 663	54.2	2 571	92	3.5	2 246
1998	4 952	2 649	53.5	2 578	71	2.7	2 303
1999	4 942	2 667	54.0	2 556	111	4.2	2 275
2000	5 097	2 707	53.1	2 546	161	5.9	2 390
2001	5 185	2 772	53.5	2 668	104	3.8	2 413
2002	5 119	2 764	54.0	2 628	136	4.9	2 355
2003	5 457	2 934	53.8	2 728	206	7.0	2 522
2004	5 551	3 052	55.0	2 855	197	6.5	2 499
2005	5 692	3 095	54.4	2 961	134	4.3	2 597
2006	5 693	3 088	54.2	2 945	143	4.6	2 604
2007	5 823	3 124	53.7	2 990	134	4.3	2 699
2008	6 022	3 352	55.7	3 167	185	5.5	2 670
2009	6 068	3 332	54.9	3 075	258	7.7	2 735
2010	6 414	3 417	53.3	3 131	286	8.4	2 997
2011	6 403	3 455	54.0	3 131	324	9.4	2 948
Women with Children Under 18 Years							
1995	8 152	5 720	70.2	5 132	588	10.3	2 431
1996	8 146	5 908	72.5	5 370	538	9.1	2 237
1997	8 348	6 335	75.9	5 621	714	11.3	2 014
1998	8 151	6 327	77.6	5 731	596	9.4	1 823
1999	8 248	6 546	79.4	6 040	506	7.7	1 702
2000	8 048	6 520	81.0	6 046	474	7.3	1 528
2001	7 746	6 261	80.8	5 785	476	7.6	1 484
2002	8 370	6 759	80.8	6 127	632	9.4	1 611
2003	8 543	6 825	79.9	6 170	655	9.6	1 718
2004	8 614	6 817	79.1	6 199	618	9.1	1 798
2005	8 699	6 846	78.7	6 179	667	9.7	1 853
2006	8 793	6 878	78.2	6 282	596	8.7	1 915
2007	9 010	7 047	78.2	6 520	527	7.5	1 963
2008	8 798	6 814	77.4	6 280	535	7.8	1 984
2009	8 745	6 807	77.8	5 959	848	12.5	1 938
2010	8 800	6 789	77.1	5 896	893	13.2	2 011
2011	9 059	7 007	77.4	6 009	998	14.2	2 052
Single Women with No Children Under 18 Years							
1995	779	534	68.5	508	26	4.9	245
1996	895	588	65.7	572	16	2.7	308
1997	860	585	68.0	563	22	3.8	275
1998	893	637	71.3	613	24	3.8	256
1999	969	674	69.6	638	36	5.3	295
2000	1 004	720	71.7	642	78	10.8	284
2001	1 096	787	71.8	756	31	3.9	309
2002	1 154	796	69.0	747	49	6.2	358
2003	1 254	814	64.9	713	101	12.4	440
2004	1 381	977	70.7	887	90	9.2	404
2005	1 388	926	66.7	855	71	7.7	463
2006	1 370	933	68.1	861	72	7.7	437
2007	1 413	986	69.8	930	57	5.7	427
2008	1 515	1 057	69.8	989	68	6.5	458
2009	1 531	1 069	69.8	967	102	9.6	462
2010	1 718	1 166	67.9	1 041	125	10.7	552
2011	1 729	1 178	68.2	1 047	132	11.2	551

Note: See notes and definitions for information on historical comparability.

Table 1-48. Employment Status of Women Who Maintain Families, by Marital Status and Presence and Age of Children, March 1995–March 2011—*Continued*

(Thousands of women, percent.)

Marital status, age of children, and year	Civilian noninstitutional population	Civilian labor force					Not in the labor force
		Number	Percent of the population	Employed	Unemployed		
					Number	Percent of the labor force	
Single Women with Children Under 18 Years							
1995	2 613	1 510	57.8	1 261	249	16.5	1 102
1996	2 639	1 633	61.9	1 346	287	17.6	1 006
1997	3 012	2 087	69.3	1 749	338	16.2	925
1998	3 083	2 280	74.0	1 960	320	14.0	803
1999	3 163	2 415	76.4	2 146	269	11.1	748
2000	3 167	2 413	76.2	2 151	262	10.9	754
2001	3 097	2 351	75.9	2 055	296	12.6	745
2002	3 315	2 566	77.4	2 241	325	12.7	749
2003	3 421	2 584	75.5	2 272	312	12.1	837
2004	3 414	2 568	75.2	2 233	335	13.0	846
2005	3 591	2 708	75.4	2 325	383	14.1	882
2006	3 671	2 710	73.8	2 370	340	12.5	961
2007	3 748	2 782	74.2	2 491	291	10.4	966
2008	3 721	2 743	73.7	2 448	295	10.8	978
2009	3 872	2 877	74.3	2 448	429	14.9	995
2010	3 948	2 868	72.6	2 379	488	17.0	1 081
2011	4 193	3 072	73.3	2 522	550	17.9	1 120
Widowed, Divorced, or Separated Women with No Children Under 18 Years							
1995	3 831	1 938	50.6	1 887	51	2.6	1 894
1996	3 952	1 964	49.7	1 890	74	3.8	1 988
1997	4 049	2 077	51.3	2 008	69	3.3	1 971
1998	4 058	2 011	49.6	1 965	46	2.3	2 047
1999	3 974	1 993	50.2	1 918	75	3.8	1 980
2000	4 093	1 987	48.5	1 904	83	4.2	2 106
2001	4 088	1 985	48.6	1 912	73	3.7	2 104
2002	3 964	1 968	49.6	1 882	86	4.4	1 997
2003	4 203	2 121	50.5	2 016	105	5.0	2 082
2004	4 170	2 075	49.8	1 968	107	5.2	2 095
2005	4 304	2 170	50.4	2 106	64	2.9	2 135
2006	4 323	2 156	49.9	2 084	72	3.3	2 168
2007	4 410	2 138	48.5	2 061	77	3.6	2 272
2008	4 507	2 295	50.9	2 178	117	5.1	2 213
2009	4 536	2 263	49.9	2 108	155	6.9	2 273
2010	4 696	2 251	47.9	2 090	161	7.1	2 445
2011	4 674	2 276	48.7	2 084	192	8.4	2 397
Widowed, Divorced, or Separated Women with Children Under 18 Years							
1995	5 539	4 210	76.0	3 871	339	8.1	1 329
1996	5 507	4 275	77.6	4 024	251	5.9	1 231
1997	5 337	4 248	79.6	3 872	376	8.9	1 089
1998	5 068	4 047	79.9	3 771	276	6.8	1 020
1999	5 086	4 131	81.2	3 894	237	5.7	955
2000	4 881	4 107	84.1	3 895	212	5.2	774
2001	4 649	3 910	84.1	3 730	180	4.6	739
2002	5 056	4 193	82.9	3 886	307	7.3	862
2003	5 122	4 241	82.8	3 898	343	8.1	881
2004	5 201	4 249	81.7	3 966	283	6.7	952
2005	5 108	4 137	81.0	3 854	283	6.8	971
2006	5 121	4 167	81.4	3 912	255	6.1	955
2007	5 262	4 266	81.1	4 029	237	5.5	997
2008	5 077	4 071	80.2	3 832	239	5.9	1 006
2009	4 873	3 930	80.7	3 511	420	10.7	943
2010	4 852	3 922	80.8	3 517	405	10.3	931
2011	4 866	3 935	80.9	3 487	448	11.4	931

Note: See notes and definitions for information on historical comparability.

Table 1-49. Number and Age of Children in Families, by Type of Family and Labor Force Status of Mother, March 1990–March 2011

(Thousands of children.)

Age of children and year	Total children	Mother in labor force	Mother not in labor force	Married-couple families			Families maintained by women			Families maintained by men
				Total	Mother in labor force	Mother not in labor force	Total	Mother in labor force	Mother not in labor force	
Children Under 18 Years										
1990	59 596	36 712	21 110	45 898	29 077	16 820	11 925	7 635	4 290	1 774
1991	60 330	36 968	21 526	45 912	29 056	16 856	12 582	7 912	4 670	1 836
1992	61 262	38 081	21 176	45 966	29 882	16 084	13 291	8 199	5 093	2 005
1993	62 020	38 542	21 444	46 499	30 054	16 445	13 487	8 488	4 999	2 034
1994	63 407	40 186	21 188	47 247	31 279	15 968	14 127	8 907	5 220	2 033
1995	63 989	41 365	20 421	47 675	32 190	15 486	14 111	9 176	4 935	2 202
1996	64 506	41 573	20 449	47 484	31 764	15 720	14 538	9 809	4 729	2 484
1997	64 710	42 747	19 223	47 529	32 263	15 265	14 441	10 483	3 958	2 740
1998	65 043	43 156	19 069	47 909	32 533	15 376	14 317	10 623	3 694	2 818
1999	65 191	43 419	19 074	47 945	32 193	15 752	14 547	11 226	3 322	2 699
2000	65 601	44 188	18 674	48 902	33 149	15 753	13 960	11 039	2 921	2 739
2001	65 777	44 051	18 864	49 352	33 436	15 916	13 563	10 615	2 948	2 862
2002	65 978	43 821	19 243	48 836	32 673	16 163	14 228	11 149	3 079	2 914
2003	66 521	43 769	19 782	49 004	32 411	16 593	14 547	11 359	3 189	2 970
2004	66 386	43 144	20 229	48 656	31 892	16 764	14 717	11 252	3 465	3 014
2005	66 526	43 239	20 179	48 688	31 886	16 802	14 729	11 352	3 377	3 108
2006	66 883	43 278	20 440	48 853	31 946	16 908	14 865	11 332	3 532	3 165
2007	67 228	44 116	20 073	48 927	32 496	16 431	15 263	11 620	3 643	3 038
2008	67 153	43 798	19 966	48 303	32 110	16 193	15 461	11 688	3 773	3 388
2009	66 913	43 509	20 074	48 384	32 065	16 315	15 204	11 444	3 759	3 326
2010	66 811	43 335	19 913	47 730	31 686	16 044	15 518	11 649	3 869	3 563
2011	66 804	42 882	20 260	47 051	30 902	16 149	16 091	11 980	4 111	3 662
Children 6 to 17 Years										
1990	39 095	25 805	12 079	29 726	20 067	9 659	8 157	5 737	2 420	1 211
1991	39 470	25 806	12 392	29 598	19 907	9 691	8 599	5 899	2 701	1 272
1992	40 064	26 666	12 067	29 673	20 586	9 087	9 060	6 079	2 980	1 331
1993	40 622	27 046	12 291	30 233	20 796	9 437	9 104	6 249	2 854	1 285
1994	41 795	28 179	12 287	30 895	21 663	9 233	9 570	6 516	3 054	1 329
1995	42 423	28 931	12 000	31 298	22 239	9 059	9 633	6 692	2 941	1 492
1996	42 964	29 381	11 897	31 231	22 092	9 139	10 047	7 289	2 758	1 685
1997	43 488	30 308	11 400	31 509	22 602	8 906	10 199	7 705	2 493	1 781
1998	43 771	30 579	11 367	31 707	22 706	9 001	10 238	7 873	2 365	1 826
1999	44 110	30 885	11 370	31 975	22 706	9 269	10 281	8 179	2 101	1 855
2000	44 562	31 531	11 198	32 732	23 393	9 339	9 997	8 138	1 859	1 833
2001	44 458	31 411	11 153	32 957	23 599	9 358	9 608	7 813	1 795	1 894
2002	44 865	31 437	11 510	32 799	23 296	9 504	10 148	8 142	2 006	1 918
2003	45 273	31 559	11 635	32 782	23 160	9 622	10 412	8 399	2 013	2 080
2004	45 066	31 040	11 968	32 506	22 736	9 769	10 502	8 304	2 199	2 058
2005	45 027	30 930	11 995	32 412	22 565	9 847	10 514	8 366	2 148	2 102
2006	45 039	30 591	12 250	32 311	22 315	9 996	10 530	8 276	2 254	2 198
2007	45 155	31 252	11 855	32 417	22 788	9 629	10 690	8 464	2 226	2 048
2008	44 909	30 853	11 874	31 990	22 413	9 577	10 737	8 440	2 297	2 182
2009	44 595	30 600	11 811	31 966	22 425	9 537	10 449	8 175	2 274	2 180
2010	44 456	30 209	11 922	31 468	21 957	9 510	10 663	8 251	2 412	2 325
2011	44 471	29 904	12 244	31 072	21 365	9 707	11 076	8 539	2 537	2 323
Children Under 6 Years										
1990	20 502	10 907	9 031	16 171	9 010	7 161	3 767	1 897	1 870	563
1991	20 860	11 162	9 134	16 313	9 148	7 165	3 983	2 013	1 969	563
1992	21 198	11 415	9 109	16 293	9 296	6 997	4 232	2 119	2 112	674
1993	21 398	11 496	9 153	16 266	9 258	7 008	4 383	2 239	2 145	749
1994	21 612	12 007	8 901	16 352	9 617	6 735	4 556	2 391	2 166	704
1995	21 566	12 435	8 421	16 377	9 951	6 427	4 478	2 484	1 995	710
1996	21 542	12 192	8 552	16 253	9 672	6 581	4 491	2 520	1 971	799
1997	21 222	12 439	7 823	16 020	9 661	6 359	4 243	2 778	1 464	959
1998	21 272	12 577	7 703	16 201	9 827	6 375	4 079	2 751	1 328	992
1999	21 081	12 533	7 704	15 971	9 487	6 484	4 267	3 046	1 220	844
2000	21 039	12 657	7 476	16 170	9 757	6 413	3 963	2 901	1 062	906
2001	21 318	12 640	7 711	16 395	9 837	6 558	3 956	2 802	1 153	968
2002	21 113	12 384	7 733	16 037	9 377	6 660	4 080	3 007	1 073	996
2003	21 248	12 210	8 147	16 222	9 251	6 971	4 136	2 960	1 176	890
2004	21 321	12 104	8 261	16 151	9 156	6 995	4 214	2 948	1 266	956
2005	21 498	12 308	8 184	16 276	9 321	6 955	4 216	2 987	1 229	1 006
2006	21 844	12 687	8 190	16 542	9 631	6 911	4 335	3 057	1 278	968
2007	22 073	12 864	8 218	16 509	9 708	6 802	4 572	3 156	1 416	991
2008	22 244	12 946	8 092	16 313	9 697	6 616	4 724	3 248	1 476	1 207
2009	22 318	12 909	8 263	16 418	9 640	6 778	4 755	3 270	1 485	1 146
2010	22 355	13 127	7 991	16 262	9 729	6 533	4 855	3 398	1 457	1 237
2011	22 333	12 978	8 015	15 979	9 537	6 442	5 015	3 441	1 573	1 340

Note: See notes and definitions for information on historical comparability.

Table 1-50. Number of Families and Median Family Income, by Type of Family and Earner Status of Members, 1990–2010

(Thousands of families, dollars.)

Number and type of families and median family income	1990	1991	1992	1993	1994	1995	1996	1997	1998	1999
NUMBER OF FAMILIES										
Married-Couple Families, Total	52 241	52 549	53 254	53 248	53 929	53 621	53 654	54 362	54 829	55 352
No earners	6 765	7 101	7 250	7 281	7 225	7 276	7 145	7 286	7 257	7 160
One earner	11 630	11 553	12 053	11 806	11 715	11 708	11 493	11 700	12 246	12 290
Husband	9 110	8 907	9 182	8 715	8 673	8 792	8 611	8 770	9 173	9 062
Wife	1 816	1 987	2 145	2 405	2 364	2 251	2 207	2 298	2 411	2 585
Other family member	703	659	726	686	678	666	674	632	662	643
Two earners	25 896	26 037	26 344	26 742	27 263	27 180	27 260	27 712	27 593	28 010
Husband and wife	23 697	23 880	24 255	24 543	25 123	25 274	25 274	25 731	25 696	26 134
Husband and other family member	1 711	1 633	1 447	1 582	1 565	1 393	1 483	1 406	1 306	1 325
Husband not an earner	487	524	642	617	574	513	502	575	590	552
Three earners or more	7 950	7 858	7 606	7 419	7 727	7 456	7 756	7 664	7 733	7 892
Husband and wife	7 029	7 052	6 882	6 723	6 987	6 770	7 126	7 023	7 102	7 220
Husband, not wife	756	595	550	535	543	531	479	478	456	528
Husband not an earner	165	211	175	162	196	155	150	163	176	144
Families Maintained by Women, Total	11 771	12 214	12 504	12 982	12 771	13 007	13 277	13 115	13 206	13 164
No earners	2 623	2 925	2 968	3 100	2 848	2 664	2 574	2 332	2 143	1 883
One earner	5 672	5 926	6 184	6 407	6 506	6 815	7 027	7 091	7 351	7 441
Householder	4 585	4 812	5 042	5 278	5 415	5 590	5 817	5 841	6 167	6 127
Other family member	1 087	1 114	1 142	1 129	1 091	1 225	1 211	1 251	1 183	1 314
Two earners or more	3 476	3 363	3 352	3 476	3 417	3 527	3 675	3 692	3 712	3 840
Householder and other family member(s)	3 146	3 058	2 998	3 139	3 126	3 225	3 431	3 398	3 399	3 508
Householder not an earner	330	305	354	337	291	302	245	294	313	332
Families Maintained by Men, Total	2 948	3 079	3 094	2 992	3 287	3 557	3 924	3 982	4 041	4 086
No earners	296	310	345	329	383	357	359	344	381	376
One earner	1 396	1 541	1 544	1 593	1 705	1 800	1 972	2 104	2 027	2 044
Householder	1 133	1 289	1 305	1 352	1 428	1 548	1 667	1 791	1 725	1 721
Other family member	263	253	239	241	277	253	305	313	302	323
Two earners or more	1 257	1 228	1 204	1 070	1 198	1 400	1 593	1 534	1 634	1 666
Householder and other family member(s)	1 180	1 157	1 117	1 002	1 128	1 302	1 469	1 427	1 532	1 522
Householder not an earner	76	71	88	67	71	98	124	107	102	143
MEDIAN FAMILY INCOME										
Married-Couple Families, Total	39 802	40 746	42 000	43 000	44 893	47 000	49 614	51 475	54 043	56 792
No earners	19 221	20 415	20 023	19 983	20 604	21 888	22 622	23 782	24 525	25 262
One earner	31 020	31 671	32 500	32 084	33 393	35 100	36 468	39 140	40 519	41 261
Husband	32 422	33 208	34 714	34 401	35 000	36 052	38 150	40 300	42 000	44 200
Wife	25 228	26 500	27 343	27 502	28 661	32 098	30 301	34 050	35 625	35 546
Other family member	33 262	33 042	33 622	30 254	32 578	37 784	39 644	40 317	42 414	41 120
Two earners	44 000	45 359	47 737	49 650	51 190	53 500	56 000	58 020	61 300	64 007
Husband and wife	44 031	45 516	48 050	49 980	51 500	53 626	56 392	58 564	61 900	64 950
Husband and other family member	42 602	45 000	45 694	48 862	48 517	52 530	49 610	53 854	57 680	53 541
Husband not an earner	39 494	40 495	40 124	38 800	42 800	47 121	46 990	47 979	50 955	52 466
Three earners or more	59 336	61 120	61 640	63 535	66 172	68 996	70 400	75 593	78 973	81 940
Husband and wife	55 846	61 448	62 674	64 099	66 674	69 371	71 148	76 105	79 907	83 000
Husband, not wife	59 675	60 592	57 015	60 712	63 633	60 360	61 824	68 890	71 001	69 561
Husband not an earner	49 107	44 874	47 551	54 805	54 655	61 196	55 495	62 684	63 205	69 275
Families Maintained by Women, Total	16 351	16 054	16 431	16 800	17 600	19 306	19 416	20 470	21 875	23 100
No earners	5 880	6 060	5 964	6 492	6 805	7 440	7 092	7 476	7 737	8 010
One earner	15 987	16 284	16 468	16 745	17 226	18 824	18 500	19 000	20 000	20 092
Householder	15 001	15 542	15 905	15 700	16 603	17 890	18 000	18 000	18 800	19 000
Other family member	20 173	20 220	19 709	20 800	21 300	23 166	21 000	22 870	25 981	26 800
Two earners or more	30 500	31 508	32 705	33 300	33 820	35 000	36 400	39 275	40 000	41 144
Householder and other family member(s)	30 367	31 550	33 280	33 165	33 357	34 674	36 400	39 000	39 713	40 855
Householder not an earner	32 800	29 477	30 460	35 394	37 531	39 444	38 249	47 471	43 725	48 004
Families Maintained by Men, Total	28 493	28 000	27 400	25 856	27 486	30 000	31 500	32 984	35 000	37 000
No earners	11 386	11 196	9 416	10 900	11 293	12 240	12 030	14 252	15 468	13 752
One earner	25 000	23 715	23 020	22 300	24 011	25 337	26 100	26 897	29 125	31 038
Householder	24 150	23 309	23 000	22 079	24 000	25 069	25 874	27 000	29 125	30 483
Other family member	27 620	25 720	24 359	26 916	26 253	27 291	28 584	25 486	28 241	34 756
Two earners or more	40 000	37 700	39 000	38 000	41 439	43 100	44 275	49 900	51 288	51 040
Householder and other family member(s)	40 256	37 550	39 300	38 363	41 534	43 000	43 065	50 000	50 954	50 960
Householder not an earner	34 064	40 000	36 445	33 700	37 386	55 133	47 001	44 786	68 257	57 407

Note: See notes and definitions for information on historical comparability.

Table 1-50. Number of Families and Median Family Income, by Type of Family and Earner Status of Members, 1990–2010—*Continued*

(Thousands of families, dollars.)

Number and type of families and median family income	2000	2001	2002	2003	2004	2005	2006	2007	2008	2009	2010
NUMBER OF FAMILIES											
Married-Couple Families, Total	55 650	56 798	57 362	57 767	58 180	58 225	59 050	58 490	59 181	58 521	58 135
No earners	7 297	7 662	7 803	8 043	7 998	8 017	8 091	7 914	8 083	8 467	8 626
One earner	12 450	12 852	13 503	14 061	14 385	14 301	14 562	14 272	14 625	15 046	15 421
Husband	9 319	9 573	10 121	10 478	10 853	10 611	10 706	10 396	10 567	10 570	10 895
Wife	2 545	2 689	2 821	3 027	2 993	3 097	3 264	3 267	3 437	3 854	3 935
Other family member	586	590	560	557	539	593	591	608	620	621	591
Two earners	28 329	28 779	28 891	28 693	28 806	28 802	29 216	29 256	29 466	28 371	27 821
Husband and wife	26 447	26 829	26 966	26 860	26 758	26 833	27 241	27 264	27 531	26 298	25 801
Husband and other family member	1 277	1 424	1 391	1 322	1 462	1 376	1 358	1 393	1 308	1 363	1 317
Husband not an earner	605	526	534	511	586	594	616	599	627	710	703
Three earners or more	7 575	7 504	7 165	6 970	6 991	7 104	7 181	7 048	7 008	6 638	6 267
Husband and wife	6 917	6 859	6 565	6 349	6 459	6 535	6 620	6 452	6 393	6 024	5 609
Husband, not wife	537	530	455	467	381	445	397	452	432	425	466
Husband not an earner	120	115	145	154	152	124	165	144	182	189	192
Families Maintained by Women, Total	12 950	13 517	14 033	14 196	14 404	14 505	14 852	14 846	14 842	15 236	15 491
No earners	1 786	2 076	2 228	2 451	2 610	2 616	2 627	2 502	2 678	3 076	3 297
One earner	7 462	7 693	8 153	8 012	8 074	8 052	8 303	8 418	8 381	8 475	8 638
Householder	6 132	6 436	6 832	6 725	6 788	6 724	6 904	7 020	6 978	6 941	7 158
Other family member	1 331	1 257	1 321	1 286	1 285	1 329	1 398	1 398	1 404	1 533	1 480
Two earners or more	3 702	3 748	3 652	3 733	3 720	3 836	3 923	3 925	3 783	3 685	3 555
Householder and other family member(s)	3 376	3 442	3 290	3 364	3 399	3 468	3 547	3 572	3 467	3 281	3 149
Householder not an earner	325	306	362	369	321	368	376	353	316	405	406
Families Maintained by Men, Total	4 316	4 499	4 747	4 778	4 953	5 193	5 119	5 181	5 301	5 630	5 649
No earners	380	461	466	530	492	537	555	532	611	539	775
One earner	2 223	2 319	2 434	2 466	2 573	2 661	2 584	2 703	2 636	2 801	2 911
Householder	1 879	1 911	2 026	2 053	2 152	2 196	2 155	2 297	2 199	2 261	2 389
Other family member	344	408	408	413	421	464	429	406	437	539	521
Two earners or more	1 713	1 719	1 847	1 782	1 888	1 995	1 979	1 947	2 054	2 030	1 963
Householder and other family member(s)	1 585	1 629	1 709	1 625	1 736	1 848	1 828	1 812	1 889	1 822	1 751
Householder not an earner	128	90	138	157	152	147	152	134	165	208	212
MEDIAN FAMILY INCOME											
Married-Couple Families, Total	59 200	60 100	61 000	62 388	63 627	65 586	69 300	72 802	72 805	71 464	72 224
No earners	25 356	25 900	25 954	26 312	26 798	28 376	30 000	30 134	31 164	32 093	32 350
One earner	44 424	44 400	45 000	46 546	47 749	50 000	50 400	52 686	53 865	53 087	55 000
Husband	47 010	47 500	48 004	48 948	50 000	52 000	53 360	55 350	56 000	55 333	56 533
Wife	36 458	36 140	39 072	41 180	41 000	43 505	45 000	47 000	47 015	47 550	50 150
Other family member	45 492	44 270	40 927	45 936	46 324	50 263	49 352	48 922	55 114	55 166	57 264
Two earners	67 500	69 543	71 282	73 309	75 100	76 960	81 500	85 012	85 500	86 361	88 500
Husband and wife	68 132	70 000	72 150	74 500	76 000	77 539	82 762	86 000	86 842	87 939	90 000
Husband and other family member	56 503	65 240	62 848	60 100	66 120	67 350	68 828	71 573	68 755	73 720	74 973
Husband not an earner	53 430	58 725	54 840	58 000	63 050	65 622	63 657	68 032	66 445	70 017	72 317
Three earners or more	83 990	86 090	88 632	93 000	94 212	98 000	103 803	106 747	105 618	107 000	107 542
Husband and wife	84 634	87 000	89 962	94 353	95 524	99 800	104 045	107 630	106 493	108 703	108 714
Husband, not wife	79 050	76 230	82 180	77 316	87 000	79 417	91 965	101 771	99 731	85 574	93 000
Husband not an earner	68 050	80 661	68 400	91 771	73 137	84 638	97 510	92 428	93 961	95 251	100 105
Families Maintained by Women, Total	25 000	25 064	26 000	26 000	26 400	27 000	28 218	30 000	29 698	29 025	28 774
No earners	8 988	8 160	8 808	8 344	8 400	8 228	8 657	8 873	9 404	10 037	9 600
One earner	22 306	23 008	24 597	24 752	25 040	25 308	26 393	27 795	28 060	29 000	29 009
Householder	21 400	22 001	23 760	23 832	24 801	24 505	25 381	26 644	27 000	27 928	27 924
Other family member	27 524	28 476	29 524	28 857	29 700	31 700	31 462	31 950	34 814	34 421	33 957
Two earners or more	43 035	45 244	46 580	47 576	48 549	50 000	52 400	55 749	54 369	54 500	55 047
Householder and other family member(s)	43 000	44 842	46 000	46 701	47 974	48 989	51 479	55 010	54 306	54 448	54 000
Householder not an earner	45 600	51 000	51 248	57 267	56 799	64 805	61 699	64 094	54 978	56 203	61 781
Families Maintained by Men, Total	37 040	36 000	37 440	37 914	40 000	40 293	41 130	44 001	43 050	41 000	42 500
No earners	14 946	12 840	15 200	15 408	14 167	13 950	15 462	12 921	15 557	15 653	16 176
One earner	30 160	30 800	30 139	32 097	35 000	35 001	35 100	37 716	36 806	35 116	37 707
Householder	30 816	30 500	30 014	31 355	35 000	35 075	35 011	37 720	37 569	35 117	37 990
Other family member	29 118	31 052	32 000	35 525	35 438	35 000	37 840	37 522	34 404	35 086	37 041
Two earners or more	55 010	55 024	55 000	57 840	57 600	60 024	61 000	63 600	64 077	64 747	66 000
Householder and other family member(s)	55 400	54 850	55 220	57 400	57 058	60 000	61 000	64 000	63 416	64 743	65 200
Householder not an earner	51 945	61 824	49 852	64 658	65 400	70 879	62 000	60 498	69 794	65 618	71 962

Note: See notes and definitions for information on historical comparability.

Table 1-51. Employment Status of the Foreign-Born and Native-Born Populations, by Selected Characteristics, 2009–2010

(Thousands of people, percent.)

Year and characteristic	Civilian noninstitutional population	Civilian labor force				
		Total	Participation rate	Employed	Unemployed	
					Number	Rate
2009						
TOTAL						
Both sexes, 16 years and over	235 801	154 142	65.4	139 877	14 265	9.3
Men	114 136	82 123	72.0	73 670	8 453	10.3
Women	121 665	72 019	59.2	66 208	5 811	8.1
FOREIGN BORN						
Both sexes, 16 years and over	35 216	23 926	67.9	21 608	2 317	9.7
Men	17 628	14 190	80.5	12 765	1 426	10.0
Women	17 588	9 735	55.4	8 844	891	9.2
Age						
16 to 24 years	3 542	1 986	56.1	1 681	304	15.3
25 to 34 years	7 637	5 907	77.3	5 330	577	9.8
35 to 44 years	8 379	6 847	81.7	6 210	637	9.3
45 to 54 years	6 819	5 588	81.9	5 096	491	8.8
55 to 64 years	4 321	2 838	65.7	2 590	249	8.8
65 years and over	4 517	760	16.8	701	59	7.8
Race and Hispanic Origin						
White, non-Hispanic	7 249	4 334	59.8	4 002	332	7.7
Black, non-Hispanic	2 812	2 037	72.4	1 807	231	11.3
Asian, non-Hispanic	7 876	5 332	67.7	4 967	365	6.8
Hispanic[1]	16 933	11 982	70.8	10 612	1 370	11.4
Educational Attainment						
Total, 25 years and over	31 674	21 940	69.3	19 927	2 013	9.2
Less than a high school diploma	9 542	5 862	61.4	5 122	740	12.6
High school graduate, no college[2]	7 992	5 371	67.2	4 875	496	9.2
Some college or associate's degree	5 070	3 735	73.7	3 406	328	8.8
Bachelor's degree or higher[3]	9 070	6 972	76.9	6 524	448	6.4
NATIVE BORN						
Both sexes, 16 years and over	200 585	130 216	64.9	118 269	11 947	9.2
Men	96 508	67 933	70.4	60 905	7 028	10.3
Women	104 077	62 284	59.8	57 364	4 920	7.9
Age						
16 to 24 years	34 025	19 375	56.9	15 920	3 455	17.8
25 to 34 years	32 643	27 392	83.9	24 684	2 707	9.9
35 to 44 years	32 540	27 391	84.2	25 307	2 085	7.6
45 to 54 years	37 546	30 617	81.5	28 517	2 101	6.9
55 to 64 years	30 349	19 667	64.8	18 429	1 238	6.3
65 years and over	33 481	5 774	17.2	5 413	362	6.3
Race and Hispanic Origin						
White, non-Hispanic	153 104	100 525	66.0	92 681	7 844	7.8
Black, non-Hispanic	24 466	14 971	61.2	12 700	2 271	15.2
Asian, non-Hispanic	2 756	1 681	61.0	1 542	138	8.2
Hispanic[1]	15 958	10 370	65.0	9 034	1 336	12.9
Educational Attainment						
Total, 25 years and over	166 560	110 842	66.5	102 349	8 492	7.7
Less than a high school diploma	16 587	6 284	37.9	5 249	1 035	16.5
High school graduates, no college[2]	53 477	32 815	61.4	29 612	3 203	9.8
Some college or associate's degree	46 657	33 080	70.9	30 482	2 599	7.9
Bachelor's degree or higher[3]	49 839	38 662	77.6	37 007	1 655	4.3

Note: Due to the introduction of revised population controls in January 2010, estimated levels for 2010 are not strictly comparable with those for 2009.

[1] May be of any race.
[2] Includes persons with a high school diploma or equivalent.
[3] Includes persons with bachelor's, master's, professional, and doctoral degrees.

Table 1-51. Employment Status of the Foreign-Born and Native-Born Populations, by Selected Characteristics, 2009–2010—*Continued*

(Thousands of people, percent.)

Year and characteristic	Civilian noninstitutional population	Civilian labor force				
		Total	Participation rate	Employed	Unemployed	
					Number	Rate
2010						
TOTAL						
Both sexes, 16 years and over	237 830	153 889	64.7	139 064	14 825	9.6
Men	115 174	81 985	71.2	73 359	8 626	10.5
Women	122 656	71 904	58.6	65 705	6 199	8.6
FOREIGN BORN						
Both sexes, 16 years and over	35 869	24 356	67.9	21 969	2 387	9.8
Men	17 936	14 375	80.1	12 946	1 429	9.9
Women	17 934	9 981	55.7	9 023	958	9.6
Age						
16 to 24 years	3 533	1 975	55.9	1 661	314	15.9
25 to 34 years	7 714	5 936	77.0	5 387	550	9.3
35 to 44 years	8 470	6 884	81.3	6 265	619	9.0
45 to 54 years	6 949	5 719	82.3	5 172	547	9.6
55 to 64 years	4 528	3 011	66.5	2 727	284	9.4
65 years and over	4 674	831	17.8	757	74	8.9
Race and Hispanic Origin						
White, non-Hispanic	7 363	4 470	60.7	4 138	332	7.4
Black, non-Hispanic	2 898	2 162	74.6	1 893	269	12.4
Asian, non-Hispanic	8 073	5 315	65.8	4 928	386	7.3
Hispanic[1]	17 162	12 152	70.8	10 776	1 376	11.3
Educational Attainment						
Total, 25 years and over	32 336	22 381	69.2	20 308	2 073	9.3
Less than a high school diploma	9 620	5 930	61.6	5 219	712	12.0
High school graduates, no college[2]	8 284	5 663	68.4	5 087	576	10.2
Some college or associate degree	5 200	3 818	73.4	3 463	355	9.3
Bachelor's degree and higher[3]	9 232	6 970	75.5	6 539	431	6.2
NATIVE BORN						
Both sexes, 16 years and over	201 960	129 533	64.1	117 095	12 438	9.6
Men	97 238	67 610	69.5	60 414	7 196	10.6
Women	104 722	61 923	59.1	56 682	5 242	8.5
Age						
16 to 24 years	34 415	18 960	55.1	15 417	3 543	18.7
25 to 34 years	33 189	27 678	83.4	24 842	2 836	10.2
35 to 44 years	31 620	26 482	83.8	24 398	2 084	7.9
45 to 54 years	37 348	30 242	81.0	28 019	2 223	7.4
55 to 64 years	31 357	20 286	64.7	18 909	1 377	6.8
65 years and over	34 032	5 886	17.3	5 511	375	6.4
Race and Hispanic Origin						
White, non-Hispanic	153 448	99 478	64.8	91 483	7 994	8.0
Black, non-Hispanic	24 691	14 996	60.7	12 529	2 467	16.5
Asian, non-Hispanic	2 900	1 782	61.5	1 641	141	7.9
Hispanic[1]	16 551	10 596	64.0	9 130	1 467	13.8
Educational Attainment						
Total, 25 years and over	167 546	110 573	66.0	101 679	8 895	8.0
Less than a high school diploma	16 046	5 949	37.1	4 896	1 053	17.7
High school graduates, no college[2]	53 753	32 573	60.6	29 206	3 367	10.3
Some college or associate degree	47 022	33 022	70.2	30 284	2 738	8.3
Bachelor's degree or higher[3]	50 724	39 029	76.9	37 293	1 736	4.4

Note: Due to the introduction of revised population controls in January 2010, estimated levels for 2010 are not strictly comparable with those for 2009.

[1]May be of any race.
[2]Includes persons with a high school diploma or equivalent.
[3]Includes persons with bachelor's, master's, professional, and doctoral degrees.

Table 1-52. Employment Status of the Foreign-Born and Native-Born Populations Age 16 Years and Over, by Sex and Presence and Age of Youngest Child, Annual Averages, 2009–2010

(Thousands of people, percent.)

Characteristic	2009			2010		
	Both sexes	Men	Women	Both sexes	Men	Women
FOREIGN BORN						
With Own Children Under 18 Years						
Civilian noninstitutional population	13 723	6 585	7 138	14 385	6 896	7 490
Civilian labor force	10 577	6 209	4 368	11 032	6 480	4 552
Participation rate	77.1	94.3	61.2	76.7	94.0	60.8
Employed	9 573	5 645	3 928	10 008	5 913	4 095
Employment-population ratio	69.8	85.7	55.0	69.6	85.7	54.7
Unemployed	1 003	563	440	1 025	568	457
Unemployment rate	9.5	9.1	10.1	9.3	8.8	10.0
With Own Children 6 to 17 Years, None Younger						
Civilian noninstitutional population	7 180	3 395	3 785	7 338	3 423	3 915
Civilian labor force	5 834	3 176	2 658	5 908	3 184	2 725
Participation rate	81.2	93.5	70.2	80.5	93.0	69.6
Employed	5 292	2 876	2 416	5 373	2 903	2 470
Employment-population ratio	73.7	84.7	63.8	73.2	84.8	63.1
Unemployed	542	299	242	536	281	255
Unemployment rate	9.3	9.4	9.1	9.1	8.8	9.4
With Own Children Under 6 Years						
Civilian noninstitutional population	6 543	3 190	3 353	7 047	3 473	3 574
Civilian labor force	4 743	3 033	1 710	5 124	3 296	1 827
Participation rate	72.5	95.1	51.0	72.7	94.9	51.1
Employed	4 281	2 769	1 512	4 635	3 010	1 625
Employment-population ratio	65.4	86.8	45.1	65.8	86.7	45.5
Unemployed	461	264	198	489	287	202
Unemployment rate	9.7	8.7	11.6	9.5	8.7	11.1
With Own Children Under 3 Years						
Civilian noninstitutional population	3 758	1 852	1 907	4 074	2 022	2 053
Civilian labor force	2 632	1 758	874	2 871	1 916	955
Participation rate	70.0	95.0	45.8	70.5	94.8	46.5
Employed	2 379	1 612	767	2 585	1 748	837
Employment-population ratio	63.3	87.0	40.2	63.4	86.4	40.8
Unemployed	253	146	107	286	168	118
Unemployment rate	9.6	8.3	12.2	10.0	8.8	12.3
With No Own Children Under 18 Years						
Civilian noninstitutional population	21 493	11 043	10 450	21 484	11 040	10 444
Civilian labor force	13 349	7 982	5 367	13 323	7 895	5 429
Participation rate	62.1	72.3	51.4	62.0	71.5	52.0
Employed	12 035	7 119	4 916	11 961	7 033	4 928
Employment-population ratio	56.0	64.5	47.0	55.7	63.7	47.2
Unemployed	1 314	862	452	1 362	862	501
Unemployment rate	9.8	10.8	8.4	10.2	10.9	9.2

Note: Due to the introduction of revised population controls in January 2010, estimated levels for 2010 are not strictly comparable with those for 2009.

Table 1-52. Employment Status of the Foreign-Born and Native-Born Populations Age 16 Years and Over, by Sex and Presence and Age of Youngest Child, Annual Averages, 2009–2010—*Continued*

(Thousands of people, percent.)

Characteristic	2009			2010		
	Both sexes	Men	Women	Both sexes	Men	Women
NATIVE BORN						
With Own Children Under 18 Years						
Civilian noninstitutional population	50 974	22 132	28 841	51 801	22 530	29 270
Civilian labor force	42 050	20 720	21 330	42 459	21 018	21 441
Participation rate	82.5	93.6	74.0	82.0	93.3	73.2
Employed	38 934	19 291	19 642	38 981	19 430	19 551
Employment-population ratio	76.4	87.2	68.1	75.3	86.2	66.8
Unemployed	3 116	1 429	1 687	3 478	1 588	1 890
Unemployment rate	7.4	6.9	7.9	8.2	7.6	8.8
With Own Children 6 to 17 Years, None Younger						
Civilian noninstitutional population	28 548	12 527	16 021	28 468	12 426	16 042
Civilian labor force	24 244	11 589	12 655	24 033	11 503	12 530
Participation rate	84.9	92.5	79.0	84.4	92.6	78.1
Employed	22 653	10 847	11 806	22 337	10 735	11 601
Employment-population ratio	79.4	86.6	73.7	78.5	86.4	72.3
Unemployed	1 591	743	848	1 697	768	929
Unemployment rate	6.6	6.4	6.7	7.1	6.7	7.4
With Own Children Under 6 Years						
Civilian noninstitutional population	22 426	9 606	12 820	23 333	10 104	13 229
Civilian labor force	17 806	9 131	8 675	18 426	9 515	8 911
Participation rate	79.4	95.1	67.7	79.0	94.2	67.4
Employed	16 281	8 445	7 836	16 644	8 695	7 949
Employment-population ratio	72.6	87.9	61.1	71.3	86.1	60.1
Unemployed	1 525	686	839	1 781	820	961
Unemployment rate	8.6	7.5	9.7	9.7	8.6	10.8
With Own Children Under 3 Years						
Civilian noninstitutional population	13 293	5 723	7 570	13 859	6 006	7 853
Civilian labor force	10 350	5 438	4 913	10 725	5 658	5 067
Participation rate	77.9	95.0	64.9	77.4	94.2	64.5
Employed	9 442	5 018	4 424	9 638	5 146	4 492
Employment-population ratio	71.0	87.7	58.4	69.5	85.7	57.2
Unemployed	908	420	488	1 087	511	575
Unemployment rate	8.8	7.7	9.9	10.1	9.0	11.4
With No Own Children Under 18 Years						
Civilian noninstitutional population	149 611	74 375	75 236	150 159	74 708	75 452
Civilian labor force	88 167	47 213	40 954	87 074	46 591	40 483
Participation rate	58.9	63.5	54.4	58.0	62.4	53.7
Employed	79 335	41 614	37 722	78 115	40 983	37 131
Employment-population ratio	53.0	56.0	50.1	52.0	54.9	49.2
Unemployed	8 831	5 599	3 232	8 960	5 608	3 352
Unemployment rate	10.0	11.9	7.9	10.3	12.0	8.3

Note: Due to the introduction of revised population controls in January 2010, estimated levels for 2010 are not strictly comparable with those for 2009.

Table 1-53. Employment Status of the Foreign-Born and Native-Born Populations Age 25 Years and Over, by Educational Attainment, Race, and Hispanic Origin, Annual Averages, 2009–2010

(Thousands of people, percent.)

Characteristic	2009				2010			
	Less than a high school diploma	High school graduate, no college[1]	Some college or associate's degree	Bachelor's degree or higher[2]	Less than a high school diploma	High school graduate, no college[1]	Some college or associate's degree	Bachelor's degree or higher[2]
FOREIGN BORN								
White, Non-Hispanic								
Civilian noninstitutional population	832	1 729	1 370	2 763	870	1 773	1 364	2 832
Civilian labor force	266	899	865	2 004	307	937	883	2 053
Participation rate	32.0	52.0	63.1	72.5	35.3	52.8	64.8	72.5
Employed	238	823	804	1 877	282	851	818	1 935
Employment-population ratio	28.6	47.6	58.6	67.9	32.4	48.0	60.0	68.3
Unemployed	28	77	61	127	25	85	66	118
Unemployment rate	10.7	8.5	7.1	6.4	8.0	9.1	7.4	5.7
Black, Non-Hispanic								
Civilian noninstitutional population	347	748	661	719	420	739	685	740
Civilian labor force	194	544	525	615	246	556	568	623
Participation rate	56.0	72.7	79.5	85.5	58.5	75.3	82.9	84.2
Employed	164	482	474	563	203	481	508	570
Employment-population ratio	47.2	64.4	71.7	78.3	48.3	65.1	74.2	77.1
Unemployed	30	62	52	52	43	75	60	53
Unemployment rate	15.7	11.4	9.8	8.5	17.4	13.6	10.6	8.5
Asian, Non-Hispanic								
Civilian noninstitutional population	936	1 425	1 032	3 881	931	1 536	1 088	3 877
Civilian labor force	419	878	759	3 016	414	977	767	2 889
Participation rate	44.8	61.6	73.6	77.7	44.5	63.6	70.6	74.5
Employed	386	814	696	2 841	368	901	703	2 724
Employment-population ratio	41.3	57.2	67.5	73.2	39.5	58.6	64.7	70.3
Unemployed	33	64	64	175	46	76	64	165
Unemployment rate	7.9	7.3	8.4	5.8	11.2	7.8	8.3	5.7
Hispanic[3]								
Civilian noninstitutional population	7 376	4 020	1 929	1 596	7 351	4 146	1 989	1 667
Civilian labor force	4 959	3 002	1 526	1 247	4 937	3 134	1 542	1 316
Participation rate	67.2	74.7	79.1	78.1	67.2	75.6	77.5	78.9
Employed	4 314	2 712	1 378	1 158	4 341	2 802	1 383	1 225
Employment-population ratio	58.5	67.5	71.5	72.5	59.1	67.6	69.5	73.5
Unemployed	644	289	147	89	595	332	159	91
Unemployment rate	13.0	9.6	9.7	7.1	12.1	10.6	10.3	6.9
NATIVE BORN								
White, Non-Hispanic								
Civilian noninstitutional population	10 507	41 552	36 165	42 586	10 172	41 667	36 307	43 147
Civilian labor force	3 860	24 975	25 328	32 751	3 654	24 684	25 135	32 916
Participation rate	36.7	60.1	70.0	76.9	35.9	59.2	69.2	76.3
Employed	3 295	22 797	23 543	31 445	3 086	22 458	23 275	31 582
Employment-population ratio	31.4	54.9	65.1	73.8	30.3	53.9	64.1	73.2
Unemployed	565	2 178	1 785	1 306	568	2 225	1 860	1 334
Unemployment rate	14.6	8.7	7.0	4.0	15.5	9.0	7.4	4.1
Black, Non-Hispanic								
Civilian noninstitutional population	3 112	6 897	5 738	3 659	3 036	6 895	5 826	3 798
Civilian labor force	1 099	4 392	4 158	2 923	1 057	4 304	4 214	2 986
Participation rate	35.3	63.7	72.5	79.9	34.8	62.4	72.3	78.6
Employed	851	3 760	3 673	2 717	798	3 605	3 682	2 752
Employment-population ratio	27.4	54.5	64.0	74.3	26.3	52.3	63.2	72.5
Unemployed	248	631	486	206	259	698	532	235
Unemployment rate	22.6	14.4	11.7	7.0	24.5	16.2	12.6	7.9
Asian, Non-Hispanic								
Civilian noninstitutional population	126	360	465	962	133	387	471	1 008
Civilian labor force	51	201	315	779	54	228	329	817
Participation rate	40.2	55.7	67.8	81.0	40.5	58.9	69.9	81.0
Employed	47	186	291	743	49	212	304	777
Employment-population ratio	37.3	51.5	62.5	77.2	37.1	54.7	64.6	77.1
Unemployed	4	15	25	36	4	16	25	40
Unemployment rate	7.4	7.6	7.8	4.7	8.3	7.1	7.5	4.9
Hispanic[3]								
Civilian noninstitutional population	2 388	3 716	3 174	1 947	2 295	3 769	3 314	2 059
Civilian labor force	1 105	2 656	2 501	1 648	1 033	2 714	2 583	1 728
Participation rate	46.3	71.5	78.8	84.7	45.0	72.0	77.9	83.9
Employed	918	2 357	2 278	1 571	842	2 373	2 343	1 637
Employment-population ratio	38.5	63.4	71.8	80.7	36.7	63.0	70.7	79.5
Unemployed	186	299	223	77	191	342	240	91
Unemployment rate	16.9	11.3	8.9	4.7	18.5	12.6	9.3	5.3

Note: Due to the introduction of revised population controls in January 2010, estimated levels for 2010 are not strictly comparable with those for 2009.

[1]Includes persons with a high school diploma or equivalent.
[2]Includes persons with bachelor's, master's, professional, and doctoral degrees.
[3]May be of any race.

Table 1-54. Employed Foreign-Born and Native-Born Persons Age 16 Years and Over, by Occupation and Sex, 2009–2010 Annual Averages

(Thousands of people, percent.)

Occupation	2009					
	Foreign born			Native born		
	Both sexes	Male	Female	Both sexes	Male	Female
TOTAL EMPLOYED	21 608	12 765	8 844	118 269	60 905	57 364
Percent Employed	100.0	100.0	100.0	100.0	100.0	100.0
Management, professional, and related	28.9	26.5	32.5	38.9	36.1	41.8
Management, business, and financial operations	10.7	10.7	10.7	16.3	18.0	14.4
Management	7.6	8.6	6.3	11.7	14.1	9.1
Business and financial operations	3.0	2.1	4.3	4.6	3.9	5.3
Professional and related	18.2	15.8	21.8	22.6	18.1	27.4
Computer and mathematical	3.3	4.2	2.1	2.3	3.4	1.2
Architecture and engineering	2.1	3.1	0.7	1.9	3.2	0.5
Life, physical, and social sciences	1.2	1.2	1.3	0.9	0.9	0.9
Community and social services	1.0	0.7	1.4	1.8	1.3	2.4
Legal	0.5	0.4	0.6	1.4	1.3	1.4
Education, training, and library	3.5	2.1	5.5	6.7	3.2	10.3
Arts, design, entertainment, sports, and media	1.3	1.3	1.5	2.1	2.1	2.0
Health care practitioner and technical	5.3	2.8	8.7	5.6	2.6	8.7
Services	24.7	19.0	32.8	16.3	13.3	19.5
Health care support	2.6	0.6	5.6	2.3	0.4	4.3
Protective services	1.0	1.3	0.6	2.5	3.8	1.1
Food preparation and serving related	8.0	8.0	8.0	5.1	3.9	6.3
Building and grounds cleaning and maintenance	8.5	7.4	10.2	3.0	3.7	2.2
Personal care and services	4.5	1.7	8.5	3.4	1.5	5.6
Sales and office	17.0	12.8	23.1	25.5	17.8	33.5
Sales and related	8.9	8.1	10.0	11.6	11.2	12.0
Office and administrative support	8.2	4.7	13.1	13.9	6.6	21.6
Natural resources, construction, and maintenance	13.5	21.9	1.4	8.8	16.3	0.8
Farming, fishing, and forestry	1.6	2.2	0.8	0.5	0.7	0.2
Construction and extraction	8.8	14.8	0.3	4.7	8.8	0.3
Installation, maintenance, and repair	3.0	4.9	0.3	3.6	6.8	0.3
Production, transportation, and material moving	15.8	19.8	10.1	10.6	16.4	4.4
Production	8.5	9.2	7.5	4.9	7.1	2.6
Transportation and material moving	7.4	10.6	2.7	5.7	9.3	1.8

Occupation	2010					
	Foreign born			Native born		
	Both sexes	Male	Female	Both sexes	Male	Female
TOTAL EMPLOYED	21 969	12 946	9 023	117 095	60 414	56 682
Percent Employed	100.0	100.0	100.0	100.0	100.0	100.0
Management, professional, and related	28.0	25.3	31.7	38.9	36.1	42.0
Management, business, and financial operations	10.3	10.4	10.2	15.9	17.5	14.2
Management	7.5	8.2	6.5	11.4	13.6	9.1
Business and financial operations	2.8	2.2	3.7	4.5	4.0	5.2
Professional and related	17.6	14.9	21.5	23.0	18.5	27.8
Computer and mathematical	3.3	4.2	2.0	2.4	3.4	1.3
Architecture and engineering	1.8	2.6	0.7	1.9	3.2	0.5
Life, physical, and social sciences	1.1	1.0	1.3	1.0	1.0	1.0
Community and social services	1.0	0.6	1.5	1.8	1.2	2.4
Legal	0.5	0.4	0.6	1.4	1.4	1.4
Education, training, and library	3.6	2.1	5.7	6.7	3.3	10.3
Arts, design, entertainment, sports, and media	1.4	1.3	1.5	2.1	2.2	2.0
Health care practitioner and technical	5.0	2.6	8.4	5.7	2.8	8.9
Services	25.0	19.1	33.4	16.4	13.5	19.4
Health care support	2.8	0.7	6.0	2.3	0.5	4.3
Protective services	1.1	1.4	0.6	2.6	4.0	1.1
Food preparation and serving related	7.9	7.9	8.0	5.1	4.0	6.2
Building and grounds cleaning and maintenance	8.7	7.6	10.3	2.9	3.6	2.2
Personal care and services	4.4	1.6	8.5	3.5	1.5	5.6
Sales and office	17.3	12.8	23.8	25.3	17.8	33.3
Sales and related	8.9	7.8	10.5	11.5	11.1	11.9
Office and administrative support	8.4	5.0	13.4	13.8	6.7	21.4
Natural resources, construction, and maintenance	13.6	22.0	1.5	8.6	15.9	0.8
Farming, fishing, and forestry	1.8	2.4	1.0	0.5	0.7	0.2
Construction and extraction	8.6	14.4	0.3	4.5	8.5	0.3
Installation, maintenance, and repair	3.2	5.3	0.2	3.6	6.7	0.3
Production, transportation, and material moving	16.1	20.7	9.6	10.8	16.7	4.5
Production	8.7	10.0	6.9	5.2	7.5	2.8
Transportation and material moving	7.4	10.8	2.6	5.6	9.2	1.7

Note: Due to the introduction of revised population controls in January 2010, estimated levels for 2010 are not strictly comparable with those for 2009.

Table 1-55. Median Usual Weekly Earnings of Full-Time Wage and Salary Workers for the Foreign-Born and Native-Born Populations, by Selected Characteristics, 2009–2010 Annual Averages

(Thousands of people, dollars, percent.)

Year and characteristic	Foreign born		Native born		Earnings of foreign born as a percent of earnings of native born[1]
	Number	Median weekly earnings	Number	Median weekly earnings	
2009					
Both Sexes, 16 Years and Over	15 965	602	83 855	761	79.1
Men	9 867	620	45 241	864	71.7
Women	6 099	567	38 614	670	84.6
Age					
16 to 24 years	1 085	400	7 873	452	88.5
25 to 34 years	4 185	555	19 675	704	78.8
35 to 44 years	4 709	647	19 659	856	75.5
45 to 54 years	3 718	679	21 605	866	78.4
55 to 64 years	1 886	672	12 842	865	77.7
65 years and over	383	574	2 201	703	81.6
Race and Hispanic Origin					
White, non-Hispanic	2 693	863	64 497	808	106.7
Black, non-Hispanic	1 397	613	9 956	601	102.1
Asian, non-Hispanic	3 726	877	1 101	908	96.6
Hispanic[2]	7 964	479	6 660	632	75.8
Educational Attainment					
Total, 25 years and over	14 881	621	75 982	805	77.1
Less than a high school diploma	3 817	415	3 472	498	83.3
High school graduate, no college[3]	3 611	530	21 766	644	82.3
Some college	2 460	641	22 657	733	87.4
Bachelor's degree or higher[4]	4 993	1 129	28 088	1 138	99.2
2010					
Both Sexes, 16 Years and Over	16 253	598	83 278	771	77.5
Men	10 056	610	45 003	873	69.9
Women	6 197	577	38 275	686	84.1
Age					
16 to 24 years	1 037	392	7 515	443	88.5
25 to 34 years	4 288	551	19 813	709	77.7
35 to 44 years	4 784	649	19 038	864	75.2
45 to 54 years	3 810	643	21 396	878	73.2
55 to 64 years	1 911	651	13 230	887	73.4
65 years and over	422	584	2 287	708	82.4
Race and Hispanic Origin					
White, non-Hispanic	2 809	850	64 060	824	103.2
Black, non-Hispanic	1 490	614	9 696	613	100.1
Asian, non-Hispanic	3 665	871	1 179	841	103.5
Hispanic[2]	8 092	480	6 745	629	76.4
Educational Attainment					
Total, 25 years and over	15 216	615	75 764	818	75.2
Less than a high school diploma	3 895	416	3 258	486	85.5
High school graduates, no college[3]	3 687	521	21 512	648	80.4
Some college	2 560	656	22 335	741	88.4
Bachelor's degree and higher[4]	5 073	1 119	28 658	1 147	97.6

Note: Due to the introduction of revised population controls in January 2010, estimated levels for 2010 are not strictly comparable with those for 2009.

[1]These figures are computed using unrounded medians and may differ slightly from percentages computed using the rounded medians displayed in this table.
[2]May be of any race.
[3]Includes persons with a high school diploma or equivalent.
[4]Includes persons with bachelor's, master's, professional, and doctoral degrees.

Table 1-56. Percent Distribution of the Civilian Labor Force Age 25 to 64 Years, by Educational Attainment, Sex, and Race, March 1990–March 2011

(Thousands of people, percent.)

Sex, race, and year	Civilian labor force	Percent distribution				
		Total	Less than a high school diploma	4 years of high school only	1 to 3 years of college	4 or more years of college
Both Sexes						
1990	99 175	100.0	13.4	39.5	20.7	26.4
1991	100 480	100.0	13.0	39.4	21.1	26.5
1992	102 387	100.0	12.2	36.2	25.2	26.4
1993	103 504	100.0	11.5	35.2	26.3	27.0
1994	104 868	100.0	11.0	34.0	27.7	27.3
1995	106 519	100.0	10.8	33.1	27.8	28.3
1996	108 037	100.0	10.9	32.9	27.7	28.5
1997	110 514	100.0	10.9	33.0	27.4	28.6
1998	111 857	100.0	10.7	32.8	27.4	29.1
1999	112 542	100.0	10.3	32.3	27.4	30.0
2000	114 052	100.0	9.8	31.8	27.9	30.4
2001	115 073	100.0	9.8	31.4	28.1	30.7
2002	117 738	100.0	10.1	30.6	27.7	31.6
2003	119 261	100.0	10.1	30.1	27.8	31.9
2004	119 392	100.0	9.7	30.1	27.8	32.4
2005	120 461	100.0	9.8	30.1	27.8	32.3
2006	122 541	100.0	9.8	29.6	28.0	32.6
2007	124 581	100.0	9.8	29.3	27.3	33.6
2008	125 493	100.0	9.0	28.8	27.9	34.4
2009	125 655	100.0	9.0	28.7	27.9	34.3
2010	126 363	100.0	8.8	29.1	27.5	34.5
2011	125 385	100.0	8.5	28.2	28.0	35.4
Men						
1990	54 476	100.0	15.1	37.2	19.7	28.0
1991	55 165	100.0	14.7	37.5	20.2	27.6
1992	55 917	100.0	13.9	34.7	23.8	27.5
1993	56 544	100.0	13.2	33.9	24.7	28.1
1994	56 633	100.0	12.7	32.9	25.8	28.6
1995	57 454	100.0	12.2	32.3	25.7	29.7
1996	58 121	100.0	12.7	32.2	26.0	29.1
1997	59 268	100.0	12.8	32.2	25.8	29.2
1998	59 905	100.0	12.3	32.3	25.8	29.6
1999	60 030	100.0	11.7	32.0	25.8	30.5
2000	60 510	100.0	11.1	31.8	26.1	30.9
2001	61 091	100.0	11.0	31.6	26.3	31.1
2002	62 794	100.0	11.8	30.6	25.9	31.7
2003	63 466	100.0	12.0	30.1	25.8	32.1
2004	63 699	100.0	11.5	30.5	25.8	32.2
2005	64 562	100.0	11.6	31.4	25.4	31.6
2006	65 708	100.0	11.8	30.7	25.7	31.8
2007	66 742	100.0	11.7	30.6	25.1	32.7
2008	66 957	100.0	11.0	30.3	25.8	33.0
2009	66 843	100.0	10.8	30.4	26.0	32.8
2010	67 261	100.0	10.6	31.2	25.3	32.9
2011	66 801	100.0	10.2	30.4	25.5	33.9
Women						
1990	44 699	100.0	11.3	42.4	21.9	24.5
1991	45 315	100.0	10.9	41.6	22.2	25.2
1992	46 469	100.0	10.2	37.9	26.9	25.0
1993	46 961	100.0	9.3	36.7	28.2	25.8
1994	48 235	100.0	9.1	35.3	29.8	25.8
1995	49 065	100.0	9.1	34.1	30.2	26.6
1996	49 916	100.0	8.8	33.7	29.7	27.8
1997	51 246	100.0	8.7	34.0	29.3	28.0
1998	51 953	100.0	8.8	33.3	29.3	28.6
1999	52 512	100.0	8.7	32.7	29.2	29.5
2000	53 541	100.0	8.4	31.8	30.0	29.8
2001	53 982	100.0	8.5	31.1	30.1	30.2
2002	54 944	100.0	8.2	30.6	29.7	31.5
2003	55 795	100.0	8.0	30.1	30.1	31.8
2004	55 693	100.0	7.7	29.6	30.2	32.5
2005	55 899	100.0	7.8	28.6	30.5	33.1
2006	56 833	100.0	7.6	28.2	30.6	33.6
2007	57 839	100.0	7.5	27.9	29.9	34.6
2008	58 536	100.0	6.7	27.0	30.4	35.9
2009	58 811	100.0	7.0	26.9	30.2	35.9
2010	59 102	100.0	6.8	26.8	30.1	36.3
2011	58 584	100.0	6.5	25.7	30.7	37.1

Table 1-56. Percent Distribution of the Civilian Labor Force Age 25 to 64 Years, by Educational Attainment, Sex, and Race, March 1990–March 2011—*Continued*

(Thousands of people, percent.)

Sex, race, and year	Civilian labor force	Percent distribution				
		Total	Less than a high school diploma	4 years of high school only	1 to 3 years of college	4 or more years of college
White[1]						
1990	85 238	100.0	12.6	39.6	20.6	27.1
1991	86 344	100.0	12.2	39.3	21.1	27.4
1992	87 656	100.0	11.3	36.1	25.5	27.1
1993	88 457	100.0	10.7	35.0	26.4	27.9
1994	89 009	100.0	10.5	33.7	27.7	28.1
1995	90 192	100.0	10.0	32.8	27.8	29.3
1996	91 506	100.0	10.4	32.8	27.5	29.3
1997	93 179	100.0	10.4	32.8	27.3	29.5
1998	93 527	100.0	10.2	32.7	27.4	29.8
1999	94 216	100.0	9.8	32.2	27.2	30.8
2000	95 073	100.0	9.5	31.8	27.7	31.0
2001	95 562	100.0	9.5	31.0	28.0	31.4
2002	97 699	100.0	9.8	30.6	27.6	32.0
2003	98 241	100.0	9.9	30.0	27.7	32.4
2004	98 030	100.0	9.5	29.8	27.8	32.9
2005	98 581	100.0	9.7	29.8	27.8	32.7
2006	100 205	100.0	9.7	29.3	28.1	32.9
2007	101 548	100.0	9.7	29.1	27.3	33.9
2008	102 077	100.0	8.9	28.7	27.8	34.6
2009	102 261	100.0	9.1	28.6	27.7	34.6
2010	102 634	100.0	8.8	29.0	27.4	34.8
2011	101 707	100.0	8.4	27.8	27.9	35.8
Black[1]						
1990	10 537	100.0	19.9	42.5	22.1	15.5
1991	10 650	100.0	19.5	42.9	22.1	15.4
1992	10 936	100.0	19.2	40.3	24.9	15.6
1993	11 051	100.0	16.8	39.5	27.6	16.1
1994	11 368	100.0	14.5	39.3	29.2	17.0
1995	11 695	100.0	14.1	38.6	29.6	17.7
1996	11 891	100.0	14.2	37.2	31.2	17.4
1997	12 253	100.0	14.3	37.8	31.3	16.6
1998	12 893	100.0	14.3	37.3	30.1	18.2
1999	12 945	100.0	13.0	37.2	30.4	19.5
2000	13 383	100.0	11.8	36.1	31.5	20.7
2001	13 617	100.0	12.0	37.1	31.1	19.8
2002	13 319	100.0	12.4	34.5	32.0	21.0
2003	13 315	100.0	11.3	35.6	31.5	21.6
2004	13 372	100.0	11.0	36.6	30.5	21.9
2005	13 635	100.0	11.2	37.3	29.9	21.6
2006	13 855	100.0	10.9	35.6	30.4	23.0
2007	14 186	100.0	10.1	35.4	31.4	23.1
2008	14 356	100.0	9.5	34.3	32.1	24.1
2009	14 325	100.0	8.5	35.1	33.0	23.5
2010	14 483	100.0	8.9	34.5	32.4	24.2
2011	14 377	100.0	8.5	33.8	33.1	24.6

[1]Beginning in 2003, persons who selected this race group only; persons who selected more than one race group are not included. Prior to 2003, persons who reported more than one race group were included in the group they identified as their main race.

Table 1-57. Labor Force Participation Rates of Persons Age 25 to 64 Years, by Educational Attainment, Sex, and Race, March 1990–March 2011

(Civilian labor force as a percent of the civilian noninstitutional population.)

Sex, race, and year	Participation rates				
	Total	Less than a high school diploma	4 years of high school only	1 to 3 years of college	4 or more years of college
Both Sexes					
1990	78.6	60.7	78.2	83.3	88.4
1991	78.6	60.7	78.1	83.2	88.4
1992	79.0	60.3	78.3	83.5	88.4
1993	78.9	59.6	77.7	82.9	88.3
1994	78.9	58.3	77.8	83.2	88.2
1995	79.3	59.8	77.3	83.2	88.7
1996	79.4	60.2	77.9	83.7	87.8
1997	80.1	61.7	78.5	83.7	88.5
1998	80.2	63.0	78.4	83.5	88.0
1999	80.0	62.7	78.1	83.0	87.6
2000	80.3	62.7	78.4	83.2	87.8
2001	80.2	63.5	78.4	83.0	87.0
2002	79.7	63.5	77.7	82.1	86.7
2003	79.4	64.1	76.9	81.9	86.2
2004	78.8	63.2	76.1	81.2	85.9
2005	78.5	62.9	75.7	81.1	85.7
2006	78.7	63.2	75.9	81.0	85.9
2007	79.0	63.7	76.3	81.1	85.9
2008	79.0	62.5	76.0	80.9	86.1
2009	78.6	62.3	75.7	80.3	85.9
2010	78.7	62.7	76.2	79.7	85.7
2011	77.6	61.0	74.3	78.6	85.3
Men					
1990	88.8	75.1	89.9	91.5	94.5
1991	88.6	75.1	89.3	92.0	94.2
1992	88.6	75.1	89.0	91.8	93.7
1993	88.1	74.9	88.1	90.6	93.7
1994	87.0	71.5	86.8	90.3	93.2
1995	87.4	72.0	86.9	90.1	93.8
1996	87.5	74.3	86.9	90.0	92.9
1997	87.7	75.2	86.4	90.6	93.5
1998	87.8	75.3	86.7	90.0	93.4
1999	87.5	74.4	86.6	89.4	93.0
2000	87.5	74.9	86.2	88.9	93.3
2001	87.4	75.4	85.8	89.1	92.9
2002	87.0	75.5	85.3	88.8	92.4
2003	86.4	76.1	84.3	87.5	92.2
2004	85.9	75.2	83.8	87.0	91.9
2005	86.0	75.7	83.7	87.5	91.7
2006	86.0	76.3	83.4	87.8	91.7
2007	86.2	75.7	83.9	87.2	92.4
2008	85.8	74.8	83.6	86.5	91.9
2009	85.1	73.7	82.3	86.0	91.9
2010	85.3	74.5	83.2	85.3	91.5
2011	84.0	73.3	81.8	83.2	91.1
Women					
1990	68.9	46.2	68.7	75.9	81.1
1991	69.1	46.2	68.6	75.2	81.8
1992	70.0	45.6	69.1	76.2	82.2
1993	70.0	44.2	68.8	76.1	82.2
1994	71.1	44.7	70.0	77.0	82.5
1995	71.5	47.2	68.9	77.3	82.8
1996	71.8	45.7	69.8	78.1	82.3
1997	72.8	47.1	71.4	77.6	83.2
1998	73.0	49.8	70.9	77.8	82.3
1999	72.8	50.5	70.4	77.4	81.9
2000	73.5	50.4	71.2	78.3	82.0
2001	73.4	51.7	71.3	77.7	80.9
2002	72.7	50.4	70.4	76.4	81.0
2003	72.6	50.5	69.8	77.1	80.1
2004	72.0	49.7	68.6	76.2	80.0
2005	71.4	48.7	67.4	75.8	79.8
2006	71.7	48.3	68.2	75.3	80.4
2007	72.1	49.6	68.4	76.0	79.7
2008	72.5	47.9	68.2	76.1	80.9
2009	72.4	49.0	68.7	75.4	80.5
2010	72.3	48.9	68.6	75.0	80.4
2011	71.3	46.8	66.1	74.7	80.0

Table 1-57. Labor Force Participation Rates of Persons Age 25 to 64 Years, by Educational Attainment, Sex, and Race, March 1990–March 2011—*Continued*

(Civilian labor force as a percent of the civilian noninstitutional population.)

Sex, race, and year	Participation rates				
	Total	Less than a high school diploma	4 years of high school only	1 to 3 years of college	4 or more years of college
White[1]					
1990	79.2	62.5	78.4	83.3	88.3
1991	79.4	62.5	78.3	83.1	88.6
1992	79.8	61.5	78.7	83.8	88.7
1993	79.7	61.1	78.2	83.1	88.8
1994	79.8	60.3	78.3	83.5	88.5
1995	80.1	61.6	77.9	83.4	88.8
1996	80.4	62.5	78.6	83.9	88.2
1997	81.0	63.8	79.2	83.9	89.0
1998	80.6	63.8	78.6	83.5	88.3
1999	80.6	64.2	78.5	83.3	87.9
2000	80.8	64.2	78.7	83.1	87.9
2001	80.7	64.5	78.7	83.1	87.2
2002	80.3	65.0	78.2	82.4	87.0
2003	80.1	65.7	77.5	82.3	86.5
2004	79.5	64.6	76.7	81.6	86.2
2005	79.2	63.8	76.4	81.5	86.1
2006	79.5	65.1	76.5	81.4	86.2
2007	79.6	65.1	77.2	81.4	86.1
2008	79.6	63.8	76.8	81.2	86.3
2009	79.4	64.7	76.4	80.7	86.2
2010	79.5	64.5	77.1	80.4	86.0
2011	78.5	62.9	75.3	79.3	85.5
Black[1]					
1990	74.6	54.5	78.2	84.2	92.0
1991	73.9	53.9	77.1	84.1	90.2
1992	74.4	55.4	76.9	83.4	89.1
1993	73.8	53.4	74.7	83.0	89.6
1994	73.5	49.4	75.2	82.4	89.5
1995	74.2	51.0	74.5	82.8	90.9
1996	73.7	50.1	74.3	83.0	87.9
1997	74.9	52.9	75.0	83.8	89.0
1998	77.7	59.3	77.0	85.0	88.8
1999	76.5	55.1	76.5	82.9	88.6
2000	77.9	55.5	77.0	84.2	90.3
2001	78.1	58.7	76.8	83.0	90.5
2002	76.4	56.6	75.0	81.7	88.9
2003	75.8	55.4	73.9	81.2	88.2
2004	75.0	55.2	73.4	79.0	87.9
2005	75.2	58.2	72.6	79.5	87.2
2006	75.0	54.0	73.3	79.6	87.7
2007	75.6	55.3	72.5	80.7	88.0
2008	75.6	54.3	72.8	80.0	87.5
2009	74.4	50.0	72.6	78.7	86.2
2010	74.2	52.2	71.7	77.5	87.0
2011	72.4	49.0	69.6	76.3	85.5

[1]Beginning in 2003, persons who selected this race group only; persons who selected more than one race group are not included. Prior to 2003, persons who reported more than one race group were included in the group they identified as their main race.

Table 1-58. Unemployment Rates of Persons Age 25 to 64 Years, by Educational Attainment and Sex, March 1990–March 2011

(Unemployment as a percent of the civilian labor force.)

Sex, race, and year	Unemployment rates				
	Total	Less than a high school diploma	4 years of high school only	1 to 3 years of college	4 or more years of college
Both Sexes					
1990	4.5	9.6	4.9	3.7	1.9
1991	6.1	12.3	6.7	5.0	2.9
1992	6.7	13.5	7.7	5.9	2.9
1993	6.4	13.0	7.3	5.5	3.2
1994	5.8	12.6	6.7	5.0	2.9
1995	4.8	10.0	5.2	4.5	2.5
1996	4.8	10.9	5.5	4.1	2.2
1997	4.4	10.4	5.1	3.8	2.0
1998	4.0	8.5	4.8	3.6	1.8
1999	3.5	7.7	4.0	3.1	1.9
2000	3.3	7.9	3.8	3.0	1.5
2001	3.5	8.1	4.2	2.9	2.0
2002	5.0	10.2	6.1	4.5	2.8
2003	5.3	9.9	6.4	5.2	3.0
2004	5.1	10.5	5.9	4.9	2.9
2005	4.4	9.0	5.5	4.1	2.3
2006	4.1	8.3	4.7	3.9	2.3
2007	3.9	8.5	4.7	3.7	1.8
2008	4.4	10.1	5.8	4.2	2.1
2009	8.1	15.8	10.4	8.0	4.3
2010	9.1	16.8	12.1	8.8	4.7
2011	8.3	16.2	10.9	8.1	4.4
Men					
1990	4.8	9.6	5.3	3.9	2.1
1991	6.8	13.4	7.7	5.2	3.2
1992	7.5	14.8	8.8	6.4	3.2
1993	7.3	14.1	8.7	6.3	3.4
1994	6.2	12.8	7.2	5.3	2.9
1995	5.1	10.9	5.7	4.4	2.6
1996	5.3	11.0	6.4	4.5	2.3
1997	4.7	9.9	5.6	4.0	2.1
1998	4.1	8.0	5.1	3.7	1.7
1999	3.5	7.0	4.1	3.2	1.9
2000	3.3	7.1	3.9	3.1	1.6
2001	3.7	7.5	4.6	3.2	1.9
2002	5.5	9.9	6.7	4.9	3.0
2003	5.8	9.5	6.9	6.0	3.2
2004	5.4	9.4	6.6	5.4	3.0
2005	4.7	7.9	6.0	4.3	2.5
2006	4.3	7.6	5.0	4.2	2.4
2007	4.3	8.4	5.5	3.9	1.9
2008	4.9	10.9	6.3	4.2	2.0
2009	9.5	16.5	12.4	9.3	4.7
2010	10.5	17.8	13.8	10.2	5.1
2011	9.2	16.7	12.2	8.7	4.6
Women					
1990	4.2	9.5	4.6	3.5	1.7
1991	5.2	10.7	5.5	4.8	2.5
1992	5.7	11.4	6.5	5.3	2.5
1993	5.2	11.2	5.8	4.6	2.9
1994	5.4	12.4	6.2	4.7	2.9
1995	4.4	8.6	4.6	4.5	2.4
1996	4.1	10.7	4.4	3.8	2.1
1997	4.1	11.3	4.5	3.6	2.0
1998	3.9	9.3	4.4	3.5	1.9
1999	3.5	8.8	3.9	3.0	1.9
2000	3.2	9.1	3.6	2.9	1.4
2001	3.3	8.9	3.8	2.6	2.0
2002	4.6	10.6	5.4	4.1	2.6
2003	4.8	10.6	5.9	4.4	2.8
2004	4.7	12.2	5.2	4.3	2.9
2005	4.2	10.9	4.8	4.0	2.2
2006	3.8	9.4	4.4	3.7	2.1
2007	3.4	8.5	3.8	3.6	1.8
2008	4.0	8.5	5.1	4.2	2.1
2009	6.6	14.5	7.9	6.7	4.0
2010	7.5	15.0	9.8	7.5	4.3
2011	7.2	15.2	9.1	7.5	4.3

Table 1-58. Unemployment Rates of Persons Age 25 to 64 Years, by Educational Attainment and Sex, March 1990–March 2011—*Continued*

(Unemployment as a percent of the civilian labor force.)

Sex, race, and year	Unemployment rates				
	Total	Less than a high school diploma	4 years of high school only	1 to 3 years of college	4 or more years of college
White[1]					
1990	4.0	8.3	4.4	3.3	1.8
1991	5.6	11.6	6.2	4.6	2.7
1992	6.0	12.9	6.8	5.3	2.7
1993	5.8	12.4	6.5	5.0	3.1
1994	5.2	11.7	5.8	4.5	2.6
1995	4.3	9.2	4.6	4.2	2.3
1996	4.2	10.2	4.6	3.7	2.1
1997	3.9	9.4	4.6	3.4	1.8
1998	3.5	7.5	4.2	3.2	1.7
1999	3.1	7.0	3.4	2.8	1.7
2000	3.0	7.5	3.3	2.7	1.4
2001	3.1	7.2	3.6	2.7	1.8
2002	4.6	9.1	5.5	4.1	2.6
2003	4.7	9.0	5.7	4.5	2.7
2004	4.6	9.6	5.4	4.4	2.8
2005	3.9	7.7	4.9	3.6	2.2
2006	3.5	7.1	4.0	3.5	2.1
2007	3.5	7.8	4.2	3.3	1.7
2008	4.0	9.2	5.1	3.7	1.9
2009	7.6	15.2	9.9	7.4	4.0
2010	8.4	16.3	11.3	8.1	4.3
2011	7.5	15.1	9.9	7.2	4.0
Black[1]					
1990	8.6	15.9	8.6	6.5	1.9
1991	10.1	15.9	10.3	8.0	5.2
1992	12.4	17.2	14.1	10.7	4.8
1993	10.9	17.3	12.4	8.7	4.1
1994	10.6	17.4	12.2	8.3	4.9
1995	7.7	13.7	8.4	6.3	4.1
1996	8.9	15.3	10.8	6.9	3.3
1997	8.1	16.6	8.2	6.1	4.4
1998	7.3	13.4	8.4	6.4	2.1
1999	6.3	12.0	6.7	5.2	3.3
2000	5.4	10.4	6.3	4.3	2.5
2001	6.5	14.0	7.7	4.3	3.3
2002	8.1	15.4	9.7	6.0	4.1
2003	9.0	14.7	9.9	8.9	4.7
2004	8.4	15.8	9.3	7.9	3.7
2005	8.3	17.9	8.6	7.5	3.6
2006	7.8	16.4	9.0	6.5	3.6
2007	6.5	14.0	7.7	5.7	2.5
2008	7.6	16.7	9.3	6.5	3.3
2009	12.1	22.0	14.0	11.2	7.2
2010	14.1	22.4	17.5	12.9	7.9
2011	13.9	25.0	16.6	12.7	7.7

[1]Beginning in 2003, persons who selected this race group only; persons who selected more than one race group are not included. Prior to 2003, persons who reported more than one race group were included in the group they identified as their main race.

Table 1-59. Workers Age 25 to 64 Years, by Educational Attainment, Occupation of Longest Job Held, and Sex, 2009–2010

(Thousands of people with work experience during the year.)

Year, sex, and occupation	Total	Less than a high school diploma	4 years of high school only	1 to 3 years of college	4 or more years of college
2009					
Both Sexes	126 188	10 799	36 267	35 059	44 064
Management, business, and financial operations	19 958	420	3 371	4 832	11 335
Management	14 294	368	2 697	3 519	7 711
Business and financial operations	5 664	52	674	1 313	3 624
Professional and related	28 756	147	2 304	6 412	19 893
Computer and mathematical	3 465	13	269	920	2 263
Architecture and engineering	2 425	. . .	220	582	1 623
Life, physical, and social sciences	1 261	4	99	130	1 028
Community and social services	2 156	20	170	399	1 566
Legal	1 530	6	76	230	1 218
Education, training, and library	8 235	35	615	1 074	6 510
Arts, design, entertainment, sports, and media	2 487	46	309	577	1 555
Health care practitioner and technical	7 197	23	545	2 500	4 128
Services	19 912	3 435	7 580	6 097	2 800
Health care support	2 941	280	1 047	1 274	340
Protective services	2 838	88	796	1 197	757
Food preparation and serving related	5 026	1 099	2 026	1 277	624
Building and grounds cleaning and maintenance	4 946	1 495	2 182	904	365
Personal care and services	4 161	473	1 528	1 445	714
Sales and office	28 602	1 320	9 438	10 268	7 576
Sales and related	12 528	726	3 771	3 768	4 263
Office and administrative support	16 074	594	5 668	6 500	3 313
Natural resources, construction, and maintenance	13 406	2 710	6 154	3 518	1 025
Farming, fishing, and forestry	930	433	304	128	64
Construction and extraction	7 854	1 810	3 745	1 767	532
Installation, maintenance, and repair	4 622	466	2 104	1 623	429
Production, transportation, and material moving	14 866	2 760	7 269	3 626	1 211
Production	7 502	1 496	3 553	1 830	623
Transportation and material moving	7 364	1 264	3 716	1 796	588
Armed forces	689	6	151	306	225
Men	66 826	6 847	20 605	17 084	22 290
Management, business, and financial operations	11 359	306	1 892	2 580	6 581
Management	8 870	283	1 678	2 103	4 807
Business and financial operations	2 489	24	214	476	1 774
Professional and related	11 980	65	865	2 281	8 769
Computer and mathematical	2 462	9	171	650	1 633
Architecture and engineering	2 108	. . .	194	503	1 412
Life, physical, and social sciences	628	3	59	65	501
Community and social services	746	9	63	133	541
Legal	735	. . .	17	27	691
Education, training, and library	2 128	8	79	165	1 876
Arts, design, entertainment, sports, and media	1 367	32	189	342	804
Health care practitioner and technical	1 805	4	94	396	1 312
Services	8 351	1 403	3 124	2 483	1 341
Health care support	300	27	83	122	68
Protective services	2 186	58	593	961	574
Food preparation and serving related	2 246	496	906	539	305
Building and grounds cleaning and maintenance	2 794	739	1 260	576	219
Personal care and services	825	83	281	286	175
Sales and office	10 284	528	2 940	3 291	3 525
Sales and related	6 419	315	1 648	1 907	2 549
Office and administrative support	3 865	213	1 292	1 384	975
Natural resources, construction, and maintenance	12 731	2 542	5 919	3 334	936
Farming, fishing, and forestry	661	298	249	72	42
Construction and extraction	7 633	1 785	3 638	1 707	504
Installation, maintenance, and repair	4 436	459	2 032	1 556	390
Production, transportation, and material moving	11 512	1 999	5 720	2 843	950
Production	5 370	968	2 613	1 353	437
Transportation and material moving	6 141	1 031	3 107	1 490	513
Armed forces	610	5	144	272	188
Women	59 362	3 952	15 662	17 975	21 774
Management, business, and financial operations	8 598	114	1 479	2 252	4 753
Management	5 424	85	1 019	1 416	2 904
Business and financial operations	3 175	29	459	837	1 850
Professional and related	16 776	82	1 439	4 132	11 124
Computer and mathematical	1 003	3	99	270	631
Architecture and engineering	317	. . .	26	80	211
Life, physical, and social sciences	633	2	40	64	527
Community and social services	1 410	11	108	266	1 026
Legal	795	6	60	203	527
Education, training, and library	6 107	27	536	909	4 634
Arts, design, entertainment, sports, and media	1 120	14	120	235	751
Health care practitioner and technical	5 391	19	451	2 105	2 816
Services	11 561	2 033	4 456	3 614	1 459
Health care support	2 641	253	964	1 152	272
Protective services	652	30	203	237	183
Food preparation and serving related	2 780	603	1 120	738	319
Building and grounds cleaning and maintenance	2 153	756	923	329	145
Personal care and services	3 336	391	1 247	1 159	539
Sales and office	18 319	793	6 498	6 977	4 051
Sales and related	6 109	412	2 122	1 861	1 714
Office and administrative support	12 210	381	4 376	5 116	2 337
Natural resources, construction, and maintenance	675	168	234	184	88
Farming, fishing, and forestry	268	135	55	56	22
Construction and extraction	221	25	108	60	27
Installation, maintenance, and repair	186	8	71	68	39
Production, transportation, and material moving	3 354	761	1 549	782	261
Production	2 132	528	940	477	186
Transportation and material moving	1 222	232	609	306	75
Armed forces	79	2	6	34	37

. . . = Not available.

Table 1-59. Workers Age 25 to 64 Years, by Educational Attainment, Occupation of Longest Job Held, and Sex, 2009–2010—*Continued*

(Thousands of people with work experience during the year.)

Year, sex, and occupation	Total	Less than a high school diploma	4 years of high school only	1 to 3 years of college	4 or more years of college
2010					
Both Sexes	125 135	10 202	34 760	35 442	44 731
Management, business, and financial operations	20 133	397	3 178	4 911	11 647
Management	14 113	361	2 537	3 547	7 668
Business and financial operations	6 020	36	641	1 363	3 980
Professional and related	28 996	149	2 075	6 380	20 391
Computer and mathematical	3 298	11	231	753	2 303
Architecture and engineering	2 687	8	231	612	1 836
Life, physical, and social sciences	1 241	3	62	127	1 049
Community and social services	2 264	15	185	398	1 665
Legal	1 554	4	70	255	1 225
Education, training, and library	8 176	49	598	1 075	6 455
Arts, design, entertainment, sports, and media	2 433	37	234	601	1 562
Health care practitioner and technical	7 342	23	464	2 559	4 296
Services	19 674	3 238	7 313	6 393	2 730
Health care support	2 888	259	926	1 312	390
Protective services	2 822	75	720	1 237	790
Food preparation and serving related	5 064	1 048	2 065	1 448	503
Building and grounds cleaning and maintenance	4 919	1 404	2 095	1 026	394
Personal care and services	3 982	451	1 508	1 370	653
Sales and office	28 106	1 262	9 060	10 275	7 509
Sales and related	12 206	670	3 733	3 838	3 965
Office and administrative support	15 901	593	5 327	6 437	3 543
Natural resources, construction, and maintenance	12 683	2 574	5 662	3 455	993
Farming, fishing, and forestry	838	412	278	100	48
Construction and extraction	7 407	1 753	3 406	1 717	531
Installation, maintenance, and repair	4 438	409	1 978	1 638	414
Production, transportation, and material moving	14 887	2 577	7 327	3 739	1 245
Production	7 618	1 391	3 663	1 923	641
Transportation and material moving	7 270	1 186	3 664	1 816	604
Armed forces	654	4	145	289	216
Men	66 276	6 488	19 756	17 286	22 746
Management, business, and financial operations	11 312	276	1 798	2 502	6 736
Management	8 625	261	1 592	2 047	4 724
Business and financial operations	2 687	14	206	455	2 012
Professional and related	12 128	62	746	2 287	9 033
Computer and mathematical	2 414	11	158	543	1 702
Architecture and engineering	2 320	8	194	548	1 570
Life, physical, and social sciences	679	. . .	40	83	555
Community and social services	767	2	64	127	574
Legal	742	2	10	29	701
Education, training, and library	2 120	14	79	192	1 834
Arts, design, entertainment, sports, and media	1 346	19	132	362	833
Health care practitioner and technical	1 740	6	69	402	1 263
Services	8 389	1 360	3 004	2 690	1 336
Health care support	297	28	82	124	61
Protective services	2 212	53	540	998	621
Food preparation and serving related	2 235	486	863	660	226
Building and grounds cleaning and maintenance	2 866	731	1 216	670	249
Personal care and services	779	62	302	237	178
Sales and office	10 309	481	3 012	3 271	3 544
Sales and related	6 276	259	1 737	1 857	2 424
Office and administrative support	4 032	223	1 275	1 414	1 120
Natural resources, construction, and maintenance	12 093	2 420	5 444	3 299	929
Farming, fishing, and forestry	629	296	220	78	35
Construction and extraction	7 216	1 734	3 316	1 670	496
Installation, maintenance, and repair	4 247	391	1 909	1 551	397
Production, transportation, and material moving	11 463	1 884	5 624	2 971	985
Production	5 370	880	2 557	1 460	472
Transportation and material moving	6 093	1 004	3 066	1 510	513
Armed forces	583	4	128	267	184
Women	58 859	3 714	15 004	18 155	21 985
Management, business, and financial operations	8 821	122	1 380	2 409	4 911
Management	5 489	100	944	1 501	2 944
Business and financial operations	3 333	22	435	908	1 968
Professional and related	16 869	87	1 329	4 093	11 359
Computer and mathematical	884	. . .	73	210	601
Architecture and engineering	368	. . .	37	64	266
Life, physical, and social sciences	563	3	21	44	494
Community and social services	1 496	13	122	271	1 091
Legal	812	2	60	226	524
Education, training, and library	6 056	35	518	882	4 621
Arts, design, entertainment, sports, and media	1 087	18	102	238	729
Health care practitioner and technical	5 602	17	395	2 157	3 033
Services	11 285	1 878	4 310	3 703	1 394
Health care support	2 591	231	843	1 188	329
Protective services	610	23	179	238	169
Food preparation and serving related	2 828	562	1 202	788	277
Building and grounds cleaning and maintenance	2 053	673	879	356	145
Personal care and services	3 202	389	1 206	1 132	475
Sales and office	17 798	781	6 048	7 004	3 965
Sales and related	5 929	411	1 996	1 981	1 541
Office and administrative support	11 868	370	4 052	5 023	2 423
Natural resources, construction, and maintenance	590	154	217	155	64
Farming, fishing, and forestry	209	116	58	22	13
Construction and extraction	191	19	90	47	35
Installation, maintenance, and repair	191	18	69	87	16
Production, transportation, and material moving	3 425	693	1 704	768	260
Production	2 248	510	1 106	463	169
Transportation and material moving	1 177	182	598	305	91
Armed forces	72	. . .	17	23	32

. . . = Not available.

Table 1-60. Percent Distribution of Workers Age 25 to 64 Years, by Educational Attainment, Occupation of Longest Job Held, and Sex, 2009–2010

(Percent of total workers in occupation.)

Year, sex, and occupation	Total	Less than a high school diploma	4 years of high school only	1 to 3 years of college	4 or more years of college
2009					
Both Sexes	100.0	8.6	28.7	27.8	34.9
Management, business, and financial operations	100.0	2.1	16.9	24.2	56.8
Management	100.0	2.6	18.9	24.6	53.9
Business and financial operations	100.0	0.9	11.9	23.2	64.0
Professional and related	100.0	0.5	8.0	22.3	69.2
Computer and mathematical	100.0	0.4	7.8	26.6	65.3
Architecture and engineering	100.0	0.0	9.1	24.0	66.9
Life, physical, and social sciences	100.0	0.4	7.8	10.3	81.5
Community and social services	100.0	0.9	7.9	18.5	72.7
Legal	100.0	0.4	5.0	15.0	79.6
Education, training, and library	100.0	0.4	7.5	13.0	79.1
Arts, design, entertainment, sports, and media	100.0	1.9	12.4	23.2	62.5
Health care practitioner and technical	100.0	0.3	7.6	34.7	57.4
Services	100.0	17.3	38.1	30.6	14.1
Health care support	100.0	9.5	35.6	43.3	11.6
Protective services	100.0	3.1	28.0	42.2	26.7
Food preparation and serving related	100.0	21.9	40.3	25.4	12.4
Building and grounds cleaning and maintenance	100.0	30.2	44.1	18.3	7.4
Personal care and services	100.0	11.4	36.7	34.7	17.2
Sales and office	100.0	4.6	33.0	35.9	26.5
Sales and related	100.0	5.8	30.1	30.1	34.0
Office and administrative support	100.0	3.7	35.3	40.4	20.6
Natural resources, construction, and maintenance	100.0	20.2	45.9	26.2	7.6
Farming, fishing, and forestry	100.0	46.6	32.7	13.7	6.9
Construction and extraction	100.0	23.0	47.7	22.5	6.8
Installation, maintenance, and repair	100.0	10.1	45.5	35.1	9.3
Production, transportation, and material moving	100.0	18.6	48.9	24.4	8.1
Production	100.0	19.9	47.4	24.4	8.3
Transportation and material moving	100.0	17.2	50.5	24.4	8.0
Armed forces	100.0	0.9	21.9	44.4	32.7
Men	100.0	10.2	30.8	25.6	33.4
Management, business, and financial operations	100.0	2.7	16.7	22.7	57.9
Management	100.0	3.2	18.9	23.7	54.2
Business and financial operations	100.0	1.0	8.6	19.1	71.3
Professional and related	100.0	0.5	7.2	19.0	73.2
Computer and mathematical	100.0	0.4	6.9	26.4	66.3
Architecture and engineering	100.0	0.0	9.2	23.8	67.0
Life, physical, and social sciences	100.0	0.4	9.4	10.4	79.8
Community and social services	100.0	1.2	8.4	17.9	72.5
Legal	100.0	0.0	2.3	3.7	94.0
Education, training, and library	100.0	0.4	3.7	7.7	88.2
Arts, design, entertainment, sports, and media	100.0	2.4	13.8	25.0	58.8
Health care practitioner and technical	100.0	0.2	5.2	21.9	72.7
Services	100.0	16.8	37.4	29.7	16.1
Health care support	100.0	9.1	27.6	40.7	22.6
Protective services	100.0	2.7	27.1	43.9	26.3
Food preparation and serving related	100.0	22.1	40.4	24.0	13.6
Building and grounds cleaning and maintenance	100.0	26.5	45.1	20.6	7.9
Personal care and services	100.0	10.0	34.1	34.7	21.2
Sales and office	100.0	5.1	28.6	32.0	34.3
Sales and related	100.0	4.9	25.7	29.7	39.7
Office and administrative support	100.0	5.5	33.4	35.8	25.2
Natural resources, construction, and maintenance	100.0	20.0	46.5	26.2	7.4
Farming, fishing, and forestry	100.0	45.1	37.7	10.8	6.4
Construction and extraction	100.0	23.4	47.7	22.4	6.6
Installation, maintenance, and repair	100.0	10.3	45.8	35.1	8.8
Production, transportation, and material moving	100.0	17.4	49.7	24.7	8.2
Production	100.0	18.0	48.7	25.2	8.1
Transportation and material moving	100.0	16.8	50.6	24.3	8.4
Armed forces	100.0	0.8	23.7	44.7	30.9
Women	100.0	6.7	26.4	30.3	36.7
Management, business, and financial operations	100.0	1.3	17.2	26.2	55.3
Management	100.0	1.6	18.8	26.1	53.5
Business and financial operations	100.0	0.9	14.5	26.4	58.3
Professional and related	100.0	0.5	8.6	24.6	66.3
Computer and mathematical	100.0	0.3	9.8	26.9	62.9
Architecture and engineering	100.0	0.0	8.2	25.1	66.7
Life, physical, and social sciences	100.0	0.3	6.3	10.1	83.3
Community and social services	100.0	0.8	7.6	18.9	72.7
Legal	100.0	0.7	7.5	25.5	66.2
Education, training, and library	100.0	0.4	8.8	14.9	75.9
Arts, design, entertainment, sports, and media	100.0	1.3	10.7	21.0	67.1
Health care practitioner and technical	100.0	0.3	8.4	39.0	52.2
Services	100.0	17.6	38.5	31.3	12.6
Health care support	100.0	9.6	36.5	43.6	10.3
Protective services	100.0	4.6	31.1	36.3	28.0
Food preparation and serving related	100.0	21.7	40.3	26.5	11.5
Building and grounds cleaning and maintenance	100.0	35.1	42.9	15.3	6.8
Personal care and services	100.0	11.7	37.4	34.7	16.2
Sales and office	100.0	4.3	35.5	38.1	22.1
Sales and related	100.0	6.7	34.7	30.5	28.1
Office and administrative support	100.0	3.1	35.8	41.9	19.1
Natural resources, construction, and maintenance	100.0	24.9	34.8	27.3	13.1
Farming, fishing, and forestry	100.0	50.3	20.6	20.9	8.1
Construction and extraction	100.0	11.4	48.9	27.2	12.4
Installation, maintenance, and repair	100.0	4.1	38.4	36.4	21.1
Production, transportation, and material moving	100.0	22.7	46.2	23.3	7.8
Production	100.0	24.8	44.1	22.4	8.7
Transportation and material moving	100.0	19.0	49.8	25.0	6.1
Armed forces	100.0	2.2	8.2	42.6	46.9

Table 1-60. Percent Distribution of Workers Age 25 to 64 Years, by Educational Attainment, Occupation of Longest Job Held, and Sex, 2009–2010—*Continued*

(Percent of total workers in occupation.)

Year, sex, and occupation	Total	Less than a high school diploma	4 years of high school only	1 to 3 years of college	4 or more years of college
2010					
Both Sexes	100.0	8.2	27.8	28.3	35.7
Management, business, and financial operations	100.0	2.0	15.8	24.4	57.9
Management	100.0	2.6	18.0	25.1	54.3
Business and financial operations	100.0	0.6	10.6	22.6	66.1
Professional and related	100.0	0.5	7.2	22.0	70.3
Computer and mathematical	100.0	0.3	7.0	22.8	69.8
Architecture and engineering	100.0	0.3	8.6	22.8	68.3
Life, physical, and social sciences	100.0	0.2	5.0	10.3	84.5
Community and social services	100.0	0.7	8.2	17.6	73.6
Legal	100.0	0.3	4.5	16.4	78.8
Education, training, and library	100.0	0.6	7.3	13.1	79.0
Arts, design, entertainment, sports, and media	100.0	1.5	9.6	24.7	64.2
Health care practitioner and technical	100.0	0.3	6.3	34.9	58.5
Services	100.0	16.5	37.2	32.5	13.9
Health care support	100.0	9.0	32.1	45.4	13.5
Protective services	100.0	2.7	25.5	43.8	28.0
Food preparation and serving related	100.0	20.7	40.8	28.6	9.9
Building and grounds cleaning and maintenance	100.0	28.5	42.6	20.9	8.0
Personal care and services	100.0	11.3	37.9	34.4	16.4
Sales and office	100.0	4.5	32.2	36.6	26.7
Sales and related	100.0	5.5	30.6	31.4	32.5
Office and administrative support	100.0	3.7	33.5	40.5	22.3
Natural resources, construction, and maintenance	100.0	20.3	44.6	27.2	7.8
Farming, fishing, and forestry	100.0	49.2	33.1	11.9	5.7
Construction and extraction	100.0	23.7	46.0	23.2	7.2
Installation, maintenance, and repair	100.0	9.2	44.6	36.9	9.3
Production, transportation, and material moving	100.0	17.3	49.2	25.1	8.4
Production	100.0	18.3	48.1	25.2	8.4
Transportation and material moving	100.0	16.3	50.4	25.0	8.3
Armed forces	100.0	0.7	22.1	44.2	33.0
Men	100.0	9.8	29.8	26.1	34.3
Management, business, and financial operations	100.0	2.4	15.9	22.1	59.5
Management	100.0	3.0	18.5	23.7	54.8
Business and financial operations	100.0	0.5	7.7	16.9	74.9
Professional and related	100.0	0.5	6.1	18.9	74.5
Computer and mathematical	100.0	0.4	6.6	22.5	70.5
Architecture and engineering	100.0	0.3	8.4	23.6	67.7
Life, physical, and social sciences	100.0	0.0	6.0	12.2	81.8
Community and social services	100.0	0.3	8.3	16.6	74.8
Legal	100.0	0.3	1.3	3.9	94.5
Education, training, and library	100.0	0.7	3.8	9.1	86.5
Arts, design, entertainment, sports, and media	100.0	1.4	9.8	26.9	61.9
Health care practitioner and technical	100.0	0.3	3.9	23.1	72.6
Services	100.0	16.2	35.8	32.1	15.9
Health care support	100.0	9.6	27.8	41.9	20.7
Protective services	100.0	2.4	24.4	45.1	28.1
Food preparation and serving related	100.0	21.8	38.6	29.5	10.1
Building and grounds cleaning and maintenance	100.0	25.5	42.4	23.4	8.7
Personal care and services	100.0	7.9	38.8	30.5	22.8
Sales and office	100.0	4.7	29.2	31.7	34.4
Sales and related	100.0	4.1	27.7	29.6	38.6
Office and administrative support	100.0	5.5	31.6	35.1	27.8
Natural resources, construction, and maintenance	100.0	20.0	45.0	27.3	7.7
Farming, fishing, and forestry	100.0	47.0	35.0	12.4	5.6
Construction and extraction	100.0	24.0	45.9	23.1	6.9
Installation, maintenance, and repair	100.0	9.2	44.9	36.5	9.4
Production, transportation, and material moving	100.0	16.4	49.1	25.9	8.6
Production	100.0	16.4	47.6	27.2	8.8
Transportation and material moving	100.0	16.5	50.3	24.8	8.4
Armed forces	100.0	0.7	22.0	45.7	31.6
Women	100.0	6.3	25.5	30.8	37.4
Management, business, and financial operations	100.0	1.4	15.6	27.3	55.7
Management	100.0	1.8	17.2	27.3	53.6
Business and financial operations	100.0	0.6	13.1	27.3	59.0
Professional and related	100.0	0.5	7.9	24.3	67.3
Computer and mathematical	100.0	0.0	8.3	23.8	67.9
Architecture and engineering	100.0	0.0	10.2	17.5	72.3
Life, physical, and social sciences	100.0	0.5	3.8	7.8	87.8
Community and social services	100.0	0.9	8.1	18.1	72.9
Legal	100.0	0.2	7.4	27.9	64.5
Education, training, and library	100.0	0.6	8.6	14.6	76.3
Arts, design, entertainment, sports, and media	100.0	1.6	9.4	21.9	67.1
Health care practitioner and technical	100.0	0.3	7.1	38.5	54.1
Services	100.0	16.6	38.2	32.8	12.4
Health care support	100.0	8.9	32.5	45.8	12.7
Protective services	100.0	3.7	29.4	39.1	27.7
Food preparation and serving related	100.0	19.9	42.5	27.9	9.8
Building and grounds cleaning and maintenance	100.0	32.8	42.8	17.4	7.1
Personal care and services	100.0	12.2	37.7	35.4	14.8
Sales and office	100.0	4.4	34.0	39.4	22.3
Sales and related	100.0	6.9	33.7	33.4	26.0
Office and administrative support	100.0	3.1	34.1	42.3	20.4
Natural resources, construction, and maintenance	100.0	26.0	36.8	26.3	10.9
Farming, fishing, and forestry	100.0	55.6	27.7	10.4	6.3
Construction and extraction	100.0	10.0	47.4	24.4	18.2
Installation, maintenance, and repair	100.0	9.6	36.3	45.6	8.5
Production, transportation, and material moving	100.0	20.2	49.7	22.4	7.6
Production	100.0	22.7	49.2	20.6	7.5
Transportation and material moving	100.0	15.5	50.8	26.0	7.8
Armed forces	100.0	. . .	23.6	31.9	44.5

. . . = Not available.

Table 1-61. Median Annual Earnings of Year-Round, Full-Time Wage and Salary Workers Age 25 to 64 Years, by Educational Attainment and Sex, 2000–2010

(Thousands of workers, dollars.)

Year and sex	Total	Less than a high school diploma	4 years of high school only	1 to 3 years of college	4 or more years of college
2000					
Both Sexes					
Number of workers	84 337	7 354	26 144	24 064	26 775
Median annual earnings	35 000	20 000	28 600	34 000	50 000
Men					
Number of workers	48 816	4 738	15 057	13 242	15 780
Median annual earnings	40 000	22 500	33 000	40 000	60 000
Women					
Number of workers	35 521	2 616	11 087	10 822	10 995
Median annual earnings	29 000	16 000	24 000	28 000	40 000
2001					
Both Sexes					
Number of workers	84 743	7 623	25 522	23 719	27 879
Median annual earnings	35 000	20 800	29 000	35 000	50 000
Men					
Number of workers	48 887	5 049	14 655	12 968	16 215
Median annual earnings	40 000	24 000	33 800	40 000	60 000
Women					
Number of workers	35 856	2 574	10 867	10 751	11 664
Median annual earnings	30 000	17 000	24 000	30 000	42 000
2002					
Both Sexes					
Number of workers	84 702	7 578	25 078	23 604	28 443
Median annual earnings	36 000	21 000	30 000	35 100	52 000
Men					
Number of workers	48 687	5 102	14 306	12 677	16 602
Median annual earnings	41 000	23 400	34 000	41 500	61 000
Women					
Number of workers	36 015	2 476	10 772	10 927	11 841
Median annual earnings	30 000	18 000	25 000	30 000	43 500
2003					
Both Sexes					
Number of workers	85 058	7 245	25 352	23 702	28 759
Median annual earnings	37 752	21 000	30 000	36 000	53 000
Men					
Number of workers	48 988	4 879	14 657	12 766	16 686
Median annual earnings	42 000	24 000	35 000	42 000	62 000
Women					
Number of workers	36 070	2 366	10 695	10 936	12 073
Median annual earnings	32 000	18 000	25 111	31 000	45 000
2004					
Both Sexes					
Number of workers	86 306	7 648	25 786	23 897	28 976
Median annual earnings	38 000	21 840	30 000	37 000	55 000
Men					
Number of workers	49 904	5 178	15 263	12 822	16 642
Median annual earnings	42 900	24 000	35 000	43 000	65 000
Women					
Number of workers	36 402	2 470	10 523	11 074	12 334
Median annual earnings	32 000	18 000	25 280	31 200	45 000
2005					
Both Sexes					
Number of workers	88 415	7 758	26 023	24 623	30 012
Median annual earnings	39 768	22 880	31 000	38 000	55 000
Men					
Number of workers	51 022	5 376	15 451	13 199	16 996
Median annual earnings	44 000	25 000	35 360	45 000	65 000
Women					
Number of workers	37 393	2 381	10 571	11 424	13 016
Median annual earnings	33 644	18 200	26 000	32 000	46 700

Table 1-61. Median Annual Earnings of Year-Round, Full-Time Wage and Salary Workers Age 25 to 64 Years, by Educational Attainment and Sex, 2000–2010—*Continued*

(Thousands of workers, dollars.)

Year and sex	Total	Less than a high school diploma	4 years of high school only	1 to 3 years of college	4 or more years of college
2006					
Both Sexes					
Number of workers	90 733	7 951	26 233	24 737	31 812
Median annual earnings	40 000	23 000	32 000	39 482	57 588
Men					
Number of workers	52 252	5 485	15 525	13 204	18 038
Median annual earnings	45 000	25 000	36 665	45 000	68 000
Women					
Number of workers	38 481	2 466	10 708	11 533	13 774
Median annual earnings	35 000	19 000	26 800	33 000	49 000
2007					
Both Sexes					
Number of workers	91 540	7 123	25 925	25 574	32 918
Median annual earnings	41 000	24 000	33 000	40 000	60 000
Men					
Number of workers	52 262	4 902	15 390	13 655	18 316
Median annual earnings	47 000	25 000	38 000	45 188	70 000
Women					
Number of workers	39 277	2 221	10 535	11 919	14 603
Median annual earnings	35 000	19 200	27 120	35 000	50 000
2008					
Both Sexes					
Number of workers	88 373	6 600	24 531	24 887	32 355
Median annual earnings	42 000	24 000	34 000	40 000	60 000
Men					
Number of workers	50 141	4 503	14 480	13 283	17 876
Median annual earnings	49 564	27 000	39 040	47 000	72 000
Women					
Number of workers	38 231	2 097	10 051	11 604	14 479
Median annual earnings	36 000	19 567	28 000	35 000	50 000
2009					
Both Sexes					
Number of workers	84 730	5 847	23 277	23 515	32 091
Median annual earnings	43 000	24 000	34 320	40 000	60 000
Men					
Number of workers	47 135	3 809	13 620	12 283	17 424
Median annual earnings	50 000	26 000	40 000	49 000	71 000
Women					
Number of workers	37 595	2 037	9 657	11 233	14 667
Median annual earnings	38 000	20 000	29 000	35 000	52 000
2010					
Both Sexes					
Number of workers	84 902	5 548	22 768	23 725	32 861
Median annual earnings	44 217	24 000	35 000	40 000	60 000
Men					
Number of workers	47 549	3 653	13 526	12 405	17 965
Median annual earnings	50 000	26 500	40 000	48 000	72 000
Women					
Number of workers	37 353	1 895	9 241	11 321	14 896
Median annual earnings	38 000	20 000	30 000	35 000	51 000

Table 1-62. Employment Status of the Civilian Noninstitutional Population by Disability Status and Selected Characteristics, 2010 Annual Averages

(Thousands of people, percent.)

Characteristic	Civilian noninstitutional population	Civilian labor force						Not in labor force
		Total	Participation rate	Employed		Unemployed		
				Total	Percent	Total	Rate	
TOTAL								
Total, 16 Years and Over	237 830	153 889	64.7	139 064	58.5	14 825	9.6	83 941
Men	115 174	81 985	71.2	73 359	63.7	8 626	10.5	33 189
Women	122 656	71 904	58.6	65 705	53.6	6 199	8.6	50 752
PERSONS WITH A DISABILITY	26 592	5 795	21.8	4 939	18.6	857	14.8	20 797
Total, 16 Years and Over	12 147	3 142	25.9	2 665	21.9	477	15.2	9 005
Men	14 445	2 653	18.4	2 274	15.7	379	14.3	11 792
16 to 64 years	14 730	4 995	33.9	4 210	28.6	786	15.7	9 735
16 to 19 years	593	134	22.7	87	14.6	48	35.6	458
20 to 24 years	777	350	45.1	265	34.1	86	24.4	427
25 to 34 years	1 534	682	44.5	535	34.9	147	21.5	852
35 to 44 years	2 148	826	38.4	699	32.6	126	15.3	1 322
45 to 54 years	4 217	1 477	35.0	1 267	30.0	210	14.2	2 740
55 to 64 years	5 462	1 526	27.9	1 356	24.8	169	11.1	3 936
65 years and over	11 862	800	6.7	729	6.1	71	8.9	11 062
Race and Hispanic Origin								
White	21 787	4 870	22.4	4 206	19.3	664	13.6	16 917
Black or African American	3 340	591	17.7	460	13.8	130	22.0	2 750
Asian	623	113	18.2	100	16.0	14	12.0	509
Hispanic[1]	2 572	599	23.3	488	19.0	110	18.4	1 973
Educational Attainment								
Total, 25 years and over	25 222	5 311	21.1	4 587	18.2	723	13.6	19 912
Less than a high school diploma	6 102	627	10.3	517	8.5	110	17.6	5 474
High school graduates, no college[2]	9 249	1 750	18.9	1 493	16.1	257	14.7	7 499
Some college or associate degree	6 059	1 666	27.5	1 421	23.5	245	14.7	4 393
Bachelor's degree and higher[3]	3 813	1 268	33.3	1 157	30.3	111	8.7	2 545

[1]May be of any race.
[2]Includes persons with a high school diploma or equivalent.
[3]Includes persons with bachelor's, master's, professional, and doctoral degrees.

Table 1-63. Employed Full- and Part-Time Workers by Disability Status and Age, 2010 Annual Averages

(Thousands of people.)

Disability status and age	Employed			At work part-time for economic reasons[1]
	Total	Usually work full-time	Usually work part-time	
TOTAL				
Total, 16 Years and Over	139 064	111 714	27 350	8 874
16 to 64 years	132 796	108 104	24 692	8 626
65 years and over	6 268	3 611	2 658	249
Persons With a Disability				
16 years and over	4 939	3 337	1 602	400
16 to 64 years	4 210	2 999	1 211	369
65 years and over	729	338	391	31
Persons Without a Disability				
16 years and over	134 125	108 378	25 748	8 474
16 to 64 years	128 586	105 105	23 481	8 256
65 years and over	5 539	3 273	2 267	218

Note: Full time refers to persons who usually work 35 hours or more per week; part time refers to persons who usually work less than 35 hours per week.

[1]Refers to persons who, whether they usually work full or part time, worked 1 to 34 hours during the reference week for an economic reason such as slack work or unfavorable business conditions, inability to find full-time work, or seasonal declines in demand.

Table 1-64. Employed Persons by Disability Status, Occupation, and Sex, 2010 Annual Averages

(Number in thousands, percent.)

Occupation	Persons with a disability			Persons with no disability		
	Total	Men	Women	Total	Men	Women
TOTAL EMPLOYED	4 939	2 665	2 274	134 125	70 694	63 431
Occupation as a Percent of Total Employed						
Management, professional, and related	31.4	29.5	33.5	37.4	34.3	40.8
Management, business, and financial operations	13.6	15.7	11.2	15.1	16.3	13.8
Management	10.2	12.6	7.3	10.8	12.6	8.8
Business and financial operations	3.5	3.1	3.9	4.3	3.7	5.0
Professional and related	17.7	13.9	22.3	22.3	18.0	27.1
Computer and mathematical	1.9	2.5	1.1	2.6	3.6	1.4
Architecture and engineering	1.5	2.3	0.5	1.9	3.1	0.5
Life, physical, and social science	0.8	0.9	0.7	1.0	1.0	1.0
Community and social services	1.9	1.5	2.3	1.7	1.1	2.3
Legal	1.1	0.9	1.4	1.2	1.2	1.3
Education, training, and library	5.3	2.6	8.4	6.2	3.1	9.7
Arts, design, entertainment, sports, and media	1.7	1.4	2.1	2.0	2.0	1.9
Healthcare practitioner and technical	3.6	1.7	5.7	5.7	2.8	8.9
Service	19.4	16.1	23.3	17.7	14.5	21.2
Healthcare support	2.0	1.0	5.0	2.0	1.0	5.0
Protective service	2	3	1	2	4	1
Food preparation and serving related	5.4	4.4	6.5	5.5	4.7	6.4
Building and grounds cleaning and maintenance	5.4	6.6	4.1	3.8	4.2	3.3
Personal care and service	4.3	1.8	7.3	3.6	1.5	5.9
Sales and office	25.1	16.9	34.8	24.0	16.9	31.9
Sales and related	11.1	9.8	12.7	11.1	10.5	11.7
Office and administrative support	14.0	7.1	22.1	12.9	6.4	20.2
Natural resources, construction, and maintenance	9.6	17.0	0.9	9.4	17.0	0.9
Farming, fishing, and forestry	0.8	1.3	0.3	0.7	1.0	0.4
Construction and extraction	5.0	9.0	0.2	5.2	9.5	0.3
Installation, maintenance, and repair	3.8	6.7	0.4	3.5	6.4	0.3
Production, transportation, and material moving	14.5	20.5	7.5	11.5	17.3	5.1
Production	7.4	9.8	4.6	5.7	7.8	3.3
Transportation and material moving	7.1	10.7	2.9	5.8	9.4	1.8

Table 1-65. Persons Not in the Labor Force by Disability Status, Age, and Sex, 2010 Annual Averages

(Thousands of people, percent distribution.)

Category	Total, 16 years and over	16 to 64 years			Total, 65 years and over
		Total	Men	Women	
Persons With a Disability					
Total not in the labor force	20 797	9 735	4 609	5 126	11 062
Persons who currently want a job	570	429	209	220	141
Marginally attached to the labor force[1]	209	178	95	83	31
Discouraged workers[2]	106	85	52	33	21
Other persons marginally attached to the labor force[3]	104	93	44	49	10
Persons Without a Disability					
Total not in the labor force	63 144	42 218	15 512	26 705	20 926
Persons who currently want a job	5 489	5 015	2 375	2 640	474
Marginally attached to the labor force[1]	2 278	2 141	1 148	993	137
Discouraged workers[2]	1 067	986	618	368	81
Other persons marginally attached to the labor force[3]	1 211	1 155	530	625	56

[1]Data refer to persons who want a job, have searched for work during the prior 12 months, and were available to take a job during the reference week, but had not looked for work in the past 4 weeks.
[2]Includes those who did not actively look for work in the prior 4 weeks for reasons such as thinks no work available, could not find work, lacks schooling or training, employer thinks too young or old, and other types of discrimination.
[3]Includes those who did not actively look for work in the prior 4 weeks for such reasons as school or family responsibilities, ill health, and transportation problems, as well as a number for whom reason for nonparticipation was not determined.

Chapter Two

EMPLOYMENT AND HOURS

EMPLOYMENT AND HOURS

HIGHLIGHTS

The employment, hours, and earnings data in this section are presented by industry and state and are derived from the Current Employment Statistics (CES) survey, which covers approximately 486,000 individual worksites and 141,000 business and government agencies. The employment numbers differ from those presented in the household survey in Chapter 1 because of dissimilarities in methodology, concepts, definitions, and coverage. As the CES survey data are obtained from payroll records, they are consistent for industry classifications.

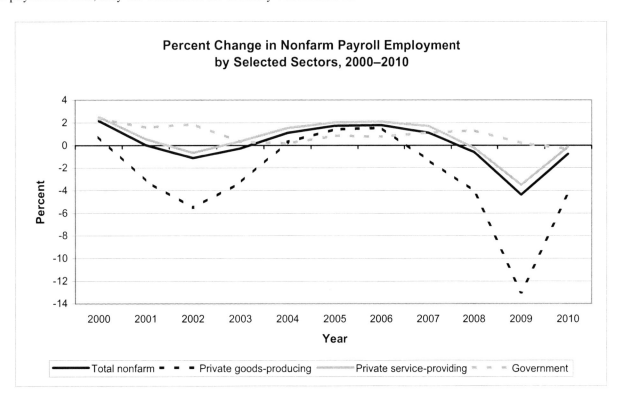

In 2010, total employment declined for the third consecutive year. Employment fell 4.3 percent in the goods-producing sector but only 0.1 percent in the private service-providing sector. Within the goods-producing industries, employment declined 8.2 percent in construction and 2.7 percent in manufacturing. (See Table 2-1.)

OTHER HIGHLIGHTS:

* While most super sectors experienced a decline in employment in 2010, employment increased 1.9 percent in education and heath services and 0.7 percent in professional and business services. Within the education and heath services sector, employment increased the fastest in ambulatory health care (3.2 percent) followed by social assistance (2.5 percent). (See Table 2-1.)

* Government employment declined 0.3 percent in 2010 after increasing each year from 2000 through 2009. However, federal government employment increased 4.8 percent. (See Table 2-1.)

* Average weekly hours of all employees on private nonfarm payrolls increased slightly in 2010 after gradually declining from 2007 through 2009. Employees in mining and logging worked the longest week (43.3 hours) while those in leisure and hospitality worked the shortest (25.7 hours). (See Table 2-6.)

* From 2009 to 2010, total nonfarm employment declined in 41 states, remained the same in West Virginia, and increased in eight states and the District of Columbia. (See Table 2-8.)

NOTES AND DEFINITIONS

EMPLOYMENT, HOURS, AND EARNINGS

Collection and Coverage

The Bureau of Labor Statistics (BLS) works with State Employment Security Agencies (SESAs) to conduct the Current Employment Statistics (CES), or establishment, survey. This survey collects monthly data on employment, hours, and earnings from a sample of nonfarm establishments (including government). The CES sample includes about 141,000 businesses and government agencies and covers approximately 486,000 individual worksites. Each month the BLS publishes over 2,300 not seasonally adjusted employment series for all employees, production and nonsupervisory employees, and women employees. The series for all employees include over 900 industries at various levels of aggregation.

In addition, BLS also publishes approximately 3,100 all employees and production and nonsupervisory employees series for average hourly earnings, average weekly hours, and, in manufacturing, average weekly overtime hours each month on a non-seasonally adjusted basis which cover about 700 industries.

BLS collects data on employment, payroll, and paid hours from a sample of establishments. Establishments reporting information are classified into industries based on their principal product or activity. Data are submitted each month by the respondent and edited by the state agency. Data submitted are used in developing national, statewide, and major metropolitan area estimates. Samples from all states are combined to form a collective sample for developing national industry estimates. Statewide samples range from nearly 30,000 sample units in California to about 1,000 units in smaller states. It should be noted that state estimation procedures are designed to produce accurate data for each individual state. BLS independently develops the national employment series and does not force state estimates to sum to national totals nor vice versa.

Data are collected by telephone, touch-tone self response, computer-assisted interviews, fax technology, voice recognition, and mail. The use of electronic media has resulted in more rapid response times and higher response rates.

Industry Classification

The CES survey completed a conversion from its original quota sample design to a probability-based sample survey design, and switched from the Standard Industrial Classification (SIC) system to the North American Industry Classification System (NAICS) in 2003. The industry-coding update included reconstruction of historical estimates in order to preserve time series for data users. The foundation of industrial classification with NAICS has changed how establishments are classified into industries and how businesses, as they exist today, are recognized. With the release of January 2008 data on February 1, 2008, the CES National Nonfarm Payroll series was updated to the 2007 North American Industry Classification System (NAICS) from the 2002 NAICS basis. This resulted in relatively minor changes.

Industry Employment

Employment data refer to persons on establishment payrolls who received pay for any part of the pay period containing the 12th day of the month. The data exclude proprietors, the self-employed, unpaid volunteer or family workers, farm workers, and domestic workers. Salaried officers of corporations are included. Government employment covers only civilian employees; military personnel are excluded. Employees of the Central Intelligence Agency, the National Security Agency, the National Imagery and Mapping Agency, and the Defense Intelligence Agency are also excluded.

Persons on establishment payrolls who were on paid sick leave (for cases in which pay is received directly from the firm), paid holiday, or vacation leave, or who work during part of the pay period despite being unemployed or on strike during the rest of the period were counted as employed. Not counted as employed were persons on layoff, on leave without pay, on strike for the entire period, or who had been hired but had not yet reported to their new jobs.

Beginning with the June 2003 publication of May 2003 data, the CES national federal government employment series has been estimated from a sample of federal establishments and benchmarked annually to counts from unemployment insurance tax records. It reflects employee counts as of the pay period containing the 12th day of the month, which is consistent with other CES industry series. Previously, the national series was an end-of-month count produced by the Office of Personnel Management.

The exclusion of farm employment, self-employment, and domestic service employment accounts from the payroll survey accounts for the differences in employment figures between the household and payroll surveys. The payroll survey also excludes workers on leave without pay. (These workers are counted as employed in the household survey.) Persons who worked in more than one establishment during the reporting period are counted each time their names appear on payrolls; these persons are only counted once in the household survey.

Concepts and Definitions

Production and related workers. This category includes working supervisors and all nonsupervisory workers (including group leaders and trainees) engaged in fabricating, processing, assembling, inspecting, receiving, storing, handling, packing, warehousing, shipping, trucking, hauling, maintenance, repair, janitorial, guard services, product development, auxiliary production for plant's own use (such as a power plant), record-keeping, and other services closely associated with production operations.

Construction workers. This group includes the following employees in the construction division: working supervisors, qualified craft workers, mechanics, apprentices, helpers, and laborers engaged in new work, alterations, demolition, repair, maintenance, and the like, whether working at the site of construction or at jobs in shops or yards at jobs (such as precutting and pre-assembling) ordinarily performed by members of the construction trades.

Nonsupervisory workers. This category consists of employees such as office and clerical workers, repairers, salespersons, operators, drivers, physicians, lawyers, accountants, nurses, social workers, research aides, teachers, drafters, photographers, beauticians, musicians, restaurant workers, custodial workers, attendants, line installers and repairers, laborers, janitors, guards, and other employees at similar occupational levels whose services are closely associated with those of the employees listed. It excludes persons in executive, managerial, and supervisory positions.

Payroll. This refers to payments made to full- and part-time production, construction, or nonsupervisory workers who received pay for any part of the pay period containing the 12th day of the month. The payroll is reported before deductions of any kind, such as those for old age and unemployment insurance, group insurance, withholding tax, bonds, or union dues. Also included is pay for overtime, holidays, and vacation, as well as for sick leave paid directly by the firm. Bonuses (unless earned and paid regularly each pay period), other pay not earned in the pay period reported (such as retroactive pay), tips, and the value of free rent, fuel, meals, or other payment-in-kind are excluded. Employee benefits (such as health and other types of insurance and contributions to retirement, as paid by the employer) are also excluded.

Total hours. During the pay period, total hours include all hours worked (including overtime hours), hours paid for standby or reporting time, and equivalent hours for which employees received pay directly from the employer for sick leave, holidays, vacations, and other leave. Overtime and other premium pay hours are not converted to straight-time equivalent hours. The concept of total hours differs from those of scheduled hours and hours worked. The average weekly hours derived from paid total hours reflect the effects of such factors as unpaid absenteeism, labor turnover, part-time work, and work stoppages, as well as fluctuations in work schedules.

Average weekly hours. The workweek information relates to the average hours for which pay was received and is different from standard or scheduled hours. Such factors as unpaid absenteeism, labor turnover, part-time work, and work stoppages cause average weekly hours to be lower than scheduled hours of work for an establishment. Group averages further reflect changes in the workweeks of component industries.

Overtime hours. These are hours worked by production or related workers for which overtime premiums were paid because the hours were in excess of the number of hours of either the straight-time workday or the total workweek. Weekend and holiday hours are included only if overtime premiums were paid. Hours for which only shift differential, hazard, incentive, or other similar types of premiums were paid are excluded.

Average overtime hours. Overtime hours represent the portion of average weekly hours that exceeded regular hours and for which overtime premiums were paid. If an employee worked during a paid holiday at regular rates, receiving as total compensation his or her holiday pay plus straight-time pay for hours worked that day, no overtime hours would be reported.

Since overtime hours are premium hours by definition, weekly hours and overtime hours do not necessarily move in the same direction from month to month. Factors such as work stoppages, absenteeism, and labor turnover may not have the same influence on overtime hours as on average hours. Diverse trends at the industry group level may also be caused by a marked change in hours for a component industry in which little or no overtime was worked in both the previous and current months.

Industry hours and earnings. Average hours and earnings data are derived from reports of payrolls and hours for production and related workers in manufacturing and natural resources and mining, construction workers in construction, and nonsupervisory employees in private service-providing industries.

Indexes of aggregate weekly hours and payrolls. The indexes of aggregate weekly hours are calculated by dividing the current month's aggregate by the average of the 12 monthly figures for 2007. For basic industries, the hours aggregates are the product of average weekly hours and production worker or nonsupervisory worker employment. At all higher levels of industry aggregation, hours aggregates are the sum of the component aggregates.

The indexes of aggregate weekly payrolls are calculated by dividing the current month's aggregate by the average of the 12 monthly figures for 2007. For basic industries, the payroll aggregates are the product of average hourly earnings and aggregate weekly hours. At all higher levels of industry aggregation, payroll aggregates are the sum of the component aggregates.

Average hourly earnings. Average hourly earnings are on a "gross" basis. They reflect not only changes in basic hourly and incentive wage rates, but also such variable factors as premium pay for overtime and late-shift work and changes in output of workers paid on an incentive plan. They also reflect shifts in the number of employees between relatively high-paid and low-paid work and changes in workers' earnings in individual establishments. Averages for groups and divisions further reflect changes in average hourly earnings for individual industries.

Averages of hourly earnings differ from wage rates. Earnings are the actual return to the worker for a stated period; rates are the amount stipulated for a given unit of work or time. The earnings series do not measure the level of total labor costs on the part of the employer because the following items are excluded: irregular bonuses, retroactive items, payroll taxes paid by employers, and earnings for those employees not covered under the definitions of production workers, construction workers, or nonsupervisory employees.

Average hourly earnings, excluding overtime-premium pay, are computed by dividing the total production worker payroll for the industry group by the sum of total production worker hours and one-half of total overtime hours. No adjustments are made for other premium payment provisions, such as holiday pay, late-shift premiums, and overtime rates other than time and one-half.

Average weekly earnings. These estimates are derived by multiplying average weekly hours estimates by average hourly earnings estimates. Therefore, weekly earnings are affected not only by changes in average hourly earnings but also by changes in the length of the workweek. Monthly variations in factors, such as the proportion of part-time workers, work stoppages, labor turnover during the survey period, and absenteeism for which employees are not paid may cause the average workweek to fluctuate.

Long-term trends of average weekly earnings can be affected by structural changes in the makeup of the workforce. For example, persistent long-term increases in the proportion of part-time workers in retail trade and many of the services industries have reduced average workweeks in these industries and have affected the average weekly earnings series.

These earnings are in constant dollars and are calculated from the earnings averages for the current month using a deflator derived from the Consumer Price Index for Urban Wage Earnings and Clerical Workers (CPI-W). The reference year for these series is 1982.

Seasonally adjusted. This removes the change in employment that is due to normal seasonal hiring or layoffs, thus leaving an over-the-month change that reflects only employment changes due to trend and irregular movements. Seasonally adjusted estimates of employment and other series are generated using the X-12 ARIMA program developed by the United States Census Bureau.

Benchmarks

Employment estimates are adjusted annually to a complete count of jobs—called benchmarks—which are primarily derived from tax reports submitted by employers covered by state unemployment laws (which cover most establishments). A comprehensive account of employment is derived in March. In this re-anchoring of sample-based employment estimates to full population counts, the original sample-based estimates are replaced with the benchmark data from the previous year. The benchmark information is used to adjust monthly estimates between the new benchmark and the preceding benchmark, thereby preserving the continuity of the series and establishing the level of employment for the new benchmark month.

Sources of Additional Information

For further information on sampling and estimation methods for national data visit the Employment, Hours, and Earnings homepage on the BLS Web site at <http://www.bls.gov/ces>. For more information on state and area data, please visit the BLS Web site at <http://www.bls.gov/sae>.

Table 2-1. Employees on Nonfarm Payrolls, by Super Sector and Selected Component Groups, NAICS Basis, 2000–2010

(Thousands of people.)

Industry	2000	2001	2002	2003	2004	2005	2006	2007	2008	2009	2010
TOTAL	131 785	131 826	130 341	129 999	131 435	133 703	136 086	137 598	136 790	130 807	129 818
Total Private	110 995	110 708	108 828	108 416	109 814	111 899	114 113	115 380	114 281	108 252	107 337
Goods-Producing	24 649	23 873	22 557	21 816	21 882	22 190	22 531	22 233	21 334	18 557	17 755
Mining and Logging	599	606	583	572	591	628	684	724	767	694	705
Mining	520	533	512	503	523	562	620	664	710	643	656
Logging	79	74	70	69	68	65	64	60	57	50	50
Construction	6 787	6 826	6 716	6 735	6 976	7 336	7 691	7 630	7 162	6 016	5 526
Construction of buildings	1 633	1 589	1 575	1 576	1 630	1 712	1 805	1 774	1 642	1 357	1 232
Heavy and civil engineering	937	953	931	903	907	951	985	1 005	965	851	829
Specialty trade contractors	4 217	4 284	4 210	4 256	4 439	4 673	4 901	4 850	4 556	3 808	3 466
Manufacturing	17 263	16 441	15 259	14 510	14 315	14 226	14 155	13 879	13 406	11 847	11 524
Durable goods	10 877	10 336	9 485	8 964	8 925	8 956	8 981	8 808	8 463	7 284	7 067
Wood product	613	574	555	538	550	559	559	515	456	359	341
Nonmetallic mineral product	554	545	516	494	506	505	510	501	465	394	372
Primary metals	622	571	509	477	467	466	464	456	442	362	361
Fabricated metal product	1 753	1 676	1 549	1 479	1 497	1 522	1 553	1 563	1 528	1 312	1 285
Machinery	1 457	1 371	1 232	1 152	1 145	1 166	1 183	1 187	1 188	1 029	993
Computer and electronic product	1 820	1 749	1 507	1 355	1 323	1 316	1 308	1 273	1 244	1 137	1 100
Electrical equipment and appliances	591	557	497	460	445	434	433	429	424	374	361
Transportation equipment	2 057	1 939	1 830	1 775	1 767	1 772	1 769	1 712	1 608	1 348	1 330
Furniture and related product	683	645	607	576	576	568	560	531	480	386	357
Miscellaneous manufacturing	728	710	683	658	651	647	644	642	629	584	568
Nondurable goods	6 386	6 105	5 774	5 546	5 390	5 271	5 174	5 071	4 943	4 563	4 457
Food manufacturing	1 553	1 551	1 526	1 518	1 494	1 478	1 479	1 484	1 481	1 456	1 447
Beverage and tobacco product	207	209	207	200	195	192	194	198	198	187	182
Textile mills	378	333	291	261	237	218	195	170	151	124	119
Textile product mills	230	217	204	188	183	176	167	158	147	126	118
Apparel	484	415	350	304	278	251	232	215	199	168	158
Paper and paper product	605	578	547	516	496	484	471	458	445	407	397
Printing and related support activities	807	768	707	681	663	646	634	622	594	522	487
Petroleum and coal product	123	121	118	114	112	112	113	115	117	115	114
Chemicals	980	959	928	906	887	872	866	861	847	804	784
Plastics and rubber product	951	896	847	814	805	802	786	757	729	625	623
Private Service-Providing	86 346	86 834	86 271	86 600	87 932	89 709	91 582	93 147	92 947	89 695	89 582
Trade, Transportation, and Utilities	26 225	25 983	25 497	25 287	25 533	25 959	26 276	26 630	26 293	24 906	24 605
Wholesale Trade	5 933	5 773	5 652	5 608	5 663	5 764	5 905	6 015	5 943	5 587	5 456
Durable goods	3 251	3 130	3 008	2 941	2 951	2 999	3 075	3 122	3 052	2 810	2 719
Nondurable goods	2 065	2 031	2 015	2 005	2 010	2 022	2 041	2 062	2 048	1 966	1 932
Electronic markets, agents, and brokers	618	611	629	662	702	743	789	832	843	811	805
Retail Trade	15 280	15 239	15 025	14 917	15 058	15 280	15 353	15 520	15 283	14 522	14 414
Motor vehicle and parts dealers	1 847	1 855	1 879	1 883	1 902	1 919	1 910	1 908	1 831	1 638	1 624
Furniture and home furnishing stores	544	541	539	547	563	576	587	575	531	449	436
Electronic and appliance stores	564	555	525	512	516	536	541	549	541	491	498
Building material and garden supply stores	1 142	1 152	1 177	1 185	1 227	1 276	1 324	1 309	1 248	1 156	1 126
Food and beverage stores	2 993	2 951	2 882	2 838	2 822	2 818	2 821	2 844	2 862	2 830	2 810
Health and personal care stores	928	952	939	938	941	954	961	993	1 003	986	979
Gasoline stations	936	925	896	882	876	871	864	862	842	826	816
Clothing and clothing accessories stores	1 322	1 321	1 313	1 305	1 364	1 415	1 451	1 500	1 468	1 364	1 376
Sporting goods, hobby, and music stores	686	679	661	647	641	647	646	656	651	614	601
General merchandise stores	2 820	2 842	2 812	2 822	2 863	2 934	2 935	3 021	3 026	2 966	2 971
Miscellaneous store retailers	1 007	993	960	931	914	900	881	865	843	782	760
Nonstore retailers	492	474	444	427	429	435	433	438	438	421	416
Transportation and Warehousing	4 410	4 372	4 224	4 185	4 249	4 361	4 470	4 541	4 508	4 236	4 184
Air transportation	614	615	564	528	515	501	487	492	491	463	464
Rail transportation	232	227	218	218	226	228	228	234	231	218	215
Water transportation	56	54	53	55	56	61	63	66	67	63	63
Truck transportation	1 406	1 387	1 339	1 326	1 352	1 398	1 436	1 439	1 389	1 268	1 244
Transit and ground passenger transportation	372	375	381	382	385	389	399	412	423	422	432
Pipeline transportation	46	45	42	40	38	38	39	40	42	43	42
Scenic and sightseeing transportation	28	29	26	27	27	29	28	29	28	28	27
Support activities for transportation	537	539	525	520	535	552	571	584	592	549	540
Couriers and messengers	605	587	561	562	557	571	582	581	573	546	527
Warehousing and storage	514	514	517	528	558	595	638	665	672	637	628
Utilities	601	599	596	577	564	554	549	553	559	560	552
Information	3 630	3 629	3 395	3 188	3 118	3 061	3 038	3 032	2 984	2 804	2 711
Publishing industries, except Internet	1 035	1 021	964	925	909	904	902	901	880	796	761
Motion picture and sound recording industry	383	377	388	376	385	378	376	381	371	358	372
Broadcasting, except Internet	344	345	334	324	325	328	328	328	325	319	294
Internet publishing and broadcasting and web search portals	111	100	76	67	66	67	69	73	81	83	91
Telecommunications	1 397	1 424	1 281	1 167	1 115	1 071	1 048	1 031	1 019	966	900
Other information services	157	147	124	116	117	118	121	126	134	135	142

Table 2-1. Employees on Nonfarm Payrolls, by Super Sector and Selected Component Groups, NAICS Basis, 2000–2010—*Continued*

(Thousands of people.)

Industry	2000	2001	2002	2003	2004	2005	2006	2007	2008	2009	2010
Financial Activities	7 687	7 808	7 847	7 977	8 031	8 153	8 328	8 301	8 145	7 769	7 630
Finance and insurance	5 677	5 769	5 814	5 919	5 945	6 019	6 156	6 132	6 015	5 775	5 691
Monetary authorities, central bank	23	23	23	23	22	21	21	22	22	21	21
Credit intermediation	2 548	2 598	2 686	2 792	2 817	2 869	2 925	2 866	2 733	2 590	2 545
Securities, commodity contracts, and investments	805	831	789	758	766	786	818	849	864	811	801
Insurance carriers and related activities	2 221	2 234	2 233	2 266	2 259	2 259	2 304	2 307	2 305	2 264	2 238
Funds, trusts, and other financial vehicles	81	84	82	80	82	84	88	89	91	88	87
Real estate and rental and leasing	2 011	2 038	2 033	2 058	2 086	2 134	2 173	2 169	2 130	1 994	1 939
Real estate	1 316	1 343	1 357	1 387	1 419	1 461	1 499	1 500	1 485	1 420	1 396
Rental and leasing services	667	666	649	643	641	646	646	640	617	547	518
Lessors of nonfinancial intangible assets	28	29	28	27	26	27	28	28	28	27	25
Professional and Business Services	16 666	16 476	15 976	15 987	16 394	16 954	17 566	17 942	17 735	16 579	16 688
Professional and technical services	6 702	6 871	6 649	6 603	6 747	7 025	7 357	7 660	7 799	7 509	7 424
Management of companies and enterprises	1 796	1 779	1 705	1 687	1 724	1 759	1 811	1 866	1 905	1 867	1 863
Administrative and waste services	8 168	7 826	7 622	7 697	7 923	8 170	8 398	8 416	8 032	7 203	7 401
Administrative and support services	7 855	7 509	7 304	7 375	7 594	7 833	8 050	8 061	7 675	6 852	7 044
Waste management and remediation services	313	317	318	322	329	338	348	355	357	352	357
Education and Health Services	15 109	15 645	16 199	16 588	16 953	17 372	17 826	18 322	18 838	19 193	19 564
Education services	2 390	2 511	2 643	2 695	2 763	2 836	2 901	2 941	3 040	3 090	3 150
Health care and social assistance	12 718	13 134	13 556	13 893	14 190	14 536	14 925	15 380	15 798	16 103	16 414
Ambulatory health care services	4 320	4 462	4 633	4 786	4 952	5 114	5 286	5 474	5 647	5 793	5 976
Hospitals	3 954	4 051	4 160	4 245	4 285	4 345	4 423	4 515	4 627	4 667	4 685
Nursing and residential health facilities	2 583	2 676	2 743	2 786	2 818	2 855	2 893	2 958	3 016	3 082	3 129
Social assistance	1 860	1 946	2 020	2 075	2 135	2 222	2 324	2 433	2 508	2 560	2 624
Leisure and Hospitality	11 862	12 036	11 986	12 173	12 493	12 816	13 110	13 427	13 436	13 077	13 020
Arts, entertainment, and recreation	1 788	1 824	1 783	1 813	1 850	1 892	1 929	1 969	1 970	1 916	1 909
Performing arts and spectator sports	382	382	364	372	368	376	399	405	406	397	410
Museums, historical sites	110	115	114	115	118	121	124	130	132	129	127
Amusements, gambling, and recreation	1 296	1 327	1 305	1 327	1 364	1 395	1 406	1 434	1 433	1 389	1 371
Accommodation and food services	10 074	10 211	10 203	10 360	10 643	10 923	11 181	11 457	11 466	11 162	11 111
Accommodation	1 884	1 852	1 779	1 775	1 790	1 819	1 832	1 867	1 869	1 763	1 759
Food services and drinking places	8 189	8 359	8 425	8 584	8 854	9 104	9 349	9 590	9 598	9 399	9 352
Other Services	5 168	5 258	5 372	5 401	5 409	5 395	5 438	5 494	5 515	5 367	5 364
Repair and maintenance	1 242	1 257	1 247	1 234	1 229	1 236	1 249	1 253	1 227	1 150	1 137
Personal and laundry services	1 243	1 255	1 257	1 264	1 273	1 277	1 288	1 310	1 323	1 281	1 265
Membership associations and organizations	2 683	2 746	2 868	2 904	2 908	2 882	2 901	2 931	2 966	2 936	2 962
Government	20 790	21 118	21 513	21 583	21 621	21 804	21 974	22 218	22 509	22 555	22 482
Federal	2 865	2 764	2 766	2 761	2 730	2 732	2 732	2 734	2 762	2 832	2 968
Federal, excluding U.S. Postal Service	1 985	1 891	1 924	1 952	1 948	1 957	1 963	1 965	2 014	2 129	2 312
State	4 786	4 905	5 029	5 002	4 982	5 032	5 075	5 122	5 177	5 169	5 142
State, excluding education	2 756	2 792	2 786	2 748	2 744	2 772	2 782	2 804	2 823	2 809	2 764
Local	13 139	13 449	13 718	13 820	13 909	14 041	14 167	14 362	14 571	14 554	14 372
Local, excluding education	5 845	5 970	6 063	6 110	6 144	6 185	6 254	6 376	6 487	6 475	6 361

Table 2-2. Women Employees on Nonfarm Payrolls, by Super Sector and Selected Component Groups, NAICS Basis, 2000–2010

(Thousands of people.)

Industry	2000	2001	2002	2003	2004	2005	2006	2007	2008	2009	2010
TOTAL NONFARM	63 223	63 684	63 360	63 237	63 739	64 718	65 525	66 805	67 084	65 207	64 648
Total Private	51 452	51 669	51 033	50 901	51 404	52 329	53 307	54 227	54 175	52 308	51 857
Goods-Producing	6 297	5 961	5 486	5 192	5 117	5 104	5 082	5 041	4 866	4 289	4 089
Mining and logging	92	90	85	80	80	79	82	93	101	98	98
Construction	846	832	827	822	841	890	944	947	916	801	724
Manufacturing	5 359	5 039	4 574	4 290	4 197	4 135	4 057	4 001	3 848	3 390	3 268
Private Service-Providing	45 155	45 708	45 547	45 709	46 287	47 225	48 224	49 186	49 310	48 019	47 768
Trade, transportation, and utilities	10 859	10 768	10 466	10 321	10 364	10 535	10 627	10 849	10 782	10 233	10 001
Wholesale trade	1 827	1 770	1 718	1 700	1 714	1 738	1 796	1 831	1 820	1 705	1 642
Retail trade	7 680	7 635	7 449	7 339	7 387	7 524	7 587	7 758	7 713	7 361	7 219
Transportation and warehousing	1 202	1 212	1 149	1 134	1 117	1 130	1 098	1 110	1 098	1 024	1 002
Utilities	151	151	150	147	146	143	146	150	151	143	138
Information	1 697	1 684	1 554	1 428	1 366	1 333	1 306	1 285	1 260	1 170	1 106
Financial activities	4 638	4 726	4 755	4 830	4 831	4 896	5 031	4 959	4 813	4 606	4 491
Professional and business services	7 680	7 591	7 314	7 248	7 360	7 574	7 779	8 007	7 946	7 472	7 438
Education and health services	11 586	12 037	12 474	12 786	13 073	13 408	13 764	14 178	14 574	14 851	15 089
Leisure and hospitality	6 082	6 224	6 215	6 319	6 516	6 708	6 903	7 054	7 056	6 861	6 804
Other services	2 614	2 677	2 769	2 779	2 776	2 772	2 814	2 854	2 880	2 824	2 839
Government	11 771	12 015	12 327	12 337	12 335	12 389	12 218	12 578	12 908	12 899	12 792
Federal	1 231	1 148	1 155	1 173	1 168	1 177	1 194	1 202	1 224	1 257	1 288
State	2 464	2 534	2 621	2 599	2 562	2 575	2 630	2 651	2 684	2 628	2 643
Local	8 076	8 333	8 551	8 565	8 606	8 637	8 395	8 725	9 000	9 014	8 861

Table 2-3. Production Workers on Private Nonfarm Payrolls, by Super Sector, NAICS Basis, 2000–2010

(Thousands of people.)

Industry	2000	2001	2002	2003	2004	2005	2006	2007	2008	2009	2010
TOTAL PRIVATE	90 336	89 983	88 393	87 658	88 937	91 135	93 451	94 903	94 270	89 173	88 472
Goods-Producing	18 169	17 466	16 400	15 732	15 821	16 145	16 559	16 405	15 724	13 399	12 779
Mining and logging	446	457	436	420	440	473	519	547	574	510	526
Construction	5 295	5 332	5 196	5 123	5 309	5 611	5 903	5 883	5 521	4 567	4 179
Manufacturing	12 428	11 677	10 768	10 189	10 072	10 060	10 137	9 975	9 629	8 322	8 075
Private Service-Providing	72 167	72 517	71 993	71 926	73 116	74 990	76 893	78 498	78 546	75 774	75 692
Trade, transportation, and utilities	21 965	21 709	21 337	21 078	21 319	21 830	22 166	22 546	22 337	21 116	20 846
Wholesale trade	4 686	4 555	4 474	4 396	4 444	4 584	4 724	4 851	4 822	4 506	4 381
Retail trade	13 040	12 952	12 774	12 655	12 788	13 030	13 110	13 317	13 134	12 472	12 402
Transportation and warehousing	3 753	3 718	3 611	3 563	3 637	3 774	3 889	3 935	3 931	3 688	3 621
Utilities	485	483	478	464	450	443	443	444	450	451	443
Information	2 502	2 531	2 398	2 347	2 371	2 386	2 399	2 403	2 388	2 240	2 172
Financial activities	5 737	5 810	5 872	5 967	5 989	6 090	6 281	6 326	6 269	6 008	5 887
Professional and business services	13 790	13 588	13 049	12 911	13 287	13 854	14 446	14 784	14 585	13 520	13 667
Education and health services	13 362	13 846	14 311	14 532	14 771	15 129	15 539	15 999	16 488	16 841	17 154
Leisure and hospitality	10 516	10 662	10 576	10 666	10 955	11 263	11 568	11 861	11 873	11 560	11 481
Other services	4 296	4 373	4 449	4 426	4 425	4 438	4 494	4 578	4 606	4 488	4 485

Table 2-4. Production Workers on Manufacturing Payrolls, by Industry, NAICS Basis, 2000–2010

(Thousands of people.)

Industry	2000	2001	2002	2003	2004	2005	2006	2007	2008	2009	2010
Total Manufacturing	12 428	11 677	10 768	10 189	10 072	10 060	10 137	9 975	9 629	8 322	8 075
Durable Goods	7 659	7 164	6 530	6 152	6 140	6 220	6 355	6 250	5 975	4 990	4 831
Wood products	506	468	449	433	444	453	450	406	356	277	268
Nometallic mineral products	440	427	399	375	388	387	391	384	363	303	284
Primary metals	490	447	396	370	364	363	363	358	348	273	274
Fabricated metal products	1 326	1 254	1 147	1 093	1 109	1 129	1 162	1 171	1 143	961	937
Machinery	961	891	787	732	730	749	770	774	772	641	614
Computer and electronic products	949	876	744	673	656	700	756	744	730	654	633
Electrical equipment and appliances	433	402	352	320	307	300	303	305	305	266	252
Transportation equipment	1 498	1 399	1 310	1 269	1 265	1 277	1 304	1 275	1 177	948	935
Furniture and related products	546	511	477	446	446	437	434	410	365	285	263
Miscellaneous manufacturing	510	490	469	442	432	424	423	425	416	382	371
Nondurable Goods	4 769	4 513	4 238	4 037	3 932	3 841	3 782	3 725	3 653	3 332	3 244
Food manufacturing	1 228	1 221	1 202	1 193	1 178	1 170	1 172	1 184	1 184	1 161	1 150
Beverage and tobacco products	117	116	120	106	107	112	115	118	112	112	106
Textile mills	315	276	242	217	194	174	158	137	122	99	96
Textile products mills	183	174	162	148	147	143	135	123	115	98	91
Apparel	404	341	286	242	219	193	182	173	163	132	121
Leather and allied products	55	47	40	35	33	31	29	27	28	24	22
Paper and paper products	468	446	421	393	374	365	357	351	344	313	304
Printing and related support	576	544	493	471	460	447	447	443	425	369	341
Petroleum and coal products	83	81	78	74	77	75	72	73	77	70	70
Chemicals	588	562	532	525	520	510	508	504	513	479	472
Plastics and rubber products	753	704	662	633	626	620	608	592	572	477	471

Table 2-5. Total Employees on Manufacturing Payrolls, by Industry, NAICS Basis, 2000–2010

(Thousands of people.)

Industry	2000	2001	2002	2003	2004	2005	2006	2007	2008	2009	2010
Total Manufacturing	17 263	16 441	15 259	14 510	14 315	14 226	14 155	13 879	13 406	11 847	11 524
Durable Goods	10 877	10 336	9 485	8 964	8 925	8 956	8 981	8 808	8 463	7 284	7 067
Wood products	613	574	555	538	550	559	559	515	456	359	341
Nometallic mineral products	554	545	516	494	506	505	510	501	465	394	372
Primary metals	622	571	509	477	467	466	464	456	442	362	361
Fabricated metal products	1 753	1 676	1 549	1 479	1 497	1 522	1 553	1 563	1 528	1 312	1 285
Machinery	1 457	1 371	1 232	1 152	1 145	1 166	1 183	1 187	1 188	1 029	993
Computer and electronic products	1 820	1 749	1 507	1 355	1 323	1 316	1 308	1 273	1 244	1 137	1 100
Electrical equipment and appliances	591	557	497	460	445	434	433	429	424	374	361
Transportation equipment	2 057	1 939	1 830	1 775	1 767	1 772	1 769	1 712	1 608	1 348	1 330
Furniture and related products	683	645	607	576	576	568	560	531	480	386	357
Miscellaneous manufacturing	728	710	683	658	651	647	644	642	629	584	568
Nondurable Goods	6 386	6 105	5 774	5 546	5 390	5 271	5 174	5 071	4 943	4 563	4 457
Food manufacturing	1 553	1 551	1 526	1 518	1 494	1 478	1 479	1 484	1 481	1 456	1 447
Beverage and tobacco products	207	209	207	200	195	192	194	198	198	187	182
Textile mills	378	333	291	261	237	218	195	170	151	124	119
Textile products mills	230	217	204	188	183	176	167	158	147	126	118
Apparel	484	415	350	304	278	251	232	215	199	168	158
Leather and allied products	69	58	50	45	42	40	37	34	33	29	28
Paper and paper products	605	578	547	516	496	484	471	458	445	407	397
Printing and related support	807	768	707	681	663	646	634	622	594	522	487
Petroleum and coal products	123	121	118	114	112	112	113	115	117	115	114
Chemicals	980	959	928	906	887	872	866	861	847	804	784
Plastics and rubber products	951	896	847	814	805	802	786	757	729	625	623

Table 2-6. Average Weekly Hours of All Employees on Private Nonfarm Payrolls by NAICS Super Sector, 2006–2010

(Hours per week, seasonally adjusted.)

| Year and month | Total private | Mining and logging | Construc-tion | Manufac-turing | Trade, transportation, and utilities | | | | Informa-tion | Financial activities | Profes-sional and business services | Education and health services | Leisure and hospitality | Other services |
					Total	Wholesale trade	Retail trade	Utilities						
2007	34.6	44.0	38.0	40.0	34.6	38.1	31.7	41.8	36.1	36.6	35.4	33.5	26.1	32.9
2008	34.5	43.7	37.8	39.8	34.4	38.4	31.4	42.0	36.5	36.5	35.2	33.7	25.9	32.9
2009	33.9	42.1	37.1	39.0	34.1	37.9	31.2	40.9	36.5	36.6	35.0	33.0	25.6	31.6
2010	34.1	43.4	37.8	40.2	34.2	38.1	31.3	41.1	36.5	36.9	35.4	32.8	25.7	31.6
2006														
January	. . .	. . .	. . .	. . .	. . .	. . .	. . .	. . .	. . .	. . .	. . .	. . .	. . .	. . .
February	. . .	. . .	. . .	. . .	. . .	. . .	. . .	. . .	. . .	. . .	. . .	. . .	. . .	. . .
March	34.4	42.6	37.7	39.9	34.1	37.6	31.3	41.0	36.3	36.7	35.1	33.4	26.1	33.3
April	34.5	43.1	37.7	39.9	34.1	37.5	31.4	41.3	36.4	36.6	35.3	33.4	26.1	33.1
May	34.5	42.7	37.7	40.0	34.1	37.5	31.4	41.2	36.5	36.7	35.2	33.4	26.2	33.1
June	34.6	43.0	37.9	40.1	34.3	37.8	31.5	41.4	36.5	36.7	35.5	33.4	26.3	33.3
July	34.5	43.2	37.7	40.1	34.2	37.7	31.5	42.0	36.5	36.6	35.3	33.4	26.2	33.2
August	34.5	42.4	37.8	39.9	34.2	37.5	31.5	41.5	36.5	36.4	35.2	33.4	26.2	33.0
September	34.5	42.6	37.7	39.9	34.3	37.7	31.6	41.4	36.3	36.7	35.4	33.5	26.2	32.9
October	34.6	42.5	38.0	40.0	34.4	37.8	31.7	41.6	36.2	36.7	35.2	33.4	26.3	32.9
November	34.5	41.5	37.8	39.7	34.4	37.8	31.7	41.4	36.1	36.7	35.3	33.3	26.3	33.0
December	34.7	42.9	38.6	39.9	34.6	37.9	32.0	41.6	36.1	36.8	35.5	33.4	26.4	32.9
2007														
January	34.4	42.3	37.8	39.9	34.4	37.6	31.7	41.3	36.0	36.5	35.0	33.3	26.3	32.6
February	34.6	43.0	37.8	39.9	34.5	37.9	31.7	41.5	36.1	36.5	35.6	33.4	26.0	32.9
March	34.6	43.3	38.1	40.0	34.6	38.0	31.8	41.7	36.1	36.4	35.4	33.5	26.1	33.0
April	34.6	45.0	37.6	40.1	34.6	38.0	31.8	41.8	36.1	36.3	35.4	33.5	26.1	32.9
May	34.6	44.2	38.2	40.0	34.5	38.1	31.7	42.0	35.9	36.4	35.5	33.6	26.1	32.9
June	34.7	44.3	38.1	40.1	34.7	38.2	31.9	42.0	36.0	36.6	35.5	33.5	26.2	33.0
July	34.6	44.3	37.9	40.1	34.5	38.2	31.7	42.0	36.0	36.6	35.4	33.6	26.1	32.8
August	34.5	43.4	37.7	40.0	34.5	38.0	31.7	41.9	36.1	36.4	35.5	33.6	26.0	32.7
September	34.6	44.8	38.2	40.1	34.6	38.1	31.7	42.4	36.0	36.5	35.4	33.6	25.9	32.7
October	34.5	44.3	38.1	39.8	34.4	38.1	31.6	41.3	36.0	36.5	35.4	33.5	26.0	32.8
November	34.5	43.5	38.2	39.9	34.5	38.2	31.7	41.5	36.2	36.6	35.3	33.5	26.1	32.9
December	34.6	44.3	38.3	40.2	34.6	38.4	31.7	42.1	36.3	36.6	35.3	33.6	26.1	32.7
2008														
January	34.5	43.5	38.1	39.9	34.5	38.3	31.6	42.6	36.5	36.4	35.0	33.5	26.1	32.5
February	34.6	43.8	38.4	40.1	34.7	38.4	31.8	42.0	36.5	36.5	35.3	33.7	25.9	32.9
March	34.6	44.9	38.3	40.3	34.6	38.4	31.6	42.8	36.6	36.6	35.2	33.7	26.0	33.1
April	34.5	43.5	37.8	40.0	34.5	38.4	31.5	42.2	36.6	36.6	35.2	33.8	26.0	33.0
May	34.5	43.6	37.7	39.9	34.4	38.4	31.5	42.0	36.5	36.7	35.3	33.8	26.0	32.9
June	34.6	43.9	38.0	40.2	34.5	38.5	31.5	42.5	36.6	36.5	35.3	33.8	26.0	32.9
July	34.5	43.4	37.7	39.8	34.4	38.6	31.4	41.9	36.6	36.5	35.3	33.8	25.8	32.8
August	34.5	43.1	37.7	39.8	34.4	38.5	31.4	41.4	36.6	36.5	35.4	33.8	25.8	32.9
September	34.4	43.0	37.6	39.5	34.4	38.4	31.4	41.9	36.7	36.5	35.2	33.7	25.8	32.8
October	34.4	44.0	37.5	39.6	34.3	38.4	31.2	41.4	36.7	36.5	35.4	33.6	25.9	32.8
November	34.3	44.0	37.4	39.4	34.4	38.4	31.3	41.7	36.7	36.5	35.1	33.6	25.7	32.8
December	34.1	43.3	37.3	39.1	34.1	38.3	30.9	41.5	36.6	36.6	35.0	33.5	25.6	32.7
2009														
January	34.1	43.3	37.4	38.9	34.4	38.4	31.3	41.7	36.5	36.6	34.9	33.5	25.6	32.5
February	34.1	42.9	37.9	39.1	34.2	38.3	31.1	42.0	36.4	36.6	35.0	33.3	25.7	32.3
March	34.0	42.4	37.2	38.6	34.2	38.1	31.3	41.2	36.4	36.6	35.0	33.2	25.6	31.8
April	33.9	42.2	37.5	38.6	34.1	37.9	31.2	40.8	36.3	36.6	35.0	33.0	25.5	31.5
May	33.8	41.6	37.3	38.5	34.2	37.9	31.3	40.8	36.5	36.5	35.1	32.9	25.5	31.5
June	33.7	41.8	37.2	38.7	34.0	37.8	31.1	40.5	36.4	36.3	35.0	32.8	25.5	31.5
July	33.8	41.8	37.5	38.9	34.0	37.7	31.2	40.7	36.5	36.6	35.0	32.9	25.5	31.4
August	33.9	42.3	37.4	39.1	34.0	37.7	31.2	40.9	36.4	36.7	35.0	32.8	25.7	31.4
September	33.9	42.0	37.3	39.2	34.2	37.6	31.5	40.5	36.5	36.6	35.0	32.9	25.6	31.3
October	33.8	41.8	36.4	39.2	34.0	37.7	31.2	40.6	36.4	36.7	35.0	32.7	25.5	31.4
November	34.0	42.5	37.6	39.7	34.2	37.7	31.4	41.0	36.5	36.7	35.1	32.9	25.5	31.4
December	33.9	42.4	37.1	39.7	34.1	37.7	31.3	40.6	36.4	36.7	35.1	32.8	25.6	31.4
2010														
January	34.0	43.4	37.6	40.0	34.1	37.8	31.3	40.5	36.6	36.7	35.2	32.9	25.6	31.5
February	34.0	43.0	36.9	39.7	34.1	37.8	31.4	40.6	36.4	36.8	35.2	32.8	25.7	31.5
March	34.1	43.3	37.3	40.0	34.2	37.9	31.4	40.6	36.5	36.9	35.3	32.8	25.8	31.6
April	34.1	43.3	38.1	40.2	34.2	38.1	31.3	40.8	36.5	36.9	35.3	32.8	25.8	31.7
May	34.2	44.1	37.8	40.5	34.3	38.1	31.4	41.6	36.6	37.0	35.4	32.8	25.7	31.8
June	34.1	43.3	37.7	40.1	34.2	38.1	31.3	41.1	36.6	37.1	35.2	32.8	25.7	31.7
July	34.2	43.6	37.8	40.2	34.3	38.2	31.4	41.1	36.6	37.0	35.5	32.8	25.8	31.7
August	34.2	43.9	38.0	40.2	34.3	38.3	31.4	41.4	36.7	37.0	35.5	32.8	25.9	31.9
September	34.2	43.7	38.0	40.3	34.3	38.4	31.3	41.3	36.7	37.1	35.6	32.8	25.8	31.8
October	34.3	43.6	38.2	40.4	34.4	38.4	31.4	41.7	36.8	37.0	35.8	32.8	25.9	31.7
November	34.2	43.3	38.1	40.4	34.3	38.3	31.2	41.5	36.6	37.1	35.5	32.8	25.9	31.6
December	34.2	43.5	38.0	40.3	34.5	38.3	31.5	41.3	36.4	37.0	35.6	32.7	25.8	31.6

. . . = Not available.

Table 2-7. Average Weekly Hours of Production Workers on Private Nonfarm Payrolls, by Super Sector, NAICS Basis, 2000–2010

(Hours.)

Industry	2000	2001	2002	2003	2004	2005	2006	2007	2008	2009	2010
TOTAL PRIVATE	34.3	34.0	33.9	33.7	33.7	33.8	33.9	33.9	33.6	33.1	33.4
Goods-Producing	40.7	39.9	39.9	39.8	40.0	40.1	40.5	40.6	40.2	39.2	40.4
Mining and logging	44.4	44.6	43.2	43.6	44.5	45.6	45.6	45.9	45.1	43.2	44.6
Construction	39.2	38.7	38.4	38.4	38.3	38.6	39.0	39.0	38.5	37.6	38.4
Manufacturing	41.3	40.3	40.5	40.4	40.8	40.7	41.1	41.2	40.8	39.8	41.1
Private Service-Providing	32.7	32.5	32.5	32.3	32.3	32.4	32.5	32.4	32.3	32.1	32.2
Trade, transportation, and utilities	33.8	33.5	33.6	33.6	33.5	33.4	33.4	33.3	33.2	32.9	33.3
Wholesale trade	38.8	38.4	38.0	37.9	37.8	37.7	38.0	38.2	38.2	37.6	37.9
Retail trade	30.7	30.7	30.9	30.9	30.7	30.6	30.5	30.2	30.0	29.9	30.2
Transportation and warehousing	37.4	36.7	36.8	36.8	37.2	37.0	36.9	37.0	36.4	36.0	37.1
Utilities	42.0	41.4	40.9	41.1	40.9	41.1	41.4	42.4	42.7	42.0	42.1
Information	36.8	36.9	36.5	36.2	36.3	36.5	36.6	36.5	36.7	36.6	36.3
Financial activities	35.9	35.8	35.6	35.5	35.5	35.9	35.7	35.9	35.8	36.1	36.1
Professional and business services	34.5	34.2	34.2	34.1	34.2	34.2	34.6	34.8	34.8	34.7	35.1
Education and health services	32.2	32.3	32.4	32.3	32.4	32.6	32.5	32.6	32.5	32.2	32.1
Leisure and hospitality	26.1	25.8	25.8	25.6	25.7	25.7	25.7	25.5	25.2	24.8	24.8
Other services	32.5	32.3	32.0	31.4	31.0	30.9	30.9	30.9	30.8	30.5	30.7

Table 2-8. Employees on Total Nonfarm Payrolls, by State and Selected Territory, 1970–2010

(Thousands of people.)

State	1970	1971	1972	1973	1974	1975	1976	1977	1978	1979	1980	1981	1982	1983	1984
UNITED STATES	71 006	71 335	73 798	76 912	78 389	77 069	79 502	82 593	86 826	89 932	90 528	91 289	89 677	90 280	94 530
Alabama	1 010	1 022	1 072	1 136	1 170	1 155	1 207	1 269	1 336	1 362	1 356	1 348	1 312	1 329	1 388
Alaska	93	98	104	110	128	162	172	163	164	167	169	186	200	214	226
Arizona	547	581	646	714	746	729	759	809	895	980	1 014	1 041	1 030	1 078	1 182
Arkansas	536	551	582	614	641	624	660	696	733	750	742	740	720	741	780
California	6 946	6 917	7 210	7 622	7 834	7 847	8 154	8 600	9 200	9 665	9 849	9 985	9 810	9 918	10 390
Colorado	750	787	869	936	960	964	1 003	1 058	1 150	1 218	1 251	1 295	1 317	1 327	1 402
Connecticut	1 198	1 164	1 190	1 239	1 264	1 223	1 240	1 282	1 346	1 398	1 427	1 438	1 428	1 444	1 517
Delaware	217	225	232	239	233	230	237	239	248	257	259	259	259	266	280
District of Columbia	567	567	572	574	580	576	576	579	596	612	616	611	598	597	614
Florida	2 152	2 276	2 513	2 779	2 864	2 746	2 784	2 933	3 181	3 381	3 576	3 736	3 762	3 905	4 204
Georgia	1 558	1 603	1 695	1 802	1 828	1 756	1 839	1 926	2 050	2 128	2 159	2 199	2 202	2 280	2 449
Hawaii	294	302	313	328	336	343	349	359	377	394	404	405	399	406	413
Idaho	208	217	236	252	267	273	291	307	331	338	330	328	312	318	330
Illinois	4 346	4 296	4 315	4 467	4 546	4 419	4 565	4 656	4 789	4 880	4 850	4 732	4 593	4 531	4 672
Indiana	1 849	1 841	1 922	2 028	2 031	1 942	2 024	2 114	2 206	2 236	2 130	2 114	2 028	2 030	2 122
Iowa	877	883	912	961	999	999	1 037	1 079	1 119	1 132	1 110	1 089	1 042	1 040	1 075
Kansas	679	678	718	763	790	801	835	871	912	947	945	950	921	922	961
Kentucky	910	932	988	1 039	1 066	1 058	1 103	1 148	1 210	1 245	1 210	1 196	1 161	1 152	1 214
Louisiana	1 034	1 056	1 129	1 176	1 221	1 250	1 314	1 365	1 464	1 517	1 579	1 630	1 607	1 565	1 602
Maine	332	332	344	355	362	357	375	388	406	416	418	419	416	425	446
Maryland	1 349	1 372	1 415	1 472	1 494	1 479	1 498	1 546	1 626	1 691	1 712	1 716	1 676	1 724	1 814
Massachusetts	2 244	2 211	2 252	2 333	2 354	2 273	2 324	2 416	2 526	2 604	2 654	2 672	2 642	2 696	2 856
Michigan	2 999	2 995	3 119	3 284	3 278	3 137	3 283	3 442	3 609	3 637	3 443	3 364	3 193	3 223	3 381
Minnesota	1 315	1 310	1 357	1 436	1 481	1 474	1 521	1 597	1 689	1 767	1 770	1 761	1 707	1 718	1 820
Mississippi	584	602	649	693	711	692	728	766	814	838	829	819	791	793	821
Missouri	1 668	1 661	1 700	1 771	1 789	1 741	1 798	1 862	1 953	2 011	1 970	1 956	1 922	1 937	2 033
Montana	199	205	215	224	234	238	251	265	280	284	280	282	274	276	281
Nebraska	484	491	517	541	562	558	572	594	610	631	628	623	610	611	635
Nevada	203	210	224	245	256	263	280	308	350	384	400	411	401	403	426
New Hampshire	258	260	278	298	300	293	313	337	360	378	385	395	394	410	442
New Jersey	2 606	2 608	2 672	2 760	2 783	2 700	2 754	2 837	2 962	3 027	3 060	3 099	3 093	3 165	3 329
New Mexico	293	306	328	346	360	370	390	415	444	461	465	476	474	480	503
New York	7 156	7 011	7 038	7 132	7 077	6 830	6 790	6 858	7 044	7 179	7 207	7 287	7 255	7 313	7 570
North Carolina	1 783	1 814	1 912	2 018	2 048	1 980	2 083	2 171	2 278	2 373	2 380	2 392	2 347	2 419	2 565
North Dakota	164	167	176	184	194	204	215	221	234	244	245	249	250	251	252
Ohio	3 881	3 840	3 938	4 113	4 169	4 016	4 095	4 230	4 395	4 485	4 367	4 318	4 124	4 092	4 260
Oklahoma	762	774	812	852	887	900	931	972	1 036	1 088	1 138	1 201	1 217	1 171	1 180
Oregon	711	729	775	816	838	837	878	937	1 009	1 056	1 044	1 019	961	967	1 007
Pennsylvania	4 352	4 291	4 400	4 506	4 515	4 436	4 513	4 565	4 716	4 806	4 753	4 729	4 580	4 524	4 655
Rhode Island	344	343	358	366	367	349	367	382	396	400	398	401	390	396	416
South Carolina	842	863	920	984	1 016	983	1 038	1 082	1 138	1 176	1 189	1 196	1 162	1 189	1 262
South Dakota	175	179	190	199	207	209	219	227	237	241	238	236	230	235	247
Tennessee	1 328	1 357	1 450	1 531	1 558	1 506	1 575	1 648	1 737	1 777	1 747	1 755	1 703	1 719	1 812
Texas	3 625	3 684	3 884	4 142	4 360	4 463	4 684	4 907	5 272	5 602	5 851	6 180	6 263	6 194	6 492
Utah	357	369	393	415	434	440	463	489	525	548	551	558	561	567	601
Vermont	148	148	154	161	163	162	168	178	191	198	200	204	203	206	215
Virginia	1 519	1 567	1 656	1 753	1 805	1 779	1 848	1 930	2 034	2 115	2 157	2 161	2 146	2 207	2 333
Washington	1 079	1 064	1 100	1 152	1 199	1 226	1 283	1 367	1 485	1 581	1 608	1 612	1 569	1 586	1 660
West Virginia	516	520	540	562	572	575	596	612	633	659	646	628	608	582	597
Wisconsin	1 530	1 525	1 581	1 660	1 703	1 677	1 726	1 799	1 887	1 960	1 938	1 923	1 867	1 867	1 949
Wyoming	108	111	117	126	136	146	157	171	187	201	210	224	218	202	204
Puerto Rico	. . .	. . .	. . .	. . .	. . .	. . .	. . .	. . .	. . .	. . .	693	680	642	646	684
Virgin Islands	. . .	. . .	. . .	. . .	. . .	33	31	32	34	36	37	38	36	36	37

. . . = Not available.

Table 2-8. Employees on Total Nonfarm Payrolls, by State and Selected Territory, 1970–2010—*Continued*

(Thousands of people.)

State	1985	1986	1987	1988	1989	1990	1991	1992	1993	1994	1995	1996	1997
UNITED STATES	97 511	99 474	102 088	105 345	108 014	109 487	108 375	108 726	110 844	114 291	117 298	119 708	122 776
Alabama	1 427	1 463	1 508	1 559	1 601	1 636	1 642	1 674	1 717	1 758	1 804	1 829	1 866
Alaska	231	221	210	214	227	238	243	247	253	259	262	264	269
Arizona	1 279	1 338	1 386	1 419	1 454	1 483	1 491	1 517	1 584	1 692	1 793	1 892	1 985
Arkansas	797	814	837	865	893	924	937	963	994	1 034	1 070	1 087	1 105
California	10 770	11 086	11 473	11 912	12 238	12 500	12 359	12 154	12 045	12 160	12 422	12 743	13 130
Colorado	1 419	1 408	1 413	1 436	1 482	1 521	1 545	1 597	1 671	1 756	1 835	1 901	1 980
Connecticut	1 558	1 598	1 638	1 667	1 666	1 620	1 557	1 526	1 531	1 544	1 562	1 582	1 608
Delaware	293	303	321	334	344	347	342	341	349	356	366	376	388
District of Columbia	629	640	656	674	681	686	677	674	670	659	659	643	618
Florida	4 410	4 599	4 848	5 067	5 261	5 376	5 283	5 348	5 560	5 788	5 985	6 172	6 403
Georgia	2 570	2 672	2 782	2 876	2 941	2 992	2 938	2 987	3 109	3 266	3 402	3 527	3 614
Hawaii	426	439	460	478	506	528	539	543	539	536	533	531	532
Idaho	336	328	333	349	366	385	398	414	433	459	475	489	506
Illinois	4 755	4 791	4 928	5 098	5 214	5 288	5 233	5 235	5 330	5 463	5 593	5 685	5 771
Indiana	2 169	2 222	2 305	2 396	2 479	2 522	2 507	2 554	2 627	2 713	2 786	2 814	2 858
Iowa	1 074	1 074	1 109	1 156	1 200	1 226	1 238	1 252	1 278	1 320	1 358	1 383	1 407
Kansas	968	985	1 005	1 035	1 064	1 092	1 097	1 116	1 135	1 167	1 200	1 228	1 270
Kentucky	1 250	1 274	1 328	1 382	1 433	1 470	1 475	1 508	1 548	1 597	1 643	1 672	1 711
Louisiana	1 591	1 518	1 484	1 512	1 538	1 588	1 611	1 625	1 656	1 720	1 770	1 808	1 848
Maine	458	477	501	527	542	535	514	512	519	532	538	542	554
Maryland	1 888	1 952	2 028	2 102	2 155	2 173	2 102	2 084	2 104	2 148	2 184	2 213	2 269
Massachusetts	2 931	2 992	3 071	3 138	3 118	2 988	2 824	2 798	2 843	2 907	2 980	3 039	3 114
Michigan	3 562	3 657	3 736	3 819	3 922	3 946	3 884	3 919	3 999	4 141	4 268	4 352	4 439
Minnesota	1 866	1 892	1 962	2 028	2 087	2 136	2 146	2 194	2 252	2 320	2 388	2 442	2 500
Mississippi	839	848	864	896	919	936	938	960	1 002	1 056	1 074	1 089	1 107
Missouri	2 095	2 143	2 198	2 259	2 315	2 345	2 309	2 334	2 395	2 470	2 521	2 567	2 639
Montana	279	275	274	283	291	297	304	317	326	340	352	362	367
Nebraska	650	652	667	688	708	731	740	752	769	798	819	837	856
Nevada	446	468	500	538	581	621	629	639	672	738	786	843	891
New Hampshire	466	490	513	529	529	508	482	487	502	523	540	554	570
New Jersey	3 414	3 488	3 576	3 651	3 690	3 635	3 499	3 458	3 493	3 553	3 600	3 639	3 724
New Mexico	520	526	529	548	562	580	585	602	626	657	682	694	708
New York	7 751	7 908	8 059	8 187	8 247	8 214	7 888	7 732	7 762	7 833	7 894	7 941	8 069
North Carolina	2 651	2 744	2 863	2 987	3 074	3 122	3 076	3 140	3 243	3 351	3 451	3 536	3 653
North Dakota	252	250	252	257	260	266	271	277	285	295	302	309	314
Ohio	4 373	4 472	4 583	4 701	4 818	4 882	4 819	4 848	4 918	5 076	5 221	5 296	5 392
Oklahoma	1 165	1 124	1 108	1 132	1 164	1 189	1 204	1 215	1 240	1 273	1 309	1 347	1 387
Oregon	1 030	1 058	1 100	1 153	1 206	1 256	1 254	1 276	1 318	1 372	1 428	1 485	1 537
Pennsylvania	4 730	4 791	4 915	5 042	5 138	5 170	5 084	5 076	5 123	5 192	5 253	5 306	5 406
Rhode Island	429	443	452	459	462	454	424	424	430	434	439	441	450
South Carolina	1 296	1 338	1 392	1 449	1 500	1 540	1 510	1 525	1 568	1 605	1 644	1 676	1 721
South Dakota	249	252	257	266	276	288	296	308	318	331	342	347	353
Tennessee	1 868	1 930	2 012	2 092	2 167	2 193	2 184	2 245	2 328	2 423	2 499	2 533	2 584
Texas	6 663	6 564	6 517	6 678	6 840	7 101	7 181	7 275	7 488	7 757	8 029	8 263	8 614
Utah	624	634	640	660	691	724	745	769	810	860	908	954	994
Vermont	225	234	246	256	262	258	249	251	257	264	270	275	279
Virginia	2 455	2 558	2 680	2 772	2 862	2 894	2 829	2 848	2 919	3 004	3 070	3 136	3 232
Washington	1 710	1 770	1 852	1 941	2 047	2 143	2 177	2 222	2 253	2 304	2 347	2 416	2 515
West Virginia	597	598	599	610	615	630	629	640	652	674	688	699	708
Wisconsin	1 983	2 024	2 090	2 168	2 236	2 292	2 302	2 358	2 413	2 491	2 559	2 601	2 656
Wyoming	207	196	183	189	193	198	203	206	210	217	219	221	224
Puerto Rico	692	728	764	818	837	846	838	858	872	898	930	973	989
Virgin Islands	37	38	40	42	42	43	44	45	48	44	42	41	42

Table 2-8. Employees on Total Nonfarm Payrolls, by State and Selected Territory, 1970–2010—*Continued*

(Thousands of people.)

State	1998	1999	2000	2001	2002	2003	2004	2005	2006	2007	2008	2009	2010
UNITED STATES	125 930	128 993	131 785	131 826	130 341	129 999	131 435	133 703	136 086	137 598	136 790	130 807	129 818
Alabama	1 898	1 920	1 931	1 909	1 883	1 876	1 902	1 945	1 980	2 006	1 992	1 886	1 869
Alaska	275	278	284	289	295	299	304	310	315	318	322	321	324
Arizona	2 075	2 163	2 243	2 265	2 267	2 298	2 383	2 511	2 637	2 677	2 620	2 429	2 377
Arkansas	1 122	1 142	1 159	1 154	1 146	1 145	1 158	1 178	1 199	1 204	1 202	1 165	1 163
California	13 596	13 992	14 488	14 602	14 458	14 393	14 533	14 801	15 060	15 174	14 981	14 085	13 892
Colorado	2 058	2 133	2 214	2 227	2 184	2 153	2 180	2 226	2 279	2 331	2 350	2 246	2 220
Connecticut	1 643	1 669	1 693	1 681	1 665	1 644	1 650	1 662	1 681	1 698	1 699	1 627	1 608
Delaware	400	413	420	420	415	416	425	433	438	439	437	417	413
District of Columbia	614	627	650	654	664	666	674	682	688	694	704	702	711
Florida	6 625	6 816	7 070	7 160	7 169	7 250	7 499	7 800	8 002	8 018	7 736	7 254	7 175
Georgia	3 741	3 855	3 949	3 943	3 870	3 845	3 898	4 001	4 089	4 146	4 102	3 880	3 826
Hawaii	531	535	551	555	557	568	583	602	617	625	619	592	587
Idaho	521	539	560	568	568	572	588	611	638	655	649	610	603
Illinois	5 899	5 958	6 045	5 995	5 884	5 811	5 816	5 862	5 933	5 980	5 949	5 657	5 611
Indiana	2 917	2 970	3 000	2 933	2 901	2 895	2 929	2 955	2 974	2 986	2 957	2 787	2 793
Iowa	1 443	1 469	1 478	1 466	1 447	1 440	1 457	1 480	1 504	1 519	1 524	1 479	1 469
Kansas	1 314	1 328	1 346	1 349	1 336	1 313	1 325	1 333	1 354	1 380	1 391	1 343	1 323
Kentucky	1 753	1 795	1 827	1 805	1 789	1 783	1 799	1 824	1 847	1 867	1 852	1 769	1 770
Louisiana	1 887	1 894	1 918	1 915	1 896	1 906	1 918	1 892	1 853	1 916	1 938	1 902	1 884
Maine	569	586	604	608	606	607	612	612	615	618	617	596	592
Maryland	2 326	2 392	2 455	2 472	2 480	2 487	2 518	2 556	2 589	2 608	2 600	2 523	2 513
Massachusetts	3 184	3 243	3 329	3 339	3 259	3 198	3 195	3 212	3 246	3 280	3 290	3 181	3 186
Michigan	4 514	4 585	4 676	4 564	4 487	4 416	4 399	4 390	4 326	4 268	4 162	3 872	3 861
Minnesota	2 564	2 622	2 685	2 690	2 664	2 660	2 681	2 723	2 758	2 771	2 763	2 655	2 637
Mississippi	1 134	1 153	1 154	1 130	1 124	1 115	1 124	1 130	1 141	1 153	1 148	1 096	1 090
Missouri	2 684	2 727	2 749	2 730	2 699	2 680	2 694	2 735	2 774	2 795	2 789	2 684	2 647
Montana	376	384	391	392	396	401	411	421	432	445	446	430	428
Nebraska	878	894	911	917	908	910	918	930	942	957	965	945	939
Nevada	926	983	1 027	1 051	1 052	1 088	1 153	1 223	1 280	1 292	1 264	1 148	1 116
New Hampshire	589	606	622	627	618	618	627	637	643	648	648	626	623
New Jersey	3 801	3 901	3 994	3 997	3 984	3 979	3 999	4 039	4 071	4 079	4 051	3 895	3 854
New Mexico	720	730	745	757	766	776	790	809	832	844	847	812	802
New York	8 239	8 458	8 638	8 595	8 462	8 410	8 465	8 537	8 618	8 734	8 793	8 556	8 553
North Carolina	3 758	3 849	3 915	3 894	3 836	3 788	3 836	3 915	4 041	4 145	4 135	3 909	3 862
North Dakota	319	324	328	330	330	333	338	345	352	358	367	367	376
Ohio	5 482	5 564	5 625	5 543	5 445	5 398	5 408	5 427	5 436	5 428	5 362	5 073	5 031
Oklahoma	1 432	1 453	1 480	1 494	1 474	1 445	1 461	1 500	1 540	1 568	1 593	1 542	1 526
Oregon	1 562	1 586	1 618	1 606	1 585	1 574	1 607	1 654	1 704	1 731	1 718	1 612	1 600
Pennsylvania	5 495	5 586	5 691	5 682	5 641	5 611	5 644	5 702	5 756	5 798	5 799	5 615	5 616
Rhode Island	458	466	477	478	479	484	488	491	493	493	482	460	459
South Carolina	1 784	1 831	1 860	1 824	1 806	1 809	1 834	1 868	1 908	1 946	1 928	1 815	1 805
South Dakota	360	370	378	379	378	378	384	390	399	406	411	404	403
Tennessee	2 638	2 685	2 729	2 688	2 664	2 663	2 706	2 743	2 783	2 797	2 775	2 620	2 612
Texas	8 943	9 160	9 432	9 514	9 416	9 370	9 497	9 740	10 066	10 395	10 607	10 307	10 342
Utah	1 023	1 048	1 075	1 081	1 073	1 074	1 104	1 148	1 204	1 253	1 252	1 189	1 181
Vermont	285	292	299	302	299	299	303	306	308	308	307	297	298
Virginia	3 320	3 412	3 516	3 517	3 494	3 498	3 584	3 664	3 726	3 761	3 763	3 642	3 627
Washington	2 595	2 649	2 711	2 697	2 654	2 658	2 701	2 777	2 859	2 934	2 959	2 821	2 777
West Virginia	719	726	736	735	733	728	737	746	756	758	762	746	746
Wisconsin	2 718	2 784	2 834	2 814	2 782	2 775	2 807	2 842	2 866	2 884	2 878	2 752	2 735
Wyoming	228	233	239	245	248	250	255	264	277	289	298	286	283
Puerto Rico	997	1 011	1 025	1 009	1 005	1 022	1 046	1 048	1 041	1 028	1 010	961	927
Virgin Islands	42	41	42	44	43	42	43	44	46	46	46	44	44

Table 2-9. Employees on Total Private Payrolls, by State and Selected Territory, 1995–2010

(Thousands of people.)

State	1995	1996	1997	1998	1999	2000	2001	2002	2003	2004	2005	2006	2007	2008	2009	2010
UNITED STATES	97 865	100 169	103 113	106 021	108 686	110 995	110 708	108 828	108 416	109 814	111 899	114 113	115 380	114 281	108 252	107 337
Alabama	1 461	1 486	1 520	1 551	1 569	1 580	1 557	1 529	1 517	1 542	1 582	1 609	1 629	1 608	1 503	1 482
Alaska	190	191	196	202	205	210	211	215	218	223	229	234	237	240	237	239
Arizona	1 483	1 574	1 656	1 733	1 809	1 876	1 888	1 876	1 905	1 984	2 108	2 229	2 256	2 187	2 006	1 961
Arkansas	893	907	921	937	954	968	960	951	947	958	974	991	994	989	948	945
California	10 315	10 630	10 989	11 430	11 752	12 170	12 220	12 011	11 967	12 135	12 381	12 608	12 679	12 463	11 605	11 469
Colorado	1 531	1 592	1 665	1 735	1 804	1 877	1 883	1 829	1 797	1 821	1 863	1 912	1 957	1 966	1 855	1 827
Connecticut	1 341	1 360	1 382	1 416	1 434	1 451	1 437	1 416	1 399	1 407	1 418	1 435	1 449	1 447	1 378	1 363
Delaware	316	324	335	346	358	364	363	358	358	367	373	377	377	374	353	349
District of Columbia	. . .	383	385	388	405	426	428	433	435	443	449	455	463	469	462	465
Florida	5 067	5 244	5 461	5 671	5 850	6 068	6 136	6 129	6 197	6 433	6 719	6 903	6 896	6 609	6 139	6 060
Georgia	2 832	2 958	3 037	3 155	3 265	3 352	3 334	3 246	3 214	3 264	3 355	3 430	3 473	3 412	3 191	3 148
Hawaii	421	420	420	419	422	437	441	439	449	463	482	496	503	494	466	462
Idaho	380	392	406	419	434	451	458	456	459	474	496	522	538	530	490	484
Illinois	4 795	4 875	4 963	5 083	5 133	5 205	5 145	5 023	4 958	4 971	5 016	5 087	5 131	5 094	4 800	4 754
Indiana	2 399	2 428	2 471	2 523	2 572	2 595	2 523	2 484	2 473	2 503	2 529	2 548	2 555	2 516	2 349	2 355
Iowa	1 128	1 151	1 172	1 207	1 229	1 235	1 220	1 203	1 196	1 213	1 235	1 257	1 269	1 272	1 224	1 216
Kansas	963	995	1 035	1 074	1 089	1 101	1 101	1 085	1 063	1 074	1 082	1 099	1 122	1 131	1 082	1 061
Kentucky	1 356	1 383	1 420	1 458	1 494	1 519	1 493	1 474	1 471	1 489	1 511	1 529	1 543	1 529	1 445	1 438
Louisiana	1 412	1 446	1 484	1 520	1 524	1 544	1 542	1 521	1 526	1 535	1 518	1 505	1 560	1 573	1 532	1 518
Maine	445	450	461	475	490	504	506	503	503	507	507	510	514	513	493	489
Maryland	1 761	1 791	1 846	1 893	1 948	2 005	2 015	2 016	2 025	2 055	2 090	2 118	2 130	2 112	2 029	2 012
Massachusetts	2 577	2 630	2 700	2 762	2 815	2 894	2 899	2 823	2 773	2 774	2 787	2 817	2 848	2 853	2 743	2 748
Michigan	3 628	3 709	3 792	3 858	3 917	3 995	3 879	3 800	3 731	3 719	3 716	3 661	3 612	3 512	3 226	3 226
Minnesota	2 001	2 054	2 111	2 174	2 226	2 277	2 280	2 251	2 248	2 269	2 308	2 342	2 357	2 344	2 238	2 221
Mississippi	860	872	888	910	926	920	892	884	874	882	889	902	909	900	847	841
Missouri	2 131	2 167	2 227	2 270	2 306	2 323	2 302	2 268	2 248	2 265	2 306	2 340	2 355	2 343	2 232	2 197
Montana	274	283	288	295	301	307	308	311	315	325	335	347	358	358	340	338
Nebraska	668	686	704	727	743	756	760	749	751	758	769	779	795	801	776	770
Nevada	689	742	784	814	866	905	925	921	954	1 014	1 079	1 129	1 136	1 101	990	961
New Hampshire	464	476	491	509	524	539	541	530	528	537	545	551	554	553	530	526
New Jersey	3 027	3 068	3 154	3 230	3 324	3 406	3 395	3 370	3 357	3 366	3 398	3 424	3 431	3 402	3 243	3 212
New Mexico	516	523	532	542	549	562	572	575	581	592	607	635	649	649	613	602
New York	6 478	6 541	6 663	6 816	7 014	7 171	7 127	6 970	6 923	6 981	7 048	7 133	7 233	7 277	7 032	7 043
North Carolina	2 908	2 982	3 084	3 172	3 252	3 300	3 265	3 202	3 154	3 191	3 259	3 368	3 457	3 429	3 200	3 158
North Dakota	231	239	244	249	253	255	257	256	257	263	270	277	283	291	289	296
Ohio	4 472	4 544	4 635	4 719	4 791	4 840	4 749	4 645	4 595	4 607	4 627	4 636	4 631	4 566	4 285	4 248
Oklahoma	1 040	1 076	1 111	1 154	1 170	1 193	1 197	1 173	1 150	1 160	1 187	1 219	1 243	1 264	1 202	1 187
Oregon	1 178	1 228	1 277	1 296	1 314	1 339	1 324	1 300	1 295	1 324	1 369	1 417	1 442	1 420	1 313	1 300
Pennsylvania	4 541	4 594	4 692	4 783	4 871	4 966	4 954	4 902	4 866	4 900	4 957	5 011	5 053	5 050	4 858	4 859
Rhode Island	378	379	387	395	402	412	413	413	418	423	426	428	428	418	398	397
South Carolina	1 350	1 378	1 419	1 474	1 515	1 536	1 500	1 479	1 481	1 508	1 539	1 576	1 608	1 580	1 468	1 460
South Dakota	273	278	284	291	300	307	305	303	304	309	315	323	331	335	326	324
Tennessee	2 126	2 152	2 204	2 253	2 295	2 330	2 285	2 254	2 252	2 291	2 330	2 366	2 376	2 347	2 191	2 181
Texas	6 583	6 805	7 130	7 439	7 625	7 870	7 928	7 790	7 724	7 841	8 056	8 359	8 660	8 828	8 486	8 482
Utah	744	788	821	847	869	890	891	879	878	905	946	999	1 046	1 041	974	965
Vermont	225	230	234	239	244	249	252	249	247	251	253	254	255	253	243	243
Virginia	2 472	2 540	2 635	2 718	2 801	2 892	2 888	2 859	2 860	2 933	3 003	3 052	3 078	3 069	2 942	2 924
Washington	1 903	1 965	2 057	2 129	2 174	2 228	2 192	2 138	2 137	2 177	2 250	2 329	2 400	2 413	2 272	2 231
West Virginia	551	560	569	579	585	593	594	590	585	594	603	611	613	615	596	593
Wisconsin	2 180	2 217	2 269	2 325	2 385	2 428	2 400	2 368	2 362	2 395	2 427	2 451	2 468	2 456	2 332	2 315
Wyoming	162	163	167	170	174	179	184	185	187	191	199	212	222	229	215	210
Puerto Rico	625	657	679	690	720	739	726	710	721	739	743	741	730	710	672	657
Virgin Islands	28	27	28	28	27	29	32	30	29	31	32	33	33	33	31	31

. . . = Not available.

Table 2-10. Employees on Manufacturing Payrolls, by State and Selected Territory, NAICS Basis, 1995–2010

(Thousands of people.)

State	1995	1996	1997	1998	1999	2000	2001	2002	2003	2004	2005	2006	2007	2008	2009	2010
UNITED STATES	17 241	17 237	17 419	17 560	17 322	17 263	16 441	15 259	14 510	14 315	14 226	14 155	13 879	13 406	11 847	11 524
Alabama	370	362	364	365	358	351	326	307	294	292	299	303	296	284	247	236
Alaska	15	14	14	13	12	12	12	11	12	12	13	13	13	13	13	13
Arizona	191	199	205	211	207	210	202	184	175	177	182	186	182	173	154	148
Arkansas	246	241	241	242	241	240	227	214	206	204	202	200	191	184	164	160
California	1 719	1 777	1 826	1 856	1 829	1 856	1 781	1 634	1 545	1 523	1 505	1 490	1 464	1 425	1 282	1 242
Colorado	179	181	187	191	187	189	180	164	154	152	150	149	147	144	130	125
Connecticut	249	245	245	248	240	236	227	211	200	197	195	194	191	187	171	166
Delaware	43	41	43	44	44	42	39	37	36	35	33	34	33	32	28	26
District of Columbia	5	5	4	4	4	4	3	3	3	2	2	2	2	2	1	1
Florida	479	485	486	482	478	477	455	428	410	411	416	416	399	371	324	307
Georgia	547	552	555	553	550	538	505	471	452	448	450	448	431	409	358	344
Hawaii	16	16	16	16	16	16	16	15	15	15	15	15	15	15	14	13
Idaho	63	66	68	69	69	70	69	66	62	62	64	66	66	63	55	53
Illinois	894	899	902	906	882	871	815	754	714	697	688	683	675	657	577	559
Indiana	653	647	652	658	666	665	615	588	573	572	571	565	550	521	442	446
Iowa	237	235	239	251	253	251	240	227	220	223	229	231	230	227	203	200
Kansas	180	186	198	206	204	201	195	184	175	177	180	183	186	187	167	160
Kentucky	299	298	302	307	309	310	292	275	265	264	262	261	256	245	213	209
Louisiana	182	183	185	185	181	177	172	161	156	153	152	153	157	153	142	138
Maine	83	81	81	81	81	80	75	68	64	63	61	60	59	59	52	51
Maryland	175	172	173	173	172	172	166	155	145	141	139	135	132	128	119	115
Massachusetts	412	411	412	413	400	403	389	349	324	313	305	300	295	286	259	254
Michigan	874	867	874	890	899	897	822	762	718	699	679	650	619	574	465	474
Minnesota	375	381	391	397	395	397	379	356	343	343	347	346	342	336	300	292
Mississippi	241	231	228	234	233	223	201	188	179	180	178	176	170	160	141	136
Missouri	377	376	377	378	373	365	345	325	315	311	309	307	300	289	254	243
Montana	21	22	22	22	23	23	21	20	19	19	20	20	21	20	17	16
Nebraska	110	111	112	114	113	114	111	106	102	101	101	102	101	101	93	92
Nevada	36	38	40	41	41	43	44	43	44	46	48	50	50	48	40	38
New Hampshire	97	99	102	104	101	103	97	85	80	80	80	78	78	76	68	66
New Jersey	449	437	435	429	422	422	401	368	350	338	330	324	311	299	266	258
New Mexico	43	43	43	43	41	42	41	38	37	36	36	38	37	35	30	29
New York	809	795	796	790	771	749	707	651	612	596	579	566	552	532	476	457
North Carolina	828	809	800	796	777	758	704	644	599	577	565	553	539	516	448	431
North Dakota	20	21	22	23	23	24	24	24	24	25	26	26	26	26	24	23
Ohio	1 037	1 030	1 027	1 030	1 028	1 021	953	885	843	822	812	796	771	739	629	620
Oklahoma	161	162	168	175	177	177	170	152	143	142	145	149	151	150	129	123
Oregon	211	218	227	229	224	225	216	202	195	200	204	207	204	195	167	164
Pennsylvania	881	867	871	874	864	864	822	760	712	691	679	670	659	644	574	561
Rhode Island	80	77	76	75	72	71	68	62	59	57	55	53	51	48	42	40
South Carolina	347	339	339	341	336	336	314	290	276	268	261	253	250	242	214	207
South Dakota	44	44	44	44	44	44	41	38	38	39	40	42	42	43	38	37
Tennessee	524	507	503	504	500	493	454	429	413	412	409	399	380	361	309	298
Texas	994	1 016	1 044	1 077	1 063	1 067	1 026	948	899	890	897	924	934	924	838	811
Utah	117	122	126	127	126	126	122	114	112	115	118	123	128	126	113	111
Vermont	41	43	44	45	45	46	46	41	38	37	37	36	36	35	31	31
Virginia	373	371	374	376	367	364	341	320	305	299	296	288	278	265	239	230
Washington	311	325	350	361	343	332	316	285	267	264	273	286	293	291	266	258
West Virginia	78	78	77	78	77	76	72	69	65	63	62	61	59	57	51	49
Wisconsin	567	568	579	593	595	594	560	528	504	503	505	506	501	493	436	431
Wyoming	10	10	10	10	10	10	10	10	9	9	10	10	10	10	9	9
Puerto Rico	159	158	155	148	144	143	132	121	118	118	115	110	107	101	92	86
Virgin Islands	2	2	2	2	2	2	2	2	2	2	2	2	2	2	2	2

Table 2-11. Employees on Government Payrolls, by State and Selected Territory, NAICS Basis, 1995–2010

(Thousands of people.)

State	1995	1996	1997	1998	1999	2000	2001	2002	2003	2004	2005	2006	2007	2008	2009	2010
UNITED STATES	19 432	19 539	19 664	19 909	20 307	20 790	21 118	21 513	21 583	21 621	21 804	21 974	22 218	22 509	22 555	22 482
Alabama	343	343	346	347	351	352	352	355	358	359	363	370	377	384	384	387
Alaska	73	73	73	73	73	74	79	80	81	81	81	81	81	82	84	85
Arizona	310	318	328	341	354	367	378	390	394	399	403	409	421	432	423	417
Arkansas	177	180	183	185	187	191	194	195	199	200	204	208	211	214	217	218
California	2 107	2 113	2 141	2 166	2 239	2 318	2 382	2 447	2 426	2 398	2 420	2 452	2 495	2 519	2 480	2 423
Colorado	304	309	316	322	328	337	344	355	356	359	363	367	375	384	391	393
Connecticut	221	223	226	228	235	242	244	249	246	243	244	246	249	253	248	245
Delaware	51	52	53	54	55	57	57	57	57	57	60	61	62	63	63	64
District of Columbia	255	240	233	226	222	224	226	232	231	231	234	233	231	235	240	246
Florida	918	928	942	955	966	1 002	1 023	1 039	1 053	1 066	1 081	1 099	1 123	1 127	1 115	1 115
Georgia	570	570	577	586	590	597	610	624	631	635	647	660	673	691	688	678
Hawaii	111	111	112	112	113	115	115	118	119	120	120	121	122	125	126	125
Idaho	96	97	100	103	105	109	110	112	113	114	115	116	117	119	120	119
Illinois	799	809	808	816	826	840	850	861	853	845	846	846	849	856	858	857
Indiana	387	386	387	394	398	405	410	417	423	426	426	426	431	441	438	438
Iowa	230	233	235	236	239	243	245	244	245	245	245	247	250	253	255	254
Kansas	237	234	236	240	240	245	248	251	250	251	251	255	258	260	261	262
Kentucky	287	289	291	295	301	308	312	315	313	310	314	318	323	323	325	331
Louisiana	358	362	364	367	370	373	374	375	379	382	374	348	356	365	369	366
Maine	93	93	93	95	97	100	102	103	104	105	105	104	104	104	104	103
Maryland	423	423	423	433	444	450	457	465	462	463	466	471	478	488	494	501
Massachusetts	404	409	414	422	428	435	440	436	426	422	425	429	433	437	438	438
Michigan	641	644	647	656	667	681	685	687	685	680	674	665	656	650	647	636
Minnesota	387	389	389	391	397	408	409	414	413	412	415	416	415	419	417	417
Mississippi	215	217	219	223	227	234	238	240	241	242	241	239	244	248	250	249
Missouri	390	401	413	414	421	426	429	431	432	429	429	434	440	446	452	451
Montana	78	79	80	81	82	84	84	85	86	87	86	86	87	88	90	91
Nebraska	151	151	152	151	151	154	157	159	160	160	161	162	162	164	169	169
Nevada	97	101	107	112	117	122	127	131	135	139	144	150	157	162	159	155
New Hampshire	76	78	79	80	82	84	86	88	90	90	91	92	93	95	97	97
New Jersey	573	571	570	572	578	589	603	614	622	633	642	647	648	649	652	643
New Mexico	166	171	177	178	180	183	186	191	195	198	201	198	199	198	199	199
New York	1 416	1 400	1 406	1 424	1 445	1 467	1 467	1 492	1 487	1 484	1 489	1 485	1 501	1 516	1 524	1 510
North Carolina	544	554	569	587	597	615	629	634	634	645	656	672	688	706	709	704
North Dakota	71	70	70	70	71	73	73	74	75	75	75	76	76	76	78	80
Ohio	749	752	758	763	772	785	794	800	803	802	800	800	797	796	788	782
Oklahoma	270	271	276	278	283	288	296	301	296	302	312	321	325	329	340	340
Oregon	250	257	260	266	272	279	282	286	280	282	285	286	290	298	300	300
Pennsylvania	712	713	715	712	716	725	728	739	746	744	745	746	745	749	757	757
Rhode Island	61	61	63	63	63	64	65	66	66	66	65	65	64	64	62	62
South Carolina	294	297	301	310	316	324	324	327	328	326	329	332	339	348	348	345
South Dakota	70	69	69	69	70	71	73	74	75	75	75	75	76	76	78	79
Tennessee	373	382	380	386	390	399	403	410	411	415	413	417	421	428	429	432
Texas	1 446	1 458	1 483	1 504	1 535	1 562	1 586	1 626	1 646	1 656	1 684	1 707	1 735	1 779	1 821	1 860
Utah	164	167	172	177	180	185	190	195	197	199	202	205	207	212	215	216
Vermont	45	45	46	46	48	49	50	51	52	52	53	54	54	54	55	55
Virginia	598	596	597	602	611	625	629	635	638	651	662	675	683	694	700	703
Washington	444	451	458	466	474	483	505	516	521	524	527	530	534	546	550	547
West Virginia	136	139	139	141	141	143	141	143	143	143	144	145	145	147	150	153
Wisconsin	58	58	58	58	59	61	62	63	64	65	65	65	67	69	72	73
Wyoming	58	58	58	58	59	61	62	63	64	65	65	65	67	69	72	73
Puerto Rico	305	317	310	308	291	286	282	295	301	307	305	300	297	299	289	270
Virgin Islands	14	14	14	14	13	13	12	13	13	12	12	13	13	13	13	13

EARNINGS

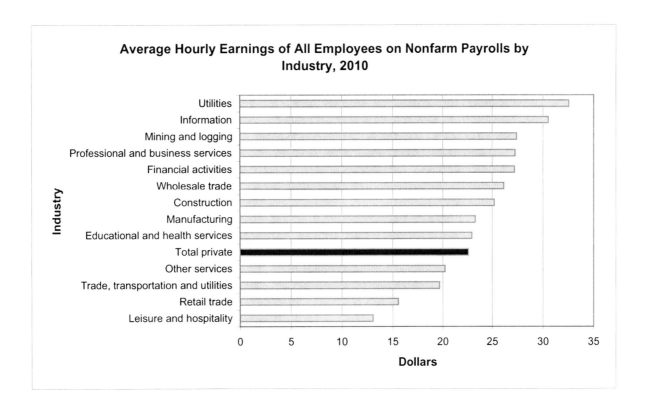

Average hourly earnings of all employees on total private payrolls increased 1.7 percent to $22.59 in 2010. Utilities had the highest average hourly earnings ($32.55) followed by information ($30.52), mining and logging ($27.40), and professional and business services ($27.24). Although utilities remained high paying, it was the only major super sector that suffered a decline in earnings from 2009 to 2010. (See Table 2-12.)

OTHER HIGHLIGHTS

- In 2010, average hourly earnings for all employees also varied significantly by state. Earnings were highest in the District of Columbia ($34.18) followed by Connecticut ($28.08) and Massachusetts ($27.13). Average hourly earnings were the lowest in Mississippi ($18.05), Arkansas ($18.08), and South Dakota ($18.55). (See Table 2-13.)

- Average weekly earnings for production workers increased 3.2 percent; however, when adjusted for inflation, average weekly earnings only increased 1.1 percent. (See Table 2-16.)

- From 2007 to 2010, average weekly earnings increased 6.3 percent nationwide but declined in the following states: Nevada (-9.9 percent), Alaska (-3.9 percent), Delaware (-2.1 percent), Alabama (-1.7 percent), Ohio (-1.2 percent), Michigan (-0.3 percent), and Texas (0.3 percent) (See Table 2-17.)

Table 2-12. Average Hourly Earnings of All Employees on Total Private Payrolls by NAICS Super Sector, 2006–2010

(Dollars, seasonally adjusted.)

Year and month	Total private	Mining and logging	Construction	Manufacturing	Trade, transportation, and utilities				Information	Financial activities	Professional and business services	Education and health services	Leisure and hospitality	Other services
					Total	Wholesale trade	Retail trade	Utilities						
2007	20.97	24.91	23.02	21.50	18.58	23.96	15.13	30.27	28.09	25.62	24.68	21.35	12.39	17.62
2008	21.62	26.20	23.96	22.16	18.93	24.37	15.21	32.22	28.66	26.16	25.82	22.12	12.77	18.17
2009	22.21	27.29	24.83	23.04	19.32	25.41	15.39	32.84	29.40	26.50	27.03	22.41	12.97	19.54
2010	22.59	27.40	25.19	23.32	19.65	26.12	15.56	32.55	30.52	27.18	27.24	22.96	13.08	20.20
2006														
January	...	...	...	...	...	...	...	...	...	...	...	...	...	...
February	...	...	...	...	...	...	...	...	...	...	...	...	...	...
March	20.05	22.61	21.79	20.69	18.22	22.92	15.24	29.15	26.79	24.05	23.36	20.31	11.49	17.08
April	20.15	23.58	22.08	20.92	18.22	22.94	15.19	29.75	26.98	24.19	23.38	20.31	11.58	17.16
May	20.13	23.39	22.02	20.70	18.23	23.08	15.14	29.12	26.99	24.31	23.38	20.34	11.66	17.19
June	20.23	23.72	22.25	20.81	18.36	23.22	15.27	29.09	27.17	24.41	23.38	20.42	11.69	17.19
July	20.28	23.87	22.31	20.97	18.29	23.09	15.16	29.41	27.26	24.63	23.43	20.49	11.75	17.21
August	20.31	23.56	22.26	20.93	18.28	23.18	15.13	29.07	27.23	24.85	23.60	20.50	11.77	17.27
September	20.41	23.93	22.44	21.01	18.36	23.61	15.11	29.18	27.33	24.87	23.84	20.53	11.82	17.35
October	20.47	24.45	22.46	21.19	18.35	23.58	15.12	29.51	27.39	24.92	23.95	20.52	11.93	17.40
November	20.49	24.78	22.48	21.08	18.39	23.72	15.10	29.34	27.34	25.10	23.98	20.59	11.94	17.44
December	20.58	24.60	22.56	21.30	18.42	23.77	15.14	29.21	27.65	25.14	24.11	20.63	11.98	17.49
2007														
January	20.60	24.69	22.56	21.23	18.35	23.47	15.11	29.37	28.04	25.14	24.23	20.71	12.07	17.54
February	20.67	24.94	22.60	21.22	18.43	23.60	15.14	29.43	27.94	25.32	24.30	20.74	12.16	17.51
March	20.78	24.70	22.67	21.27	18.44	23.72	15.10	29.76	27.99	25.41	24.41	21.31	12.18	17.36
April	20.85	25.12	22.86	21.49	18.45	23.74	15.09	30.49	28.18	25.44	24.51	21.26	12.29	17.34
May	20.89	24.89	22.98	21.41	18.48	23.91	15.05	30.12	28.09	25.54	24.61	21.28	12.36	17.44
June	21.00	25.13	23.06	21.54	18.64	24.15	15.18	30.07	28.08	25.68	24.71	21.38	12.42	17.56
July	21.04	24.98	23.13	21.60	18.60	24.02	15.10	30.51	28.15	25.72	24.73	21.43	12.51	17.66
August	21.03	24.77	23.10	21.59	18.56	23.91	15.08	30.27	28.13	25.75	24.74	21.44	12.48	17.74
September	21.12	24.95	23.27	21.68	18.67	24.12	15.14	30.64	28.11	25.77	24.81	21.59	12.51	17.77
October	21.11	24.91	23.12	21.57	18.71	24.15	15.17	30.66	28.14	25.76	24.89	21.56	12.53	17.78
November	21.17	24.75	23.30	21.63	18.77	24.32	15.17	30.58	28.16	25.82	24.98	21.66	12.54	17.81
December	21.27	25.13	23.48	21.80	18.78	24.24	15.17	31.26	28.35	25.89	25.07	21.73	12.70	17.84
2008														
January	21.25	25.49	23.38	21.75	18.68	23.94	15.10	31.49	28.47	25.96	25.14	21.81	12.63	17.86
February	21.30	24.92	23.45	21.76	18.76	24.07	15.18	32.17	28.32	26.06	25.21	21.82	12.70	17.90
March	21.42	26.28	23.55	21.97	18.82	24.21	15.18	31.75	28.50	26.09	25.29	22.05	12.74	17.95
April	21.44	25.23	23.66	21.92	18.85	24.23	15.19	31.58	28.70	26.13	25.43	21.95	12.77	18.01
May	21.52	25.31	23.83	22.03	18.90	24.29	15.22	31.75	28.50	26.17	25.62	22.01	12.78	18.04
June	21.62	25.85	23.91	22.23	19.02	24.46	15.27	32.80	28.48	26.19	25.74	22.06	12.81	18.14
July	21.66	26.50	24.00	22.14	19.00	24.48	15.23	32.10	28.79	26.17	25.84	22.12	12.80	18.25
August	21.73	26.82	24.19	22.20	19.02	24.46	15.26	32.47	28.91	26.27	25.98	22.18	12.83	18.29
September	21.80	26.68	24.28	22.26	19.05	24.50	15.28	32.61	28.75	26.38	26.11	22.31	12.85	18.32
October	21.82	26.49	24.25	22.44	19.00	24.47	15.21	32.41	28.67	26.29	26.30	22.26	12.81	18.37
November	21.92	27.32	24.43	22.59	19.08	24.61	15.27	32.78	28.76	26.25	26.50	22.40	12.81	18.42
December	21.99	27.30	24.59	22.63	19.13	24.68	15.29	32.81	28.90	26.27	26.62	22.48	12.82	18.48
2009														
January	22.01	27.25	24.58	22.78	19.11	24.71	15.30	32.83	28.89	26.24	26.68	22.49	12.84	18.64
February	22.07	27.43	24.53	22.92	19.19	24.90	15.31	33.05	28.77	26.24	26.80	22.53	12.86	18.93
March	22.08	27.55	24.75	23.00	19.21	25.04	15.31	33.05	28.80	26.23	26.92	22.22	12.88	19.26
April	22.13	27.50	24.81	23.02	19.23	25.19	15.30	32.92	28.98	26.28	26.99	22.23	12.90	19.49
May	22.14	27.60	24.78	23.01	19.27	25.30	15.35	32.91	29.21	26.41	27.00	22.26	12.87	19.55
June	22.18	27.39	24.86	23.05	19.28	25.34	15.37	32.89	29.38	26.49	27.02	22.34	12.93	19.56
July	22.21	27.13	24.86	23.05	19.30	25.41	15.41	32.70	29.63	26.43	27.10	22.35	12.96	19.63
August	22.26	27.42	24.92	23.12	19.37	25.58	15.44	32.88	29.65	26.48	27.19	22.39	13.01	19.73
September	22.31	27.23	24.92	23.15	19.44	25.75	15.52	32.60	29.51	26.65	27.20	22.43	13.06	19.84
October	22.34	27.17	25.00	23.12	19.43	25.80	15.40	32.68	29.73	26.77	27.14	22.53	13.10	19.91
November	22.37	26.79	25.05	23.17	19.46	25.81	15.46	32.83	29.88	26.81	27.08	22.56	13.15	19.99
December	22.39	26.92	25.02	23.13	19.49	25.88	15.47	32.73	29.89	26.87	27.06	22.61	13.12	20.05
2010														
January	22.44	26.89	25.14	23.17	19.56	26.04	15.50	32.59	29.95	26.97	27.11	22.66	13.11	20.07
February	22.48	27.08	25.19	23.22	19.56	26.10	15.51	32.12	30.14	27.01	27.20	22.72	13.09	20.09
March	22.48	27.04	25.17	23.16	19.58	26.08	15.54	32.28	30.25	27.10	27.15	22.73	13.09	20.11
April	22.52	27.19	25.12	23.18	19.66	26.15	15.62	32.24	30.25	27.20	27.11	22.82	13.07	20.09
May	22.57	27.53	25.15	23.33	19.66	26.13	15.58	32.85	30.41	27.16	27.17	22.89	13.08	20.14
June	22.57	27.35	25.13	23.26	19.64	26.11	15.55	32.48	30.42	27.18	27.24	22.92	13.07	20.19
July	22.61	27.40	25.18	23.33	19.67	26.17	15.59	32.51	30.43	27.27	27.32	22.97	13.07	20.14
August	22.67	27.60	25.20	23.43	19.72	26.21	15.60	32.73	30.66	27.28	27.37	23.06	13.10	20.14
September	22.70	27.89	25.19	23.43	19.76	26.23	15.61	32.75	30.84	27.29	27.41	23.06	13.10	20.22
October	22.77	27.71	25.25	23.49	19.79	26.29	15.63	32.84	31.03	27.38	27.47	23.15	13.12	20.36
November	22.76	27.62	25.32	23.43	19.77	26.20	15.61	32.50	31.05	27.37	27.40	23.21	13.11	20.48
December	22.77	27.59	25.33	23.46	19.76	26.17	15.63	32.78	31.06	27.45	27.34	23.29	13.12	20.46

. . . = Not available.

Table 2-13. Average Hourly Earnings of All Employees on Total Private Payrolls, by State, NAICS Basis, 2007–2010

(Dollars.)

State	2007	2008	2009	2010
UNITED STATES	20.97	21.62	22.21	22.59
Alabama	19.37	19.56	19.68	19.86
Alaska	24.70	25.01	24.79	23.87
Arizona	19.84	20.69	22.03	22.16
Arkansas	16.27	17.21	17.97	18.08
California	24.69	24.70	25.47	26.39
Colorado	23.13	23.80	23.78	23.79
Connecticut	26.59	27.71	27.81	28.08
Delaware	21.98	22.73	22.30	22.71
District of Columbia	. . .	32.37	31.37	34.18
Florida	20.58	21.00	21.61	21.44
Georgia	20.43	20.77	21.08	21.57
Hawaii	20.68	20.80	21.11	21.65
Idaho	16.51	17.53	19.26	21.03
Illinois	22.94	22.67	23.05	23.14
Indiana	19.94	20.30	20.56	20.57
Iowa	18.01	18.35	20.01	20.38
Kansas	19.64	20.13	20.18	20.08
Kentucky	17.73	18.07	18.82	19.40
Louisiana	18.73	19.22	19.46	19.55
Maine	18.74	18.96	19.16	19.45
Maryland	24.04	24.56	25.42	26.17
Massachusetts	26.07	26.38	26.84	27.13
Michigan	21.55	21.62	21.89	22.26
Minnesota	23.13	23.23	23.41	23.85
Mississippi	16.46	16.89	17.87	18.05
Missouri	19.78	20.57	20.94	21.19
Montana	17.80	18.43	19.86	20.19
Nebraska	19.92	19.79	20.19	20.89
Nevada	19.64	19.75	19.56	19.13
New Hampshire	22.06	22.66	22.70	22.98
New Jersey	24.84	25.32	25.92	25.96
New Mexico	18.57	18.73	18.92	19.57
New York	25.26	25.48	25.70	26.06
North Carolina	19.25	19.90	20.59	20.60
North Dakota	18.34	18.75	19.21	20.19
Ohio	20.22	20.11	19.95	20.21
Oklahoma	17.33	17.43	18.07	19.19
Oregon	20.61	20.93	21.33	21.56
Pennsylvania	20.07	20.43	20.75	21.21
Rhode Island	22.17	22.50	22.52	22.67
South Carolina	18.76	18.80	19.17	19.89
South Dakota	16.47	16.53	17.94	18.55
Tennessee	19.01	19.40	19.52	19.94
Texas	21.07	21.30	21.39	21.36
Utah	21.41	21.10	22.48	24.31
Vermont	20.42	21.35	22.41	23.01
Virginia	22.46	22.31	22.58	23.54
Washington	24.19	25.23	26.32	26.95
West Virginia	17.04	17.70	18.09	18.65
Wisconsin	20.45	20.67	21.12	21.35
Wyoming	20.03	20.83	21.06	21.46

. . . = Not available.

Table 2-14. Average Hourly Earnings of Production Workers on Private Nonfarm Payrolls, by Super Sector, NAICS Basis, 2000–2010

(Dollars.)

Industry	2000	2001	2002	2003	2004	2005	2006	2007	2008	2009	2010
TOTAL PRIVATE	14.02	14.54	14.97	15.37	15.69	16.13	16.76	17.43	18.08	18.63	19.07
Goods-Producing	15.27	15.78	16.33	16.80	17.19	17.60	18.02	18.67	19.33	19.90	20.28
Mining and logging	16.55	17.00	17.19	17.56	18.07	18.72	19.90	20.97	22.50	23.29	23.83
Construction	17.48	18.00	18.52	18.95	19.23	19.46	20.02	20.95	21.87	22.66	23.22
Manufacturing	14.32	14.76	15.29	15.74	16.14	16.56	16.81	17.26	17.75	18.24	18.61
Private Service-Providing	13.62	14.18	14.59	14.99	15.29	15.74	16.42	17.11	17.77	18.35	18.81
Trade, transportation, and utilities	13.31	13.70	14.02	14.34	14.58	14.92	15.39	15.78	16.16	16.48	16.83
Wholesale trade	16.28	16.77	16.98	17.36	17.65	18.16	18.91	19.59	20.13	20.84	21.53
Retail trade	10.86	11.29	11.67	11.90	12.08	12.36	12.57	12.75	12.87	13.01	13.24
Transportation and warehousing	15.05	15.33	15.76	16.25	16.52	16.70	17.28	17.72	18.41	18.81	19.17
Utilities	22.75	23.58	23.96	24.77	25.61	26.68	27.40	27.88	28.83	29.48	30.04
Information	19.07	19.80	20.20	21.01	21.40	22.06	23.23	23.96	24.78	25.45	25.86
Financial activities	14.98	15.59	16.17	17.14	17.52	17.95	18.80	19.64	20.28	20.85	21.49
Professional and business services	15.52	16.33	16.81	17.21	17.48	18.08	19.13	20.15	21.18	22.35	22.78
Education and health services	13.95	14.64	15.21	15.64	16.15	16.71	17.38	18.11	18.87	19.49	20.12
Leisure and hospitality	8.32	8.57	8.81	9.00	9.15	9.38	9.75	10.41	10.84	11.12	11.31
Other services	12.73	13.27	13.72	13.84	13.98	14.34	14.77	15.42	16.09	16.59	17.08

Table 2-15. Average Weekly Earnings of All Employees on Nonfarm Payrolls, by Industry, in Current and 1982–1984 Dollars, NAICS Basis, 2007–2010

(Dollars.)

Industry	2007	2008	2009	2010
TOTAL PRIVATE				
Current dollars	725.22	744.80	753.18	770.74
1982–1984 dollars	349.77	345.93	351.07	353.46
Goods-Producing				
Current dollars	873.51	899.62	916.04	952.00
1982–1984 dollars	421.29	417.84	426.98	436.59
Mining and logging				
Current dollars	1 094.85	1 144.59	1 150.12	1 189.98
1982–1984 dollars	528.04	531.62	536.09	545.72
Construction				
Current dollars	875.28	905.68	922.54	952.84
1982–1984 dollars	422.14	420.65	430.01	436.97
Manufacturing				
Current dollars	861.22	882.19	898.64	937.47
1982–1984 dollars	415.36	409.74	418.87	429.92
Private Service-Providing				
Current dollars	689.95	709.65	719.10	734.84
1982–1984 dollars	332.76	329.61	335.19	337.00
Trade, transportation, and utilities				
Current dollars	641.97	651.96	659.78	672.66
1982–1984 dollars	309.62	302.81	307.54	308.48
Wholesale trade				
Current dollars	913.00	936.17	963.44	994.27
1982–1984 dollars	440.34	434.82	449.08	455.97
Retail trade				
Current dollars	479.91	477.87	481.06	487.47
1982–1984 dollars	231.46	221.95	224.23	223.55
Transportation and warehousing				
Current dollars	758.26	780.55	780.53	803.73
1982–1984 dollars	365.70	362.54	363.82	368.59
Utilities				
Current dollars	1 264.45	1 352.50	1 343.90	1 338.09
1982–1984 dollars	609.84	628.18	626.42	613.65
Information				
Current dollars	1 014.38	1 047.50	1 073.27	1 113.96
1982–1984 dollars	489.23	486.52	500.27	510.86
Financial activities				
Current dollars	936.56	954.82	970.00	1 002.18
1982–1984 dollars	451.70	443.48	452.14	459.60
Professional and business services				
Current dollars	874.68	909.23	947.10	963.59
1982–1984 dollars	421.85	422.30	441.46	441.90
Education and health services				
Current dollars	715.84	745.03	739.27	752.07
1982–1984 dollars	345.25	346.04	344.59	344.90
Leisure and hospitality				
Current dollars	323.54	330.32	331.64	336.87
1982–1984 dollars	156.04	153.42	154.58	154.49
Other services				
Current dollars	578.84	597.13	618.18	638.98
1982–1984 dollars	279.17	277.34	288.15	293.03

Table 2-16. Average Weekly Earnings of Production Workers on Nonfarm Payrolls, by Industry, in Current and 1982–1984 Dollars, NAICS Basis, 2000–2010

(Dollars.)

Industry	2000	2001	2002	2003	2004	2005	2006	2007	2008	2009	2010
TOTAL PRIVATE											
Current dollars	481.01	493.79	506.75	518.06	529.09	544.33	567.87	590.04	607.95	617.18	636.91
1982–1984 dollars	284.79	284.61	288.09	288.13	286.77	284.99	288.11	290.99	288.06	294.41	297.67
Goods-Producing											
Current dollars	621.86	630.01	651.61	669.13	688.13	705.31	730.16	757.34	776.66	779.68	819.18
1982–1984 dollars	368.18	363.12	370.44	372.15	372.97	369.27	370.45	373.50	367.99	371.93	382.85
Mining and logging											
Current dollars	734.92	757.92	741.97	765.94	803.82	853.71	907.95	962.64	1 014.69	1 006.67	1 063.28
1982–1984 dollars	435.12	436.84	421.81	426.00	435.67	446.97	460.65	474.75	480.77	480.21	496.94
Construction											
Current dollars	685.78	695.89	711.82	726.83	735.55	750.22	781.21	816.66	842.61	851.76	891.85
1982–1984 dollars	406.03	401.09	404.67	404.24	398.67	392.79	396.35	402.76	399.24	406.32	416.82
Manufacturing											
Current dollars	590.77	595.19	618.75	635.99	658.49	673.30	691.02	711.56	724.46	726.12	765.08
1982–1984 dollars	349.78	343.05	351.76	353.72	356.91	352.51	350.59	350.92	343.26	346.38	357.57
Private Service-Providing											
Current dollars	445.74	461.08	473.80	484.68	494.22	509.58	532.78	554.89	574.35	588.20	606.11
1982–1984 dollars	263.91	265.75	269.36	269.57	267.87	266.80	270.31	273.66	272.14	280.59	283.27
Trade, transportation, and utilities											
Current dollars	449.88	459.53	471.27	481.14	488.42	498.43	514.34	526.07	536.06	541.88	559.62
1982–1984 dollars	266.36	264.86	267.92	267.60	264.73	260.96	260.95	259.45	253.99	258.49	261.55
Wholesale trade											
Current dollars	631.40	643.45	644.38	657.29	667.09	685.00	718.63	748.94	769.62	784.49	816.15
1982–1984 dollars	373.83	370.86	366.33	365.57	361.57	358.64	364.60	369.36	364.66	374.23	381.44
Retail trade											
Current dollars	333.38	346.16	360.81	367.15	371.13	377.58	383.02	385.11	386.21	388.57	399.74
1982–1984 dollars	197.38	199.52	205.12	204.20	201.15	197.69	194.33	189.93	182.99	185.36	186.82
Transportation and warehousing											
Current dollars	562.31	562.70	579.88	598.41	614.96	618.58	636.97	654.95	670.37	677.56	710.63
1982–1984 dollars	332.92	324.32	329.66	332.82	333.31	323.86	323.17	323.01	317.63	323.22	332.12
Utilities											
Current dollars	955.66	977.18	979.09	1 017.27	1 048.44	1 095.90	1 135.34	1 182.65	1 230.69	1 239.37	1 263.33
1982–1984 dollars	565.81	563.22	556.62	565.78	568.26	573.77	576.02	583.26	583.12	591.22	590.43
Information											
Current dollars	700.86	730.88	737.77	760.45	777.25	805.08	850.42	874.65	908.99	931.08	938.89
1982–1984 dollars	414.96	421.26	419.43	422.94	421.27	421.51	431.47	431.36	430.69	444.15	438.80
Financial activities											
Current dollars	537.37	557.92	575.54	609.08	622.87	644.99	672.21	705.13	727.07	752.03	776.82
1982–1984 dollars	318.16	321.57	327.20	338.75	337.60	337.69	341.05	347.75	344.50	358.74	363.06
Professional and business services											
Current dollars	535.07	557.84	574.66	587.02	597.56	618.87	662.27	700.82	737.70	775.81	798.59
1982–1984 dollars	316.80	321.52	326.70	326.48	323.88	324.02	336.01	345.63	349.53	370.09	373.23
Education and health services											
Current dollars	449.29	473.39	492.74	505.69	523.78	544.59	564.94	590.09	613.73	628.45	646.52
1982–1984 dollars	266.01	272.85	280.13	281.25	283.89	285.13	286.63	291.02	290.79	299.79	302.16
Leisure and hospitality											
Current dollars	217.20	220.73	227.17	230.42	234.86	241.36	250.34	265.52	273.39	275.95	280.87
1982–1984 dollars	128.60	127.22	129.15	128.15	127.30	126.37	127.01	130.95	129.54	131.64	131.27
Other services											
Current dollars	413.41	428.64	439.76	434.41	433.04	443.37	456.50	477.06	495.57	506.26	524.01
1982–1984 dollars	244.77	247.05	250.01	241.61	234.71	232.13	231.61	235.27	234.81	241.50	244.90

Table 2-17. Average Weekly Earnings of All Employees on Total Private Payrolls, by State, NAICS Basis, 2007–2010

(Dollars.)

State	2007	2008	2009	2010
UNITED STATES	725.22	744.80	753.18	770.74
Alabama	708.94	704.16	686.83	697.09
Alaska	876.85	882.85	867.65	842.61
Arizona	698.37	720.01	766.64	780.03
Arkansas	569.45	605.79	621.76	630.99
California	851.81	844.74	860.89	897.26
Colorado	807.24	828.24	815.65	816.00
Connecticut	912.04	942.14	917.73	935.06
Delaware	753.91	768.27	729.21	738.08
District of Columbia	1 217.50	1 158.85	1 138.73	1 203.14
Florida	728.53	739.20	756.35	758.98
Georgia	727.31	733.18	729.37	748.48
Hawaii	674.17	678.08	686.08	710.12
Idaho	566.29	594.27	647.14	704.51
Illinois	789.14	777.58	792.92	796.02
Indiana	707.87	710.50	711.38	722.01
Iowa	615.94	620.23	668.33	694.96
Kansas	681.51	700.52	690.16	684.73
Kentucky	652.46	654.13	666.23	684.82
Louisiana	670.53	701.53	702.51	713.58
Maine	640.91	650.33	638.03	657.41
Maryland	836.59	852.23	876.99	892.40
Massachusetts	873.35	889.01	901.82	911.57
Michigan	752.10	739.40	728.94	750.16
Minnesota	781.79	778.21	763.17	787.05
Mississippi	587.62	601.28	632.60	648.00
Missouri	680.43	709.67	709.87	718.34
Montana	633.68	595.29	619.63	658.19
Nebraska	667.32	666.92	680.40	712.35
Nevada	732.57	730.75	702.20	659.99
New Hampshire	734.60	743.25	742.29	760.64
New Jersey	844.56	850.75	870.91	877.45
New Mexico	642.52	663.04	664.09	684.95
New York	861.37	868.87	868.66	883.43
North Carolina	669.90	682.57	695.94	702.46
North Dakota	605.22	607.50	614.72	660.21
Ohio	685.46	681.73	658.35	677.04
Oklahoma	606.55	618.77	634.26	683.16
Oregon	704.86	707.43	708.16	724.42
Pennsylvania	678.37	688.49	684.75	706.29
Rhode Island	742.70	767.25	763.43	768.51
South Carolina	675.36	669.28	665.20	692.17
South Dakota	543.51	543.84	597.40	628.85
Tennessee	671.05	682.88	687.10	703.88
Texas	769.06	773.19	755.07	766.82
Utah	747.21	730.06	804.78	863.01
Vermont	696.32	734.44	764.18	786.94
Virginia	790.59	780.85	781.27	833.32
Washington	853.91	872.96	905.41	921.69
West Virginia	599.81	623.04	622.30	650.89
Wisconsin	672.81	682.11	680.06	700.28
Wyoming	725.09	764.46	749.74	770.41

NOTES AND DEFINITIONS

QUARTERLY CENSUS OF EMPLOYMENT AND WAGES

The Quarterly Census of Employment and Wages (QCEW), often referred to as the ES-202 program, is a cooperative endeavor of the Bureau of Labor Statistics (BLS) and the State Employment Security Agencies (SESAs). Using quarterly data submitted by the agencies, BLS summarizes the employment and wage data for workers covered by state unemployment insurance laws and civilian workers covered by the Unemployment Compensation for Federal Employees (UCFE) program.

Since the introduction of 2001 data, the QCEW data have been coded according to the North American Classification System, either NAICS 2002, which was used for the data up through 2006, or NAICS 2007 which will be used for data for the period from 2007 forward. NAICS is the statistical classification standard underlying all establishment-based federal economic statistics classified by industry. Before 2001, QCEW data were coded according to the Standard Industrial Classification (SIC) system. Due to the differences in the classification systems, data coded according to NAICS are often not directly comparable to SIC coded data.

Most industry definitions remained the same under NAICS 2007 as they were under NAICS 2002. However, there were a few industries with substantial changes. As QCEW data coded to the NAICS 2007 system become available, users will need to exercise caution in making comparisons that span the transition.

The QCEW data series is the most complete universe of employment and wage information by industry, county, and state. It includes 98 percent of all wage and salary civilian employment. These data serve as the basic source of benchmark information for employment by industry in the Current Employment Statistics (CES) survey, which is described in the first section of notes in this chapter. Therefore, the entire employment series is not presented here. The wage series is presented because the CES provides earnings for production and nonsupervisory employees only. The QCEW is more comprehensive. BLS aggregates the data by industry and ownership; these aggregations are available at the national, state, county, and metropolitan statistical area (MSA) levels.

Collection and Coverage

Employment data under the QCEW program represent the number of covered workers who worked during, or received pay for, the pay period including the 12th of the month. Excluded are members of the armed forces, the self-employed, proprietors, domestic workers, unpaid family workers, and railroad workers covered by the railroad unemployment insurance system. Wages represent total compensation paid during the calendar quarter, regardless of when services were performed. Included in wages are pay for vacation and other paid leave, bonuses, stock options, tips, the cash value of meals and lodging, and in some states, contributions to deferred compensation plans (such as 401(k) plans). The QCEW program does provide partial information on agricultural industries and employees in private households.

Data from the QCEW program serve as an important input to many BLS programs. The QCEW data are used as the benchmark source for employment by the Current Employment Statistics program and the Occupational employment statistics program. The UI administrative records collected under the QCEW program serve as a sampling frame for BLS establishment surveys.

In addition, data from the QCEW program serve as an input to other federal and state programs. The Bureau of Economic Analysis (BEA) of the Department of Commerce uses QCEW data as the base for developing the wage and salary component of personal income. The Employment and Training Administration (ETA) of the Department of Labor and the SESAs use QCEW data to administer the employment security program. The QCEW data accurately reflect the extent of coverage of the state UI laws and are used to measure UI revenues; national, state and local area employment; and total and UI taxable wage trends.

Sources of Additional Information

Additional information is available on the BLS Web site at <http://www.bls.gov/cew>.

Table 2-18. Employment and Average Annual Pay for Covered Workers,[1] by Industry, NAICS Basis, 2005–2010

(Number, dollars.)

Industry	2005		2006		2007	
	Employment	Average annual pay	Employment	Average annual pay	Employment	Average annual pay
Total Private	110 611 016	40 505	112 718 858	42 414	114 012 221	44 362
Natural resources and mining	1 724 044	39 080	1 776 777	42 904	1 826 609	45 733
Agriculture, forestry, fishing, and hunting	1 163 629	23 117	1 160 179	24 132	1 166 333	25 191
Construction	7 269 317	42 100	7 602 148	44 496	7 562 732	46 784
Manufacturing	14 190 394	49 287	14 110 663	51 427	13 833 022	53 489
Wholesale trade	5 752 802	55 262	5 885 194	58 046	5 987 206	60 719
Retail trade	15 256 340	24 930	15 370 040	25 567	15 509 017	26 124
Transportation and warehousing	4 098 553	39 515	4 204 514	40 848	4 292 445	42 615
Utilities	550 593	75 208	546 521	78 341	549 539	82 275
Information	3 056 431	62 853	3 040 577	65 962	3 029 789	69 140
Financial activities	8 037 850	64 398	8 162 063	68 901	8 145 981	73 980
Professional and business services	16 869 852	49 574	17 469 679	51 974	17 859 796	55 139
Education and health services	16 479 482	37 654	16 916 228	39 115	17 433 162	40 528
Leisure and hospitality	12 739 466	17 068	13 024 615	17 781	13 327 559	18 495
Other services	4 324 015	25 883	4 364 889	26 923	4 438 439	27 970
Total Government	20 960 607	41 585	21 114 976	43 180	21 353 885	44 968
Federal	2 733 675	59 864	2 728 974	62 274	2 726 300	64 871
State	4 527 514	42 249	4 565 908	43 875	4 611 395	45 903
Local	13 699 418	37 718	13 820 093	39 179	14 016 190	40 790

Industry	2008		2009		2010	
	Employment	Average annual pay	Employment	Average annual pay	Employment	Average annual pay
Total Private	113 188 643	45 371	106 947 104	45 155	106 201 232	46 455
Natural resources and mining	1 882 426	49 170	1 783 558	47 425	1 798 592	49 820
Agriculture, forestry, fishing, and hunting	1 169 029	25 986	1 142 192	26 031	1 146 962	26 636
Construction	7 124 886	49 013	5 948 837	49 322	5 489 499	49 597
Manufacturing	13 382 697	54 400	11 810 371	54 873	11 487 496	57 526
Wholesale trade	5 954 915	61 843	5 561 787	61 595	5 466 463	63 629
Retail trade	15 307 933	26 179	14 544 111	26 162	14 481 324	26 652
Transportation and warehousing	4 271 969	42 962	3 985 037	42 823	3 943 659	44 197
Utilities	557 983	84 153	560 713	84 877	551 287	86 791
Information	2 989 161	70 787	2 807 721	71 191	2 703 886	74 395
Financial activities	7 968 376	74 133	7 589 821	70 045	7 401 812	73 977
Professional and business services	17 705 280	57 476	16 488 835	58 344	16 712 011	60 145
Education and health services	17 954 103	41 984	18 321 635	43 042	18 656 160	43 604
Leisure and hospitality	13 395 477	18 946	13 001 028	18 899	13 006 814	19 387
Other services	4 484 907	28 773	4 369 780	28 814	4 349 563	29 370
Total Government	21 617 017	46 568	21 660 738	47 552	21 619 210	48 202
Federal	2 762 055	66 293	2 826 713	67 756	2 980 813	69 198
State	4 642 650	47 980	4 639 715	48 742	4 606 001	48 960
Local	14 212 311	42 274	14 194 311	43 140	14 032 396	43 493

[1]Includes workers covered by unemployment insurance (UI) and Unemployment Compensation for Federal Employees (UCFE) programs.

Table 2-19. Employment and Average Annual Pay for Covered Workers,[1] by State and Selected Territory, 2005–2010

(Number, dollars.)

State	2005		2006		2007	
	Employment	Average annual pay	Employment	Average annual pay	Employment	Average annual pay
UNITED STATES	131 571 623	40 677	133 833 834	42 535	135 366 106	44 458
Alabama	1 894 616	34 598	1 928 281	36 204	1 952 091	37 492
Alaska	302 330	40 216	307 637	41 750	310 810	43 972
Arizona	2 489 462	38 154	2 614 344	40 019	2 647 691	41 551
Arkansas	1 147 615	31 266	1 167 925	32 389	1 173 852	34 118
California	15 234 188	46 211	15 503 144	48 345	15 640 575	50 538
Colorado	2 189 516	41 601	2 242 012	43 506	2 292 630	45 396
Connecticut	1 644 274	52 954	1 672 109	54 814	1 686 043	58 029
Delaware	417 692	44 622	422 187	46 285	423 412	47 308
District of Columbia	667 512	66 696	671 143	70 151	678 119	73 450
Florida	7 747 729	36 800	7 952 023	38 485	7 945 162	39 746
Georgia	3 932 315	39 096	4 024 699	40 370	4 077 184	42 178
Hawaii	603 668	36 353	618 178	37 799	625 862	39 466
Idaho	614 548	30 777	643 671	32 580	660 683	33 544
Illinois	5 748 355	43 744	5 821 022	45 650	5 869 157	47 685
Indiana	2 873 795	35 431	2 892 419	36 553	2 905 725	37 528
Iowa	1 446 568	33 070	1 470 742	34 320	1 485 627	35 738
Kansas	1 305 440	33 864	1 327 677	35 696	1 356 966	37 044
Kentucky	1 757 997	33 965	1 779 202	35 201	1 801 907	36 480
Louisiana	1 841 046	33 566	1 807 563	36 604	1 868 986	38 229
Maine	594 481	32 701	598 525	33 794	602 321	35 129
Maryland	2 497 487	44 368	2 530 011	46 162	2 547 351	48 241
Massachusetts	3 159 934	50 095	3 194 914	52 435	3 234 357	55 244
Michigan	4 297 017	41 214	4 235 650	42 157	4 179 122	43 357
Minnesota	2 640 326	40 800	2 670 222	42 185	2 687 482	44 375
Mississippi	1 111 269	29 763	1 122 474	31 194	1 135 336	32 291
Missouri	2 664 447	35 951	2 699 860	37 143	2 719 380	38 603
Montana	413 460	29 150	426 182	30 596	436 656	32 224
Nebraska	892 397	32 422	902 383	33 814	916 580	35 238
Nevada	1 215 783	38 763	1 271 634	40 070	1 284 502	42 149
New Hampshire	620 893	40 551	627 371	42 447	630 204	43 863
New Jersey	3 917 397	49 471	3 951 210	51 645	3 961 341	53 853
New Mexico	778 233	32 605	807 063	34 567	821 484	36 379
New York	8 348 739	51 937	8 429 519	55 479	8 554 012	59 439
North Carolina	3 856 748	35 912	3 965 479	37 439	4 062 955	38 909
North Dakota	328 097	29 956	335 718	31 316	341 705	33 086
Ohio	5 308 808	37 333	5 314 572	38 568	5 306 812	39 917
Oklahoma	1 465 969	31 721	1 507 196	34 022	1 534 802	35 491
Oregon	1 652 773	36 588	1 699 932	38 077	1 727 886	39 569
Pennsylvania	5 552 301	39 661	5 607 139	41 349	5 652 547	43 239
Rhode Island	477 420	38 751	480 570	40 454	480 132	41 646
South Carolina	1 819 217	32 927	1 855 842	34 281	1 891 255	35 393
South Dakota	375 707	29 149	383 876	30 291	392 060	31 655
Tennessee	2 685 491	35 879	2 728 694	37 564	2 745 099	39 082
Texas	9 583 457	40 150	9 922 313	42 458	10 231 906	44 695
Utah	1 115 375	33 328	1 170 587	35 130	1 219 207	37 054
Vermont	300 919	34 197	303 205	35 542	303 448	36 956
Virginia	3 578 558	42 287	3 636 417	44 051	3 672 958	45 995
Washington	2 766 451	40 721	2 850 073	42 897	2 925 908	45 021
West Virginia	695 382	31 347	705 189	32 728	706 172	34 106
Wisconsin	2 744 006	35 471	2 767 141	36 821	2 780 924	38 050
Wyoming	254 418	33 251	266 894	36 662	277 721	39 254
Puerto Rico	1 048 004	22 859	1 036 802	23 707	1 016 362	24 741
Virgin Islands	44 464	44 464	45 114	45 114	45 922	45 922

[1]Includes workers covered by the unemployment insurance (UI) and Unemployment Compensation for Federal Employees (UCFE) programs.

Table 2-19. Employment and Average Annual Pay for Covered Workers,[1] by State and Selected Territory, 2005–2010—*Continued*

(Number, dollars.)

State	2008 Employment	2008 Average annual pay	2009 Employment	2009 Average annual pay	2010 Employment	2010 Average annual pay
UNITED STATES	134 805 659	45 563	128 607 842	45 559	127 820 442	46 751
Alabama	1 936 489	38 734	1 829 487	39 422	1 813 155	40 289
Alaska	315 285	45 805	313 802	47 103	316 691	48 230
Arizona	2 583 215	42 518	2 396 362	42 832	2 356 789	43 299
Arkansas	1 172 208	34 919	1 134 488	35 692	1 134 071	36 254
California	15 494 915	51 487	14 629 953	51 566	14 414 461	53 285
Colorado	2 310 865	46 614	2 201 427	46 861	2 176 986	47 868
Connecticut	1 687 902	58 395	1 615 356	57 771	1 595 713	59 465
Delaware	423 083	47 569	402 343	47 770	399 078	48 669
District of Columbia	685 069	76 518	681 875	77 483	693 274	80 200
Florida	7 666 374	40 568	7 182 815	40 970	7 109 630	41 581
Georgia	4 031 467	42 585	3 796 429	42 902	3 753 934	43 899
Hawaii	619 703	40 675	592 171	41 328	586 772	41 709
Idaho	653 108	33 897	613 814	34 124	605 571	34 900
Illinois	5 841 692	48 719	5 551 930	48 358	5 502 322	49 497
Indiana	2 872 442	38 403	2 705 331	38 270	2 709 831	39 256
Iowa	1 490 575	36 964	1 445 627	37 158	1 436 340	38 146
Kansas	1 366 878	38 178	1 317 029	38 154	1 297 779	38 936
Kentucky	1 791 017	37 434	1 710 677	37 996	1 712 178	38 720
Louisiana	1 890 007	40 381	1 849 303	40 579	1 832 357	41 461
Maine	602 074	36 317	581 796	36 617	577 790	37 338
Maryland	2 537 752	49 535	2 461 109	50 579	2 453 197	51 739
Massachusetts	3 245 983	56 746	3 135 497	56 267	3 149 169	57 770
Michigan	4 070 914	44 245	3 775 435	43 645	3 770 225	44 439
Minnesota	2 679 527	45 826	2 569 651	45 319	2 558 310	46 787
Mississippi	1 131 096	33 508	1 081 138	33 847	1 074 617	34 343
Missouri	2 715 183	40 361	2 607 595	40 022	2 573 703	40 679
Montana	437 591	33 305	421 566	33 762	419 231	34 595
Nebraska	922 929	36 243	901 470	36 644	896 936	37 324
Nevada	1 252 987	42 984	1 138 036	42 743	1 108 238	42 512
New Hampshire	628 763	44 912	605 004	44 932	600 697	45 957
New Jersey	3 934 789	55 280	3 771 296	55 168	3 735 703	56 382
New Mexico	825 736	37 910	791 509	38 529	781 694	39 264
New York	8 608 351	60 288	8 343 862	57 739	8 340 732	60 291
North Carolina	4 043 486	39 740	3 823 299	39 844	3 788 581	41 119
North Dakota	350 440	35 075	349 560	35 970	358 635	38 128
Ohio	5 235 972	40 784	4 943 970	40 900	4 908 571	41 788
Oklahoma	1 550 489	37 284	1 497 855	37 238	1 485 400	38 237
Oregon	1 713 764	40 500	1 607 915	40 757	1 598 173	41 675
Pennsylvania	5 658 771	44 381	5 468 176	44 829	5 472 171	45 733
Rhode Island	469 701	43 029	448 842	43 439	447 408	44 645
South Carolina	1 876 081	36 252	1 765 739	36 759	1 758 204	37 553
South Dakota	397 108	32 822	389 360	33 352	389 198	34 331
Tennessee	2 721 990	39 996	2 565 288	40 242	2 558 438	41 572
Texas	10 452 907	45 939	10 149 694	45 692	10 182 150	46 952
Utah	1 221 052	37 980	1 157 704	38 614	1 150 737	39 389
Vermont	302 627	38 328	292 406	38 778	293 058	39 434
Virginia	3 665 654	47 241	3 545 623	48 239	3 536 676	49 651
Washington	2 950 773	46 569	2 836 283	47 470	2 808 698	48 516
West Virginia	709 657	35 987	691 998	36 897	692 448	37 675
Wisconsin	2 772 889	39 119	2 644 190	39 131	2 633 572	39 966
Wyoming	286 333	41 487	274 758	40 709	271 151	41 963
Puerto Rico	1 001 120	25 554	954 555	26 359	930 319	26 617
Virgin Islands	45 796	45 796	43 799	43 799	44 267	38 936

[1]Includes workers covered by the unemployment insurance (UI) and Unemployment Compensation for Federal Employees (UCFE) programs.

BUSINESS EMPLOYMENT DYNAMICS

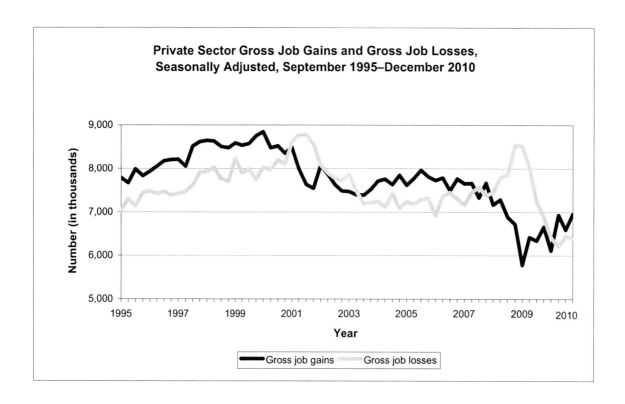

The change in the number of jobs is the net result of the gross increase in the number of jobs from expanding and opening establishments and the gross decrease in jobs from contracting and closing establishments. The net gain of 563,000 jobs in the fourth quarter of 2010 resulted from 6.954 million gross job gains and 6.391 million gross job losses. There was a net loss of jobs in nine consecutive quarters from the first quarter in 2008 through the first quarter in March 2010. However, in the last three quarters in 2010, there was a net gain. (See Table 2-20.)

OTHER HIGHLIGHTS

- Of 6.391 million job losses in the fourth quarter of 2010, nearly 81 percent resulted from contracting establishments while 19.2 percent were the result of establishments closing. (See Table 2-20.)

- In the fourth quarter of 2010, the service-providing industries experienced a net job gain of 613,000 while the goods-producing industries suffered a net job loss of 50,000. (See Table 2-22.)

- In professional and business services, gross job gains exceeded gross job losses by 193,000 in the fourth quarter of 2010—higher than in any other sector. (Table 2-22.)

- Gross job losses exceeded gross job losses in eight states in December 2010 including: Michigan (-6.4 million), Rhode Island (-2.0 million), Arkansas (-1.8 million), Maine (-1.3 million), Minnesota (-1.2 million), West Virginia (-1.1 million), Delaware (-520,000) and Alaska (-505,000). (See Table 2-23.)

NOTES AND DEFINITIONS

BUSINESS EMPLOYMENT DYNAMICS (BED)

The Business Employment Dynamics (BED) data are a set of statistics generated from the federal-state cooperative program known as the Quarterly Census of Employment and Wages (QCEW), or the ES-202 program. These quarterly data series consist of gross job gains and gross job losses statistics from 1992 forward.

The Bureau of Labor Statistics (BLS) compiles the BED data from existing quarterly state unemployment insurance (UI) records. Most employers in the United States are required to file quarterly reports on the employment and wages of workers covered by UI laws and to pay quarterly UI taxes. The quarterly UI reports are sent by the State Workforce Agencies (SWAs) to BLS. These reports form the basis of the BLS establishment universe-sampling frame.

In the BED program, the quarterly UI records are linked across quarters to provide a longitudinal history for each establishment. The linkage process allows the tracking of net employment changes at the establishment level, which in turn allows estimations of jobs gained at opening and expanding establishments and of jobs lost at closing and contracting establishments. BLS publishes three different establishment-based employment measures for every given quarter. Each of these measures—the Current Employment Statistics (CES) survey, the QCEW program, and the BED data each make use of the quarterly UI employment reports. However, each measure has somewhat different types of universal coverage, estimation procedures, and publication products. (See the notes and corresponding tables for CES and QCEW in earlier sections of this chapter.)

Concepts and Definitions

The BED data measure the net change in employment at the establishment level. These changes can come about in four different ways. A net increase in employment can come from either opening establishments or expanding establishments. A net decrease in employment can come from either closing establishments or contracting establishments.

Gross job gains include the sum of all jobs added at either opening or expanding establishments.

Gross job losses include the sum of all jobs lost in either closing or contracting establishments. The net change in employment is the difference between gross job gains and gross job losses.

Openings consist of establishments with positive third-month employment for the first time in the current quarter, with no links to the prior quarter, or with positive third-month employment in the current quarter, following zero employment in the previous quarter.

Expansions include establishments with positive employment in the third month in both the previous and current quarters, with a net increase in employment over this period.

Closings consist of establishments with positive third-month employment in the previous quarter, with no employment or zero employment reported in the current quarter.

Contractions include establishments with positive employment in the third month in both the previous and current quarters, with a net decrease in employment over this period.

Sources of Additional Information

For additional information, see BLS news release 11-1149, "Business Employment Dynamics: Fourth Quarter 2010." An extensive article on the BED data appeared in the April 2004 edition of the *Monthly Labor Review*. These resources can be found on the BLS Web site at <http://www.bls.gov>.

Table 2-20. Private Sector Gross Job Gains and Job Losses, Seasonally Adjusted, March 1995–December 2010

(Thousands of jobs.)

Year and month	Net change[1]	Gross job gains			Gross job losses		
		Total	Expanding establishments	Opening establishments	Total	Contracting establishments	Closing establishments
1995							
March	758	7 787	6 124	1 663	7 029	5 652	1 377
June	358	7 666	6 006	1 660	7 308	5 840	1 468
September	845	7 983	6 341	1 642	7 138	5 645	1 493
December	378	7 830	6 140	1 690	7 452	5 929	1 523
1996							
March	457	7 933	6 179	1 754	7 476	5 967	1 509
June	631	8 051	6 282	1 769	7 420	5 903	1 517
September	704	8 177	6 373	1 804	7 473	5 942	1 531
December	816	8 206	6 396	1 810	7 390	5 875	1 515
1997							
March	784	8 214	6 407	1 807	7 430	5 886	1 544
June	584	8 055	6 330	1 725	7 471	5 931	1 540
September	901	8 515	6 718	1 797	7 614	5 927	1 687
December	708	8 617	6 697	1 920	7 909	6 024	1 885
1998							
March	711	8 648	6 599	2 049	7 937	6 077	1 860
June	610	8 629	6 552	2 077	8 019	6 224	1 795
September	742	8 508	6 607	1 901	7 766	6 093	1 673
December	768	8 475	6 737	1 738	7 707	6 025	1 682
1999							
March	353	8 585	6 626	1 959	8 232	6 395	1 837
June	644	8 539	6 661	1 878	7 895	6 210	1 685
September	588	8 571	6 734	1 837	7 983	6 250	1 733
December	1 005	8 749	6 956	1 793	7 744	6 076	1 668
2000							
March	827	8 849	6 960	1 889	8 022	6 342	1 680
June	503	8 479	6 794	1 685	7 976	6 373	1 603
September	324	8 525	6 756	1 769	8 201	6 479	1 722
December	251	8 351	6 673	1 678	8 100	6 444	1 656
2001							
March	-119	8 491	6 728	1 763	8 610	6 717	1 893
June	-780	7 991	6 302	1 689	8 771	7 036	1 735
September	-1 148	7 630	5 945	1 685	8 778	6 990	1 788
December	-1 009	7 547	5 912	1 635	8 556	6 870	1 686
2002							
March	-10	8 071	6 298	1 773	8 081	6 434	1 647
June	-30	7 868	6 145	1 723	7 898	6 274	1 624
September	-151	7 630	6 039	1 591	7 781	6 248	1 533
December	-241	7 483	5 938	1 545	7 724	6 185	1 539
2003							
March	-393	7 467	5 928	1 539	7 860	6 307	1 553
June	-90	7 398	5 929	1 469	7 488	6 030	1 458
September	204	7 392	5 923	1 469	7 188	5 828	1 360
December	297	7 521	6 005	1 516	7 224	5 800	1 424
2004							
March	470	7 715	6 204	1 511	7 245	5 795	1 450
June	644	7 754	6 235	1 519	7 110	5 639	1 471
September	206	7 633	6 060	1 573	7 427	5 888	1 539
December	757	7 844	6 243	1 601	7 087	5 663	1 424
2005							
March	384	7 620	6 131	1 489	7 236	5 801	1 435
June	593	7 774	6 231	1 543	7 181	5 776	1 405
September	677	7 965	6 387	1 578	7 288	5 844	1 444
December	494	7 807	6 252	1 555	7 313	5 948	1 365
2006							
March	806	7 726	6 293	1 433	6 920	5 635	1 285
June	424	7 789	6 273	1 516	7 365	5 998	1 367
September	45	7 495	6 057	1 438	7 450	6 098	1 352
December	462	7 765	6 241	1 524	7 303	5 954	1 349
2007							
March	491	7 657	6 243	1 414	7 166	5 870	1 296
June	207	7 661	6 250	1 411	7 454	6 056	1 398
September	-249	7 328	5 855	1 473	7 577	6 223	1 354
December	286	7 670	6 197	1 473	7 384	6 028	1 356
2008							
March	-275	7 172	5 778	1 394	7 447	6 083	1 364
June	-520	7 285	5 878	1 407	7 805	6 332	1 473
September	-966	6 888	5 521	1 367	7 854	6 469	1 385
December	-1 814	6 720	5 357	1 363	8 534	7 041	1 493
2009							
March	-2 741	5 783	4 611	1 172	8 524	7 109	1 415
June	-1 604	6 421	5 117	1 304	8 025	6 644	1 381
September	-900	6 341	5 124	1 217	7 241	5 883	1 358
December	-228	6 662	5 326	1 336	6 890	5 598	1 292
2010							
March	-311	6 110	4 996	1 114	6 421	5 231	1 190
June	728	6 935	5 682	1 253	6 207	5 064	1 143
September	151	6 593	5 388	1 205	6 442	5 226	1 216
December	563	6 954	5 609	1 345	6 391	5 162	1 229

[1]Net change is the difference between total gross job gains and total gross job losses.

Table 2-21. Private Sector Gross Job Gains and Job Losses, as a Percent of Employment,[1] Seasonally Adjusted, March 1995–December 2010

(Percent.)

Year and month	Net change[2]	Gross job gains			Gross job losses		
		Total	Expanding establishments	Opening establishments	Total	Contracting establishments	Closing establishments
1995							
March	0.8	8.1	6.4	1.7	7.3	5.9	1.4
June	0.3	7.9	6.2	1.7	7.6	6.1	1.5
September	0.9	8.2	6.5	1.7	7.3	5.8	1.5
December	0.3	8.0	6.3	1.7	7.7	6.1	1.6
1996							
March	0.5	8.1	6.3	1.8	7.6	6.1	1.5
June	0.7	8.2	6.4	1.8	7.5	6.0	1.5
September	0.7	8.2	6.4	1.8	7.5	6.0	1.5
December	0.8	8.2	6.4	1.8	7.4	5.9	1.5
1997							
March	0.9	8.2	6.4	1.8	7.3	5.8	1.5
June	0.6	7.9	6.2	1.7	7.3	5.8	1.5
September	1.0	8.4	6.6	1.8	7.4	5.8	1.6
December	0.8	8.4	6.5	1.9	7.6	5.8	1.8
1998							
March	0.7	8.4	6.4	2.0	7.7	5.9	1.8
June	0.6	8.3	6.3	2.0	7.7	6.0	1.7
September	0.7	8.1	6.3	1.8	7.4	5.8	1.6
December	0.7	8.0	6.4	1.6	7.3	5.7	1.6
1999							
March	0.3	8.0	6.2	1.8	7.7	6.0	1.7
June	0.6	8.0	6.2	1.8	7.4	5.8	1.6
September	0.6	8.0	6.3	1.7	7.4	5.8	1.6
December	1.0	8.1	6.4	1.7	7.1	5.6	1.5
2000							
March	0.8	8.1	6.4	1.7	7.3	5.8	1.5
June	0.4	7.7	6.2	1.5	7.3	5.8	1.5
September	0.2	7.7	6.1	1.6	7.5	5.9	1.6
December	0.2	7.5	6.0	1.5	7.3	5.8	1.5
2001							
March	-0.1	7.7	6.1	1.6	7.8	6.1	1.7
June	-0.8	7.2	5.7	1.5	8.0	6.4	1.6
September	-1.1	6.9	5.4	1.5	8.0	6.4	1.6
December	-1.0	7.0	5.5	1.5	8.0	6.4	1.6
2002							
March	0.0	7.5	5.9	1.6	7.5	6.0	1.5
June	0.0	7.3	5.7	1.6	7.3	5.8	1.5
September	-0.1	7.1	5.6	1.5	7.2	5.8	1.4
December	-0.3	6.9	5.5	1.4	7.2	5.8	1.4
2003							
March	-0.5	6.9	5.5	1.4	7.4	5.9	1.5
June	0.0	7.0	5.6	1.4	7.0	5.6	1.4
September	0.1	6.9	5.5	1.4	6.8	5.5	1.3
December	0.3	7.0	5.6	1.4	6.7	5.4	1.3
2004							
March	0.5	7.2	5.8	1.4	6.7	5.4	1.3
June	0.6	7.2	5.8	1.4	6.6	5.2	1.4
September	0.3	7.1	5.6	1.5	6.8	5.4	1.4
December	0.7	7.2	5.7	1.5	6.5	5.2	1.3
2005							
March	0.4	7.0	5.6	1.4	6.6	5.3	1.3
June	0.6	7.1	5.7	1.4	6.5	5.2	1.3
September	0.6	7.2	5.8	1.4	6.6	5.3	1.3
December	0.4	7.0	5.6	1.4	6.6	5.4	1.2
2006							
March	0.8	6.9	5.6	1.3	6.1	5.0	1.1
June	0.4	6.9	5.6	1.3	6.5	5.3	1.2
September	0.1	6.7	5.4	1.3	6.6	5.4	1.2
December	0.3	6.8	5.5	1.3	6.5	5.3	1.2
2007							
March	0.4	6.7	5.5	1.2	6.3	5.2	1.1
June	0.2	6.7	5.5	1.2	6.5	5.3	1.2
September	-0.3	6.4	5.1	1.3	6.7	5.5	1.2
December	0.2	6.7	5.4	1.3	6.5	5.3	1.2
2008							
March	-0.2	6.3	5.1	1.2	6.5	5.3	1.2
June	-0.5	6.4	5.2	1.2	6.9	5.6	1.3
September	-0.8	6.1	4.9	1.2	6.9	5.7	1.2
December	-1.6	6.0	4.8	1.2	7.6	6.3	1.3
2009							
March	-2.5	5.3	4.2	1.1	7.8	6.5	1.3
June	-1.5	6.0	4.8	1.2	7.5	6.2	1.3
September	-1.0	5.9	4.8	1.1	6.9	5.6	1.3
December	-0.1	6.4	5.1	1.3	6.5	5.3	1.2
2010							
March	-0.3	5.8	4.7	1.1	6.1	5.0	1.1
June	0.7	6.6	5.4	1.2	5.9	4.8	1.1
September	0.2	6.2	5.1	1.1	6.0	4.9	1.1
December	0.5	6.6	5.3	1.3	6.1	4.9	1.2

[1] The rates measure gross job gains and job losses as a percentage of the average of the previous and current employment.
[2] Net change is the difference between total gross job gains and total gross job losses.

Table 2-22. Three-Month Private Sector Job Gains and Losses, by Industry, Seasonally Adjusted, December 2009–December 2010

(Thousands of jobs.)

Industry	Gross job gains and job losses (3 months ended)					Gross job gains and losses as a percent of employment (3 months ended)				
	December 2009	March 2010	June 2010	September 2010	December 2010	December 2009	March 2010	June 2010	September 2010	December 2010
TOTAL PRIVATE[1]										
Gross job gains	6 662	6 110	6 935	6 593	6 954	6.4	5.8	6.6	6.2	6.6
Gross job losses	6 890	6 421	6 207	6 442	6 391	6.5	6.1	5.9	6.0	6.1
Net employment change	-228	-311	728	151	563	-0.1	-0.3	0.7	0.2	0.5
Goods-Producing										
Gross job gains	1 313	1 266	1 461	1 360	1 350	6.9	6.7	7.8	7.3	7.2
Gross job losses	1 590	1 459	1 305	1 315	1 400	8.4	7.8	7.0	7.0	7.4
Net employment change	-277	-193	156	45	-50	-1.5	-1.1	0.8	0.3	-0.2
Natural Resources and Mining										
Gross job gains	285	270	305	268	279	16.3	15.4	17.2	14.8	15.4
Gross job losses	292	271	235	263	277	16.7	15.4	13.2	14.5	15.2
Net employment change	-7	-1	70	5	2	-0.4	0.0	4.0	0.3	0.2
Construction										
Gross job gains	615	591	677	644	631	10.9	10.7	12.3	11.8	11.5
Gross job losses	773	728	676	647	694	13.6	13.1	12.3	11.8	12.7
Net employment change	-158	-137	1	-3	-63	-2.7	-2.4	0.0	0.0	-1.2
Manufacturing										
Gross job gains	413	405	479	448	440	3.6	3.5	4.1	3.9	3.9
Gross job losses	525	460	394	405	429	4.5	4.0	3.4	3.5	3.8
Net employment change	-112	-55	85	43	11	-0.9	-0.5	0.7	0.4	0.1
Service-Providing[1]										
Gross job gains	5 349	4 844	5 474	5 233	5 604	6.2	5.6	6.3	6.1	6.4
Gross job losses	5 300	4 962	4 902	5 127	4 991	6.2	5.8	5.7	5.9	5.7
Net employment change	49	-118	572	106	613	0.0	-0.2	0.6	0.2	0.7
Wholesale Trade										
Gross job gains	259	248	280	263	278	4.7	4.6	5.2	4.8	5.0
Gross job losses	283	274	248	259	252	5.1	5.0	4.5	4.7	4.6
Net employment change	-24	-26	32	4	26	-0.4	-0.4	0.7	0.1	0.4
Retail Trade										
Gross job gains	816	784	892	788	889	5.7	5.4	6.2	5.4	6.2
Gross job losses	936	805	769	884	807	6.5	5.6	5.3	6.1	5.5
Net employment change	-120	-21	123	-96	82	-0.8	-0.2	0.9	-0.7	0.7
Transportation and Warehousing										
Gross job gains	220	183	216	211	250	5.5	4.7	5.4	5.4	6.2
Gross job losses	222	223	189	195	192	5.7	5.6	4.8	4.9	4.8
Net employment change	-2	-40	27	16	58	-0.2	-0.9	0.6	0.5	1.4
Utilities										
Gross job gains	11	9	11	9	11	2.0	1.6	2.0	1.7	2.0
Gross job losses	14	9	12	12	10	2.5	1.6	2.2	2.2	1.8
Net employment change	-3	0	-1	-3	1	-0.5	0.0	-0.2	-0.5	0.2
Information										
Gross job gains	123	106	128	135	126	4.4	3.8	4.7	5.0	4.7
Gross job losses	144	130	129	136	131	5.2	4.7	4.7	5.0	4.9
Net employment change	-21	-24	-1	-1	-5	-0.8	-0.9	0.0	0.0	-0.2
Financial Activities										
Gross job gains	356	326	347	346	368	4.8	4.3	4.6	4.7	4.9
Gross job losses	400	369	372	369	346	5.4	5.0	5.0	5.0	4.6
Net employment change	-44	-43	-25	-23	22	-0.6	-0.7	-0.4	-0.3	0.3
Professional and Business Services										
Gross job gains	1 368	1 125	1 340	1 258	1 364	8.3	6.8	8.1	7.5	8.0
Gross job losses	1 184	1 130	1 144	1 185	1 171	7.2	6.8	6.9	7.1	6.9
Net employment change	184	-5	196	73	193	1.1	0.0	1.2	0.4	1.1
Education and Health Services										
Gross job gains	825	730	767	784	835	4.5	3.9	4.1	4.2	4.4
Gross job losses	677	690	718	729	698	3.7	3.7	3.8	3.9	3.8
Net employment change	148	40	49	55	137	0.8	0.2	0.3	0.3	0.6
Leisure and Hospitality										
Gross job gains	1 032	1 000	1 143	1 089	1 116	7.9	7.7	8.8	8.4	8.6
Gross job losses	1 141	1 037	1 043	1 062	1 097	8.8	8.0	8.0	8.2	8.4
Net employment change	-109	-37	100	27	19	-0.9	-0.3	0.8	0.2	0.2
Other Services										
Gross job gains	262	247	278	259	266	7.0	6.7	7.5	7.0	7.2
Gross job losses	272	263	253	274	266	7.3	7.1	6.8	7.3	7.1
Net employment change	-10	-16	25	-15	0	-0.3	-0.4	0.7	-0.3	0.1

[1]Includes unclassified sector, not shown separately.

Table 2-23. Private Sector Gross Job Gains and Losses, by State and Selected Territory, Seasonally Adjusted, December 2009–December 2010

(Number.)

State	Gross job gains (3 months ended)					Gross job losses (3 months ended)				
	December 2009	March 2010	June 2010	September 2010	December 2010	December 2009	March 2010	June 2010	September 2010	December 2010
UNITED STATES	6 662 000	6 110 000	6 935 000	6 593 000	6 954 000	6 890 000	6 421 000	6 207 000	6 442 000	6 391 000
Alabama	86 379	82 695	90 438	88 544	90 702	92 544	83 327	83 971	93 826	89 501
Alaska	24 288	25 078	26 302	22 312	24 643	25 288	23 147	21 772	23 678	25 148
Arizona	131 273	116 334	120 892	125 191	141 383	140 298	123 728	126 749	128 620	113 291
Arkansas	57 989	52 233	59 161	54 065	51 200	54 247	49 809	52 001	57 243	52 965
California	845 478	759 025	877 920	778 595	865 213	831 793	816 085	775 156	808 688	764 402
Colorado	122 327	117 669	134 977	123 839	130 646	132 705	124 210	125 355	123 841	119 650
Connecticut	70 946	66 227	84 589	71 786	73 898	77 470	81 300	67 402	66 409	71 286
Delaware	20 397	19 505	23 200	22 394	21 906	24 289	20 984	18 817	20 947	22 426
District of Columbia	26 592	23 480	26 793	24 765	27 063	24 332	21 514	23 153	28 738	25 329
Florida	440 522	362 571	417 808	404 527	448 586	448 286	370 546	398 220	419 712	409 980
Georgia	204 380	197 155	210 870	214 910	212 882	215 423	195 344	206 776	201 871	199 578
Hawaii	24 368	23 639	23 154	27 664	26 011	25 953	25 062	27 020	25 508	23 225
Idaho	38 431	35 560	36 170	39 190	40 627	40 220	38 578	39 976	35 182	37 883
Illinois	255 104	229 254	268 855	254 225	280 923	275 576	243 415	231 470	248 499	254 352
Indiana	134 249	129 707	144 840	138 311	144 007	135 204	125 181	130 048	129 856	131 387
Iowa	68 771	63 734	66 021	67 723	73 723	74 300	65 573	64 302	68 074	67 678
Kansas	62 377	55 897	62 950	60 969	70 888	67 646	61 303	60 033	64 595	60 301
Kentucky	89 347	77 786	86 562	82 611	92 103	86 416	83 376	80 238	81 243	80 087
Louisiana	100 019	95 060	103 774	99 254	103 225	103 173	94 395	99 189	99 829	102 496
Maine	35 430	30 442	37 089	35 485	34 589	37 779	34 497	35 250	34 301	35 896
Maryland	119 515	124 598	137 676	125 059	127 919	132 550	125 093	118 452	129 294	124 842
Massachusetts	145 704	145 413	161 032	155 260	153 871	160 961	143 996	137 623	152 522	152 222
Michigan	210 533	183 635	221 292	216 561	207 002	228 170	191 162	184 025	191 483	213 459
Minnesota	123 644	120 648	137 671	122 151	128 848	132 265	131 091	113 426	123 654	130 063
Mississippi	51 744	50 450	55 735	55 347	56 747	52 347	49 877	53 286	57 549	54 639
Missouri	122 278	123 242	131 143	128 842	126 065	132 033	129 143	129 992	124 464	122 341
Montana	27 841	25 855	26 844	27 113	27 675	29 098	27 670	26 442	24 859	27 566
Nebraska	40 153	39 893	44 594	43 235	42 866	46 789	40 899	39 950	42 344	42 597
Nevada	68 915	51 824	60 877	54 879	68 041	66 626	65 187	55 657	62 955	58 121
New Hampshire	33 650	34 318	36 515	32 944	35 973	36 107	35 737	33 092	33 520	34 008
New Jersey	196 657	176 313	224 190	191 225	204 741	210 510	193 790	190 949	197 695	195 727
New Mexico	37 662	37 821	40 218	38 901	40 319	42 496	37 739	40 379	40 590	37 219
New York	420 489	373 307	460 370	427 213	453 107	428 924	390 777	398 109	410 850	420 427
North Carolina	196 885	182 350	203 715	197 026	202 887	213 043	188 187	187 704	193 011	193 221
North Dakota	19 816	19 787	20 384	22 672	23 787	19 189	18 824	18 476	17 083	17 984
Ohio	234 522	219 390	249 715	240 319	256 936	255 910	228 984	217 712	222 822	246 148
Oklahoma	68 999	66 668	74 136	74 038	75 680	76 133	66 249	63 918	75 077	63 113
Oregon	89 357	87 342	87 560	93 583	94 073	96 934	87 279	85 849	82 215	91 616
Pennsylvania	267 074	249 634	280 379	265 581	280 004	274 524	248 312	234 954	252 791	256 214
Rhode Island	23 191	22 628	26 103	24 288	23 465	24 865	21 893	25 469	23 157	25 506
South Carolina	85 984	87 466	96 184	91 029	89 047	92 731	82 707	86 190	85 292	84 617
South Dakota	19 762	19 139	21 984	20 768	21 260	21 189	21 608	19 021	19 553	19 800
Tennessee	121 455	108 572	134 652	122 885	127 894	119 337	111 023	118 770	125 005	112 694
Texas	476 502	467 608	492 190	494 933	513 948	484 059	434 114	448 103	449 143	440 853
Utah	65 512	63 614	66 317	66 278	70 287	67 768	63 688	63 939	63 404	62 171
Vermont	19 496	15 542	17 791	18 480	19 035	18 017	17 756	20 659	16 402	16 968
Virginia	166 982	151 244	186 533	173 108	177 916	168 916	162 007	166 993	176 544	167 012
Washington	151 742	153 771	156 299	161 355	166 765	181 151	155 633	146 072	145 950	161 011
West Virginia	37 101	33 246	37 055	36 236	34 319	34 836	34 478	35 887	33 719	35 458
Wisconsin	130 553	125 693	134 910	131 286	137 195	138 015	129 422	121 104	126 228	132 336
Wyoming	16 108	17 159	17 405	19 989	18 898	18 573	18 274	17 953	16 365	18 402
Puerto Rico	45 647	38 617	37 160	39 838	44 957	41 169	44 755	43 997	40 417	36 329
Virgin Islands	2 361	2 632	2 006	2 327	2 249	1 899	1 897	2 825	1 758	1 800

Table 2-24. Private Sector Gross Job Gains and Losses as a Percent of Total Employment, by State and Selected Territory, Seasonally Adjusted, December 2009–December 2010

(Percent.)

State	Gross job gains (3 months ended)					Gross job losses (3 months ended)				
	December 2009	March 2010	June 2010	September 2010	December 2010	December 2009	March 2010	June 2010	September 2010	December 2010
UNITED STATES	6.4	5.8	6.6	6.2	6.6	6.5	6.1	5.9	6.0	6.1
Alabama	6.0	5.8	6.3	6.1	6.3	6.4	5.8	5.8	6.5	6.2
Alaska	10.3	10.6	11.1	9.4	10.3	10.8	9.8	9.2	10.0	10.6
Arizona	6.7	5.9	6.2	6.4	7.2	7.1	6.3	6.4	6.5	5.7
Arkansas	6.3	5.7	6.3	5.8	5.5	5.9	5.4	5.6	6.1	5.7
California	7.2	6.5	7.5	6.6	7.3	7.1	7.0	6.6	6.8	6.4
Colorado	6.8	6.5	7.5	6.9	7.2	7.3	6.9	7.0	6.9	6.6
Connecticut	5.3	4.9	6.3	5.3	5.4	5.7	6.0	5.0	4.9	5.3
Delaware	6.0	5.8	6.9	6.6	6.4	7.2	6.3	5.6	6.1	6.5
District of Columbia	6.0	5.3	6.0	5.6	6.1	5.5	4.9	5.2	6.5	5.7
Florida	7.3	6.1	7.0	6.7	7.4	7.4	6.2	6.6	6.9	6.8
Georgia	6.6	6.4	6.9	7.0	6.9	7.0	6.4	6.7	6.6	6.4
Hawaii	5.2	5.1	5.0	6.0	5.6	5.5	5.4	5.8	5.5	4.9
Idaho	7.8	7.2	7.4	8.0	8.2	8.1	7.8	8.2	7.2	7.7
Illinois	5.5	4.9	5.7	5.4	6.0	5.9	5.3	4.9	5.3	5.4
Indiana	5.8	5.7	6.3	6.0	6.2	5.9	5.5	5.7	5.6	5.7
Iowa	5.8	5.4	5.5	5.7	6.1	6.2	5.5	5.4	5.7	5.7
Kansas	6.0	5.4	6.0	5.9	6.7	6.5	5.8	5.7	6.2	5.7
Kentucky	6.4	5.6	6.2	5.8	6.5	6.2	5.9	5.7	5.8	5.6
Louisiana	6.7	6.4	7.0	6.7	6.9	7.0	6.4	6.7	6.7	6.9
Maine	7.4	6.4	7.8	7.5	7.2	8.0	7.3	7.4	7.2	7.5
Maryland	6.1	6.4	7.0	6.4	6.4	6.8	6.4	6.0	6.5	6.4
Massachusetts	5.5	5.4	6.0	5.7	5.7	6.0	5.4	5.1	5.7	5.6
Michigan	6.7	5.9	7.0	6.8	6.5	7.2	6.1	5.8	6.0	6.7
Minnesota	5.7	5.6	6.3	5.6	5.8	6.1	6.1	5.2	5.7	6.0
Mississippi	6.3	6.1	6.7	6.6	6.8	6.4	6.0	6.4	6.9	6.6
Missouri	5.7	5.8	6.1	6.0	5.9	6.2	6.0	6.1	5.9	5.7
Montana	8.3	7.7	8.1	8.1	8.2	8.6	8.2	7.9	7.5	8.2
Nebraska	5.5	5.4	6.0	5.9	5.8	6.3	5.6	5.4	5.7	5.8
Nevada	7.2	5.4	6.4	5.8	7.1	6.9	6.7	5.8	6.6	6.1
New Hampshire	6.6	6.7	7.1	6.4	7.0	7.0	7.0	6.5	6.5	6.6
New Jersey	6.2	5.6	7.2	6.0	6.5	6.7	6.2	6.1	6.2	6.2
New Mexico	6.3	6.4	6.8	6.6	6.8	7.1	6.4	6.8	6.9	6.3
New York	6.1	5.5	6.7	6.2	6.5	6.3	5.7	5.7	6.0	6.1
North Carolina	6.4	5.9	6.6	6.4	6.5	6.9	6.1	6.0	6.2	6.2
North Dakota	7.0	7.0	7.1	7.7	8.0	6.7	6.5	6.4	5.8	6.1
Ohio	5.6	5.3	6.0	5.7	6.1	6.2	5.5	5.3	5.4	5.9
Oklahoma	6.0	5.8	6.4	6.3	6.5	6.6	5.8	5.5	6.4	5.4
Oregon	6.8	6.7	6.7	7.1	7.2	7.4	6.6	6.6	6.3	6.9
Pennsylvania	5.7	5.3	5.9	5.6	5.9	5.9	5.3	5.0	5.3	5.4
Rhode Island	6.1	5.9	6.8	6.2	6.1	6.5	5.6	6.6	6.0	6.6
South Carolina	6.1	6.3	6.8	6.4	6.3	6.6	5.9	6.0	6.0	6.0
South Dakota	6.3	6.1	7.0	6.6	6.7	6.7	6.8	6.0	6.1	6.2
Tennessee	5.7	5.1	6.3	5.7	5.9	5.6	5.2	5.6	5.8	5.3
Texas	5.8	5.7	5.9	5.9	6.1	5.8	5.3	5.4	5.4	5.2
Utah	6.9	6.8	7.1	7.0	7.4	7.2	6.8	6.8	6.7	6.6
Vermont	8.2	6.5	7.5	7.7	7.9	7.5	7.4	8.8	6.8	7.1
Virginia	5.9	5.4	6.6	6.1	6.3	5.9	5.8	5.9	6.2	5.9
Washington	6.7	6.9	7.0	7.2	7.5	8.1	7.0	6.6	6.5	7.2
West Virginia	6.8	6.0	6.7	6.6	6.2	6.4	6.3	6.6	6.2	6.4
Wisconsin	5.9	5.6	6.1	5.9	6.1	6.2	5.8	5.5	5.7	5.9
Wyoming	7.8	8.4	8.6	9.8	9.1	9.0	8.9	8.8	8.0	8.9
Puerto Rico	6.7	5.7	5.5	6.0	6.7	6.1	6.7	6.5	6.1	5.5
Virgin Islands	7.8	8.5	6.5	7.5	7.1	6.3	6.1	9.1	5.6	5.7

Chapter Three

OCCUPATIONAL EMPLOYMENT AND WAGES

OCCUPATIONAL EMPLOYMENT AND WAGES

HIGHLIGHTS

This chapter presents employment and wage statistics from the Bureau of Labor Statistics Occupational Employment Statistics (OES) program.

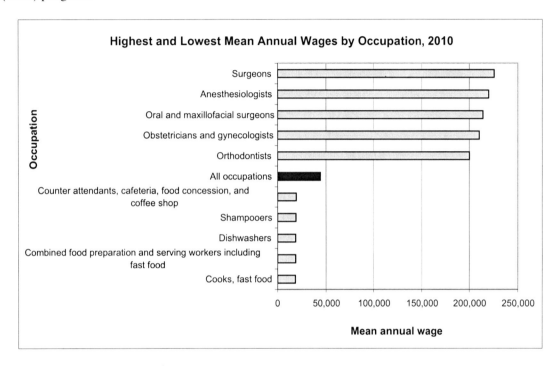

In 2010, the mean annual wage was $44,410. Nine of the top ten paying occupations were either medical doctors or orthodontists. Chief executives were the lone occupation not in the health profession. Meanwhile, workers in the food preparation and serving related occupations had the lowest mean annual wages. (See Table 3-1.)

OTHER HIGHLIGHTS

- The following occupational groups all had a mean hourly wage above $35.00 in 2010: legal ($46.60), management ($43.96) architecture and engineering ($36.32) and computer and mathematical sciences ($35.44). (See Table 3-1.)

- In the legal profession, 28.6 percent of workers had a hourly wage $49.75 or more while only 2.2 percent had an hourly wage under $9.50. (See Table 3-2.)

- The mean annual wage increased for all the major occupational groups in 2010 except for personal care and services which experienced a slight decline of 0.4 percent. Wages grew the fastest in business and finance at 2.7 percent. (See Table 3-1.)

- The mean average wages of those in the education, training, or library professions ranged from $24,880 for teacher assistants to $107,990 for postsecondary law teachers. (See Table 3-3.)

NOTES AND DEFINITIONS

Collection and Coverage

The Occupational Employment Statistics (OES) survey is a federal-state cooperative program conducted by the Bureau of Labor Statistics (BLS) and the State Workforce Agencies (SWAs). The OES program collects data on wage and salary workers in nonfarm establishments in order to produce employment and wage estimates for about 801 detailed occupations. Data from self-employed persons are not collected and are not included in the estimates. BLS funds the survey and provides procedural and technical support, while the SWAs collect the necessary data.

OES estimates are created from a sample of 1.2 million establishments. In March and November of each year, forms are mailed to two semiannual panels of around 200,000 establishments. May 2010 estimates are based on responses from six semiannual panels collected over a 3-year period: May 2010, November 2009, May 2009, November 2008, May 2008, and November 2007.

The May 2010 OES estimates are the first estimates based in part on data collected using the 2010 Standard Occupational Classification (SOC) system. Nearly all the occupations listed in Table 3-3 are 2010 SOC occupations; however, some are not. In these cases, an estimate for a temporary occupation was created from data reported for one or more occupations in the 2000 SOC combined with data reported for one or more 2010 SOC occupations.

Scope of the Survey

Prior to 1996, the OES program collected only occupational employment data for selected industries in each year of the three-year survey cycle, and produced only industry-specific estimates of occupational employment. The 1996 survey round was the first year that the OES program began collecting occupational employment and wage data in every State. In addition, the program's three-year survey cycle was modified to collect data from all covered industries each year. In 1997, the OES program began producing estimates of cross-industry as well as industry-specific occupational employment and wages.

In 1999, the OES survey began using the Standard Occupational Classification (SOC) system. The SOC system is the first occupational classification system for federal agencies required by the Office of Management and Budget (OMB). The SOC system consists of 821 detailed occupations grouped into 449 broad occupations, 96 minor occupational groups, and 23 major occupational groups. The OES survey uses 22 of the 23 major occupational groups from the SOC to categorize workers into 801 detailed occu-

pations. Military-specific occupations, which are not covered by the OES survey, are not included.

In 2002, the OES survey switched from the Standard Industrial Classification System (SIC) to the North American Industry Classification System (NAICS). In 2008, the OES survey switched to the 2007 NAICS from the 2002 NAICS. The most significant revisions were in the information sector, particularly within the telecommunications area. More information about NAICS can be found on the BLS Web site at <http://www.bls.gov/bls/naics.htm>.

Concepts and Definitions

Employment is the estimate of total wage and salary employment in an occupation across the industries in which it was reported. The OES survey defines employment as the number of workers who can be classified as full-time or part-time employees, including workers on paid vacations or other types of leave; workers on unpaid short-term absences; employees who are salaried officers, executives, or staff members of incorporated firms; employees temporarily assigned to other units; and employees for whom the reporting unit is their permanent duty station regardless of whether that unit prepares their paycheck. Self-employed owners, partners in unincorporated firms, household workers, and unpaid family workers are excluded.

Occupations are classified based on work performed and required skills. Employees are assigned to an occupation based on the work they perform and not on their education or training. For example, an employee trained as an engineer but working as a drafter is reported as a drafter. Employees who perform the duties of two or more occupations are reported as being in either the occupation that requires the highest level of skill or the occupation in which the most time is spent (if there is no measurable difference in skill requirements).

Wages are money that is paid or received for work or services performed in a specified period. Base rate, cost-of-living allowances, guaranteed pay, hazardous-duty pay, incentive pay (including commissions and production bonuses), tips, and on-call pay are included. Excluded are back pay, jury duty pay, overtime pay, severance pay, shift differentials, nonproduction bonuses, employer cost of supplementary benefits, and tuition reimbursements.

Mean wage refers to an average wage; an occupational mean wage estimate is calculated by summing the wages of all the employees in a given occupation and then dividing the total wages by the number of employees.

An *establishment* is defined as an economic unit that processes goods or provides services, such as a factory, store, or mine. The establishment is generally at a single physical location and is primarily engaged in one type of economic activity.

An *industry* is a group of establishments that produce similar products or provide similar services. For example, all establishments that manufacture automobiles are in the same industry. A given industry, or even a particular establishment in that industry, might have employees in dozens of occupations. The North American Industry Classification System (NAICS) groups similar establishments into industries.

Additional Information
For additional data including area data, see BLS news release USDL 11-0722, "Occupational Employment and Wages, May 2010," and special reports on the BLS Web site at <http://www.bls.gov/OES/>.

Table 3-1. Employment and Wages, by Major Occupational Group, May 2007–May 2010

(Number, percent, dollars.)

Occupation	May 2007				May 2008			
	Employment		Mean hourly wage	Mean annual wage[1]	Employment		Mean hourly wage	Mean annual wage[1]
	Number	Percent			Number	Percent		
All Occupations	134 354 250	100.0	19.56	40 690	135 185 230	100.0	20.32	42 270
Management	6 003 930	4.5	46.22	96 150	6 152 650	4.6	48.23	100 310
Business and financial operations	6 015 500	4.5	30.01	62 410	6 135 520	4.5	31.12	64 720
Computer and mathematical sciences	3 191 360	2.4	34.71	72 190	3 308 260	2.4	35.82	74 500
Architecture and engineering	2 486 020	1.9	33.11	68 880	2 521 630	1.9	34.34	71 430
Life, physical, and social sciences	1 255 670	0.9	29.82	62 020	1 296 840	1.0	30.90	64 280
Community and social services	1 793 040	1.3	19.49	40 540	1 861 750	1.4	20.09	41 790
Legal	998 590	0.7	42.53	88 450	1 003 270	0.7	44.36	92 270
Education, training, and library	8 316 360	6.2	22.41	46 610	8 451 250	6.3	23.30	48 460
Arts, design, entertainment, sports, and media	1 761 270	1.3	23.27	48 410	1 804 940	1.3	24.36	50 670
Health care practitioner and technical	6 877 680	5.1	31.26	65 020	7 076 800	5.2	32.64	67 890
Health care support	3 625 240	2.7	12.31	25 600	3 779 280	2.8	12.66	26 340
Protective services	3 087 650	2.3	18.63	38 750	3 128 960	2.3	19.33	40 200
Food preparation and serving related	11 273 850	8.4	9.35	19 440	11 438 550	8.5	9.72	20 220
Building and grounds cleaning and maintenance	4 403 900	3.3	11.33	23 560	4 429 870	3.3	11.72	24 370
Personal care and services	3 339 510	2.5	11.53	23 980	3 437 520	2.5	11.59	24 120
Sales and related	14 332 020	10.7	11.41	35 240	14 336 430	10.6	17.35	36 080
Office and administrative support	23 270 810	17.3	15.00	31 200	23 231 750	17.2	15.49	32 220
Farming, fishing, and forestry	448 000	0.3	10.89	22 640	438 490	0.3	11.32	23 560
Construction and extraction	6 708 200	5.0	19.53	40 620	6 548 760	4.8	20.36	42 350
Installation, maintenance, and repair	5 390 090	4.0	19.20	39 930	5 374 850	4.0	19.82	41 230
Production	10 146 560	7.6	15.05	31 310	9 919 120	7.3	15.54	32 320
Transportation and material moving	9 629 030	7.2	14.75	30 680	9 508 750	7.0	15.12	31 450

Occupation	May 2009				May 2010			
	Employment		Mean hourly wage	Mean annual wage[1]	Employment		Mean hourly wage	Mean annual wage[1]
	Number	Percent			Number	Percent		
All Occupations	130 647 610	100.0	20.90	43 460	127 097 160	100.0	16.27	44 410
Management	6 116 380	4.7	49.47	102 900	6 022 860	4.7	43.96	105 440
Business and financial operations	6 063 670	4.6	31.68	65 900	6 090 910	4.8	29.17	67 690
Computer and mathematical sciences	3 303 690	2.5	36.68	76 290	3 283 950	2.6	35.44	77 230
Architecture and engineering	2 412 730	1.8	35.38	73 590	2 305 530	1.8	36.32	75 550
Life, physical, and social sciences	1 308 380	1.0	31.57	65 660	1 064 510	0.8	31.92	66 390
Community and social services	1 891 320	1.4	20.55	42 750	1 901 180	1.5	20.76	43 180
Legal	999 020	0.8	46.07	95 820	992 650	0.8	46.60	96 940
Education, training, and library	8 488 740	6.5	23.81	49 530	8 457 870	6.7	24.25	50 440
Arts, design, entertainment, sports, and media	1 745 670	1.3	24.87	51 720	1 716 640	1.4	25.14	52 290
Health care practitioner and technical	7 200 950	5.5	33.51	69 690	7 346 580	5.8	34.27	71 280
Health care support	3 886 690	3.0	12.84	26 710	3 962 930	3.1	12.94	26 920
Protective services	3 172 420	2.4	20.07	41 740	3 187 810	2.5	20.43	42 490
Food preparation and serving related	11 218 260	8.6	10.04	20 880	11 027 340	8.7	10.21	21 240
Building and grounds cleaning and maintenance	4 269 480	3.3	12.00	24 970	4 175 550	3.3	12.16	25 300
Personal care and services	3 461 910	2.6	11.87	24 680	3 425 220	2.7	11.82	24 590
Sales and related	13 715 050	10.5	17.32	36 020	13 437 980	10.6	17.69	36 790
Office and administrative support	22 336 450	17.1	15.86	32 990	21 503 800	16.9	16.09	33 470
Farming, fishing, and forestry	419 200	0.3	11.53	23 990	408 040	0.3	11.70	24 330
Construction and extraction	5 751 630	4.4	20.84	43 350	5 072 530	4.0	21.09	43 870
Installation, maintenance, and repair	5 114 150	3.9	20.30	42 210	4 928 960	3.9	20.58	42 810
Production	8 927 130	6.8	16.01	33 290	8 236 340	6.5	16.24	33 770
Transportation and material moving	8 844 700	6.8	15.47	32 180	8 547 980	6.7	15.70	32 660

[1]The annual wage has been calculated by multiplying the hourly mean wage by a "year-round, full-time" hours figure of 2,080 hours; for occupations with no published hourly mean wage, the annual wage has been directly calculated from the reported survey data.

Table 3-2. Distribution of Employment, by Wage Range and Occupational Group, May 2010

(Percent distribution.)

Occupation	Total	Under $9.50	$9.50 to $11.99	$12.00 to $15.24	$15.25 to $19.24	$19.25 to $24.49	$24.50 to $30.99	$31.00 to $39.24	$39.25 to $49.74	$49.75 and over
Management	100.0	1.3	1.3	3.1	5.8	9.8	13.9	17.0	16.7	31.0
Business and financial operations	100.0	2.2	3.6	8.5	14.4	19.9	19.7	15.7	9.0	6.8
Computer and mathematical sciences	100.0	1.1	2.4	5.3	9.3	14.4	19.0	21.4	16.4	10.8
Architecture and engineering	100.0	1.0	2.6	5.8	9.8	16.2	20.1	19.7	14.8	10.0
Life, physical, and social sciences	100.0	3.1	6.1	10.3	14.8	17.4	17.0	13.9	9.4	7.9
Community and social services	100.0	12.0	14.6	20.4	19.0	16.6	10.6	5.0	1.5	0.3
Legal	100.0	2.2	3.8	8.3	10.9	13.0	12.2	11.1	10.0	28.6
Education, training, and library	100.0	15.2	9.1	12.2	16.4	18.7	13.8	8.4	3.5	2.7
Arts, design, entertainment, sports, and media	100.0	17.3	10.7	13.9	15.0	14.2	11.7	8.1	4.3	4.8
Health care practitioner and technical	100.0	4.2	6.1	9.7	13.3	18.6	18.1	12.4	7.0	10.6
Health care support	100.0	45.9	25.6	17.1	7.4	2.8	0.9	0.2	0.1	-
Protective services	100.0	23.4	14.0	15.0	13.6	13.5	10.9	6.0	2.4	1.2
Food preparation and serving related	100.0	77.9	11.8	6.0	2.7	1.1	0.3	0.1	-	-
Building and grounds cleaning and maintenance	100.0	57.0	19.5	12.9	6.4	3.1	0.8	0.2	-	-
Personal care and services	100.0	66.1	15.1	8.5	4.9	3.0	1.5	0.6	0.2	0.1
Sales and related	100.0	48.7	12.3	10.1	8.2	6.6	5.0	3.6	2.3	3.2
Office and administrative support	100.0	26.7	21.5	21.4	15.3	10.3	3.3	1.1	0.3	0.1
Farming, fishing, and forestry	100.0	68.0	12.5	9.1	5.4	3.1	1.4	0.4	0.1	-
Construction and extraction	100.0	12.1	15.6	19.9	17.1	15.6	11.0	6.1	2.1	0.5
Installation, maintenance, and repair	100.0	12.8	13.5	18.9	19.4	18.4	11.6	4.2	1.0	0.2
Production	100.0	29.4	20.1	20.1	14.3	9.4	4.7	1.6	0.4	0.1
Transportation and material moving	100.0	36.4	18.7	17.4	12.9	8.2	4.0	1.3	0.6	0.6

- = Quantity represents or rounds to zero.

Table 3-3. Employment and Wages, by Occupation, May 2010

(Number of people, dollars.)

Occupation	May 2010			
	Employment	Median hourly wage	Mean hourly wage	Mean annual wage[1]
ALL OCCUPATIONS	127 097 160	16.27	21.35	44 410
Management				
Chief executives	273 500	79.37	83.34	173 350
General and operations managers	1 708 080	45.38	54.38	113 100
Legislators	65 710	([2])	([2])	38 470
Advertising and promotions managers	32 240	40.33	47.46	98 720
Marketing managers	164 590	54.23	59.00	122 720
Sales managers	319 300	47.37	54.86	114 110
Public relations and fundraising managers	53 460	44.14	50.19	104 390
Administrative services managers	240 320	37.45	40.57	84 390
Computer and information systems managers	288 660	55.67	59.27	123 280
Financial managers	478 940	49.96	56.24	116 970
Industrial production managers	143 310	41.91	45.99	95 660
Purchasing managers	65 220	45.71	48.36	100 600
Transportation, storage, and distribution managers	90 280	38.56	41.65	86 630
Compensation and benefits managers	29 830	42.92	46.61	96 940
Human resources managers	67 700	47.68	52.21	108 600
Training and development managers	28 070	42.87	46.06	95 800
Farmers, ranchers, and other agricultural managers	3 680	29.21	31.71	65 960
Construction managers	191 430	40.32	45.31	94 240
Education administrators, preschool and childcare center/program	50 700	20.65	24.23	50 410
Education administrators, elementary and secondary school ...	222 270	([2])	([2])	89 990
Education administrators, postsecondary	110 360	40.24	46.48	96 680
Education administrators, all other	28 100	36.39	39.36	81 870
Architectural and engineering managers	174 720	57.34	60.53	125 900
Food service managers	186 830	23.14	25.11	52 220
Gaming managers	3 230	32.19	35.55	73 940
Lodging managers	29 920	22.54	26.23	54 570
Medical and health services managers	282 990	40.52	45.03	93 670
Natural sciences managers	45 920	55.78	62.17	129 320
Postmasters and mail superintendents	25 160	28.99	29.09	60 500
Property, real estate, and community association managers ...	147 110	24.75	30.00	62 400
Social and community service managers	116 480	27.86	29.98	62 360
Emergency management directors	11 800	26.61	29.00	60 330
Managers, all other	342 960	46.37	49.12	102 160
Business and Financial Operations				
Agents and business managers of artists, performers, and athletes	11 790	30.35	43.19	89 840
Buyers and purchasing agents, farm products	10 250	26.07	30.55	63 540
Wholesale and retail buyers, except farm products	108 220	23.87	27.07	56 300
Purchasing agents, except wholesale, retail, and farm products	272 370	27.20	28.92	60 160
Claims adjusters, examiners, and investigators	262 540	28.18	28.94	60 200
Insurance appraisers, auto damage	10 280	27.03	27.75	57 710
Compliance officers	204 000	28.23	29.88	62 140
Cost estimators	183 790	27.82	29.84	62 060
Farm labor contractors	830	14.42	17.25	35 890
Human resources, training, and labor relations specialists, all other	417 880	25.33	27.80	57 830
Logisticians	104 800	34.04	35.34	73 510
Management analysts	536 310	37.58	41.95	87 260
Meeting, convention, and event planners	56 950	21.76	23.45	48 780
Compensation, benefits, and job analysis specialists	102 830	27.41	28.65	59 590
Training and development specialists	203 870	26.04	27.54	57 280
Market research analysts and marketing specialists	261 780	29.12	32.14	66 850
Business operations specialists, all other	993 980	30.02	32.55	67 710
Accountants and auditors	1 072 490	29.66	33.15	68 960
Appraisers and assessors of real estate	62 560	23.32	26.07	54 230
Budget analysts	58 290	32.79	33.97	70 660
Credit analysts	62 680	28.29	32.78	68 180
Financial analysts	220 810	35.75	41.36	86 040
Personal financial advisors	155 360	31.13	43.85	91 220
Insurance underwriters	95 350	28.51	31.35	65 220
Financial examiners	27 860	36.03	39.58	82 320
Credit counselors	29 560	18.34	20.05	41 700
Loan officers	283 330	27.16	31.68	65 900
Tax examiners and collectors, and revenue agents	68 530	23.73	26.36	54 830
Tax preparers	56 990	14.90	17.82	37 060
Financial specialists, all other	154 640	29.32	32.17	66 920

[1]Annual wages have been calculated by multiplying the hourly mean wage by a "year-round, full-time" hours figure of 2,080 hours; for occupations with no published hourly mean wage, the annual wage has been directly calculated from the reported survey data.
[2]Wages for some occupations that do not generally entail year-round, full-time employment are reported as either hourly wages or annual salaries (depending on how employees are typically paid).

Table 3-3. Employment and Wages, by Occupation, May 2010—*Continued*

(Number of people, dollars.)

Occupation	May 2010			
	Employment	Median hourly wage	Mean hourly wage	Mean annual wage[1]
Computer and Mathematical Science				
Computer and information research scientists	24 900	48.39	49.59	103 150
Computer systems analysts	495 800	37.38	39.06	81 250
Computer programmers	333 620	34.32	36.01	74 900
Software developers, applications	499 280	42.21	43.47	90 410
Software developers, systems software	378 920	45.28	47.10	97 960
Database administrators	104 080	35.33	36.41	75 730
Network and computer systems administrators	333 210	33.25	34.71	72 200
Computer support specialists	579 270	22.24	24.00	49 930
Information security analysts, web developers, and computer network architects	243 330	36.37	38.16	79 370
Computer occupations, all other	183 110	38.10	38.36	79 790
Actuaries	18 320	42.14	47.41	98 620
Mathematicians	2 830	47.78	48.20	100 260
Operations research analysts	62 210	34.12	37.01	76 980
Statisticians	22 830	35.02	36.57	76 070
Mathematical technicians	960	21.58	23.64	49 170
Mathematical science occupations, all other	1 290	26.21	34.02	70 760
Architecture and Engineering				
Architects, except landscape and naval	87 700	34.88	37.75	78 530
Landscape architects	16 680	29.85	32.15	66 880
Cartographers and photogrammetrists	11 670	26.21	29.31	60 970
Surveyors	43 950	26.39	27.95	58 140
Aerospace engineers	78 450	46.86	47.59	99 000
Agricultural engineers	2 520	34.18	35.96	74 790
Biomedical engineers	15 280	39.20	40.76	84 780
Chemical engineers	28 720	43.42	45.48	94 590
Civil engineers	249 120	37.29	39.56	82 280
Computer hardware engineers	66 960	47.50	48.85	101 600
Electrical engineers	148 770	40.65	42.20	87 770
Electronics engineers, except computer	133 660	43.35	44.58	92 730
Environmental engineers	49 800	37.86	39.98	83 160
Health and safety engineers, except mining safety engineers and inspectors	23 390	36.26	37.60	78 210
Industrial engineers	202 990	36.59	37.72	78 450
Marine engineers and naval architects	5 720	38.42	42.20	87 770
Materials engineers	21 830	39.96	41.28	85 860
Mechanical engineers	234 400	37.58	39.65	82 480
Mining and geological engineers, including mining safety engineers	6 270	39.84	41.99	87 350
Nuclear engineers	18 610	48.04	48.80	101 500
Petroleum engineers	28 210	54.85	61.53	127 970
Engineers, all other	139 610	43.40	44.12	91 770
Architectural and civil drafters	89 670	22.32	23.43	48 740
Electrical and electronics drafters	27 960	25.49	26.90	55 960
Mechanical drafters	64 440	23.46	24.62	51 200
Drafters, all other	15 210	21.68	23.17	48 190
Aerospace engineering and operations technicians	8 480	27.93	28.84	59 990
Civil engineering technicians	77 050	22.26	23.05	47 940
Electrical and electronics engineering technicians	147 750	26.94	27.26	56 690
Electro-mechanical technicians	15 970	23.82	24.60	51 160
Environmental engineering technicians	18 450	20.86	22.51	46 820
Industrial engineering technicians	61 630	23.18	24.30	50 540
Mechanical engineering technicians	44 170	24.09	24.74	51 450
Engineering technicians, except drafters, all other	66 560	27.89	28.39	59 060
Surveying and mapping technicians	53 870	18.22	19.41	40 370
Life, Physical, and Social Sciences				
Animal scientists	2 440	28.00	32.77	68 170
Food scientists and technologists	10 480	28.93	31.43	65 380
Soil and plant scientists	12 120	27.57	30.09	62 600
Biochemists and biophysicists	22 800	38.17	41.63	86 580
Microbiologists	18 330	31.69	34.63	72 030
Zoologists and wildlife biologists	17 440	27.61	29.64	61 660
Biological scientists, all other	30 430	32.80	34.28	71 310
Conservation scientists	18 880	28.51	29.42	61 200
Foresters	9 470	26.22	26.82	55 790
Epidemiologists	4 710	30.29	32.83	68 280
Medical scientists, except epidemiologists	93 560	36.87	41.69	86 710
Life scientists, all other	10 610	29.97	34.67	72 120
Astronomers	1 840	41.95	44.88	93 340
Physicists	16 860	51.14	53.86	112 020
Atmospheric and space scientists	8 640	42.20	42.31	88 010
Chemists	80 180	32.85	35.21	73 240
Materials scientists	8 390	40.73	41.49	86 300
Environmental scientists and specialists, including health	81 690	29.66	32.60	67 810
Geoscientists, except hydrologists and geographers	30 830	39.66	44.89	93 380
Hydrologists	6 910	36.39	38.11	79 280

[1]Annual wages have been calculated by multiplying the hourly mean wage by a "year-round, full-time" hours figure of 2,080 hours; for occupations with no published hourly mean wage, the annual wage has been directly calculated from the reported survey data.

Table 3-3. Employment and Wages, by Occupation, May 2010—*Continued*

(Number of people, dollars.)

Occupation	May 2010			
	Employment	Median hourly wage	Mean hourly wage	Mean annual wage[1]
Life, Physical, and Social Sciences—*Continued*				
Physical scientists, all other	24 690	45.57	46.05	95 780
Economists	13 250	43.00	47.77	99 350
Survey researchers	17 850	17.33	20.89	43 450
Clinical, counseling, and school psychologists	100 700	32.12	34.87	72 540
Industrial-organizational psychologists	1 420	41.99	54.82	114 040
Psychologists, all other	10 690	43.22	41.59	86 510
Sociologists	3 710	34.79	38.53	80 130
Urban and regional planners	38 830	30.31	31.74	66 020
Anthropologists and archeologists	5 100	26.07	27.90	58 040
Geographers	1 300	35.00	35.05	72 890
Historians	3 320	25.73	27.81	57 840
Political scientists	4 470	51.65	51.89	107 930
Social scientists and related workers, all other	28 420	35.88	37.45	77 890
Agricultural and food science technicians	16 890	15.75	16.89	35 140
Biological technicians	72 940	18.76	20.07	41 740
Chemical technicians	59 440	20.21	21.25	44 200
Geological and petroleum technicians	13 560	25.97	29.04	60 410
Nuclear technicians	6 960	32.73	32.37	67 330
Social science research assistants	25 830	17.90	19.28	40 090
Environmental science and protection technicians, including health	28 480	19.90	21.36	44 440
Forensic science technicians	12 390	24.79	26.46	55 040
Forest and conservation technicians	32 290	16.05	17.72	36 860
Life, physical, and social science technicians, all other	55 360	20.84	22.10	45 980
Community and Social Science				
Substance abuse and behavioral disorder counselors	77 940	18.33	19.62	40 810
Educational, guidance, school, and vocational counselors	246 890	25.67	26.91	55 970
Marriage and family therapists	33 050	21.98	22.85	47 530
Mental health counselors	110 300	18.34	19.88	41 360
Rehabilitation counselors	111 490	15.55	17.24	35 850
Counselors, all other	28 140	20.02	21.33	44 380
Child, family, and school social workers	276 100	19.33	21.08	43 850
Healthcare social workers	143 080	22.71	23.65	49 200
Mental health and substance abuse social workers	119 960	18.56	20.13	41 880
Social workers, all other	69 920	24.76	25.13	52 270
Health educators	58 150	22.03	24.17	50 270
Probation officers and correctional treatment specialists	89 900	22.69	24.64	51 240
Social and human service assistants	357 500	13.56	14.47	30 100
Community and social service specialists, all other	112 010	18.32	19.83	41 250
Clergy	42 820	21.14	23.22	48 290
Directors, religious activities and education	16 840	17.39	19.52	40 600
Religious workers, all other	7 090	12.87	15.42	32 070
Legal				
Lawyers	561 350	54.21	62.23	129 440
Judicial law clerks	25 150	19.12	21.18	44 060
Administrative law judges, adjudicators, and hearing officers	14 310	41.11	43.14	89 740
Arbitrators, mediators, and conciliators	6 920	26.83	31.95	66 460
Judges, magistrate judges, and magistrates	25 900	57.34	50.67	105 390
Paralegals and legal assistants	247 940	22.44	23.87	49 640
Court reporters	18 430	22.93	25.61	53 270
Title examiners, abstractors, and searchers	50 490	18.75	20.85	43 370
Legal support workers, all other	42 160	24.91	28.51	59 310
Education, Training, and Library				
Business teachers, postsecondary	79 070	(2)	(2)	85 470
Computer science teachers, postsecondary	33 080	(2)	(2)	78 190
Mathematical science teachers, postsecondary	51 980	(2)	(2)	73 480
Architecture teachers, postsecondary	7 620	(2)	(2)	79 300
Engineering teachers, postsecondary	34 400	(2)	(2)	96 480
Agricultural sciences teachers, postsecondary	10 600	(2)	(2)	81 760
Biological science teachers, postsecondary	54 540	(2)	(2)	86 570
Forestry and conservation science teachers, postsecondary	2 410	(2)	(2)	81 120
Atmospheric, earth, marine, and space sciences teachers, postsecondary	10 680	(2)	(2)	90 660
Chemistry teachers, postsecondary	21 150	(2)	(2)	80 070
Environmental science teachers, postsecondary	5 090	(2)	(2)	78 490
Physics teachers, postsecondary	13 500	(2)	(2)	86 560
Anthropology and archeology teachers, postsecondary	5 850	(2)	(2)	80 040
Area, ethnic, and cultural studies teachers, postsecondary	8 980	(2)	(2)	76 720
Economics teachers, postsecondary	13 020	(2)	(2)	92 870
Geography teachers, postsecondary	4 250	(2)	(2)	71 230
Political science teachers, postsecondary	15 930	(2)	(2)	78 620
Psychology teachers, postsecondary	34 350	(2)	(2)	74 320
Sociology teachers, postsecondary	17 430	(2)	(2)	71 830
Social sciences teachers, postsecondary, all other	7 410	(2)	(2)	85 400

[1]Annual wages have been calculated by multiplying the hourly mean wage by a "year-round, full-time" hours figure of 2,080 hours; for occupations with no published hourly mean wage, the annual wage has been directly calculated from the reported survey data.
[2]Wages for some occupations that do not generally entail year-round, full-time employment are reported as either hourly wages or annual salaries (depending on how employees are typically paid).

Table 3-3. Employment and Wages, by Occupation, May 2010—*Continued*

(Number of people, dollars.)

Occupation	May 2010			
	Employment	Median hourly wage	Mean hourly wage	Mean annual wage[1]
Education, Training, and Library —*Continued*				
Health specialties teachers, postsecondary	144 780	(^{2})	(^{2})	103 960
Nursing instructors and teachers, postsecondary	54 050	(^{2})	(^{2})	66 010
Education teachers, postsecondary	61 450	(^{2})	(^{2})	64 370
Library science teachers, postsecondary	4 370	(^{2})	(^{2})	66 950
Criminal justice and law enforcement teachers, postsecondary	13 860	(^{2})	(^{2})	65 590
Law teachers, postsecondary	14 620	(^{2})	(^{2})	107 990
Social work teachers, postsecondary	9 370	(^{2})	(^{2})	68 630
Art, drama, and music teachers, postsecondary	86 860	(^{2})	(^{2})	70 850
Communications teachers, postsecondary	28 590	(^{2})	(^{2})	67 820
English language and literature teachers, postsecondary	69 880	(^{2})	(^{2})	67 920
Foreign language and literature teachers, postsecondary	28 100	(^{2})	(^{2})	66 520
History teachers, postsecondary	23 240	(^{2})	(^{2})	70 860
Philosophy and religion teachers, postsecondary	21 250	(^{2})	(^{2})	69 150
Graduate teaching assistants	107 790	(^{2})	(^{2})	34 660
Home economics teachers, postsecondary	5 910	(^{2})	(^{2})	69 060
Recreation and fitness studies teachers, postsecondary	17 720	(^{2})	(^{2})	63 760
Vocational education teachers, postsecondary	120 290	23.18	25.38	52 790
Postsecondary teachers, all other	183 160	(^{2})	(^{2})	71 280
Preschool teachers, except special education	369 380	12.35	14.04	29 200
Kindergarten teachers, except special education	173 330	(^{2})	(^{2})	51 550
Elementary school teachers, except special education	1 485 600	(^{2})	(^{2})	54 330
Middle school teachers, except special and career/technical education	655 090	(^{2})	(^{2})	54 880
Career/technical education teachers, middle school	14 600	(^{2})	(^{2})	54 160
Secondary school teachers, except special and career/technical education	1 053 140	(^{2})	(^{2})	55 990
Career/technical education teachers, secondary school	91 690	(^{2})	(^{2})	56 010
Special education teachers, preschool, kindergarten, and elementary school	226 920	(^{2})	(^{2})	55 220
Special education teachers, middle school	100 510	(^{2})	(^{2})	56 500
Special education teachers, secondary school	141 420	(^{2})	(^{2})	58 080
Adult basic and secondary education and literacy teachers and instructors	68 510	22.37	24.56	51 080
Self-enrichment education teachers	160 990	17.47	19.81	41 210
Teachers and instructors, all other	710 230	(^{2})	(^{2})	38 940
Archivists	5 030	21.73	23.65	49 190
Curators	10 550	23.29	25.56	53 160
Museum technicians and conservators	10 390	17.94	20.16	41 940
Librarians	148 240	26.20	27.09	56 360
Library technicians	109 240	14.36	15.10	31 410
Audio-visual and multimedia collections specialists	7 740	20.53	22.07	45 910
Farm and home management advisors	10 670	21.89	22.90	47 640
Instructional coordinators	128 780	28.28	29.46	61 270
Teacher assistants	1 249 380	(^{2})	(^{2})	24 880
Education, training, and library workers, all other	99 820	18.07	20.63	42 900
Arts, Design, Entertainment, Sports, and Media				
Art directors	29 700	38.77	45.24	94 100
Craft artists	4 790	12.95	15.39	32 010
Fine artists, including painters, sculptors, and illustrators	10 320	21.56	25.52	53 080
Multimedia artists and animators	26 560	28.13	30.50	63 440
Artists and related workers, all other	7 560	28.29	29.69	61 760
Commercial and industrial designers	28 670	27.99	29.76	61 890
Fashion designers	15 060	31.02	35.79	74 440
Floral designers	47 850	11.35	12.04	25 030
Graphic designers	192 240	20.92	23.14	48 140
Interior designers	40 120	22.25	25.05	52 100
Merchandise displayers and window trimmers	64 330	12.48	13.69	28 480
Set and exhibit designers	8 120	22.44	24.81	51 600
Designers, all other	8 560	21.70	24.25	50 440
Actors	54 740	17.44	28.44	(^{2})
Producers and directors	83 520	32.90	42.60	88 610
Athletes and sports competitors	12 660	(^{2})	(^{2})	87 340
Coaches and scouts	184 280	(^{2})	(^{2})	35 950
Umpires, referees, and other sports officials	15 250	(^{2})	(^{2})	28 900
Dancers	11 200	13.16	16.55	(^{2})
Choreographers	12 390	18.11	20.25	42 110
Music directors and composers	20 640	22.10	25.36	52 750
Musicians and singers	43 350	22.39	30.22	(^{2})
Entertainers and performers, sports and related workers, all other	23 510	14.34	18.60	(^{2})
Radio and television announcers	32 520	12.91	19.19	39 910
Public address system and other announcers	7 580	13.42	18.19	37 840
Broadcast news analysts	5 670	26.03	34.96	72 710
Reporters and correspondents	45 130	16.60	21.05	43 780
Public relations specialists	225 590	25.05	28.44	59 150
Editors	99 160	24.75	28.53	59 340
Technical writers	43 990	30.42	31.85	66 240

[1]Annual wages have been calculated by multiplying the hourly mean wage by a "year-round, full-time" hours figure of 2,080 hours; for occupations with no published hourly mean wage, the annual wage has been directly calculated from the reported survey data.

[2]Wages for some occupations that do not generally entail year-round, full-time employment are reported as either hourly wages or annual salaries (depending on how employees are typically paid).

Table 3-3. Employment and Wages, by Occupation, May 2010—*Continued*

(Number of people, dollars.)

Occupation	May 2010			
	Employment	Median hourly wage	Mean hourly wage	Mean annual wage[1]
Arts, Design, Entertainment, Sports, and Media—*Continued*				
Writers and authors	40 980	26.64	31.71	65 960
Interpreters and translators	44 200	20.82	23.94	49 790
Media and communication workers, all other	23 740	20.72	24.27	50 490
Audio and video equipment technicians	47 510	19.49	21.38	44 460
Broadcast technicians	30 520	16.89	19.79	41 170
Radio operators	920	21.46	21.40	44 510
Sound engineering technicians	15 650	22.63	25.98	54 030
Photographers	54 550	17.30	14.00	35 980
Camera operators, television, video, and motion picture	16 760	19.42	23.29	48 450
Film and video editors	19 930	24.49	29.75	61 890
Media and communication equipment workers, all other	16 820	29.65	30.54	63 530
Healthcare Practitioners and Technical				
Chiropractors	26 250	32.31	38.38	79 820
Dentists, general	87 700	67.81	76.33	158 770
Oral and maxillofacial surgeons	5 330	(³)	102.94	214 120
Orthodontists	5 580	(³)	96.29	200 290
Prosthodontists	670	56.92	67.12	139 620
Dentists, all other specialists	5 010	77.41	77.98	162 190
Dietitians and nutritionists	53 510	25.60	26.13	54 340
Optometrists	26 480	45.67	51.32	106 750
Pharmacists	268 030	53.64	52.59	109 380
Anesthesiologists	34 820	(³)	105.82	220 100
Family and general practitioners	97 820	78.61	83.59	173 860
Internists, general	50 070	(³)	91.10	189 480
Obstetricians and gynecologists	19 940	(³)	101.13	210 340
Pediatricians, general	30 100	74.70	79.67	165 720
Psychiatrists	22 690	78.95	80.58	167 610
Surgeons	43 230	(³)	108.36	225 390
Physicians and surgeons, all other	293 740	(³)	86.96	180 870
Physician assistants	81 420	41.54	41.89	87 140
Podiatrists	9 310	56.75	64.14	133 410
Registered nurses	2 655 020	31.10	32.56	67 720
Occupational therapists	100 300	34.77	35.28	73 380
Physical therapists	180 280	36.69	37.50	77 990
Radiation therapists	16 590	36.05	37.64	78 290
Recreational therapists	20 830	18.95	19.92	41 440
Respiratory therapists	109 270	26.10	26.54	55 200
Speech-language pathologists	112 530	32.17	33.60	69 880
Therapists, all other	16 170	23.05	24.99	51 980
Veterinarians	54 480	39.44	44.51	92 570
Audiologists	12 860	32.05	33.58	69 840
Health diagnosing and treating practitioners, all other	31 390	33.32	39.34	81 830
Medical and clinical laboratory technologists	164 430	26.98	27.34	56 870
Medical and clinical laboratory technicians	156 480	17.44	18.36	38 190
Dental hygienists	177 520	32.81	33.02	68 680
Cardiovascular technologists and technicians	48 720	23.75	24.38	50 720
Diagnostic medical sonographers	53 010	30.95	31.20	64 900
Nuclear medicine technologists	21 600	32.96	33.20	69 050
Radiologic technologists and technicians	216 730	26.13	26.80	55 730
Emergency medical technicians and paramedics	221 760	14.60	16.01	33 300
Dietetic technicians	23 890	13.01	13.86	28 820
Pharmacy technicians	333 500	13.65	14.10	29 330
Psychiatric technicians	72 650	13.80	15.15	31 520
Respiratory therapy technicians	13 570	21.74	22.28	46 340
Surgical technologists	92 260	19.19	19.86	41 310
Veterinary technologists and technicians	79 870	14.28	14.92	31 030
Licensed practical and licensed vocational nurses	730 290	19.42	19.88	41 360
Medical records and health information technicians	176 090	15.55	16.83	35 010
Opticians, dispensing	62 200	15.84	16.73	34 800
Orthotists and prosthetists	5 940	31.28	33.14	68 930
Health technologists and technicians, all other	87 900	18.49	20.31	42 240
Occupational health and safety specialists	54 680	31.09	31.54	65 610
Occupational health and safety technicians	10 040	21.79	22.85	47 520
Athletic trainers	16 290	(²)	(²)	44 030
Healthcare practitioners and technical workers, all other	55 720	21.14	25.28	52 580

[1]Annual wages have been calculated by multiplying the hourly mean wage by a "year-round, full-time" hours figure of 2,080 hours; for occupations with no published hourly mean wage, the annual wage has been directly calculated from the reported survey data.
[2]Wages for some occupations that do not generally entail year-round, full-time employment are reported as either hourly wages or annual salaries (depending on how employees are typically paid).
[3]Median hourly wage is equal to or greater than $80.00 per hour.

Table 3-3. Employment and Wages, by Occupation, May 2010—*Continued*

(Number of people, dollars.)

Occupation	May 2010			
	Employment	Median hourly wage	Mean hourly wage	Mean annual wage[1]
Healthcare Support				
Home health aides	982 840	9.89	10.46	21 760
Nursing aides, orderlies, and attendants	1 451 090	11.54	12.09	25 140
Psychiatric aides	64 730	12.00	12.84	26 710
Occupational therapy assistants	27 720	24.52	24.66	51 300
Occupational therapy aides	7 180	13.19	14.95	31 090
Physical therapist assistants	65 960	23.89	23.95	49 810
Physical therapist aides	45 900	11.39	12.02	25 000
Massage therapists	60 040	16.78	19.12	39 770
Dental assistants	294 030	16.09	16.41	34 140
Medical assistants	523 260	13.87	14.31	29 760
Medical equipment preparers	47 310	14.18	14.59	30 350
Medical transcriptionists	78 780	15.82	16.12	33 530
Pharmacy aides	49 580	10.31	10.98	22 830
Veterinary assistants and laboratory animal caretakers	70 530	10.60	11.38	23 660
Healthcare support workers, all other	193 980	14.56	15.23	31 670
Protective Service				
First-line supervisors of correctional officers	39 920	26.88	28.02	58 290
First-line supervisors of police and detectives	102 200	37.62	38.83	80 770
First-line supervisors of fire fighting and prevention workers	58 800	32.81	34.56	71 890
First-line supervisors of protective service workers, all other	55 190	22.17	23.40	48 670
Firefighters	302 400	21.76	22.95	47 730
Fire inspectors and investigators	13 050	25.11	27.00	56 160
Forest fire inspectors and prevention specialists	1 530	16.78	19.33	40 200
Bailiffs	17 310	18.54	19.67	40 910
Correctional officers and jailers	457 550	18.77	20.57	42 780
Detectives and criminal investigators	110 640	33.08	35.10	73 010
Fish and game wardens	7 240	23.91	26.75	55 650
Parking enforcement workers	9 430	17.01	17.37	36 130
Police and sheriff's patrol officers	644 300	25.74	26.74	55 620
Transit and railroad police	3 540	26.12	26.89	55 930
Animal control workers	15 040	15.41	16.35	34 020
Private detectives and investigators	28 210	20.61	22.99	47 830
Gaming surveillance officers and gaming investigators	6 620	14.75	15.87	33 020
Security guards	1 006 880	11.50	12.92	26 870
Crossing guards	68 740	11.35	12.43	25 850
Lifeguards, ski patrol, and other recreational protective service workers	117 540	9.06	9.98	20 750
Transportation security screeners (federal only)	42 430	17.82	18.10	37 650
Protective service workers, all other	79 280	14.37	16.07	33 420
Food Preparation and Serving Related				
Chefs and head cooks	90 510	19.53	21.53	44 780
First-line supervisors of food preparation and serving workers	773 400	14.21	15.28	31 770
Cooks, fast food	525 350	8.70	8.91	18 540
Cooks, institution and cafeteria	387 700	10.93	11.62	24 180
Cooks, private household	400	14.96	12.29	31 110
Cooks, restaurant	901 310	10.65	11.18	23 260
Cooks, short order	171 780	9.42	10.11	21 030
Cooks, all other	19 460	10.93	11.82	24 590
Food preparation workers	802 650	9.18	9.93	20 660
Bartenders	495 350	8.98	10.25	21 310
Combined food preparation and serving workers, including fast food	2 692 170	8.63	8.95	18 610
Counter attendants, cafeteria, food concession, and coffee shop	446 660	8.83	9.27	19 280
Waiters and waitresses	2 244 480	8.81	9.99	20 790
Food servers, nonrestaurant	205 330	9.34	10.40	21 640
Dining room and cafeteria attendants and bartender helpers	390 920	8.75	9.29	19 320
Dishwashers	505 950	8.73	8.98	18 680
Hosts and hostesses, restaurant, lounge, and coffee shop	329 020	8.87	9.43	19 600
Food preparation and serving related workers, all other	44 890	9.61	10.94	22 760
Building and Grounds Cleaning and Maintenance				
First-line supervisors of housekeeping and janitorial workers	172 610	16.87	18.02	37 480
First-line supervisors of landscaping, lawn service, and groundskeeping workers	100 630	20.13	21.50	44 730
Janitors and cleaners, except maids and housekeeping cleaners	2 058 610	10.68	11.81	24 560
Maids and housekeeping cleaners	865 960	9.28	10.17	21 150
Building cleaning workers, all other	12 280	12.72	13.38	27 830
Pest control workers	62 490	14.59	15.62	32 480
Landscaping and groundskeeping workers	829 350	11.25	12.23	25 430
Pesticide handlers, sprayers, and applicators, vegetation	23 200	14.37	15.13	31 470
Tree trimmers and pruners	37 540	14.64	15.49	32 220
Grounds maintenance workers, all other	12 890	11.61	13.92	28 960

[1] Annual wages have been calculated by multiplying the hourly mean wage by a "year-round, full-time" hours figure of 2,080 hours; for occupations with no published hourly mean wage, the annual wage has been directly calculated from the reported survey data.

Table 3-3. Employment and Wages, by Occupation, May 2010—*Continued*

(Number of people, dollars.)

Occupation	May 2010			
	Employment	Median hourly wage	Mean hourly wage	Mean annual wage[1]
Personal Care and Service				
Gaming supervisors	22 960	23.33	23.69	49 270
Slot supervisors	12 020	12.81	14.47	30 110
First-line supervisors of personal service workers	131 800	16.97	18.48	38 430
Animal trainers	9 740	12.78	14.96	31 110
Nonfarm animal caretakers	135 070	9.40	10.61	22 070
Gaming dealers	85 430	8.70	10.49	21 820
Gaming and sports book writers and runners	13 450	10.02	11.57	24 060
Gaming service workers, all other	11 620	11.51	12.65	26 320
Motion picture projectionists	9 440	9.79	10.83	22 530
Ushers, lobby attendants, and ticket takers	107 200	8.92	9.76	20 290
Amusement and recreation attendants	254 630	8.87	9.50	19 750
Costume attendants	5 490	14.02	16.62	34 580
Locker room, coatroom, and dressing room attendants	17 280	9.35	10.43	21 700
Entertainment attendants and related workers, all other	36 340	9.41	10.51	21 850
Embalmers	6 780	20.91	21.29	44 280
Funeral attendants	29 810	11.05	11.82	24 590
Funeral service managers, directors, morticians, and undertakers	27 280	26.12	30.04	62 490
Barbers	9 360	11.45	13.43	27 930
Hairdressers, hairstylists, and cosmetologists	349 420	10.94	12.74	26 510
Makeup artists, theatrical and performance	2 240	18.33	24.51	50 980
Manicurists and pedicurists	51 990	9.45	10.61	22 060
Shampooers	14 220	8.78	9.20	19 140
Skincare specialists	30 230	13.90	15.40	32 030
Baggage porters and bellhops	44 740	9.74	11.40	23 720
Concierges	19 650	13.40	14.17	29 480
Tour guides and escorts	29 690	11.20	12.54	26 090
Travel guides	3 620	14.32	15.33	31 900
Childcare workers	611 280	9.28	10.15	21 110
Personal care aides	686 030	9.44	9.82	20 420
Fitness trainers and aerobics instructors	225 490	14.95	17.27	35 920
Recreation workers	293 430	10.70	12.15	25 270
Residential advisors	65 610	11.75	12.69	26 400
Personal care and service workers, all other	71 860	9.79	11.09	23 070
Sales and Related				
First-line supervisors of retail sales workers	1 172 070	17.22	19.18	39 890
First-line supervisors of non-retail sales workers	244 320	33.11	39.00	81 120
Cashiers	3 354 170	8.89	9.52	19 810
Gaming change persons and booth cashiers	19 570	11.14	11.74	24 420
Counter and rental clerks	414 730	10.63	12.32	25 620
Parts salespersons	201 610	13.88	15.09	31 380
Retail salespersons	4 155 190	9.94	12.02	25 000
Advertising sales agents	145 160	21.80	26.45	55 020
Insurance sales agents	318 800	22.48	30.06	62 520
Securities, commodities, and financial services sales agents	276 290	33.75	45.73	95 130
Travel agents	70 930	15.32	16.32	33 950
Sales representatives, services, all other	531 410	24.34	29.06	60 430
Sales representatives, wholesale and manufacturing, technical and scientific products	381 080	35.44	40.56	84 360
Sales representatives, wholesale and manufacturing, except technical and scientific products	1 367 210	25.21	30.16	62 720
Demonstrators and product promoters	75 790	11.11	13.28	27 630
Models	1 020	15.83	20.46	42 560
Real estate brokers	41 210	26.40	36.57	76 060
Real estate sales agents	153 740	19.24	25.24	52 490
Sales engineers	66 060	42.01	45.56	94 760
Telemarketers	288 760	10.73	12.24	25 470
Door-to-door sales workers, news and street vendors, and related workers	7 590	10.67	13.13	27 300
Sales and related workers, all other	151 280	16.53	19.90	41 400
Office and Administrative Support				
First-line supervisors of office and administrative support workers	1 359 950	22.82	24.41	50 770
Switchboard operators, including answering service	138 200	11.98	12.63	26 280
Telephone operators	18 650	15.37	16.06	33 400
Communications equipment operators, all other	2 780	17.60	18.25	37 960
Bill and account collectors	399 950	15.05	15.91	33 100
Billing and posting clerks	483 440	15.47	16.00	33 270
Bookkeeping, accounting, and auditing clerks	1 675 250	16.36	16.99	35 340
Gaming cage workers	15 640	12.35	12.96	26 950
Payroll and timekeeping clerks	180 280	17.47	17.82	37 070
Procurement clerks	73 650	17.69	17.86	37 150
Tellers	556 310	11.59	12.01	24 980
Brokerage clerks	57 600	19.31	20.50	42 640
Correspondence clerks	9 470	16.06	16.56	34 440
Court, municipal, and license clerks	123 510	16.53	17.39	36 170
Credit authorizers, checkers, and clerks	53 770	15.62	16.67	34 670

[1]Annual wages have been calculated by multiplying the hourly mean wage by a "year-round, full-time" hours figure of 2,080 hours; for occupations with no published hourly mean wage, the annual wage has been directly calculated from the reported survey data.

Table 3-3. Employment and Wages, by Occupation, May 2010—*Continued*

(Number of people, dollars.)

Occupation	May 2010			
	Employment	Median hourly wage	Mean hourly wage	Mean annual wage[1]
Office and Administrative Support—*Continued*				
Customer service representatives	2 146 120	14.64	15.76	32 780
Eligibility interviewers, government programs	118 920	19.21	19.67	40 900
File clerks	174 910	12.06	12.88	26 800
Hotel, motel, and resort desk clerks	222 540	9.58	10.30	21 430
Interviewers, except eligibility and loan	204 730	13.86	14.48	30 120
Library assistants, clerical	110 210	11.12	12.07	25 120
Loan interviewers and clerks	181 600	16.33	16.91	35 180
New accounts clerks	67 170	14.63	15.17	31 540
Order clerks	211 370	13.80	14.58	30 320
Human resources assistants, except payroll and timekeeping	150 090	17.69	18.22	37 900
Receptionists and information clerks	997 080	12.14	12.63	26 260
Reservation and transportation ticket agents and travel clerks	121 250	15.26	15.69	32 640
Information and record clerks, all other	200 410	17.80	18.00	37 450
Cargo and freight agents	81 390	17.86	18.76	39 020
Couriers and messengers	85 620	11.58	12.55	26 100
Police, fire, and ambulance dispatchers	97 740	17.00	17.74	36 900
Dispatchers, except police, fire, and ambulance	180 540	16.62	18.00	37 430
Meter readers, utilities	40 160	16.74	17.69	36 800
Postal service clerks	67 320	25.53	25.25	52 520
Postal service mail carriers	324 990	25.90	24.16	50 250
Postal service mail sorters, processors, and processing machine operators	145 690	25.52	23.24	48 340
Production, planning, and expediting clerks	266 170	20.30	21.19	44 070
Shipping, receiving, and traffic clerks	687 850	13.64	14.46	30 070
Stock clerks and order fillers	1 795 970	10.24	11.44	23 790
Weighers, measurers, checkers, and samplers, recordkeeping	66 480	13.06	13.94	28 990
Executive secretaries and executive administrative assistants	1 132 070	20.92	22.05	45 860
Legal secretaries	228 700	19.95	20.80	43 270
Medical secretaries	494 650	14.68	15.30	31 820
Secretaries and administrative assistants, except legal, medical, and executive	1 841 020	14.82	15.38	32 000
Computer operators	82 410	17.75	18.43	38 340
Data entry keyers	219 530	13.20	13.65	28 400
Word processors and typists	101 450	16.06	16.55	34 420
Desktop publishers	20 060	17.60	18.78	39 060
Insurance claims and policy processing clerks	231 570	16.71	17.49	36 390
Mail clerks and mail machine operators, except postal service	119 960	12.54	13.23	27 530
Office clerks, general	2 789 590	12.79	13.58	28 240
Office machine operators, except computer	66 580	13.02	13.76	28 610
Proofreaders and copy markers	12 770	15.08	16.13	33 550
Statistical assistants	15 490	16.60	17.83	37 090
Office and administrative support workers, all other	253 190	14.56	15.67	32 600
Farming, Fishing, and Forestry				
First-line supervisors of farming, fishing, and forestry workers	19 540	20.10	21.65	45 040
Agricultural inspectors	13 560	20.03	20.36	42 340
Animal breeders	1 380	15.07	17.13	35 620
Graders and sorters, agricultural products	38 950	9.22	10.18	21 180
Agricultural equipment operators	24 110	11.71	12.49	25 970
Farmworkers and laborers, crop, nursery, and greenhouse	228 600	8.98	9.64	20 040
Farmworkers, farm, ranch, and aquacultural animals	31 880	10.56	11.56	24 040
Agricultural workers, all other	7 490	11.65	13.35	27 780
Fishers and related fishing workers	700	12.30	13.41	27 880
Forest and conservation workers	7 040	11.49	13.34	27 740
Fallers	6 260	16.57	18.59	38 660
Logging equipment operators	22 880	15.57	16.06	33 400
Log graders and scalers	2 480	15.59	16.50	34 330
Logging workers, all other	3 130	16.62	16.59	34 510
Construction and Extraction				
First-line supervisors of construction trades and extraction workers	474 510	28.21	29.93	62 260
Boilermakers	19 030	26.27	26.80	55 750
Brickmasons and blockmasons	68 520	22.56	24.09	50 110
Stonemasons	11 920	17.87	19.16	39 850
Carpenters	620 410	19.00	21.10	43 890
Carpet installers	25 580	17.35	19.39	40 320
Floor layers, except carpet, wood, and hard tiles	9 480	17.36	18.99	39 490
Floor sanders and finishers	5 740	15.07	16.45	34 220
Tile and marble setters	31 670	18.32	20.11	41 830
Cement masons and concrete finishers	140 950	17.04	18.89	39 290
Terrazzo workers and finishers	3 640	18.62	19.97	41 530
Construction laborers	777 700	14.08	16.15	33 590
Paving, surfacing, and tamping equipment operators	51 830	16.42	18.28	38 020
Pile-driver operators	4 230	23.01	25.01	52 020
Operating engineers and other construction equipment operators	334 730	19.42	21.55	44 830
Drywall and ceiling tile installers	82 320	17.94	19.99	41 570
Tapers	17 690	21.87	23.35	48 560
Electricians	514 760	23.20	24.91	51 810
Glaziers	40 880	17.61	19.49	40 540
Insulation workers, floor, ceiling, and wall	23 380	15.30	17.37	36 120

[1]Annual wages have been calculated by multiplying the hourly mean wage by a "year-round, full-time" hours figure of 2,080 hours; for occupations with no published hourly mean wage, the annual wage has been directly calculated from the reported survey data.

Table 3-3. Employment and Wages, by Occupation, May 2010—*Continued*

(Number of people, dollars.)

Occupation	May 2010			
	Employment	Median hourly wage	Mean hourly wage	Mean annual wage[1]
Construction and Extraction—*Continued*				
Insulation workers, mechanical	28 100	18.10	20.49	42 620
Painters, construction and maintenance	189 840	16.48	18.08	37 610
Paperhangers	4 040	18.08	19.82	41 230
Pipelayers	45 320	16.73	18.38	38 230
Plumbers, pipefitters, and steamfitters	358 790	22.43	24.21	50 360
Plasterers and stucco masons	26 430	17.89	19.75	41 080
Reinforcing iron and rebar workers	19 590	18.48	21.48	44 690
Roofers	99 280	16.45	18.21	37 880
Sheet metal workers	131 600	20.05	21.98	45 710
Structural iron and steel workers	58 460	21.42	23.42	48 710
Helpers–brickmasons, blockmasons, stonemasons, and tile and marble setters	31 160	13.35	14.65	30 470
Helpers–carpenters	46 910	12.38	12.93	26 890
Helpers–electricians	72 390	13.08	13.61	28 300
Helpers–painters, paperhangers, plasterers, and stucco masons	12 320	11.20	11.89	24 730
Helpers–pipelayers, plumbers, pipefitters, and steamfitters	57 660	12.85	13.44	27 950
Helpers–roofers	12 310	11.21	11.75	24 450
Helpers, construction trades, all other	19 570	12.12	13.29	27 650
Construction and building inspectors	89 270	25.18	26.11	54 320
Elevator installers and repairers	20 430	34.09	33.66	70 010
Fence erectors	20 810	13.93	14.99	31 170
Hazardous materials removal workers	36 910	18.08	19.61	40 800
Highway maintenance workers	142 530	16.72	17.23	35 830
Rail-track laying and maintenance equipment operators	15 520	22.10	22.23	46 230
Septic tank servicers and sewer pipe cleaners	24 350	16.14	17.05	35 460
Segmental pavers	1 280	14.63	15.61	32 480
Construction and related workers, all other	42 140	16.59	18.03	37 510
Derrick operators, oil and gas	16 930	20.90	21.53	44 790
Rotary drill operators, oil and gas	20 230	24.99	28.84	59 980
Service unit operators, oil, gas, and mining	36 620	18.71	20.58	42 810
Earth drillers, except oil and gas	16 200	18.92	20.22	42 050
Explosives workers, ordnance handling experts, and blasters	15 710	21.03	22.30	46 370
Continuous mining machine operators	13 060	23.44	23.22	48 300
Mine cutting and channeling machine operators	6 630	21.61	21.41	44 530
Mining machine operators, all other	3 200	21.08	21.16	44 010
Rock splitters, quarry	3 390	14.48	14.84	30 860
Roof bolters, mining	5 610	23.97	24.18	50 290
Roustabouts, oil and gas	48 880	15.27	16.35	34 020
Helpers–extraction workers	23 400	16.43	17.82	37 060
Extraction workers, all other	6 660	18.80	19.52	40 600
Installation, Maintenance, and Repair				
First-line supervisors of mechanics, installers, and repairers	415 900	28.44	29.50	61 350
Computer, automated teller, and office machine repairers	110 320	17.92	18.79	39 080
Radio, cellular, and tower equipment installers and repairs	9 590	19.11	20.23	42 090
Telecommunications equipment installers and repairers, except line installers	190 100	26.30	25.41	52 850
Avionics technicians	18 320	25.15	25.02	52 050
Electric motor, power tool, and related repairers	18 740	17.39	18.20	37 860
Electrical and electronics installers and repairers, transportation equipment	12 830	23.27	23.91	49 730
Electrical and electronics repairers, commercial and industrial equipment	67 550	24.91	25.06	52 120
Electrical and electronics repairers, powerhouse, substation, and relay	23 220	31.36	30.83	64 120
Electronic equipment installers and repairers, motor vehicles	15 630	13.68	14.65	30 460
Electronic home entertainment equipment installers and repairers	30 840	15.84	16.87	35 100
Security and fire alarm systems installers	57 390	18.51	19.59	40 760
Aircraft mechanics and service technicians	117 510	25.68	25.62	53 280
Automotive body and related repairers	129 730	18.33	19.84	41 270
Automotive glass installers and repairers	14 020	15.94	16.41	34 120
Automotive service technicians and mechanics	587 510	17.21	18.36	38 200
Bus and truck mechanics and diesel engine specialists	1 222 770	19.64	20.31	42 250
Farm equipment mechanics and service technicians	30 300	16.17	16.67	34 680
Mobile heavy equipment mechanics, except engines	108 540	21.55	22.18	46 140
Rail car repairers	19 280	22.80	22.31	46 400
Motorboat mechanics and service technicians	16 850	17.11	17.96	37 360
Motorcycle mechanics	14 750	15.37	16.32	33 950
Outdoor power equipment and other small engine mechanics	25 010	14.22	14.80	30 790
Bicycle repairers	9 530	11.38	11.77	24 490
Recreational vehicle service technicians	9 540	15.66	16.78	34 900
Tire repairers and changers	94 120	11.14	11.98	24 920
Mechanical door repairers	13 240	17.20	18.16	37 780
Control and valve installers and repairers, except mechanical door	43 430	23.28	23.74	49 380
Heating, air conditioning, and refrigeration mechanics and installers	224 320	20.45	21.57	44 860
Home appliance repairers	33 180	16.70	17.54	36 490
Industrial machinery mechanics	275 370	21.84	22.65	47 100
Maintenance workers, machinery	69 480	18.49	19.38	40 310
Millwrights	36 670	23.25	23.95	49 820
Refractory materials repairers, except brickmasons	2 060	20.36	21.37	44 450
Electrical power-line installers and repairers	105 540	27.90	27.65	57 510

[1]Annual wages have been calculated by multiplying the hourly mean wage by a "year-round, full-time" hours figure of 2,080 hours; for occupations with no published hourly mean wage, the annual wage has been directly calculated from the reported survey data.

Table 3-3. Employment and Wages, by Occupation, May 2010—*Continued*

(Number of people, dollars.)

Occupation	May 2010			
	Employment	Median hourly wage	Mean hourly wage	Mean annual wage[1]
Installation, Maintenance, and Repair—*Continued*				
Telecommunications line installers and repairers	156 350	24.45	24.08	50 080
Camera and photographic equipment repairers	2 810	17.87	19.82	41 220
Medical equipment repairers	32 980	21.39	22.30	46 380
Musical instrument repairers and tuners	5 650	15.27	16.75	34 830
Watch repairers	2 240	17.87	18.73	38 960
Precision instrument and equipment repairers, all other	12 640	24.48	24.66	51 290
Maintenance and repair workers, general	1 217 820	16.70	17.61	36 630
Coin, vending, and amusement machine servicers and repairers	36 240	14.66	15.36	31 950
Commercial divers	3 720	24.69	27.12	56 400
Fabric menders, except garment	690	12.68	13.16	27 370
Locksmiths and safe repairers	15 850	17.09	18.05	37 550
Manufactured building and mobile home installers	5 760	13.83	14.46	30 070
Riggers	13 660	20.57	21.37	44 440
Signal and track switch repairers	7 400	25.59	24.80	51 580
Helpers–installation, maintenance, and repair workers	123 220	11.66	12.80	26 620
Installation, maintenance, and repair workers, all other	118 740	17.51	18.91	39 330
Production				
First-line supervisors of production and operating workers	555 260	25.53	27.01	56 170
Aircraft structure, surfaces, rigging, and systems assemblers	36 320	21.55	21.74	45 230
Coil winders, tapers, and finishers	14 930	13.77	14.42	29 980
Electrical and electronic equipment assemblers	180 440	13.99	14.96	31 110
Electromechanical equipment assemblers	48 980	15.21	15.57	32 380
Engine and other machine assemblers	33 310	17.46	18.75	38 990
Structural metal fabricators and fitters	79 540	16.60	17.26	35 900
Fiberglass laminators and fabricators	19 060	13.75	14.24	29 620
Team assemblers	928 170	13.07	14.05	29 220
Timing device assemblers and adjusters	1 560	15.02	15.53	32 300
Assemblers and fabricators, all other	248 090	13.00	14.92	31 040
Bakers	140 790	11.27	12.19	25 350
Butchers and meat cutters	125 910	13.75	14.51	30 190
Meat, poultry, and fish cutters and trimmers	163 080	10.74	11.27	23 440
Slaughterers and meat packers	88 500	11.24	11.55	24 010
Food and tobacco roasting, baking, and drying machine operators and tenders	18 710	13.05	13.91	28 940
Food batchmakers	97 220	11.85	12.90	26 820
Food cooking machine operators and tenders	32 220	11.24	12.19	25 360
Computer-controlled machine tool operators, metal and plastic	123 600	16.70	17.26	35 890
Computer numerically controlled machine tool programmers, metal and plastic	16 360	22.07	23.27	48 400
Extruding and drawing machine setters, operators, and tenders, metal and plastic	76 260	15.26	16.30	33 900
Forging machine setters, operators, and tenders, metal and plastic	22 110	16.13	16.40	34 100
Rolling machine setters, operators, and tenders, metal and plastic	31 900	17.63	18.00	37 450
Cutting, punching, and press machine setters, operators, and tenders, metal and plastic	182 170	14.12	14.76	30 690
Drilling and boring machine tool setters, operators, and tenders, metal and plast	22 390	15.56	16.16	33 620
Grinding, lapping, polishing, and buffing machine tool setters, operators, and tenders, metal and plastic	70 120	14.74	15.54	32 310
Lathe and turning machine tool setters, operators, and tenders, metal and plastic	40 970	16.66	17.23	35 830
Milling and planing machine setters, operators, and tenders, metal and plastic	20 520	17.47	18.05	37 540
Machinists	352 650	18.52	19.13	39 780
Metal-refining furnace operators and tenders	15 210	18.49	19.28	40 100
Pourers and casters, metal	11 190	16.36	16.99	35 350
Model makers, metal and plastic	6 000	20.55	21.50	44 730
Patternmakers, metal and plastic	4 390	17.88	19.04	39 600
Foundry mold and coremakers	10 040	14.66	15.36	31 940
Molding, coremaking, and casting machine setters, operators, and tenders, metal and plastic	114 760	13.54	14.44	30 030
Multiple machine tool setters, operators, and tenders, metal and plastic	69 330	15.30	15.99	33 250
Tool and die makers	66 530	22.56	23.42	48 710
Welders, cutters, solderers, and brazers	314 260	17.04	17.96	37 370
Welding, soldering, and brazing machine setters, operators, and tenders	38 530	16.26	16.93	35 220
Heat treating equipment setters, operators, and tenders, metal and plastic	18 300	15.86	16.42	34 150
Layout workers, metal and plastic	8 770	19.15	19.18	39 890
Plating and coating machine setters, operators, and tenders, metal and plastic	30 580	13.93	14.88	30 940
Tool grinders, filers, and sharpeners	11 930	16.56	17.15	35 660
Metal workers and plastic workers, all other	24 150	14.83	16.44	34 190
Prepress technicians and workers	48 070	17.44	18.26	37 970
Printing press operators	191 130	16.19	17.00	35 370
Print binding and finishing workers	54 230	13.90	14.81	30 800
Laundry and dry-cleaning workers	204 820	9.40	10.21	21 230
Pressers, textile, garment, and related materials	56 600	9.33	9.85	20 480
Sewing machine operators	147 030	9.90	10.88	22 630
Shoe and leather workers and repairers	6 010	11.06	11.87	24 690
Shoe machine operators and tenders	3 180	12.63	12.96	26 960
Sewers, hand	5 770	11.13	12.11	25 200
Tailors, dressmakers, and custom sewers	26 250	12.77	13.63	28 360
Textile bleaching and dyeing machine operators and tenders	12 700	11.04	11.89	24 720

[1]Annual wages have been calculated by multiplying the hourly mean wage by a "year-round, full-time" hours figure of 2,080 hours; for occupations with no published hourly mean wage, the annual wage has been directly calculated from the reported survey data.

Table 3-3. Employment and Wages, by Occupation, May 2010—*Continued*

(Number of people, dollars.)

Occupation	May 2010			
	Employment	Median hourly wage	Mean hourly wage	Mean annual wage[1]
Production—*Continued*				
Textile cutting machine setters, operators, and tenders	15 000	11.29	12.00	24 950
Textile knitting and weaving machine setters, operators, and tenders	21 190	12.44	12.68	26 360
Textile winding, twisting, and drawing out machine setters, operators, and tenders	27 840	12.33	12.60	26 200
Extruding and forming machine setters, operators, and tenders, synthetic and glass fibers	14 670	15.58	15.79	32 840
Fabric and apparel patternmakers	6 060	18.74	21.25	44 190
Upholsterers	30 210	14.40	15.20	31 620
Textile, apparel, and furnishings workers, all other	13 300	11.94	13.81	28 720
Cabinetmakers and bench carpenters	84 170	14.48	15.29	31 790
Furniture finishers	15 400	13.37	14.06	29 230
Model makers, wood	1 660	14.12	16.22	33 730
Patternmakers, wood	1 240	16.65	19.57	40 700
Sawing machine setters, operators, and tenders, wood	37 050	12.59	13.13	27 310
Woodworking machine setters, operators, and tenders, except sawing	61 130	12.75	13.29	27 650
Woodworkers, all other	8 610	11.79	13.42	27 910
Nuclear power reactor operators	5 080	36.37	37.17	77 310
Power distributors and dispatchers	10 100	33.13	33.24	69 130
Power plant operators	39 930	30.33	29.94	62 270
Stationary engineers and boiler operators	35 800	25.07	25.30	52 620
Water and wastewater treatment plant and system operators	108 330	19.60	20.45	42 530
Chemical plant and system operators	43 130	26.68	26.30	54 700
Gas plant operators	13 480	27.50	27.72	57 660
Petroleum pump system operators, refinery operators, and gaugers	42 850	28.87	28.64	59 580
Plant and system operators, all other	10 870	24.99	25.00	52 010
Chemical equipment operators and tenders	46 250	21.71	22.02	45 790
Separating, filtering, clarifying, precipitating, and still machine setters, operators, and tenders	38 050	18.19	18.65	38 800
Crushing, grinding, and polishing machine setters, operators, and tenders	33 140	15.60	16.21	33 720
Grinding and polishing workers, hand	27 420	13.16	13.80	28 710
Mixing and blending machine setters, operators, and tenders	123 840	15.80	16.40	34 120
Cutters and trimmers, hand	17 420	11.74	12.57	26 140
Cutting and slicing machine setters, operators, and tenders	61 360	14.42	14.95	31 090
Extruding, forming, pressing, and compacting machine setters, operators, and tenders	65 100	15.01	15.74	32 740
Furnace, kiln, oven, drier, and kettle operators and tenders	18 470	16.54	17.08	35 520
Inspectors, testers, sorters, samplers, and weighers	410 750	15.88	17.09	35 550
Jewelers and precious stone and metal workers	21 510	16.91	18.52	38 520
Dental laboratory technicians	38 360	16.90	18.26	37 980
Medical appliance technicians	13 320	17.15	18.56	38 610
Ophthalmic laboratory technicians	27 880	13.45	14.24	29 610
Packaging and filling machine operators and tenders	342 280	12.15	13.26	27 580
Coating, painting, and spraying machine setters, operators, and tenders	77 870	14.28	14.93	31 050
Painters, transportation equipment	43 300	18.77	20.27	42 160
Painting, coating, and decorating workers	23 970	11.73	12.83	26 680
Semiconductor processors	20 930	15.93	16.64	34 610
Photographic process workers and processing machine operators	57 540	10.58	11.90	24 760
Adhesive bonding machine operators and tenders	15 060	14.09	14.68	30 520
Cleaning, washing, and metal pickling equipment operators and tenders	18 320	12.34	13.50	28 090
Cooling and freezing equipment operators and tenders	8 960	14.09	14.82	30 830
Etchers and engravers	8 090	13.55	14.53	30 210
Molders, shapers, and casters, except metal and plastic	32 250	13.86	14.56	30 270
Paper goods machine setters, operators, and tenders	88 390	16.41	16.81	34 970
Tire builders	15 020	18.87	18.19	37 840
Helpers–production workers	394 270	10.79	11.66	24 240
Production workers, all other	229 240	13.42	14.89	30 980
Transportation and Material Moving				
Aircraft cargo handling supervisors	6 160	23.65	24.81	51 610
First-line supervisors of helpers, laborers, and material movers, hand	166 360	21.06	22.08	45 930
First-line supervisors of transportation and material-moving machine and vehicle operators	196 420	25.34	26.42	54 950
Airline pilots, copilots, and flight engineers	68 580	(2)	(2)	115 300
Commercial pilots	29 900	(2)	(2)	73 490
Air traffic controllers	23 970	51.94	53.02	110 280
Airfield operations specialists	6 790	21.67	22.47	46 740
Flight attendants	88 020	(2)	(2)	41 630
Ambulance drivers and attendants, except emergency medical technicians	19 440	11.03	11.60	24 130
Bus drivers, transit and intercity	179 700	17.08	17.82	37 060
Bus drivers, school or special client	467 610	13.26	13.78	28 660
Driver/sales workers	371 670	10.84	13.02	27 070
Heavy and tractor-trailer truck drivers	1 466 740	18.16	18.97	39 450
Light truck or delivery services drivers	780 260	13.77	15.45	32 140
Taxi drivers and chauffeurs	161 940	10.79	11.82	24 580
Motor vehicle operators, all other	61 230	13.58	15.83	32 920
Locomotive engineers	40 750	22.42	24.46	50 870
Locomotive firers	1 130	20.92	22.62	47 040
Rail yard engineers, dinkey operators, and hostlers	5 600	17.06	18.18	37 810
Railroad brake, signal, and switch operators	22 760	22.92	23.47	48 820
Railroad conductors and yardmasters	42 700	23.93	25.18	52 370

[1] Annual wages have been calculated by multiplying the hourly mean wage by a "year-round, full-time" hours figure of 2,080 hours; for occupations with no published hourly mean wage, the annual wage has been directly calculated from the reported survey data.
[2] Wages for some occupations that do not generally entail year-round, full-time employment are reported as either hourly wages or annual salaries (depending on how employees are typically paid).

Table 3-3. Employment and Wages, by Occupation, May 2010—*Continued*

(Number of people, dollars.)

Occupation	May 2010			
	Employment	Median hourly wage	Mean hourly wage	Mean annual wage[1]
Transportation and Material Moving—*Continued*				
Subway and streetcar operators	6 360	27.35	25.69	53 440
Rail transportation workers, all other	3 210	22.95	23.09	48 030
Sailors and marine oilers	31 690	17.44	18.28	38 030
Captains, mates, and pilots of water vessels	29 280	30.86	33.89	70 500
Motorboat operators	2 480	18.52	19.31	40 170
Ship engineers	9 470	31.67	34.09	70 920
Bridge and lock tenders	3 250	22.08	20.72	43 090
Parking lot attendants	124 590	9.39	10.21	21 250
Automotive and watercraft service attendants	86 440	9.40	10.20	21 210
Traffic technicians	6 730	19.77	20.94	43 550
Transportation inspectors	24 280	27.71	30.31	63 050
Transportation attendants, except flight attendants	25 150	10.06	11.21	23 320
Transportation workers, all other	32 760	15.83	17.31	36 010
Conveyor operators and tenders	36 810	14.07	14.69	30 550
Crane and tower operators	39 510	22.23	24.03	49 980
Dredge operators	1 720	16.20	17.59	36 580
Excavating and loading machine and dragline operators	49 140	17.75	19.19	39 910
Loading machine operators, underground mining	3 050	22.07	22.20	46 170
Hoist and winch operators	2 810	18.11	19.76	41 110
Industrial truck and tractor operators	518 350	14.32	15.15	31 500
Cleaners of vehicles and equipment	288 110	9.46	10.74	22 340
Laborers and freight, stock, and material movers, hand	2 024 180	11.28	12.36	25 710
Machine feeders and offbearers	119 730	12.98	13.54	28 170
Packers and packagers, hand	676 870	9.44	10.63	22 100
Gas compressor and gas pumping station operators	4 040	24.32	24.48	50 920
Pump operators, except wellhead pumpers	9 440	21.03	22.14	46 060
Wellhead pumpers	12 960	19.54	20.45	42 540
Refuse and recyclable material collectors	126 360	15.69	16.50	34 310
Mine shuttle car operators	3 080	23.13	23.43	48 730
Tank car, truck, and ship loaders	10 390	20.57	21.40	44 510
Material moving workers, all other	28 040	16.35	18.02	37 480

[1]Annual wages have been calculated by multiplying the hourly mean wage by a "year-round, full-time" hours figure of 2,080 hours; for occupations with no published hourly mean wage, the annual wage has been directly calculated from the reported survey data.

Chapter Four

LABOR FORCE AND EMPLOYMENT PROJECTIONS BY INDUSTRY AND OCCUPATION

LABOR FORCE AND EMPLOYMENT PROJECTIONS
BY INDUSTRY AND OCCUPATION

HIGHLIGHTS

Every two years, the Bureau of Labor Statistics (BLS) develops decade-long projections for industry output, employment, and occupations. This chapter presents the employment outlook for the 2010–2020 period. The projections are based on a set of explicit assumptions and an application of a model of economic relationships.

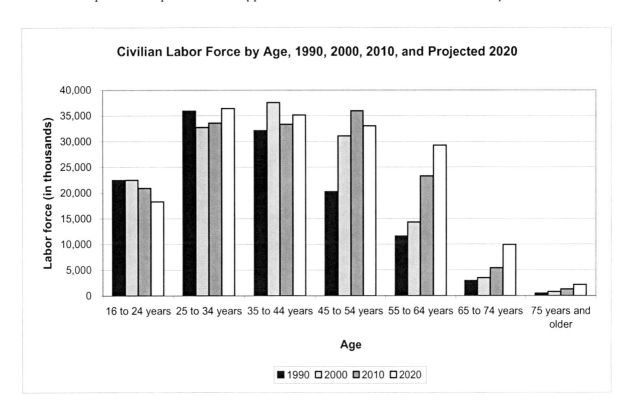

From 2010 to 2020, the civilian labor force is projected to grow by 6.8 percent, a much slower rate than the 7.9 percent increase from 2000 to 2010 or the 13.3 percent increase from 1990 to 2000. The aging of baby boomers has lead to a significant increase of older workers in the labor force. By 2020, persons 55 years of age and over are expected to make up 25.2 percent of the labor force, an increase from 19.5 percent in 2010 and 13.1 percent in 2000. (See Table 4-1.)

OTHER HIGHLIGHTS

- While the number of persons 55 years and over in the labor force is expected to increase, the number of 16- to 24-year-olds in the labor force is expected to decline. In 1990, 16- to 24-year-olds made up 17.9 percent of the labor force. It is projected that by 2020, this age group will only comprise 11.2 percent of the labor force. (See Table 4-1.)

- The labor force in 2020 is expected to be more diverse. From 2010 to 2020, the number of Hispanics in the labor force is projected to increase by 34.0 percent, followed by the number of Asians at 30.1 percent and the number of Blacks at 10.2 percent. Meanwhile, the number of non-Hispanic Whites in the labor force is projected to decrease by 1.5 percent. (Hispanics may be of any race.) (See Table 4-1.)

- The number of women in the labor force is expected to increase 7.4 percent from 2010 to 2020, significantly lower than the 8.4 percent increase from 2000 to 2010, or the 16.7 percent increase from 1990 to 2000. (See Table 4-1.)

NOTES AND DEFINITIONS

The Bureau of Labor Statistics (BLS) develops long-term projections of likely employment patterns in the U.S. economy. Since the early 1970s, projections have been prepared on a 2-year cycle. The projections cover the future size and composition of the labor force, aggregate economic growth, detailed estimates of industry production, and industry and occupational employment. The resulting data serve a variety of users who need information about expected patterns of economic growth and the effects these patterns are expected to have on employment. For example, information about future employment opportunities by occupation is used by counselors, educators, and others helping people choose a career and by officials who plan education and training programs.

The labor force projections are a function of two components—projections of the population and projections of labor force participation rates. Population projections are provided by the Census Bureau for detailed age, sex, race, and ethnicity groupings. BLS extrapolates participation rates for these same categories by applying well-specified smoothing and time series techniques to historical time series for the detailed participation rates.

Concepts and Definitions

Economic dependency ratio. This ratio is measured by estimating the number of persons in the total population (including all Armed Forces personnel overseas and children) who are *not* in the labor force per hundred of those who are.

Employment. In the employment projections survey, employment is defined as a count of jobs, not a count of individual workers.

Employment change. The numerical change in employment measures the projected number of job gains or losses.

Employment change, percent. The percent change in employment measures the projected rate of change of employment in an occupation. A rapidly growing occupation usually indicates favorable prospects for employment. However, even modest employment growth in a large occupation can result in many more job openings than rapid growth in a small occupation.

Job openings due to growth and replacement needs. Estimates of the projected number of net entrants into an occupation. For occupations that require training, the data may be used to assess the minimum number of workers who will need to be trained. The number of openings due to growth is the positive employment change from 2010 to 2020. If employment declines, then there are no job openings due to growth. The number of openings due to replacement needs is the net number of workers leaving an occupation who will need to be replaced.

On-the-Job Training Terms

Apprenticeship. An apprenticeship is a formal relationship between a worker and sponsor that combines technical instruction and on-the-job training. The typical programs provide at least 2,000 hours of on-the-job training per year over a 3-to-5 year period and 144 hours of technical instruction. Apprenticeship programs are sponsored by individual employers, joint employer-and-labor groups, and employer associations.

Internship/residency. An internship or residency typically involves supervised training in a professional setting such as a classroom or hospital. Internships and/or residency programs are often required for certification or to obtain a license in fields such as architecture, counseling, medicine, and teaching. This does not include internships that are recommended for advancement.

Short-term on-the-job training. Skills needed for a worker to become fully qualified can be acquired during a short demonstration of job duties or during 1 month or less of on-the-job experience or instruction. Examples include retail salespersons and waiters and waitresses.

Moderate-term on-the-job training. Skills needed for a worker to become fully qualified can be acquired during 1 to 12 months of combined on-the-job experience and informal training. Examples include heavy and tractor-trailer truck drivers and medical secretaries.

Long-term on-the-job training. More than 12 months of on-the-job training or, alternatively, combined work experience and formal classroom instruction are needed for workers to develop the skills to become fully qualified. This category includes formal or informal apprenticeships that may last up to 5 years. Long-term on-the-job training also includes intensive occupation-specific, employer-sponsored programs that workers must complete. Such programs include those offered by fire and police academies and schools for air traffic controllers and flight attendants. Individuals undergoing training usually are considered to be employed in the occupation. Also included in this category is the development of some natural ability—such as that possessed by musicians, athletes, actors, and other entertainers.

Sources of Additional Information

A complete presentation of the projections, including analysis of results and additional tables and a comprehensive description of the methodology, can be found in the January 2012 edition of the *Monthly Labor Review* which is available on the BLS Web site at www.bls.gov/opub/mlr/mlrhome.htm. In addition, more information on employment projections can be found on the BLS Web site at <http://www.bls.gov/emp/>.

Table 4-1. Civilian Labor Force, by Age, Sex, Race, and Hispanic Origin, 1990, 2000, 2010, and Projected 2020

(Numbers in thousands, percent.)

Age, sex, race, and Hispanic origin	Labor force				Change			Percent change		
	1990	2000	2010	2020	1990–2000	2000–2010	1990–2020	1990–2000	2000–2010	2010–2020
Both Sexes, 16 Years and Over	125 840	142 583	153 889	164 360	16 743	11 306	10 471	13.3	7.9	6.8
16 to 24 years	22 492	22 520	20 934	18 330	28	-1 586	-2 604	0.1	-7.0	-12.4
16 to 19 years	7 792	8 270	5 906	4 548	478	-2 364	-1 358	6.1	-28.6	-23.0
20 to 24 years	14 700	14 250	15 028	13 783	-450	778	-1 245	-3.1	5.5	-8.3
25 to 54 years	88 322	101 394	102 940	104 619	13 072	1 546	1 679	14.8	1.5	1.6
25 to 34 years	35 929	32 756	33 614	36 421	-3 173	858	2 807	-8.8	2.6	8.4
35 to 44 years	32 145	37 566	33 366	35 147	5 421	-4 200	1 781	16.9	-11.2	5.3
45 to 54 years	20 248	31 072	35 960	33 051	10 824	4 888	-2 909	53.5	15.7	-8.1
55 years and over	15 026	18 669	30 014	41 411	3 643	11 345	11 397	24.2	60.8	38.0
55 to 64 years	11 575	14 357	23 297	29 298	2 782	8 940	6 001	24.0	62.3	25.8
65 to 74 years	2 952	3 505	5 424	9 945	553	1 919	4 521	18.7	54.8	83.4
75 years and over	498	807	1 293	2 168	309	486	875	62.0	60.2	67.7
Men, 16 Years and Over	69 011	76 280	81 985	87 128	7 269	5 705	5 143	10.5	7.5	6.3
16 to 24 years	11 960	11 789	10 855	9 690	-171	-934	-1 165	-1.4	-7.9	-10.7
16 to 19 years	4 094	4 268	2 991	2 413	174	-1 277	-578	4.3	-29.9	-19.3
20 to 24 years	7 866	7 521	7 864	7 276	-345	343	-588	-4.4	4.6	-7.5
25 to 54 years	48 456	54 206	55 326	56 386	5 750	1 120	1 060	11.9	2.1	1.9
25 to 34 years	19 872	17 844	18 352	19 667	-2 028	508	1 315	-10.2	2.8	7.2
35 to 44 years	17 481	20 093	18 119	19 303	2 612	-1 974	1 184	14.9	-9.8	6.5
45 to 54 years	11 103	16 269	18 856	17 415	5 166	2 587	-1 441	46.5	15.9	-7.6
55 years and over	8 594	10 285	15 803	21 052	1 691	5 518	5 249	19.7	53.7	33.2
55 to 64 years	6 627	7 796	12 103	14 662	1 169	4 307	2 559	17.6	55.2	21.1
65 to 74 years	1 664	2 018	2 971	5 236	354	953	2 265	21.3	47.2	76.2
75 years and over	303	471	729	1 155	168	258	426	55.4	54.8	58.4
Women, 16 Years and Over	56 829	66 303	71 904	77 232	9 474	5 601	5 328	16.7	8.4	7.4
16 to 24 years	10 532	10 731	10 079	8 641	199	-652	-1 438	1.9	-6.1	-14.3
16 to 19 years	3 698	4 002	2 914	2 134	304	-1 088	-780	8.2	-27.2	-26.8
20 to 24 years	6 834	6 729	7 164	6 506	-105	435	-658	-1.5	6.5	-9.2
25 to 54 years	39 866	47 188	47 614	48 233	7 322	426	619	18.4	0.9	1.3
25 to 34 years	16 058	14 912	15 263	16 754	-1 146	351	1 491	-7.1	2.4	9.8
35 to 44 years	14 663	17 473	15 247	15 844	2 810	-2 226	597	19.2	-12.7	3.9
45 to 54 years	9 145	14 803	17 104	15 635	5 658	2 301	-1 469	61.9	15.5	-8.6
55 years and over	6 431	8 384	14 211	20 358	1 953	5 827	6 147	30.4	69.5	43.3
55 to 64 years	4 948	6 561	11 194	14 637	1 613	4 633	3 443	32.6	70.6	30.8
65 to 74 years	1 288	1 487	2 453	4 709	199	966	2 256	15.5	65.0	92.0
75 years and over	195	336	564	1 012	141	228	448	72.3	67.9	79.4
White, 16 Years and Over	107 447	118 545	125 084	130 516	11 098	6 539	5 432	10.3	5.5	4.3
Men	59 638	64 466	67 728	70 379	4 828	3 262	2 651	8.1	5.1	3.9
Women	47 809	54 079	57 356	60 137	6 270	3 277	2 781	13.1	6.1	4.8
Black, 16 Years and Over	13 740	16 397	17 862	19 676	2 657	1 465	1 814	19.3	8.9	10.2
Men	6 802	7 702	8 415	9 393	900	713	978	13.2	9.3	11.6
Women	6 938	8 695	9 447	10 283	1 757	752	836	25.3	8.6	8.8
Asian, 16 Years and Over	4 653	6 270	7 248	9 430	1 617	978	2 182	34.8	15.6	30.1
Men	2 570	3 362	3 893	4 968	792	531	1 075	30.8	15.8	27.6
Women	2 083	2 908	3 355	4 462	825	447	1 107	39.6	15.4	33.0
All Other Groups,[1] 16 Years and Over	. . .	1 371	3 694	4 738	. . .	2 323	1 044	. . .	169.4	28.3
Men	. . .	750	1 949	2 388	. . .	1 199	439	. . .	159.9	22.5
Women	. . .	621	1 746	2 350	. . .	1 125	604	. . .	181.2	34.6
Hispanic,[2] 16 Years and Over	10 720	16 689	22 748	30 493	5 969	6 059	7 745	55.7	36.3	34.0
Men	6 546	9 923	13 511	17 859	3 377	3 588	4 348	51.6	36.2	32.2
Women	4 174	6 767	9 238	12 634	2 593	2 471	3 396	62.1	36.5	36.8
Non-Hispanic, 16 Years and Over	115 120	125 894	131 141	133 867	10 774	5 247	2 726	9.4	4.2	2.1
Men	62 465	66 357	68 474	69 269	3 892	2 117	795	6.2	3.2	1.2
Women	52 655	59 536	62 666	64 598	6 881	3 130	1 932	13.1	5.3	3.1
White Non-Hispanic, 16 Years and Over	97 818	102 729	103 947	102 371	4 911	1 218	-1 576	5.0	1.2	-1.5
Men	53 731	55 040	55 116	53 867	1 309	76	-1 249	2.4	0.1	-2.3
Women	44 087	47 689	48 831	48 504	3 602	1 142	-327	8.2	2.4	-0.7

[1]The "All other groups" category includes respondents who reported the racial categories of "American Indian and Alaska Native" or "Native Hawaiian and Other Pacific Islander," as well as those who reported two or more races. This category was not defined prior to 2003.
[2]May be of any race.
. . . = Not available.

Table 4-1. Civilian Labor Force, by Age, Sex, Race, and Hispanic Origin, 1990, 2000, 2010, and Projected 2020—*Continued*

(Numbers in thousands, percent.)

Age, sex, race, and Hispanic origin	Percent distribution				Annual growth rate (percent)		
	1990	2000	2010	2020	1990–2000	2000–2010	2010–2020
Both Sexes, 16 Years and Over	100.0	100.0	100.0	100.0	1.3	0.8	0.7
16 to 24 years	17.9	15.8	13.6	11.2	0.0	-0.7	-1.3
16 to 19 years	6.2	5.8	3.8	2.8	0.6	-3.3	-2.6
20 to 24 years	11.7	10.0	9.8	8.4	-0.3	0.5	-0.9
25 to 54 years	70.2	71.1	66.9	63.7	1.4	0.2	0.2
25 to 34 years	28.6	23.0	21.8	22.2	-0.9	0.3	0.8
35 to 44 years	25.5	26.3	21.7	21.4	1.6	-1.2	0.5
45 to 54 years	16.1	21.8	23.4	20.1	4.4	1.5	-0.8
55 years and over	11.9	13.1	19.5	25.2	2.2	4.9	3.3
55 to 64 years	9.2	10.1	15.1	17.8	2.2	5.0	2.3
65 to 74 years	2.3	2.5	3.5	6.1	1.7	4.5	6.2
75 years and over	0.4	0.6	0.8	1.3	4.9	4.8	5.3
Men, 16 Years and Over	54.8	53.5	53.3	53.0	1.0	0.7	0.6
16 to 24 years	9.5	8.3	7.1	5.9	-0.1	-0.8	-1.1
16 to 19 years	3.3	3.0	1.9	1.5	0.4	-3.5	-2.1
20 to 24 years	6.3	5.3	5.1	4.4	-0.4	0.4	-0.8
25 to 54 years	38.5	38.0	36.0	34.3	1.1	0.2	0.2
25 to 34 years	15.8	12.5	11.9	12.0	-1.1	0.3	0.7
35 to 44 years	13.9	14.1	11.8	11.7	1.4	-1.0	0.6
45 to 54 years	8.8	11.4	12.3	10.6	3.9	1.5	-0.8
55 years and over	6.8	7.2	10.3	12.8	1.8	4.4	2.9
55 to 64 years	5.3	5.5	7.9	8.9	1.6	4.5	1.9
65 to 74 years	1.3	1.4	1.9	3.2	1.9	3.9	5.8
75 years and over	0.2	0.3	0.5	0.7	4.5	4.5	4.7
Women, 16 Years and Over	45.2	46.5	46.7	47.0	1.6	0.8	0.7
16 to 24 years	8.4	7.5	6.5	5.3	0.2	-0.6	-1.5
16 to 19 years	2.9	2.8	1.9	1.3	0.8	-3.1	-3.1
20 to 24 years	5.4	4.7	4.7	4.0	-0.2	0.6	-1.0
25 to 54 years	31.7	33.1	30.9	29.3	1.7	0.1	0.1
25 to 34 years	12.8	10.5	9.9	10.2	-0.7	0.2	0.9
35 to 44 years	11.7	12.3	9.9	9.6	1.8	-1.4	0.4
45 to 54 years	7.3	10.4	11.1	9.5	4.9	1.5	-0.9
55 years and over	5.1	5.9	9.2	12.4	2.7	5.4	3.7
55 to 64 years	3.9	4.6	7.3	8.9	2.9	5.5	2.7
65 to 74 years	1.0	1.0	1.6	2.9	1.4	5.1	6.7
75 years and over	0.2	0.2	0.4	0.6	5.6	5.3	6.0
White, 16 Years and Over	85.4	83.1	81.3	79.4	1.0	0.5	0.4
Men	47.4	45.2	44.0	42.8	0.8	0.5	0.4
Women	38.0	37.9	37.3	36.6	1.2	0.6	0.5
Black, 16 Years and Over	10.9	11.5	11.6	12.0	1.8	0.9	1.0
Men	5.4	5.4	5.5	5.7	1.3	0.9	1.1
Women	5.5	6.1	6.1	6.3	2.3	0.8	0.9
Asian, 16 Years and Over	3.7	4.4	4.7	5.7	3.0	1.5	2.7
Men	2.0	2.4	2.5	3.0	2.7	1.5	2.5
Women	1.7	2.0	2.2	2.7	3.4	1.4	2.9
All Other Groups,[1] 16 Years and Over	. . .	1.0	2.4	2.9	. . .	10.4	2.5
Men	. . .	0.5	1.3	1.5	. . .	10.0	2.1
Women	. . .	0.4	1.1	1.4	. . .	10.9	3.0
Hispanic,[2] 16 Years and Over	8.5	11.7	14.8	18.6	4.5	3.1	3.0
Men	5.2	7.0	8.8	10.9	4.2	3.1	2.8
Women	3.3	4.7	6.0	7.7	5.0	3.2	3.2
Non-Hispanic, 16 Years and Over	91.5	88.3	85.2	81.4	0.9	0.4	0.2
Men	49.6	46.5	44.5	42.1	0.6	0.3	0.1
Women	41.8	41.8	40.7	39.3	1.2	0.5	0.3
White Non-Hispanic, 16 Years and Over	77.7	72.0	67.5	62.3	0.5	0.1	-0.2
Men	42.7	38.6	35.8	32.8	0.2	0.0	-0.2
Women	35.0	33.4	31.7	29.5	0.8	0.2	-0.1

[1]The "All other groups" category includes respondents who reported the racial categories of "American Indian and Alaska Native" or "Native Hawaiian and Other Pacific Islander," as well as those who reported two or more races. This category was not defined prior to 2003.
[2]May be of any race.
. . . = Not available.

PROJECTED EMPLOYMENT

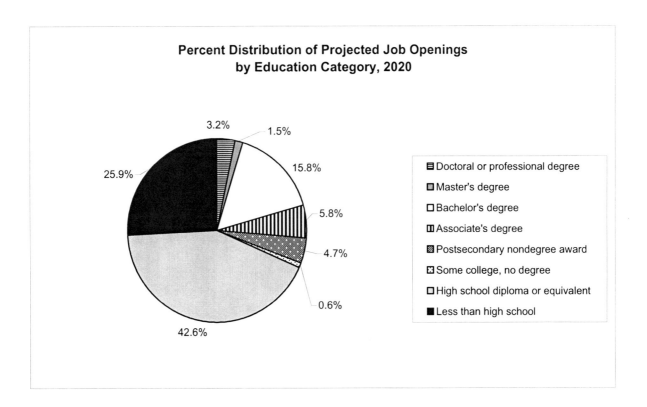

In 2020, only 1.5 percent of job openings will require a Master's degree. However, the number of job openings that require a Master's degree will grow by 21.7 percent—more than any other education category. Nearly 16 percent of jobs in 2020 will require a Bachelor's degree while 42.6 percent will require a high school diploma or equivalent. (See Table 4-9.)

OTHER HIGHLIGHTS:

• Personal health care aides and home health care aids are projected to be the fastest-growing occupations between 2010 and 2020 at 70.5 percent and 69.4 percent respectively. Postal service mail sorters, processors, and processing machine operators are expected to experience the fastest decline, dropping 48.5 percent (See Table 4-2.)

• The occupations projected to add the highest number of jobs from 2008 to 2018 are registered nurses (711,900), retail salespersons (706,800), and home health aides (706,300). (See Table 4-3.)

• Of the ten occupations with the largest wage and salary growth in 2020, five of them are in health care and social assistance sector. Meanwhile, four of the top ten occupations with the largest declines are in the manufacturing sector while another three are in the federal government. (See Table 4-5.)

• The median age of the labor force has gradually increased each decade from 1980 (34.6 years) to 2010 (41.7 years). In 2020, the median age is expected to increase even further to 42.8 years. (See Table 4-6.)

Table 4-2. Fastest-Growing Occupations, 2010 and Projected 2020

(Numbers in thousands, percent.)

Occupation	Employment		Change, 2010–2020		Mean annual wage, 2010
	2010	2020	Number	Percent	
TOTAL, ALL OCCUPATIONS	143 068.1	163 537.1	20 468.9	14.3	33 840
Personal care aides	861.0	1 468.0	607.0	70.5	19 640
Home health aides	1 017.7	1 723.9	706.3	69.4	20 560
Biomedical engineers	15.7	25.4	9.7	61.7	81 540
Helpers–brickmasons, blockmasons, stonemasons, and tile and marble setters	29.4	47.0	17.6	60.1	27 780
Helpers–carpenters	46.5	72.4	25.9	55.7	25 760
Veterinary technologists and technicians	80.2	121.9	41.7	52.0	29 710
Reinforcing iron and rebar workers	19.1	28.4	9.3	48.6	38 430
Physical therapist assistants	67.4	98.2	30.8	45.7	49 690
Helpers–pipelayers, plumbers, pipefitters, and steamfitters	57.9	84.2	26.3	45.4	26 740
Meeting, convention, and event planners	71.6	102.9	31.3	43.7	45 260
Diagnostic medical sonographers	53.7	77.1	23.4	43.5	64 380
Occupational therapy assistants	28.5	40.8	12.3	43.3	51 010
Physical therapist aides	47.0	67.3	20.3	43.1	23 680
Glaziers	41.9	59.6	17.7	42.4	36 640
Interpreters and translators	58.4	83.1	24.6	42.2	43 300
Medical secretaries	508.7	718.9	210.2	41.3	30 530
Market research analysts and marketing specialists	282.7	399.3	116.6	41.2	60 570
Marriage and family therapists	36.0	50.8	14.8	41.2	45 720
Brickmasons and blockmasons	89.2	125.3	36.1	40.5	46 930
Physical therapists	198.6	276.0	77.4	39.0	76 310
Dental hygienists	181.8	250.3	68.5	37.7	68 250
Bicycle repairers	9.9	13.6	3.7	37.6	23 660
Audiologists	13.0	17.8	4.8	36.8	66 660
Health educators	63.4	86.6	23.2	36.5	45 830
Stonemasons	15.6	21.4	5.7	36.5	37 180
Cost estimators	185.4	252.9	67.5	36.4	57 860
Medical scientists, except epidemiologists	100.0	136.5	36.4	36.4	76 700
Mental health counselors	120.3	163.9	43.6	36.3	38 150
Pile-driver operators	4.1	5.6	1.5	36.0	47 860
Veterinarians	61.4	83.4	22.0	35.9	82 040

Table 4-3. Occupations with the Largest Job Growth, 2010–2020

(Numbers in thousands, percent.)

Occupation	Employment		Change, 2010–2020		Mean annual wage, 2010
	2010	2020	Number	Percent	
TOTAL, ALL OCCUPATIONS	143 068.2	163 537.1	20 468.9	14.3	33 840
Registered nurses	2 737.4	3 449.3	711.9	26.0	64 690
Retail salespersons	4 261.6	4 968.4	706.8	16.6	20 670
Home health aides	1 017.7	1 723.9	706.3	69.4	20 560
Personal care aides	861.0	1 468.0	607.0	70.5	19 640
Office clerks, general	2 950.7	3 440.2	489.5	16.6	26 610
Combined food preparation and serving workers, including fast food	2 682.1	3 080.1	398.0	14.8	17 950
Customer service representatives	2 187.3	2 525.6	338.4	15.5	30 460
Heavy and tractor-trailer truck drivers	1 604.8	1 934.9	330.1	20.6	37 770
Laborers and freight, stock, and material movers, hand	2 068.2	2 387.3	319.1	15.4	23 460
Postsecondary teachers	1 756.0	2 061.7	305.7	17.4	45 690
Nursing aides, orderlies, and attendants	1 505.3	1 807.2	302.0	20.1	24 010
Childcare workers	1 282.3	1 544.3	262.0	20.4	19 300
Bookkeeping, accounting, and auditing clerks	1 898.3	2 157.4	259.0	13.6	34 030
Cashiers	3 362.6	3 612.8	250.2	7.4	18 500
Elementary school teachers, except special education	1 476.5	1 725.3	248.8	16.8	51 660
Receptionists and information clerks	1 048.5	1 297.0	248.5	23.7	25 240
Janitors and cleaners, except maids and housekeeping cleaners	2 310.4	2 556.8	246.4	10.7	22 210
Landscaping and groundskeeping workers	1 151.5	1 392.3	240.8	20.9	23 400
Sales representatives, wholesale and manufacturing, except technical and scientific products	1 430.0	1 653.4	223.4	15.6	52 440
Construction laborers	998.8	1 211.2	212.4	21.3	29 280
Medical secretaries	508.7	718.9	210.2	41.3	30 530
First-line supervisors of office and administrative support workers	1 424.4	1 627.8	203.4	14.3	47 460
Carpenters	1 001.7	1 197.6	196.0	19.6	39 530
Waiters and waitresses	2 260.3	2 456.2	195.9	8.7	18 330
Security guards	1 035.7	1 230.7	195.0	18.8	23 920
Teacher assistants	1 288.3	1 479.3	191.1	14.8	23 220
Accountants and auditors	1 216.9	1 407.6	190.7	15.7	61 690
Licensed practical and licensed vocational nurses	752.3	920.8	168.5	22.4	40 380
Physicians and surgeons	691.0	859.3	168.3	24.4	111 570
Medical assistants	527.6	690.4	162.9	30.9	28 860

Table 4-4. Economic Dependency Ratio, 1980, 1990, 2000, 2010, and Projected 2020

(Number.)

Group	1980	1990	2000	2010	2020
TOTAL POPULATION	108.9	98.3	93.9	100.6	107.0
Under age 16	50.7	45.8	44.1	43.3	44.0
Ages 16 to 64	37.4	30.5	28.3	36.5	38.0
Ages 65 and older	20.8	22.1	21.6	21.8	26.0

Table 4-5. Industries with the Largest Wage and Salary Employment Growth and Declines, 2010–2020

(Number in thousands, percent.)

Industry	Sector	Employment		Change, 2010–2020	Annual rate of change, 2010–2020
		2010	2020		
Largest Growth					
Construction	Construction	5 525.6	7 365.1	1 839.5	2.9
Retail trade	Retail trade	14 413.7	16 182.2	1 768.5	1.2
Offices of health practitioners	Health care and social assistance	3 818.2	5 209.6	1 391.4	3.2
Hospitals	Health care and social assistance	4 685.3	5 563.6	878.3	1.7
Home health care services	Health care and social assistance	1 080.6	1 952.4	871.8	6.1
Food services and drinking places	Leisure and hospitality	9 351.8	10 212.2	860.4	0.9
Individual and family services	Health care and social assistance	1 215.0	2 066.4	851.4	5.5
Nursing and residential care facilities	Health care and social assistance	3 129.0	3 951.0	822.0	2.4
Wholesale trade	Wholesale trade	5 456.1	6 200.2	744.1	1.3
General local government educational services compensation	State and local government	8 010.4	8 751.4	741.0	0.9
Largest Declines					
Postal service	Federal government	656.4	474.6	-181.8	-3.2
General federal non-defense government compensation	Federal government	1 667.5	1 545.7	-121.8	-0.8
Apparel knitting mills	Manufacturing	157.7	66.1	-91.6	-8.3
Newspaper, periodical, book, and directory publishers	Information	501.3	439.7	-61.6	-1.3
Other miscellaneous manufacturing	Federal government	266.0	210.3	-55.7	-2.3
General federal defense government compensation	Manufacturing	545.5	496.0	-49.5	-0.9
Computer and peripheral equipment manufacturing	Manufacturing	161.6	117.5	-44.1	-3.1
Navigational, measuring, electromedical, and control instruments manufacturing	Manufacturing	406.0	363.2	-42.8	-1.1
Crop production	Agriculture, forestry, fishing and hunting	629.5	589.3	-40.2	-0.7
Drycleaning and laundry services	Other services	302.1	265.7	-36.4	-1.3

Table 4-6. Median Age of the Labor Force, by Sex, Race, and Ethnicity, 1980, 1990, 2000, 2010, and Projected 2020

(Number.)

	1980	1990	2000	2010	2020
TOTAL	34.6	36.4	39.3	41.7	42.8
Sex					
Men	35.1	36.5	39.2	41.5	42.4
Women	33.9	36.2	39.3	42.0	43.3
Race					
White	34.8	36.6	39.6	42.3	43.3
Black	33.3	34.8	37.4	39.3	40.4
Asian	34.1	35.8	37.9	41.2	44.0
Ethnicity					
Hispanic origin[1]	32.0	31.2	33.7	36.9	38.7
White non-Hispanic	35.2	37.1	40.5	43.6	44.8

[1]May be of any race.

Table 4-7. Employment and Output, by Industry, 2000, 2010, and Projected 2020

(Number, percent, dollars.)

Industry	Employment							Output				
	Number of jobs (thousands)			Change		Average annual rate of change (percent)		Billions of chained (2005) dollars			Average annual rate of change (percent)	
	2000	2010	2020	2000–2020	2010–2020	2000–2010	2010–2020	2000	2010	2020	2000–2010	2010–2020
TOTAL	146 236	143 068	163 537	-3 168	20 469	-0.2	1.3	20 979	23 171	30 876	1.0	2.9
Nonagriculture Wage and Salary	132 425	130 436	150 177	-1 989	19 741	-0.2	1.4	20 694	22 870	30 507	1.0	2.9
Mining	520	656	681	136	25	2.3	0.4	393	388	441	-0.1	1.3
Oil and gas extraction	125	159	182	34	23	2.4	1.4	252	251	260	0.0	0.4
Mining, except oil and gas	225	203	203	-22	0	-1.0	0.0	72	52	69	-3.2	2.8
Coal mining	72	81	78	8	-3.0	1.1	-0.4	31	21	28	-3.9	2.9
Metal ore mining	38	36	28	-2	-8	-0.4	-2.5	19	7	9	-10.0	3.0
Nonmetallic mineral mining and quarrying	115	86	98	-29	12	-2.9	1.3	22	25	34	1.1	3.0
Support activities for mining	171	294	295	124	1	5.6	0.0	69	85	112	2.1	2.8
Utilities	601	552	516	-50	-36	-0.9	-0.7	478	354	432	-3.0	2.0
Electric power generation, transmission and distribution	434	397	361	-38	-36	-0.9	-0.9	321	237	300	-3.0	2.4
Natural gas distribution	121	108	96	-13	-12	-1.1	-1.2	147	109	122	-3.0	1.1
Water, sewage and other systems	46	47	59	1	12	0.2	2.3	10	9	12	-1.4	2.5
Construction	6 786	5 526	7 365	-1 261	1 840	-2.0	2.9	1 240	815	1 183	-4.1	3.8
Manufacturing	17 263	11 524	11 451	-5 739	-73	-4.0	-0.1	4 585	4 363	5 723	-0.5	2.8
Food manufacturing	1 553	1 447	1 470	-107	23	-0.7	0.2	498	531	610	0.6	1.4
Animal food manufacturing	55	50	47	-4	-4	-0.8	-0.8	30	26	32	-1.4	1.9
Grain and oilseed milling	65	58	56	-7	-2	-1.1	-0.4	63	53	63	-1.8	1.9
Sugar and confectionery product manufacturing	92	70	67	-23	-2	-2.8	-0.3	29	27	30	-0.4	0.9
Fruit and vegetable preserving and specialty food manufacturing	197	171	160	-26	-12	-1.4	-0.7	54	64	71	1.7	1.1
Dairy product manufacturing	136	128	122	-8	-6	-0.6	-0.5	71	75	89	0.6	1.6
Animal slaughtering and processing	507	490	537	-17	47	-0.3	0.9	138	150	175	0.8	1.6
Seafood product preparation and packaging	45	38	41	-7	3	-1.6	0.7	8	10	11	2.6	1.3
Bakeries and tortilla manufacturing	306	276	275	-30	-2	-1.0	-0.1	51	55	63	0.8	1.3
Other food manufacturing	150	165	166	14	2	0.9	0.1	55	71	78	2.6	1.0
Beverage and tobacco product	207	182	181	-25	-2	-1.3	-0.1	129	142	146	0.9	0.3
Beverage manufacturing	175	166	166	-9	0	-0.5	0.0	76	88	95	1.4	0.8
Tobacco manufacturing	32	17	15	-16	-2	-6.5	-1.0	53	54	52	0.3	-0.4
Textile mills and textile product mills	608	238	206	-370	-32	-9.0	-1.4	88	44	40	-6.7	-1.0
Apparel manufacturing	484	158	66	-326	-92	-10.6	-8.3	58	15	7	-12.7	-7.1
Leather and allied product manufacturing	69	28	13	-41	-15	-8.6	-7.6	9	4	3	-7.0	-3.3
Wood product manufacturing	613	341	424	-272	83	-5.7	2.2	104	89	118	-1.6	2.9
Sawmills and wood preservation	134	81	105	-53	24	-4.9	2.6	33	27	36	-2.0	3.1
Veneer, plywood, and engineered wood product manufacturing	122	65	95	-58	30	-6.2	3.9	24	23	31	-0.2	2.9
Other wood product manufacturing	357	195	224	-162	29	-5.9	1.4	48	39	51	-2.0	2.8
Paper manufacturing	605	397	366	-208	-31	-4.1	-0.8	170	140	167	-1.9	1.8
Pulp, paper, and paperboard mills	191	113	97	-79	-15	-5.2	-1.4	78	65	78	-1.8	1.8
Converted paper product manufacturing	413	284	269	-129	-15	-3.7	-0.5	92	75	89	-2.0	1.7
Printing and related support activities	807	487	455	-320	-32	-4.9	-0.7	111	85	112	-2.6	2.7
Petroleum and coal products manufacturing	123	114	100	-9	-14	-0.8	-1.3	419	441	543	0.5	2.1
Chemical manufacturing	980	784	728	-197	-56	-2.2	-0.7	519	548	725	0.5	2.9
Basic chemical manufacturing	188	142	122	-46	-21	-2.8	-1.6	139	126	172	-1.0	3.2
Resin, synthetic rubber, and artificial synthetic fibers and filaments manufacturing	136	90	84	-46	-5	-4.0	-0.6	86	71	95	-1.9	2.9
Pesticide, fertilizer, and other agricultural chemical manufacturing	48	35	28	-13	-8	-3.0	-2.5	26	23	28	-1.5	2.0
Pharmaceutical and medicine manufacturing	274	277	282	2	5	0.1	0.2	136	169	219	2.2	2.6
Paint, coating, and adhesive manufacturing	79	56	49	-23	-6	-3.4	-1.2	31	25	33	-1.8	2.7
Soap, cleaning compound, and toilet preparation manufacturing	129	101	95	-27	-6	-2.4	-0.6	61	86	111	3.6	2.5
Other chemical product and preparation manufacturing	127	83	69	-44	-14	-4.2	-1.9	40	47	68	1.6	3.8
Plastics and rubber products manufacturing	951	623	714	-328	91	-4.1	1.4	198	157	209	-2.3	2.9
Plastics product manufacturing	737	500	600	-237	100	-3.8	1.8	159	129	173	-2.1	3.0
Rubber product manufacturing	214	124	115	-90	-9	-5.3	-0.8	40	28	37	-3.3	2.7
Nonmetallic mineral product manufacturing	554	372	432	-182	60	-3.9	1.5	107	91	121	-1.6	2.9
Clay product and refractory manufacturing	82	40	44	-42	3	-6.8	0.8	10	8	10	-2.9	2.6
Glass and glass product manufacturing	141	81	69	-60	-12	-5.4	-1.6	25	22	28	-1.2	2.5
Cement and concrete product manufacturing	234	172	236	-62	64	-3.0	3.2	49	40	56	-2.0	3.4
Lime, gypsum and other nonmetallic mineral product manufacturing	97	79	83	-18	4	-2.0	0.5	23	21	28	-0.8	2.6
Primary metal manufacturing	622	361	366	-261	6	-5.3	0.2	198	175	231	-1.2	2.8
Iron and steel mills and ferroalloy manufacturing	135	85	74	-50	-11	-4.5	-1.4	75	74	98	-0.1	2.9
Steel product manufacturing from purchased steel	73	52	56	-21	4	-3.4	0.7	26	19	24	-2.8	2.1
Alumina and aluminum production and processing	101	55	52	-46	-3	-5.9	-0.5	33	31	43	-0.5	3.3
Nonferrous metal (except aluminum) production and processing	96	58	54	-38	-4	-5.0	-0.7	33	25	30	-3.0	2.0
Foundries	217	111	130	-106	20	-6.5	1.7	31	26	36	-2.0	3.5
Fabricated metal product manufacturing	1 753	1 285	1 436	-468	152	-3.1	1.1	294	285	381	-0.3	2.9
Forging and stamping	138	89	92	-49	3	-4.3	0.3	27	27	37	-0.3	3.4
Cutlery and handtool manufacturing	79	41	41	-38	1	-6.4	0.2	13	13	17	0.4	2.3
Architectural and structural metals manufacturing	428	320	403	-108	83	-2.9	2.3	67	71	98	0.5	3.3
Boiler, tank, and shipping container manufacturing	107	86	92	-20	6	-2.1	0.6	28	28	33	-0.1	1.8
Hardware manufacturing	50	23	22	-27	-2	-7.4	-0.8	13	13	16	-0.2	2.8
Spring and wire product manufacturing	81	42	39	-39	-3	-6.3	-0.8	13	9	12	-3.0	2.6
Machine shops; turned product; and screw, nut, and bolt manufacturing	365	312	330	-53	18	-1.6	0.5	51	49	66	-0.5	3.1
Coating, engraving, heat treating, and allied activities	175	122	144	-53	22	-3.5	1.7	22	20	28	-0.7	3.3
Other fabricated metal product manufacturing	330	249	275	-81	26	-2.8	1.0	60	56	74	-0.7	2.9
Machinery manufacturing	1 457	993	978	-464	-15	-3.8	-0.2	294	262	370	-1.1	3.5
Agriculture, construction, and mining machinery manufacturing	222	208	241	-14	32	-0.6	1.5	62	48	73	-2.6	4.3
Industrial machinery manufacturing	164	100	108	-65	9	-4.9	0.8	37	30	42	-1.9	3.4
Commercial and service industry machinery manufacturing	147	91	81	-56	-11	-4.7	-1.2	28	21	31	-2.8	4.0
Ventilation, heating, air-conditioning, and commercial refrigeration equipment manufacturing	194	123	118	-71	-5	-4.4	-0.4	38	30	42	-2.2	3.4
Metalworking machinery manufacturing	274	153	131	-120	-23	-5.6	-1.6	32	26	35	-1.9	3.0
Engine, turbine, and power transmission equipment manufacturing	111	91	81	-20	-11	-2.0	-1.2	40	34	45	-1.5	2.7
Other general purpose machinery manufacturing	344	226	220	-118	-6	-4.1	-0.3	58	73	103	2.3	3.5

Table 4-7. Employment and Output, by Industry, 2000, 2010, and Projected 2020—*Continued*

(Number, percent, dollars.)

Industry	Employment Number of jobs (thousands) 2000	2010	2020	Change 2000–2020	2010–2020	Average annual rate of change (percent) 2000–2010	2010–2020	Output Billions of chained (2005) dollars 2000	2010	2020	Average annual rate of change (percent) 2000–2010	2010–2020
Manufacturing—*Continued*												
Computer and electronic product manufacturing	1 820	1 100	943	-720	-157	-4.9	-1.5	417	466	896	1.1	6.8
Computer and peripheral equipment manufacturing	302	162	118	-140	-44	-6.1	-3.1	60	132	513	8.3	14.5
Communications equipment manufacturing	239	118	86	-121	-32	-6.8	-3.1	82	63	106	-2.6	5.3
Audio and video equipment manufacturing	52	20	18	-32	-2	-9.2	-0.9	10	12	16	2.1	3.1
Semiconductor and other electronic component manufacturing	676	370	337	-307	-33	-5.9	-0.9	133	144	290	0.8	7.3
Navigational, measuring, electromedical, and control instruments manufacturing	488	406	363	-82	-43	-1.8	-1.1	124	108	145	-1.4	3.0
Manufacturing and reproducing magnetic and optical media	63	25	22	-39	-3	-8.9	-1.3	10	7	11	-2.6	4.2
Electrical equipment, appliance, and component manufacturing	591	361	331	-230	-30	-4.8	-0.8	128	96	123	-2.8	2.5
Electric lighting equipment manufacturing	85	46	41	-39	-5	-6.0	-1.0	14	12	15	-1.6	1.8
Household appliance manufacturing	106	61	61	-45	0	-5.4	0.0	24	22	26	-0.8	1.9
Electrical equipment manufacturing	210	136	117	-73	-19	-4.2	-1.5	41	30	37	-3.1	2.2
Other electrical equipment and component manufacturing	191	118	112	-73	-6	-4.7	-0.5	49	32	45	-4.0	3.3
Transportation equipment manufacturing	2 057	1 330	1 333	-727	3	-4.3	0.0	640	586	801	-0.9	3.2
Motor vehicle manufacturing	291	151	166	-140	15	-6.3	0.9	233	186	267	-2.2	3.7
Motor vehicle body and trailer manufacturing	183	108	115	-75	7	-5.2	0.6	28	20	29	-3.2	3.6
Motor vehicle parts manufacturing	840	415	395	-424	-20	-6.8	-0.5	199	151	207	-2.7	3.2
Aerospace product and parts manufacturing	517	477	462	-40	-15	-0.8	-0.3	138	163	214	1.7	2.7
Railroad rolling stock manufacturing	33	20	25	-13	5	-4.8	2.1	10	11	16	1.1	4.0
Ship and boat building	154	126	128	-29	3	-2.0	0.2	21	30	35	3.4	1.6
Other transportation equipment manufacturing	40	33	42	-7	9	-1.8	2.4	11	25	32	8.5	2.4
Furniture and related product manufacturing	683	357	392	-325	34	-6.3	0.9	81	62	76	-2.6	2.1
Household and institutional furniture and kitchen cabinet manufacturing	443	223	234	-220	11	-6.6	0.5	46	35	41	-2.7	1.7
Office furniture (including fixtures) manufacturing	181	98	117	-84	19	-6.0	1.8	26	19	25	-3.2	2.9
Other furniture related product manufacturing	58	37	41	-22	5	-4.5	1.2	9	8	10	-0.5	2.2
Miscellaneous manufacturing	728	568	517	-160	-51	-2.5	-0.9	123	144	181	1.6	2.3
Medical equipment and supplies manufacturing	305	302	306	-3	5	-0.1	0.2	56	72	92	2.5	2.5
Other miscellaneous manufacturing	423	266	210	-157	-56	-4.5	-2.3	67	72	89	0.8	2.1
Wholesale Trade	5 934	5 456	6 200	-477	744	-0.8	1.3	897	1 176	1 649	2.8	3.4
Retail Trade	15 280	14 414	16 182	-866	1 769	-0.6	1.2	1 019	1 165	1 671	1.3	3.7
Transportation and Warehousing	4 410	4 183	5 036	-227	853	-0.5	1.9	640	709	978	1.0	3.3
Air transportation	614	464	480	-150	16	-2.8	0.3	146	130	166	-1.1	2.5
Rail transportation	232	215	214	-17	-1	-0.7	0.0	53	62	84	1.7	3.1
Water transportation	56	63	79	7	16	1.2	2.3	35	30	41	-1.6	3.0
Truck transportation	1 406	1 244	1 544	-162	300	-1.2	2.2	200	252	350	2.4	3.3
Transit and ground passenger transportation	372	432	536	60	103	1.5	2.2	28	33	44	1.6	2.9
Pipeline transportation	46	42	33	-4	-10	-0.8	-2.6	29	16	20	-5.9	2.7
Scenic and sightseeing transportation and support activities for transportation	565	567	689	2	121	0.0	2.0	58	63	93	0.8	4.0
Postal Service	880	656	475	-223	-182	-2.9	-3.2	74	62	58	-1.8	-0.8
Couriers and messengers	605	527	669	-78	142	-1.4	2.4	54	74	111	3.2	4.1
Warehousing and storage	514	628	794	114	165	2.0	2.4	38	49	71	2.6	3.6
Information	3 631	2 711	2 851	-920	140	-2.9	0.5	951	1 196	1 893	2.3	4.7
Publishing industries	1 035	761	791	-274	30	-3.0	0.4	265	321	556	1.9	5.7
Newspaper, periodical, book, and directory publishers	774	501	440	-273.0	-62	-4.3	-1.3	172	164	210	-0.5	2.5
Software publishers	261	260	352	-1	92	0.0	3.1	93	157	368	5.4	8.9
Motion picture, video, and sound recording industries	383	372	347	-11	-25	-0.3	-0.7	80	97	130	1.9	3.0
Broadcasting (except Internet)	344	295	325	-49	30	-1.5	1.0	88	99	137	1.2	3.2
Telecommunications	1 397	900	974	-497	74	-4.3	0.8	419	511	775	2.0	4.2
Data processing, hosting, related services, and other information services	473	384	415	-89	31	-2.1	0.8	99	168	303	5.4	6.1
Finance and Insurance	5 677	5 691	6 196	15	505	0.0	0.9	1 621	2 029	2 804	2.3	3.3
Monetary authorities, credit intermediation, and related activities	2 571	2 566	2 651	-5	85	0.0	0.3	597	917	1 303	4.4	3.6
Securities, commodity contracts, and other financial investments and related activities	805	801	1 002	-4	201	0.0	2.3	384	411	637	0.7	4.5
Insurance carriers and related activities	2 221	2 238	2 433	18	195	0.1	0.8	533	595	743	1.1	2.2
Insurance carriers	1 433	1 368	1 415	-65	47	-0.5	0.3	415	441	546	0.6	2.2
Agencies, brokerages, and other insurance related activities	788	871	1 018	83	148	1.0	1.6	118	155	198	2.7	2.5
Funds, trusts, and other financial vehicles	81	87	111	6	24	0.7	2.4	107	107	139	0.0	2.7
Real estate, rental, and leasing	2 011	1 939	2 214	-72	275	-0.4	1.3	1 066	1 300	1 765	2.0	3.1
Real estate	1 316	1 396	1 563	80	167	0.6	1.1	842	1 017	1 334	1.9	2.8
Rental and leasing services and lessors of intangible assets	695	543	651	-151	108	-2.4	1.8	224	283	434	2.4	4.3
Automotive equipment rental and leasing	208	163	177	-46	14	-2.4	0.8	43	50	72	1.5	3.8
Consumer goods rental and general rental centers	356	242	290	-114	48	-3.8	1.8	26	37	52	3.7	3.5
Commercial and industrial machinery and equipment rental and leasing	103	114	151	11	38	1.0	2.9	47	63	90	3.0	3.7
Lessors of nonfinancial intangible assets (except copyrighted works)	28	25	33	-3	8	-1.0	2.9	109	134	220	2.1	5.1
Professional, Scientific, and Technical Services	6 702	7 424	9 551	722	2 127	1.0	2.6	1 131	1 444	2 057	2.5	3.6
Legal services	1 066	1 114	1 178	48	64	0.4	0.6	229	244	293	0.6	1.9
Accounting, tax preparation, bookkeeping, and payroll services	866	888	975	22	87	0.2	0.9	119	129	178	0.8	3.3
Architectural, engineering, and related services	1 238	1 277	1 635	39	359	0.3	2.5	191	264	366	3.3	3.3
Specialized design services	132	111	140	-21	29	-1.7	2.4	24	31	43	2.5	3.4
Computer systems design and related services	1 254	1 442	2 113	187	671	1.4	3.9	165	259	467	4.6	6.1
Management, scientific, and technical consulting services	673	991	1 567	319	576	4.0	4.7	128	167	243	2.7	3.8
Scientific research and development services	515	620	694	105	74	1.9	1.1	103	141	194	3.2	3.3
Advertising and related services	497	408	490	-88	81	-1.9	1.8	84	120	171	3.6	3.7
Other professional, scientific, and technical services	462	573	760	112	187	2.2	2.9	88	92	125	0.5	3.1
Management of companies and enterprises	1 796	1 863	1 966	67	103	0.4	0.5	274	319	495	1.5	4.5
Administrative and support and waste management and remediation services	8 168	7 401	8 980	-767	1 579	-1.0	2.0	530	592	819	1.1	3.3
Administrative and support services	7 855	7 044	8 545	-811	1 501	-1.1	2.0	472	518	724	0.9	3.4
Office administrative services	264	412	504	148	93	4.6	2.1	45	44	63	-0.2	3.5
Facilities support services	97	134	178	37	44	3.3	2.9	15	17	20	1.1	1.8
Employment services	3 849	2 717	3 348	-1 133	631	-3.4	2.1	118	158	229	2.9	3.8
Business support services	787	807	973	20	166	0.2	1.9	63	66	91	0.4	3.3
Travel arrangement and reservation services	299	187	219	-112	33	-4.6	1.6	36	36	47	-0.2	2.8
Investigation and security services	689	777	969	88	192	1.2	2.2	39	44	62	1.3	3.5
Services to buildings and dwellings	1 571	1 743	2 045	172	302	1.0	1.6	110	118	164	0.7	3.4
Other support services	301	269	309	-32	40	-1.1	1.4	46	35	49	-2.5	3.3

Table 4-7. Employment and Output, by Industry, 2000, 2010, and Projected 2020—*Continued*

(Number, percent, dollars.)

Industry	Number of jobs (thousands)			Change		Average annual rate of change (percent)		Billions of chained (2005) dollars			Average annual rate of change (percent)	
	2000	2010	2020	2000–2020	2010–2020	2000–2010	2010–2020	2000	2010	2020	2000–2010	2010–2020
Professional, Scientific, and Technical Services —*Continued*												
Waste management and remediation services	313	357	434	44	78	1.3	2.0	58	74	95	2.6	2.5
Education services	2 391	3 150	3 969	759	819	2.8	2.3	202	199	236	-0.2	1.7
Elementary and secondary schools	716	851	1 011	135	159	1.7	1.7	35	33	36	-0.6	0.8
Junior colleges, colleges, universities, and professional schools	1 275	1 694	2 171	419	477	2.9	2.5	123	123	146	0.0	1.7
Other educational services	399	604	787	205	183	4.2	2.7	43	43	53	-0.1	2.2
Health care and social assistance	12 718	16 415	22 054	3 696	5 639	2.6	3.0	1 142	1 526	2 026	2.9	2.9
Ambulatory health care services	4 320	5 976	8 633	1 656	2 657	3.3	3.7	508	708	982	3.4	3.3
Offices of health practitioners	2 966	3 818	5 210	853	1 391	2.6	3.2	369	513	693	3.4	3.0
Outpatient, laboratory, and other ambulatory care services	721	1 077	1 471	356	394	4.1	3.2	100	146	216	3.9	4.0
Home health care services	633	1 081	1 952	447	872	5.5	6.1	39	49	74	2.2	4.3
Hospitals, private	3 954	4 685	5 564	731	878	1.7	1.7	403	508	638	2.3	2.3
Nursing and residential care facilities	2 583	3 129	3 951	546	822	1.9	2.4	133	169	222	2.4	2.7
Social assistance	1 860	2 624	3 906	764	1 282	3.5	4.1	98	140	187	3.7	2.9
Individual and family services	678	1 215	2 066	537	851	6.0	5.5	41	65	89	4.8	3.2
Community, and vocational rehabilitation services	487	558	738	71	181	1.4	2.9	20	35	47	5.5	3.1
Child day care services	696	852	1 101	156	250	2.0	2.6	37	41	52	1.1	2.5
Arts, entertainment, and recreation	1 788	1 909	2 249	121	340	0.7	1.7	174	193	254	1.0	2.8
Performing arts, spectator sports, and related industries	382	410	487	28	77	0.7	1.7	80	99	136	2.2	3.2
Performing arts companies	132	111	124	-22	13	-1.8	1.1	13	14	18	0.1	2.8
Spectator sports	131	140	163	10	23	0.7	1.5	27	34	47	2.1	3.3
Promoters of events, and agents and managers	83	116	149	33	33	3.4	2.5	17	23	31	2.8	3.1
Independent artists, writers, and performers	36	44	51	8	8	1.9	1.7	22	29	40	2.9	3.3
Museums, historical sites, and similar institutions	110	127	151	17	23	1.4	1.7	9	14	19	4.9	3.2
Amusement, gambling, and recreation industries	1 296	1 371	1 612	76	240	0.6	1.6	86	80	99	-0.7	2.2
Accommodation and food services	10 074	11 111	12 113	1 037	1 002	1.0	0.9	580	677	869	1.6	2.5
Accommodation	1 884	1 759	1 901	-125	142	-0.7	0.8	164	197	254	1.8	2.6
Food services and drinking places	8 189	9 352	10 212	1 163	860	1.3	0.9	416	481	615	1.4	2.5
Other services	5 886	6 031	6 851	146	819	0.2	1.3	514	515	652	0.0	2.4
Repair and maintenance	1 242	1 137	1 400	-105	264	-0.9	2.1	184	175	235	-0.5	3.0
Automotive repair and maintenance	888	800	1 037	-88	238	-1.0	2.6	114	104	145	-0.9	3.4
Electronic and precision equipment repair and maintenance	107	98	101	-9	4	-0.9	0.4	21	27	35	2.5	2.7
Commercial and industrial machinery and equipment (except automotive and electronic) repair and maintenance	161	171	193	11	22	0.6	1.2	27	25	32	-0.7	2.5
Personal and household goods repair and maintenance	86	68	69	-18	1	-2.3	0.1	22	19	23	-1.6	2.1
Personal and laundry services	1 243	1 265	1 346	22	81	0.2	0.6	134	117	150	-1.3	2.5
Personal care services	490	600	699	111	98	2.1	1.5	43	42	54	-0.3	2.6
Death care services	136	132	141	-5	10	-0.3	0.7	19	14	17	-3.0	2.3
Drycleaning and laundry services	388	302	266	-86	-36	-2.5	-1.3	27	23	28	-1.5	2.2
Other personal services	229	231	240	1	10	0.1	0.4	46	39	50	-1.5	2.5
Religious, grantmaking, civic, professional, and similar organizations	2 683	2 962	3 406	279	443	1.0	1.4	180	207	250	1.4	1.9
Religious organizations	1 547	1 682	1 929	135	247	0.8	1.4	65	72	83	1.0	1.4
Grantmaking and giving services and social advocacy organizations	259	395	511	136	116	4.3	2.6	39	56	69	3.6	2.0
Civic, social, professional, and similar organizations	877	886	966	8	80	0.1	0.9	75	79	99	0.4	2.3
Private households	718	667	699	-51	32	-0.7	0.5	17	15	19	-0.8	2.2
Federal Government	2 865	2 968	2 596	103	-372	0.4	-1.3	732	1 012	939	3.3	-0.7
Postal Service	880	656	475	-223	-182	-2.9	-3.2	74	62	58	-1.8	-0.8
Federal electric utilities	30	22	19	-8	-3	-3.1	-1.2	11	13	16	1.6	2.4
Federal enterprises except the Postal Service and electric utilities	67	77	60	9	-16	1.3	-2.4	8	8	9	-0.1	1.1
Federal defense government compensation	510	546	496	36	-50	0.7	-0.9	197	242	225	2.1	-0.7
Federal defense government consumption of fixed capital	0	0	0	0	0	0.0	0.0	66	83	77	2.4	-0.7
Federal defense government except compensation and consumption of fixed capital	0	0	0	0	0	0.0	0.0	149	289	272	6.8	-0.6
Federal non-defense government compensation-except enterprises	1 379	1 668	1 546	289	-122	1.9	-0.8	125	147	129	1.7	-1.3
Federal non-defense government consumption of fixed capital	0	0	0	0	0	0.0	0.0	22	31	27	3.4	-1.3
Federal non-defense government except compensation and consumption of fixed capital	0	0	0	0	0	0.0	0.0	81	139	127	5.5	-0.8
Federal government except enterprises	1 888	2 213	2 042	325	-171	1.6	-0.8	640	930	857	3.8	-0.8
State and Local Government	17 925	19 513	21 155	1 588	1 642	0.9	0.8	1 574	1 759	2 120	1.1	1.9
Local government passenger transit	230	264	282	34	18	1.4	0.7	11	11	14	0.0	2.9
Local government enterprises except passenger transit	1 154	1 327	1 533	173	206	1.4	1.5	140	163	211	1.5	2.6
Local government hospitals-compensation	622	654	703	32	50.0	0.5	0.7	44	44	52	0.0	1.7
Local government educational services-compensation	7 294	8 010	8 751	717	741	0.9	0.9	358	373	442	0.4	1.7
Local government excluding enterprises, educational services, and hospitals-compensation	3 840	4 117	4 350	278	233	0.7	0.6	195	222	262	1.3	1.7
State government enterprises	528	518	485	-11	-33	-0.2	-0.7	20	24	31	1.9	2.6
State government hospitals-compensation	343	357	371	14	14	0.4	0.4	35	30	28	-1.5	-0.5
State government educational services-compensation	2 031	2 377	2 662	347	285	1.6	1.1	100	112	132	1.1	1.7
State government, other compensation	1 885	1 890	2 018	5	128	0.0	0.7	112	116	137	0.3	1.7
State and local government capital services	0	0	0	0	0	0.0	0.0	96	131	155	3.1	1.7
General state and local government except compensation and capital services	0	0	0	0	0	0.0	0.0	465	535	656	1.4	2.1
Owner-Occupied Dwellings	0	0	0	0	0	0.0	0.0	950	1 138	1 521	1.8	2.9
Agriculture, Forestry, Fishing, and Hunting	2 396	2 136	2 005	-261	-130	-1.1	-0.6	285	301	365	0.5	1.9
Crop production	1 036	982	913	-55	-69	-0.5	-0.7	124	123	143	-0.1	1.5
Animal production	1 036	833	785	-204	-47	-2.2	-0.6	119	139	175	1.5	2.4
Forestry	14	15	19	1	5	0.6	2.7	6	8	10	2.3	2.5
Logging	126	73	76	-53	4	-5.4	0.5	14	15	19	0.4	2.3
Fishing, hunting and trapping	55	47	39	-9	-8.0	-1.7	-1.8	6	6	6	0.1	-0.3
Support activities for agriculture and forestry	129	188	173	59	-15	3.8	-0.8	16	11	13	-3.7	2.0
Nonagriculture Self-Employed and Unpaid Family Worker	9 314	8 944	9 721	-370	777	-0.4	0.8	. . .	. . .	. . .	. . .	. . .
Secondary Wage and Salary Jobs in Agriculture and Private Household Industries	142	112	113	-30	1	-2.4	0.1	. . .	. . .	. . .	. . .	. . .
Secondary Jobs as a Self-Employed or Unpaid Family Worker	1 959	1 442	1 522	-518	81	-3.0	0.5	. . .	. . .	. . .	. . .	. . .

. . . = Not available.

Table 4-8. Employment, by Occupation, 2010 and Projected 2020

(Numbers in thousands, percent.)

Occupation	Employment				Change, 2010–2020		Total job openings due to growth and net replacements, 2010–2020[1]
	Number		Percent distribution		Number	Percent	
	2010	2020	2010	2020			
TOTAL, ALL OCCUPATIONS	143 068	163 537	100.0	100.0	20 469	14.3	54 787
Management, Business, and Financial	15 565	17 354	10.9	10.6	1 788	11.5	5 123
Management occupations	8 776	9 392	6.1	5.7	616	7.0	2 568
Top executives	2 205	2 302	1.5	1.4	97	4.4	537
Chief executives	370	385	0.3	0.2	15	4.2	112
General and operations managers	1 767	1 849	1.2	1.1	82	4.6	410
Legislators	68	68	0.0	0.0	0	0.3	16
Advertising, marketing, promotions, public relations, and sales managers	621	701	0.4	0.4	80	12.8	260
Advertising and promotions managers	39	44	0.0	0.0	5	13.3	16
Marketing and sales managers	520	585	0.4	0.4	64	12.4	216
Marketing managers	178	202	0.1	0.1	24	13.6	76
Sales managers	342	382	0.2	0.2	40	11.7	140
Public relations and fundraising managers	62	72	0.0	0.0	10	16.4	28
Operations specialties managers	1 540	1 722	1.1	1.1	182	11.8	501
Administrative services managers	254	291	0.2	0.2	37	14.5	100
Computer and information systems managers	308	364	0.2	0.2	56	18.1	103
Financial managers	527	573	0.4	0.4	46	8.8	143
Industrial production managers	150	164	0.1	0.1	14	9.1	49
Purchasing managers	68	73	0.0	0.0	5	7.2	26
Transportation, storage, and distribution managers	99	109	0.1	0.1	10	10.0	34
Compensation and benefits managers	32	33	0.0	0.0	1	2.8	9
Human resources managers	72	81	0.1	0.0	9	12.9	27
Training and development managers	30	34	0.0	0.0	4	14.6	12
Other management occupations	4 411	4 668	3.1	2.9	257	5.8	1 270
Farmers, ranchers, and other agricultural managers	1 203	1 106	0.8	0.7	-96	-8.0	235
Construction managers	523	610	0.4	0.4	87	16.6	120
Education administrators	478	550	0.3	0.3	71	14.9	206
Education administrators, preschool and childcare center/program	64	80	0.0	0.0	16	24.9	34
Education administrators, elementary and secondary school	236	259	0.2	0.2	23	9.8	90
Education administrators, postsecondary	146	174	0.1	0.1	28	19.0	69
Education administrators, all other	33	37	0.0	0.0	4	13.6	14
Architectural and engineering managers	177	192	0.1	0.1	15	8.6	50
Food service managers	321	310	0.2	0.2	-11	-3.3	59
Gaming managers	3	4	0.0	0.0	0	11.5	1
Lodging managers	51	56	0.0	0.0	4	8.3	18
Medical and health services managers	303	371	0.2	0.2	68	22.4	142
Natural sciences managers	49	53	0.0	0.0	4	7.7	34
Postmasters and mail superintendents	25	18	0.0	0.0	-7	-27.8	5
Property, real estate, and community association managers	304	322	0.2	0.2	18	6.0	82
Social and community service managers	134	170	0.1	0.1	36	26.7	65
Emergency management directors	12	14	0.0	0.0	2	12.8	4
Managers, all other	828	894	0.6	0.5	65	7.9	249
Business and Financial Operations	6 789	7 962	4.7	4.9	1 173	17.3	2 555
Business operations specialists	4 152	4 903	2.9	3.0	751	18.1	1 563
Agents and business managers of artists, performers, and athletes	24	28	0.0	0.0	3	14.0	8
Buyers and purchasing agents	419	446	0.3	0.3	27	6.4	136
Buyers and purchasing agents, farm products	13	14	0.0	0.0	1	5.5	3
Wholesale and retail buyers, except farm products	122	133	0.1	0.1	11	9.0	42
Purchasing agents, except wholesale, retail, and farm products	284	299	0.2	0.2	15	5.3	91
Claims adjusters, appraisers, examiners, and investigators	291	298	0.2	0.2	8	2.6	83
Claims adjusters, examiners, and investigators	280	288	0.2	0.2	8	3.0	80
Insurance appraisers, auto damage	11	10	0.0	0.0	-1	-7.5	3
Compliance officers	217	249	0.2	0.2	32	15.0	59
Cost estimators	185	253	0.1	0.2	68	36.4	103
Human resources workers	443	533	0.3	0.3	91	20.5	165
Farm labor contractors	0	0	0.0	0.0	0	-0.7	0
Human resources, training, and labor relations specialists, all other	442	533	0.3	0.3	91	20.5	165
Logisticians	109	137	0.1	0.1	28	25.5	49
Management analysts	719	876	0.5	0.5	157	21.9	274
Meeting, convention, and event planners	72	103	0.1	0.1	31	43.7	45
Compensation, benefits, and job analysis specialists	110	115	0.1	0.1	6	5.0	24
Training and development specialists	218	279	0.2	0.2	62	28.3	98
Market research analysts and marketing specialists	283	399	0.2	0.2	117	41.2	192
Business operations specialists, all other	1 064	1 187	0.7	0.7	123	11.6	327
Financial specialists	2 637	3 058	1.8	1.9	421	16.0	992
Accountants and auditors	1 217	1 408	0.9	0.9	191	15.7	452
Appraisers and assessors of real estate	78	84	0.1	0.1	6	7.4	22
Budget analysts	62	69	0.0	0.0	7	10.4	20
Credit analysts	63	76	0.0	0.0	13	19.7	26
Financial analysts and advisors	545	671	0.4	0.4	127	23.2	234
Financial analysts	236	290	0.2	0.2	54	23.0	104
Personal financial advisors	207	273	0.1	0.2	66	32.1	90
Insurance underwriters	102	108	0.1	0.1	6	5.9	39
Financial examiners	29	37	0.0	0.0	8	27.0	14
Credit counselors and loan officers	323	370	0.2	0.2	48	14.8	130
Credit counselors	33	40	0.0	0.0	7	20.3	15
Loan officers	289	330	0.2	0.2	41	14.2	115
Tax examiners, collectors and preparers, and revenue agents	156	169	0.1	0.1	13	8.6	49
Tax examiners and collectors, and revenue agents	75	80	0.1	0.0	6	7.3	23
Tax preparers	82	90	0.1	0.1	8	9.8	26
Financial specialists, all other	165	175	0.1	0.1	10	6.1	45

Note: Data may not sum to totals or 100 percent due to rounding.

[1]Total job openings represent the sum of employment increases and net replacements. If employment change is negative, job openings due to growth are zero and total job openings equal net replacements.

Table 4-8. Employment, by Occupation, 2010 and Projected 2020—*Continued*

(Numbers in thousands, percent.)

Occupation	Employment				Change, 2010–2020		Total job openings due to growth and net replacements, 2010–2020[1]
	Number		Percent distribution		Number	Percent	
	2010	2020	2010	2020			
Computer, Engineering, and Science	7 205	8 427	5.0	5.2	1 222	17.0	2 782
Computer and mathematical occupations	3 543	4 321	2.5	2.6	778	22.0	1 438
Computer occupations	3 426	4 185	2.4	2.6	759	22.1	1 366
Computer and information research scientists	28	34	0.0	0.0	5	18.7	11
Computer systems analysts	544	665	0.4	0.4	120	22.1	223
Software developers and programmers	1 276	1 591	0.9	1.0	315	24.6	494
Computer programmers	363	407	0.3	0.2	44	12.0	128
Software developers, applications	521	665	0.4	0.4	144	27.6	198
Software developers, systems software	392	519	0.3	0.3	127	32.4	168
Database and systems administrators and network architects	458	589	0.3	0.4	131	28.5	208
Database administrators	111	145	0.1	0.1	34	30.6	53
Network and computer systems administrators	347	444	0.2	0.3	97	27.8	155
Computer support specialists	607	717	0.4	0.4	110	18.1	270
Information security analysts, web developers, and computer network architects	302	368	0.2	0.2	66	21.7	110
Computer occupations, all other	210	222	0.1	0.1	12	5.9	52
Mathematical science occupations	117	136	0.1	0.1	20	16.7	72
Actuaries	22	28	0.0	0.0	6	26.7	19
Mathematicians	3	4	0.0	0.0	1	15.7	2
Operations research analysts	65	74	0.0	0.0	9	14.6	30
Statisticians	25	29	0.0	0.0	4	14.1	19
Miscellaneous mathematical science occupations	2	3	0.0	0.0	0	11.0	2
Mathematical technicians	1	1	0.0	0.0	0	6.2	1
Mathematical science occupations, all other	1	2	0.0	0.0	0	14.7	1
Architecture and Engineering	2 433	2 686	1.7	1.6	253	10.4	798
Architects, surveyors, and cartographers	200	248	0.1	0.2	47	23.7	89
Architects, except naval	135	167	0.1	0.1	31	23.1	59
Architects, except landscape and naval	114	142	0.1	0.1	28	24.5	51
Landscape architects	22	25	0.0	0.0	4	16.0	8
Surveyors, cartographers, and photogrammetrists	65	81	0.0	0.0	16	24.8	30
Cartographers and photogrammetrists	14	17	0.0	0.0	3	22.2	6
Surveyors	51	64	0.0	0.0	13	25.4	24
Engineers	1 519	1 679	1.1	1.0	160	10.6	526
Aerospace engineers	81	85	0.1	0.1	4	4.9	22
Agricultural engineers	3	3	0.0	0.0	0	9.1	1
Biomedical engineers	16	25	0.0	0.0	10	61.7	13
Chemical engineers	30	32	0.0	0.0	2	5.9	11
Civil engineers	263	314	0.2	0.2	51	19.4	104
Computer hardware engineers	70	76	0.0	0.0	6	9.0	23
Electrical and electronics engineers	294	312	0.2	0.2	18	6.0	88
Electrical engineers	154	165	0.1	0.1	11	7.0	48
Electronics engineers, except computer	140	147	0.1	0.1	7	4.9	41
Environmental engineers	51	63	0.0	0.0	11	21.9	23
Industrial engineers, including health and safety	228	244	0.2	0.1	16	7.1	66
Health and safety engineers, except mining safety engineers and inspectors	24	27	0.0	0.0	3	13.0	8
Industrial engineers	204	217	0.1	0.1	13	6.4	58
Marine engineers and naval architects	6	7	0.0	0.0	1	17.5	2
Materials engineers	22	24	0.0	0.0	2	8.7	8
Mechanical engineers	243	265	0.2	0.2	21	8.8	100
Mining and geological engineers, including mining safety engineers	6	7	0.0	0.0	1	9.6	2
Nuclear engineers	19	21	0.0	0.0	2	10.2	6
Petroleum engineers	30	35	0.0	0.0	5	17.0	12
Engineers, all other	157	167	0.1	0.1	10	6.6	45
Drafters, engineering technicians, and mapping technicians	714	759	0.5	0.5	45	6.3	183
Drafters	205	217	0.1	0.1	11	5.6	52
Architectural and civil drafters	93	96	0.1	0.1	3	3.2	21
Electrical and electronics drafters	29	31	0.0	0.0	2	5.4	7
Mechanical drafters	67	75	0.0	0.0	8	11.1	21
Drafters, all other	16	15	0.0	0.0	-1	-4.0	3
Engineering technicians, except drafters	452	477	0.3	0.3	25	5.4	111
Aerospace engineering and operations technicians	9	9	0.0	0.0	0	-1.6	2
Civil engineering technicians	79	89	0.1	0.1	9	12.0	25
Electrical and electronics engineering technicians	151	154	0.1	0.1	3	1.9	32
Electro-mechanical technicians	16	17	0.0	0.0	0	0.5	3
Environmental engineering technicians	19	23	0.0	0.0	5	24.3	8
Industrial engineering technicians	63	65	0.0	0.0	3	4.2	15
Mechanical engineering technicians	45	47	0.0	0.0	2	3.9	10
Engineering technicians, except drafters, all other	71	74	0.0	0.0	3	4.7	17
Surveying and mapping technicians	57	66	0.0	0.0	9	15.9	20
Life, Physical, and Social Science	1 229	1 420	0.9	0.9	191	15.5	546
Life scientists	286	344	0.2	0.2	58	20.4	106
Agricultural and food scientists	34	37	0.0	0.0	4	10.4	17
Animal scientists	3	4	0.0	0.0	0	12.8	2
Food scientists and technologists	14	15	0.0	0.0	1	8.0	7
Soil and plant scientists	16	18	0.0	0.0	2	12.1	9
Biological scientists	101	115	0.1	0.1	14	14.0	37
Biochemists and biophysicists	25	33	0.0	0.0	8	30.8	13
Microbiologists	20	23	0.0	0.0	3	13.3	7
Zoologists and wildlife biologists	20	21	0.0	0.0	2	7.4	6
Biological scientists, all other	36	38	0.0	0.0	2	6.3	10
Conservation scientists and foresters	35	37	0.0	0.0	2	5.0	6
Conservation scientists	23	25	0.0	0.0	1	5.2	4
Foresters	12	12	0.0	0.0	1	4.7	2
Medical scientists	105	143	0.1	0.1	38	35.8	44
Epidemiologists	5	6	0.0	0.0	1	23.6	2
Medical scientists, except epidemiologists	100	137	0.1	0.1	36	36.4	43
Life scientists, all other	12	13	0.0	0.0	1	11.7	2

Note: Data may not sum to totals or 100 percent due to rounding.

[1] Total job openings represent the sum of employment increases and net replacements. If employment change is negative, job openings due to growth are zero and total job openings equal net replacements.

Table 4-8. Employment, by Occupation, 2010 and Projected 2020—*Continued*

(Numbers in thousands, percent.)

Occupation	Employment				Change, 2010–2020		Total job openings due to growth and net replacements, 2010–2020[1]
	Number		Percent distribution		Number	Percent	
	2010	2020	2010	2020			
Life, Physical, and Social Science—*Continued*							
Physical scientists	282	318	0.2	0.2	36	12.7	122
Astronomers and physicists	21	23	0.0	0.0	3	13.8	9
Astronomers	2	3	0.0	0.0	0	11.0	1
Physicists	18	21	0.0	0.0	3	14.2	8
Atmospheric and space scientists	10	10	0.0	0.0	1	10.6	2
Chemists and materials scientists	91	95	0.1	0.1	4	4.5	34
Chemists	82	85	0.1	0.1	3	3.8	30
Materials scientists	9	10	0.0	0.0	1	10.2	4
Environmental scientists and geoscientists	131	156	0.1	0.1	25	19.3	64
Environmental scientists and specialists, including health	89	106	0.1	0.1	17	18.7	43
Geoscientists, except hydrologists and geographers	34	41	0.0	0.0	7	21.2	17
Hydrologists	8	9	0.0	0.0	1	17.8	4
Physical scientists, all other	30	33	0.0	0.0	3	8.5	13
Social scientists and related workers	306	363	0.2	0.2	57	18.4	155
Economists	15	16	0.0	0.0	1	6.1	6
Survey researchers	20	24	0.0	0.0	5	24.1	10
Psychologists	174	212	0.1	0.1	38	21.6	93
Clinical, counseling, and school psychologists	154	188	0.1	0.1	34	21.9	82
Industrial-organizational psychologists	2	3	0.0	0.0	1	34.9	2
Psychologists, all other	18	21	0.0	0.0	3	18.2	9
Sociologists	4	5	0.0	0.0	1	18.1	2
Urban and regional planners	40	47	0.0	0.0	7	16.2	17
Miscellaneous social scientists and related workers	53	59	0.0	0.0	6	11.2	28
Anthropologists and archeologists	6	7	0.0	0.0	1	20.7	4
Geographers	2	2	0.0	0.0	1	35.4	1
Historians	4	5	0.0	0.0	1	17.9	2
Political scientists	6	6	0.0	0.0	0	7.9	3
Social scientists and related workers, all other	35	38	0.0	0.0	3	8.1	18
Life, physical, and social science technicians	355	395	0.2	0.2	40	11.4	163
Agricultural and food science technicians	21	23	0.0	0.0	2	7.0	9
Biological technicians	80	91	0.1	0.1	11	13.5	38
Chemical technicians	61	65	0.0	0.0	4	6.7	13
Geological and petroleum technicians	14	17	0.0	0.0	2	14.7	7
Nuclear technicians	7	8	0.0	0.0	1	13.5	3
Social science research assistants	30	34	0.0	0.0	4	15.0	17
Miscellaneous life, physical, and social science technicians	141	157	0.1	0.1	16	11.6	76
Environmental science and protection technicians, including health	30	37	0.0	0.0	7	23.6	20
Forensic science technicians	13	15	0.0	0.0	2	18.6	8
Forest and conservation technicians	37	36	0.0	0.0	0	-1.0	15
Life, physical, and social science technicians, all other	62	69	0.0	0.0	7	11.8	34
Education, Legal, Community Service, Arts, and Media	15 517	17 976	10.8	11.0	2 460	15.9	5 906
Community and social service occupations	2 403	2 985	1.7	1.8	582	24.2	1 098
Counselors, social workers, and other community and social service specialists	1 997	2 510	1.4	1.5	512	25.7	957
Counselors	685	863	0.5	0.5	179	26.1	325
Substance abuse and behavioral disorder counselors	86	109	0.1	0.1	23	27.3	42
Educational, guidance, school, and vocational counselors	281	335	0.2	0.2	53	19.0	114
Marriage and family therapists	36	51	0.0	0.0	15	41.2	23
Mental health counselors	120	164	0.1	0.1	44	36.3	69
Rehabilitation counselors	130	166	0.1	0.1	37	28.2	64
Counselors, all other	32	38	0.0	0.0	7	21.3	14
Social workers	651	812	0.5	0.5	161	24.8	315
Child, family, and school social workers	296	354	0.2	0.2	58	19.7	128
Healthcare social workers	153	204	0.1	0.1	51	33.5	87
Mental health and substance abuse social workers	126	166	0.1	0.1	40	31.3	69
Social workers, all other	76	88	0.1	0.1	12	16.2	30
Miscellaneous community and social service specialists	662	835	0.5	0.5	173	26.1	316
Health educators	63	87	0.0	0.1	23	36.5	37
Probation officers and correctional treatment specialists	93	110	0.1	0.1	17	18.4	37
Social and human service assistants	384	490	0.3	0.3	106	27.6	189
Community and social service specialists, all other	121	148	0.1	0.1	26	21.8	53
Religious workers	405	475	0.3	0.3	70	17.2	142
Clergy	231	271	0.2	0.2	41	17.5	80
Directors, religious activities and education	126	147	0.1	0.1	21	16.8	45
Religious workers, all other	49	57	0.0	0.0	8	17.0	17
Legal	1 212	1 343	0.8	0.8	131	10.8	344
Lawyers, judges, and related workers	821	901	0.6	0.6	80	9.8	235
Lawyers and judicial law clerks	758	834	0.5	0.5	76	10.0	219
Lawyers	728	802	0.5	0.5	74	10.1	212
Judicial law clerks	30	32	0.0	0.0	2	7.7	7
Judges, magistrates, and other judicial workers	63	67	0.0	0.0	5	7.3	17
Administrative law judges, adjudicators, and hearing officers	19	19	0.0	0.0	0	-0.1	4
Arbitrators, mediators, and conciliators	9	11	0.0	0.0	2	15.5	3
Judges, magistrate judges, and magistrates	34	37	0.0	0.0	3	9.2	10
Legal support workers	391	442	0.3	0.3	51	12.9	108
Paralegals and legal assistants	256	303	0.2	0.2	47	18.3	83
Miscellaneous legal support workers	135	139	0.1	0.1	4	2.7	25
Court reporters	22	25	0.0	0.0	3	14.1	6
Title examiners, abstractors, and searchers	59	58	0.0	0.0	-1	-1.4	9
Legal support workers, all other	54	56	0.0	0.0	1	2.6	10

Note: Data may not sum to totals or 100 percent due to rounding.

[1]Total job openings represent the sum of employment increases and net replacements. If employment change is negative, job openings due to growth are zero and total job openings equal net replacements.

Table 4-8. Employment, by Occupation, 2010 and Projected 2020—*Continued*

(Numbers in thousands, percent.)

Occupation	Employment				Change, 2010–2020		Total job openings due to growth and net replacements, 2010–2020[1]
	Number		Percent distribution		Number	Percent	
	2010	2020	2010	2020			
Education, Training, and Library	9 194	10 597	6.4	6.5	1 404	15.3	3 398
Postsecondary teachers	1 756	2 062	1.2	1.3	306	17.4	586
Preschool, Primary, secondary, and special education school teachers	4 354	5 009	3.0	3.1	655	15.0	1 733
Preschool and kindergarten teachers	636	782	0.4	0.5	146	23.0	312
Preschool teachers, except special education	457	570	0.3	0.3	114	24.9	232
Kindergarten teachers, except special education	179	212	0.1	0.1	33	18.2	79
Elementary and middle school teachers	2 133	2 491	1.5	1.5	358	16.8	827
Elementary school teachers, except special education	1 477	1 725	1.0	1.1	249	16.8	573
Middle school teachers, except special and career/technical education	642	750	0.4	0.5	108	16.9	249
Career/technical education teachers, middle school	14	16	0.0	0.0	1	8.9	5
Secondary school teachers	1 126	1 199	0.8	0.7	73	6.5	381
Secondary school teachers, except special and career/technical education	1 038	1 110	0.7	0.7	72	6.9	356
Career/technical education teachers, secondary school	89	90	0.1	0.1	1	1.1	25
Special education teachers	460	537	0.3	0.3	77	16.8	213
Special education teachers, preschool, kindergarten, and elementary school	223	270	0.2	0.2	47	21.3	113
Special education teachers, middle school	98	118	0.1	0.1	20	20.2	49
Special education teachers, secondary school	139	149	0.1	0.1	10	7.3	51
Other Teachers and instructors	1 220	1 402	0.9	0.9	182	14.9	368
Adult basic and secondary education and literacy teachers and instructors	87	100	0.1	0.1	13	14.6	26
Self-enrichment education teachers	253	306	0.2	0.2	53	20.9	92
Teachers and instructors, all other	881	997	0.6	0.6	116	13.2	251
Librarians, Curators, and archivists	301	327	0.2	0.2	26	8.5	124
Archivists, curators, and museum technicians	30	34	0.0	0.0	5	15.0	13
Archivists	6	7	0.0	0.0	1	11.7	2
Curators	12	15	0.0	0.0	3	24.8	6
Museum technicians and conservators	12	13	0.0	0.0	1	6.8	4
Librarians	156	167	0.1	0.1	11	6.9	51
Library technicians	115	126	0.1	0.1	10	8.9	60
Other Education, training, and library occupations	1 562	1 798	1.1	1.1	236	15.1	587
Audio-visual and multimedia collections specialists	8	10	0.0	0.0	1	12.7	3
Farm and home management advisors	13	15	0.0	0.0	2	16.6	5
Instructional coordinators	140	167	0.1	0.1	27	19.5	58
Teacher assistants	1 288	1 479	0.9	0.9	191	14.8	482
Education, training, and library workers, all other	112	127	0.1	0.1	14	12.8	39
Arts, Design, Entertainment, Sports, and Media	2 709	3 051	1.9	1.9	343	12.6	1 067
Art and design workers	777	853	0.5	0.5	76	9.8	309
Artists and related workers	197	213	0.1	0.1	15	7.7	62
Art directors	74	81	0.1	0.0	7	9.0	24
Craft artists	12	13	0.0	0.0	1	7.3	4
Fine artists, including painters, sculptors, and illustrators	26	28	0.0	0.0	2	7.8	8
Multimedia artists and animators	67	72	0.0	0.0	6	8.3	21
Artists and related workers, all other	19	20	0.0	0.0	0	1.0	5
Designers	580	640	0.4	0.4	61	10.5	247
Commercial and industrial designers	41	45	0.0	0.0	4	10.5	17
Fashion designers	22	22	0.0	0.0	0	0.2	7
Floral designers	67	60	0.0	0.0	-6	-9.3	21
Graphic designers	279	317	0.2	0.2	37	13.4	124
Interior designers	57	67	0.0	0.0	11	19.3	28
Merchandise displayers and window trimmers	91	103	0.1	0.1	12	12.8	40
Set and exhibit designers	12	13	0.0	0.0	1	9.9	5
Designers, all other	12	14	0.0	0.0	2	13.1	5
Entertainers and performers, sports and related workers	806	935	0.6	0.6	129	16.0	340
Actors, producers, and directors	189	205	0.1	0.1	16	8.5	70
Actors	67	69	0.0	0.0	3	3.9	20
Producers and directors	123	136	0.1	0.1	14	11.0	50
Athletes, coaches, umpires, and related workers	279	358	0.2	0.2	79	28.3	150
Athletes and sports competitors	17	20	0.0	0.0	4	21.6	8
Coaches and scouts	243	314	0.2	0.2	71	29.4	133
Umpires, referees, and Other Sports Officials	20	23	0.0	0.0	4	19.9	9
Dancers and choreographers	26	30	0.0	0.0	5	18.0	15
Dancers	12	14	0.0	0.0	1	11.2	6
Choreographers	13	16	0.0	0.0	3	24.2	8
Musicians, singers, and related workers	269	297	0.2	0.2	27	10.2	93
Music directors and composers	93	103	0.1	0.1	10	10.2	32
Musicians and singers	176	194	0.1	0.1	18	10.1	61
Entertainers and performers, sports and related workers, all other	43	45	0.0	0.0	2	4.4	13
Media and communication workers	792	898	0.6	0.5	106	13.4	325
Announcers	62	66	0.0	0.0	4	6.6	21
Radio and television announcers	50	54	0.0	0.0	4	6.9	17
Public address system and other announcers	12	12	0.0	0.0	1	5.2	4
News analysts, reporters and correspondents	59	55	0.0	0.0	-3	-5.5	21
Broadcast news analysts	7	7	0.0	0.0	1	10.2	3
Reporters and correspondents	52	48	0.0	0.0	-4	-7.5	18
Public relations specialists	258	316	0.2	0.2	58	22.5	127
Writers and editors	323	341	0.2	0.2	19	5.8	103
Editors	127	128	0.1	0.1	1	0.6	37
Technical writers	50	58	0.0	0.0	9	17.2	18
Writers and authors	146	155	0.1	0.1	10	6.5	48
Miscellaneous media and communication workers	91	119	0.1	0.1	28	31.2	53
Interpreters and translators	58	83	0.0	0.1	25	42.2	40
Media and communication workers, all other	33	36	0.0	0.0	4	11.4	12

Note: Data may not sum to totals or 100 percent due to rounding.

[1]Total job openings represent the sum of employment increases and net replacements. If employment change is negative, job openings due to growth are zero and total job openings equal net replacements.

Table 4-8. Employment, by Occupation, 2010 and Projected 2020—*Continued*

(Numbers in thousands, percent.)

Occupation	Employment				Change, 2010–2020		Total job openings due to growth and net replacements, 2010–2020[1]
	Number		Percent distribution		Number	Percent	
	2010	2020	2010	2020			
Arts, Design, Entertainment, Sports, and Media—*Continued*							
Media and communication equipment workers	334	366	0.2	0.2	31	9.4	92
Broadcast and sound engineering technicians and radio operators	118	130	0.1	0.1	12	9.9	45
Audio and video equipment technicians	61	69	0.0	0.0	8	13.4	26
Broadcast technicians	37	40	0.0	0.0	3	9.0	14
Radio operators	1	1	0.0	0.0	0	7.0	0
Sound engineering technicians	19	19	0.0	0.0	0	0.6	6
Photographers	140	157	0.1	0.1	18	12.5	31
Television, video, and motion picture camera operators and editors	58	61	0.0	0.0	2	3.8	13
Camera operators, television, video, and motion picture	27	27	0.0	0.0	1	2.1	5
Film and video editors	32	33	0.0	0.0	2	5.2	7
Media and communication equipment workers, all other	18	18	0.0	0.0	0	0.3	3
Healthcare Practitioners and Technical	7 799	9 819	5.5	6.0	2 020	25.9	3 591
Health diagnosing and treating practitioners	4 852	6 128	3.4	3.7	1 276	26.3	2 219
Chiropractors	53	67	0.0	0.0	15	28.3	25
Dentists	156	188	0.1	0.1	32	20.7	78
Dentists, general	131	158	0.1	0.1	28	21.1	66
Oral and maxillofacial surgeons	8	10	0.0	0.0	2	21.3	4
Orthodontists	8	10	0.0	0.0	2	21.1	4
Prosthodontists	1	1	0.0	0.0	0	21.4	1
Dentists, all other specialists	8	9	0.0	0.0	1	11.7	3
Dietitians and nutritionists	64	77	0.0	0.0	13	19.7	35
Optometrists	34	46	0.0	0.0	11	33.1	23
Pharmacists	275	345	0.2	0.2	70	25.4	140
Physicians and surgeons	691	859	0.5	0.5	168	24.4	305
Physician assistants	84	108	0.1	0.1	25	29.5	41
Podiatrists	13	16	0.0	0.0	3	20.0	5
Registered nurses	2 737	3 449	1.9	2.1	712	26.0	1 207
Therapists	616	806	0.4	0.5	190	30.9	298
Occupational therapists	109	145	0.1	0.1	36	33.5	57
Physical therapists	199	276	0.1	0.2	77	39.0	101
Radiation therapists	17	20	0.0	0.0	3	20.3	7
Recreational therapists	22	26	0.0	0.0	4	17.1	12
Respiratory therapists	113	144	0.1	0.1	31	27.7	53
Speech-language pathologists	123	152	0.1	0.1	29	23.4	52
Therapists, all other	33	42	0.0	0.0	9	27.9	16
Veterinarians	61	83	0.0	0.1	22	35.9	34
Audiologists	13	18	0.0	0.0	5	36.8	6
Health diagnosing and treating practitioners, all other	56	66	0.0	0.0	11	19.0	21
Health technologists and technicians	2 799	3 519	2.0	2.2	720	25.7	1 297
Clinical laboratory technologists and technicians	331	374	0.2	0.2	43	13.0	107
Medical and clinical laboratory technologists	169	189	0.1	0.1	19	11.3	52
Medical and clinical laboratory technicians	161	185	0.1	0.1	24	14.7	55
Dental hygienists	182	250	0.1	0.2	69	37.7	105
Diagnostic related technologists and technicians	345	448	0.2	0.3	103	29.9	157
Cardiovascular technologists and technicians	49	64	0.0	0.0	15	29.3	22
Diagnostic medical sonographers	54	77	0.0	0.0	23	43.5	32
Nuclear medicine technologists	22	26	0.0	0.0	4	18.9	8
Radiologic technologists and technicians	220	281	0.2	0.2	61	27.8	95
Emergency medical technicians and paramedics	227	302	0.2	0.2	75	33.3	121
Health practitioner support technologists and technicians	621	805	0.4	0.5	184	29.6	292
Dietetic technicians	24	28	0.0	0.0	4	16.0	8
Pharmacy technicians	334	443	0.2	0.3	108	32.4	166
Psychiatric technicians	75	86	0.1	0.1	12	15.5	25
Respiratory therapy technicians	14	14	0.0	0.0	1	4.1	3
Surgical technologists	94	111	0.1	0.1	18	18.9	34
Veterinary technologists and technicians	80	122	0.1	0.1	42	52.0	56
Licensed practical and licensed vocational nurses	752	921	0.5	0.6	169	22.4	369
Medical records and health information technicians	180	217	0.1	0.1	38	21.0	74
Opticians, dispensing	63	81	0.0	0.0	18	28.9	31
Orthotists and prosthetists	6	7	0.0	0.0	1	12.1	2
Health technologists and technicians, all other	94	115	0.1	0.1	22	23.2	40
Other healthcare practitioners and technical occupations	148	171	0.1	0.1	23	15.8	75
Occupational health and safety specialists and technicians	69	76	0.0	0.0	6	9.2	31
Occupational health and safety specialists	59	64	0.0	0.0	5	8.5	26
Occupational health and safety technicians	11	12	0.0	0.0	1	12.9	5
Miscellaneous health practitioners and technical workers	79	96	0.1	0.1	17	21.6	45
Athletic trainers	18	24	0.0	0.0	6	30.0	12
Healthcare practitioners and technical workers, all other	60	72	0.0	0.0	12	19.0	33
Service	29 136	34 037	20.4	20.8	4 901	16.8	12 577
Healthcare support occupations	4 190	5 634	2.9	3.4	1 444	34.5	2 042
Nursing, psychiatric, and home health aides	2 591	3 609	1.8	2.2	1 019	39.3	1 353
Home health aides	1 018	1 724	0.7	1.1	706	69.4	838
Nursing aides, orderlies, and attendants	1 505	1 807	1.1	1.1	302	20.1	496
Psychiatric aides	68	78	0.0	0.0	10	15.1	19
Occupational therapy and physical therapist assistants and aides	150	216	0.1	0.1	66	43.8	89
Occupational therapy assistants and aides	36	51	0.0	0.0	15	41.2	20
Occupational therapy assistants	29	41	0.0	0.0	12	43.3	17
Occupational therapy aides	8	10	0.0	0.0	3	33.0	4
Physical therapist assistants and aides	114	166	0.1	0.1	51	44.6	69
Physical therapist assistants	67	98	0.0	0.1	31	45.7	41
Physical therapist aides	47	67	0.0	0.0	20	43.1	28

Note: Data may not sum to totals or 100 percent due to rounding.

[1]Total job openings represent the sum of employment increases and net replacements. If employment change is negative, job openings due to growth are zero and total job openings equal net replacements.

Table 4-8. Employment, by Occupation, 2010 and Projected 2020—*Continued*

(Numbers in thousands, percent.)

Occupation	Employment				Change, 2010–2020		Total job openings due to growth and net replacements, 2010–2020[1]
	Number		Percent distribution		Number	Percent	
	2010	2020	2010	2020			
Service—*Continued*							
Other healthcare support occupations	1 449	1 808	1.0	1.1	359	24.8	600
Massage therapists	154	185	0.1	0.1	31	20.1	56
Miscellaneous healthcare support occupations	1 295	1 624	0.9	1.0	329	25.4	544
Dental assistants	297	389	0.2	0.2	92	30.8	154
Medical assistants	528	690	0.4	0.4	163	30.9	244
Medical equipment preparers	49	58	0.0	0.0	9	17.5	16
Medical transcriptionists	95	101	0.1	0.1	6	5.9	20
Pharmacy aides	51	65	0.0	0.0	15	28.6	22
Veterinary assistants and laboratory animal caretakers	73	84	0.1	0.1	10	14.2	22
Healthcare support workers, all other	202	237	0.1	0.1	35	17.2	66
Protective service occupations	3 303	3 667	2.3	2.2	365	11.0	1 196
Supervisors of protective service workers	267	282	0.2	0.2	15	5.8	114
First-line supervisors of law enforcement workers	148	152	0.1	0.1	5	3.1	55
First-line supervisors of correctional officers	42	44	0.0	0.0	2	5.6	17
First-line supervisors of police and detectives	106	108	0.1	0.1	2	2.1	39
First-line supervisors of fire fighting and prevention workers	60	65	0.0	0.0	5	8.2	33
First-line supervisors of protective service workers, all other	59	65	0.0	0.0	6	9.9	26
Fire fighting and prevention workers	326	354	0.2	0.2	28	8.6	118
Firefighters	310	337	0.2	0.2	27	8.6	112
Fire inspectors	15	17	0.0	0.0	1	8.8	5
Fire inspectors and investigators	14	15	0.0	0.0	1	9.2	5
Forest fire inspectors and prevention specialists	2	2	0.0	0.0	0	5.8	1
Law enforcement workers	1 297	1 383	0.9	0.8	86	6.6	399
Bailiffs, correctional officers, and jailers	493	519	0.3	0.3	26	5.3	113
Bailiffs	18	19	0.0	0.0	1	8.0	5
Correctional officers and jailers	475	500	0.3	0.3	25	5.2	108
Detectives and criminal investigators	119	123	0.1	0.1	4	2.9	30
Fish and game wardens	8	8	0.0	0.0	0	4.7	2
Parking enforcement workers	10	11	0.0	0.0	1	9.6	3
Police officers	667	722	0.5	0.4	55	8.2	251
Police and sheriff's patrol officers	664	719	0.5	0.4	55	8.2	249
Transit and railroad police	4	4	0.0	0.0	0	6.5	1
Other protective service workers	1 413	1 649	1.0	1.0	236	16.7	565
Animal control workers	16	17	0.0	0.0	2	11.7	6
Private detectives and investigators	35	42	0.0	0.0	7	20.5	15
Security guards and gaming surveillance officers	1 043	1 238	0.7	0.8	196	18.8	361
Gaming surveillance officers and gaming investigators	7	7	0.0	0.0	1	9.1	2
Security guards	1 036	1 231	0.7	0.8	195	18.8	360
Miscellaneous protective service workers	321	352	0.2	0.2	31	9.7	183
Crossing guards	69	70	0.0	0.0	1	1.1	17
Lifeguards, ski patrol, and other recreational protective service workers	122	136	0.1	0.1	15	12.3	93
Transportation security screeners (federal only)	48	53	0.0	0.0	5	9.5	10
Protective service workers, all other	82	92	0.1	0.1	11	13.2	63
Food Preparation and Serving Related	11 150	12 243	7.8	7.5	1 093	9.8	5 103
Supervisors of food preparation and serving workers	902	979	0.6	0.6	78	8.6	266
Chefs and head cooks	101	100	0.1	0.1	-1	-0.8	18
First-line supervisors of food preparation and serving workers	801	880	0.6	0.5	79	9.8	248
Cooks and food preparation workers	2 865	3 111	2.0	1.9	246	8.6	995
Cooks	2 051	2 213	1.4	1.4	162	7.9	618
Cooks, fast food	530	511	0.4	0.3	-19	-3.6	113
Cooks, institution and cafeteria	405	455	0.3	0.3	50	12.3	136
Cooks, private household	4	4	0.0	0.0	1	14.4	1
Cooks, restaurant	915	1 033	0.6	0.6	118	12.9	313
Cooks, short order	174	184	0.1	0.1	9	5.4	47
Cooks, all other	22	25	0.0	0.0	3	15.0	8
Food preparation workers	814	898	0.6	0.5	84	10.3	377
Food and beverage serving workers	6 100	6 804	4.3	4.2	704	11.5	3 139
Bartenders	503	549	0.4	0.3	46	9.0	221
Fast food and counter workers	3 128	3 553	2.2	2.2	425	13.6	1 497
Combined food preparation and serving workers, including fast food	2 682	3 080	1.9	1.9	398	14.8	1 147
Counter attendants, cafeteria, food concession, and coffee shop	446	473	0.3	0.3	27	6.2	350
Waiters and waitresses	2 260	2 456	1.6	1.5	196	8.7	1 324
Food servers, nonrestaurant	209	247	0.1	0.2	38	18.0	97
Other food preparation and serving related workers	1 284	1 349	0.9	0.8	65	5.0	703
Dining room and cafeteria attendants and bartender helpers	397	415	0.3	0.3	18	4.5	165
Dishwashers	510	546	0.4	0.3	36	7.0	269
Hosts and hostesses, restaurant, lounge, and coffee shop	331	344	0.2	0.2	14	4.1	246
Food preparation and serving related workers, all other	46	44	0.0	0.0	-3	-5.8	23
Building and Grounds Cleaning and Maintenance	5 499	6 163	3.8	3.8	664	12.1	1 655
Supervisors of building and grounds cleaning and maintenance workers	430	462	0.3	0.3	33	7.6	93
First-line supervisors of housekeeping and janitorial workers	227	229	0.2	0.1	2	0.8	33
First-line supervisors of landscaping, lawn service, and groundskeeping workers	203	234	0.1	0.1	31	15.1	60
Building cleaning and pest control workers	3 819	4 196	2.7	2.6	377	9.9	1 086
Building cleaning workers	3 751	4 110	2.6	2.5	359	9.6	1 037
Janitors and cleaners, except maids and housekeeping cleaners	2 310	2 557	1.6	1.6	246	10.7	682
Maids and housekeeping cleaners	1 427	1 539	1.0	0.9	112	7.8	352
Building cleaning workers, all other	13	14	0.0	0.0	1	7.3	3
Pest control workers	68	86	0.0	0.1	18	26.1	49
Grounds maintenance workers	1 250	1 504	0.9	0.9	255	20.4	476
Landscaping and groundskeeping workers	1 152	1 392	0.8	0.9	241	20.9	444
Pesticide handlers, sprayers, and applicators, vegetation	30	33	0.0	0.0	3	10.2	8
Tree trimmers and pruners	51	60	0.0	0.0	9	17.9	18
Grounds maintenance workers, all other	18	20	0.0	0.0	2	9.5	5

Note: Data may not sum to totals or 100 percent due to rounding.

[1]Total job openings represent the sum of employment increases and net replacements. If employment change is negative, job openings due to growth are zero and total job openings equal net replacements.

Table 4-8. Employment, by Occupation, 2010 and Projected 2020—*Continued*

(Numbers in thousands, percent.)

Occupation	Employment				Change, 2010–2020		Total job openings due to growth and net replacements, 2010–2020[1]
	Number		Percent distribution		Number	Percent	
	2010	2020	2010	2020			
Personal Care and Service	4 995	6 331	3.5	3.9	1 337	26.8	2 583
Supervisors of personal care and service workers	274	307	0.2	0.2	33	12.1	96
First-line supervisors of gaming workers	55	59	0.0	0.0	4	6.5	14
Gaming supervisors	36	39	0.0	0.0	3	6.9	9
Slot supervisors	19	20	0.0	0.0	1	5.7	5
First-line supervisors of personal service workers	219	249	0.2	0.2	30	13.5	83
Animal care and service workers	235	289	0.2	0.2	54	23.0	100
Animal trainers	46	47	0.0	0.0	2	3.2	6
Nonfarm animal caretakers	189	242	0.1	0.1	53	27.8	94
Entertainment attendants and related workers	560	637	0.4	0.4	78	13.9	382
Gaming services workers	119	138	0.1	0.1	19	16.0	70
Gaming dealers	91	107	0.1	0.1	16	17.1	55
Gaming and sports book writers and runners	15	17	0.0	0.0	2	12.1	8
Gaming service workers, all other	12	14	0.0	0.0	2	12.9	7
Motion picture projectionists	10	9	0.0	0.0	-1	-11.1	4
Ushers, lobby attendants, and ticket takers	109	120	0.1	0.1	11	10.2	75
Miscellaneous entertainment attendants and related workers	321	370	0.2	0.2	49	15.1	233
Amusement and recreation attendants	261	299	0.2	0.2	37	14.2	187
Costume attendants	6	6	0.0	0.0	1	9.9	4
Locker room, coatroom, and dressing room attendants	18	20	0.0	0.0	3	14.6	13
Entertainment attendants and related workers, all other	37	45	0.0	0.0	8	22.5	30
Funeral service workers	67	75	0.0	0.0	7	10.9	31
Embalmers	7	7	0.0	0.0	0	5.3	4
Funeral attendants	31	33	0.0	0.0	2	5.2	16
Funeral service managers, directors, morticians, and undertakers	29	35	0.0	0.0	5	18.2	11
Personal appearance workers	845	971	0.6	0.6	126	15.0	288
Barbers, hairdressers, hairstylists and cosmetologists	690	793	0.5	0.5	103	14.9	234
Barbers	62	67	0.0	0.0	5	7.2	16
Hairdressers, hairstylists, and cosmetologists	628	726	0.4	0.4	98	15.7	218
Miscellaneous personal appearance workers	155	179	0.1	0.1	23	15.1	54
Makeup artists, theatrical and performance	4	4	0.0	0.0	0	3.4	1
Manicurists and pedicurists	82	95	0.1	0.1	14	16.7	29
Shampooers	22	20	0.0	0.0	-2	-9.0	4
Skincare specialists	48	59	0.0	0.0	12	24.6	20
Baggage porters, bellhops, and concierges	66	74	0.0	0.0	8	12.2	25
Baggage porters and bellhops	46	52	0.0	0.0	6	12.4	17
Concierges	20	23	0.0	0.0	2	11.9	7
Tour and travel guides	39	46	0.0	0.0	7	18.5	22
Tour guides and escorts	35	41	0.0	0.0	6	17.9	20
Travel guides	4	5	0.0	0.0	1	23.6	3
Other personal care and service workers	2 909	3 932	2.0	2.4	1 023	35.2	1 639
Childcare workers	1 282	1 544	0.9	0.9	262	20.4	666
Personal care aides	861	1 468	0.6	0.9	607	70.5	675
Recreation and fitness workers	591	715	0.4	0.4	125	21.1	219
Fitness trainers and aerobics instructors	251	312	0.2	0.2	60	24.0	101
Recreation workers	339	403	0.2	0.2	64	19.0	119
Residential advisors	73	91	0.1	0.1	18	25.0	46
Personal care and service workers, all other	102	114	0.1	0.1	11	10.9	33
Sales and Related	14 916	16 785	10.4	10.3	1 869	12.5	6 454
Supervisors of sales workers	2 042	2 196	1.4	1.3	153	7.5	637
First-line supervisors of retail sales workers	1 620	1 756	1.1	1.1	136	8.4	514
First-line supervisors of non-retail sales workers	423	440	0.3	0.3	17	4.0	124
Retail sales workers	8 268	9 306	5.8	5.7	1 038	12.6	3 998
Cashiers	3 383	3 630	2.4	2.2	248	7.3	1 785
Cashiers	3 363	3 613	2.4	2.2	250	7.4	1 776
Gaming change persons and booth cashiers	20	18	0.0	0.0	-2	-12.1	9
Counter and rental clerks and parts salespersons	623	707	0.4	0.4	84	13.4	254
Counter and rental clerks	420	471	0.3	0.3	51	12.2	147
Parts salespersons	204	237	0.1	0.1	33	16.0	107
Retail salespersons	4 262	4 968	3.0	3.0	707	16.6	1 959
Sales representatives, services	1 528	1 800	1.1	1.1	272	17.8	675
Advertising sales agents	160	181	0.1	0.1	21	13.0	70
Insurance sales agents	412	502	0.3	0.3	90	21.9	184
Securities, commodities, and financial services sales agents	312	360	0.2	0.2	48	15.2	134
Travel agents	83	91	0.1	0.1	8	10.0	17
Sales representatives, services, all other	561	667	0.4	0.4	105	18.8	270
Sales Representatives, wholesale and manufacturing	1 830	2 119	1.3	1.3	289	15.8	720
Sales representatives, wholesale and manufacturing, technical and scientific products	400	466	0.3	0.3	66	16.4	160
Sales representatives, wholesale and manufacturing, except technical and scientific products	1 430	1 653	1.0	1.0	223	15.6	560
Other sales and related workers	1 247	1 364	0.9	0.8	117	9.4	424
Models, demonstrators, and product promoters	91	107	0.1	0.1	16	17.5	43
Demonstrators and product promoters	90	106	0.1	0.1	16	17.5	42
Models	1	2	0.0	0.0	0	14.5	1
Real estate brokers and sales agents	466	519	0.3	0.3	53	11.3	157
Real estate brokers	99	106	0.1	0.1	8	7.6	30
Real estate sales agents	368	413	0.3	0.3	45	12.2	128
Sales engineers	66	76	0.0	0.0	10	14.4	32
Telemarketers	291	312	0.2	0.2	22	7.4	84
Door-to-door sales workers, news and street vendors, and related workers	154	142	0.1	0.1	-12	-7.5	34
Sales and related workers, all other	179	208	0.1	0.1	29	16.0	74

Note: Data may not sum to totals or 100 percent due to rounding.

[1]Total job openings represent the sum of employment increases and net replacements. If employment change is negative, job openings due to growth are zero and total job openings equal net replacements.

Table 4-8. Employment, by Occupation, 2010 and Projected 2020—*Continued*

(Numbers in thousands, percent.)

Occupation	Employment				Change, 2010–2020		Total job openings due to growth and net replacements, 2010–2020[1]
	Number		Percent distribution		Number	Percent	
	2010	2020	2010	2020			
Office and Administrative Support	22 603	24 938	15.8	15.2	2 336	10.3	7 450
Supervisors of office and administrative support workers	1 424	1 628	1.0	1.0	203	14.3	584
First-line supervisors of office and administrative support workers	1 424	1 628	1.0	1.0	203	14.3	584
Communications equipment operators	164	128	0.1	0.1	-36	-22.0	34
Switchboard operators, including answering service	143	109	0.1	0.1	-33	-23.3	28
Telephone operators	19	15	0.0	0.0	-3	-16.6	5
Communications equipment operators, all other	3	3	0.0	0.0	0	4.1	1
Financial clerks	3 645	4 097	2.5	2.5	453	12.4	1 133
Bill and account collectors	402	459	0.3	0.3	57	14.2	136
Billing and posting clerks	505	604	0.4	0.4	100	19.7	188
Bookkeeping, accounting, and auditing clerks	1 898	2 157	1.3	1.3	259	13.6	468
Gaming cage workers	16	14	0.0	0.0	-2	-12.7	3
Payroll and timekeeping clerks	187	214	0.1	0.1	27	14.6	66
Procurement clerks	77	81	0.1	0.0	4	5.7	36
Tellers	560	567	0.4	0.3	7	1.3	238
Information and record clerks	5 320	6 029	3.7	3.7	709	13.3	2 244
Brokerage clerks	58	61	0.0	0.0	3	5.9	20
Correspondence clerks	10	9	0.0	0.0	-1	-12.1	3
Court, municipal, and license clerks	130	140	0.1	0.1	10	8.0	47
Credit authorizers, checkers, and clerks	54	57	0.0	0.0	3	4.8	18
Customer service representatives	2 187	2 526	1.5	1.5	338	15.5	960
Eligibility interviewers, government programs	126	130	0.1	0.1	4	3.1	37
File clerks	185	176	0.1	0.1	-9	-4.8	49
Hotel, motel, and resort desk clerks	228	253	0.2	0.2	25	11.1	116
Interviewers, except eligibility and loan	214	250	0.1	0.2	37	17.3	80
Library assistants, clerical	116	128	0.1	0.1	12	10.3	64
Loan interviewers and clerks	183	177	0.1	0.1	-6	-3.1	34
New accounts clerks	68	69	0.0	0.0	1	2.0	20
Order clerks	212	228	0.1	0.1	16	7.4	75
Human resources assistants, except payroll and timekeeping	157	175	0.1	0.1	18	11.2	62
Receptionists and information clerks	1 049	1 297	0.7	0.8	249	23.7	566
Reservation and transportation ticket agents and travel clerks	124	132	0.1	0.1	7	5.8	31
Information and record clerks, all other	221	223	0.2	0.1	2	1.0	64
Material recording, scheduling, dispatching, and distributing workers	3 861	3 857	2.7	2.4	-5	-0.1	1 092
Cargo and freight agents	82	106	0.1	0.1	24	29.3	44
Couriers and messengers	116	131	0.1	0.1	15	12.6	43
Dispatchers	285	331	0.2	0.2	46	16.2	100
Police, fire, and ambulance dispatchers	100	112	0.1	0.1	12	11.7	31
Dispatchers, except police, fire, and ambulance	185	220	0.1	0.1	34	18.6	70
Meter readers, utilities	41	41	0.0	0.0	1	1.2	13
Postal service workers	524	386	0.4	0.2	-139	-26.4	126
Postal service clerks	66	34	0.0	0.0	-32	-48.2	16
Postal service mail carriers	317	279	0.2	0.2	-38	-12.0	103
Postal service mail sorters, processors, and processing machine operators	142	73	0.1	0.0	-69	-48.5	8
Production, planning, and expediting clerks	271	289	0.2	0.2	18	6.6	89
Shipping, receiving, and traffic clerks	688	690	0.5	0.4	2	0.3	177
Stock clerks and order fillers	1 787	1 808	1.2	1.1	21	1.2	465
Weighers, measurers, checkers, and samplers, recordkeeping	67	75	0.0	0.0	8	12.0	34
Secretaries and administrative assistants	4 010	4 503	2.8	2.8	493	12.3	1 031
Executive secretaries and executive administrative assistants	1 236	1 392	0.9	0.9	156	12.6	322
Legal secretaries	233	241	0.2	0.1	8	3.5	39
Medical secretaries	509	719	0.4	0.4	210	41.3	278
Secretaries and administrative assistants, except legal, medical, and executive	2 032	2 151	1.4	1.3	119	5.8	391
Other office and administrative support workers	4 178	4 696	2.9	2.9	518	12.4	1 333
Computer operators	86	79	0.1	0.0	-7	-8.6	8
Data entry and information processing workers	350	321	0.2	0.2	-29	-8.3	48
Data entry keyers	235	219	0.2	0.1	-16	-6.8	41
Word processors and typists	115	102	0.1	0.1	-13	-11.5	7
Desktop publishers	23	19	0.0	0.0	-3	-14.7	4
Insurance claims and policy processing clerks	248	270	0.2	0.2	22	8.7	96
Mail clerks and mail machine operators, except postal service	126	142	0.1	0.1	15	12.1	40
Office clerks, general	2 951	3 440	2.1	2.1	490	16.6	1 012
Office machine operators, except computer	70	63	0.0	0.0	-7	-9.7	20
Proofreaders and copy markers	14	15	0.0	0.0	1	4.8	3
Statistical assistants	17	18	0.0	0.0	1	6.0	4
Office and administrative support workers, all other	294	330	0.2	0.2	37	12.4	99
Farming, Fishing, and Forestry	972	953	0.7	0.6	-19	-2.0	291
Supervisors of farming, fishing, and forestry workers	47	46	0.0	0.0	-1	-1.5	14
First-line supervisors of farming, fishing, and forestry workers	47	46	0.0	0.0	-1	-1.5	14
Agricultural workers	826	806	0.6	0.5	-19	-2.3	249
Agricultural inspectors	19	20	0.0	0.0	0	1.5	6
Animal breeders	12	11	0.0	0.0	-1	-7.5	4
Graders and sorters, agricultural products	48	49	0.0	0.0	-1	1.2	12
Miscellaneous agricultural workers	746	727	0.5	0.4	-19	-2.6	227
Fishing and hunting workers	33	31	0.0	0.0	-2	-6.2	9
Fishers and related fishing workers	32	30	0.0	0.0	-2	-6.3	9
Forest, conservation, and logging workers	67	69	0.0	0.0	2	3.6	19
Forest and conservation workers	14	14	0.0	0.0	0	1.0	4
Logging workers	53	56	0.0	0.0	2	4.3	15
Fallers	10	10	0.0	0.0	0	3.3	3
Logging equipment operators	35	36	0.0	0.0	1	3.7	10
Log graders and scalers	4	4	0.0	0.0	1	13.3	1
Logging workers, all other	5	5	0.0	0.0	0	3.0	1

Note: Data may not sum to totals or 100 percent due to rounding.

[1]Total job openings represent the sum of employment increases and net replacements. If employment change is negative, job openings due to growth are zero and total job openings equal net replacements.

Table 4-8. Employment, by Occupation, 2010 and Projected 2020—*Continued*

(Numbers in thousands, percent.)

Occupation	Employment				Change, 2010–2020		Total job openings due to growth and net replacements, 2010–2020[1]
	Number		Percent distribution		Number	Percent	
	2010	2020	2010	2020			
Construction and Extraction	6 328	7 735	4.4	4.7	1 407	22.2	2 760
Supervisors of construction and extraction workers	559	690	0.4	0.4	131	23.5	260
First-line supervisors of construction trades and extraction workers	559	690	0.4	0.4	131	23.5	260
Construction trades workers	4 865	5 961	3.4	3.6	1 096	22.5	2 085
Boilermakers	20	24	0.0	0.0	4	21.3	12
Brickmasons, blockmasons, and stonemasons	105	147	0.1	0.1	42	39.9	63
Brickmasons and blockmasons	89	125	0.1	0.1	36	40.5	55
Stonemasons	16	21	0.0	0.0	6	36.5	9
Carpenters	1 002	1 198	0.7	0.7	196	19.6	408
Carpet, floor, and tile installers and finishers	135	158	0.1	0.1	23	17.1	52
Carpet installers	48	52	0.0	0.0	5	10.4	15
Floor layers, except carpet, wood, and hard tiles	18	19	0.0	0.0	1	6.8	5
Floor sanders and finishers	11	13	0.0	0.0	2	18.2	4
Tile and marble setters	59	74	0.0	0.0	15	25.4	28
Cement masons, concrete finishers, and terrazzo workers	148	199	0.1	0.1	51	34.1	74
Cement masons and concrete finishers	145	195	0.1	0.1	50	34.6	73
Terrazzo workers and finishers	4	4	0.0	0.0	1	15.0	1
Construction laborers	999	1 211	0.7	0.7	212	21.3	292
Construction equipment operators	405	500	0.3	0.3	95	23.4	187
Paving, surfacing, and tamping equipment operators	52	63	0.0	0.0	11	22.1	22
Pile-driver operators	4	6	0.0	0.0	2	36.0	2
Operating engineers and other construction equipment operators	349	431	0.2	0.3	82	23.5	163
Drywall installers, ceiling tile installers, and tapers	130	167	0.1	0.1	37	28.8	73
Drywall and ceiling tile installers	107	136	0.1	0.1	29	27.5	59
Tapers	23	31	0.0	0.0	8	34.7	14
Electricians	577	711	0.4	0.4	134	23.2	289
Glaziers	42	60	0.0	0.0	18	42.4	33
Insulation workers	51	66	0.0	0.0	14	28.0	35
Insulation workers, floor, ceiling, and wall	23	29	0.0	0.0	5	23.4	15
Insulation workers, mechanical	28	37	0.0	0.0	9	31.8	20
Painters and paperhangers	400	473	0.3	0.3	73	18.3	159
Painters, construction and maintenance	391	463	0.3	0.3	72	18.5	157
Paperhangers	9	10	0.0	0.0	1	10.3	2
Pipelayers, plumbers, pipefitters, and steamfitters	473	594	0.3	0.4	121	25.6	258
Pipelayers	53	67	0.0	0.0	13	25.3	29
Plumbers, pipefitters, and steamfitters	420	528	0.3	0.3	108	25.6	229
Plasterers and stucco masons	28	33	0.0	0.0	5	17.1	11
Reinforcing iron and rebar workers	19	28	0.0	0.0	9	48.6	13
Roofers	137	161	0.1	0.1	24	17.8	53
Sheet metal workers	136	160	0.1	0.1	24	17.5	47
Structural iron and steel workers	60	73	0.0	0.0	13	21.9	25
Helpers, Construction trades	251	353	0.2	0.2	102	40.5	169
Helpers–brickmasons, blockmasons, stonemasons, and tile and marble setters	29	47	0.0	0.0	18	60.1	25
Helpers–carpenters	47	72	0.0	0.0	26	55.7	38
Helpers–electricians	74	96	0.1	0.1	23	30.6	42
Helpers–painters, paperhangers, plasterers, and stucco masons	12	15	0.0	0.0	3	22.0	6
Helpers–pipelayers, plumbers, pipefitters, and steamfitters	58	84	0.0	0.1	26	45.4	42
Helpers–roofers	13	14	0.0	0.0	1	9.6	5
Helpers, construction trades, all other	20	25	0.0	0.0	6	28.7	11
Other construction and related workers	428	491	0.3	0.3	63	14.8	184
Construction and building inspectors	102	121	0.1	0.1	18	17.9	49
Elevator installers and repairers	20	22	0.0	0.0	2	11.3	8
Fence erectors	32	40	0.0	0.0	8	23.8	16
Hazardous materials removal workers	38	47	0.0	0.0	9	23.1	19
Highway maintenance workers	149	161	0.1	0.1	12	8.2	51
Rail-track laying and maintenance equipment operators	15	15	0.0	0.0	0	1.9	4
Septic tank servicers and sewer pipe cleaners	25	31	0.0	0.0	5	20.7	12
Miscellaneous construction and related workers	1	2	0.0	0.0	0	33.1	1
Segmental pavers	1	2	0.0	0.0	0	33.1	1
Construction and related workers, all other	45	53	0.0	0.0	8	17.9	23
Extraction workers	225	241	0.2	0.1	16	6.9	63
Derrick, rotary drill, and service unit operators, oil, gas, and mining	82	89	0.1	0.1	7	8.4	24
Derrick operators, oil and gas	19	21	0.0	0.0	2	9.3	6
Rotary drill operators, oil and gas	23	24	0.0	0.0	2	7.2	6
Service unit operators, oil, gas, and mining	41	44	0.0	0.0	4	8.6	12
Earth drillers, except oil and gas	18	20	0.0	0.0	3	13.8	6
Explosives workers, ordnance handling experts, and blasters	7	7	0.0	0.0	0	0.2	1
Mining machine operators	24	25	0.0	0.0	0	0.7	5
Continuous mining machine operators	14	14	0.0	0.0	0	0.4	3
Mine cutting and channeling machine operators	7	7	0.0	0.0	0	2.1	2
Mining machine operators, all other	3	3	0.0	0.0	0	-1.1	1
Rock splitters, quarry	4	4	0.0	0.0	0	11.7	1
Roof bolters, mining	6	6	0.0	0.0	0	2.0	1
Roustabouts, oil and gas	53	57	0.0	0.0	4	8.3	16
Helpers–extraction workers	25	26	0.0	0.0	1	5.5	7
Extraction workers, all other	8	7	0.0	0.0	0	-2.9	2
Installation, Maintenance, and Repair	5 429	6 229	3.8	3.8	800	14.7	2 026
Supervisors of installation, maintenance, and repair workers	431	483	0.3	0.3	51	11.9	165
First-line supervisors of mechanics, installers, and repairers	431	483	0.3	0.3	51	11.9	165
Electrical and electronic equipment mechanics, installers, and repairers	611	683	0.4	0.4	72	11.8	201
Computer, automated teller, and office machine repairers	146	156	0.1	0.1	10	6.5	45
Radio and telecommunications equipment installers and repairers	205	236	0.1	0.1	31	15.3	64
Radio, cellular, and tower equipment installers and repairs	10	13	0.0	0.0	3	29.4	5
Telecommunications equipment installers and repairers, except line installers	195	223	0.1	0.1	28	14.6	59

Note: Data may not sum to totals or 100 percent due to rounding.

[1]Total job openings represent the sum of employment increases and net replacements. If employment change is negative, job openings due to growth are zero and total job openings equal net replacements.

Table 4-8.　Employment, by Occupation, 2010 and Projected 2020—*Continued*

(Numbers in thousands, percent.)

Occupation	Employment				Change, 2010–2020		Total job openings due to growth and net replacements, 2010–2020[1]
	Number		Percent distribution		Number	Percent	
	2010	2020	2010	2020			
Installation, Maintenance, and Repair—*Continued*							
Miscellaneous electrical and electronic equipment mechanics, installers, and repairers	260	291	0.2	0.2	31	11.9	92
Avionics technicians	19	20	0.0	0.0	1	6.9	6
Electric motor, power tool, and related repairers	20	21	0.0	0.0	1	4.9	3
Electrical and electronics installers and repairers, transportation equipment	13	13	0.0	0.0	0	2.1	3
Electrical and electronics repairers, commercial and industrial equipment	69	70	0.0	0.0	1	1.1	18
Electrical and electronics repairers, powerhouse, substation, and relay	23	25	0.0	0.0	1	4.9	7
Electronic equipment installers and repairers, motor vehicles	16	16	0.0	0.0	0	2.8	4
Electronic home entertainment equipment installers and repairers	37	42	0.0	0.0	5	13.9	14
Security and fire alarm systems installers	64	85	0.0	0.1	21	33.0	37
Vehicle and mobile equipment mechanics, installers, and repairers	1 627	1 894	1.1	1.2	267	16.4	681
Aircraft mechanics and service technicians	124	132	0.1	0.1	8	6.3	45
Automotive technicians and repairers	894	1 052	0.6	0.6	158	17.6	386
Automotive body and related repairers	153	181	0.1	0.1	28	18.4	65
Automotive glass installers and repairers	18	23	0.0	0.0	5	25.0	9
Automotive service technicians and mechanics	723	848	0.5	0.5	125	17.2	312
Bus and truck mechanics and diesel engine specialists	242	277	0.2	0.2	35	14.5	88
Heavy vehicle and mobile equipment service technicians and mechanics	179	208	0.1	0.1	28	15.8	75
Farm equipment mechanics and service technicians	33	37	0.0	0.0	4	13.4	13
Mobile heavy equipment mechanics, except engines	125	145	0.1	0.1	20	16.2	53
Rail car repairers	22	25	0.0	0.0	4	16.9	9
Small engine mechanics	69	83	0.0	0.1	14	20.7	32
Motorboat mechanics and service technicians	21	25	0.0	0.0	4	20.6	10
Motorcycle mechanics	18	22	0.0	0.0	4	23.6	9
Outdoor power equipment and other small engine mechanics	30	36	0.0	0.0	6	19.1	14
Miscellaneous vehicle and mobile equipment mechanics, installers, and repairers	119	143	0.1	0.1	24	20.4	55
Bicycle repairers	10	14	0.0	0.0	4	37.6	6
Recreational vehicle service technicians	10	12	0.0	0.0	2	22.3	5
Tire repairers and changers	99	117	0.1	0.1	18	18.5	44
Other installation, maintenance, and repair occupations	2 759	3 169	1.9	1.9	410	14.8	979
Control and valve installers and repairers	57	60	0.0	0.0	3	5.5	14
Mechanical door repairers	13	16	0.0	0.0	3	24.6	6
Control and valve installers and repairers, except mechanical door	44	44	0.0	0.0	0	-0.1	8
Heating, air conditioning, and refrigeration mechanics and installers	268	358	0.2	0.2	90	33.7	138
Home appliance repairers	48	51	0.0	0.0	3	6.5	12
Industrial machinery installation, repair, and maintenance workers	396	461	0.3	0.3	65	16.4	143
Industrial machinery mechanics	287	349	0.2	0.2	62	21.6	117
Maintenance workers, machinery	70	74	0.0	0.0	5	6.5	17
Millwrights	37	35	0.0	0.0	-2	-4.8	8
Refractory materials repairers, except brickmasons	2	2	0.0	0.0	0	8.6	1
Line installers and repairers	269	305	0.2	0.2	36	13.5	104
Electrical power-line installers and repairers	108	123	0.1	0.1	14	13.2	53
Telecommunications line installers and repairers	161	183	0.1	0.1	22	13.6	51
Precision instrument and equipment repairers	65	79	0.0	0.0	14	21.4	32
Camera and photographic equipment repairers	3	4	0.0	0.0	0	10.3	1
Medical equipment repairers	38	50	0.0	0.0	12	31.5	22
Musical instrument repairers and tuners	6	6	0.0	0.0	0	1.9	2
Watch repairers	3	3	0.0	0.0	0	5.9	1
Precision instrument and equipment repairers, all other	15	16	0.0	0.0	1	9.3	6
Maintenance and repair workers, general	1 289	1 431	0.9	0.9	142	11.0	379
Miscellaneous installation, maintenance, and repair workers	225	264	0.2	0.2	39	17.5	115
Coin, vending, and amusement machine servicers and repairers	39	48	0.0	0.0	9	22.1	16
Commercial divers	4	4	0.0	0.0	1	16.2	1
Fabric menders, except garment	1	1	0.0	0.0	0	-6.3	0
Locksmiths and safe repairers	26	30	0.0	0.0	5	17.7	9
Manufactured building and mobile home installers	8	9	0.0	0.0	1	13.9	2
Riggers	15	17	0.0	0.0	2	10.6	4
Signal and track switch repairers	7	7	0.0	0.0	0	-2.0	1
Helpers–installation, maintenance, and repair workers	125	148	0.1	0.1	23	18.4	80
Installation, maintenance, and repair workers, all other	144	160	0.1	0.1	17	11.7	43
Production	8 594	8 951	6.0	5.5	357	4.2	2 231
Supervisors of production workers	589	599	0.4	0.4	11	1.9	88
First-line supervisors of production and operating workers	589	599	0.4	0.4	11	1.9	88
Assemblers and fabricators	1 627	1 715	1.1	1.0	88	5.4	409
Aircraft structure, surfaces, rigging, and systems assemblers	36	42	0.0	0.0	5	14.3	12
Electrical, electronics, and electromechanical assemblers	247	235	0.2	0.1	-12	-5.0	36
Coil winders, tapers, and finishers	15	13	0.0	0.0	-2	-15.9	2
Electrical and electronic equipment assemblers	183	172	0.1	0.1	-10	-5.7	26
Electromechanical equipment assemblers	49	50	0.0	0.0	0	0.8	8
Engine and other machine assemblers	34	36	0.0	0.0	2	5.3	8
Structural metal fabricators and fitters	81	94	0.1	0.1	13	15.7	28
Miscellaneous assemblers and fabricators	1 228	1 309	0.9	0.8	81	6.6	324
Fiberglass laminators and fabricators	19	19	0.0	0.0	0	-1.8	4
Team assemblers	953	1 005	0.7	0.6	52	5.5	241
Timing device assemblers and adjusters	2	2	0.0	0.0	0	1.2	0
Assemblers and fabricators, all other	255	283	0.2	0.2	29	11.3	79
Food processing workers	681	732	0.5	0.4	51	7.4	247
Bakers	150	153	0.1	0.1	4	2.3	47
Butchers and other meat, poultry, and fish processing workers	382	425	0.3	0.3	43	11.3	154
Butchers and meat cutters	127	137	0.1	0.1	10	7.9	47
Meat, poultry, and fish cutters and trimmers	166	192	0.1	0.1	26	15.5	74
Slaughterers and meat packers	89	97	0.1	0.1	7	8.3	33
Miscellaneous food processing workers	149	153	0.1	0.1	4	2.6	46
Food and tobacco roasting, baking, and drying machine operators and tenders	18	20	0.0	0.0	2	8.1	7
Food batchmakers	99	99	0.1	0.1	1	0.7	28
Food cooking machine operators and tenders	32	34	0.0	0.0	2	5.1	11
Metal workers and plastic workers	1 764	1 903	1.2	1.2	139	7.9	482

Note: Data may not sum to totals or 100 percent due to rounding.

[1]Total job openings represent the sum of employment increases and net replacements. If employment change is negative, job openings due to growth are zero and total job openings equal net replacements.

Table 4-8. Employment, by Occupation, 2010 and Projected 2020—*Continued*

(Numbers in thousands, percent.)

Occupation	Employment				Change, 2010–2020		Total job openings due to growth and net replacements, 2010–2020[1]
	Number		Percent distribution		Number	Percent	
	2010	2020	2010	2020			
Production—*Continued*							
Computer control programmers and operators	142	167	0.1	0.1	26	18.2	53
Computer-controlled machine tool operators, metal and plastic	125	149	0.1	0.1	24	19.2	48
Computer numerically controlled machine tool programmers, metal and plastic	17	18	0.0	0.0	2	10.8	5
Forming machine setters, operators, and tenders, metal and plastic	131	141	0.1	0.1	10	7.4	35
Extruding and drawing machine setters, operators, and tenders, metal and plastic	77	83	0.1	0.1	6	8.3	21
Forging machine setters, operators, and tenders, metal and plastic	23	23	0.0	0.0	1	3.0	5
Rolling machine setters, operators, and tenders, metal and plastic	32	35	0.0	0.0	3	8.2	9
Machine tool cutting setters, operators, and tenders, metal and plastic	342	345	0.2	0.2	3	0.8	52
Cutting, punching, and press machine setters, operators, and tenders, metal and plastic	184	189	0.1	0.1	5	2.5	18
Drilling and boring machine tool setters, operators, and tenders, metal and plastic	23	21	0.0	0.0	-2	-7.0	1
Grinding, lapping, polishing, and buffing machine tool setters, operators, and tenders, metal and plastic	73	74	0.1	0.0	1	1.4	12
Lathe and turning machine tool setters, operators, and tenders, metal and plastic	42	40	0.0	0.0	-2	-4.7	15
Milling and planing machine setters, operators, and tenders, metal and plastic	21	22	0.0	0.0	1	3.6	5
Machinists	370	402	0.3	0.2	32	8.5	100
Metal furnace operators, tenders, pourers, and casters	27	30	0.0	0.0	3	11.3	8
Metal-refining furnace operators and tenders	16	18	0.0	0.0	3	16.3	6
Pourers and casters, metal	12	12	0.0	0.0	1	4.5	3
Model makers and patternmakers, metal and plastic	11	10	0.0	0.0	-1	-5.5	1
Model makers, metal and plastic	6	6	0.0	0.0	-1	-8.2	0
Patternmakers, metal and plastic	5	4	0.0	0.0	0	-1.9	0
Molders and molding machine setters, operators, and tenders, metal and plastic	125	132	0.1	0.1	7	5.6	28
Foundry mold and coremakers	10	11	0.0	0.0	1	11.5	3
Molding, coremaking, and casting machine setters, operators, and tenders, metal and plastic	115	121	0.1	0.1	6	5.1	25
Multiple machine tool setters, operators, and tenders, metal and plastic	70	73	0.0	0.0	3	3.8	16
Tool and die makers	68	66	0.0	0.0	-2	-2.3	4
Welding, soldering, and brazing workers	379	432	0.3	0.3	53	14.1	155
Welders, cutters, solderers, and brazers	337	388	0.2	0.2	51	15.0	141
Welding, soldering, and brazing machine setters, operators, and tenders	42	44	0.0	0.0	3	6.6	14
Miscellaneous metal workers and plastic workers	99	104	0.1	0.1	6	5.7	33
Heat treating equipment setters, operators, and tenders, metal and plastic	19	19	0.0	0.0	0	0.8	15
Layout workers, metal and plastic	9	10	0.0	0.0	1	13.7	3
Plating and coating machine setters, operators, and tenders, metal and plastic	31	34	0.0	0.0	3	9.3	10
Tool grinders, filers, and sharpeners	13	14	0.0	0.0	1	7.0	2
Metal workers and plastic workers, all other	27	27	0.0	0.0	0	1.6	3
Printing workers	305	292	0.2	0.2	-13	-4.2	69
Prepress technicians and workers	51	43	0.0	0.0	-8	-15.9	12
Printing press operators	200	197	0.1	0.1	-3	-1.5	39
Print binding and finishing workers	54	52	0.0	0.0	-2	-3.1	18
Textile, apparel, and furnishings workers	682	616	0.5	0.4	-66	-9.6	98
Laundry and dry-cleaning workers	225	227	0.2	0.1	2	0.7	44
Pressers, textile, garment, and related materials	58	51	0.0	0.0	-7	-11.8	4
Sewing machine operators	163	121	0.1	0.1	-42	-25.8	9
Shoe and leather workers	13	10	0.0	0.0	-3	-23.1	4
Shoe and leather workers and repairers	10	9	0.0	0.0	-1	-13.6	3
Shoe machine operators and tenders	3	2	0.0	0.0	-2	-53.4	0
Tailors, dressmakers, and sewers	58	58	0.0	0.0	0	0.6	9
Sewers, hand	10	10	0.0	0.0	-1	-5.4	1
Tailors, dressmakers, and custom sewers	47	48	0.0	0.0	1	2.0	7
Textile machine setters, operators, and tenders	80	67	0.1	0.0	-13	-16.2	10
Textile bleaching and dyeing machine operators and tenders	14	12	0.0	0.0	-2	-15.2	2
Textile cutting machine setters, operators, and tenders	15	12	0.0	0.0	-3	-21.8	4
Textile knitting and weaving machine setters, operators, and tenders	23	18	0.0	0.0	-4	-18.2	1
Textile winding, twisting, and drawing out machine setters, operators, and tenders	29	25	0.0	0.0	-4	-12.4	3
Miscellaneous textile, apparel, and furnishings workers	84	82	0.1	0.1	-2	-2.9	18
Extruding and forming machine setters, operators, and tenders, synthetic and glass fibers	15	14	0.0	0.0	0	-1.6	2
Fabric and apparel patternmakers	6	4	0.0	0.0	-2	-35.6	1
Upholsterers	47	49	0.0	0.0	2	4.2	14
Textile, apparel, and furnishings workers, all other	17	15	0.0	0.0	-2	-12.1	1
Woodworkers	235	275	0.2	0.2	40	17.1	87
Cabinetmakers and bench carpenters	97	113	0.1	0.1	16	16.8	40
Furniture finishers	21	22	0.0	0.0	1	5.5	6
Model makers and patternmakers, wood	3	3	0.0	0.0	0	8.3	1
Model makers, wood	2	2	0.0	0.0	0	11.3	1
Patternmakers, wood	1	1	0.0	0.0	0	4.3	0
Woodworking machine setters, operators, and tenders	100	122	0.1	0.1	22	21.9	36
Sawing machine setters, operators, and tenders, wood	39	49	0.0	0.0	10	24.7	18
Woodworking machine setters, operators, and tenders, except sawing	61	73	0.0	0.0	12	20.2	17
Woodworkers, all other	15	16	0.0	0.0	1	4.4	4
Plant and system operators	317	318	0.2	0.2	2	0.5	109
Power plant operators, distributors, and dispatchers	56	55	0.0	0.0	-1	-2.0	20
Nuclear power reactor operators	5	5	0.0	0.0	0	3.6	2
Power distributors and dispatchers	10	10	0.0	0.0	0	-3.0	4
Power plant operators	41	40	0.0	0.0	-1	-2.5	14
Stationary engineers and boiler operators	38	40	0.0	0.0	2	6.2	11
Water and wastewater treatment plant and system operators	111	124	0.1	0.1	13	11.6	42
Miscellaneous plant and system operators	113	100	0.1	0.1	-12	-11.0	37
Chemical plant and system operators	43	38	0.0	0.0	-5	-12.2	14
Gas plant operators	14	13	0.0	0.0	-1	-6.5	5
Petroleum pump system operators, refinery operators, and gaugers	44	38	0.0	0.0	-6	-14.0	14
Plant and system operators, all other	11	11	0.0	0.0	0	-0.1	4

Note: Data may not sum to totals or 100 percent due to rounding.

[1]Total job openings represent the sum of employment increases and net replacements. If employment change is negative, job openings due to growth are zero and total job openings equal net replacements.

Table 4-8. Employment, by Occupation, 2010 and Projected 2020—*Continued*

(Numbers in thousands, percent.)

Occupation	Employment				Change, 2010–2020		Total job openings due to growth and net replacements, 2010–2020[1]
	Number		Percent distribution		Number	Percent	
	2010	2020	2010	2020			
Production—*Continued*							
Other production occupations	2 396	2 500	1.7	1.5	104	4.3	642
Chemical processing machine setters, operators, and tenders	86	84	0.1	0.1	-2	-1.9	16
Chemical equipment operators and tenders	47	44	0.0	0.0	-4	-7.5	8
Separating, filtering, clarifying, precipitating, and still machine setters, operators, and tenders	38	40	0.0	0.0	2	5.1	8
Crushing, grinding, polishing, mixing, and blending workers	186	187	0.1	0.1	1	0.6	59
Crushing, grinding, and polishing machine setters, operators, and tenders	33	35	0.0	0.0	2	5.1	12
Grinding and polishing workers, hand	28	30	0.0	0.0	2	7.7	11
Mixing and blending machine setters, operators, and tenders	125	122	0.1	0.1	-3	-2.2	37
Cutting workers	79	78	0.1	0.0	-1	-1.4	17
Cutters and trimmers, hand	17	16	0.0	0.0	-1	-5.7	4
Cutting and slicing machine setters, operators, and tenders	61	61	0.0	0.0	0	-0.1	14
Extruding, forming, pressing, and compacting machine setters, operators, and tenders	65	67	0.0	0.0	1	1.9	17
Furnace, kiln, oven, drier, and kettle operators and tenders	20	21	0.0	0.0	0	1.1	6
Inspectors, testers, sorters, samplers, and weighers	416	449	0.3	0.3	33	8.0	124
Jewelers and precious stone and metal workers	39	37	0.0	0.0	-2	-5.2	9
Medical, dental, and ophthalmic laboratory technicians	85	90	0.1	0.1	5	5.5	31
Dental laboratory technicians	41	41	0.0	0.0	0	0.8	13
Medical appliance technicians	14	15	0.0	0.0	1	3.7	5
Ophthalmic laboratory technicians	30	34	0.0	0.0	4	12.8	13
Packaging and filling machine operators and tenders	337	350	0.2	0.2	13	3.8	68
Painting workers	155	169	0.1	0.1	14	8.9	47
Coating, painting, and spraying machine setters, operators, and tenders	84	89	0.1	0.1	5	6.1	23
Painters, transportation equipment	46	51	0.0	0.0	4	9.4	14
Painting, coating, and decorating workers	25	30	0.0	0.0	4	17.2	10
Semiconductor processors	21	17	0.0	0.0	-4	-17.9	5
Photographic process workers and processing machine operators	59	54	0.0	0.0	-5	-7.7	15
Miscellaneous production workers	597	630	0.4	0.4	32	5.4	145
Adhesive bonding machine operators and tenders	15	16	0.0	0.0	1	4.5	3
Cleaning, washing, and metal pickling equipment operators and tenders	18	18	0.0	0.0	0	1.1	4
Cooling and freezing equipment operators and tenders	9	9	0.0	0.0	0	1.0	2
Etchers and engravers	11	11	0.0	0.0	0	-2.7	1
Molders, shapers, and casters, except metal and plastic	43	47	0.0	0.0	4	8.0	19
Paper goods machine setters, operators, and tenders	91	85	0.1	0.1	-6	-6.1	9
Tire builders	16	15	0.0	0.0	-1	-5.7	7
Helpers–production workers	395	430	0.3	0.3	34	8.7	100
Production workers, all other	250	268	0.2	0.2	18	7.1	83
Transportation and Material Moving	9 005	10 333	6.3	6.3	1 329	14.8	3 597
Supervisors of transportation and material moving workers	372	448	0.3	0.3	75	20.2	152
Aircraft cargo handling supervisors	6	8	0.0	0.0	1	20.3	3
First-line supervisors of helpers, laborers, and material movers, hand	167	213	0.1	0.1	46	27.2	80
First-line supervisors of transportation and material-moving machine and vehicle operators	199	227	0.1	0.1	28	14.3	69
Air transportation workers	228	239	0.2	0.1	11	4.9	81
Aircraft pilots and flight engineers	104	115	0.1	0.1	12	11.1	51
Airline pilots, copilots, and flight engineers	71	75	0.0	0.0	5	6.4	31
Commercial pilots	33	40	0.0	0.0	7	21.2	19
Air traffic controllers and airfield operations specialists	34	34	0.0	0.0	0	-0.6	13
Air traffic controllers	27	26	0.0	0.0	-1	-2.9	10
Airfield operations specialists	7	8	0.0	0.0	1	8.4	3
Flight attendants	91	90	0.1	0.1	0	-0.2	17
Motor vehicle operators	3 839	4 480	2.7	2.7	641	16.7	1 383
Ambulance drivers and attendants, except emergency medical technicians	20	26	0.0	0.0	6	32.1	10
Bus drivers	647	730	0.5	0.4	83	12.8	208
Bus drivers, transit and intercity	186	214	0.1	0.1	28	14.8	64
Bus drivers, school or special client	461	516	0.3	0.3	56	12.0	145
Driver/sales workers and truck drivers	2 867	3 365	2.0	2.1	498	17.4	1 068
Driver/sales workers	407	449	0.3	0.3	42	10.3	123
Heavy and tractor-trailer truck drivers	1 605	1 935	1.1	1.2	330	20.6	649
Light truck or delivery services drivers	856	982	0.6	0.6	126	14.7	296
Taxi drivers and chauffeurs	240	287	0.2	0.2	47	19.6	77
Motor vehicle operators, all other	65	72	0.0	0.0	7	11.1	20
Rail transportation workers	118	121	0.1	0.1	3	2.7	43
Locomotive engineers and operators	45	47	0.0	0.0	1	3.2	18
Locomotive engineers	39	40	0.0	0.0	2	4.4	16
Locomotive firers	1	1	0.0	0.0	0	-5.1	0
Rail yard engineers, dinkey operators, and hostlers	6	5	0.0	0.0	0	-3.6	2
Railroad brake, signal, and switch operators	22	21	0.0	0.0	-1	-4.2	7
Railroad conductors and yardmasters	41	43	0.0	0.0	2	4.7	14
Subway and streetcar operators	7	7	0.0	0.0	1	9.8	3
Rail transportation workers, all other	3	3	0.0	0.0	0	1.3	1
Water transportation workers	83	99	0.1	0.1	17	20.3	50
Sailors and marine oilers	33	41	0.0	0.0	7	21.3	22
Ship and boat captains and operators	39	47	0.0	0.0	8	19.9	22
Captains, mates, and pilots of water vessels	36	43	0.0	0.0	7	20.4	21
Motorboat operators	3	4	0.0	0.0	1	14.9	2
Ship engineers	10	12	0.0	0.0	2	18.0	6
Other transportation workers	308	336	0.2	0.2	29	9.4	121
Bridge and lock tenders	4	3	0.0	0.0	0	-1.1	1
Parking lot attendants	125	123	0.1	0.1	-2	-1.7	37
Automotive and watercraft service attendants	86	106	0.1	0.1	19	22.2	48
Traffic technicians	7	8	0.0	0.0	1	11.2	3
Transportation inspectors	27	31	0.0	0.0	4	14.4	11
Transportation attendants, except flight attendants	25	28	0.0	0.0	3	11.1	8
Transportation workers, all other	33	38	0.0	0.0	4	13.2	14

Note: Data may not sum to totals or 100 percent due to rounding.

[1]Total job openings represent the sum of employment increases and net replacements. If employment change is negative, job openings due to growth are zero and total job openings equal net replacements.

Table 4-8. Employment, by Occupation, 2010 and Projected 2020—*Continued*

(Numbers in thousands, percent.)

Occupation	Employment				Change, 2010–2020		Total job openings due to growth and net replacements, 2010–2020[1]
	Number		Percent distribution		Number	Percent	
	2010	2020	2010	2020			
Transportation and Material Moving—*Continued*							
Material moving workers	4 058	4 611	2.8	2.8	553	13.6	1 767
Conveyor operators and tenders	36	41	0.0	0.0	4	11.5	15
Crane and tower operators	40	46	0.0	0.0	6	15.7	17
Dredge, excavating, and loading machine operators	68	78	0.0	0.0	11	16.1	31
Dredge operators	2	2	0.0	0.0	0	14.8	1
Excavating and loading machine and dragline operators	62	72	0.0	0.0	11	17.3	29
Loading machine operators, underground mining	4	4	0.0	0.0	0	-2.4	1
Hoist and winch operators	3	3	0.0	0.0	0	6.5	1
Industrial truck and tractor operators	522	584	0.4	0.4	62	11.8	210
Laborers and material movers, hand	3 176	3 613	2.2	2.2	437	13.8	1 403
Cleaners of vehicles and equipment	311	371	0.2	0.2	60	19.4	152
Laborers and freight, stock, and material movers, hand	2 068	2 387	1.4	1.5	319	15.4	980
Machine feeders and offbearers	119	120	0.1	0.1	0	0.1	19
Packers and packagers, hand	677	735	0.5	0.4	58	8.6	252
Pumping station operators	30	31	0.0	0.0	1	2.1	10
Gas compressor and gas pumping station operators	5	4	0.0	0.0	-1	-10.1	1
Pump operators, except wellhead pumpers	11	11	0.0	0.0	0	3.7	4
Wellhead pumpers	15	16	0.0	0.0	1	4.6	5
Refuse and recyclable material collectors	140	168	0.1	0.1	28	20.2	70
Mine shuttle car operators	3	3	0.0	0.0	0	-6.2	1
Tank car, truck, and ship loaders	10	11	0.0	0.0	0	2.1	3
Material moving workers, all other	30	33	0.0	0.0	3	11.4	6

Note: Data may not sum to totals or 100 percent due to rounding.

[1]Total job openings represent the sum of employment increases and net replacements. If employment change is negative, job openings due to growth are zero and total job openings equal net replacements.

Table 4-9. Employment and Total Job Openings by Education, Work Experience, and On-the-Job Training Category, 2010 and Projected 2020

(Numbers in thousands, percent.)

Education, work experience, and on-the-job training	Employment				Change, 2010–2020		Total job openings due to growth and repalcement needs, 2010–2020[1]	
	Number		Percent distribution		Number	Percent	Number	Percent distribution
	2010	2020	2010	2020				
TOTAL, ALL OCCUPATIONS	143 068.2	163 537.1	100.0	100.0	20 468.9	14.3	54 787.4	100.0
Typical Education Needed for Entry								
Doctoral or professional degree	4 409.7	5 286.3	3.1	3.2	876.6	19.9	1 701.8	3.1
Master's degree	1 986.0	2 417.2	1.4	1.5	431.2	21.7	903.9	1.6
Bachelor's degree	22 171.1	25 827.2	15.5	15.8	3 656.1	16.5	8 562.4	15.6
Associate's degree	7 994.6	9 434.6	5.6	5.8	1 440.0	18.0	2 941.0	5.4
Postsecondary non-degree award	6 524.0	7 624.9	4.6	4.7	1 100.9	16.9	2 389.6	4.4
Some college, no degree	811.6	953.8	0.6	0.6	142.2	17.5	362.0	0.7
High school diploma or equivalent	62 089.6	69 665.7	43.4	42.6	7 576.1	12.2	21 745.9	39.7
Less than high school	37 081.7	42 327.4	25.9	25.9	5 245.7	14.1	16 180.8	29.5
Work Experience in a Related Occupation[2]								
More than 5 years	4 612.4	4 956.0	3.2	3.0	343.6	7.4	1 368.5	2.5
1 to 5 years	17 103.0	19 078.2	12.0	11.7	1 975.2	11.5	5 638.7	10.3
Less than 1 year	3 129.6	3 535.2	2.2	2.2	405.6	13.0	1 125.2	2.1
None	118 223.3	135 967.7	82.6	83.1	17 744.5	15.0	46 654.9	85.2
Typical On-the-Job Training								
Internship/residency	5 374.2	6 271.5	3.8	3.8	897.3	16.7	2 193.6	4.0
Apprenticeship	2 539.0	3 109.2	1.8	1.9	570.2	22.5	1 183.0	2.2
Long-term	7 039.0	7 920.5	4.9	4.8	881.5	12.5	2 545.5	4.6
Moderate-term	25 007.0	28 244.5	17.5	17.3	3 237.5	12.9	8 682.0	15.8
Short-term	58 171.0	66 040.0	40.7	40.4	7 869.0	13.5	23 767.8	43.4
None	44 937.9	51 951.3	31.4	31.8	7 013.4	15.6	16 415.5	30.0

[1]Total job openings represent the sum of employment increases and replacement needs. If employment change is negative, then job openings due to growth are zero and total job openings equals replacements.
[2]Indicates if work experience in a related occupation is commonly considered necessary by employers for entry, or is a commonly accepted subtitute for formal types of training.

Chapter Five

PRODUCTIVITY AND COSTS

PRODUCTIVITY AND COSTS

HIGHLIGHTS

This chapter covers two kinds of productivity measures produced by the Bureau of Labor Statistics (BLS): output per hour (or labor productivity) and multifactor productivity. Multifactor productivity is designed to combine the joint influence of technological change, efficiency improvements, returns to scale, and other factors on economic growth. Industry data are based on the North American Industry Classification System (NAICS).

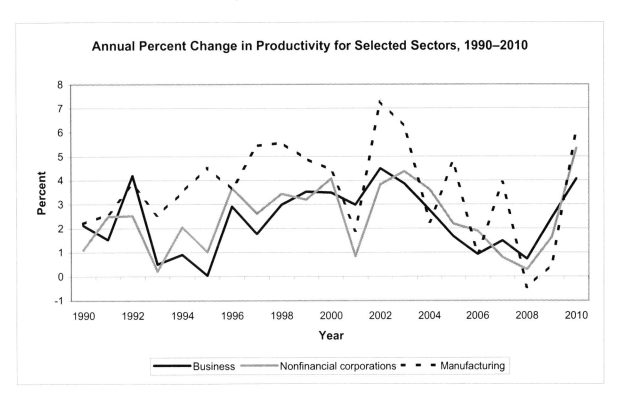

The levels of the output indexes for business, nonfinancial corporations, and manufacturing are not directly comparable because of different sources of the data. However, trends can be examined in output per hour or labor productivity. In 2010, labor productivity grew in each major sector. Manufacturing experienced the fastest growth at 6.1 percent, followed by nonfinancial corporations at 5.3 percent, and buisness at 4.1 percent. (See Table 5-1.)

OTHER HIGHLIGHTS

• Employment and hours generally remained steady in the manufacturing, business, and nonfinancial sectors in 2010 after declining sharply in 2009. (See Table 5-1.)

• Although labor productivity increased in retail trade and wholesale trade between 2009 and 2010, it did not increase in every industry within those sectors. In wholesale trade, productivity declined in paper and paper products, petroleum, and alcoholic beverages. In retail trade, productivity declined in auto parts, specialty food stores, department stores, and direct selling establishments. (See Table 5-3.)

• Between 1987 and 2010 productivity increased 3.2 percent in wholesale trade, 2.9 percent in retail trade, but only 0.7 percent in food services and drinking places. (See Table 5-3.)

NOTES AND DEFINITIONS

PRODUCTIVITY AND COSTS

The Bureau of Labor Statistics (BLS) publishes three sets of productivity measures for the major sectors and subsectors of the U.S. economy, each using a distinct methodology. One measure includes labor productivity for the major sectors of business, nonfarm business, and nonfinancial corporations and for the subsectors of total, durable, and nondurable manufacturing. The second set includes multifactor productivity for major sectors; and the third measures multifactor productivity for total industries. Each set of measures involves a comparison of output and input measures.

Indexes of labor productivity show changes in the ratio of output to hours of labor input. These measures are used in economic analysis, public and private policymaking, and forecasting and analysis of prices, wages, and technological change.

Concepts and Definitions

Business sector output is constructed by excluding the following outputs from gross domestic product (GDP): general government, nonprofit institutions, paid employees of private households, and the rental value of owner-occupied dwellings. Corresponding exclusions are also made in labor inputs. These activities are excluded because theoretical or practical difficulties make it impossible to use them as a basis for the computation of meaningful productivity measures.

Hourly compensation costs are defined as the sum of wage and salary accruals and supplements to wages and salaries. Wage and salary accruals consist of the monetary remuneration of employees, including the compensation of corporate officers; commissions, tips, and bonuses; voluntary employee contributions to certain deferred compensation plans, such as 401(k) plans; employee gains from exercising nonqualified stock options; and receipts in kind that represent income. Supplements to wages and salaries consist of employer contributions for social insurance and employer payments (including payments in kind) to private pension and profit-sharing plans, group health and life insurance plans, privately administered workers' compensation plans. For employees (wage and salary workers), hourly compensation is measured relative to hours at work and includes payments made by employers for time not at work, such as vacation, holiday, and sick pay. Because compensation costs for the business and nonfarm business sectors would otherwise be severely understated, an estimate of the hourly compensation of proprietors of unincorporated businesses is made by assuming that their hourly compensation is equal to that of employees in the same sector.

Hours at work include paid time working, traveling between job sites, coffee breaks, and machine downtime.

Hours at work, however, exclude hours for which employees are paid but not at work.

The *nonfarm business sector* is a subset of the domestic economy and excludes the economic activities of the following: general government, private households, nonprofit organizations serving individuals, and farms.

Nonfinancial corporations are a subset of the domestic economy and excludes the economic activities of the following: general government, private households, nonprofit organizations serving individuals, and those corporations classified as offices of bank holding companies, offices of other holding companies, or offices in the finance and insurance sector.

Nonlabor payments include profits, consumption of fixed capital, taxes on production and imports less subsidies, net interest and miscellaneous payments, business current transfer payments, rental income of persons, and the current surplus of government enterprises.

Output is measured as an annual-weighted index of the changes in the various products or services (in real terms) provided for sale outside the industry. Real industry output is usually derived by deflating nominal sales or values of production using BLS price indexes, but for some industries it is measured by physical quantities of output. Industry output measures are constructed primarily using data from the economic censuses and annual surveys of the U.S. Census Bureau, U.S. Department of Commerce, together with information on price changes primarily from BLS. Output measures for some mining and utilities industries are based on physical quantity data from the Energy Information Administration, U.S. Department of Energy, while output measures for some transportation industries are based on physical quantity data from the Bureau of Transportation Statistics, U.S. Department of Transportation. Other data sources for some industries include the U.S. Geological Survey, U.S. Department of the Interior; the U.S. Postal Service; the Federal Deposit Insurance Corporation; and the Postal Rate Commission.

Productivity measures describe the relationship between industry output and the labor time involved in its production. They show the changes from period to period in the amount of goods and services produced per hour. Although the labor productivity measures relate output to hours of employees or all persons in an industry, they do not measure the specific contribution of labor or any other factor of production. Rather, they reflect the joint effects of many influences, including changes in technology; capital investment; utilization of capacity, energy, and materials; the use of purchased services inputs, including contract employment services; the organization of production; managerial skill; and the characteristics and effort of the workforce.

Unit labor costs show the growth in compensation relative to that of real output. These costs are calculated by dividing total labor compensation by real output. Changes in unit labor costs can be approximated by subtracting the change in productivity from the change in hourly compensation.

Multifactor Productivity Concepts and Definitions

Multifactor productivity indexes for private business and private nonfarm business are derived by dividing an output index by an index of labor input and capital services. The output indexes are computed as chained superlative indexes of components of real output. BLS adjusts output measures from the Bureau of Economic Analysis (BEA) to remove the output of government enterprises.

Capital services measures the services derived from the stock of physical assets and software. The assets included are computers, software, communications and other information processing equipment, other fixed business equipment, structures, inventories, rental residences, and land. Investments, depreciation, capital income, and rental prices are estimated for each of these eight aggregates. Rental prices reflect the nominal rates of return and rates of economic depreciation and revaluation for the specific asset. Rental prices are adjusted for the effects of taxes. Data on investments in physical assets are obtained from BEA. Capital input measures constructed for the preliminary MFP measures are based on less detail than those for full MFP measure.

Combined inputs involve combining labor and capital inputs using a Tornqvist index. Growth rates of labor and capital input are combined with weights that represent each component's share of total costs. Total costs are defined as the value of output (Gross Product Originating) less a portion of taxes on production and imports. Most taxes on production and imports, such as excise taxes, are excluded from costs; however, property and motor vehicle taxes remain in

total costs. The index uses changing weights: The share in each year is averaged with the preceding year's share.

Labor input is total hours worked multiplied by a labor composition index. Hours paid of employees are largely obtained from BLS's Current Employment Survey (CES). These hours of employees are then converted to an at-work basis by using information from the Employment Cost Index (ECI) of the National Compensation Survey (NCS) and the Hours at Work Survey. Hours at work for non-production and supervisory workers are derived using data from the CPS, the CES, and the NCS. The hours at work of proprietors, unpaid family workers, and farm employees are derived from the Current Population Survey.

Multifactor productivity measures describe the relationship between output in real terms and the inputs involved in its production. They do not measure the specific contributions of labor, capital, or any other factor of production. Rather, multifactor productivity is designed to measure the joint influences of output, capital, and labor on economic growth of technological change, efficiency improvements, returns to scale, reallocation of resources due to shifts in factor inputs across industries, and other factors. The multifactor productivity indexes for private business and private nonfarm business are derived by dividing an output index by an index of labor input and capital services. The output indexes are computed as chained superlative indexes (Fisher Ideal indexes) of components of real output. BLS adjusts BEA output measures to remove the output of government enterprises.

Sources of Additional Information

Productivity concepts and methodology are described in Chapters 10 and 11 of the *BLS Handbook of Methods*. More information on productivity can be found in BLS news releases on the BLS Web site at <http://www.bls.gov/lpc/>.

Table 5-1. Indexes of Productivity and Related Data, 1947–2010

(2005 = 100.)

Year	Business											
	Output per hour	Output	Hours	Hourly compensation	Real hourly compensation	Unit labor costs	Unit nonlabor payments	Implicit price deflator	Employment	Output per person	Compensation in current dollars	Nonlabor payments in current dollars
1947	23.5	12.6	53.6	4.3	34.3	18.2	14.1	16.6	46.3	27.3	2.3	1.8
1948	24.6	13.3	54.0	4.7	34.4	18.9	15.7	17.6	46.9	28.4	2.5	2.1
1949	25.2	13.2	52.3	4.7	35.3	18.7	15.5	17.5	45.8	28.8	2.5	2.0
1950	27.3	14.5	53.0	5.1	37.3	18.5	16.3	17.7	46.3	31.3	2.7	2.4
1951	28.1	15.4	54.7	5.5	37.9	19.7	18.0	19.0	47.5	32.4	3.0	2.8
1952	28.9	15.9	54.8	5.9	39.5	20.3	17.6	19.2	47.7	33.3	3.2	2.8
1953	30.0	16.7	55.5	6.3	41.7	20.9	17.2	19.4	48.4	34.4	3.5	2.9
1954	30.6	16.4	53.7	6.5	42.7	21.1	17.1	19.5	47.2	34.8	3.5	2.8
1955	31.9	17.8	55.7	6.6	44.0	20.7	18.2	19.7	48.6	36.6	3.7	3.2
1956	32.0	18.1	56.5	7.1	46.2	22.1	17.8	20.4	49.6	36.4	4.0	3.2
1957	33.0	18.4	55.7	7.5	47.6	22.8	18.3	21.0	49.5	37.1	4.2	3.4
1958	33.9	18.0	53.2	7.8	48.3	23.1	18.7	21.4	47.6	37.9	4.2	3.4
1959	35.2	19.5	55.4	8.2	50.0	23.2	19.1	21.6	49.1	39.8	4.5	3.7
1960	35.8	19.9	55.5	8.5	51.2	23.7	18.8	21.8	49.3	40.3	4.7	3.7
1961	37.1	20.3	54.7	8.8	52.6	23.8	19.1	22.0	48.8	41.6	4.8	3.9
1962	38.8	21.6	55.7	9.2	54.4	23.8	19.7	22.2	49.4	43.7	5.1	4.3
1963	40.3	22.6	56.1	9.6	55.6	23.7	20.2	22.3	49.7	45.5	5.4	4.6
1964	41.7	24.0	57.7	9.9	57.0	23.8	20.7	22.6	50.6	47.4	5.7	5.0
1965	43.1	25.7	59.6	10.3	58.2	23.9	21.5	22.9	52.1	49.4	6.1	5.5
1966	44.9	27.5	61.2	11.0	60.4	24.5	22.0	23.5	53.6	51.2	6.7	6.0
1967	45.9	28.0	61.0	11.6	61.9	25.3	22.3	24.1	54.4	51.5	7.1	6.3
1968	47.4	29.4	61.9	12.5	64.2	26.4	23.0	25.1	55.4	53.0	7.8	6.8
1969	47.7	30.3	63.5	13.4	65.1	28.1	23.3	26.2	57.2	53.0	8.5	7.1
1970	48.6	30.3	62.2	14.5	66.3	29.7	23.8	27.4	57.0	53.1	9.0	7.2
1971	50.6	31.4	62.1	15.4	67.5	30.3	25.8	28.5	57.1	55.0	9.5	8.1
1972	52.3	33.5	64.0	16.3	69.6	31.2	27.0	29.6	58.8	56.9	10.5	9.0
1973	53.9	35.8	66.5	17.7	71.0	32.9	28.4	31.1	61.3	58.4	11.8	10.2
1974	53.0	35.3	66.6	19.4	70.1	36.6	30.2	34.1	62.3	56.6	12.9	10.7
1975	54.8	34.9	63.7	21.4	70.8	39.0	35.0	37.4	60.4	57.8	13.6	12.2
1976	56.6	37.2	65.8	23.2	72.7	41.1	36.8	39.4	62.3	59.8	15.3	13.7
1977	57.5	39.3	68.3	25.1	73.7	43.6	39.0	41.8	65.0	60.5	17.1	15.3
1978	58.2	41.8	71.8	27.3	74.9	46.9	41.4	44.7	68.5	61.0	19.6	17.3
1979	58.1	43.2	74.3	29.9	74.9	51.4	44.1	48.5	71.2	60.6	22.2	19.1
1980	58.0	42.7	73.6	33.1	74.6	57.0	46.6	52.9	71.4	59.8	24.3	19.9
1981	59.2	43.9	74.1	36.2	74.5	61.1	52.6	57.8	72.1	60.9	26.8	23.1
1982	58.7	42.6	72.5	38.8	75.4	66.1	53.3	61.1	70.9	60.0	28.1	22.7
1983	60.8	44.8	73.7	40.4	75.3	66.4	58.1	63.1	71.5	62.7	29.8	26.1
1984	62.5	48.7	78.0	42.1	75.4	67.4	61.2	65.0	75.1	64.9	32.9	29.8
1985	63.9	51.0	79.8	44.1	76.3	69.0	62.7	66.5	77.0	66.2	35.2	32.0
1986	65.7	52.9	80.5	46.4	78.8	70.5	63.1	67.6	78.3	67.6	37.3	33.4
1987	65.9	54.6	82.9	48.0	79.0	72.9	63.7	69.2	80.4	68.0	39.8	34.8
1988	66.9	57.0	85.2	50.5	80.1	75.5	65.1	71.4	82.9	68.8	43.0	37.1
1989	67.6	59.1	87.4	51.9	78.9	76.7	69.9	74.0	84.7	69.8	45.4	41.3
1990	69.0	60.0	86.9	55.2	80.0	80.0	71.6	76.7	85.2	70.4	48.0	43.0
1991	70.1	59.5	84.9	58.0	81.1	82.8	73.6	79.2	83.9	70.9	49.3	43.8
1992	73.0	61.8	84.7	61.1	83.3	83.7	76.1	80.7	83.4	74.1	51.7	47.0
1993	73.4	63.8	86.9	62.5	83.1	85.1	77.9	82.3	85.2	74.9	54.3	49.7
1994	74.1	67.0	90.4	63.4	82.6	85.6	80.7	83.7	88.0	76.0	57.3	54.1
1995	74.1	68.8	92.9	64.7	82.4	87.4	81.9	85.2	90.5	76.0	60.1	56.4
1996	76.3	72.0	94.4	66.9	82.9	87.8	84.7	86.6	92.5	77.8	63.2	61.0
1997	77.6	75.7	97.5	69.1	83.8	89.1	86.2	87.9	95.0	79.7	67.4	65.3
1998	79.9	79.5	99.4	73.3	87.7	91.7	83.6	88.5	97.0	82.0	72.9	66.4
1999	82.7	83.9	101.4	76.6	89.8	92.6	84.0	89.2	98.5	85.2	77.7	70.5
2000	85.6	87.7	102.4	82.3	93.3	96.1	82.9	90.9	100.2	87.5	84.3	72.7
2001	88.2	88.4	100.3	86.1	95.0	97.7	84.5	92.5	99.4	89.0	86.4	74.7
2002	92.2	90.2	97.8	88.8	96.4	96.4	88.4	93.2	97.2	92.8	86.9	79.7
2003	95.7	93.0	97.2	93.0	98.7	97.2	90.3	94.5	97.0	95.9	90.4	83.9
2004	98.4	96.7	98.3	96.2	99.5	97.8	95.4	96.9	98.2	98.5	94.6	92.3
2005	100.0	100.0	100.0	100.0	100.0	100.0	100.0	100.0	100.0	100.0	100.0	100.0
2006	100.9	103.0	102.1	103.8	100.5	102.8	103.0	102.9	101.9	101.2	106.0	106.1
2007	102.4	105.1	102.6	108.1	101.7	105.5	105.6	105.6	102.6	102.4	110.9	111.0
2008	103.2	103.7	100.5	111.7	101.2	108.2	106.3	107.5	101.1	102.6	112.2	110.2
2009	105.7	98.7	93.4	113.5	103.3	107.4	109.6	108.3	95.3	103.5	105.9	108.1
2010	110.0	102.5	93.2	115.8	103.6	105.3	116.3	109.6	94.2	108.9	107.9	119.3

Table 5-1. Indexes of Productivity and Related Data, 1947–2010—*Continued*

(2005 = 100.)

| Year | Nonfarm business | | | | | | | | | | | |
	Output per hour	Output	Hours	Hourly compensation	Real hourly compensation	Unit labor costs	Unit nonlabor payments	Implicit price deflator	Employment	Output per person	Compensation in current dollars	Nonlabor payments in current dollars
1947	27.2	12.4	45.5	4.6	36.7	16.9	13.4	15.5	38.9	31.9	2.1	1.7
1948	28.0	12.9	46.3	5.0	36.9	17.9	14.5	16.5	39.7	32.6	2.3	1.9
1949	28.9	12.9	44.5	5.1	38.5	17.8	15.0	16.7	38.6	33.3	2.3	1.9
1950	30.8	14.2	45.9	5.4	40.2	17.7	15.6	16.9	39.5	35.8	2.5	2.2
1951	31.7	15.2	48.1	5.9	40.5	18.7	16.8	18.0	41.3	36.9	2.8	2.6
1952	32.2	15.7	48.6	6.2	42.0	19.4	16.7	18.3	41.8	37.5	3.0	2.6
1953	33.0	16.4	49.8	6.6	44.0	20.0	16.6	18.7	43.1	38.2	3.3	2.7
1954	33.6	16.2	48.1	6.8	45.0	20.2	16.7	18.8	41.9	38.6	3.3	2.7
1955	35.0	17.5	50.1	7.1	46.9	20.1	17.7	19.2	43.2	40.6	3.5	3.1
1956	34.8	17.8	51.3	7.5	49.0	21.5	17.3	19.9	44.4	40.2	3.8	3.1
1957	35.7	18.2	51.0	7.9	50.2	22.2	17.8	20.5	44.6	40.8	4.0	3.2
1958	36.5	17.8	48.9	8.2	50.7	22.6	18.0	20.8	43.1	41.4	4.0	3.2
1959	37.9	19.4	51.1	8.6	52.3	22.6	18.7	21.0	44.6	43.4	4.4	3.6
1960	38.3	19.7	51.4	8.9	53.7	23.3	18.2	21.3	45.1	43.7	4.6	3.6
1961	39.5	20.1	50.9	9.2	54.9	23.3	18.6	21.5	44.8	44.9	4.7	3.7
1962	41.3	21.5	52.0	9.6	56.5	23.2	19.3	21.7	45.6	47.1	5.0	4.1
1963	42.7	22.5	52.6	9.9	57.7	23.2	19.7	21.8	46.1	48.8	5.2	4.4
1964	44.0	24.0	54.5	10.2	58.7	23.2	20.3	22.1	47.2	50.8	5.6	4.9
1965	45.4	25.7	56.6	10.6	59.7	23.3	21.0	22.4	48.9	52.5	6.0	5.4
1966	47.0	27.5	58.6	11.2	61.5	23.8	21.5	22.9	50.8	54.2	6.6	5.9
1967	47.8	28.0	58.6	11.8	63.1	24.8	21.9	23.6	51.7	54.2	6.9	6.1
1968	49.4	29.5	59.6	12.8	65.3	25.8	22.6	24.6	52.9	55.7	7.6	6.7
1969	49.5	30.4	61.3	13.6	66.2	27.5	22.8	25.7	54.8	55.4	8.4	6.9
1970	50.2	30.3	60.4	14.6	67.1	29.1	23.3	26.8	54.8	55.3	8.8	7.1
1971	52.3	31.5	60.2	15.5	68.4	29.8	25.2	28.0	55.0	57.2	9.4	7.9
1972	54.0	33.6	62.2	16.6	70.5	30.7	26.0	28.8	56.6	59.3	10.3	8.7
1973	55.7	36.0	64.7	17.9	71.8	32.2	26.3	29.9	59.2	60.9	11.6	9.5
1974	54.8	35.5	64.8	19.7	71.0	35.9	28.4	32.9	60.1	59.0	12.7	10.1
1975	56.3	34.9	62.0	21.6	71.6	38.4	33.5	36.5	58.4	59.8	13.4	11.7
1976	58.2	37.4	64.2	23.5	73.4	40.3	35.7	38.5	60.4	61.9	15.1	13.3
1977	59.1	39.5	66.8	25.4	74.5	42.9	37.8	40.9	63.1	62.5	16.9	14.9
1978	59.9	42.1	70.3	27.6	75.8	46.1	39.9	43.7	66.6	63.1	19.4	16.8
1979	59.6	43.4	72.8	30.2	75.7	50.7	42.3	47.4	69.5	62.4	22.0	18.4
1980	59.5	42.9	72.2	33.4	75.4	56.2	45.3	51.9	69.7	61.6	24.1	19.5
1981	60.3	43.8	72.7	36.7	75.5	60.8	50.9	56.9	70.5	62.2	26.6	22.3
1982	59.7	42.4	71.1	39.3	76.3	65.8	52.1	60.4	69.3	61.2	27.9	22.1
1983	62.3	45.1	72.5	40.9	76.2	65.7	57.2	62.4	70.0	64.5	29.6	25.8
1984	63.5	48.9	76.9	42.6	76.2	67.0	59.7	64.1	73.8	66.2	32.7	29.2
1985	64.6	51.0	78.9	44.5	76.9	68.9	61.5	66.0	75.9	67.1	35.1	31.3
1986	66.6	52.9	79.5	46.8	79.5	70.3	62.1	67.1	77.2	68.5	37.2	32.9
1987	66.8	54.7	81.9	48.5	79.7	72.7	62.6	68.7	79.4	68.9	39.7	34.3
1988	67.9	57.2	84.3	50.9	80.8	75.1	64.2	70.8	81.9	69.8	42.9	36.7
1989	68.4	59.2	86.6	52.2	79.4	76.4	68.7	73.4	83.8	70.7	45.2	40.7
1990	69.6	60.1	86.3	55.5	80.3	79.7	70.5	76.1	84.4	71.2	47.9	42.4
1991	70.7	59.5	84.2	58.4	81.6	82.6	72.8	78.7	83.0	71.7	49.1	43.3
1992	73.5	61.8	84.0	61.5	83.9	83.7	75.1	80.3	82.5	74.8	51.7	46.4
1993	73.9	63.9	86.4	62.7	83.5	84.9	77.3	81.9	84.5	75.6	54.2	49.4
1994	74.7	66.9	89.6	63.9	83.2	85.5	80.1	83.4	87.2	76.7	57.2	53.6
1995	75.0	69.0	92.0	65.2	82.9	86.9	81.6	84.8	89.7	76.9	60.0	56.3
1996	76.9	72.1	93.7	67.4	83.4	87.5	83.7	86.0	91.8	78.5	63.1	60.3
1997	78.1	75.7	96.9	69.4	84.2	88.9	85.6	87.6	94.4	80.2	67.3	64.8
1998	80.4	79.6	99.0	73.6	88.0	91.5	83.3	88.3	96.5	82.5	72.9	66.3
1999	83.1	84.1	101.2	76.8	89.9	92.4	84.1	89.1	98.2	85.6	77.7	70.7
2000	85.9	87.8	102.2	82.5	93.5	96.0	83.0	90.9	100.0	87.8	84.3	72.8
2001	88.4	88.6	100.2	86.2	95.0	97.5	84.6	92.4	99.3	89.2	86.3	74.9
2002	92.4	90.3	97.6	88.9	96.5	96.2	88.7	93.2	97.0	93.0	86.8	80.1
2003	95.8	93.0	97.1	93.1	98.8	97.1	90.1	94.4	96.9	96.0	90.4	83.9
2004	98.4	96.7	98.3	96.2	99.4	97.8	94.8	96.6	98.2	98.5	94.6	91.7
2005	100.0	100.0	100.0	100.0	100.0	100.0	100.0	100.0	100.0	100.0	100.0	100.0
2006	100.9	103.1	102.2	103.8	100.5	102.8	103.2	103.0	101.9	101.2	106.0	106.4
2007	102.4	105.3	102.7	107.9	101.6	105.3	105.4	105.4	102.7	102.5	110.9	111.0
2008	103.1	103.7	100.6	111.6	101.2	108.2	105.8	107.3	101.1	102.6	112.3	109.7
2009	105.5	98.5	93.3	113.4	103.3	107.5	109.8	108.4	95.3	103.3	105.9	108.1
2010	109.8	102.4	93.2	115.8	103.7	105.4	116.1	109.6	94.1	108.7	107.9	118.8

Table 5-1. Indexes of Productivity and Related Data, 1947–2010—*Continued*

(2005 = 100.)

Year	Nonfinancial corporations												
	Output per hour	Output	Hours	Hourly compensation	Real hourly compensation	Unit labor costs	Unit nonlabor costs	Unit profits	Implicit price deflator	Employment	Output per person	Compensation in current dollars	Nonlabor payments in current dollars
1947	...	...	...	...	...	...	...	...	...	...	...	...	...
1948	...	...	...	...	...	...	...	...	...	...	...	...	...
1949	...	...	...	...	...	...	...	...	...	...	...	...	...
1950	...	...	...	...	...	...	...	...	...	...	...	...	...
1951	...	...	...	...	...	...	...	...	...	...	...	...	...
1952	...	...	...	...	...	...	...	...	...	...	...	...	...
1953	...	...	...	...	...	...	...	...	...	...	...	...	...
1954	...	...	...	...	...	...	...	...	...	...	...	...	...
1955	...	...	...	...	...	...	...	...	...	...	...	...	...
1956	...	...	...	...	...	...	...	...	...	...	...	...	...
1957	...	...	...	...	...	...	...	...	...	...	...	...	...
1958	36.6	15.0	41.0	9.5	58.7	26.0	21.0	28.3	25.1	36.5	41.1	3.9	3.5
1959	38.4	16.7	43.5	9.9	60.5	25.7	20.1	32.9	25.3	38.2	43.7	4.3	4.1
1960	39.0	17.2	44.2	10.3	61.8	26.3	20.6	30.3	25.4	39.0	44.2	4.5	4.1
1961	40.3	17.6	43.8	10.6	63.2	26.3	21.0	30.4	25.5	38.8	45.5	4.6	4.3
1962	42.1	19.1	45.5	11.0	65.0	26.2	20.6	32.8	25.7	40.1	47.8	5.0	4.8
1963	43.6	20.3	46.5	11.4	66.1	26.0	20.5	34.7	25.8	40.9	49.6	5.3	5.1
1964	44.3	21.7	49.0	11.6	66.5	26.1	20.5	36.0	26.0	42.4	51.2	5.7	5.6
1965	45.4	23.5	51.8	11.9	67.3	26.2	20.3	38.7	26.4	44.6	52.7	6.2	6.3
1966	46.2	25.2	54.6	12.6	69.1	27.2	20.4	38.5	27.0	47.2	53.5	6.9	6.7
1967	47.0	25.9	55.1	13.3	70.8	28.3	21.7	36.0	27.6	48.5	53.4	7.3	6.9
1968	48.7	27.6	56.7	14.3	73.1	29.4	23.0	35.9	28.6	50.2	54.9	8.1	7.6
1969	48.7	28.7	58.9	15.3	74.0	31.3	24.8	32.5	29.9	52.5	54.7	9.0	7.9
1970	49.1	28.5	58.0	16.3	74.9	33.3	28.0	26.5	31.1	52.6	54.1	9.5	7.8
1971	51.2	29.6	57.9	17.3	76.3	33.9	29.3	30.0	32.3	52.7	56.2	10.0	8.8
1972	52.2	31.9	61.1	18.3	77.9	35.0	29.3	32.5	33.3	55.4	57.6	11.2	9.7
1973	52.8	33.9	64.2	19.7	78.9	37.3	30.8	32.9	35.2	58.4	58.0	12.6	10.7
1974	51.7	33.3	64.5	21.5	77.8	41.7	35.4	29.1	38.6	59.5	56.0	13.9	11.1
1975	53.7	32.8	61.2	23.7	78.3	44.1	40.3	37.8	42.4	57.3	57.3	14.5	12.9
1976	55.5	35.5	64.0	25.6	80.1	46.1	40.0	42.7	44.2	59.8	59.4	16.4	14.5
1977	57.0	38.2	66.9	27.6	81.2	48.5	41.5	46.6	46.6	62.9	60.7	18.5	16.5
1978	57.7	40.6	70.4	30.2	82.9	52.3	43.6	48.4	49.7	66.4	61.2	21.3	18.4
1979	57.2	41.9	73.2	32.9	82.5	57.5	47.5	45.4	53.5	69.7	60.1	24.1	19.6
1980	57.1	41.5	72.7	36.2	81.7	63.5	55.6	40.7	58.7	70.0	59.3	26.3	20.9
1981	58.5	43.1	73.8	39.5	81.3	67.5	63.3	48.5	64.1	71.2	60.6	29.1	25.1
1982	58.7	42.1	71.8	42.1	81.7	71.7	70.2	44.7	67.9	69.6	60.5	30.2	25.9
1983	60.6	44.2	72.8	43.6	81.3	71.9	70.3	54.3	69.3	69.9	63.2	31.8	28.6
1984	62.0	48.1	77.5	45.4	81.3	73.2	69.6	65.2	71.3	74.0	65.0	35.2	32.7
1985	63.3	50.1	79.3	47.5	82.1	75.0	71.5	62.4	72.6	76.1	65.9	37.6	34.3
1986	64.6	51.4	79.5	49.8	84.7	77.1	74.9	53.6	73.6	77.2	66.5	39.6	34.7
1987	65.9	54.0	82.0	51.5	84.6	78.1	74.2	60.3	74.9	79.3	68.1	42.2	37.5
1988	67.6	57.1	84.6	53.7	85.1	79.4	75.1	66.8	76.8	82.0	69.7	45.4	41.3
1989	66.6	58.1	87.2	55.0	83.6	82.5	80.0	61.2	79.2	84.0	69.1	47.9	42.7
1990	67.4	59.0	87.5	57.6	83.4	85.6	83.5	58.8	81.7	85.5	69.0	50.4	44.3
1991	69.0	58.7	85.0	60.5	84.6	87.6	87.9	58.0	83.9	83.7	70.1	51.4	45.5
1992	70.8	60.4	85.4	63.4	86.5	89.6	85.8	61.4	85.1	83.7	72.2	54.1	46.8
1993	70.9	62.0	87.4	64.6	85.9	91.0	85.1	70.3	87.0	85.3	72.6	56.4	49.6
1994	72.4	66.0	91.1	65.7	85.6	90.8	85.5	82.4	88.4	88.5	74.6	59.9	55.7
1995	73.1	69.0	94.4	66.9	85.1	91.5	85.8	85.4	89.3	91.6	75.4	63.2	59.2
1996	75.8	72.9	96.1	68.8	85.3	90.8	85.4	92.5	89.7	94.0	77.5	66.2	64.0
1997	77.8	77.6	99.8	71.0	86.0	91.2	85.3	94.7	90.2	96.9	80.1	70.8	68.7
1998	80.5	82.0	102.0	75.2	90.0	93.5	85.7	83.1	90.3	99.3	82.6	76.7	69.6
1999	83.0	86.6	104.3	78.6	92.0	94.6	88.1	77.3	90.8	101.4	85.4	81.9	73.0
2000	86.4	91.2	105.6	84.4	95.6	97.6	91.1	64.2	91.8	103.4	88.2	89.1	74.7
2001	87.1	89.5	102.7	87.1	96.1	100.0	96.7	51.8	93.1	102.1	87.7	89.5	72.8
2002	90.5	90.1	99.6	89.5	97.1	98.9	97.0	59.4	93.5	99.1	90.9	89.1	75.8
2003	94.4	92.3	97.8	93.9	99.7	99.5	96.8	66.0	94.6	97.8	94.5	91.8	79.6
2004	97.8	96.5	98.7	96.5	99.7	98.6	95.7	88.0	96.6	98.5	98.0	95.2	89.9
2005	100.0	100.0	100.0	100.0	100.0	100.0	100.0	100.0	100.0	100.0	100.0	100.0	100.0
2006	101.9	103.8	101.9	103.3	100.0	101.3	103.0	111.6	103.0	101.5	102.3	105.2	110.0
2007	102.7	105.0	102.2	107.3	101.0	104.5	109.0	99.8	105.0	102.0	102.9	109.7	111.1
2008	103.0	103.5	100.5	111.2	100.8	108.0	113.5	91.5	107.2	100.6	102.9	111.7	109.6
2009	104.7	97.0	92.6	113.4	103.2	108.4	119.5	83.0	107.9	94.1	103.1	105.1	103.8
2010	110.3	102.2	92.7	115.6	103.5	104.9	108.0	116.7	107.1	93.0	109.9	107.2	113.4

... = Not available.

Table 5-1. Indexes of Productivity and Related Data, 1947–2010—*Continued*

(2005 = 100.)

Year	Manufacturing											
	Output per hour	Output	Hours	Hourly compen- sation	Real hourly compen- sation	Unit labor costs	Unit nonlabor payments	Implicit price deflator	Employment	Output per person	Compen- sation in current dollars	Nonlabor payments in current dollars
1947	. . .	. . .	. . .	. . .	. . .	. . .	. . .	. . .	. . .	. . .	. . .	. . .
1948	. . .	. . .	. . .	. . .	. . .	. . .	. . .	. . .	. . .	. . .	. . .	. . .
1949	. . .	. . .	. . .	. . .	. . .	. . .	. . .	. . .	. . .	. . .	. . .	. . .
1950	. . .	. . .	. . .	. . .	. . .	. . .	. . .	. . .	. . .	. . .	. . .	. . .
1951	. . .	. . .	. . .	. . .	. . .	. . .	. . .	. . .	. . .	. . .	. . .	. . .
1952	. . .	. . .	. . .	. . .	. . .	. . .	. . .	. . .	. . .	. . .	. . .	. . .
1953	. . .	. . .	. . .	. . .	. . .	. . .	. . .	. . .	. . .	. . .	. . .	. . .
1954	. . .	. . .	. . .	. . .	. . .	. . .	. . .	. . .	. . .	. . .	. . .	. . .
1955	. . .	. . .	. . .	. . .	. . .	. . .	. . .	. . .	. . .	. . .	. . .	. . .
1956	. . .	. . .	. . .	. . .	. . .	. . .	. . .	. . .	. . .	. . .	. . .	. . .
1957	. . .	. . .	. . .	. . .	. . .	. . .	. . .	. . .	. . .	. . .	. . .	. . .
1958	. . .	. . .	. . .	. . .	. . .	. . .	. . .	. . .	. . .	. . .	. . .	. . .
1959	. . .	. . .	. . .	. . .	. . .	. . .	. . .	. . .	. . .	. . .	. . .	. . .
1960	. . .	. . .	. . .	. . .	. . .	. . .	. . .	. . .	. . .	. . .	. . .	. . .
1961	. . .	. . .	. . .	. . .	. . .	. . .	. . .	. . .	. . .	. . .	. . .	. . .
1962	. . .	. . .	. . .	. . .	. . .	. . .	. . .	. . .	. . .	. . .	. . .	. . .
1963	. . .	. . .	. . .	. . .	. . .	. . .	. . .	. . .	. . .	. . .	. . .	. . .
1964	. . .	. . .	. . .	. . .	. . .	. . .	. . .	. . .	. . .	. . .	. . .	. . .
1965	. . .	. . .	. . .	. . .	. . .	. . .	. . .	. . .	. . .	. . .	. . .	. . .
1966	. . .	. . .	. . .	. . .	. . .	. . .	. . .	. . .	. . .	. . .	. . .	. . .
1967	. . .	. . .	. . .	. . .	. . .	. . .	. . .	. . .	. . .	. . .	. . .	. . .
1968	. . .	. . .	. . .	. . .	. . .	. . .	. . .	. . .	. . .	. . .	. . .	. . .
1969	. . .	. . .	. . .	. . .	. . .	. . .	. . .	. . .	. . .	. . .	. . .	. . .
1970	. . .	. . .	. . .	. . .	. . .	. . .	. . .	. . .	. . .	. . .	. . .	. . .
1971	. . .	. . .	. . .	. . .	. . .	. . .	. . .	. . .	. . .	. . .	. . .	. . .
1972	. . .	. . .	. . .	. . .	. . .	. . .	. . .	. . .	. . .	. . .	. . .	. . .
1973	. . .	. . .	. . .	. . .	. . .	. . .	. . .	. . .	. . .	. . .	. . .	. . .
1974	. . .	. . .	. . .	. . .	. . .	. . .	. . .	. . .	. . .	. . .	. . .	. . .
1975	. . .	. . .	. . .	. . .	. . .	. . .	. . .	. . .	. . .	. . .	. . .	. . .
1976	. . .	. . .	. . .	. . .	. . .	. . .	. . .	. . .	. . .	. . .	. . .	. . .
1977	. . .	. . .	. . .	. . .	. . .	. . .	. . .	. . .	. . .	. . .	. . .	. . .
1978	. . .	. . .	. . .	. . .	. . .	. . .	. . .	. . .	. . .	. . .	. . .	. . .
1979	. . .	. . .	. . .	. . .	. . .	. . .	. . .	. . .	. . .	. . .	. . .	. . .
1980	. . .	. . .	. . .	. . .	. . .	. . .	. . .	. . .	. . .	. . .	. . .	. . .
1981	. . .	. . .	. . .	. . .	. . .	. . .	. . .	. . .	. . .	. . .	. . .	. . .
1982	. . .	. . .	. . .	. . .	. . .	. . .	. . .	. . .	. . .	. . .	. . .	. . .
1983	. . .	. . .	. . .	. . .	. . .	. . .	. . .	. . .	. . .	. . .	. . .	. . .
1984	. . .	. . .	. . .	. . .	. . .	. . .	. . .	. . .	. . .	. . .	. . .	. . .
1985	. . .	. . .	. . .	. . .	. . .	. . .	. . .	. . .	. . .	. . .	. . .	. . .
1986	. . .	. . .	. . .	. . .	. . .	. . .	. . .	. . .	. . .	. . .	. . .	. . .
1987	51.0	62.9	123.2	49.4	81.2	96.8	72.0	78.7	123.2	51.0	60.8	45.2
1988	52.1	66.1	126.9	51.2	81.1	98.2	74.7	81.1	125.4	52.7	64.9	49.4
1989	52.6	67.2	127.7	52.7	80.1	100.1	78.8	84.6	126.1	53.3	67.3	53.0
1990	53.8	67.0	124.5	55.2	80.0	102.7	81.7	87.4	124.2	53.9	68.8	54.7
1991	55.2	65.8	119.3	58.5	81.8	106.0	81.1	87.9	119.9	54.9	69.8	53.4
1992	57.3	68.0	118.7	61.3	83.5	106.9	82.2	88.9	117.9	57.7	72.7	55.9
1993	58.8	70.7	120.3	62.7	83.4	106.6	83.0	89.4	118.0	59.9	75.3	58.7
1994	60.8	74.9	123.1	64.2	83.7	105.6	84.3	90.1	119.5	62.7	79.0	63.1
1995	63.6	78.8	123.9	65.2	83.0	102.6	87.3	91.5	121.2	65.0	80.8	68.8
1996	65.9	81.5	123.6	66.4	82.2	100.7	88.7	92.0	121.0	67.3	82.0	72.3
1997	69.5	87.4	125.9	68.0	82.4	97.8	88.3	90.9	122.1	71.6	85.6	77.2
1998	73.3	92.1	125.5	72.2	86.3	98.4	84.2	88.0	123.1	74.8	90.6	77.5
1999	76.9	95.9	124.7	75.4	88.3	97.9	84.5	88.2	121.2	79.1	94.0	81.1
2000	80.4	98.9	123.1	81.2	92.0	101.0	85.5	89.8	120.9	81.8	99.9	84.6
2001	81.9	94.2	115.0	84.3	92.9	102.9	83.9	89.1	115.3	81.7	96.9	79.1
2002	87.8	93.9	106.9	88.9	96.5	101.2	83.4	88.2	107.0	87.8	95.0	78.3
2003	93.3	94.9	101.7	96.0	101.9	102.9	84.9	89.8	101.9	93.1	97.6	80.6
2004	95.4	96.5	101.1	96.8	100.0	101.4	91.4	94.1	100.5	96.0	97.9	88.2
2005	100.0	100.0	100.0	100.0	100.0	100.0	100.0	100.0	100.0	100.0	100.0	100.0
2006	100.9	101.6	100.7	102.0	98.8	101.1	104.3	103.5	99.4	102.2	102.8	106.1
2007	104.9	103.8	99.0	105.3	99.2	100.4	110.4	107.7	97.7	106.3	104.3	114.7
2008	104.4	99.2	95.1	109.8	99.6	105.2	118.7	115.0	94.2	105.3	104.4	117.8
2009	104.9	86.8	82.7	114.8	104.5	109.4	110.0	109.9	83.6	103.8	95.0	95.5
2010	111.3	92.0	82.7	116.6	104.4	104.8	. . .	. . .	81.3	113.2	96.5	. . .

. . . = Not available.

Table 5-2. Average Annual Percent Change in Output Per Hour and Related Series, Selected Industries, 1987–2009 and 2008–2009

(Number, percent.)

Industry	NAICS code	2009 employment (thousands)	Average annual percent change, 1987–2009			Annual percent change, 2008–2009		
			Output per hour	Output	Hours	Output per hour	Output	Hours
Mining								
Mining	21	661	0.2	-0.2	-0.4	14.2	0.4	-12.1
Oil and gas extraction	211	162	0.7	-0.5	-1.2	6.3	5.4	-0.9
Mining, except oil and gas	212	212	1.8	0.2	-1.6	-2.4	-13.6	-11.5
Coal mining	2121	82	2.0	-0.3	-2.3	-6.2	-8.8	-2.7
Metal ore mining	2122	35	2.4	1.7	-0.7	11.0	-11.5	-20.3
Nonmetallic mineral mining and quarrying	2123	95	0.7	-0.5	-1.2	-6.8	-21.3	-15.5
Support activities for mining	213	287	2.6	4.1	1.4	-6.2	-22.6	-17.5
Utilities								
Power generation and supply	2211	404	2.2	0.9	-1.3	-2.4	-3.6	-1.3
Natural gas distribution	2212	109	2.5	1.1	-1.3	-3.8	-2.1	1.8
Transportation and Warehousing								
Air transportation	481	399	2.8	2.7	-0.1	0.1	-6.5	-6.6
Line-haul railroads	482111	172	4.0	1.4	-2.4	-3.9	-17.2	-13.8
General freight trucking	484	1 501	0.1	1.2	1.1	-4.5	-14.4	-10.4
General freight trucking	4841	1 096	0.8	1.8	1.0	-5.0	-14.8	-10.3
General freight trucking, local	48411	289	2.3	3.1	0.7	-4.5	-14.7	-10.7
General freight trucking, long-distance	48412	807	0.9	1.9	0.9	-5.2	-14.8	-10.1
Used household and office goods moving	48421	86	-0.5	-1.0	-0.4	-0.3	-16.8	-16.6
Postal service	491	703	1.0	0.1	-0.8	1.4	-11.7	-12.9
Couriers and messengers	492	579	-0.4	1.6	2.0	-4.9	-11.0	-6.3
Warehousing and storage	493	645	2.6	5.5	2.8	1.4	-4.0	-5.4
General warehousing and storage	49311	538	5.0	7.9	2.8	2.2	-3.6	-5.7
Refrigerated warehousing and storage	49312	51	-0.6	2.8	3.4	-8.4	-2.6	6.2
Information								
Publishing	511	833	3.7	3.6	-0.1	1.3	-8.0	-9.2
Newspaper, book, and directory publishers	5111	576	-0.1	-1.6	-1.5	-1.6	-14.2	-12.8
Software publishers	5112	258	13.9	20.9	6.2	-0.8	-1.8	-1.0
Motion picture and video exhibition	51213	134	1.6	2.0	0.4	6.6	1.3	-5.0
Broadcasting, except Internet	515	316	1.6	2.5	0.9	1.7	-1.7	-3.3
Radio and television broadcasting	5151	227	0.5	0.4	-0.1	-0.1	-4.1	-4.0
Cable and other subscription programming	5152	89	3.5	7.9	4.2	2.6	0.7	-1.8
Wired telecommunications carriers	5171	643	4.1	3.4	-0.7	1.7	-2.9	-4.6
Wireless telecommunications carriers	5172	192	10.2	21.8	10.5	24.3	6.4	-14.4
Finance and Insurance								
Commercial banking	52211	1 317	3.6	3.5	-0.1	2.2	-0.6	-2.8
Real Estate and Rental and Leasing								
Passenger car rental	532111	106	1.8	2.2	0.4	-4.1	-16.0	-12.4
Truck, trailer, and RV rental and leasing	53212	58	2.9	2.1	-0.8	-13.3	-14.3	-1.2
Video tape and disc rental	53223	88	4.3	3.2	-1.0	8.4	-15.9	-22.4
Professional and Technical Services								
Tax preparation services	541213	149	0.4	2.9	2.5	-2.3	-1.0	1.4
Architectural services	54131	194	1.3	2.6	1.2	-1.2	-20.1	-19.1
Engineering services	54133	917	1.2	3.0	1.8	-5.4	-11.9	-6.9
Advertising agencies	54181	184	1.8	2.0	0.1	1.9	-5.6	-7.3
Photography studios, portrait	541921	74	-0.2	2.0	2.2	-5.8	-4.7	1.2
Administrative and Waste Services								
Employment placement agencies	561311	219	6.8	6.9	0.1	0.3	-16.4	-16.7
Travel agencies	56151	100	5.5	3.6	-1.8	2.8	-14.9	-17.2
Janitorial services	56172	1 214	1.9	3.6	1.7	-3.7	-7.5	-4.0
Healthcare and Social Assistance								
Medical and diagnostic laboratories	6215	232	3.7	6.7	2.8	2.7	4.3	1.6
Medical laboratories	621511	155	3.3	5.8	2.4	5.0	6.7	1.6
Diagnostic imaging centers	621512	76	4.1	8.2	4.0	-0.7	1.0	1.7
Arts, Entertainment, and Recreation								
Amusement and theme parks	71311	136	-0.3	2.5	2.7	-7.8	-7.9	-0.1
Bowling centers	71395	72	0.2	-1.8	-2.0	-2.9	-7.6	-4.8
Accommodation and Food Services								
Accommodation and food services	72	11 412	0.8	2.1	1.2	-0.6	-4.9	-4.4
Accommodation	721	1 793	1.5	2.3	0.8	-1.6	-8.6	-7.1
Traveler accommodation	7211	1 719	1.6	2.4	0.8	-1.9	-9.0	-7.2
Food services and drinking places	722	9 619	0.6	2.0	1.4	0.3	-3.5	-3.8
Full-service restaurants	7221	4 511	0.6	2.0	1.4	0.3	-3.5	-3.8
Limited-service eating places	7222	4 098	0.6	2.2	1.6	1.2	-2.5	-3.6
Special food services	7223	653	1.4	2.4	0.9	-5.2	-8.3	-3.2
Drinking places (alcoholic beverages)	7224	358	-0.4	-0.8	-0.4	3.8	-2.7	-6.3

Table 5-2. Average Annual Percent Change in Output Per Hour and Related Series, Selected Industries, 1987–2009 and 2008–2009—*Continued*

(Number, percent.)

Industry	NAICS code	2009 employment (thousands)	Average annual percent change, 1987–2009			Annual percent change, 2008–2009		
			Output per hour	Output	Hours	Output per hour	Output	Hours
Other Services								
Automotive repair and maintenance	8111	1 074	0.7	1.1	0.4	-4.7	-9.2	-4.7
Reupholstery and furniture repair	81142	22	-0.7	-3.2	-2.4	-2.7	-15.6	-13.3
Hair, nail, and skin care services	81211	956	1.9	2.9	0.9	-6.0	-2.9	3.3
Funeral homes and funeral services	81221	104	-0.6	-0.5	0.0	1.6	-5.0	-6.5
Drycleaning and laundry services	8123	340	1.3	0.4	-0.9	10.1	-3.2	-12.1
Coin-operated laundries and drycleaners	81231	44	2.1	0.3	-1.7	7.7	-4.0	-10.9
Drycleaning and laundry services	81232	167	1.0	-0.9	-1.9	11.6	-5.7	-15.5
Linen and uniform supply	81233	129	0.7	1.6	0.9	8.5	-0.9	-8.6
Photofinishing	81292	19	1.5	-5.0	-6.4	24.7	-5.6	-24.3
Manufacturing								
Food	311	1 491	1.2	1.3	0.2	3.5	0.5	-2.9
Animal food	3111	53	3.0	2.2	-0.8	5.9	3.5	-2.3
Grain and oilseed milling	3112	60	2.3	1.5	-0.9	8.4	6.4	-1.8
Sugar and confectionery products	3113	73	0.8	-0.5	-1.2	3.0	-4.6	-7.4
Fruit and vegetable preserving and specialty	3114	175	1.3	1.1	-0.2	-5.4	-3.3	2.2
Dairy products	3115	133	1.8	1.1	-0.7	6.2	1.9	-4.1
Animal slaughtering and processing	3116	500	1.0	2.2	1.2	3.1	0.6	-2.4
Seafood product preparation and packaging	3117	38	1.6	0.3	-1.2	18.3	5.7	-10.6
Bakeries and tortilla manufacturing	3118	296	0.5	0.2	-0.3	1.7	-1.4	-3.0
Other food products	3119	163	0.6	1.9	1.2	4.6	-1.1	-5.5
Beverages and tobacco products	312	195	0.7	-0.7	-1.4	3.7	-8.0	-11.3
Beverages	3121	176	2.2	1.3	-0.9	9.1	-1.9	-10.1
Tobacco and tobacco products	3122	19	0.4	-4.1	-4.5	-1.9	-22.2	-20.7
Textile mills	313	135	3.4	-3.3	-6.5	-0.2	-18.1	-18.0
Fiber, yarn, and thread mills	3131	31	3.5	-2.8	-6.0	-7.2	-24.4	-18.5
Fabric mills	3132	60	4.9	-3.1	-7.6	3.7	-14.9	-17.9
Textile and fabric finishing mills	3133	44	0.4	-4.4	-4.8	-3.4	-20.4	-17.6
Textile product mills	314	144	0.5	-2.2	-2.7	-11.5	-24.7	-14.9
Textile furnishings mills	3141	69	0.1	-2.9	-2.9	-14.6	-27.9	-15.5
Other textile product mills	3149	75	1.4	-1.1	-2.4	-5.9	-19.3	-14.3
Apparel	315	192	-2.3	-9.3	-7.1	-16.8	-27.6	-13.0
Apparel knitting mills	3151	24	-0.6	-7.8	-7.3	-0.4	-25.8	-25.6
Cut and sew apparel	3152	153	-2.8	-9.9	-7.3	-22.0	-30.3	-10.6
Accessories and other apparel	3159	15	-2.8	-7.3	-4.6	0.1	-12.0	-12.1
Leather and allied products	316	33	1.4	-5.5	-6.9	-11.4	-22.5	-12.5
Leather and hide tanning and finishing	3161	4	-0.6	-6.6	-6.0	-16.9	-29.2	-14.8
Footwear	3162	15	2.1	-6.3	-8.2	-5.5	-19.1	-14.4
Other leather products	3169	14	0.6	-4.5	-5.0	-15.2	-23.4	-9.7
Wood products	321	389	1.1	-1.2	-2.3	-2.5	-23.9	-21.9
Sawmills and wood preservation	3211	84	2.7	-0.6	-3.2	7.3	-14.3	-20.1
Plywood and engineered wood products	3212	68	0.6	-1.6	-2.1	-2.2	-28.2	-26.6
Other wood products	3219	237	0.7	-1.3	-2.0	-6.3	-26.1	-21.1
Paper and paper products	322	408	1.9	-0.3	-2.2	0.7	-10.7	-11.3
Pulp, paper, and paperboard mills	3221	118	2.8	-0.6	-3.3	-1.4	-9.2	-7.9
Converted paper products	3222	290	1.5	-0.1	-1.6	1.6	-11.3	-12.7
Printing and related support activities	323	550	1.2	-0.6	-1.8	-4.1	-14.9	-11.3
Petroleum and coal products	324	117	2.6	1.0	-1.5	2.8	-2.6	-5.3
Chemicals	325	807	1.4	0.5	-0.9	-5.4	-10.7	-5.6
Basic chemicals	3251	146	1.9	-0.4	-2.3	-12.1	-16.7	-5.3
Resin, rubber, and artificial fibers	3252	92	1.7	-0.4	-2.1	-7.3	-17.3	-10.9
Agricultural chemicals	3253	37	2.9	0.8	-2.0	14.1	12.3	-1.5
Pharmaceuticals and medicines	3254	285	0.4	2.5	2.1	-4.6	-6.7	-2.3
Paints, coatings, and adhesives	3255	57	0.7	-1.2	-1.8	-6.3	-17.1	-11.5
Soaps, cleaning compounds, and toiletries	3256	103	2.9	1.8	-1.0	-0.5	-7.6	-7.1
Other chemical products and preparations	3259	87	2.1	-0.4	-2.5	-4.8	-10.6	-6.1
Plastics and rubber products	326	631	1.9	0.8	-1.1	-1.0	-17.2	-16.4
Plastics products	3261	506	1.8	1.1	-0.7	-1.1	-17.3	-16.4
Rubber products	3262	124	2.0	-0.4	-2.4	-0.5	-16.8	-16.4
Nonmetallic mineral products	327	409	0.8	-0.5	-1.3	-7.0	-23.0	-17.3
Clay products and refractories	3271	51	0.5	-2.5	-3.0	-14.6	-28.1	-15.9
Glass and glass products	3272	89	2.1	-0.2	-2.2	3.1	-14.4	-17.0
Cement and concrete products	3273	186	-0.1	-0.5	-0.4	-10.4	-27.6	-19.2
Lime and gypsum products	3274	15	0.7	-1.1	-1.8	-7.1	-22.1	-16.2
Other nonmetallic mineral products	3279	69	1.3	0.5	-0.8	-5.7	-18.3	-13.4
Primary metals	331	365	1.9	-1.2	-3.0	-13.1	-30.3	-19.7
Iron and steel mills and ferroalloy production	3311	86	3.8	0.4	-3.3	-22.4	-34.7	-15.8
Steel products from purchased steel	3312	51	-1.6	-3.2	-1.6	-15.6	-31.6	-19.0
Alumina and aluminum production	3313	56	2.1	-1.2	-3.2	-5.1	-21.8	-17.5
Other nonferrous metal production	3314	58	0.7	-2.1	-2.8	-14.5	-24.6	-11.8
Foundries	3315	114	1.9	-1.3	-3.2	1.8	-26.2	-27.5

Table 5-2. Average Annual Percent Change in Output Per Hour and Related Series, Selected Industries, 1987–2009 and 2008–2009—*Continued*

(Number, percent.)

Industry	NAICS code	2009 employment (thousands)	Average annual percent change, 1987–2009			Annual percent change, 2008–2009		
			Output per hour	Output	Hours	Output per hour	Output	Hours
Manufacturing—*Continued*								
Fabricated metal products	332	1 344	1.2	0.2	-1.0	-8.3	-23.3	-16.3
Forging and stamping	3321	89	2.5	0.3	-2.1	-6.8	-26.7	-21.3
Cutlery and hand tools	3322	45	0.8	-1.9	-2.6	-11.8	-19.5	-8.7
Architectural and structural metals	3323	351	0.7	0.5	-0.1	-9.2	-23.5	-15.8
Boilers, tanks, and shipping containers	3324	89	0.6	-0.4	-1.1	-4.4	-16.4	-12.6
Hardware	3325	25	0.4	-4.0	-4.4	-13.2	-27.6	-16.7
Spring and wire products	3326	44	2.4	-0.5	-2.8	-4.3	-22.2	-18.7
Machine shops and threaded products	3327	323	1.8	1.8	0.0	-11.6	-25.7	-15.9
Coating, engraving, and heat treating metals	3328	123	2.5	1.7	-0.8	-6.2	-26.5	-21.6
Other fabricated metal products	3329	255	1.3	-0.2	-1.5	-7.3	-21.4	-15.2
Machinery	333	1 037	2.1	0.6	-1.5	-6.1	-22.3	-17.3
Agriculture, construction, and mining machinery	3331	215	2.3	2.2	-0.1	-11.2	-23.5	-13.8
Industrial machinery	3332	103	1.8	-0.1	-1.9	-8.5	-27.5	-20.8
Commercial and service industry machinery	3333	97	1.3	-0.9	-2.1	-3.1	-13.3	-10.6
HVAC and commercial refrigeration equipment	3334	129	2.1	0.7	-1.3	0.9	-17.5	-18.3
Metalworking machinery	3335	160	1.6	-1.1	-2.6	-8.6	-29.9	-23.4
Turbine and power transmission equipment	3336	95	1.2	0.4	-0.9	-13.0	-24.5	-13.3
Other general purpose machinery	3339	238	2.4	0.8	-1.6	-3.3	-20.7	-18.0
Computer and electronic products	334	1 145	11.2	8.4	-2.5	-2.1	-12.0	-10.1
Computer and peripheral equipment	3341	168	23.3	18.3	-4.1	-0.3	-10.3	-10.0
Communications equipment	3342	122	5.4	2.5	-2.8	-15.4	-18.8	-4.0
Audio and video equipment	3343	24	1.8	-2.5	-4.2	-33.3	-45.6	-18.5
Semiconductors and electronic components	3344	381	15.9	13.6	-2.0	-3.9	-17.2	-13.8
Electronic instruments	3345	422	3.9	1.7	-2.1	1.0	-6.1	-7.1
Magnetic media manufacturing and reproduction	3346	29	2.4	1.0	-1.4	10.7	-12.5	-21.0
Electrical equipment and appliances	335	376	2.3	-0.6	-2.8	-4.6	-19.8	-15.9
Electric lighting equipment	3351	49	2.0	-0.7	-2.6	-0.9	-19.8	-19.1
Household appliances	3352	60	3.7	-0.1	-3.7	1.3	-17.2	-18.2
Electrical equipment	3353	146	2.3	-0.4	-2.7	-6.3	-19.9	-14.4
Other electrical equipment and components	3359	122	1.6	-0.9	-2.4	-7.0	-21.1	-15.1
Transportation equipment	336	1 362	2.7	0.5	-2.1	-2.6	-19.0	-16.8
Motor vehicles	3361	147	3.0	-0.6	-3.5	-4.3	-30.2	-27.1
Motor vehicle bodies and trailers	3362	106	0.8	-0.6	-1.4	-7.1	-30.9	-25.6
Motor vehicle parts	3363	420	2.7	0.6	-2.1	-0.5	-25.6	-25.2
Aerospace products and parts	3364	496	2.0	-0.2	-2.1	3.0	0.8	-2.1
Railroad rolling stock	3365	23	5.0	4.2	-0.8	2.1	-25.9	-27.4
Ship and boat building	3366	132	2.3	0.6	-1.7	5.0	-14.3	-18.4
Other transportation equipment	3369	40	6.2	6.4	0.2	-15.3	-18.6	-3.8
Furniture and related products	337	420	1.3	-0.8	-2.1	-9.6	-26.5	-18.7
Household and institutional furniture	3371	273	1.2	-1.2	-2.4	-10.2	-28.3	-20.1
Office furniture and fixtures	3372	108	1.1	-0.7	-1.8	-13.0	-29.2	-18.6
Other furniture-related products	3379	39	2.0	1.1	-0.9	-2.8	-10.5	-7.9
Miscellaneous manufacturing	339	649	2.9	2.4	-0.4	0.3	-8.6	-8.9
Medical equipment and supplies	3391	321	3.4	4.6	1.2	-0.7	-2.1	-1.4
Other miscellaneous manufacturing	3399	328	2.1	0.4	-1.7	-0.7	-16.4	-15.8

Table 5-3. Average Annual Percent Change in Output Per Hour and Related Series, Wholesale Trade, Retail Trade, Food Service, and Drinking Places, 1987–2010 and 2009–2010

(Number, percent.)

Industry	NAICS code	2010 employment (thousands)	Average annual percent change, 1987–2010			Annual percent change, 2009–2010		
			Output per hour	Output	Hours	Output per hour	Output	Hours
Wholesale Trade								
Wholesale trade	42	5 628	3.2	3.4	0.2	9.0	7.2	-1.7
Durable goods	423	2 807	4.9	4.8	-0.1	14.4	11.5	-2.5
Motor vehicles and parts	4231	318	3.3	2.7	-0.6	21.7	19.0	-2.2
Furniture and furnishings	4232	98	1.9	1.2	-0.7	10.1	6.0	-3.7
Lumber and construction supplies	4233	192	1.5	1.4	0.0	11.1	3.1	-7.2
Commercial equipment	4234	615	14.7	14.9	0.1	15.4	11.4	-3.4
Metals and minerals	4235	111	-0.9	-1.3	-0.4	8.3	4.9	-3.1
Electric goods	4236	320	8.5	7.8	-0.7	20.4	16.9	-2.9
Hardware and plumbing	4237	222	1.6	1.9	0.3	11.6	6.3	-4.7
Machinery and supplies	4238	621	1.9	1.6	-0.3	11.1	8.7	-2.2
Miscellaneous durable goods	4239	308	0.8	1.6	0.8	0.0	4.3	4.3
Nondurable goods	424	2 011	1.5	1.6	0.0	3.7	2.8	-0.8
Paper and paper products	4241	128	1.3	0.3	-1.0	-2.6	-2.6	0.0
Druggists' goods	4242	193	3.9	5.3	1.3	1.8	-2.3	-4.1
Apparel and piece goods	4243	149	2.5	2.1	-0.4	1.0	3.3	2.2
Grocery and related products	4244	735	1.4	2.0	0.6	8.2	6.4	-1.7
Farm product raw materials	4245	81	2.1	-0.1	-2.1	9.5	12.4	2.6
Chemicals	4246	122	0.6	0.8	0.2	13.8	7.6	-5.5
Petroleum	4247	97	2.5	0.3	-2.2	-0.8	1.3	2.1
Alcoholic beverages	4248	162	0.0	1.8	1.8	-6.8	-0.3	7.0
Miscellaneous nondurable goods	4249	344	0.1	-0.3	-0.3	2.3	0.3	-2.0
Electronic markets and agents and brokers	425	810	1.8	4.0	2.2	9.2	8.5	-0.6
Retail Trade								
Retail trade	44	15 300	2.9	3.3	0.3	3.9	4.5	0.5
Motor vehicle and parts dealers	441	1 685	1.9	2.1	0.2	4.4	4.6	0.2
Automobile dealers	4411	1 040	2.0	2.0	0.1	6.6	5.5	-1.0
Other motor vehicle dealers	4412	133	2.5	2.9	0.4	7.1	-1.5	-8.1
Auto parts, accessories, and tire stores	4413	512	1.4	2.0	0.5	-3.1	1.5	4.8
Furniture and home furnishings stores	442	481	3.8	3.3	-0.4	5.2	6.0	0.7
Furniture stores	4421	233	3.1	2.8	-0.3	3.9	6.8	2.8
Home furnishings stores	4422	248	4.6	3.9	-0.6	6.8	5.1	-1.6
Electronics and appliance stores	443	520	13.1	14.0	0.9	5.7	11.6	5.6
Building material and garden supply stores	444	1 168	2.8	3.5	0.7	10.6	6.9	-3.4
Building material and supplies dealers	4441	1 024	2.5	3.5	0.9	9.9	6.8	-2.9
Lawn and garden equipment and supplies stores	4442	144	4.4	3.4	-1.0	16.0	7.7	-7.2
Food and beverage stores	445	2 912	0.4	0.2	-0.2	1.6	1.3	-0.3
Grocery stores	4451	2 522	0.2	0.1	-0.1	1.2	1.2	0.0
Specialty food stores	4452	239	0.0	-0.6	-0.5	-0.5	0.4	0.9
Beer, wine and liquor stores	4453	151	2.4	0.8	-1.5	11.7	2.9	-7.9
Health and personal care stores	446	1 009	2.4	3.5	1.1	1.3	1.3	0.0
Gasoline stations	447	828	2.1	1.2	-0.8	1.5	1.0	-0.5
Clothing and clothing accessories stores	448	1 480	4.6	4.1	-0.5	4.9	4.8	-0.1
Clothing stores	4481	1 114	4.9	4.7	-0.2	3.2	5.1	1.8
Shoe stores	4482	189	3.3	2.2	-1.1	5.8	5.0	-0.8
Jewelry, luggage, and leather goods stores	4483	176	3.9	2.8	-1.0	11.2	2.9	-7.5
Sporting goods, hobby, book, and music stores	451	669	4.2	4.1	-0.1	9.3	5.6	-3.4
Sporting goods and musical instrument store	4511	515	4.9	5.1	0.3	8.6	8.1	-0.4
Book, periodical, and music stores	4512	155	2.6	1.6	-1.0	11.7	-1.9	-12.2
General merchandise stores	452	2 983	3.3	5.0	1.7	0.3	4.2	3.9
Department stores	4521	1 488	0.6	1.7	1.1	-2.8	1.2	4.2
Other general merchandise stores	4529	1 495	6.3	8.8	2.3	1.9	5.6	3.6
Miscellaneous store retailers	453	934	3.8	3.5	-0.2	6.9	5.6	-1.2
Florists	4531	93	3.5	0.1	-3.4	17.9	10.8	-6.1
Office supplies, stationery and gift stores	4532	335	5.9	5.0	-0.9	4.0	0.2	-3.6
Used merchandise stores	4533	174	5.0	6.2	1.1	16.5	19.3	2.4
Other miscellaneous store retailers	4539	332	1.4	2.5	1.1	5.4	5.8	0.4
Nonstore retailers	454	633	8.7	8.9	0.2	8.3	12.2	3.5
Electronic shopping and mail-order houses	4541	304	11.3	15.2	3.5	10.9	16.2	4.8
Vending machine operators	4542	52	0.8	-2.0	-2.8	11.5	5.8	-5.1
Direct selling establishments	4543	277	2.9	1.3	-1.5	-4.0	-0.1	4.0
Food Services and Drinking Places								
Food services and drinking places	722	9 566	0.7	1.9	1.3	1.9	1.3	-0.6
Full-service restaurants	7221	4 500	0.7	2.0	1.3	2.8	1.9	-0.8
Limited-service eating places	7222	4 041	0.7	2.2	1.5	2.7	1.7	-0.9
Special food services	7223	661	1.1	2.1	1.0	-4.9	-3.5	1.6
Drinking places, alcoholic beverages	7224	364	-0.4	-0.7	-0.3	-1.0	1.1	2.1

Table 5-4. Indexes of Multifactor Productivity and Related Measures, 1990–2010

(2005 = 100.)

Sector	1990	1991	1992	1993	1994	1995	1996	1997	1998	1999
PRIVATE BUSINESS										
Productivity										
Output per hour of all persons	68.6	69.7	72.6	73.0	73.7	73.8	75.9	77.3	79.6	82.4
Output per unit of capital services	107.9	104.2	106.1	106.3	107.8	106.4	106.5	106.4	105.2	104.2
Multifactor productivity	82.7	81.9	84.0	84.1	84.8	84.5	86.0	86.7	88.0	89.6
Real value-added output	59.5	59.0	61.4	63.4	66.6	68.5	71.6	75.3	79.2	83.6
Inputs										
Labor input	81.4	80.6	81.4	83.9	87.7	90.0	91.8	95.4	97.6	99.9
Capital services	55.2	56.7	57.9	59.7	61.8	64.3	67.3	70.8	75.2	80.2
Combined input quantity	72.0	72.1	73.1	75.4	78.5	81.0	83.3	86.9	90.0	93.3
Capital hours ratio	63.6	66.9	68.4	68.7	68.4	69.3	71.3	72.6	75.6	79.0
PRIVATE NONFARM BUSINESS										
Productivity										
Output per hour of all persons	68.6	69.7	72.6	73.0	73.7	73.8	75.9	77.3	79.6	82.4
Output per unit of capital services	107.9	104.2	106.1	106.3	107.8	106.4	106.5	106.4	105.2	104.2
Multifactor productivity	82.7	81.9	84.0	84.1	84.8	84.5	86.0	86.7	88.0	89.6
Real value-added output	59.5	59.0	61.4	63.4	66.6	68.5	71.6	75.3	79.2	83.6
Inputs										
Labor input	81.4	80.6	81.4	83.9	87.7	90.0	91.8	95.4	97.6	99.9
Capital services	55.2	56.7	57.9	59.7	61.8	64.3	67.3	70.8	75.2	80.2
Combined input quantity	72.0	72.1	73.1	75.4	78.5	81.0	83.3	86.9	90.0	93.3
Capital hours ratio	63.6	66.9	68.4	68.7	68.4	69.3	71.3	72.6	75.6	79.0
MANUFACTURING										
Productivity										
Output per unit of labor	62.8	61.2	62.4	64.5	68.1	69.4	71.7	72.3	74.8	76.5
Output per unit of capital	168.2	153.8	151.9	157.6	164.0	164.4	156.7	149.7	137.7	122.4
Sector output	78.4	73.1	73.2	78.7	86.2	92.2	94.7	99.5	102.2	99.7
Inputs										
Labor hours	80.8	79.9	80.7	83.4	86.9	89.2	91.1	94.8	97.1	99.6
Combined input quantity	71.4	71.4	72.4	74.8	77.8	80.3	82.7	86.5	89.6	93.1
Energy	88.6	88.4	87.5	90.4	93.7	96.4	93.8	91.9	95.4	117.7
Materials	66.9	66.6	72.3	72.9	76.0	80.2	87.4	94.4	102.4	108.7
Capital services	70.2	71.8	73.4	75.1	77.0	79.7	83.0	86.7	90.7	94.1
Purchased services	82.9	82.3	88.4	89.1	92.6	97.1	96.8	100.8	104.2	105.2

Table 5-4. Indexes of Multifactor Productivity and Related Measures, 1990–2010—*Continued*

(2005 = 100.)

Sector	2000	2001	2002	2003	2004	2005	2006	2007	2008	2009	2010
PRIVATE BUSINESS											
Productivity											
Output per hour of all persons	85.3	88.0	92.1	95.6	98.4	100.0	101.0	102.6	103.8	107.6	111.4
Output per unit of capital services	102.5	98.8	97.5	98.0	99.6	100.0	100.2	99.4	95.8	91.5	94.2
Multifactor productivity	91.2	91.8	94.0	96.5	98.9	100.0	100.5	100.9	99.9	100.2	103.3
Real value-added output	87.4	88.2	90.0	92.8	96.7	100.0	103.1	105.3	104.3	100.6	104.3
Inputs											
Labor input	101.1	99.3	97.4	97.0	98.1	100.0	102.4	103.6	102.1	95.6	96.1
Capital services	85.3	89.3	92.2	94.7	97.1	100.0	102.9	106.0	108.8	109.9	110.6
Combined input quantity	95.9	96.1	95.7	96.2	97.7	100.0	102.6	104.4	104.4	100.4	101.0
Capital hours ratio	83.2	89.1	94.4	97.6	98.8	100.0	100.8	103.3	108.3	117.6	118.2
PRIVATE NONFARM BUSINESS											
Productivity											
Output per hour of all persons	85.3	88.0	92.1	95.6	98.4	100.0	101.0	102.6	103.8	107.6	111.4
Output per unit of capital services	102.5	98.8	97.5	98.0	99.6	100.0	100.2	99.4	95.8	91.5	94.2
Multifactor productivity	91.2	91.8	94.0	96.5	98.9	100.0	100.5	100.9	99.9	100.2	103.3
Real value-added output	87.4	88.2	90.0	92.8	96.7	100.0	103.1	105.3	104.3	100.6	104.3
Inputs											
Labor input	101.1	99.3	97.4	97.0	98.1	100.0	102.4	103.6	102.1	95.6	96.1
Capital services	85.3	89.3	92.2	94.7	97.1	100.0	102.9	106.0	108.8	109.9	110.6
Combined input quantity	95.9	96.1	95.7	96.2	97.7	100.0	102.6	104.4	104.4	100.4	101.0
Capital hours ratio	83.2	89.1	94.4	97.6	98.8	100.0	100.8	103.3	108.3	117.6	118.2
MANUFACTURING											
Productivity											
Output per unit of labor	83.1	81.5	87.5	93.5	94.8	100.0	102.3	102.9	104.0	95.2	. . .
Output per unit of capital	118.7	98.6	90.4	90.2	94.5	100.0	102.8	102.7	96.6	72.4	. . .
Sector output	105.2	93.7	89.5	89.7	93.5	100.0	105.1	107.6	105.4	82.2	. . .
Inputs											
Labor hours	100.8	99.2	97.2	96.9	98.1	100.0	102.5	103.8	102.2	95.8	96.3
Combined input quantity	95.7	96.0	95.6	96.2	97.7	100.0	102.8	104.6	104.6	100.6	101.1
Energy	128.4	140.3	108.6	97.0	90.8	100.0	92.2	100.1	104.0	92.2	. . .
Materials	106.7	100.0	101.0	99.3	98.5	100.0	98.2	98.3	93.4	85.9	. . .
Capital services	96.8	98.4	99.3	99.7	99.4	100.0	100.8	102.2	105.1	106.4	. . .
Purchased services	103.8	102.0	98.7	98.1	91.8	100.0	98.4	105.6	93.0	88.1	. . .

. . . = Not available.

Chapter Six

COMPENSATION OF EMPLOYEES

COMPENSATION OF EMPLOYEES

HIGHLIGHTS

This chapter discusses the Employment Cost Index (ECI), which covers changes in wages and salaries and benefits; the Employer Costs for Employee Compensation (ECEC); employee participation in various benefit plans; and occupational and hourly wage percentiles wages from the National Compensation Survey.

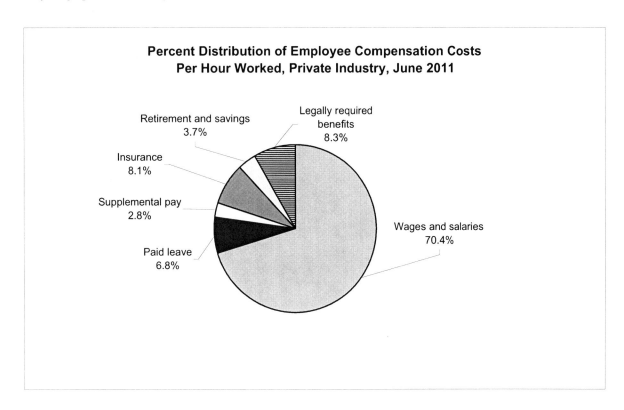

Percent Distribution of Employee Compensation Costs Per Hour Worked, Private Industry, June 2011

Wages and salaries made up 70.4 percent of employee compensation for private industry workers in June 2011, a slight decrease from 70.6 percent in June 2010. Legally required benefits, which include Social Security and Medicare, made up the second largest category at 8.3 percent followed by insurance at 8.1 percent. Supplemental pay including overtime and premium pay, shift differentials, and nonproduction bonuses comprised the smallest catgory at 2.8 percent. (See Table 6-6.)

OTHER HIGHLIGHTS

- Total employer compensation costs per hour varied among the different Census divisions, ranging from $33.27 in the New England states (Connecticut, Maine, Massachusetts, New Hampshire, Rhode Island and Vermont) to $22.70 in the East South Central states (Alabama, Kentucky, Mississippi, and Tennessee). (See Table 6-7.)

- In March 2011, 69 percent of all workers had access to medical care benefits in private industry compared to 87 percent in state and local government. In the private sector, 92 percent of union workers had access to medical benefits compared to only 67 percent of non-union workers. (See Table 6-12.)

- Among private industry workers, 29 percent of same-sex unmarried domestic partners had access to medical care benefits compared with 25 percent of opposite-sex unmarried domestic partners in March 2011. (See Table 6-13.)

- Workers in state and local government also had greater access to retirement benefits than workers in private industry— 90 percent compared to 64 percent. (See Tables 6-11.)

NOTES AND DEFINITIONS

NATIONAL COMPENSATION SURVEY

The National Compensation Survey (NCS) is an establishment-based survey that provides data for the Employment Cost Index (ECI), the Employer Costs for Employee Compensation (ECEC), an experimental series, the occupational earnings series, and the employee benefits survey.

The NCS surveys workers in private industry establishments, and in state and local government, in each state and the District of Columbia. For the NCS, the term *civilian workers* denotes workers in private industry and workers in state and local government. Establishments with one or more workers are included in the survey. Major exclusions from the survey are workers in the federal government, military personnel, agricultural workers, workers in private households, the self-employed, volunteers, unpaid workers, individuals receiving long-term disability compensation, and U.S. citizens working overseas. Currently, the NCS also excludes individuals who set their own pay (for example, proprietors, owners, major stockholders, and partners in unincorporated firms) and family members being paid token wages; however, these exclusions are being reevaluated.

The NCS, which originally used the Standard Industrial Classification (SIC) system, began a transition from SIC to the 2002 version of North American Industry Classification System (NAICS) in 2004; the transition was completed in July 2007. NAICS revises its industry classifications every 5 years to stay current with industrial taxonomy in North America. In August 2007, the NCS began collecting and coding data under the 2007 NAICS. The 2007 NAICS includes revisions across several sectors. The most significant revisions are in the information sector, particularly within the telecommunications area; overall, the change from 2002 NAICS to 2007 NAICS had little effect on the resulting NCS estimates.

EMPLOYMENT COST INDEX

The Employment Cost Index (ECI) is a measure of the change in the cost of labor, free from the influence of employment shifts among occupations and industries. The compensation series includes changes in wages and salaries and employer costs for employee benefits. The wage and salary series and the benefit cost series are the two components of compensation.

The ECI provides data for the civilian economy, which includes the total private nonfarm economy excluding private households, and the public sector excluding the federal government. The private industry series and the state and local government series provide data for the two sectors separately.

To be included in the ECI, employees in occupations must receive cash payments from the establishment for services performed and the establishment must pay the employer's portion of Medicare taxes on that individual's wages. Major exclusions from the survey are the self-employed, individuals who set their own pay (for example, proprietors, owners, major stockholders, and partners in unincorporated firms), volunteers, unpaid workers, family members being paid token wages, individuals receiving long-term disability compensation, and U.S. citizens working overseas.

Data for the June 2011 reference period were collected from a probability sample of approximately 62,100 occupational observations selected from a sample of about 12,700 establishments in private industry and approximately 11,500 occupations from a sample of about 1,800 establishments in state and local governments. The state and local government sample, which is replaced less frequently than the private industry sample, was replaced in its entirety in September 2007. The private industry sample is rotated over approximately 5 years, which makes the sample more representative of the economy and reduces respondent burden. Data are collected for the pay period including the 12th day of the survey months of March, June, September, and December. The sample is replaced on a cross-area, cross-industry basis.

Beginning with the release of the March 2006 data, indexes were rebased to December 2005 = 100 from June 1989 = 100. The percentage changes shown in the current and constant-dollar historical tables were calculated from the rebased indexes. Thus, changes may differ from those published in the previous edition of the handbook because of rounding.

Concepts and Definitions

Wages and salaries are defined as the hourly straight-time wage rate or, for workers not paid on an hourly basis, straight-time earnings divided by the corresponding hours. Straight-time wage and salary rates are total earnings before payroll deductions, excluding premium pay for overtime and for work on weekends and holidays, shift differentials, and nonproduction bonuses such as lump-sum payments provided in lieu of wage increases. Production bonuses, incentive earnings, commission payments, and cost-of-living adjustments are included in straight-time wage and salary rates.

Benefits covered by the ECI are: paid leave—vacations, holidays, sick leave, and personal leave; supplemental pay—premium pay for work in addition to the regular work schedule (such as overtime, weekends, and holidays), shift differentials, and nonproduction bonuses (such as referral bonuses and attendance bonuses); insurance benefits—life, health, short-term disability, and long-term disability; retirement and savings benefits—defined benefit and defined contribution plans; and legally required benefits—Social Security, Medicare, federal and state unemployment insurance, and workers' compensation.

Sources of Additional Information

Additional information on ECI methodology and more tables are available in Chapter 8 of the *BLS Handbook of Methods* and BLS new releases. The BLS publication *Compensation and Working Conditions* contains articles on all aspects of the NCS. All of these resources are on the BLS Web site at <http://www.bls.gov/ncs/ect/>.

Table 6-1. Employment Cost Index, Private Industry Workers, Total Compensation[1] and Wages and Salaries, by Industry and Occupation, 2001–2011

(December 2005 = 100.)

Characteristic and year	Total compensation					Wages and salaries				
	Indexes				Percent change for 12 months (ended December)	Indexes				Percent change for 12 months (ended December)
	March	June	September	December		March	June	September	December	
WORKERS BY INDUSTRY										
Total Private										
2001	85.0	85.8	86.7	87.3	4.1	87.6	88.4	89.2	89.9	3.8
2002	88.2	89.2	89.7	90.0	3.1	90.7	91.6	92.0	92.2	2.6
2003	91.4	92.3	93.2	93.6	4.0	93.3	94.0	94.8	95.1	3.1
2004	94.9	95.9	96.7	97.2	3.8	95.7	96.5	97.3	97.6	2.6
2005	98.2	98.9	99.5	100.0	2.9	98.3	98.9	99.5	100.0	2.5
2006	100.8	101.7	102.5	103.2	3.2	100.7	101.7	102.5	103.2	3.2
2007	104.0	104.9	105.7	106.3	3.0	104.3	105.1	106.0	106.6	3.3
2008	107.3	108.0	108.7	108.9	2.4	107.6	108.4	109.1	109.4	2.6
2009	109.3	109.6	110.0	110.2	1.2	109.8	110.1	110.6	110.8	1.3
2010	111.1	111.7	112.2	112.5	2.1	111.4	111.9	112.4	112.8	1.8
2011	113.3	114.3	. . .	. . .	. . .	113.2	113.8	. . .	. . .	. . .
Goods-Producing[2]										
2001	83.9	84.7	85.3	86.0	3.6	87.9	88.8	89.3	90.0	3.6
2002	87.0	87.7	88.2	89.0	3.5	90.7	91.4	91.9	92.6	2.9
2003	90.5	91.5	92.1	92.6	4.0	93.3	94.1	94.6	94.9	2.5
2004	94.5	95.4	96.5	96.9	4.6	95.6	96.2	97.2	97.2	2.4
2005	98.0	99.0	99.8	100.0	3.2	97.9	98.7	99.5	100.0	2.9
2006	100.3	101.3	102.0	102.5	2.5	100.7	101.8	102.3	102.9	2.9
2007	102.9	103.9	104.4	105.0	2.4	103.9	104.7	105.4	106.0	3.0
2008	106.1	106.8	107.2	107.5	2.4	107.1	108.0	108.6	109.0	2.8
2009	107.9	108.2	108.4	108.6	1.0	109.2	109.5	109.8	110.0	0.9
2010	109.7	110.3	111.0	111.1	2.3	110.5	110.9	111.5	111.6	1.5
2011	112.0	113.2	. . .	. . .	. . .	112.2	112.7	. . .	. . .	. . .
Service-Providing[3]										
2001	85.4	86.2	87.1	87.8	4.4	87.4	88.3	89.2	89.8	3.8
2002	88.7	89.7	90.2	90.4	3.0	90.7	91.7	92.0	92.1	2.6
2003	91.7	92.5	93.6	94.0	4.0	93.3	93.9	94.9	95.2	3.4
2004	95.1	96.1	96.8	97.3	3.5	95.8	96.6	97.3	97.7	2.6
2005	98.3	98.9	99.5	100.0	2.8	98.4	99.0	99.5	100.0	2.4
2006	101.0	101.8	102.7	103.4	3.4	100.8	101.7	102.6	103.3	3.3
2007	104.3	105.2	106.1	106.7	3.2	104.4	105.3	106.1	106.8	3.4
2008	107.7	108.5	109.1	109.4	2.5	107.7	108.6	109.3	109.6	2.6
2009	109.8	110.1	110.5	110.8	1.3	110.0	110.3	110.8	111.1	1.4
2010	111.6	112.1	112.6	113.0	2.0	111.7	112.3	112.7	113.1	1.8
2011	113.8	114.6	. . .	. . .	. . .	113.5	114.1	. . .	. . .	. . .
WORKERS BY OCCUPATION										
Management, Professional, and Related[4]										
2001	85.0	86.0	86.8	87.4	4.5	87.0	88.0	88.9	89.5	4.1
2002	88.3	89.2	89.5	89.7	2.6	90.4	91.3	91.6	91.7	2.5
2003	91.6	92.3	93.3	93.8	4.6	93.3	94.0	94.8	95.3	3.9
2004	94.9	95.7	96.5	97.1	3.5	96.0	96.5	97.3	97.8	2.6
2005	98.5	99.1	99.6	100.0	3.0	98.6	99.2	99.6	100.0	2.2
2006	101.1	101.9	102.9	103.5	3.5	101.1	102.0	103.0	103.6	3.6
2007	104.6	105.5	106.4	106.8	3.2	104.9	105.8	106.7	107.2	3.5
2008	108.1	108.9	109.6	109.9	2.9	108.5	109.3	110.1	110.5	3.1
2009	110.4	110.5	110.6	110.7	0.7	111.1	111.1	111.3	111.5	0.9
2010	111.8	112.2	112.7	113.0	2.1	112.5	112.9	113.4	113.7	2.0
2011	114.1	114.8	. . .	. . .	. . .	114.4	114.9	. . .	. . .	. . .
Management, Business, and Financial										
2001	86.1	87.1	87.8	88.5	4.4	87.3	88.3	89.1	89.8	4.1
2002	89.5	90.7	90.7	90.6	2.4	90.8	92.2	92.4	92.1	2.6
2003	93.3	93.9	94.9	95.4	5.3	94.8	95.5	96.4	96.7	5.0
2004	95.9	96.8	97.3	97.9	2.6	96.8	97.5	98.1	98.5	1.9
2005	99.1	99.6	99.7	100.0	2.1	99.2	99.7	99.5	100.0	1.5
2006	101.3	102.0	102.7	103.1	3.1	101.3	102.2	102.8	103.1	3.1
2007	104.3	105.1	106.0	106.3	3.1	104.7	105.5	106.3	106.6	3.4
2008	108.0	108.7	109.3	109.5	3.0	108.2	109.0	109.7	110.0	3.2
2009	109.6	109.7	109.7	109.9	0.4	110.3	110.3	110.4	110.8	0.7
2010	111.3	111.7	112.0	112.3	2.2	112.0	112.6	112.8	113.2	2.2
2011	113.6	114.5	. . .	. . .	. . .	113.9	114.4	. . .	. . .	. . .

[1] Includes wages, salaries, and employer costs for employee benefits.
[2] Includes mining, construction, and manufacturing.
[3] Includes the following industries: wholesale trade; retail trade; transportation and warehousing; utilities; information; finance and insurance; real estate and rental and leasing; professional, scientific, and technical services; management of companies and enterprises; administrative and support and waste management and remediation services; education services; health care and social assistance; arts, entertainment, and recreation; accommodation and food services; and other services, except public administration.
[4] Includes the following occupational groups: management, business, and financial; professional and related; sales and related; and office and administrative support.
. . . = Not available.

Table 6-1. Employment Cost Index, Private Industry Workers, Total Compensation[1] and Wages and Salaries, by Industry and Occupation, 2001–2011—*Continued*

(December 2005 = 100.)

Characteristic and year	Total compensation					Wages and salaries				
	Indexes				Percent change for 12 months (ended December)	Indexes				Percent change for 12 months (ended December)
	March	June	September	December		March	June	September	December	
Professional and Related										
2001	84.1	85.0	86.0	86.5	4.7	86.9	87.8	88.7	89.3	4.1
2002	87.3	87.9	88.5	89.1	3.0	90.1	90.5	91.0	91.4	2.4
2003	90.3	91.0	92.0	92.6	3.9	92.1	92.7	93.6	94.2	3.1
2004	94.1	94.8	95.8	96.5	4.2	95.3	95.7	96.7	97.2	3.2
2005	98.0	98.8	99.5	100.0	3.6	98.2	98.8	99.6	100.0	2.9
2006	101.0	101.8	103.1	103.9	3.9	100.9	101.8	103.1	104.0	4.0
2007	104.9	105.9	106.7	107.3	3.3	105.1	106.0	107.0	107.6	3.5
2008	108.3	109.0	109.9	110.3	2.8	108.7	109.5	110.4	110.9	3.1
2009	111.0	111.1	111.4	111.4	1.0	111.6	111.8	112.1	112.1	1.1
2010	112.2	112.6	113.3	113.5	1.9	112.8	113.2	113.9	114.1	1.8
2011	114.6	115.1	. . .	. . .	. . .	114.8	115.2	. . .	. . .	. . .
Sales and Office										
2001	84.5	85.4	86.1	86.9	4.1	86.9	87.8	88.4	89.1	3.5
2002	87.8	89.0	89.5	89.8	3.3	90.0	91.2	91.5	91.7	2.9
2003	90.8	91.9	93.0	93.1	3.7	92.4	93.3	94.4	94.3	2.8
2004	94.4	95.7	96.6	96.8	4.0	95.1	96.1	97.2	97.2	3.1
2005	97.8	98.5	99.3	100.0	3.3	97.8	98.5	99.3	100.0	2.9
2006	100.5	101.6	102.3	102.9	2.9	100.4	101.6	102.4	103.0	3.0
2007	103.7	104.7	105.3	106.1	3.1	103.8	104.8	105.3	106.2	3.1
2008	106.6	107.5	107.9	107.9	1.7	106.7	107.7	108.0	108.0	1.7
2009	107.9	108.3	108.8	109.2	1.2	107.9	108.3	109.0	109.4	1.3
2010	109.8	110.8	111.1	111.6	2.2	109.6	110.7	110.9	111.5	1.9
2011	112.1	113.3	. . .	. . .	. . .	111.6	112.7	. . .	. . .	. . .
Sales and Related										
2001	84.9	86.0	86.3	87.2	3.3	86.8	88.0	87.9	88.6	2.4
2002	87.7	89.7	89.7	89.7	2.9	89.2	91.0	91.0	90.9	2.6
2003	90.6	91.7	93.2	92.9	3.6	91.5	92.5	94.3	93.8	3.2
2004	94.0	95.4	96.8	96.2	3.6	94.4	95.7	97.4	96.6	3.0
2005	97.2	97.9	99.2	100.0	4.0	97.3	97.8	99.2	100.0	3.5
2006	99.9	101.1	101.7	102.3	2.3	99.8	101.3	102.0	102.6	2.6
2007	102.4	103.6	104.2	105.2	2.8	102.8	104.0	104.4	105.5	2.8
2008	105.0	106.2	106.0	105.5	0.3	105.3	106.6	106.4	105.7	0.2
2009	104.3	104.5	105.3	105.8	0.3	104.3	104.7	105.7	106.2	0.5
2010	105.8	107.5	107.4	108.1	2.2	106.2	108.0	107.8	108.7	2.4
2011	107.8	109.8	. . .	. . .	. . .	107.8	109.8	. . .	. . .	. . .
Office and Administrative Support										
2001	84.2	84.9	85.9	86.6	4.6	87.0	87.7	88.8	89.4	4.2
2002	87.9	88.6	89.3	89.9	3.8	90.7	91.3	91.8	92.4	3.4
2003	91.0	92.0	92.8	93.3	3.8	93.1	93.9	94.4	94.7	2.5
2004	94.7	95.8	96.5	97.2	4.2	95.6	96.4	97.1	97.6	3.1
2005	98.1	98.9	99.5	100.0	2.9	98.2	99.0	99.4	100.0	2.5
2006	100.9	101.9	102.7	103.4	3.4	100.9	101.9	102.6	103.3	3.3
2007	104.5	105.4	106.0	106.7	3.2	104.5	105.4	106.0	106.7	3.3
2008	107.8	108.5	109.2	109.6	2.7	107.7	108.5	109.2	109.7	2.8
2009	110.5	110.9	111.3	111.6	1.8	110.6	111.1	111.4	111.8	1.9
2010	112.6	113.1	113.7	114.0	2.2	112.2	112.6	113.3	113.6	1.6
2011	115.1	115.8	. . .	. . .	. . .	114.4	114.8	. . .	. . .	. . .
Natural Resources, Construction, and Maintenance										
2001	84.3	85.0	86.4	86.6	4.0	87.6	88.4	89.9	90.0	3.8
2002	87.4	88.5	89.3	89.7	3.6	90.5	91.7	92.3	92.6	2.9
2003	90.8	92.0	92.8	93.3	4.0	93.2	94.1	94.8	95.2	2.8
2004	94.8	96.1	96.5	97.1	4.1	95.8	96.7	97.1	97.5	2.4
2005	97.9	98.9	99.5	100.0	3.0	97.8	98.7	99.4	100.0	2.6
2006	100.8	102.1	103.0	103.6	3.6	100.7	101.8	102.8	103.4	3.4
2007	104.0	105.0	105.9	106.7	3.0	104.2	105.1	106.2	107.1	3.6
2008	107.6	108.3	109.0	109.6	2.7	108.1	109.0	109.8	110.5	3.2
2009	109.9	110.3	110.8	111.2	1.5	110.6	111.0	111.6	112.0	1.4
2010	112.2	112.7	113.1	113.3	1.9	112.5	112.8	113.1	113.3	1.2
2011	113.8	114.9	. . .	. . .	. . .	113.7	114.4	. . .	. . .	. . .

[1]Includes wages, salaries, and employer costs for employee benefits.
. . . = Not available.

Table 6-1. Employment Cost Index, Private Industry Workers, Total Compensation[1] and Wages and Salaries, by Industry and Occupation, 2001–2011—*Continued*

(December 2005 = 100.)

Characteristic and year	Total compensation					Wages and salaries				
	Indexes				Percent change for 12 months (ended December)	Indexes				Percent change for 12 months (ended December)
	March	June	September	December		March	June	September	December	
Construction, Extraction, Farming, Fishing, and Forestry										
2001	84.2	85.1	86.2	86.4	3.8	87.8	88.9	89.8	90.0	3.6
2002	87.3	88.1	88.8	89.5	3.6	90.6	91.3	91.9	92.4	2.7
2003	90.3	91.6	92.5	93.1	4.0	92.7	93.7	94.6	94.9	2.7
2004	94.7	95.8	96.4	97.2	4.4	95.8	96.6	96.9	97.5	2.7
2005	97.7	98.7	99.5	100.0	2.9	97.8	98.5	99.3	100.0	2.6
2006	100.7	102.2	103.1	103.7	3.7	100.7	102.0	103.0	103.7	3.7
2007	104.4	105.7	106.5	107.4	3.6	104.7	105.8	106.7	107.8	4.0
2008	108.6	109.7	110.3	110.8	3.2	109.2	110.1	110.8	111.5	3.4
2009	110.9	111.5	112.0	112.4	1.4	111.4	111.7	112.3	112.7	1.1
2010	113.1	113.6	114.3	114.4	1.8	112.9	113.3	113.9	114.0	1.2
2011	114.8	115.5	...	...	...	114.5	114.9	...	...	...
Installation, Maintenance, and Repair										
2001	84.4	84.9	86.8	86.8	4.1	87.4	87.9	90.1	90.1	4.3
2002	87.4	89.1	90.0	90.1	3.8	90.4	92.2	92.9	92.9	3.1
2003	91.4	92.5	93.1	93.6	3.9	93.8	94.6	95.1	95.5	2.8
2004	95.0	96.3	96.7	97.0	3.6	95.9	96.8	97.3	97.4	2.0
2005	98.1	99.3	99.6	100.0	3.1	97.8	99.1	99.5	100.0	2.7
2006	100.9	102.1	103.0	103.4	3.4	100.7	101.6	102.6	103.0	3.0
2007	103.5	104.1	105.2	105.8	2.3	103.7	104.2	105.6	106.1	3.0
2008	106.3	106.6	107.4	108.1	2.2	106.8	107.6	108.5	109.3	3.0
2009	108.6	108.9	109.4	109.8	1.6	109.7	110.2	110.7	111.2	1.7
2010	111.1	111.5	111.6	111.9	1.9	112.1	112.1	112.1	112.5	1.2
2011	112.6	114.2	...	...	...	112.7	113.9	...	...	...
Production, Transportation, and Material Moving										
2001	85.3	85.8	86.7	87.4	3.6	88.7	89.4	90.2	91.0	3.9
2002	88.4	89.1	89.7	90.3	3.3	91.9	92.4	92.8	93.3	2.5
2003	91.5	92.4	93.2	93.6	3.7	94.0	94.6	95.1	95.4	2.3
2004	95.5	96.5	97.4	97.8	4.5	96.0	96.7	97.6	97.8	2.5
2005	98.5	99.0	99.7	100.0	2.2	98.3	98.9	99.6	100.0	2.2
2006	100.4	101.1	101.7	102.3	2.3	100.6	101.2	101.8	102.4	2.4
2007	102.5	103.3	103.9	104.5	2.2	103.1	103.8	104.5	105.0	2.5
2008	105.5	106.0	106.6	106.9	2.3	106.0	106.8	107.5	107.8	2.7
2009	107.7	108.1	108.6	108.9	1.9	108.3	108.8	109.4	109.6	1.7
2010	109.9	110.5	111.3	111.5	2.4	109.8	110.3	111.1	111.3	1.6
2011	112.2	113.5	...	...	...	111.6	112.0	...	...	...
Production										
2001	84.9	85.2	86.0	86.7	3.2	88.4	89.1	89.7	90.5	3.7
2002	87.7	88.3	88.8	89.4	3.1	91.3	91.8	92.3	92.8	2.5
2003	91.0	91.7	92.5	93.0	4.0	93.6	94.1	94.8	95.1	2.5
2004	95.3	96.4	97.4	97.7	5.1	95.6	96.5	97.4	97.5	2.5
2005	98.6	99.1	99.6	100.0	2.4	98.3	98.9	99.5	100.0	2.6
2006	100.4	101.0	101.6	102.0	2.0	100.7	101.2	101.7	102.2	2.2
2007	102.1	102.8	103.2	104.0	2.0	103.1	103.6	104.2	104.6	2.3
2008	104.8	105.2	105.8	106.1	2.0	105.6	106.4	107.2	107.4	2.7
2009	107.1	107.6	108.0	108.2	2.0	108.1	108.5	109.0	109.3	1.8
2010	109.5	110.0	110.7	110.8	2.4	109.6	110.0	110.5	110.5	1.1
2011	111.7	113.2	...	...	...	111.1	111.5	...	...	...
Transportation and Material Moving										
2001	85.8	86.7	87.7	88.5	4.2	89.0	89.9	90.8	91.6	4.1
2002	89.5	90.2	90.9	91.4	3.3	92.6	93.1	93.6	94.0	2.6
2003	92.4	93.4	94.0	94.4	3.3	94.7	95.3	95.6	95.8	1.9
2004	95.7	96.7	97.5	97.9	3.7	96.4	97.1	97.9	98.2	2.5
2005	98.3	99.0	99.8	100.0	2.1	98.5	98.9	99.7	100.0	1.8
2006	100.4	101.2	102.0	102.6	2.6	100.4	101.2	102.0	102.6	2.6
2007	103.1	104.1	104.9	105.3	2.6	103.2	104.1	105.0	105.4	2.7
2008	106.4	107.2	107.7	107.9	2.5	106.5	107.4	108.0	108.3	2.8
2009	108.4	108.9	109.6	109.7	1.7	108.5	109.2	109.9	110.1	1.7
2010	110.4	111.2	112.2	112.5	2.6	110.2	110.8	111.8	112.2	1.9
2011	113.0	114.0	...	...	...	112.2	112.8	...	...	...
Service										
2001	87.1	87.7	88.2	89.4	3.8	89.7	90.2	90.6	91.7	3.4
2002	90.2	90.6	91.5	92.0	2.9	92.5	92.8	93.4	93.9	2.4
2003	93.0	93.4	94.4	95.0	3.3	94.5	94.8	95.6	96.1	2.3
2004	95.9	96.7	97.2	97.7	2.8	96.4	96.9	97.4	97.9	1.9
2005	98.5	99.0	99.5	100.0	2.4	98.6	99.0	99.6	100.0	2.1
2006	100.8	101.5	102.3	103.1	3.1	100.6	101.3	102.0	102.9	2.9
2007	104.5	105.2	106.4	107.0	3.8	104.6	105.3	106.5	107.1	4.1
2008	107.8	108.7	109.4	109.8	2.6	107.9	108.8	109.7	110.1	2.8
2009	110.7	110.9	111.7	111.8	1.8	111.0	111.2	112.1	112.3	2.0
2010	112.4	112.7	113.3	113.5	1.5	112.6	112.7	113.3	113.5	1.1
2011	114.5	114.7	...	...	...	114.2	114.2	...	...	...

[1]Includes wages, salaries, and employer costs for employee benefits.
. . . = Not available.

Table 6-2. Employment Cost Index, Private Industry Workers, Total Compensation[1] and Wages and Salaries, by Bargaining Status and Industry, 2001–2011

(December 2005 = 100.)

Characteristic and year	Total compensation					Wages and salaries				
	Indexes				Percent change for 12 months (ended December)	Indexes				Percent change for 12 months (ended December)
	March	June	September	December		March	June	September	December	
WORKERS BY BARGAINING STATUS AND INDUSTRY										
Union Workers										
2001	82.0	82.9	83.7	84.8	4.2	86.5	87.4	88.3	89.6	4.3
2002	85.7	86.5	87.5	88.2	4.0	90.2	91.1	91.9	92.6	3.3
2003	89.5	90.7	91.6	92.3	4.6	93.0	93.8	94.4	94.9	2.5
2004	94.5	95.9	96.7	97.3	5.4	95.6	96.4	97.1	97.6	2.8
2005	97.9	98.8	99.6	100.0	2.8	97.9	98.7	99.5	100.0	2.5
2006	100.5	101.8	102.4	103.0	3.0	100.3	101.2	101.7	102.3	2.3
2007	102.7	103.9	104.4	105.1	2.0	102.8	103.7	104.4	104.7	2.3
2008	105.9	106.7	107.4	108.0	2.8	105.5	106.7	107.4	108.1	3.2
2009	109.1	109.8	110.5	111.1	2.9	108.8	109.6	110.2	110.9	2.6
2010	112.8	113.7	114.6	114.8	3.3	111.5	112.1	112.7	112.9	1.8
2011	115.6	117.1	...	...	...	113.6	114.0	...	...	...
Union Workers, Goods-Producing[2]										
2001	81.9	82.7	83.4	84.0	2.9	87.2	88.2	88.9	89.5	3.5
2002	84.8	85.5	86.4	87.1	3.7	90.0	90.9	91.7	92.4	3.2
2003	88.9	90.2	90.9	91.7	5.3	92.9	94.0	94.5	95.0	2.8
2004	94.6	95.9	96.7	97.2	6.0	95.4	96.3	96.9	97.1	2.2
2005	97.7	98.8	99.6	100.0	2.9	97.5	98.5	99.2	100.0	3.0
2006	99.9	101.2	101.8	102.2	2.2	100.5	101.6	101.9	102.3	2.3
2007	101.5	102.8	103.1	104.0	1.8	102.7	103.6	104.3	104.3	2.0
2008	104.6	105.6	106.2	106.9	2.8	105.2	106.4	107.1	107.7	3.3
2009	108.0	108.9	109.5	110.0	2.9	108.2	108.8	109.5	109.8	1.9
2010	111.9	112.6	113.8	113.9	3.5	110.2	110.7	111.1	111.2	1.3
2011	114.3	116.4	...	...	...	111.7	112.1	...	...	...
Union Workers, Manufacturing										
2001	81.1	81.4	82.0	83.0	2.7	87.3	88.1	88.8	89.7	3.7
2002	84.1	84.7	85.4	86.5	4.2	90.3	90.8	91.6	92.5	3.1
2003	88.6	89.5	90.1	91.0	5.2	93.3	94.2	94.5	95.0	2.7
2004	95.6	96.7	97.5	97.8	7.5	95.5	96.2	97.0	97.1	2.2
2005	98.3	99.1	99.7	100.0	2.2	97.6	98.3	99.0	100.0	3.0
2006	99.3	100.1	100.5	100.8	0.8	100.6	101.2	101.4	101.7	1.7
2007	99.2	100.0	100.0	101.0	0.2	102.0	102.5	102.9	102.6	0.9
2008	101.4	101.7	102.1	102.8	1.8	103.4	104.4	104.9	105.5	2.8
2009	104.4	104.8	105.3	105.8	2.9	106.0	106.4	107.0	107.3	1.7
2010	108.6	109.1	110.5	110.5	4.4	107.8	108.2	108.6	108.7	1.3
2011	110.9	113.8	...	...	...	109.4	109.8	...	...	...
Union Workers, Service-Providing[3]										
2001	82.0	83.0	84.0	85.5	5.2	85.9	86.8	87.8	89.6	4.9
2002	86.4	87.3	88.4	89.1	4.2	90.3	91.2	92.0	92.7	3.5
2003	90.1	91.1	92.3	92.8	4.2	93.1	93.6	94.4	94.8	2.3
2004	94.4	95.8	96.6	97.3	4.8	95.7	96.5	97.3	98.0	3.4
2005	98.1	98.8	99.6	100.0	2.8	98.2	99.0	99.7	100.0	2.0
2006	101.0	102.2	102.9	103.6	3.6	100.1	100.9	101.6	102.2	2.2
2007	103.7	104.7	105.4	106.0	2.3	102.9	103.8	104.6	104.9	2.6
2008	107.0	107.5	108.3	108.8	2.6	105.8	106.9	107.7	108.3	3.2
2009	109.9	110.6	111.3	111.9	2.8	109.2	110.1	110.8	111.6	3.0
2010	113.4	114.5	115.2	115.5	3.2	112.4	113.1	113.8	114.2	2.3
2011	116.8	117.7	...	...	...	115.0	115.3	...	...	...
Nonunion Workers										
2001	85.5	86.3	87.2	87.8	4.2	87.7	88.6	89.3	89.9	3.7
2002	88.7	89.6	90.0	90.3	2.8	90.8	91.7	92.0	92.2	2.6
2003	91.8	92.5	93.5	93.9	4.0	93.3	94.0	94.9	95.1	3.1
2004	95.0	95.9	96.7	97.2	3.5	95.8	96.5	97.3	97.6	2.6
2005	98.3	98.9	99.5	100.0	2.9	98.3	98.9	99.5	100.0	2.5
2006	100.9	101.7	102.6	103.2	3.2	100.8	101.8	102.7	103.3	3.3
2007	104.2	105.1	105.9	106.5	3.2	104.5	105.3	106.2	106.9	3.5
2008	107.5	108.3	108.9	109.1	2.4	107.9	108.7	109.4	109.6	2.5
2009	109.4	109.6	109.9	110.1	0.9	110.0	110.2	110.6	110.9	1.2
2010	110.9	111.4	111.8	112.1	1.8	111.4	111.9	112.4	112.7	1.6
2011	113.0	113.8	...	...	...	113.2	113.8	...	...	...

[1]Includes wages, salaries, and employer costs for employee benefits.
[2]Includes mining, construction, and manufacturing.
[3]Includes the following industries: wholesale trade; retail trade; transportation and warehousing; utilities; information; finance and insurance; real estate and rental and leasing; professional, scientific, and technical services; management of companies and enterprises; administrative and support and waste management and remediation services; education services; health care and social assistance; arts, entertainment, and recreation; accommodation and food services; and other services, except public administration.
. . . = Not available.

Table 6-2. Employment Cost Index, Private Industry Workers, Total Compensation[1] and Wages and Salaries, by Bargaining Status and Industry, 2001–2011—*Continued*

(December 2005 = 100.)

Characteristic and year	Total compensation					Wages and salaries				
	Indexes				Percent change for 12 months (ended December)	Indexes				Percent change for 12 months (ended December)
	March	June	September	December		March	June	September	December	
Nonunion, Goods-Producing[2]										
2001	84.7	85.5	86.0	86.7	3.8	88.1	89.0	89.5	90.1	3.6
2002	87.8	88.5	88.8	89.7	3.5	91.0	91.6	91.9	92.7	2.9
2003	91.1	91.9	92.6	92.9	3.6	93.4	94.1	94.6	94.9	2.4
2004	94.5	95.2	96.4	96.8	4.2	95.6	96.2	97.3	97.3	2.5
2005	98.1	99.0	99.9	100.0	3.3	98.0	98.7	99.6	100.0	2.8
2006	100.5	101.4	102.0	102.5	2.5	100.7	101.9	102.4	103.0	3.0
2007	103.3	104.2	104.8	105.4	2.8	104.2	105.0	105.8	106.4	3.3
2008	106.5	107.1	107.6	107.7	2.2	107.7	108.4	109.0	109.3	2.7
2009	107.9	108.0	108.0	108.2	0.5	109.5	109.7	109.9	110.1	0.7
2010	109.1	109.5	110.1	110.2	1.8	110.6	111.0	111.6	111.7	1.5
2011	111.3	112.2	. . .	. . .	. . .	112.3	112.9	. . .	. . .	. . .
Nonunion Workers, Manufacturing										
2001	84.5	85.3	85.8	86.3	3.6	88.5	89.4	89.8	90.3	3.4
2002	87.6	88.4	88.7	89.4	3.6	91.4	92.0	92.4	92.9	2.9
2003	91.2	91.9	92.6	92.8	3.8	93.9	94.5	94.9	95.2	2.5
2004	94.4	95.3	96.4	96.6	4.1	95.8	96.5	97.5	97.5	2.4
2005	98.2	99.1	99.8	100.0	3.5	98.4	99.0	99.8	100.0	2.6
2006	100.3	101.3	101.7	102.1	2.1	100.7	101.8	102.0	102.5	2.5
2007	102.8	103.7	104.1	104.6	2.4	103.6	104.2	104.9	105.5	2.9
2008	105.6	106.2	106.6	106.8	2.1	106.6	107.3	108.0	108.2	2.6
2009	107.1	107.3	107.3	107.5	0.7	108.6	108.9	109.1	109.3	1.0
2010	108.5	109.2	109.9	110.0	2.3	109.8	110.5	111.1	111.2	1.7
2011	111.6	112.5	. . .	. . .	. . .	112.1	112.6	. . .	. . .	. . .
Nonunion, Service-Providing[3]										
2001	85.7	86.5	87.5	88.0	4.1	87.6	88.5	89.3	89.9	3.8
2002	88.9	89.9	90.4	90.5	2.8	90.8	91.7	92.0	92.1	2.4
2003	91.9	92.7	93.7	94.1	4.0	93.3	94.0	94.9	95.2	3.4
2004	95.2	96.1	96.9	97.3	3.4	95.8	96.6	97.3	97.7	2.6
2005	98.3	98.9	99.4	100.0	2.8	98.4	99.0	99.5	100.0	2.4
2006	101.0	101.8	102.7	103.4	3.4	100.8	101.7	102.7	103.4	3.4
2007	104.4	105.3	106.2	106.8	3.3	104.6	105.4	106.3	107.0	3.5
2008	107.7	108.6	109.2	109.4	2.4	107.9	108.8	109.4	109.7	2.5
2009	109.8	110.0	110.4	110.6	1.1	110.1	110.3	110.8	111.0	1.2
2010	111.3	111.9	112.3	112.7	1.9	111.6	112.2	112.6	113.0	1.8
2011	113.5	114.3	. . .	. . .	. . .	113.4	114.0	. . .	. . .	. . .

[1]Includes wages, salaries, and employer costs for employee benefits.
[2]Includes mining, construction, and manufacturing.
[3]Includes the following industries: wholesale trade; retail trade; transportation and warehousing; utilities; information; finance and insurance; real estate and rental and leasing; professional, scientific, and technical services; management of companies and enterprises; administrative and support and waste management and remediation services; education services; health care and social assistance; arts, entertainment, and recreation; accommodation and food services; and other services, except public administration.
. . . = Not available.

Table 6-3. Employment Cost Index, Private Industry Workers, Total Compensation[1] and Wages and Salaries, by Region, and Metropolitan Area Status, 2001–2011

(December 2005 = 100.)

Geography type and year	Total compensation					Wages and salaries				
	Indexes				Percent change for 12 months (ended December)	Indexes				Percent change for 12 months (ended December)
	March	June	September	December		March	June	September	December	
CENSUS REGIONS AND DIVISIONS[1]										
Northeast										
2001	84.3	85.3	86.2	86.7	3.8	86.8	87.8	88.6	89.2	3.8
2002	87.7	88.6	88.9	89.3	3.0	90.2	91.0	91.1	91.5	2.6
2003	90.6	91.4	92.4	92.9	4.0	92.4	93.2	94.1	94.5	3.3
2004	94.2	95.5	96.3	96.6	4.0	95.3	96.3	97.1	97.2	2.9
2005	97.6	98.5	99.2	100.0	3.5	97.8	98.6	99.2	100.0	2.9
2006	100.9	101.8	102.5	103.3	3.3	100.8	101.7	102.5	103.1	3.1
2007	104.0	105.1	106.2	106.8	3.4	104.0	105.0	106.1	106.6	3.4
2008	107.4	108.1	108.7	109.5	2.5	107.5	108.2	108.7	109.6	2.8
2009	109.8	110.2	110.7	111.0	1.4	109.9	110.3	110.8	111.1	1.4
2010	111.8	112.7	113.1	113.6	2.3	111.7	112.6	112.9	113.4	2.1
2011	114.4	115.3	. . .	. . .	. . .	113.7	114.6	. . .	. . .	. . .
New England										
2006	100.7	101.4	102.1	103.1	3.1	100.7	101.5	102.3	103.1	3.1
2007	103.6	104.8	105.4	106.1	2.9	103.6	104.8	105.7	106.3	3.1
2008	106.7	107.1	107.8	109.5	3.2	107.1	107.6	108.3	110.3	3.8
2009	109.9	110.2	111.2	111.5	1.8	110.5	110.6	111.7	112.1	1.6
2010	112.3	113.1	113.4	114.1	2.3	112.6	113.4	113.5	114.3	2.0
2011	114.8	116.0	. . .	. . .	. . .	114.5	115.9	. . .	. . .	. . .
Middle Atlantic										
2006	100.9	101.9	102.6	103.3	3.3	100.8	101.7	102.5	103.1	3.1
2007	104.2	105.3	106.5	107.1	3.7	104.2	105.1	106.4	106.7	3.5
2008	107.8	108.6	109.1	109.5	2.2	107.6	108.4	109.0	109.4	2.5
2009	109.8	110.2	110.6	110.8	1.2	109.7	110.1	110.4	110.7	1.2
2010	111.6	112.5	113.0	113.4	2.3	111.3	112.3	112.7	113.1	2.2
2011	114.3	115.1	. . .	. . .	. . .	113.4	114.0	. . .	. . .	. . .
South										
2001	86.4	87.2	88.1	88.7	4.2	88.9	89.7	90.5	91.0	3.6
2002	89.5	90.5	91.2	91.2	2.8	91.8	92.7	93.3	93.2	2.4
2003	92.0	92.7	93.6	93.9	3.0	93.5	94.1	94.9	95.0	1.9
2004	95.2	96.2	97.1	97.7	4.0	95.8	96.7	97.5	98.0	3.2
2005	98.9	99.3	99.7	100.0	2.4	98.9	99.3	99.7	100.0	2.0
2006	101.0	101.6	102.8	103.5	3.5	101.0	101.6	102.9	103.6	3.6
2007	104.3	105.3	106.1	106.7	3.1	104.6	105.6	106.5	107.0	3.3
2008	107.8	108.5	109.1	109.3	2.4	108.1	109.1	109.8	110.0	2.8
2009	109.8	110.1	110.6	110.7	1.3	110.4	110.7	111.3	111.5	1.4
2010	111.5	112.0	112.5	112.8	1.9	111.9	112.4	112.9	113.4	1.7
2011	113.4	114.3	. . .	. . .	. . .	113.7	114.4	. . .	. . .	. . .
South Atlantic										
2006	101.2	101.9	103.1	103.8	3.8	101.3	101.9	103.2	103.9	3.9
2007	104.9	106.0	106.8	107.3	3.4	105.0	106.1	106.9	107.5	3.5
2008	108.5	109.1	109.7	109.8	2.3	108.6	109.5	110.2	110.3	2.6
2009	110.3	110.7	111.3	111.5	1.5	110.8	111.3	111.9	112.2	1.7
2010	112.2	112.6	113.0	113.3	1.6	112.5	112.9	113.3	113.7	1.3
2011	113.8	114.6	. . .	. . .	. . .	114.0	114.6	. . .	. . .	. . .
East South Central										
2006	100.7	100.9	101.5	102.3	2.3	100.7	101.5	102.1	103.1	3.1
2007	103.3	103.8	104.8	105.4	3.0	104.2	104.5	105.6	106.3	3.1
2008	106.5	107.2	108.0	108.0	2.5	107.2	107.9	109.0	109.0	2.5
2009	108.5	108.7	109.2	109.3	1.2	109.2	109.5	110.1	110.2	1.1
2010	110.0	110.8	111.0	110.9	1.5	110.8	111.4	111.6	111.5	1.2
2011	112.1	112.7	. . .	. . .	. . .	112.6	112.9	. . .	. . .	. . .
West South Central										
2006	100.7	101.4	102.7	103.4	3.4	100.6	101.2	102.7	103.4	3.4
2007	103.7	104.8	105.6	106.1	2.6	104.1	105.3	106.1	106.6	3.1
2008	107.3	108.2	108.7	109.0	2.7	107.8	108.8	109.4	109.8	3.0
2009	109.4	109.5	109.9	109.9	0.8	110.1	110.2	110.8	110.9	1.0
2010	110.8	111.4	112.2	112.7	2.5	111.3	111.9	112.8	113.5	2.3
2011	113.2	114.4	. . .	. . .	. . .	113.7	114.5	. . .	. . .	. . .

[1]Includes wages, salaries, and employer costs for employee benefits.
. . . = Not available.

Table 6-3. Employment Cost Index, Private Industry Workers, Total Compensation[1] and Wages and Salaries, by Region, and Metropolitan Area Status, 2001–2011—Continued

(December 2005 = 100.)

Geography type and year	Total compensation					Wages and salaries				
	Indexes				Percent change for 12 months (ended December)	Indexes				Percent change for 12 months (ended December)
	March	June	September	December		March	June	September	December	
Midwest										
2001	84.8	85.4	86.1	86.7	3.5	86.8	87.6	88.3	88.9	3.3
2002	88.0	88.7	89.0	89.5	3.2	90.3	91.0	91.3	91.7	3.1
2003	92.1	92.8	93.6	94.0	5.0	94.2	94.7	95.2	95.5	4.1
2004	95.0	95.9	96.6	96.9	3.1	95.6	96.1	96.9	97.1	1.7
2005	97.8	98.4	99.5	100.0	3.2	97.8	98.2	99.4	100.0	3.0
2006	100.7	101.7	102.3	102.8	2.8	100.4	101.4	102.0	102.6	2.6
2007	103.3	104.2	104.6	105.3	2.4	103.6	104.4	105.0	105.6	2.9
2008	106.0	107.0	107.4	107.6	2.2	106.3	107.5	107.9	108.0	2.3
2009	107.9	108.1	108.4	108.6	0.9	108.4	108.6	108.9	109.2	1.1
2010	109.9	110.4	111.0	111.3	2.5	109.9	110.4	110.9	111.2	1.8
2011	112.2	113.3	. . .	. . .	. . .	111.8	112.2	. . .	. . .	. . .
East North Central										
2006	100.7	101.7	102.3	102.8	2.8	100.3	101.4	101.9	102.5	2.5
2007	103.2	104.1	104.4	105.0	2.1	103.6	104.4	104.7	105.3	2.7
2008	105.5	106.5	106.9	107.0	1.9	105.8	107.0	107.3	107.4	2.0
2009	107.0	107.3	107.5	107.8	0.7	107.5	107.7	108.0	108.3	0.8
2010	109.2	109.8	110.3	110.5	2.5	109.1	109.7	110.1	110.3	1.8
2011	111.6	112.7	. . .	. . .	. . .	110.9	111.3	. . .	. . .	. . .
West North Central										
2006	100.6	101.5	102.4	102.7	2.7	100.6	101.5	102.4	102.7	2.7
2007	103.5	104.3	105.3	105.9	3.1	103.8	104.5	105.6	106.3	3.5
2008	107.3	108.4	108.8	109.0	2.9	107.9	108.9	109.5	109.7	3.2
2009	109.9	110.2	110.6	110.7	1.6	110.7	110.8	111.2	111.4	1.5
2010	111.6	112.0	112.8	113.2	2.3	111.9	112.4	113.1	113.5	1.9
2011	113.9	114.8	. . .	. . .	. . .	114.0	114.5	. . .	. . .	. . .
West										
2001	84.1	85.0	85.9	86.9	5.2	87.4	88.3	89.2	90.2	4.8
2002	87.4	88.5	89.1	89.8	3.3	90.4	91.5	92.0	92.4	2.4
2003	90.9	92.0	93.2	93.8	4.5	93.0	93.9	95.1	95.5	3.4
2004	95.3	96.2	96.9	97.4	3.8	96.4	97.0	97.7	98.0	2.6
2005	98.4	99.3	99.7	100.0	2.7	98.4	99.3	99.6	100.0	2.0
2006	100.6	101.8	102.5	103.0	3.0	100.7	102.1	102.7	103.2	3.2
2007	104.2	104.9	105.7	106.5	3.4	104.8	105.4	106.2	107.0	3.7
2008	107.8	108.4	109.3	109.4	2.7	108.3	108.9	109.9	110.1	2.9
2009	109.9	110.0	110.3	110.6	1.1	110.5	110.8	111.2	111.6	1.4
2010	111.3	111.7	112.3	112.5	1.7	112.0	112.4	112.9	113.0	1.3
2011	113.5	114.3	. . .	. . .	. . .	113.6	114.1	. . .	. . .	. . .
Mountain										
2006	101.0	101.8	102.7	103.1	3.1	100.6	101.7	102.8	103.2	3.2
2007	105.2	105.2	106.6	107.5	4.3	105.3	105.5	106.7	107.8	4.5
2008	108.4	109.4	110.3	110.4	2.7	108.9	109.9	110.8	111.0	3.0
2009	110.5	110.6	110.9	111.0	0.5	111.1	111.4	111.9	111.9	0.8
2010	111.3	112.3	113.0	112.8	1.6	112.3	113.2	114.1	113.7	1.6
2011	113.4	113.9	. . .	. . .	. . .	113.7	114.1	. . .	. . .	. . .
Pacific										
2006	100.5	101.8	102.5	103.0	3.0	100.8	102.2	102.7	103.3	3.3
2007	103.9	104.8	105.4	106.1	3.0	104.6	105.3	106.0	106.8	3.4
2008	107.6	108.1	108.9	109.1	2.8	108.1	108.6	109.6	109.8	2.8
2009	109.7	109.9	110.1	110.5	1.3	110.3	110.6	110.9	111.5	1.5
2010	111.4	111.5	112.0	112.4	1.7	112.0	112.1	112.4	112.8	1.2
2011	113.6	114.5	. . .	. . .	. . .	113.6	114.1	. . .	. . .	. . .

[1]Includes wages, salaries, and employer costs for employee benefits.
. . . = Not available.

Table 6-4. Employment Cost Index, State and Local Government Workers, Total Compensation[1] and Wages and Salaries, by Industry and Occupation, 2001–2011

(December 2005 = 100.)

Characteristic and year	Total compensation					Wages and salaries				
	Indexes				Percent change for 12 months (ended December)	Indexes				Percent change for 12 months (ended December)
	March	June	September	December		March	June	September	December	
WORKERS BY INDUSTRY[1]										
Total State and Local Government										
2001	83.6	84.1	85.8	86.2	4.1	87.6	88.0	89.7	90.2	3.8
2002	86.7	87.0	89.0	89.7	4.1	90.5	90.8	92.4	93.0	3.1
2003	90.4	90.7	92.3	92.8	3.5	93.4	93.6	94.6	95.0	2.2
2004	93.5	93.9	95.4	96.1	3.6	95.4	95.6	96.6	97.0	2.1
2005	96.9	97.2	99.1	100.0	4.1	97.6	97.8	99.1	100.0	3.1
2006	100.5	100.9	103.2	104.1	4.1	100.3	100.8	102.8	103.5	3.5
2007	105.1	105.7	107.6	108.4	4.1	104.1	104.6	106.4	107.1	3.5
2008	108.9	109.4	111.3	111.6	3.0	107.7	108.2	110.1	110.4	3.1
2009	112.3	112.8	113.9	114.2	2.3	110.9	111.4	112.2	112.5	1.9
2010	114.5	114.7	115.9	116.2	1.8	112.7	112.9	113.6	113.8	1.2
2011	116.6	116.7	. . .	. . .	. . .	114.1	114.2	. . .	. . .	. . .
Education and Health Services										
2001	84.3	84.7	86.9	87.1	3.9	87.8	88.1	90.2	90.4	3.6
2002	87.4	87.6	89.7	90.4	3.8	90.6	90.8	92.8	93.3	3.2
2003	90.8	91.1	92.7	93.2	3.1	93.5	93.6	94.7	95.0	1.8
2004	93.7	93.8	95.5	96.1	3.1	95.3	95.4	96.6	97.0	2.1
2005	96.7	97.0	99.0	100.0	4.1	97.4	97.6	99.0	100.0	3.1
2006	100.3	100.8	103.7	104.3	4.3	100.2	100.7	103.1	103.6	3.6
2007	104.8	105.3	107.5	108.2	3.7	104.0	104.2	106.3	107.1	3.4
2008	108.6	109.1	111.2	111.5	3.0	107.5	108.1	110.2	110.5	3.2
2009	111.9	112.4	113.7	113.9	2.2	110.7	111.1	112.0	112.3	1.6
2010	114.0	114.2	115.4	115.6	1.5	112.5	112.6	113.4	113.6	1.2
2011	115.9	115.9	. . .	. . .	. . .	113.8	113.8	. . .	. . .	. . .
Education Services										
2001	84.4	84.7	86.9	87.2	3.9	87.9	88.2	90.3	90.5	3.4
2002	87.3	87.5	89.7	90.4	3.7	90.6	90.8	92.9	93.3	3.1
2003	90.8	91.1	92.7	93.1	3.0	93.4	93.6	94.7	95.0	1.8
2004	93.6	93.8	95.4	96.1	3.2	95.3	95.4	96.6	96.9	2.0
2005	96.6	96.9	98.9	100.0	4.1	97.3	97.5	98.9	100.0	3.2
2006	100.2	100.5	103.5	104.1	4.1	100.1	100.4	103.0	103.4	3.4
2007	104.6	105.0	107.4	108.0	3.7	103.7	103.9	106.1	106.8	3.3
2008	108.4	108.8	111.0	111.2	3.0	107.2	107.7	109.9	110.1	3.1
2009	111.8	112.1	113.5	113.7	2.2	110.4	110.7	111.7	111.9	1.6
2010	113.8	113.9	115.1	115.3	1.4	112.1	112.2	113.0	113.2	1.2
2011	115.5	115.5	. . .	. . .	. . .	113.4	113.4	. . .	. . .	. . .
Schools[2]										
2001	84.4	84.7	87.0	87.2	3.9	87.9	88.2	90.3	90.5	3.4
2002	87.3	87.5	89.7	90.4	3.7	90.6	90.8	92.9	93.3	3.1
2003	90.8	91.1	92.7	93.1	3.0	93.4	93.6	94.7	95.0	1.8
2004	93.6	93.8	95.5	96.1	3.2	95.3	95.4	96.6	96.9	2.0
2005	96.6	96.9	98.9	100.0	4.1	97.3	97.5	98.9	100.0	3.2
2006	100.2	100.5	103.5	104.1	4.1	100.1	100.4	103.0	103.4	3.4
2007	104.6	104.9	107.4	108.0	3.7	103.6	103.9	106.1	106.8	3.3
2008	108.4	108.8	111.0	111.2	3.0	107.2	107.7	109.9	110.1	3.1
2009	111.8	112.1	113.5	113.7	2.2	110.4	110.7	111.7	111.9	1.6
2010	113.8	113.9	115.1	115.3	1.4	112.1	112.2	113.0	113.2	1.2
2011	115.5	115.5	. . .	. . .	. . .	113.4	113.4	. . .	. . .	. . .
Elementary and Secondary Schools										
2001	84.1	84.3	86.5	86.7	3.5	87.8	88.2	90.0	90.3	3.1
2002	86.8	87.0	89.3	89.9	3.7	90.5	90.6	92.8	93.2	3.2
2003	90.3	90.6	92.4	92.7	3.1	93.2	93.4	94.6	94.8	1.7
2004	93.2	93.4	95.3	96.0	3.6	95.1	95.2	96.5	96.9	2.2
2005	96.4	96.6	98.8	100.0	4.2	97.1	97.2	98.9	100.0	3.2
2006	100.2	100.5	103.6	104.2	4.2	100.0	100.3	103.0	103.4	3.4
2007	104.7	105.0	107.4	108.0	3.6	103.6	103.8	106.0	106.6	3.1
2008	108.3	108.8	111.1	111.4	3.1	106.9	107.5	109.8	110.1	3.3
2009	112.0	112.2	114.0	114.1	2.4	110.3	110.5	112.0	112.1	1.8
2010	114.1	114.3	115.6	115.6	1.3	112.3	112.5	113.4	113.5	1.2
2011	115.8	115.8	. . .	. . .	. . .	113.6	113.6	. . .	. . .	. . .

[1]Includes wages, salaries, and employer costs for employee benefits.
[2]Includes elementary and secondary schools, junior colleges, colleges, universities, and professional schools.
. . . = Not available.

Table 6-4. Employment Cost Index, State and Local Government Workers, Total Compensation[1] and Wages and Salaries, by Industry and Occupation, 2001–2011—*Continued*

(December 2005 = 100.)

Characteristic and year	Total compensation					Wages and salaries				
	Indexes				Percent change for 12 months (ended December)	Indexes				Percent change for 12 months (ended December)
	March	June	September	December		March	June	September	December	
Health Care and Social Assistance[3]										
2001	83.4	84.5	86.0	86.8	5.0	86.1	87.1	88.6	89.5	4.8
2002	87.8	88.2	89.5	90.6	4.4	90.7	91.1	92.2	93.0	3.9
2003	91.2	91.4	92.9	93.5	3.2	93.5	93.9	94.7	95.3	2.5
2004	94.2	94.7	96.3	96.5	3.2	95.7	96.0	97.1	97.3	2.1
2005	97.6	98.0	99.5	100.0	3.6	98.1	98.5	99.4	100.0	2.8
2006	101.3	102.9	105.1	105.7	5.7	101.0	103.0	104.8	105.5	5.5
2007	107.1	107.6	108.6	109.3	3.4	106.6	107.2	108.2	109.2	3.5
2008	110.1	111.1	112.7	113.2	3.6	110.1	111.0	112.8	113.4	3.8
2009	113.3	114.6	115.1	115.4	1.9	113.1	114.6	115.0	115.2	1.6
2010	115.9	116.3	117.2	117.9	2.2	115.5	115.8	116.2	116.8	1.4
2011	119.0	119.2	. . .	. . .	. . .	117.3	117.4	. . .	. . .	. . .
Hospitals										
2001	83.0	84.4	85.9	86.6	4.5	85.3	86.6	88.0	88.8	4.3
2002	87.6	88.1	89.3	90.6	4.6	90.0	90.6	91.7	92.8	4.5
2003	91.0	91.1	92.8	93.4	3.1	93.1	93.5	94.5	95.2	2.6
2004	93.9	94.4	96.1	96.7	3.5	95.6	95.9	97.1	97.7	2.6
2005	97.6	98.0	99.5	100.0	3.4	98.3	98.6	99.4	100.0	2.4
2006	100.9	101.3	103.3	104.3	4.3	100.9	101.4	103.1	104.4	4.4
2007	105.6	106.3	107.5	108.2	3.7	105.7	106.5	107.6	108.6	4.0
2008	109.2	109.7	110.8	111.3	2.9	109.8	110.3	111.4	112.1	3.2
2009	112.4	113.4	113.9	114.3	2.7	112.8	113.9	114.2	114.7	2.3
2010	115.1	115.6	116.1	117.0	2.4	115.2	115.5	115.7	116.3	1.4
2011	118.2	118.3	. . .	. . .	. . .	117.0	116.9	. . .	. . .	. . .
WORKERS BY OCCUPATION										
Management, Professional, and Related[4]										
2001	84.1	84.6	86.5	86.8	4.1	87.5	88.0	89.8	90.2	3.8
2002	87.2	87.4	89.5	90.3	4.0	90.4	90.6	92.5	93.1	3.2
2003	90.8	91.1	92.6	93.1	3.1	93.4	93.6	94.6	95.0	2.0
2004	93.8	94.0	95.5	96.2	3.3	95.3	95.5	96.6	97.0	2.1
2005	97.0	97.3	99.0	100.0	4.0	97.5	97.8	99.0	100.0	3.1
2006	100.3	100.8	103.3	104.0	4.0	100.2	100.7	102.9	103.5	3.5
2007	104.9	105.4	107.5	108.3	4.1	104.0	104.3	106.3	107.0	3.4
2008	108.8	109.3	111.3	111.6	3.0	107.6	108.2	110.1	110.4	3.2
2009	112.0	112.5	113.6	113.8	2.0	110.7	111.1	112.0	112.2	1.6
2010	114.0	114.2	115.3	115.5	1.5	112.4	112.6	113.3	113.5	1.2
2011	115.9	116.0	. . .	. . .	. . .	113.8	113.8	. . .	. . .	. . .
Professional and Related										
2001	84.0	84.4	86.4	86.7	4.0	87.5	87.9	89.8	90.1	3.7
2002	87.0	87.2	89.4	90.2	4.0	90.2	90.5	92.4	93.0	3.2
2003	90.7	91.0	92.5	93.0	3.1	93.3	93.4	94.5	94.9	2.0
2004	93.6	93.9	95.5	96.1	3.3	95.3	95.4	96.6	96.9	2.1
2005	96.8	97.1	98.9	100.0	4.1	97.4	97.7	98.9	100.0	3.2
2006	100.2	100.8	103.4	104.0	4.0	100.2	100.7	103.0	103.6	3.6
2007	104.8	105.3	107.5	108.2	4.0	103.9	104.2	106.3	107.0	3.3
2008	108.6	109.1	111.1	111.4	3.0	107.5	108.1	110.1	110.3	3.1
2009	111.9	112.4	113.6	113.9	2.2	110.6	111.0	112.0	112.3	1.8
2010	114.0	114.2	115.3	115.5	1.4	112.4	112.6	113.3	113.6	1.2
2011	115.9	115.9	. . .	. . .	. . .	113.8	113.8	. . .	. . .	. . .
Sales and Office										
2001	82.8	83.1	84.5	85.2	3.9	87.4	87.8	89.1	89.6	3.1
2002	86.1	86.5	88.3	89.1	4.6	90.4	90.8	92.3	92.9	3.7
2003	89.8	90.3	92.4	92.8	4.2	93.5	93.8	95.1	95.4	2.7
2004	93.7	94.4	95.7	96.5	4.0	96.0	96.2	97.3	97.6	2.3
2005	97.5	97.6	99.3	100.0	3.6	98.1	98.0	99.4	100.0	2.5
2006	100.9	101.5	103.3	104.1	4.1	100.6	101.2	102.6	103.2	3.2
2007	105.6	106.2	107.9	108.6	4.3	104.5	104.8	106.3	107.0	3.7
2008	108.8	109.3	111.0	111.3	2.5	107.4	107.9	109.3	109.7	2.5
2009	112.4	112.8	114.1	114.4	2.8	110.5	111.0	111.9	112.1	2.2
2010	115.0	115.2	116.4	116.6	1.9	112.5	112.5	113.1	113.2	1.0
2011	117.1	117.3	. . .	. . .	. . .	113.5	113.7	. . .	. . .	. . .

[1]Includes wages, salaries, and employer costs for employee benefits.
[3]Includes ambulatory health care services and social assistance, not shown separately.
[4]Includes the following occupational groups: management, business, and financial; professional and related; sales and related; and office and administrative support.
. . . = Not available.

Table 6-4. Employment Cost Index, State and Local Government Workers, Total Compensation[1] and Wages and Salaries, by Industry and Occupation, 2001–2011—*Continued*

(December 2005 = 100.)

Characteristic and year	Total compensation				Percent change for 12 months (ended December)	Wages and salaries				Percent change for 12 months (ended December)
	March	June	September	December		March	June	September	December	
Office and Administration Support										
2001	82.6	82.9	84.4	85.1	3.9	87.4	87.8	89.1	89.7	3.1
2002	86.0	86.5	88.2	88.9	4.5	90.5	91.0	92.4	92.8	3.5
2003	89.6	90.0	92.1	92.6	4.2	93.4	93.7	95.0	95.3	2.7
2004	93.5	94.2	95.6	96.4	4.1	95.9	96.1	97.1	97.5	2.3
2005	97.4	97.5	99.2	100.0	3.7	98.0	97.9	99.3	100.0	2.6
2006	101.0	101.6	103.5	104.2	4.2	100.7	101.4	102.7	103.4	3.4
2007	105.7	106.4	108.2	108.9	4.5	104.7	105.0	106.5	107.3	3.8
2008	109.3	109.8	111.4	111.8	2.7	107.8	108.3	109.7	110.1	2.6
2009	112.0	113.1	114.4	114.7	2.6	111.0	111.4	112.3	112.5	2.2
2010	115.3	115.6	116.8	116.9	1.9	113.0	113.0	113.5	113.6	1.0
2011	117.5	117.7	. . .	. . .	. . .	113.9	114.1	. . .	. . .	. . .
Service										
2001	82.1	82.6	84.1	84.7	4.7	87.8	88.3	89.7	90.3	3.8
2002	85.2	85.8	87.4	88.0	3.9	90.8	91.2	92.1	92.4	2.3
2003	88.8	89.3	91.0	91.6	4.1	93.1	93.6	94.3	94.9	2.7
2004	92.3	92.7	94.9	95.5	4.3	95.3	95.4	96.4	96.8	2.0
2005	96.2	96.7	99.1	100.0	4.7	97.3	97.7	99.3	100.0	3.3
2006	100.6	101.2	103.1	104.5	4.5	100.3	100.8	102.4	103.9	3.9
2007	105.4	106.3	108.0	109.1	4.4	104.5	105.2	106.5	107.7	3.7
2008	109.7	110.0	111.9	112.4	3.0	108.3	108.6	110.4	110.9	3.0
2009	113.4	113.8	114.7	115.3	2.6	112.0	112.4	113.1	113.5	2.3
2010	115.8	116.2	117.6	118.0	2.3	114.0	114.2	114.9	115.1	1.4
2011	118.5	118.6	. . .	. . .	. . .	115.4	115.5	. . .	. . .	. . .

[1]Includes wages, salaries, and employer costs for employee benefits.
. . . = Not available.

Table 6-5. Employment Cost Index, Benefits, by Industry and Occupation, 2001–2011

(December 2005 = 100.)

Characteristic and year	Indexes				Percent change for 12 months (ended December)
	March	June	September	December	
Civilian Workers					
2001	78.0	78.8	79.9	80.8	1.1
2002	81.5	82.5	83.5	84.6	1.3
2003	86.3	87.5	88.9	90.0	1.2
2004	92.1	93.7	94.8	95.9	1.2
2005	97.5	98.4	99.4	100.2	0.8
2006	100.8	101.7	102.7	103.7	1.0
2007	103.9	105.2	106.0	106.9	0.8
2008	107.5	108.1	108.8	109.2	0.4
2009	109.6	110.0	110.4	110.9	0.5
2010	112.0	112.7	113.5	114.1	0.5
2011	115.4	116.9	...	...	...
Total Private					
2001	78.8	79.5	80.6	81.5	1.1
2002	82.3	83.3	84.1	85.0	1.1
2003	87.0	88.1	89.4	90.5	1.2
2004	92.9	94.4	95.4	96.5	1.2
2005	98.0	98.8	99.7	100.3	0.6
2006	100.8	101.6	102.5	103.4	0.9
2007	103.1	104.2	105.0	105.9	0.9
2008	106.4	106.9	107.5	107.9	0.4
2009	108.0	108.3	108.6	109.0	0.4
2010	110.3	110.9	111.6	112.2	0.5
2011	113.5	115.3	...	...	...
State and Local Government Workers					
2001	75.2	76.3	77.4	78.0	0.8
2002	78.8	79.9	81.4	82.9	1.8
2003	84.1	85.4	86.9	88.0	1.3
2004	89.5	91.1	92.5	93.9	1.5
2005	95.6	96.8	98.4	99.9	1.5
2006	100.8	102.0	103.5	105.1	1.5
2007	107.1	108.7	109.7	110.9	1.1
2008	111.5	112.4	113.3	114.0	0.6
2009	115.3	116.3	116.8	117.6	0.7
2010	118.2	119.2	120.2	121.0	0.7
2011	122.1	122.7	...	...	...
WORKERS BY OCCUPATION					
Management, Professional, and Related					
2002	82.7	83.7	84.2	85.2	1.2
2003	87.1	88.0	89.5	90.7	1.3
2004	91.9	93.4	94.5	95.9	1.5
2005	97.9	98.8	99.8	100.4	0.6
2006	101.0	101.7	102.8	103.8	1.0
2007	103.5	104.8	105.6	106.4	0.8
2008	107.0	107.8	108.5	108.9	0.4
2009	108.5	108.8	108.9	109.2	0.3
2010	109.9	110.4	110.9	111.6	0.6
2011	113.1	114.7	...	...	...
Sales and Office					
2002	81.8	83.2	84.2	85.1	1.1
2003	86.6	88.0	89.3	90.4	1.2
2004	92.5	94.2	95.2	96.1	0.9
2005	97.5	98.4	99.3	100.2	0.9
2006	100.7	101.5	102.1	103.0	0.9
2007	103.3	104.2	105.2	106.1	0.9
2008	106.4	107.0	107.6	108.0	0.4
2009	107.9	108.1	108.6	108.9	0.3
2010	110.1	111.0	111.7	112.0	0.3
2011	113.3	115.0	...	...	...
Natural Resources, Construction, and Maintenance					
2002	81.2	82.1	83.3	84.6	1.6
2003	86.0	87.6	88.7	90.3	1.8
2004	92.9	94.5	95.4	96.9	1.6
2005	98.0	98.9	99.7	100.4	0.7
2006	101.1	102.4	103.4	104.4	1.0
2007	103.5	104.4	105.2	106.3	1.0
2008	106.5	106.7	107.4	108.1	0.7
2009	108.2	108.5	109.2	109.9	0.6
2010	111.5	112.1	112.9	113.7	0.7
2011	114.0	115.6	...	...	...

. . . = Not available.

Table 6-5. Employment Cost Index, Benefits, by Industry and Occupation, 2001–2011—*Continued*

(December 2005 = 100.)

Characteristic and year	Indexes				Percent change for 12 months (ended December)
	March	June	September	December	
Production, Transportation, and Material Moving					
2002	81.8	82.7	83.7	84.8	1.3
2003	86.7	88.1	89.4	90.4	1.1
2004	94.4	96.0	97.1	98.0	0.9
2005	98.7	99.2	99.9	100.1	0.2
2006	100.0	100.8	101.6	102.3	0.7
2007	101.0	102.3	102.8	104.0	1.2
2008	104.2	104.4	104.8	105.5	0.7
2009	106.1	106.6	107.2	107.9	0.7
2010	109.5	110.6	111.8	112.7	0.8
2011	113.1	116.3	. . .	. . .	. . .
Service					
2002	83.5	84.4	86.0	86.8	0.9
2003	88.5	89.4	90.8	92.0	1.3
2004	94.3	95.9	96.7	97.3	0.6
2005	98.0	98.8	99.5	100.3	0.8
2006	101.3	102.1	103.0	103.9	0.9
2007	104.0	105.0	106.0	107.0	0.9
2008	107.4	108.4	108.7	109.1	0.4
2009	109.5	109.9	110.4	110.8	0.4
2010	111.5	112.4	113.2	113.8	0.5
2011	115.3	116.0	. . .	. . .	. . .
WORKERS BY INDUSTRY					
Goods-Producing					
2001	76.5	77.0	77.8	78.7	1.1
2002	79.9	80.6	81.2	82.5	1.6
2003	85.2	86.5	87.5	88.4	1.0
2004	92.4	93.8	95.0	96.5	1.6
2005	98.3	99.5	100.3	100.2	-0.1
2006	99.4	100.3	101.3	102.0	0.7
2007	100.8	102.1	102.4	103.5	1.1
2008	103.9	104.3	104.6	105.1	0.5
2009	105.2	105.5	105.6	106.3	0.7
2010	108.0	108.8	110.0	110.7	0.6
2011	111.4	114.0	. . .	. . .	. . .
Manufacturing					
2001	75.4	75.8	76.4	77.4	1.2
2002	78.8	79.7	80.3	81.5	1.5
2003	84.7	85.7	86.8	87.5	0.8
2004	92.7	94.1	95.4	96.1	0.7
2005	98.2	99.4	100.1	100.1	0.0
2006	98.6	99.6	100.7	101.1	0.4
2007	99.3	100.8	100.8	102.0	1.2
2008	102.0	102.1	102.4	102.9	0.5
2009	103.1	103.5	103.5	104.2	0.7
2010	106.1	107.3	108.7	109.6	0.8
2011	110.6	113.8	. . .	. . .	. . .
Service-Providing					
2001	79.7	80.5	81.7	82.6	1.1
2002	83.2	84.4	85.2	86.0	0.9
2003	87.7	88.8	90.2	91.4	1.3
2004	93.0	94.6	95.5	96.5	1.0
2005	97.9	98.6	99.4	100.3	0.9
2006	101.3	102.2	103.0	104.0	1.0
2007	104.0	105.1	106.0	106.8	0.8
2008	107.4	108.0	108.7	109.1	0.4
2009	109.2	109.4	109.9	110.1	0.2
2010	111.2	111.8	112.3	112.8	0.4
2011	114.4	115.8	. . .	. . .	. . .

. . . = Not available.

NOTES AND DEFINITIONS

EMPLOYER COSTS FOR EMPLOYEE COMPENSATION

The Employer Costs for Employee Compensation (ECEC) measures the average cost per employee hour worked that employers pay for wages and salaries and benefits.

Survey Scope

The ECEC consists of data for the civilian economy, obtained from both private industry and state and local government. Excluded from private industry are the self-employed and farm and private household workers. Federal government workers are excluded from the public sector. The private industry series and the state and local government series provide separate data for the two sectors.

The cost levels for June 2011 were collected from a probability sample of 62,100 occupations selected from a sample of about 12,700 establishments in private industry and approximately 11,500 occupations from a sample of about 1,800 establishments in state and local governments. The state and local government sample, which is replaced less frequently than the private industry sample, was replaced in its entirety in September 2007. The private industry sample is rotated over approximately 5 years, which makes the sample more representative of the economy and reduces respondent burden. Data are collected for the pay period including the 12th day of the survey months of March, June, September, and December. The sample is replaced on a cross-area, cross-industry basis.

To be included in the ECEC, employees in occupations must receive cash payments from the establishment for services performed and the establishment must pay the employer's portion of Medicare taxes on that individual's wages. Major exclusions from the survey are the self-employed, individuals who set their own pay (for example, proprietors, owners, major stockholders, and partners in unincorporated firms), volunteers, unpaid workers, family members being paid token wages, individuals receiving long-term disability compensation, and U.S. citizens working overseas.

Current employment weights are used to calculate cost levels. These weights are derived from two BLS programs: the Quarterly Census of Employment and Wages (QCEW) and the Current Employment Statistics (CES). Combined, these programs provide the appropriate industry coverage and currency of data needed to match the ECEC.

Sources of Additional Information

Additional information may be obtained from BLS news release 11-1305 "Employer Costs for Employee Compensation—June 2011," and in various articles in the BLS e-publication, *Compensation and Working Conditions*. These resources are available on the BLS Web site at <http://www.bls.gov/ncs/ect/>.

Table 6-6. Employer Compensation Costs Per Hour Worked for Employee Compensation and Costs as a Percent of Total Compensation: Private Industry Workers, by Major Industry Group, June 2011

(Dollars, percent of total cost.)

Compensation component	All workers Cost	All workers Percent	All goods-producing[1] Cost	Percent	Construction Cost	Percent	Manufacturing Cost	Percent	All service-providing[2] Cost	Percent	Trade, transportation, and utilities Cost	Percent
TOTAL COMPENSATION	28.13	100.0	33.26	100.0	31.77	100.0	33.04	100.0	27.05	100.0	23.84	100.0
Wages and Salaries	19.81	70.4	22.02	66.2	22.01	69.3	21.49	65.1	19.34	71.5	16.76	70.3
Total Benefits	8.32	29.6	11.24	33.8	9.76	30.7	11.54	34.9	7.71	28.5	7.08	29.7
Paid leave	1.90	6.7	2.10	6.3	1.17	3.7	2.45	7.4	1.85	6.8	1.43	6.0
Vacation	0.97	3.4	1.12	3.4	0.63	2.0	1.28	3.9	0.94	3.5	0.73	3.1
Holiday	0.60	2.1	0.74	2.2	0.41	1.3	0.87	2.6	0.57	2.1	0.44	1.8
Sick	0.24	0.8	0.19	0.6	0.09	0.3	0.22	0.7	0.25	0.9	0.19	0.8
Personal	0.09	0.3	0.06	0.2	0.04	0.1	0.07	0.2	0.10	0.4	0.07	0.3
Supplemental pay	0.80	2.8	1.32	4.0	0.98	3.1	1.39	4.2	0.69	2.5	0.56	2.4
Overtime and premium pay[3]	0.26	0.9	0.56	1.7	0.63	2.0	0.52	1.6	0.19	0.7	0.26	1.1
Shift differentials	0.07	0.2	0.08	0.3	([4])	([5])	0.12	0.4	0.06	0.2	0.02	0.1
Nonproduction bonuses	0.47	1.7	0.67	2.0	0.35	1.1	0.75	2.3	0.43	1.6	0.28	1.2
Insurance	2.27	8.1	3.14	9.5	2.38	7.5	3.42	10.3	2.09	7.7	2.12	8.9
Life insurance	0.04	0.2	0.07	0.2	0.05	0.2	0.07	0.2	0.04	0.1	0.04	0.2
Health insurance	2.14	7.6	2.95	8.9	2.25	7.1	3.21	9.7	1.97	7.3	2.01	8.4
Short-term disability	0.05	0.2	0.08	0.2	0.06	0.2	0.09	0.3	0.04	0.2	0.03	0.1
Long-term disability	0.04	0.2	0.05	0.1	0.02	0.1	0.05	0.2	0.04	0.2	0.04	0.2
Retirement and savings	1.03	3.7	1.70	5.1	1.71	5.4	1.57	4.8	0.89	3.3	0.87	3.6
Defined benefit plans	0.46	1.6	1.03	3.1	1.13	3.6	0.90	2.7	0.34	1.3	0.43	1.8
Defined contribution plans	0.57	2.0	0.67	2.0	0.58	1.8	0.67	2.0	0.54	2.0	0.44	1.8
Legally required benefits	2.33	8.3	2.98	8.9	3.51	11.1	2.72	8.2	2.19	8.1	2.10	8.8
Social Security and Medicare	1.65	5.9	1.87	5.6	1.82	5.7	1.85	5.6	1.61	5.9	1.39	5.8
Social Security[6]	1.33	4.7	1.50	4.5	1.47	4.6	1.49	4.5	1.29	4.8	1.12	4.7
Medicare	0.33	1.2	0.37	1.1	0.35	1.1	0.36	1.1	0.32	1.2	0.27	1.1
Federal unemployment insurance	0.03	0.1	0.03	0.1	0.03	0.1	0.03	0.1	0.03	0.1	0.04	0.2
State unemployment insurance	0.21	0.7	0.29	0.9	0.35	1.1	0.27	0.8	0.19	0.7	0.19	0.8
Workers' compensation	0.43	1.5	0.79	2.4	1.32	4.2	0.56	1.7	0.36	1.3	0.48	2.0

Compensation component	Information Cost	Percent	Financial activities Cost	Percent	Professional and business services Cost	Percent	Education and health services Cost	Percent	Leisure and hospitality Cost	Percent	Other services Cost	Percent
TOTAL COMPENSATION	42.73	100.0	38.62	100.0	33.84	100.0	30.13	100.0	12.35	100.0	24.75	100.0
Wages and Salaries	29.10	68.1	25.96	67.2	24.64	72.8	21.56	71.6	9.74	78.9	18.27	73.8
Total Benefits	13.63	31.9	12.66	32.8	9.19	27.2	8.57	28.4	2.61	21.1	6.48	26.2
Paid leave	3.91	9.2	3.12	8.1	2.41	7.1	2.29	7.6	0.41	3.3	1.49	6.0
Vacation	2.01	4.7	1.58	4.1	1.23	3.6	1.14	3.8	0.23	1.9	0.68	2.7
Holiday	1.04	2.4	0.93	2.4	0.78	2.3	0.67	2.2	0.13	1.0	0.55	2.2
Sick	0.49	1.1	0.45	1.2	0.29	0.9	0.35	1.2	0.04	0.3	0.20	0.8
Personal	0.38	0.9	0.16	0.4	0.10	0.3	0.14	0.5	0.02	0.1	0.06	0.2
Supplemental pay	1.15	2.7	2.01	5.2	0.87	2.6	0.57	1.9	0.13	1.0	0.54	2.2
Overtime and premium pay[3]	0.34	0.8	0.14	0.4	0.19	0.6	0.21	0.7	0.07	0.6	0.13	0.5
Shift differentials	0.06	0.1	([4])	([5])	0.03	0.1	0.21	0.7	([4])	([5])	([4])	([5])
Nonproduction bonuses	0.76	1.8	1.86	4.8	0.65	1.9	0.15	0.5	0.05	0.4	0.40	1.6
Insurance	4.02	9.4	3.27	8.5	2.26	6.7	2.37	7.9	0.62	5.0	1.58	6.4
Life insurance	0.06	0.1	0.06	0.1	0.06	0.2	0.03	0.1	([4])	([5])	0.05	0.2
Health insurance	3.73	8.7	3.06	7.9	2.09	6.2	2.25	7.5	0.60	4.8	1.48	6.0
Short-term disability	0.16	0.4	0.10	0.3	0.05	0.2	0.03	0.1	([4])	([5])	0.03	0.1
Long-term disability	0.07	0.2	0.06	0.2	0.05	0.2	0.05	0.2	([4])	([5])	0.03	0.1
Retirement and savings	1.59	3.7	1.69	4.4	1.02	3.0	1.01	3.3	0.12	1.0	0.69	2.8
Defined benefit plans	0.55	1.3	0.69	1.8	0.36	1.1	0.30	1.0	0.04	0.3	0.30	1.2
Defined contribution plans	1.04	2.4	1.00	2.6	0.67	2.0	0.70	2.3	0.08	0.6	0.39	1.6
Legally required benefits	2.97	6.9	2.55	6.6	2.64	7.8	2.32	7.7	1.33	10.7	2.18	8.8
Social Security and Medicare	2.45	5.7	2.13	5.5	2.01	6.0	1.79	5.9	0.87	7.0	1.52	6.1
Social Security[6]	1.96	4.6	1.69	4.4	1.61	4.8	1.44	4.8	0.70	5.7	1.22	4.9
Medicare	0.49	1.2	0.45	1.2	0.40	1.2	0.35	1.2	0.16	1.3	0.29	1.2
Federal unemployment insurance	0.03	0.1	0.03	0.1	0.03	0.1	0.03	0.1	0.04	0.3	0.03	0.1
State unemployment insurance	0.22	0.5	0.20	0.5	0.24	0.7	0.16	0.5	0.17	1.4	0.21	0.9
Workers' compensation	0.26	0.6	0.19	0.5	0.36	1.1	0.35	1.2	0.25	2.0	0.41	1.7

Note: Individual items may not sum to totals due to rounding.

[1]Includes mining, construction, and manufacturing. The agriculture, forestry, farming, and hunting sector is excluded.
[2]Includes utilities; wholesale trade; retail trade; transportation and warehousing; information; finance and insurance; real estate and rental and leasing; professional and technical services; management of companies and enterprises; administrative and waste services; education services; health care and social assistance; arts, entertainment, and recreation; accommodation and food services; and other services, except public administration.
[3]Includes premium pay for work in addition to the regular work schedule (such as overtime, weekends, and holidays).
[4]Cost per hour worked is $0.01 or less.
[5]Less than 0.05 percent.
[6]Comprises the Old Age, Survivors, and Disability Insurance (OASDI) program.

Table 6-7. Employer Compensation Costs Per Hour Worked for Employee Compensation and Costs as a Percent of Total Compensation: Private Industry Workers, by Census Region and Area, June 2011

(Dollars, percent of total costs.)

Compensation component	Census region and division[1]					
	Northeast		Northeast divisions			
			New England		Middle Atlantic	
	Cost	Percent	Cost	Percent	Cost	Percent
TOTAL COMPENSATION	32.20	100.0	33.27	100.0	31.79	100.0
Wages and Salaries	22.30	69.3	23.44	70.5	21.87	68.8
Total Benefits	9.90	30.7	9.83	29.5	9.92	31.2
Paid leave	2.35	7.3	2.41	7.2	2.33	7.3
Vacation	1.17	3.6	1.22	3.7	1.15	3.6
Holiday	0.74	2.3	0.78	2.3	0.72	2.3
Sick	0.32	1.0	0.29	0.9	0.33	1.0
Personal	0.13	0.4	0.12	0.4	0.14	0.4
Supplemental pay	1.03	3.2	0.92	2.8	1.07	3.4
Overtime and premium pay[2]	0.25	0.8	0.24	0.7	0.25	0.8
Shift differentials	0.07	0.2	0.07	0.2	0.07	0.2
Nonproduction bonuses	0.71	2.2	0.60	1.8	0.75	2.4
Insurance	2.68	8.3	2.64	7.9	2.69	8.5
Life insurance	0.05	0.2	0.05	0.2	0.05	0.1
Health insurance	2.50	7.8	2.46	7.4	2.52	7.9
Short-term disability	0.08	0.2	0.07	0.2	0.08	0.3
Long-term disability	0.05	0.2	0.06	0.2	0.05	0.1
Retirement and savings	1.20	3.7	1.18	3.5	1.21	3.8
Defined benefit plans	0.53	1.6	0.49	1.5	0.54	1.7
Defined contribution plans	0.67	2.1	0.69	2.1	0.67	2.1
Legally required benefits	2.63	8.2	2.68	8.0	2.62	8.2
Social Security and Medicare	1.86	5.8	1.95	5.9	1.83	5.7
Social Security	1.49	4.6	1.56	4.7	1.46	4.6
Medicare	0.37	1.2	0.39	1.2	0.37	1.1
Federal unemployment insurance	0.03	0.1	0.03	0.1	0.03	0.1
State unemployment insurance	0.29	0.9	0.31	0.9	0.29	0.9
Workers' compensation	0.44	1.4	0.39	1.2	0.47	1.5

Compensation component	Census region and division[1]							
	South		South divisions					
			South Atlantic		East South Central		West South Central	
	Cost	Percent	Cost	Percent	Cost	Percent	Cost	Percent
TOTAL COMPENSATION	24.94	100.0	25.36	100.0	22.70	100.0	25.26	100.0
Wages and Salaries	17.88	71.7	18.32	72.2	16.02	70.6	18.01	71.3
Total Benefits	7.06	28.3	7.04	27.8	6.69	29.4	7.25	28.7
Paid leave	1.62	6.5	1.66	6.6	1.43	6.3	1.62	6.4
Vacation	0.82	3.3	0.84	3.3	0.74	3.3	0.82	3.2
Holiday	0.52	2.1	0.53	2.1	0.46	2.0	0.53	2.1
Sick	0.20	0.8	0.21	0.8	0.16	0.7	0.20	0.8
Personal	0.08	0.3	0.08	0.3	0.07	0.3	0.07	0.3
Supplemental pay	0.72	2.9	0.61	2.4	0.62	2.7	0.94	3.7
Overtime and premium pay[2]	0.26	1.0	0.23	0.9	0.26	1.1	0.30	1.2
Shift differentials	0.07	0.3	0.07	0.3	0.08	0.3	0.06	0.2
Nonproduction bonuses	0.39	1.6	0.31	1.2	0.29	1.3	0.58	2.3
Insurance	1.92	7.7	1.92	7.6	2.02	8.9	1.86	7.4
Life insurance	0.04	0.2	0.04	0.2	0.05	0.2	0.04	0.2
Health insurance	1.80	7.2	1.80	7.1	1.91	8.4	1.75	6.9
Short-term disability	0.04	0.2	0.04	0.2	0.04	0.2	0.03	0.1
Long-term disability	0.04	0.1	0.04	0.2	0.04	0.2	0.03	0.1
Retirement and savings	0.78	3.1	0.77	3.1	0.68	3.0	0.84	3.3
Defined benefit plans	0.30	1.2	0.26	1.0	0.29	1.3	0.36	1.4
Defined contribution plans	0.49	1.9	0.51	2.0	0.39	1.7	0.49	1.9
Legally required benefits	2.02	8.1	2.07	8.2	1.92	8.5	1.99	7.9
Social Security and Medicare	1.50	6.0	1.53	6.0	1.40	6.2	1.51	6.0
Social Security	1.21	4.9	1.23	4.9	1.13	5.0	1.21	4.8
Medicare	0.29	1.2	0.30	1.2	0.27	1.2	0.30	1.2
Federal unemployment insurance	0.03	0.1	0.03	0.1	0.03	0.1	0.03	0.1
State unemployment insurance	0.14	0.6	0.14	0.6	0.14	0.6	0.13	0.5
Workers' compensation	0.35	1.4	0.37	1.4	0.35	1.5	0.31	1.2

Note: Individual items may not sum to totals due to rounding.

[1]The states that comprise the Census divisions are: New England—Connecticut, Maine, Massachusetts, New Hampshire, Rhode Island, and Vermont; Middle Atlantic—New Jersey, New York, and Pennsylvania; South Atlantic—Delaware, District of Columbia, Florida, Georgia, Maryland, North Carolina, South Carolina, Virginia, and West Virginia; East South Central—Alabama, Kentucky, Mississippi, and Tennessee; West South Central—Arkansas, Louisiana, Oklahoma, and Texas; East North Central—Illinois, Indiana, Michigan, Ohio, and Wisconsin; West North Central—Iowa, Kansas, Minnesota, Missouri, Nebraska, North Dakota, and South Dakota; Mountain—Arizona, Colorado, Idaho, Montana, Nevada, New Mexico, Utah, and Wyoming; and Pacific—Alaska, California, Hawaii, Oregon, and Washington.
[2]Comprises the Old-Age, Survivors, and Disability Insurance (OASDI) program.

Table 6-7. Employer Compensation Costs Per Hour Worked for Employee Compensation and Costs as a Percent of Total Compensation: Private Industry Workers, by Census Region and Area, June 2011—*Continued*

(Dollars, percent of total costs.)

Compensation component	Census region and division[1]					
	Midwest		Midwest divisions			
			East North Central		West North Central	
	Cost	Percent	Cost	Percent	Cost	Percent
TOTAL COMPENSATION	27.45	100.0	27.74	100.0	26.84	100.0
Wages and Salaries	19.08	69.5	19.10	68.9	19.03	70.9
Total Benefits	8.37	30.5	8.63	31.1	7.81	29.1
Paid leave	1.80	6.6	1.82	6.6	1.77	6.6
Vacation	0.96	3.5	0.95	3.4	0.98	3.7
Holiday	0.57	2.1	0.58	2.1	0.53	2.0
Sick	0.19	0.7	0.19	0.7	0.20	0.7
Personal	0.08	0.3	0.10	0.3	0.06	0.2
Supplemental pay	0.74	2.7	0.80	2.9	0.60	2.2
Overtime and premium pay[2]	0.27	1.0	0.27	1.0	0.25	0.9
Shift differentials	0.08	0.3	0.09	0.3	0.06	0.2
Nonproduction bonuses	0.39	1.4	0.44	1.6	0.29	1.1
Insurance	2.43	8.9	2.53	9.1	2.22	8.3
Life insurance	0.04	0.2	0.04	0.2	0.04	0.1
Health insurance	2.29	8.3	2.38	8.6	2.08	7.8
Short-term disability	0.05	0.2	0.06	0.2	0.04	0.1
Long-term disability	0.05	0.2	0.04	0.2	0.06	0.2
Retirement and savings	1.15	4.2	1.21	4.3	1.04	3.9
Defined benefit plans	0.60	2.2	0.68	2.5	0.42	1.6
Defined contribution plans	0.55	2.0	0.52	1.9	0.62	2.3
Legally required benefits	2.25	8.2	2.27	8.2	2.18	8.1
Social Security and Medicare	1.60	5.8	1.61	5.8	1.56	5.8
Social Security	1.28	4.7	1.30	4.7	1.25	4.6
Medicare	0.31	1.1	0.31	1.1	0.31	1.2
Federal unemployment insurance	0.03	0.1	0.03	0.1	0.04	0.1
State unemployment insurance	0.22	0.8	0.22	0.8	0.20	0.8
Workers' compensation	0.40	1.5	0.41	1.5	0.39	1.4

Compensation component	Census region and division[1]					
	West		West divisions			
			Mountain		Pacific	
	Cost	Percent	Cost	Percent	Cost	Percent
TOTAL COMPENSATION	30.12	100.0	28.10	100.0	31.02	100.0
Wages and Salaries	21.32	70.8	20.31	72.3	21.77	70.2
Total Benefits	8.80	29.2	7.80	27.7	9.25	29.8
Paid leave	2.01	6.7	1.84	6.6	2.09	6.7
Vacation	1.04	3.5	0.95	3.4	1.08	3.5
Holiday	0.62	2.1	0.56	2.0	0.65	2.1
Sick	0.27	0.9	0.24	0.9	0.28	0.9
Personal	0.08	0.2	0.09	0.3	0.07	0.2
Supplemental pay	0.78	2.6	0.69	2.5	0.81	2.6
Overtime and premium pay[2]	0.24	0.8	0.21	0.7	0.26	0.8
Shift differentials	0.05	0.2	0.04	0.2	0.06	0.2
Nonproduction bonuses	0.48	1.6	0.44	1.6	0.50	1.6
Insurance	2.28	7.6	2.05	7.3	2.39	7.7
Life insurance	0.04	0.1	0.06	0.2	0.03	0.1
Health insurance	2.16	7.2	1.92	6.8	2.27	7.3
Short-term disability	0.03	0.1	0.03	0.1	0.04	0.1
Long-term disability	0.04	0.1	0.04	0.2	0.04	0.1
Retirement and savings	1.12	3.7	0.98	3.5	1.18	3.8
Defined benefit plans	0.51	1.7	0.34	1.2	0.59	1.9
Defined contribution plans	0.60	2.0	0.63	2.3	0.59	1.9
Legally required benefits	2.61	8.7	2.23	7.9	2.78	9.0
Social Security and Medicare	1.76	5.8	1.64	5.8	1.82	5.9
Social Security	1.41	4.7	1.30	4.6	1.46	4.7
Medicare	0.35	1.2	0.33	1.2	0.36	1.2
Federal unemployment insurance	0.03	0.1	0.03	0.1	0.03	0.1
State unemployment insurance	0.23	0.8	0.17	0.6	0.26	0.8
Workers' compensation	0.59	1.9	0.40	1.4	0.67	2.2

Note: Individual items may not sum to totals due to rounding.

[1]The states that comprise the Census divisions are: New England—Connecticut, Maine, Massachusetts, New Hampshire, Rhode Island, and Vermont; Middle Atlantic—New Jersey, New York, and Pennsylvania; South Atlantic—Delaware, District of Columbia, Florida, Georgia, Maryland, North Carolina, South Carolina, Virginia, and West Virginia; East South Central—Alabama, Kentucky, Mississippi, and Tennessee; West South Central—Arkansas, Louisiana, Oklahoma, and Texas; East North Central—Illinois, Indiana, Michigan, Ohio, and Wisconsin; West North Central—Iowa, Kansas, Minnesota, Missouri, Nebraska, North Dakota, and South Dakota; Mountain—Arizona, Colorado, Idaho, Montana, Nevada, New Mexico, Utah, and Wyoming; and Pacific—Alaska, California, Hawaii, Oregon, and Washington.
[2]Comprises the Old-Age, Survivors, and Disability Insurance (OASDI) program.

Table 6-8. Employer Compensation Costs Per Hour Worked for Employee Compensation and Costs as a Percent of Total Compensation: State and Local Government Workers, by Major Occupational and Industry Group, June 2011

(Dollars, percent of total cost.)

Compensation component	All workers		Occupational group[1]						Industry group	
	Cost	Percent	Management, professional, and related		Sales and office		Service		Service-providing[2]	
			Cost	Percent	Cost	Percent	Cost	Percent	Cost	Percent
TOTAL COMPENSATION	40.40	100.0	49.07	100.0	27.97	100.0	30.58	100.0	40.45	100.0
Wages and Salaries	26.41	65.4	33.38	68.0	17.01	60.8	18.25	59.7	26.46	65.4
Total Benefits	13.99	34.6	15.69	32.0	10.96	39.2	12.33	40.3	14.00	34.6
Paid leave	3.03	7.5	3.36	6.8	2.48	8.9	2.69	8.8	3.02	7.5
Vacation	1.15	2.8	1.14	2.3	1.10	4.0	1.17	3.8	1.14	2.8
Holiday	0.88	2.2	0.92	1.9	0.78	2.8	0.86	2.8	0.88	2.2
Sick	0.78	1.9	1.00	2.0	0.49	1.7	0.54	1.8	0.79	1.9
Personal	0.22	0.5	0.30	0.6	0.11	0.4	0.12	0.4	0.22	0.5
Supplemental pay	0.34	0.8	0.24	0.5	0.20	0.7	0.57	1.9	0.34	0.8
Overtime and premium pay[3]	0.18	0.4	0.07	0.1	0.11	0.4	0.38	1.2	0.17	0.4
Shift differentials	0.05	0.1	0.03	0.1	0.02	0.1	0.09	0.3	0.05	0.1
Nonproduction bonuses	0.11	0.3	0.14	0.3	0.06	0.2	0.11	0.4	0.12	0.3
Insurance	4.83	12.0	5.38	11.0	4.34	15.5	3.95	12.9	4.84	12.0
Life insurance	0.08	0.2	0.12	0.2	0.04	0.2	0.04	0.1	0.08	0.2
Health insurance	4.68	11.6	5.18	10.6	4.24	15.2	3.86	12.6	4.69	11.6
Short-term disability	0.03	0.1	0.03	0.1	0.03	0.1	0.02	0.1	0.03	0.1
Long-term disability	0.04	0.1	0.05	0.1	0.03	0.1	0.02	0.1	0.04	0.1
Retirement and savings	3.32	8.2	3.88	7.9	2.09	7.5	3.06	10.0	3.32	8.2
Defined benefit plans	3.00	7.4	3.48	7.1	1.86	6.7	2.85	9.3	3.00	7.4
Defined contribution plans	0.32	0.8	0.40	0.8	0.23	0.8	0.21	0.7	0.32	0.8
Legally required benefits	2.47	6.1	2.83	5.8	1.85	6.6	2.06	6.7	2.47	6.1
Social Security and Medicare	1.87	4.6	2.28	4.7	1.34	4.8	1.34	4.4	1.87	4.6
Social Security[4]	1.45	3.6	1.76	3.6	1.06	3.8	1.03	3.4	1.45	3.6
Medicare	0.42	1.0	0.53	1.1	0.28	1.0	0.30	1.0	0.42	1.0
State unemployment insurance	0.11	0.3	0.10	0.2	0.16	0.6	0.10	0.3	0.11	0.3
Workers' compensation	0.49	1.2	0.45	0.9	0.35	1.2	0.62	2.0	0.49	1.2

Note: Individual items may not sum to totals due to rounding.

[1]This table presents data for the three major occupational groups in state and local government: management, professional, and related occupations, including teachers; sales and office occupations, including clerical workers; and service occupations, including police and firefighters.
[2]Service-providing industries, which include health and education services, employ a large proportion of the state and local government workforce.
[3]Includes premium pay for work in addition to the regular work schedule (such as overtime, weekends, and holidays).
[4]Comprises the Old Age, Survivors, and Disability Insurance (OASDI) program.

Table 6-9. Employer Compensation Costs Per Hour Worked for Employee Compensation and Costs as a Percent of Total Compensation: State and Local Government, by Major Occupational and Industry Group, June 2011

(Dollars, percent of total compensation.)

Characteristic	Total compensation	Wages and salaries	Benefit costs					
			Total	Paid leave	Supplemental pay	Insurance	Retirement and savings	Legally required benefits
COSTS PER HOUR WORKED								
State and Local Government Workers	40.40	26.41	13.99	3.03	0.34	4.83	3.32	2.47
Occupational Group								
Management, professional, and related	49.07	33.38	15.69	3.36	0.24	5.38	3.88	2.83
Professional and related	48.09	32.92	15.17	3.03	0.23	5.37	3.82	2.71
Teachers[1]	55.59	39.30	16.29	2.80	0.14	5.89	4.44	3.02
Primary, secondary, and special education school teachers	56.43	39.68	16.75	2.57	0.15	6.48	4.64	2.92
Sales and office	27.97	17.01	10.96	2.48	0.20	4.34	2.09	1.85
Office and administrative support	28.24	17.12	11.13	2.52	0.20	4.42	2.14	1.86
Service	30.58	18.25	12.33	2.69	0.57	3.95	3.06	2.06
Industry Group								
Education and health services	42.48	28.81	13.68	2.71	0.21	5.07	3.27	2.41
Education services	43.55	29.79	13.76	2.62	0.15	5.14	3.41	2.42
Elementary and secondary schools	43.18	29.60	13.57	2.29	0.16	5.34	3.44	2.35
Junior colleges, colleges, and universities	45.23	30.72	14.51	3.84	0.13	4.46	3.38	2.69
Health care and social assistance	35.71	22.53	13.18	3.27	0.61	4.61	2.35	2.33
Hospitals	38.02	24.00	14.02	3.53	0.74	4.95	2.39	2.42
Public administration	38.64	23.53	15.11	3.65	0.55	4.65	3.64	2.61
PERCENT OF TOTAL COMPENSATION								
State and Local Government Workers	100.0	65.4	34.6	7.5	0.8	12.0	8.2	6.1
Occupational Group								
Management, professional, and related	100.0	68.0	32.0	6.8	0.5	11.0	7.9	5.8
Professional and related	100.0	68.5	31.5	6.3	0.5	11.2	8.0	5.6
Teachers[1]	100.0	70.7	29.3	5.0	0.2	10.6	8.0	5.4
Primary, secondary, and special education school teachers	100.0	70.3	29.7	4.5	0.3	11.5	8.2	5.2
Sales and office	100.0	60.8	39.2	8.9	0.7	15.5	7.5	6.6
Office and administrative support	100.0	60.6	39.4	8.9	0.7	15.6	7.6	6.6
Service	100.0	59.7	40.3	8.8	1.9	12.9	10.0	6.7
Industry Group								
Education and health services	100.0	67.8	32.2	6.4	0.5	11.9	7.7	5.7
Education services	100.0	68.4	31.6	6.0	0.3	11.8	7.8	5.6
Elementary and secondary schools	100.0	68.6	31.4	5.3	0.4	12.4	8.0	5.4
Junior colleges, colleges, and universities	100.0	67.9	32.1	8.5	0.3	9.9	7.5	6.0
Health care and social assistance	100.0	63.1	36.9	9.2	1.7	12.9	6.6	6.5
Hospitals	100.0	63.1	36.9	9.3	2.0	13.0	6.3	6.4
Public administration	100.0	60.9	39.1	9.5	1.4	12.0	9.4	6.8

Note: Individual items may not sum to totals due to rounding.

[1]Includes postsecondary teachers; primary, secondary, and special education teachers; and other teachers and instructors.

Table 6-10. Employer Costs Per Hour Worked for Employee Compensation and Costs as a Percent of Total Compensation: Private Industry Workers, by Establishment Employment Size, June 2011

(Dollars, percent.)

Compensation component	1–99 workers					
	1–99 workers		1–49 workers		50–99 workers	
	Cost	Percent	Cost	Percent	Cost	Percent
TOTAL COMPENSATION	23.25	100.0	22.47	100.0	25.65	100.0
Wages and Salaries	17.16	73.8	16.74	74.5	18.44	71.9
Total Benefits	6.09	26.2	5.73	25.5	7.21	28.1
Paid leave	1.29	5.6	1.21	5.4	1.56	6.1
Vacation	0.64	2.8	0.60	2.7	0.78	3.0
Holiday	0.43	1.9	0.41	1.8	0.51	2.0
Sick	0.16	0.7	0.14	0.6	0.20	0.8
Personal	0.06	0.3	0.05	0.2	0.08	0.3
Supplemental pay	0.52	2.2	0.49	2.2	0.63	2.4
Overtime and premium pay[1]	0.19	0.8	0.17	0.7	0.24	1.0
Shift differentials	0.02	0.1	([2])	([3])	0.03	0.1
Nonproduction bonuses	0.32	1.4	0.31	1.4	0.35	1.4
Insurance	1.57	6.8	1.45	6.4	1.94	7.6
Life insurance	0.03	0.1	0.03	0.1	0.04	0.1
Health insurance	1.48	6.4	1.37	6.1	1.83	7.1
Short-term disability	0.03	0.1	0.03	0.1	0.04	0.2
Long-term disability	0.02	0.1	0.02	0.1	0.03	0.1
Retirement and savings	0.61	2.6	0.53	2.4	0.85	3.3
Defined benefit plans	0.23	1.0	0.20	0.9	0.34	1.3
Defined contribution plans	0.38	1.6	0.33	1.5	0.51	2.0
Legally required benefits	2.10	9.0	2.05	9.1	2.23	8.7
Social Security and Medicare	1.42	6.1	1.38	6.2	1.53	6.0
Social Security[4]	1.14	4.9	1.11	5.0	1.23	4.8
Medicare	0.28	1.2	0.27	1.2	0.30	1.2
Federal unemployment insurance ...	0.04	0.2	0.04	0.2	0.03	0.1
State unemployment insurance	0.21	0.9	0.21	0.9	0.21	0.8
Workers' compensation	0.43	1.9	0.43	1.9	0.46	1.8

[1]Includes premium pay for work in addition to the regular work schedule (such as overtime, weekends, and holidays).
[2]Cost per hour worked is $0.01 or less.
[3]Less than .05 percent.
[4]Comprises the Old-Age, Survivors, and Disability Insurance (OASDI) program.

Table 6-10. Employer Costs Per Hour Worked for Employee Compensation and Costs as a Percent of Total Compensation: Private Industry Workers, by Establishment Employment Size, June 2011—*Continued*

(Dollars, percent.)

Compensation component	100 workers or more					
	100 workers or more		100–499 workers		500 workers or more	
	Cost	Percent	Cost	Percent	Cost	Percent
TOTAL COMPENSATION	33.76	100.0	28.77	100.0	40.68	100.0
Wages and Salaries	22.87	67.7	20.10	69.8	26.70	65.6
Total Benefits	10.90	32.3	8.68	30.2	13.98	34.4
Paid leave	2.59	7.7	1.97	6.9	3.44	8.5
Vacation	1.35	4.0	1.01	3.5	1.81	4.5
Holiday	0.78	2.3	0.63	2.2	1.00	2.5
Sick	0.33	1.0	0.24	0.8	0.46	1.1
Personal	0.13	0.4	0.09	0.3	0.17	0.4
Supplemental pay	1.12	3.3	0.76	2.6	1.61	4.0
Overtime and premium pay[1]	0.34	1.0	0.30	1.1	0.38	0.9
Shift differentials	0.13	0.4	0.07	0.2	0.21	0.5
Nonproduction bonuses	0.65	1.9	0.39	1.3	1.02	2.5
Insurance	3.08	9.1	2.54	8.8	3.83	9.4
Life insurance	0.06	0.2	0.05	0.2	0.07	0.2
Health insurance	2.89	8.6	2.39	8.3	3.57	8.8
Short-term disability	0.07	0.2	0.06	0.2	0.10	0.2
Long-term disability	0.06	0.2	0.04	0.1	0.09	0.2
Retirement and savings	1.51	4.5	1.03	3.6	2.18	5.4
Defined benefit plans	0.73	2.2	0.43	1.5	1.14	2.8
Defined contribution plans	0.78	2.3	0.60	2.1	1.04	2.6
Legally required benefits	2.59	7.7	2.37	8.2	2.91	7.2
Social Security and Medicare	1.93	5.7	1.66	5.8	2.29	5.6
Social Security[4]	1.54	4.6	1.33	4.6	1.83	4.5
Medicare	0.38	1.1	0.33	1.1	0.46	1.1
Federal unemployment insurance	0.03	0.1	0.03	0.1	0.03	0.1
State unemployment insurance	0.21	0.6	0.22	0.8	0.19	0.5
Workers' compensation	0.43	1.3	0.45	1.6	0.40	1.0

[1]Includes premium pay for work in addition to the regular work schedule (such as overtime, weekends, and holidays).
[4]Comprises the Old-Age, Survivors, and Disability Insurance (OASDI) program.

NOTES AND DEFINITIONS

EMPLOYEE BENEFITS SURVEY

The Employee Benefits Survey provides data on the incidence and provisions of selected employee benefit plans.

Collection and Coverage

The March 2011 National Compensation Survey (NCS) benefits survey represented approximately 120 million civilian workers; of this number, about 101 million were private industry workers and 19 million were state and local government workers. It included a sample of 17,585 establishments.

Definitions

Access to a benefit is determined on an occupational basis within an establishment. An employee is considered to have access to a benefit if it is available for his or her use.

Participation refers to the proportion of employees covered by a benefit. There will be cases where employees with access to a plan will not participate. For example, some employees may decline to participate in a health insurance plan if there is an employee cost involved.

A *private establishment* is an economic unit that produces goods or services, a central administrative office, or an auxiliary unit providing support services to a company. For private industries, the establishment is usually at a single physical location. For state and local governments, an establishment is defined as an agency or entity such as a school district, college, university, hospital, nursing home, administrative body, court, police department, fire department, health or social service operation, highway maintenance operation, urban transit operation, or other governmental unit. It provides services under the authority of a specific state or local government organization within a defined geographic area or jurisdiction.

Take-up rates are the percentage of workers with access to a plan who participate in the plan. They are computed by using the number of workers participating in a plan divided by the number of workers with access to the plan, times 100 and rounded to the nearest one percent. Since the computation of take-up rates is based on the number of workers collected, rather the rounded percentage estimates, the take-up rates in the tables may not equal the ratio of participation to access estimates.

An employee is considered to be a *union worker* when all the following conditions are met: (1) a labor organization is recognized as the bargaining agent for all workers in the occupation; (2) wage and salary rates are determined through collective bargaining or negotiations; (3) settlement terms, which must include earnings provisions and may include benefit provisions, are embodied in a signed, mutually binding collective bargaining agreement.

Sources of Additional Information

For more information, see Bureau of Labor Statistics (BLS) news release 11-1112 "Employee Benefits in the United States–March 2011." For a listing of selected benefit definitions, see the *Glossary of Compensation Terms*. These resources are available on the BLS Web site at <http://www.bls.gov/ncs/ebs/>.

Table 6-11. Retirement Benefits:[1] Access, Participation, and Take-Up Rates,[2] March 2011

(Percent.)

Characteristic	Civilian[3]			Private industry			State and local government		
	Access	Participation	Take-up rate	Access	Participation	Take-up rate	Access	Participation	Take-up rate
ALL WORKERS	68	55	80	64	49	76	90	85	95
Worker Characteristics									
Management, professional, and related	83	74	88	80	68	85	92	87	95
Management, business, and financial	86	78	91	84	75	90	. . .	. . .	. . .
Professional and related	82	72	88	78	65	83	92	87	95
Teachers	86	81	94	. . .	. . .	. . .	91	86	95
Primary, secondary, and special education school teachers	95	90	96	. . .	. . .	. . .	99	95	96
Registered nurses	83	69	83	. . .	. . .	. . .	. . .	. . .	. . .
Service	47	31	66	40	22	56	84	79	95
Protective service	74	62	84	49	24	50	91	87	96
Sales and office	71	55	78	69	52	76	90	86	95
Sales and related	66	44	67	66	44	66	. . .	. . .	. . .
Office and administrative support	73	61	84	71	58	81	92	87	95
Natural resources, construction, and maintenance	65	53	81	62	49	79	94	90	96
Construction, extraction, farming, fishing, and forestry	63	50	80	59	45	76	. . .	. . .	. . .
Installation, maintenance, and repair	68	57	83	66	53	82	. . .	. . .	. . .
Production, transportation, and material moving	67	52	78	66	51	77	87	84	96
Production	67	53	79	67	53	79	. . .	. . .	. . .
Transportation and material moving	66	51	77	65	49	76	. . .	. . .	. . .
Full-time workers	78	65	84	73	59	80	99	94	95
Part-time workers	38	22	58	37	20	54	41	37	91
Union workers	93	88	94	90	83	93	97	92	95
Nonunion workers	64	49	77	61	45	74	84	79	95
Average Wage Within the Following Percentiles[4]									
Lowest 25 percent	41	23	56	39	19	50	74	70	94
Lowest 10 percent	29	12	40	28	10	35	60	56	94
Second 25 percent	70	54	78	66	48	73	94	89	95
Third 25 percent	78	67	86	74	61	83	95	91	96
Highest 25 percent	88	80	91	84	75	89	98	93	95
Highest 10 percent	90	83	92	87	79	90	97	92	94
Establishment Characteristics									
Goods-producing industries	73	61	83	73	60	83	. . .	. . .	. . .
Service-providing industries	67	54	80	62	47	75	90	85	95
Education and health services	79	67	85	71	55	77	91	86	95
Educational services	87	82	93	73	63	86	91	87	95
Elementary and secondary schools	91	86	95	. . .	. . .	. . .	92	88	96
Junior colleges, colleges, and universities	88	80	91	90	79	88	86	80	93
Health care and social assistance	73	56	77	71	54	76	93	86	92
Hospitals	90	78	87	. . .	. . .	. . .	95	86	90
Public administration	90	86	95	. . .	. . .	. . .	90	86	95
Number of Workers									
1 to 99 workers	51	36	71	49	34	69	78	75	96
1 to 49 workers	46	33	72	45	32	70	73	70	95
50 to 99 workers	64	44	69	62	41	66	87	84	97
100 workers or more	84	72	85	81	66	82	91	87	95
100 to 499 workers	79	62	79	77	59	76	87	84	96
500 workers or more	89	81	91	86	76	88	93	88	95
Geographic Areas[5]									
New England	63	53	83	60	48	80	84	81	97
Middle Atlantic	70	58	83	66	53	80	92	85	92
East North Central	70	57	82	68	53	79	85	81	95
West North Central	70	58	83	66	53	80	89	81	91
South Atlantic	69	52	76	64	46	72	91	85	93
East South Central	71	56	80	65	47	73	92	89	96
West South Central	67	52	78	63	45	72	90	87	98
Mountain	68	53	78	65	48	74	89	86	97
Pacific	65	53	82	60	46	77	92	90	98

[1]Includes defined benefit pension plans and defined contribution retirement plans. Workers are considered as having access or as participating if they have access to or participate in at least one of these plan types.
[2]The take-up rate is an estimate of the percentage of workers with access to a plan who participate in the plan, rounded for presentation.
[3]Includes workers in the private nonfarm economy except those in private households, and workers in the public sector, except the federal government.
[4]The percentile groupings are based on the average wage for each occupation surveyed, which may include workers both above and below the threshold.
[5]The states that comprise the Census divisions are: New England—Connecticut, Maine, Massachusetts, New Hampshire, Rhode Island, and Vermont; Middle Atlantic—New Jersey, New York, and Pennsylvania; South Atlantic—Delaware, District of Columbia, Florida, Georgia, Maryland, North Carolina, South Carolina, Virginia, and West Virginia; East South Central—Alabama, Kentucky, Mississippi, and Tennessee; West South Central—Arkansas, Louisiana, Oklahoma, and Texas; East North Central—Illinois, Indiana, Michigan, Ohio, and Wisconsin; West North Central—Iowa, Kansas, Minnesota, Missouri, Nebraska, North Dakota, and South Dakota; Mountain—Arizona, Colorado, Idaho, Montana, Nevada, New Mexico, Utah, and Wyoming; and Pacific—Alaska, California, Hawaii, Oregon, and Washington.
. . . = Not available or not applicable.

Table 6-12. Medical Care Benefits: Access, Participation, and Take-Up Rates,[1] March 2011

(Percent.)

Characteristic	Civilian[2]			Private industry			State and local government		
	Access	Participation	Take-up rate	Access	Participation	Take-up rate	Access	Participation	Take-up rate
ALL WORKERS	72	54	75	69	51	73	87	72	83
Worker Characteristics									
Management, professional, and related	88	68	78	87	66	77	89	73	82
Management, business, and financial	94	73	78	94	72	76	...	...	...
Professional and related	85	67	78	83	64	77	89	73	82
Teachers	85	68	80	...	...	...	89	73	82
Primary, secondary, and special education school teachers	95	77	81	...	...	...	98	81	82
Registered nurses	82	63	77	...	...	...	...	...	...
Service	48	33	70	42	27	65	81	68	84
Protective service	72	58	81	47	32	68	88	76	86
Sales and office	72	52	72	71	50	70	88	73	82
Sales and related	63	42	67	63	42	66	...	...	...
Office and administrative support	78	58	74	76	55	73	89	73	82
Natural resources, construction, and maintenance	77	59	77	75	56	75	95	82	86
Construction, extraction, farming, fishing, and forestry	71	57	80	69	54	79	...	...	...
Installation, maintenance, and repair	83	61	73	81	58	72	...	...	...
Production, transportation, and material moving	76	59	78	75	58	77	82	69	84
Production	82	65	80	82	65	80	...	...	...
Transportation and material moving	70	53	76	69	52	75	...	...	...
Full-time workers	88	67	77	85	64	75	99	82	83
Part-time workers	24	14	58	23	13	57	26	18	69
Union workers	93	77	82	92	75	82	95	78	82
Nonunion workers	69	50	73	67	48	72	81	67	83
Average Wage Within the Following Percentiles[3]									
Lowest 25 percent	39	24	62	36	21	59	69	57	82
Lowest 10 percent	22	12	56	20	11	53	54	43	81
Second 25 percent	77	56	73	74	53	71	91	77	84
Third 25 percent	87	69	79	85	66	77	94	79	84
Highest 25 percent	93	74	80	91	71	79	97	79	81
Highest 10 percent	94	75	79	93	73	79	97	79	82
Establishment Characteristics									
Goods-producing industries	85	69	81	85	68	81	...	...	...
Service-providing industries	70	52	74	66	47	71	87	72	83
Education and health services	79	60	76	74	53	72	89	72	81
Educational services	86	69	80	78	56	73	88	72	81
Elementary and secondary schools	88	70	79	...	...	...	89	72	80
Junior colleges, colleges, and universities	87	72	82	90	70	78	86	73	84
Health care and social assistance	75	54	73	73	52	72	91	75	83
Hospitals	89	71	80	...	...	...	94	77	82
Public administration	88	74	85	...	...	...	88	74	85
Number of Workers									
1 to 99 workers	57	42	73	56	41	72	74	63	85
1 to 49 workers	53	38	72	53	38	71	67	57	85
50 to 99 workers	69	51	74	68	50	73	84	72	86
100 workers or more	86	66	77	84	63	74	89	74	82
100 to 499 workers	82	60	74	81	58	72	85	71	84
500 workers or more	90	71	79	89	69	77	91	74	82
Geographic Areas[4]									
New England	70	51	72	68	47	70	84	68	81
Middle Atlantic	73	57	78	71	53	76	87	77	88
East North Central	72	54	75	71	53	75	79	61	77
West North Central	70	53	75	67	50	74	84	66	79
South Atlantic	73	53	72	69	48	70	90	75	84
East South Central	79	62	79	74	55	74	95	86	91
West South Central	71	53	74	67	48	72	90	74	82
Mountain	72	52	72	70	49	71	87	65	75
Pacific	72	56	77	69	52	76	90	75	83

[1]The take-up rate is an estimate of the percentage of workers with access to a plan who participate in the plan, rounded for presentation.
[2]Includes workers in the private nonfarm economy except those in private households, and workers in the public sector, except the federal government.
[3]The percentile groupings are based on the average wage for each occupation surveyed, which may include workers both above and below the threshold.
[4]The states that comprise the Census divisions are: New England—Connecticut, Maine, Massachusetts, New Hampshire, Rhode Island, and Vermont; Middle Atlantic—New Jersey, New York, and Pennsylvania; South Atlantic—Delaware, District of Columbia, Florida, Georgia, Maryland, North Carolina, South Carolina, Virginia, and West Virginia; East South Central—Alabama, Kentucky, Mississippi, and Tennessee; West South Central—Arkansas, Louisiana, Oklahoma, and Texas; East North Central—Illinois, Indiana, Michigan, Ohio, and Wisconsin; West North Central—Iowa, Kansas, Minnesota, Missouri, Nebraska, North Dakota, and South Dakota; Mountain—Arizona, Colorado, Idaho, Montana, Nevada, New Mexico, Utah, and Wyoming; and Pacific—Alaska, California, Hawaii, Oregon, and Washington.
. . . = Not available or not applicable.

Table 6-13. Medical Care Benefits: Access[1] for Unmarried Domestic Partners, March 2011

(Percent.)

Characteristic	Civilian[2]		Private industry		State and local government	
	Same sex	Opposite sex	Same sex	Opposite sex	Same sex	Opposite sex
ALL WORKERS	30	25	29	25	33	28
Worker Characteristics						
Management, professional, and related	42	36	46	38	34	29
Management, business, and financial	50	43	52	45	. . .	. . .
Professional and related	40	33	43	35	34	29
Teachers	31	26	. . .	. . .	31	26
Primary, secondary, and special education school teachers	28	24	. . .	. . .	30	25
Registered nurses	31	24	. . .	. . .	. . .	. . .
Service	19	15	17	14	30	24
Protective service	29	20	20	10	35	26
Sales and office	30	26	30	26	36	31
Sales and related	24	20	24	20	. . .	. . .
Office and administrative support	34	30	34	29	37	32
Natural resources, construction, and maintenance	23	18	22	18	29	22
Construction, extraction, farming, fishing, and forestry	17	17	16	16	. . .	. . .
Installation, maintenance, and repair	29	20	29	20	. . .	. . .
Production, transportation, and material moving	25	21	25	21	29	26
Production	24	20	24	20	. . .	. . .
Transportation and material moving	26	22	26	22	. . .	. . .
Full-time workers	37	31	36	31	37	31
Part-time workers	10	8	9	8	13	12
Union workers	49	38	46	31	53	45
Nonunion workers	27	23	28	24	17	14
Average Wage Within the Following Percentiles[3]						
Lowest 25 percent	11	9	11	9	15	13
Lowest 10 percent	7	5	6	4	8	7
Second 25 percent	26	23	26	23	35	29
Third 25 percent	37	31	35	30	37	31
Highest 25 percent	49	40	50	41	47	39
Highest 10 percent	57	48	59	49	57	49
Establishment Characteristics						
Goods-producing industries	27	23	27	24	. . .	. . .
Service-providing industries	31	25	30	25	33	28
Education and health services	30	26	29	25	32	27
Educational services	33	27	38	29	32	26
Elementary and secondary schools	28	24	. . .	. . .	28	24
Junior colleges, colleges, and universities	49	37	58	43	43	33
Health care and social assistance	28	25	28	24	35	31
Hospitals	34	26	. . .	. . .	36	32
Public administration	37	31	. . .	. . .	37	31
Number of Workers						
1 to 99 workers	18	16	18	16	16	15
1 to 49 workers	17	15	17	15	12	11
50 to 99 workers	23	20	23	20	22	21
100 workers or more	41	33	42	34	36	30
100 to 499 workers	32	28	34	30	22	19
500 workers or more	49	38	54	41	40	34
Geographic Areas[4]						
New England	37	33	38	33	34	28
Middle Atlantic	34	28	31	24	54	49
East North Central	22	14	22	15	23	. . .
West North Central	19	16	20	16	. . .	. . .
South Atlantic	21	16	22	18	12	7
East South Central	17	12	21	14	2	3
West South Central	19	18	20	19	10	11
Mountain	41	34	39	33	51	36
Pacific	57	53	52	48	84	82

[1]The percentage of workers with access to the benefit reflects both the availability of the benefits and the employer's policy on providing the benefit to unmarried domestic partners.
[2]Includes workers in the private nonfarm economy except those in private households, and workers in the private sector, except the federal government.
[3]The categories are based on the average wage for each occupation surveyed, which may include workers with earnings both above and below the threshold.
[4]The states that comprise the Census divisions are: New England—Connecticut, Maine, Massachusetts, New Hampshire, Rhode Island, and Vermont; Middle Atlantic—New Jersey, New York, and Pennsylvania; South Atlantic—Delaware, District of Columbia, Florida, Georgia, Maryland, North Carolina, South Carolina, Virginia, and West Virginia; East South Central—Alabama, Kentucky, Mississippi, and Tennessee; West South Central—Arkansas, Louisiana, Oklahoma, and Texas; East North Central—Illinois, Indiana, Michigan, Ohio, and Wisconsin; West North Central—Iowa, Kansas, Minnesota, Missouri, Nebraska, North Dakota, and South Dakota; Mountain—Arizona, Colorado, Idaho, Montana, Nevada, New Mexico, Utah, and Wyoming; and Pacific—Alaska, California, Hawaii, Oregon, and Washington.
. . . = Not available or not applicable.

Table 6-14. Medical Plans: Share of Premiums Paid by Employer and Employee for Single Coverage, March 2011

(Percent.)

Characteristic	Civilian[1]		Private industry		State and local government	
	Employer share of premium	Employee share of premium	Employer share of premium	Employee share of premium	Employer share of premium	Employee share of premium
ALL WORKERS	81	19	80	20	88	12
Worker Characteristics						
Management, professional, and related	83	17	81	19	88	12
Management, business, and financial	82	18	80	20	. . .	. . .
Professional and related	83	17	81	19	88	12
Teachers	87	13	. . .	. . .	89	11
Primary, secondary, and special education school teachers	88	12	. . .	. . .	88	12
Registered nurses	81	19	. . .	. . .	. . .	. . .
Service	81	19	78	22	88	12
Protective service	85	15	75	25	88	12
Sales and office	79	21	78	22	89	11
Sales and related	75	25	75	25	. . .	. . .
Office and administrative support	81	19	79	21	88	12
Natural resources, construction, and maintenance	82	18	81	19	89	11
Construction, extraction, farming, fishing, and forestry	83	17	82	18	. . .	. . .
Installation, maintenance, and repair	81	19	80	20	. . .	. . .
Production, transportation, and material moving	81	19	81	19	88	12
Production	81	19	81	19	. . .	. . .
Transportation and material moving	81	19	81	19	. . .	. . .
Full-time workers	82	18	80	20	88	12
Part-time workers	78	22	77	23	84	16
Union workers	89	11	89	11	89	11
Nonunion workers	79	21	78	22	88	12
Average Wage Within the Following Percentiles[2]						
Lowest 25 percent	78	22	76	24	88	12
Lowest 10 percent	75	25	72	28	89	11
Second 25 percent	80	20	78	22	89	11
Third 25 percent	82	18	80	20	89	11
Highest 25 percent	83	17	82	18	88	12
Highest 10 percent	84	16	82	18	90	10
Establishment Characteristics						
Goods-producing industries	82	18	82	18	. . .	. . .
Service-providing industries	81	19	79	21	88	12
Education and health services	84	16	80	20	88	12
Educational services	87	13	80	20	88	12
Elementary and secondary schools	88	12	. . .	. . .	88	12
Junior colleges, colleges, and universities	86	14	79	21	89	11
Health care and social assistance	81	19	81	19	85	15
Hospitals	81	19	. . .	. . .	85	15
Public administration	89	11	. . .	. . .	89	11
Number of Workers						
1 to 99 workers	80	20	79	21	91	9
1 to 49 workers	80	20	79	21	91	9
50 to 99 workers	79	21	78	22	90	10
100 workers or more	82	18	80	20	88	12
100 to 499 workers	80	20	79	21	89	11
500 workers or more	84	16	81	19	88	12
Geographic Areas[3]						
New England	79	21	77	23	86	14
Middle Atlantic	83	17	81	19	91	9
East North Central	82	18	80	20	90	10
West North Central	83	17	80	20	92	8
South Atlantic	80	20	77	23	88	12
East South Central	80	20	77	23	88	12
West South Central	81	19	80	20	86	14
Mountain	81	19	79	21	89	11
Pacific	83	17	82	18	86	14

[1]Includes workers in the private nonfarm economy except those in private households, and workers in the public sector, except the federal government.
[2]The percentile groupings are based on the average wage for each occupation surveyed, which may include workers both above and below the threshold.
[3]The states that comprise the Census divisions are: New England—Connecticut, Maine, Massachusetts, New Hampshire, Rhode Island, and Vermont; Middle Atlantic—New Jersey, New York, and Pennsylvania; South Atlantic—Delaware, District of Columbia, Florida, Georgia, Maryland, North Carolina, South Carolina, Virginia, and West Virginia; East South Central—Alabama, Kentucky, Mississippi, and Tennessee; West South Central—Arkansas, Louisiana, Oklahoma, and Texas; East North Central—Illinois, Indiana, Michigan, Ohio, and Wisconsin; West North Central—Iowa, Kansas, Minnesota, Missouri, Nebraska, North Dakota, and South Dakota; Mountain—Arizona, Colorado, Idaho, Montana, Nevada, New Mexico, Utah, and Wyoming; and Pacific—Alaska, California, Hawaii, Oregon, and Washington.
. . . = Not available or not applicable.

Table 6-15. Medical Plans: Share of Premiums Paid by Employer and Employee for Family Coverage, March 2011

(Percent.)

Characteristic	Civilian[1]		Private industry		State and local government	
	Employer share of premium	Employee share of premium	Employer share of premium	Employee share of premium	Employer share of premium	Employee share of premium
ALL WORKERS	70	30	69	31	71	29
Worker Characteristics						
Management, professional, and related	71	29	71	29	70	30
Management, business, and financial	71	29	70	30	. . .	. . .
Professional and related	70	30	71	29	69	31
Teachers	67	33	. . .	. . .	69	31
Primary, secondary, and special education school teachers	66	34	. . .	. . .	67	33
Registered nurses	72	28	. . .	. . .	. . .	. . .
Service	66	34	63	37	73	27
Protective service	74	26	62	38	77	23
Sales and office	68	32	67	33	73	27
Sales and related	65	35	65	35	. . .	. . .
Office and administrative support	69	31	68	32	73	27
Natural resources, construction, and maintenance	69	31	68	32	73	27
Construction, extraction, farming, fishing, and forestry	68	32	66	34	. . .	. . .
Installation, maintenance, and repair	70	30	69	31	. . .	. . .
Production, transportation, and material moving	73	27	73	27	73	27
Production	74	26	73	27	. . .	. . .
Transportation and material moving	72	28	72	28	. . .	. . .
Full-time workers	70	30	69	31	71	29
Part-time workers	70	30	70	30	71	29
Union workers	82	18	83	17	80	20
Nonunion workers	66	34	67	33	64	36
Average Wage Within the Following Percentiles[2]						
Lowest 25 percent	63	37	63	37	64	36
Lowest 10 percent	62	38	61	39	58	42
Second 25 percent	67	33	66	34	74	26
Third 25 percent	70	30	69	31	71	29
Highest 25 percent	73	27	73	27	75	25
Highest 10 percent	75	25	74	26	80	20
Establishment Characteristics						
Goods-producing industries	73	27	73	27	. . .	. . .
Service-providing industries	69	31	68	32	71	29
Education and health services	67	33	67	33	68	32
Educational services	67	33	64	36	67	33
Elementary and secondary schools	65	35	. . .	. . .	66	34
Junior colleges, colleges, and universities	70	30	69	31	71	29
Health care and social assistance	68	32	67	33	72	28
Hospitals	74	26	. . .	. . .	73	27
Public administration	78	22	. . .	. . .	78	22
Number of Workers						
1 to 99 workers	64	36	64	36	71	29
1 to 49 workers	64	36	63	37	72	28
50 to 99 workers	65	35	65	35	70	30
100 workers or more	72	28	73	27	72	28
100 to 499 workers	70	30	70	30	72	28
500 workers or more	74	26	76	24	72	28
Geographic Areas[3]						
New England	74	26	72	28	82	18
Middle Atlantic	76	24	73	27	89	11
East North Central	75	25	73	27	85	15
West North Central	71	29	72	28	69	31
South Atlantic	65	35	64	36	66	34
East South Central	62	38	65	35	54	46
West South Central	62	38	65	35	52	48
Mountain	67	33	67	33	66	34
Pacific	70	30	68	32	77	23

[1]Includes workers in the private nonfarm economy except those in private households, and workers in the public sector, except the federal government.
[2]The percentile groupings are based on the average wage for each occupation surveyed, which may include workers both above and below the threshold.
[3]The states that comprise the Census divisions are: New England—Connecticut, Maine, Massachusetts, New Hampshire, Rhode Island, and Vermont; Middle Atlantic—New Jersey, New York, and Pennsylvania; South Atlantic—Delaware, District of Columbia, Florida, Georgia, Maryland, North Carolina, South Carolina, Virginia, and West Virginia; East South Central—Alabama, Kentucky, Mississippi, and Tennessee; West South Central—Arkansas, Louisiana, Oklahoma, and Texas; East North Central—Illinois, Indiana, Michigan, Ohio, and Wisconsin; West North Central—Iowa, Kansas, Minnesota, Missouri, Nebraska, North Dakota, and South Dakota; Mountain—Arizona, Colorado, Idaho, Montana, Nevada, New Mexico, Utah, and Wyoming; and Pacific—Alaska, California, Hawaii, Oregon, and Washington.
. . . = Not available or not applicable.

Table 6-16. Access to Paid Sick Leave, Vacation, and Holidays, March 2011

(Percent.)

Characteristic	Civilian[1]			Private industry			State and local government		
	Paid sick leave	Paid vacation	Paid holidays	Paid sick leave	Paid vacation	Paid holidays	Paid sick leave	Paid vacation	Paid holidays
ALL WORKERS	67	74	42	63	77	38	89	60	59
Worker Characteristics									
Management, professional, and related	87	74	59	86	87	56	90	43	64
Management, business, and financial	91	94	59	91	96	59	...	...	...
Professional and related	85	67	59	83	83	55	90	36	65
Teachers	84	17	64	...	...	...	88	12	69
Primary, secondary, and special education school teachers	94	12	75	...	...	...	96	9	78
Registered nurses	81	82	63	...	...	...	...	...	...
Service	50	61	28	43	58	24	84	75	51
Protective service	69	77	42	39	62	25	89	87	53
Sales and office	68	80	42	66	79	41	90	85	54
Sales and related	56	69	33	55	69	33	...	...	...
Office and administrative support	76	86	48	74	86	46	91	86	55
Natural resources, construction, and maintenance	56	81	28	51	80	26	94	94	45
Construction, extraction, farming, fishing, and forestry	44	72	22	38	69	19	...	...	...
Installation, maintenance, and repair	67	91	35	64	90	33	...	...	...
Production, transportation, and material moving	55	82	33	54	83	32	87	63	59
Production	55	90	31	54	90	31	...	...	...
Transportation and material moving	56	74	35	54	75	33	...	...	...
Full-time workers	79	87	48	75	91	45	98	67	64
Part-time workers	28	35	20	27	37	19	41	21	29
Union workers	84	74	59	71	90	49	97	57	70
Nonunion workers	64	74	38	62	76	37	83	62	49
Average Wage Within the Following Percentiles[2]									
Lowest 25 percent	36	53	21	32	51	18	75	56	44
Lowest 10 percent	23	40	13	21	38	11	62	41	37
Second 25 percent	69	83	43	66	84	41	93	84	57
Third 25 percent	79	89	47	74	90	43	94	70	63
Highest 25 percent	88	78	60	85	89	56	96	36	71
Highest 10 percent	90	75	61	87	90	58	98	34	64
Establishment Characteristics									
Goods-producing industries	56	88	31	56	88	31	...	...	...
Service-providing industries	69	72	43	64	75	40	89	59	59
Education and health services	83	66	58	78	80	54	90	43	64
Educational services	87	40	61	76	57	46	90	36	65
Elementary and secondary schools	90	27	70	...	...	...	91	27	72
Junior colleges, colleges, and universities	86	68	47	82	72	54	88	66	43
Health care and social assistance	79	84	55	78	84	55	91	90	55
Hospitals	89	90	70	...	...	...	93	93	49
Public administration	89	88	53	...	...	...	89	88	53
Number of Workers									
1 to 99 workers	55	70	28	54	70	27	78	66	44
1 to 49 workers	53	68	25	52	68	25	72	68	37
50 to 99 workers	60	75	35	58	76	33	87	64	56
100 workers or more	78	79	54	73	86	51	91	59	61
100 to 499 workers	69	79	47	67	82	45	87	59	60
500 workers or more	86	78	61	82	90	60	92	59	61
Geographic Areas[3]									
New England	72	71	49	70	75	44	84	48	81
Middle Atlantic	71	74	52	67	76	49	90	58	70
East North Central	62	74	44	58	78	41	85	52	63
West North Central	66	72	34	61	76	30	89	56	50
South Atlantic	65	77	40	60	79	36	93	68	56
East South Central	65	76	38	58	78	38	92	67	38
West South Central	68	75	39	64	80	35	86	52	59
Mountain	66	74	38	63	77	35	84	55	52
Pacific	69	74	37	65	75	33	93	68	58

[1]Includes workers in the private nonfarm economy except those in private households, and workers in the public sector, except the federal government.
[2]The percentile groupings are based on the average wage for each occupation surveyed, which may include workers both above and below the threshold.
[3]The states that comprise the Census divisions are: New England—Connecticut, Maine, Massachusetts, New Hampshire, Rhode Island, and Vermont; Middle Atlantic—New Jersey, New York, and Pennsylvania; South Atlantic—Delaware, District of Columbia, Florida, Georgia, Maryland, North Carolina, South Carolina, Virginia, and West Virginia; East South Central—Alabama, Kentucky, Mississippi, and Tennessee; West South Central—Arkansas, Louisiana, Oklahoma, and Texas; East North Central—Illinois, Indiana, Michigan, Ohio, and Wisconsin; West North Central—Iowa, Kansas, Minnesota, Missouri, Nebraska, North Dakota, and South Dakota; Mountain—Arizona, Colorado, Idaho, Montana, Nevada, New Mexico, Utah, and Wyoming; and Pacific—Alaska, California, Hawaii, Oregon, and Washington.
. . . = Not available or not applicable.

NOTES AND DEFINITIONS

OCCUPATIONAL EARNINGS

Collection and Coverage

Tables 6-17 through 6-22 present occupational pay estimates for the nation. The data were compiled from locality data collected between December 2009 and January 2011. The average reference period is July 2010.

Concepts and Definitions

Earnings are regular payments from the employer to the employee as compensation for straight-time hourly work, or for any salaried work performed. The following components were included as part of earnings:

- Incentive pay, including commissions, production bonuses, and piece rates
- Cost-of-living allowances
- Hazard pay
- Payments of income deferred due to participation in a salary reduction plan
- Deadhead pay, defined as pay given to transportation workers returning in a vehicle without freight or passengers

Work levels are standardized measures of duties and responsibilities that apply to all occupations.

Percentiles designate position in the earnings distribution and are calculated from individual worker earnings and the hours those workers are scheduled to work. Table 6-22 provides estimates on the mean hourly wage for the 10th percentile, the 25th percentile, the 50th percentile (the median), the 75th percentile, and the 90th percentile of occupational wages, by ownership sector and for full- and part-time workers within the sectors.

An *incentive worker* is any employee whose earnings are at least partly tied to commissions, piece rates, production bonuses, or other incentives based on production or sales.

A *time-based worker* is any employee whose earnings are tied to an hourly rate or salary, and not to a specific level of production.

Sources of Additional Information

An extensive description of the sampling, weighting, and estimation steps and many additional detailed tables are available in BLS Bulletin 2753, "National Compensation Survey: Occupational Earnings in the United States, 2010," which is available on the BLS Web site at <http://www.bls.gov>.

Table 6-17. Mean Hourly Earnings[1] and Weekly Hours, by Selected Worker and Establishment Characteristics, National Compensation Survey, 2010

(Dollars, number of hours.)

Characteristic	Civilian workers		Private workers		State and local government workers	
	Mean hourly earnings	Mean weekly hours[2]	Mean hourly earnings	Mean weekly hours[2]	Mean hourly earnings	Mean weekly hours[2]
TOTAL	21.29	35.1	20.47	34.9	26.08	36.2
Worker Characteristics[3]						
Management, professional, and related occupations	34.49	36.7	34.99	37.0	33.02	35.9
Management, business, and financial occupations	38.81	39.3	39.42	39.7	35.32	37.4
Professional and related occupations	32.55	35.6	32.57	35.7	32.50	35.6
Service occupations	12.14	30.7	10.62	29.7	19.32	36.4
Sales and office occupations	16.44	34.7	16.35	34.5	17.39	36.4
Sales and related occupations	17.11	32.3	17.11	32.3	16.65	33.9
Office and administrative support occupations	16.09	36.1	15.90	36.0	17.42	36.5
Natural resources, construction, and maintenance occupations	21.21	39.0	21.24	39.0	20.97	38.8
Construction and extraction occupations	21.18	39.0	21.31	39.0	20.13	38.7
Installation, maintenance, and repair occupations	21.40	39.2	21.34	39.2	21.98	39.2
Production, transportation, and material moving occupations	16.00	37.1	15.88	37.2	19.52	34.4
Production occupations	16.26	38.9	16.18	38.8	21.69	39.5
Transportation and material moving occupations	15.73	35.4	15.55	35.6	18.86	33.1
Full-time workers	22.77	39.5	22.02	39.6	26.75	38.9
Part-time workers	12.10	20.7	11.78	21.0	16.39	18.3
Union workers	26.04	36.6	23.13	36.3	29.72	37.0
Nonunion workers	20.46	34.8	20.19	34.8	23.12	35.6
Time workers	21.06	34.9	20.16	34.7	26.07	36.2
Incentive workers	26.04	38.4	26.03	38.4	. . .	. . .
Establishment Characteristics						
Goods-producing	(4)	(4)	22.04	39.4	(4)	(4)
Service-providing	(4)	(4)	20.09	34.0	(4)	(4)
Number of Workers						
1–49 workers	17.86	33.5	17.80	33.6	19.61	33.0
50–99 workers	19.24	34.3	19.10	34.2	21.40	35.8
100–499 workers	20.88	35.9	20.42	35.8	24.31	36.0
500 workers or more	27.02	36.9	26.65	37.0	27.68	36.7

[1]Earnings are the straight-time hourly wages or salaries paid to employees. They include incentive pay, cost-of-living adjustments, and hazard pay. Excluded are premium pay for overtime, vacations, and holidays; nonproduction bonuses; and tips. The mean is computed by totaling the pay of all workers and dividing by the number of workers, weighted by hours.
[2]Mean weekly hours are the hours an employee is scheduled to work in a week, not including overtime.
[3]Employees are classified as working either a full-time or part-time schedule based on the definition used by each establishment. Union workers are those whose wages are determined through collective bargaining. Wages of time workers are based solely on hourly rate or salary; incentive workers are those whose wages are at least partly based on productivity payments such as piece rates, commissions, and production bonuses.
[4]Classification of establishments into goods-producing and service-producing industries applies to private industry only.
. . . = Not available.

Table 6-18. Mean Hourly Earnings[1] for Civilian Industry Workers by Size of Establishment, National Compensation Survey, 2010

(Dollars.)

Characteristic	Civilian workers	1–49 workers	50–99 workers	100–499 workers	500 workers or more
TOTAL	21.29	17.86	19.24	20.88	27.02
Worker Characteristics					
Management, professional, and related occupations	34.49	30.52	33.18	34.48	37.02
Management, business, and financial occupations	38.81	34.09	38.80	40.52	41.51
Professional and related occupations	32.55	28.36	30.01	31.52	35.52
Service occupations	12.14	10.08	10.09	12.50	16.01
Sales and office occupations	16.44	15.93	16.82	15.92	18.06
Sales and related occupations	17.11	16.66	18.84	15.90	22.49
Office and administrative support occupations	16.09	15.39	15.69	15.92	17.43
Natural resources, construction, and maintenance occupations	21.21	19.32	21.53	22.92	24.24
Construction and extraction occupations	21.18	. . .	. . .	. . .	. . .
Installation, maintenance, and repair occupations	21.40	19.47	21.72	22.23	24.63
Production, transportation, and material moving occupations	16.00	14.36	14.63	15.57	20.28
Production occupations	16.26	14.68	15.15	16.02	19.40
Transportation and material moving occupations	15.73	14.07	14.13	15.05	21.36

[1]Earnings are the straight-time hourly wages or salaries paid to employees. They include incentive pay, cost-of-living adjustments, and hazard pay. Excluded are premium pay for overtime, vacations, and holidays; nonproduction bonuses; and tips. The mean is computed by totaling the pay of all workers and dividing by the number of workers, weighed by hours.
. . . = Not available.

Table 6-19. Mean Hourly Earnings[1] for Private Industry Workers by Size of Establishment, National Compensation Survey, 2010

(Dollars.)

Characteristic	Private industry workers	1–49 workers	50–99 workers	100–499 workers	500 workers or more
TOTAL	20.47	17.80	19.10	20.42	26.65
Worker Characteristics					
Management, professional, and related occupations	34.99	30.88	33.90	35.20	38.98
Management, business, and financial occupations	39.42	34.54	39.05	41.16	43.35
Professional and related occupations	32.57	28.66	30.79	31.80	36.98
Service occupations	10.62	9.87	9.61	11.11	12.85
Sales and office occupations	16.35	15.94	16.85	15.86	18.06
Sales and related occupations	17.11	16.67	18.87	15.91	22.77
Office and administrative support occupations	15.90	15.39	15.67	15.82	17.14
Natural resources, construction, and maintenance occupations	21.24	19.37	21.83	23.27	24.98
Construction and extraction occupations	21.31	. . .	. . .	. . .	. . .
Installation, maintenance, and repair occupations	21.34	19.47	21.91	22.33	25.26
Production, transportation, and material moving occupations	15.88	14.32	14.60	15.54	20.19
Production occupations	16.18	14.64	15.11	15.97	19.24
Transportation and material moving occupations	15.55	14.04	14.10	15.03	21.62

[1]Earnings are the straight-time hourly wages or salaries paid to employees. They include incentive pay, cost-of-living adjustments, and hazard pay. Excluded are premium pay for overtime, vacations, and holidays; nonproduction bonuses; and tips. The mean is computed by totaling the pay of all workers and dividing by the number of workers, weighed by hours.
. . . = Not available.

Table 6-20. Mean Hourly Earnings[1] by Major Occupational Groups for Full and Part-Time Workers,[2] National Compensation Survey, 2010

(Dollars.)

Characteristic	Full-time			Part-time		
	Civilian workers	Private industry workers	State and local government workers	Civilian workers	Private industry workers	State and local government workers
TOTAL	22.77	22.02	26.75	12.10	11.78	16.39
Worker Characteristics						
Management, professional, and related occupations	35.02	35.50	33.61	26.63	27.79	22.19
Management, business, and financial occupations	38.87	39.48	35.39	35.01	35.75	30.86
Professional and related occupations	33.16	33.14	33.19	25.96	27.10	21.70
Service occupations	13.62	11.69	20.10	8.81	8.65	11.67
Sales and office occupations	17.59	17.57	17.75	10.66	10.59	12.49
Sales and related occupations	19.97	19.99	17.80	9.39	9.38	10.60
Office and administrative support occupations	16.57	16.38	17.74	12.27	12.24	12.67
Natural resources, construction, and maintenance occupations	21.39	21.42	21.14	13.97	13.99	13.81
Construction and extraction occupations	21.29	21.41	20.26	14.91	15.13	13.29
Installation, maintenance, and repair occupations	21.61	21.54	22.18	13.98	14.10	12.55
Production, transportation, and material moving occupations	16.53	16.40	20.14	10.94	10.73	15.17
Production occupations	16.48	16.39	21.68	10.73	10.69	22.09
Transportation and material moving occupations	16.58	16.41	19.59	11.00	10.75	15.07

[1]Earnings are the straight-time hourly wages or salaries paid to employees. They include incentive pay, cost-of-living adjustments, and hazard pay. Excluded are premium pay for overtime, vacations, and holidays; nonproduction bonuses; and tips. The mean is computed by totaling the pay of all workers and dividing by the number of workers, weighted by hours.
[2]Employees are classified as working either a full-time or part-time schedule based on the definition used by each establishment. Union workers are those whose wages are determined through collective bargaining. Wages of time workers are based solely on hourly rate or salary; incentive workers are those whose wages are at least partly based on productivity payments such as piece rates, commissions, and production bonuses.

Table 6-21. Mean Hourly Earnings[1] for Civilian and Private Industry Workers Paid on Time or Incentive Basis,[2] National Compensation Survey, 2010

(Dollars.)

Characteristic	Time		Incentive	
	Civilian workers	Private industry workers	Civilian workers	Private industry workers
TOTAL	21.06	20.16	26.04	26.03
Worker Characteristics				
Management, professional, and related occupations	34.20	34.61	48.78	48.70
Management, business, and financial occupations	38.54	39.14	44.38	44.38
Professional and related occupations	32.32	32.25	59.68	59.48
Service occupations	12.09	10.54	15.42	15.42
Sales and office occupations	15.54	15.34	25.00	25.00
Sales and related occupations	14.25	14.22	27.48	27.49
Office and administrative support occupations	16.09	15.89	16.08	16.08
Natural resources, construction, and maintenance occupations	21.14	21.16	22.58	22.58
Construction and extraction occupations	. . .	21.33	. . .	19.30
Installation, maintenance, and repair occupations	21.23	21.14	23.19	23.19
Production, transportation, and material moving occupations	15.90	15.77	17.91	17.91
Production occupations	16.24	16.15	17.03	17.03
Transportation and material moving occupations	15.54	15.33	18.30	18.30

[1]Earnings are the straight-time hourly wages or salaries paid to employees. They include incentive pay, cost-of-living adjustments, and hazard pay. Excluded are premium pay for overtime, vacations, and holidays; nonproduction bonuses; and tips. The mean is computed by totaling the pay of all workers and dividing by the number of workers, weighed by hours.
[2]Earnings of time workers are based solely on hourly rate or salary. Incentive workers are those whose earnings are at least partially based on productivity payments such as piece rates, commissions, and production bonuses.
. . . = Not available.

Table 6-22. Private Industry Workers: Hourly Wage Percentiles,[1] 2010

(Dollars.)

Occupation	Wages fall at or below the following percentiles:				
	10	25	50	75	90
ALL OCCUPATIONS	8.25	10.69	15.87	24.81	37.89
Management	21.64	29.11	40.14	55.74	72.81
Chief executives	26.22	50.06	83.67	119.58	158.82
General and operations managers	21.88	29.81	40.62	60.94	86.86
Advertising and promotions managers	18.09	21.94	32.53	46.95	61.78
Marketing and sales managers	25.15	34.40	46.89	63.46	86.72
Marketing managers	28.00	35.83	46.15	62.02	76.92
Sales managers	24.16	32.51	47.31	67.40	93.05
Public relations managers	18.67	21.64	30.00	40.87	52.82
Administrative services managers	20.20	25.40	32.40	39.38	48.56
Computer and information systems managers	36.32	43.27	54.90	65.27	77.27
Financial managers	23.18	29.63	41.67	57.69	75.77
Human resources managers	24.43	29.59	37.92	51.41	67.88
Compensation and benefits managers	20.67	27.53	32.76	49.41	56.66
Training and development managers	32.83	33.89	42.71	57.69	74.87
Industrial production managers	27.92	34.10	41.39	49.89	63.04
Purchasing managers	23.40	30.29	39.09	56.07	70.34
Transportation, storage, and distribution managers	22.49	25.96	33.31	48.28	62.34
Agricultural managers	15.00	21.64	37.11	46.82	57.73
Farm, ranch, and other agricultural managers	15.00	21.64	37.11	46.82	57.73
Construction managers	23.38	29.57	38.44	48.08	55.72
Education administrators	17.92	22.56	29.76	38.16	55.11
Education administrators, preschool and child care center/program	14.68	18.09	27.54	31.35	31.35
Education administrators, elementary and secondary school	19.00	26.63	33.74	42.31	50.18
Education administrators, postsecondary	21.45	24.84	31.84	49.82	66.76
Engineering managers	36.29	48.89	58.84	68.30	76.68
Food service managers	16.10	19.45	22.85	30.14	37.35
Funeral directors	14.00	21.64	28.75	32.75	34.75
Gaming managers	31.50	33.00	33.75	34.10	35.91
Lodging managers	15.17	15.17	17.48	24.60	33.95
Medical and health services managers	23.35	30.65	37.97	48.32	59.47
Natural sciences managers	29.78	33.65	41.14	48.75	67.60
Property, real estate, and community association managers	16.10	20.00	29.25	33.65	48.08
Social and community service managers	15.06	21.06	26.44	32.79	38.32
Business and Financial Operations	18.47	22.77	28.97	37.64	49.15
Buyers and purchasing agents	19.48	22.21	27.19	34.10	43.26
Purchasing agents and buyers, farm products	20.94	23.41	28.85	34.98	44.53
Wholesale and retail buyers, except farm products	19.48	20.90	26.69	33.65	42.62
Purchasing agents, except wholesale, retail, and farm products	19.21	22.60	27.90	34.20	43.46
Claims adjusters, appraisers, examiners, and investigators	18.14	22.10	28.33	33.41	38.94
Claims adjusters, examiners, and investigators	18.14	22.10	28.32	33.33	38.94
Insurance appraisers, auto damage	18.67	24.53	28.81	33.81	38.23
Compliance officers, except agriculture, construction, health and safety, and transportation	20.19	23.02	28.85	36.53	44.73
Cost estimators	19.75	21.85	29.57	39.42	49.04
Human resources, training, and labor relations specialists	17.88	21.61	27.73	36.13	45.13
Employment, recruitment, and placement specialists	15.39	19.00	23.44	31.82	39.71
Compensation, benefits, and job analysis specialists	20.19	21.99	27.46	33.99	42.07
Training and development specialists	16.88	24.51	31.25	41.30	45.58
Logisticians	20.09	24.04	32.22	39.85	49.23
Management analysts	22.83	29.35	37.50	51.98	63.40
Meeting and convention planners	15.87	20.19	25.38	36.64	42.31
Accountants and auditors	18.32	22.57	27.51	34.62	44.60
Appraisers and assessors of real estate	16.83	17.63	26.44	36.06	45.68
Budget analysts	22.42	28.63	34.77	39.60	50.70
Credit analysts	19.37	21.56	27.40	36.55	48.46
Financial analysts and advisors	20.31	25.64	33.41	45.61	58.81
Financial analysts	23.95	27.40	35.31	45.67	62.57
Personal financial advisors	15.38	19.82	26.43	47.36	58.01
Insurance underwriters	19.73	23.08	29.51	40.29	50.38
Financial examiners	21.12	23.21	31.19	34.99	62.09
Loan counselors and officers	16.41	20.25	27.98	36.51	49.42
Loan counselors	12.02	13.78	21.42	30.33	38.67
Loan officers	16.41	20.60	28.24	37.17	49.57
Tax examiners, collectors, preparers, and revenue agents	15.50	17.82	27.64	30.77	30.77
Tax preparers	15.50	15.50	18.84	30.77	30.77
Computer and Mathematical Science	20.25	26.44	36.06	45.89	55.91
Computer and information scientists, research	35.48	43.83	52.55	63.50	82.71
Computer programmers	20.91	26.04	34.28	39.20	46.93
Computer software engineers	28.18	35.81	43.40	52.49	60.67
Computer software engineers, applications	27.89	34.40	42.06	50.96	57.69
Computer software engineers, systems software	30.47	37.52	44.74	54.62	64.31
Computer support specialists	15.06	19.09	23.70	30.30	39.64
Computer systems analysts	26.57	32.07	39.46	47.12	54.69
Database administrators	22.16	26.72	39.81	50.60	60.90
Network and computer systems administrators	19.98	25.27	32.08	40.76	48.78
Network systems and data communications analysts	19.10	23.08	31.25	41.68	49.80
Actuaries	27.80	32.45	40.96	54.21	66.34
Operations research analysts	21.39	25.63	34.90	49.15	60.10
Statisticians	31.72	36.25	44.71	49.79	65.03

[1]Percentiles designate position in the earnings distribution and are calculated from individual worker earnings and the hours they are scheduled to work.

Table 6-22. Private Industry Workers: Hourly Wage Percentiles,[1] 2010—*Continued*

(Dollars.)

Occupation	Wages fall at or below the following percentiles:				
	10	25	50	75	90
Architecture and Engineering	19.64	26.00	34.00	44.46	56.24
Architects, except naval	18.33	22.60	29.57	33.65	48.08
Architects, except landscape and naval	18.00	22.53	29.99	36.06	48.08
Landscape architects	18.80	23.74	25.63	30.92	32.79
Surveyors, cartographers, and photogrammetrists	20.44	24.19	30.29	38.46	56.00
Surveyors	20.44	25.33	31.75	38.46	56.82
Engineers	26.92	32.16	39.89	49.84	61.50
Aerospace engineers	34.28	39.31	48.13	59.95	70.03
Biomedical engineers	24.04	27.25	32.34	43.42	46.50
Chemical engineers	30.53	35.51	41.11	57.65	68.25
Civil engineers	22.75	28.28	36.29	44.48	54.21
Computer hardware engineers	31.42	37.72	46.64	57.68	71.99
Electrical and electronics engineers	26.64	32.00	39.41	47.31	58.17
Electrical engineers	25.67	30.46	38.32	45.16	56.21
Electronics engineers, except computer	27.38	33.45	41.45	49.40	63.47
Environmental engineers	20.84	28.13	34.37	50.97	51.65
Industrial engineers, including health and safety	25.82	29.03	35.78	43.19	54.08
Health and safety engineers, except mining safety engineers and inspectors	26.83	30.36	36.37	52.53	60.05
Industrial engineers	25.13	28.85	35.35	41.60	50.49
Materials engineers	28.89	30.84	39.57	54.57	61.82
Mechanical engineers	25.96	30.80	37.39	45.26	54.25
Mining and geological engineers, including mining safety engineers	26.89	30.50	39.67	53.61	113.46
Nuclear engineers	33.63	38.97	44.62	47.99	59.63
Petroleum engineers	30.29	40.39	51.62	62.26	82.05
Drafters	16.20	18.82	23.54	30.00	36.56
Architectural and civil drafters	16.34	18.75	23.60	31.25	36.54
Electrical and electronics drafters	15.75	18.61	27.00	28.96	34.18
Mechanical drafters	17.11	19.46	23.08	26.87	32.00
Engineering technicians, except drafters	15.43	20.17	25.72	31.13	37.09
Aerospace engineering and operations technicians	22.82	25.24	30.29	33.75	39.10
Civil engineering technicians	12.00	13.00	15.95	22.50	31.00
Electrical and electronic engineering technicians	17.77	21.45	26.04	31.13	36.73
Electro-mechanical technicians	18.68	20.37	26.83	30.59	30.59
Environmental engineering technicians	14.90	18.00	19.00	22.50	30.78
Industrial engineering technicians	17.11	20.93	26.02	31.25	36.40
Mechanical engineering technicians	19.00	21.35	26.71	29.27	34.55
Surveying and mapping technicians	11.00	14.84	20.20	29.86	38.52
Life, Physical, and Social Science	16.83	21.71	28.89	39.62	52.50
Life scientists	21.23	26.09	37.14	44.34	56.49
Agricultural and food scientists	36.67	37.39	43.27	43.99	47.52
Food scientists and technologists	36.67	37.39	43.27	43.99	47.52
Biological scientists	20.14	23.60	36.32	42.32	52.46
Biochemists and biophysicists	20.12	33.65	42.32	50.03	59.71
Microbiologists	27.62	29.27	36.01	40.48	44.34
Medical scientists	21.58	26.92	37.86	47.51	66.22
Physical scientists	21.64	25.81	35.13	46.32	60.67
Astronomers and physicists	33.36	48.57	56.50	69.21	108.94
Physicists	31.28	48.00	55.14	70.43	108.94
Chemists and materials scientists	23.01	26.78	34.21	46.21	57.31
Chemists	22.31	25.75	31.97	41.80	55.59
Materials scientists	35.10	39.23	46.21	55.05	62.60
Environmental scientists and geoscientists	19.33	24.61	32.43	39.56	49.46
Environmental scientists and specialists, including health	18.67	21.65	30.13	35.31	49.46
Geoscientists, except hydrologists and geographers	23.46	28.48	36.54	40.34	51.92
Economists	18.38	28.03	36.23	43.27	51.96
Market and survey researchers	19.23	24.51	32.15	42.14	57.35
Market research analysts	19.23	24.51	30.89	39.31	54.55
Psychologists	18.11	21.76	28.44	40.63	56.81
Clinical, counseling, and school psychologists	18.11	24.49	28.83	40.63	56.81
Miscellaneous social scientists and related workers	14.00	15.24	26.73	30.87	50.37
Agricultural and food science technicians	14.63	15.50	19.41	20.72	28.35
Biological technicians	13.51	15.58	19.65	25.48	31.92
Chemical technicians	14.78	17.36	22.59	27.29	32.78
Geological and petroleum technicians	18.91	21.16	32.57	33.17	47.89
Nuclear technicians	28.48	33.99	34.94	39.78	48.36
Social science research assistants	15.98	17.01	18.68	25.00	26.04
Miscellaneous life, physical, and social science technicians	13.93	16.77	21.33	25.00	34.90
Environmental science and protection technicians, including health	11.41	18.00	23.48	25.00	34.90
Community and Social Services	11.25	13.80	17.31	21.78	28.16
Counselors	11.59	14.14	18.37	22.01	26.82
Substance abuse and behavioral disorder counselors	12.26	13.46	17.48	22.01	25.00
Educational, vocational, and school counselors	14.14	17.09	20.19	25.49	39.19
Marriage and family therapists	15.39	17.93	18.80	20.00	26.67
Mental health counselors	14.55	17.37	18.55	23.28	28.25
Rehabilitation counselors	10.50	11.59	14.91	19.71	21.22
Social workers	13.46	15.76	19.19	24.45	29.71
Child, family, and school social workers	12.00	14.09	16.35	20.30	24.45
Medical and public health social workers	17.34	20.35	24.42	29.28	31.00
Mental health and substance abuse social workers	13.46	15.96	18.27	22.59	26.92
Miscellaneous community and social service specialists	9.99	11.38	14.23	17.24	20.00
Health educators	12.91	15.32	18.99	33.52	40.26
Social and human service assistants	9.55	10.73	12.69	15.00	18.62
Clergy	13.25	14.10	17.05	23.26	25.74
Directors, religious activities and education	16.76	18.46	23.48	25.68	44.19

[1]Percentiles designate position in the earnings distribution and are calculated from individual worker earnings and the hours they are scheduled to work.

Table 6-22. Private Industry Workers: Hourly Wage Percentiles,[1] 2010—*Continued*

(Dollars.)

Occupation	Wages fall at or below the following percentiles:				
	10	25	50	75	90
Legal	15.00	19.92	29.92	48.08	75.00
Lawyers	23.71	33.65	50.25	72.12	96.46
Paralegals and legal assistants	12.00	16.48	21.64	28.85	34.62
Miscellaneous legal support workers	13.59	16.15	21.15	24.28	33.78
Law clerks	12.00	15.87	20.00	28.05	28.05
Title examiners, abstractors, and searchers	14.94	17.14	21.13	24.28	33.20
Education, Training, and Library	9.90	12.17	22.09	35.63	52.10
Postsecondary teachers	22.39	29.88	40.43	58.06	85.86
Business teachers, postsecondary	24.08	26.71	47.69	69.05	95.19
Math and computer teachers, postsecondary	28.04	33.08	45.59	58.51	79.68
Computer science teachers, postsecondary	33.40	40.05	50.96	63.18	87.88
Mathematical science teachers, postsecondary	28.04	33.08	37.42	53.03	75.47
Engineering and architecture teachers, postsecondary	39.52	48.90	72.16	92.72	103.40
Engineering teachers, postsecondary	39.52	48.90	75.00	92.72	103.40
Life sciences teachers, postsecondary	31.65	42.31	49.67	60.45	150.95
Biological science teachers, postsecondary	31.65	42.31	49.67	60.45	150.95
Physical sciences teachers, postsecondary	31.97	46.24	52.91	62.13	89.20
Chemistry teachers, postsecondary	31.97	36.01	46.33	55.08	78.17
Physics teachers, postsecondary	49.87	54.68	57.62	84.96	89.20
Social sciences teachers, postsecondary	32.37	35.47	47.22	56.54	75.59
Anthropology and archeology teachers, postsecondary	42.57	43.42	45.74	51.31	52.15
Economics teachers, postsecondary	38.87	50.53	64.49	76.49	105.38
Political science teachers, postsecondary	46.40	49.04	50.79	51.13	64.89
Psychology teachers, postsecondary	28.87	33.00	43.76	51.51	67.60
Sociology teachers, postsecondary	35.47	36.70	43.98	96.12	96.12
Health teachers, postsecondary	25.75	35.77	51.63	80.85	100.51
Health specialties teachers, postsecondary	23.34	37.73	65.21	90.21	112.64
Nursing instructors and teachers, postsecondary	31.43	35.77	39.39	42.27	48.96
Education and library science teachers, postsecondary	25.25	31.93	34.86	41.55	50.38
Education teachers, postsecondary	25.25	31.93	34.86	41.55	50.38
Law, criminal justice, and social work teachers, postsecondary	34.15	46.70	69.06	82.18	100.45
Law teachers, postsecondary	54.08	64.05	74.22	97.09	106.87
Arts, communications, and humanities teachers, postsecondary	25.00	31.08	37.76	49.99	67.80
Art, drama, and music teachers, postsecondary	24.28	27.71	34.48	40.85	44.83
Communications teachers, postsecondary	23.12	26.07	32.67	54.83	76.79
English language and literature teachers, postsecondary	25.30	35.63	42.26	52.35	74.32
Foreign language and literature teachers, postsecondary	29.81	37.76	49.99	60.59	88.20
History teachers, postsecondary	26.92	36.23	45.09	55.83	70.70
Philosophy and religion teachers, postsecondary	24.95	30.94	38.39	47.46	60.70
Miscellaneous postsecondary teachers	18.03	22.10	30.36	42.35	55.94
Vocational education teachers, postsecondary	15.93	20.00	25.29	33.25	37.29
Primary, secondary, and special education school teachers	10.50	14.07	21.98	31.92	40.34
Preschool and kindergarten teachers	9.70	11.00	14.00	18.62	25.19
Preschool teachers, except special education	9.65	10.97	13.82	17.25	23.31
Kindergarten teachers, except special education	14.07	14.07	22.51	28.99	33.30
Elementary and middle school teachers	16.00	20.39	25.66	32.15	40.29
Elementary school teachers, except special education	16.13	20.36	25.13	31.85	39.33
Middle school teachers, except special and vocational education	16.90	23.12	27.41	35.56	41.17
Secondary school teachers	19.89	25.29	33.25	40.54	53.75
Secondary school teachers, except special and vocational education	21.41	25.96	33.52	40.98	54.28
Special education teachers	17.95	22.36	29.29	35.13	63.62
Special education teachers, preschool, kindergarten, and elementary school	18.87	22.30	28.10	31.25	40.37
Special education teachers, secondary school	33.94	33.94	67.65	67.65	67.65
Other teachers and instructors	11.50	12.64	20.00	28.00	34.78
Self-enrichment education teachers	10.90	15.78	20.00	20.67	25.00
Archivists, curators, and museum technicians	19.02	22.07	27.30	40.87	40.87
Archivists	13.60	15.03	19.02	22.60	33.67
Curators	23.85	25.24	31.04	40.87	40.87
Librarians	19.44	22.24	28.37	34.01	44.39
Library technicians	12.79	15.23	17.71	21.04	27.47
Instructional coordinators	21.02	23.08	29.00	38.87	49.76
Teacher assistants	8.03	9.25	10.39	12.05	14.47
Arts, Design, Entertainment, Sports, and Media	12.00	16.83	23.73	32.52	45.67
Artists and related workers	15.00	16.98	26.11	37.50	49.60
Art directors	16.00	18.00	30.49	49.45	50.48
Multi-media artists and animators	16.98	16.98	23.54	33.52	39.79
Designers	11.99	16.25	22.43	31.25	39.70
Commercial and industrial designers	19.61	27.89	34.35	42.51	50.48
Fashion designers	20.37	24.04	40.14	49.81	49.81
Floral designers	7.50	8.76	10.50	11.99	15.00
Graphic designers	13.46	16.25	21.54	27.12	36.54
Interior designers	16.83	19.28	26.44	32.48	32.48
Merchandise displayers and window trimmers	13.45	14.46	19.77	22.43	24.67
Set and exhibit designers	13.65	13.65	19.23	29.62	33.69
Actors, producers, and directors	13.39	17.83	29.81	55.16	70.80
Producers and directors	14.42	19.59	34.54	55.35	79.11
Athletes, coaches, umpires, and related workers	8.50	10.64	18.00	29.08	37.12
Coaches and scouts	8.75	10.64	18.00	29.08	37.12
Umpires, referees, and other sports officials	5.88	6.99	9.50	13.43	22.41
Dancers and choreographers	15.00	18.59	25.00	26.65	50.00
Choreographers	15.00	18.59	18.59	25.00	26.00
Musicians, singers, and related workers	13.65	18.55	23.37	40.67	55.59
Music directors and composers	15.63	17.86	22.46	23.96	40.00
Musicians and singers	13.65	18.75	28.52	53.09	65.35
Announcers	8.17	13.14	20.74	24.12	69.71
Radio and television announcers	8.17	13.14	20.74	24.12	69.71

[1]Percentiles designate position in the earnings distribution and are calculated from individual worker earnings and the hours they are scheduled to work.

Table 6-22. Private Industry Workers: Hourly Wage Percentiles,[1] 2010—*Continued*

(Dollars.)

Occupation	Wages fall at or below the following percentiles:				
	10	25	50	75	90
Arts, Design, Entertainment, Sports, and Media—*Continued*					
News analysts, reporters and correspondents	15.23	18.27	27.57	36.49	68.24
Reporters and correspondents	14.84	17.50	25.96	33.79	57.08
Public relations specialists	16.06	21.26	26.44	37.05	51.15
Writers and editors	16.83	19.67	26.76	33.32	41.34
Editors	15.61	18.67	25.55	33.68	43.10
Technical writers	20.06	23.50	29.66	33.33	39.90
Writers and authors	15.25	19.50	25.72	33.17	41.34
Miscellaneous media and communication workers	15.38	17.99	22.52	24.83	27.57
Interpreters and translators	12.06	15.50	19.34	26.00	34.00
Broadcast and sound engineering technicians and radio operators	11.27	14.96	21.53	38.94	44.84
Audio and video equipment technicians	12.50	15.48	19.75	26.50	41.59
Broadcast technicians	9.22	12.25	18.02	33.41	38.94
Sound engineering technicians	12.00	32.65	41.21	49.86	53.82
Photographers	7.25	8.50	11.12	17.31	28.16
Television, video, and motion picture camera operators and editors	16.00	18.54	26.44	29.14	32.56
Camera operators, television, video, and motion picture	13.64	18.54	24.02	26.57	32.56
Healthcare Practitioner and Technical	15.09	20.06	27.28	36.00	50.89
Dentists	54.69	56.96	75.01	75.01	111.01
Dentists, general	52.88	56.96	75.01	75.01	144.38
Dietitians and nutritionists	19.90	21.15	24.08	26.53	31.54
Optometrists	36.76	40.63	46.42	55.00	55.77
Pharmacists	46.63	51.00	54.75	57.25	60.33
Physicians and surgeons	25.56	53.76	85.58	120.19	181.73
Anesthesiologists	86.54	103.84	132.48	184.73	197.80
Family and general practitioners	26.17	61.42	76.92	102.27	139.12
Internists, general	39.46	64.90	76.93	120.19	192.31
Obstetricians and gynecologists	66.33	95.70	105.56	109.14	130.23
Pediatricians, general	24.37	52.89	80.11	95.83	100.96
Psychiatrists	67.50	71.81	79.16	89.05	102.14
Surgeons	83.33	102.16	181.73	181.73	204.33
Physician assistants	32.69	36.75	43.20	49.51	55.57
Registered nurses	22.50	26.04	30.79	37.25	44.57
Therapists	21.01	25.21	31.23	37.85	45.46
Audiologists	16.83	25.23	28.85	33.65	37.22
Occupational therapists	26.93	30.09	35.62	41.00	50.58
Physical therapists	25.21	28.13	34.33	40.00	45.67
Radiation therapists	22.78	29.11	32.96	42.46	50.46
Recreational therapists	11.69	12.60	16.92	19.50	20.35
Respiratory therapists	19.99	23.31	25.37	28.97	33.90
Speech-language pathologists	22.21	24.56	30.87	40.34	55.25
Veterinarians	34.59	40.52	44.23	48.93	53.51
Clinical laboratory technologists and technicians	13.62	16.82	22.56	28.00	32.00
Medical and clinical laboratory technologists	18.55	22.75	26.57	30.45	34.00
Medical and clinical laboratory technicians	12.57	14.41	17.11	21.54	27.00
Dental hygienists	23.25	28.00	33.00	37.50	46.15
Diagnostic related technologists and technicians	17.00	21.49	27.54	33.25	38.10
Cardiovascular technologists and technicians	13.33	14.90	23.39	30.41	39.02
Diagnostic medical sonographers	25.55	29.56	34.00	38.61	44.52
Nuclear medicine technologists	31.00	31.73	34.60	36.77	39.46
Radiologic technologists and technicians	17.53	20.81	26.60	30.81	36.19
Emergency medical technicians and paramedics	10.00	11.28	12.75	15.50	19.02
Health diagnosing and treating practitioner support technicians	10.50	13.05	15.75	19.76	23.94
Dietetic technicians	7.50	8.00	11.47	13.15	29.57
Pharmacy technicians	10.00	12.24	14.49	16.30	18.94
Psychiatric technicians	10.00	12.05	13.05	15.89	20.00
Respiratory therapy technicians	18.72	21.72	26.52	30.00	31.52
Surgical technologists	14.56	17.00	19.50	22.90	25.00
Veterinary technologists and technicians	10.50	13.30	15.81	19.06	22.00
Licensed practical and licensed vocational nurses	15.00	17.00	19.28	22.13	25.78
Medical records and health information technicians	10.35	12.62	15.70	18.88	23.09
Opticians, dispensing	10.51	14.71	19.25	25.13	28.00
Miscellaneous health technologists and technicians	11.00	13.75	17.20	21.56	25.53
Occupational health and safety specialists and technicians	16.19	26.44	30.68	34.94	41.68
Occupational health and safety specialists	16.13	22.67	29.93	35.84	41.68
Occupational health and safety technicians	22.55	28.64	30.68	31.80	32.82
Miscellaneous healthcare practitioner and technical workers	14.61	19.50	27.06	28.95	31.68
Healthcare Support	8.75	10.00	11.92	14.75	18.00
Nursing, psychiatric, and home health aides	8.31	9.50	10.77	12.85	15.02
Home health aides	7.50	8.53	10.00	11.25	13.37
Nursing aides, orderlies, and attendants	9.00	10.00	11.40	13.42	15.69
Psychiatric aides	8.30	9.00	10.54	12.25	14.81
Occupational therapist assistants and aides	12.50	16.73	25.00	30.70	33.65
Occupational therapist assistants	15.72	22.00	25.00	30.70	33.65
Physical therapist assistants and aides	10.00	11.55	14.64	25.17	29.95
Physical therapist assistants	10.90	17.25	22.47	28.37	32.00
Physical therapist aides	9.26	10.35	12.20	13.42	14.27
Massage therapists	10.00	14.00	17.00	19.00	24.69
Miscellaneous healthcare support	9.55	11.47	14.00	17.00	20.31
Dental assistants	9.55	12.64	16.65	19.45	22.00
Medical assistants	10.07	11.62	13.86	16.31	18.66
Medical equipment preparers	10.55	12.16	14.50	18.32	21.56
Medical transcriptionists	11.67	13.74	15.57	17.88	20.85
Pharmacy aides	8.60	9.44	11.75	15.00	20.50
Veterinary assistants and laboratory animal caretakers	8.00	9.00	10.75	13.00	15.25

[1]Percentiles designate position in the earnings distribution and are calculated from individual worker earnings and the hours they are scheduled to work.

Table 6-22. Private Industry Workers: Hourly Wage Percentiles,[1] 2010—*Continued*

(Dollars.)

Occupation	Wages fall at or below the following percentiles:				
	10	25	50	75	90
Protective Service	8.00	9.22	10.95	14.07	18.10
Bailiffs, correctional officers, and jailers	8.50	8.86	10.00	12.05	20.68
Correctional officers and jailers	8.50	8.86	10.00	11.67	20.68
Police officers	15.05	16.54	20.34	23.05	24.84
Police and sheriff's patrol officers	15.05	16.54	20.34	23.05	24.84
Private detectives and investigators	11.03	13.50	14.77	19.36	26.51
Security guards and gaming surveillance officers	8.15	9.22	10.68	13.00	16.83
Security guards	8.15	9.22	10.68	12.97	16.92
Miscellaneous protective service workers	7.30	7.85	8.75	11.25	14.07
Lifeguards, ski patrol, and other recreational protective service workers	7.26	7.50	8.25	9.75	13.10
Food Preparation and Serving Related	3.72	7.25	8.00	10.00	13.16
First-line supervisors/managers, food preparation and serving workers	9.65	12.00	15.00	19.20	23.85
Chefs and head cooks	10.50	12.95	17.12	21.89	27.14
First-line supervisors/managers of food preparation and serving workers	9.50	11.97	14.80	18.41	23.13
Cooks	7.50	8.25	10.00	12.11	14.35
Cooks, fast food	7.25	7.27	8.00	8.85	10.00
Cooks, institution and cafeteria	8.50	9.75	11.83	14.26	17.84
Cooks, restaurant	8.00	9.00	10.75	12.50	14.31
Cooks, short order	7.25	8.00	9.00	10.90	13.25
Food preparation workers	7.25	7.80	8.64	10.68	13.00
Food service, tipped	2.13	3.09	4.85	8.00	9.00
Bartenders	3.65	4.65	7.25	8.50	10.00
Waiters and waitresses	2.13	2.65	4.23	7.25	8.16
Dining room and cafeteria attendants and bartender helpers	4.60	7.25	8.00	9.00	11.12
Fast food and counter workers	7.25	7.40	8.00	9.00	10.61
Combined food preparation and serving workers, including fast food	7.25	7.36	8.00	8.95	10.50
Counter attendants, cafeteria, food concession, and coffee shop	7.25	7.50	8.38	9.62	11.54
Food servers, nonrestaurant	4.00	7.25	8.40	10.20	13.57
Dishwashers	7.25	7.65	8.50	9.50	11.37
Hosts and hostesses, restaurant, lounge, and coffee shop	4.50	7.25	8.00	9.69	11.74
Building and Grounds Cleaning and Maintenance	8.00	8.75	10.41	13.63	17.92
First-line supervisors/managers, building and grounds cleaning and maintenance workers	11.85	14.16	16.83	21.17	24.02
First-line supervisors/managers of housekeeping and janitorial workers	11.50	14.00	16.73	20.85	23.76
First-line supervisors/managers of landscaping, lawn service, and groundskeeping workers	11.85	14.76	17.16	21.22	24.59
Building cleaning workers	7.75	8.50	10.00	12.75	16.93
Janitors and cleaners, except maids and housekeeping cleaners	7.92	8.75	10.50	13.49	17.91
Maids and housekeeping cleaners	7.52	8.12	9.18	11.01	14.00
Pest control workers	13.64	15.72	16.83	16.83	20.00
Grounds maintenance workers	8.00	9.14	10.65	13.28	16.48
Landscaping and groundskeeping workers	8.00	9.06	10.25	12.75	16.01
Pesticide handlers, sprayers, and applicators, vegetation	11.37	14.00	16.19	16.19	18.65
Tree trimmers and pruners	12.73	14.00	17.00	21.60	22.50
Personal Care and Service	7.25	8.00	9.50	12.28	17.58
First-line supervisors/managers of gaming workers	10.41	12.06	14.74	18.03	22.60
Gaming supervisors	11.94	13.70	16.73	22.22	25.63
Slot key persons	8.95	10.80	12.13	13.68	14.20
First-line supervisors/managers of personal service workers	10.59	12.88	15.51	17.55	20.64
Animal trainers	8.00	9.39	15.39	15.91	15.91
Nonfarm animal caretakers	7.50	8.25	9.69	12.00	16.41
Gaming services workers	5.64	6.07	7.00	8.00	8.93
Gaming dealers	5.57	6.00	6.89	7.84	8.29
Gaming and sports book writers and runners	7.25	7.50	8.25	10.00	14.76
Ushers, lobby attendants, and ticket takers	7.28	8.00	9.00	14.38	14.38
Miscellaneous entertainment attendants and related workers	7.25	7.50	8.25	10.39	13.19
Amusement and recreation attendants	7.25	7.31	8.00	9.25	13.19
Locker room, coatroom, and dressing room attendants	8.00	8.92	10.94	12.48	18.74
Funeral attendants	8.50	9.00	11.88	13.19	14.00
Barbers and cosmetologists	7.44	9.00	11.25	18.26	26.14
Hairdressers, hairstylists, and cosmetologists	7.37	9.00	11.25	18.27	26.14
Miscellaneous personal appearance workers	7.28	8.06	11.85	17.51	21.10
Manicurists and pedicurists	7.50	7.79	12.11	13.54	17.78
Shampooers	7.25	7.28	8.06	8.50	11.00
Skin care specialists	9.99	15.46	19.23	21.10	24.04
Baggage porters, bellhops, and concierges	7.25	8.25	10.30	13.00	16.53
Baggage porters and bellhops	7.25	7.73	8.60	10.50	13.00
Concierges	9.58	10.63	12.83	15.05	17.45
Tour and travel guides	7.75	8.41	10.50	17.32	17.32
Tour guides and escorts	7.75	8.41	10.00	17.32	17.32
Transportation attendants	9.00	17.50	32.30	42.48	48.77
Flight attendants	21.16	32.30	39.50	45.11	51.10
Transportation attendants, except flight attendants and baggage porters	7.25	7.25	10.37	12.81	14.57
Child care workers	7.25	8.00	9.00	10.50	12.50
Personal and home care aides	7.60	8.05	9.00	10.37	11.75
Recreation and fitness workers	7.87	9.00	11.58	15.99	22.28
Fitness trainers and aerobics instructors	8.00	10.00	15.48	22.00	30.00
Recreation workers	7.50	8.65	10.45	13.72	18.05
Residential advisors	10.73	12.50	14.19	16.39	21.29

[1]Percentiles designate position in the earnings distribution and are calculated from individual worker earnings and the hours they are scheduled to work.

Table 6-22. Private Industry Workers: Hourly Wage Percentiles,[1] 2010—*Continued*

(Dollars.)

Occupation	Wages fall at or below the following percentiles:				
	10	25	50	75	90
Sales and Related	7.77	9.00	12.00	19.23	30.91
First-line supervisors/managers, sales workers	10.84	13.93	17.89	23.52	33.38
First-line supervisors/managers of retail sales workers	10.84	13.70	17.36	21.64	28.85
First-line supervisors/managers of non-retail sales workers	10.11	16.84	22.60	37.01	53.26
Retail sales workers	7.50	8.25	9.85	12.50	16.88
Cashiers, all workers	7.33	8.00	8.90	10.55	13.04
Cashiers	7.33	8.00	8.88	10.50	12.82
Gaming change persons and booth cashiers	9.26	12.29	13.04	14.50	15.67
Counter and rental clerks and parts salespersons	7.84	9.00	12.00	16.72	21.42
Counter and rental clerks	7.25	8.00	9.56	12.56	17.75
Parts salespersons	8.81	11.00	14.71	17.93	21.64
Retail salespersons	7.75	8.75	10.71	13.95	19.19
Advertising sales agents	10.00	13.47	20.10	29.28	36.00
Insurance sales agents	12.79	16.56	22.84	32.48	47.34
Securities, commodities, and financial services sales agents	16.08	22.48	38.89	69.38	110.10
Travel agents	10.97	13.24	16.86	21.09	23.08
Sales representatives, wholesale and manufacturing	14.38	19.11	25.64	38.09	53.99
Sales representatives, wholesale and manufacturing, technical and scientific products ...	15.70	23.56	35.12	48.08	58.45
Sales representatives, wholesale and manufacturing, except technical and scientific products	13.26	17.50	23.22	31.49	45.10
Models, demonstrators, and product promoters	9.38	11.25	13.62	20.43	26.88
Demonstrators and product promoters	9.38	11.25	13.62	20.43	26.88
Real estate brokers and sales agents	11.00	12.40	14.86	21.65	44.25
Real estate brokers	3.63	12.30	17.72	31.86	38.83
Real estate sales agents	11.00	12.46	14.72	21.22	46.15
Sales engineers	19.14	29.11	32.27	39.30	55.06
Telemarketers	8.15	10.00	11.65	14.52	19.22
Miscellaneous sales and related workers	8.08	9.63	14.65	20.00	26.90
Door-to-door sales workers, news and street vendors, and related workers	8.00	8.00	8.50	12.00	12.00
Office and Administrative Support	9.60	11.80	14.90	18.75	23.37
First-line supervisors/managers of office and administrative support workers	15.00	17.90	21.63	26.98	31.53
Switchboard operators, including answering service	7.85	8.40	10.00	12.27	15.14
Telephone operators	9.00	9.50	12.60	15.00	23.23
Financial clerks	10.50	12.20	15.00	18.26	21.65
Bill and account collectors	9.37	12.02	14.50	17.93	23.89
Billing and posting clerks and machine operators	11.25	13.13	15.53	18.00	20.90
Bookkeeping, accounting, and auditing clerks	11.28	13.52	16.22	19.40	22.69
Gaming cage workers	9.32	9.71	10.50	12.60	13.50
Payroll and timekeeping clerks	13.50	15.95	18.17	21.38	25.08
Procurement clerks	11.38	14.00	16.57	19.95	22.21
Tellers	9.88	10.75	11.91	13.56	15.95
Brokerage clerks	13.71	15.42	18.20	21.15	27.03
Correspondence clerks	13.10	15.27	16.70	19.20	22.34
Credit authorizers, checkers, and clerks	11.80	13.60	16.97	19.81	24.45
Customer service representatives	9.87	12.00	14.69	18.19	22.60
Eligibility interviewers, government programs	11.25	14.19	17.00	17.90	22.76
File clerks	9.00	10.00	12.00	16.26	17.01
Hotel, motel, and resort desk clerks	7.76	8.50	9.84	11.30	13.67
Interviewers, except eligibility and loan	8.81	10.80	13.37	15.94	18.26
Library assistants, clerical	9.69	11.54	13.75	16.38	17.63
Loan interviewers and clerks	12.00	13.38	16.15	19.00	21.82
New accounts clerks	10.93	12.69	14.42	16.51	18.90
Order clerks	9.90	11.31	14.00	17.60	21.42
Human resources assistants, except payroll and timekeeping	12.50	14.75	18.17	20.67	23.23
Receptionists and information clerks	9.00	10.32	12.50	15.00	17.66
Reservation and transportation ticket agents and travel clerks	9.99	11.52	16.08	21.54	21.84
Cargo and freight agents	11.46	13.85	18.13	27.13	39.00
Couriers and messengers	8.25	8.44	10.40	12.24	14.53
Dispatchers	11.50	13.38	15.88	20.56	24.13
Police, fire, and ambulance dispatchers	11.20	11.56	12.52	14.25	17.88
Dispatchers, except police, fire, and ambulance	11.59	13.44	16.00	20.89	25.00
Meter readers, utilities	12.02	15.58	19.66	25.06	27.50
Production, planning, and expediting clerks	12.98	15.56	19.15	24.00	27.91
Shipping, receiving, and traffic clerks	9.00	10.30	12.52	15.53	18.86
Stock clerks and order fillers	7.75	8.63	10.56	13.78	17.00
Weighers, measurers, checkers, and samplers, recordkeeping	9.50	11.25	13.50	15.50	18.38
Secretaries and administrative assistants	12.11	14.85	18.27	23.17	28.69
Executive secretaries and administrative assistants	15.15	17.83	21.64	25.95	30.33
Legal secretaries	13.00	16.00	21.92	28.64	33.33
Medical secretaries	10.94	13.00	15.13	18.00	21.45
Secretaries, except legal, medical, and executive	10.80	13.20	16.09	18.77	22.84
Computer operators	12.03	14.28	18.00	21.63	24.76
Data entry and information processing workers	10.00	11.01	13.21	15.75	18.31
Data entry keyers	10.00	11.00	13.00	15.10	16.97
Word processors and typists	10.80	12.95	15.80	19.32	22.99
Desktop publishers	11.12	12.00	18.99	22.53	27.27
Insurance claims and policy processing clerks	11.54	13.50	16.75	19.69	23.08
Mail clerks and mail machine operators, except postal service	8.58	10.05	12.05	14.88	17.22
Office clerks, general	9.59	11.40	14.05	17.00	21.00
Office machine operators, except computer	9.00	10.19	12.50	14.82	16.47
Proofreaders and copy markers	10.00	11.01	19.20	21.11	22.62
Statistical assistants	12.96	16.63	19.02	20.43	24.86

[1]Percentiles designate position in the earnings distribution and are calculated from individual worker earnings and the hours they are scheduled to work.

Table 6-22. Private Industry Workers: Hourly Wage Percentiles,[1] 2010—*Continued*

(Dollars.)

Occupation	Wages fall at or below the following percentiles:				
	10	25	50	75	90
Farming, Fishing, and Forestry	7.25	8.13	10.67	16.14	21.65
First-line supervisors/managers of farming, fishing, and forestry workers	13.50	17.34	21.65	21.65	26.43
Graders and sorters, agricultural products	6.92	7.25	8.55	10.30	16.14
Miscellaneous agricultural workers	7.25	8.00	10.15	13.05	15.30
Farmworkers and laborers, crop, nursery, and greenhouse	7.25	8.25	10.00	12.22	16.25
Farmworkers, farm and ranch animals	7.25	7.50	7.58	10.80	15.00
Logging workers	8.71	13.67	17.76	18.65	25.24
Construction and Extraction	11.00	14.00	19.00	26.33	36.22
First-line supervisors/managers of construction trades and extraction workers	18.95	22.33	28.63	38.46	43.63
Boilermakers	15.78	15.78	23.35	30.27	30.65
Brickmasons, blockmasons, and stonemasons	12.47	16.00	24.82	28.59	39.03
Brickmasons and blockmasons	12.47	18.32	25.59	29.34	39.03
Stonemasons	10.00	11.00	14.50	16.00	25.50
Carpenters	13.53	16.00	20.23	26.38	36.99
Carpet, floor, and tile installers and finishers	13.03	16.00	18.50	20.00	24.00
Carpet installers	18.75	20.00	20.00	24.00	27.02
Tile and marble setters	13.03	15.00	17.07	20.00	24.00
Cement masons, concrete finishers, and terrazzo workers	13.50	16.00	20.13	24.81	29.50
Cement masons and concrete finishers	13.50	16.00	20.13	24.81	29.50
Construction laborers	9.01	10.50	14.00	19.98	27.85
Construction equipment operators	11.00	14.00	18.00	25.79	32.54
Paving, surfacing, and tamping equipment operators	10.87	12.39	15.89	20.67	23.67
Operating engineers and other construction equipment operators	11.50	14.50	19.35	28.00	33.96
Drywall installers, ceiling tile installers, and tapers	13.53	15.71	16.69	28.75	35.66
Drywall and ceiling tile installers	13.53	15.24	16.69	25.00	36.34
Tapers	15.71	15.71	18.50	32.29	34.31
Electricians	14.00	16.75	21.91	31.08	38.26
Glaziers	7.74	15.00	21.75	31.62	34.03
Insulation workers	10.26	13.00	16.00	19.53	22.31
Insulation workers, floor, ceiling, and wall	9.50	10.26	13.00	16.90	19.00
Insulation workers, mechanical	12.50	15.00	16.75	20.44	22.31
Painters and paperhangers	11.40	13.00	16.00	20.00	24.00
Painters, construction and maintenance	11.40	13.47	16.00	20.00	24.00
Pipelayers, plumbers, pipefitters, and steamfitters	14.00	17.87	23.75	32.45	40.89
Pipelayers	12.00	13.78	15.25	21.92	25.00
Plumbers, pipefitters, and steamfitters	15.00	18.64	24.42	33.37	42.27
Plasterers and stucco masons	12.67	14.00	15.50	21.72	33.99
Reinforcing iron and rebar workers	11.96	15.41	30.24	33.00	35.50
Roofers	10.00	12.00	15.00	19.89	24.00
Sheet metal workers	13.00	16.80	21.37	30.19	38.00
Structural iron and steel workers	11.00	16.00	23.51	34.01	57.58
Helpers, construction trades	9.50	10.25	12.66	15.00	20.00
Helpers–brickmasons, blockmasons, stonemasons, and tile and marble setters	9.84	10.00	16.00	26.33	26.33
Helpers–carpenters	10.00	11.00	13.97	15.00	16.34
Helpers–electricians	10.00	11.00	12.21	14.50	20.00
Helpers–painters, paperhangers, plasterers, and stucco masons	9.00	9.50	10.00	12.75	13.21
Helpers–pipelayers, plumbers, pipefitters, and steamfitters	10.00	11.52	12.21	14.38	19.55
Helpers–roofers	9.62	10.00	11.37	14.26	15.42
Construction and building inspectors	16.64	21.55	24.35	34.35	40.71
Hazardous materials removal workers	11.86	15.00	19.00	22.00	42.95
Highway maintenance workers	10.00	13.00	21.42	26.18	35.20
Miscellaneous construction and related workers	10.35	11.50	15.00	18.97	31.00
Derrick, rotary drill, and service unit operators, oil, gas, and mining	12.83	17.03	21.50	26.70	35.97
Service unit operators, oil, gas, and mining	16.01	17.03	18.90	24.12	33.55
Mining machine operators	16.00	20.47	24.05	24.50	32.55
Roustabouts, oil and gas	11.43	14.00	15.00	19.75	31.77
Helpers–extraction workers	12.50	13.50	15.75	22.85	22.94
Installation, Maintenance, and Repair	11.40	15.00	20.00	26.45	32.59
First-line supervisors/managers of mechanics, installers, and repairers	17.50	21.15	27.62	35.65	43.69
Computer, automated teller, and office machine repairers	12.80	14.74	17.21	20.00	23.58
Radio and telecommunications equipment installers and repairers	13.40	20.08	29.50	32.71	35.32
Telecommunications equipment installers and repairers, except line installers	13.40	20.25	29.50	32.71	35.32
Miscellaneous electrical and electronic equipment mechanics, installers, and repairers	13.00	15.06	20.04	26.12	33.45
Avionics technicians	15.36	19.23	23.61	27.59	38.29
Electric motor, power tool, and related repairers	10.00	11.50	12.50	16.23	23.68
Electrical and electronics repairers, commercial and industrial equipment	15.50	18.97	23.76	29.01	32.82
Electrical and electronics repairers, powerhouse, substation, and relay	25.99	29.50	34.85	37.81	40.51
Electronic equipment installers and repairers, motor vehicles	16.00	16.17	18.00	18.00	25.84
Electronic home entertainment equipment installers and repairers	10.17	14.00	14.48	14.92	17.01
Security and fire alarm systems installers	13.86	17.08	20.05	24.13	26.80
Aircraft mechanics and service technicians	18.35	21.99	26.69	30.90	36.12
Automotive technicians and repairers	10.00	13.55	18.50	23.61	29.60
Automotive body and related repairers	12.65	15.00	19.00	24.29	31.25
Automotive service technicians and mechanics	9.75	13.25	18.50	23.40	29.27
Bus and truck mechanics and diesel engine specialists	14.50	16.39	20.51	24.60	29.25
Heavy vehicle and mobile equipment service technicians and mechanics	15.55	17.96	20.85	24.40	28.50
Farm equipment mechanics	12.00	13.00	18.34	19.96	26.45
Mobile heavy equipment mechanics, except engines	15.55	18.50	22.11	25.50	29.31
Rail car repairers	16.50	17.60	18.60	21.34	25.21
Small engine mechanics	10.00	14.00	15.00	18.25	20.80
Motorboat mechanics	10.00	13.00	16.00	17.31	18.00
Motorcycle mechanics	10.00	12.00	14.49	16.90	21.79
Outdoor power equipment and other small engine mechanics	13.09	14.00	17.00	19.23	20.80
Miscellaneous vehicle and mobile equipment mechanic, installers, and repairers	8.00	9.00	11.00	14.00	16.95
Recreational vehicle service technicians	11.06	13.00	16.00	24.04	27.50
Tire repairers and changers	8.00	9.00	10.63	12.75	15.20
Control and valve installers and repairers	15.00	17.50	21.66	27.10	33.99
Mechanical door repairers	13.00	16.28	18.75	22.68	30.00
Control and valve installers and repairers, except mechanical door	17.50	21.50	26.82	32.60	37.94
Heating, air conditioning, and refrigeration mechanics and installers	13.00	16.00	20.00	29.00	33.00

[1]Percentiles designate position in the earnings distribution and are calculated from individual worker earnings and the hours they are scheduled to work.

Table 6-22. Private Industry Workers: Hourly Wage Percentiles,[1] 2010—*Continued*

(Dollars.)

Occupation	Wages fall at or below the following percentiles:				
	10	25	50	75	90
Installation, Maintenance and Repair—*Continued*					
Home appliance repairers	13.00	15.00	19.43	22.08	24.20
Industrial machinery installation, repair, and maintenance workers	12.24	15.39	19.45	23.97	29.70
Industrial machinery mechanics	17.34	20.00	22.95	27.25	32.62
Maintenance and repair workers, general	10.56	13.50	17.15	20.77	27.20
Maintenance workers, machinery	12.50	14.50	17.15	20.50	25.99
Millwrights	18.00	21.00	24.50	29.82	40.77
Line installers and repairers	14.15	20.93	27.94	32.00	34.20
Electrical power-line installers and repairers	20.58	26.22	31.25	35.92	41.93
Telecommunications line installers and repairers	13.68	19.25	27.00	30.28	32.79
Precision instrument and equipment repairers	13.28	16.30	21.91	29.31	36.33
Medical equipment repairers	14.06	15.85	22.07	28.35	29.94
Musical instrument repairers and tuners	10.67	14.42	20.00	20.50	20.50
Miscellaneous installation, maintenance, and repair workers	9.00	11.12	14.43	19.00	25.86
Coin, vending, and amusement machine servicers and repairers	11.33	11.33	14.45	18.01	19.94
Manufactured building and mobile home installers	9.00	10.75	11.25	12.80	12.80
Riggers	12.00	17.00	19.32	24.00	27.07
Helpers–installation, maintenance, and repair workers	8.30	9.00	11.75	14.51	17.00
Production	9.00	11.00	14.63	19.40	25.90
First-line supervisors/managers of production and operating workers	14.66	19.08	24.00	31.48	37.10
Aircraft structure, surfaces, rigging, and systems assemblers	16.07	18.29	23.03	30.77	32.70
Electrical, electronics, and electromechanical assemblers	8.86	10.50	12.73	16.50	20.63
Coil winders, tapers, and finishers	9.00	10.65	13.15	15.16	21.08
Electrical and electronic equipment assemblers	8.50	10.10	12.59	15.80	20.84
Electromechanical equipment assemblers	9.97	11.38	14.67	18.00	20.63
Engine and other machine assemblers	12.47	13.00	16.79	22.23	28.49
Structural metal fabricators and fitters	9.77	12.00	15.00	18.00	23.55
Miscellaneous assemblers and fabricators	8.45	10.40	13.55	18.00	25.90
Fiberglass laminators and fabricators	9.95	10.00	12.50	15.66	16.00
Team assemblers	10.00	11.90	13.60	18.25	28.59
Bakers	8.70	10.00	12.00	14.38	18.22
Butchers and other meat, poultry, and fish processing workers	8.75	10.34	12.60	14.25	18.05
Butchers and meat cutters	9.50	11.52	14.40	18.40	21.22
Meat, poultry, and fish cutters and trimmers	7.64	8.75	10.34	12.60	13.30
Slaughterers and meat packers	10.50	12.15	12.76	14.25	15.74
Miscellaneous food processing workers	9.35	9.85	12.95	16.96	20.00
Food and tobacco roasting, baking, and drying machine operators and tenders	8.50	10.00	13.00	18.00	20.99
Food batchmakers	9.82	11.00	14.01	18.10	21.30
Food cooking machine operators and tenders	9.30	9.66	10.00	11.95	18.30
Computer control programmers and operators	11.18	14.25	18.70	21.94	26.37
Computer-controlled machine tool operators, metal and plastic	11.00	13.58	17.75	21.00	25.65
Numerical tool and process control programmers	19.50	20.00	22.00	25.00	32.67
Forming machine setters, operators, and tenders, metal and plastic	10.47	11.84	15.00	19.03	21.78
Extruding and drawing machine setters, operators, and tenders, metal and plastic	10.40	12.17	14.30	18.19	20.16
Forging machine setters, operators, and tenders, metal and plastic	11.44	11.47	17.85	21.38	23.25
Rolling machine setters, operators, and tenders, metal and plastic	9.30	11.63	15.33	20.56	21.78
Machine tool cutting setters, operators, and tenders, metal and plastic	9.80	12.25	14.98	18.25	21.31
Cutting, punching, and press machine setters, operators, and tenders, metal and plastic	9.58	11.80	14.19	17.49	20.36
Drilling and boring machine tool setters, operators, and tenders, metal and plastic	10.50	13.03	16.00	19.81	29.72
Grinding, lapping, polishing, and buffing machine tool setters, operators, and tenders, metal and plastic	9.73	12.35	14.60	17.46	20.37
Lathe and turning machine tool setters, operators, and tenders, metal and plastic	10.00	13.00	17.94	20.59	23.00
Milling and planing machine setters, operators, and tenders, metal and plastic	11.20	13.12	18.54	21.66	22.82
Machinists	15.00	18.00	20.73	25.45	30.90
Metal furnace and kiln operators and tenders	9.63	11.00	18.15	20.37	22.32
Metal-refining furnace operators and tenders	9.63	10.00	15.50	20.91	25.12
Pourers and casters, metal	10.15	15.50	18.15	19.78	20.78
Model makers and patternmakers, metal and plastic	9.56	16.00	23.19	32.94	34.52
Model makers, metal and plastic	16.00	18.70	23.77	33.75	36.47
Patternmakers, metal and plastic	9.00	14.00	16.50	32.94	34.52
Molders and molding machine setters, operators, and tenders, metal and plastic	8.50	9.51	12.37	16.02	19.92
Foundry mold and coremakers	10.19	10.19	16.68	17.92	20.04
Molding, coremaking, and casting machine setters, operators, and tenders, metal and plastic	8.35	9.25	12.19	15.30	19.07
Multiple machine tool setters, operators, and tenders, metal and plastic	10.75	11.81	14.75	18.92	24.75
Tool and die makers	18.52	20.70	24.65	27.92	32.91
Welding, soldering, and brazing workers	11.51	14.00	16.86	20.00	24.00
Welders, cutters, solderers, and brazers	11.69	14.00	16.85	20.00	24.07
Welding, soldering, and brazing machine setters, operators, and tenders	11.50	13.77	17.00	19.75	21.57
Miscellaneous metalworkers and plastic workers	9.00	11.79	15.00	17.50	22.13
Heat treating equipment setters, operators, and tenders, metal and plastic	9.00	11.00	15.28	18.31	20.78
Lay-out workers, metal and plastic	11.33	15.00	16.00	20.80	26.40
Plating and coating machine setters, operators, and tenders, metal and plastic	9.46	12.20	14.50	19.50	27.29
Tool grinders, filers, and sharpeners	8.25	9.08	17.00	22.13	23.19
Bookbinders and bindery workers	8.29	10.00	12.67	16.25	22.00
Bindery workers	8.29	10.00	12.67	16.25	22.00
Printers	9.50	11.70	17.00	22.38	27.00
Job printers	10.00	14.00	18.95	20.00	23.10
Prepress technicians and workers	9.50	13.50	19.23	24.30	27.83
Printing machine operators	9.14	11.53	15.75	21.00	27.00
Laundry and dry-cleaning workers	7.55	8.50	9.92	11.56	13.75
Pressers, textile, garment, and related materials	7.60	8.00	9.00	10.07	11.99
Sewing machine operators	8.00	9.48	11.00	14.35	16.94
Tailors, dressmakers, and sewers	9.14	11.00	13.00	19.50	25.91
Tailors, dressmakers, and custom sewers	9.14	11.00	12.14	19.00	25.91
Textile machine setters, operators, and tenders	8.41	9.42	11.05	13.91	15.98
Textile bleaching and dyeing machine operators and tenders	8.00	8.10	9.00	11.50	16.11
Textile cutting machine setters, operators, and tenders	9.00	9.27	11.00	12.76	13.65
Textile knitting and weaving machine setters, operators, and tenders	8.73	10.35	13.54	15.50	19.83
Textile winding, twisting, and drawing out machine setters, operators, and tenders	10.03	10.38	10.66	13.92	16.86

[1]Percentiles designate position in the earnings distribution and are calculated from individual worker earnings and the hours they are scheduled to work.

Table 6-22. Private Industry Workers: Hourly Wage Percentiles,[1] 2010—*Continued*

(Dollars.)

Occupation	Wages fall at or below the following percentiles:				
	10	25	50	75	90
Production—*Continued*					
Miscellaneous textile, apparel, and furnishings workers	8.50	10.58	15.15	18.35	21.83
Extruding and forming machine setters, operators, and tenders, synthetic and glass fibers	10.58	12.30	17.75	20.04	21.80
Fabric and apparel patternmakers	13.13	13.13	17.57	19.30	22.00
Upholsterers	8.50	14.85	16.08	20.00	24.14
Cabinetmakers and bench carpenters	11.00	13.50	15.30	19.00	23.00
Furniture finishers	9.00	11.07	13.77	17.67	20.00
Woodworking machine setters, operators, and tenders	8.50	10.75	13.36	15.70	17.63
Sawing machine setters, operators, and tenders, wood	8.25	9.80	12.12	15.00	17.15
Woodworking machine setters, operators, and tenders, except sawing	9.18	11.30	14.07	16.00	17.85
Power plant operators, distributors, and dispatchers	27.81	29.16	34.29	36.06	40.92
Power distributors and dispatchers	33.61	37.55	39.92	43.25	51.40
Power plant operators	25.65	28.43	30.89	34.29	39.36
Stationary engineers and boiler operators	17.92	24.81	27.61	33.92	34.03
Water and liquid waste treatment plant and system operators	17.67	17.80	19.82	23.10	33.98
Miscellaneous plant and system operators	17.61	22.08	28.58	32.64	35.61
Chemical plant and system operators	17.44	20.60	23.33	29.35	32.20
Gas plant operators	26.74	29.17	34.40	35.61	37.65
Petroleum pump system operators, refinery operators, and gaugers	19.00	28.65	32.46	35.31	36.58
Chemical processing machine setters, operators, and tenders	12.50	17.02	21.65	31.25	34.00
Chemical equipment operators and tenders	12.50	16.04	21.10	26.09	29.75
Separating, filtering, clarifying, precipitating, and still machine setters, operators, and tenders	12.84	18.34	26.53	33.42	36.43
Crushing, grinding, polishing, mixing, and blending workers	9.50	11.23	14.45	17.85	22.27
Crushing, grinding, and polishing machine setters, operators, and tenders	8.65	11.50	16.07	18.00	22.86
Grinding and polishing workers, hand	9.00	10.40	12.40	15.40	17.00
Mixing and blending machine setters, operators, and tenders	10.09	11.25	15.00	19.70	22.91
Cutting workers	9.00	11.25	14.50	17.60	20.80
Cutters and trimmers, hand	8.66	9.45	11.95	15.00	20.55
Cutting and slicing machine setters, operators, and tenders	9.80	11.50	14.81	17.84	21.17
Extruding, forming, pressing, and compacting machine setters, operators, and tenders	8.96	10.87	13.20	17.02	21.22
Furnace, kiln, oven, drier, and kettle operators and tenders	11.93	12.23	15.97	19.13	26.37
Inspectors, testers, sorters, samplers, and weighers	9.84	12.37	16.00	20.00	26.00
Jewelers and precious stone and metal workers	11.50	14.00	18.00	23.50	28.00
Medical, dental, and ophthalmic laboratory technicians	10.00	12.50	15.25	19.60	25.00
Dental laboratory technicians	9.00	13.50	17.00	22.68	25.50
Ophthalmic laboratory technicians	10.37	11.71	14.47	15.00	17.15
Packaging and filling machine operators and tenders	8.25	10.38	13.89	18.24	21.51
Painting workers	10.00	12.35	15.39	18.82	25.00
Coating, painting, and spraying machine setters, operators, and tenders	10.00	12.00	15.06	16.98	19.49
Painters, transportation equipment	12.00	17.40	19.15	25.00	36.06
Painting, coating, and decorating workers	8.00	9.50	11.61	13.05	18.24
Photographic process workers and processing machine operators	8.00	8.85	12.00	15.00	18.28
Photographic process workers	9.99	12.00	12.00	18.28	25.57
Photographic processing machine operators	7.95	8.36	11.12	14.48	15.45
Semiconductor processors	12.80	15.09	18.24	20.13	23.80
Miscellaneous production workers	8.25	9.83	12.25	16.65	20.95
Cementing and gluing machine operators and tenders	10.30	12.39	15.12	16.91	20.91
Cleaning, washing, and metal pickling equipment operators and tenders	10.57	13.36	15.00	23.44	29.28
Cooling and freezing equipment operators and tenders	9.30	9.80	17.35	19.17	25.17
Etchers and engravers	10.00	13.31	14.00	15.69	23.50
Molders, shapers, and casters, except metal and plastic	9.25	10.22	13.13	16.00	21.77
Paper goods machine setters, operators, and tenders	9.18	12.00	18.57	21.88	26.80
Tire builders	11.00	11.85	15.14	17.32	20.40
Helpers–production workers	8.00	9.32	11.25	13.35	17.45
Transportation and Material Moving	8.24	10.00	13.56	18.32	23.39
First-line supervisors/managers of helpers, laborers, and material movers, hand	14.67	16.28	20.42	25.00	29.09
First-line supervisors/managers of transportation and material-moving machine and vehicle operators	16.70	20.00	23.08	29.38	37.58
Aircraft pilots and flight engineers	25.63	28.06	87.43	145.44	171.41
Airline pilots, copilots, and flight engineers	26.55	72.21	120.53	165.74	172.40
Commercial pilots	25.63	26.39	27.42	39.55	55.00
Ambulance drivers and attendants, except emergency medical technicians	9.79	10.20	11.00	13.25	16.90
Bus drivers	9.75	11.30	14.75	17.50	22.00
Bus drivers, transit and intercity	9.75	12.60	15.69	19.84	23.35
Bus drivers, school	9.60	11.03	13.65	16.50	18.32
Driver/sales workers and truck drivers	9.74	12.65	16.54	20.77	26.98
Driver/sales workers	7.25	7.33	10.75	16.83	21.60
Truck drivers, heavy and tractor-trailer	12.30	14.66	18.15	21.36	25.62
Truck drivers, light or delivery services	9.07	11.02	14.50	20.77	29.66
Taxi drivers and chauffeurs	7.63	8.50	9.85	11.08	16.44
Railroad conductors and yardmasters	21.48	28.56	32.46	35.87	41.43
Sailors and marine oilers	9.25	9.30	12.08	13.00	14.17
Ship and boat captains and operators	6.98	17.50	29.58	38.50	41.67
Captains, mates, and pilots of water vessels	6.98	26.02	30.00	38.67	41.67
Parking lot attendants	7.25	8.00	8.81	10.00	12.10
Service station attendants	7.50	8.00	9.00	11.00	15.75
Transportation inspectors	23.02	25.04	32.78	33.52	39.33
Conveyor operators and tenders	11.98	12.95	16.70	18.86	19.13
Crane and tower operators	13.16	16.28	19.79	26.50	32.08
Dredge, excavating, and loading machine operators	13.00	14.00	17.99	21.50	27.65
Excavating and loading machine and dragline operators	12.75	14.00	16.00	20.12	24.78
Hoist and winch operators	9.04	15.84	19.22	21.03	21.03
Industrial truck and tractor operators	9.75	11.50	14.15	16.85	20.66
Laborers and material movers, hand	7.85	8.60	10.55	13.63	17.30
Cleaners of vehicles and equipment	8.00	8.50	10.75	13.56	16.75
Laborers and freight, stock, and material movers, hand	8.00	9.00	11.00	14.13	18.25
Machine feeders and offbearers	8.00	9.00	10.61	13.93	16.65
Packers and packagers, hand	7.35	8.00	9.30	11.84	14.45
Pumping station operators	18.64	18.75	23.77	26.85	29.66
Refuse and recyclable material collectors	9.10	9.70	11.00	17.00	20.55
Tank car, truck, and ship loaders	15.00	15.25	20.39	21.30	24.90

[1]Percentiles designate position in the earnings distribution and are calculated from individual worker earnings and the hours they are scheduled to work.

Chapter Seven

RECENT TRENDS IN THE LABOR MARKET

RECENT TRENDS IN THE LABOR MARKET

HIGHLIGHTS

This chapter contains information on mass layoff events, initial claimants for unemployment insurance, movement of work, job openings, hires, and separations.

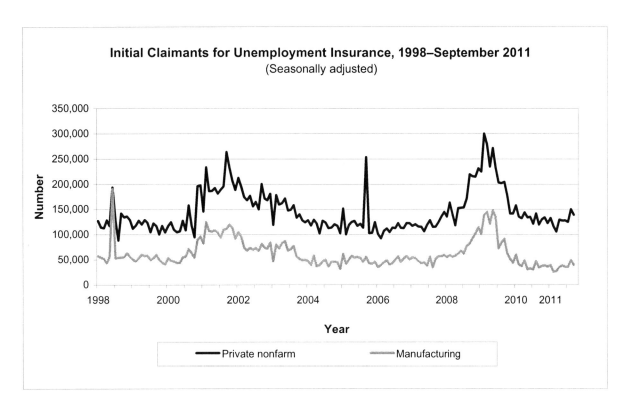

Initial Claimants for Unemployment Insurance, 1998–September 2011
(Seasonally adjusted)

The National Bureau of Economic Research (NBER) determined that the recession began in December 2007 and ended in June 2009. During that time period, there were a total of 39,108 mass layoff events and 4,003,211 initial claims filed for unemployment insurance. (See Table 7-1.)

OTHER HIGHLIGHTS

• From January 2011 to September 2011, the number of mass layoff events (seasonally adjusted), reached 13,597 while the number of initial claims rose to 1,293,827. During the same time period in 2010 there were 14,639 mass layoff events and 1,376,397 initial claims. (See Table 7-1.)

• The manufacturing sector accounted for 23.1 percent of all mass layoff events and 27.1 percent of initial claims filed in 2010. In contrast, government only made up 8.6 percent of mass layoff events and 8.1 percent of initial claimants. (See Table 7-3.)

• Of the four census regions, the West had the highest number of mass layoff events in September 2011 (373), followed by the South (311), the Northeast (286), and the Midwest (219). (See Table 7-4.)

• In September 2011, the number of job openings reached 3,354,000, which is the highest level since August 2008. The number of job openings were the highest in professional and business services (684,000), educational and health services (616,000) and trade, transportation, and utilities (546,000) and lowest in manufacturing (242,000) and construction (75,000). (See Table 7-7.)

NOTES AND DEFINITIONS

MASS LAYOFFS

Collection and Coverage

The Mass Layoff Statistics (MLS) program is a federal-state program that identifies, describes, and tracks the effects of major job cutbacks, using data from each state's unemployment insurance database. Employers that have at least 50 initial claims filed against them during a consecutive 5-week period are contacted by the state agency to determine whether these separations are of at least 31 days duration, and, if so, information is obtained on the total number of persons separated, the reasons for these separations, and recall expectations. Employers are identified according to industry classification and location, and unemployment insurance claimants are identified by such demographic factors as age, race, gender, ethnic group, and place of residence. The program yields information on an individual's entire spell of unemployment, to the point when regular unemployment insurance benefits are exhausted.

A given month contains an aggregation of the weekly unemployment insurance claims filings for the Sunday through Saturday weeks in that month. All weeks are included for the particular month, except if the first day of the month falls on Saturday. In this case, the week is included in the prior month's tabulations. This means that some months will contain 4 weeks and others, 5 weeks, the number of weeks in a given month may be different from year to year, and the number of weeks in a year may vary. Therefore, analysis of over-the-month and over-the-year change in not seasonally adjusted series should take this calendar effect into consideration.

The latest quarterly data in these tables are considered preliminary. After the initial publication of quarterly information, more data are collected as remaining employer interviews for the quarter are completed and additional initial claimant information associated with extended layoff events is received.

The MLS program discontinued the collection of "domestic relocation" and "overseas relocation" as standard reasons for layoff beginning with data for the first quarter 2004. It was felt these reasons do not reflect an economic reason, and instead relate to the effect of the actual reason.

Concepts and Definitions

Employers in the MLS program include those covered by state unemployment insurance laws. Information on employers is obtained from the Quarterly Census of Employment and Wages (QCEW) program.

Extended layoff event is when there are fifty or more initial claims for unemployment insurance benefits from an employer during a 5-week period, with at least 50 workers separated for more than 30 days.

Initial claimant is a person who files any notice of unemployment to initiate a request either for a determination of entitlement to and eligibility for compensation, or for a subsequent period of unemployment within a benefit year or period of eligibility.

Layoff is the separation of persons from an employer as part of a mass layoff event. Such layoffs involve both persons subject to recall and those who are terminated by the establishment.

Mass layoff event is when there are fifty or more initial claims for unemployment insurance benefits from an employer during a five-week period, regardless of duration.

Movement-of-work action is relocation of work within the same company or to other companies, domestically or outside the United States. Because employers may cite more than one location to which work is moving, a layoff event may have more than one action associated with it.

Movement-of-work separations is the number of separations specifically associated with movement-of-work actions.

Outsourcing is the movement of work that was formerly conducted in-house by employees paid directly by a company to a different company under a contractual arrangement.

Seasonal adjustment is the process of estimating and removing the effect on time series data of regularly recurring seasonal events such as changes in the weather, holidays, and the beginning and ending of the school year. The use of seasonal adjustment makes it easier to observe fundamental changes in time series, particularly those associated with general economic expansions and contractions.

Separations is the total number of people laid-off in an extended mass layoff event for more than 30 days, according to the employer.

Worksite closure is the complete closure of either multi-unit or single-unit employers or the partial closure of a multi-unit employer where entire worksites affected by layoffs are closed or planned to be closed.

Sources of Additional Information

For more extensive information and the latest edition of the Mass Layoffs news release, please see <http://www.bls.gov/news.release/mmls.nr0.htm>.

Table 7-1. Mass Layoff Events and Initial Claimants for Unemployment Insurance, 1998–September 2011, Seasonally Adjusted

(Number.)

Year and month	Total		Private nonfarm		Manufacturing	
	Events	Initial claimants	Events	Initial claimants	Events	Initial claimants
1998						
January	1 316	143 061	1 089	126 988	406	57 309
February	1 234	129 602	1 046	114 166	438	54 440
March	1 181	124 912	1 030	112 851	436	52 061
April	1 362	145 440	1 142	128 241	428	43 403
May	1 248	129 030	1 089	117 332	466	56 728
June	1 332	205 228	1 162	193 631	684	190 810
July	1 422	147 574	1 187	128 085	444	53 057
August	1 076	100 917	887	88 347	433	54 085
September	1 268	150 904	1 139	141 911	450	54 589
October	1 389	153 632	1 174	134 417	468	55 517
November	1 331	151 957	1 138	135 741	467	63 022
December	1 400	150 760	1 115	128 451	415	55 676
1999						
January	1 399	129 104	1 122	111 713	429	50 593
February	1 321	136 296	1 074	117 827	404	46 526
March	1 354	148 022	1 112	127 562	460	53 087
April	1 251	134 118	1 058	120 142	457	60 125
May	1 278	146 682	1 063	128 874	438	57 589
June	1 217	138 397	1 053	123 191	446	58 202
July	1 136	117 941	951	104 930	358	49 567
August	1 188	140 981	1 000	122 361	408	53 579
September	1 355	134 430	1 152	116 756	374	59 783
October	995	115 894	797	100 478	344	50 194
November	1 258	138 992	1 025	117 116	337	44 140
December	1 174	119 033	973	104 519	298	40 825
2000						
January	1 100	126 440	968	116 846	371	53 270
February	1 280	151 107	1 018	124 497	379	48 372
March	1 159	126 309	965	109 445	393	46 564
April	1 030	115 068	913	104 865	407	43 829
May	1 196	126 525	976	106 893	376	44 019
June	1 220	145 766	1 020	127 239	406	54 672
July	1 065	118 649	922	108 499	417	56 465
August	1 282	178 789	1 060	157 762	423	71 141
September	1 260	134 153	1 045	117 266	407	63 394
October	938	107 676	798	94 783	385	54 006
November	1 643	215 381	1 447	196 166	599	89 869
December	1 691	214 601	1 514	197 944	575	96 295
2001						
January	1 288	158 580	1 144	145 584	529	82 504
February	1 912	253 943	1 684	233 524	828	124 430
March	1 761	202 344	1 569	186 565	800	107 481
April	1 622	200 683	1 484	186 898	776	106 255
May	1 676	206 062	1 523	192 500	750	108 773
June	1 608	195 802	1 432	181 264	740	103 468
July	1 710	201 363	1 574	189 030	721	93 949
August	1 732	207 416	1 568	195 777	791	109 611
September	2 407	277 955	2 236	263 773	841	111 520
October	2 177	242 507	2 051	232 371	923	119 873
November	2 104	218 378	1 940	206 999	948	113 776
December	1 824	200 677	1 673	188 836	746	92 019
2002						
January	1 841	224 765	1 711	212 461	764	104 909
February	1 823	207 788	1 663	194 840	701	95 406
March	1 697	187 212	1 525	174 281	604	74 492
April	1 666	183 005	1 494	167 848	584	68 282
May	1 730	190 129	1 561	176 744	613	73 612
June	1 632	171 213	1 436	155 960	547	70 137
July	1 632	179 407	1 461	164 741	557	73 479
August	1 468	161 431	1 324	149 847	563	67 831
September	1 918	217 299	1 737	200 635	615	81 292
October	1 749	187 851	1 573	171 346	611	73 940
November	1 651	178 739	1 507	167 723	590	72 329
December	1 834	194 852	1 646	180 976	676	84 247
2003						
January	1 336	132 819	1 160	119 199	382	46 839
February	1 831	191 434	1 650	178 003	650	80 285
March	1 784	175 384	1 589	159 467	609	72 679
April	1 702	172 252	1 555	162 323	637	83 268
May	1 744	185 159	1 556	171 221	646	87 077
June	1 726	164 597	1 518	147 553	640	68 197
July	1 661	165 130	1 450	149 233	567	71 319
August	1 546	171 996	1 383	157 968	563	77 405
September	1 571	149 250	1 370	133 276	479	56 454
October	1 525	157 759	1 319	140 086	422	51 872
November	1 370	139 572	1 225	127 963	379	49 219
December	1 395	136 166	1 226	124 009	428	49 789
2004						
January	1 414	145 593	1 221	128 305	396	47 882
February	1 257	130 205	1 111	117 788	365	39 214
March	1 362	138 397	1 222	129 094	396	58 213
April	1 349	136 837	1 175	121 841	347	37 115
May	1 240	116 392	1 077	102 443	340	39 208
June	1 397	139 975	1 231	127 229	370	46 998
July	1 315	135 186	1 165	123 768	371	49 945
August	1 417	127 814	1 226	112 867	344	36 298
September	1 275	124 279	1 149	113 689	337	45 732
October	1 265	129 312	1 153	120 337	366	46 319
November	1 306	129 014	1 161	117 300	374	44 939
December	1 163	114 258	1 009	102 732	285	31 445

Table 7-1. Mass Layoff Events and Initial Claimants for Unemployment Insurance, 1998–September 2011, Seasonally Adjusted—*Continued*

(Number.)

Year and month	Total		Private nonfarm		Manufacturing	
	Events	Initial claimants	Events	Initial claimants	Events	Initial claimants
2005						
January	1 509	161 805	1 367	151 530	413	61 483
February	1 075	111 437	948	100 564	344	42 035
March	1 193	129 288	1 045	118 827	361	50 086
April	1 238	135 353	1 107	124 881	384	58 255
May	1 266	139 915	1 124	127 071	395	54 052
June	1 185	125 919	1 072	117 229	359	55 621
July	1 257	133 036	1 116	121 311	392	53 945
August	1 118	124 738	996	113 784	340	46 067
September	2 241	299 151	2 028	253 431	423	55 855
October	1 113	111 868	994	102 840	323	43 326
November	1 176	115 215	1 040	103 701	328	41 868
December	1 272	135 737	1 142	124 459	356	46 211
2006						
January	1 086	111 484	955	101 462	290	35 030
February	935	100 482	837	92 542	299	39 328
March	1 044	115 705	942	107 238	308	45 044
April	1 162	122 174	1 028	112 014	351	48 735
May	1 106	114 200	995	104 870	302	40 491
June	1 128	122 783	1 021	113 724	352	42 960
July	1 181	122 246	1 058	112 645	367	50 719
August	1 231	131 837	1 095	122 479	370	57 150
September	1 140	121 613	1 031	113 304	365	45 207
October	1 184	121 126	1 071	112 667	404	53 017
November	1 223	132 407	1 107	122 718	412	57 192
December	1 196	132 153	1 094	122 556	367	50 644
2007						
January	1 235	128 523	1 082	117 096	403	54 843
February	1 198	129 244	1 072	120 459	371	53 420
March	1 202	124 521	1 092	115 835	384	47 658
April	1 238	126 334	1 102	115 271	358	42 989
May	1 159	113 578	1 064	106 573	347	44 637
June	1 207	127 776	1 097	119 007	342	37 552
July	1 295	136 168	1 193	128 208	401	55 906
August	1 217	122 450	1 126	115 305	312	34 877
September	1 233	121 998	1 140	115 675	430	51 731
October	1 330	133 063	1 210	124 455	439	56 970
November	1 397	145 339	1 269	135 651	408	56 985
December	1 553	154 275	1 435	144 785	463	59 445
2008						
January	1 437	146 900	1 302	135 622	431	55 562
February	1 604	175 128	1 441	163 475	471	59 118
March	1 500	150 502	1 388	140 424	435	56 156
April	1 292	128 901	1 162	118 016	449	58 402
May	1 582	161 944	1 444	152 230	468	62 452
June	1 631	164 508	1 488	153 014	491	68 198
July	1 581	164 497	1 443	153 720	463	62 425
August	1 791	181 107	1 653	171 705	583	77 874
September	2 192	233 034	2 024	219 532	635	82 471
October	2 221	229 254	2 062	215 787	697	92 408
November	2 415	228 107	2 256	214 631	900	102 284
December	2 443	245 661	2 264	231 138	927	114 280
2009						
January	2 272	238 717	2 103	224 850	756	100 927
February	2 801	315 507	2 636	300 042	1 194	138 583
March	2 950	295 543	2 758	279 027	1 205	144 713
April	2 579	251 032	2 368	234 796	997	121 435
May	2 758	288 319	2 557	271 425	1 187	147 548
June	2 506	250 275	2 293	232 814	1 048	135 389
July	2 192	223 697	1 977	203 365	620	72 932
August	2 419	220 262	2 177	201 951	778	83 837
September	2 305	219 924	2 095	204 596	799	91 665
October	1 975	195 347	1 780	177 977	570	63 646
November	1 754	154 223	1 585	141 439	464	51 891
December	1 725	156 274	1 545	141 649	420	43 584
2010						
January	1 716	171 633	1 541	157 597	494	60 059
February	1 492	149 369	1 318	135 490	351	40 564
March	1 635	146 901	1 436	131 953	347	37 273
April	1 675	159 358	1 498	143 814	371	48 646
May	1 665	155 352	1 405	133 913	314	30 967
June	1 729	153 937	1 504	134 837	326	32 646
July	1 528	138 581	1 316	121 378	296	30 752
August	1 658	163 325	1 453	141 489	409	47 668
September	1 541	137 941	1 331	119 654	336	34 641
October	1 649	147 204	1 445	130 264	353	37 394
November	1 579	148 800	1 397	133 845	350	39 072
December	1 483	137 992	1 272	122 688	319	35 977
2011						
January	1 534	149 799	1 344	132 730	341	39 189
February	1 421	130 818	1 220	116 190	291	26 060
March	1 286	118 523	1 128	105 636	253	27 619
April	1 564	143 927	1 401	129 702	327	35 022
May	1 599	143 540	1 405	127 494	373	38 673
June	1 532	143 444	1 348	128 105	341	35 693
July	1 579	145 000	1 363	124 745	342	35 460
August	1 587	165 547	1 373	150 136	391	48 997
September	1 495	153 229	1 347	139 151	376	39 929

Table 7-2. Mass Layoff Events and Initial Claimants for Unemployment Insurance, 1998–September 2011, Not Seasonally Adjusted

(Number.)

Year and month	Total Events	Total Initial claimants	Private nonfarm Events	Private nonfarm Initial claimants	Manufacturing Events	Manufacturing Initial claimants
1998						
January	2 360	255 203	2 117	235 263	823	104 790
February	970	81 455	773	68 345	315	31 692
March	762	78 210	673	71 258	289	31 369
April	1 253	132 476	1 076	117 601	342	37 312
May	1 180	107 952	1 038	97 493	365	38 553
June	1 208	183 590	1 012	169 411	409	103 501
July	2 220	286 055	1 903	255 245	1 014	152 044
August	617	53 665	558	50 149	259	26 593
September	637	79 629	564	74 941	248	25 134
October	1 553	160 830	1 220	132 258	507	60 529
November	1 368	144 343	1 076	123 066	478	62 829
December	1 776	207 661	1 552	188 787	618	82 871
1999						
January	2 421	226 995	2 142	206 615	861	94 887
February	1 067	89 800	810	73 846	289	28 322
March	880	91 890	737	80 063	302	31 317
April	1 270	136 885	1 100	123 987	450	56 668
May	1 032	102 738	895	93 006	303	32 958
June	1 140	130 951	925	109 848	268	32 610
July	1 741	221 334	1 496	201 412	808	137 688
August	698	75 691	638	70 285	246	26 606
September	717	75 288	592	64 942	212	28 968
October	1 098	118 938	814	97 984	373	55 222
November	1 336	139 508	977	110 200	347	45 431
December	1 509	162 381	1 353	150 171	446	60 349
2000						
January	1 934	223 322	1 807	212 805	741	100 397
February	1 045	103 898	780	81 103	268	30 358
March	986	106 748	827	92 565	329	38 434
April	924	101 359	838	93 631	323	34 061
May	984	92 193	841	81 125	262	25 838
June	1 597	192 025	1 269	160 685	404	60 258
July	1 333	164 978	1 159	152 243	664	100 874
August	751	97 215	679	90 877	256	35 687
September	936	106 842	767	93 327	319	46 865
October	874	103 755	684	84 922	321	48 877
November	1 697	216 514	1 397	190 626	617	93 966
December	2 677	326 743	2 477	311 623	1 074	166 928
2001						
January	1 522	200 343	1 405	188 504	632	107 028
February	1 501	172 908	1 285	156 183	576	79 784
March	1 527	171 466	1 371	158 108	659	86 874
April	1 450	176 265	1 353	166 167	608	78 845
May	1 434	159 365	1 331	151 186	528	64 887
June	2 107	253 826	1 784	226 022	737	116 005
July	2 117	273 807	1 952	259 128	1 144	168 877
August	1 490	166 148	1 386	158 307	603	79 515
September	1 327	160 402	1 214	151 161	485	58 544
October	1 831	215 483	1 676	202 053	742	107 030
November	2 721	295 956	2 373	270 268	1 122	151 969
December	2 440	268 893	2 319	259 497	1 103	136 820
2002						
January	2 146	263 777	2 028	252 245	892	128 825
February	1 382	138 808	1 253	129 849	481	58 784
March	1 460	161 316	1 335	151 305	500	59 613
April	1 506	165 814	1 378	153 216	461	50 897
May	1 723	179 799	1 571	166 801	488	52 720
June	1 584	162 189	1 266	136 424	336	42 130
July	2 042	245 294	1 819	226 892	907	135 271
August	1 248	128 103	1 151	119 874	427	48 668
September	1 062	124 522	957	114 736	352	43 755
October	1 497	171 100	1 270	149 327	493	64 655
November	2 153	240 171	1 860	216 237	719	92 712
December	2 474	264 158	2 324	252 807	984	126 826
2003						
January	2 315	225 430	2 130	210 918	822	90 244
February	1 363	124 965	1 222	116 264	435	48 161
March	1 207	113 026	1 099	104 468	390	41 063
April	1 581	161 412	1 470	152 937	499	62 349
May	1 703	174 204	1 538	160 729	499	61 278
June	1 691	157 552	1 336	127 743	389	40 845
July	2 087	226 435	1 815	206 901	946	136 410
August	1 258	133 839	1 163	124 131	405	52 620
September	868	82 647	756	73 914	271	31 428
October	1 523	158 240	1 265	137 706	438	53 741
November	1 438	138 543	1 234	123 524	408	48 419
December	1 929	192 633	1 793	182 750	648	77 915
2004						
January	2 428	239 454	2 226	220 687	848	89 551
February	941	84 201	832	76 577	240	23 043
March	920	92 554	847	87 782	258	34 686
April	1 458	157 314	1 316	142 657	343	36 172
May	988	87 501	878	78 786	219	22 141
June	1 379	134 588	1 077	110 804	222	27 307
July	2 094	253 929	1 860	234 877	885	145 895
August	809	69 033	745	63 876	194	17 698
September	708	68 972	637	63 102	189	25 808
October	1 242	127 918	1 101	117 375	372	48 265
November	1 399	130 423	1 201	115 549	412	44 243
December	1 614	161 271	1 487	152 092	436	50 726

Table 7-2. Mass Layoff Events and Initial Claimants for Unemployment Insurance, 1998–September 2011, Not Seasonally Adjusted—*Continued*

(Number.)

Year and month	Total		Private nonfarm		Manufacturing	
	Events	Initial claimants	Events	Initial claimants	Events	Initial claimants
2005						
January	2 564	263 952	2 421	253 409	823	108 985
February	810	74 644	722	68 372	230	24 931
March	806	88 937	733	83 793	246	33 030
April	1 373	158 582	1 263	148 133	395	59 129
May	986	101 358	891	93 332	249	30 424
June	1 157	120 463	941	103 307	216	32 783
July	1 981	244 216	1 745	222 377	856	136 210
August	645	67 582	598	63 484	188	22 531
September	1 662	213 281	1 505	179 042	318	47 497
October	905	91 941	757	80 694	249	37 276
November	1 254	116 127	1 079	102 182	363	41 442
December	2 323	254 258	2 168	242 753	706	96 382
2006						
January	1 245	117 946	1 123	108 701	331	35 097
February	719	66 555	658	62 208	210	24 892
March	921	111 838	856	106 177	285	44 688
April	1 140	121 589	1 038	112 964	296	39 538
May	872	84 809	794	78 663	192	23 570
June	1 489	164 761	1 224	140 687	319	41 095
July	1 511	166 857	1 335	154 342	648	96 152
August	708	72 844	656	69 054	203	28 494
September	865	87 699	785	81 274	296	39 076
October	964	98 804	820	88 133	311	46 737
November	1 315	136 186	1 172	125 009	455	58 473
December	2 249	254 503	2 126	244 783	735	105 462
2007						
January	1 407	134 984	1 263	124 475	456	53 615
February	935	86 696	861	82 097	273	36 170
March	1 082	123 974	1 015	118 431	367	49 886
April	1 219	127 444	1 115	118 040	309	35 229
May	923	85 816	856	81 153	224	26 527
June	1 599	172 810	1 318	148 669	313	36 571
July	1 599	175 419	1 450	164 939	684	101 390
August	963	93 458	908	88 345	220	23 361
September	717	67 385	667	64 026	246	29 381
October	1 083	108 455	929	97 716	338	50 918
November	1 799	198 220	1 593	181 184	514	75 413
December	2 167	224 214	2 071	216 898	699	91 754
2008						
January	1 647	154 503	1 520	144 191	488	54 418
February	1 269	119 508	1 178	113 587	361	42 527
March	1 089	114 541	1 039	110 147	333	43 740
April	1 272	130 810	1 172	121 625	394	48 188
May	1 552	159 471	1 438	150 462	388	51 698
June	1 622	166 742	1 315	140 916	309	42 097
July	1 891	200 382	1 687	186 018	760	108 733
August	1 427	139 999	1 343	133 146	414	51 912
September	1 292	129 586	1 202	122 505	361	46 391
October	2 125	221 784	1 917	205 553	689	100 457
November	2 574	241 589	2 389	226 657	997	107 620
December	3 377	351 305	3 232	340 220	1 378	172 529
2009						
January	3 806	388 813	3 633	375 293	1 461	172 757
February	2 262	218 438	2 173	210 755	945	103 588
March	2 191	228 387	2 107	221 397	940	114 747
April	2 547	256 930	2 385	243 321	887	100 872
May	2 738	289 628	2 572	274 047	1 005	123 683
June	2 519	256 357	2 051	216 063	674	85 726
July	3 054	336 654	2 659	296 589	1 133	154 208
August	1 428	125 024	1 334	117 193	436	41 151
September	1 371	123 177	1 258	115 141	448	51 126
October	1 934	193 904	1 678	172 883	566	69 655
November	1 870	164 496	1 679	150 751	517	55 053
December	2 310	214 648	2 166	203 655	615	64 540
2010						
January	2 860	278 679	2 682	265 074	962	104 846
February	1 183	102 818	1 091	96 022	282	30 728
March	1 197	111 727	1 111	105 514	273	29 745
April	1 840	199 690	1 697	184 654	424	55 178
May	1 354	123 333	1 170	109 203	216	19 334
June	1 861	171 190	1 355	125 872	212	21 083
July	2 124	206 254	1 732	172 248	532	64 200
August	976	92 435	897	83 021	230	23 088
September	920	77 654	806	67 987	187	19 403
October	1 642	148 638	1 373	127 865	351	40 861
November	1 676	158 048	1 477	142 591	389	41 383
December	1 931	184 130	1 763	172 881	465	52 816
2011						
January	2 558	246 463	2 372	229 765	693	75 006
February	1 024	85 585	919	78 718	222	18 471
March	908	85 095	844	80 014	191	20 869
April	1 750	189 919	1 625	176 478	397	47 104
May	1 367	119 911	1 221	108 531	270	25 199
June	1 661	159 930	1 238	122 821	226	22 986
July	2 176	216 774	1 759	174 078	602	71 814
August	961	99 213	875	93 159	228	26 916
September	1 189	117 232	1 095	107 300	296	32 058

Table 7-3. Industry Distribution: Mass Layoff Events and Initial Claimants for Unemployment Insurance, 1998–September 2011

(Number, not seasonally adjusted.)

Industry	1998	1999	2000	2001	2002	2003	2004	2005	2006	2007	2008	2009
	Mass layoff events											
ALL INDUSTRIES	15 904	14 909	15 738	21 467	20 277	18 963	15 980	16 466	13 998	15 493	21 137	28 030
Total, Private	15 098	14 197	15 028	20 763	19 376	17 846	15 018	15 534	13 238	14 714	20 130	26 437
Agriculture, forestry, fishing and hunting	1 536	1 718	1 503	1 314	1 164	1 025	811	711	651	668	698	742
Total, private nonfarm	13 562	12 479	13 525	19 449	18 212	16 821	14 207	14 823	12 587	14 046	19 432	25 695
Mining, quarrying, and oil and gas extraction	152	176	102	115	176	101	69	75	58	66	103	314
Utilities	40	31	37	33	44	40	25	25	20	20	28	39
Construction	1 477	1 509	1 638	1 688	1 939	2 013	1 821	1 975	1 546	1 952	2 393	2 833
Manufacturing	5 667	4 905	5 578	8 939	7 040	6 150	4 618	4 839	4 281	4 643	6 872	9 627
Food	909	830	826	879	826	850	797	751	648	595	678	771
Beverage and tobacco products	79	68	61	74	79	82	75	66	56	58	78	78
Textile mills	245	218	209	352	272	245	169	160	143	146	179	195
Textile product mills	84	70	83	91	113	111	93	86	66	63	69	76
Apparel	605	463	424	433	346	295	220	179	128	131	149	201
Leather and allied products	94	83	76	79	48	48	42	41	26	27	22	28
Wood products	271	240	377	355	377	345	225	273	339	418	557	552
Paper	142	91	148	212	167	156	82	98	86	78	146	241
Printing and related support activities	103	93	95	156	156	125	118	98	74	90	132	235
Petroleum and coal products	30	32	39	25	39	30	27	24	34	28	37	49
Chemicals	82	92	84	156	122	105	101	77	69	75	122	193
Plastics and rubber products	268	200	278	482	331	328	282	300	250	265	501	559
Nonmetallic mineral products	159	150	186	239	219	233	167	204	172	215	316	400
Primary metals	256	214	274	568	399	366	194	222	184	225	352	686
Fabricated metal products	284	268	327	675	482	397	322	311	288	293	574	949
Machinery	321	349	324	781	555	425	235	272	255	287	402	1 046
Computer and electronic products	489	344	231	1 050	817	481	230	217	173	190	285	626
Electrical equipment and appliance manufacturing	202	152	195	391	313	231	137	167	136	135	220	397
Transportation equipment	756	678	1 004	1 410	961	927	821	1 034	925	1 068	1 647	1 827
Furniture and related products	125	130	187	329	255	223	169	164	150	184	288	324
Miscellaneous manufacturing	163	140	150	202	163	147	112	95	79	72	118	194
Wholesale trade	234	228	236	334	336	318	222	251	184	220	363	653
Retail trade	935	830	906	1 249	1 351	1 327	1 165	1 196	991	1 048	1 457	1 965
Transportation and warehousing	661	595	717	908	947	965	853	1 011	934	982	1 267	1 491
Information	412	336	358	736	719	598	454	383	350	383	545	752
Finance and insurance	187	229	218	325	432	384	322	272	310	510	552	677
Real estate and rental and leasing	49	42	64	99	91	91	79	92	54	71	118	165
Professional and technical services	332	324	348	591	634	522	420	427	352	420	564	800
Management of companies and enterprises	26	43	40	47	40	35	38	27	28	42	61	104
Administrative and waste services	1 649	1 536	1 644	2 333	2 428	2 266	2 035	1 989	1 741	1 862	2 699	3 205
Educational services	36	35	34	51	69	82	60	70	63	67	100	149
Health care and social assistance	472	434	405	374	480	499	522	585	415	450	580	675
Arts, entertainment, and recreation	213	205	162	229	277	285	287	293	245	240	311	389
Accommodation and food services	790	738	729	1 032	916	886	980	1 083	844	905	1 238	1 606
Other services, except public administration	146	148	148	171	221	217	198	201	148	155	174	242
Unclassified	84	135	161	195	72	42	39	29	23	10	7	9
Government	806	712	710	704	901	1 117	962	932	760	779	1 007	1 593
Local	466	393	386	396	605	778	643	582	511	509	705	1 122

Table 7-3. Industry Distribution: Mass Layoff Events and Initial Claimants for Unemployment Insurance, 1998–September 2011—*Continued*

(Number, not seasonally adjusted.)

Industry	2010	January 2011	February 2011	March 2011	April 2011	May 2011	June 2011	July 2011	August 2011	September 2011
					Mass layoff events					
ALL INDUSTRIES	19 564	2 558	1 024	908	1 750	1 367	1 661	2 176	961	1 189
Total, Private	17 887	2 438	976	874	1 685	1 243	1 282	1 867	904	1 108
Agriculture, forestry, fishing and hunting	733	66	57	30	60	22	44	108	29	13
Total, private nonfarm	17 154	2 372	919	844	1 625	1 221	1 238	1 759	875	1 095
Mining, quarrying, and oil and gas extraction	102	15	4	3	4	5	(1)	...	(1)	(1)
Utilities	30	5	3	4	(1)	(1)	3	(1)	...	3
Construction	2 262	325	104	99	161	137	84	118	65	150
Manufacturing	4 523	693	222	191	397	270	226	602	228	296
Food	745	94	58	45	84	64	51	84	51	58
Beverage and tobacco products	73	5	5	4	6	(1)	...	3	6	7
Textile mills	109	31	5	3	5	12	8	29	8	11
Textile product mills	59	9	4	3	6	5	6	9	3	(1)
Apparel	134	20	5	4	10	10	10	14	10	11
Leather and allied products	17	(1)	(1)	...	...	(1)	(1)	3	...	...
Wood products	309	43	22	24	19	10	12	28	11	21
Paper	93	14	12	7	6	9	5	4	7	6
Printing and related support activities	131	12	6	5	8	14	5	9	6	6
Petroleum and coal products	43	4	(1)	(1)	...	(1)	(1)	(1)	...	(1)
Chemicals	116	18	7	(1)	5	8	5	12	6	5
Plastics and rubber products	199	51	5	4	21	14	11	36	8	14
Nonmetallic mineral products	224	56	16	5	9	6	5	13	11	3
Primary metals	210	23	8	8	12	11	11	24	5	8
Fabricated metal products	292	51	8	12	21	11	10	27	11	20
Machinery	331	46	11	11	16	12	16	34	16	22
Computer and electronic products	198	14	13	10	18	12	10	19	10	19
Electrical equipment and appliance manufacturing	152	15	4	8	16	7	9	19	12	17
Transportation equipment	811	128	19	19	117	45	34	193	30	38
Furniture and related products	198	44	9	10	9	12	7	31	7	18
Miscellaneous manufacturing	79	14	(1)	5	9	5	9	9	10	7
Wholesale trade	328	32	24	18	27	21	18	21	17	16
Retail trade	1 574	241	114	89	147	108	82	165	79	120
Transportation and warehousing	1 160	212	49	44	194	38	144	114	74	49
Information	548	53	58	36	42	36	41	52	58	36
Finance and insurance	430	31	22	19	42	24	18	43	26	22
Real estate and rental and leasing	117	17	7	6	15	7	7	10	4	(1)
Professional and technical services	599	52	43	35	80	50	32	51	24	39
Management of companies and enterprises	60	6	(1)	3	7	3	5	5	4	3
Administrative and waste services	2 579	381	166	151	262	203	170	320	162	186
Educational services	161	19	8	4	17	15	26	29	11	12
Health care and social assistance	709	56	28	33	46	102	177	104	30	39
Arts, entertainment, and recreation	363	55	11	13	45	24	30	30	17	27
Accommodation and food services	1 386	158	50	88	127	148	120	74	65	82
Other services, except public administration	218	21	4	8	9	28	53	17	8	12
Unclassified	5	...	...	...	1	...	...	3	1	...
Government	1 677	120	48	34	65	124	379	309	57	81
Local	1 181	65	26	19	41	80	332	221	32	31

[1] Data do not meet BLS or state agency disclosure standards.
. . . = Not available.

Table 7-3. Industry Distribution: Mass Layoff Events and Initial Claimants for Unemployment Insurance, 1998–September 2011—Continued

(Number, not seasonally adjusted.)

Industry	1998	1999	2000	2001	2002	2003	2004	2005	2006	2007	2008	2009
						Initial claimants						
ALL INDUSTRIES	1 771 069	1 572 399	1 835 592	2 514 862	2 245 051	1 888 926	1 607 158	1 795 341	1 484 391	1 598 875	2 130 220	2 796 456
Total, Private	1 695 163	1 509 503	1 768 743	2 447 154	2 158 413	1 790 713	1 520 157	1 691 217	1 418 452	1 533 920	2 046 011	2 650 289
Agriculture, forestry, fishing and hunting	111 346	127 144	123 211	100 570	88 700	68 728	55 993	50 339	46 457	47 947	50 984	53 201
Total, private nonfarm	1 583 817	1 382 359	1 645 532	2 346 584	2 069 713	1 721 985	1 464 164	1 640 878	1 371 995	1 485 973	1 995 027	2 597 088
Mining, quarrying, and oil and gas extraction	12 206	19 537	9 271	14 887	16 672	9 852	5 985	6 483	5 582	5 327	9 273	27 872
Utilities	3 257	2 224	3 361	3 898	4 275	2 963	2 827	3 173	1 336	1 462	2 299	3 355
Construction	110 128	119 706	136 328	139 958	158 366	146 602	134 486	149 893	116 283	142 618	173 627	205 765
Manufacturing	757 217	631 026	782 543	1 236 178	904 856	744 473	565 535	670 620	583 274	610 215	870 310	1 137 106
Food	93 292	87 309	90 972	98 013	98 251	87 353	82 114	76 926	62 852	62 141	72 081	78 345
Beverage and tobacco products	6 421	7 229	5 955	6 242	6 564	6 775	6 594	4 714	4 404	4 679	6 466	7 205
Textile mills	32 403	33 744	33 064	57 009	43 511	37 734	19 669	22 213	19 070	19 527	21 620	23 439
Textile product mills	8 264	6 977	8 542	10 233	16 234	11 611	11 101	9 801	6 044	6 681	6 810	8 306
Apparel	65 714	47 715	40 474	50 423	41 320	29 887	24 729	21 889	14 170	11 508	13 970	18 545
Leather and allied products	12 343	8 492	8 204	7 867	3 903	5 170	4 733	4 960	2 757	3 077	2 862	2 280
Wood products	28 639	22 964	42 774	37 390	42 177	34 820	26 220	32 590	34 728	41 604	56 278	49 686
Paper	13 789	9 191	14 592	25 345	17 165	14 031	6 686	8 430	7 468	6 439	14 707	23 238
Printing and related support activities	8 624	8 981	9 030	13 799	15 019	9 976	10 534	8 005	6 131	7 414	12 000	22 793
Petroleum and coal products	2 500	2 761	3 609	2 518	3 611	2 292	2 343	2 262	2 874	2 333	3 114	3 689
Chemicals	8 980	9 338	8 960	15 659	11 161	10 811	8 707	7 713	6 164	6 665	10 227	15 692
Plastics and rubber products	27 693	26 551	35 828	59 024	38 596	35 054	28 409	30 714	26 098	24 611	49 196	58 926
Nonmetallic mineral products	16 125	16 035	19 272	25 246	21 712	22 031	15 389	18 956	15 980	19 204	27 834	32 179
Primary metals	29 975	26 928	38 835	81 601	48 671	40 641	23 193	27 469	21 866	27 016	37 765	76 288
Fabricated metal products	27 657	28 437	34 543	66 862	49 228	35 884	30 672	28 137	26 090	26 674	49 757	84 702
Machinery	43 662	72 480	57 793	121 724	87 710	60 370	28 407	33 713	40 069	45 831	53 673	164 176
Computer and electronic products	51 875	33 422	24 638	133 552	85 958	46 888	21 230	20 249	15 326	16 439	26 270	58 693
Electrical equipment and appliance manufacturing	30 547	31 223	39 205	60 387	48 413	36 496	24 443	30 804	24 503	23 274	37 732	48 250
Transportation equipment	214 826	123 741	228 380	303 139	176 505	178 282	163 026	253 681	221 257	228 213	323 622	304 693
Furniture and related products	15 887	14 799	23 821	40 267	34 743	25 225	16 379	18 168	17 499	19 510	33 617	39 591
Miscellaneous manufacturing	18 001	12 709	14 052	19 878	14 404	13 142	10 957	9 226	7 924	7 375	10 709	16 390
Wholesale trade	22 232	19 091	20 576	27 973	31 224	25 422	19 861	20 780	13 856	17 922	28 849	54 003
Retail trade	98 261	83 419	95 451	131 316	149 363	138 457	114 588	113 748	96 999	96 787	136 209	193 492
Transportation and warehousing	97 816	70 147	79 430	106 358	124 699	103 499	94 588	113 279	106 708	109 104	136 178	157 661
Information	99 124	55 890	80 618	103 122	100 982	80 715	72 820	72 100	64 365	64 404	70 066	96 127
Finance and insurance	14 619	17 804	17 532	27 881	36 099	27 870	24 954	20 884	22 213	40 917	42 152	55 876
Real estate and rental and leasing	2 816	2 991	4 564	7 611	7 324	6 412	6 329	7 615	4 082	5 139	8 754	11 567
Professional and technical services	33 922	47 941	57 135	77 862	82 223	52 700	49 547	49 719	40 739	49 223	57 144	72 962
Management of companies and enterprises	2 653	3 845	4 601	5 540	5 668	3 777	4 729	2 864	2 310	3 258	5 818	11 064
Administrative and waste services	175 144	154 902	191 073	258 542	257 530	206 765	184 369	187 156	153 655	168 460	246 670	294 709
Educational services	2 251	2 611	2 486	3 571	4 855	5 862	4 315	5 641	5 081	5 667	9 025	13 670
Health care and social assistance	36 658	36 229	36 759	32 255	40 364	38 108	40 118	51 371	33 972	38 848	44 139	52 058
Arts, entertainment, and recreation	17 040	16 629	14 399	20 542	23 517	21 387	21 191	27 564	16 531	16 874	21 550	29 853
Accommodation and food services	76 129	68 550	71 713	110 234	92 575	83 856	96 509	117 107	89 947	94 928	118 247	160 464
Other services, except public administration	11 802	12 806	13 287	15 742	20 049	18 617	18 226	18 753	13 478	13 936	14 310	18 889
Unclassified	10 542	17 011	24 405	23 114	9 072	4 648	3 187	2 128	1 584	884	407	595
Government	75 906	62 896	66 849	67 708	86 638	98 213	87 001	104 124	65 939	64 955	84 209	146 167
Local	38 545	30 264	32 271	35 003	53 323	66 279	57 331	69 351	41 689	40 690	58 272	103 273

Table 7-3. Industry Distribution: Mass Layoff Events and Initial Claimants for Unemployment Insurance, 1998–September 2011—*Continued*

(Number, not seasonally adjusted.)

Industry	2010	January 2011	February 2011	March 2011	April 2011	May 2011	June 2011	July 2011	August 2011	September 2011
						Initial claimants				
ALL INDUSTRIES	1 854 596	246 463	85 585	85 095	189 919	119 911	159 930	216 774	99 213	117 232
Total, Private	1 704 320	234 708	82 230	82 046	183 436	109 881	125 944	182 960	94 711	108 119
Agriculture, forestry, fishing and hunting	51 388	4 943	3 512	2 032	6 958	1 350	3 123	8 882	1 552	819
Total, private nonfarm	1 652 932	229 765	78 718	80 014	176 478	108 531	122 821	174 078	93 159	107 300
Mining, quarrying, and oil and gas extraction	8 192	1 188	322	247	270	308	(^{1})	. . .	(^{1})	(^{1})
Utilities	2 684	390	208	547	(^{1})	(^{1})	206	(^{1})	. . .	159
Construction	169 377	23 906	7 003	7 569	12 121	9 875	6 847	8 990	4 628	10 813
Manufacturing	502 665	75 006	18 471	20 869	47 104	25 199	22 986	71 814	26 916	32 058
Food	76 351	9 313	5 115	4 338	9 064	6 036	5 011	9 998	4 585	6 532
Beverage and tobacco products	5 952	752	287	242	438	(^{1})	. . .	288	472	656
Textile mills	13 872	4 455	468	328	792	1 045	1 131	3 341	944	1 784
Textile product mills	6 946	793	270	481	536	313	(^{1})	1 107	200	(^{1})
Apparel	11 663	1 776	693	374	964	1 174	1 119	1 526	1 024	993
Leather and allied products	2 187	(^{1})	(^{1})	. . .	. . .	(^{1})	(^{1})	869	. . .	(^{1})
Wood products	28 361	4 930	1 872	2 354	1 681	755	1 083	2 826	1 242	1 662
Paper	7 399	1 049	750	622	590	934	427	298	512	544
Printing and related support activities	11 396	983	679	359	858	1 182	383	930	569	451
Petroleum and coal products	3 405	412	(^{1})	(^{1})	. . .	(^{1})	(^{1})	(^{1})	. . .	(^{1})
Chemicals	9 880	1 612	759	(^{1})	453	503	371	935	303	376
Plastics and rubber products	17 354	4 569	262	321	2 113	1 082	880	3 359	705	1 011
Nonmetallic mineral products	18 013	4 239	1 141	404	926	635	380	1 612	685	363
Primary metals	20 467	3 046	794	536	944	1 053	914	2 450	415	869
Fabricated metal products	24 651	4 174	446	916	1 758	848	607	2 980	1 051	2 010
Machinery	44 916	5 446	897	1 077	2 552	2 054	2 042	4 799	4 407	3 069
Computer and electronic products	16 796	1 020	847	808	1 675	731	716	1 735	884	1 235
Electrical equipment and appliance manufacturing	20 199	1 572	1 078	2 886	1 736	1 049	915	2 628	2 537	1 872
Transportation equipment	133 554	19 478	1 275	2 887	18 328	4 146	4 871	26 488	4 688	6 006
Furniture and related products	22 467	4 263	533	1 099	831	888	771	2 770	952	1 342
Miscellaneous manufacturing	6 836	1 073	(^{1})	530	865	456	826	726	741	912
Wholesale trade	24 600	2 839	2 187	1 393	2 005	1 777	1 440	1 594	1 347	1 316
Retail trade	155 299	27 038	9 346	9 012	16 501	8 244	7 177	17 189	6 804	12 805
Transportation and warehousing	130 607	22 440	5 630	5 133	26 537	3 371	19 513	9 326	7 181	4 611
Information	75 518	7 915	8 959	3 788	5 689	5 394	5 721	5 289	18 813	6 431
Finance and insurance	33 122	2 758	1 407	1 354	3 482	1 616	1 158	2 769	1 647	1 821
Real estate and rental and leasing	7 861	1 150	369	452	1 389	457	779	856	235	(^{1})
Professional and technical services	56 713	4 019	3 729	3 771	8 572	4 062	3 378	4 372	1 737	6 476
Management of companies and enterprises	6 864	439	(^{1})	194	550	136	351	654	269	182
Administrative and waste services	221 024	34 996	13 894	11 303	23 380	15 938	16 582	31 193	13 158	17 285
Educational services	14 200	2 672	474	265	2 522	1 201	1 604	1 993	1 329	791
Health care and social assistance	55 205	3 880	1 685	2 038	3 397	11 059	14 975	7 079	2 279	2 711
Arts, entertainment, and recreation	28 366	5 494	629	893	4 650	1 835	1 664	2 867	1 438	2 092
Accommodation and food services	144 356	12 107	4 088	10 491	17 269	15 483	14 179	6 445	4 533	6 357
Other services, except public administration	15 849	1 528	161	695	845	2 361	4 129	1 336	654	1 067
Unclassified	430	. . .	. . .	. . .	76	. . .	. . .	184	70	. . .
Government	150 276	11 755	3 355	3 049	6 483	10 030	33 986	33 814	4 502	9 113
Local	104 733	5 561	1 942	1 128	4 187	6 734	29 958	20 810	2 402	4 571

^{1}Data do not meet BLS or state agency disclosure standards.
. . . = Not available.

Table 7-4. Mass Layoff Events and Initial Claimants for Unemployment Insurance, by Region and State, 1998–September 2011

(Number.)

Region and state	1998	1999	2000	2001	2002	2003	2004	2005	2006	2007	2008	2009
	\multicolumn{12}{c}{Mass layoff events}											
UNITED STATES[1]	15 904	14 909	15 738	21 467	20 277	18 963	15 980	16 466	13 998	15 493	21 137	28 030
Northeast	2 550	2 058	2 226	3 157	3 073	3 139	2 630	2 806	2 514	2 775	3 257	4 864
New England	395	383	427	691	615	493	359	426	352	358	427	745
Middle Atlantic	2 155	1 675	1 799	2 466	2 458	2 646	2 271	2 380	2 162	2 417	2 830	4 119
South	3 107	2 930	3 166	4 601	4 829	4 198	3 587	4 035	2 789	3 260	5 153	7 089
South Atlantic	1 608	1 423	1 538	2 249	2 275	2 068	1 802	1 585	1 475	1 727	2 561	3 782
East South Central	436	413	626	902	1 060	858	798	893	699	857	1 392	1 694
West South Central	1 063	1 094	1 002	1 450	1 494	1 272	987	1 557	615	676	1 200	1 613
Midwest	3 336	3 520	4 223	5 945	4 828	4 644	4 135	4 512	4 026	4 258	5 751	7 434
East North Central	2 591	2 710	3 309	4 682	3 679	3 622	3 292	3 585	3 183	3 381	4 551	5 734
West North Central	745	810	914	1 263	1 149	1 022	843	927	843	877	1 200	1 700
West	6 911	6 401	6 123	7 764	7 547	6 982	5 628	5 113	4 669	5 200	6 976	8 643
Mountain	481	508	596	836	726	638	512	537	443	558	831	1 291
Pacific	6 430	5 893	5 527	6 928	6 821	6 344	5 116	4 576	4 226	4 642	6 145	7 352
Alabama	90	105	119	169	428	332	274	244	138	276	444	493
Alaska	41	37	30	31	36	36	35	24	30	19	27	72
Arizona	105	103	107	161	170	146	110	109	72	99	146	255
Arkansas	105	103	85	95	76	60	54	52	40	69	116	117
California	5 881	5 342	5 008	6 145	6 045	5 651	4 547	4 104	3 702	4 130	5 403	6 377
Colorado	72	69	62	143	126	104	74	72	65	80	93	188
Connecticut	35	41	45	73	73	80	49	55	60	51	65	125
Delaware	13	13	13	33	19	23	13	9	9	17	38	57
District of Columbia	16	20	14	24	14	14	8	7	5	6	11	17
Florida	579	503	525	870	936	866	876	700	593	795	1 333	1 748
Georgia	155	165	164	215	310	403	323	323	317	350	476	618
Hawaii	53	62	38	77	74	55	37	33	48	46	88	106
Idaho	106	101	117	144	126	122	90	82	65	92	145	137
Illinois	532	549	647	870	824	775	663	647	600	641	871	1 309
Indiana	235	236	333	497	460	506	434	443	403	375	680	730
Iowa	153	196	230	319	251	249	169	212	188	192	303	423
Kansas	56	71	92	110	129	119	102	103	88	92	136	211
Kentucky	130	124	261	409	363	277	289	328	330	346	540	719
Louisiana	155	129	185	225	241	204	206	956	134	107	311	282
Maine	91	58	48	50	45	44	48	43	33	40	33	68
Maryland	67	57	68	73	85	94	80	55	120	128	85	141
Massachusetts	186	188	188	356	325	262	152	178	123	128	162	275
Michigan	489	791	969	1 359	612	604	866	1 032	922	949	1 156	1 305
Minnesota	172	162	198	304	279	260	213	237	205	199	245	377
Mississippi	95	53	102	121	82	81	61	155	71	80	167	135
Missouri	336	344	352	432	374	292	256	276	289	329	433	551
Montana	30	16	25	35	32	46	36	48	40	49	54	93
Nebraska	15	14	24	50	80	65	71	72	48	32	47	66
Nevada	92	148	214	246	178	148	121	138	117	135	251	369
New Hampshire	32	27	37	79	61	31	29	40	29	31	42	90
New Jersey	402	317	405	427	509	481	449	485	452	503	518	690
New Mexico	47	39	31	37	40	44	42	44	49	55	73	123
New York	446	311	244	441	765	932	836	806	717	733	897	1 367
North Carolina	124	123	172	288	245	246	167	166	129	93	196	325
North Dakota	6	12	10	30	24	22	22	14	18	22	26	47
Ohio	635	527	653	963	901	913	699	761	608	716	1 027	1 205
Oklahoma	74	74	61	122	122	121	86	58	55	69	79	150
Oregon	255	244	277	410	368	342	282	202	246	258	367	472
Pennsylvania	1 307	1 047	1 150	1 598	1 184	1 233	986	1 089	993	1 181	1 415	2 062
Rhode Island	47	58	71	82	72	41	51	65	52	54	64	90
South Carolina	369	334	288	452	364	170	159	142	140	177	284	493
South Dakota	7	11	8	18	12	15	10	13	7	11	10	25
Tennessee	121	131	144	203	187	168	174	166	160	155	241	347
Texas	729	788	671	1 008	1 055	887	641	491	386	431	694	1 064
Utah	29	30	39	66	50	24	33	37	30	43	61	113
Vermont	. . .	11	38	51	39	35	30	45	55	54	61	97
Virginia	258	200	271	275	263	229	156	170	143	142	116	330
Washington	200	208	174	265	298	260	215	213	200	189	260	325
West Virginia	27	8	23	19	39	23	20	13	19	19	22	53
Wisconsin	700	607	707	993	882	824	630	702	650	700	817	1 185
Wyoming	. . .	(²)	(²)	4	4	4	6	7	5	(²)	8	13

[1]Data for all states and the District of Columbia.
[2]Data do not meet BLS or state agency disclosure standards.
. . . = Not available.

Table 7-4. Mass Layoff Events and Initial Claimants for Unemployment Insurance, by Region and State, 1998–September 2011—*Continued*

(Number.)

Region and state	2010	January 2011	February 2011	March 2011	April 2011	May 2011	June 2011	July 2011	August 2011	September 2011
					Mass layoff events					
UNITED STATES[1]	19 564	2 558	1 024	908	1 750	1 367	1 661	2 176	961	1 189
Northeast	3 493	591	173	169	402	210	276	363	187	286
New England	504	81	32	22	67	30	53	44	23	23
Middle Atlantic	2 989	510	141	147	335	180	223	319	164	263
South	4 948	687	260	250	431	468	482	624	277	311
South Atlantic	2 753	431	166	116	210	234	273	358	174	183
East South Central	1 091	156	44	61	125	131	60	164	47	52
West South Central	1 104	100	50	73	96	103	149	102	56	76
Midwest	4 409	613	180	172	383	288	326	505	181	219
East North Central	3 286	464	130	124	310	217	236	359	132	178
West North Central	1 123	149	50	48	73	71	90	146	49	41
West	6 714	667	411	317	534	401	577	684	316	373
Mountain	947	66	35	46	118	68	64	67	36	43
Pacific	5 767	601	376	271	416	333	513	617	280	330
Alabama	365	70	12	18	28	37	20	60	14	14
Alaska	70	4	(2)	(2)	9	6	(2)	(2)	4	6
Arizona	192	13	12	11	40	15	18	23	5	9
Arkansas	71	6	3	3	(2)	15	29	17	10	9
California	5 110	530	349	230	348	285	462	571	251	297
Colorado	153	11	4	5	15	10	9	8	6	7
Connecticut	101	11	4	5	10	11	10	8	3	4
Delaware	47	5	3	...	8	5	6	3	(2)	(2)
District of Columbia	16	4	(2)	...	(2)	5	(2)	(2)	(2)	(2)
Florida	1 231	128	85	56	98	102	114	147	78	69
Georgia	429	84	28	16	40	40	43	45	30	28
Hawaii	56	6	3	5	6	5	4	(2)	(2)	(2)
Idaho	113	8	4	10	10	6	8	9	4	5
Illinois	804	86	35	37	56	47	61	48	35	48
Indiana	353	43	15	12	41	28	28	31	13	22
Iowa	243	39	9	10	17	6	14	19	9	8
Kansas	119	23	5	5	5	12	8	12	9	3
Kentucky	373	47	13	20	56	33	22	54	13	20
Louisiana	240	29	6	11	22	29	28	21	7	16
Maine	46	11	(2)	5	7	4	7	9	(2)	3
Maryland	128	25	4	4	5	5	12	13	4	9
Massachusetts	170	34	6	7	17	10	16	16	12	8
Michigan	634	127	17	21	50	38	55	130	21	31
Minnesota	221	19	10	9	16	10	17	68	7	6
Mississippi	147	13	8	14	27	40	5	25	10	8
Missouri	420	55	17	21	23	32	42	36	17	21
Montana	76	6	(2)	(2)	7	4	6	4	(2)	3
Nebraska	83	9	9	3	9	8	5	8	4	3
Nevada	240	12	5	7	23	13	12	10	11	13
New Hampshire	66	9	4	(2)	7	3	3	5	(2)	(2)
New Jersey	569	109	19	19	70	34	44	81	23	40
New Mexico	84	7	3	7	9	10	8	9	5	(2)
New York	1 121	207	45	49	153	56	55	142	71	91
North Carolina	315	100	27	18	14	40	45	80	21	44
North Dakota	30	3	...	...	(2)	(2)	(2)	3	3	...
Ohio	712	93	30	22	87	63	42	67	25	37
Oklahoma	71	11	9	5	6	9	6	6	(2)	3
Oregon	301	36	9	20	25	21	28	27	10	14
Pennsylvania	1 299	194	77	79	112	90	124	96	70	132
Rhode Island	71	8	10	(2)	9	(2)	10	4	4	(2)
South Carolina	272	41	5	7	19	11	23	28	20	20
South Dakota	7	(2)	...	...	(2)	(2)	(2)	...	...	...
Tennessee	206	26	11	9	14	21	13	25	10	10
Texas	722	54	32	54	67	50	86	58	37	48
Utah	77	7	6	3	13	8	3	4	(2)	4
Vermont	50	8	6	(2)	17	(2)	(2)	(2)	(2)	4
Virginia	290	42	10	13	23	21	25	41	17	8
Washington	230	25	13	14	28	16	17	15	14	11
West Virginia	25	(2)	3	(2)	(2)	5	3	...	(2)	(2)
Wisconsin	783	115	33	32	76	41	50	83	38	40
Wyoming	12	(2)	...	(2)	(2)	(2)	...	...	...	...

[1] Data for all states and the District of Columbia.
[2] Data do not meet BLS or state agency disclosure standards.
. . . = Not available.

Table 7-4. Mass Layoff Events and Initial Claimants for Unemployment Insurance, by Region and State, 1998–September 2011—*Continued*

(Number.)

Region and state	1998	1999	2000	2001	2002	2003	2004	2005	2006	2007	2008	2009
	Initial claimants											
UNITED STATES[1]	1 771 069	1 572 399	1 835 592	2 514 862	2 245 051	1 888 926	1 607 158	1 795 341	1 484 391	1 598 875	2 130 220	2 796 456
Northeast	264 063	207 057	235 083	340 246	338 965	306 462	270 788	280 628	254 684	273 079	316 191	465 208
New England	40 074	40 473	56 909	75 283	67 846	50 708	35 020	45 064	37 359	34 860	40 915	70 288
Middle Atlantic	223 989	166 584	178 174	264 963	271 119	255 754	235 768	235 564	217 325	238 219	275 276	394 920
South	347 332	314 556	360 330	546 222	545 907	435 387	355 561	485 505	312 892	356 812	533 687	691 460
South Atlantic	173 436	155 192	185 615	257 113	247 353	206 290	165 280	159 131	152 443	163 761	225 596	344 284
East South Central	48 496	41 403	69 619	107 661	127 477	98 450	91 565	131 138	95 861	115 114	180 702	183 287
West South Central	125 400	117 961	105 096	181 448	171 077	130 647	98 716	195 236	64 588	77 937	127 389	163 889
Midwest	504 413	474 132	583 290	841 597	614 121	552 140	485 255	571 950	508 798	509 431	676 591	892 202
East North Central	390 667	359 364	465 917	663 997	457 002	414 489	387 065	457 592	406 432	414 919	538 429	706 233
West North Central	113 746	114 768	117 373	177 600	157 119	137 651	98 190	114 358	102 366	94 512	138 162	185 969
West	655 261	576 654	656 889	786 797	746 058	594 937	495 554	457 258	408 017	459 553	603 751	747 586
Mountain	45 541	51 863	61 090	94 490	76 484	58 247	47 929	50 830	41 696	49 308	75 567	117 890
Pacific	609 720	524 791	595 799	692 307	669 574	536 690	447 625	406 428	366 321	410 245	528 184	629 696
Alabama	10 721	10 175	13 491	18 228	59 821	44 523	34 012	29 603	14 530	30 543	57 324	56 284
Alaska	3 246	3 565	2 706	2 814	2 846	2 973	2 930	2 326	2 770	1 798	2 888	7 056
Arizona	11 350	11 710	10 782	16 148	17 775	12 566	11 020	11 831	7 950	10 839	14 274	24 316
Arkansas	11 819	13 896	9 050	11 328	6 868	6 131	5 926	7 611	5 056	8 647	11 914	12 353
California	556 078	469 814	536 673	600 501	576 110	467 573	394 114	360 138	317 907	357 994	446 480	532 028
Colorado	7 181	7 024	5 967	14 127	12 601	9 422	6 856	6 759	5 905	6 567	8 200	16 424
Connecticut	3 084	3 847	4 393	6 122	7 360	7 054	4 203	4 972	6 595	4 975	5 505	10 559
Delaware	5 764	3 477	8 271	8 200	4 927	8 084	3 764	5 034	4 185	4 522	6 335	5 513
District of Columbia	1 514	2 052	1 572	2 301	1 688	1 160	807	565	346	418	1 195	1 504
Florida	43 184	36 724	39 407	70 889	71 635	61 863	63 087	51 535	42 593	55 696	94 656	131 190
Georgia	16 992	15 903	16 967	22 141	41 888	49 009	33 406	40 854	35 947	39 624	48 603	64 642
Hawaii	5 148	5 107	3 042	7 803	7 467	5 151	2 938	2 692	3 706	3 988	9 590	9 173
Idaho	9 845	11 264	13 121	17 144	15 579	13 690	8 148	7 233	5 665	8 245	13 591	12 405
Illinois	74 206	86 768	108 726	135 126	116 592	90 181	75 763	71 399	75 118	80 477	103 685	193 495
Indiana	35 329	38 252	50 892	71 521	67 134	70 393	58 853	62 574	56 395	47 923	80 027	84 555
Iowa	19 467	30 779	32 479	44 997	35 460	32 744	18 126	30 291	27 804	23 637	43 574	54 587
Kansas	8 198	8 189	13 145	21 657	18 186	16 102	10 782	9 740	9 785	10 654	17 243	27 741
Kentucky	14 988	14 485	33 975	60 327	42 094	34 709	37 809	55 078	61 246	59 399	89 953	87 321
Louisiana	15 544	9 869	14 799	28 373	22 113	17 329	16 519	120 600	12 915	13 042	31 664	26 098
Maine	7 471	5 875	7 407	4 713	4 377	3 828	4 293	3 445	2 622	3 035	2 536	5 922
Maryland	10 295	4 527	5 868	6 259	9 386	7 911	7 951	4 998	11 771	12 172	7 116	11 932
Massachusetts	20 599	19 879	27 907	36 693	33 705	25 352	13 960	18 114	11 188	10 785	14 911	25 608
Michigan	101 297	99 284	129 640	196 459	63 350	66 866	99 124	131 411	127 964	125 942	132 468	153 361
Minnesota	29 806	19 936	24 169	38 739	33 348	27 725	24 607	26 689	25 729	19 231	23 370	34 255
Mississippi	9 651	4 576	8 684	10 501	7 162	5 239	4 384	29 971	5 524	9 647	13 818	10 116
Missouri	52 631	51 518	43 765	60 026	57 373	50 379	35 034	37 005	29 324	33 557	43 451	54 046
Montana	2 744	1 501	3 489	4 048	3 570	4 379	3 600	4 567	3 726	3 873	4 731	8 260
Nebraska	2 045	1 325	2 102	6 363	8 371	6 761	6 764	8 332	5 907	3 440	5 204	7 371
Nevada	7 652	14 611	21 976	32 414	19 115	12 897	11 795	13 224	11 130	11 344	22 389	34 364
New Hampshire	2 790	3 279	4 615	10 903	8 080	3 030	2 726	4 666	2 996	3 053	3 873	8 548
New Jersey	48 119	34 439	45 173	52 530	63 369	49 815	51 252	48 732	51 128	52 738	51 623	68 149
New Mexico	3 536	3 036	2 243	3 045	2 894	3 129	3 071	3 469	4 226	4 619	6 253	9 680
New York	50 700	30 753	22 318	46 404	85 578	93 583	95 228	87 649	76 638	77 353	95 612	144 247
North Carolina	11 723	18 592	23 902	33 021	27 324	28 977	14 435	16 670	13 316	10 694	21 037	37 488
North Dakota	961	2 022	912	4 303	3 140	2 577	1 980	1 184	3 065	2 992	4 354	5 870
Ohio	92 045	65 449	94 419	139 218	103 577	102 864	86 850	113 165	80 291	83 429	131 813	147 712
Oklahoma	9 646	9 889	7 531	21 086	16 203	17 502	14 124	10 090	7 234	9 627	10 187	16 986
Oregon	25 005	24 260	32 159	55 449	44 944	35 508	28 401	22 231	24 386	29 391	42 780	52 900
Pennsylvania	125 170	101 392	110 683	166 029	122 172	112 356	89 288	99 183	89 559	108 128	128 041	182 524
Rhode Island	5 675	6 788	8 441	10 851	9 567	5 251	6 907	9 151	8 211	7 362	7 040	10 159
South Carolina	49 051	46 724	45 084	74 891	51 006	21 001	22 241	17 450	16 909	21 787	32 063	53 172
South Dakota	638	999	801	1 515	1 241	1 363	897	1 117	752	1 001	966	2 099
Tennessee	13 136	12 167	13 469	18 605	18 400	13 979	15 360	16 486	14 561	15 525	19 607	29 566
Texas	88 391	84 307	73 716	120 661	125 893	89 685	62 147	56 935	39 383	46 621	73 624	108 452
Utah	3 233	2 590	3 457	7 260	4 642	1 892	2 959	3 266	2 765	3 464	5 604	11 255
Vermont	. . .	805	4 146	6 001	4 757	6 193	2 931	4 716	5 747	5 650	7 050	9 492
Virginia	32 636	26 515	42 651	37 911	36 059	26 377	17 802	20 927	25 642	17 496	12 738	33 637
Washington	20 243	22 045	21 219	25 740	38 207	25 485	19 242	19 041	17 552	17 074	26 446	28 539
West Virginia	2 277	678	1 893	1 500	3 440	1 908	1 787	1 098	1 734	1 352	1 853	5 206
Wisconsin	87 790	69 611	82 240	121 673	106 349	84 185	66 475	79 043	66 664	77 148	90 436	127 110
Wyoming	. . .	. . .	. . .	304	308	272	480	481	329	. . .	525	1 186

[1]Data for all states and the District of Columbia.
[2]Data do not meet BLS or state agency disclosure standards.
. . . = Not available.

Table 7-4. Mass Layoff Events and Initial Claimants for Unemployment Insurance, by Region and State, 1998–September 2011—*Continued*

(Number.)

Region and state	2010	January 2011	February 2011	March 2011	April 2011	May 2011	June 2011	July 2011	August 2011	September 2011
					Initial claimants					
UNITED STATES[1]	1 854 596	246 463	85 585	85 095	189 919	119 911	159 930	216 774	99 213	117 232
Northeast	350 507	58 802	16 047	15 540	54 129	17 726	30 513	34 691	29 937	26 131
New England	50 632	7 047	4 259	1 883	8 926	2 505	5 004	3 808	7 784	2 245
Middle Atlantic	299 875	51 755	11 788	13 657	45 203	15 221	25 509	30 883	22 153	23 886
South	469 957	66 552	19 998	26 112	42 685	43 457	45 180	62 261	25 771	28 956
South Atlantic	245 720	40 880	11 371	9 765	17 371	18 785	24 626	33 888	15 565	16 747
East South Central	113 934	16 508	4 343	6 539	16 048	14 830	5 603	17 365	4 879	4 988
West South Central	110 303	9 164	4 284	9 808	9 266	9 842	14 951	11 008	5 327	7 221
Midwest	466 753	63 468	15 075	17 168	44 126	26 017	33 813	62 114	20 541	21 885
East North Central	358 694	45 790	11 550	11 640	37 250	18 948	26 402	41 262	14 839	18 293
West North Central	108 059	17 678	3 525	5 528	6 876	7 069	7 411	20 852	5 702	3 592
West	567 379	57 641	34 465	26 275	48 979	32 711	50 424	57 708	22 964	40 260
Mountain	85 395	6 046	2 440	4 292	12 547	5 948	6 011	6 339	3 048	3 678
Pacific	481 984	51 595	32 025	21 983	36 432	26 763	44 413	51 369	19 916	36 582
Alabama	39 152	7 730	1 583	2 072	3 080	3 604	1 922	6 904	1 310	1 419
Alaska	6 796	392	(2)	(2)	1 137	489	(2)	(2)	307	532
Arizona	19 280	1 075	838	1 045	5 635	1 394	1 561	2 137	341	678
Arkansas	7 748	768	283	232	(2)	1 647	3 185	1 607	909	825
California	419 809	44 274	29 769	17 478	29 264	22 874	39 788	46 009	17 552	33 690
Colorado	13 915	1 126	383	557	1 750	1 171	708	704	547	680
Connecticut	8 835	1 048	331	410	1 056	769	807	713	280	242
Delaware	3 271	411	239	...	551	334	415	233	(2)	(2)
District of Columbia	1 352	452	(2)	...	(2)	276	(2)	(2)	(2)	(2)
Florida	88 776	9 464	5 071	4 060	7 600	6 363	9 161	12 098	5 176	4 538
Georgia	44 512	8 952	2 221	1 593	3 380	4 038	4 789	5 152	2 447	3 256
Hawaii	4 629	388	232	659	420	351	275	(2)	(2)	(2)
Idaho	9 267	698	225	886	896	370	832	1 220	255	365
Illinois	91 277	7 516	3 508	3 495	6 701	4 749	6 436	5 599	5 514	5 092
Indiana	42 895	6 487	1 471	1 336	4 689	2 189	2 722	5 700	1 215	2 179
Iowa	31 028	4 007	870	2 060	2 143	1 069	1 359	2 397	1 796	741
Kansas	13 212	5 440	308	727	381	1 365	682	1 372	1 497	334
Kentucky	46 854	5 472	1 682	2 387	9 722	3 431	2 003	6 294	1 935	2 202
Louisiana	20 739	2 309	518	1 239	1 669	2 531	2 056	1 936	378	1 554
Maine	4 058	900	(2)	575	818	318	458	667	(2)	194
Maryland	11 022	1 888	306	431	365	462	1 102	1 486	812	617
Massachusetts	15 749	3 225	534	624	2 040	1 068	1 133	1 632	6 030	617
Michigan	74 773	10 398	1 091	2 359	6 813	3 368	5 413	14 164	1 986	2 186
Minnesota	20 543	1 988	675	707	1 023	932	1 249	11 406	607	419
Mississippi	11 410	1 163	446	1 413	1 987	5 957	240	1 853	613	521
Missouri	32 586	4 713	1 038	1 755	2 259	2 620	3 176	4 068	1 145	1 520
Montana	6 094	560	(2)	(2)	438	414	531	306	(2)	228
Nebraska	7 061	1 086	634	279	768	860	441	1 026	247	578
Nevada	21 704	1 299	394	524	1 703	1 133	1 292	875	1 158	1 274
New Hampshire	7 214	722	537	(2)	1 107	233	614	363	(2)	(2)
New Jersey	61 398	9 853	2 243	1 494	11 776	2 937	6 432	7 381	6 817	3 922
New Mexico	6 509	467	164	640	711	783	663	568	338	(2)
New York	125 909	24 950	4 161	5 159	22 636	4 743	5 185	14 892	7 506	7 664
North Carolina	32 337	9 865	1 984	1 917	1 240	3 928	4 871	8 083	1 624	5 449
North Dakota	3 098	390	...	...	(2)	(2)	(2)	583	410	...
Ohio	71 382	9 241	2 473	1 891	11 082	5 170	6 150	7 739	2 420	4 985
Oklahoma	8 271	1 048	1 015	367	392	902	481	1 206	(2)	372
Oregon	31 404	4 390	896	2 337	2 886	1 586	2 967	3 435	836	1 178
Pennsylvania	112 568	16 952	5 384	7 004	10 791	7 541	13 892	8 610	7 830	12 300
Rhode Island	10 046	555	2 125	(2)	2 105	(2)	1 276	323	882	(2)
South Carolina	32 332	5 124	340	489	1 913	949	1 878	2 724	2 871	1 944
South Dakota	531	(2)	467	...	(2)	(2)	(2)	...	...	...
Tennessee	16 518	2 143	632	667	1 259	1 838	1 438	2 314	1 021	846
Texas	73 545	5 039	2 468	7 970	7 118	4 762	9 229	6 259	3 836	4 470
Utah	7 339	720	370	423	1 232	554	424	529	218	329
Vermont	4 730	597	558	(2)	1 800	(2)	716	(2)	(2)	537
Virginia	29 924	4 497	899	1 102	2 063	2 050	2 071	4 028	1 988	569
Washington	19 346	2 151	955	1 099	2 725	1 463	1 231	1 537	1 170	1 006
West Virginia	2 194	(2)	216	(2)	(2)	385	189	...	(2)	(2)
Wisconsin	78 367	12 148	3 007	2 559	7 965	3 472	5 681	8 060	3 704	3 851
Wyoming	1 287	(2)	...	(2)	(2)	(2)	...	...	...	...

[1]Data for all states and the District of Columbia.
[2]Data do not meet BLS or state agency disclosure standards.
. . . = Not available.

Table 7-5. Extended Mass Layoff Events and Separations, Selected Measures, 2006–2011

(Number.)

Year and quarter	Layoff events					
	Total, private nonfarm	Total, excluding seasonal and vacation events[1]	Total, movement of work[2]	Movement of work actions		
				Total	With separations reported	With separations unknown
2006						
Quarter 1	963	715	53	80	51	29
Quarter 2	1 353	750	72	103	66	37
Quarter 3	929	752	58	72	49	23
Quarter 4	1 640	943	69	94	66	28
2007						
Quarter 1	1 110	849	70	86	61	25
Quarter 2	1 421	772	65	89	66	23
Quarter 3	1 018	800	63	87	60	27
Quarter 4	1 814	1 062	69	90	66	24
2008						
Quarter 1	1 340	1 094	59	76	41	35
Quarter 2	1 756	1 105	71	100	78	22
Quarter 3	1 581	1 365	84	106	78	28
Quarter 4	3 582	2 713	118	161	122	39
2009						
Quarter 1	3 979	3 639	92	124	87	37
Quarter 2	3 395	2 638	116	158	102	56
Quarter 3	2 034	1 748	77	109	73	36
Quarter 4	2 416	1 588	66	100	55	45
2010						
Quarter 1	1 870	1 452	72	101	67	34
Quarter 2	2 008	1 207	56	74	47	27
Quarter 3	1 370	998	51	75	41	34
Quarter 4	1 999	1 173	50	68	46	22
2011						
Quarter 1	1 490	1 099	50	74	34	40
Quarter 2[3]	1 810	1 037	42	50	25	25
Quarter 3[3]	1 226	994	35	49	28	21

Year and quarter	Separations					
	Total, private nonfarm	Total, excluding seasonal and vacation events[1]	Total, movement of work[2]	Movement of work actions		
				Total	With separations reported	With separations unknown
2006						
Quarter 1	183 089	141 448	10 519	. . .	7 080	. . .
Quarter 2	295 964	139 737	16 610	. . .	9 674	. . .
Quarter 3	160 254	132 563	12 840	. . .	6 820	. . .
Quarter 4	296 662	167 130	15 782	. . .	10 462	. . .
2007						
Quarter 1	225 600	186 345	11 438	. . .	8 467	. . .
Quarter 2	278 719	123 843	11 352	. . .	7 401	. . .
Quarter 3	160 024	119 663	12 367	. . .	7 159	. . .
Quarter 4	301 592	171 808	11 302	. . .	7 152	. . .
2008						
Quarter 1	230 098	186 991	13 314	. . .	6 180	. . .
Quarter 2	354 713	198 389	12 317	. . .	7 346	. . .
Quarter 3	290 453	246 532	14 943	. . .	9 631	. . .
Quarter 4	641 714	491 941	20 382	. . .	11 919	. . .
2009						
Quarter 1	705 141	648 916	15 501	. . .	9 089	. . .
Quarter 2	651 318	491 273	21 365	. . .	11 478	. . .
Quarter 3	345 531	289 220	12 854	. . .	7 088	. . .
Quarter 4	406 212	269 005	11 974	. . .	4 573	. . .
2010						
Quarter 1	314 512	245 887	11 491	. . .	5 949	. . .
Quarter 2	381 622	210 491	10 987	. . .	4 677	. . .
Quarter 3	222 357	169 744	7 553	. . .	3 574	. . .
Quarter 4	338 643	201 165	9 073	. . .	4 422	. . .
2011						
Quarter 1	225 136	169 671	10 789	. . .	5 951	. . .
Quarter 2[3]	317 422	165 706	6 922	. . .	3 293	. . .
Quarter 3[3]	184 493	145 730	6 216	. . .	2 905	. . .

[1]The questions on movement of work were not asked of employers when the reason for layoff was either seasonal work or vacation period.
[2]Movement of work can involve more than one action.
[3]Preliminary.
. . . = Not available.

Table 7-6. Movement of Work Actions by Type of Separation Where Number of Separations Is Known by Employers, 2006–2011

(Number.)

Actions[1]

Year and quarter	With separations reported	Location — Out-of-country relocations Total	Within company	Different company	Location — Domestic relocations Total	Within company	Different company	Unable to assign place of relocation	Company — Within company Total	Domestic	Out of country	Unable to assign	Company — Different company Total	Domestic	Out of country	Unable to assign
2006																
Quarter 1	51	22	17	5	29	24	5	...	41	24	17	...	10	5	5	...
Quarter 2	66	23	21	2	43	35	8	...	56	35	21	...	10	8	2	...
Quarter 3	49	12	9	3	37	31	6	...	40	31	9	...	9	6	3	...
Quarter 4	66	27	24	3	39	35	4	...	59	35	24	...	7	4	3	...
2007																
Quarter 1	61	14	13	1	46	41	5	1	55	41	13	1	6	5	1	...
Quarter 2	66	23	22	1	43	34	9	...	56	34	22	...	10	9	1	...
Quarter 3	60	21	11	10	38	34	4	1	46	34	11	1	14	4	10	...
Quarter 4	66	27	26	1	39	38	1	...	64	38	26	...	2	1	1	...
2008																
Quarter 1	41	15	12	3	26	24	2	...	36	24	12	...	5	2	3	...
Quarter 2	78	25	23	2	52	47	5	1	70	47	23	...	8	5	2	1
Quarter 3	78	19	17	2	59	50	9	...	67	50	17	...	11	9	2	...
Quarter 4	122	36	31	5	86	79	7	...	110	79	31	...	12	7	5	...
2009																
Quarter 1	87	25	23	2	62	57	5	...	80	57	23	...	7	5	2	...
Quarter 2	102	22	21	1	80	73	7	...	94	73	21	...	8	7	1	...
Quarter 3	73	19	16	3	54	42	12	...	58	42	16	...	15	12	3	...
Quarter 4	55	15	12	3	38	34	4	2	48	34	12	2	7	4	3	...
2010																
Quarter 1	67	14	11	3	53	47	6	...	58	47	11	...	9	6	3	...
Quarter 2	47	11	10	1	36	34	2	...	44	34	10	...	3	2	1	...
Quarter 3	41	8	4	4	33	28	5	...	32	28	4	...	9	5	4	...
Quarter 4	46	13	11	2	33	28	5	...	39	28	11	...	7	5	2	...
2011																
Quarter 1	34	11	10	1	22	17	5	1	28	17	10	1	6	5	1	...
Quarter 2[2]	25	6	4	2	19	17	2	...	21	17	4	...	4	2	2	...
Quarter 3[3]	28	2	...	2	26	23	3	...	23	23	...	...	5	3	2	...

Separations

Year and quarter	With separations reported	Location — Out-of-country relocations Total	Within company	Different company	Location — Domestic relocations Total	Within company	Different company	Unable to assign place of relocation	Company — Within company Total	Domestic	Out of country	Unable to assign	Company — Different company Total	Domestic	Out of country	Unable to assign
2006																
Quarter 1	7 080	2 682	2 408	274	4 398	3 873	525	...	6 281	3 873	2 408	...	799	525	274	...
Quarter 2	9 674	3 033	2 912	121	6 641	5 823	818	...	8 735	5 823	2 912	...	939	818	121	...
Quarter 3	6 820	2 071	1 030	1 041	4 749	4 020	729	...	5 050	4 020	1 030	...	1 770	729	1 041	...
Quarter 4	10 462	5 581	5 426	155	4 881	4 494	387	...	9 920	4 494	5 426	...	542	387	155	...
2007																
Quarter 1	8 467	2 135	2 086	49	6 261	5 221	1 040	71	7 378	5 221	2 086	71	1 089	1 040	49	...
Quarter 2	7 401	3 537	3 387	150	3 864	3 254	610	...	6 641	3 254	3 387	...	760	610	150	...
Quarter 3	7 159	3 187	1 504	1 683	3 793	3 396	397	179	5 079	3 396	1 504	179	2 080	397	1 683	...
Quarter 4	7 152	2 997	2 910	87	4 155	3 975	180	...	6 885	3 975	2 910	...	267·	180	87	...
2008																
Quarter 1	6 180	1 901	1 602	299	4 279	3 364	915	...	4 966	3 364	1 602	...	1 214	915	299	...
Quarter 2	7 346	3 159	2 935	224	3 912	3 694	218	275	6 629	3 694	2 935	...	717	218	224	275
Quarter 3	9 631	2 312	2 135	177	7 319	6 522	797	...	8 657	6 522	2 135	...	974	797	177	...
Quarter 4	11 919	4 059	3 720	339	7 860	7 363	497	...	11 083	7 363	3 720	...	836	497	339	...
2009																
Quarter 1	9 089	3 967	3 794	173	5 122	4 776	346	...	8 570	4 776	3 794	...	519	346	173	...
Quarter 2	11 478	2 849	2 759	90	8 629	7 406	1 223	...	10 165	7 406	2 759	...	1 313	1 223	90	...
Quarter 3	7 088	2 006	1 786	220	5 082	3 642	1 440	...	5 428	3 642	1 786	...	1 660	1 440	220	...
Quarter 4	4 573	1 556	1 291	265	2 722	2 360	362	295	3 946	2 360	1 291	295	627	362	265	...
2010																
Quarter 1	5 949	1 023	933	90	4 926	3 992	934	...	4 925	3 992	933	...	1 024	934	90	...
Quarter 2	4 677	1 200	1 160	40	3 477	3 018	459	...	4 178	3 018	1 160	...	499	459	40	...
Quarter 3	3 574	1 198	340	858	2 376	1 824	552	...	2 164	1 824	340	...	1 410	552	858	...
Quarter 4	4 422	1 915	1 115	800	2 507	2 294	213	...	3 409	2 294	1 115	...	1 013	213	800	...
2011																
Quarter 1	5 951	2 409	2 309	100	3 395	3 186	209	147	5 642	3 186	2 309	147	309	209	100	...
Quarter 2[2]	3 293	916	733	183	2 377	2 119	258	...	2 852	2 119	733	...	441	258	183	...
Quarter 3[3]	2 905	110	...	110	2 795	2 498	297	...	2 498	2 498	...	...	407	297	110	...

[1] Only actions for which separations associated with the movement of work were reported are shown.
[2] Revised.
[3] Preliminary.
... = Not available.

NOTES AND DEFINITIONS

JOB OPENINGS AND LABOR TURNOVER SURVEY

The data for the Job Openings and Labor Turnover Survey (JOLTS) are collected and compiled monthly from a sample of business establishments by the Bureau of Labor Statistics (BLS). Each month, data are collected in a survey of business establishments for total employment, job openings, hires, quits, layoffs and discharges, and other separations. Data collection methods include computer-assisted telephone interviewing, touchtone data entry, fax, and mail.

Concepts and Definitions

The JOLTS program covers all private nonfarm establishments such as factories, offices, and stores, as well as federal, state, and local government entities in the 50 states and the District of Columbia.

Industry classification is in accordance with the 2007 version of the North American Industry Classification System (NAICS). In order to ensure the highest possible quality of data, state workforce agencies verify with employers and update, if necessary, the industry code, location, and ownership classification of all establishments on a 3-year cycle. Changes in establishment characteristics resulting from the verification process are always introduced into the JOLTS sampling frame with the data reported for the first month of the year.

Employment includes persons on the payroll who worked or received pay for the pay period that includes the 12th day of the reference month. Full-time, part-time, permanent, short-term, seasonal, salaried, and hourly employees are included, as are employees on paid vacations or other paid leave. Proprietors or partners of unincorporated businesses, unpaid family workers, or persons on leave without pay or on strike for the entire pay period, are not counted as employed. Employees of temporary help agencies, employee leasing companies, outside contractors, and consultants are counted by their employer of record, not by the establishment where they are working.

Job openings information is submitted by establishments for the last business day of the reference month. A job opening requires that: 1) a specific position exists and there is work available for that position, 2) work could start within 30 days regardless of whether a suitable candidate is found, and 3) the employer is actively recruiting from outside the establishment to fill the position. Included are full-time, part-time, permanent, short-term, and seasonal openings. Active recruiting means that the establishment is taking steps to fill a position by advertising in newspapers or on the Internet, posting help-wanted signs, accepting applications, or using other similar methods.

Jobs to be filled only by internal transfers, promotions, demotions, or recall from layoffs are excluded. Also excluded are jobs with start dates more than 30 days in the future, jobs for which employees have been hired but have not yet reported for work, and jobs to be filled by employees of temporary help agencies, employee leasing companies, outside contractors, or consultants. The job openings rate is computed by dividing the number of job openings by the sum of employment and job openings and multiplying that quotient by 100.

Hires are the total number of additions to the payroll occurring at any time during the reference month, including both new and rehired employees, full-time and part-time, permanent, short-term and seasonal employees, employees recalled to the location after a layoff lasting more than 7 days, on-call or intermittent employees who returned to work after having been formally separated, and transfers from other locations. The hires count does not include transfers or promotions within the reporting site, employees returning from strike, employees of temporary help agencies or employee leasing companies, outside contractors, or consultants. The hires rate is computed by dividing the number of hires by employment and multiplying that quotient by 100.

Separations are the total number of terminations of employment occurring at any time during the reference month, and are reported by type of separation—quits, layoffs and discharges, and other separations. Quits are voluntary separations by employees (except for retirements, which are reported as other separations). Layoffs and discharges are involuntary separations initiated by the employer and include layoffs with no intent to rehire, formal layoffs lasting or expected to last more than 7 days, discharges resulting from mergers, downsizing, or closings, firings or other discharges for cause, terminations of permanent or short-term employees, and terminations of seasonal employees. Other separations include retirements, transfers to other locations, deaths, and separations due to disability. Separations do not include transfers within the same location or employees on strike.

The separations rate is computed by dividing the number of separations by employment and multiplying that quotient by 100. The quits, layoffs and discharges, and other separations rates are computed similarly, dividing the number by employment and multiplying by 100.

The JOLTS annual level estimates for hires, quits, layoffs and discharges, other separations, and total separations are the sum of the 12 published monthly levels. The annual rate estimates are computed by dividing the annual level by the Current Employment Statistics (CES) annual average employment level, and multiplying that quotient by 100.

This figure will be approximately equal to the sum of the 12 monthly rates.

Annual estimates are not calculated for job openings because job openings are a stock, or point-in-time, measurement for the last business day of each month. Only jobs still open on the last day of the month are counted. For the same reason job openings cannot be cumulated throughout each month, annual figures for job openings cannot be created by summing the monthly estimates.

Hires and separations are flow measures and are cumulated over the month with a total reported for the month. Therefore, the annual figures can be created by summing the monthly estimates.

Sources of Additional Information

For more extensive information see the Job Openings and Labor Turnover Survey (JOLTS) page on the BLS Web site at <http://www.bls.gov/jlt/>.

Table 7-7. Job Openings Levels and Rates, by Industry, December 2000–September 2011

(Seasonally adjusted, levels in thousands, rates per 100.)

Year and month	Level											
	Total[1]	Total private[1]	Construction	Manufacturing	Trade, transportation, and utilities[2]	Retail trade	Professional and business services	Education and health services	Leisure and hospitality[3]	Accommodation and food services	Government[4]	State and local government
2000												
December	5 111	4 716	226	467	879	543	830	842	591	555	396	322
2001												
January	5 082	4 601	189	422	929	496	689	782	658	597	481	401
February	4 885	4 394	228	417	877	519	796	808	617	567	491	421
March	4 992	4 511	200	405	699	430	1 044	787	678	569	481	422
April	4 803	4 307	232	322	894	550	836	709	600	547	496	433
May	4 560	4 063	221	313	699	464	813	791	585	521	498	430
June	4 491	3 953	188	347	694	436	746	770	526	467	538	475
July	4 392	3 859	191	304	665	408	623	795	599	511	534	482
August	4 293	3 792	112	277	626	404	594	921	595	533	501	450
September	4 165	3 724	146	313	587	362	647	757	638	560	441	385
October	3 726	3 264	128	262	615	362	511	771	440	381	461	408
November	3 670	3 216	140	231	566	353	563	709	491	421	455	408
December	3 621	3 163	121	220	567	369	520	728	466	411	458	405
2002												
January	3 702	3 299	110	260	570	374	564	759	429	370	403	367
February	3 505	3 040	109	259	542	350	495	750	424	359	464	418
March	3 687	3 243	128	242	598	354	597	740	428	355	444	393
April	3 485	3 058	98	244	567	352	537	709	412	353	427	384
May	3 614	3 161	111	249	556	340	655	673	429	364	453	397
June	3 429	3 030	130	257	544	339	525	742	391	342	400	369
July	3 466	3 045	103	259	516	345	599	698	402	362	421	374
August	3 506	3 048	112	249	535	322	597	702	405	351	457	405
September	3 371	2 954	132	241	497	319	588	720	380	346	417	364
October	3 698	3 289	134	230	593	395	724	680	407	354	409	355
November	3 646	3 181	120	238	503	298	677	736	427	382	465	397
December	3 127	2 752	86	218	436	246	556	659	383	321	375	334
2003												
January	3 622	3 203	109	216	518	313	853	642	395	360	420	359
February	3 444	3 035	101	202	555	358	774	609	342	286	409	355
March	3 180	2 784	87	199	481	301	660	590	362	332	396	328
April	3 260	2 883	137	206	455	293	523	626	440	353	377	341
May	3 190	2 854	92	203	497	308	624	669	378	344	335	282
June	3 339	2 932	114	195	510	333	618	609	482	411	407	341
July	3 249	2 895	155	189	522	322	706	574	345	289	354	283
August	3 223	2 901	109	225	539	336	729	559	365	316	322	260
September	3 140	2 819	66	209	553	361	651	551	393	342	321	270
October	3 305	2 958	85	225	558	360	597	626	416	372	347	300
November	3 338	3 011	90	267	584	382	613	586	408	365	327	275
December	3 293	2 964	100	217	607	345	619	524	459	404	329	279
2004												
January	3 524	3 111	141	235	556	349	592	639	425	360	413	347
February	3 502	3 135	122	224	561	390	657	604	445	386	368	307
March	3 514	3 148	127	251	620	388	589	611	436	393	366	317
April	3 574	3 207	136	265	607	386	669	617	416	377	367	305
May	3 728	3 337	138	288	639	427	661	617	439	375	391	348
June	3 500	3 148	102	269	637	402	729	528	463	420	352	297
July	3 894	3 510	117	277	681	428	759	608	474	430	385	339
August	3 734	3 371	129	283	649	431	674	608	506	426	362	315
September	3 817	3 447	124	274	702	479	708	610	466	398	371	316
October	3 961	3 539	156	290	656	450	746	675	451	403	422	361
November	3 464	3 076	144	255	553	320	593	624	420	365	389	336
December	3 916	3 490	153	274	669	412	709	636	465	393	426	351
2005												
January	3 895	3 515	154	292	657	447	689	637	522	459	381	352
February	3 864	3 482	153	283	711	443	695	618	502	443	382	336
March	3 943	3 568	150	286	697	462	734	672	496	436	375	322
April	4 191	3 797	135	294	731	472	801	651	600	525	393	340
May	3 912	3 531	138	281	696	411	776	693	495	436	381	324
June	4 161	3 779	144	294	690	415	888	653	529	450	382	334
July	4 175	3 769	158	320	686	417	801	693	523	421	407	354
August	4 112	3 711	154	302	680	424	825	669	482	415	402	350
September	4 290	3 862	171	330	678	396	824	694	499	453	428	364
October	4 276	3 889	182	286	759	453	813	660	497	429	387	338
November	4 465	4 067	199	395	826	542	847	661	532	466	398	348
December	4 433	3 977	174	362	736	467	872	669	547	489	456	396

[1]Includes natural resources and mining, information, financial activities, and other services, not shown separately.
[2]Includes wholesale trade and transportation, warehousing, and utilities, not shown separately.
[3]Includes arts, entertainment, and recreation, not shown separately.
[4]Includes federal government, not shown separately.

Table 7-7. Job Openings Levels and Rates, by Industry, December 2000–September 2011—*Continued*

(Seasonally adjusted, levels in thousands, rates per 100.)

Year and month	Rate											
	Total[1]	Total private[1]	Construction	Manufacturing	Trade, transportation, and utilities[2]	Retail trade	Professional and business services	Education and health services	Leisure and hospitality[3]	Accommodation and food services	Government[4]	State and local government
2000												
December	3.7	4.1	3.2	2.6	3.2	3.4	4.7	5.2	4.7	5.2	1.9	1.8
2001												
January	3.7	4.0	2.7	2.4	3.4	3.1	3.9	4.8	5.2	5.5	2.3	2.2
February	3.6	3.8	3.2	2.4	3.2	3.3	4.5	5.0	4.9	5.3	2.3	2.3
March	3.6	3.9	2.8	2.3	2.6	2.7	5.9	4.8	5.3	5.3	2.2	2.3
April	3.5	3.7	3.3	1.9	3.3	3.5	4.8	4.4	4.7	5.1	2.3	2.3
May	3.3	3.5	3.1	1.8	2.6	3.0	4.7	4.8	4.6	4.8	2.3	2.3
June	3.3	3.4	2.7	2.1	2.6	2.8	4.3	4.7	4.2	4.4	2.5	2.5
July	3.2	3.4	2.7	1.8	2.5	2.6	3.6	4.8	4.7	4.7	2.5	2.6
August	3.2	3.3	1.6	1.7	2.4	2.6	3.5	5.5	4.7	4.9	2.3	2.4
September	3.1	3.3	2.1	1.9	2.2	2.3	3.8	4.6	5.0	5.2	2.0	2.0
October	2.8	2.9	1.8	1.6	2.3	2.3	3.1	4.6	3.5	3.6	2.1	2.2
November	2.7	2.9	2.0	1.4	2.2	2.3	3.4	4.3	3.9	4.0	2.1	2.1
December	2.7	2.8	1.7	1.4	2.2	2.4	3.1	4.4	3.8	3.9	2.1	2.1
2002												
January	2.8	2.9	1.6	1.6	2.2	2.4	3.4	4.5	3.5	3.5	1.9	1.9
February	2.6	2.7	1.6	1.6	2.1	2.3	3.0	4.5	3.4	3.4	2.1	2.2
March	2.7	2.9	1.9	1.5	2.3	2.3	3.6	4.4	3.5	3.4	2.0	2.1
April	2.6	2.7	1.4	1.6	2.2	2.3	3.2	4.2	3.3	3.4	2.0	2.0
May	2.7	2.8	1.6	1.6	2.1	2.2	3.9	4.0	3.5	3.5	2.1	2.1
June	2.6	2.7	1.9	1.7	2.1	2.2	3.2	4.4	3.2	3.3	1.8	1.9
July	2.6	2.7	1.5	1.7	2.0	2.2	3.6	4.1	3.3	3.4	1.9	2.0
August	2.6	2.7	1.6	1.6	2.1	2.1	3.6	4.1	3.3	3.3	2.1	2.1
September	2.5	2.6	1.9	1.6	1.9	2.1	3.6	4.2	3.1	3.3	1.9	1.9
October	2.8	2.9	2.0	1.5	2.3	2.6	4.3	4.0	3.3	3.3	1.9	1.9
November	2.7	2.8	1.8	1.6	1.9	2.0	4.1	4.3	3.4	3.6	2.1	2.1
December	2.3	2.5	1.3	1.4	1.7	1.6	3.4	3.9	3.1	3.0	1.7	1.7
2003												
January	2.7	2.9	1.6	1.4	2.0	2.0	5.1	3.8	3.1	3.4	1.9	1.9
February	2.6	2.7	1.5	1.3	2.1	2.3	4.6	3.6	2.7	2.7	1.9	1.9
March	2.4	2.5	1.3	1.3	1.9	2.0	4.0	3.5	2.9	3.1	1.8	1.7
April	2.4	2.6	2.0	1.4	1.8	1.9	3.2	3.6	3.5	3.3	1.7	1.8
May	2.4	2.6	1.4	1.4	1.9	2.0	3.8	3.9	3.0	3.2	1.5	1.5
June	2.5	2.6	1.7	1.3	2.0	2.2	3.7	3.5	3.8	3.8	1.8	1.8
July	2.4	2.6	2.3	1.3	2.0	2.1	4.2	3.3	2.8	2.7	1.6	1.5
August	2.4	2.6	1.6	1.5	2.1	2.2	4.4	3.3	2.9	3.0	1.5	1.4
September	2.4	2.5	1.0	1.4	2.1	2.4	3.9	3.2	3.1	3.2	1.5	1.4
October	2.5	2.7	1.2	1.5	2.2	2.3	3.6	3.6	3.3	3.4	1.6	1.6
November	2.5	2.7	1.3	1.8	2.3	2.5	3.7	3.4	3.2	3.4	1.5	1.4
December	2.5	2.7	1.4	1.5	2.3	2.3	3.7	3.0	3.6	3.7	1.5	1.5
2004												
January	2.6	2.8	2.0	1.6	2.1	2.3	3.5	3.7	3.3	3.3	1.9	1.8
February	2.6	2.8	1.7	1.5	2.2	2.5	3.9	3.5	3.5	3.5	1.7	1.6
March	2.6	2.8	1.8	1.7	2.4	2.5	3.5	3.5	3.4	3.6	1.7	1.7
April	2.7	2.8	1.9	1.8	2.3	2.5	3.9	3.5	3.2	3.4	1.7	1.6
May	2.8	3.0	1.9	2.0	2.4	2.8	3.9	3.5	3.4	3.4	1.8	1.8
June	2.6	2.8	1.4	1.8	2.4	2.6	4.3	3.0	3.6	3.8	1.6	1.5
July	2.9	3.1	1.6	1.9	2.6	2.8	4.4	3.5	3.7	3.9	1.7	1.8
August	2.8	3.0	1.8	1.9	2.5	2.8	3.9	3.5	3.9	3.8	1.6	1.6
September	2.8	3.0	1.7	1.9	2.7	3.1	4.1	3.5	3.6	3.6	1.7	1.6
October	2.9	3.1	2.2	2.0	2.5	2.9	4.3	3.8	3.5	3.6	1.9	1.9
November	2.6	2.7	2.0	1.8	2.1	2.1	3.5	3.5	3.2	3.3	1.8	1.7
December	2.9	3.1	2.1	1.9	2.5	2.7	4.1	3.6	3.6	3.5	1.9	1.8
2005												
January	2.9	3.1	2.1	2.0	2.5	2.9	4.0	3.6	4.0	4.1	1.7	1.8
February	2.8	3.0	2.1	1.9	2.7	2.8	4.0	3.5	3.8	3.9	1.7	1.7
March	2.9	3.1	2.0	2.0	2.6	3.0	4.2	3.8	3.8	3.9	1.7	1.7
April	3.1	3.3	1.8	2.0	2.7	3.0	4.5	3.6	4.5	4.6	1.8	1.8
May	2.8	3.1	1.9	1.9	2.6	2.6	4.4	3.8	3.7	3.8	1.7	1.7
June	3.0	3.3	1.9	2.0	2.6	2.6	5.0	3.6	4.0	4.0	1.7	1.7
July	3.0	3.3	2.1	2.2	2.6	2.6	4.5	3.8	3.9	3.7	1.8	1.8
August	3.0	3.2	2.0	2.1	2.5	2.7	4.6	3.7	3.6	3.6	1.8	1.8
September	3.1	3.3	2.3	2.3	2.5	2.5	4.6	3.8	3.7	4.0	1.9	1.9
October	3.1	3.3	2.4	2.0	2.8	2.9	4.5	3.6	3.7	3.8	1.7	1.7
November	3.2	3.5	2.6	2.7	3.1	3.4	4.7	3.6	4.0	4.1	1.8	1.8
December	3.2	3.4	2.3	2.5	2.7	3.0	4.8	3.7	4.1	4.3	2.0	2.0

[1]Includes natural resources and mining, information, financial activities, and other services, not shown separately.
[2]Includes wholesale trade and transportation, warehousing, and utilities, not shown separately.
[3]Includes arts, entertainment, and recreation, not shown separately.
[4]Includes federal government, not shown separately.

Table 7-7. Job Openings Levels and Rates, by Industry, December 2000–September 2011—*Continued*

(Seasonally adjusted, levels in thousands, rates per 100.)

Year and month	Level											
	Total[1]	Total private[1]	Construction	Manufacturing	Trade, transportation, and utilities[2]	Retail trade	Professional and business services	Education and health services	Leisure and hospitality[3]	Accommodation and food services	Government[4]	State and local government
2006												
January	4 308	3 948	143	324	717	455	834	694	560	494	360	313
February	4 372	3 942	145	377	698	425	838	732	563	518	430	372
March	4 613	4 164	192	389	740	429	803	750	567	499	449	398
April	4 662	4 206	188	378	823	466	732	736	584	515	456	410
May	4 589	4 140	177	315	791	461	923	694	560	504	449	396
June	4 409	3 948	196	357	723	426	696	720	523	464	461	408
July	4 197	3 699	197	321	702	391	624	654	562	490	498	437
August	4 529	4 068	206	341	754	438	735	774	573	523	460	413
September	4 613	4 145	180	349	861	445	729	785	556	435	468	426
October	4 665	4 220	181	372	803	435	774	836	600	517	446	393
November	4 655	4 200	137	339	763	420	783	776	722	637	455	411
December	4 653	4 200	117	374	917	554	702	759	613	548	453	411
2007												
January	4 658	4 214	270	361	865	466	775	753	552	478	444	400
February	4 488	4 029	279	375	753	435	662	683	548	472	459	406
March	4 755	4 286	209	387	835	416	864	729	585	517	469	422
April	4 674	4 210	191	369	870	408	812	757	579	492	464	409
May	4 539	4 070	198	372	709	367	798	769	577	517	470	413
June	4 740	4 279	168	359	802	453	805	792	605	533	462	417
July	4 537	4 072	173	377	814	444	723	741	612	551	465	418
August	4 563	4 094	155	324	804	414	792	787	616	556	469	416
September	4 514	4 081	121	324	750	407	766	841	643	570	433	383
October	4 429	3 979	148	294	741	368	761	759	638	570	449	403
November	4 484	4 016	128	333	772	428	773	721	702	596	468	409
December	4 354	3 901	129	302	809	426	748	764	602	557	453	390
2008												
January	4 392	3 963	126	307	732	367	771	771	588	534	428	387
February	4 080	3 651	130	281	691	364	765	768	555	483	429	386
March	4 064	3 637	99	253	640	388	795	769	555	492	427	372
April	3 673	3 288	92	267	583	348	722	652	499	443	386	351
May	3 931	3 487	156	282	611	352	658	726	534	470	443	386
June	3 681	3 250	109	253	562	316	703	714	465	416	431	369
July	3 556	3 145	97	236	582	356	625	710	404	354	411	342
August	3 516	3 078	85	253	559	363	621	668	396	345	438	358
September	3 161	2 724	104	215	476	279	589	579	372	334	437	369
October	3 039	2 656	66	210	524	348	538	601	353	312	383	317
November	3 034	2 679	72	168	555	394	527	620	301	268	355	328
December	2 938	2 608	71	159	453	304	535	618	313	278	331	289
2009												
January	2 566	2 186	32	98	447	320	496	551	215	187	380	288
February	2 771	2 403	66	136	426	305	507	543	304	282	368	299
March	2 529	2 149	52	121	393	250	422	501	284	260	379	262
April	2 237	1 846	21	94	299	185	419	460	280	258	390	301
May	2 366	2 069	42	94	448	314	386	514	266	246	297	251
June	2 423	2 090	49	100	425	286	374	525	283	267	333	274
July	2 112	1 808	40	96	294	182	383	525	219	205	304	247
August	2 202	1 921	59	123	392	242	347	526	205	182	281	253
September	2 464	2 158	65	126	393	280	422	523	294	269	306	228
October	2 307	1 905	62	119	326	212	368	486	233	208	403	265
November	2 262	1 927	64	134	325	214	376	503	230	206	335	240
December	2 376	1 996	69	165	341	223	388	508	204	188	380	265
2010												
January	2 411	2 020	61	118	316	218	381	519	221	208	391	226
February	2 523	2 159	62	156	373	257	396	523	245	223	364	235
March	2 697	2 248	100	162	429	294	420	522	247	219	449	253
April	3 043	2 396	77	176	402	248	480	503	259	234	647	250
May	2 790	2 423	79	189	398	249	574	516	266	226	367	239
June	2 685	2 370	72	197	410	266	468	486	313	245	315	229
July	2 848	2 516	89	219	416	262	517	504	304	266	333	248
August	2 862	2 556	54	173	409	250	613	477	350	313	306	228
September	2 756	2 429	68	183	419	239	554	510	284	248	326	239
October	2 905	2 560	69	193	445	272	575	569	274	247	345	272
November	2 966	2 639	94	213	430	248	647	528	253	224	327	244
December	2 921	2 500	44	184	463	268	609	510	270	229	421	319
2011												
January	2 741	2 418	60	207	470	263	459	482	301	262	323	259
February	3 025	2 695	55	209	448	232	606	553	378	330	330	260
March	3 123	2 793	68	235	472	254	613	609	340	299	331	274
April	2 953	2 635	90	226	524	312	497	550	305	269	319	268
May	3 034	2 725	100	211	484	276	615	594	298	264	309	261
June	3 169	2 835	68	217	515	332	616	596	360	305	334	279
July	3 213	2 905	75	252	540	312	640	604	338	276	309	253
August	3 129	2 799	102	232	490	324	621	609	351	307	329	287
September	3 354	2 988	75	242	546	344	684	616	362	309	366	313

[1]Includes natural resources and mining, information, financial activities, and other services, not shown separately.
[2]Includes wholesale trade and transportation, warehousing, and utilities, not shown separately.
[3]Includes arts, entertainment, and recreation, not shown separately.
[4]Includes federal government, not shown separately.

Table 7-7. Job Openings Levels and Rates, by Industry, December 2000–September 2011—*Continued*

(Seasonally adjusted, levels in thousands, rates per 100.)

Year and month	Total[1]	Total private[1]	Construction	Manufacturing	Trade, transportation, and utilities[2]	Retail trade	Professional and business services	Education and health services	Leisure and hospitality[3]	Accommodation and food services	Government[4]	State and local government
2006												
January	3.1	3.4	1.8	2.2	2.7	2.9	4.6	3.8	4.1	4.3	1.6	1.6
February	3.1	3.4	1.9	2.6	2.6	2.7	4.6	4.0	4.2	4.5	1.9	1.9
March	3.3	3.5	2.4	2.7	2.7	2.7	4.4	4.1	4.2	4.3	2.0	2.0
April	3.3	3.6	2.4	2.6	3.0	2.9	4.0	4.0	4.3	4.4	2.0	2.1
May	3.3	3.5	2.2	2.2	2.9	2.9	5.0	3.8	4.1	4.3	2.0	2.0
June	3.1	3.3	2.5	2.5	2.7	2.7	3.8	3.9	3.9	4.0	2.1	2.1
July	3.0	3.1	2.5	2.2	2.6	2.5	3.4	3.5	4.1	4.2	2.2	2.2
August	3.2	3.4	2.6	2.3	2.8	2.8	4.0	4.2	4.2	4.5	2.0	2.1
September	3.3	3.5	2.3	2.4	3.2	2.8	4.0	4.2	4.1	3.7	2.1	2.2
October	3.3	3.6	2.3	2.6	3.0	2.8	4.2	4.4	4.4	4.4	2.0	2.0
November	3.3	3.5	1.8	2.4	2.8	2.7	4.2	4.1	5.2	5.3	2.0	2.1
December	3.3	3.5	1.5	2.6	3.3	3.5	3.8	4.0	4.4	4.6	2.0	2.1
2007												
January	3.3	3.5	3.4	2.5	3.2	2.9	4.2	4.0	4.0	4.0	2.0	2.0
February	3.2	3.4	3.5	2.6	2.8	2.7	3.6	3.6	3.9	4.0	2.0	2.1
March	3.3	3.6	2.6	2.7	3.0	2.6	4.6	3.9	4.2	4.3	2.1	2.1
April	3.3	3.5	2.4	2.6	3.2	2.6	4.3	4.0	4.1	4.1	2.1	2.1
May	3.2	3.4	2.5	2.6	2.6	2.3	4.3	4.0	4.1	4.3	2.1	2.1
June	3.3	3.6	2.1	2.5	2.9	2.8	4.3	4.1	4.3	4.4	2.0	2.1
July	3.2	3.4	2.2	2.6	3.0	2.8	3.9	3.9	4.4	4.6	2.1	2.1
August	3.2	3.4	2.0	2.3	2.9	2.6	4.2	4.1	4.4	4.6	2.1	2.1
September	3.2	3.4	1.6	2.3	2.7	2.6	4.1	4.4	4.6	4.7	1.9	1.9
October	3.1	3.3	1.9	2.1	2.7	2.3	4.1	3.9	4.5	4.7	2.0	2.0
November	3.1	3.4	1.7	2.4	2.8	2.7	4.1	3.7	4.9	4.9	2.1	2.0
December	3.1	3.3	1.7	2.2	2.9	2.7	4.0	4.0	4.3	4.6	2.0	2.0
2008												
January	3.1	3.3	1.7	2.2	2.7	2.3	4.1	4.0	4.2	4.4	1.9	1.9
February	2.9	3.1	1.7	2.0	2.5	2.3	4.1	4.0	3.9	4.0	1.9	1.9
March	2.9	3.1	1.3	1.8	2.3	2.4	4.2	4.0	3.9	4.1	1.9	1.9
April	2.6	2.8	1.2	1.9	2.1	2.2	3.9	3.4	3.6	3.7	1.7	1.8
May	2.8	2.9	2.1	2.0	2.3	2.2	3.5	3.7	3.8	3.9	1.9	1.9
June	2.6	2.8	1.5	1.8	2.1	2.0	3.8	3.7	3.3	3.5	1.9	1.8
July	2.5	2.7	1.3	1.7	2.2	2.3	3.4	3.6	2.9	3.0	1.8	1.7
August	2.5	2.6	1.2	1.9	2.1	2.3	3.4	3.4	2.9	2.9	1.9	1.8
September	2.3	2.3	1.5	1.6	1.8	1.8	3.2	3.0	2.7	2.8	1.9	1.8
October	2.2	2.3	0.9	1.6	2.0	2.3	3.0	3.1	2.6	2.7	1.7	1.6
November	2.2	2.3	1.0	1.3	2.1	2.6	2.9	3.2	2.2	2.3	1.6	1.6
December	2.1	2.3	1.0	1.2	1.7	2.0	3.0	3.1	2.3	2.4	1.4	1.4
2009												
January	1.9	1.9	0.5	0.8	1.7	2.1	2.8	2.8	1.6	1.6	1.7	1.4
February	2.0	2.1	1.0	1.1	1.7	2.0	2.9	2.8	2.3	2.4	1.6	1.5
March	1.9	1.9	0.8	1.0	1.5	1.7	2.5	2.6	2.1	2.3	1.7	1.3
April	1.7	1.7	0.3	0.8	1.2	1.3	2.5	2.4	2.1	2.3	1.7	1.5
May	1.8	1.9	0.7	0.8	1.8	2.1	2.3	2.6	2.0	2.2	1.3	1.3
June	1.8	1.9	0.8	0.8	1.7	1.9	2.2	2.7	2.1	2.3	1.5	1.4
July	1.6	1.7	0.7	0.8	1.2	1.2	2.3	2.7	1.6	1.8	1.3	1.2
August	1.7	1.8	1.0	1.0	1.6	1.6	2.1	2.7	1.5	1.6	1.2	1.3
September	1.9	2.0	1.1	1.1	1.6	1.9	2.5	2.6	2.2	2.4	1.3	1.1
October	1.8	1.7	1.1	1.0	1.3	1.5	2.2	2.5	1.8	1.8	1.8	1.3
November	1.7	1.8	1.1	1.2	1.3	1.5	2.2	2.5	1.7	1.8	1.5	1.2
December	1.8	1.8	1.2	1.4	1.4	1.5	2.3	2.6	1.6	1.7	1.7	1.3
2010												
January	1.8	1.9	1.1	1.0	1.3	1.5	2.3	2.6	1.7	1.8	1.7	1.1
February	1.9	2.0	1.1	1.3	1.5	1.8	2.3	2.6	1.9	2.0	1.6	1.2
March	2.0	2.1	1.8	1.4	1.7	2.0	2.5	2.6	1.9	1.9	2.0	1.3
April	2.3	2.2	1.4	1.5	1.6	1.7	2.8	2.5	2.0	2.1	2.8	1.3
May	2.1	2.2	1.4	1.6	1.6	1.7	3.3	2.6	2.0	2.0	1.6	1.2
June	2.0	2.2	1.3	1.7	1.6	1.8	2.7	2.4	2.4	2.2	1.4	1.2
July	2.1	2.3	1.6	1.9	1.7	1.8	3.0	2.5	2.3	2.3	1.5	1.3
August	2.2	2.3	1.0	1.5	1.6	1.7	3.5	2.4	2.6	2.7	1.3	1.2
September	2.1	2.2	1.2	1.6	1.7	1.6	3.2	2.5	2.1	2.2	1.4	1.2
October	2.2	2.3	1.2	1.6	1.8	1.8	3.3	2.8	2.1	2.2	1.5	1.4
November	2.2	2.4	1.7	1.8	1.7	1.7	3.7	2.6	1.9	2.0	1.4	1.2
December	2.2	2.3	0.8	1.6	1.8	1.8	3.5	2.5	2.0	2.0	1.9	1.6
2011												
January	2.1	2.2	1.1	1.7	1.9	1.8	2.6	2.4	2.3	2.3	1.4	1.3
February	2.3	2.4	1.0	1.8	1.8	1.6	3.4	2.7	2.8	2.9	1.5	1.3
March	2.3	2.5	1.2	2.0	1.9	1.7	3.5	3.0	2.5	2.6	1.5	1.4
April	2.2	2.4	1.6	1.9	2.1	2.1	2.8	2.7	2.3	2.3	1.4	1.4
May	2.3	2.4	1.8	1.8	1.9	1.9	3.5	2.9	2.2	2.3	1.4	1.3
June	2.4	2.5	1.2	1.8	2.0	2.2	3.5	2.9	2.6	2.6	1.5	1.4
July	2.4	2.6	1.3	2.1	2.1	2.1	3.6	2.9	2.5	2.4	1.4	1.3
August	2.3	2.5	1.8	1.9	1.9	2.2	3.5	2.9	2.6	2.6	1.5	1.5
September	2.5	2.7	1.3	2.0	2.1	2.3	3.8	3.0	2.7	2.7	1.6	1.6

[1] Includes natural resources and mining, information, financial activities, and other services, not shown separately.
[2] Includes wholesale trade and transportation, warehousing, and utilities, not shown separately.
[3] Includes arts, entertainment, and recreation, not shown separately.
[4] Includes federal government, not shown separately.

Table 7-8. Hires Levels[1] and Rates,[2] by Industry, December 2000–September 2011

(Seasonally adjusted, levels in thousands, rates per 100.)

Year and month	Level[3]											
	Total[4]	Total private[4]	Construc-tion	Manufac-turing	Trade, transpor-tation, and utilities[5]	Retail trade	Profes-sional and business services	Education and health services	Leisure and hospitality[6]	Accommo-dation and food services	Govern-ment[7]	State and local govern-ment
2000												
December	5 484	5 078	424	536	1 152	861	953	514	944	803	406	360
2001												
January	5 622	5 257	473	499	1 166	841	1 064	467	943	815	365	309
February	5 552	5 153	468	450	1 115	763	978	530	953	803	399	366
March	5 893	5 526	539	469	1 151	832	1 183	564	976	839	368	327
April	5 407	5 044	448	436	1 143	800	810	507	1 082	921	363	327
May	5 454	5 072	442	408	1 236	888	1 027	492	948	797	382	339
June	5 193	4 819	444	397	1 092	810	931	513	925	768	375	329
July	5 223	4 873	456	360	1 113	792	902	530	935	771	350	302
August	5 154	4 750	402	362	1 057	764	933	530	881	738	405	365
September	5 119	4 802	413	356	1 085	794	910	531	955	804	317	287
October	5 097	4 729	425	388	1 078	776	913	514	840	704	368	333
November	5 069	4 718	497	365	1 014	719	878	501	850	727	351	317
December	4 877	4 525	443	373	948	665	897	471	844	714	352	301
2002												
January	4 991	4 645	405	371	1 022	726	890	503	858	746	346	309
February	4 982	4 633	426	398	1 051	701	911	483	848	725	348	300
March	4 799	4 452	402	364	958	653	957	472	812	674	346	299
April	5 055	4 699	420	408	1 060	729	929	500	835	711	356	309
May	5 054	4 678	403	416	1 025	726	998	478	823	698	376	321
June	4 919	4 576	432	397	1 025	719	858	501	811	680	343	301
July	5 190	4 868	475	410	1 052	739	1 005	493	883	716	322	281
August	4 950	4 577	399	379	997	700	950	464	836	705	373	319
September	4 991	4 672	449	401	1 023	720	946	466	837	703	319	256
October	4 881	4 537	432	368	990	702	953	467	796	691	344	286
November	5 018	4 618	424	384	1 012	715	995	453	813	675	401	343
December	4 997	4 680	440	370	1 035	734	972	488	834	687	317	272
2003												
January	5 078	4 718	447	409	953	674	952	512	891	738	360	307
February	4 806	4 495	359	362	1 002	737	946	459	811	682	311	266
March	4 528	4 202	405	343	935	642	748	454	781	644	326	266
April	4 739	4 433	446	330	921	653	930	450	824	684	306	275
May	4 684	4 391	443	324	929	656	820	480	856	699	293	254
June	4 771	4 443	431	341	960	681	880	478	831	709	328	281
July	4 659	4 340	427	338	946	639	894	459	744	635	319	280
August	4 741	4 482	494	357	1 003	686	857	461	837	704	259	220
September	4 894	4 602	470	344	1 022	688	883	510	821	702	292	252
October	5 058	4 715	413	363	1 126	786	920	499	853	720	343	301
November	4 796	4 493	445	378	972	674	875	482	827	695	303	255
December	5 098	4 767	449	374	1 070	739	901	470	910	782	332	282
2004												
January	5 033	4 644	441	369	1 117	761	886	483	842	707	389	332
February	4 823	4 493	432	374	1 049	727	742	482	882	723	330	282
March	5 340	4 982	516	409	1 142	760	945	486	904	771	358	318
April	5 180	4 866	428	413	1 141	798	979	478	870	742	314	263
May	5 072	4 766	451	395	1 072	740	920	463	891	753	305	277
June	5 031	4 719	470	374	1 051	692	924	451	860	731	313	274
July	4 972	4 632	419	386	1 084	760	891	471	859	723	340	300
August	5 181	4 859	451	409	1 100	742	950	497	880	745	321	288
September	5 146	4 791	438	394	1 083	740	911	475	926	743	355	322
October	5 248	4 895	486	388	1 114	775	922	504	909	765	352	308
November	5 283	4 919	452	384	1 159	815	941	501	872	764	365	322
December	5 321	4 982	461	372	1 164	815	1 011	509	874	751	339	286
2005												
January	5 552	5 165	482	371	1 164	790	1 036	511	969	818	387	355
February	5 342	5 008	508	366	1 155	794	1 045	498	852	730	334	294
March	5 355	5 026	459	378	1 164	831	1 023	529	883	760	329	286
April	5 353	5 002	511	365	1 156	799	990	532	878	738	351	303
May	5 356	5 022	498	373	1 160	799	1 001	514	863	737	335	293
June	5 419	5 100	471	355	1 159	804	1 080	522	964	798	319	276
July	5 337	4 993	427	382	1 155	828	1 045	505	908	775	344	306
August	5 538	5 203	534	381	1 158	828	1 091	519	914	780	336	295
September	5 511	5 186	523	390	1 127	785	1 066	541	973	801	325	275
October	5 150	4 829	519	409	1 091	756	886	493	874	764	321	283
November	5 382	5 026	488	394	1 093	705	920	521	954	829	356	310
December	5 238	4 886	461	364	1 143	747	932	512	917	794	353	302

[1]Hires are the number of hires during the entire month.
[2]The hires rate is the number of hires during the entire month as a percent of total employment.
[3]Detail will not necessarily add to totals because of the independent seasonal adjustment of the various series.
[4]Includes natural resources and mining, information, financial activities, and other services, not shown separately.
[5]Includes wholesale trade and transportation, warehousing, and utilities, not shown separately.
[6]Includes arts, entertainment, and recreation, not shown separately.
[7]Includes federal government, not shown separately.

Table 7-8. Hires Levels[1] and Rates,[2] by Industry, December 2000–September 2011—*Continued*

(Seasonally adjusted, levels in thousands, rates per 100.)

Year and month	Rate											
	Total[4]	Total private[4]	Construction	Manufacturing	Trade, transportation, and utilities[5]	Retail trade	Professional and business services	Education and health services	Leisure and hospitality[6]	Accommodation and food services	Government[7]	State and local government
2000												
December	4.1	4.5	6.2	3.1	4.4	5.6	5.7	3.4	7.9	7.9	2.0	2.0
2001												
January	4.2	4.7	6.9	2.9	4.4	5.5	6.3	3.0	7.9	8.0	1.7	1.7
February	4.2	4.6	6.8	2.6	4.2	5.0	5.8	3.4	7.9	7.9	1.9	2.0
March	4.4	5.0	7.9	2.8	4.4	5.4	7.1	3.6	8.1	8.2	1.8	1.8
April	4.1	4.5	6.5	2.6	4.4	5.2	4.9	3.3	9.0	9.0	1.7	1.8
May	4.1	4.6	6.4	2.4	4.7	5.8	6.2	3.2	7.9	7.8	1.8	1.9
June	3.9	4.3	6.5	2.4	4.2	5.3	5.6	3.3	7.7	7.5	1.8	1.8
July	4.0	4.4	6.7	2.2	4.3	5.2	5.5	3.4	7.7	7.5	1.7	1.6
August	3.9	4.3	5.9	2.2	4.1	5.0	5.7	3.4	7.3	7.2	1.9	2.0
September	3.9	4.4	6.1	2.2	4.2	5.2	5.6	3.4	7.9	7.9	1.5	1.6
October	3.9	4.3	6.2	2.4	4.2	5.1	5.6	3.2	7.0	6.9	1.7	1.8
November	3.9	4.3	7.3	2.3	3.9	4.7	5.4	3.2	7.1	7.2	1.6	1.7
December	3.7	4.1	6.5	2.4	3.7	4.4	5.6	3.0	7.1	7.0	1.7	1.6
2002												
January	3.8	4.3	6.0	2.4	4.0	4.8	5.6	3.2	7.1	7.3	1.6	1.7
February	3.8	4.2	6.3	2.6	4.1	4.7	5.7	3.0	7.1	7.1	1.6	1.6
March	3.7	4.1	6.0	2.4	3.8	4.3	6.0	2.9	6.8	6.6	1.6	1.6
April	3.9	4.3	6.3	2.7	4.1	4.8	5.8	3.1	7.0	7.0	1.7	1.7
May	3.9	4.3	6.0	2.7	4.0	4.8	6.2	3.0	6.9	6.9	1.7	1.7
June	3.8	4.2	6.5	2.6	4.0	4.8	5.4	3.1	6.8	6.7	1.6	1.6
July	4.0	4.5	7.1	2.7	4.1	4.9	6.3	3.0	7.4	7.0	1.5	1.5
August	3.8	4.2	5.9	2.5	3.9	4.7	6.0	2.8	7.0	6.9	1.7	1.7
September	3.8	4.3	6.7	2.7	4.0	4.8	5.9	2.9	7.0	6.9	1.5	1.4
October	3.7	4.2	6.5	2.4	3.9	4.7	6.0	2.9	6.6	6.7	1.6	1.5
November	3.9	4.2	6.3	2.6	4.0	4.8	6.2	2.8	6.7	6.6	1.9	1.8
December	3.8	4.3	6.6	2.5	4.1	4.9	6.1	3.0	6.9	6.7	1.5	1.4
2003												
January	3.9	4.3	6.7	2.8	3.8	4.5	6.0	3.1	7.3	7.1	1.7	1.6
February	3.7	4.1	5.4	2.4	4.0	4.9	5.9	2.8	6.7	6.6	1.4	1.4
March	3.5	3.9	6.1	2.3	3.7	4.3	4.7	2.8	6.5	6.3	1.5	1.4
April	3.6	4.1	6.7	2.3	3.6	4.4	5.9	2.7	6.8	6.6	1.4	1.5
May	3.6	4.1	6.6	2.2	3.7	4.4	5.2	2.9	7.1	6.8	1.4	1.4
June	3.7	4.1	6.4	2.4	3.8	4.6	5.5	2.9	6.9	6.9	1.5	1.5
July	3.6	4.0	6.3	2.4	3.8	4.3	5.6	2.8	6.1	6.1	1.5	1.5
August	3.7	4.1	7.3	2.5	4.0	4.6	5.4	2.8	6.9	6.8	1.2	1.2
September	3.8	4.2	6.9	2.4	4.0	4.6	5.5	3.1	6.7	6.7	1.4	1.3
October	3.9	4.3	6.1	2.5	4.4	5.3	5.7	3.0	7.0	6.9	1.6	1.6
November	3.7	4.1	6.5	2.6	3.8	4.5	5.4	2.9	6.7	6.6	1.4	1.4
December	3.9	4.4	6.6	2.6	4.2	5.0	5.6	2.8	7.4	7.5	1.5	1.5
2004												
January	3.9	4.3	6.4	2.6	4.4	5.1	5.5	2.9	6.8	6.7	1.8	1.8
February	3.7	4.1	6.3	2.6	4.1	4.9	4.6	2.9	7.1	6.9	1.5	1.5
March	4.1	4.6	7.5	2.9	4.5	5.1	5.8	2.9	7.3	7.3	1.7	1.7
April	4.0	4.4	6.2	2.9	4.5	5.3	6.0	2.8	7.0	7.0	1.5	1.4
May	3.9	4.3	6.5	2.8	4.2	4.9	5.6	2.7	7.1	7.1	1.4	1.5
June	3.8	4.3	6.7	2.6	4.1	4.6	5.6	2.7	6.9	6.9	1.4	1.5
July	3.8	4.2	6.0	2.7	4.2	5.0	5.4	2.8	6.9	6.8	1.6	1.6
August	3.9	4.4	6.4	2.9	4.3	4.9	5.8	2.9	7.0	7.0	1.5	1.5
September	3.9	4.4	6.2	2.8	4.2	4.9	5.5	2.8	7.4	6.9	1.6	1.7
October	4.0	4.4	6.9	2.7	4.3	5.1	5.6	2.9	7.2	7.1	1.6	1.6
November	4.0	4.5	6.4	2.7	4.5	5.4	5.7	2.9	6.9	7.1	1.7	1.7
December	4.0	4.5	6.5	2.6	4.5	5.4	6.1	3.0	6.9	7.0	1.6	1.5
2005												
January	4.2	4.7	6.8	2.6	4.5	5.2	6.2	3.0	7.6	7.6	1.8	1.9
February	4.0	4.5	7.1	2.6	4.5	5.2	6.3	2.9	6.7	6.7	1.5	1.5
March	4.0	4.5	6.4	2.7	4.5	5.5	6.1	3.1	6.9	7.0	1.5	1.5
April	4.0	4.5	7.0	2.6	4.5	5.2	5.9	3.1	6.9	6.8	1.6	1.6
May	4.0	4.5	6.8	2.6	4.5	5.2	5.9	3.0	6.7	6.8	1.5	1.5
June	4.1	4.6	6.4	2.5	4.5	5.3	6.4	3.0	7.5	7.3	1.5	1.5
July	4.0	4.5	5.8	2.7	4.4	5.4	6.1	2.9	7.1	7.1	1.6	1.6
August	4.1	4.6	7.2	2.7	4.4	5.4	6.4	3.0	7.1	7.1	1.5	1.5
September	4.1	4.6	7.1	2.7	4.3	5.1	6.2	3.1	7.6	7.3	1.5	1.4
October	3.8	4.3	7.0	2.9	4.2	4.9	5.2	2.8	6.8	7.0	1.5	1.5
November	4.0	4.5	6.5	2.8	4.2	4.6	5.3	3.0	7.4	7.6	1.6	1.6
December	3.9	4.3	6.1	2.6	4.4	4.9	5.4	2.9	7.1	7.2	1.6	1.6

[1]Hires are the number of hires during the entire month.
[2]The hires rate is the number of hires during the entire month as a percent of total employment.
[4]Includes natural resources and mining, information, financial activities, and other services, not shown separately.
[5]Includes wholesale trade and transportation, warehousing, and utilities, not shown separately.
[6]Includes arts, entertainment, and recreation, not shown separately.
[7]Includes federal government, not shown separately.

Table 7-8. Hires Levels[1] and Rates,[2] by Industry, December 2000–September 2011—*Continued*

(Seasonally adjusted, levels in thousands, rates per 100.)

Year and month	Level[3]											
	Total[4]	Total private[4]	Construction	Manufacturing	Trade, transportation, and utilities[5]	Retail trade	Professional and business services	Education and health services	Leisure and hospitality[6]	Accommodation and food services	Government[7]	State and local government
2006												
January	5 148	4 858	472	378	1 120	782	923	489	929	819	290	243
February	5 474	5 109	473	377	1 197	833	973	500	974	858	365	309
March	5 359	4 971	466	416	1 118	789	925	491	958	826	388	329
April	5 295	4 925	461	380	1 167	823	880	520	913	789	370	313
May	5 563	5 188	484	394	1 175	817	1 148	579	868	733	375	309
June	5 401	5 021	406	422	1 206	854	993	500	917	780	381	318
July	5 604	5 237	469	397	1 180	798	1 024	583	963	813	368	304
August	5 341	4 960	425	387	1 169	777	968	529	908	778	381	311
September	5 373	4 951	405	351	1 132	786	1 023	546	882	769	422	348
October	5 385	5 043	415	350	1 152	796	1 014	552	941	811	342	301
November	5 586	5 219	474	366	1 121	785	1 095	528	1 038	898	366	313
December	5 343	5 004	450	374	1 074	760	1 003	527	996	855	338	292
2007												
January	5 373	5 010	412	388	1 145	802	997	543	944	802	363	304
February	5 217	4 829	328	395	1 126	785	982	518	923	784	387	317
March	5 385	4 999	455	374	1 139	780	973	536	906	770	387	309
April	5 397	5 016	396	378	1 112	741	945	544	1 025	879	381	312
May	5 355	4 948	403	391	1 127	798	967	546	905	777	408	321
June	5 271	4 889	425	401	1 098	713	847	544	941	800	382	311
July	5 281	4 936	423	384	1 065	718	979	532	932	811	344	254
August	5 180	4 771	397	377	1 050	737	934	539	903	779	409	321
September	5 162	4 783	385	376	1 068	751	956	526	912	768	379	297
October	5 382	5 034	401	392	1 132	781	1 011	547	962	820	348	315
November	5 187	4 833	389	392	1 101	776	963	536	920	773	354	306
December	4 975	4 605	357	349	1 033	735	909	495	915	787	371	319
2008												
January	5 115	4 769	371	350	1 073	731	902	594	893	754	345	309
February	4 895	4 558	369	319	1 021	706	842	564	913	770	337	292
March	4 820	4 494	398	317	968	670	884	564	839	708	326	291
April	4 688	4 379	373	322	962	650	871	536	824	714	309	279
May	4 669	4 360	373	328	927	615	816	542	857	715	309	286
June	4 665	4 342	398	317	983	677	863	504	782	681	323	296
July	4 240	3 955	347	250	914	627	767	500	747	649	285	262
August	4 493	4 168	388	272	938	638	787	520	783	639	324	300
September	4 258	3 965	332	282	880	610	743	486	771	672	293	271
October	4 111	3 826	343	275	867	590	721	501	713	599	285	260
November	3 836	3 567	318	251	736	523	719	478	665	585	269	242
December	4 113	3 829	315	267	902	596	760	500	679	570	284	254
2009												
January	3 979	3 674	329	161	863	527	715	503	665	561	305	266
February	3 996	3 732	348	245	773	523	712	512	684	590	264	241
March	3 776	3 519	304	244	811	533	620	459	659	576	257	230
April	3 825	3 431	298	202	818	605	677	446	627	543	394	234
May	3 793	3 529	343	181	817	560	683	467	645	562	264	242
June	3 621	3 356	252	196	705	494	619	492	628	537	265	235
July	3 665	3 393	308	235	681	460	639	481	610	493	271	233
August	3 683	3 415	255	241	749	515	627	520	641	530	269	245
September	3 796	3 537	316	263	794	512	659	494	610	504	258	235
October	3 581	3 275	280	222	682	468	665	475	579	477	306	260
November	3 918	3 644	290	270	771	504	775	476	673	558	274	237
December	3 731	3 468	325	248	790	524	617	463	594	503	263	231
2010												
January	3 596	3 311	344	231	698	507	681	409	593	504	284	233
February	3 784	3 484	297	254	778	534	717	457	584	503	300	248
March	4 139	3 763	382	262	855	618	721	495	656	542	377	265
April	3 967	3 613	340	275	773	534	740	459	642	524	355	240
May	4 347	3 613	312	251	766	527	755	467	624	518	734	239
June	3 952	3 660	267	251	811	551	792	497	639	513	292	240
July	3 937	3 650	323	278	798	549	752	497	630	517	287	247
August	3 886	3 627	332	259	749	528	777	471	628	527	259	221
September	3 869	3 614	327	240	776	539	747	487	645	535	255	224
October	3 865	3 580	331	259	777	545	730	465	596	508	285	250
November	3 943	3 668	324	272	799	548	761	491	590	496	275	243
December	3 905	3 631	356	264	756	476	780	465	596	498	274	242
2011												
January	3 769	3 494	254	246	783	536	810	437	588	504	275	242
February	3 986	3 729	369	250	816	547	791	468	632	531	257	218
March	4 067	3 807	338	269	803	553	840	470	681	560	260	229
April	4 001	3 733	355	257	791	556	831	468	653	546	269	244
May	4 129	3 870	371	263	804	557	902	480	629	517	259	232
June	4 058	3 797	360	260	802	553	806	485	689	585	261	238
July	3 976	3 733	334	259	767	552	819	472	682	586	243	219
August	4 060	3 785	309	249	779	526	863	481	679	569	275	247
September	4 245	3 984	404	239	758	537	1 002	470	699	573	262	233

[1]Hires are the number of hires during the entire month.
[2]The hires rate is the number of hires during the entire month as a percent of total employment.
[3]Detail will not necessarily add to totals because of the independent seasonal adjustment of the various series.
[4]Includes natural resources and mining, information, financial activities, and other services, not shown separately.
[5]Includes wholesale trade and transportation, warehousing, and utilities, not shown separately.
[6]Includes arts, entertainment, and recreation, not shown separately.
[7]Includes federal government, not shown separately.

Table 7-8. Hires Levels[1] and Rates,[2] by Industry, December 2000–September 2011—*Continued*

(Seasonally adjusted, levels in thousands, rates per 100.)

Year and month	Rate											
	Total[4]	Total private[4]	Construction	Manufacturing	Trade, transportation, and utilities[5]	Retail trade	Professional and business services	Education and health services	Leisure and hospitality[6]	Accommodation and food services	Government[7]	State and local government
2006												
January	3.8	4.3	6.2	2.7	4.3	5.1	5.3	2.8	7.2	7.4	1.3	1.3
February	4.0	4.5	6.2	2.7	4.6	5.4	5.6	2.8	7.5	7.7	1.7	1.6
March	3.9	4.4	6.1	2.9	4.3	5.1	5.3	2.8	7.4	7.4	1.8	1.7
April	3.9	4.3	6.0	2.7	4.4	5.4	5.0	2.9	7.0	7.1	1.7	1.6
May	4.1	4.6	6.3	2.8	4.5	5.3	6.6	3.3	6.7	6.6	1.7	1.6
June	4.0	4.4	5.3	3.0	4.6	5.6	5.7	2.8	7.0	7.0	1.7	1.7
July	4.1	4.6	6.1	2.8	4.5	5.2	5.8	3.3	7.3	7.3	1.7	1.6
August	3.9	4.3	5.5	2.7	4.4	5.1	5.5	3.0	6.9	6.9	1.7	1.6
September	3.9	4.3	5.2	2.5	4.3	5.1	5.8	3.0	6.7	6.9	1.9	1.8
October	3.9	4.4	5.4	2.5	4.4	5.2	5.7	3.1	7.1	7.2	1.5	1.6
November	4.1	4.6	6.2	2.6	4.2	5.1	6.2	2.9	7.8	7.9	1.7	1.6
December	3.9	4.4	5.9	2.7	4.1	4.9	5.6	2.9	7.5	7.5	1.5	1.5
2007												
January	3.9	4.4	5.3	2.8	4.3	5.2	5.6	3.0	7.1	7.1	1.6	1.6
February	3.8	4.2	4.3	2.8	4.2	5.1	5.5	2.9	6.9	6.9	1.8	1.6
March	3.9	4.3	5.9	2.7	4.3	5.0	5.4	3.0	6.8	6.8	1.7	1.6
April	3.9	4.4	5.2	2.7	4.2	4.8	5.3	3.0	7.7	7.7	1.7	1.6
May	3.9	4.3	5.3	2.8	4.2	5.1	5.4	3.0	6.7	6.8	1.8	1.6
June	3.8	4.2	5.5	2.9	4.1	4.6	4.7	3.0	7.0	7.0	1.7	1.6
July	3.8	4.3	5.5	2.8	4.0	4.6	5.5	2.9	6.9	7.1	1.6	1.3
August	3.8	4.1	5.2	2.7	3.9	4.8	5.2	2.9	6.7	6.8	1.8	1.6
September	3.7	4.1	5.1	2.7	4.0	4.8	5.3	2.9	6.8	6.7	1.7	1.5
October	3.9	4.4	5.3	2.9	4.2	5.0	5.6	3.0	7.1	7.1	1.6	1.6
November	3.8	4.2	5.2	2.9	4.1	5.0	5.3	2.9	6.8	6.7	1.6	1.6
December	3.6	4.0	4.8	2.5	3.9	4.7	5.0	2.7	6.8	6.8	1.7	1.6
2008												
January	3.7	4.1	5.0	2.6	4.0	4.7	5.0	3.2	6.6	6.5	1.5	1.6
February	3.5	3.9	5.0	2.3	3.8	4.5	4.7	3.0	6.7	6.7	1.5	1.5
March	3.5	3.9	5.4	2.3	3.6	4.3	4.9	3.0	6.2	6.1	1.5	1.5
April	3.4	3.8	5.1	2.4	3.6	4.2	4.8	2.9	6.1	6.2	1.4	1.4
May	3.4	3.8	5.1	2.4	3.5	4.0	4.6	2.9	6.4	6.2	1.4	1.4
June	3.4	3.8	5.5	2.3	3.7	4.4	4.8	2.7	5.8	5.9	1.4	1.5
July	3.1	3.5	4.8	1.9	3.5	4.1	4.3	2.6	5.6	5.7	1.3	1.3
August	3.3	3.7	5.5	2.0	3.6	4.2	4.4	2.7	5.8	5.6	1.4	1.5
September	3.1	3.5	4.7	2.1	3.4	4.0	4.2	2.6	5.8	5.9	1.3	1.4
October	3.0	3.4	4.9	2.1	3.3	3.9	4.1	2.6	5.3	5.3	1.3	1.3
November	2.8	3.2	4.7	1.9	2.9	3.5	4.1	2.5	5.0	5.2	1.2	1.2
December	3.1	3.4	4.7	2.1	3.5	4.0	4.4	2.6	5.1	5.0	1.3	1.3
2009												
January	3.0	3.3	5.0	1.3	3.4	3.6	4.2	2.6	5.0	5.0	1.3	1.3
February	3.0	3.4	5.4	2.0	3.1	3.6	4.2	2.7	5.2	5.3	1.2	1.2
March	2.9	3.2	4.8	2.0	3.2	3.6	3.7	2.4	5.0	5.1	1.1	1.2
April	2.9	3.2	4.8	1.7	3.3	4.2	4.1	2.3	4.8	4.9	1.7	1.2
May	2.9	3.3	5.6	1.5	3.3	3.8	4.1	2.4	4.9	5.0	1.2	1.2
June	2.8	3.1	4.2	1.7	2.8	3.4	3.8	2.6	4.8	4.8	1.2	1.2
July	2.8	3.2	5.2	2.0	2.7	3.2	3.9	2.5	4.7	4.4	1.2	1.2
August	2.8	3.2	4.4	2.1	3.0	3.6	3.8	2.7	4.9	4.8	1.2	1.2
September	2.9	3.3	5.5	2.3	3.2	3.5	4.0	2.6	4.7	4.5	1.1	1.2
October	2.8	3.1	4.9	1.9	2.8	3.3	4.1	2.5	4.5	4.3	1.4	1.3
November	3.0	3.4	5.1	2.4	3.1	3.5	4.7	2.5	5.2	5.0	1.2	1.2
December	2.9	3.2	5.8	2.2	3.2	3.7	3.7	2.4	4.6	4.6	1.2	1.2
2010												
January	2.8	3.1	6.2	2.0	2.8	3.5	4.1	2.1	4.6	4.6	1.3	1.2
February	2.9	3.3	5.4	2.2	3.2	3.7	4.3	2.4	4.5	4.6	1.3	1.3
March	3.2	3.5	6.9	2.3	3.5	4.3	4.4	2.5	5.1	4.9	1.7	1.4
April	3.1	3.4	6.1	2.4	3.1	3.7	4.5	2.4	4.9	4.7	1.6	1.2
May	3.3	3.4	5.6	2.2	3.1	3.7	4.5	2.4	4.8	4.7	3.2	1.2
June	3.0	3.4	4.8	2.2	3.3	3.8	4.7	2.5	4.9	4.6	1.3	1.2
July	3.0	3.4	5.9	2.4	3.2	3.8	4.5	2.5	4.8	4.7	1.3	1.3
August	3.0	3.4	6.0	2.2	3.0	3.7	4.6	2.4	4.8	4.7	1.2	1.1
September	3.0	3.4	5.9	2.1	3.2	3.7	4.5	2.5	4.9	4.8	1.1	1.2
October	3.0	3.3	6.0	2.2	3.1	3.8	4.4	2.4	4.6	4.5	1.3	1.3
November	3.0	3.4	5.9	2.4	3.2	3.8	4.5	2.5	4.5	4.4	1.2	1.3
December	3.0	3.4	6.5	2.3	3.1	3.3	4.6	2.4	4.6	4.5	1.2	1.2
2011												
January	2.9	3.2	4.6	2.1	3.2	3.7	4.8	2.2	4.5	4.5	1.2	1.3
February	3.1	3.4	6.7	2.1	3.3	3.8	4.7	2.4	4.8	4.7	1.2	1.1
March	3.1	3.5	6.1	2.3	3.2	3.8	4.9	2.4	5.2	5.0	1.2	1.2
April	3.1	3.4	6.4	2.2	3.2	3.8	4.9	2.4	4.9	4.8	1.2	1.3
May	3.2	3.6	6.7	2.2	3.2	3.8	5.3	2.4	4.8	4.6	1.2	1.2
June	3.1	3.5	6.5	2.2	3.2	3.8	4.7	2.4	5.2	5.2	1.2	1.2
July	3.0	3.4	6.0	2.2	3.1	3.8	4.8	2.4	5.2	5.2	1.1	1.1
August	3.1	3.5	5.6	2.1	3.1	3.6	5.0	2.4	5.1	5.0	1.2	1.3
September	3.2	3.6	7.3	2.0	3.0	3.7	5.8	2.3	5.3	5.1	1.2	1.2

[1]Hires are the number of hires during the entire month.
[2]The hires rate is the number of hires during the entire month as a percent of total employment.
[4]Includes natural resources and mining, information, financial activities, and other services, not shown separately.
[5]Includes wholesale trade and transportation, warehousing, and utilities, not shown separately.
[6]Includes arts, entertainment, and recreation, not shown separately.
[7]Includes federal government, not shown separately.

Table 7-9. Separations Levels[1] and Rates,[2] by Industry, December 2000–September 2011

(Seasonally adjusted, levels in thousands, rates per 100.)

Year and month	Level[3]											
	Total[4]	Total private[4]	Construction	Manufacturing	Trade, transportation, and utilities[5]	Retail trade	Professional and business services	Education and health services	Leisure and hospitality[6]	Accommodation and food services	Government[7]	State and local government
2000												
December	5 441	5 044	432	540	1 127	837	946	521	928	793	397	359
2001												
January	5 683	5 330	441	547	1 256	868	1 076	427	960	821	353	290
February	5 455	5 126	465	533	1 146	774	994	491	876	733	329	293
March	5 912	5 588	493	562	1 245	904	1 229	498	980	852	324	288
April	5 598	5 284	459	559	1 241	873	909	464	1 020	895	314	277
May	5 559	5 214	443	554	1 231	866	1 123	438	910	774	345	307
June	5 378	5 092	460	559	1 155	818	1 027	480	885	733	286	257
July	5 455	5 142	453	508	1 179	834	978	473	945	787	313	272
August	5 240	4 875	408	502	1 056	755	979	461	894	744	364	325
September	5 309	5 046	427	465	1 149	805	994	466	996	835	262	226
October	5 496	5 160	429	560	1 169	813	1 004	485	909	768	336	293
November	5 317	5 023	522	494	1 084	723	946	462	906	753	294	259
December	5 002	4 692	443	487	1 014	707	923	425	847	712	310	258
2002												
January	5 170	4 829	420	472	1 082	753	952	461	834	709	341	299
February	5 095	4 758	443	473	1 083	726	933	443	847	720	337	289
March	4 818	4 518	399	436	1 021	687	940	427	815	679	300	254
April	5 078	4 732	462	450	1 043	712	899	462	853	710	346	297
May	5 116	4 810	432	478	1 032	733	1 050	450	806	680	305	267
June	4 926	4 604	424	451	1 040	727	887	409	817	685	322	275
July	5 391	5 050	491	468	1 040	730	1 098	459	909	726	341	293
August	4 912	4 592	374	458	1 048	750	912	437	808	673	320	274
September	4 989	4 663	444	445	1 048	736	962	434	789	686	325	274
October	4 792	4 464	439	445	980	698	922	441	733	643	329	280
November	4 956	4 585	403	437	1 031	716	967	415	797	666	371	318
December	5 099	4 797	447	452	1 004	707	1 031	479	823	684	303	261
2003												
January	5 038	4 697	453	444	1 008	708	903	469	846	699	342	286
February	4 941	4 628	401	443	1 054	791	917	436	822	685	313	268
March	4 747	4 411	409	403	1 019	697	819	436	805	655	337	281
April	4 756	4 431	410	437	907	622	930	392	827	679	326	271
May	4 735	4 414	428	381	963	663	805	462	843	694	321	270
June	4 806	4 515	423	412	996	685	883	471	787	669	292	251
July	4 713	4 398	416	442	966	640	858	455	741	642	314	275
August	4 736	4 406	453	377	976	662	858	451	801	666	330	283
September	4 734	4 420	443	371	977	661	824	465	792	672	314	276
October	4 874	4 588	406	387	1 095	767	870	452	817	687	286	236
November	4 734	4 412	435	384	988	690	816	450	815	675	323	263
December	4 912	4 598	411	385	1 059	731	845	441	866	742	315	280
2004												
January	4 919	4 505	434	375	1 033	728	878	451	826	699	414	340
February	4 757	4 440	447	383	1 048	731	732	473	835	688	317	267
March	5 028	4 713	456	402	1 104	740	920	442	852	728	315	277
April	4 930	4 635	413	384	1 101	770	893	445	844	706	295	262
May	4 803	4 501	406	374	1 033	708	847	447	844	719	301	255
June	4 975	4 651	463	387	1 015	667	924	429	840	710	324	282
July	4 990	4 623	404	396	1 092	775	873	438	873	736	367	329
August	5 024	4 731	411	395	1 075	736	925	456	884	747	293	261
September	4 924	4 604	409	406	1 022	708	871	484	847	692	320	289
October	4 897	4 571	432	389	1 070	748	806	403	889	748	326	276
November	5 171	4 844	440	398	1 146	801	920	485	849	730	327	289
December	5 134	4 795	429	387	1 128	820	976	467	846	714	339	286
2005												
January	5 432	5 079	521	395	1 126	757	984	476	943	804	354	318
February	5 087	4 767	457	354	1 083	755	972	492	821	700	320	282
March	5 263	4 932	423	388	1 178	857	1 003	514	858	740	331	293
April	5 016	4 670	424	379	1 069	739	964	495	783	669	346	285
May	5 253	4 947	473	378	1 127	778	983	480	875	741	306	276
June	5 154	4 829	436	383	1 107	765	996	464	928	764	325	279
July	5 029	4 743	408	400	1 093	791	976	446	885	764	286	245
August	5 313	4 991	480	396	1 125	806	1 034	487	885	767	322	285
September	5 374	5 048	497	417	1 142	806	966	501	978	813	327	280
October	5 043	4 712	466	392	1 074	755	869	469	901	778	331	294
November	5 013	4 687	427	388	1 050	686	819	484	902	783	326	287
December	5 040	4 706	450	348	1 121	747	889	484	892	763	334	274

[1]Total separations are the number of separations during the entire month.
[2]The total separations rate is the number of total separations during the entire month as a percent of total employment.
[3]Detail will not necessarily add to totals because of the independent seasonal adjustment of the various series.
[4]Includes natural resources and mining, information, financial activities, and other services, not shown separately.
[5]Includes wholesale trade and transportation, warehousing, and utilities, not shown separately.
[6]Includes arts, entertainment, and recreation, not shown separately.
[7]Includes federal government, not shown separately.

Table 7-9. Separations Levels[1] and Rates,[2] by Industry, December 2000–September 2011—*Continued*

(Seasonally adjusted, levels in thousands, rates per 100.)

Year and month	Rate											
	Total[4]	Total private[4]	Construction	Manufacturing	Trade, transportation, and utilities[5]	Retail trade	Professional and business services	Education and health services	Leisure and hospitality[6]	Accommodation and food services	Government[7]	State and local government
2000												
December	4.1	4.5	6.4	3.1	4.3	3.4	4.7	5.2	7.7	7.8	1.9	2.0
2001												
January	4.3	4.8	6.5	3.2	4.8	3.1	3.9	4.8	8.0	8.1	1.7	1.6
February	4.1	4.6	6.8	3.1	4.4	3.3	4.5	5.0	7.3	7.2	1.6	1.6
March	4.5	5.0	7.2	3.3	4.8	2.7	5.9	4.8	8.2	8.4	1.5	1.6
April	4.2	4.8	6.7	3.3	4.8	3.5	4.8	4.4	8.5	8.8	1.5	1.5
May	4.2	4.7	6.5	3.3	4.7	3.0	4.7	4.8	7.5	7.6	1.6	1.7
June	4.1	4.6	6.7	3.4	4.4	2.8	4.3	4.7	7.3	7.2	1.4	1.4
July	4.1	4.6	6.6	3.1	4.5	2.6	3.6	4.8	7.8	7.7	1.5	1.5
August	4.0	4.4	6.0	3.1	4.1	2.6	3.5	5.5	7.4	7.3	1.7	1.8
September	4.0	4.6	6.3	2.9	4.4	2.3	3.8	4.6	8.3	8.2	1.2	1.2
October	4.2	4.7	6.3	3.5	4.5	2.3	3.1	4.6	7.6	7.5	1.6	1.6
November	4.1	4.6	7.7	3.1	4.2	2.3	3.4	4.3	7.6	7.4	1.4	1.4
December	3.8	4.3	6.5	3.1	4.0	2.4	3.1	4.4	7.1	7.0	1.5	1.4
2002												
January	4.0	4.4	6.2	3.0	4.2	2.4	3.4	4.5	6.9	7.0	1.6	1.6
February	3.9	4.4	6.6	3.1	4.2	2.3	3.0	4.5	7.1	7.1	1.6	1.5
March	3.7	4.1	5.9	2.8	4.0	2.3	3.6	4.4	6.8	6.7	1.4	1.4
April	3.9	4.3	6.9	2.9	4.1	2.3	3.2	4.2	7.2	7.0	1.6	1.6
May	3.9	4.4	6.5	3.1	4.0	2.2	3.9	4.0	6.8	6.7	1.4	1.4
June	3.8	4.2	6.3	2.9	4.1	2.2	3.2	4.4	6.9	6.8	1.5	1.5
July	4.1	4.6	7.3	3.1	4.1	2.2	3.6	4.1	7.6	7.1	1.6	1.6
August	3.8	4.2	5.6	3.0	4.1	2.1	3.6	4.1	6.8	6.6	1.5	1.5
September	3.8	4.3	6.6	2.9	4.1	2.1	3.6	4.2	6.6	6.7	1.5	1.5
October	3.7	4.1	6.6	3.0	3.9	2.6	4.3	4.0	6.1	6.3	1.5	1.5
November	3.8	4.2	6.0	2.9	4.1	2.0	4.1	4.3	6.6	6.5	1.7	1.7
December	3.9	4.4	6.7	3.0	3.9	1.6	3.4	3.9	6.8	6.6	1.4	1.4
2003												
January	3.9	4.3	6.8	3.0	4.0	2.0	5.1	3.8	6.9	6.8	1.6	1.5
February	3.8	4.3	6.0	3.0	4.2	2.3	4.6	3.6	6.8	6.6	1.4	1.4
March	3.7	4.1	6.2	2.7	4.0	2.0	4.0	3.5	6.6	6.4	1.6	1.5
April	3.7	4.1	6.1	3.0	3.6	1.9	3.2	3.6	6.8	6.6	1.5	1.4
May	3.6	4.1	6.4	2.6	3.8	2.0	3.8	3.9	7.0	6.7	1.5	1.4
June	3.7	4.2	6.3	2.8	3.9	2.2	3.7	3.5	6.5	6.5	1.4	1.3
July	3.6	4.1	6.2	3.1	3.8	2.1	4.2	3.3	6.1	6.2	1.5	1.5
August	3.6	4.1	6.7	2.6	3.9	2.2	4.4	3.3	6.6	6.4	1.5	1.5
September	3.6	4.1	6.5	2.6	3.9	2.4	3.9	3.2	6.5	6.5	1.5	1.5
October	3.7	4.2	6.0	2.7	4.3	2.3	3.6	3.6	6.7	6.6	1.3	1.3
November	3.6	4.1	6.4	2.7	3.9	2.5	3.7	3.4	6.6	6.5	1.5	1.4
December	3.8	4.2	6.0	2.7	4.2	2.3	3.7	3.0	7.0	7.1	1.5	1.5
2004												
January	3.8	4.1	6.3	2.6	4.1	2.3	3.5	3.7	6.7	6.7	1.9	1.8
February	3.6	4.1	6.5	2.7	4.1	2.5	3.9	3.5	6.7	6.5	1.5	1.4
March	3.8	4.3	6.6	2.8	4.3	2.5	3.5	3.5	6.9	6.9	1.5	1.5
April	3.8	4.2	6.0	2.7	4.3	2.5	3.9	3.5	6.8	6.7	1.4	1.4
May	3.7	4.1	5.8	2.6	4.1	2.8	3.9	3.5	6.8	6.8	1.4	1.3
June	3.8	4.2	6.6	2.7	4.0	2.6	4.3	3.0	6.7	6.7	1.5	1.5
July	3.8	4.2	5.8	2.8	4.3	2.8	4.4	3.5	7.0	6.9	1.7	1.7
August	3.8	4.3	5.9	2.8	4.2	2.8	3.9	3.5	7.1	7.0	1.4	1.4
September	3.7	4.2	5.8	2.8	4.0	3.1	4.1	3.5	6.8	6.5	1.5	1.5
October	3.7	4.1	6.1	2.7	4.2	2.9	4.3	3.8	7.1	7.0	1.5	1.5
November	3.9	4.4	6.2	2.8	4.5	2.1	3.5	3.5	6.7	6.8	1.5	1.5
December	3.9	4.3	6.0	2.7	4.4	2.7	4.1	3.6	6.7	6.6	1.6	1.5
2005												
January	4.1	4.6	7.3	2.8	4.4	2.9	4.0	3.6	7.4	7.4	1.6	1.7
February	3.8	4.3	6.4	2.5	4.2	2.8	4.0	3.5	6.5	6.5	1.5	1.5
March	4.0	4.4	5.9	2.7	4.6	3.0	4.2	3.8	6.7	6.8	1.5	1.5
April	3.8	4.2	5.8	2.7	4.1	3.0	4.5	3.6	6.1	6.1	1.6	1.5
May	3.9	4.4	6.5	2.6	4.3	2.6	4.4	3.8	6.8	6.8	1.4	1.4
June	3.9	4.3	5.9	2.7	4.3	2.6	5.0	3.6	7.2	7.0	1.5	1.5
July	3.8	4.2	5.5	2.8	4.2	2.6	4.5	3.8	6.9	7.0	1.3	1.3
August	4.0	4.4	6.5	2.8	4.3	2.7	4.6	3.7	6.9	7.0	1.5	1.5
September	4.0	4.5	6.7	2.9	4.4	2.5	4.6	3.8	7.6	7.4	1.5	1.5
October	3.8	4.2	6.3	2.8	4.1	2.9	4.5	3.6	7.0	7.1	1.5	1.5
November	3.7	4.2	5.7	2.7	4.0	3.4	4.7	3.6	7.0	7.1	1.5	1.5
December	3.7	4.2	6.0	2.5	4.3	3.0	4.8	3.7	6.9	6.9	1.5	1.4

[1]Total separations are the number of separations during the entire month.
[2]The total separations rate is the number of total separations during the entire month as a percent of total employment.
[4]Includes natural resources and mining, information, financial activities, and other services, not shown separately.
[5]Includes wholesale trade and transportation, warehousing, and utilities, not shown separately.
[6]Includes arts, entertainment, and recreation, not shown separately.
[7]Includes federal government, not shown separately.

Table 7-9. Separations Levels[1] and Rates,[2] by Industry, December 2000–September 2011—*Continued*

(Seasonally adjusted, levels in thousands, rates per 100.)

Year and month	Level[3]											
	Total[4]	Total private[4]	Construction	Manufacturing	Trade, transportation, and utilities[5]	Retail trade	Professional and business services	Education and health services	Leisure and hospitality[6]	Accommodation and food services	Government[7]	State and local government
2006												
January	4 874	4 548	424	363	1 061	769	882	428	894	781	327	276
February	5 142	4 807	406	377	1 149	813	909	447	941	829	336	284
March	5 123	4 769	436	419	1 113	796	864	457	915	785	354	294
April	5 162	4 807	429	366	1 157	839	885	503	874	772	355	294
May	5 576	5 211	489	429	1 185	848	1 082	572	905	763	365	302
June	5 298	4 926	433	402	1 168	831	937	500	914	779	372	307
July	5 462	5 116	455	437	1 164	808	979	551	895	766	346	286
August	5 123	4 777	418	406	1 146	762	902	483	879	754	346	273
September	5 205	4 846	407	385	1 103	773	1 021	459	875	756	359	270
October	5 330	5 000	450	393	1 105	766	1 004	514	902	778	330	292
November	5 325	4 980	475	392	1 084	776	1 008	489	955	821	344	293
December	5 147	4 814	420	401	1 024	746	981	490	948	807	333	287
2007												
January	5 134	4 787	396	392	1 078	750	933	495	914	775	347	294
February	5 131	4 773	419	420	1 067	744	944	483	902	765	358	289
March	5 202	4 846	359	404	1 103	746	958	493	903	763	357	280
April	5 349	4 994	418	401	1 093	741	959	498	997	853	354	285
May	5 248	4 873	412	412	1 098	784	929	517	900	779	375	291
June	5 162	4 809	430	418	1 095	727	842	505	930	793	353	270
July	5 394	4 952	444	412	1 063	729	969	494	935	808	441	351
August	5 208	4 860	449	422	1 056	736	919	494	907	780	348	273
September	5 091	4 760	424	418	1 056	748	944	457	870	745	330	233
October	5 223	4 918	413	415	1 113	770	975	494	904	771	305	270
November	5 053	4 736	408	397	1 061	736	947	523	867	724	317	283
December	4 887	4 561	402	362	1 022	720	873	452	905	775	325	285
2008												
January	5 036	4 708	400	361	1 063	731	904	527	890	749	328	275
February	4 971	4 680	401	362	1 065	739	879	523	914	766	291	259
March	4 894	4 595	416	356	1 002	694	927	522	848	718	299	271
April	4 871	4 573	442	373	1 026	704	900	488	832	720	298	274
May	4 925	4 625	420	369	1 005	679	881	500	920	770	300	275
June	4 859	4 579	489	379	1 047	707	894	464	797	692	280	257
July	4 525	4 254	395	329	995	692	829	462	768	660	272	252
August	4 789	4 504	435	345	1 045	704	863	477	818	668	285	264
September	4 693	4 401	406	370	1 011	680	811	465	825	711	292	272
October	4 574	4 287	415	398	978	651	844	480	725	623	287	262
November	4 613	4 338	472	365	958	652	901	446	706	617	276	253
December	4 749	4 481	433	448	1 050	680	880	472	707	600	268	242
2009												
January	4 723	4 451	481	442	1 010	627	856	437	701	591	273	248
February	4 707	4 440	443	425	913	591	894	499	710	610	267	248
March	4 540	4 282	452	413	979	618	724	464	722	626	258	238
April	4 453	4 181	437	371	928	637	852	448	677	571	272	239
May	4 224	3 901	390	372	862	575	749	414	637	556	323	240
June	4 125	3 796	365	355	778	512	708	461	655	544	329	251
July	4 031	3 729	383	301	793	519	669	472	613	501	301	272
August	3 949	3 654	339	280	793	533	658	481	667	559	295	268
September	4 016	3 743	385	311	872	563	663	469	621	544	273	254
October	3 788	3 514	332	272	769	522	675	443	616	504	274	240
November	3 973	3 688	326	313	806	511	716	443	675	555	285	241
December	3 889	3 595	381	266	822	537	598	441	639	533	293	256
2010												
January	3 543	3 274	410	218	696	475	640	373	597	498	269	248
February	3 795	3 486	344	263	773	523	684	430	571	496	309	267
March	3 877	3 561	344	245	819	587	680	438	629	514	315	269
April	3 642	3 343	323	233	715	497	684	439	595	490	298	252
May	3 929	3 603	338	235	755	531	745	429	656	544	326	259
June	4 173	3 620	307	250	830	565	724	467	617	510	554	272
July	4 032	3 588	334	252	794	558	760	478	619	511	445	257
August	3 996	3 556	320	279	769	545	757	429	601	498	440	289
September	3 904	3 526	330	245	763	531	742	460	607	503	379	266
October	3 702	3 436	323	266	741	527	709	408	613	507	265	220
November	3 869	3 568	342	265	773	541	687	460	595	497	300	263
December	3 836	3 539	393	252	718	470	735	450	583	485	297	269
2011												
January	3 612	3 337	281	184	769	527	756	394	596	505	275	245
February	3 825	3 538	324	234	800	549	760	441	582	495	287	255
March	3 805	3 534	334	245	772	541	719	429	650	528	271	247
April	3 833	3 528	357	241	725	511	785	428	621	512	304	278
May	4 145	3 844	376	272	799	562	892	450	652	528	301	271
June	3 993	3 687	371	252	785	538	766	459	653	552	306	273
July	3 962	3 659	327	239	770	547	806	431	670	573	302	271
August	3 960	3 688	320	250	762	521	824	444	689	576	272	240
September	4 149	3 861	367	246	757	534	946	407	707	563	288	255

[1]Total separations are the number of separations during the entire month.
[2]The total separations rate is the number of total separations during the entire month as a percent of total employment.
[3]Detail will not necessarily add to totals because of the independent seasonal adjustment of the various series.
[4]Includes natural resources and mining, information, financial activities, and other services, not shown separately.
[5]Includes wholesale trade and transportation, warehousing, and utilities, not shown separately.
[6]Includes arts, entertainment, and recreation, not shown separately.
[7]Includes federal government, not shown separately.

Table 7-9. Separations Levels[1] and Rates,[2] by Industry, December 2000–September 2011—*Continued*

(Seasonally adjusted, levels in thousands, rates per 100.)

Year and month	Rate											
	Total[4]	Total private[4]	Construction	Manufacturing	Trade, transportation, and utilities[5]	Retail trade	Professional and business services	Education and health services	Leisure and hospitality[6]	Accommodation and food services	Government[7]	State and local government
2006												
January	3.6	4.0	5.6	2.6	4.1	2.9	4.6	3.8	6.9	7.1	1.5	1.4
February	3.8	4.2	5.3	2.7	4.4	2.7	4.6	4.0	7.2	7.5	1.5	1.5
March	3.8	4.2	5.7	2.9	4.2	2.7	4.4	4.1	7.0	7.1	1.6	1.5
April	3.8	4.2	5.6	2.6	4.4	2.9	4.0	4.0	6.7	6.9	1.6	1.5
May	4.1	4.6	6.3	3.0	4.5	2.9	5.0	3.8	6.9	6.9	1.7	1.6
June	3.9	4.3	5.6	2.8	4.4	2.7	3.8	3.9	7.0	7.0	1.7	1.6
July	4.0	4.5	5.9	3.1	4.4	2.5	3.4	3.5	6.8	6.8	1.6	1.5
August	3.8	4.2	5.4	2.9	4.4	2.8	4.0	4.2	6.7	6.7	1.6	1.4
September	3.8	4.2	5.3	2.7	4.2	2.8	4.0	4.2	6.7	6.7	1.6	1.4
October	3.9	4.4	5.9	2.8	4.2	2.8	4.2	4.4	6.8	6.9	1.5	1.5
November	3.9	4.3	6.2	2.8	4.1	2.7	4.2	4.1	7.2	7.3	1.6	1.5
December	3.8	4.2	5.5	2.9	3.9	3.5	3.8	4.0	7.1	7.1	1.5	1.5
2007												
January	3.7	4.2	5.1	2.8	4.1	2.9	4.2	4.0	6.9	6.8	1.6	1.5
February	3.7	4.1	5.5	3.0	4.0	2.7	3.6	3.6	6.8	6.7	1.6	1.5
March	3.8	4.2	4.7	2.9	4.1	2.6	4.6	3.9	6.8	6.7	1.6	1.4
April	3.9	4.3	5.4	2.9	4.1	2.6	4.3	4.0	7.5	7.5	1.6	1.5
May	3.8	4.2	5.4	3.0	4.1	2.3	4.3	4.0	6.7	6.8	1.7	1.5
June	3.7	4.2	5.6	3.0	4.1	2.8	4.3	4.1	6.9	6.9	1.6	1.4
July	3.9	4.3	5.8	3.0	4.0	2.8	3.9	3.9	7.0	7.1	2.0	1.8
August	3.8	4.2	5.9	3.1	4.0	2.6	4.2	4.1	6.8	6.8	1.6	1.4
September	3.7	4.1	5.6	3.0	4.0	2.6	4.1	4.4	6.5	6.5	1.5	1.2
October	3.8	4.3	5.5	3.0	4.2	2.3	4.1	3.9	6.7	6.7	1.4	1.4
November	3.7	4.1	5.4	2.9	4.0	2.7	4.1	3.7	6.4	6.3	1.4	1.4
December	3.5	3.9	5.4	2.6	3.8	2.7	4.0	4.0	6.7	6.7	1.5	1.5
2008												
January	3.6	4.1	5.3	2.6	4.0	2.3	4.1	4.0	6.6	6.5	1.5	1.4
February	3.6	4.1	5.4	2.6	4.0	2.3	4.1	4.0	6.8	6.6	1.3	1.3
March	3.6	4.0	5.6	2.6	3.8	2.4	4.2	4.0	6.3	6.2	1.3	1.4
April	3.5	4.0	6.0	2.7	3.9	2.2	3.9	3.4	6.2	6.2	1.3	1.4
May	3.6	4.0	5.8	2.7	3.8	2.2	3.5	3.7	6.8	6.7	1.3	1.4
June	3.5	4.0	6.8	2.8	4.0	2.0	3.8	3.7	5.9	6.0	1.2	1.3
July	3.3	3.7	5.5	2.4	3.8	2.3	3.4	3.6	5.7	5.7	1.2	1.3
August	3.5	3.9	6.1	2.6	4.0	2.3	3.4	3.4	6.1	5.8	1.3	1.3
September	3.4	3.9	5.8	2.8	3.9	1.8	3.2	3.0	6.2	6.2	1.3	1.4
October	3.4	3.8	6.0	3.0	3.8	2.3	3.0	3.1	5.4	5.5	1.3	1.3
November	3.4	3.9	6.9	2.8	3.7	2.6	2.9	3.2	5.3	5.4	1.2	1.3
December	3.5	4.0	6.5	3.5	4.1	2.0	3.0	3.1	5.3	5.3	1.2	1.2
2009												
January	3.5	4.0	7.3	3.5	4.0	2.1	2.8	2.8	5.3	5.2	1.2	1.3
February	3.5	4.0	6.9	3.4	3.6	2.0	2.9	2.8	5.4	5.4	1.2	1.3
March	3.4	3.9	7.2	3.4	3.9	1.7	2.5	2.6	5.5	5.6	1.1	1.2
April	3.4	3.8	7.1	3.1	3.7	1.3	2.5	2.4	5.2	5.1	1.2	1.2
May	3.2	3.6	6.4	3.1	3.5	2.1	2.3	2.6	4.9	5.0	1.4	1.2
June	3.2	3.5	6.1	3.0	3.1	1.9	2.2	2.7	5.0	4.9	1.5	1.3
July	3.1	3.5	6.5	2.6	3.2	1.2	2.3	2.7	4.7	4.5	1.3	1.4
August	3.0	3.4	5.8	2.4	3.2	1.6	2.1	2.7	5.1	5.0	1.3	1.4
September	3.1	3.5	6.7	2.7	3.5	1.9	2.5	2.6	4.8	4.9	1.2	1.3
October	2.9	3.3	5.8	2.4	3.1	1.5	2.2	2.5	4.7	4.5	1.2	1.2
November	3.1	3.4	5.7	2.7	3.3	1.5	2.2	2.5	5.2	5.0	1.3	1.2
December	3.0	3.4	6.8	2.3	3.3	1.5	2.3	2.6	4.9	4.8	1.3	1.3
2010												
January	2.7	3.1	7.3	1.9	2.8	1.5	2.3	2.6	4.6	4.5	1.2	1.3
February	2.9	3.3	6.2	2.3	3.2	1.8	2.3	2.6	4.4	4.5	1.4	1.4
March	3.0	3.3	6.2	2.1	3.3	2.0	2.5	2.6	4.9	4.6	1.4	1.4
April	2.8	3.1	5.8	2.0	2.9	1.7	2.8	2.5	4.6	4.4	1.3	1.3
May	3.0	3.4	6.1	2.0	3.1	1.7	3.3	2.6	5.0	4.9	1.4	1.3
June	3.2	3.4	5.6	2.2	3.4	1.8	2.7	2.4	4.7	4.6	2.4	1.4
July	3.1	3.3	6.1	2.2	3.2	1.8	3.0	2.5	4.8	4.6	2.0	1.3
August	3.1	3.3	5.8	2.4	3.1	1.7	3.5	2.4	4.6	4.5	2.0	1.5
September	3.0	3.3	6.0	2.1	3.1	1.6	3.2	2.5	4.6	4.5	1.7	1.4
October	2.8	3.2	5.9	2.3	3.0	1.8	3.3	2.8	4.7	4.5	1.2	1.1
November	3.0	3.3	6.2	2.3	3.1	1.7	3.7	2.6	4.6	4.4	1.3	1.4
December	2.9	3.3	7.2	2.2	2.9	1.8	3.5	2.5	4.5	4.3	1.3	1.4
2011												
January	2.8	3.1	5.1	1.6	3.1	1.8	2.6	2.4	4.6	4.5	1.2	1.3
February	2.9	3.3	5.9	2.0	3.2	1.6	3.4	2.7	4.4	4.4	1.3	1.3
March	2.9	3.3	6.0	2.1	3.1	1.7	3.5	3.0	4.9	4.7	1.2	1.3
April	2.9	3.2	6.5	2.1	2.9	2.1	2.8	2.7	4.7	4.5	1.4	1.4
May	3.2	3.5	6.8	2.3	3.2	1.9	3.5	2.9	4.9	4.7	1.4	1.4
June	3.0	3.4	6.7	2.2	3.1	2.2	3.5	2.9	4.9	4.9	1.4	1.4
July	3.0	3.4	5.9	2.0	3.1	2.1	3.6	2.9	5.1	5.1	1.4	1.4
August	3.0	3.4	5.8	2.1	3.1	2.2	3.5	2.9	5.2	5.1	1.2	1.2
September	3.2	3.5	6.6	2.1	3.0	2.3	3.8	3.0	5.3	5.0	1.3	1.3

[1] Total separations are the number of separations during the entire month.
[2] The total separations rate is the number of total separations during the entire month as a percent of total employment.
[4] Includes natural resources and mining, information, financial activities, and other services, not shown separately.
[5] Includes wholesale trade and transportation, warehousing, and utilities, not shown separately.
[6] Includes arts, entertainment, and recreation, not shown separately.
[7] Includes federal government, not shown separately.

Table 7-10. Quits Levels[1] and Rates,[2] by Industry, December 2000–September 2011

(Seasonally adjusted, levels in thousands, rates per 100.)

Year and month	Level[3]											
	Total[4]	Total private[4]	Construction	Manufacturing	Trade, transportation, and utilities[5]	Retail trade	Professional and business services	Education and health services	Leisure and hospitality[6]	Accommodation and food services	Government[7]	State and local government
2000												
December	3 145	2 915	89	339	697	569	408	324	674	637	231	211
2001												
January	3 353	3 151	159	286	693	483	708	273	668	631	203	172
February	3 320	3 136	165	245	825	583	551	335	608	554	183	166
March	3 144	2 965	177	244	728	514	539	339	609	560	179	162
April	3 224	3 060	214	230	794	585	537	326	623	551	164	147
May	3 136	2 948	158	206	777	549	552	315	625	559	188	169
June	2 988	2 849	174	200	754	553	481	330	596	536	139	124
July	3 008	2 849	176	177	721	539	528	283	592	535	160	140
August	2 930	2 751	147	194	656	480	497	274	598	533	179	162
September	2 858	2 704	141	176	670	489	461	304	632	575	153	138
October	2 904	2 747	142	192	685	522	520	283	578	514	157	137
November	2 704	2 542	166	176	613	463	485	280	491	434	163	144
December	2 671	2 496	131	170	654	490	443	282	508	445	175	147
2002												
January	2 999	2 832	170	180	697	512	556	274	612	538	166	147
February	2 686	2 509	159	189	552	408	480	272	539	472	177	156
March	2 617	2 469	137	188	586	441	481	236	568	499	148	127
April	2 751	2 561	180	197	593	403	471	278	560	496	190	169
May	2 723	2 574	143	209	546	393	560	285	520	453	149	130
June	2 697	2 531	137	196	651	499	457	256	527	465	165	133
July	2 722	2 581	161	206	581	419	494	295	532	477	141	120
August	2 671	2 515	148	205	573	423	483	279	506	455	157	135
September	2 651	2 496	176	195	550	412	491	249	512	459	155	132
October	2 556	2 401	155	168	555	388	475	281	491	445	154	130
November	2 577	2 383	127	178	570	449	490	275	460	427	194	169
December	2 635	2 492	137	165	545	421	513	303	500	446	143	119
2003												
January	2 504	2 348	147	183	504	373	445	286	485	438	157	131
February	2 567	2 419	152	169	565	438	431	276	524	474	148	125
March	2 453	2 307	131	156	559	398	423	254	473	428	146	122
April	2 402	2 258	100	161	517	383	423	245	495	454	145	120
May	2 366	2 220	158	182	530	400	336	263	455	426	147	125
June	2 410	2 273	158	166	502	377	415	270	506	459	137	117
July	2 351	2 206	140	182	509	371	366	249	506	459	145	125
August	2 378	2 232	162	172	522	388	352	267	485	433	147	125
September	2 463	2 313	147	170	549	415	377	305	476	425	151	132
October	2 529	2 385	137	172	579	425	375	282	544	490	144	127
November	2 484	2 347	169	193	544	369	351	263	493	438	138	121
December	2 498	2 350	193	212	534	368	376	277	463	421	148	130
2004												
January	2 465	2 284	149	184	552	429	353	280	472	434	181	153
February	2 505	2 345	170	189	537	401	362	273	507	479	160	133
March	2 689	2 538	174	204	574	426	444	280	550	509	152	133
April	2 670	2 520	173	207	628	490	377	289	510	452	149	137
May	2 534	2 386	167	180	559	404	343	280	547	503	148	127
June	2 709	2 555	197	201	577	420	441	271	511	472	154	141
July	2 682	2 520	118	194	615	456	433	309	503	456	162	148
August	2 635	2 496	150	170	602	467	452	275	535	490	139	126
September	2 647	2 509	177	202	608	452	440	267	513	465	138	127
October	2 672	2 531	164	187	608	450	435	263	519	476	141	125
November	2 879	2 738	186	218	665	495	477	292	577	521	141	127
December	2 806	2 650	159	212	581	420	489	278	572	519	156	143
2005												
January	3 013	2 849	204	193	684	483	518	295	600	544	165	152
February	2 733	2 589	171	188	585	435	482	302	518	468	145	132
March	2 887	2 728	205	190	664	494	484	327	522	465	160	147
April	2 835	2 672	158	185	625	474	509	321	536	478	163	139
May	2 869	2 720	181	186	662	519	479	292	577	521	150	137
June	2 874	2 717	167	204	675	501	460	311	555	498	157	141
July	2 804	2 679	171	195	638	486	439	299	595	538	125	109
August	3 002	2 849	198	196	680	499	483	312	615	567	153	138
September	3 112	2 953	242	217	648	474	517	326	649	598	159	142
October	2 964	2 786	231	216	644	480	395	305	677	610	178	160
November	2 963	2 798	202	206	644	481	398	316	638	590	166	147
December	2 859	2 708	250	177	687	515	408	298	580	530	151	130

[1]Quits are the number of quits during the entire month.
[2]The quits rate is the number of quits during the entire month as a percent of total employment.
[3]Detail will not necessarily add to totals because of the independent seasonal adjustment of the various series.
[4]Includes natural resources and mining, information, financial activities, and other services, not shown separately.
[5]Includes wholesale trade and transportation, warehousing, and utilities, not shown separately.
[6]Includes arts, entertainment, and recreation, not shown separately.
[7]Includes federal government, not shown separately.

Table 7-10. Quits Levels[1] and Rates,[2] by Industry, December 2000–September 2011—*Continued*

(Seasonally adjusted, levels in thousands, rates per 100.)

Year and month	Rate											
	Total[4]	Total private[4]	Construction	Manufacturing	Trade, transportation, and utilities[5]	Retail trade	Professional and business services	Education and health services	Leisure and hospitality[6]	Accommodation and food services	Government[7]	State and local government
2000												
December	2.4	2.6	1.3	2.0	2.6	3.7	2.4	2.1	5.6	6.3	1.1	1.2
2001												
January	2.5	2.8	2.3	1.7	2.6	3.1	4.2	1.8	5.6	6.2	1.0	0.9
February	2.5	2.8	2.4	1.4	3.1	3.8	3.3	2.2	5.1	5.4	0.9	0.9
March	2.4	2.7	2.6	1.4	2.8	3.3	3.2	2.2	5.1	5.5	0.9	0.9
April	2.4	2.8	3.1	1.4	3.0	3.8	3.2	2.1	5.2	5.4	0.8	0.8
May	2.4	2.7	2.3	1.2	3.0	3.6	3.3	2.0	5.2	5.5	0.9	0.9
June	2.3	2.6	2.5	1.2	2.9	3.6	2.9	2.1	4.9	5.2	0.7	0.7
July	2.3	2.6	2.6	1.1	2.8	3.5	3.2	1.8	4.9	5.2	0.8	0.8
August	2.2	2.5	2.1	1.2	2.5	3.2	3.0	1.7	4.9	5.2	0.8	0.9
September	2.2	2.5	2.1	1.1	2.6	3.2	2.8	1.9	5.2	5.6	0.7	0.7
October	2.2	2.5	2.1	1.2	2.7	3.4	3.2	1.8	4.8	5.0	0.7	0.7
November	2.1	2.3	2.5	1.1	2.4	3.1	3.0	1.8	4.1	4.3	0.8	0.8
December	2.0	2.3	1.9	1.1	2.6	3.2	2.8	1.8	4.2	4.4	0.8	0.8
2002												
January	2.3	2.6	2.5	1.2	2.7	3.4	3.5	1.7	5.1	5.3	0.8	0.8
February	2.1	2.3	2.3	1.2	2.2	2.7	3.0	1.7	4.5	4.6	0.8	0.8
March	2.0	2.3	2.0	1.2	2.3	2.9	3.0	1.5	4.7	4.9	0.7	0.7
April	2.1	2.4	2.7	1.3	2.3	2.7	2.9	1.7	4.7	4.9	0.9	0.9
May	2.1	2.4	2.1	1.4	2.1	2.6	3.5	1.8	4.4	4.5	0.7	0.7
June	2.1	2.3	2.0	1.3	2.6	3.3	2.9	1.6	4.4	4.6	0.8	0.7
July	2.1	2.4	2.4	1.3	2.3	2.8	3.1	1.8	4.5	4.7	0.7	0.6
August	2.1	2.3	2.2	1.4	2.2	2.8	3.0	1.7	4.2	4.5	0.7	0.7
September	2.0	2.3	2.6	1.3	2.2	2.8	3.1	1.5	4.3	4.5	0.7	0.7
October	2.0	2.2	2.3	1.1	2.2	2.6	3.0	1.7	4.1	4.3	0.7	0.7
November	2.0	2.2	1.9	1.2	2.2	3.0	3.1	1.7	3.8	4.1	0.9	0.9
December	2.0	2.3	2.0	1.1	2.1	2.8	3.2	1.8	4.1	4.3	0.7	0.6
2003												
January	1.9	2.2	2.2	1.2	2.0	2.5	2.8	1.7	4.0	4.2	0.7	0.7
February	2.0	2.2	2.3	1.1	2.2	2.9	2.7	1.7	4.3	4.6	0.7	0.7
March	1.9	2.1	2.0	1.1	2.2	2.7	2.7	1.5	3.9	4.2	0.7	0.6
April	1.8	2.1	1.5	1.1	2.0	2.6	2.7	1.5	4.1	4.4	0.7	0.6
May	1.8	2.1	2.4	1.3	2.1	2.7	2.1	1.6	3.8	4.1	0.7	0.7
June	1.9	2.1	2.3	1.1	2.0	2.5	2.6	1.6	4.2	4.4	0.6	0.6
July	1.8	2.0	2.1	1.3	2.0	2.5	2.3	1.5	4.2	4.4	0.7	0.7
August	1.8	2.1	2.4	1.2	2.1	2.6	2.2	1.6	4.0	4.2	0.7	0.7
September	1.9	2.1	2.2	1.2	2.2	2.8	2.4	1.8	3.9	4.1	0.7	0.7
October	1.9	2.2	2.0	1.2	2.3	2.8	2.3	1.7	4.4	4.7	0.7	0.7
November	1.9	2.2	2.5	1.3	2.2	2.5	2.2	1.6	4.0	4.2	0.6	0.6
December	1.9	2.2	2.8	1.5	2.1	2.5	2.3	1.7	3.8	4.0	0.7	0.7
2004												
January	1.9	2.1	2.2	1.3	2.2	2.9	2.2	1.7	3.8	4.1	0.8	0.8
February	1.9	2.2	2.5	1.3	2.1	2.7	2.2	1.6	4.1	4.5	0.7	0.7
March	2.1	2.3	2.5	1.4	2.3	2.8	2.7	1.7	4.4	4.8	0.7	0.7
April	2.0	2.3	2.5	1.4	2.5	3.3	2.3	1.7	4.1	4.3	0.7	0.7
May	1.9	2.2	2.4	1.3	2.2	2.7	2.1	1.7	4.4	4.7	0.7	0.7
June	2.1	2.3	2.8	1.4	2.3	2.8	2.7	1.6	4.1	4.4	0.7	0.7
July	2.0	2.3	1.7	1.4	2.4	3.0	2.6	1.8	4.0	4.3	0.8	0.8
August	2.0	2.3	2.1	1.2	2.4	3.1	2.7	1.6	4.3	4.6	0.6	0.7
September	2.0	2.3	2.5	1.4	2.4	3.0	2.7	1.6	4.1	4.3	0.6	0.7
October	2.0	2.3	2.3	1.3	2.4	3.0	2.6	1.5	4.1	4.4	0.7	0.7
November	2.2	2.5	2.6	1.5	2.6	3.3	2.9	1.7	4.6	4.8	0.7	0.7
December	2.1	2.4	2.2	1.5	2.3	2.8	2.9	1.6	4.5	4.8	0.7	0.8
2005												
January	2.3	2.6	2.9	1.4	2.7	3.2	3.1	1.7	4.7	5.0	0.8	0.8
February	2.1	2.3	2.4	1.3	2.3	2.9	2.9	1.8	4.1	4.3	0.7	0.7
March	2.2	2.5	2.8	1.3	2.6	3.3	2.9	1.9	4.1	4.3	0.7	local
April	2.1	2.4	2.2	1.3	2.4	3.1	3.0	1.9	4.2	4.4	0.7	0.7
May	2.2	2.4	2.5	1.3	2.6	3.4	2.8	1.7	4.5	4.8	0.7	0.7
June	2.2	2.4	2.3	1.4	2.6	3.3	2.7	1.8	4.3	4.5	0.7	0.7
July	2.1	2.4	2.3	1.4	2.5	3.2	2.6	1.7	4.6	4.9	0.6	0.6
August	2.2	2.5	2.7	1.4	2.6	3.2	2.8	1.8	4.8	5.2	0.7	0.7
September	2.3	2.6	3.3	1.5	2.5	3.1	3.0	1.9	5.0	5.5	0.7	0.7
October	2.2	2.5	3.1	1.5	2.5	3.1	2.3	1.7	5.3	5.6	0.8	0.8
November	2.2	2.5	2.7	1.4	2.5	3.1	2.3	1.8	5.0	5.4	0.8	0.8
December	2.1	2.4	3.3	1.2	2.6	3.4	2.4	1.7	4.5	4.8	0.7	0.7

[1]Quits are the number of quits during the entire month.
[2]The quits rate is the number of quits during the entire month as a percent of total employment.
[4]Includes natural resources and mining, information, financial activities, and other services, not shown separately.
[5]Includes wholesale trade and transportation, warehousing, and utilities, not shown separately.
[6]Includes arts, entertainment, and recreation, not shown separately.
[7]Includes federal government, not shown separately.

Table 7-10. Quits Levels[1] and Rates,[2] by Industry, December 2000–September 2011—*Continued*

(Seasonally adjusted, levels in thousands, rates per 100.)

Year and month	Level[3]											
	Total[4]	Total private[4]	Construc-tion	Manufac-turing	Trade, transpor-tation, and utilities[5]	Retail trade	Profes-sional and business services	Education and health services	Leisure and hospitality[6]	Accommo-dation and food services	Govern-ment[7]	State and local govern-ment
2006												
January	2 914	2 762	213	201	656	491	428	275	662	592	153	134
February	3 024	2 855	195	203	699	522	458	305	645	596	170	148
March	3 071	2 903	202	203	701	528	492	288	646	588	168	143
April	2 863	2 690	209	189	712	522	464	299	545	492	173	146
May	3 088	2 904	205	231	702	509	487	340	619	574	184	158
June	3 081	2 894	204	193	647	476	496	335	678	623	187	152
July	3 095	2 928	182	226	686	524	502	338	608	565	167	141
August	3 018	2 833	168	205	701	476	487	325	611	564	185	155
September	2 975	2 801	154	180	652	483	551	298	613	567	173	131
October	3 030	2 863	180	208	653	483	526	335	603	551	166	145
November	3 126	2 958	164	236	716	527	550	313	631	570	168	143
December	3 133	2 961	172	254	652	470	567	345	662	608	172	150
2007												
January	3 046	2 874	167	235	661	477	540	311	621	584	172	153
February	3 005	2 843	134	216	682	492	524	324	621	568	162	139
March	3 040	2 860	146	224	659	468	508	308	622	568	181	152
April	3 002	2 831	157	215	668	483	481	315	653	606	172	148
May	3 067	2 885	161	220	704	503	478	345	604	563	182	153
June	2 812	2 645	132	208	656	475	422	297	621	572	167	140
July	3 018	2 836	186	195	594	437	538	328	663	607	182	153
August	2 941	2 783	176	209	599	443	480	320	643	579	157	135
September	2 612	2 449	137	184	591	430	461	266	479	430	163	128
October	2 929	2 772	162	207	642	471	470	297	648	590	156	140
November	2 764	2 605	155	183	558	406	480	322	632	580	159	146
December	2 826	2 680	165	214	648	478	408	294	643	576	146	134
2008												
January	2 921	2 766	148	213	662	488	439	341	598	536	154	140
February	2 824	2 678	166	190	616	428	479	307	588	534	146	134
March	2 662	2 530	121	190	571	406	459	310	573	527	131	123
April	2 723	2 573	160	179	576	411	492	298	556	510	150	141
May	2 696	2 547	137	162	588	395	469	272	633	578	149	142
June	2 578	2 442	150	159	556	397	461	279	552	507	137	130
July	2 357	2 226	140	138	519	378	416	286	524	473	131	124
August	2 353	2 213	144	138	536	390	347	277	500	458	140	131
September	2 393	2 248	102	140	545	397	386	274	532	488	145	138
October	2 239	2 107	103	143	485	335	392	272	485	453	132	124
November	2 063	1 941	91	123	457	340	361	237	446	416	122	116
December	1 987	1 862	77	99	484	361	352	232	415	391	125	119
2009												
January	1 878	1 775	77	104	426	332	343	226	411	383	103	97
February	1 932	1 826	85	95	396	298	307	262	410	376	106	102
March	1 842	1 740	96	87	455	325	274	241	393	362	102	99
April	1 692	1 589	66	78	353	252	283	213	382	346	104	97
May	1 739	1 633	79	90	358	264	309	244	365	325	106	98
June	1 707	1 606	72	92	382	291	254	250	378	332	101	93
July	1 624	1 520	63	84	367	263	257	225	350	312	104	99
August	1 663	1 551	59	77	383	291	247	240	378	344	112	102
September	1 605	1 511	70	88	371	263	253	253	312	299	94	88
October	1 589	1 487	56	76	352	255	263	247	323	296	103	96
November	1 764	1 655	93	73	391	261	275	244	372	334	109	99
December	1 604	1 495	65	72	364	278	229	250	340	310	109	97
2010												
January	1 482	1 387	71	68	306	223	251	214	342	299	95	91
February	1 782	1 659	75	98	427	331	288	237	361	327	124	110
March	1 803	1 683	78	89	398	295	299	241	365	332	120	103
April	1 739	1 635	62	89	397	301	294	256	352	314	104	93
May	1 816	1 712	63	90	413	313	307	238	391	355	105	91
June	1 847	1 714	66	99	411	307	332	249	347	321	133	105
July	1 788	1 673	69	86	405	311	337	240	349	320	115	94
August	1 846	1 726	77	101	398	299	363	230	366	330	120	103
September	1 843	1 723	80	93	411	319	337	235	358	320	120	106
October	1 755	1 654	77	95	376	291	342	228	357	314	101	89
November	1 756	1 653	56	103	388	292	317	248	335	297	102	91
December	1 838	1 731	81	107	373	274	335	244	368	327	107	98
2011												
January	1 679	1 572	56	83	338	240	361	206	352	324	107	100
February	1 910	1 793	62	94	442	317	396	241	353	317	117	108
March	1 924	1 820	72	115	443	342	357	251	382	337	104	97
April	1 887	1 771	91	105	410	315	360	239	386	344	117	108
May	2 000	1 877	92	109	463	351	372	253	388	343	123	114
June	1 904	1 786	75	109	432	333	330	264	395	353	117	108
July	1 969	1 839	71	101	412	316	391	238	401	357	130	121
August	2 006	1 889	66	98	422	319	383	268	432	384	117	108
September	2 048	1 933	84	95	432	327	425	243	421	378	115	105

[1]Quits are the number of quits during the entire month.
[2]The quits rate is the number of quits during the entire month as a percent of total employment.
[3]Detail will not necessarily add to totals because of the independent seasonal adjustment of the various series.
[4]Includes natural resources and mining, information, financial activities, and other services, not shown separately.
[5]Includes wholesale trade and transportation, warehousing, and utilities, not shown separately.
[6]Includes arts, entertainment, and recreation, not shown separately.
[7]Includes federal government, not shown separately.

Table 7-10. Quits Levels[1] and Rates,[2] by Industry, December 2000–September 2011—*Continued*

(Seasonally adjusted, levels in thousands, rates per 100.)

Year and month	Rate											
	Total[4]	Total private[4]	Construction	Manufacturing	Trade, transportation, and utilities[5]	Retail trade	Professional and business services	Education and health services	Leisure and hospitality[6]	Accommodation and food services	Government[7]	State and local government
2006												
January	2.2	2.4	2.8	1.4	2.5	3.2	2.5	1.6	5.1	5.4	0.7	0.7
February	2.2	2.5	2.5	1.4	2.7	3.4	2.6	1.7	5.0	5.4	0.8	0.8
March	2.3	2.6	2.6	1.4	2.7	3.4	2.8	1.6	5.0	5.3	0.8	0.7
April	2.1	2.4	2.7	1.3	2.7	3.4	2.7	1.7	4.2	4.4	0.8	0.8
May	2.3	2.5	2.7	1.6	2.7	3.3	2.8	1.9	4.7	5.2	0.8	0.8
June	2.3	2.5	2.6	1.4	2.5	3.1	2.8	1.9	5.2	5.6	0.9	0.8
July	2.3	2.6	2.4	1.6	2.6	3.4	2.8	1.9	4.6	5.1	0.8	0.7
August	2.2	2.5	2.2	1.4	2.7	3.1	2.8	1.8	4.6	5.0	0.8	0.8
September	2.2	2.4	2.0	1.3	2.5	3.1	3.1	1.7	4.7	5.0	0.8	0.7
October	2.2	2.5	2.3	1.5	2.5	3.1	3.0	1.9	4.6	4.9	0.8	0.7
November	2.3	2.6	2.1	1.7	2.7	3.4	3.1	1.7	4.8	5.0	0.8	0.7
December	2.3	2.6	2.2	1.8	2.5	3.1	3.2	1.9	5.0	5.4	0.8	0.8
2007												
January	2.2	2.5	2.2	1.7	2.5	3.1	3.0	1.7	4.7	5.1	0.8	0.8
February	2.2	2.5	1.8	1.5	2.6	3.2	2.9	1.8	4.7	5.0	0.7	0.7
March	2.2	2.5	1.9	1.6	2.5	3.0	2.8	1.7	4.7	5.0	0.8	0.8
April	2.2	2.5	2.0	1.5	2.5	3.1	2.7	1.7	4.9	5.3	0.8	0.8
May	2.2	2.5	2.1	1.6	2.6	3.2	2.7	1.9	4.5	4.9	0.8	0.8
June	2.0	2.3	1.7	1.5	2.5	3.1	2.3	1.6	4.6	5.0	0.8	0.7
July	2.2	2.5	2.4	1.4	2.2	2.8	3.0	1.8	4.9	5.3	0.8	0.8
August	2.1	2.4	2.3	1.5	2.2	2.9	2.7	1.7	4.8	5.1	0.7	0.7
September	1.9	2.1	1.8	1.3	2.2	2.8	2.6	1.4	3.6	3.7	0.7	0.7
October	2.1	2.4	2.1	1.5	2.4	3.0	2.6	1.6	4.8	5.1	0.7	0.7
November	2.0	2.3	2.1	1.3	2.1	2.6	2.7	1.7	4.7	5.0	0.7	0.7
December	2.0	2.3	2.2	1.6	2.4	3.1	2.3	1.6	4.7	5.0	0.7	0.7
2008												
January	2.1	2.4	2.0	1.6	2.5	3.1	2.4	1.8	4.4	4.6	0.7	0.7
February	2.0	2.3	2.2	1.4	2.3	2.8	2.7	1.6	4.3	4.6	0.7	0.7
March	1.9	2.2	1.6	1.4	2.1	2.6	2.6	1.7	4.2	4.6	0.6	0.6
April	2.0	2.2	2.2	1.3	2.2	2.7	2.7	1.6	4.1	4.4	0.7	0.7
May	2.0	2.2	1.9	1.2	2.2	2.6	2.6	1.4	4.7	5.0	0.7	0.7
June	1.9	2.1	2.1	1.2	2.1	2.6	2.6	1.5	4.1	4.4	0.6	0.7
July	1.7	1.9	2.0	1.0	2.0	2.5	2.3	1.5	3.9	4.1	0.6	0.6
August	1.7	1.9	2.0	1.0	2.0	2.6	2.0	1.5	3.7	4.0	0.6	0.7
September	1.8	2.0	1.5	1.1	2.1	2.6	2.2	1.4	4.0	4.3	0.6	0.7
October	1.6	1.9	1.5	1.1	1.9	2.2	2.2	1.4	3.6	4.0	0.6	0.6
November	1.5	1.7	1.3	0.9	1.8	2.3	2.1	1.3	3.4	3.7	0.5	0.6
December	1.5	1.7	1.2	0.8	1.9	2.4	2.0	1.2	3.1	3.5	0.6	0.6
2009												
January	1.4	1.6	1.2	0.8	1.7	2.2	2.0	1.2	3.1	3.4	0.5	0.5
February	1.5	1.7	1.3	0.8	1.6	2.0	1.8	1.4	3.1	3.3	0.5	0.5
March	1.4	1.6	1.5	0.7	1.8	2.2	1.6	1.3	3.0	3.2	0.5	0.5
April	1.3	1.5	1.1	0.7	1.4	1.7	1.7	1.1	2.9	3.1	0.5	0.5
May	1.3	1.5	1.3	0.8	1.4	1.8	1.9	1.3	2.8	2.9	0.5	0.5
June	1.3	1.5	1.2	0.8	1.5	2.0	1.5	1.3	2.9	3.0	0.4	0.5
July	1.2	1.4	1.1	0.7	1.5	1.8	1.6	1.2	2.7	2.8	0.5	0.5
August	1.3	1.4	1.0	0.7	1.5	2.0	1.5	1.2	2.9	3.1	0.5	0.5
September	1.2	1.4	1.2	0.8	1.5	1.8	1.5	1.3	2.4	2.7	0.4	0.4
October	1.2	1.4	1.0	0.7	1.4	1.8	1.6	1.3	2.5	2.7	0.5	0.5
November	1.4	1.5	1.6	0.6	1.6	1.8	1.7	1.3	2.9	3.0	0.5	0.5
December	1.2	1.4	1.1	0.6	1.5	1.9	1.4	1.3	2.6	2.8	0.5	0.5
2010												
January	1.1	1.3	1.3	0.6	1.2	1.5	1.5	1.1	2.6	2.7	0.4	0.5
February	1.4	1.6	1.4	0.9	1.7	2.3	1.7	1.2	2.8	3.0	0.6	0.6
March	1.4	1.6	1.4	0.8	1.6	2.0	1.8	1.2	2.8	3.0	0.5	0.5
April	1.3	1.5	1.1	0.8	1.6	2.1	1.8	1.3	2.7	2.8	0.5	0.5
May	1.4	1.6	1.1	0.8	1.7	2.2	1.8	1.2	3.0	3.2	0.5	0.5
June	1.4	1.6	1.2	0.9	1.7	2.1	2.0	1.3	2.7	2.9	0.6	0.5
July	1.4	1.6	1.2	0.7	1.6	2.2	2.0	1.2	2.7	2.9	0.5	0.5
August	1.4	1.6	1.4	0.9	1.6	2.1	2.2	1.2	2.8	3.0	0.5	0.5
September	1.4	1.6	1.5	0.8	1.7	2.2	2.0	1.2	2.7	2.9	0.5	0.5
October	1.4	1.5	1.4	0.8	1.5	2.0	2.0	1.2	2.7	2.8	0.5	0.5
November	1.3	1.5	1.0	0.9	1.6	2.0	1.9	1.3	2.6	2.7	0.5	0.5
December	1.4	1.6	1.5	0.9	1.5	1.9	2.0	1.2	2.8	2.9	0.5	0.5
2011												
January	1.3	1.5	1.0	0.7	1.4	1.7	2.1	1.0	2.7	2.9	0.5	0.5
February	1.5	1.7	1.1	0.8	1.8	2.2	2.3	1.2	2.7	2.8	0.5	0.6
March	1.5	1.7	1.3	1.0	1.8	2.4	2.1	1.3	2.9	3.0	0.5	0.5
April	1.4	1.6	1.7	0.9	1.6	2.2	2.1	1.2	2.9	3.0	0.5	0.6
May	1.5	1.7	1.7	0.9	1.9	2.4	2.2	1.3	2.9	3.0	0.6	0.6
June	1.5	1.6	1.3	0.9	1.7	2.3	1.9	1.3	3.0	3.1	0.5	0.6
July	1.5	1.7	1.3	0.9	1.7	2.2	2.3	1.2	3.0	3.2	0.6	0.6
August	1.5	1.7	1.2	0.8	1.7	2.2	2.2	1.3	3.3	3.4	0.5	0.6
September	1.6	1.8	1.5	0.8	1.7	2.2	2.5	1.2	3.2	3.3	0.5	0.5

[1]Quits are the number of quits during the entire month.
[2]The quits rate is the number of quits during the entire month as a percent of total employment.
[4]Includes natural resources and mining, information, financial activities, and other services, not shown separately.
[5]Includes wholesale trade and transportation, warehousing, and utilities, not shown separately.
[6]Includes arts, entertainment, and recreation, not shown separately.
[7]Includes federal government, not shown separately.

Table 7-11. Layoffs and Discharges Levels[1] and Rates,[2] by Industry, December 2000–September 2011

(Not seasonally adjusted, levels in thousands, rates per 100.)

Year and month	Level												
	Total	Total private	Mining and logging	Construc-tion	Manufac-turing	Durable goods	Non-durable goods	Trade, transpor-tation, and utilities	Whole-sale trade	Retail trade	Transpor-tation, ware-housing, and utilities	Infor-mation	Financial activities
2001	24 351	23 209	106	3 192	3 311	1 992	1 320	4 557	854	2 986	717	572	838
2002	23 325	22 124	106	3 118	2 690	1 653	1 038	4 536	810	2 990	735	534	950
2003	23 959	22 666	107	3 145	2 326	1 414	914	4 783	836	3 141	805	426	771
2004	23 389	22 011	83	2 945	1 998	1 219	782	4 809	790	3 070	946	390	785
2005	22 774	21 476	78	2 928	1 847	1 154	693	4 641	761	2 922	957	272	863
2006	21 468	20 097	75	2 639	1 821	1 023	796	4 171	645	2 849	679	257	873
2007	22 577	21 209	91	2 857	1 974	1 210	763	4 284	822	2 759	704	312	1 113
2008	23 737	22 571	114	3 330	2 222	1 422	797	4 720	987	2 963	768	356	1 035
2009	26 318	24 709	178	3 737	2 860	1 844	1 017	4 929	1 096	2 822	1 011	405	1 217
2010	21 243	19 156	93	3 138	1 643	929	713	3 621	713	2 274	634	271	730
2000													
December	2 140	2 058	23	364	210	110	99	444	91	317	37	23	30
2001													
January	3 184	3 083	11	372	378	253	125	927	135	685	107	86	192
February	1 411	1 362	4	271	202	120	81	232	64	149	19	37	45
March	1 887	1 844	7	248	234	131	103	330	36	264	30	21	51
April	1 872	1 813	5	164	323	211	112	301	73	174	54	61	64
May	1 585	1 493	5	202	254	147	107	312	46	211	54	38	38
June	1 780	1 621	9	206	287	153	135	301	43	206	53	45	38
July	1 949	1 857	9	192	298	166	132	371	100	222	49	43	54
August	1 857	1 656	8	229	224	140	84	267	51	173	43	41	41
September	2 173	2 065	7	261	224	128	96	349	63	227	59	39	82
October	2 480	2 354	11	329	349	230	120	391	108	222	61	63	99
November	2 097	2 048	13	359	259	158	101	365	71	195	99	62	70
December	2 076	2 013	17	359	279	155	124	411	64	258	89	36	64
2002													
January	2 920	2 805	11	347	399	247	153	687	85	505	97	131	195
February	1 596	1 548	6	254	195	107	88	396	69	261	66	23	53
March	1 429	1 387	11	201	189	132	57	276	59	162	55	32	41
April	1 860	1 796	13	212	243	151	92	338	57	224	57	59	63
May	1 592	1 501	8	214	182	107	75	366	81	248	36	32	70
June	1 722	1 569	5	224	196	116	80	257	47	153	57	38	83
July	2 210	2 062	15	289	216	128	88	334	90	199	45	38	77
August	1 870	1 721	8	207	189	133	56	319	51	210	58	36	78
September	1 978	1 810	6	244	188	120	69	353	63	229	61	25	70
October	2 097	2 010	7	326	249	159	89	369	50	271	48	41	92
November	1 837	1 764	6	276	194	116	78	335	86	196	53	49	65
December	2 214	2 151	10	324	250	137	113	506	72	332	102	30	63
2003													
January	3 132	3 014	18	403	352	218	135	758	102	575	81	94	156
February	1 571	1 518	9	220	179	109	70	350	44	273	33	32	41
March	1 476	1 418	8	217	183	111	73	283	45	192	46	37	61
April	1 931	1 854	8	264	261	143	117	296	65	181	49	25	45
May	1 594	1 496	5	198	135	78	57	313	95	171	47	25	47
June	1 906	1 756	8	185	196	122	74	362	48	233	80	41	46
July	2 022	1 887	8	228	223	123	100	372	95	199	78	32	106
August	2 072	1 894	12	287	149	105	44	359	62	202	95	24	44
September	1 981	1 822	3	285	148	93	56	290	91	155	44	16	68
October	2 213	2 126	7	309	186	103	83	447	92	285	71	32	60
November	1 798	1 703	5	275	152	108	44	353	41	258	54	33	41
December	2 263	2 178	16	274	162	101	61	600	56	417	127	35	56
2004													
January	3 028	2 879	12	362	267	153	114	771	99	543	129	63	110
February	1 510	1 465	10	244	136	80	57	397	65	281	51	29	33
March	1 567	1 516	5	221	151	95	56	303	55	179	69	40	56
April	1 857	1 800	6	190	167	90	77	348	95	201	52	29	51
May	1 495	1 412	6	171	130	65	65	353	61	202	90	35	35
June	1 732	1 574	4	190	133	89	44	290	55	166	69	40	54
July	1 940	1 758	6	247	167	102	65	368	69	230	69	24	55
August	2 080	1 933	7	248	191	131	60	325	73	170	82	19	98
September	2 017	1 815	4	195	152	99	53	302	50	188	64	38	68
October	2 056	1 948	7	276	193	115	78	350	67	214	68	35	90
November	1 847	1 757	8	281	156	104	53	377	60	237	79	17	66
December	2 260	2 154	8	320	155	96	60	625	41	459	124	21	69
2005													
January	3 035	2 923	12	457	273	178	94	717	96	505	116	57	174
February	1 558	1 506	6	250	112	73	39	373	50	264	59	12	66
March	1 633	1 584	5	174	151	87	63	307	40	216	51	23	60
April	1 788	1 719	7	218	183	128	55	341	80	196	65	20	93
May	1 581	1 477	4	209	131	89	43	359	84	176	99	20	58
June	1 810	1 653	4	188	128	80	48	321	46	198	77	16	28
July	1 864	1 731	6	187	153	99	54	358	62	229	67	25	59
August	1 976	1 798	6	250	146	96	50	323	48	221	53	17	51
September	2 013	1 842	8	226	141	81	60	370	33	259	78	19	66
October	1 908	1 816	8	257	149	94	55	349	74	205	71	19	94
November	1 624	1 551	4	239	143	72	72	321	73	169	79	24	53
December	1 984	1 876	8	273	137	77	60	502	75	284	142	20	61

[1] Layoffs and discharges are the number of layoffs and discharges during the entire month.
[2] The layoffs and discharges rate is the number of layoffs and discharges during the entire month as a percent of total employment.

Table 7-11. Layoffs and Discharges Levels[1] and Rates,[2] by Industry, December 2000–September 2011
—Continued

(Not seasonally adjusted, levels in thousands, rates per 100.)

Year and month	Level												
	Finance and insurance	Real estate and rental and leasing	Professional and business services	Education and health services	Educational services	Health care and social assistance	Leisure and hospitality	Arts, entertainment, and recreation	Accommodation and food services	Other services	Government	Federal	State and local government
2001	538	300	4 848	1 537	264	1 274	3 554	963	2 590	686	1 147	112	1 031
2002	577	374	4 637	1 626	247	1 380	3 090	804	2 286	841	1 202	143	1 058
2003	421	349	4 924	1 732	359	1 372	3 408	966	2 442	1 042	1 292	160	1 134
2004	427	358	4 907	1 655	287	1 370	3 584	1 061	2 522	853	1 380	162	1 217
2005	474	389	5 080	1 680	301	1 381	3 232	907	2 328	855	1 298	166	1 134
2006	467	405	4 586	1 686	338	1 350	3 055	835	2 220	935	1 369	192	1 178
2007	611	502	4 751	1 741	386	1 352	3 168	902	2 268	913	1 370	226	1 141
2008	612	423	4 881	1 982	385	1 597	3 015	865	2 152	913	1 171	111	1 059
2009	666	552	4 846	2 123	445	1 680	3 237	810	2 427	1 179	1 610	236	1 374
2010	423	305	4 113	2 022	388	1 632	2 663	774	1 891	864	2 087	763	1 325
2000													
December	26	5	635	119	43	76	174	53	121	36	81	7	75
2001													
January	172	20	542	184	29	156	288	79	209	103	102	28	73
February	23	22	323	84	9	75	138	44	94	25	49	5	44
March	22	29	546	92	11	81	243	37	205	73	43	6	37
April	48	16	324	96	24	72	397	62	335	76	59	7	53
May	28	10	360	98	18	80	159	25	133	26	93	7	86
June	20	18	336	138	23	115	212	41	172	48	159	5	154
July	45	9	314	220	35	185	293	73	220	61	93	7	85
August	27	14	320	172	59	113	257	97	161	95	201	8	193
September	30	52	434	113	13	100	500	248	251	57	107	12	95
October	60	38	461	168	24	144	435	101	334	48	127	12	114
November	34	37	378	95	10	85	401	115	286	46	50	6	43
December	29	35	510	77	9	68	231	41	190	28	64	9	54
2002													
January	152	43	471	227	33	193	253	43	209	85	116	26	90
February	39	14	287	103	9	94	188	26	162	42	47	8	39
March	23	19	344	116	19	98	146	30	116	31	42	9	32
April	44	19	368	135	20	115	275	91	184	90	64	12	53
May	51	19	283	135	24	110	171	21	150	42	91	7	84
June	57	26	329	148	24	124	210	23	187	79	153	9	144
July	45	33	468	177	27	150	335	103	232	113	149	12	136
August	41	37	312	148	29	119	292	114	179	131	150	8	141
September	26	44	370	136	31	105	346	129	217	73	168	16	152
October	30	61	424	125	10	116	326	62	264	51	86	14	72
November	33	32	399	71	3	69	320	111	209	49	73	14	60
December	36	27	582	105	18	87	228	51	177	55	63	8	55
2003													
January	89	67	548	199	25	173	362	83	279	123	118	26	92
February	32	9	345	98	13	86	177	46	131	66	53	7	46
March	33	28	283	103	9	94	202	54	148	42	57	9	49
April	27	18	457	113	20	93	312	115	196	74	77	10	68
May	28	19	301	166	41	124	265	78	187	41	98	9	88
June	23	23	383	201	61	140	224	33	191	111	150	11	139
July	50	56	389	229	63	166	196	33	163	106	134	11	124
August	21	23	404	190	56	134	297	97	201	126	178	11	167
September	36	32	377	112	17	96	405	169	236	117	159	13	146
October	36	24	485	135	22	112	367	103	264	99	87	20	67
November	23	17	392	102	15	87	294	101	193	54	95	27	68
December	23	33	560	84	17	67	307	54	253	83	86	6	80
2004													
January	62	48	673	187	26	161	357	74	282	78	149	27	122
February	23	10	260	110	13	97	196	66	131	49	45	9	36
March	27	29	385	111	19	92	206	42	164	38	51	6	45
April	28	23	487	135	14	121	308	89	219	79	57	7	50
May	22	13	314	134	28	106	181	49	132	52	84	9	75
June	26	28	373	163	48	115	279	49	230	47	158	21	137
July	34	21	368	134	24	110	322	62	260	68	182	12	170
August	61	37	374	170	34	137	336	125	211	164	148	10	138
September	32	36	360	171	35	136	440	234	206	86	202	12	190
October	46	44	353	107	9	98	498	136	361	40	108	14	94
November	38	28	387	109	17	93	249	80	169	106	90	7	82
December	28	41	573	124	20	104	212	55	157	46	106	28	78
2005													
January	115	60	581	199	22	177	344	69	275	109	112	14	98
February	24	42	324	117	10	107	187	39	149	59	51	8	43
March	35	24	436	137	14	123	233	29	205	59	49	7	42
April	63	30	432	155	23	132	221	59	162	49	69	13	56
May	35	23	266	156	45	112	191	48	143	84	104	9	95
June	19	8	451	148	30	119	320	59	261	49	157	18	140
July	35	24	507	142	31	110	236	31	206	57	133	13	120
August	40	11	436	165	24	141	252	89	163	153	178	15	163
September	24	42	362	127	34	93	442	243	199	80	171	18	153
October	41	53	428	122	19	103	325	92	234	66	92	9	83
November	18	36	367	93	12	81	268	92	175	38	73	10	64
December	25	36	490	119	37	83	213	57	156	52	109	32	77

[1]Layoffs and discharges are the number of layoffs and discharges during the entire month.
[2]The layoffs and discharges rate is the number of layoffs and discharges during the entire month as a percent of total employment.

Table 7-11. Layoffs and Discharges Levels[1] and Rates,[2] by Industry, December 2000–September 2011
—Continued

(Not seasonally adjusted, levels in thousands, rates per 100.)

Year and month	Rate												
	Total	Total private	Mining and logging	Construction	Manufacturing	Durable goods	Non-durable goods	Trade, transportation, and utilities	Whole-sale trade	Retail trade	Transportation, warehousing, and utilities	Information	Financial activities
2001	18.5	21.0	17.5	46.8	20.1	19.3	21.6	17.5	14.8	19.6	14.4	15.8	10.7
2002	17.9	20.3	18.2	46.4	17.6	17.4	18.0	17.8	14.3	19.9	15.2	15.7	12.1
2003	18.4	20.9	18.7	46.7	16.0	15.8	16.5	18.9	14.9	21.1	16.9	13.4	9.7
2004	17.8	20.0	14.0	42.2	14.0	13.7	14.5	18.8	14.0	20.4	19.7	12.5	9.8
2005	17.0	19.2	12.4	39.9	13.0	12.9	13.1	17.9	13.2	19.1	19.5	8.9	10.6
2006	15.8	17.6	11.0	34.3	12.9	11.4	15.4	15.9	10.9	18.6	13.5	8.5	10.5
2007	16.4	18.4	12.6	37.4	14.2	13.7	15.0	16.1	13.7	17.8	13.8	10.3	13.4
2008	17.4	19.8	14.9	46.5	16.6	16.8	16.1	18.0	16.6	19.4	15.2	11.9	12.7
2009	20.1	22.8	25.6	62.1	24.1	25.3	22.3	19.8	19.6	19.4	21.1	14.4	15.7
2010	16.4	17.8	13.2	56.8	14.3	13.1	16.0	14.7	13.1	15.8	13.4	10.0	9.6
2000													
December	1.6	1.8	3.9	5.4	1.2	1.0	1.6	1.6	1.5	2.0	0.7	0.6	0.4
2001													
January	2.4	2.8	1.9	5.8	2.2	2.4	2.0	3.6	2.3	4.5	2.1	2.3	2.5
February	1.1	1.2	0.7	4.2	1.2	1.1	1.3	0.9	1.1	1.0	0.4	1.0	0.6
March	1.4	1.7	1.2	3.8	1.4	1.2	1.7	1.3	0.6	1.8	0.6	0.6	0.7
April	1.4	1.6	0.9	2.5	1.9	2.0	1.8	1.2	1.3	1.2	1.1	1.7	0.8
May	1.2	1.3	0.9	2.9	1.5	1.4	1.7	1.2	0.8	1.4	1.1	1.0	0.5
June	1.3	1.4	1.5	2.9	1.7	1.5	2.2	1.2	0.7	1.3	1.1	1.2	0.5
July	1.5	1.7	1.4	2.7	1.8	1.6	2.2	1.4	1.7	1.5	1.0	1.2	0.7
August	1.4	1.5	1.3	3.2	1.4	1.4	1.4	1.0	0.9	1.1	0.9	1.1	0.5
September	1.6	1.9	1.2	3.7	1.4	1.3	1.6	1.4	1.1	1.5	1.2	1.1	1.0
October	1.9	2.1	1.8	4.7	2.2	2.3	2.0	1.5	1.9	1.5	1.2	1.8	1.3
November	1.6	1.9	2.1	5.2	1.6	1.6	1.7	1.4	1.2	1.3	2.0	1.7	0.9
December	1.6	1.8	2.8	5.4	1.8	1.6	2.1	1.6	1.1	1.6	1.8	1.0	0.8
2002													
January	2.3	2.6	2.0	5.5	2.6	2.6	2.6	2.7	1.5	3.4	2.0	3.8	2.5
February	1.2	1.4	1.1	4.0	1.3	1.1	1.5	1.6	1.2	1.8	1.4	0.7	0.7
March	1.1	1.3	1.9	3.1	1.2	1.4	1.0	1.1	1.0	1.1	1.2	0.9	0.5
April	1.4	1.7	2.3	3.2	1.6	1.6	1.6	1.3	1.0	1.5	1.2	1.7	0.8
May	1.2	1.4	1.3	3.2	1.2	1.1	1.3	1.4	1.4	1.7	0.8	0.9	0.9
June	1.3	1.4	0.9	3.2	1.3	1.2	1.4	1.0	0.8	1.0	1.2	1.1	1.1
July	1.7	1.9	2.5	4.1	1.4	1.4	1.5	1.3	1.6	1.3	0.9	1.1	1.0
August	1.4	1.6	1.4	3.0	1.2	1.4	1.0	1.3	0.9	1.4	1.2	1.1	1.0
September	1.5	1.7	1.0	3.5	1.2	1.3	1.2	1.4	1.1	1.5	1.3	0.7	0.9
October	1.6	1.8	1.3	4.7	1.6	1.7	1.6	1.4	0.9	1.8	1.0	1.2	1.2
November	1.4	1.6	1.0	4.1	1.3	1.2	1.4	1.3	1.5	1.3	1.1	1.5	0.8
December	1.7	2.0	1.7	4.9	1.7	1.5	2.0	1.9	1.3	2.1	2.1	0.9	0.8
2003													
January	2.4	2.8	3.3	6.4	2.4	2.4	2.4	3.0	1.8	3.9	1.7	2.9	2.0
February	1.2	1.4	1.5	3.5	1.2	1.2	1.3	1.4	0.8	1.9	0.7	1.0	0.5
March	1.1	1.3	1.4	3.4	1.3	1.2	1.3	1.1	0.8	1.3	1.0	1.1	0.8
April	1.5	1.7	1.4	4.0	1.8	1.6	2.1	1.2	1.2	1.2	1.0	0.8	0.6
May	1.2	1.4	0.9	2.9	0.9	0.9	1.0	1.2	1.7	1.2	1.0	0.8	0.6
June	1.5	1.6	1.3	2.7	1.3	1.4	1.3	1.4	0.9	1.6	1.7	1.3	0.6
July	1.6	1.7	1.3	3.2	1.5	1.4	1.8	1.5	1.7	1.3	1.7	1.0	1.3
August	1.6	1.7	2.1	4.1	1.0	1.2	0.8	1.4	1.1	1.4	2.0	0.8	0.5
September	1.5	1.7	0.6	4.1	1.0	1.0	1.0	1.1	1.6	1.0	0.9	0.5	0.8
October	1.7	1.9	1.2	4.4	1.3	1.2	1.5	1.8	1.6	1.9	1.5	1.0	0.7
November	1.4	1.6	0.9	4.0	1.1	1.2	0.8	1.4	0.7	1.7	1.1	1.1	0.5
December	1.7	2.0	2.8	4.1	1.1	1.1	1.1	2.3	1.0	2.7	2.6	1.1	0.7
2004													
January	2.4	2.7	2.1	5.6	1.9	1.7	2.1	3.1	1.8	3.7	2.7	2.0	1.4
February	1.2	1.4	1.8	3.8	1.0	0.9	1.1	1.6	1.2	1.9	1.1	0.9	0.4
March	1.2	1.4	0.8	3.4	1.1	1.1	1.0	1.2	1.0	1.2	1.5	1.3	0.7
April	1.4	1.6	1.1	2.8	1.2	1.0	1.4	1.4	1.7	1.4	1.1	0.9	0.6
May	1.1	1.3	0.9	2.4	0.9	0.7	1.2	1.4	1.1	1.3	1.9	1.1	0.4
June	1.3	1.4	0.7	2.6	0.9	1.0	0.8	1.1	1.0	1.1	1.4	1.3	0.7
July	1.5	1.6	0.9	3.4	1.2	1.1	1.2	1.4	1.2	1.5	1.4	0.8	0.7
August	1.6	1.7	1.1	3.4	1.3	1.5	1.1	1.3	1.3	1.1	1.7	0.6	1.2
September	1.5	1.6	0.7	2.7	1.1	1.1	1.0	1.2	0.9	1.3	1.3	1.2	0.8
October	1.5	1.8	1.2	3.8	1.3	1.3	1.4	1.4	1.2	1.4	1.4	1.1	1.1
November	1.4	1.6	1.4	3.9	1.1	1.2	1.0	1.4	1.1	1.5	1.6	0.6	0.8
December	1.7	1.9	1.4	4.6	1.1	1.1	1.1	2.4	0.7	2.9	2.5	0.7	0.9
2005													
January	2.3	2.7	2.1	6.8	1.9	2.0	1.8	2.8	1.7	3.4	2.4	1.9	2.2
February	1.2	1.4	1.0	3.7	0.8	0.8	0.7	1.5	0.9	1.8	1.2	0.4	0.8
March	1.2	1.4	0.8	2.5	1.1	1.0	1.2	1.2	0.7	1.4	1.1	0.8	0.7
April	1.3	1.5	1.2	3.1	1.3	1.4	1.0	1.3	1.4	1.3	1.3	0.6	1.2
May	1.2	1.3	0.6	2.8	0.9	1.0	0.8	1.4	1.5	1.2	2.0	0.6	0.7
June	1.3	1.5	0.7	2.5	0.9	0.9	0.9	1.2	0.8	1.3	1.6	0.5	0.3
July	1.4	1.5	0.9	2.4	1.1	1.1	1.0	1.4	1.1	1.5	1.4	0.8	0.7
August	1.5	1.6	1.0	3.2	1.0	1.1	0.9	1.2	0.8	1.4	1.1	0.6	0.6
September	1.5	1.6	1.3	2.9	1.0	0.9	1.1	1.4	0.6	1.7	1.6	0.6	0.8
October	1.4	1.6	1.2	3.3	1.0	1.1	1.0	1.3	1.3	1.3	1.4	0.6	1.1
November	1.2	1.4	0.6	3.1	1.0	0.8	1.4	1.2	1.3	1.1	1.6	0.8	0.6
December	1.5	1.7	1.2	3.7	1.0	0.9	1.2	1.9	1.3	1.8	2.9	0.6	0.7

[1]Layoffs and discharges are the number of layoffs and discharges during the entire month.
[2]The layoffs and discharges rate is the number of layoffs and discharges during the entire month as a percent of total employment.

Table 7-11. Layoffs and Discharges Levels[1] and Rates,[2] by Industry, December 2000–September 2011
—Continued

(Not seasonally adjusted, levels in thousands, rates per 100.)

Year and month	Rate												
	Finance and insurance	Real estate and rental and leasing	Professional and business services	Education and health services	Educational services	Health care and social assistance	Leisure and hospitality	Arts, entertainment, and recreation	Accommodation and food services	Other services	Government	Federal	State and local government
2001	9.3	14.7	29.4	9.8	10.5	9.7	29.5	52.8	25.4	13.0	5.4	4.1	5.6
2002	9.9	18.4	29.0	10.0	9.3	10.2	25.8	45.1	22.4	15.7	5.6	5.2	5.6
2003	7.1	17.0	30.8	10.4	13.3	9.9	28.0	53.3	23.6	19.3	6.0	5.8	6.0
2004	7.2	17.2	29.9	9.8	10.4	9.7	28.7	57.4	23.7	15.8	6.4	5.9	6.4
2005	7.9	18.2	30.0	9.7	10.6	9.5	25.2	47.9	21.3	15.8	6.0	6.1	5.9
2006	7.6	18.6	26.1	9.5	11.7	9.0	23.3	43.3	19.9	17.2	6.2	7.0	6.1
2007	10.0	23.1	26.5	9.5	13.1	8.8	23.6	45.8	19.8	16.6	6.2	8.3	5.9
2008	10.2	19.9	27.5	10.5	12.7	10.1	22.4	43.9	18.8	16.6	5.2	4.0	5.4
2009	11.5	27.7	29.2	11.1	14.4	10.4	24.8	42.3	21.7	22.0	7.1	8.3	7.0
2010	7.4	15.7	24.6	10.3	12.3	9.9	20.5	40.5	17.0	16.1	9.3	25.7	6.8
2000													
December	0.5	0.2	3.8	0.8	1.7	0.6	1.5	3.3	1.2	0.7	0.4	0.2	0.4
2001													
January	3.0	1.0	3.3	1.2	1.2	1.2	2.5	5.0	2.1	2.0	0.5	1.0	0.4
February	0.4	1.1	2.0	0.5	0.3	0.6	1.2	2.8	1.0	0.5	0.2	0.2	0.2
March	0.4	1.4	3.3	0.6	0.4	0.6	2.1	2.3	2.1	1.4	0.2	0.2	0.2
April	0.8	0.8	2.0	0.6	0.9	0.6	3.3	3.5	3.3	1.5	0.3	0.2	0.3
May	0.5	0.5	2.2	0.6	0.7	0.6	1.3	1.3	1.3	0.5	0.4	0.2	0.5
June	0.4	0.9	2.0	0.9	1.0	0.9	1.7	1.9	1.6	0.9	0.8	0.2	0.8
July	0.8	0.4	1.9	1.4	1.6	1.4	2.3	3.4	2.1	1.2	0.5	0.3	0.5
August	0.5	0.7	1.9	1.1	2.7	0.9	2.0	4.6	1.5	1.8	1.0	0.3	1.1
September	0.5	2.5	2.6	0.7	0.5	0.8	4.1	13.1	2.4	1.1	0.5	0.4	0.5
October	1.0	1.9	2.8	1.1	0.9	1.1	3.6	5.6	3.3	0.9	0.6	0.4	0.6
November	0.6	1.8	2.3	0.6	0.4	0.6	3.4	6.9	2.8	0.9	0.2	0.2	0.2
December	0.5	1.7	3.2	0.5	0.3	0.5	2.0	2.5	1.9	0.5	0.3	0.3	0.3
2002													
January	2.6	2.1	3.0	1.4	1.3	1.4	2.2	2.7	2.1	1.6	0.5	1.0	0.5
February	0.7	0.7	1.8	0.6	0.3	0.7	1.6	1.6	1.6	0.8	0.2	0.3	0.2
March	0.4	0.9	2.2	0.7	0.7	0.7	1.3	1.8	1.2	0.6	0.2	0.3	0.2
April	0.8	0.9	2.3	0.8	0.7	0.9	2.3	5.3	1.8	1.7	0.3	0.4	0.3
May	0.9	0.9	1.8	0.8	0.9	0.8	1.4	1.2	1.5	0.8	0.4	0.2	0.4
June	1.0	1.3	2.0	0.9	1.0	0.9	1.7	1.2	1.8	1.5	0.7	0.3	0.8
July	0.8	1.6	2.9	1.1	1.1	1.1	2.7	5.1	2.2	2.1	0.7	0.4	0.8
August	0.7	1.8	1.9	0.9	1.2	0.9	2.3	5.7	1.7	2.4	0.7	0.3	0.8
September	0.5	2.1	2.3	0.8	1.2	0.8	2.8	7.0	2.1	1.4	0.8	0.6	0.8
October	0.5	3.0	2.6	0.8	0.3	0.8	2.7	3.5	2.6	0.9	0.4	0.5	0.4
November	0.6	1.6	2.5	0.4	0.1	0.5	2.7	6.7	2.1	0.9	0.3	0.5	0.3
December	0.6	1.3	3.7	0.6	0.6	0.6	1.9	3.1	1.7	1.0	0.3	0.3	0.3
2003													
January	1.5	3.4	3.5	1.2	1.0	1.3	3.1	5.1	2.8	2.3	0.5	0.9	0.5
February	0.5	0.5	2.2	0.6	0.4	0.6	1.5	2.8	1.3	1.2	0.2	0.3	0.2
March	0.6	1.4	1.8	0.6	0.3	0.7	1.7	3.2	1.5	0.8	0.3	0.3	0.3
April	0.5	0.9	2.9	0.7	0.7	0.7	2.6	6.6	1.9	1.4	0.4	0.3	0.4
May	0.5	0.9	1.9	1.0	1.5	0.9	2.2	4.2	1.8	0.7	0.4	0.3	0.5
June	0.4	1.1	2.4	1.2	2.4	1.0	1.8	1.6	1.8	2.0	0.7	0.4	0.7
July	0.8	2.6	2.4	1.4	2.6	1.2	1.5	1.6	1.5	1.9	0.7	0.4	0.7
August	0.4	1.1	2.5	1.2	2.4	1.0	2.3	4.7	1.9	2.3	0.9	0.4	0.9
September	0.6	1.5	2.3	0.7	0.6	0.7	3.3	9.0	2.2	2.2	0.7	0.5	0.8
October	0.6	1.1	3.0	0.8	0.8	0.8	3.0	5.9	2.5	1.8	0.4	0.7	0.4
November	0.4	0.8	2.4	0.6	0.5	0.6	2.4	6.0	1.9	1.0	0.4	1.0	0.4
December	0.4	1.6	3.5	0.5	0.6	0.5	2.5	3.2	2.4	1.5	0.4	0.2	0.4
2004													
January	1.0	2.4	4.3	1.1	1.0	1.2	3.0	4.6	2.8	1.5	0.7	1.0	0.6
February	0.4	0.5	1.6	0.7	0.4	0.7	1.7	4.0	1.3	0.9	0.2	0.3	0.2
March	0.5	1.4	2.4	0.7	0.7	0.6	1.7	2.5	1.6	0.7	0.2	0.2	0.2
April	0.5	1.1	3.0	0.8	0.5	0.9	2.5	4.9	2.1	1.5	0.3	0.3	0.3
May	0.4	0.6	1.9	0.8	1.0	0.7	1.4	2.6	1.2	1.0	0.4	0.3	0.4
June	0.4	1.3	2.3	1.0	1.9	0.8	2.1	2.4	2.1	0.9	0.7	0.8	0.7
July	0.6	1.0	2.2	0.8	1.0	0.8	2.5	2.9	2.4	1.2	0.9	0.4	1.0
August	1.0	1.7	2.2	1.0	1.4	1.0	2.6	5.9	1.9	3.0	0.7	0.4	0.8
September	0.5	1.7	2.2	1.0	1.3	1.0	3.5	12.1	1.9	1.6	0.9	0.4	1.0
October	0.8	2.1	2.1	0.6	0.3	0.7	4.0	7.5	3.4	0.7	0.5	0.5	0.5
November	0.6	1.3	2.3	0.6	0.6	0.6	2.0	4.6	1.6	2.0	0.4	0.3	0.4
December	0.5	2.0	3.5	0.7	0.7	0.7	1.7	3.2	1.5	0.9	0.5	1.0	0.4
2005													
January	1.9	2.9	3.6	1.2	0.8	1.2	2.8	4.2	2.6	2.1	0.5	0.5	0.5
February	0.4	2.0	2.0	0.7	0.4	0.7	1.5	2.3	1.4	1.1	0.2	0.3	0.2
March	0.6	1.2	2.6	0.8	0.5	0.9	1.9	1.7	1.9	1.1	0.2	0.3	0.2
April	1.1	1.4	2.6	0.9	0.8	0.9	1.7	3.2	1.5	0.9	0.3	0.5	0.3
May	0.6	1.1	1.6	0.9	1.6	0.8	1.5	2.4	1.3	1.5	0.5	0.3	0.5
June	0.3	0.4	2.6	0.9	1.1	0.8	2.4	2.7	2.3	0.9	0.7	0.6	0.7
July	0.6	1.1	3.0	0.8	1.2	0.8	1.7	1.4	1.8	1.1	0.6	0.5	0.7
August	0.7	0.5	2.5	1.0	1.0	1.0	1.9	4.1	1.4	2.8	0.9	0.5	0.9
September	0.4	2.0	2.1	0.7	1.2	0.6	3.4	12.3	1.8	1.5	0.8	0.7	0.8
October	0.7	2.5	2.5	0.7	0.6	0.7	2.5	4.9	2.1	1.2	0.4	0.3	0.4
November	0.3	1.7	2.1	0.5	0.4	0.6	2.1	5.2	1.6	0.7	0.3	0.3	0.3
December	0.4	1.7	2.8	0.7	1.2	0.6	1.7	3.3	1.4	1.0	0.5	1.2	0.4

[1]Layoffs and discharges are the number of layoffs and discharges during the entire month.
[2]The layoffs and discharges rate is the number of layoffs and discharges during the entire month as a percent of total employment.

Table 7-11. Layoffs and Discharges Levels[1] and Rates,[2] by Industry, December 2000–September 2011
—Continued

(Not seasonally adjusted, levels in thousands, rates per 100.)

Year and month	Level												
	Total	Total private	Mining and logging	Construction	Manufacturing	Durable goods	Non-durable goods	Trade, transportation, and utilities	Wholesale trade	Retail trade	Transportation, warehousing, and utilities	Information	Financial activities
2006													
January	2 364	2 251	8	326	201	99	103	641	54	492	95	21	108
February	1 388	1 338	6	178	115	61	53	310	47	230	33	17	64
March	1 314	1 254	8	173	162	78	84	222	36	150	36	15	69
April	1 756	1 686	10	147	160	69	91	311	50	235	27	32	83
May	1 634	1 517	3	170	139	83	56	315	47	208	59	13	52
June	1 613	1 410	2	127	133	71	62	341	48	240	53	13	53
July	1 881	1 720	4	209	150	93	57	352	101	194	58	25	82
August	1 748	1 610	5	209	150	90	60	305	50	197	58	19	79
September	1 876	1 689	10	208	156	98	58	302	55	186	62	16	63
October	2 039	1 940	6	262	162	96	65	347	68	203	76	30	75
November	1 840	1 759	6	325	142	92	49	288	46	189	53	23	63
December	2 015	1 923	7	305	151	93	58	437	43	325	69	33	82
2007													
January	2 475	2 365	13	335	221	135	86	600	67	420	113	73	124
February	1 402	1 354	6	231	148	94	54	279	37	205	38	25	65
March	1 466	1 415	4	152	139	91	48	256	51	150	55	18	98
April	1 825	1 762	6	223	152	93	59	301	65	178	58	20	104
May	1 506	1 386	6	170	128	76	51	295	54	196	45	21	72
June	1 790	1 629	4	217	135	87	48	289	78	164	47	20	58
July	1 934	1 691	7	198	179	109	70	362	91	212	60	35	106
August	1 951	1 775	9	233	159	93	66	339	64	221	55	28	103
September	2 161	2 016	7	264	172	108	65	343	68	231	44	19	100
October	2 096	2 007	9	260	201	122	78	390	90	235	64	20	114
November	1 938	1 875	10	278	189	118	71	390	69	248	73	14	78
December	2 033	1 934	10	296	151	84	67	440	88	299	52	19	91
2008													
January	2 617	2 506	15	374	217	146	71	625	121	416	88	49	160
February	1 481	1 447	9	199	136	77	58	315	57	217	42	17	59
March	1 524	1 471	6	221	119	77	42	266	59	161	45	30	68
April	1 624	1 574	8	220	178	111	67	288	71	169	48	15	85
May	1 608	1 500	4	206	143	89	54	311	74	193	44	15	64
June	1 808	1 658	5	233	159	93	65	367	75	240	51	30	69
July	1 856	1 728	10	218	151	105	46	375	55	239	81	20	103
August	2 238	2 081	5	249	165	118	47	391	70	251	69	17	116
September	1 971	1 829	6	286	176	110	66	344	69	212	63	32	78
October	2 131	2 049	10	322	244	152	91	414	90	255	69	46	73
November	2 176	2 111	17	398	222	138	84	385	75	236	74	38	74
December	2 703	2 617	19	404	312	206	106	639	171	374	94	47	86
2009													
January	3 371	3 262	18	548	466	332	134	782	242	431	109	70	202
February	2 035	1 981	17	307	280	192	87	398	95	229	74	32	114
March	1 993	1 935	21	284	277	207	70	361	82	188	91	33	116
April	2 284	2 209	14	327	281	207	74	428	83	283	62	37	95
May	1 889	1 710	13	251	217	145	71	360	101	202	58	25	90
June	2 019	1 746	10	223	193	126	67	310	70	170	70	26	93
July	2 232	2 048	21	311	188	101	87	346	78	191	77	54	108
August	2 208	1 992	8	268	180	94	86	321	82	180	59	19	107
September	2 165	1 985	11	300	175	101	75	404	63	238	103	15	68
October	2 012	1 919	15	294	205	118	88	330	59	208	62	21	106
November	1 907	1 824	12	262	229	121	108	346	64	206	76	29	44
December	2 203	2 098	18	362	169	100	70	543	77	296	170	44	74
2010													
January	2 353	2 244	11	467	206	149	57	515	72	365	78	44	103
February	1 394	1 337	8	221	137	80	57	240	68	133	39	21	50
March	1 429	1 357	7	203	120	70	50	306	58	218	30	20	54
April	1 455	1 375	7	221	123	61	62	221	50	137	34	14	52
May	1 523	1 356	9	216	95	59	36	221	55	125	41	23	66
June	1 920	1 476	4	175	105	50	55	316	52	199	65	20	41
July	2 009	1 707	6	247	131	68	63	302	73	185	45	21	66
August	1 947	1 620	6	218	143	78	64	247	47	167	34	21	53
September	1 761	1 529	6	229	120	67	53	249	72	137	40	16	46
October	1 762	1 663	6	256	174	95	79	298	48	186	63	19	84
November	1 755	1 661	10	305	161	84	77	299	54	200	44	22	55
December	1 935	1 831	13	380	128	68	60	407	64	222	121	30	60
2011													
January	2 112	2 025	9	320	139	70	69	551	48	393	110	35	102
February	1 287	1 238	4	224	107	59	48	251	48	171	32	16	46
March	1 269	1 217	3	198	90	53	37	226	43	146	37	34	36
April	1 413	1 344	8	235	107	53	54	187	32	126	29	21	28
May	1 566	1 438	5	224	112	60	52	203	65	114	25	22	31
June	1 696	1 492	7	225	92	54	38	242	64	139	39	21	56
July	1 761	1 585	6	237	96	56	40	251	41	165	46	26	47
August	1 783	1 627	6	227	121	77	44	230	33	150	46	21	54
September	1 855	1 679	8	257	120	74	47	215	36	136	43	21	65

[1]Layoffs and discharges are the number of layoffs and discharges during the entire month.
[2]The layoffs and discharges rate is the number of layoffs and discharges during the entire month as a percent of total employment.

Table 7-11. Layoffs and Discharges Levels[1] and Rates,[2] by Industry, December 2000–September 2011
—Continued

(Not seasonally adjusted, levels in thousands, rates per 100.)

Year and month	Level												
	Finance and insurance	Real estate and rental and leasing	Professional and business services	Education and health services	Educational services	Health care and social assistance	Leisure and hospitality	Arts, entertainment, and recreation	Accommodation and food services	Other services	Government	Federal	State and local government
2006													
January	66	42	413	176	28	149	266	37	229	90	113	18	95
February	43	21	335	87	8	79	178	32	146	50	50	9	41
March	31	38	286	111	20	92	180	38	142	29	60	11	49
April	45	38	377	151	25	126	257	46	211	157	70	12	57
May	29	23	363	226	49	177	188	68	120	49	117	12	105
June	29	24	313	172	54	118	191	43	148	64	203	19	184
July	37	45	404	184	41	143	228	55	173	80	160	22	138
August	43	35	329	146	26	120	266	92	174	102	138	26	112
September	36	27	399	118	26	92	327	153	174	89	187	27	160
October	34	41	433	123	22	101	398	110	288	106	99	10	90
November	23	40	422	88	13	75	341	96	245	61	80	9	72
December	51	31	512	104	26	78	235	65	170	58	92	17	75
2007													
January	68	56	442	180	43	137	307	88	219	70	110	21	89
February	34	31	295	97	20	76	183	47	137	25	48	11	37
March	49	49	384	129	18	110	186	48	137	48	51	14	37
April	53	51	442	142	32	110	257	85	172	114	63	13	50
May	28	44	286	158	40	117	220	55	165	30	120	17	103
June	40	18	326	214	69	145	263	52	211	102	161	25	136
July	63	44	365	144	23	121	186	29	157	108	243	28	215
August	73	30	340	184	61	123	250	58	192	130	176	25	150
September	55	44	389	149	18	131	477	155	322	95	145	31	113
October	71	43	472	131	15	116	349	117	233	60	89	11	77
November	22	56	468	105	21	83	268	117	152	76	64	9	55
December	55	36	542	108	26	83	222	51	171	55	100	21	79
2008													
January	104	55	504	208	35	173	271	69	202	82	111	28	83
February	34	25	309	128	15	114	221	51	170	54	35	6	29
March	49	20	377	145	15	130	187	54	134	51	54	5	49
April	57	28	403	130	33	98	194	56	138	53	50	7	43
May	31	33	262	201	37	164	206	65	141	87	109	5	103
June	50	19	348	202	56	146	195	31	164	50	150	9	141
July	61	42	367	194	47	146	172	27	144	117	128	6	122
August	71	45	420	206	50	155	369	142	228	142	158	7	151
September	40	38	341	143	20	123	351	125	226	73	142	8	134
October	34	39	406	135	26	109	322	107	216	78	83	10	72
November	34	40	538	105	22	83	278	73	205	55	65	6	60
December	47	39	606	185	29	156	249	65	184	71	86	14	72
2009													
January	118	84	553	190	23	167	291	66	225	142	109	13	96
February	66	48	443	142	17	124	192	36	156	57	54	5	48
March	68	47	390	140	14	126	229	40	189	85	58	6	52
April	59	37	537	175	29	146	237	59	178	78	75	15	60
May	66	25	315	144	51	94	215	25	190	79	179	63	117
June	55	39	361	210	58	152	223	38	185	97	273	63	210
July	64	44	365	293	95	199	216	48	168	147	184	10	174
August	47	60	363	251	71	180	323	95	228	151	217	9	208
September	25	43	339	172	29	143	362	116	246	139	180	8	172
October	42	64	358	134	24	111	378	127	251	78	94	10	83
November	20	23	397	124	11	113	327	100	227	55	82	21	62
December	36	38	425	148	23	125	244	60	184	71	105	13	92
2010													
January	40	63	410	150	19	130	250	45	205	89	109	9	100
February	28	22	304	133	10	123	129	19	110	95	57	9	48
March	31	23	305	123	13	109	174	55	119	45	72	15	57
April	34	18	379	128	15	113	179	57	123	51	80	20	60
May	40	26	310	157	40	118	199	49	150	60	167	39	128
June	24	16	293	235	71	164	223	55	169	63	443	241	203
July	34	32	376	281	64	217	207	56	151	71	302	154	148
August	38	15	312	221	66	155	243	87	155	156	327	129	198
September	38	8	309	200	36	163	298	123	175	56	232	92	140
October	54	30	312	108	13	95	326	103	223	80	99	31	68
November	26	28	344	129	17	112	267	81	187	69	94	15	79
December	36	24	459	157	24	133	168	44	124	29	105	9	96
2011													
January	47	56	415	137	23	114	235	49	186	82	87	13	74
February	26	20	285	111	19	92	125	18	108	70	49	6	43
March	26	10	283	105	14	91	198	52	146	45	51	6	46
April	11	17	401	105	16	88	161	54	107	92	69	9	61
May	22	9	403	154	37	117	208	58	150	75	128	8	120
June	32	24	348	209	74	135	218	35	183	73	205	10	195
July	27	20	364	215	57	158	218	32	187	124	176	10	167
August	28	26	371	212	36	176	275	84	191	110	155	21	134
September	43	22	419	132	33	98	376	198	178	67	175	20	155

[1] Layoffs and discharges are the number of layoffs and discharges during the entire month.
[2] The layoffs and discharges rate is the number of layoffs and discharges during the entire month as a percent of total employment.

Table 7-11. Layoffs and Discharges Levels[1] and Rates,[2] by Industry, December 2000–September 2011
—Continued

(Not seasonally adjusted, levels in thousands, rates per 100.)

Year and month	Rate												
	Total	Total private	Mining and logging	Construction	Manufacturing	Durable goods	Non-durable goods	Trade, transportation, and utilities	Wholesale trade	Retail trade	Transportation, warehousing, and utilities	Information	Financial activities
2006													
January	1.8	2.0	1.2	4.5	1.4	1.1	2.0	2.5	0.9	3.2	1.9	0.7	1.3
February	1.0	1.2	1.0	2.5	0.8	0.7	1.0	1.2	0.8	1.5	0.7	0.5	0.8
March	1.0	1.1	1.2	2.4	1.1	0.9	1.6	0.9	0.6	1.0	0.7	0.5	0.8
April	1.3	1.5	1.4	1.9	1.1	0.8	1.8	1.2	0.8	1.5	0.5	1.1	1.0
May	1.2	1.3	0.4	2.2	1.0	0.9	1.1	1.2	0.8	1.4	1.2	0.4	0.6
June	1.2	1.2	0.3	1.6	0.9	0.8	1.2	1.3	0.8	1.6	1.1	0.4	0.6
July	1.4	1.5	0.6	2.6	1.1	1.0	1.1	1.3	1.7	1.3	1.2	0.8	1.0
August	1.3	1.4	0.8	2.6	1.1	1.0	1.1	1.2	0.8	1.3	1.2	0.6	0.9
September	1.4	1.5	1.4	2.6	1.1	1.1	1.1	1.2	0.9	1.2	1.2	0.5	0.8
October	1.5	1.7	0.8	3.3	1.1	1.1	1.3	1.3	1.1	1.3	1.5	1.0	0.9
November	1.3	1.5	0.8	4.2	1.0	1.0	1.0	1.1	0.8	1.2	1.0	0.8	0.8
December	1.5	1.7	1.0	4.0	1.1	1.0	1.1	1.6	0.7	2.0	1.3	1.1	1.0
2007													
January	1.8	2.1	2.0	4.6	1.6	1.5	1.7	2.3	1.1	2.7	2.2	2.4	1.5
February	1.0	1.2	0.8	3.2	1.1	1.1	1.1	1.1	0.6	1.3	0.8	0.8	0.8
March	1.1	1.2	0.6	2.1	1.0	1.0	0.9	1.0	0.9	1.0	1.1	0.6	1.2
April	1.3	1.5	0.8	3.0	1.1	1.1	1.2	1.1	1.1	1.2	1.2	0.7	1.3
May	1.1	1.2	0.8	2.2	0.9	0.9	1.0	1.1	0.9	1.3	0.9	0.7	0.9
June	1.3	1.4	0.5	2.7	1.0	1.0	0.9	1.1	1.3	1.1	0.9	0.7	0.7
July	1.4	1.5	1.0	2.5	1.3	1.2	1.4	1.4	1.5	1.4	1.2	1.2	1.3
August	1.4	1.5	1.2	2.9	1.1	1.1	1.3	1.3	1.1	1.4	1.1	0.9	1.2
September	1.6	1.7	1.0	3.4	1.2	1.2	1.3	1.3	1.1	1.5	0.8	0.6	1.2
October	1.5	1.7	1.3	3.3	1.5	1.4	1.5	1.5	1.5	1.5	1.2	0.7	1.4
November	1.4	1.6	1.3	3.6	1.4	1.3	1.4	1.4	1.1	1.5	1.4	0.5	1.0
December	1.5	1.7	1.3	4.0	1.1	1.0	1.3	1.6	1.5	1.9	1.0	0.6	1.1
2008													
January	1.9	2.2	2.1	5.3	1.6	1.7	1.4	2.4	2.0	2.7	1.7	1.6	2.0
February	1.1	1.3	1.3	2.9	1.0	0.9	1.2	1.2	0.9	1.4	0.8	0.6	0.7
March	1.1	1.3	0.8	3.1	0.9	0.9	0.8	1.0	1.0	1.1	0.9	1.0	0.8
April	1.2	1.4	1.0	3.1	1.3	1.3	1.3	1.1	1.2	1.1	0.9	0.5	1.0
May	1.2	1.3	0.5	2.8	1.1	1.0	1.1	1.2	1.2	1.3	0.9	0.5	0.8
June	1.3	1.4	0.7	3.1	1.2	1.1	1.3	1.4	1.3	1.6	1.0	1.0	0.8
July	1.4	1.5	1.3	2.9	1.1	1.2	0.9	1.4	0.9	1.6	1.6	0.7	1.3
August	1.6	1.8	0.6	3.4	1.2	1.4	0.9	1.5	1.2	1.6	1.4	0.6	1.4
September	1.4	1.6	0.7	3.9	1.3	1.3	1.3	1.3	1.2	1.4	1.2	1.1	1.0
October	1.6	1.8	1.3	4.5	1.8	1.8	1.9	1.6	1.5	1.7	1.4	1.6	0.9
November	1.6	1.9	2.2	5.7	1.7	1.7	1.7	1.5	1.3	1.5	1.5	1.3	0.9
December	2.0	2.3	2.4	6.1	2.4	2.5	2.2	2.4	2.9	2.4	1.9	1.6	1.1
2009													
January	2.6	3.0	2.4	8.9	3.7	4.3	2.9	3.1	4.2	2.9	2.2	2.4	2.6
February	1.5	1.8	2.3	5.1	2.3	2.5	1.9	1.6	1.7	1.6	1.5	1.1	1.5
March	1.5	1.8	3.0	4.8	2.3	2.7	1.5	1.5	1.5	1.3	1.9	1.2	1.5
April	1.7	2.0	2.0	5.4	2.3	2.8	1.6	1.7	1.5	2.0	1.3	1.3	1.2
May	1.4	1.6	1.9	4.1	1.8	2.0	1.6	1.4	1.8	1.4	1.2	0.9	1.2
June	1.5	1.6	1.5	3.6	1.6	1.7	1.5	1.2	1.2	1.2	1.5	0.9	1.2
July	1.7	1.9	3.1	5.0	1.6	1.4	1.9	1.4	1.4	1.3	1.6	1.9	1.4
August	1.7	1.8	1.2	4.4	1.5	1.3	1.9	1.3	1.5	1.2	1.2	0.7	1.4
September	1.7	1.8	1.6	5.0	1.5	1.4	1.6	1.6	1.1	1.7	2.1	0.5	0.9
October	1.5	1.8	2.2	4.9	1.8	1.7	1.9	1.3	1.1	1.4	1.3	0.7	1.4
November	1.5	1.7	1.8	4.5	2.0	1.7	2.4	1.4	1.2	1.4	1.6	1.0	0.6
December	1.7	2.0	2.7	6.5	1.5	1.4	1.6	2.2	1.4	2.0	3.6	1.6	1.0
2010													
January	1.8	2.1	1.7	9.0	1.8	2.1	1.3	2.1	1.3	2.6	1.7	1.6	1.3
February	1.1	1.3	1.2	4.3	1.2	1.2	1.3	1.0	1.3	0.9	0.8	0.8	0.7
March	1.1	1.3	1.1	3.9	1.1	1.0	1.1	1.3	1.1	1.5	0.7	0.8	0.7
April	1.1	1.3	1.1	4.1	1.1	0.9	1.4	0.9	0.9	1.0	0.7	0.5	0.7
May	1.2	1.3	1.3	3.9	0.8	0.8	0.8	0.9	1.0	0.9	0.9	0.8	0.9
June	1.5	1.4	0.6	3.1	0.9	0.7	1.2	1.3	0.9	1.4	1.4	0.7	0.5
July	1.6	1.6	0.8	4.3	1.1	1.0	1.4	1.2	1.3	1.3	0.9	0.8	0.9
August	1.5	1.5	0.9	3.7	1.2	1.1	1.4	1.0	0.8	1.2	0.7	0.8	0.7
September	1.4	1.4	0.9	4.0	1.0	0.9	1.2	1.0	1.3	1.0	0.8	0.6	0.6
October	1.3	1.5	0.8	4.4	1.5	1.3	1.8	1.2	0.9	1.3	1.3	0.7	1.1
November	1.3	1.5	1.3	5.4	1.4	1.2	1.7	1.2	1.0	1.4	0.9	0.8	0.7
December	1.5	1.7	1.8	7.0	1.1	1.0	1.4	1.6	1.2	1.5	2.5	1.1	0.8
2011													
January	1.6	1.9	1.2	6.3	1.2	1.0	1.6	2.2	0.9	2.7	2.3	1.3	1.4
February	1.0	1.2	0.5	4.4	0.9	0.8	1.1	1.0	0.9	1.2	0.7	0.6	0.6
March	1.0	1.1	0.4	3.8	0.8	0.7	0.8	0.9	0.8	1.0	0.8	1.3	0.5
April	1.1	1.2	1.0	4.4	0.9	0.7	1.2	0.8	0.6	0.9	0.6	0.8	0.4
May	1.2	1.3	0.7	4.0	1.0	0.8	1.2	0.8	1.2	0.8	0.5	0.8	0.4
June	1.3	1.4	0.9	3.9	0.8	0.7	0.8	1.0	1.1	1.0	0.8	0.8	0.7
July	1.3	1.4	0.7	4.1	0.8	0.8	0.9	1.0	0.7	1.1	1.0	1.0	0.6
August	1.4	1.5	0.8	3.9	1.0	1.1	1.0	0.9	0.6	1.0	1.0	0.8	0.7
September	1.4	1.5	0.9	4.4	1.0	1.0	1.0	0.9	0.6	0.9	0.9	0.8	0.9

[1]Layoffs and discharges are the number of layoffs and discharges during the entire month.
[2]The layoffs and discharges rate is the number of layoffs and discharges during the entire month as a percent of total employment.

Table 7-11. Layoffs and Discharges Levels[1] and Rates,[2] by Industry, December 2000–September 2011 —Continued

(Not seasonally adjusted, levels in thousands, rates per 100.)

Year and month	Rate												
	Finance and insurance	Real estate and rental and leasing	Professional and business services	Education and health services	Educational services	Health care and social assistance	Leisure and hospitality	Arts, entertainment, and recreation	Accommodation and food services	Other services	Government	Federal	State and local government
2006													
January	1.1	2.0	2.4	1.0	1.0	1.0	2.2	2.2	2.2	1.7	0.5	0.7	0.5
February	0.7	1.0	2.0	0.5	0.3	0.5	1.4	1.9	1.4	0.9	0.2	0.3	0.2
March	0.5	1.8	1.7	0.6	0.6	0.6	1.4	2.2	1.3	0.5	0.3	0.4	0.3
April	0.7	1.7	2.2	0.8	0.8	0.8	2.0	2.5	1.9	2.9	0.3	0.5	0.3
May	0.5	1.1	2.1	1.3	1.7	1.2	1.4	3.4	1.1	0.9	0.5	0.4	0.5
June	0.5	1.1	1.8	1.0	2.0	0.8	1.4	2.0	1.3	1.2	0.9	0.7	1.0
July	0.6	2.0	2.3	1.1	1.6	1.0	1.7	2.4	1.5	1.5	0.8	0.8	0.8
August	0.7	1.6	1.8	0.8	1.0	0.8	1.9	4.2	1.5	1.9	0.7	0.9	0.6
September	0.6	1.2	2.2	0.7	0.9	0.6	2.5	7.7	1.5	1.6	0.9	1.0	0.8
October	0.6	1.9	2.4	0.7	0.7	0.7	3.0	5.8	2.6	1.9	0.4	0.4	0.5
November	0.4	1.9	2.4	0.5	0.4	0.5	2.6	5.3	2.2	1.1	0.4	0.3	0.4
December	0.8	1.4	2.9	0.6	0.8	0.5	1.8	3.6	1.5	1.1	0.4	0.6	0.4
2007													
January	1.1	2.6	2.5	1.0	1.5	0.9	2.4	5.1	2.0	1.3	0.5	0.8	0.5
February	0.5	1.4	1.7	0.5	0.7	0.5	1.4	2.6	1.2	0.5	0.2	0.4	0.2
March	0.8	2.3	2.2	0.7	0.6	0.7	1.4	2.7	1.2	0.9	0.2	0.5	0.2
April	0.9	2.4	2.5	0.8	1.1	0.7	1.9	4.5	1.5	2.1	0.3	0.5	0.3
May	0.5	2.0	1.6	0.9	1.4	0.8	1.6	2.7	1.4	0.5	0.5	0.6	0.5
June	0.7	0.8	1.8	1.2	2.5	0.9	1.9	2.3	1.8	1.8	0.7	0.9	0.7
July	1.0	2.0	2.0	0.8	0.9	0.8	1.3	1.3	1.3	1.9	1.2	1.0	1.2
August	1.2	1.4	1.9	1.0	2.3	0.8	1.8	2.6	1.6	2.3	0.8	0.9	0.8
September	0.9	2.0	2.2	0.8	0.6	0.8	3.5	7.6	2.8	1.7	0.7	1.1	0.6
October	1.2	2.0	2.6	0.7	0.5	0.7	2.6	6.0	2.0	1.1	0.4	0.4	0.4
November	0.4	2.6	2.6	0.6	0.7	0.5	2.0	6.3	1.3	1.4	0.3	0.3	0.3
December	0.9	1.7	3.0	0.6	0.8	0.5	1.7	2.8	1.5	1.0	0.4	0.8	0.4
2008													
January	1.7	2.6	2.9	1.1	1.2	1.1	2.1	3.9	1.8	1.5	0.5	1.0	0.4
February	0.6	1.2	1.7	0.7	0.5	0.7	1.7	2.8	1.5	1.0	0.2	0.2	0.1
March	0.8	0.9	2.1	0.8	0.5	0.8	1.4	2.9	1.2	0.9	0.2	0.2	0.2
April	0.9	1.3	2.3	0.7	1.0	0.6	1.4	2.9	1.2	1.0	0.2	0.3	0.2
May	0.5	1.5	1.5	1.1	1.2	1.0	1.5	3.2	1.2	1.6	0.5	0.2	0.5
June	0.8	0.9	1.9	1.1	2.0	0.9	1.4	1.4	1.4	0.9	0.7	0.3	0.7
July	1.0	1.9	2.1	1.0	1.7	0.9	1.2	1.2	1.2	2.1	0.6	0.2	0.7
August	1.2	2.1	2.4	1.1	1.8	1.0	2.6	6.4	1.9	2.6	0.7	0.2	0.8
September	0.7	1.8	1.9	0.8	0.7	0.8	2.6	6.2	2.0	1.3	0.6	0.3	0.7
October	0.6	1.8	2.3	0.7	0.8	0.7	2.4	5.6	1.9	1.4	0.4	0.4	0.4
November	0.6	1.9	3.1	0.5	0.7	0.5	2.1	4.1	1.8	1.0	0.3	0.2	0.3
December	0.8	1.9	3.5	1.0	0.9	1.0	1.9	3.6	1.7	1.3	0.4	0.5	0.4
2009													
January	2.0	4.2	3.3	1.0	0.8	1.0	2.3	3.8	2.1	2.7	0.5	0.5	0.5
February	1.1	2.4	2.7	0.7	0.5	0.8	1.5	2.1	1.4	1.1	0.2	0.2	0.2
March	1.2	2.4	2.4	0.7	0.4	0.8	1.8	2.3	1.7	1.6	0.3	0.2	0.3
April	1.0	1.8	3.2	0.9	0.9	0.9	1.8	3.2	1.6	1.5	0.3	0.5	0.3
May	1.1	1.2	1.9	0.8	1.6	0.6	1.6	1.2	1.7	1.5	0.8	2.2	0.6
June	0.9	1.9	2.2	1.1	2.0	0.9	1.6	1.8	1.6	1.8	1.2	2.2	1.1
July	1.1	2.2	2.2	1.6	3.4	1.2	1.6	2.2	1.5	2.7	0.9	0.4	0.9
August	0.8	3.0	2.2	1.3	2.6	1.1	2.4	4.4	2.0	2.8	1.0	0.3	1.1
September	0.4	2.2	2.1	0.9	1.0	0.9	2.7	5.8	2.2	2.6	0.8	0.3	0.9
October	0.7	3.2	2.2	0.7	0.7	0.7	2.9	6.8	2.3	1.5	0.4	0.4	0.4
November	0.4	1.2	2.4	0.6	0.3	0.7	2.6	5.7	2.1	1.0	0.4	0.7	0.3
December	0.6	2.0	2.6	0.8	0.7	0.8	1.9	3.4	1.7	1.3	0.5	0.5	0.5
2010													
January	0.7	3.3	2.5	0.8	0.6	0.8	2.0	2.7	1.9	1.7	0.5	0.3	0.5
February	0.5	1.1	1.9	0.7	0.3	0.8	1.0	1.1	1.0	1.8	0.2	0.3	0.2
March	0.5	1.2	1.9	0.6	0.4	0.7	1.4	3.1	1.1	0.9	0.3	0.5	0.3
April	0.6	0.9	2.3	0.7	0.5	0.7	1.4	3.1	1.1	0.9	0.3	0.7	0.3
May	0.7	1.3	1.9	0.8	1.2	0.7	1.5	2.5	1.3	1.1	0.7	1.1	0.6
June	0.4	0.8	1.7	1.2	2.4	1.0	1.6	2.5	1.5	1.2	2.0	7.5	1.0
July	0.6	1.6	2.2	1.5	2.2	1.3	1.5	2.5	1.3	1.3	1.4	5.0	0.8
August	0.7	0.8	1.9	1.1	2.3	0.9	1.8	4.0	1.4	2.9	1.5	4.4	1.1
September	0.7	0.4	1.8	1.0	1.2	1.0	2.2	6.1	1.6	1.0	1.1	3.2	0.7
October	1.0	1.5	1.8	0.5	0.4	0.6	2.5	5.5	2.0	1.5	0.4	1.1	0.3
November	0.5	1.5	2.0	0.6	0.5	0.7	2.1	4.6	1.7	1.3	0.4	0.5	0.4
December	0.6	1.2	2.7	0.8	0.7	0.8	1.3	2.5	1.1	0.5	0.5	0.3	0.5
2011													
January	0.8	2.9	2.5	0.7	0.7	0.7	1.9	3.0	1.7	1.5	0.4	0.5	0.4
February	0.5	1.1	1.7	0.6	0.6	0.6	1.0	1.0	1.0	1.3	0.2	0.2	0.2
March	0.5	0.5	1.7	0.5	0.4	0.5	1.5	3.0	1.3	0.8	0.2	0.2	0.2
April	0.2	0.9	2.3	0.5	0.5	0.5	1.2	2.9	0.9	1.7	0.3	0.3	0.3
May	0.4	0.5	2.3	0.8	1.1	0.7	1.6	3.0	1.3	1.4	0.6	0.3	0.6
June	0.6	1.2	2.0	1.1	2.5	0.8	1.6	1.6	1.6	1.3	0.9	0.3	1.0
July	0.5	1.0	2.1	1.1	2.0	0.9	1.6	1.4	1.6	2.2	0.9	0.3	0.9
August	0.5	1.3	2.1	1.1	1.2	1.0	2.0	3.9	1.6	2.0	0.7	0.8	0.7
September	0.8	1.1	2.4	0.7	1.1	0.6	2.8	10.1	1.6	1.2	0.8	0.7	0.8

[1]Layoffs and discharges are the number of layoffs and discharges during the entire month.
[2]The layoffs and discharges rate is the number of layoffs and discharges during the entire month as a percent of total employment.

Table 7-12. Other Separations Levels[1] and Rates,[2] by Industry, December 2000–September 2011

(Not seasonally adjusted, levels in thousands, rates per 100.)

Year and month	Total[3]	Total private[3]	Construction	Manufacturing	Trade, transportation, and utilities[4]	Retail trade	Professional and business services	Education and health services	Leisure and hospitality[5]	Accommodation and food services	Government[6]	State and local government
Level												
2001	4 851	4 145	270	515	850	549	990	70	452	382	707	547
2002	4 711	3 901	215	495	897	543	964	50	369	333	807	661
2003	4 537	3 766	181	462	871	492	768	50	410	364	772	610
2004	4 425	3 634	231	349	952	551	669	51	406	369	791	610
2005	4 369	3 646	199	429	797	469	796	54	365	340	723	576
2006	4 875	4 130	355	431	1 105	665	852	53	325	282	748	544
2007	4 466	3 593	220	392	960	625	645	50	324	266	874	562
2008	3 875	3 236	224	338	925	628	585	46	302	265	639	525
2009	3 652	3 005	118	275	847	569	602	52	267	234	645	522
2010	3 810	3 019	144	245	802	498	606	53	349	312	788	660
2000												
December	348	297	24	47	86	35	46	28	30	20	51	41
2001												
January	642	540	33	67	155	120	66	46	67	61	102	54
February	270	234	8	33	69	50	17	28	37	35	36	27
March	343	307	16	51	53	33	88	31	30	27	36	28
April	462	402	29	47	89	60	82	36	30	23	60	49
May	318	263	17	36	62	36	75	21	27	22	55	47
June	479	400	17	46	35	18	172	49	30	30	79	71
July	492	401	41	44	61	32	88	29	56	48	92	79
August	442	386	40	60	53	31	104	44	42	23	56	44
September	368	306	21	29	67	45	72	35	36	30	62	53
October	384	338	22	44	95	53	67	33	40	32	46	35
November	271	235	17	22	49	32	49	27	22	18	36	27
December	380	333	9	36	62	39	110	28	35	33	47	33
2002												
January	636	530	20	72	118	74	146	51	35	31	106	79
February	300	253	10	37	65	33	62	27	19	18	47	35
March	324	280	16	34	38	21	79	33	30	29	44	35
April	421	368	24	40	67	43	91	47	38	36	52	40
May	316	256	11	39	54	30	75	26	26	23	60	50
June	381	284	7	37	66	38	69	28	42	38	96	88
July	499	402	7	47	113	83	100	37	37	34	97	83
August	367	299	23	39	94	62	60	30	25	24	68	57
September	401	340	18	30	92	56	76	39	35	26	60	47
October	366	297	19	46	62	30	63	37	29	26	69	60
November	303	263	17	40	68	40	46	25	25	23	41	29
December	397	329	43	34	60	33	97	27	28	25	67	58
2003												
January	746	624	29	71	164	88	121	72	64	61	121	82
February	292	249	11	44	83	54	36	19	20	19	43	33
March	331	278	11	36	53	31	82	41	38	37	53	40
April	381	324	14	49	58	22	79	34	33	30	58	43
May	333	265	10	28	61	37	54	35	29	28	68	53
June	367	283	22	27	66	36	53	42	27	26	84	74
July	428	345	19	40	81	47	90	35	26	25	83	75
August	357	291	9	42	45	27	71	25	45	26	67	57
September	364	301	8	29	89	54	48	35	31	28	63	54
October	355	310	16	42	66	37	46	32	33	27	45	34
November	268	232	19	25	53	31	43	24	41	37	36	26
December	315	264	13	29	52	28	45	41	23	20	51	39
2004												
January	649	501	46	47	110	61	48	57	60	58	147	84
February	258	213	12	25	46	25	38	37	19	18	46	37
March	300	256	11	29	89	56	55	18	17	15	44	36
April	346	304	13	31	86	38	57	27	34	33	42	34
May	344	280	9	31	66	48	57	39	39	35	63	50
June	400	296	11	31	87	48	75	31	21	18	104	95
July	428	332	18	31	85	57	68	28	38	34	96	82
August	378	313	15	26	94	47	52	40	49	48	65	56
September	359	309	30	29	61	33	50	33	39	31	50	39
October	379	329	46	20	99	56	57	30	20	16	50	35
November	265	232	8	16	62	45	48	22	44	39	34	23
December	319	269	12	33	67	37	64	23	26	24	50	39
2005												
January	584	481	12	52	101	53	59	53	60	55	103	75
February	311	262	10	29	63	39	77	25	20	19	48	36
March	283	233	7	28	72	55	46	15	19	19	50	39
April	342	289	16	35	72	37	54	27	22	20	53	37
May	339	287	12	32	48	26	79	41	34	32	51	45
June	342	230	21	25	56	32	41	35	21	20	113	99
July	357	285	10	47	64	40	41	38	20	18	72	58
August	370	312	26	42	58	35	66	39	38	35	59	50
September	320	263	18	33	67	35	65	31	16	13	57	40
October	351	313	27	34	60	37	88	32	26	24	38	31
November	303	273	28	33	49	27	57	19	23	22	30	25
December	467	418	12	39	87	53	123	34	66	63	49	41

[1]Other separations are the number of other separations during the entire month.
[2]The other separations rate is the number of other separations during the entire month as a percent of total employment.
[3]Includes natural resources and mining, information, financial activities, and other services, not shown separately.
[4]Includes wholesale trade and transportation, warehousing, and utilities, not shown separately.
[5]Includes arts, entertainment, and recreation, not shown separately.
[6]Includes federal government, not shown separately.

Table 7-12. Other Separations Levels[1] and Rates,[2] by Industry, December 2000–September 2011—*Continued*

(Not seasonally adjusted, levels in thousands, rates per 100.)

Year and month	Rate											
	Total[3]	Total private[3]	Construction	Manufacturing	Trade, transportation, and utilities[4]	Retail trade	Professional and business services	Education and health services	Leisure and hospitality[5]	Accommodation and food services	Government[6]	State and local government
2001	3.7	3.7	4.0	3.1	3.3	3.6	6.0	2.6	3.8	3.7	3.3	3.0
2002	3.6	3.6	3.2	3.2	3.5	3.6	6.0	2.5	3.1	3.3	3.8	3.5
2003	3.5	3.5	2.7	3.2	3.4	3.3	4.8	2.6	3.4	3.5	3.6	3.2
2004	3.4	3.3	3.3	2.4	3.7	3.7	4.1	2.3	3.2	3.5	3.7	3.2
2005	3.3	3.3	2.7	3.0	3.1	3.1	4.7	2.2	2.8	3.1	3.3	3.0
2006	3.6	3.6	4.6	3.0	4.2	4.3	4.9	2.4	2.5	2.5	3.4	2.8
2007	3.2	3.1	2.9	2.8	3.6	4.0	3.6	2.4	2.4	2.3	3.9	2.9
2008	2.8	2.8	3.1	2.5	3.5	4.1	3.3	2.3	2.2	2.3	2.8	2.7
2009	2.8	2.8	2.0	2.3	3.4	3.9	3.6	2.6	2.0	2.1	2.9	2.6
2010	2.9	2.8	2.6	2.1	3.3	3.5	3.6	2.1	2.7	2.8	3.5	3.4
2000												
December	0.3	0.3	0.4	0.3	0.3	0.2	0.3	0.2	0.3	0.2	0.2	0.2
2001												
January	0.5	0.5	0.5	0.4	0.6	0.8	0.4	0.3	0.6	0.6	0.5	0.3
February	0.2	0.2	0.1	0.2	0.3	0.3	0.1	0.2	0.3	0.4	0.2	0.1
March	0.3	0.3	0.2	0.3	0.2	0.2	0.5	0.2	0.3	0.3	0.2	0.1
April	0.3	0.4	0.4	0.3	0.3	0.4	0.5	0.2	0.3	0.2	0.3	0.3
May	0.2	0.2	0.2	0.2	0.2	0.2	0.5	0.1	0.2	0.2	0.3	0.3
June	0.4	0.4	0.2	0.3	0.1	0.1	1.0	0.3	0.2	0.3	0.4	0.4
July	0.4	0.4	0.6	0.3	0.2	0.2	0.5	0.2	0.4	0.5	0.5	0.5
August	0.3	0.3	0.6	0.4	0.2	0.2	0.6	0.3	0.3	0.2	0.3	0.3
September	0.3	0.3	0.3	0.2	0.3	0.3	0.4	0.2	0.3	0.3	0.3	0.3
October	0.3	0.3	0.3	0.3	0.4	0.3	0.4	0.2	0.3	0.3	0.2	0.2
November	0.2	0.2	0.3	0.1	0.2	0.2	0.3	0.2	0.2	0.2	0.2	0.1
December	0.3	0.3	0.1	0.2	0.2	0.2	0.7	0.2	0.3	0.3	0.2	0.2
2002												
January	0.5	0.5	0.3	0.5	0.5	0.5	0.9	0.3	0.3	0.3	0.5	0.4
February	0.2	0.2	0.2	0.2	0.3	0.2	0.4	0.2	0.2	0.2	0.2	0.2
March	0.2	0.3	0.2	0.2	0.2	0.1	0.5	0.2	0.3	0.3	0.2	0.2
April	0.3	0.3	0.4	0.3	0.3	0.3	0.6	0.3	0.3	0.4	0.2	0.2
May	0.2	0.2	0.2	0.3	0.2	0.2	0.5	0.2	0.2	0.2	0.3	0.3
June	0.3	0.3	0.1	0.2	0.3	0.3	0.4	0.2	0.3	0.4	0.4	0.5
July	0.4	0.4	0.1	0.3	0.4	0.6	0.6	0.2	0.3	0.3	0.5	0.5
August	0.3	0.3	0.3	0.3	0.4	0.4	0.4	0.2	0.2	0.2	0.3	0.3
September	0.3	0.3	0.3	0.2	0.4	0.4	0.5	0.2	0.3	0.3	0.3	0.3
October	0.3	0.3	0.3	0.3	0.2	0.2	0.4	0.2	0.2	0.3	0.3	0.3
November	0.2	0.2	0.2	0.3	0.3	0.3	0.3	0.1	0.2	0.2	0.2	0.2
December	0.3	0.3	0.7	0.2	0.2	0.2	0.6	0.2	0.2	0.2	0.3	0.3
2003												
January	0.6	0.6	0.5	0.5	0.6	0.6	0.8	0.4	0.6	0.6	0.6	0.4
February	0.2	0.2	0.2	0.3	0.3	0.4	0.2	0.1	0.2	0.2	0.2	0.2
March	0.3	0.3	0.2	0.2	0.2	0.2	0.5	0.2	0.3	0.4	0.2	0.2
April	0.3	0.3	0.2	0.3	0.2	0.2	0.5	0.2	0.3	0.3	0.3	0.2
May	0.3	0.2	0.1	0.2	0.2	0.2	0.3	0.2	0.2	0.3	0.3	0.3
June	0.3	0.3	0.3	0.2	0.3	0.2	0.3	0.3	0.2	0.2	0.4	0.4
July	0.3	0.3	0.3	0.3	0.3	0.3	0.6	0.2	0.2	0.2	0.4	0.4
August	0.3	0.3	0.1	0.3	0.2	0.2	0.4	0.2	0.4	0.2	0.3	0.3
September	0.3	0.3	0.1	0.2	0.4	0.4	0.3	0.2	0.3	0.3	0.3	0.3
October	0.3	0.3	0.2	0.3	0.3	0.2	0.3	0.2	0.3	0.3	0.2	0.2
November	0.2	0.2	0.3	0.2	0.2	0.2	0.3	0.1	0.3	0.4	0.2	0.1
December	0.2	0.2	0.2	0.2	0.2	0.2	0.3	0.2	0.2	0.2	0.2	0.2
2004												
January	0.5	0.5	0.7	0.3	0.4	0.4	0.3	0.3	0.5	0.6	0.7	0.4
February	0.2	0.2	0.2	0.2	0.2	0.2	0.2	0.2	0.2	0.2	0.2	0.2
March	0.2	0.2	0.2	0.2	0.4	0.4	0.3	0.1	0.1	0.1	0.2	0.2
April	0.3	0.3	0.2	0.2	0.3	0.3	0.3	0.2	0.3	0.3	0.2	0.2
May	0.3	0.3	0.1	0.2	0.3	0.3	0.3	0.2	0.3	0.3	0.3	0.3
June	0.3	0.3	0.2	0.2	0.3	0.3	0.5	0.2	0.2	0.2	0.5	0.5
July	0.3	0.3	0.2	0.2	0.3	0.4	0.4	0.2	0.3	0.3	0.5	0.5
August	0.3	0.3	0.2	0.2	0.4	0.3	0.3	0.2	0.4	0.4	0.3	0.3
September	0.3	0.3	0.4	0.2	0.2	0.2	0.3	0.2	0.3	0.3	0.2	0.2
October	0.3	0.3	0.6	0.1	0.4	0.4	0.3	0.2	0.2	0.1	0.2	0.2
November	0.2	0.2	0.1	0.1	0.2	0.3	0.3	0.1	0.4	0.4	0.2	0.1
December	0.2	0.2	0.2	0.2	0.3	0.2	0.4	0.1	0.2	0.2	0.2	0.2
2005												
January	0.4	0.4	0.2	0.4	0.4	0.4	0.4	0.3	0.5	0.5	0.5	0.4
February	0.2	0.2	0.2	0.2	0.2	0.3	0.5	0.1	0.2	0.2	0.2	0.2
March	0.2	0.2	0.1	0.2	0.3	0.4	0.3	0.1	0.2	0.2	0.2	0.2
April	0.3	0.3	0.2	0.2	0.3	0.2	0.3	0.2	0.2	0.2	0.2	0.2
May	0.3	0.3	0.2	0.2	0.2	0.2	0.5	0.2	0.3	0.3	0.2	0.2
June	0.3	0.2	0.3	0.2	0.2	0.2	0.2	0.2	0.2	0.2	0.5	0.5
July	0.3	0.3	0.1	0.3	0.2	0.3	0.2	0.2	0.1	0.2	0.4	0.3
August	0.3	0.3	0.3	0.3	0.2	0.2	0.4	0.2	0.3	0.3	0.3	0.3
September	0.2	0.2	0.2	0.2	0.3	0.2	0.4	0.2	0.1	0.1	0.3	0.2
October	0.3	0.3	0.4	0.2	0.2	0.2	0.5	0.2	0.2	0.2	0.2	0.2
November	0.2	0.2	0.4	0.2	0.2	0.2	0.3	0.1	0.2	0.2	0.1	0.1
December	0.3	0.4	0.2	0.3	0.3	0.3	0.7	0.2	0.5	0.6	0.2	0.2

[1]Other separations are the number of other separations during the entire month.
[2]The other separations rate is the number of other separations during the month as a percent of total employment.
[3]Includes natural resources and mining, information, financial activities, and other services, not shown separately.
[4]Includes wholesale trade and transportation, warehousing, and utilities, not shown separately.
[5]Includes arts, entertainment, and recreation, not shown separately.
[6]Includes federal government, not shown separately.

Table 7-12. Other Separations Levels[1] and Rates,[2] by Industry, December 2000–September 2011—*Continued*

(Not seasonally adjusted, levels in thousands, rates per 100.)

Year and month	Level											
	Total[3]	Total private[3]	Construc-tion	Manufac-turing	Trade, transpor-tation, and utilities[4]	Retail trade	Profes-sional and business services	Education and health services	Leisure and hospitality[5]	Accommo-dation and food services	Govern-ment[6]	State and local govern-ment
2006												
January	606	514	25	67	108	59	176	39	26	20	92	56
February	318	281	20	41	86	49	36	21	32	28	38	25
March	341	293	20	35	86	47	62	27	23	21	48	34
April	424	375	41	33	90	48	62	52	37	34	49	35
May	431	363	44	29	118	73	62	28	33	28	67	48
June	479	373	25	42	114	74	84	37	25	24	106	93
July	488	411	27	47	97	53	85	62	24	23	77	60
August	363	282	18	32	73	46	44	35	33	27	82	61
September	366	301	36	27	84	59	43	26	18	15	65	36
October	422	384	45	31	91	53	79	36	30	27	39	32
November	299	266	32	23	66	48	68	30	16	13	34	25
December	338	287	22	24	92	56	51	31	28	22	51	39
2007												
January	585	497	30	52	139	101	66	75	28	23	88	55
February	323	265	25	37	67	41	58	21	20	19	58	38
March	313	262	22	29	86	59	45	27	22	18	51	29
April	378	320	9	48	80	53	54	30	31	26	58	32
May	311	232	22	33	51	31	38	31	18	14	79	47
June	421	291	8	37	92	59	49	43	23	20	130	97
July	472	360	23	22	76	45	73	53	43	35	112	72
August	360	270	10	26	70	43	55	28	45	31	91	53
September	339	258	11	35	70	49	63	25	17	14	81	36
October	342	307	18	23	66	37	51	42	30	26	35	26
November	281	249	23	28	76	58	38	29	23	20	32	27
December	341	282	19	22	87	49	55	40	24	20	59	50
2008												
January	433	352	18	44	82	55	65	45	59	56	80	50
February	291	253	17	25	84	71	35	41	16	15	38	30
March	326	285	21	35	79	64	73	35	15	14	41	32
April	362	321	34	27	112	94	25	39	30	27	42	35
May	288	234	18	28	60	43	46	34	27	24	54	45
June	304	213	20	23	66	41	29	29	27	25	91	84
July	335	270	12	24	70	42	50	27	37	34	65	57
August	342	286	15	24	85	50	75	43	17	14	56	48
September	337	277	9	29	81	39	53	32	24	12	59	51
October	318	276	21	41	70	43	51	37	18	17	42	35
November	262	233	21	20	73	51	32	41	20	17	30	23
December	277	236	18	18	63	35	51	37	12	10	41	35
2009												
January	453	390	21	41	115	68	59	77	22	16	63	48
February	258	229	8	18	50	34	60	47	28	27	28	23
March	288	254	9	23	80	50	45	50	17	15	34	26
April	316	276	18	21	97	76	61	35	12	11	40	30
May	291	241	4	22	92	67	44	28	23	22	50	41
June	337	248	6	34	44	33	53	54	28	26	89	82
July	317	228	10	17	61	41	52	32	25	21	89	73
August	323	265	5	20	73	59	37	52	28	24	58	50
September	294	243	6	27	74	38	40	41	31	29	51	43
October	289	234	6	18	78	45	50	21	18	14	54	36
November	218	185	8	12	38	26	67	20	17	12	33	26
December	268	212	17	22	45	32	34	37	18	17	56	44
2010												
January	380	321	18	27	92	42	55	39	25	21	59	43
February	273	232	16	15	67	42	42	28	21	19	41	31
March	283	239	16	20	52	27	62	43	19	18	43	34
April	277	225	23	22	54	37	36	24	22	22	52	37
May	303	235	9	19	68	50	54	25	27	23	68	57
June	375	247	9	18	57	37	50	42	20	17	127	117
July	365	267	14	22	64	36	46	41	45	38	98	86
August	385	292	6	21	101	78	49	36	44	39	93	84
September	341	272	13	14	79	47	62	31	39	36	69	56
October	249	208	7	24	54	36	37	29	29	27	41	33
November	268	233	10	15	58	33	53	26	35	32	35	29
December	311	248	3	28	56	33	60	42	23	20	62	53
2011												
January	462	391	12	25	116	63	83	68	27	23	71	54
February	295	258	5	21	71	38	50	54	26	23	36	26
March	271	229	13	22	55	27	54	39	15	12	41	34
April	305	258	16	22	58	28	64	46	21	19	47	38
May	311	243	4	23	82	56	44	37	20	18	68	57
June	392	256	11	22	67	39	39	53	18	15	137	123
July	383	290	13	23	90	54	48	42	48	46	94	81
August	319	261	9	22	77	35	50	38	28	27	58	51
September	329	276	16	17	79	44	74	24	30	28	53	44

[1]Other separations are the number of other separations during the entire month.
[2]The other separations rate is the number of other separations during the entire month as a percent of total employment.
[3]Includes natural resources and mining, information, financial activities, and other services, not shown separately.
[4]Includes wholesale trade and transportation, warehousing, and utilities, not shown separately.
[5]Includes arts, entertainment, and recreation, not shown separately.
[6]Includes federal government, not shown separately.

Table 7-12. Other Separations Levels[1] and Rates,[2] by Industry, December 2000–September 2011—*Continued*

(Not seasonally adjusted, levels in thousands, rates per 100.)

Year and month	Rate											
	Total[3]	Total private[3]	Construction	Manufacturing	Trade, transportation, and utilities[4]	Retail trade	Professional and business services	Education and health services	Leisure and hospitality[5]	Accommodation and food services	Government[6]	State and local government
2006												
January	0.5	0.5	0.3	0.5	0.4	0.4	1.0	0.2	0.2	0.2	0.4	0.3
February	0.2	0.3	0.3	0.3	0.3	0.3	0.2	0.1	0.3	0.3	0.2	0.1
March	0.3	0.3	0.3	0.3	0.3	0.3	0.4	0.2	0.2	0.2	0.2	0.2
April	0.3	0.3	0.5	0.2	0.3	0.3	0.4	0.3	0.3	0.3	0.2	0.2
May	0.3	0.3	0.6	0.2	0.5	0.5	0.4	0.2	0.2	0.2	0.3	0.2
June	0.3	0.3	0.3	0.3	0.4	0.5	0.5	0.2	0.2	0.2	0.5	0.5
July	0.4	0.4	0.3	0.3	0.4	0.3	0.5	0.4	0.2	0.2	0.4	0.3
August	0.3	0.2	0.2	0.2	0.3	0.3	0.2	0.2	0.2	0.2	0.4	0.3
September	0.3	0.3	0.4	0.2	0.3	0.4	0.2	0.1	0.1	0.1	0.3	0.2
October	0.3	0.3	0.6	0.2	0.3	0.3	0.4	0.2	0.2	0.2	0.2	0.2
November	0.2	0.2	0.4	0.2	0.2	0.3	0.4	0.2	0.1	0.1	0.1	0.1
December	0.2	0.2	0.3	0.2	0.3	0.3	0.3	0.2	0.2	0.2	0.2	0.2
2007												
January	0.4	0.4	0.4	0.4	0.5	0.7	0.4	0.4	0.2	0.2	0.4	0.3
February	0.2	0.2	0.3	0.3	0.3	0.3	0.3	0.1	0.2	0.2	0.3	0.2
March	0.2	0.2	0.3	0.2	0.3	0.4	0.3	0.1	0.2	0.2	0.2	0.1
April	0.3	0.3	0.1	0.3	0.3	0.3	0.3	0.2	0.2	0.2	0.3	0.2
May	0.2	0.2	0.3	0.2	0.2	0.2	0.2	0.2	0.1	0.1	0.3	0.2
June	0.3	0.2	0.1	0.3	0.3	0.4	0.3	0.2	0.2	0.2	0.6	0.5
July	0.3	0.3	0.3	0.2	0.3	0.3	0.4	0.3	0.3	0.3	0.5	0.4
August	0.3	0.2	0.1	0.2	0.3	0.3	0.3	0.2	0.3	0.3	0.4	0.3
September	0.2	0.2	0.1	0.2	0.3	0.3	0.3	0.1	0.1	0.1	0.4	0.2
October	0.2	0.3	0.2	0.2	0.2	0.2	0.3	0.2	0.2	0.2	0.2	0.1
November	0.2	0.2	0.3	0.2	0.3	0.4	0.2	0.2	0.2	0.2	0.1	0.1
December	0.2	0.2	0.3	0.2	0.3	0.3	0.3	0.2	0.2	0.2	0.3	0.3
2008												
January	0.3	0.3	0.3	0.3	0.3	0.4	0.4	0.2	0.5	0.5	0.4	0.3
February	0.2	0.2	0.2	0.2	0.3	0.5	0.2	0.2	0.1	0.1	0.2	0.2
March	0.2	0.2	0.3	0.3	0.3	0.4	0.4	0.2	0.1	0.1	0.2	0.2
April	0.3	0.3	0.5	0.2	0.4	0.6	0.1	0.2	0.2	0.2	0.2	0.2
May	0.2	0.2	0.2	0.2	0.2	0.3	0.3	0.2	0.2	0.2	0.2	0.2
June	0.2	0.2	0.3	0.2	0.2	0.3	0.2	0.2	0.2	0.2	0.4	0.4
July	0.2	0.2	0.2	0.2	0.3	0.3	0.3	0.1	0.3	0.3	0.3	0.3
August	0.3	0.2	0.2	0.2	0.3	0.3	0.4	0.2	0.1	0.1	0.3	0.3
September	0.2	0.2	0.1	0.2	0.3	0.3	0.3	0.2	0.2	0.1	0.3	0.3
October	0.2	0.2	0.3	0.3	0.3	0.3	0.3	0.2	0.1	0.1	0.2	0.2
November	0.2	0.2	0.3	0.2	0.3	0.3	0.2	0.2	0.2	0.1	0.1	0.1
December	0.2	0.2	0.3	0.1	0.2	0.2	0.3	0.2	0.1	0.1	0.2	0.2
2009												
January	0.3	0.4	0.3	0.3	0.5	0.5	0.4	0.4	0.2	0.1	0.3	0.2
February	0.2	0.2	0.1	0.1	0.2	0.2	0.4	0.2	0.2	0.3	0.1	0.1
March	0.2	0.2	0.2	0.2	0.3	0.3	0.3	0.3	0.1	0.1	0.1	0.1
April	0.2	0.3	0.3	0.2	0.4	0.5	0.4	0.2	0.1	0.1	0.2	0.1
May	0.2	0.2	0.1	0.2	0.4	0.5	0.3	0.1	0.2	0.2	0.2	0.2
June	0.3	0.2	0.1	0.3	0.2	0.2	0.3	0.3	0.2	0.2	0.4	0.4
July	0.2	0.2	0.2	0.1	0.2	0.3	0.3	0.2	0.2	0.2	0.4	0.4
August	0.2	0.2	0.1	0.2	0.3	0.4	0.2	0.3	0.2	0.2	0.3	0.3
September	0.2	0.2	0.1	0.2	0.3	0.3	0.2	0.2	0.2	0.3	0.2	0.2
October	0.2	0.2	0.1	0.2	0.3	0.3	0.3	0.1	0.1	0.1	0.2	0.2
November	0.2	0.2	0.1	0.1	0.2	0.2	0.4	0.1	0.1	0.1	0.1	0.1
December	0.2	0.2	0.3	0.2	0.2	0.2	0.2	0.2	0.1	0.2	0.2	0.2
2010												
January	0.3	0.3	0.3	0.2	0.4	0.3	0.3	0.2	0.2	0.2	0.3	0.2
February	0.2	0.2	0.3	0.1	0.3	0.3	0.3	0.1	0.2	0.2	0.2	0.2
March	0.2	0.2	0.3	0.2	0.2	0.2	0.4	0.2	0.1	0.2	0.2	0.2
April	0.2	0.2	0.4	0.2	0.2	0.3	0.2	0.1	0.2	0.2	0.2	0.2
May	0.2	0.2	0.2	0.2	0.3	0.3	0.3	0.2	0.2	0.2	0.3	0.3
June	0.3	0.2	0.2	0.2	0.2	0.3	0.3	0.2	0.1	0.2	0.6	0.6
July	0.3	0.2	0.2	0.2	0.3	0.3	0.3	0.2	0.3	0.3	0.5	0.5
August	0.3	0.3	0.1	0.2	0.4	0.5	0.3	0.2	0.3	0.3	0.4	0.5
September	0.3	0.3	0.2	0.1	0.3	0.3	0.4	0.2	0.3	0.3	0.3	0.3
October	0.2	0.2	0.1	0.2	0.2	0.2	0.2	0.1	0.2	0.2	0.2	0.2
November	0.2	0.2	0.2	0.1	0.2	0.2	0.3	0.1	0.3	0.3	0.2	0.1
December	0.2	0.2	0.1	0.2	0.2	0.2	0.4	0.2	0.2	0.2	0.3	0.3
2011												
January	0.4	0.4	0.2	0.2	0.5	0.4	0.5	0.3	0.2	0.2	0.3	0.3
February	0.2	0.2	0.1	0.2	0.3	0.3	0.3	0.3	0.2	0.2	0.2	0.1
March	0.2	0.2	0.3	0.2	0.2	0.2	0.3	0.2	0.1	0.1	0.2	0.2
April	0.2	0.2	0.3	0.2	0.2	0.2	0.4	0.2	0.2	0.2	0.2	0.2
May	0.2	0.2	0.1	0.2	0.3	0.4	0.3	0.2	0.2	0.2	0.3	0.3
June	0.3	0.2	0.2	0.2	0.3	0.3	0.2	0.3	0.1	0.1	0.6	0.6
July	0.3	0.3	0.2	0.2	0.4	0.4	0.3	0.2	0.3	0.4	0.5	0.5
August	0.2	0.2	0.2	0.2	0.3	0.2	0.3	0.2	0.2	0.2	0.3	0.3
September	0.3	0.3	0.3	0.1	0.3	0.3	0.4	0.1	0.2	0.2	0.2	0.2

[1] Other separations are the number of other separations during the entire month.
[2] The other separations rate is the number of other separations during the entire month as a percent of total employment.
[3] Includes natural resources and mining, information, financial activities, and other services, not shown separately.
[4] Includes wholesale trade and transportation, warehousing, and utilities, not shown separately.
[5] Includes arts, entertainment, and recreation, not shown separately.
[6] Includes federal government, not shown separately.

Chapter Eight

LABOR-MANAGEMENT RELATIONS

LABOR-MANAGEMENT RELATIONS

HIGHLIGHTS

This chapter contains information on historical trends in union membership, earnings, and work stoppages.

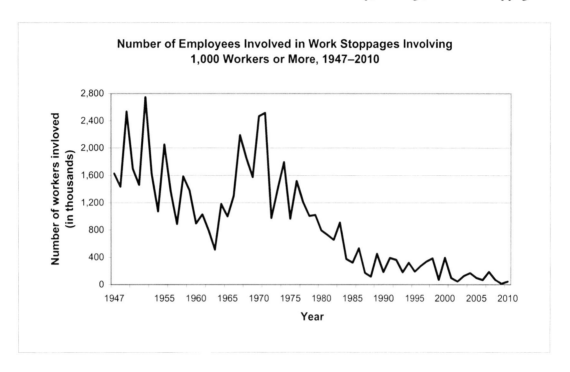

Number of Employees Involved in Work Stoppages Involving 1,000 Workers or More, 1947–2010

While the number of work stoppages and the number of employees involved in them has declined dramatically since 1947, the number of work stoppages increased from five in 2009 to eleven in 2010, affecting 45,000 workers who were idle for a total of 302,000 days. A record-high 470 work stoppages involving 1,000 workers or more took place in 1952. (See Table 8-1.)

OTHER HIGHLIGHTS

- In 2010, the number of workers belonging to a union declined for the second straight year after increasing in 2007 and 2008. Approximately 14.7 million workers were union members in 2010 compared with 15.3 million in 2009. Union members accounted for 11.9 percent of employed wage and salary workers in 2010, down from 12.3 percent in 2009 and 12.4 percent in 2008. (See Table 8-2.)

- Workers in the public sector were far more likely to be in a union than those in the private sector (36.2 percent compared with 6.9 percent). In the private sector, workers in utilities had the highest unionization rate (28.3 percent) while those in finance and food services and drinking places (both at 1.1 percent) had the lowest. (See Table 8-3.)

- The median weekly earnings of union members were significantly higher than that of non-union members in both the private and public sector. In the private sector, the median weekly earnings of union members were $864 compared with $703 of non-union members. In the public sector, union members had a median weekly earning of $961 compared with $801 for non-union members. (See Table 8-4.)

- Seven states had a union membership rates below five percent with North Carolina reporting the lowest union membership rate at 3.2 percent. Meanwhile, three states had union membership rates over 20 percent in 2010—New York (24.2 percent), Alaska (22.9 percent), and Hawaii (21.8 percent). (See Table 8-6.)

NOTES AND DEFINITIONS

WORK STOPPAGES

Collection and Coverage

Data on work stoppages measure the number and duration of major strikes or lockouts (involving 1,000 workers or more) during the year, the number of workers involved in these stoppages, and the amount of time lost due to these stoppages.

Information on work stoppages is obtained from reports issued by the Federal Mediation and Conciliation Service, state labor market information offices, Bureau of Labor Statistics (BLS) Strike Reports from the Office of Employment and Unemployment Statistics, and media sources such as the *Daily Labor Report* and the *Wall Street Journal*. One or both parties involved in the work stoppage (employer and/or union) is contacted to verify the duration of the stoppage and number of workers idled by the stoppage.

Concepts and Definitions

Major work stoppage includes both worker-initiated strikes and employer-initiated lockouts involving 1,000 workers or more. BLS does not distinguish between lockouts and strikes in its statistics.

Workers involved consists of workers directly involved in the stoppage. This category does not measure the indirect or secondary effect of stoppages on other establishments whose employees are idle from material shortages or lack of service.

Days of idleness is calculated by taking the number of workers involved in the strike or lockout and multiplying it by the number of days workers are off the job. The number of working days lost for every major work stoppage is based on a 5-day workweek (Monday through Friday), excluding federal holidays.

Sources of Additional Information

Additional information is available in BLS news release USDL 11-0153, "Major Work Stoppages in 2010" on the BLS Web site at <http://www.bls.gov/wsp/home.htm>.

UNION MEMBERSHIP

Collection and Coverage

The estimates of union membership are obtained from the Current Population Survey (CPS), which provides basic information on the labor force, employment, and unemployment. The survey is conducted monthly for the Bureau of Labor Statistics by the U.S. Census Bureau from a scientifically selected national sample of about 60,000 households. The union membership and earnings data are tabulated from one-quarter of the CPS monthly sample and are limited to wage and salary workers. All self-employed workers are excluded. The data in these tables are annual averages.

Union membership data for 2010 are not strictly comparable with data for 2009 because of the introduction of updated population controls with the release of January data. The effect of the revised population controls on the union membership estimates should be negligible. However, the effect of the new controls on the monthly CPS estimates was to decrease the December 2009 employment level by 243,000. The updated controls had little or no effect on unemployment rates and other ratios.

Concepts and Definitions

Union members are members of a labor union or an employee association similar to a union.

Represented by unions refers to union members, as well as to workers who have no union affiliation but whose jobs are covered by a union contract.

Usual weekly earnings represent earnings before taxes and other deductions and include any overtime pay, commissions, or tips usually received (at the main job in the case of multiple jobholders). Prior to 1994, respondents were asked how much they usually earned per week. Since January 1994, respondents have been asked to identify the easiest way for them to report earnings (hourly, weekly, biweekly, twice monthly, monthly, annually, other) and how much they usually earn in the reported time period. Earnings reported on a basis other than weekly are converted to a weekly equivalent. The term "usual" is as perceived by the respondent. If the respondent asks for a definition of "usual," interviewers are instructed to define the term as more than half of the weeks worked during the past 4 or 5 months.

Median earnings is the amount which divides a given earnings distribution into two equal groups, one having earnings above the median and the other having earnings below the median. The estimating procedure places each reported or calculated weekly earnings value into $50-wide intervals which are centered around multiples of $50. The actual value is estimated through the linear interpolation of the interval in which the median lies.

Wage and salary workers are workers who receive wages, salaries, commissions, tips, payment in kind, or piece rates. The group includes employees in both the private and public sectors, but, for the purposes of the union membership and earnings series, excludes all self-employed persons, regardless of whether or not their businesses are incorporated.

Full-time workers are workers who usually work 35 hours or more per week at their sole or principal job.

Part-time workers are workers who usually work fewer than 35 hours per week at their sole or principal job.

Hispanic or Latino ethnicity refers to persons who identified themselves in the enumeration process as being Spanish, Hispanic, or Latino. Persons whose ethnicity is identified as Hispanic or Latino may be of any race.

Sources of Additional Information

For additional information see BLS news release USDL 11-0063, "Union Members–2010."

Table 8-1. Work Stoppages Involving 1,000 Workers or More, 1947–2010

(Number, percent.)

Year	Stoppages beginning during the year		Days idle during the year[1]	
	Number	Workers involved (thousands)[2]	Number (thousands)	Percent of estimated total working time[3]
1947	270	1 629	25 720	. . .
1948	245	1 435	26 127	0.22
1949	262	2 537	43 420	0.38
1950	424	1 698	30 390	0.26
1951	415	1 462	15 070	0.12
1952	470	2 746	48 820	0.38
1953	437	1 623	18 130	0.14
1954	265	1 075	16 630	0.13
1955	363	2 055	21 180	0.16
1956	287	1 370	26 840	0.20
1957	279	887	10 340	0.07
1958	332	1 587	17 900	0.13
1959	245	1 381	60 850	0.43
1960	222	896	13 260	0.09
1961	195	1 031	10 140	0.07
1962	211	793	11 760	0.08
1963	181	512	10 020	0.07
1964	246	1 183	16 220	0.11
1965	268	999	15 140	0.10
1966	321	1 300	16 000	0.10
1967	381	2 192	31 320	0.18
1968	392	1 855	35 367	0.20
1969	412	1 576	29 397	0.16
1970	381	2 468	52 761	0.29
1971	298	2 516	35 538	0.19
1972	250	975	16 764	0.09
1973	317	1 400	16 260	0.08
1974	424	1 796	31 809	0.16
1975	235	965	17 563	0.09
1976	231	1 519	23 962	0.12
1977	298	1 212	21 258	0.10
1978	219	1 006	23 774	0.11
1979	235	1 021	20 409	0.09
1980	187	795	20 844	0.09
1981	145	729	16 908	0.07
1982	96	656	9 061	0.04
1983	81	909	17 461	0.08
1984	62	376	8 499	0.04
1985	54	324	7 079	0.03
1986	69	533	11 861	0.05
1987	46	174	4 481	0.02
1988	40	118	4 381	0.02
1989	51	452	16 996	0.07
1990	44	185	5 926	0.02
1991	40	392	4 584	0.02
1992	35	364	3 989	0.01
1993	35	182	3 981	0.01
1994	45	322	5 021	0.02
1995	31	192	5 771	0.02
1996	37	273	4 889	0.02
1997	29	339	4 497	0.01
1998	34	387	5 116	0.02
1999	17	73	1 996	0.01
2000	39	394	20 419	0.06
2001	29	99	1 151	([4])
2002	19	46	660	([4])
2003	14	129	4 091	0.01
2004	17	171	3 344	0.01
2005	22	100	1 736	0.01
2006	20	70	2 688	0.01
2007	21	189	1 265	([4])
2008	15	72	1 954	0.01
2009	5	13	124	([4])
2010	11	45	302	([4])

[1]Days idle include all stoppages in effect during the reference period. For work stoppages that are still ongoing at the end of the calendar year, only those days of idleness during the calendar year are counted.
[2]Workers are counted more than once if involved in more than one stoppage during the reference period.
[3]Agricultural and government workers are included in the calculation of estimated working time; private household, forestry, and fishery workers are excluded.
[4]Less than 0.005 percent.
. . . = Not available.

Table 8-2. Union Affiliation of Employed Wage and Salary Workers, by Selected Characteristics, 2005–2010

(Numbers in thousands, percent.)

Characteristic	2005					2006					2007				
	Total employed	Member of union[1]		Represented by union[2]		Total employed	Member of union[1]		Represented by union[2]		Total employed	Member of union[1]		Represented by union[2]	
		Total	Percent of employed	Total	Percent of employed		Total	Percent of employed	Total	Percent of employed		Total	Percent of employed	Total	Percent of employed
SEX AND AGE															
Both Sexes, 16 Years and Over	125 889	15 685	12.5	17 223	13.7	128 237	15 359	12.0	16 860	13.1	129 767	15 670	12.1	17 243	13.3
16 to 24 years	19 283	878	4.6	1 019	5.3	19 538	857	4.4	978	5.0	19 395	939	4.8	1 068	5.5
25 years and over	106 606	14 808	13.9	16 204	15.2	108 699	14 502	13.3	15 883	14.6	110 372	14 731	13.3	16 176	14.7
25 to 34 years	28 450	3 044	10.7	3 368	11.8	28 805	2 899	10.1	3 195	11.1	29 409	3 050	10.4	3 358	11.4
35 to 44 years	30 654	4 211	13.7	4 579	14.9	30 526	3 997	13.1	4 356	14.3	30 296	3 972	13.1	4 362	14.4
45 to 54 years	28 714	4 731	16.5	5 158	18.0	29 401	4 710	16.0	5 131	17.5	29 731	4 664	15.7	5 087	17.1
55 to 64 years	15 158	2 496	16.5	2 732	18.0	16 095	2 568	16.0	2 832	17.6	16 752	2 691	16.1	2 967	17.7
65 years and over	3 631	325	8.9	366	10.1	3 872	328	8.5	370	9.5	4 183	355	8.5	402	9.6
Men, 16 Years and Over	65 466	8 870	13.5	9 597	14.7	66 811	8 657	13.0	9 360	14.0	67 468	8 767	13.0	9 494	14.1
16 to 24 years	9 860	523	5.3	603	6.1	10 130	543	5.4	608	6.0	9 959	551	5.5	627	6.3
25 years and over	55 606	8 347	15.0	8 994	16.2	56 682	8 114	14.3	8 752	15.4	57 509	8 217	14.3	8 867	15.4
25 to 34 years	15 559	1 754	11.3	1 915	12.3	15 677	1 650	10.5	1 793	11.4	15 994	1 736	10.9	1 884	11.8
35 to 44 years	16 196	2 422	15.0	2 582	15.9	16 159	2 309	14.3	2 488	15.4	16 070	2 318	14.4	2 501	15.6
45 to 54 years	14 421	2 658	18.4	2 849	19.8	14 867	2 617	17.6	2 807	18.9	15 040	2 578	17.1	2 745	18.3
55 to 64 years	7 606	1 346	17.7	1 458	19.2	7 990	1 370	17.1	1 474	18.4	8 286	1 403	16.9	1 532	18.5
65 years and over	1 824	167	9.1	190	10.4	1 989	167	8.4	190	9.6	2 119	181	8.5	205	9.7
Women, 16 Years and Over	60 423	6 815	11.3	7 626	12.6	61 426	6 702	10.9	7 501	12.2	62 299	6 903	11.1	7 749	12.4
16 to 24 years	9 423	354	3.8	417	4.4	9 408	315	3.3	370	3.9	9 436	388	4.1	441	4.7
25 years and over	51 000	6 461	12.7	7 210	14.1	52 018	6 388	12.3	7 131	13.7	52 863	6 514	12.3	7 308	13.8
25 to 34 years	12 891	1 290	10.0	1 454	11.3	13 127	1 249	9.5	1 401	10.7	13 416	1 313	9.8	1 474	11.0
35 to 44 years	14 457	1 790	12.4	1 997	13.8	14 368	1 687	11.7	1 867	13.0	14 226	1 653	11.6	1 861	13.1
45 to 54 years	14 293	2 073	14.5	2 309	16.2	14 534	2 093	14.4	2 325	16.0	14 691	2 086	14.2	2 341	15.9
55 to 64 years	7 552	1 150	15.2	1 274	16.9	8 106	1 198	14.8	1 358	16.8	8 466	1 288	15.2	1 435	17.0
65 years and over	1 806	158	8.8	176	9.8	1 883	160	8.5	180	9.5	2 065	174	8.4	197	9.5
RACE, HISPANIC ORIGIN, AND SEX															
White, 16 Years and Over[3]	102 967	12 520	12.2	13 755	13.4	104 668	12 259	11.7	13 424	12.8	105 515	12 487	11.8	13 715	13.0
Men	54 462	7 275	13.4	7 858	14.4	55 459	7 115	12.8	7 668	13.8	55 771	7 134	12.8	7 708	13.8
Women	48 505	5 245	10.8	5 897	12.2	49 209	5 144	10.5	5 756	11.7	49 743	5 352	10.8	6 007	12.1
Black, 16 Years and Over[3]	14 459	2 178	15.1	2 391	16.5	14 878	2 163	14.5	2 391	16.1	15 177	2 165	14.3	2 403	15.8
Men	6 603	1 062	16.1	1 166	17.7	6 788	1 056	15.6	1 158	17.1	6 945	1 097	15.8	1 205	17.3
Women	7 857	1 115	14.2	1 225	15.6	8 090	1 107	13.7	1 233	15.2	8 232	1 067	13.0	1 198	14.6
Asian, 16 Years and Over[3]	5 479	614	11.2	666	12.2	5 703	592	10.4	657	11.5	6 016	654	10.9	720	12.0
Men	2 881	314	10.9	337	11.7	3 015	286	9.5	316	10.5	3 168	324	10.2	348	11.0
Women	2 598	299	11.5	329	12.7	2 688	306	11.4	340	12.7	2 849	330	11.6	372	13.1
Hispanic, 16 Years and Over[4]	17 191	1 793	10.4	1 981	11.5	18 121	1 770	9.8	1 935	10.7	18 778	1 837	9.8	2 026	10.8
Men	10 324	1 093	10.6	1 185	11.5	10 842	1 064	9.8	1 144	10.6	11 163	1 108	9.9	1 208	10.8
Women	6 866	700	10.2	796	11.6	7 279	706	9.7	791	10.9	7 615	728	9.6	818	10.7
FULL- OR PART-TIME STATUS[5]															
Full-time workers	103 560	14 207	13.7	15 551	15.0	106 106	13 938	13.1	15 244	14.4	107 339	14 201	13.2	15 570	14.5
Part-time workers	22 052	1 441	6.5	1 630	7.4	21 863	1 382	6.3	1 573	7.2	22 172	1 437	6.5	1 635	7.4

[1]Data refer to members of a labor union or to an employee association similar to a union.

[2]Data refer to members of a labor union or to an employee association similar to a union, as well as to workers who report no union affiliation but whose jobs are covered by a union or an employee association contract.

[3]Beginning in 2003, persons who selected this race group only; persons who selected more than one race group are not included. Prior to 2003, persons who reported more than one race group were included in the group they identified as their main race. Additionally, estimates for the above race groups (White, Black, and Asian) do not sum to totals because data are not presented for all races.

[4]May be of any race.

[5]The distinction between full- and part-time workers is based on hours usually worked. Data will not sum to totals because full- or part-time status on the principal job is not identifiable for a small number of multiple job holders.

Table 8-2. Union Affiliation of Employed Wage and Salary Workers, by Selected Characteristics, 2005–2010
—Continued

(Numbers in thousands, percent.)

Characteristic	2008					2009					2010				
	Total employed	Member of union[1]		Represented by union[2]		Total employed	Member of union[1]		Represented by union[2]		Total employed	Member of union[1]		Represented by union[2]	
		Total	Percent of employed	Total	Percent of employed		Total	Percent of employed	Total	Percent of employed		Total	Percent of employed	Total	Percent of employed
SEX AND AGE															
Both Sexes, 16 Years and Over	129 377	16 098	12.4	17 761	13.7	124 490	15 327	12.3	16 904	13.6	124 073	14 715	11.9	16 290	13.1
16 to 24 years	18 705	930	5.0	1 062	5.7	17 173	813	4.7	941	5.5	16 638	722	4.3	836	5.0
25 years and over	110 672	15 168	13.7	16 699	15.1	107 317	14 514	13.5	15 962	14.9	107 435	13 993	13.0	15 453	14.4
25 to 34 years	29 276	3 120	10.7	3 443	11.8	28 067	2 942	10.5	3 262	11.6	28 363	2 860	10.1	3 179	11.2
35 to 44 years	29 708	3 993	13.4	4 365	14.7	28 066	3 669	13.1	4 035	14.4	27 356	3 512	12.8	3 888	14.2
45 to 54 years	29 787	4 767	16.0	5 228	17.6	29 054	4 551	15.7	4 994	17.2	28 860	4 340	15.0	4 774	16.5
55 to 64 years	17 430	2 887	16.6	3 209	18.4	17 599	2 926	16.6	3 186	18.1	18 199	2 849	15.7	3 126	17.2
65 years and over	4 471	401	9.0	454	10.2	4 530	425	9.4	485	10.7	4 657	432	9.3	486	10.4
Men, 16 Years and Over	66 846	8 938	13.4	9 724	14.5	63 539	8 441	13.3	9 176	14.4	63 531	7 994	12.6	8 761	13.8
16 to 24 years	9 537	555	5.8	617	6.5	8 555	493	5.8	560	6.5	8 291	419	5.0	476	5.7
25 years and over	57 309	8 383	14.6	9 107	15.9	54 984	7 947	14.5	8 616	15.7	55 240	7 575	13.7	8 286	15.0
25 to 34 years	15 780	1 750	11.1	1 909	12.1	14 952	1 633	10.9	1 786	11.9	15 148	1 603	10.6	1 759	11.6
35 to 44 years	15 653	2 307	14.7	2 491	15.9	14 679	2 077	14.1	2 250	15.3	14 430	1 966	13.6	2 151	14.9
45 to 54 years	14 988	2 608	17.4	2 812	18.8	14 421	2 492	17.3	2 693	18.7	14 423	2 349	16.3	2 554	17.7
55 to 64 years	8 657	1 525	17.6	1 682	19.4	8 647	1 536	17.8	1 654	19.1	8 895	1 430	16.1	1 566	17.6
65 years and over	2 230	193	8.7	213	9.6	2 285	211	9.2	233	10.2	2 343	227	9.7	256	10.9
Women, 16 Years and Over	62 532	7 160	11.4	8 036	12.9	60 951	6 887	11.3	7 727	12.7	60 542	6 722	11.1	7 528	12.4
16 to 24 years	9 168	374	4.1	445	4.8	8 619	320	3.7	381	4.4	8 347	303	3.6	361	4.3
25 years and over	53 364	6 785	12.7	7 592	14.2	52 333	6 567	12.5	7 346	14.0	52 195	6 418	12.3	7 167	13.7
25 to 34 years	13 496	1 370	10.1	1 534	11.4	13 116	1 309	10.0	1 476	11.3	13 215	1 257	9.5	1 420	10.7
35 to 44 years	14 055	1 685	12.0	1 874	13.3	13 387	1 593	11.9	1 785	13.3	12 926	1 546	12.0	1 737	13.4
45 to 54 years	14 799	2 159	14.6	2 416	16.3	14 633	2 060	14.1	2 302	15.7	14 437	1 991	13.8	2 219	15.4
55 to 64 years	8 773	1 363	15.5	1 527	17.4	8 952	1 390	15.5	1 532	17.1	9 303	1 419	15.3	1 560	16.8
65 years and over	2 241	208	9.3	241	10.7	2 245	215	9.6	252	11.2	2 314	205	8.8	230	10.0
RACE, HISPANIC ORIGIN, AND SEX															
White, 16 Years and Over[3]	105 052	12 863	12.2	14 222	13.5	101 581	12 330	12.1	13 595	13.4	101 042	11 865	11.7	13 111	13.0
Men	55 197	7 309	13.2	7 961	14.4	52 691	6 918	13.1	7 512	14.3	52 565	6 588	12.5	7 208	13.7
Women	49 855	5 555	11.1	6 261	12.6	48 889	5 412	11.1	6 083	12.4	48 477	5 277	10.9	5 903	12.2
Black, 16 Years and Over[3]	15 030	2 178	14.5	2 370	15.8	14 127	1 966	13.9	2 172	15.4	14 195	1 896	13.4	2 115	14.9
Men	6 809	1 081	15.9	1 159	17.0	6 257	964	15.4	1 046	16.7	6 347	938	14.8	1 031	16.2
Women	8 221	1 097	13.3	1 211	14.7	7 870	1 002	12.7	1 126	14.3	7 848	958	12.2	1 085	13.8
Asian, 16 Years and Over[3]	6 157	653	10.6	714	11.6	5 847	664	11.4	730	12.5	5 900	645	10.9	713	12.1
Men	3 216	310	9.6	339	10.6	3 075	332	10.8	370	12.0	3 112	292	9.4	325	10.4
Women	2 941	344	11.7	374	12.7	2 772	333	12.0	361	13.0	2 787	353	12.6	388	13.9
Hispanic, 16 Years and Over[4]	18 572	1 960	10.6	2 168	11.7	18 034	1 841	10.2	2 036	11.3	18 263	1 820	10.0	2 021	11.1
Men	10 998	1 204	11.0	1 317	12.0	10 518	1 108	10.5	1 199	11.4	10 646	1 090	10.2	1 196	11.2
Women	7 574	756	10.0	852	11.2	7 515	733	9.7	836	11.1	7 616	730	9.6	825	10.8
FULL- OR PART-TIME STATUS[5]															
Full-time workers	106 648	14 561	13.7	16 029	15.0	99 820	13 602	13.6	14 960	15.0	99 531	13 125	13.2	14 498	14.6
Part-time workers	22 497	1 505	6.7	1 697	7.5	24 431	1 698	7.0	1 913	7.8	24 351	1 560	6.4	1 760	7.2

[1] Data refer to members of a labor union or to an employee association similar to a union.

[2] Data refer to members of a labor union or to an employee association similar to a union, as well as to workers who report no union affiliation but whose jobs are covered by a union or an employee association contract.

[3] Beginning in 2003, persons who selected this race group only; persons who selected more than one race group are not included. Prior to 2003, persons who reported more than one race group were included in the group they identified as their main race. Additionally, estimates for the above race groups (White, Black, and Asian) do not sum to totals because data are not presented for all races.

[4] May be of any race.

[5] The distinction between full- and part-time workers is based on hours usually worked. Data will not sum to totals because full- or part-time status on the principal job is not identifiable for a small number of multiple job holders.

Table 8-3. Union Affiliation of Wage and Salary Workers, by Occupation and Industry, 2009–2010

(Thousands of people, percent.)

Occupation and industry	2009					2010				
	Total employed	Member of union[1]		Represented by union[2]		Total employed	Member of union[1]		Represented by union[2]	
		Total	Percent of employed	Total	Percent of employed		Total	Percent of employed	Total	Percent of employed
OCCUPATION										
Management, professional, and related	44 845	6 027	13.4	6 821	15.2	44 871	5 867	13.1	6 674	14.9
Management, business, and financial operations	16 978	822	4.8	997	5.9	16 684	782	4.7	973	5.8
Management	11 548	473	4.1	585	5.1	11 386	476	4.2	599	5.3
Business and financial operations	5 430	348	6.4	412	7.6	5 299	306	5.8	373	7.0
Professional and related	27 867	5 206	18.7	5 824	20.9	28 187	5 085	18.0	5 701	20.2
Computer and mathematical	3 306	175	5.3	207	6.3	3 350	136	4.0	180	5.4
Architecture and engineering	2 512	194	7.7	228	9.1	2 468	197	8.0	244	9.9
Life, physical, and social science	1 220	122	10.0	141	11.6	1 256	126	10.1	145	11.5
Community and social service	2 269	366	16.1	396	17.5	2 260	362	16.0	390	17.3
Legal	1 335	79	5.9	97	7.3	1 352	72	5.3	87	6.4
Education, training, and library	8 318	3 172	38.1	3 503	42.1	8 415	3 123	37.1	3 441	40.9
Arts, design, entertainment, sports, and media	1 840	136	7.4	157	8.5	1 899	112	5.9	139	7.3
Health care practitioner and technical	7 067	962	13.6	1 096	15.5	7 188	957	13.3	1 076	15.0
Services	22 364	2 588	11.6	2 830	12.7	22 463	2 467	11.0	2 683	11.9
Health care support	3 159	317	10.0	353	11.2	3 214	268	8.4	296	9.2
Protective service	3 120	1 111	35.6	1 180	37.8	3 287	1 122	34.1	1 202	36.6
Food preparation and serving related	7 621	334	4.4	389	5.1	7 555	297	3.9	328	4.3
Building and grounds cleaning and maintenance	4 592	521	11.3	570	12.4	4 549	469	10.3	518	11.4
Personal care and service	3 873	306	7.9	338	8.7	3 858	311	8.0	338	8.8
Sales and office	30 998	2 231	7.2	2 499	8.1	30 673	2 113	6.9	2 388	7.8
Sales and related	13 331	411	3.1	480	3.6	13 033	418	3.2	496	3.8
Office and administrative support	17 667	1 820	10.3	2 019	11.4	17 641	1 695	9.6	1 892	10.7
Natural resources, construction, and maintenance	11 231	1 989	17.7	2 088	18.6	10 879	1 808	16.6	1 912	17.6
Farming, fishing, and forestry	880	24	2.8	26	2.9	869	30	3.4	36	4.1
Construction and extraction	5 820	1 220	21.0	1 269	21.8	5 579	1 050	18.8	1 100	19.7
Installation, maintenance, and repair	4 531	744	16.4	793	17.5	4 431	728	16.4	776	17.5
Production, transportation, and material moving	15 052	2 492	16.6	2 666	17.7	15 186	2 460	16.2	2 633	17.3
Production	7 309	1 082	14.8	1 164	15.9	7 540	1 144	15.2	1 210	16.1
Transportation and material moving	7 742	1 410	18.2	1 502	19.4	7 647	1 316	17.2	1 423	18.6
INDUSTRY										
Private sector	103 357	7 431	7.2	8 226	8.0	103 040	7 092	6.9	7 884	7.7
Agriculture and related industries	1 045	12	1.1	14	1.4	1 131	18	1.6	23	2.0
Nonagricultural industries	102 312	7 419	7.3	8 212	8.0	101 909	7 074	6.9	7 861	7.7
Mining	662	57	8.6	63	9.5	695	55	8.0	61	8.8
Construction	6 613	958	14.5	993	15.0	6 103	801	13.1	838	13.7
Manufacturing	13 454	1 470	10.9	1 595	11.9	13 252	1 418	10.7	1 538	11.6
Durable goods	8 438	907	10.8	985	11.7	8 268	835	10.1	909	11.0
Nondurable goods	5 016	562	11.2	610	12.2	4 984	584	11.7	629	12.6
Wholesale and retail trade	17 851	937	5.3	1 032	5.8	17 800	860	4.8	949	5.3
Wholesale trade	3 386	167	4.9	185	5.5	3 321	173	5.2	186	5.6
Retail trade	14 465	770	5.3	847	5.9	14 479	687	4.7	763	5.3
Transportation and utilities	5 162	1 144	22.2	1 210	23.4	5 195	1 134	21.8	1 203	23.2
Transportation and warehousing	4 256	908	21.3	960	22.6	4 286	877	20.5	928	21.6
Utilities	906	237	26.1	249	27.5	909	257	28.3	275	30.3
Information[3]	2 790	280	10.0	312	11.2	2 743	265	9.6	299	10.9
Publishing, except Internet	633	34	5.3	41	6.5	577	29	5.0	38	6.5
Motion pictures and sound recording	331	42	12.8	43	13.0	341	32	9.3	36	10.6
Broadcasting, except Internet	534	25	4.7	30	5.5	561	29	5.1	38	6.8
Telecommunications	1 088	174	16.0	192	17.7	1 054	167	15.8	177	16.8
Financial activities	8 236	150	1.8	193	2.3	8 072	160	2.0	206	2.5
Finance and insurance	6 199	88	1.4	120	1.9	6 108	79	1.3	110	1.8
Finance	4 043	56	1.4	73	1.8	3 985	44	1.1	65	1.6
Insurance	2 155	32	1.5	48	2.2	2 123	35	1.6	45	2.1
Real estate and rental and leasing	2 037	61	3.0	73	3.6	1 964	81	4.1	95	4.9
Professional and business services	11 325	256	2.3	314	2.8	11 738	315	2.7	388	3.3
Professional and technical services	6 915	78	1.1	107	1.5	6 980	98	1.4	134	1.9
Management, administrative, and waste services	4 410	178	4.0	207	4.7	4 757	217	4.6	254	5.3
Education and health services	19 269	1 655	8.6	1 912	9.9	19 804	1 608	8.1	1 858	9.4
Education services	3 816	494	12.9	580	15.2	3 964	517	13.0	599	15.1
Health care and social assistance	15 454	1 161	7.5	1 332	8.6	15 840	1 091	6.9	1 259	7.9
Leisure and hospitality	11 352	349	3.1	407	3.6	11 111	301	2.7	337	3.0
Arts, entertainment, and recreation	2 143	138	6.4	152	7.1	2 111	113	5.3	126	5.9
Accommodation and food services	9 209	211	2.3	255	2.8	8 999	188	2.1	212	2.4
Accommodation	1 390	108	7.8	115	8.3	1 345	106	7.9	112	8.3
Food services and drinking places	7 819	103	1.3	140	1.8	7 654	82	1.1	100	1.3
Other services[3]	5 598	164	2.9	182	3.2	5 397	158	2.9	184	3.4
Other services, except private households	4 775	147	3.1	163	3.4	4 726	152	3.2	178	3.8
Public sector	21 133	7 896	37.4	8 677	41.1	21 033	7 623	36.2	8 406	40.0
Federal government	3 594	1 005	28.0	1 192	33.2	3 670	984	26.8	1 154	31.4
State government	6 294	2 025	32.2	2 222	35.3	6 328	1 969	31.1	2 191	34.6
Local government	11 244	4 867	43.3	5 263	46.8	11 035	4 670	42.3	5 061	45.9

Note: Updated population controls are introduced annually with the release of January data. Data refer to the sole or principal job of full- and part-time workers. Excluded are all self-employed workers, regardless of whether or not their businesses are incorporated.

[1]Data refer to members of a labor union or an employee association similar to a union.
[2]Data refer to members of a labor union or an employee association similar to a union, as well as to workers who report no union affiliation but whose jobs are covered by a union or an employee association contract.
[3]Includes other industries, not shown separately.

Table 8-4. Median Weekly Earnings of Full-Time Wage and Salary Workers, by Union Affiliation, Occupation, and Industry, 2009–2010

(Dollars.)

Occupation and industry	2009				2010			
	Total	Member of union[1]	Represented by union[2]	Non-union	Total	Member of union[1]	Represented by union[2]	Non-union
OCCUPATION								
Management, professional, and related	1 044	1 047	1 040	1 045	1 063	1 059	1 055	1 064
Management, business, and financial operations	1 138	1 116	1 123	1 139	1 155	1 138	1 145	1 156
Management	1 208	1 192	1 208	1 208	1 230	1 161	1 187	1 231
Business and financial operations	996	1 002	1 009	995	1 036	1 082	1 048	1 035
Professional and related	994	1 036	1 026	983	1 008	1 047	1 040	998
Computer and mathematical	1 253	1 078	1 107	1 263	1 289	1 062	1 074	1 311
Architecture and engineering	1 266	1 230	1 210	1 271	1 255	1 238	1 285	1 252
Life, physical, and social science	1 059	1 099	1 135	1 040	1 062	1 166	1 160	1 038
Community and social service	783	957	948	746	802	980	955	759
Legal	1 200	1 266	1 258	1 191	1 213	1 329	1 358	1 199
Education, training, and library	887	1 010	996	782	913	1 023	1 008	811
Arts, design, entertainment, sports, and media	888	1 105	1 059	877	920	999	1 015	915
Health care practitioner and technical	970	1 089	1 070	952	986	1 095	1 098	967
Services	470	702	682	435	479	723	707	447
Health care support	472	518	518	464	471	514	503	467
Protective service	747	992	980	611	747	995	980	629
Food preparation and serving related	398	463	456	395	406	508	503	402
Building and grounds cleaning and maintenance	444	597	588	418	446	595	590	421
Personal care and service	440	576	567	429	455	575	564	440
Sales and office	624	768	761	613	631	752	745	621
Sales and related	665	678	673	665	666	683	678	665
Office and administrative support	612	782	773	595	619	762	754	607
Natural resources, construction, and maintenance	719	1 009	1 003	657	719	1 013	1 006	664
Farming, fishing, and forestry	416	([3])	([3])	411	416	([3])	([3])	412
Construction and extraction	718	1 023	1 011	643	709	1 029	1 019	633
Installation, maintenance, and repair	781	999	999	733	794	1 005	1 001	745
Production, transportation, and material moving	605	786	780	578	599	817	809	564
Production	610	783	778	587	599	811	801	569
Transportation and material moving	599	789	782	563	599	824	816	557
INDUSTRY								
Private sector	711	856	845	697	717	864	855	703
Agriculture and related industries	462	([3])	([3])	457	465	([3])	([3])	463
Nonagricultural industries	715	857	846	701	721	865	856	707
Mining	1 050	1 013	1 015	1 058	1 032	1 076	1 053	1 026
Construction	744	1 072	1 052	698	735	1 051	1 046	692
Manufacturing	767	800	799	762	767	828	817	759
Durable goods	806	836	832	801	806	878	866	796
Nondurable goods	706	735	741	698	700	760	749	690
Wholesale and retail trade	611	648	641	609	612	669	657	610
Wholesale trade	760	761	767	760	777	770	774	777
Retail trade	577	612	607	575	575	613	608	572
Transportation and utilities	798	975	964	748	823	1 000	994	765
Transportation and warehousing	749	923	911	707	765	934	928	725
Utilities	1 043	1 120	1 104	1 008	1 102	1 199	1 193	1 014
Information[4]	905	1 105	1 083	883	912	1 018	998	895
Publishing, except Internet	847	([3])	([3])	843	876	([3])	([3])	871
Motion pictures and sound recording	1 047	([3])	([3])	924	917	([3])	([3])	893
Broadcasting, except Internet	827	([3])	([3])	828	821	([3])	([3])	814
Telecommunications	964	1 095	1 079	924	987	1 039	1 023	974
Financial activities	839	843	831	839	849	806	799	852
Finance and insurance	881	845	837	882	902	819	829	905
Finance	889	842	817	892	902	([3])	870	903
Insurance	868	([3])	([3])	868	902	([3])	([3])	908
Real estate and rental and leasing	726	842	822	718	702	786	713	701
Professional and business services	864	761	748	868	855	751	754	859
Professional and technical services	1 094	1 081	1 096	1 094	1 124	1 157	1 147	1 123
Management, administrative, and waste services	560	658	640	553	542	598	592	536
Education and health services	715	839	838	698	731	849	846	717
Education services	819	886	879	795	852	900	875	846
Health care and social assistance	685	801	802	673	698	817	823	686
Leisure and hospitality	464	583	576	458	469	580	575	461
Arts, entertainment, and recreation	601	673	671	593	616	636	632	614
Accommodation and food services	423	526	505	421	430	530	524	424
Accommodation	505	582	582	496	508	547	553	502
Food services and drinking places	412	424	423	412	417	517	509	416
Other services[4]	605	886	862	599	615	866	862	609
Other services, except private households	627	893	868	620	636	880	874	627
Public sector	865	947	943	782	878	961	956	801
Federal government	1 002	981	989	1 019	1 012	977	987	1 040
State government	829	906	899	767	829	922	917	769
Local government	834	956	948	720	854	971	962	743

Note: Updated population controls are introduced annually with the release of January data. Data refer to the sole or principal job of full- and part-time workers. Excluded are all self-employed workers, regardless of whether or not their businesses are incorporated.

[1]Data refer to members of a labor union or an employee association similar to a union.
[2]Data refer to members of a labor union or an employee association similar to a union, as well as to workers who report no union affiliation but whose jobs are covered by a union or an employee association contract.
[3]Data not shown where base is less than 50,000.
[4]Includes other industries, not shown separately.

Table 8-5. Union or Employee Association Members Among Wage and Salary Employees, 1977–2010

(Numbers in thousands, percent.)

Year	Total wage and salary employment	Union or employee association member	Union or association members as a percent of total wage and salary employment
1977	81 334	19 335	23.8
1978	84 968	19 548	23.0
1979	87 117	20 986	24.1
1980	87 480	20 095	23.0
1981	. . .	. . .	. . .
1982	. . .	. . .	. . .
1983[1]	88 290	17 717	20.1
1984	92 194	17 340	18.8
1985	94 521	16 996	18.0
1986	96 903	16 975	17.5
1987	99 303	16 913	17.0
1988	101 407	17 002	16.8
1989	103 480	16 980	16.4
1990	103 905	16 740	16.1
1991	102 786	16 568	16.1
1992	103 688	16 390	15.8
1993	105 087	16 598	15.8
1994[2]	107 989	16 748	15.5
1995	110 038	16 360	14.9
1996	111 960	16 269	14.5
1997	114 533	16 110	14.1
1998	116 730	16 211	13.9
1999	118 963	16 477	13.9
2000	120 786	16 258	13.5
2001	122 482	16 387	13.4
2002	121 826	16 145	13.3
2003	122 358	15 776	12.9
2004	123 554	15 472	12.5
2005	125 889	15 685	12.5
2006	128 237	15 359	12.0
2007	129 767	15 670	12.1
2008	129 377	16 098	12.4
2009	124 490	15 327	12.3
2010	124 073	14 715	11.9

[1]Annual average data beginning in 1983 are not directly comparable with the data for 1977–1980.
[2]Data beginning in 1994 are not strictly comparable with data for 1993 and earlier years because of the introduction of a major redesign of the Current Population Survey questionnaire and collection methodology and the introduction of 1990 census–based population controls.
. . . = Not available.

Table 8-6. Union Affiliation of Employed Wage and Salary Workers, by State, 2009–2010

(Numbers in thousands, percent.)

State	2009					2010				
	Total employed	Member of union[1]		Represented by union[2]		Total employed	Member of union[1]		Represented by union[2]	
		Total	Percent of employed	Total	Percent of employed		Total	Percent of employed	Total	Percent of employed
UNITED STATES	124 490	15 327	12.3	16 904	13.6	124 073	14 715	11.9	16 290	13.1
Alabama	1 763	191	10.9	212	12.0	1 809	183	10.1	203	11.2
Alaska	293	65	22.3	69	23.6	295	68	22.9	73	24.8
Arizona	2 471	162	6.5	194	7.9	2 507	161	6.4	203	8.1
Arkansas	1 103	47	4.2	55	5.0	1 082	44	4.0	59	5.4
California	14 297	2 453	17.2	2 622	18.3	13 892	2 431	17.5	2 578	18.6
Colorado	2 175	153	7.0	181	8.3	2 130	140	6.6	171	8.0
Connecticut	1 538	265	17.3	282	18.4	1 549	258	16.7	270	17.4
Delaware	367	44	11.9	47	12.8	352	40	11.4	44	12.5
District of Columbia	276	29	10.4	35	12.5	287	26	9.0	30	10.5
Florida	7 097	411	5.8	489	6.9	7 033	392	5.6	488	6.9
Georgia	3 869	177	4.6	226	5.9	3 792	153	4.0	191	5.0
Hawaii	526	123	23.5	128	24.3	511	111	21.8	120	23.5
Idaho	577	36	6.3	46	7.9	584	42	7.1	50	8.6
Illinois	5 435	951	17.5	997	18.3	5 434	844	15.5	891	16.4
Indiana	2 612	277	10.6	319	12.2	2 554	279	10.9	313	12.2
Iowa	1 398	156	11.1	185	13.3	1 393	158	11.4	192	13.8
Kansas	1 249	77	6.2	104	8.4	1 222	84	6.8	111	9.1
Kentucky	1 657	142	8.6	173	10.5	1 642	147	8.9	166	10.1
Louisiana	1 704	99	5.8	110	6.5	1 742	76	4.3	96	5.5
Maine	543	63	11.7	74	13.7	543	63	11.6	71	13.0
Maryland	2 555	323	12.6	366	14.3	2 558	296	11.6	329	12.9
Massachusetts	2 864	476	16.6	516	18.0	2 866	415	14.5	446	15.6
Michigan	3 785	710	18.8	752	19.9	3 806	627	16.5	659	17.3
Minnesota	2 400	362	15.1	377	15.7	2 468	385	15.6	397	16.1
Mississippi	1 029	49	4.8	66	6.4	1 037	46	4.5	58	5.6
Missouri	2 481	234	9.4	264	10.6	2 469	244	9.9	274	11.1
Montana	374	52	13.9	68	18.1	364	46	12.7	52	14.4
Nebraska	823	76	9.2	94	11.4	813	75	9.3	96	11.8
Nevada	1 097	173	15.7	188	17.2	1 012	151	15.0	170	16.8
New Hampshire	616	67	10.8	76	12.3	622	63	10.2	73	11.7
New Jersey	3 734	721	19.3	742	19.9	3 734	637	17.1	660	17.7
New Mexico	759	51	6.7	77	10.2	750	55	7.3	72	9.7
New York	8 021	2 019	25.2	2 182	27.2	8 078	1 959	24.2	2 099	26.0
North Carolina	3 707	115	3.1	162	4.4	3 686	117	3.2	180	4.9
North Dakota	301	21	6.8	30	9.8	313	23	7.4	28	9.1
Ohio	4 827	685	14.2	742	15.4	4 787	655	13.7	702	14.7
Oklahoma	1 456	83	5.7	107	7.3	1 418	77	5.5	99	6.9
Oregon	1 471	250	17.0	272	18.5	1 515	245	16.2	268	17.7
Pennsylvania	5 220	782	15.0	844	16.2	5 224	770	14.7	831	15.9
Rhode Island	444	80	17.9	83	18.7	456	75	16.4	79	17.4
South Carolina	1 672	75	4.5	91	5.4	1 713	80	4.6	107	6.2
South Dakota	357	20	5.5	24	6.6	357	20	5.6	24	6.6
Tennessee	2 387	121	5.1	156	6.6	2 477	115	4.7	142	5.8
Texas	9 920	508	5.1	615	6.2	10 025	545	5.4	677	6.7
Utah	1 136	79	6.9	90	8.0	1 144	75	6.5	96	8.4
Vermont	285	35	12.3	40	14.1	289	34	11.8	40	13.6
Virginia	3 503	166	4.7	191	5.4	3 473	161	4.6	196	5.7
Washington	2 847	574	20.2	612	21.5	2 837	552	19.4	605	21.3
West Virginia	699	97	13.9	108	15.4	677	100	14.8	111	16.5
Wisconsin	2 528	385	15.2	400	15.8	2 508	355	14.2	380	15.1
Wyoming	239	18	7.7	20	8.3	246	18	7.4	21	8.4

Note: Updated population controls are introduced annually with the release of January data. Data refer to the sole or principal job of full- and part-time workers. Excluded are all self-employed workers, regardless of whether or not their businesses are incorporated.

[1]Data refer to members of a labor union or an employee association similar to a union.
[2]Data refer to members of a labor union or an employee association similar to a union, as well as to workers who report no union affiliation but whose jobs are covered by a union or an employee association contract.

Chapter Nine

PRICES

PRICES

HIGHLIGHTS

This chapter examines the movement of prices, which is one of the most important indicators of the state of the economy. Several indexes are covered: the Producer Price Index (PPI), which gives information about prices received by producers; the Consumer Price Index (CPI), which gives information about prices paid by consumers; and the Import Price Index (MPI) and the Export Price Index (XPI), which give information about prices involved in various foreign trade, export, and import price indexes.

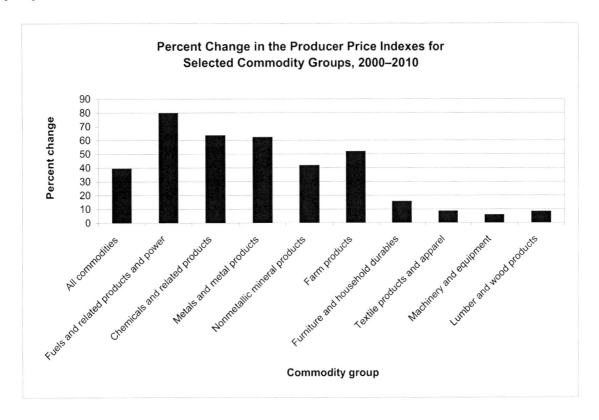

From 2000 through 2010, the producer price index for all commodities grew 39.2 percent. Fuels and related products and power (79.5 percent), chemicals and related products (63.3 percent), and metals and metal products (62.1 percent) experienced the fastest growth while textile products (8.5 percent), lumber and wood products (8.1 percent), and machinery and equipment (5.7 percent) grew at a far slower pace. (See Table 9-2.)

OTHER HIGHLIGHTS

- The PPI for all commodities grew 6.8 percent in 2010 after declining in 2009 for the first time since 2002. (See Table 9-2.)

- While the PPI for most commodities increased in 2010, it decreased for nonmetallic mineral products (-0.3 percent) and machinery and equipment (-0.2 percent). Fuels and related products and power (17.1 percent) and hides, leather and related products (15.5 percent) experienced the greatest increase between 2009 and 2010. (See Table 9-2.)

- The PPI for finished capital equipment continued to grow at a much slower rate (0.4 percent) than the PPI for consumer goods (5.6 percent) and the PPI for all finished goods (4.2 percent) in 2010. (See Table 9-1.)

NOTES AND DEFINITIONS

PRODUCER PRICE INDEX

Coverage

The *Producer Price Index (PPI)* measures average changes in prices received by domestic producers of goods and services. PPIs measure price change from the perspective of the seller. This contrasts with other measures, such as the Consumer Price Index (CPI). CPIs measure price change from the purchaser's perspective. Sellers' and purchasers' prices can differ due to government subsidies, sales and excise taxes, and distribution costs.

Over 25,000 establishments provide approximately 100,000 price quotations per month. Establishments report selling prices on the Tuesday that includes the 13th of each month and they usually respond by mail.

PPIs are typically organized into one of three groups: (1) stage-of-processing indexes, (2) commodity indexes, and (3) indexes for the net output of industries and their products. The stage-of-processing structure organizes products by class of buyer and degree of fabrication. The commodity structure organizes products by similarity of end use or material composition. The entire output of various industries is sampled to derive price indexes for the net output of industries and their products.

Within the stage-of-processing system, finished goods are commodities that will not undergo further processing and that are ready for sale to the final demand user—either an individual consumer or a business firm. Consumer foods include unprocessed foods, such as eggs and fresh vegetables, and processed foods, such as bakery products and meats. Other finished consumer goods include durable goods, such as automobiles, household furniture, and appliances; and

nondurable goods, such as apparel and home heating oil. Capital equipment includes producer durable goods, such as heavy motor trucks, tractors, and machine tools.

The stage-of-processing category for intermediate materials, supplies, and components includes commodities that have been processed but require further processing, such as flour, cotton, yarn, steel mill products, and lumber. The intermediate goods category also encompasses physically complete nondurable goods purchased by business firms as inputs for their operations, such as diesel fuel, belts and belting, paper boxes, and fertilizers.

Crude materials for further processing are products entering the market for the first time that have not been manufactured or fabricated; these products will not be sold directly to consumers. Crude foodstuffs and feedstuffs includes items such as grains and livestock; examples of crude nonfood materials include raw cotton, crude petroleum, coal, hides and skins, and iron and steel scrap.

PPIs for the net output of industries and their products are grouped according to the North American Industry Classification System (NAICS). Prior to the release of January 2004, industry-based PPIs were published according to the Standard Industrial Classification (SIC) system. Industry price indexes are compatible with other economic time series organized by industry, such as data on employment, wages, and productivity.

Sources of Additional Information

For more information on the underlying concepts and methodology of the Producer Price Index, see Chapter 14 in the *BLS Handbook of Methods*, which is available on the BLS Web site at <http://www.bls.gov/opub/hom/>.

Table 9-1. Producer Price Indexes, by Stage of Processing, 1947–2010

(1982 = 100.)

Year	Crude materials for further processing				Intermediate materials, supplies, and components						Finished goods		
	Total	Foodstuffs and feedstuffs	Nonfood materials, except fuel	Fuel	Total	Materials and components for construction	Components for manufacturing	Processed fuels and lubricants	Containers	Supplies	Total	Consumer goods	Capital equipment
1947	31.7	45.1	24.0	7.5	23.3	22.5	21.3	14.4	23.4	28.5	26.4	28.6	19.8
1948	34.7	48.8	26.7	8.9	25.2	24.9	23.0	16.4	24.4	29.8	28.5	30.8	21.6
1949	30.1	40.5	24.3	8.8	24.2	24.9	23.4	14.9	24.5	28.0	27.7	29.4	22.7
1950	32.7	43.4	27.8	8.8	25.3	26.2	24.3	15.2	25.2	29.0	28.2	29.9	23.2
1951	37.6	50.2	32.0	9.0	28.4	28.7	27.6	15.9	29.6	32.6	30.8	32.7	25.5
1952	34.5	47.3	27.8	9.0	27.5	28.5	27.6	15.7	28.0	32.6	30.6	32.3	25.9
1953	31.9	42.3	26.6	9.3	27.7	29.0	28.1	15.8	28.0	31.0	30.3	31.7	26.3
1954	31.6	42.3	26.1	8.9	27.9	29.1	28.3	15.8	28.5	31.7	30.4	31.7	26.7
1955	30.4	38.4	27.5	8.9	28.4	30.3	29.5	15.8	28.9	31.2	30.5	31.5	27.4
1956	30.6	37.6	28.6	9.5	29.6	31.8	32.2	16.3	31.0	32.0	31.3	32.0	29.5
1957	31.2	39.2	28.2	10.1	30.3	32.0	33.5	17.2	32.4	32.3	32.5	32.9	31.3
1958	31.9	41.6	27.1	10.2	30.4	32.0	33.8	16.2	33.2	33.1	33.2	33.6	32.1
1959	31.1	38.8	28.1	10.4	30.8	32.9	34.2	16.2	33.0	33.5	33.1	33.3	32.7
1960	30.4	38.4	26.9	10.5	30.8	32.7	34.0	16.6	33.4	33.3	33.4	33.6	32.8
1961	30.2	37.9	27.2	10.5	30.6	32.2	33.7	16.8	33.2	33.7	33.4	33.6	32.9
1962	30.5	38.6	27.1	10.4	30.6	32.1	33.4	16.7	33.6	34.5	33.5	33.7	33.0
1963	29.9	37.5	26.7	10.5	30.7	32.2	33.4	16.6	33.2	35.0	33.4	33.5	33.1
1964	29.6	36.6	27.2	10.5	30.8	32.5	33.7	16.2	32.9	34.7	33.5	33.6	33.4
1965	31.1	39.2	27.7	10.6	31.2	32.8	34.2	16.5	33.5	35.0	34.1	34.2	33.8
1966	33.1	42.7	28.3	10.9	32.0	33.6	35.4	16.8	34.5	36.5	35.2	35.4	34.6
1967	31.3	40.3	26.5	11.3	32.2	34.0	36.5	16.9	35.0	36.8	35.6	35.6	35.8
1968	31.8	40.9	27.1	11.5	33.0	35.7	37.3	16.5	35.9	37.1	36.6	36.5	37.0
1969	33.9	44.1	28.4	12.0	34.1	37.7	38.5	16.6	37.2	37.8	38.0	37.9	38.3
1970	35.2	45.2	29.1	13.8	35.4	38.3	40.6	17.7	39.0	39.7	39.3	39.1	40.1
1971	36.0	46.1	29.4	15.7	36.8	40.8	41.9	19.5	40.8	40.8	40.5	40.2	41.7
1972	39.9	51.5	32.3	16.8	38.2	43.0	42.9	20.1	42.7	42.5	41.8	41.5	42.8
1973	54.5	72.6	42.9	18.6	42.4	46.5	44.3	22.2	45.2	51.7	45.6	46.0	44.2
1974	61.4	76.4	54.5	24.8	52.5	55.0	51.1	33.6	53.3	56.8	52.6	53.1	50.5
1975	61.6	77.4	50.0	30.6	58.0	60.1	57.8	39.4	60.0	61.8	58.2	58.2	58.2
1976	63.4	76.8	54.9	34.5	60.9	64.1	60.8	42.3	63.1	65.8	60.8	60.4	62.1
1977	65.5	77.5	56.3	42.0	64.9	69.3	64.5	47.7	65.9	69.3	64.7	64.3	66.1
1978	73.4	87.3	61.9	48.2	69.5	76.5	69.2	49.9	71.0	72.9	69.8	69.4	71.3
1979	85.9	100.0	75.5	57.3	78.4	84.2	75.8	61.6	79.4	80.2	77.6	77.5	77.5
1980	95.3	104.6	91.8	69.4	90.3	91.3	84.6	85.0	89.1	89.9	88.0	88.6	85.8
1981	103.0	103.9	109.8	84.8	98.6	97.9	94.7	100.6	96.7	96.9	96.1	96.6	94.6
1982	100.0	100.0	100.0	100.0	100.0	100.0	100.0	100.0	100.0	100.0	100.0	100.0	100.0
1983	101.3	101.8	98.8	105.1	100.6	102.8	102.4	95.4	100.4	101.8	101.6	101.3	102.8
1984	103.5	104.7	101.0	105.1	103.1	105.6	105.0	95.7	105.9	104.1	103.7	103.3	105.2
1985	95.8	94.8	94.3	102.7	102.7	107.3	106.4	92.8	109.0	104.4	104.7	103.8	107.5
1986	87.7	93.2	76.0	92.2	99.1	108.1	107.5	72.7	110.3	105.6	103.2	101.4	109.7
1987	93.7	96.2	88.5	84.1	101.5	109.8	108.8	73.3	114.5	107.7	105.4	103.6	111.7
1988	96.0	106.1	85.9	82.1	107.1	116.1	112.3	71.2	120.1	113.7	108.0	106.2	114.3
1989	103.1	111.2	95.8	85.3	112.0	121.3	116.4	76.4	125.4	118.1	113.6	112.1	118.8
1990	108.9	113.1	107.3	84.8	114.5	122.9	119.0	85.9	127.7	119.4	119.2	118.2	122.9
1991	101.2	105.5	97.5	82.9	114.4	124.5	121.0	85.3	128.1	121.4	121.7	120.5	126.7
1992	100.4	105.1	94.2	84.0	114.7	126.5	122.0	84.5	127.7	122.7	123.2	121.7	129.1
1993	102.4	108.4	94.1	87.1	116.2	132.0	123.0	84.7	126.4	125.0	124.7	123.0	131.4
1994	101.8	106.5	97.0	82.4	118.5	136.6	124.3	83.1	129.7	127.0	125.5	123.3	134.1
1995	102.7	105.8	105.8	72.1	124.9	142.1	126.5	84.2	148.8	132.1	127.9	125.6	136.7
1996	113.8	121.5	105.7	92.6	125.7	143.6	126.9	90.0	141.1	135.9	131.3	129.5	138.3
1997	111.1	112.2	103.5	101.3	125.6	146.5	126.4	89.3	136.0	135.9	131.8	130.2	138.2
1998	96.8	103.9	84.5	86.7	123.0	146.8	125.9	81.1	140.8	134.8	130.7	128.9	137.6
1999	98.2	98.7	91.1	91.2	123.2	148.9	125.7	84.6	142.5	134.2	133.0	132.0	137.6
2000	120.6	100.2	118.0	136.9	129.2	150.7	126.2	102.0	151.6	136.9	138.0	138.2	138.8
2001	121.0	106.1	101.5	151.4	129.7	150.6	126.4	104.5	153.1	138.7	140.7	141.5	139.7
2002	108.1	99.5	101.0	117.3	127.8	151.3	126.1	96.3	152.1	138.9	138.9	139.4	139.1
2003	135.3	113.5	116.9	185.7	133.7	153.6	125.9	112.6	153.7	141.5	143.3	145.3	139.5
2004	159.0	127.0	149.2	211.4	142.6	166.4	127.4	124.3	159.3	146.7	148.5	151.7	141.4
2005	182.2	122.7	176.7	279.7	154.0	176.6	129.9	150.0	167.1	151.9	155.7	160.4	144.6
2006	184.8	119.3	210.0	241.5	164.0	188.4	134.5	162.8	175.0	157.0	160.4	166.0	146.9
2007	207.1	146.7	238.7	236.8	170.7	192.5	136.3	173.9	180.3	161.7	166.6	173.5	149.5
2008	251.8	163.4	308.5	298.3	188.3	205.4	140.3	206.2	191.8	173.8	177.1	186.3	153.8
2009	175.2	134.5	211.1	166.3	172.5	202.9	141.0	161.9	195.8	172.2	172.5	179.1	156.7
2010	212.2	152.4	280.8	188.0	183.4	205.7	142.2	185.2	201.2	175.0	179.8	189.1	157.3

Table 9-2. Producer Price Indexes, by Commodity Group, 1913–2010

(1982 = 100.)

Year	All commodities	Farm products	Processed foods and feeds	Industrial commodities													
				Total	Textile products and apparel	Hides, leather, and related products	Fuels and related products and power	Chemicals and related products	Rubber and plastics products	Lumber and wood products	Pulp, paper, and allied products	Metals and metal products	Machinery and equipment	Furniture and household durables	Nonmetallic mineral products	Transportation equipment	Miscellaneous products
1913	12.0	18.0	...	11.9	...	...	...	...	...	...	...	...	...	...	...	...	...
1914	11.8	17.9	...	11.3	...	...	...	...	...	...	...	...	...	...	...	...	...
1915	12.0	18.0	...	11.6	...	...	...	...	...	...	...	...	...	...	...	...	...
1916	14.7	21.3	...	15.0	...	...	...	...	...	...	...	...	...	...	...	...	...
1917	20.2	32.6	...	19.5	...	...	...	...	...	...	...	...	...	...	...	...	...
1918	22.6	37.4	...	21.1	...	...	...	...	...	...	...	...	...	...	...	...	...
1919	23.9	39.8	...	22.0	...	...	...	...	...	...	...	...	...	...	...	...	...
1920	26.6	38.0	...	27.4	...	...	...	...	...	...	...	...	...	...	...	...	...
1921	16.8	22.3	...	17.8	...	...	...	...	...	...	...	...	...	...	...	...	...
1922	16.7	23.7	...	17.4	...	...	...	...	...	...	...	...	...	...	...	...	...
1923	17.3	24.9	...	17.8	...	...	...	...	...	...	...	...	...	...	...	...	...
1924	16.9	25.2	...	17.0	...	...	...	...	...	...	...	...	...	...	...	...	...
1925	17.8	27.7	...	17.5	...	...	...	...	...	...	...	...	...	...	...	...	...
1926	17.2	25.3	...	17.0	...	17.1	10.3	...	47.1	9.3	...	13.7	...	28.6	16.4	...	...
1927	16.5	25.1	...	16.0	...	18.4	9.1	...	35.7	8.8	...	12.9	...	27.9	15.7	...	...
1928	16.7	26.7	...	15.8	...	20.7	8.7	...	28.3	8.5	...	12.9	...	27.2	16.2	...	...
1929	16.4	26.4	...	15.6	...	18.6	8.6	...	24.6	8.8	...	13.3	...	27.0	16.0	...	...
1930	14.9	22.4	...	14.5	...	17.1	8.1	...	21.5	8.0	...	12.0	...	26.5	15.9	...	...
1931	12.6	16.4	...	12.8	...	14.7	7.0	...	18.3	6.5	...	10.8	...	24.4	14.9	...	...
1932	11.2	12.2	...	11.9	...	12.5	7.3	...	15.9	5.6	...	9.9	...	21.5	13.9	...	...
1933	11.4	13.0	...	12.1	...	13.8	6.9	16.2	16.7	6.7	...	10.2	...	21.6	14.7	...	...
1934	12.9	16.5	...	13.3	...	14.8	7.6	17.0	19.5	7.8	...	11.2	...	23.4	15.7	...	...
1935	13.8	19.8	...	13.3	...	15.3	7.6	17.7	19.6	7.5	...	11.2	...	23.2	15.7	...	...
1936	13.9	20.4	...	13.5	...	16.3	7.9	17.8	21.1	7.9	...	11.4	...	23.6	15.8	...	...
1937	14.9	21.8	...	14.5	...	17.9	8.0	18.6	24.9	9.3	...	13.1	...	26.1	16.1	...	...
1938	13.5	17.3	...	13.9	...	15.8	7.9	17.7	24.4	8.5	...	12.6	...	25.5	15.6	...	...
1939	13.3	16.5	...	13.9	...	16.3	7.5	17.6	25.4	8.7	...	12.5	14.8	25.4	15.3	...	...
1940	13.5	17.1	...	14.1	...	17.2	7.4	17.9	23.7	9.6	...	12.5	14.9	26.0	15.3	...	...
1941	15.1	20.8	...	15.1	...	18.4	7.9	19.5	25.5	11.5	...	12.8	15.1	27.6	15.7	...	...
1942	17.0	26.7	...	16.2	...	20.1	8.1	21.7	29.7	12.5	...	13.0	15.4	29.9	16.3	...	...
1943	17.8	30.9	...	16.5	...	20.1	8.3	21.9	30.5	13.2	...	12.9	15.2	29.7	16.4	...	...
1944	17.9	31.2	...	16.7	...	19.9	8.6	22.2	30.1	14.3	...	12.9	15.1	30.5	16.7	...	...
1945	18.2	32.4	...	17.0	...	20.1	8.7	22.3	29.2	14.5	...	13.1	15.1	30.5	17.4	...	...
1946	20.8	37.5	...	18.6	...	23.3	9.3	24.1	29.3	16.6	...	14.7	16.6	32.4	18.5	...	...
1947	25.6	45.1	33.0	22.7	50.6	31.7	11.1	32.1	29.2	25.8	25.1	18.2	19.3	37.2	20.7	...	26.6
1948	27.7	48.5	35.3	24.6	52.8	32.1	13.1	32.8	30.2	29.5	26.2	20.7	20.9	39.4	22.4	...	27.7
1949	26.3	41.9	32.1	24.1	48.3	30.4	12.4	30.0	29.2	27.3	25.1	20.9	21.9	40.1	23.0	...	28.2
1950	27.3	44.0	33.2	25.0	50.2	32.9	12.6	30.4	35.6	31.4	25.7	22.0	22.6	40.9	23.5	...	28.6
1951	30.4	51.2	36.9	27.6	56.0	37.7	13.0	34.8	43.7	34.1	30.5	24.5	25.3	44.4	25.0	...	30.3
1952	29.6	48.4	36.4	26.9	50.5	30.5	13.0	33.0	39.6	33.2	29.7	24.5	25.3	43.5	25.0	...	30.2
1953	29.2	43.8	34.8	27.2	49.3	31.0	13.4	33.4	36.9	33.1	29.6	25.3	25.9	44.4	26.0	...	31.0
1954	29.3	43.2	35.4	27.2	48.2	29.5	13.2	33.8	37.5	32.5	29.6	25.5	26.3	44.9	26.6	...	31.3
1955	29.3	40.5	33.8	27.8	48.2	29.4	13.2	33.7	42.4	34.1	30.4	27.2	27.2	45.1	27.3	...	31.3
1956	30.3	40.0	33.8	29.1	48.2	31.2	13.6	33.9	43.0	34.6	32.4	29.6	29.3	46.3	28.5	...	31.7
1957	31.2	41.1	34.8	29.9	48.3	31.2	14.3	34.6	42.8	32.8	33.0	30.2	31.4	47.5	29.6	...	32.6
1958	31.6	42.9	36.5	30.0	47.4	31.6	13.7	34.9	42.8	32.5	33.4	30.0	32.1	47.9	29.9	...	33.3
1959	31.7	40.2	35.6	30.5	48.1	35.9	13.7	34.8	42.6	34.7	33.7	30.6	32.8	48.0	30.3	...	33.4
1960	31.7	40.1	35.6	30.5	48.6	34.6	13.9	34.8	42.7	33.5	34.0	30.6	33.0	47.8	30.4	...	33.6
1961	31.6	39.7	36.2	30.4	47.8	34.9	14.0	34.5	41.1	32.0	33.0	30.5	33.0	47.5	30.5	...	33.7
1962	31.7	40.4	36.5	30.4	48.2	35.3	14.0	33.9	39.9	32.2	33.4	30.2	33.0	47.2	30.5	...	33.9
1963	31.6	39.6	36.8	30.3	48.2	34.3	13.9	33.5	40.1	32.8	33.1	30.3	33.1	46.9	30.3	...	34.2
1964	31.6	39.0	36.7	30.5	48.5	34.4	13.5	33.6	39.6	33.5	33.0	31.1	33.3	47.1	30.4	...	34.4

. . . = Not available.

Table 9-2. Producer Price Indexes, by Commodity Group, 1913–2010—*Continued*

(1982 = 100.)

Year	All commodities	Farm products	Processed foods and feeds	Industrial commodities													
				Total	Textile products and apparel	Hides, leather, and related products	Fuels and related products and power	Chemicals and related products	Rubber and plastics products	Lumber and wood products	Pulp, paper, and allied products	Metals and metal products	Machinery and equipment	Furniture and household durables	Non-metallic mineral products	Transportation equipment	Miscellaneous products
1965	32.3	40.7	38.0	30.9	48.8	35.9	13.8	33.9	39.7	33.7	33.3	32.0	33.7	46.8	30.4	. . .	34.7
1966	33.3	43.7	40.2	31.5	48.9	39.4	14.1	34.0	40.5	35.2	34.2	32.8	34.7	47.4	30.7	. . .	35.3
1967	33.4	41.3	39.8	32.0	48.9	38.1	14.4	34.2	41.4	35.1	34.6	33.2	35.9	48.3	31.2	. . .	36.2
1968	34.2	42.3	40.6	32.8	50.7	39.3	14.3	34.1	42.8	39.8	35.0	34.0	37.0	49.7	32.4	. . .	37.0
1969	35.6	45.0	42.7	33.9	51.8	41.5	14.6	34.2	43.6	44.0	36.0	36.0	38.2	50.7	33.6	40.4	38.1
1970	36.9	45.8	44.6	35.2	52.4	42.0	15.3	35.0	44.9	39.9	37.5	38.7	40.0	51.9	35.3	41.9	39.8
1971	38.1	46.6	45.5	36.5	53.3	43.4	16.6	35.6	45.2	44.7	38.1	39.4	41.4	53.1	38.2	44.2	40.8
1972	39.8	51.6	48.0	37.8	55.5	50.0	17.1	35.6	45.3	50.7	39.3	40.9	42.3	53.8	39.4	45.5	41.5
1973	45.0	72.7	58.9	40.3	60.5	54.5	19.4	37.6	46.6	62.2	42.3	44.0	43.7	55.7	40.7	46.1	43.3
1974	53.5	77.4	68.0	49.2	68.0	55.2	30.1	50.2	56.4	64.5	52.5	57.0	50.0	61.8	47.8	50.3	48.1
1975	58.4	77.0	72.6	54.9	67.4	56.5	35.4	62.0	62.2	62.1	59.0	61.5	57.9	67.5	54.4	56.7	53.4
1976	61.1	78.8	70.8	58.4	72.4	63.9	38.3	64.0	66.0	72.2	62.1	65.0	61.3	70.3	58.2	60.5	55.6
1977	64.9	79.4	74.0	62.5	75.3	68.3	43.6	65.9	69.4	83.0	64.6	69.3	65.2	73.2	62.6	64.6	59.4
1978	69.9	87.7	80.6	67.0	78.1	76.1	46.5	68.0	72.4	96.9	67.7	75.3	70.3	77.5	69.6	69.5	66.7
1979	78.7	99.6	88.5	75.7	82.5	96.1	58.9	76.0	80.5	105.5	75.9	86.0	76.7	82.8	77.6	75.3	75.5
1980	89.8	102.9	95.9	88.0	89.7	94.7	82.8	89.0	90.1	101.5	86.3	95.0	86.0	90.7	88.4	82.9	93.6
1981	98.0	105.2	98.9	97.4	97.6	99.3	100.2	98.4	96.4	102.8	94.8	99.6	94.4	95.9	96.7	94.3	96.1
1982	100.0	100.0	100.0	100.0	100.0	100.0	100.0	100.0	100.0	100.0	100.0	100.0	100.0	100.0	100.0	100.0	100.0
1983	101.3	102.4	101.8	101.1	100.3	103.2	95.9	100.3	100.8	107.9	103.3	101.8	102.7	103.4	101.6	102.8	104.8
1984	103.7	105.5	105.4	103.3	102.7	109.0	94.8	102.9	102.3	108.0	110.3	104.8	105.1	105.7	105.4	105.2	107.0
1985	103.2	95.1	103.5	103.7	102.9	108.9	91.4	103.7	101.9	106.6	113.3	104.4	107.2	107.1	108.6	107.9	109.4
1986	100.2	92.9	105.4	100.0	103.2	113.0	69.8	102.6	101.9	107.2	116.1	103.2	108.8	108.2	110.0	110.5	111.6
1987	102.8	95.5	107.9	102.6	105.1	120.4	70.2	106.4	103.0	112.8	121.8	107.1	110.4	109.9	110.0	112.5	114.9
1988	106.9	104.9	112.7	106.3	109.2	131.4	66.7	116.3	109.3	118.9	130.4	118.7	113.2	113.1	111.2	114.3	120.2
1989	112.2	110.9	117.8	111.6	112.3	136.3	72.9	123.0	112.6	126.7	137.8	124.1	117.4	116.9	112.6	117.7	126.5
1990	116.3	112.2	121.9	115.8	115.0	141.7	82.3	123.6	113.6	129.7	141.2	122.9	120.7	119.2	114.7	121.5	134.2
1991	116.5	105.7	121.9	116.5	116.3	138.9	81.2	125.6	115.1	132.1	142.9	120.2	123.0	121.2	117.2	126.4	140.8
1992	117.2	103.6	122.1	117.4	117.8	140.4	80.4	125.9	115.1	146.6	145.2	119.2	123.4	122.2	117.3	130.4	145.3
1993	118.9	107.1	124.0	119.0	118.0	143.7	80.0	128.2	116.0	174.0	147.3	119.2	124.0	123.7	120.0	133.7	145.4
1994	120.4	106.3	125.5	120.7	118.3	148.5	77.8	132.1	117.6	180.0	152.5	124.8	125.1	126.1	124.2	137.2	141.9
1995	124.7	107.4	127.0	125.5	120.8	153.7	78.0	142.5	124.3	178.1	172.2	134.5	126.6	128.2	129.0	139.7	145.4
1996	127.7	122.4	133.3	127.3	122.4	150.5	85.8	142.1	123.8	176.1	168.7	131.0	126.5	130.4	131.0	141.7	147.7
1997	127.6	112.9	134.0	127.7	122.6	154.2	86.1	143.6	123.2	183.8	167.9	131.8	125.9	130.8	133.2	141.6	150.9
1998	124.4	104.6	131.6	124.8	122.9	148.0	75.3	143.9	122.6	179.1	171.7	127.8	124.9	131.3	135.4	141.2	156.0
1999	125.5	98.4	131.1	126.5	121.1	146.0	80.5	144.2	122.5	183.6	174.1	124.6	124.3	131.7	138.9	141.8	166.6
2000	132.7	99.5	133.1	134.8	121.4	151.5	103.5	151.0	125.5	178.2	183.7	128.1	124.0	132.6	142.5	143.8	170.8
2001	134.2	103.8	137.3	135.7	121.3	158.4	105.3	151.8	127.2	174.4	184.8	125.4	123.7	133.2	144.3	145.2	181.3
2002	131.1	99.0	136.2	132.4	119.9	157.6	93.2	151.9	126.8	173.3	185.9	125.9	122.9	133.5	146.2	144.6	182.4
2003	138.1	111.5	143.4	139.1	119.8	162.3	112.9	161.8	130.1	177.4	190.0	129.2	121.9	133.9	148.2	145.7	179.6
2004	146.7	123.3	151.2	147.6	121.0	164.5	126.9	174.4	133.8	195.6	195.7	149.6	122.1	135.1	153.2	148.6	183.2
2005	157.4	118.5	153.1	160.2	122.8	165.4	156.4	192.0	143.8	196.5	202.6	160.8	123.7	139.4	164.2	151.0	195.1
2006	164.7	117.0	153.8	168.8	124.5	168.4	166.7	205.8	153.8	194.4	209.8	181.6	126.2	142.6	179.9	152.6	205.6
2007	172.6	143.4	165.1	175.1	125.8	173.6	177.6	214.8	155.0	192.4	216.9	193.5	127.3	144.7	186.2	155.0	210.3
2008	189.6	161.3	180.5	192.3	128.9	173.1	214.6	245.5	165.9	191.3	226.8	213.0	129.7	148.9	197.1	158.6	216.6
2009	172.9	134.6	176.2	174.8	129.5	157.0	158.7	229.4	165.2	182.8	225.6	186.8	131.3	153.1	202.4	162.2	217.5
2010	184.7	151.0	182.3	187.0	131.7	181.4	185.8	246.6	170.7	192.7	236.9	207.6	131.1	153.2	201.8	163.4	221.5

. . . = Not available.

Table 9-3. Producer Price Indexes for the Net Output of Selected Industries, 2000–2010

(December 2003 = 100, unless otherwise specified.)

Industry	2000	2001	2002	2003	2004	2005	2006	2007	2008	2009	2010
Agriculture, Forestry, Fishing, and Hunting											
Logging[1]	177.5	167.5	165.0	168.7	175.2	179.0	176.6	175.0	171.5	160.3	177.1
Mining											
Oil and gas extraction[2]	126.8	127.5	107.0	160.1	192.7	262.0	252.5	267.1	347.5	187.3	240.5
Mining (except oil and gas)	...	...	...	...	109.5	126.6	147.9	158.4	180.8	187.3	203.5
Coal mining [2]	84.8	91.3	93.9	94.4	104.1	118.2	126.9	130.6	162.2	185.7	192.8
Metal ore mining[3]	73.8	70.8	73.6	81.6	111.8	146.0	204.6	226.4	232.6	203.4	270.3
Iron ore mining[3]	93.9	95.2	94.2	95.0	97.2	115.7	131.2	127.5	141.0	143.5	145.6
Gold ore and silver ore mining[3]	57.0	55.2	62.6	72.6	82.6	89.5	121.3	138.8	143.9	161.9	206.7
Copper, nickel, lead, and zinc mining[4]	88.7	81.7	80.1	90.1	147.7	195.2	350.2	386.5	390.3	288.6	407.4
Other metal ore mining[2]	26.4	24.7	28.9	34.9	80.0	159.1	128.7	145.5	147.8	110.9	171.7
Nonmetallic mineral mining and quarrying[3]	137.0	141.0	143.5	146.4	151.2	161.3	176.0	191.1	217.6	228.9	224.6
Stone mining and quarrying[3]	147.3	152.2	156.1	160.2	166.1	176.7	192.7	210.2	224.7	236.8	241.3
Sand, gravel, clay, and refractory minerals mining	...	...	...	...	102.4	108.8	117.6	126.1	135.1	142.2	143.4
Other nonmetallic mineral mining and quarrying[3]	106.8	107.1	107.7	108.4	111.4	120.8	133.8	148.3	222.5	233.3	200.8
Mining support activities	...	...	...	...	68.0	86.8	111.5	110.8	112.8	103.2	102.0
Utilities	...	...	...	...	104.9	117.6	123.1	127.0	136.5	130.2	133.4
Electric power generation, transmission, and distribution	...	...	...	...	103.3	111.3	118.8	122.7	130.7	129.3	133.0
Electric power generation	...	...	...	...	105.2	121.6	128.0	132.0	145.5	132.3	137.9
Electric power transmission, control, and distribution	...	...	...	...	103.3	111.3	118.8	122.7	130.7	129.3	133.0
Natural gas distribution	...	...	...	...	107.3	126.6	129.3	129.0	142.9	117.9	119.2
Manufacturing											
Food[3]	128.5	132.8	132.0	137.4	144.3	146.1	146.8	158.6	173.8	169.5	175.5
Animal food	...	...	...	...	103.3	98.2	101.8	118.6	147.8	142.1	140.8
Grain and oilseed milling	...	...	...	...	103.1	99.8	104.7	121.2	157.4	136.3	133.5
Flour milling and malt	...	...	...	...	102.6	100.5	109.1	128.5	178.8	145.3	140.5
Starch and vegetable fats and oils	...	...	...	...	103.6	97.9	102.4	122.2	163.1	138.9	135.7
Breakfast cereal manufacturing	...	...	...	...	101.7	105.0	106.9	108.9	112.1	115.7	116.9
Sugar and confectionery product[3]	127.5	129.3	133.7	139.5	141.4	147.3	154.7	155.4	166.7	180.2	187.9
Sugar	...	...	...	...	99.7	105.6	123.4	111.1	114.4	129.1	154.1
Chocolate and confectionery from cacao beans	...	...	...	...	100.1	101.7	103.9	107.2	116.9	125.2	128.1
Confectionery from purchased chocolate	...	...	...	...	100.1	102.2	103.8	109.1	120.0	127.6	129.0
Non-chocolate confectionery	...	...	...	...	104.0	111.0	113.0	114.9	121.1	131.1	130.9
Fruit and vegetable preserving and specialty food[3]	132.1	133.3	135.2	136.6	139.2	141.7	144.5	147.6	156.5	165.2	164.5
Frozen food	...	...	...	...	101.6	103.9	107.7	108.9	113.5	118.7	120.7
Fruit and vegetable canning, pickling, and drying	...	...	...	...	100.5	104.0	107.3	112.5	120.5	128.0	125.9
Dairy product[3]	129.9	141.2	133.3	135.8	151.0	151.3	147.4	174.5	179.1	157.9	173.6
Dairy product (except frozen)	...	...	...	...	108.4	108.5	105.0	126.9	130.0	112.1	125.0
Ice cream and frozen dessert	...	...	...	...	103.3	104.7	106.9	110.6	114.8	115.8	116.4
Animal slaughtering and processing[3]	115.0	120.3	114.0	125.8	134.2	135.8	130.8	139.1	145.8	140.3	152.8
Seafood product preparation and packaging	...	...	...	...	102.4	106.2	107.0	112.8	123.6	124.8	129.7
Bakery and tortilla	...	...	...	...	100.8	102.6	105.3	109.8	123.5	127.7	127.0
Bread and bakery product	...	...	...	...	101.1	103.4	106.6	111.1	125.0	129.6	128.4
Cookie, cracker, and pasta	...	...	...	...	100.5	101.3	103.2	107.3	120.3	124.8	124.8
Tortilla	...	...	...	...	100.4	102.5	103.9	113.3	129.6	126.0	125.6
Other food	...	...	...	...	101.1	105.4	107.0	110.6	119.9	122.3	124.6
Snack food	...	...	...	...	101.4	108.4	108.5	109.5	119.2	127.1	132.4
Coffee and tea	...	...	...	...	101.7	115.1	117.3	124.3	135.4	137.1	142.7
Flavoring syrup and concentrate	...	...	...	...	101.0	103.1	105.6	109.1	113.4	117.1	115.3
Seasoning and dressing	...	...	...	...	101.1	101.3	102.7	106.7	116.2	121.8	120.8
All other food	...	...	...	...	100.4	100.8	103.1	108.2	118.5	112.8	114.8
Beverage and tobacco product	...	...	...	...	101.0	104.8	106.3	109.6	114.4	119.8	123.4
Beverage[3]	134.4	138.6	140.8	142.7	146.4	150.4	153.3	155.2	162.2	168.4	170.8
Soft drink and ice	...	...	...	...	102.1	104.1	106.8	109.3	114.5	119.1	120.4
Breweries	...	...	...	...	101.3	105.6	105.6	104.0	108.7	114.4	118.1
Wineries	...	...	...	...	100.7	104.2	109.8	112.0	114.6	116.8	116.4
Distilleries	...	...	...	...	100.1	100.6	101.9	106.5	113.7	114.5	112.9
Tobacco[3]	345.8	386.1	401.9	377.9	379.7	401.0	403.8	429.5	446.9	474.8	502.9
Tobacco stemming and redrying[5]	109.0	112.3	114.7	117.5	119.4	119.9	109.4	112.6	113.4	115.2	115.9
Tobacco product[6]	379.3	425.8	442.8	411.7	412.5	436.3	440.2	468.4	487.6	518.2	549.5
Textile mills	...	...	...	...	101.1	103.6	106.6	108.2	112.4	112.3	115.9
Fiber, yarn, and thread mills[3]	105.5	103.0	99.8	100.9	105.6	108.8	111.1	114.0	121.1	117.6	126.7
Fabric mills	...	...	...	...	101.0	103.0	105.8	106.2	109.7	109.2	112.3
Broadwoven fabric mills	...	...	...	...	101.1	103.2	106.7	108.1	111.7	108.0	113.2
Narrow fabric mills and schiffli mach embroidery[5]	125.3	126.2	126.0	125.1	126.2	129.3	131.1	132.5	134.6	136.9	138.3
Nonwoven fabric mills	...	...	...	...	101.5	105.6	108.1	108.2	112.8	113.7	115.1
Knit fabric mills	...	...	...	...	100.4	100.5	101.3	99.4	101.2	107.4	108.1
Textile and fabric finishing mills	...	...	...	...	99.9	102.8	106.5	109.5	113.4	116.3	116.8
Fabric coating mills	...	...	...	...	100.2	104.9	113.4	116.5	123.9	126.2	127.0
Textile product mills	...	...	...	...	101.4	105.3	108.4	109.6	112.4	115.4	117.3
Textile furnishings mills	...	...	...	...	101.1	105.1	108.6	110.0	112.0	116.3	118.1
Carpet and rug mills[3]	117.8	118.9	119.0	121.8	124.6	132.9	140.2	141.6	144.6	151.0	152.4
Curtain and linen mills	...	...	...	...	100.2	100.3	100.5	102.1	103.5	106.3	109.1
Other textile product mills	...	...	...	...	102.0	105.4	107.9	108.8	113.3	113.4	115.4
Textile bag and canvas mills	...	...	...	...	102.7	104.9	107.5	111.5	115.1	116.3	115.8
All other textile product mills	...	...	...	...	101.7	105.6	108.0	107.8	112.7	112.4	115.2

[1] December 1981 = 100.
[2] December 1985 = 100.
[3] December 1984 = 100.
[4] June 1988 = 100.
[5] June 1984 = 100.
[6] December 1982 = 100.
... = Not available.

Table 9-3. Producer Price Indexes for the Net Output of Selected Industries, 2000–2010—*Continued*

(December 2003 = 100, unless otherwise specified.)

Industry	2000	2001	2002	2003	2004	2005	2006	2007	2008	2009	2010
Manufacturing—*Continued*											
Apparel	. . .	. . .	. . .	. . .	100.0	100.0	100.5	101.5	102.4	103.5	103.4
Apparel knitting mills[3]	113.9	113.7	112.7	111.6	110.3	109.6	110.5	110.9	112.9	113.9	115.3
Cut and sew apparel	. . .	. . .	. . .	. . .	100.2	100.2	100.6	101.7	102.4	103.5	103.3
Cut and sew apparel contractors	. . .	. . .	. . .	. . .	100.2	103.0	105.3	105.9	106.3	106.3	106.1
Men's and boys' cut and sew apparel	. . .	. . .	. . .	. . .	99.9	98.4	98.0	98.2	99.2	101.6	102.5
Women's and girls' cut and sew apparel	. . .	. . .	. . .	. . .	100.4	100.8	101.0	102.2	102.6	103.1	102.2
Other cut and sew apparel	. . .	. . .	. . .	. . .	100.2	102.3	107.1	111.8	114.7	116.5	117.0
Accessories and other apparel	. . .	. . .	. . .	. . .	100.5	101.6	102.2	103.5	106.5	106.9	106.7
Leather and allied product[3]	137.9	141.3	141.1	142.8	143.6	144.5	146.6	149.7	153.5	153.8	156.2
Leather and hide tanning and finishing[7]	174.6	191.7	191.4	200.5	205.7	204.8	208.4	215.9	221.3	212.1	217.0
Footwear	. . .	. . .	. . .	. . .	100.1	101.1	102.2	103.3	106.3	107.7	108.7
Other leather and allied product	. . .	. . .	. . .	. . .	99.8	100.7	102.6	104.7	106.6	109.8	111.0
Wood product	. . .	. . .	. . .	. . .	106.7	108.6	108.5	107.0	107.4	103.2	107.7
Sawmills and wood preservation	. . .	. . .	. . .	. . .	110.5	110.7	107.9	103.8	99.3	88.7	98.3
Plywood, and engineered wood product	. . .	. . .	. . .	. . .	107.0	105.2	99.6	94.6	95.8	90.6	96.2
Other wood product	. . .	. . .	. . .	. . .	104.7	108.3	111.4	112.4	114.3	113.5	115.2
Millwork	. . .	. . .	. . .	. . .	104.8	105.4	106.7	107.3	107.5	106.3	108.6
Wood container and pallet	. . .	. . .	. . .	. . .	102.8	107.1	110.9	109.9	111.7	110.8	114.7
All other wood product	. . .	. . .	. . .	. . .	105.0	111.3	115.9	118.0	122.3	122.1	122.1
Paper	. . .	. . .	. . .	. . .	102.6	106.9	112.3	115.7	122.8	123.3	127.2
Pulp, paper, and paperboard mills	. . .	. . .	. . .	. . .	103.8	109.4	115.7	119.3	129.0	126.6	131.8
Pulp mills[6]	143.4	122.9	116.5	120.9	131.3	137.4	144.8	163.2	175.5	162.1	191.9
Paper mills[7]	148.8	150.5	144.1	145.7	151.1	161.0	168.1	170.8	184.6	183.9	186.1
Paperboard mills[6]	192.2	187.3	179.5	180.2	189.9	196.0	212.7	224.1	242.4	230.9	251.9
Converted paper product	. . .	. . .	. . .	. . .	101.9	105.5	110.5	113.9	119.4	121.8	125.4
Paper container[3]	157.1	158.9	157.0	157.3	161.5	167.1	177.1	182.9	192.3	195.0	202.8
Paper bag and coated and treated paper	. . .	. . .	. . .	. . .	101.7	105.8	110.4	113.3	117.8	120.3	123.1
Stationery product	. . .	. . .	. . .	. . .	101.7	106.8	110.5	114.7	120.2	122.9	123.7
Other converted paper product	. . .	. . .	. . .	. . .	97.0	98.7	100.0	102.8	107.9	112.0	114.1
Printing and related support activities	. . .	. . .	. . .	. . .	101.1	103.1	105.6	106.7	109.4	109.3	109.8
Printing	. . .	. . .	. . .	. . .	101.2	103.3	105.9	107.1	109.9	109.8	110.4
Printing support activities	. . .	. . .	. . .	. . .	100.4	100.0	100.4	100.9	101.2	101.2	100.9
Petroleum and coal product[3]	112.8	105.3	98.8	122.0	149.9	200.4	235.5	260.3	329.2	218.8	285.8
Petroleum refineries[8]	111.6	103.1	96.3	121.2	151.5	205.3	241.0	266.9	338.3	217.0	289.4
Asphalt paving, roofing, and saturated materials[3]	113.5	116.9	119.7	125.1	127.1	138.6	164.8	174.2	213.5	229.9	235.7
Other petroleum and coal product[3]	150.3	159.3	160.5	165.3	172.0	197.8	238.3	253.5	320.2	313.4	323.7
Chemical[3]	156.7	158.4	157.3	164.6	172.8	187.3	196.8	203.3	228.2	224.7	233.7
Basic chemical[3]	177.3	173.5	170.6	183.0	197.7	225.9	244.3	254.4	309.0	290.3	307.1
Petrochemical	. . .	. . .	. . .	. . .	120.7	151.0	164.7	168.5	212.6	141.2	182.5
Industrial gas	. . .	. . .	. . .	. . .	108.3	118.3	123.0	123.2	140.9	129.0	127.2
Synthetic dye and pigment	. . .	. . .	. . .	. . .	104.2	108.7	112.0	118.1	125.5	118.4	120.7
Other basic inorganic chemical	. . .	. . .	. . .	. . .	103.1	120.4	149.4	159.5	206.6	219.7	220.1
Other basic organic chemical	. . .	. . .	. . .	. . .	. . .	. . .	. . .	. . .	. . .	. . .	. . .
Resin, synthetic rubber, and artificial and synthetic fiber and filament[3]	128.0	126.2	119.7	131.0	145.5	169.4	175.2	174.6	193.0	174.3	191.8
Resin and synthetic rubber	. . .	. . .	. . .	. . .	115.1	136.5	141.2	140.4	156.3	140.6	155.8
Artificial and synthetic fiber and filament	. . .	. . .	. . .	. . .	101.2	107.8	111.1	110.6	113.7	107.2	109.5
Pesticide, fertilizer, and other agricultural chemical[3]	124.9	132.0	127.0	135.3	142.7	151.3	156.6	179.4	278.7	198.8	200.2
Fertilizer	. . .	. . .	. . .	. . .	107.3	118.1	123.5	151.8	277.5	162.1	169.9
Pesticide and other agricultural chemical	. . .	. . .	. . .	. . .	100.6	102.2	104.4	106.9	115.5	125.9	118.4
Pharmaceutical and medicine[3]	215.7	220.5	226.3	235.4	244.2	255.2	266.3	276.0	293.3	311.7	327.9
Paint, coating, and adhesive	. . .	. . .	. . .	. . .	101.9	108.8	116.9	121.5	129.8	137.4	138.3
Adhesive	. . .	. . .	. . .	. . .	100.5	106.4	114.8	119.0	127.4	133.6	136.3
Soap, cleaners, and toilet preparation[3]	132.5	134.2	134.2	134.9	136.9	140.5	144.6	147.2	153.0	157.0	156.4
Soap and cleaning compound	. . .	. . .	. . .	. . .	102.0	105.8	110.5	112.5	120.8	126.1	124.4
Toilet preparation	. . .	. . .	. . .	. . .	100.0	101.2	102.1	103.9	104.3	104.7	105.5
Other chemical product and preparation	. . .	. . .	. . .	. . .	101.6	108.6	114.2	118.0	126.5	128.0	128.3
Printing ink	. . .	. . .	. . .	. . .	100.0	103.0	107.2	114.2	123.5	131.8	131.9
Explosives[9]	. . .	. . .	. . .	. . .	. . .	. . .	. . .	103.1	113.1	106.8	105.5
All other chemical product and preparation	. . .	. . .	. . .	. . .	101.8	109.4	115.3	118.7	127.0	127.8	128.2
Plastics and rubber product[3]	124.6	125.9	125.5	128.4	131.7	141.2	149.7	150.6	161.3	161.3	166.1
Plastics product[10]	109.8	111.0	110.2	113.0	116.2	125.8	134.1	133.9	143.4	142.4	146.5
Unsupported plastics film, sheet, and bag	. . .	. . .	. . .	. . .	104.2	116.9	124.4	123.8	137.9	132.2	140.9
Plastics pipe, fitting, and unsupported shape	. . .	. . .	. . .	. . .	108.5	122.6	142.8	136.2	147.6	142.7	149.2
Laminated plastics plate, sheet, and shape	. . .	. . .	. . .	. . .	101.7	105.0	108.4	107.7	112.5	113.2	113.9
Polystyrene foam product	. . .	. . .	. . .	. . .	104.6	117.0	120.8	125.7	136.1	135.4	134.3
Foam product (except polystyrene)	. . .	. . .	. . .	. . .	100.2	110.0	136.6	132.5	140.0	142.4	140.6
Plastics bottle	. . .	. . .	. . .	. . .	103.1	114.8	119.5	118.3	126.8	114.3	115.4
Other plastics product	. . .	. . .	. . .	. . .	101.3	107.1	111.7	112.5	118.6	120.6	123.5
Rubber product	. . .	. . .	. . .	. . .	102.1	106.7	111.8	115.2	123.6	127.1	131.5
Tire[7]	100.4	101.5	102.7	105.6	110.5	116.9	123.8	128.6	140.2	143.5	150.6
Rubber and plastics hose and belting	. . .	. . .	. . .	. . .	102.3	107.4	111.0	113.6	120.1	127.1	130.1
Other rubber product	120.5	121.3	121.4	121.8	121.9	125.1	130.2	133.0	140.4	143.9	146.6
Nonmetallic mineral product[3]	134.7	136.0	137.1	138.0	142.7	152.0	163.4	166.8	170.9	174.0	172.5
Clay product and refractory	. . .	. . .	. . .	. . .	101.5	105.1	110.4	113.1	116.0	119.4	120.2
Pottery, ceramics, and plumbing fixture[3]	139.7	150.2	150.1	150.6	152.1	154.3	159.8	163.3	164.1	168.5	170.8
Clay building material and refractories	. . .	. . .	. . .	. . .	102.2	107.8	114.5	117.5	122.1	125.8	126.2
Glass and glass product	. . .	. . .	. . .	. . .	100.1	101.6	103.7	105.8	108.6	110.2	109.6

[3]December 1984 = 100.
[6]December 1982 = 100.
[7]June 1981 = 100.
[8]June 1985 = 100.
[9]December 2006 = 100.
[10]June 1993 = 100.
. . . = Not available.

Table 9-3. Producer Price Indexes for the Net Output of Selected Industries, 2000–2010—*Continued*

(December 2003 = 100, unless otherwise specified.)

Industry	2000	2001	2002	2003	2004	2005	2006	2007	2008	2009	2010
Manufacturing—*Continued*											
Cement and concrete product	...	...	...	...	104.2	114.8	126.6	131.9	136.4	138.0	135.3
Cement[11]	148.6	148.7	151.1	150.5	155.4	175.2	197.7	208.4	207.8	204.3	192.8
Ready-mix concrete	...	...	...	...	104.5	117.3	130.6	135.6	139.7	143.3	139.7
Concrete pipe, brick, and block	...	...	...	...	102.5	109.2	116.7	121.0	127.9	128.5	126.0
Other concrete products	...	...	...	...	104.7	111.3	121.0	126.6	132.2	131.3	132.4
Lime and gypsum product	...	...	...	...	110.0	124.5	145.1	128.1	119.4	123.6	121.4
Lime	...	...	...	...	103.5	112.4	121.8	129.1	136.5	161.5	163.5
Gypsum product	...	...	...	...	111.9	127.9	151.6	128.6	116.0	115.3	112.1
Other nonmetallic mineral product[3]	130.9	132.0	132.6	133.4	137.2	142.5	150.2	152.0	154.9	160.6	162.7
Abrasive product	...	...	...	...	100.2	103.1	107.2	110.4	118.1	124.6	124.9
All other nonmetallic mineral product	...	...	...	...	103.5	108.0	114.5	115.2	115.7	119.3	121.3
Primary metal[3]	119.8	116.1	116.2	118.4	142.8	156.3	179.3	190.5	211.9	172.5	196.1
Iron and steel mills and ferroalloy	...	...	...	...	127.7	136.7	150.9	160.8	189.7	138.1	163.4
Steel product from purchased steel	...	...	...	...	133.1	146.2	148.2	151.1	189.8	156.8	168.9
Iron/steel pipe and tube from purchased steel	...	...	...	...	147.9	160.1	164.1	168.1	206.6	164.7	190.6
Rolling and drawing of purchased steel	...	...	...	...	123.7	137.5	138.1	140.8	180.6	154.0	155.0
Alumina and aluminum production and processing	...	...	...	...	...	114.0	131.2	136.3	139.0	111.3	124.4
Nonferrous (except aluminum) production and processing	...	...	...	...	113.6	137.6	202.8	223.0	218.6	186.0	223.2
Copper rolling, drawing, extruding, and alloying	...	...	...	...	118.2	138.9	222.0	232.8	232.9	196.9	244.2
Other nonferrous rolling, drawing, extruding, and alloying	...	...	...	...	110.3	136.2	181.2	206.0	195.8	168.3	191.1
Foundries	...	...	...	...	103.9	110.9	118.7	126.3	138.6	133.5	139.6
Ferrous metal foundries[3]	132.1	132.7	133.0	133.5	140.4	152.5	160.1	168.5	188.7	183.5	191.6
Nonferrous metal foundries[3]	133.5	134.1	134.4	135.6	140.0	145.0	160.4	173.2	185.6	176.4	184.8
Fabricated metal product[3]	130.3	131.0	131.7	132.9	141.3	149.5	155.7	162.3	174.4	175.2	176.5
Forging and stamping	...	...	...	...	107.0	113.3	116.8	120.9	130.8	128.0	130.3
Cuttlery and handtool	...	...	...	...	...	105.5	108.9	111.8	115.8	119.7	120.4
Architectural and structural metals	...	...	...	...	111.2	118.0	122.6	127.4	140.9	135.6	134.2
Plate work and fabricated structural product	...	...	...	...	115.2	124.2	128.9	135.2	155.4	143.2	139.7
Ornamental and architectural metal product	...	...	...	...	108.3	113.5	118.1	121.7	129.9	130.1	130.5
Boiler, tank, and shipping container	...	...	...	...	106.8	115.7	120.3	126.2	136.5	143.0	142.5
Power boiler and heat exchanger	...	...	...	...	...	124.2	132.4	136.9	147.3	143.3	144.7
Metal tank (heavy gauge)	...	...	...	...	...	120.8	125.6	132.3	143.2	142.3	140.0
Light gauge metal container[3]	101.0	100.8	102.7	105.4	110.4	117.5	120.5	127.1	137.8	149.9	149.5
Hardware	...	...	...	...	103.4	107.2	110.7	115.3	122.4	125.1	126.7
Spring and wire product	...	...	...	...	108.9	114.4	117.9	120.7	138.4	140.8	145.1
Machine shops; turned product; and screw, nut, and bolt	...	...	...	...	102.8	108.4	113.0	118.8	125.2	126.4	126.7
Machine shops	...	...	...	...	102.4	107.4	109.8	112.4	119.4	122.7	122.5
Turned product and screw, nut, and bolt[3]	122.9	122.8	123.4	123.6	128.4	136.6	147.1	161.2	167.9	165.3	166.6
Coating, engraving, heat treating, and other activity	...	...	...	...	102.0	104.2	110.6	115.5	119.5	118.9	122.4
Other fabricated metal product	...	...	...	...	103.8	109.8	115.7	121.5	128.4	133.0	136.0
Metal valve	...	...	...	...	103.0	109.8	118.1	126.6	132.8	136.5	138.2
All other fabricated metal product	...	...	...	...	104.5	109.9	113.7	117.1	124.7	129.9	134.0
Machinery	...	...	...	...	101.9	105.6	108.8	112.1	117.0	120.3	120.5
Agricultural, construction, and mining machinery	...	...	...	...	102.4	107.4	111.7	115.4	120.3	124.2	124.8
Agricultural implement	...	...	...	...	101.8	105.8	107.8	110.5	114.5	117.8	119.5
Construction machinery	...	...	...	...	102.9	107.7	112.5	115.8	119.4	123.7	123.4
Mining and oil and gas field machinery	...	...	...	...	102.7	110.6	119.5	127.3	137.9	142.1	141.9
Industrial machinery[3]	148.7	149.9	149.6	150.1	153.0	155.9	158.9	162.8	166.4	166.2	165.0
Sawmill and woodworking machinery	...	...	...	...	101.5	105.0	108.2	110.6	115.4	117.4	118.0
Plastics and rubber industry machinery	...	...	...	...	102.8	106.3	109.4	111.4	115.2	118.7	119.7
Other industrial machinery[3]	148.7	149.9	149.6	150.1	152.7	155.3	158.0	162.0	165.2	164.2	162.5
Commercial and service industry machinery	...	...	...	...	101.3	102.9	103.9	106.0	109.3	111.8	112.2
HVAC and commercial refrigeration equipment	...	...	...	...	101.9	108.0	112.1	117.8	123.0	124.1	123.8
Metalworking machinery	...	...	...	...	100.8	103.3	105.8	106.8	108.8	109.2	109.1
Turbine, and power transmission equipment[3]	136.6	137.7	138.9	139.1	140.8	143.2	148.0	152.6	162.9	174.6	174.6
Other general purpose machinery	...	...	...	...	103.0	107.6	111.2	115.0	121.4	125.4	126.5
Pump and compressor	...	...	...	...	102.2	108.4	112.6	117.9	123.6	127.5	129.0
Material handling equipment	...	...	...	...	104.6	110.6	114.4	118.2	125.3	129.5	129.1
All other general purpose machinery	...	...	...	...	102.5	105.7	108.7	112.0	118.1	122.2	123.8
Computer and electronic product	...	...	...	...	99.0	97.5	96.5	94.2	92.7	92.1	91.0
Computer and peripheral equipment[9]	162.2	153.1	139.5	123.9	115.4	107.8	102.1	94.5	86.4	81.1	76.5
Communications equipment[2]	110.4	108.6	105.0	101.7	98.4	97.0	95.9	95.8	97.1	97.2	96.9
Telephone apparatus	...	...	...	...	95.3	93.2	91.1	90.5	91.3	90.7	89.6
Radio/TV broadcast and wireless communication equipment	...	...	...	...	99.4	98.7	98.2	98.6	100.3	100.8	101.0
Other communications equipment	...	...	...	...	99.8	99.7	101.2	101.6	103.5	104.9	105.8
Audio and video equipment	...	...	...	...	98.1	95.6	93.7	90.9	89.3	85.5	84.4
Semiconductor and other electronic component[3]	88.8	86.4	84.9	81.1	78.3	76.5	75.1	70.2	66.3	65.4	63.9
Navigation, measuring, medical, and control instruments	...	...	...	...	100.6	101.9	103.5	104.9	106.5	108.2	108.9
Manufacturing and reproducing magnetic and optical media	...	...	...	...	98.0	97.0	95.5	92.2	93.8	92.4	88.8
Electrical equipment, appliance and component	...	...	...	...	103.2	108.0	116.6	122.2	127.8	128.6	131.9
Electric lighting equipment	...	...	...	...	100.8	103.5	105.9	108.2	110.9	112.7	112.8
Electric lamp bulb and part	...	...	...	...	98.1	100.2	98.6	98.8	99.6	100.7	102.0
Lighting fixture	...	...	...	...	101.7	104.6	107.2	108.2	111.2	114.3	116.1
Household appliance[3]	106.2	104.6	104.2	103.1	103.1	106.3	107.7	109.3	112.6	117.7	117.3
Small electrical appliance	...	...	...	...	99.9	101.8	103.0	105.3	106.0	109.2	109.2
Major appliance	...	...	...	...	100.6	104.2	105.6	106.8	110.8	116.1	115.7
Electrical equipment	...	...	...	...	101.9	107.2	113.7	120.6	127.3	129.5	133.1
Other electrical equipment and component	...	...	...	...	106.6	112.5	129.1	136.7	144.0	140.5	147.0
Battery	...	...	...	...	102.2	105.7	112.6	126.2	139.8	138.2	140.9
Communications and energy wire and cable	...	...	...	...	106.8	115.8	150.3	161.3	167.9	154.8	172.8
Wiring device	...	...	...	...	113.6	118.9	128.6	133.9	140.9	139.9	142.1
All other electrical equipment and component	...	...	...	...	101.7	105.4	109.3	110.3	114.0	119.5	117.4

[2] December 1985 = 100.
[3] December 1984 = 100.
[9] December 2006 = 100.
[11] June 1982 = 100.
... = Not available.

Table 9-3. Producer Price Indexes for the Net Output of Selected Industries, 2000–2010—*Continued*

(December 2003 = 100, unless otherwise specified.)

Industry	2000	2001	2002	2003	2004	2005	2006	2007	2008	2009	2010
Manufacturing—*Continued*											
Transportation equipment	...	...	...	...	100.9	102.5	103.2	104.9	107.3	109.5	110.4
Motor vehicle	...	...	...	...	99.4	98.7	96.1	96.6	98.0	100.9	101.2
Automobile and light truck motor vehicle	...	...	...	...	99.2	98.2	95.1	95.3	96.6	99.4	99.4
Motor vehicle body and trailer	...	...	...	...	104.0	109.7	113.7	117.2	121.5	122.4	122.7
Motor vehicle parts	...	...	...	...	101.4	102.7	104.8	106.8	108.8	108.5	109.8
Motor vehicle steering and suspension parts	...	...	...	...	101.8	105.1	106.3	105.0	106.5	105.3	105.9
Aerospace product and parts[8]	149.9	154.7	157.3	162.2	168.0	176.0	182.8	188.6	196.2	200.6	203.4
Railroad rolling stock[5]	128.6	128.3	127.7	129.0	135.8	150.5	158.4	165.6	169.3	171.5	174.0
Ship and boat building[3]	149.0	152.6	156.8	163.0	169.6	175.0	181.4	188.3	193.8	199.2	203.0
Other transportation equipment	...	...	...	...	101.1	103.6	104.8	106.3	106.4	107.2	107.7
Furniture and related product[3]	143.3	145.1	146.3	147.4	151.5	157.8	162.5	165.7	171.7	176.6	177.1
Household and institutional furniture and kitchen cabinet[3]	142.5	144.4	146.2	147.0	148.6	152.6	157.4	160.8	166.5	171.1	171.6
Wood kitchen cabinet and countertop	...	...	...	...	101.1	103.2	106.3	108.4	111.2	113.4	113.4
Household and institutional furniture	...	...	...	...	101.1	104.0	107.4	109.7	114.0	117.6	118.1
Office furniture (including fixtures)	...	...	...	...	105.1	111.5	113.8	116.7	121.2	124.6	125.7
Other furniture-related product	...	...	...	...	104.0	110.6	115.2	114.9	118.5	122.9	121.1
Mattress	...	...	...	...	105.6	115.0	120.6	119.2	123.9	127.7	126.0
Blind and shade	...	...	...	...	101.3	103.9	106.9	108.3	109.9	115.5	113.7
Miscellaneous	...	...	...	...	101.2	102.9	104.7	107.0	109.9	111.5	113.0
Medical equipment and supplies	...	...	...	...	101.3	102.5	103.8	105.1	107.4	108.9	110.2
Other miscellaneous[2]	130.9	132.4	133.3	133.9	135.2	138.4	142.0	146.5	151.1	153.5	155.6
Jewelry and silverware[2]	127.1	128.0	129.1	131.0	134.6	138.7	146.5	152.6	161.7	165.6	178.3
Sporting and athletic goods	...	...	...	...	101.3	102.0	103.6	107.6	106.2	108.2	109.1
Doll, toy, and game	...	...	...	...	100.3	101.7	102.7	104.9	107.9	113.9	112.5
Office supplies (except paper)[2]	132.0	131.4	132.8	132.9	133.1	135.8	136.2	139.0	141.1	144.1	143.1
Sign	...	...	...	...	100.9	104.6	106.9	109.1	111.2	111.5	112.0
All other miscellaneous	...	...	...	...	101.0	103.7	106.7	110.2	115.4	116.4	116.8
Wholesale Trade											
Merchant wholesalers, durable goods[12]	...	...	...	...	...	102.0	106.3	110.4	116.4	119.8	118.0
Merchant wholesalers, nondurable goods[13]	...	...	...	...	...	...	106.2	112.2	120.5	133.4	140.1
Wholesale trade agents and brokers[13]	...	...	...	...	...	...	102.4	105.5	110.4	110.9	113.8
Retail Trade											
Motor vehicle and parts dealers	...	...	...	...	103.5	106.9	112.8	115.5	118.0	120.0	124.4
Automobile dealers	...	...	...	...	102.9	105.4	110.8	113.2	113.8	116.2	121.2
New car dealers[14]	99.7	103.1	108.7	111.5	113.5	116.3	122.3	125.0	125.7	128.2	133.8
Recreational vehicle dealers[15]	...	98.8	112.2	109.7	121.4	133.6	133.8	142.4	143.5	119.1	120.3
Automotive parts, accessories, and tire stores[16]	...	...	100.9	104.2	109.4	115.1	124.3	128.2	142.0	148.2	149.0
Automotive parts and accessories stores	...	...	...	...	106.8	110.9	119.7	125.6	140.3	148.1	148.9
Tire dealers	...	...	...	...	102.0	110.7	119.3	117.5	128.1	130.5	131.2
Furniture and home furnishings stores	...	...	...	...	102.4	110.7	116.6	117.4	120.3	121.5	121.1
Furniture stores	...	...	...	...	100.8	108.0	111.0	110.6	113.7	117.2	117.0
Floor covering stores	...	...	...	...	104.6	114.4	124.3	127.0	129.8	128.2	127.5
Electronics and appliance stores	...	...	...	...	99.0	98.9	99.4	106.1	110.8	104.5	102.0
Appliance, TV, and other electronics stores	...	...	...	...	101.8	103.5	103.8	104.9	112.8	109.6	105.9
Computer and software stores	...	...	...	...	95.2	92.4	91.7	91.7	84.6	61.9	60.6
Camera and photographic supplies stores	...	...	...	...	88.6	82.0	95.5	91.3	86.7	89.2	100.5
Building material and garden equipment and supplies dealers	...	...	...	...	108.3	109.9	118.4	120.1	119.2	119.5	119.5
Building material and supplies dealers	...	...	...	...	108.7	109.9	119.8	122.4	121.0	120.8	121.5
Home centers	...	...	...	...	107.0	109.6	122.5	121.8	115.7	118.4	115.9
Paint and wallpaper stores	...	...	...	...	99.5	104.4	106.2	110.3	121.8	129.7	127.8
Hardware stores	...	...	...	...	103.1	108.2	112.3	114.3	114.3	118.2	127.1
Other building material dealers	...	...	...	...	111.4	110.8	121.3	128.9	130.6	125.7	128.1
Lawn and garden equipment and supplies stores	...	...	...	...	105.8	110.3	111.5	106.8	110.1	114.5	108.5
Nursery, garden, and farm supply stores	...	...	...	...	105.8	110.3	111.5	106.8	110.1	114.5	108.5
Food and beverage stores[14]	103.8	109.6	113.4	117.6	123.2	131.0	134.7	139.6	149.3	151.2	148.2
Grocery stores	...	...	...	...	103.5	110.7	114.0	117.9	126.1	127.4	124.3
Grocery (except convenience) stores	...	...	...	...	103.5	110.7	114.0	117.9	126.1	127.4	124.3
Specialty food stores	...	...	...	...	107.1	110.2	114.1	122.9	132.4	141.0	138.9
Beer, wine, and liquor stores[17]	...	102.9	103.5	106.9	110.7	111.0	111.3	113.2	120.6	119.8	125.3
Health and personal care stores	...	...	...	...	101.7	107.6	118.7	123.1	130.5	137.9	137.9
Pharmacies and drug stores[17]	...	102.4	112.4	116.6	119.8	127.9	142.0	148.5	158.7	169.4	169.3
Optical goods stores	...	...	...	...	99.8	100.1	101.5	103.0	104.8	107.0	107.9
Gasoline stations[15]	...	105.6	66.8	54.1	51.3	51.0	50.9	74.0	70.3	68.5	71.8
Gasoline stations with convenience stores	...	...	...	...	102.5	104.3	110.0	123.0	135.0	129.7	138.7
Other gasoline stations	...	...	...	...	132.8	118.1	84.2	216.2	151.4	152.7	152.2
Clothing and clothing accessories stores	...	...	...	...	100.5	103.3	105.4	107.0	110.7	111.9	117.0
Clothing stores	...	...	...	...	99.3	102.4	104.4	105.3	107.5	108.3	114.4
Men's clothing stores	...	...	...	...	100.2	102.1	98.9	99.8	98.3	91.1	80.3
Women's clothing stores	...	...	...	...	102.9	103.3	108.6	110.7	114.6	122.7	126.0
Family clothing stores	...	...	...	...	97.8	102.2	104.3	104.0	105.9	103.8	113.8
Shoe stores	...	...	...	...	103.9	105.0	105.7	109.7	114.0	114.7	112.6
Jewelry, luggage, and leather goods stores	...	...	...	...	101.8	104.9	108.7	110.9	120.4	123.7	129.9
Jewelry stores	...	...	...	...	101.8	104.8	108.6	110.8	120.7	124.1	130.6
Luggage and leather goods stores	...	...	...	...	101.4	106.5	111.0	113.5	116.8	118.9	120.3

[2]December 1985 = 100.
[3]December 1984 = 100.
[5]June 1984 = 100.
[8]June 1985 = 100.
[12]June 2004 = 100.
[13]June 2005 = 100.
[14]December 1999 = 100.
[15]June 2001 = 100.
[16]December 2001 = 100.
[17]June 2000 = 100.
. . . = Not available.

Table 9-3. Producer Price Indexes for the Net Output of Selected Industries, 2000–2010—*Continued*

(December 2003 = 100, unless otherwise specified.)

Industry	2000	2001	2002	2003	2004	2005	2006	2007	2008	2009	2010
Retail Trade—*Continued*											
Sporting goods, hobby, book, and music stores	...	...	...	...	96.6	96.6	98.4	103.4	111.6	113.9	112.6
Sporting goods, hobby, and musical instrument stores	...	...	...	...	97.8	99.0	102.5	107.7	119.5	123.2	121.4
Sporting goods stores	...	...	...	...	95.0	96.1	99.2	112.7	130.7	134.5	132.9
Hobby, toy, and game stores	...	...	...	...	100.5	101.7	105.7	101.9	108.5	112.2	110.1
Sewing, needlework, and piece goods stores	...	...	...	...	103.2	104.7	109.0	108.2	110.5	113.7	111.5
Book, periodical, and music stores	...	...	...	...	94.7	92.5	91.6	95.4	96.2	95.6	95.3
Bookstores and news dealers	...	...	...	...	95.0	92.0	94.2	97.1	98.0	101.3	102.8
Prerecorded tape, CD, and record stores	...	...	...	...	93.9	93.8	84.4	91.0	91.5	80.2	74.6
General merchandise stores	...	...	...	...	103.1	103.4	106.6	110.0	112.9	105.7	114.7
Department stores	...	...	...	...	105.4	105.1	105.6	111.4	117.8	111.3	122.6
Other general merchandise stores	...	...	...	...	97.7	99.5	108.9	110.0	107.9	99.5	105.3
Florists	...	...	...	...	100.2	100.2	102.8	107.3	108.6	107.5	107.2
Office supplies, stationery, and gift stores	...	...	...	...	99.7	101.7	104.3	107.8	112.0	116.5	121.6
Office supplies and stationery stores	...	...	...	...	100.4	102.9	107.1	113.6	119.4	130.7	140.4
Gift, novelty, and souvenir stores	...	...	...	...	98.7	100.0	100.1	101.2	104.0	102.8	103.9
Manufactured (mobile) home dealers	...	...	...	...	107.7	116.7	123.2	118.3	113.6	113.5	108.8
Nonstore retailers	...	...	...	...	107.5	119.8	118.9	129.2	144.1	147.7	140.9
Vending machine operators	...	...	...	...	101.5	104.4	105.7	106.4	110.6	111.9	112.9
Fuel dealers[17]	...	120.5	113.8	122.7	129.4	147.3	138.9	138.3	174.2	179.2	157.9
Transportation and Warehousing											
Air transportation[18]	147.7	157.2	157.8	162.1	162.3	171.0	180.4	183.7	203.8	188.5	202.9
Scheduled air transportation[19]	180.1	193.0	193.3	198.5	198.6	209.3	220.5	224.5	248.9	229.1	247.7
Nonscheduled air transportation[20]	107.3	112.7	114.7	117.8	119.9	126.7	136.8	148.5	165.8	160.4	165.4
Rail transportation[20]	102.6	104.5	106.6	108.8	113.4	125.2	135.9	140.9	157.3	148.5	156.2
Water transportation	...	...	...	...	101.3	106.4	111.1	113.5	127.0	116.1	125.5
Inland water transportation	...	...	...	...	103.2	119.3	144.1	146.7	172.0	166.7	171.4
Truck transportation	...	...	...	...	103.1	109.0	113.2	115.4	123.0	117.3	119.4
General freight trucking	...	...	...	...	103.5	110.0	114.1	116.5	123.6	117.5	119.3
General freight trucking, local	...	...	...	...	105.2	111.5	115.3	119.6	130.2	126.0	127.2
General freight trucking, long distance	...	...	...	...	103.2	109.7	113.8	115.9	122.2	115.5	117.5
Specialized freight trucking	...	...	...	...	102.3	107.0	111.4	113.1	122.1	117.4	119.9
Used household and office goods moving	...	...	...	...	102.6	106.0	107.8	108.8	112.2	112.8	114.7
Specialized freight (except used) trucking, local	...	...	...	...	102.7	107.1	112.3	114.2	126.7	123.9	126.5
Specialized freight (except used) trucking, long distance	...	...	...	...	101.7	107.5	112.8	114.8	123.6	113.2	115.8
Pipeline transportation of crude oil	...	...	...	...	103.9	113.3	122.0	125.4	137.1	141.0	183.4
Other pipeline transportation	...	...	...	...	101.4	105.2	108.2	115.0	121.6	128.7	133.8
Pipeline transportation of refined petroleum products	...	...	...	...	101.4	105.2	108.2	115.0	121.6	128.7	133.8
Transportation support activities	...	...	...	...	101.1	104.1	106.5	108.5	111.7	108.6	110.7
Air transportation support activities[20]	114.2	117.5	121.4	125.1	128.1	134.2	138.6	141.0	145.4	149.2	154.5
Airport operations	...	...	...	...	101.1	104.8	108.6	109.6	112.3	117.9	122.1
Other air transportation support activities	...	...	...	...	102.0	107.5	110.8	112.9	117.0	117.5	121.8
Water transportation support activities	...	...	...	...	101.0	103.5	107.7	112.7	117.3	116.8	120.2
Port and harbor operations	...	...	...	...	102.4	105.9	108.8	114.8	117.7	120.5	127.7
Marine cargo handling	...	...	...	...	100.5	102.2	105.1	109.0	110.7	113.3	116.8
Navigational services to shipping	...	...	...	...	101.5	105.7	113.9	120.6	133.8	122.9	122.9
Freight transportation arrangement[20]	98.3	98.2	97.5	97.9	98.9	99.1	98.8	100.2	102.5	94.8	95.2
Postal service[21]	135.2	143.4	150.2	155.0	155.0	155.0	164.7	171.9	178.9	185.0	187.7
Couriers and messengers	...	...	...	...	106.1	113.8	121.5	131.5	142.0	141.5	153.4
Couriers	...	...	...	...	106.6	115.0	123.2	133.5	144.4	143.8	156.6
Local messengers and local delivery	...	...	...	...	101.1	102.7	104.4	108.1	112.2	114.3	112.7
Warehousing and storage[9]	90.8	93.2	94.5	95.8	...	...	...	102.5	106.5	107.2	105.5
General warehousing and storage	...	...	...	...	100.3	101.5	103.8	107.3	111.9	112.2	109.7
Refrigerated warehousing and storage	...	...	...	...	100.5	101.0	102.4	104.0	106.7	109.5	110.5
Farm product warehousing and storage	...	...	...	...	100.2	101.5	103.8	104.0	108.7	108.1	107.4
Information											
Publishing industries, except Internet	...	...	...	...	101.5	104.1	106.2	108.1	110.6	111.3	110.3
Newspaper, book, and directory publishers	...	...	...	...	102.1	105.5	108.3	111.8	115.1	117.6	119.3
Newspaper publishers[22]	351.3	367.9	381.9	395.7	409.7	426.2	439.0	450.3	459.2	466.3	471.0
Periodical publishers[22]	292.6	305.9	320.4	332.4	339.1	347.6	354.4	369.5	383.1	391.7	396.0
Book publishers[3]	190.2	195.6	201.5	208.2	215.7	224.3	232.8	240.2	250.9	260.7	268.2
Directory and mailing list publishers	...	...	...	...	101.3	103.3	105.4	108.4	111.1	113.0	114.4
Other publishers	...	...	...	...	100.7	103.9	104.9	107.9	108.8	109.2	109.2
Software publishers	...	...	...	...	99.8	99.8	100.1	99.6	100.7	98.9	94.1
Broadcasting, except Internet	...	...	...	...	101.2	102.1	102.8	101.4	106.7	105.3	109.7
Radio and television broadcasting[15]	...	98.2	97.1	99.8	102.8	101.9	101.1	101.3	101.7	92.5	95.6
Radio broadcasting	...	...	...	...	102.7	106.3	105.8	104.3	103.7	99.5	100.3
Television broadcasting	...	...	...	...	100.5	97.3	96.3	97.3	98.0	85.8	90.6
Cable networks	...	...	...	...	101.4	104.3	106.7	103.6	111.9	115.2	120.5
Telecommunications	...	...	...	...	99.8	98.1	98.3	100.8	101.1	101.1	101.0
Wired telecommunications carriers[23]	96.4	93.6	89.9	88.1	86.3	85.8	86.6	89.3	90.7	91.1	91.8
Wireless telecommunications carriers	...	...	...	...	98.4	86.4	80.9	80.4	76.1	73.6	70.4
Cable and other program distribution	...	...	...	...	102.2	106.5	109.6	113.7	116.2	118.7	120.4
ISPs and Web search portals[12]	...	...	...	...	...	95.9	87.6	72.8	73.4	71.1	69.3
Data processing and related services	...	...	...	...	98.8	98.8	99.7	100.3	100.9	100.9	101.1

[3]December 1984 = 100.
[9]December 2006 = 100.
[12]June 2004 = 100.
[15]June 2001 = 100.
[17]June 2000 = 100.
[18]December 1992 = 100.
[19]December 1989 = 100.
[20]December 1996 = 100.
[21]June 1989 = 100.
[22]December 1979 = 100.
[23]June 1999 = 100.
. . . = Not available.

Table 9-3. Producer Price Indexes for the Net Output of Selected Industries, 2000–2010—*Continued*

(December 2003 = 100, unless otherwise specified.)

Industry	2000	2001	2002	2003	2004	2005	2006	2007	2008	2009	2010
Other Services											
Depository credit intermediation	. . .	. . .	. . .	. . .	102.5	105.0	111.2	112.8	102.6	97.5	103.2
Security, commodity contracts, and like activity	. . .	. . .	. . .	. . .	103.4	109.4	113.8	119.9	119.5	112.2	119.5
Security and commodity contracts, intermediation, and brokerage[17]	. . .	88.1	81.8	82.5	84.2	88.1	90.1	92.8	94.2	90.1	93.5
Investment banking and securities dealing	. . .	. . .	. . .	. . .	102.6	109.1	111.0	113.6	125.4	119.0	127.9
Securities brokerage	. . .	. . .	. . .	. . .	100.0	102.2	105.2	109.7	103.4	99.6	99.8
Portfolio management	. . .	. . .	. . .	. . .	108.1	117.8	124.8	137.1	131.2	116.0	132.7
Investment advice	. . .	. . .	. . .	. . .	102.0	104.8	119.4	129.7	133.4	134.7	133.4
Insurance carriers and related activities	. . .	. . .	. . .	. . .	101.9	104.5	106.3	107.7	110.1	113.3	116.6
Insurance carriers	. . .	. . .	. . .	. . .	101.9	104.5	106.4	107.7	110.2	113.4	116.7
Direct life/health/medical insurance carriers	. . .	. . .	. . .	. . .	102.2	105.1	107.6	109.5	112.6	116.2	120.3
Other direct insurance carriers[24]	101.9	104.3	108.7	115.0	118.7	121.0	121.7	122.1	123.6	126.7	128.8
Insurance agencies and brokerages	. . .	. . .	. . .	. . .	100.8	101.8	102.2	102.9	103.4	103.7	103.8
Lessors of nonresidential building (except miniwarehouse)	. . .	. . .	. . .	. . .	102.3	105.1	107.7	107.2	110.6	109.4	109.4
Lessors of miniwarehouse and self-storage units	. . .	. . .	. . .	. . .	102.0	105.6	109.2	110.6	113.4	112.9	111.1
Offices of real estate agents and brokers	. . .	. . .	. . .	. . .	101.8	108.1	110.9	110.8	106.5	101.9	100.2
Real estate property managers	. . .	. . .	. . .	. . .	100.9	102.2	102.9	103.8	108.1	108.5	107.1
Automotive equipment rental and leasing[15]	. . .	. . .	103.9	106.6	107.8	109.0	115.2	118.0	126.4	135.2	133.5
Passenger car rental and leasing	. . .	. . .	. . .	. . .	98.2	99.9	108.0	108.2	116.5	131.0	126.8
Truck, utility trailer, and RV rental and leasing	. . .	. . .	. . .	. . .	99.9	99.9	101.2	107.7	114.7	111.8	114.6
Legal services[20]	112.5	117.9	121.7	125.6	131.8	138.5	145.2	153.6	161.6	166.2	171.9
Offices of lawyers[20]	112.5	117.9	121.7	125.6	131.8	138.5	145.2	153.6	161.6	166.2	171.9
Architectural, engineering, and related services[20]	111.8	115.9	121.1	124.3	126.8	129.2	134.4	140.0	141.0	142.9	143.5
Architectural services	. . .	. . .	. . .	. . .	99.7	102.0	106.0	109.3	110.5	110.2	109.8
Engineering services	. . .	. . .	. . .	. . .	101.5	103.4	107.6	112.2	113.0	114.9	115.5
Management and technical consulting services[25]	. . .	. . .	. . .	. . .	. . .	. . .	. . .	102.8	105.7	107.3	108.5
Advertising agencies	. . .	. . .	. . .	. . .	100.1	101.4	104.1	105.0	106.0	105.1	105.1
Employment services[20]	107.3	108.2	108.9	111.4	113.9	116.3	119.2	121.7	123.2	123.5	124.9
Employee leasing services	. . .	. . .	. . .	. . .	101.3	102.9	105.4	107.6	109.0	110.2	112.1
Professional employer organizations	. . .	. . .	. . .	. . .	101.3	102.9	105.4	107.6	109.0	110.2	112.1
Staffing services	. . .	. . .	. . .	. . .	. . .	. . .	. . .	. . .	. . .	. . .	100.0
Travel agencies	. . .	. . .	. . .	. . .	96.9	95.9	99.5	101.0	99.7	99.6	100.2
Janitorial services	. . .	. . .	. . .	. . .	100.9	101.9	103.7	106.0	109.1	110.0	110.7
Waste collection	. . .	. . .	. . .	. . .	101.3	102.5	104.5	107.6	112.4	115.5	118.0
Amusement and theme parks[25]	. . .	. . .	. . .	. . .	. . .	. . .	. . .	105.2	109.8	112.5	118.2
Accommodations[20]	116.2	121.3	121.3	122.0	125.2	131.9	136.7	142.9	146.0	141.5	140.6
Hotels (except casino hotels) and motels	. . .	. . .	. . .	. . .	103.5	110.0	114.1	119.8	124.2	120.8	119.7
Casino hotels	. . .	. . .	. . .	. . .	105.0	107.5	110.8	113.0	110.9	106.3	106.3
Health Care and Social Assistance											
Offices of physicians[20]	107.3	110.4	110.3	112.1	114.3	116.4	117.5	122.3	123.6	126.6	129.7
Medical and diagnostic laboratories	. . .	. . .	. . .	. . .	100.0	104.1	104.4	107.0	107.3	108.4	108.3
Home health care services[20]	111.1	114.0	116.6	117.0	119.8	121.1	121.8	124.0	126.1	128.0	129.5
Hospitals[18]	119.4	123.0	127.5	134.9	141.5	146.9	153.3	158.6	163.4	168.3	173.3
General medical and surgical hospitals	. . .	. . .	. . .	. . .	102.9	106.7	111.2	115.1	118.6	122.3	125.9
Psychiatric and substance abuse hospitals	. . .	. . .	. . .	. . .	101.1	103.7	106.2	110.0	113.4	115.2	116.3
Other specialty hospitals	. . .	. . .	. . .	. . .	103.8	109.6	122.8	126.7	128.4	130.7	138.0
Nursing care facilities	. . .	. . .	. . .	. . .	102.6	106.4	109.6	114.7	119.2	123.2	125.7
Residential mental retardation facilities	. . .	. . .	. . .	. . .	101.2	104.5	108.5	112.7	118.3	123.0	130.6

[15]June 2001 = 100.
[17]June 2000 = 100.
[18]December 1992 = 100.
[20]December 1996 = 100.
[24]December 1998 = 100.
[25]June 2006 = 100.
. . . = Not available.

CONSUMER PRICE INDEX

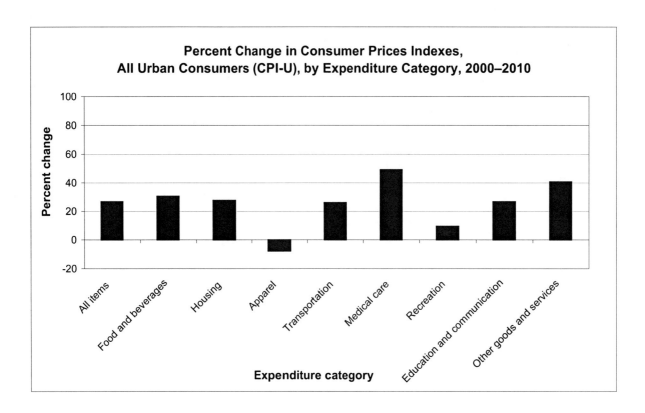

While the Consumer Price Index for all Urban Consumers (CPI-U) for all items increased by 26.7 percent from 2000 to 2010, the CPI-U for medical care increased by 48.9 percent. The CPI-U also increased rapidly for food and beverages (30.6 percent) and housing (27.5 percent) from 2000 to 2010. The CPI-U for apparel declined by 7.8 percent from 2000 to 2010 with men's and boy's apparel experiencing the greatest decline at 13.7 percent. (See Table 9-8.)

OTHER HIGHLIGHTS

• The CPI-U for energy commodities increased 18.2 percent in 2010 after decreasing 27.8 percent from 2008 to 2009. (See Table 9-5.)

• Among all medical care components between 2000 and 2010, hospitals and related services grew the fastest (91.5 percent) followed by medical care services (54.6 percent) and professional services (38.1 percent). Although medical care commodities grew the slowest among all medical care components, it still grew rapidly at 32.2 percent. (See Table 9-8.)

• The CPI-U in Milwaukee increased 3.3 percent in 2010—faster than any other MSA listed in Table 9-10. The CPI-U grew by less than 1 percent in Detroit-Ann Arbor-Flint, MI (0.8 percent); Miami-Fort Lauderdale, FL (0.8 percent); Dallas-Fort Worth, TX (0.5 percent); and Seattle-Tacoma-Bremerton, WA (0.3 percent). (See Table 9-10.)

• The Consumer Price Index, Urban Wage Earners and Clerical Workers (CPI-W) increased 2.1 percent in 2010 after declining in 2009 for the first time since 1955. (See Table 9-7.)

NOTES AND DEFINITIONS

CONSUMER PRICE INDEX

The Consumer Price Index (CPI) is a measure of the average change over time in the prices of consumer items—goods and services that people buy for day-to-day living. The CPI is a complex construct that combines economic theory with sampling and other statistical techniques and uses data from several surveys to produce a timely and precise measure of average price change for the consumption sector of the American economy.

The Bureau of Labor Statistics (BLS) publishes CPIs for two population groups: (1) the CPI for Urban Wage Earners and Clerical Workers (CPI-W), which covers households of wage earners and clerical workers that comprise approximately 32 percent of the total population and (2) the CPI for All Urban Consumers (CPI-U) and the Chained CPI for All Urban Consumers (C-CPI-U), which cover approximately 87 percent of the total population and include in addition to wage earners and clerical worker households, groups such as professional, managerial, and technical workers, the self-employed, short-term workers, the unemployed, and retirees and others not in the labor force. BLS began publishing the CPI-U in January 1978, but did not begin publishing the C-CPI-U until August 2002 with data beginning in January 2000. The CPI-W is much older than either the CPI-U or C-CPI-U.

The CPIs are based on prices of food, clothing, shelter, and fuels, transportation fares, charges for doctors' and dentists' services, drugs, and other goods and services that people buy for day-to-day living. Prices are collected each month in 87 urban areas across the country from about 4,000 housing units and approximately 26,000 retail establishments-department stores, supermarkets, hospitals, filling stations, and other types of stores and service establishments. All taxes directly associated with the purchase and use of items are included in the index. Prices of fuels and a few other items are obtained every month in all 87 locations. Prices of most other commodities and services are collected every month in the three largest geographic areas and every other month in other areas. Prices of most goods and services are obtained by personal visits or telephone calls from BLS trained representatives.

In calculating the index, price changes for the various items in each location are averaged together with weights, which represent their importance in the spending of the appropriate population group. Local data are then combined to obtain a U.S. city average. For the CPI-U and CPI-W, separate indexes are also published by size of city, by region of the country, for cross-classifications of regions and population-size classes, and for 27 local areas. Area indexes do not measure differences in the level of prices among cities; they only measure the average change in prices for each area since the base period. For the C-CPI-U data are issued only at the national level. It is important to note that the CPI-U and CPI-W are considered final when released, but the C-CPI-U is issued in preliminary form and subject to two annual revisions. The prices used in the C-CPI-U are the same as those used to produce the CPI-U and the CPI-W, but the C-CPI-U uses a different formula and different weights to combine basic indexes.

The Consumer Price Index Research Series Using Current Methods (CPI-U-RS), shown in Table 9-11, provides estimates for the period since 1977 of what the CPI would have been had the most current methods been in effect. Each time there are new methods introduced into the CPI, the CPI-U-RS is revised from 1978 forward.

Sources of Additional Information

An extensive description of the methodology is available in the updated version of Chapter 17 in the *BLS Handbook of Methods*. Additional detailed data can be found in the *Consumer Price Index Detailed Report* and in special reports. These resources can be found on the BLS Web site at <http://www.bls.gov>.

Table 9-4. Consumer Price Indexes, All Urban Consumers (CPI-U): U.S. City Average, Major Groups, 1957–2010

(1982–1984 = 100, unless otherwise specified.)

Year	All items	Food and beverages	Housing	Apparel	Transportation	Medical care	Recreation[1]	Education and communication[1]	Other goods and services
1957	28.1	...	...	44.5	27.7	19.7	...	...	...
1958	28.9	...	...	44.6	28.6	20.6	...	...	...
1959	29.1	...	...	45.0	29.8	21.5	...	...	...
1960	29.6	...	...	45.7	29.8	22.3	...	...	...
1961	29.9	...	...	46.1	30.1	22.9	...	...	...
1962	30.2	...	...	46.3	30.8	23.5	...	...	...
1963	30.6	...	...	46.9	30.9	24.1	...	...	...
1964	31.0	...	...	47.3	31.4	24.6	...	...	...
1965	31.5	...	...	47.8	31.9	25.2	...	...	...
1966	32.4	...	...	49.0	32.3	26.3	...	...	...
1967	33.4	35.0	30.8	51.0	33.3	28.2	...	...	35.1
1968	34.8	36.2	32.0	53.7	34.3	29.9	...	...	36.9
1969	36.7	38.1	34.0	56.8	35.7	31.9	...	...	38.7
1970	38.8	40.1	36.4	59.2	37.5	34.0	...	...	40.9
1971	40.5	41.4	38.0	61.1	39.5	36.1	...	...	42.9
1972	41.8	43.1	39.4	62.3	39.9	37.3	...	...	44.7
1973	44.4	48.8	41.2	64.6	41.2	38.8	...	...	46.4
1974	49.3	55.5	45.8	69.4	45.8	42.4	...	...	49.8
1975	53.8	60.2	50.7	72.5	50.1	47.5	...	...	53.9
1976	56.9	62.1	53.8	75.2	55.1	52.0	...	...	57.0
1977	60.6	65.8	57.4	78.6	59.0	57.0	...	...	60.4
1978	65.2	72.2	62.4	81.4	61.7	61.8	...	...	64.3
1979	72.6	79.9	70.1	84.9	70.5	67.5	...	...	68.9
1980	82.4	86.7	81.1	90.9	83.1	74.9	...	...	75.2
1981	90.9	93.5	90.4	95.3	93.2	82.9	...	...	82.6
1982	96.5	97.3	96.9	97.8	97.0	92.5	...	...	91.1
1983	99.6	99.5	99.5	100.2	99.3	100.6	...	...	101.1
1984	103.9	103.2	103.6	102.1	103.7	106.8	...	...	107.9
1985	107.6	105.6	107.7	105.0	106.4	113.5	...	...	114.5
1986	109.6	109.1	110.9	105.9	102.3	122.0	...	...	121.4
1987	113.6	113.5	114.2	110.6	105.4	130.1	...	...	128.5
1988	118.3	118.2	118.5	115.4	108.7	138.6	...	...	137.0
1989	124.0	124.9	123.0	118.6	114.1	149.3	...	...	147.7
1990	130.7	132.1	128.5	124.1	120.5	162.8	...	...	159.0
1991	136.2	136.8	133.6	128.7	123.8	177.0	...	...	171.6
1992	140.3	138.7	137.5	131.9	126.5	190.1	...	...	183.3
1993	144.5	141.6	141.2	133.7	130.4	201.4	90.7	85.5	192.9
1994	148.2	144.9	144.8	133.4	134.3	211.0	92.7	88.8	198.5
1995	152.4	148.9	148.5	132.0	139.1	220.5	94.5	92.2	206.9
1996	156.9	153.7	152.8	131.7	143.0	228.2	97.4	95.3	215.4
1997	160.5	157.7	156.8	132.9	144.3	234.6	99.6	98.4	224.8
1998	163.0	161.1	160.4	133.0	141.6	242.1	101.1	100.3	237.7
1999	166.6	164.6	163.9	131.3	144.4	250.6	102.0	101.2	258.3
2000	172.2	168.4	169.6	129.6	153.3	260.8	103.3	102.5	271.1
2001	177.1	173.6	176.4	127.3	154.3	272.8	104.9	105.2	282.6
2002	179.9	176.8	180.3	124.0	152.9	285.6	106.2	107.9	293.2
2003	184.0	180.5	184.8	120.9	157.6	297.1	107.5	109.8	298.7
2004	188.9	186.6	189.5	120.4	163.1	310.1	108.6	111.6	304.7
2005	195.3	191.2	195.7	119.5	173.9	323.2	109.4	113.7	313.4
2006	201.6	195.7	203.2	119.5	180.9	336.2	110.9	116.8	321.7
2007	207.3	203.3	209.6	119.0	184.7	351.1	111.4	119.6	333.3
2008	215.3	214.2	216.3	118.9	195.5	364.1	113.3	123.6	345.4
2009	214.5	218.2	217.1	120.1	179.3	375.6	114.3	127.4	368.6
2010	218.1	220.0	216.3	119.5	193.4	388.4	113.3	129.9	381.3

[1]December 1997 = 100.
. . . = Not available.

Table 9-5. Consumer Price Indexes, All Urban Consumers (CPI-U): U.S. City Average, Commodity, Service, and Special Groups, 1957–2010

(1982–1984 = 100, unless otherwise specified.)

Year	All items less food	All items less shelter	All items less medical care	All items less energy	All items less food and energy	Commodities	Commodities less food and beverages	Commodities less food and energy	Energy commodities	Nondurables	Nondurables less food	Nondurables less food and apparel
1957	28.0	29.7	28.7	28.9	28.9	32.6	. . .	37.4	21.6	30.9	32.9	28.5
1958	28.6	30.6	29.5	29.7	29.6	33.3	. . .	37.9	21.3	31.7	33.1	28.8
1959	29.2	30.8	29.8	29.9	30.2	33.3	. . .	38.4	21.5	31.5	33.5	29.2
1960	29.7	31.3	30.2	30.4	30.6	33.6	. . .	38.5	21.9	32.0	34.1	29.7
1961	30.0	31.7	30.5	30.7	31.0	33.8	. . .	38.6	21.9	32.2	34.3	29.8
1962	30.3	32.0	30.8	31.1	31.4	34.1	. . .	38.9	22.0	32.5	34.5	30.1
1963	30.7	32.4	31.1	31.5	31.8	34.4	. . .	39.2	22.1	32.9	34.8	30.4
1964	31.1	32.8	31.5	32.0	32.3	34.8	. . .	39.6	21.9	33.2	35.1	30.6
1965	31.6	33.3	32.0	32.5	32.7	35.2	. . .	39.8	22.6	33.8	35.6	31.2
1966	32.3	34.3	33.0	33.5	33.5	36.1	. . .	40.3	23.2	35.1	36.4	31.8
1967	33.4	35.2	33.7	34.4	34.7	36.8	38.3	41.3	23.9	35.7	37.6	32.6
1968	34.9	36.7	35.1	35.9	36.3	38.1	39.7	42.9	24.4	37.1	39.1	33.7
1969	36.8	38.4	37.0	38.0	38.4	39.9	41.4	44.7	25.2	38.9	40.9	34.9
1970	39.0	40.3	39.2	40.3	40.8	41.7	43.1	46.7	25.6	40.8	42.5	36.3
1971	40.8	42.0	40.8	42.0	42.7	43.2	44.7	48.5	26.1	42.1	44.0	37.6
1972	42.0	43.3	42.1	43.4	44.0	44.5	45.8	49.7	26.4	43.5	45.0	38.6
1973	43.7	46.2	44.8	46.1	45.6	47.8	47.3	51.1	29.1	47.5	46.9	40.3
1974	48.0	51.4	49.8	50.6	49.4	53.5	52.4	55.0	40.4	54.0	52.9	46.9
1975	52.5	56.0	54.3	55.1	53.9	58.2	57.3	60.1	43.4	58.3	57.0	51.5
1976	56.0	59.3	57.2	58.2	57.4	60.7	60.2	63.2	45.4	60.5	59.5	54.1
1977	59.6	63.1	60.8	61.9	61.0	64.2	63.6	66.5	48.7	64.0	62.5	57.2
1978	63.9	67.4	65.4	66.7	65.5	68.8	67.3	70.5	51.0	68.6	65.5	60.4
1979	71.2	74.2	72.9	73.4	71.9	76.6	75.2	76.4	68.7	77.2	74.6	71.2
1980	81.5	82.9	82.8	81.9	80.8	86.0	85.7	83.5	95.2	87.6	88.4	87.1
1981	90.4	91.0	91.4	90.1	89.2	93.2	93.1	90.0	107.6	95.2	96.7	96.8
1982	96.3	96.2	96.8	96.1	95.8	97.0	96.9	95.3	102.9	97.8	98.3	98.2
1983	99.7	99.8	99.6	99.6	99.6	99.8	100.0	100.2	99.0	99.7	100.0	100.0
1984	104.0	103.9	103.7	104.3	104.6	103.2	103.1	104.4	98.1	102.5	101.7	101.8
1985	108.0	107.0	107.2	108.4	109.1	105.4	105.2	107.1	98.2	104.8	104.1	104.1
1986	109.8	108.0	108.8	112.6	113.5	104.4	101.4	108.6	77.2	103.5	98.5	96.9
1987	113.6	111.6	112.6	117.2	118.2	107.7	104.0	111.8	80.2	107.5	101.8	100.3
1988	118.3	115.9	117.0	122.3	123.4	111.5	107.3	115.8	80.8	111.8	105.8	104.0
1989	123.7	121.6	122.4	128.1	129.0	116.7	111.6	119.6	87.9	118.2	111.7	111.3
1990	130.3	128.2	128.8	134.7	135.5	122.8	117.0	123.6	101.2	126.0	119.9	120.9
1991	136.1	133.5	133.8	140.9	142.1	126.6	120.4	128.8	99.1	130.3	124.5	125.7
1992	140.8	137.3	137.5	145.4	147.3	129.1	123.2	132.5	98.3	132.8	127.6	128.9
1993	145.1	141.4	141.2	150.0	152.2	131.5	125.3	135.2	97.3	135.1	129.3	130.7
1994	149.0	144.8	144.7	154.1	156.5	133.8	126.9	137.1	97.6	136.8	129.7	131.6
1995	153.1	148.6	148.6	158.7	161.2	136.4	128.9	139.3	98.8	139.3	130.9	134.1
1996	157.5	152.8	152.8	163.1	165.6	139.9	131.5	141.3	105.7	143.5	134.5	139.5
1997	161.1	155.9	156.3	167.1	169.5	141.8	132.2	142.3	105.7	146.4	136.3	141.8
1998	163.4	157.2	158.6	170.9	173.4	141.9	130.5	143.2	92.1	146.9	134.6	139.2
1999	167.0	160.2	162.0	174.4	177.0	144.4	132.5	144.1	100.0	151.2	139.4	147.5
2000	173.0	165.7	167.3	178.6	181.3	149.2	137.7	144.9	129.5	158.2	149.1	162.9
2001	177.8	169.7	171.9	183.5	186.1	150.7	137.2	145.3	125.2	160.6	149.1	164.1
2002	180.5	170.8	174.3	187.7	190.5	149.7	134.2	143.7	117.1	161.1	147.4	163.3
2003	184.7	174.6	178.1	190.6	193.2	151.2	134.5	140.9	136.7	165.3	151.9	172.1
2004	189.4	179.3	182.7	194.4	196.6	154.7	136.7	139.6	161.2	172.2	159.3	183.8
2005	196.0	186.1	188.7	198.7	200.9	160.2	142.5	140.3	197.4	180.2	170.1	201.2
2006	202.7	191.9	194.7	203.7	205.9	164.0	145.9	140.6	223.0	186.7	178.2	213.9
2007	208.1	196.6	200.1	208.9	210.7	167.5	147.5	140.1	241.0	193.5	184.0	223.4
2008	215.5	205.5	207.8	214.8	215.6	174.8	153.0	140.2	284.4	205.9	197.3	244.4
2009	214.0	203.3	206.6	218.4	219.2	169.7	144.4	142.0	205.3	198.5	181.5	218.7
2010	217.8	208.6	209.7	220.5	221.3	174.6	150.4	143.6	242.6	205.3	191.9	235.6

. . . = Not available.

Table 9-5. Consumer Price Indexes, All Urban Consumers (CPI-U): U.S. City Average, Commodity, Service, and Special Groups, 1957–2010—*Continued*

(1982–1984 = 100, unless otherwise specified.)

Year	Total services[1]	Rent of shelter[2]	Gasoline, all types	Transportation services	Medical care services	Other services	Services less medical care	Energy	Services less energy
1957	21.8	. . .	23.8	24.1	17.0	. . .	22.8	21.5	21.9
1958	22.6	. . .	23.5	25.6	17.9	. . .	23.6	21.5	22.7
1959	23.3	. . .	23.7	26.5	18.7	. . .	24.2	21.9	23.4
1960	24.1	. . .	24.4	27.2	19.5	. . .	25.0	22.4	24.2
1961	24.5	. . .	24.1	27.8	20.2	. . .	25.4	22.5	24.7
1962	25.0	. . .	24.3	28.3	20.9	. . .	25.9	22.6	25.2
1963	25.5	. . .	24.2	28.6	21.5	. . .	26.3	22.6	25.7
1964	26.0	. . .	24.1	29.2	22.0	. . .	26.8	22.5	26.2
1965	26.6	. . .	25.1	30.3	22.7	. . .	27.4	22.9	26.9
1966	27.6	. . .	25.6	31.6	23.9	. . .	28.3	23.3	28.0
1967	28.8	. . .	26.4	32.6	26.0	36.0	29.3	23.8	29.3
1968	30.3	. . .	26.8	33.9	27.9	38.1	30.8	24.2	30.9
1969	32.4	. . .	27.7	36.3	30.2	40.0	32.9	24.8	33.2
1970	35.0	. . .	27.9	40.2	32.3	42.2	35.6	25.5	36.0
1971	37.0	. . .	28.1	43.4	34.7	44.4	37.5	26.5	38.0
1972	38.4	. . .	28.4	44.4	35.9	45.6	38.9	27.2	39.4
1973	40.1	. . .	31.2	44.7	37.5	47.7	40.6	29.4	41.1
1974	43.8	. . .	42.2	46.3	41.4	51.3	44.3	38.1	44.8
1975	48.0	. . .	45.1	49.8	46.6	55.1	48.3	42.1	48.8
1976	52.0	. . .	47.0	56.9	51.3	58.4	52.2	45.1	52.7
1977	56.0	. . .	49.7	61.5	56.4	62.1	55.9	49.4	56.5
1978	60.8	. . .	51.8	64.4	61.2	66.4	60.7	52.5	61.3
1979	67.5	. . .	70.2	69.5	67.2	71.9	67.5	65.7	68.2
1980	77.9	. . .	97.5	79.2	74.8	78.7	78.2	86.0	78.5
1981	88.1	. . .	108.5	88.6	82.8	86.1	88.7	97.7	88.7
1982	96.0	. . .	102.8	96.1	92.6	93.5	96.4	99.2	96.3
1983	99.4	102.7	99.4	99.1	100.7	100.0	99.2	99.9	99.2
1984	104.6	107.7	97.8	104.8	106.7	106.5	104.4	100.9	104.5
1985	109.9	113.9	98.6	110.0	113.2	113.0	109.6	101.6	110.2
1986	115.4	120.2	77.0	116.3	121.9	119.4	114.6	88.2	116.5
1987	120.2	125.9	80.1	121.9	130.0	125.7	119.1	88.6	122.0
1988	125.7	132.0	80.8	128.0	138.3	132.6	124.3	89.3	127.9
1989	131.9	138.0	88.5	135.6	148.9	140.9	130.1	94.3	134.4
1990	139.2	145.5	101.0	144.2	162.7	150.2	136.8	102.1	142.3
1991	146.3	152.1	99.2	151.2	177.1	159.8	143.3	102.5	149.8
1992	152.0	157.3	99.0	155.7	190.5	168.5	148.4	103.0	155.9
1993	157.9	162.0	97.7	162.9	202.9	177.0	153.6	104.2	161.9
1994	163.1	167.0	98.2	168.6	213.4	185.4	158.4	104.6	167.6
1995	168.7	172.4	99.8	175.9	224.2	193.3	163.5	105.2	173.7
1996	174.1	178.0	105.9	180.5	232.4	201.4	168.7	110.1	179.4
1997	179.4	183.4	105.8	185.0	239.1	209.6	173.9	111.5	185.0
1998	184.2	189.6	91.6	187.9	246.8	216.9	178.4	102.9	190.6
1999	188.8	195.0	100.1	190.7	255.1	223.1	182.7	106.6	195.7
2000	195.3	201.3	128.6	196.1	266.0	229.9	188.9	124.6	202.1
2001	203.4	208.9	124.0	201.9	278.8	238.0	196.6	129.3	209.6
2002	209.8	216.7	116.0	209.1	292.9	246.4	202.5	121.7	217.5
2003	216.5	221.9	135.1	216.3	306.0	254.4	208.7	136.5	223.8
2004	222.8	227.9	159.7	220.6	321.3	261.3	214.5	151.4	230.2
2005	230.1	233.7	194.7	225.7	336.7	268.4	221.2	177.1	236.6
2006	238.9	241.9	219.9	230.8	350.6	277.5	229.6	196.9	244.7
2007	246.8	250.8	238.0	233.7	369.3	285.6	236.8	207.7	253.1
2008	255.5	257.2	277.5	244.1	384.9	295.8	245.0	236.7	261.0
2009	259.2	259.9	201.6	251.0	397.3	304.0	248.1	193.1	265.9
2010	261.3	258.8	238.6	259.8	411.2	309.6	249.6	211.4	268.3

[1] Includes tenants, household insurance, water, sewer, trash, and household operations services, not shown separately.
[2] December 1982 = 100.
. . . = Not available.

Table 9-6. Consumer Price Indexes, All Urban Consumers (CPI-U): U.S. City Average, Selected Groups and Purchasing Power of the Consumer Dollar, 1913–2010

(1982–1984 = 100, unless otherwise specified.)

Year	All items	Food	Rent of primary residence	Owners' equivalent of primary residence[1]	Apparel	Purchasing power of the consumer dollar[2]
1913	9.9	10.0	21.0	. . .	14.9	10.08
1914	10.0	10.2	21.0	. . .	15.0	9.94
1915	10.1	10.0	21.1	. . .	15.3	9.84
1916	10.9	11.3	21.3	. . .	16.8	9.15
1917	12.8	14.5	21.2	. . .	20.2	7.79
1918	15.1	16.7	21.5	. . .	27.3	6.64
1919	17.3	18.6	23.3	. . .	36.2	5.78
1920	20.0	21.0	27.4	. . .	43.1	4.99
1921	17.9	15.9	31.5	. . .	33.2	5.59
1922	16.8	14.9	32.4	. . .	27.0	5.96
1923	17.1	15.4	33.2	. . .	27.1	5.86
1924	17.1	15.2	34.4	. . .	26.8	5.85
1925	17.5	16.5	34.6	. . .	26.3	5.70
1926	17.7	17.0	34.2	. . .	25.9	5.65
1927	17.4	16.4	33.7	. . .	25.3	5.76
1928	17.1	16.3	32.9	. . .	25.0	5.83
1929	17.1	16.5	32.1	. . .	24.7	5.83
1930	16.7	15.6	31.2	. . .	24.2	5.99
1931	15.2	12.9	29.6	. . .	22.0	6.56
1932	13.7	10.7	26.5	. . .	19.5	7.32
1933	13.0	10.4	22.9	. . .	18.8	7.71
1934	13.4	11.6	21.4	. . .	20.6	7.46
1935	13.7	12.4	21.4	. . .	20.8	7.28
1936	13.9	12.6	21.9	. . .	21.0	7.21
1937	14.4	13.1	22.9	. . .	22.0	6.96
1938	14.1	12.1	23.7	. . .	21.9	7.09
1939	13.9	11.8	23.7	. . .	21.6	7.20
1940	14.0	12.0	23.7	. . .	21.8	7.13
1941	14.7	13.1	24.2	. . .	22.8	6.79
1942	16.3	15.4	24.7	. . .	26.7	6.13
1943	17.3	17.1	24.7	. . .	27.8	5.78
1944	17.6	16.9	24.8	. . .	29.8	5.68
1945	18.0	17.3	24.8	. . .	31.4	5.55
1946	19.5	19.8	25.0	. . .	34.4	5.12
1947	22.3	24.1	25.8	. . .	39.9	4.47
1948	24.1	26.1	27.5	. . .	42.5	4.15
1949	23.8	25.0	28.7	. . .	40.8	4.19
1950	24.1	25.4	29.7	. . .	40.3	4.15
1951	26.0	28.2	30.9	. . .	43.9	3.85
1952	26.5	28.7	32.2	. . .	43.5	3.77
1953	26.7	28.3	33.9	. . .	43.1	3.74
1954	26.9	28.2	35.1	. . .	43.1	3.72
1955	26.8	27.8	35.6	. . .	42.9	3.73
1956	27.2	28.0	36.3	. . .	43.7	3.68
1957	28.1	28.9	37.0	. . .	44.5	3.55
1958	28.9	30.2	37.6	. . .	44.6	3.46
1959	29.1	29.7	38.2	. . .	45.0	3.43
1960	29.6	30.0	38.7	. . .	45.7	3.37
1961	29.9	30.4	39.2	. . .	46.1	3.34
1962	30.2	30.6	39.7	. . .	46.3	3.30
1963	30.6	31.1	40.1	. . .	46.9	3.27
1964	31.0	31.5	40.5	. . .	47.3	3.22
1965	31.5	32.2	40.9	. . .	47.8	3.17
1966	32.4	33.8	41.5	. . .	49.0	3.08
1967	33.4	34.1	42.2	. . .	51.0	2.99
1968	34.8	35.3	43.3	. . .	53.7	2.87
1969	36.7	37.1	44.7	. . .	56.8	2.73
1970	38.8	39.2	46.5	. . .	59.2	2.57
1971	40.5	40.4	48.7	. . .	61.1	2.47
1972	41.8	42.1	50.4	. . .	62.3	2.39
1973	44.4	48.2	52.5	. . .	64.6	2.25
1974	49.3	55.1	55.2	. . .	69.4	2.03
1975	53.8	59.8	58.0	. . .	72.5	1.86
1976	56.9	61.6	61.1	. . .	75.2	1.76
1977	60.6	65.5	64.8	. . .	78.6	1.65
1978	65.2	72.0	69.3	. . .	81.4	1.53
1979	72.6	79.9	74.3	. . .	84.9	1.38

[1]December 1982 = 100.
[2]Purchasing power in 1982–1984 = $1.00.
. . . = Not available.

Table 9-6. Consumer Price Indexes, All Urban Consumers (CPI-U): U.S. City Average, Selected Groups and Purchasing Power of the Consumer Dollar, 1913–2010—*Continued*

(1982–1984 = 100, unless otherwise specified.)

Year	All items	Food	Rent of primary residence	Owners' equivalent of primary residence[1]	Apparel	Purchasing power of the consumer dollar[2]
1980	82.4	86.8	80.9	. . .	90.9	1.22
1981	90.9	93.6	87.9	. . .	95.3	1.10
1982	96.5	97.4	94.6	. . .	97.8	1.04
1983	99.6	99.4	100.1	102.5	100.2	1.00
1984	103.9	103.2	105.3	107.3	102.1	0.96
1985	107.6	105.6	111.8	113.2	105.0	0.93
1986	109.6	109.0	118.3	119.4	105.9	0.91
1987	113.6	113.5	123.1	124.8	110.6	0.88
1988	118.3	118.2	127.8	131.1	115.4	0.85
1989	124.0	125.1	132.8	137.4	118.6	0.81
1990	130.7	132.4	138.4	144.8	124.1	0.77
1991	136.2	136.3	143.3	150.4	128.7	0.73
1992	140.3	137.9	146.9	155.5	131.9	0.71
1993	144.5	140.9	150.3	160.5	133.7	0.69
1994	148.2	144.3	154.0	165.8	133.4	0.68
1995	152.4	148.4	157.8	171.3	132.0	0.66
1996	156.9	153.3	162.0	176.8	131.7	0.64
1997	160.5	157.3	166.7	181.9	132.9	0.62
1998	163.0	160.7	172.1	187.8	133.0	0.61
1999	166.6	164.1	177.5	192.9	131.3	0.60
2000	172.2	167.8	183.9	198.7	129.6	0.58
2001	177.1	173.1	192.1	206.3	127.3	0.57
2002	179.9	176.2	199.7	214.7	124.0	0.56
2003	184.0	180.0	205.5	219.9	120.9	0.54
2004	188.9	186.2	211.0	224.9	120.4	0.53
2005	195.3	190.7	217.3	230.2	119.5	0.51
2006	201.6	195.2	225.1	238.2	119.5	0.50
2007	207.3	202.9	234.7	246.2	119.0	0.48
2008	215.3	214.1	243.3	252.4	118.9	0.47
2009	214.5	218.0	248.8	256.6	120.1	0.47
2010	218.1	219.6	249.4	256.6	119.5	0.46

[1]December 1982 = 100.
[2]Purchasing power in 1982–1984 = $1.00.
. . . = Not available.

Table 9-7. Consumer Price Indexes, Urban Wage Earners and Clerical Workers (CPI-W): U.S. City Average, Major Groups, 1913–2010

(1982–1984 = 100, unless otherwise specified.)

Year	All items	Food and beverages	Housing	Apparel	Transportation	Medical care	Recreation[1]	Education and communication[1]	Other goods and services
1913	10.0	. . .	. . .	15.0	. . .	. . .	. . .	. . .	. . .
1914	10.1	. . .	. . .	15.1	. . .	. . .	. . .	. . .	. . .
1915	10.2	. . .	. . .	15.4	. . .	. . .	. . .	. . .	. . .
1916	11.0	. . .	. . .	16.9	. . .	. . .	. . .	. . .	. . .
1917	12.9	. . .	. . .	20.3	. . .	. . .	. . .	. . .	. . .
1918	15.1	. . .	. . .	27.5	. . .	. . .	. . .	. . .	. . .
1919	17.4	. . .	. . .	36.4	. . .	. . .	. . .	. . .	. . .
1920	20.1	. . .	. . .	43.3	. . .	. . .	. . .	. . .	. . .
1921	18.0	. . .	. . .	33.4	. . .	. . .	. . .	. . .	. . .
1922	16.9	. . .	. . .	27.2	. . .	. . .	. . .	. . .	. . .
1923	17.2	. . .	. . .	27.2	. . .	. . .	. . .	. . .	. . .
1924	17.2	. . .	. . .	26.9	. . .	. . .	. . .	. . .	. . .
1925	17.6	. . .	. . .	26.4	. . .	. . .	. . .	. . .	. . .
1926	17.8	. . .	. . .	26.0	. . .	. . .	. . .	. . .	. . .
1927	17.5	. . .	. . .	25.5	. . .	. . .	. . .	. . .	. . .
1928	17.2	. . .	. . .	25.1	. . .	. . .	. . .	. . .	. . .
1929	17.2	. . .	. . .	24.8	. . .	. . .	. . .	. . .	. . .
1930	16.8	. . .	. . .	24.3	. . .	. . .	. . .	. . .	. . .
1931	15.3	. . .	. . .	22.1	. . .	. . .	. . .	. . .	. . .
1932	13.7	. . .	. . .	19.6	. . .	. . .	. . .	. . .	. . .
1933	13.0	. . .	. . .	18.9	. . .	. . .	. . .	. . .	. . .
1934	13.5	. . .	. . .	20.7	. . .	. . .	. . .	. . .	. . .
1935	13.8	. . .	. . .	20.9	14.1	10.2	. . .	. . .	. . .
1936	13.9	. . .	. . .	21.1	14.2	10.3	. . .	. . .	. . .
1937	14.4	. . .	. . .	22.1	14.5	10.4	. . .	. . .	. . .
1938	14.2	. . .	. . .	22.0	14.6	10.4	. . .	. . .	. . .
1939	14.0	. . .	. . .	21.7	14.2	10.4	. . .	. . .	. . .
1940	14.1	. . .	. . .	21.9	14.1	10.4	. . .	. . .	. . .
1941	14.8	. . .	. . .	23.0	14.6	10.5	. . .	. . .	. . .
1942	16.4	. . .	. . .	26.8	15.9	10.8	. . .	. . .	. . .
1943	17.4	. . .	. . .	28.0	15.8	11.3	. . .	. . .	. . .
1944	17.7	. . .	. . .	30.0	15.8	11.6	. . .	. . .	. . .
1945	18.1	. . .	. . .	31.5	15.8	11.9	. . .	. . .	. . .
1946	19.6	. . .	. . .	34.6	16.6	12.6	. . .	. . .	. . .
1947	22.5	. . .	. . .	40.1	18.4	13.6	. . .	. . .	. . .
1948	24.2	. . .	. . .	42.7	20.4	14.5	. . .	. . .	. . .
1949	24.0	. . .	. . .	41.0	22.0	14.9	. . .	. . .	. . .
1950	24.2	. . .	. . .	40.5	22.6	15.2	. . .	. . .	. . .
1951	26.1	. . .	. . .	44.1	24.0	15.9	. . .	. . .	. . .
1952	26.7	. . .	. . .	43.7	25.6	16.8	. . .	. . .	. . .
1953	26.9	. . .	. . .	43.3	26.3	17.4	. . .	. . .	. . .
1954	27.0	. . .	. . .	43.3	25.9	17.9	. . .	. . .	. . .
1955	26.9	. . .	. . .	43.1	25.6	18.3	. . .	. . .	. . .
1956	27.3	. . .	. . .	44.0	26.1	19.0	. . .	. . .	. . .
1957	28.3	. . .	. . .	44.7	27.6	19.8	. . .	. . .	. . .
1958	29.1	. . .	. . .	44.8	28.4	20.7	. . .	. . .	. . .
1959	29.3	. . .	. . .	45.2	29.6	21.6	. . .	. . .	. . .
1960	29.8	. . .	. . .	45.9	29.6	22.4	. . .	. . .	. . .
1961	30.1	. . .	. . .	46.3	30.0	23.0	. . .	. . .	. . .
1962	30.4	. . .	. . .	46.6	30.6	23.6	. . .	. . .	. . .
1963	30.8	. . .	. . .	47.1	30.8	24.2	. . .	. . .	. . .
1964	31.2	. . .	. . .	47.5	31.2	24.7	. . .	. . .	. . .
1965	31.7	. . .	. . .	48.0	31.7	25.3	. . .	. . .	. . .
1966	32.6	. . .	. . .	49.2	32.2	26.4	. . .	. . .	. . .
1967	33.6	35.0	31.1	51.2	33.1	28.3	. . .	. . .	35.4
1968	35.0	36.2	32.3	54.0	34.1	30.0	. . .	. . .	37.2
1969	36.9	38.0	34.3	57.1	35.5	32.1	. . .	. . .	39.1
1970	39.0	40.1	36.7	59.5	37.3	34.1	. . .	. . .	41.3
1971	40.7	41.3	38.3	61.4	39.2	36.3	. . .	. . .	43.3
1972	42.1	43.1	39.8	62.7	39.7	37.5	. . .	. . .	45.1
1973	44.7	48.8	41.5	65.0	41.0	39.0	. . .	. . .	46.9
1974	49.6	55.5	46.2	69.8	45.5	42.6	. . .	. . .	50.2
1975	54.1	60.2	51.1	72.9	49.8	47.7	. . .	. . .	54.4
1976	57.2	62.0	54.2	75.6	54.7	52.3	. . .	. . .	57.6
1977	60.9	65.7	57.9	79.0	58.6	57.3	. . .	. . .	60.9
1978	65.6	72.1	62.9	81.7	61.5	62.1	. . .	. . .	64.8
1979	73.1	79.9	70.7	85.2	70.4	68.0	. . .	. . .	69.4

[1]December 1997 = 100.
. . . = Not available.

Table 9-7. Consumer Price Indexes, Urban Wage Earners and Clerical Workers (CPI-W): U.S. City Average, Major Groups, 1913–2010—*Continued*

(1982–1984 = 100, unless otherwise specified.)

Year	All items	Food and beverages	Housing	Apparel	Transportation	Medical care	Recreation[1]	Education and communication[1]	Other goods and services
1980	82.9	86.9	81.7	90.9	82.9	75.6	. . .	. . .	75.6
1981	91.4	93.6	91.1	95.6	93.0	83.5	. . .	. . .	82.5
1982	96.9	97.3	97.7	97.8	97.0	92.5	. . .	. . .	90.9
1983	99.8	99.5	100.0	100.2	99.2	100.5	. . .	. . .	101.3
1984	103.3	103.2	102.2	102.0	103.8	106.9	. . .	. . .	107.9
1985	106.9	105.5	106.6	105.0	106.4	113.6	. . .	. . .	114.2
1986	108.6	108.9	109.7	105.8	101.7	122.0	. . .	. . .	120.9
1987	112.5	113.3	112.8	110.4	105.1	130.2	. . .	. . .	127.8
1988	117.0	117.9	116.8	114.9	108.3	139.0	. . .	. . .	136.5
1989	122.6	124.6	121.2	117.9	113.9	149.6	. . .	. . .	147.4
1990	129.0	131.8	126.4	123.1	120.1	162.7	. . .	. . .	158.9
1991	134.3	136.5	131.2	127.4	123.1	176.5	. . .	. . .	171.7
1992	138.2	138.3	135.0	130.7	125.8	189.6	. . .	. . .	183.3
1993	142.1	141.2	138.5	132.4	129.4	200.9	91.2	86.0	192.2
1994	145.6	144.4	142.0	132.2	133.4	210.4	93.0	89.1	196.4
1995	149.8	148.3	145.4	130.9	138.8	219.8	94.7	92.3	204.2
1996	154.1	153.2	149.6	130.9	142.8	227.6	97.5	95.4	212.2
1997	157.6	157.2	153.4	132.1	143.6	234.0	99.7	98.5	221.6
1998	159.7	160.4	156.7	131.6	140.5	241.4	100.9	100.4	236.1
1999	163.2	163.8	160.0	130.1	143.4	249.7	101.3	101.5	261.9
2000	168.9	167.7	165.4	128.3	152.8	259.9	102.4	102.7	276.5
2001	173.5	173.0	172.1	126.1	153.6	271.8	103.6	105.3	289.5
2002	175.9	176.1	175.7	123.1	151.8	284.6	104.6	107.6	302.0
2003	179.8	179.9	180.4	120.0	156.3	296.3	105.5	109.0	307.0
2004	184.5	186.2	185.0	120.0	161.5	309.5	106.3	110.0	312.6
2005	191.0	190.5	191.2	119.1	173.0	322.8	106.8	111.4	322.2
2006	197.1	194.9	198.5	119.1	180.3	335.7	108.2	113.9	330.9
2007	202.8	202.5	204.8	118.5	184.3	350.9	108.6	116.3	344.0
2008	211.1	213.5	211.8	118.7	195.7	364.2	110.1	119.8	357.9
2009	209.6	217.5	213.1	119.8	176.7	376.1	111.0	123.0	391.6
2010	214.0	219.2	212.9	118.7	192.6	389.8	109.8	124.9	409.3

[1]December 1997 = 100.
. . . = Not available.

Table 9-8. Consumer Price Indexes, All Urban Consumers (CPI-U): U.S. City Average, by Expenditure Category, 1990–2010

(1982–1984 = 100, unless otherwise specified.)

Expenditure category	1990	1991	1992	1993	1994	1995	1996	1997	1998	1999
ALL ITEMS	130.7	136.2	140.3	144.5	148.2	152.4	156.9	160.5	163.0	166.6
Food and Beverages	132.1	136.8	138.7	141.6	144.9	148.9	153.7	157.7	161.1	164.6
Food	132.4	136.3	137.9	140.9	144.3	148.4	153.3	157.3	160.7	164.1
Food at home	132.3	135.8	136.8	140.1	144.1	148.8	154.3	158.1	161.1	164.2
Cereals and bakery product	140.0	145.8	151.5	156.6	163.0	167.5	174.0	177.6	181.1	185.0
Meats, poultry, fish, and eggs	130.0	132.6	130.9	135.5	137.2	138.8	144.8	148.5	147.3	147.9
Dairy and related product	126.5	125.1	128.5	129.4	131.7	132.8	142.1	145.5	150.8	159.6
Fruits and vegetables	149.0	155.8	155.4	159.0	165.0	177.7	183.9	187.5	198.2	203.1
Nonalcoholic beverages and beverage materials	113.5	114.1	114.3	114.6	123.2	131.7	128.6	133.4	133.0	134.3
Other food at home	123.4	127.3	128.8	130.5	135.6	140.8	142.9	147.3	150.8	153.5
Sugar and sweets	124.7	129.3	133.1	133.4	135.2	137.5	143.7	147.8	150.2	152.3
Fats and oils	126.3	131.7	129.8	130.0	133.5	137.3	140.5	141.7	146.9	148.3
Other food	131.2	137.1	140.1	143.7	147.5	151.1	156.2	161.2	165.5	168.9
Other miscellaneous food[1]	. . .	. . .	. . .	. . .	. . .	. . .	. . .	. . .	102.6	104.9
Food away from home	133.4	137.9	140.7	143.2	145.7	149.0	152.7	157.0	161.1	165.1
Other food away from home[1]	. . .	. . .	. . .	. . .	. . .	. . .	. . .	. . .	101.6	105.2
Alcoholic beverages	129.3	142.8	147.3	149.6	151.5	153.9	158.5	162.8	165.7	169.7
Housing	128.5	133.6	137.5	141.2	144.8	148.5	152.8	156.8	160.4	163.9
Shelter	140.0	146.3	151.2	155.7	160.5	165.7	171.0	176.3	182.1	187.3
Rent of primary residence	138.4	143.3	146.9	150.3	154.0	157.8	162.0	166.7	172.1	177.5
Lodging away from home[1]	. . .	. . .	. . .	. . .	. . .	. . .	. . .	. . .	109.0	112.3
Owners' equivalent rent of primary residence[2]	144.8	150.4	155.5	160.5	165.8	171.3	176.8	181.9	187.8	192.9
Tenants' and household insurance[1]	. . .	. . .	. . .	. . .	. . .	. . .	. . .	. . .	99.8	101.3
Fuels and utilities	111.6	115.3	117.8	121.3	122.8	123.7	127.5	130.8	128.5	128.8
Household energy	104.5	106.7	108.1	111.2	111.7	111.5	115.2	117.9	113.7	113.5
Fuel oil and other fuels	99.3	94.6	90.7	90.3	88.8	88.1	99.2	99.8	90.0	91.4
Energy services	109.3	112.6	114.8	118.5	119.2	119.2	122.1	125.1	121.2	120.9
Water, sewer, and trash collection services[1]	. . .	. . .	. . .	. . .	. . .	. . .	. . .	. . .	101.6	104.0
Household furnishings and operations	113.3	116.0	118.0	119.3	121.0	123.0	124.7	125.4	126.6	126.7
Household operations[1]	. . .	. . .	. . .	. . .	. . .	. . .	. . .	. . .	101.5	104.5
Apparel	124.1	128.7	131.9	133.7	133.4	132.0	131.7	132.9	133.0	131.3
Men's and boys' apparel	120.4	124.2	126.5	127.5	126.4	126.2	127.7	130.1	131.8	131.1
Women's and girls' apparel	122.6	127.6	130.4	132.6	130.9	126.9	124.7	126.1	126.0	123.3
Infants' and toddlers' apparel	125.8	128.9	129.3	127.1	128.1	127.2	129.7	129.0	126.1	129.0
Footwear	117.4	120.9	125.0	125.9	126.0	125.4	126.6	127.6	128.0	125.7
Transportation	120.5	123.8	126.5	130.4	134.3	139.1	143.0	144.3	141.6	144.4
Private transportation	118.8	121.9	124.6	127.5	131.4	136.3	140.0	141.0	137.9	140.5
New and used motor vehicles[1]	. . .	. . .	. . .	91.8	95.5	99.4	101.0	100.5	100.1	100.1
New vehicles	121.4	126.0	129.2	132.7	137.6	141.0	143.7	144.3	143.4	142.9
Used cars and trucks	117.6	118.1	123.2	133.9	141.7	156.5	157.0	151.1	150.6	152.0
Motor fuel	101.2	99.4	99.0	98.0	98.5	100.0	106.3	106.2	92.2	100.7
Gasoline (all types)	101.0	99.2	99.0	97.7	98.2	99.8	105.9	105.8	91.6	100.1
Motor vehicle parts and equipment	100.9	102.2	103.1	101.6	101.4	102.1	102.2	101.9	101.1	100.5
Motor vehicle maintenance and repair	130.1	136.0	141.3	145.9	150.2	154.0	158.4	162.7	167.1	171.9
Public transportation	142.6	148.9	151.4	167.0	172.0	175.9	181.9	186.7	190.3	197.7
Medical Care	162.8	177.0	190.1	201.4	211.0	220.5	228.2	234.6	242.1	250.6
Medical care commodities	163.4	176.8	188.1	195.0	200.7	204.5	210.4	215.3	221.8	230.7
Medical care services	162.7	177.1	190.5	202.9	213.4	224.2	232.4	239.1	246.8	255.1
Professional services	156.1	165.7	175.8	184.7	192.5	201.0	208.3	215.4	222.2	229.2
Hospital and related services	178.0	196.1	214.0	231.9	245.6	257.8	269.5	278.4	287.5	299.5
Recreation[1]	. . .	. . .	. . .	90.7	92.7	94.5	97.4	99.6	101.1	102.0
Video and audio[1]	. . .	. . .	. . .	96.5	95.4	95.1	96.6	99.4	101.1	100.7
Education and Communication[1]	. . .	. . .	. . .	85.5	88.8	92.2	95.3	98.4	100.3	101.2
Education[1]	. . .	. . .	. . .	78.4	83.3	88.0	92.7	97.3	102.1	107.0
Educational books and supplies	171.3	180.3	190.3	197.6	205.5	214.4	226.9	238.4	250.8	261.7
Tuition, other school fees, and childcare	175.7	191.4	208.5	225.3	239.8	253.8	267.1	280.4	294.2	308.4
Communication[1]	. . .	. . .	. . .	. . .	. . .	. . .	. . .	. . .	. . .	. . .
Information and information processing[1]	. . .	. . .	. . .	. . .	. . .	. . .	. . .	. . .	. . .	. . .
Telephone services[1]	. . .	. . .	. . .	. . .	. . .	. . .	. . .	. . .	100.7	100.1
Information technology, hardware, and services[3]	93.5	88.6	83.7	78.8	72.0	63.8	57.2	50.1	39.9	30.5
Personal computers and peripheral equipment[1]	. . .	. . .	. . .	. . .	. . .	. . .	. . .	. . .	875.1	598.7
Other Goods and Services	159.0	171.6	183.3	192.9	198.5	206.9	215.4	224.8	237.7	258.3
Tobacco and smoking product	181.5	202.7	219.8	228.4	220.0	225.7	232.8	243.7	274.8	355.8
Personal care	130.4	134.9	138.3	141.5	144.6	147.1	150.1	152.7	156.7	161.1
Personal care product	128.2	132.8	136.5	139.0	141.5	143.1	144.3	144.2	148.3	151.8
Personal care services	132.8	137.0	140.0	144.0	147.9	151.5	156.6	162.4	166.0	171.4
Miscellaneous personal services	158.4	168.8	177.5	186.1	195.9	205.9	215.6	226.1	234.7	243.0

[1]December 1997 = 100.
[2]December 1982 = 100.
[3]December 1988 = 100.
. . . = Not available.

Table 9-8. Consumer Price Indexes, All Urban Consumers (CPI-U): U.S. City Average, by Expenditure Category, 1990–2010—*Continued*

(1982–1984 = 100, unless otherwise specified.)

Expenditure category	2000	2001	2002	2003	2004	2005	2006	2007	2008	2009	2010
ALL ITEMS	172.2	177.1	179.9	184.0	188.9	195.3	201.6	207.3	215.3	214.5	218.1
Food and Beverages	168.4	173.6	176.8	180.5	186.6	191.2	195.7	203.3	214.2	218.2	220.0
Food	167.8	173.1	176.2	180.0	186.2	190.7	195.2	202.9	214.1	218.0	219.6
Food at home	167.9	173.4	175.6	179.4	186.2	189.8	193.1	201.2	214.1	215.1	215.8
Cereals and bakery product	188.3	193.8	198.0	202.8	206.0	209.0	212.8	222.1	244.9	252.6	250.4
Meats, poultry, fish, and eggs	154.5	161.3	162.1	169.3	181.7	184.7	186.6	195.6	204.7	203.8	207.7
Dairy and related product	160.7	167.1	168.1	167.9	180.2	182.4	181.4	194.8	210.4	197.0	199.2
Fruits and vegetables	204.6	212.2	220.9	225.9	232.7	241.4	252.9	262.6	278.9	272.9	273.5
Nonalcoholic beverages and beverage materials	137.8	139.2	139.2	139.8	140.4	144.4	147.4	153.4	160.0	163.0	161.6
Other food at home	155.6	159.6	160.8	162.6	164.9	167.0	169.6	173.3	184.2	191.2	191.1
Sugar and sweets	154.0	155.7	159.0	162.0	163.2	165.2	171.5	176.8	186.6	196.9	201.2
Fats and oils	147.4	155.7	155.4	157.4	167.8	167.7	168.0	172.9	196.8	201.2	200.6
Other food	172.2	176.0	177.1	178.8	179.7	182.5	185.0	188.2	198.1	205.5	204.6
Other miscellaneous food[1]	107.5	108.9	109.2	110.3	110.4	111.3	113.9	115.1	119.9	122.4	121.7
Food away from home	169.0	173.9	178.3	182.1	187.5	193.4	199.4	206.7	215.8	223.3	226.1
Other food away from home[1]	109.0	113.4	117.7	121.3	125.3	131.3	136.6	144.1	150.6	155.9	159.3
Alcoholic beverages	174.7	179.3	183.6	187.2	192.1	195.9	200.7	207.0	214.5	220.8	223.3
Housing	169.6	176.4	180.3	184.8	189.5	195.7	203.2	209.6	216.3	217.1	216.3
Shelter	193.4	200.6	208.1	213.1	218.8	224.4	232.1	240.6	246.7	249.4	248.4
Rent of primary residence	183.9	192.1	199.7	205.5	211.0	217.3	225.1	234.7	243.3	248.8	249.4
Lodging away from home[1]	117.5	118.6	118.3	119.3	125.9	130.3	136.0	142.8	143.7	134.2	133.7
Owners' equivalent rent of primary residence[2]	198.7	206.3	214.7	219.9	224.9	230.2	238.2	246.2	252.4	256.6	256.6
Tenants' and household insurance[1]	103.7	106.2	108.7	114.8	116.2	117.6	116.5	117.0	118.8	121.5	125.7
Fuels and utilities	137.9	150.2	143.6	154.5	161.9	179.0	194.7	200.6	220.0	210.7	214.2
Household energy	122.8	135.4	127.2	138.2	144.4	161.6	177.1	181.7	200.8	188.1	189.3
Fuel oil and other fuels	129.7	129.3	115.5	139.5	160.5	208.6	234.9	251.5	334.4	239.8	275.1
Energy services	128.0	142.4	134.4	145.0	150.6	166.5	182.1	186.3	202.2	193.6	192.9
Water, sewer, and trash collection services[1]	106.5	109.6	113.0	117.2	124.0	130.3	136.8	143.7	152.1	161.1	170.9
Household furnishings and operations	128.2	129.1	128.3	126.1	125.5	126.1	127.0	126.9	127.8	128.7	125.5
Household operations[1]	110.5	115.6	119.0	121.8	125.0	130.3	136.6	140.6	147.5	150.3	150.3
Apparel	129.6	127.3	124.0	120.9	120.4	119.5	119.5	119.0	118.9	120.1	119.5
Men's and boys' apparel	129.7	125.7	121.7	118.0	117.5	116.1	114.1	112.4	113.0	113.6	111.9
Women's and girls' apparel	121.5	119.3	115.8	113.1	113.0	110.8	110.7	110.3	107.5	108.1	107.1
Infants' and toddlers' apparel	130.6	129.2	126.4	122.1	118.5	116.7	116.5	113.9	113.8	114.5	114.2
Footwear	123.8	123.0	121.4	119.6	119.3	122.6	123.5	122.4	124.2	126.9	128.0
Transportation	153.3	154.3	152.9	157.6	163.1	173.9	180.9	184.7	195.5	179.3	193.4
Private transportation	149.1	150.0	148.8	153.6	159.4	170.2	177.0	180.8	191.0	174.8	188.7
New and used motor vehicles[1]	100.8	101.3	99.2	96.5	94.2	95.6	95.6	94.3	93.3	93.5	97.1
New vehicles	142.8	142.1	140.0	137.9	137.1	137.9	137.6	136.3	134.2	135.6	138.0
Used cars and trucks	155.8	158.7	152.0	142.9	133.3	139.4	140.0	135.7	134.0	127.0	143.1
Motor fuel	129.3	124.7	116.6	135.8	160.4	195.7	221.0	239.1	279.7	202.0	239.2
Gasoline (all types)	128.6	124.0	116.0	135.1	159.7	194.7	219.9	238.0	277.5	201.6	238.6
Motor vehicle parts and equipment	101.5	104.8	106.9	107.8	108.7	111.9	117.3	121.6	128.7	134.1	137.0
Motor vehicle maintenance and repair	177.3	183.5	190.2	195.6	200.2	206.9	215.6	223.0	233.9	243.3	248.0
Public transportation	209.6	210.6	207.4	209.3	209.1	217.3	226.6	230.0	250.5	236.3	251.4
Medical Care	260.8	272.8	285.6	297.1	310.1	323.2	336.2	351.1	364.1	375.6	388.4
Medical care commodities	238.1	247.6	256.4	262.8	269.3	276.0	285.9	290.0	296.0	305.1	314.7
Medical care services	266.0	278.8	292.9	306.0	321.3	336.7	350.6	369.3	384.9	397.3	411.2
Professional services	237.7	246.5	253.9	261.2	271.5	281.7	289.3	300.8	311.0	319.4	328.2
Hospital and related services	317.3	338.3	367.8	394.8	417.9	439.9	468.1	498.9	534.0	567.9	607.7
Recreation[1]	103.3	104.9	106.2	107.5	108.6	109.4	110.9	111.4	113.3	114.3	113.3
Video and audio[1]	101.0	101.5	102.8	103.6	104.2	104.2	104.6	102.9	102.6	101.3	99.1
Education and Communication[1]	102.5	105.2	107.9	109.8	111.6	113.7	116.8	119.6	123.6	127.4	129.9
Education[1]	112.5	118.5	126.0	134.4	143.7	152.7	162.1	171.4	181.3	190.9	199.3
Educational books and supplies	279.9	295.9	317.6	335.4	351.0	365.6	388.9	420.4	450.2	482.1	505.6
Tuition, other school fees, and childcare	324.0	341.1	362.1	386.7	414.3	440.9	468.1	494.1	522.1	549.0	573.2
Communication[1]	93.6	93.3	92.3	89.7	86.7	84.7	84.1	83.4	84.2	85.0	84.7
Information and information processing[1]	92.8	92.3	90.8	87.8	84.6	82.6	81.7	80.7	81.4	81.9	81.5
Telephone services[1]	98.5	99.3	99.7	98.3	95.8	94.9	95.8	98.2	100.5	102.4	102.4
Information technology, hardware, and services[3]	25.9	21.3	18.3	16.1	14.8	13.6	12.5	10.6	10.1	9.7	9.4
Personal computers and peripheral equipment[1]	459.9	330.1	248.4	196.9	171.2	143.2	120.9	108.4	94.9	82.3	76.4
Other Goods and Services	271.1	282.6	293.2	298.7	304.7	313.4	321.7	333.3	345.4	368.6	381.3
Tobacco and smoking product	394.9	425.2	461.5	469.0	478.0	502.8	519.9	554.2	588.7	730.3	807.3
Personal care	165.6	170.5	174.7	178.0	181.7	185.6	190.2	195.6	201.3	204.6	206.6
Personal care product	153.7	155.1	154.7	153.5	153.9	154.4	155.8	158.3	159.3	162.6	161.1
Personal care services	178.1	184.3	188.4	193.2	197.6	203.9	209.7	216.6	223.7	227.6	229.6
Miscellaneous personal services	252.3	263.1	274.4	283.5	293.9	303.0	313.6	325.0	338.9	344.5	354.1

[1]December 1997 = 100.
[2]December 1982 = 100.
[3]December 1988 = 100.

Table 9-9. Relative Importance of Components in the Consumer Price Index: U.S. City Average, Selected Groups, December 1997–December 2010

(Percent distribution.)

Index and year	All items	Food and beverages	Housing	Apparel	Transportation	Medical care	Recreation	Education and communication	Other goods and services
ALL URBAN CONSUMERS (CPI-U)									
December 1997	100.0	16.3	39.6	4.9	17.6	5.6	6.1	5.5	4.3
December 1998	100.0	16.4	39.8	4.8	17.0	5.7	6.1	5.5	4.6
December 1999	100.0	16.3	39.6	4.7	17.5	5.8	6.0	5.4	4.7
December 2000	100.0	16.2	40.0	4.4	17.6	5.8	5.9	5.3	4.8
December 2001[1]	100.0	16.4	40.5	4.2	16.6	6.0	5.9	5.4	4.9
December 2001[2]	100.0	15.7	40.9	4.4	17.1	5.8	6.0	5.8	4.3
December 2002	100.0	15.6	40.9	4.2	17.3	6.0	5.9	5.8	4.4
December 2003	100.0	15.4	42.1	4.0	16.9	6.1	5.9	5.9	3.8
December 2004	100.0	15.3	42.0	3.8	17.4	6.1	5.7	5.8	3.8
December 2005	100.0	15.1	42.2	3.7	17.7	6.2	5.6	5.8	3.7
December 2006	100.0	15.0	42.7	3.7	17.2	6.3	5.6	6.0	3.5
December 2007	100.0	14.9	42.4	3.7	17.7	6.2	5.6	6.1	3.3
December 2008	100.0	15.8	43.4	3.7	15.3	6.4	5.7	6.3	3.4
December 2009	100.0	14.8	42.0	3.7	16.7	6.5	6.4	6.4	3.5
December 2010	100.0	14.8	42.0	3.7	16.7	6.5	6.4	3.0	3.5
URBAN WAGE EARNERS AND WORKERS (CPI-W)									
December 1997	100.0	17.9	36.5	5.3	19.8	4.6	6.0	5.4	4.5
December 1998	100.0	18.0	36.7	5.2	19.2	4.7	5.9	5.4	5.0
December 1999	100.0	17.9	36.5	5.0	19.7	4.7	5.8	5.3	5.1
December 2000	100.0	17.8	36.8	4.8	19.9	4.7	5.7	5.2	5.2
December 2001[1]	100.0	18.0	37.3	4.6	18.8	4.9	5.7	5.3	5.4
December 2001[2]	100.0	17.2	38.1	4.8	19.4	4.6	5.6	5.6	4.5
December 2002	100.0	17.1	38.1	4.6	19.7	4.7	5.6	5.6	4.6
December 2003	100.0	17.2	39.1	4.4	19.1	5.0	5.7	5.6	3.9
December 2004	100.0	17.0	39.0	4.2	19.8	5.0	5.5	5.5	3.9
December 2005	100.0	16.8	39.2	4.0	20.1	5.1	5.4	5.4	3.9
December 2006	100.0	16.5	40.5	4.0	19.5	5.2	5.0	5.6	3.7
December 2007	100.0	15.9	40.0	4.0	20.1	5.2	5.3	6.0	3.5
December 2008	100.0	16.9	41.3	4.0	17.1	5.4	5.5	6.2	3.7
December 2009	100.0	16.4	39.8	3.8	18.6	5.3	6.0	6.2	3.9
December 2010	100.0	16.4	39.8	3.8	18.6	5.3	6.0	6.2	3.9

[1] 1993–1995 weights.
[2] 1999–2000 weights.

Table 9-10. Consumer Price Indexes, All Urban Consumers (CPI-U), All Items: Selected Metropolitan Statistical Areas, Selected Years, 1975–2010

(1982–1984 = 100, unless otherwise specified.)

Area	1975	1980	1985	1986	1987	1988	1989	1990	1991	1992	1993	1994	1995	1996
NORTHEAST														
Boston-Brockton-Nashua, MA-NH-ME-CT	55.8	82.6	109.4	112.2	117.1	124.2	131.3	138.9	145.0	148.6	152.9	154.9	158.6	163.3
New York-Northern New Jersey-Long Island, NY-NJ-CT-PA	57.6	82.1	108.7	112.3	118.0	123.7	130.6	138.5	144.8	150.0	154.5	158.2	162.2	166.9
Philadelphia-Wilmington-Atlantic City, PA-NJ-DE-MD	56.8	83.6	108.8	111.5	116.8	122.4	128.3	135.8	142.2	146.6	150.2	154.6	158.7	162.8
Pittsburgh, PA	52.4	81.0	106.9	108.2	111.4	114.9	120.1	126.2	131.3	136.0	139.9	144.6	149.2	153.2
NORTH CENTRAL														
Chicago-Gary-Kenosha, IL-IN-WI	52.8	82.2	107.7	110.0	114.5	119.0	125.0	131.7	137.0	141.1	145.4	148.6	153.3	157.4
Cincinnati-Hamilton, OH-KY-IN	51.8	82.1	106.6	107.6	111.9	116.1	120.9	126.5	131.4	134.1	137.8	142.4	146.2	149.6
Cleveland-Akron, OH	50.2	78.9	107.8	109.4	112.7	116.7	122.7	129.0	134.2	136.8	140.3	144.4	147.9	152.0
Detroit-Ann Arbor-Flint, MI	53.9	85.3	106.8	108.3	111.7	116.1	122.3	128.6	133.1	135.9	139.6	144.0	148.6	152.5
Kansas City, MO-KS	53.2	83.6	107.7	108.7	113.1	117.4	121.6	126.0	131.2	134.3	138.1	141.3	145.3	151.6
Milwaukee-Racine, WI	50.8	81.4	107.0	107.4	111.5	115.9	120.8	126.2	132.2	137.1	142.1	147.0	151.0	154.7
Minneapolis-St. Paul, MN-WI	51.2	78.9	107.0	108.4	111.6	117.2	122.0	127.0	130.4	135.0	139.2	143.6	147.0	151.9
St. Louis, MO-IL	52.6	82.5	107.1	108.6	112.2	115.7	121.8	128.1	132.1	134.7	137.5	141.3	145.2	149.6
SOUTH														
Atlanta, GA	53.6	80.3	108.9	112.2	116.5	120.4	126.1	131.7	135.9	138.5	143.4	146.7	150.9	156.0
Dallas-Fort Worth, TX	50.4	81.5	108.2	109.9	112.9	116.1	119.5	125.1	130.8	133.9	137.3	141.2	144.9	148.8
Houston-Galveston-Brazoria, TX	51.4	82.7	104.9	103.9	106.5	109.5	114.1	120.6	125.1	129.1	133.4	137.9	139.8	142.7
Miami-Fort Lauderdale, FL	...	81.1	106.5	107.9	111.8	116.8	121.5	128.0	132.3	134.5	139.1	143.6	148.9	153.7
Tampa-St. Petersburg-Clearwater, FL[1]	...	...	...	...	100.0	103.7	107.2	111.7	116.4	119.2	124.0	126.5	129.7	131.6
Washington-Baltimore, DC-MD-VA-WV[2]	...	...	...	...	...	...	...	...	...	...	...	...	...	...
WEST														
Anchorage, AK	57.1	85.5	105.8	107.8	108.2	108.6	111.7	118.6	124.0	128.2	132.2	135.0	138.9	142.7
Denver-Boulder-Greeley, CO	48.4	78.4	107.1	107.9	110.8	113.7	115.8	120.9	125.6	130.3	135.8	141.8	147.9	153.1
Honolulu, HI	56.3	83.0	106.8	109.4	114.9	121.7	128.7	138.1	148.0	155.1	160.1	164.5	168.1	170.7
Los Angeles-Riverside-Orange County, CA	53.3	83.7	108.4	111.9	116.7	122.1	128.3	135.9	141.4	146.5	150.3	152.3	154.6	157.5
Phoenix-Mesa, AZ	...	...	...	...	...	...	...	...	...	...	...	...	...	...
Portland-Salem, OR-WA	53.5	87.2	106.7	108.2	110.9	114.7	120.4	127.4	133.9	139.8	144.7	148.9	153.2	158.6
San Diego, CA	47.6	79.4	110.4	113.5	117.5	123.4	130.6	138.4	143.4	147.4	150.6	154.5	156.8	160.9
San Francisco-Oakland-San Jose, CA	51.8	80.4	108.4	111.6	115.4	120.5	126.4	132.1	137.9	142.5	146.3	148.7	151.6	155.1
Seattle-Tacoma-Bremerton, WA	51.1	82.7	105.6	106.7	109.2	112.8	118.1	126.8	134.1	139.0	142.9	147.8	152.3	157.5

Area	1997	1998	1999	2000	2001	2002	2003	2004	2005	2006	2007	2008	2009	2010
NORTHEAST														
Boston-Brockton-Nashua, MA-NH-ME-CT	167.9	171.7	176.0	183.6	191.5	196.5	203.9	209.5	216.4	223.1	227.4	235.4	233.8	237.4
New York-Northern New Jersey-Long Island, NY-NJ-CT-PA	170.8	173.6	177.0	182.5	187.1	191.9	197.8	204.8	212.7	220.7	226.9	235.8	236.8	240.9
Philadelphia-Wilmington-Atlantic City, PA-NJ-DE-MD	166.5	168.2	171.9	176.5	181.3	184.9	188.8	196.5	204.2	212.1	216.7	224.1	223.3	227.7
Pittsburgh, PA	157.0	159.2	162.5	168.0	172.5	174.0	177.5	183.0	189.8	195.7	201.5	211.3	212.1	215.4
NORTH CENTRAL														
Chicago-Gary-Kenosha, IL-IN-WI	161.7	165.0	168.4	173.8	178.3	181.2	184.5	188.6	194.3	198.3	204.8	212.5	210.0	212.9
Cincinnati-Hamilton, OH-KY-IN	152.1	155.1	159.2	164.8	167.9	170.0	173.4	176.5	181.6	188.6	193.9	201.5	200.6	204.7
Cleveland-Akron, OH	156.1	159.8	162.5	168.0	172.9	173.3	176.2	181.6	187.9	191.1	196.0	203.0	200.5	204.6
Detroit-Ann Arbor-Flint, MI	156.3	159.8	163.9	169.8	174.4	178.9	182.5	185.4	190.8	196.6	200.1	204.7	203.5	205.1
Kansas City, MO-KS	155.8	157.8	160.1	166.6	172.2	174.0	177.0	180.7	185.3	190.1	194.5	201.2	201.0	205.4
Milwaukee-Racine, WI	157.7	160.3	163.7	168.6	171.7	174.0	177.7	180.2	185.2	189.9	194.1	203.0	203.0	209.6
Minneapolis-St. Paul, MN-WI	155.4	158.3	163.3	170.1	176.5	179.6	182.7	187.9	193.1	196.2	201.2	209.0	207.9	211.7
St. Louis, MO-IL	152.9	154.5	157.6	163.1	167.3	169.1	173.4	180.3	186.2	189.5	193.2	198.7	198.5	203.2
SOUTH														
Atlanta, GA	158.9	161.2	164.8	170.6	176.2	178.2	180.8	183.2	188.9	193.8	200.0	206.5	201.0	203.5
Dallas-Fort Worth, TX	151.4	153.6	158.0	164.7	170.4	172.7	176.2	178.7	184.7	190.1	193.2	201.8	200.5	201.6
Houston-Galveston-Brazoria, TX	145.4	146.8	148.7	154.2	158.8	159.2	163.7	169.5	175.6	180.6	183.8	190.0	190.5	194.2
Miami-Fort Lauderdale, FL	158.4	160.5	162.4	167.8	173.0	175.5	180.6	185.6	194.3	203.9	212.4	222.1	221.4	223.1
Tampa-St. Petersburg-Clearwater, FL[1]	134.0	137.5	140.6	145.7	148.8	153.9	158.1	162.0	168.5	175.2	184.3	190.1	189.9	193.5
Washington-Baltimore, DC-MD-VA-WV[2]	100.8	102.1	104.2	107.6	110.4	113.0	116.2	119.5	124.3	128.8	133.5	139.5	139.8	142.2
WEST														
Anchorage, AK	144.8	146.9	148.4	150.9	155.2	158.2	162.5	166.7	171.8	177.3	181.2	189.5	191.7	195.1
Denver-Boulder-Greeley, CO	158.1	161.9	166.6	173.2	181.3	184.8	186.8	187.0	190.9	197.7	202.0	209.9	208.5	212.4
Honolulu, HI	171.9	171.5	173.3	176.3	178.4	180.3	184.5	190.6	197.8	209.4	219.5	228.9	230.0	234.9
Los Angeles-Riverside-Orange County, CA	160.0	162.3	166.1	171.6	177.3	182.2	187.0	193.2	201.8	210.4	217.3	225.0	223.2	225.9
Phoenix-Mesa, AZ	...	...	...	...	...	101.2	103.3	105.2	108.3	111.5	115.3	119.3	117.6	118.2
Portland-Salem, OR-WA	164.0	167.1	172.6	178.0	182.4	183.8	186.3	191.1	196.0	201.1	208.6	215.4	215.6	218.3
San Diego, CA	163.7	166.9	172.8	182.8	191.2	197.9	205.3	212.8	220.6	228.1	233.3	242.3	242.3	245.5
San Francisco-Oakland-San Jose, CA	160.4	165.5	172.5	180.2	189.9	193.0	194.4	198.8	202.7	209.2	216.0	222.8	224.4	227.5
Seattle-Tacoma-Bremerton, WA	163.0	167.7	172.8	179.2	185.7	189.3	192.3	194.7	200.2	207.6	215.7	224.7	226.0	226.7

[1] 1987 = 100.
[2] November 1996 = 100.
. . . = Not available.

Table 9-11. Consumer Price Index Research Series, Using Current Methods (CPI-U-RS), by Month and Annual Average, 1977–2010

(December 1977 = 100.)

Year	January	February	March	April	May	June	July	August	September	October	November	December	Annual average
1977	. . .	. . .	. . .	. . .	. . .	. . .	. . .	. . .	. . .	. . .	. . .	100.0	. . .
1978	100.5	101.1	101.8	102.7	103.6	104.6	105.0	105.5	106.1	106.7	107.3	107.9	104.4
1979	108.7	109.7	110.7	111.8	113.0	114.1	115.2	116.0	117.1	117.9	118.5	119.5	114.4
1980	120.9	122.4	123.8	124.8	125.8	126.7	127.6	128.6	130.0	130.8	131.5	132.4	127.1
1981	133.6	135.3	136.4	137.1	137.9	138.7	139.7	140.7	141.8	142.4	142.9	143.4	139.2
1982	144.2	144.7	144.9	145.1	146.1	147.5	148.5	148.8	149.5	150.2	150.5	150.7	147.6
1983	151.1	151.2	151.3	152.4	153.2	153.8	154.4	154.8	155.6	156.0	156.2	156.4	153.9
1984	157.3	158.0	158.4	159.1	159.5	160.0	160.5	161.1	161.9	162.3	162.3	162.4	160.2
1985	162.6	163.3	164.0	164.7	165.3	165.8	166.1	166.4	167.0	167.4	167.9	168.3	165.7
1986	168.8	168.3	167.5	167.1	167.7	168.5	168.5	168.7	169.7	169.7	169.8	169.9	168.7
1987	170.9	171.6	172.3	173.2	173.7	174.3	174.6	175.6	176.4	176.8	176.9	176.8	174.4
1988	177.3	177.6	178.3	179.2	179.8	180.5	181.1	181.9	183.0	183.5	183.6	183.7	180.8
1989	184.6	185.2	186.2	187.5	188.4	188.8	189.3	189.5	190.2	190.9	191.2	191.5	188.6
1990	193.3	194.2	195.2	195.5	195.8	196.9	197.6	199.3	200.9	202.1	202.3	202.4	198.0
1991	203.3	203.5	203.6	203.9	204.4	204.9	205.0	205.6	206.4	206.6	207.1	207.2	205.1
1992	207.5	208.1	209.0	209.3	209.6	210.1	210.4	211.0	211.6	212.2	212.5	212.3	210.3
1993	212.9	213.7	214.3	214.9	215.3	215.5	215.6	216.1	216.4	217.1	217.3	217.1	215.5
1994	217.4	218.0	218.8	219.0	219.2	219.9	220.4	221.1	221.5	221.6	221.9	221.8	220.1
1995	222.6	223.3	224.0	224.7	225.1	225.6	225.7	226.1	226.5	227.1	226.9	226.8	225.4
1996	227.9	228.7	229.8	230.6	231.2	231.3	231.7	232.0	232.7	233.4	233.8	233.8	231.4
1997	234.5	235.2	235.6	235.9	235.8	236.2	236.3	236.7	237.5	237.9	237.8	237.4	236.4
1998	237.8	238.2	238.6	239.1	239.4	239.6	239.8	240.2	240.5	241.0	241.0	240.7	239.7
1999	241.4	241.7	242.4	244.1	244.1	244.2	244.9	245.6	246.7	247.2	247.3	247.3	244.7
2000	248.0	249.4	251.4	251.6	251.8	253.2	253.7	253.8	255.1	255.5	255.7	255.5	252.9
2001	257.1	258.2	258.8	259.8	260.9	261.4	260.6	260.7	261.8	260.9	260.4	259.4	260.0
2002	260.1	261.1	262.5	264.0	264.0	264.2	264.5	265.3	265.8	266.3	266.3	265.7	264.2
2003	266.8	268.9	270.5	269.9	269.5	269.8	270.1	271.1	271.9	271.7	270.9	270.6	270.1
2004	272.0	273.5	275.2	276.1	277.6	278.5	278.2	278.3	278.8	280.4	280.5	279.5	277.4
2005	280.0	281.6	283.8	285.7	285.5	285.6	286.9	288.3	291.9	292.5	290.2	288.9	286.7
2006	291.2	291.8	293.5	295.9	297.3	297.9	298.8	299.5	298.0	296.4	295.9	296.4	296.1
2007	297.2	298.8	301.6	303.5	305.4	306.0	305.9	305.3	306.2	306.8	308.6	308.4	304.5
2008	310.0	310.9	313.6	315.5	318.1	321.3	323.0	321.7	321.3	318.0	311.9	308.7	316.2
2009	310.1	311.6	312.4	313.1	314.0	316.7	316.2	316.9	317.1	317.5	317.7	317.1	315.0
2010	318.2	318.3	319.6	320.1	320.4	320.1	320.1	320.6	320.8	321.2	321.3	321.9	320.2

. . . = Not available.

NOTES AND DEFINITIONS

IMPORT AND EXPORT PRICE INDEXES

Collection and Coverage

The International Price Program (IPP) at the Bureau of Labor Statistics (BLS) produces Import/Export Price Indexes (MXP) which contain data on changes in the prices of nonmilitary goods and services traded between the U.S. and the rest of the world.

The MXP are primarily used to deflate foreign trade statistics produced by the U.S. government. The MXP are also a valuable input into the processes of measuring inflation, formulating fiscal and monetary policy, forecasting future prices, conducting elasticity studies, measuring U.S. industrial competitiveness, analyzing exchange rates, negotiating trade contracts, and analyzing import prices by locality of origin. The IPP collects prices as close as possible to the first day of each reference month.

The formula used to calculate the MXP is a modified form of the Laspeyres index. A Laspeyres index uses fixed base period quantities to aggregate prices. This means that the quality of goods and services is fixed; new goods do not appear, and the prices of goods that disappear must be observable. Because these implications are not consistent with the actual workings of the economy, adjustments must be made to the index.

The merchandise item price indexes are classified by end use for the Bureau of Economic Analysis System, by industry according to the North American Industry Classification System (NAICS), and product category according to the Harmonized System (HS). While classification by end use and product category are self-explanatory, a couple of notes are in order for classifying items by industry. In the NAICS tables, for both imports and exports, items are classified by output industry, not input industry. As an example, NAICS import index 326 (plastics and rubber products) includes outputs such as manufactured plastic rather than inputs such as petroleum. The NAICS classification structure also matches the classification system used by the PPI to produce the NAICS primary products indexes.

The Import Price Indexes (MPI) are based on U.S. dollar prices paid by the U.S. importer. The prices are generally either "free on board" (f.o.b.) foreign port or "cost, insur-ance, and freight" (c.i.f.) U.S. port transaction prices, depending on the practices of the individual industry. The index for crude petroleum is calculated from data collected by the Department of Energy.

Prices used in the import indexes by locality of origin are a subset of the data collected for the Import Price Indexes. Beginning with January 2002, the indexes are defined by locality of origin using a nomenclature based upon the North American Industry Classification System (NAICS). Nonmanufactured goods are defined as NAICS 11 and 21, and manufactured goods are defined as NAICS 31–33.

The Export Price Indexes (XPI) are classified by end use, determined by BEA. The prices used are generally either "free alongside ship" (f.a.s.) factory or "free on board" (f.o.b.) transaction prices, depending on the practices of the individual industry. Prices used in the grain index, excluding rice, are obtained from the Department of Agriculture.

Starting in September 2008 the Import Air Passenger Fares Indexes represent changes in the average revenue per passenger received by foreign carriers from U.S. residents and are calculated from data obtained from an airline consulting service. These data include tickets sold by travel agencies and travel websites. Tickets sold directly by the airlines are excluded, as are frequent flyer tickets generally. Starting in January 2008 the Export Air Passenger Fares Indexes represent changes in the average revenue per passenger received by U.S. carriers from foreign residents and are calculated from data collected directly from airlines. These data include frequent flyer tickets and those sold by consolidators. Taxes and fees are included in the Import Air Passenger Fares Index and excluded from the Export Air Passenger Fares Index. The Air Freight Indexes are calculated from data collected directly from airlines. These data exclude mail and passenger baggage. The scope of the service being priced is the movement of freight from airport to airport only, and does not include any ground transportation or port service.

Sources of Additional Information

Concepts and methodology are described in Chapter 15 of the *BLS Handbook of Methods* and in monthly BLS press releases. These resources are available on the BLS Web site at <http://www.bls.gov>.

Table 9-12. U.S. Export Price Indexes for Selected Categories of Goods, by End Use, 2000–2010

(2000 = 100, unless otherwise indicated.)

Commodity	2000				2001				2002			
	March	June	September	December	March	June	September	December	March	June	September	December
ALL COMMODITIES	100.0	100.1	100.4	100.1	100.0	99.4	99.0	97.6	97.6	98.0	98.8	98.6
Foods, Feeds, and Beverages	100.8	100.8	98.7	101.2	101.0	100.4	102.6	100.7	99.7	101.5	109.8	108.7
Agricultural foods, feeds, and beverages excluding distilled beverages	100.9	100.9	98.6	101.5	101.2	101.2	103.6	101.6	100.0	101.7	110.7	109.5
Nonagricultural foods (fish, distilled beverages)	99.6	99.9	99.7	98.2	99.4	92.6	92.9	92.1	98.3	100.7	101.3	102.3
Industrial Supplies and Materials	100.1	100.2	101.7	100.0	100.1	100.2	101.7	100.0	91.9	94.6	95.9	96.0
Industrial supplies and materials, durable	100.7	99.9	100.4	99.5	98.6	97.6	95.9	93.8	94.4	96.0	96.4	96.6
Industrial supplies and materials, nondurable	99.8	100.4	102.4	100.2	99.0	96.9	94.8	90.0	90.4	93.9	95.8	95.8
Agricultural industrial supplies and materials	98.0	98.6	103.2	104.6	101.7	99.3	96.8	93.3	93.6	95.8	98.4	101.9
Fuels and lubricants	103.1	97.3	111.3	104.9	100.3	102.8	103.2	83.5	85.6	86.7	92.9	91.3
Nonagricultural supplies and materials excluding fuels and building materials	99.8	100.2	100.2	98.8	98.5	96.1	93.8	92.3	92.6	95.7	96.4	96.4
Selected building materials	100.5	100.2	99.7	99.2	97.5	97.0	95.5	94.2	94.2	94.2	96.2	96.2
Capital Goods	99.9	99.9	100.0	100.2	100.6	100.3	100.0	99.4	99.4	98.7	98.4	98.1
Electrical generating equipment	99.6	100.0	100.7	100.5	100.9	101.7	101.6	101.5	102.1	102.0	102.0	101.9
Nonelectrical machinery	100.2	100.0	99.8	99.7	99.7	99.1	98.6	97.7	97.5	96.6	96.0	95.4
Transportation equipment excluding motor vehicles[1]	. . .	. . .	. . .	. . .	. . .	. . .	. . .	100.0	100.9	100.8	101.7	102.5
Automotive Vehicles, Parts, and Engines	99.9	99.9	100.3	100.1	100.3	100.4	100.4	100.5	100.9	100.9	101.1	101.3
Consumer Goods, Excluding Automotives	100.0	99.9	99.9	99.7	99.6	99.4	99.7	99.9	99.1	99.1	99.3	99.3
Nondurables, manufactured	100.1	99.8	99.8	99.6	99.0	99.0	99.1	99.1	98.1	98.5	98.7	98.7
Durables, manufactured	99.8	100.1	100.1	99.9	100.2	100.0	100.4	100.5	99.7	99.4	99.6	99.6
Agricultural Commodities	100.4	100.5	99.4	102.0	101.3	100.9	102.5	100.2	98.9	100.7	108.6	108.2
Nonagricultural Commodities	100.0	100.0	100.5	99.9	99.9	99.3	98.6	97.4	97.5	97.8	98.0	97.8

Commodity	2003				2004				2005			
	March	June	September	December	March	June	September	December	March	June	September	December
ALL COMMODITIES	99.7	99.5	99.8	100.8	103.0	103.4	103.8	104.8	106.4	106.7	107.5	107.7
Foods, Feeds, and Beverages	108.2	111.3	115.3	122.4	130.5	129.1	118.7	116.9	120.9	125.2	122.8	121.9
Agricultural foods, feeds, and beverages excluding distilled beverages	108.1	111.2	116.3	123.8	132.4	131.1	119.3	116.6	120.7	125.6	122.6	121.7
Nonagricultural foods (fish, distilled beverages)	110.0	113.1	106.5	108.5	112.1	110.7	113.0	118.4	121.8	120.1	123.6	123.6
Industrial Supplies and Materials	100.6	100.1	100.2	102.5	108.1	109.9	114.0	118.0	122.3	122.3	127.4	127.9
Industrial supplies and materials, durable	99.2	99.7	100.4	103.3	110.3	111.8	116.0	120.2	122.6	122.7	123.4	129.1
Industrial supplies and materials, nondurable	101.7	100.6	100.4	102.2	107.0	108.9	112.9	116.9	122.2	122.1	129.8	127.4
Agricultural industrial supplies and materials	104.8	104.4	107.3	117.5	117.2	110.7	109.4	109.5	115.6	115.8	116.4	117.4
Fuels and lubricants	108.0	97.0	97.6	99.0	108.9	114.9	121.5	125.4	143.8	148.8	184.8	163.4
Nonagricultural supplies and materials excluding fuels and building materials	99.9	100.7	100.5	102.5	108.1	110.0	114.4	118.9	121.4	120.6	122.2	125.7
Selected building materials	96.4	96.3	98.4	99.5	102.3	103.4	104.0	104.4	105.3	106.2	105.7	106.5
Capital Goods	98.3	97.6	97.5	97.5	98.0	97.8	97.8	98.2	98.4	98.4	97.6	97.7
Electrical generating equipment	101.6	101.6	101.7	101.7	102.0	102.0	102.4	103.6	103.9	103.4	102.6	103.6
Nonelectrical machinery	95.6	94.5	94.3	94.1	94.5	94.1	93.9	93.9	93.9	93.7	92.7	92.5
Transportation equipment excluding motor vehicles[1]	103.5	104.0	105.1	105.7	106.6	107.2	108.3	109.5	111.1	111.8	112.6	113.8
Automotive Vehicles, Parts, and Engines	101.5	101.6	101.8	101.8	101.9	102.3	102.5	102.9	103.3	103.4	103.7	103.9
Consumer Goods, Excluding Automotives	99.4	99.6	99.4	99.9	100.2	100.4	101.0	101.2	101.6	101.5	101.9	101.9
Nondurables, manufactured	98.7	98.8	98.5	99.2	99.9	100.0	101.0	101.0	101.5	101.2	101.5	101.6
Durables, manufactured	99.7	100.1	100.1	100.3	100.1	100.7	100.9	101.1	101.5	101.5	101.8	101.5
Agricultural Commodities	107.5	110.0	114.7	122.7	129.7	127.4	117.6	115.4	119.9	123.9	121.5	121.0
Nonagricultural Commodities	99.1	98.7	98.6	99.1	100.9	101.5	102.8	104.1	105.4	105.4	106.5	106.8

[1]December 2001 = 100.
. . . = Not available.

Table 9-12. U.S. Export Price Indexes for Selected Categories of Goods, by End Use, 2000–2010—*Continued*

(2000 = 100, unless otherwise indicated.)

Commodity	2006				2007				2008			
	March	June	September	December	March	June	September	December	March	June	September	December
ALL COMMODITIES	108.8	111.2	111.7	112.5	114.7	116.0	116.7	119.3	123.8	126.1	124.9	115.8
Foods, Feeds, and Beverages	121.7	125.6	128.8	138.7	146.9	148.6	157.8	171.1	196.9	198.0	190.4	155.1
Agricultural foods, feeds, and beverages excluding distilled beverages	121.5	125.7	129.1	140.5	149.2	151.0	160.8	175.2	202.6	204.0	195.6	156.6
Nonagricultural foods (fish, distilled beverages)	123.2	125.0	126.0	123.5	128.0	128.5	133.0	136.1	148.3	146.1	145.5	143.5
Industrial Supplies and Materials	131.3	138.8	139.5	139.4	145.5	149.0	148.8	154.1	165.5	173.2	169.4	139.6
Industrial supplies and materials, durable	135.7	146.2	146.9	150.1	160.2	160.9	155.5	159.2	172.7	172.9	167.1	141.5
Industrial supplies and materials, nondurable	129.0	134.9	135.7	133.9	137.6	142.8	145.5	151.9	162.0	174.2	171.6	139.1
Agricultural industrial supplies and materials	116.8	117.3	118.1	123.9	127.3	128.7	140.0	144.7	159.3	158.0	157.4	126.1
Fuels and lubricants	173.5	196.3	191.1	183.5	188.8	201.1	200.9	222.8	249.5	297.2	267.2	166.8
Nonagricultural supplies and materials excluding fuels and building materials	128.5	134.7	136.3	136.8	143.5	146.1	145.0	148.5	158.2	161.6	160.8	138.8
Selected building materials	108.5	109.8	110.0	111.5	112.7	113.9	114.4	113.7	114.2	113.8	115.4	115.1
Capital Goods	98.2	98.4	98.5	98.8	99.2	99.6	99.9	100.6	101.2	102.0	101.8	101.5
Electrical generating equipment	104.4	104.8	105.1	106.2	106.0	106.5	106.7	107.5	108.6	108.9	109.5	109.0
Nonelectrical machinery	92.7	92.7	92.6	92.6	92.8	92.9	93.1	93.6	93.7	94.2	93.9	93.3
Transportation equipment excluding motor vehicles[1]	116.0	117.1	117.7	119.1	121.1	122.3	123.4	125.0	128.1	130.3	130.7	131.5
Automotive Vehicles, Parts, and Engines	104.4	104.9	105.2	105.5	105.9	106.1	106.3	106.7	107.1	107.4	107.9	108.0
Consumer Goods, Excluding Automotives	102.3	103.5	104.0	104.0	104.8	105.8	106.2	107.3	108.0	108.2	109.3	109.0
Nondurables, manufactured	102.4	103.3	103.8	104.0	105.0	106.7	107.0	108.2	109.3	110.1	109.0	107.2
Durables, manufactured	101.3	102.4	103.1	102.8	103.4	103.7	104.2	105.2	105.4	105.2	108.7	109.7
Agricultural Commodities	120.7	124.1	127.1	137.3	145.0	146.7	156.8	169.3	194.3	195.2	188.3	150.8
Nonagricultural Commodities	108.0	110.3	110.6	110.7	112.6	113.8	113.8	115.7	118.8	121.2	120.4	113.2

Commodity	2009				2010			
	March	June	September	December	March	June	September	December
ALL COMMODITIES	115.5	117.8	117.9	119.7	121.2	122.2	123.7	127.5
Foods, Feeds, and Beverages	156.7	174.8	158.2	165.1	163.4	164.5	174.6	191.1
Agricultural foods, feeds, and beverages excluding distilled beverages	158.3	178.6	160.7	167.9	165.7	166.7	177.6	194.6
Nonagricultural foods (fish, distilled beverages)	144.4	141.5	137.3	140.9	145.9	147.2	149.4	161.1
Industrial Supplies and Materials	136.5	140.4	143.9	150.1	155.1	159.8	162.6	172.6
Industrial supplies and materials, durable	143.4	144.0	150.7	157.7	160.4	165.5	167.0	174.8
Industrial supplies and materials, nondurable	133.1	139.0	140.5	146.2	152.6	157.2	160.8	172.2
Agricultural industrial supplies and materials	122.9	131.0	142.2	152.5	155.7	162.5	173.2	223.0
Fuels and lubricants	146.9	175.2	171.9	189.6	197.0	208.0	213.1	233.9
Nonagricultural supplies and materials excluding fuels and building materials	138.2	138.5	142.7	147.3	152.2	155.8	158.0	164.4
Selected building materials	114.0	113.0	114.0	113.5	116.0	118.7	117.1	116.2
Capital Goods	102.3	103.1	103.5	103.3	103.8	103.5	103.5	103.9
Electrical generating equipment	106.8	107.2	107.4	109.3	109.8	109.3	108.7	109.8
Nonelectrical machinery	93.8	94.4	94.9	94.5	94.7	94.3	94.3	94.4
Transportation equipment excluding motor vehicles[1]	135.1	137.3	137.2	136.5	139.1	139.5	140.1	141.6
Automotive Vehicles, Parts, and Engines	108.2	108.0	108.0	108.2	108.6	108.5	108.7	109.1
Consumer Goods, Excluding Automotives	108.5	108.4	109.2	109.4	110.2	110.4	111.8	112.7
Nondurables, manufactured	107.1	108.5	109.4	110.0	111.9	111.5	112.9	114.0
Durables, manufactured	109.9	108.1	109.5	109.2	107.7	108.2	109.9	110.9
Agricultural Commodities	151.6	169.7	156.9	164.7	163.3	165.3	176.1	198.5
Nonagricultural Commodities	112.9	114.1	115.1	116.5	118.1	119.1	120.0	122.4

[1]December 2001 = 100.

Table 9-13. U.S. Import Price Indexes for Selected Categories of Goods, by End Use, 2000–2010

(2000 = 100, unless otherwise indicated.)

Commodity	2000				2001				2002			
	March	June	September	December	March	June	September	December	March	June	September	December
ALL COMMODITIES	99.9	100.2	101.6	100.5	98.3	97.6	95.9	91.4	92.8	94.1	95.5	95.2
Foods, Feeds, and Beverages	101.0	99.4	98.9	99.3	98.9	95.4	95.0	94.6	95.0	96.2	99.7	100.2
Agricultural foods, feeds, and beverages, excluding distilled beverages	102.1	99.2	97.3	99.3	101.0	97.0	97.8	98.3	99.5	101.3	105.4	106.0
Nonagricultural foods (fish and distilled beverages)	98.5	99.7	102.3	99.2	94.5	92.2	89.2	86.8	85.5	85.1	87.3	87.5
Industrial Supplies and Materials	99.0	100.7	105.5	102.9	96.0	95.5	91.0	77.6	84.9	89.8	95.2	94.6
Fuels and lubricants	97.2	101.3	111.3	106.1	91.1	90.9	86.1	61.6	76.4	85.8	96.2	94.7
Paper and paper base stocks	95.5	100.0	103.2	104.5	104.4	100.0	93.9	90.7	88.0	87.1	90.5	89.1
Materials associated with nondurable supplies and materials	98.5	99.9	101.1	101.5	102.8	100.3	97.9	96.2	95.9	97.1	99.4	100.1
Selected building materials	107.1	100.3	94.3	94.7	91.9	111.1	103.7	92.9	100.7	99.1	97.6	95.0
Unfinished metals related to durable goods	102.7	100.7	101.5	99.5	99.5	93.6	87.1	82.1	83.8	88.5	89.7	91.5
Finished metals related to durable goods	100.6	100.5	100.3	99.4	98.3	99.4	98.2	97.9	97.1	96.5	97.1	96.8
Nonmetals related to durable goods	100.2	99.5	99.7	99.7	101.6	100.6	100.4	99.0	97.2	96.7	96.9	97.1
Industrial Supplies and Materials, Durable	102.9	100.4	99.6	98.5	98.1	99.1	94.1	89.1	91.1	92.3	92.7	92.7
Industrial Supplies and Materials, Excluding Fuels[1]	. . .	. . .	. . .	. . .	. . .	. . .	. . .	100.0	101.0	102.1	103.4	103.6
Industrial Supplies and Materials, Excluding Petroleum	98.9	99.9	101.0	105.4	102.1	99.8	94.2	90.0	90.3	92.9	93.9	95.2
Industrial Supplies and Materials, Nondurable, Excluding Petroleum	94.6	99.3	102.6	112.9	106.4	100.7	94.2	90.9	89.3	93.4	95.2	98.1
Capital Goods	100.5	100.0	99.7	98.9	98.7	97.7	96.8	96.2	95.2	95.1	94.7	93.9
Electric generating equipment	98.7	101.1	100.3	99.8	102.1	101.8	101.4	100.6	95.5	95.1	95.7	94.9
Nonelectrical machinery	100.9	99.9	99.5	98.6	98.0	96.7	95.6	94.9	94.4	94.4	93.7	92.8
Transportation equipment, excluding motor vehicles[1]	. . .	. . .	. . .	. . .	. . .	. . .	. . .	100.0	100.5	100.4	101.0	101.0
Automotive Parts and Accessories	99.4	100.9	100.3	100.0	99.3	98.7	98.0	97.4	97.1	98.0	98.3	98.0
Consumer Goods, Excluding Automotive	99.7	100.2	100.0	100.2	100.1	99.8	99.9	100.0	99.9	100.1	100.3	100.5
Nondurables, manufactured	100.3	99.6	99.8	99.6	100.2	99.8	99.6	99.7	99.2	99.1	99.5	99.7
Nonmanufactured consumer goods	100.3	98.2	99.8	99.0	99.3	99.2	97.9	96.4	96.1	95.6	95.4	95.4
All Imports, Excluding Fuels	. . .	. . .	. . .	. . .	. . .	. . .	. . .	100.0	99.7	99.9	100.1	100.0
All Imports, Excluding Petroleum	100.0	99.9	100.0	100.7	100.0	98.9	97.3	96.2	95.8	96.2	96.4	96.5

Commodity	2003				2004				2005			
	March	June	September	December	March	June	September	December	March	June	September	December
ALL COMMODITIES	99.1	96.2	96.2	97.5	100.2	101.7	104.1	104.0	107.8	109.2	114.4	112.3
Foods, Feeds, and Beverages	102.6	100.7	101.8	103.2	105.9	106.9	108.7	111.5	115.9	114.1	114.2	117.5
Agricultural foods, feeds, and beverages, excluding distilled beverages	109.6	107.1	108.3	110.9	113.0	114.3	116.4	120.7	125.7	123.5	122.6	127.2
Nonagricultural foods (fish and distilled beverages)	86.9	86.6	87.6	86.0	90.1	90.3	91.4	91.0	94.0	93.1	95.6	95.9
Industrial Supplies and Materials	109.7	98.2	98.9	103.6	112.7	119.3	128.5	126.4	139.8	145.5	167.2	158.6
Fuels and lubricants	125.2	100.3	99.4	107.2	120.2	130.9	146.2	141.0	165.6	178.0	222.1	202.4
Paper and paper base stocks	91.0	94.1	94.0	93.9	95.6	99.0	101.1	101.3	103.8	103.8	104.3	106.1
Materials associated with nondurable supplies and materials	104.2	103.0	102.5	104.4	105.4	106.0	108.0	109.8	113.0	113.5	117.3	117.8
Selected building materials	96.3	96.7	110.3	108.0	118.4	120.5	125.6	115.6	122.7	118.1	117.6	116.9
Unfinished metals related to durable goods	92.8	92.2	93.4	99.2	114.9	124.4	133.1	138.5	140.4	139.9	138.2	145.8
Finished metals related to durable goods	96.1	97.4	99.0	101.0	104.8	108.1	112.4	114.7	115.9	116.6	117.3	117.6
Nonmetals related to durable goods	97.9	98.2	97.5	98.2	99.3	98.7	98.8	99.7	100.8	100.9	100.7	100.5
Industrial Supplies and Materials, Durable	93.6	93.7	97.3	99.5	108.5	112.8	117.8	118.0	120.8	119.7	119.1	121.4
Industrial Supplies and Materials, Excluding Fuels[1]	105.8	105.7	107.9	110.1	116.5	119.8	124.1	124.8	128.0	127.5	128.5	130.3
Industrial Supplies and Materials, Excluding Petroleum	104.3	99.9	100.3	102.1	107.9	112.5	114.4	118.8	119.9	120.2	126.8	132.2
Industrial Supplies and Materials, Nondurable, Excluding Petroleum	117.1	107.2	103.8	105.0	107.1	112.0	110.2	119.7	118.7	120.7	135.4	144.3
Capital Goods	93.7	93.8	93.5	92.9	93.1	92.2	92.0	92.2	92.3	92.3	91.5	91.0
Electric generating equipment	95.5	96.6	95.8	96.8	97.8	97.0	97.4	98.0	98.8	98.8	99.0	99.3
Nonelectrical machinery	92.5	92.3	92.1	91.1	91.2	90.1	89.8	89.9	89.8	89.8	88.7	88.1
Transportation equipment, excluding motor vehicles[1]	101.6	102.0	102.2	102.8	103.5	104.0	103.9	104.5	105.6	106.0	106.4	106.1
Automotive Parts and Accessories	98.0	98.3	97.8	98.8	99.6	100.1	100.2	101.5	101.8	102.0	102.1	101.8
Consumer Goods, Excluding Automotive	100.5	100.6	100.5	101.4	101.8	102.2	102.7	103.2	103.2	103.4	103.6	103.6
Nondurables, manufactured	99.7	99.8	99.7	100.1	101.3	100.9	100.8	101.4	102.8	102.8	103.1	102.7
Nonmanufactured consumer goods	95.7	96.2	95.7	96.2	96.4	96.8	97.9	98.2	100.3	101.8	100.6	101.2
All Imports, Excluding Fuels	100.3	100.3	100.6	101.0	102.4	102.7	103.4	104.0	105.0	104.9	104.8	105.1
All Imports, Excluding Petroleum	98.1	97.3	97.3	97.7	99.1	99.7	100.1	101.3	102.0	102.0	102.8	103.7

[1]December 2001 = 100.
. . . = Not available.

Table 9-13. U.S. Import Price Indexes for Selected Categories of Goods, by End Use, 2000–2010—Continued

(2000 = 100, unless otherwise indicated.)

Commodity	2006				2007				2008			
	March	June	September	December	March	June	September	December	March	June	September	December
ALL COMMODITIES	112.7	117.3	116.2	115.1	115.9	120.0	121.8	127.3	133.5	145.5	137.8	114.5
Foods, Feeds, and Beverages	117.0	118.0	120.9	122.6	124.6	127.8	131.8	134.4	141.8	147.7	147.9	142.3
Agricultural foods, feeds, and beverages, excluding distilled beverages	125.4	126.8	130.4	133.7	135.1	139.5	144.4	148.3	157.3	165.1	165.1	159.4
Nonagricultural foods (fish and distilled beverages)	98.3	98.5	99.8	97.9	101.3	101.5	103.5	103.0	106.8	108.4	109.1	103.8
Industrial Supplies and Materials	160.4	178.1	172.2	166.6	169.8	185.6	190.7	211.3	234.5	283.0	248.9	150.4
Fuels and lubricants	201.5	230.2	216.3	204.3	209.6	238.2	250.0	290.3	329.0	423.7	346.3	153.9
Paper and paper base stocks	107.7	111.3	113.1	112.8	111.5	110.8	111.2	109.2	114.1	117.3	119.9	113.2
Materials associated with nondurable supplies and materials	119.3	120.6	121.8	123.0	124.0	125.4	128.2	135.3	147.8	152.9	162.4	148.5
Selected building materials	118.0	117.2	115.8	110.6	111.4	113.1	116.9	116.0	114.1	119.2	122.7	118.1
Unfinished metals related to durable goods	161.1	193.2	194.4	195.9	202.9	219.7	209.1	217.2	241.5	273.2	255.4	185.7
Finished metals related to durable goods	119.2	125.3	128.4	128.9	125.4	133.7	134.8	135.0	145.8	158.7	159.9	140.8
Nonmetals related to durable goods	100.8	101.1	101.3	101.7	101.8	101.6	102.5	103.8	105.2	107.6	111.4	109.0
Industrial Supplies and Materials, Durable	127.2	139.1	139.8	139.2	141.0	148.4	146.3	149.1	158.9	173.5	169.7	141.8
Industrial Supplies and Materials, Excluding Fuels[1]	134.9	143.7	144.7	144.7	146.2	151.6	151.2	155.4	166.8	178.8	179.5	155.1
Industrial Supplies and Materials, Excluding Petroleum	128.1	133.9	135.1	138.3	139.3	144.6	141.0	147.5	159.4	173.7	167.4	146.0
Industrial Supplies and Materials, Nondurable, Excluding Petroleum	128.3	126.7	128.5	136.3	136.3	139.1	133.6	144.5	159.3	173.0	163.5	150.8
Capital Goods	91.1	91.2	91.3	91.5	91.1	91.3	91.9	92.2	92.2	93.2	93.3	92.7
Electric generating equipment	100.1	102.1	102.7	103.0	104.3	105.7	106.5	107.9	109.3	112.0	112.9	111.4
Nonelectrical machinery	88.0	87.8	87.8	87.9	87.2	87.2	87.7	87.7	87.5	88.2	88.2	87.5
Transportation equipment, excluding motor vehicles[1]	107.0	107.9	108.3	109.1	110.1	111.0	113.4	114.7	115.3	117.7	118.2	120.2
Automotive Parts and Accessories	101.6	102.7	103.2	103.0	103.5	103.3	103.6	104.8	106.2	106.7	107.4	108.8
Consumer Goods, Excluding Automotive	103.5	103.9	104.1	104.3	104.4	104.7	105.2	106.8	107.4	107.9	108.1	107.8
Nondurables, manufactured	102.8	102.6	103.0	103.4	104.1	104.3	105.0	105.5	107.5	107.9	108.2	108.2
Nonmanufactured consumer goods	98.2	98.6	100.5	101.8	102.2	102.6	103.4	103.8	104.3	106.6	106.6	103.6
All Imports, Excluding Fuels	105.7	107.2	107.8	108.1	108.4	109.5	110.1	111.4	113.9	116.5	116.8	112.7
All Imports, Excluding Petroleum	103.0	104.2	104.8	105.7	105.9	107.1	107.1	108.9	111.6	114.9	114.0	109.9

Commodity	2009				2010			
	March	June	September	December	March	June	September	December
ALL COMMODITIES	113.6	120.0	121.3	124.4	126.3	125.2	125.7	131.0
Foods, Feeds, and Beverages	137.0	139.8	140.6	143.7	147.4	148.7	153.3	162.7
Agricultural foods, feeds, and beverages, excluding distilled beverages	151.3	155.5	156.8	160.8	165.8	166.1	171.1	182.6
Nonagricultural foods (fish and distilled beverages)	104.8	104.4	104.1	104.9	105.6	109.2	113.0	117.4
Industrial Supplies and Materials	149.3	177.3	183.0	196.2	205.0	199.5	200.1	222.6
Fuels and lubricants	162.3	222.1	228.5	249.7	262.4	245.8	247.1	285.2
Paper and paper base stocks	106.6	101.8	99.1	103.1	107.6	115.5	117.5	117.5
Materials associated with nondurable supplies and materials	136.7	137.5	134.8	140.6	144.6	146.2	147.7	157.0
Selected building materials	116.2	116.0	118.9	120.9	127.6	131.9	124.6	127.0
Unfinished metals related to durable goods	171.6	178.3	204.0	221.5	233.4	244.6	244.2	266.0
Finished metals related to durable goods	132.7	133.2	137.1	140.4	142.4	146.5	147.7	152.7
Nonmetals related to durable goods	105.2	103.0	104.3	105.4	107.1	107.2	107.7	108.7
Industrial Supplies and Materials, Durable	134.7	136.0	145.7	152.5	158.4	163.7	162.5	171.2
Industrial Supplies and Materials, Excluding Fuels[1]	145.5	146.5	151.7	158.6	164.3	168.9	168.9	178.0
Industrial Supplies and Materials, Excluding Petroleum	133.1	132.1	134.4	145.2	149.7	151.6	151.0	159.4
Industrial Supplies and Materials, Nondurable, Excluding Petroleum	131.0	127.4	121.0	136.3	139.4	137.5	137.5	145.5
Capital Goods	91.8	91.9	91.9	91.9	91.4	91.5	91.8	92.0
Electric generating equipment	109.4	110.0	110.3	111.3	111.0	111.4	112.7	113.7
Nonelectrical machinery	86.6	86.5	86.5	86.4	85.9	86.0	86.1	86.2
Transportation equipment, excluding motor vehicles[1]	120.6	122.4	123.2	122.6	121.5	121.3	121.6	121.9
Automotive Parts and Accessories	108.9	108.5	109.2	110.0	109.9	110.2	111.5	112.0
Consumer Goods, Excluding Automotive	107.7	108.0	108.6	108.8	108.2	108.5	109.3	109.4
Nondurables, manufactured	108.4	108.1	107.8	107.9	109.0	109.3	110.0	110.4
Nonmanufactured consumer goods	101.2	101.4	101.2	102.1	102.5	102.4	103.0	103.7
All Imports, Excluding Fuels	110.7	111.2	111.9	113.0	113.7	114.4	114.7	116.4
All Imports, Excluding Petroleum	107.3	107.4	107.9	109.7	110.3	110.7	111.0	112.6

[1]December 2001 = 100.

Table 9-14. U.S. Import Price Indexes for Selected Categories of Goods, by Locality of Origin, 1995–2010

(2000 = 100, unless otherwise indicated.)

Category and year	Percent of U.S. imports[1]	Month			
		March	June	September	December
INDUSTRIALIZED COUNTRIES[2]					
Total Goods	41.1				
1995		97.4	99.8	100.0	100.0
1996		99.7	98.8	99.3	99.4
1997		97.4	96.5	96.4	96.1
1998		94.6	94.0	93.3	93.8
1999		94.1	94.8	96.4	97.5
2000		99.5	100.1	100.9	101.4
2001		100.2	99.0	96.5	93.7
2002		94.3	95.7	96.9	96.7
2003		100.0	98.4	98.6	100.0
2004		103.4	104.7	106.3	107.5
2005		109.7	110.0	113.5	114.1
2006		113.5	117.4	117.0	116.4
2007		117.9	119.7	120.4	124.2
2008		130.9	139.6	135.1	119.1
2009		117.5	119.3	120.4	123.9
2010		125.7	124.0	124.5	
Manufactured Goods	34.9				
1995		100.0	102.6	102.9	102.9
1996		102.1	101.1	101.4	100.7
1997		99.5	98.9	98.8	98.6
1998		97.8	97.5	96.7	97.3
1999		97.6	97.7	98.1	98.9
2000		100.2	99.9	100.2	99.8
2001		99.9	99.2	97.6	96.0
2002		95.6	96.3	96.9	96.7
2003		97.8	97.7	98.2	99.4
2004		102.1	102.8	104.0	104.6
2005		106.3	106.6	106.7	107.7
2006		109.0	111.8	111.8	111.1
2007		112.5	113.5	114.5	116.3
2008		120.1	124.3	124.2	115.7
2009		114.9	114.9	116.1	117.9
2010		118.9	118.8	119.0	
Nonmanufactured Goods	5.7				
1995		66.3	67.6	65.2	66.0
1996		71.6	72.3	76.0	84.3
1997		73.3	68.9	69.4	68.5
1998		59.3	56.8	57.2	55.7
1999		56.9	65.1	78.7	83.2
2000		92.7	102.2	107.5	118.2
2001		103.9	97.2	85.2	69.9
2002		82.9	93.8	102.4	102.7
2003		134.3	113.7	108.9	112.4
2004		122.9	133.1	138.7	147.1
2005		156.7	158.0	203.0	199.2
2006		170.9	190.0	183.7	184.9
2007		185.6	197.9	195.4	228.2
2008		275.6	346.8	279.0	154.5
2009		143.9	170.6	169.1	198.8
2010		209.7	188.0	191.7	
OTHER COUNTRIES					
Total Goods	58.9				
1995		97.5	98.7	97.4	97.6
1996		99.8	99.0	101.3	102.7
1997		100.6	99.4	98.7	96.6
1998		92.4	90.7	89.5	86.8
1999		87.7	90.3	94.5	96.9
2000		99.8	100.4	102.5	99.5
2001		97.0	96.6	95.0	88.6
2002		90.9	92.2	94.3	93.4
2003		96.7	93.1	93.3	94.1
2004		96.3	97.9	101.5	99.7
2005		105.0	107.0	112.1	109.5
2006		110.8	115.5	114.0	111.8
2007		113.1	118.0	121.1	127.5
2008		133.3	147.3	139.0	111.2
2009		110.3	118.7	120.0	122.1
2010		124.2	123.1	123.5	

[1]Based on 2008 trade values.
[2]Includes Western Europe, Canada, Japan, Australia, New Zealand and South Africa.

Table 9-14. U.S. Import Price Indexes for Selected Categories of Goods, by Locality of Origin, 1995–2010
    —Continued

(2000 = 100, unless otherwise indicated.)

Category and year	Percent of U.S. imports[1]	Month			
		March	June	September	December
Manufactured Goods	43.0				
1995		107.3	108.8	108.6	108.4
1996		108.9	108.4	107.9	108.6
1997		108.4	107.8	107.0	105.3
1998		103.5	102.2	100.6	99.6
1999		98.8	98.9	99.0	99.3
2000		99.8	99.7	100.3	100.2
2001		99.6	98.8	97.9	96.0
2002		95.6	95.9	96.2	95.8
2003		96.5	95.1	95.1	94.5
2004		95.2	96.2	97.2	97.1
2005		98.4	98.7	99.3	99.6
2006		99.4	101.2	101.2	100.7
2007		102.0	103.6	104.1	106.0
2008		107.8	111.8	111.3	103.4
2009		101.7	103.5	104.3	104.5
2010		105.0	105.3	105.4	
Nonmanufactured Goods	15.7				
1995		69.5	70.3	66.1	67.3
1996		73.7	72.1	80.9	84.5
1997		75.8	72.6	72.2	68.8
1998		57.1	54.9	54.5	46.8
1999		53.0	63.6	80.3	89.2
2000		99.9	102.4	109.2	97.4
2001		88.9	89.7	86.1	65.3
2002		81.3	88.2	99.6	96.4
2003		113.3	98.0	98.8	106.5
2004		118.1	123.2	141.5	130.3
2005		158.0	169.5	199.8	181.3
2006		191.7	215.4	204.6	191.1
2007		192.4	220.6	241.6	279.0
2008		314.6	402.3	336.0	160.2
2009		166.8	225.6	231.3	247.8
2010		260.8	248.9	251.4	
CANADA					
Total Goods	15.9				
1995		92.1	93.8	94.8	94.7
1996		94.3	93.5	93.8	95.1
1997		93.2	92.6	93.2	92.0
1998		90.1	89.7	89.3	88.7
1999		88.8	90.6	93.5	94.7
2000		97.2	99.8	102.4	105.6
2001		102.6	101.8	97.0	93.2
2002		96.1	97.8	99.6	99.2
2003		106.6	103.1	103.9	104.4
2004		110.0	112.3	114.4	116.6
2005		120.1	119.6	128.2	129.6
2006		125.4	130.6	129.7	129.2
2007		130.2	135.0	135.0	142.3
2008		152.0	171.2	160.1	129.8
2009		124.4	129.0	131.1	137.7
2010		143.7	139.3	140.6	
Manufactured Goods	10.3				
1995		98.0	99.4	100.7	100.5
1996		99.0	98.0	97.7	97.4
1997		98.0	98.0	98.3	97.3
1998		96.7	96.6	96.3	95.5
1999		95.5	96.1	96.9	97.7
2000		98.8	98.9	101.3	101.8
2001		101.6	102.8	99.9	98.1
2002		99.1	98.7	99.5	98.9
2003		100.9	101.1	103.2	103.3
2004		107.4	108.2	110.3	110.7
2005		113.7	112.9	113.1	115.6
2006		117.2	120.0	119.9	118.7
2007		119.5	123.7	125.3	127.6
2008		128.8	137.5	138.7	126.8
2009		122.7	123.0	125.8	127.3
2010		131.7	132.0	132.5	

[1]Based on 2008 trade values.

Table 9-14. U.S. Import Price Indexes for Selected Categories of Goods, by Locality of Origin, 1995–2010
—Continued

(2000 = 100, unless otherwise indicated.)

Category and year	Percent of U.S. imports[1]	Month			
		March	June	September	December
Nonmanufactured Goods	5.3				
1995		61.7	64.4	63.9	64.8
1996		70.3	70.7	74.4	84.3
1997		69.9	66.6	68.1	66.4
1998		58.4	56.6	56.5	56.3
1999		56.5	64.2	76.8	79.9
2000		89.3	103.6	107.6	124.4
2001		108.1	97.9	83.1	69.8
2002		83.8	96.8	104.1	104.9
2003		143.1	119.0	111.5	114.0
2004		126.1	138.0	138.9	150.5
2005		157.9	159.8	210.8	207.4
2006		171.3	189.2	183.1	187.1
2007		187.8	195.9	187.7	222.3
2008		273.7	345.1	273.0	150.8
2009		139.7	163.4	161.6	192.5
2010		204.6	181.3	185.7	
EUROPEAN UNION					
Total Goods	16.8				
1995		97.7	99.5	99.7	100.4
1996		101.3	101.0	101.7	101.9
1997		100.5	100.0	99.1	100.1
1998		98.9	98.8	98.7	99.4
1999		98.8	99.1	99.9	100.3
2000		100.8	100.1	100.0	98.9
2001		99.0	98.8	98.2	97.4
2002		97.4	99.2	101.0	100.9
2003		103.2	102.8	102.8	104.3
2004		107.4	108.5	110.0	111.6
2005		113.8	114.1	115.7	114.5
2006		117.7	120.4	120.5	119.6
2007		121.3	121.6	122.3	124.1
2008		129.7	133.9	131.5	124.3
2009		123.6	124.4	125.4	127.4
2010		128.3	127.7	128.0	
Manufactured Goods	16.5				
1995		98.6	100.4	100.9	101.5
1996		102.3	101.8	102.4	102.3
1997		101.0	100.8	100.1	101.0
1998		100.4	100.6	100.5	101.5
1999		100.9	100.6	100.8	100.8
2000		100.8	99.9	99.6	98.6
2001		99.2	98.8	98.7	98.4
2002		98.1	99.9	101.5	101.4
2003		103.3	103.2	103.2	104.5
2004		107.4	108.4	109.3	110.9
2005		112.8	113.0	113.8	112.9
2006		116.0	118.0	118.4	118.0
2007		119.5	119.2	119.7	121.1
2008		126.5	130.1	128.2	121.8
2009		121.5	122.1	123.0	124.9
2010		125.8	125.2	125.5	
Nonmanufactured Goods	0.2				
1995		72.8	74.5	71.2	73.0
1996		78.8	80.6	85.7	91.7
1997		89.3	82.2	76.5	78.4
1998		65.6	58.7	58.8	53.4
1999		53.6	66.6	81.3	88.7
2000		100.4	102.9	107.9	106.2
2001		96.0	99.5	89.1	75.7
2002		86.6	88.7	99.6	104.1
2003		118.8	106.7	111.5	118.8
2004		128.4	135.1	157.9	163.1
2005		177.1	177.5	209.7	191.1
2006		211.4	231.9	219.9	198.7
2007		205.2	234.6	274.9	304.8
2008		323.4	400.2	332.3	230.8
2009		188.3	230.0	235.3	250.2
2010		252.4	250.4	249.9	

[1]Based on 2008 trade values.

Table 9-14. U.S. Import Price Indexes for Selected Categories of Goods, by Locality of Origin, 1995–2010
—*Continued*

(2000 = 100, unless otherwise indicated.)

Category and year	Percent of U.S. imports[1]	Month			
		March	June	September	December
LATIN AMERICA					
Total Goods	18.0				
1998		84.3	83.9	83.0	80.4
1999		81.7	85.3	90.7	94.2
2000		98.9	100.9	103.5	99.5
2001		99.5	98.9	97.2	90.6
2002		94.0	96.2	100.0	98.9
2003		104.8	99.6	99.8	102.6
2004		106.3	108.6	114.7	113.1
2005		122.1	126.3	133.8	131.0
2006		134.0	142.8	140.2	136.4
2007		138.1	146.3	152.3	161.5
2008		171.6	193.9	181.7	135.4
2009		132.1	146.7	148.5	154.0
2010		157.4	154.5	155.9	
Manufactured Goods	11.7				
1998		94.8	95.0	93.8	93.5
1999		92.0	93.6	94.6	96.0
2000		98.3	99.6	101.6	102.3
2001		104.2	103.5	102.5	101.4
2002		101.5	102.4	104.2	103.8
2003		108.2	103.6	104.4	105.8
2004		107.5	109.1	112.0	113.9
2005		117.1	118.6	120.1	122.2
2006		123.2	128.9	128.4	125.8
2007		127.4	131.4	132.5	134.3
2008		139.3	146.0	145.4	127.7
2009		121.7	125.0	126.5	129.3
2010		130.3	130.5	130.2	
Nonmanufactured Goods	6.2				
1998		60.8	59.7	59.4	51.9
1999		59.3	67.2	82.1	90.2
2000		100.2	103.5	107.8	93.6
2001		89.3	89.0	86.0	67.3
2002		83.5	90.7	103.0	99.3
2003		111.7	103.5	100.9	109.8
2004		121.1	125.9	144.6	130.1
2005		161.0	175.1	205.1	184.6
2006		195.5	217.2	205.7	197.1
2007		199.3	225.0	250.7	289.5
2008		320.9	409.2	348.3	181.5
2009		188.9	254.3	257.1	273.9
2010		286.4	269.3	278.1	
CHINA					
Total Goods	16.4				
2004		99.5	99.7	99.6	99.0
2005		98.8	98.8	98.4	98.5
2006		97.9	97.4	97.4	97.3
2007		97.4	98.1	99.1	99.6
2008		101.1	102.8	103.7	102.4
2009		100.9	100.4	100.5	100.6
2010		100.1	100.4	100.3	
JAPAN					
Total Goods	6.7				
1995		108.6	112.5	112.0	111.0
1996		110.1	108.4	107.8	106.5
1997		104.6	103.2	102.7	101.0
1998		99.8	98.2	96.8	98.0
1999		98.2	98.2	98.6	99.6
2000		99.6	100.0	99.9	99.9
2001		99.4	98.6	97.8	97.0
2002		95.6	95.4	95.0	94.6
2003		94.4	94.2	93.8	94.7
2004		95.2	95.1	95.3	95.9
2005		95.9	95.8	95.8	95.2
2006		94.6	94.7	94.4	94.1
2007		93.9	94.0	93.9	94.2
2008		94.6	95.1	94.9	96.0
2009		96.3	96.9	97.2	97.8
2010		98.1	98.6	98.9	

[1]Based on 2008 trade values.

Table 9-14. U.S. Import Price Indexes for Selected Categories of Goods, by Locality of Origin, 1995–2010
    —*Continued*

(2000 = 100, unless otherwise indicated.)

Category and year	Percent of U.S. imports[1]	Month			
		March	June	September	December
ASIAN NEWLY INDUSTRIALIZED COUNTRIES[2]					
Total Goods	5.0				
1995		120.9	121.3	121.5	120.8
1996		120.6	119.6	118.1	117.3
1997		116.6	115.3	113.8	111.3
1998		108.7	105.2	103.0	102.0
1999		101.3	100.8	100.7	100.8
2000		100.6	99.9	100.0	99.3
2001		97.3	96.4	95.2	93.8
2002		93.3	92.6	92.5	91.3
2003		91.2	91.5	91.7	90.9
2004		90.3	90.6	91.0	90.6
2005		90.9	90.0	89.7	88.5
2006		88.8	89.2	89.3	89.1
2007		88.7	88.5	88.8	88.9
2008		89.2	91.1	93.2	89.2
2009		85.4	85.7	86.1	86.5
2010		87.0	88.1	88.6	

[1]Based on 2008 trade values.
[2]Includes Western Europe, Canada, Japan, Australia, New Zealand and South Africa.

Table 9-15. U.S. International Price Indexes for Selected Transportation Services, 1995–2010

(2000 = 100.)

Category and year	March	June	September	December
AIR FREIGHT				
Import Air Freight				
1995	115.8	118.7	112.9	115.1
1996	113.7	112.2	112.0	110.6
1997	104.1	104.5	102.5	100.1
1998	93.0	94.2	92.8	100.2
1999	101.5	98.7	100.6	102.8
2000	100.7	100.1	100.2	99.0
2001	98.9	96.0	95.9	95.6
2002	96.7	99.7	101.2	106.9
2003	110.2	111.5	116.8	114.9
2004	117.1	117.5	120.0	126.8
2005	128.6	128.4	129.7	128.9
2006	129.7	135.2	133.1	131.2
2007	130.7	132.3	134.2	141.8
2008	144.4	158.7	157.1	138.5
2009	132.9	132.8	134.8	163.9
2010	158.3	162.5	163.2	170.1
Export Air Freight				
1996	. . .	. . .	. . .	112.9
1997	111.1	110.4	109.0	105.4
1998	107.1	106.6	108.0	109.2
1999	102.1	102.5	100.8	99.1
2000	99.1	100.8	100.8	99.4
2001	99.7	98.4	98.6	97.9
2002	95.5	97.9	98.3	95.2
2003	96.3	95.2	95.1	95.4
2004	97.1	99.1	100.3	106.1
2005	106.4	110.1	110.9	112.0
2006	113.6	115.9	117.9	116.7
2007	117.0	117.0	119.8	127.1
2008	132.0	140.8	144.3	135.0
2009	124.1	117.4	121.6	122.9
2010	124.0	126.3	125.7	128.1
Inbound Air Freight				
1995	113.6	116.5	111.0	111.7
1996	108.6	107.7	108.2	107.6
1997	101.3	101.8	100.3	97.9
1998	93.9	94.4	92.7	99.0
1999	99.6	97.6	99.5	102.8
2000	100.7	100.1	100.2	99.0
2001	97.9	95.1	94.9	95.1
2002	93.9	98.3	100.3	105.9
2003	108.8	109.4	112.5	112.9
2004	116.2	116.6	118.7	125.1
2005	126.3	125.6	127.5	124.6
2006	124.6	129.2	128.9	127.1
2007	126.6	127.3	129.6	138.1
2008	140.7	152.1	151.6	136.8
2009	127.5	125.1	127.4	147.3
2010	144.3	147.1	147.2	153.4

. . . = Not available.

Table 9-15. U.S. International Price Indexes for Selected Transportation Services, 1995–2010—*Continued*

(2000 = 100.)

Category and year	March	June	September	December
Outbound Air Freight				
1995	108.2	108.1	108.6	107.8
1996	107.3	107.6	107.0	107.3
1997	108.0	107.3	107.7	105.7
1998	105.2	103.8	103.7	103.0
1999	100.3	100.4	100.3	99.2
2000	99.2	100.3	100.2	100.2
2001	100.1	98.0	97.6	97.8
2002	95.9	98.4	97.3	95.4
2003	97.2	95.4	95.5	94.9
2004	96.1	99.0	100.7	104.7
2005	103.8	107.2	112.4	112.0
2006	113.5	117.2	116.9	113.8
2007	112.3	114.3	117.0	124.3
2008	128.9	143.7	147.0	130.4
2009	119.7	112.1	111.9	114.6
2010	118.1	122.4	122.8	126.2
AIR PASSENGER FARES				
Import Air Passenger Fares				
1995	80.2	88.1	86.4	82.6
1996	82.0	88.1	86.8	84.3
1997	84.7	95.5	94.0	88.0
1998	87.1	94.9	95.1	88.6
1999	87.5	98.9	99.5	89.7
2000	92.5	103.5	105.1	98.9
2001	101.1	112.8	116.4	105.7
2002	103.1	119.1	125.2	107.2
2003	108.6	122.3	125.9	107.0
2004	103.6	123.1	121.0	111.7
2005	110.0	128.1	124.0	116.3
2006	114.9	136.7	130.9	125.4
2007	122.9	144.6	140.2	135.3
2008	131.3	171.6	161.3	157.3
2009	134.9	147.3	137.9	152.3
2010	149.8	175.3	160.9	169.9
Export Air Passenger Fares				
1995	92.4	99.4	96.4	91.6
1996	93.0	94.4	97.7	94.7
1997	85.3	97.7	95.0	87.4
1998	89.5	90.2	90.6	93.1
1999	95.5	96.8	100.6	98.6
2000	98.1	101.5	102.6	97.7
2001	99.6	100.4	102.5	98.4
2002	97.5	103.2	108.1	103.2
2003	108.4	117.0	118.0	118.4
2004	123.2	123.8	130.1	134.0
2005	136.3	136.2	139.5	128.3
2006	130.8	139.3	142.4	137.3
2007	140.2	147.3	154.6	155.7
2008	156.4	171.4	171.9	164.6
2009	141.7	138.2	141.3	156.1
2010	157.7	176.3	172.2	169.0

Chapter Ten

INTERNATIONAL LABOR COMPARISONS

INTERNATIONAL LABOR COMPARISONS

HIGHLIGHTS

This chapter compares several summary statistics of labor force status, manufacturing productivity, and consumer prices for the United States with similar statistics for other countries. Different concepts and methodologies can make comparisons between countries difficult, but the Bureau of Labor Statistics (BLS) makes adjustments to reconcile as much of the data as possible.

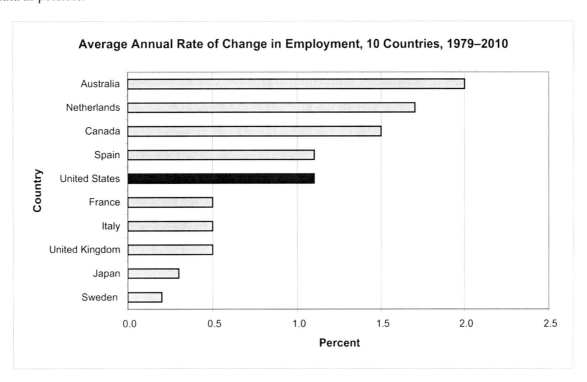

Average Annual Rate of Change in Employment, 10 Countries, 1979–2010

From 1979 to 2010, employment increased at an average rate of 1.1 percent in the United States. In comparison, it increased at a faster rate in Australia (2.0 percent) and the Netherlands (1.7 percent) but at a far slower rate in Japan (0.3 percent) and Sweden (0.2 percent). (See Table 10-1.)

OTHER HIGHLIGHTS

- For the second consecutive year in 2010, the United States had the highest unemployment rate among the 10 countries being compared in Table 10-1. In the past, unemployment rates have typically been higher in Western European countries than in the United States. (See Table 10-1.)

- Between 2009 and 2010, the unemployment rate increased for 6 of the 10 countries compared: France, Italy, Netherlands, Sweden, the United Kingdom and the United States. It declined in Canada, Australia, and Germany; and remained stable in Japan. (See Table 10-1.)

- While manufacturing only comprised 10.1 percent of employment in the United States, it made up 21.2 percent of employment in Germany and 18.8 percent in Italy. (See Table 10-8.)

- Real Gross Domestic Product (GDP) per capita, stated in U.S. dollars, increased in every country compared except for Norway and Spain between 2009 and 2010. However, Norway continued to have the highest real GDP per capita among all the countries at ($55,938) followed by the United States ($46,844) and the Netherlands ($41,512). (See Table 10-12.)

401

NOTES AND DEFINITIONS

Collection and Coverage

From its inception, the Bureau of Labor Statistics (BLS) has conducted a program of research and statistical analysis that compares labor conditions in the United States with those in selected foreign countries. The principal comparative measures of the International Labor Comparisons (ILC) program (formerly called the Foreign Labor Statistics program) cover the labor force, employment, and unemployment; trends in labor productivity and unit labor costs in manufacturing; hourly compensation costs for manufacturing production workers, and consumer prices. All of the measures are based upon statistical data and other source materials from (a) the statistical agencies of the foreign countries studied; (b) international and supranational bodies such as the United Nations, the International Labour Office (ILO), the Organisation for Economic Co-operation and Development (OECD), and the Statistical Office of the European Communities (EUROSTAT), which attempt to obtain comparable country data; and (c) private agencies such as banks, industry associations, and research institutions.

International statistical comparisons should be made with caution, as the statistical concepts and methods in each country are primarily fashioned to meet domestic (rather than international) needs. Whenever possible, BLS adjusts the data to improve comparability.

Labor Force, Employment, and Unemployment

To compare unemployment across countries, BLS publishes monthly, quarterly, and annual unemployment rates for 10 countries that have been adjusted as closely as possible to U.S. concepts. The 10 countries are the United States, Canada, Australia, Japan, France, Germany, Italy, the Netherlands, Sweden, and the United Kingdom. BLS publishes additional annual labor force statistics on a civilian basis for the same 10 countries: working-age population, labor force, employment by major economic sector (agriculture, industry, manufacturing, and services), unemployment, employment-population ratios by sex, and unemployment rates by age and sex, and women's share of the labor force.

Foreign country data are adjusted as closely as possible to the U.S. definitions. Primary areas of adjustment address conceptual differences in upper age limits and definitions of employment and unemployment, provided that reliable data are available to make these adjustments. Adjustments are made where applicable to include employed and unemployed persons above upper age limits; some European countries do not include persons older than age 64 in their labor force measures, because a large portion of this population has retired. Adjustments are made to exclude active duty military from employment figures, although a small

number of career military may be included in some European countries. Adjustments are made to exclude unpaid family workers who worked fewer than 15 hours per week from employment figures; U.S. concepts do not include them in employment; most foreign countries include all unpaid family workers regardless of the number of hours worked. Adjustments are made to include full-time students seeking work and available for work as unemployed when they are classified as not in the labor force.

Where possible, lower age limits are based on the age at which compulsory schooling ends in each country, rather than based on the U.S. standard of 16 years of age and over. Lower age limits have ranged between 13 and 16 over the years covered; currently, the lower age limits are either 15 or 16 in all 10 countries.

Some adjustments for comparability are not made because data are unavailable for adjustment purposes. For example, no adjustments to unemployment are usually made for deviations from U.S. concepts in the treatment of persons waiting to start a new job or passive job seekers. These conceptual differences have little impact on the measures. Furthermore, BLS studies have concluded that no adjustments should be made for persons on layoff who are counted as employed in some countries because of their strong job attachment as evidenced by, for example, payment of salary or the existence of a recall date. In the United States, persons on layoff have weaker job attachment and are classified as unemployed. Finally, employment data by economic sector are not fully comparable with U.S. definitions for some countries because all data required to make adjustments at the sector level are not available. Therefore, the sum of employment by sector may not equal total adjusted employment.

Hourly Compensation Costs

Measures of hourly compensation costs are prepared by BLS to assess international differences in manufacturing employer labor costs. For several reasons, comparisons based on the more readily available average earnings statistics published by many countries can be misleading. National definitions of average earnings differ considerably; average earnings do not include all items of labor compensation, and the omitted items of compensation frequently represent a large proportion of total compensation. For many years, data on hourly compensation costs covered production workers only; recently, the series has been extended to cover all employees as well.

Hourly compensation costs include (1) hourly direct pay and (2) employer social insurance expenditures and other labor taxes. Hourly direct pay includes all payments made directly to the worker, before payroll deductions of any kind, consisting of pay for time worked and other direct pay. Social insurance expenditures and other labor taxes include employer expenditures for legally required insurance programs, contractual and private benefit plans, and other labor taxes. Other labor taxes refer to taxes on payrolls or employment (or reductions to reflect subsidies), even if they do not finance programs that directly benefit workers, because such taxes are regarded as labor costs.

Productivity and Unit Labor Costs

Time series indexes of manufacturing labor productivity (output per hour) and unit labor costs are constructed from three basic aggregate measures: Total real output, hours worked, and nominal compensation. Indexes for unit labor costs are prepared on a national currency basis and, using currency exchange rates, a U.S. dollar basis. With the additional collection of annual employment in manufacturing and the use of consumer price indexes, a total of 15 time series indexes are constructed.

The employment, hours, and compensation measures refer to employees (wage and salary workers) in Belgium and Taiwan and to all employed persons (employees plus the self-employed and unpaid family workers) in all other economies.

In general, the measures relate to total manufacturing as defined by the International Standard Industrial Classification (ISIC) system. However, the measures for France include parts of mining. Data for the United States are in accordance with the North American Industry Classification System (NAICS), except compensation data before 1987, which are based on SIC 1987. Canadian data are in accordance with NAICS 97 starting in 1961.

The data for the most recent years are based on the United Nations System of National Accounts 1993 (SNA 93). For earlier years, data were compiled according to previously used systems.

To obtain historical time series, BLS sometimes links together data series that were compiled according to different accounting systems by national statistical offices.

Consumer Price Index

The indexes and percent changes in this chapter are based upon national consumer price indexes as published by each country. They have not been adjusted for comparability. National differences exist, for example, in population coverage, frequency of market basket weight changes, and treatment of homeowner costs. The data in these tables are not available in this form from the foreign statistical agencies.

The indexes in Table 10-10 are calculated by rebasing the official indexes of each country to the official U.S. base year. Because of the change in base year, the indexes may differ from the official indexes published by national statistical agencies.

Percent change in Table 10-11 is computed using the compound rate method. The figures may differ from official percent changes published by national statistical agencies because of rounding. In Sweden and Switzerland, the national statistical agencies calculate the official percent changes from more precise index values than those that they publish.

Real Gross Domestic Product per Capita and per Employed Person

Measures of gross domestic product (GDP), population, and employment are obtained from national statistical sources. While these data are generally comparable to one another, some differences remain in the countries' statistical methodologies, which may affect comparability. The GDP measures used for all countries come from their national accounts sources. For all countries, the most recent series use the 1993 United Nations System of National Accounts (SNA 93). However, some earlier series have been prepared using 1968 United Nations System of National Accounts (SNA 68). The U.S. GDP series is based on the system of national income and product accounts (NIPAs) estimated by the Bureau of Economic Analysis (BEA).

Sources of Additional Information

An extensive description of the methodology can be found in Chapter 12 in the *BLS Handbook of Methods*. For more information on international comparisons see the BLS report titled, "International Comparisons of Annual Labor Force Statistics, Adjusted to U.S. Concepts, 10 Countries, 1970–2010" and "International Comparisons of GDP per Capita and per Hour 1960–2010" on the BLS Web site at <http://www.bls.gov/fls/>.

Table 10-1. Employment Status of the Working-Age Population, Adjusted to U.S. Concepts, 10 Countries, 1975–2010

(Numbers in thousands, percent.)

Category and year	United States	Canada	Australia	Japan	France	Germany[1]	Italy	Netherlands	Sweden	United Kingdom
Employed										
1975	85 846	9 284	5 866	51 530	20 869	25 536	19 395	5 070	4 056	24 758
1976	88 752	9 652	5 946	52 030	21 041	25 396	19 504	5 100	4 082	24 611
1977	92 017	9 825	6 000	52 720	21 235	25 428	19 668	5 210	4 093	24 638
1978	96 048	10 124	6 038	53 370	21 326	25 647	19 725	5 260	4 109	24 774
1979	98 824	10 561	6 111	54 040	21 392	26 074	19 932	5 350	4 174	25 031
1980	99 303	10 872	6 284	54 600	21 443	26 486	20 195	5 520	4 226	24 917
1981	100 397	11 192	6 416	55 060	21 345	26 453	20 279	5 550	4 219	24 256
1982	99 526	10 847	6 415	55 620	22 396	26 149	20 246	5 520	4 213	23 782
1983	100 834	10 936	6 300	56 550	22 365	25 765	20 320	5 420	4 218	23 607
1984	105 005	11 211	6 494	56 870	22 161	25 826	20 392	5 490	4 249	24 115
1985	107 150	11 557	6 697	57 250	22 189	26 018	20 492	5 650	4 293	24 422
1986	109 597	11 895	6 984	57 740	22 398	26 383	20 614	5 740	4 326	24 578
1987	112 440	12 221	7 142	58 310	22 400	26 584	20 591	5 756	4 340	25 073
1988	114 968	12 591	7 413	59 300	22 481	26 799	20 868	5 917	4 410	25 905
1989	117 342	12 876	7 734	60 490	22 801	27 201	20 773	6 048	4 480	26 588
1990	118 793	12 964	7 877	61 710	22 872	27 952	21 080	6 251	4 513	26 713
1991	117 718	12 754	7 698	62 920	22 763	36 871	21 364	6 427	4 447	26 007
1992	118 492	12 643	7 660	63 630	22 721	36 390	21 233	6 559	4 265	25 388
1993	120 259	12 705	7 699	63 830	22 536	35 989	20 549	6 554	4 027	25 161
1994	123 060	12 975	7 942	63 860	22 461	35 756	20 176	6 614	3 990	25 373
1995	124 900	13 210	8 256	63 900	22 735	35 780	20 034	6 821	4 053	25 694
1996	126 708	13 337	8 364	64 200	22 858	35 637	20 124	6 966	4 014	25 941
1997	129 558	13 639	8 444	64 900	22 782	35 508	20 169	7 189	3 974	26 413
1998	131 463	13 974	8 618	64 450	22 990	36 059	20 370	7 408	4 036	26 684
1999	133 488	14 326	8 762	63 920	23 285	36 042	20 617	7 605	4 116	27 058
2000	136 891	14 677	8 989	63 790	23 928	36 236	20 973	7 762	4 230	27 375
2001	136 933	14 860	9 088	63 460	24 264	36 350	21 359	7 950	4 303	27 604
2002	136 485	15 210	9 271	62 650	24 521	36 018	21 666	8 035	4 311	27 815
2003	137 736	15 576	9 485	62 510	24 397	35 615	21 972	7 989	4 301	28 077
2004	139 252	15 835	9 662	62 640	24 464	35 604	22 124	7 960	4 279	28 380
2005	141 730	16 032	9 998	62 910	24 632	36 123	22 290	7 959	4 334	28 674
2006	144 427	16 317	10 257	63 210	24 828	36 949	22 721	8 096	4 416	28 929
2007	146 047	16 704	10 576	63 509	25 246	37 763	22 953	8 290	4 530	29 129
2008	145 362	16 985	10 873	63 250	25 614	38 345	23 144	8 412	4 581	29 346
2009	139 877	16 732	10 953	62 242	25 395	38 279	22 760	8 389	4 486	28 880
2010	139 064	16 969	11 247	62 000	25 423	38 209	22 621	8 264	4 534	28 944
Unemployed										
1975	7 929	690	303	1 000	793	890	690	270	67	1 174
1976	7 406	716	298	1 080	893	890	790	290	66	1 414
1977	6 991	836	358	1 100	1 015	900	840	270	75	1 470
1978	6 202	898	405	1 240	1 063	870	850	280	94	1 453
1979	6 137	831	408	1 170	1 212	780	920	290	88	1 432
1980	7 637	854	409	1 140	1 306	770	920	350	86	1 833
1981	8 273	887	394	1 260	1 547	1 090	1 040	540	108	2 609
1982	10 678	1 298	495	1 360	1 692	1 560	1 160	630	137	2 875
1983	10 717	1 437	697	1 560	1 766	1 900	1 270	700	151	3 081
1984	8 539	1 377	641	1 610	2 074	1 970	1 280	710	136	3 241
1985	8 312	1 293	603	1 470	2 210	2 010	1 310	600	124	3 151
1986	8 237	1 205	601	1 630	2 234	1 860	1 680	640	117	3 160
1987	7 425	1 123	612	1 570	2 272	1 800	1 760	622	100	2 940
1988	6 701	999	558	1 440	2 194	1 810	1 790	609	86	2 445
1989	6 528	982	490	1 340	2 052	1 640	1 760	558	74	2 082
1990	7 047	1 083	563	1 280	1 995	1 460	1 590	516	84	2 053
1991	8 628	1 386	788	1 270	2 047	2 204	1 580	490	147	2 530
1992	9 613	1 507	897	1 350	2 283	2 615	1 680	478	261	2 822
1993	8 940	1 533	914	1 600	2 559	3 113	2 227	437	416	2 929
1994	7 996	1 372	829	1 720	2 726	3 318	2 421	492	426	2 676
1995	7 404	1 246	739	1 920	2 584	3 200	2 544	523	404	2 441
1996	7 236	1 282	751	2 040	2 743	3 505	2 555	489	441	2 301
1997	6 739	1 247	759	2 110	2 785	3 907	2 584	423	445	1 991
1998	6 210	1 160	721	2 540	2 685	3 693	2 634	337	368	1 791
1999	5 880	1 072	652	2 810	2 630	3 333	2 559	277	313	1 728
2000	5 692	955	602	2 920	2 265	3 065	2 388	246	260	1 587
2001	6 801	1 026	658	3 020	2 075	3 110	2 164	206	227	1 489
2002	8 378	1 146	630	3 216	2 137	3 396	2 062	254	234	1 528
2003	8 774	1 146	599	2 985	2 295	3 661	2 048	341	264	1 488
2004	8 149	1 091	551	2 726	2 408	4 107	1 960	419	300	1 423
2005	7 591	1 024	531	2 476	2 429	4 573	1 889	441	360	1 463
2006	7 001	949	516	2 346	2 432	4 257	1 673	366	330	1 670
2007	7 078	922	484	2 400	2 220	3 601	1 506	306	292	1 652
2008	8 924	951	483	2 410	2 069	3 136	1 692	267	294	1 780
2009	14 265	1 326	649	3 120	2 577	3 228	1 945	327	401	2 395
2010	14 825	1 294	621	3 100	2 644	2 980	2 119	390	409	2 477

[1]Unified Germany from 1991 onward; data for previous years relate to the former West Germany.

Table 10-1. Employment Status of the Working-Age Population, Adjusted to U.S. Concepts, 10 Countries, 1975–2010—*Continued*

(Numbers in thousands, percent.)

Category and year	United States	Canada	Australia	Japan	France	Germany[1]	Italy	Netherlands	Sweden	United Kingdom
Civilian Labor Force Participation Rate										
1975	61.2	61.1	63.2	62.4	57.0	55.0	47.7	54.5	65.9	63.1
1976	61.6	62.5	62.7	62.4	57.2	54.6	48.0	54.1	66.0	63.0
1977	62.3	62.8	62.7	62.5	57.5	54.4	48.2	54.2	65.9	62.7
1978	63.2	63.7	61.9	62.8	57.4	54.4	47.8	54.0	66.1	62.6
1979	63.7	64.5	61.6	62.7	57.4	54.5	48.0	54.2	66.6	62.7
1980	63.8	65.0	62.1	62.6	57.2	54.7	48.1	55.4	66.9	62.8
1981	63.9	65.6	61.9	62.6	57.1	54.7	48.3	56.7	66.8	62.7
1982	64.0	64.9	61.7	62.7	59.5	54.6	47.7	56.6	66.8	61.9
1983	64.0	65.2	61.4	63.1	59.1	54.3	47.5	55.7	66.7	61.6
1984	64.4	65.5	61.5	62.7	58.9	54.4	47.3	55.7	66.6	62.7
1985	64.8	66.0	61.7	62.2	58.8	54.7	47.2	55.5	66.9	62.9
1986	65.3	66.4	62.8	62.1	58.9	54.9	47.8	56.0	67.0	62.9
1987	65.6	66.8	62.9	61.8	58.4	55.0	47.6	55.2	66.5	63.2
1988	65.9	67.1	63.3	61.8	57.9	55.1	47.4	55.9	67.0	63.8
1989	66.5	67.5	64.1	62.1	57.8	55.2	47.3	56.1	67.3	64.3
1990	66.5	67.4	64.7	62.6	57.4	55.0	47.2	57.0	67.4	64.3
1991	66.2	66.8	64.2	63.1	56.9	58.8	47.8	57.7	67.0	63.7
1992	66.4	65.9	63.9	63.3	57.0	58.1	47.5	58.3	65.8	62.9
1993	66.3	65.5	63.5	63.2	56.9	57.8	48.3	57.5	64.5	62.6
1994	66.6	65.2	63.9	62.9	56.8	57.4	47.6	58.0	63.7	62.4
1995	66.6	64.9	64.5	62.8	56.8	57.1	47.3	59.6	64.0	62.4
1996	66.8	64.8	64.6	62.8	57.1	57.1	47.3	60.2	63.9	62.4
1997	67.1	65.1	64.3	63.0	56.6	57.3	47.3	61.1	63.2	62.5
1998	67.1	65.4	64.3	62.6	56.5	57.7	47.7	61.8	62.8	62.4
1999	67.1	65.8	64.0	62.0	56.6	56.9	47.9	62.5	62.7	62.8
2000	67.1	66.0	64.4	61.7	56.8	56.7	48.1	63.0	63.7	62.8
2001	66.8	66.1	64.4	61.2	56.6	56.7	48.3	63.7	63.7	62.7
2002	66.6	67.1	64.3	60.4	56.8	56.4	48.5	64.3	63.9	62.9
2003	66.2	67.7	64.6	59.9	56.4	56.0	49.1	64.3	63.9	62.9
2004	66.0	67.6	64.6	59.6	56.3	56.4	49.1	64.4	63.6	63.0
2005	66.0	67.3	65.4	59.5	56.2	57.5	48.7	64.2	64.8	63.1
2006	66.2	67.2	65.8	59.6	56.2	58.1	48.9	64.5	64.9	63.5
2007	66.0	67.5	66.2	59.8	56.3	58.3	48.6	65.2	65.3	63.3
2008	66.0	67.7	66.7	59.5	56.4	58.4	49.0	65.4	65.3	63.5
2009	65.4	67.2	66.7	59.3	56.6	58.5	48.4	65.2	64.8	63.3
2010	64.7	67.0	66.5	59.0	56.5	58.1	48.2	64.3	64.7	63.1
Unemployment Rate										
1975	8.5	6.9	4.9	1.9	3.7	3.4	3.4	5.1	1.6	4.5
1976	7.7	6.9	4.8	2.0	4.1	3.4	3.9	5.4	1.6	5.4
1977	7.1	7.8	5.6	2.0	4.6	3.4	4.1	4.9	1.8	5.6
1978	6.1	8.1	6.3	2.3	4.7	3.3	4.1	5.1	2.2	5.5
1979	5.8	7.3	6.3	2.1	5.4	2.9	4.4	5.1	2.1	5.4
1980	7.1	7.3	6.1	2.0	5.7	2.8	4.4	6.0	2.0	6.9
1981	7.6	7.3	5.8	2.2	6.8	4.0	4.9	8.9	2.5	9.7
1982	9.7	10.7	7.2	2.4	7.0	5.6	5.4	10.2	3.1	10.8
1983	9.6	11.6	10.0	2.7	7.3	6.9	5.9	11.4	3.5	11.5
1984	7.5	10.9	9.0	2.8	8.6	7.1	5.9	11.5	3.1	11.8
1985	7.2	10.1	8.3	2.5	9.1	7.2	6.0	9.6	2.8	11.4
1986	7.0	9.2	7.9	2.7	9.1	6.6	7.5	10.0	2.6	11.4
1987	6.2	8.4	7.9	2.6	9.2	6.3	7.9	9.8	2.3	10.5
1988	5.5	7.4	7.0	2.4	8.9	6.3	7.9	9.3	1.9	8.6
1989	5.3	7.1	6.0	2.2	8.3	5.7	7.8	8.4	1.6	7.3
1990	5.6	7.7	6.7	2.0	8.0	5.0	7.0	7.6	1.8	7.1
1991	6.8	9.8	9.3	2.0	8.3	5.6	6.9	7.1	3.2	8.9
1992	7.5	10.6	10.5	2.1	9.1	6.7	7.3	6.8	5.8	10.0
1993	6.9	10.8	10.6	2.4	10.2	8.0	9.8	6.3	9.4	10.4
1994	6.1	9.6	9.4	2.6	10.8	8.5	10.7	6.9	9.6	9.5
1995	5.6	8.6	8.2	2.9	10.2	8.2	11.3	7.1	9.1	8.7
1996	5.4	8.8	8.2	3.1	10.7	9.0	11.3	6.6	9.9	8.1
1997	4.9	8.4	8.3	3.1	10.9	9.9	11.4	5.6	10.1	7.0
1998	4.5	7.7	7.7	3.8	10.5	9.3	11.5	4.4	8.4	6.3
1999	4.2	7.0	6.9	4.2	10.1	8.5	11.0	3.5	7.1	6.0
2000	4.0	6.1	6.3	4.4	8.6	7.8	10.2	3.1	5.8	5.5
2001	4.7	6.5	6.8	4.5	7.9	7.9	9.2	2.5	5.0	5.1
2002	5.8	7.0	6.4	4.9	8.0	8.6	8.7	3.1	5.1	5.2
2003	6.0	6.9	5.9	4.6	8.6	9.3	8.5	4.1	5.8	5.0
2004	5.5	6.4	5.4	4.2	9.0	10.3	8.1	5.0	6.6	4.8
2005	5.1	6.0	5.0	3.8	9.0	11.2	7.8	5.3	7.7	4.9
2006	4.6	5.5	4.8	3.6	8.9	10.3	6.9	4.3	7.0	5.5
2007	4.6	5.2	4.4	3.6	8.1	8.7	6.2	3.6	6.1	5.4
2008	5.8	5.3	4.2	3.7	7.5	7.6	6.8	3.1	6.0	5.7
2009	9.3	7.3	5.6	4.8	9.2	7.8	7.8	3.7	8.2	7.7
2010	9.6	7.1	5.2	4.8	9.4	7.2	8.6	4.5	8.3	7.9

[1]Unified Germany from 1991 onward; data for previous years relate to the former West Germany.

Table 10-2. Unemployment Rates by Sex and Country, Adjusted to U.S. Concepts, 10 Countries, 1975–2010

(Percent.)

Sex and year	United States	Canada	Australia	Japan	France	Germany[1]	Italy	Netherlands	Sweden	United Kingdom
Men										
1975	7.9	6.2	3.8	1.8	2.7	3.3	2.5	3.9	1.4	4.1
1976	7.1	6.3	3.9	2.2	2.9	3.0	2.7	4.1	1.3	5.2
1977	6.3	7.3	4.6	2.0	3.3	2.9	2.8	3.8	1.5	5.3
1978	5.3	7.5	5.4	2.2	3.6	2.7	2.8	3.6	2.1	5.1
1979	5.1	6.7	5.2	1.9	4.0	2.3	3.0	3.6	1.9	4.9
1980	6.9	6.9	5.1	1.7	4.0	2.3	2.9	4.2	1.7	6.7
1981	7.4	7.0	4.8	2.0	5.0	3.4	3.3	6.9	2.4	10.3
1982	9.9	11.1	6.4	2.1	5.5	5.0	3.8	8.6	3.0	11.6
1983	9.9	12.2	9.7	2.5	5.8	6.2	4.1	10.4	3.4	12.3
1984	7.4	11.1	8.7	2.5	7.1	6.2	4.2	10.4	3.0	12.0
1985	7.0	10.2	7.9	2.2	7.7	6.2	4.2	8.4	2.8	11.8
1986	6.9	9.3	7.6	2.4	7.7	5.6	5.2	7.9	2.6	11.8
1987	6.2	8.3	7.6	2.2	7.6	5.4	5.5	7.3	2.3	10.9
1988	5.5	7.2	6.6	2.0	7.1	5.3	5.5	7.3	1.9	8.8
1989	5.2	7.0	5.6	1.8	6.4	4.6	5.4	6.4	1.6	7.4
1990	5.7	7.9	6.6	1.7	6.3	4.2	4.8	5.6	1.9	7.4
1991	7.2	10.5	9.7	1.7	6.6	4.6	4.9	5.4	3.5	9.9
1992	7.9	11.6	11.2	1.8	7.5	5.5	5.3	5.4	6.8	11.8
1993	7.2	11.5	11.3	2.1	8.9	6.7	7.4	5.3	11.0	12.4
1994	6.2	10.2	9.8	2.3	9.5	7.3	8.4	6.1	11.0	11.3
1995	5.6	9.1	8.6	2.6	8.8	7.3	8.7	5.9	9.9	10.1
1996	5.4	9.2	8.5	2.8	9.4	8.4	8.8	5.3	10.4	9.5
1997	4.9	8.7	8.5	2.8	9.7	9.4	8.8	4.5	10.4	7.9
1998	4.4	8.0	8.0	3.5	9.2	8.9	8.9	3.5	8.7	7.0
1999	4.1	7.3	7.1	4.0	8.9	8.1	8.6	2.8	7.4	6.6
2000	3.9	6.3	6.5	4.1	7.4	7.6	7.9	2.4	6.2	6.0
2001	4.8	6.9	7.0	4.4	6.7	7.8	7.2	2.1	5.3	5.7
2002	5.9	7.6	6.5	4.7	7.2	8.8	6.8	2.8	5.6	5.8
2003	6.3	7.3	5.9	4.3	7.8	9.7	6.6	4.0	6.3	5.6
2004	5.6	6.8	5.3	3.9	8.1	10.6	6.5	4.9	6.9	5.2
2005	5.1	6.3	4.9	3.5	8.2	11.5	6.3	4.9	7.8	5.3
2006	4.6	5.8	4.7	3.3	8.2	10.4	5.5	3.9	6.9	5.8
2007	4.7	5.6	4.0	3.2	7.6	8.6	5.0	3.2	5.8	5.7
2008	6.1	5.8	4.0	3.2	7.1	7.5	5.6	2.9	5.8	6.2
2009	10.3	8.5	5.7	4.4	9.1	8.2	6.9	3.7	8.6	8.7
2010	10.5	7.8	5.1	4.6	9.2	7.7	7.7	4.5	8.4	8.7
Women										
1975	9.3	8.1	7.0	3.9	5.1	3.5	5.8	8.2	2.0	5.2
1976	8.6	7.9	6.4	3.9	5.9	3.9	6.5	8.6	2.0	5.8
1977	8.2	8.8	7.5	4.3	6.5	4.3	6.8	7.6	2.2	6.2
1978	7.2	9.1	7.9	4.3	6.6	4.2	6.8	8.6	2.4	6.2
1979	6.8	8.3	8.2	4.1	7.4	3.9	7.3	8.8	2.3	6.2
1980	7.4	7.9	7.9	3.3	8.3	3.6	7.4	9.7	2.3	7.1
1981	7.9	7.8	7.4	3.5	9.2	4.8	8.1	12.9	2.7	8.8
1982	9.4	10.1	8.5	3.5	9.2	6.5	8.6	13.3	3.4	9.5
1983	9.2	10.8	10.4	3.7	9.4	7.9	9.4	13.9	3.5	10.5
1984	7.6	10.7	9.5	3.3	10.5	8.5	9.4	13.9	3.2	11.6
1985	7.4	9.9	8.8	3.0	10.9	8.6	9.4	11.9	2.9	11.0
1986	7.1	9.1	8.5	3.2	10.9	8.1	11.8	13.7	2.7	10.9
1987	6.2	8.6	8.3	3.2	11.4	7.8	12.0	13.7	2.3	10.0
1988	5.6	7.6	7.5	2.9	11.1	7.8	12.3	12.6	1.9	8.3
1989	5.4	7.1	6.5	2.7	10.6	7.2	12.1	11.6	1.7	7.1
1990	5.5	7.5	6.8	2.5	10.2	6.1	10.8	10.8	1.8	6.8
1991	6.4	9.0	8.7	2.5	10.4	7.0	10.4	9.6	2.9	7.5
1992	7.0	9.4	9.5	2.5	11.2	8.4	10.8	8.9	4.6	7.7
1993	6.6	9.9	9.7	3.0	11.8	9.6	13.8	7.7	7.6	7.9
1994	6.0	8.8	9.0	3.1	12.4	10.1	14.6	8.1	8.2	7.4
1995	5.6	8.0	7.7	3.4	11.9	9.4	15.4	8.8	8.1	6.9
1996	5.4	8.2	7.8	3.5	12.2	9.6	15.3	8.4	9.3	6.4
1997	5.0	8.0	7.9	3.7	12.3	10.6	15.4	7.0	9.7	5.9
1998	4.6	7.2	7.4	4.2	11.9	9.8	15.4	5.5	8.0	5.4
1999	4.3	6.6	6.7	4.5	11.6	8.9	14.8	4.5	6.7	5.2
2000	4.1	5.8	6.1	4.8	10.1	8.1	13.7	3.9	5.4	4.9
2001	4.7	6.0	6.4	4.8	9.3	7.9	12.2	3.1	4.7	4.5
2002	5.6	6.4	6.2	5.2	8.9	8.3	11.5	3.5	4.7	4.5
2003	5.7	6.3	6.0	4.9	9.5	8.8	11.4	4.2	5.2	4.4
2004	5.4	6.0	5.5	4.6	9.9	10.0	10.6	5.1	6.1	4.3
2005	5.1	5.6	5.2	4.1	9.9	10.9	10.1	5.6	7.5	4.4
2006	4.6	5.2	4.9	4.0	9.7	10.2	8.8	4.9	7.1	5.0
2007	4.5	4.8	4.8	4.2	8.6	8.8	7.9	4.0	6.4	5.0
2008	5.4	4.8	4.6	4.3	7.9	7.7	8.5	3.4	6.3	5.1
2009	8.1	6.1	5.4	5.2	9.4	7.3	9.3	3.8	7.9	6.5
2010	8.6	6.2	5.4	5.0	9.7	6.7	9.8	4.5	8.2	6.9

[1]Unified Germany from 1991 onward; data for previous years relate to the former West Germany.

Table 10-3. Unemployment Rates Among Youth, Adjusted to U.S. Concepts, 10 Countries, 1970–2010

(Percent.)

Year	United States	Canada	Australia	Japan	France	Germany[1]	Italy	Netherlands	Sweden	United Kingdom
1970	11.0	. . .	. . .	2.0	4.9	0.4	10.4	. . .	2.9	. . .
1971	12.7	. . .	. . .	2.1	5.5	0.6	10.3	. . .	5.1	. . .
1972	12.1	. . .	. . .	2.5	5.9	0.7	13.6	. . .	5.8	. . .
1973	10.5	. . .	. . .	2.3	5.8	0.8	13.2	3.8	5.3	. . .
1974	11.9	. . .	. . .	2.4	6.3	2.2	12.0	5.1	4.5	. . .
1975	16.1	. . .	. . .	3.1	7.9	4.7	13.2	8.2	3.8	. . .
1976	14.7	12.4	. . .	3.2	9.1	4.8	15.2	9.3	3.8	. . .
1977	13.6	13.8	. . .	3.6	10.7	5.0	14.9	8.9	4.5	. . .
1978	12.3	13.9	12.6	3.8	11.2	4.5	15.4	9.6	5.6	. . .
1979	11.8	12.6	13.0	3.7	12.9	3.6	16.0	10.2	5.1	. . .
1980	13.9	12.7	12.5	3.5	14.3	3.7	15.8	11.9	5.1	. . .
1981	14.9	12.6	11.4	4.0	16.9	5.7	17.3	16.8	6.4	. . .
1982	17.8	18.1	13.8	4.3	16.4	8.2	19.4	19.8	7.7	. . .
1983	17.2	19.1	18.3	4.6	17.3	9.6	20.9	20.9	8.1	. . .
1984	13.9	17.2	16.8	4.9	20.9	10.7	21.6	20.8	6.1	19.8
1985	13.6	15.6	15.2	4.7	21.0	10.0	22.2	17.4	5.9	18.0
1986	13.3	14.5	14.8	5.2	19.5	8.0	25.5	16.8	5.7	18.2
1987	12.2	13.0	14.6	5.0	18.5	7.4	25.8	15.2	5.3	15.4
1988	11.0	11.2	13.1	4.7	17.5	6.9	24.8	14.1	4.3	12.6
1989	10.9	10.5	10.8	4.4	15.4	5.5	23.9	12.5	4.0	10.1
1990	11.2	12.0	12.6	4.3	15.6	4.6	21.3	11.5	4.6	10.6
1991	13.4	15.4	17.0	4.2	16.5	5.5	21.2	10.7	8.0	14.3
1992	14.2	16.8	18.8	4.4	17.9	6.4	22.8	9.7	13.9	16.8
1993	13.4	16.7	18.2	5.1	21.0	7.8	27.8	9.9	23.5	18.0
1994	12.5	14.9	16.5	5.2	22.5	8.5	29.4	10.4	23.8	16.8
1995	12.1	13.9	14.8	5.9	20.8	8.4	30.6	12.9	20.2	15.8
1996	12.0	14.5	15.1	6.4	22.2	9.7	30.6	12.1	21.5	15.4
1997	11.3	15.5	15.7	6.4	22.8	10.6	30.4	9.5	21.1	14.2
1998	10.4	14.6	14.6	7.4	21.2	9.4	30.1	8.2	17.1	13.6
1999	9.9	13.4	13.3	8.7	21.0	8.8	29.0	7.1	14.6	13.0
2000	9.3	11.7	12.1	8.9	16.7	8.6	27.3	6.0	12.0	12.5
2001	10.6	11.9	13.5	9.1	15.9	8.4	24.4	5.0	12.0	12.0
2002	12.0	12.9	12.8	9.5	17.0	10.0	23.4	5.5	13.1	12.2
2003	12.4	12.8	12.0	9.6	19.1	10.8	24.0	7.1	14.0	12.4
2004	11.8	12.5	11.4	9.0	20.8	12.9	23.8	8.7	17.2	12.3
2005	11.3	11.4	10.6	8.1	21.4	15.5	24.2	9.1	22.2	13.0
2006	10.5	10.6	10.0	7.5	22.6	13.8	22.0	7.3	21.1	14.2
2007	10.5	10.0	9.4	7.6	19.9	11.9	20.6	6.9	18.7	14.4
2008	12.8	10.4	8.8	7.0	19.4	10.5	21.5	6.3	19.1	15.1
2009	17.6	13.9	11.5	8.8	24.0	11.2	25.8	7.7	24.6	19.2
2010	18.4	13.6	11.5	9.0	24.1	10.2	28.0	8.8	24.8	19.8

Note: Youth are defined as 16- to 24-year-olds in the United States, Canada, France, Sweden, and the United Kingdom; otherwise, they are defined as 15- to 24-year-olds.

[1]Unified Germany from 1991 onward; data for previous years relate to the former West Germany.
. . . = Not available.

Table 10-4. Employment-Population Ratios by Sex, Adjusted to U.S. Concepts, 10 Countries, 1975–2010

(Ratio.)

Sex and year	United States	Canada	Australia	Japan	France	Germany[1]	Italy	Netherlands	Sweden	United Kingdom
Men										
1975	71.7	73.5	79.1	79.5	72.3	70.9	68.8	76.9	76.0	77.9
1976	72.0	74.2	78.3	79.2	71.9	70.3	68.5	75.9	75.6	76.7
1977	72.8	73.3	77.3	78.7	71.4	69.9	67.5	75.7	74.5	75.9
1978	73.8	73.4	75.5	78.2	70.6	69.7	66.8	75.0	73.5	75.3
1979	73.8	74.3	75.3	78.2	69.8	69.8	66.3	74.3	73.7	75.0
1980	72.0	74.0	75.1	77.9	69.1	69.6	66.0	74.1	73.6	73.3
1981	71.3	73.9	75.1	77.8	67.6	68.5	65.6	72.2	72.0	70.1
1982	69.0	69.3	73.4	77.4	69.3	67.0	64.4	69.5	71.3	68.0
1983	68.8	68.3	70.1	77.1	68.2	65.8	63.5	67.4	70.4	66.7
1984	70.7	68.9	70.5	76.4	66.4	65.7	62.9	66.6	70.2	67.2
1985	70.9	69.6	70.6	75.9	65.7	65.8	62.5	67.6	70.5	67.1
1986	71.0	70.4	70.8	75.4	65.3	66.3	61.8	66.7	70.6	66.6
1987	71.5	71.0	70.3	74.9	64.6	66.2	60.9	64.8	69.7	67.2
1988	72.0	71.6	71.0	75.0	64.1	65.9	60.4	65.0	70.3	69.0
1989	72.5	71.8	72.1	75.0	64.2	65.9	59.9	65.7	70.9	70.2
1990	72.0	70.6	71.4	75.4	63.5	65.6	60.0	66.5	70.6	70.0
1991	70.4	67.6	68.2	75.8	62.4	67.9	60.6	66.8	69.2	67.3
1992	69.8	65.7	66.6	76.1	61.5	66.3	59.8	67.2	65.7	64.8
1993	70.0	65.3	66.0	75.9	59.9	64.7	58.8	65.5	61.6	63.7
1994	70.4	65.9	67.2	75.4	59.1	63.8	57.2	65.2	60.9	64.2
1995	70.8	66.1	68.2	75.0	59.4	63.1	56.2	66.7	62.0	64.7
1996	70.9	65.8	68.1	74.9	59.2	62.1	55.8	67.5	61.5	64.9
1997	71.3	66.4	67.7	74.9	58.6	61.3	55.5	68.5	61.0	65.9
1998	71.6	66.8	67.9	73.9	58.3	61.9	55.4	69.8	62.1	66.2
1999	71.6	67.5	68.2	73.0	58.5	60.7	55.5	70.4	62.5	66.6
2000	71.9	68.2	68.4	72.5	59.5	60.6	55.8	70.8	64.2	66.9
2001	70.9	67.7	67.6	71.5	59.6	60.2	56.0	71.3	64.4	66.9
2002	69.7	67.9	67.8	70.4	59.4	58.9	56.3	71.0	64.3	66.7
2003	68.9	68.3	68.1	69.9	58.2	57.5	56.9	69.7	63.7	66.9
2004	69.2	68.5	68.8	69.6	57.6	57.3	56.9	68.9	63.0	66.9
2005	69.6	68.6	69.4	69.7	57.3	57.7	56.8	68.1	63.8	66.8
2006	70.1	68.4	69.8	69.8	57.2	58.6	57.3	68.8	64.5	66.7
2007	69.8	68.7	70.4	70.1	57.4	59.7	57.3	69.6	65.5	66.7
2008	68.5	68.8	70.7	69.6	57.7	60.5	56.9	69.8	65.5	66.4
2009	64.5	65.9	69.1	68.0	56.5	59.9	55.3	68.6	63.0	64.2
2010	63.7	66.2	69.5	67.5	56.3	60.1	54.5	66.7	63.3	63.8
Women										
1975	42.0	40.8	41.4	44.0	39.2	37.9	25.3	27.1	54.1	44.2
1976	43.2	42.6	41.5	44.1	39.7	37.8	25.8	27.3	54.7	44.0
1977	44.5	42.9	41.5	44.9	40.1	37.7	26.9	28.2	55.5	44.0
1978	46.4	44.0	41.0	45.5	40.4	37.9	26.9	28.4	56.1	44.4
1979	47.5	45.7	40.7	45.7	40.5	38.4	27.3	29.2	57.2	45.0
1980	47.7	46.9	41.9	45.7	40.4	38.9	27.9	31.0	58.0	45.1
1981	48.0	48.2	42.1	45.7	40.3	38.7	28.0	31.9	58.5	44.3
1982	47.7	47.0	41.5	45.9	42.9	38.1	27.7	32.8	58.4	43.5
1983	48.0	47.3	40.8	46.7	42.8	37.3	27.6	31.9	58.6	43.3
1984	49.5	48.2	41.8	46.5	42.6	37.3	27.6	32.7	59.1	44.4
1985	50.4	49.5	43.0	46.3	42.5	37.6	27.8	33.4	59.7	45.2
1986	51.4	50.7	45.1	46.2	43.0	38.1	28.1	34.7	60.1	45.8
1987	52.5	51.6	45.8	46.2	42.7	38.5	28.3	35.4	60.5	46.9
1988	53.4	53.0	47.0	46.6	42.6	39.0	28.3	37.0	61.2	48.4
1989	54.3	53.9	48.8	47.4	43.0	39.7	28.6	37.7	61.7	49.9
1990	54.3	54.1	49.5	48.0	43.2	40.5	29.2	39.4	61.8	50.3
1991	53.7	53.2	48.4	48.6	43.0	44.3	29.7	40.9	60.6	49.6
1992	53.8	52.4	48.0	48.7	43.0	43.4	29.7	41.9	58.4	49.1
1993	54.1	51.9	47.7	48.3	43.1	42.7	29.7	42.8	55.5	49.0
1994	55.3	52.4	48.8	48.0	43.0	42.3	29.2	43.3	54.3	49.3
1995	55.6	52.7	50.5	47.7	43.4	42.7	29.1	44.4	54.7	49.8
1996	56.0	52.6	50.6	47.7	43.6	42.8	29.4	45.3	53.9	50.3
1997	56.8	53.2	50.5	47.9	43.2	42.7	29.6	47.3	53.0	51.0
1998	57.1	54.3	51.0	47.4	43.6	43.5	30.1	48.7	53.3	51.4
1999	57.4	55.2	51.3	46.6	44.0	44.1	30.8	50.5	54.2	52.0
2000	57.5	56.0	52.5	46.4	45.0	44.4	31.6	51.7	56.1	52.5
2001	57.0	56.2	52.6	46.2	45.5	44.8	32.7	53.2	56.7	52.7
2002	56.3	57.1	52.9	45.4	45.9	44.7	33.3	54.0	57.1	53.0
2003	56.1	58.0	53.6	45.3	45.6	44.5	34.0	53.8	56.8	53.1
2004	56.0	58.2	53.7	45.5	45.6	44.3	34.2	53.6	56.1	53.4
2005	56.2	58.1	55.0	45.7	45.7	44.9	34.1	53.9	56.0	53.7
2006	56.6	58.6	55.7	46.0	45.8	46.0	34.7	54.8	56.4	53.8
2007	56.6	59.5	56.4	46.1	46.6	47.1	34.9	56.3	57.4	53.6
2008	56.2	59.6	57.2	45.9	47.2	47.8	35.3	57.2	57.4	53.7
2009	54.4	58.7	56.9	45.7	46.8	48.3	34.7	57.1	56.0	53.1
2010	53.6	58.5	56.6	45.7	46.6	48.1	34.5	56.2	55.5	52.8

[1]Unified Germany from 1991 onward; data for previous years relate to the former West Germany.
. . . = Not available.

Table 10-5. Women's Share of the Labor Force, Adjusted to U.S. Concepts, 10 Countries, 1970–2010

(Percent.)

Year	United States	Canada	Australia	Japan	France	Germany[1]	Italy	Netherlands	Sweden	United Kingdom
1970	38.1	33.6	32.8	38.9	36.6	36.5	28.2	. . .	39.6	. . .
1971	38.2	34.4	33.2	38.4	37.0	36.8	28.3	. . .	40.3	37.4
1972	38.5	34.9	33.4	37.9	37.4	37.3	28.1	. . .	40.8	37.6
1973	38.9	35.6	34.1	38.2	37.7	37.7	28.7	27.1	41.1	38.2
1974	39.4	36.1	34.8	37.4	38.0	38.0	29.1	27.2	41.9	38.7
1975	40.0	36.9	35.5	37.0	38.2	38.5	29.4	27.5	42.7	38.8
1976	40.5	37.4	35.6	37.1	38.8	38.8	30.2	28.0	43.1	38.9
1977	41.0	37.9	36.1	37.7	39.3	39.0	31.4	28.6	43.8	39.2
1978	41.7	38.6	36.3	38.1	39.8	39.2	31.5	29.2	44.4	39.7
1979	42.1	39.2	36.4	38.3	40.2	39.3	32.2	30.1	44.8	40.1
1980	42.5	39.8	37.1	38.4	40.6	39.5	32.7	31.5	45.3	40.4
1981	43.0	40.5	37.2	38.4	41.0	39.7	33.0	33.0	46.1	40.6
1982	43.3	40.9	37.3	38.7	41.9	39.8	33.2	34.1	46.4	40.7
1983	43.5	41.4	37.5	39.2	42.1	39.8	33.5	34.0	46.7	41.1
1984	43.8	41.9	38.0	39.3	42.6	39.9	33.7	34.8	47.0	41.8
1985	44.2	42.4	38.6	39.6	42.8	40.1	34.0	34.9	47.2	42.2
1986	44.5	42.7	39.6	39.6	43.2	40.2	34.9	36.7	47.3	42.7
1987	44.8	43.1	40.0	39.8	43.5	40.3	35.3	37.9	47.7	43.0
1988	45.0	43.6	40.5	40.0	43.7	40.7	35.6	38.7	47.8	43.2
1989	45.2	43.9	41.1	40.3	44.0	41.0	35.9	38.7	47.8	43.5
1990	45.2	44.2	41.6	40.5	44.2	41.5	36.2	39.5	47.8	43.7
1991	45.3	44.6	41.8	40.6	44.5	42.8	36.3	40.0	47.7	43.8
1992	45.4	44.7	41.9	40.6	44.8	42.8	36.7	40.2	47.7	44.0
1993	45.5	44.9	42.0	40.5	45.3	42.8	37.4	41.1	47.7	44.4
1994	46.0	44.9	42.4	40.5	45.5	42.9	37.6	41.3	47.6	44.5
1995	46.1	45.1	42.9	40.5	45.8	43.1	38.0	41.5	47.6	44.7
1996	46.2	45.2	43.0	40.5	45.9	43.3	38.4	41.8	47.7	44.9
1997	46.2	45.3	43.1	40.7	45.8	43.4	38.6	42.3	47.5	45.1
1998	46.3	45.5	43.3	40.7	46.2	43.5	39.1	42.4	47.2	45.3
1999	46.5	45.7	43.5	40.6	46.3	44.0	39.5	43.0	47.4	45.4
2000	46.5	45.9	44.0	40.8	46.4	44.3	39.8	43.4	47.5	45.6
2001	46.5	46.0	44.3	40.9	46.6	44.4	40.3	43.8	47.7	45.6
2002	46.5	46.2	44.4	40.9	46.7	44.7	40.5	44.1	47.8	45.7
2003	46.6	46.5	44.8	41.1	47.0	45.0	40.7	44.4	47.8	45.7
2004	46.4	46.6	44.6	41.3	47.3	45.1	40.7	44.6	47.8	45.8
2005	46.4	46.5	45.0	41.4	47.5	45.2	40.5	45.2	47.5	45.9
2006	46.3	46.8	45.2	41.6	47.6	45.5	40.6	45.5	47.5	46.0
2007	46.4	47.0	45.3	41.6	47.8	45.7	40.6	45.8	47.6	45.8
2008	46.5	47.0	45.4	41.7	47.9	45.7	41.0	46.0	47.5	45.8
2009	46.7	47.2	45.5	42.1	48.0	45.9	41.1	46.3	47.4	46.1
2010	46.7	47.2	45.4	42.2	48.1	45.6	41.3	46.5	47.2	46.1

[1]Unified Germany from 1991 onward; data for previous years relate to the former West Germany.

Table 10-6. Percent of Employment in Agriculture, Adjusted to U.S. Concepts, 10 Countries, 1970–2010

(Percent.)

Year	United States	Canada	Australia	Japan	France	Germany[1]	Italy	Netherlands	Sweden	United Kingdom[2]
1970	4.5	7.6	8.1	16.9	. . .	8.5	20.1	. . .	8.2	. . .
1971	4.4	7.5	7.7	15.5	16.0	8.0	20.1	. . .	7.8	3.2
1972	4.4	6.9	7.9	14.4	15.0	7.6	19.0	. . .	7.5	3.0
1973	4.2	6.5	7.4	13.1	14.1	7.2	18.2	6.1	7.2	3.0
1974	4.2	6.3	7.0	12.6	13.3	6.9	17.4	6.0	6.7	2.8
1975	4.1	6.1	6.9	12.4	12.9	6.7	16.7	5.9	6.5	2.8
1976	3.9	5.6	6.6	11.9	12.3	6.2	16.4	5.7	6.2	2.8
1977	3.7	5.4	6.7	11.6	11.8	5.9	15.8	5.6	6.1	2.8
1978	3.7	5.2	6.4	11.4	11.4	5.7	15.4	5.6	6.1	2.8
1979	3.5	5.1	6.5	10.8	11.1	5.3	14.9	5.4	5.8	2.7
1980	3.6	4.9	6.5	10.1	10.7	5.2	14.2	5.2	5.6	2.6
1981	3.5	4.8	6.5	9.7	10.4	5.0	13.3	5.2	5.6	2.7
1982	3.6	4.9	6.5	9.4	9.5	4.9	12.4	5.3	5.6	2.7
1983	3.5	5.0	6.6	8.9	9.2	4.8	12.3	5.3	5.5	2.7
1984	3.3	4.8	6.2	8.5	9.0	4.7	11.7	5.2	5.2	2.6
1985	3.1	4.7	6.1	8.4	8.6	4.5	11.0	5.1	4.9	2.3
1986	3.1	4.7	6.1	8.1	8.3	4.3	10.7	5.0	4.7	2.2
1987	3.0	4.5	5.8	8.0	7.9	4.1	10.4	4.9	4.5	2.3
1988	2.9	4.4	5.8	7.6	7.6	3.9	9.8	4.7	4.4	2.3
1989	2.9	4.2	5.5	7.3	7.2	3.7	9.3	4.7	4.3	2.2
1990	2.9	4.2	5.6	6.9	6.8	3.5	8.9	4.6	3.9	2.1
1991	2.9	4.3	5.5	6.4	6.5	4.1	8.5	4.5	3.8	2.3
1992	2.9	4.2	5.3	6.1	6.2	3.8	8.2	4.0	3.8	2.2
1993	2.7	4.3	5.3	5.7	6.0	3.5	7.1	3.9	3.9	2.0
1994	2.9	4.2	5.1	5.6	5.7	3.3	6.9	4.0	3.9	2.1
1995	2.9	4.0	4.9	5.5	5.4	3.1	6.6	3.8	3.5	2.1
1996	2.8	3.9	5.0	5.3	5.2	3.0	6.2	3.9	3.3	1.9
1997	2.7	3.8	5.1	5.1	5.1	2.9	6.2	3.8	3.1	1.6
1998	2.7	3.8	4.9	5.0	5.0	2.8	5.9	3.3	2.9	1.4
1999	2.6	3.5	4.9	4.9	4.8	2.8	5.5	3.2	3.1	1.3
2000	1.8	3.3	4.9	4.8	4.6	2.6	5.3	3.2	2.9	1.2
2001	1.7	2.8	4.8	4.7	4.4	2.6	5.3	3.0	2.6	1.1
2002	1.7	2.8	4.4	4.5	4.3	2.5	5.0	3.0	2.5	1.0
2003	1.7	2.7	3.9	4.4	4.2	2.5	4.9	3.0	2.5	1.0
2004	1.6	2.7	3.7	4.3	3.9	2.4	4.5	3.1	2.5	1.0
2005	1.6	2.7	3.6	4.2	3.7	2.4	4.2	3.3	2.3	1.0
2006	1.5	2.6	3.4	4.1	3.8	2.3	4.3	3.3	2.2	1.0
2007	1.4	2.5	3.3	4.1	3.5	2.3	4.0	3.0	2.2	1.0
2008	1.5	2.3	3.3	4.0	2.8	2.3	3.7	2.7	2.2	1.1
2009	1.5	2.3	3.3	4.0	3.0	2.3	3.7	2.7	2.2	1.1
2010	1.6	2.2	3.3	3.9	2.8	2.2	3.8	2.8	2.1	1.3

Note: Agriculture includes agriculture, forestry, hunting, and fishing.

[1]Unified Germany from 1991 onward; data for previous years relate to the former West Germany.
[2]Sectoral employment is only partially adjusted to U.S. concepts prior to 1984.
. . . = Not available.

Table 10-7. Percent of Employment in Industry, Adjusted to U.S. Concepts, 10 Countries, 1970–2010

(Percent.)

Year	United States	Canada	Australia	Japan	France	Germany[1]	Italy	Netherlands	Sweden	United Kingdom[2]
1970	33.1	29.8	34.6	35.7	. . .	48.7	38.8	. . .	37.9	. . .
1971	31.7	29.4	34.3	35.9	39.6	47.7	39.0	. . .	37.1	42.0
1972	31.4	29.2	33.5	36.2	39.8	47.0	38.8	. . .	36.3	41.2
1973	32.0	29.5	33.4	37.0	39.9	46.8	38.4	35.1	36.3	40.9
1974	31.4	29.5	33.0	36.8	39.6	45.9	38.4	34.3	36.3	40.6
1975	29.5	28.1	31.5	35.6	39.1	44.5	38.3	33.2	35.8	39.0
1976	29.6	27.9	31.0	35.6	38.4	44.1	37.5	32.3	34.8	38.1
1977	29.7	27.5	30.4	35.1	38.0	43.8	37.6	32.1	33.7	38.0
1978	30.0	27.3	29.3	34.8	37.4	43.5	37.4	31.8	32.4	37.7
1979	30.2	27.5	29.0	34.7	36.8	43.3	37.0	31.0	31.9	37.3
1980	29.3	27.3	28.6	35.1	36.3	42.9	37.0	29.7	31.5	36.2
1981	28.9	26.9	28.3	35.1	35.8	42.2	36.5	28.4	30.6	34.3
1982	27.2	25.0	27.4	34.5	33.4	41.3	36.1	27.5	29.5	33.1
1983	26.8	24.2	25.9	34.4	32.7	40.6	35.1	27.3	29.1	32.0
1984	27.3	24.3	25.5	34.5	31.9	40.3	33.4	27.3	29.0	34.2
1985	26.9	24.3	24.8	34.6	30.9	40.1	32.6	26.6	29.0	33.8
1986	26.6	24.2	24.1	34.2	30.1	39.9	32.0	26.1	29.1	33.1
1987	26.0	24.1	23.9	33.5	29.7	39.5	31.5	26.3	28.7	31.9
1988	25.8	24.3	23.8	33.9	29.4	39.0	31.5	25.7	28.3	31.9
1989	25.6	24.3	24.2	34.1	29.3	38.9	31.5	25.9	28.4	31.8
1990	25.1	23.6	23.2	33.9	29.3	38.9	31.4	25.9	28.2	31.2
1991	24.2	22.0	22.0	34.2	29.0	39.8	31.4	25.1	27.2	31.4
1992	23.5	21.3	21.7	34.3	28.1	38.9	31.3	24.3	25.6	29.1
1993	23.0	20.7	21.8	34.0	27.1	37.8	33.3	24.0	24.5	28.4
1994	23.0	20.9	21.8	33.7	26.4	36.6	33.2	22.9	24.0	26.8
1995	23.0	21.2	21.4	33.1	26.0	35.3	33.0	22.8	25.0	26.6
1996	22.9	21.1	21.1	32.9	25.5	34.4	32.7	22.3	25.2	26.5
1997	23.0	21.5	20.8	32.8	25.3	33.9	32.4	22.3	25.0	26.0
1998	22.7	21.6	20.6	31.7	25.0	33.6	32.3	21.7	24.9	25.7
1999	22.2	21.7	20.2	31.3	24.8	33.2	32.1	21.6	24.2	25.0
2000	22.0	21.8	20.6	30.9	24.5	32.8	31.6	21.2	23.6	24.2
2001	21.3	21.7	19.8	30.1	24.5	32.3	31.4	21.1	23.1	23.8
2002	20.3	21.8	20.0	29.0	24.1	31.7	31.3	20.2	22.5	23.3
2003	20.0	21.6	19.9	28.5	23.8	31.0	31.4	19.6	21.9	22.4
2004	20.0	21.7	20.3	27.6	23.4	30.7	30.3	19.9	21.9	21.8
2005	19.8	21.4	20.1	27.1	23.2	29.2	30.4	20.0	21.4	21.6
2006	19.9	20.9	20.2	27.1	23.1	29.0	29.8	19.7	21.4	21.5
2007	19.8	20.5	20.2	27.0	22.8	29.2	29.9	18.8	21.1	21.6
2008	19.1	20.4	20.5	26.5	22.2	29.0	28.9	17.8	21.2	20.8
2009	17.6	19.1	19.9	25.5	21.4	28.3	28.3	17.1	19.7	18.4
2010	17.2	19.0	19.7	24.9	20.6	28.0	27.7	16.5	19.5	18.1

Note: Industry includes manufacturing, mining, and construction.

[1]Unified Germany from 1991 onward; data for previous years relate to the former West Germany.
[2]Sectoral employment is only partially adjusted to U.S. concepts prior to 1984.
. . . = Not available.

Table 10-8. Percent of Employment in Manufacturing, Adjusted to U.S. Concepts, 10 Countries, 1970–2010

(Percent.)

Year	United States	Canada	Australia	Japan	France	Germany[1]	Italy	Netherlands	Sweden	United Kingdom[2]
1970	26.4	22.3	24.4	27.4	. . .	39.5	27.7	. . .	27.7	. . .
1971	24.7	21.8	24.1	27.4	28.4	37.4	28.0	. . .	27.4	33.9
1972	24.3	21.8	23.5	27.3	28.7	36.9	27.9	. . .	27.2	32.9
1973	24.8	22.0	23.3	27.8	28.8	36.7	27.9	25.3	27.6	32.3
1974	24.2	21.7	22.9	27.6	28.7	36.5	28.1	25.1	28.4	32.4
1975	22.7	20.2	21.3	26.1	28.4	35.7	28.0	24.5	28.1	31.0
1976	22.8	19.2	21.2	25.8	27.9	35.2	27.7	23.6	27.0	30.2
1977	22.7	18.8	20.9	25.3	27.6	35.1	27.6	23.2	26.0	30.4
1978	22.7	18.9	19.9	24.8	27.1	34.8	27.3	22.7	25.0	30.1
1979	22.7	19.2	19.6	24.6	26.6	34.5	26.9	22.0	24.7	29.5
1980	22.1	19.1	19.4	25.0	26.2	34.0	26.9	21.3	24.3	28.3
1981	21.7	18.5	19.2	25.1	25.7	33.4	26.3	20.8	23.4	26.5
1982	20.4	17.2	18.6	24.7	24.1	32.8	25.8	20.1	22.5	25.5
1983	19.8	16.8	17.8	24.8	23.7	32.2	25.0	19.6	22.4	24.3
1984	20.0	17.1	17.3	25.2	23.3	32.1	23.9	19.6	22.5	25.1
1985	19.5	17.0	16.1	25.3	22.7	32.3	23.2	19.5	22.6	25.0
1986	19.1	17.1	15.5	24.9	21.9	32.3	22.9	19.4	22.8	24.8
1987	18.6	16.7	15.4	24.4	21.5	32.0	22.5	19.5	22.0	23.4
1988	18.5	16.6	15.3	24.5	21.1	31.6	22.6	18.8	21.7	23.6
1989	18.5	16.5	15.1	24.5	20.9	31.6	22.8	19.1	21.7	22.8
1990	18.0	15.8	14.4	24.3	21.0	31.6	22.6	19.1	21.0	22.4
1991	17.5	14.8	13.7	24.6	20.8	30.7	22.1	18.3	19.9	22.9
1992	17.0	14.3	13.7	24.6	20.1	29.5	22.0	18.1	18.9	21.4
1993	16.4	14.0	13.5	23.9	19.5	28.1	24.6	17.7	18.3	21.2
1994	16.4	14.0	13.5	23.4	19.0	26.6	24.7	16.7	18.2	19.1
1995	16.4	14.4	13.0	22.7	18.7	25.2	24.9	16.4	19.0	19.1
1996	16.2	14.4	12.8	22.5	18.5	24.3	24.6	15.9	19.3	19.2
1997	16.1	14.8	12.9	22.2	18.4	24.0	24.2	15.7	19.3	18.0
1998	15.8	15.0	12.3	21.4	18.2	24.1	24.3	15.2	19.1	17.7
1999	15.0	15.3	11.8	21.0	18.0	23.8	24.1	15.1	18.5	17.0
2000	14.4	15.3	12.0	20.7	17.6	23.9	23.6	14.8	18.0	16.2
2001	13.5	15.0	11.6	20.2	17.6	23.7	23.1	14.5	17.5	15.5
2002	12.6	15.0	11.5	19.1	17.2	23.6	23.0	13.8	16.7	15.0
2003	12.3	14.6	11.0	18.8	17.0	23.3	22.9	13.5	16.2	13.8
2004	11.8	14.5	10.9	18.3	16.7	23.1	21.9	13.7	16.0	12.9
2005	11.5	13.8	10.4	18.1	16.3	22.2	21.6	13.7	15.3	12.6
2006	11.3	12.9	10.0	18.3	16.1	22.0	21.2	13.3	15.0	12.3
2007	11.2	12.1	9.9	18.3	15.7	22.2	21.2	12.5	14.6	12.1
2008	10.9	11.5	9.8	18.0	14.6	22.2	20.1	11.4	14.3	11.4
2009	10.2	10.6	9.3	17.2	13.9	21.4	19.5	10.7	13.0	9.8
2010	10.1	10.3	8.9	16.9	13.1	21.2	18.8	10.6	12.7	10.0

[1]Unified Germany from 1991 onward; data for previous years relate to the former West Germany.
[2]Sectoral employment is only partially adjusted to U.S. concepts prior to 1984.
. . . = Not available.

Table 10-9. Percent of Employment in Services, Adjusted to U.S. Concepts, 10 Countries, 1970–2010

(Percent.)

Category and year	United States	Canada	Australia	Japan	France	Germany[1]	Italy	Netherlands	Sweden	United Kingdom
1970	62.3	62.6	57.3	47.4	. . .	42.8	41.1	. . .	53.9	. . .
1971	63.8	63.1	57.9	48.5	44.4	44.4	40.9	. . .	55.1	54.8
1972	64.2	63.9	58.6	49.4	45.1	45.4	42.2	. . .	56.2	55.8
1973	63.8	63.9	59.3	49.9	46.0	46.0	43.4	58.9	56.6	56.1
1974	64.5	64.2	60.1	50.6	47.0	47.2	44.2	59.7	57.0	56.5
1975	66.4	65.8	61.5	52.0	48.0	48.8	45.1	60.8	57.7	58.2
1976	66.5	66.5	62.4	52.5	49.3	49.6	46.1	61.9	59.0	59.1
1977	66.6	67.2	62.9	53.3	50.2	50.3	46.6	62.3	60.2	59.2
1978	66.3	67.5	64.3	53.8	51.2	50.8	47.2	62.6	61.5	59.5
1979	66.3	67.4	64.5	54.5	52.1	51.4	48.2	63.6	62.3	60.1
1980	67.1	67.8	64.9	54.8	53.0	51.9	48.8	65.1	62.9	61.2
1981	67.6	68.3	65.2	55.3	53.9	52.8	50.2	66.4	63.8	63.0
1982	69.2	70.1	66.1	56.0	57.1	53.7	51.6	67.3	64.9	64.2
1983	69.7	70.8	67.4	56.6	58.1	54.5	52.6	67.5	65.5	65.3
1984	69.4	70.9	68.2	56.9	59.1	55.1	54.8	67.5	65.9	63.2
1985	70.0	71.0	69.1	57.0	60.4	55.4	56.4	68.3	66.1	63.9
1986	70.4	71.1	69.8	57.6	61.6	55.8	57.3	68.9	66.1	64.6
1987	71.0	71.3	70.3	58.5	62.4	56.4	58.1	68.8	66.8	65.8
1988	71.3	71.4	70.3	58.5	63.0	57.0	58.8	69.5	67.3	65.8
1989	71.5	71.5	70.3	58.7	63.6	57.4	59.3	69.4	67.3	66.0
1990	72.0	72.3	71.2	59.2	63.9	57.6	59.6	69.5	67.9	66.7
1991	72.9	73.6	72.6	59.4	64.5	56.1	60.2	70.4	69.0	66.2
1992	73.6	74.4	73.0	59.5	65.7	57.3	60.6	71.7	70.6	68.7
1993	74.3	75.0	72.9	60.3	67.0	58.7	59.5	72.0	71.6	69.5
1994	74.1	74.9	73.1	60.8	67.9	60.0	59.9	73.0	72.1	71.1
1995	74.1	74.8	73.7	61.4	68.6	61.5	60.4	73.4	71.5	71.3
1996	74.3	75.0	73.9	61.8	69.3	62.6	61.2	73.7	71.6	71.5
1997	74.3	74.7	74.1	62.1	69.6	63.2	61.4	73.9	71.9	72.4
1998	74.6	74.7	74.5	63.3	70.0	63.6	61.8	75.0	72.2	72.8
1999	75.3	74.8	74.9	63.8	70.4	64.0	62.4	75.3	72.7	73.8
2000	76.2	74.9	74.4	64.3	70.9	64.5	63.0	75.6	73.5	74.6
2001	77.1	75.5	75.4	65.2	71.1	65.1	63.4	75.9	74.3	75.1
2002	78.0	75.4	75.6	66.5	71.6	65.8	63.6	76.8	75.0	75.8
2003	78.3	75.7	76.2	67.1	72.0	66.4	63.7	77.4	75.6	76.7
2004	78.4	75.7	76.0	68.0	72.7	66.9	65.2	76.9	75.6	77.3
2005	78.6	75.8	76.3	68.7	73.2	68.5	65.4	76.7	76.3	77.3
2006	78.5	76.4	76.3	68.8	73.2	68.7	65.9	77.1	76.4	77.5
2007	78.8	77.1	76.5	68.9	73.7	68.5	66.1	78.2	76.7	77.4
2008	79.5	77.3	76.2	69.5	75.0	68.7	67.4	79.4	76.7	78.1
2009	80.9	78.7	76.8	70.5	75.6	69.4	68.0	80.2	78.1	80.5
2010	81.2	78.9	76.9	71.2	76.6	69.7	68.5	80.7	78.4	80.7

[1]Unified Germany from 1991 onward; data for previous years relate to the former West Germany.
. . . = Not available.

Table 10-10. Average Annual Hours Worked Per Employed Person, 16 Countries, 1970–2010

(Hours.)

Year	United States	Canada	Japan	Australia	Austria	Bel-gium	Den-mark	France	Ger-many[1]	Italy	Nether-lands	Norway	Spain	Sweden	Ireland	United Kingdom
1970	1 911.8	1 928.2	2 187.0	...	...	1 877.8	1 901.6	1 912.4	1 966.4	...	2 075.3	1 834.8	...	...	...	...
1971	1 896.0	1 910.4	2 162.4	...	...	1 867.3	1 870.7	1 911.9	1 934.4	...	2 047.3	1 813.4	...	...	...	1 835.1
1972	1 892.6	1 899.6	2 168.2	...	...	1 842.2	1 813.5	1 863.1	1 911.3	...	2 054.2	1 780.4	...	...	...	1 856.5
1973	1 890.8	1 895.3	2 153.2	...	...	1 814.1	1 769.2	1 849.9	1 882.7	...	2 039.8	1 766.2	...	...	...	1 865.4
1974	1 862.9	1 880.9	2 111.1	...	...	1 786.1	1 757.7	1 820.2	1 843.2	...	1 974.2	1 744.9	...	...	...	1 850.4
1975	1 830.0	1 864.7	2 080.7	...	...	1 777.1	1 688.7	1 794.9	1 806.3	...	1 929.8	1 727.9	...	...	...	1 819.0
1976	1 823.6	1 835.9	2 099.4	...	...	1 780.2	1 697.6	1 821.3	1 818.8	...	1 924.7	1 674.4	...	...	...	1 811.9
1977	1 822.5	1 829.6	2 115.2	...	...	1 754.3	1 674.1	1 785.2	1 801.3	...	1 900.6	1 638.3	1 836.9	...	...	1 821.8
1978	1 830.2	1 835.4	2 127.6	1 840.0	...	1 738.2	1 655.0	1 755.7	1 782.3	...	1 866.8	1 601.9	1 814.8	...	...	1 823.1
1979	1 828.6	1 832.3	2 131.6	1 859.5	...	1 721.1	1 647.3	1 753.3	1 770.4	...	1 854.7	1 580.1	1 766.3	...	...	1 820.4
1980	1 814.6	1 806.8	2 133.5	1 834.3	...	1 701.1	1 670.0	1 745.2	1 751.0	1 858.8	1 821.9	1 579.7	1 753.0	1 530.8	...	1 790.3
1981	1 798.3	1 807.0	2 123.7	1 843.4	...	1 678.0	1 642.5	1 726.1	1 729.4	1 865.1	1 777.0	1 570.3	1 726.5	1 522.4	...	1 754.0
1982	1 786.0	1 786.1	2 118.5	1 794.2	...	1 663.9	1 652.2	1 655.3	1 718.2	1 876.5	1 755.2	1 558.9	1 726.5	1 536.6	...	1 750.1
1983	1 794.6	1 783.5	2 114.9	1 783.9	...	1 670.0	1 647.9	1 637.7	1 705.3	1 875.8	1 744.8	1 553.2	1 695.6	1 546.0	1 981.0	1 744.2
1984	1 811.5	1 787.6	2 127.6	1 806.6	...	1 694.0	1 642.2	1 631.9	1 693.7	1 865.4	1 739.8	1 548.2	1 660.3	1 548.2	1 964.0	1 750.5
1985	1 816.3	1 801.5	2 110.2	1 799.4	...	1 700.1	1 627.4	1 599.1	1 670.6	1 861.9	1 721.5	1 542.2	1 642.6	1 552.3	1 970.0	1 752.9
1986	1 797.2	1 798.5	2 108.1	1 806.1	...	1 680.1	1 630.3	1 595.0	1 651.6	1 870.4	1 718.5	1 538.2	1 642.6	1 550.3	2 003.0	1 747.6
1987	1 800.0	1 809.4	2 113.5	1 822.0	...	1 665.0	1 595.2	1 607.9	1 629.4	1 889.5	1 551.7	1 510.6	1 595.3	1 560.5	1 984.0	1 752.4
1988	1 814.2	1 828.2	2 115.7	1 812.0	...	1 653.0	1 577.0	1 617.9	1 624.2	1 893.2	1 532.3	1 513.4	1 599.6	1 580.2	1 991.0	1 759.5
1989	1 827.6	1 822.6	2 089.4	1 810.1	...	1 644.1	1 559.4	1 604.5	1 600.7	1 877.3	1 537.1	1 510.5	1 608.2	1 579.1	1 998.0	1 763.4
1990	1 809.4	1 804.7	2 061.6	1 792.3	...	1 658.0	1 545.8	1 601.6	1 577.6	1 866.6	1 527.8	1 502.5	1 608.2	1 575.4	1 988.0	1 750.7
1991	1 800.6	1 781.0	2 015.2	1 795.3	...	1 621.0	1 540.6	1 592.8	1 548.1	1 859.6	1 508.3	1 500.3	1 599.6	1 562.0	1 954.0	1 725.4
1992	1 792.7	1 779.6	1 972.3	1 809.0	...	1 598.0	1 561.1	1 596.0	1 566.2	1 862.8	1 505.5	1 510.1	1 596.3	1 579.8	1 908.0	1 718.6
1993	1 810.3	1 805.9	1 917.7	1 796.1	...	1 554.1	1 561.8	1 583.4	1 549.9	1 862.6	1 502.8	1 506.9	1 587.4	1 596.9	1 883.0	1 715.2
1994	1 826.6	1 822.5	1 908.6	1 807.0	...	1 554.0	1 553.8	1 574.8	1 547.2	1 856.6	1 511.1	1 504.9	1 584.4	1 635.2	1 883.0	1 725.4
1995	1 845.8	1 812.4	1 910.8	1 805.2	1 699.1	1 580.0	1 546.0	1 552.2	1 533.6	1 858.9	1 512.4	1 487.7	1 592.0	1 640.3	1 875.0	1 727.6
1996	1 843.4	1 828.9	1 912.2	1 775.0	1 709.6	1 553.9	1 535.9	1 554.7	1 517.8	1 873.1	1 519.9	1 482.6	1 591.6	1 653.1	1 882.0	1 727.0
1997	1 856.8	1 811.9	1 883.1	1 801.3	1 718.0	1 567.1	1 548.7	1 546.8	1 508.7	1 863.2	1 509.2	1 477.5	1 602.2	1 658.0	1 832.0	1 725.3
1998	1 869.9	1 803.7	1 860.8	1 801.9	1 720.6	1 577.9	1 563.7	1 535.0	1 503.3	1 879.7	1 493.4	1 475.6	1 614.0	1 656.3	1 754.0	1 721.8
1999	1 878.3	1 807.9	1 843.0	1 797.0	1 711.9	1 580.9	1 573.3	1 525.6	1 491.7	1 875.6	1 488.5	1 473.7	1 629.4	1 664.8	1 725.0	1 713.3
2000	1 856.9	1 803.0	1 857.2	1 799.1	1 720.6	1 544.9	1 585.5	1 488.8	1 473.0	1 861.3	1 479.6	1 455.2	1 653.1	1 642.0	1 719.0	1 697.6
2001	1 833.1	1 793.5	1 838.5	1 749.3	1 719.1	1 577.0	1 587.7	1 480.0	1 458.4	1 843.1	1 461.3	1 429.1	1 649.0	1 618.2	1 713.0	1 700.0
2002	1 814.1	1 776.6	1 823.1	1 754.9	1 716.1	1 579.9	1 578.8	1 443.2	1 445.4	1 831.0	1 435.2	1 414.0	1 646.9	1 594.8	1 698.0	1 682.5
2003	1 786.9	1 762.1	1 823.4	1 763.0	1 728.1	1 575.0	1 576.5	1 440.3	1 438.9	1 825.6	1 428.8	1 398.6	1 631.9	1 581.6	1 671.0	1 673.2
2004	1 787.4	1 780.2	1 826.8	1 743.7	1 716.5	1 548.9	1 579.4	1 468.1	1 441.5	1 826.1	1 417.4	1 417.3	1 617.5	1 605.4	1 668.0	1 670.5
2005	1 784.1	1 770.0	1 813.6	1 754.0	1 698.9	1 565.1	1 578.8	1 462.6	1 434.1	1 818.7	1 417.3	1 420.2	1 597.5	1 605.0	1 654.0	1 673.4
2006	1 783.8	1 767.0	1 822.1	1 727.2	1 690.0	1 566.0	1 585.6	1 440.8	1 429.6	1 814.8	1 413.8	1 413.9	1 583.2	1 599.1	1 645.0	1 667.7
2007	1 776.6	1 759.5	1 816.1	1 699.1	1 677.8	1 560.1	1 569.6	1 448.1	1 429.6	1 816.4	1 411.9	1 419.0	1 563.9	1 611.5	1 634.0	1 670.0
2008	1 765.4	1 748.3	1 795.0	1 749.7	1 673.2	1 568.0	1 570.1	1 464.1	1 426.4	1 802.8	1 414.6	1 422.4	1 573.9	1 616.9	1 601.0	1 664.9
2009	1 732.3	1 717.2	1 744.5	1 711.4	1 634.4	1 550.0	1 559.1	1 444.0	1 390.2	1 772.4	1 395.5	1 403.0	1 579.2	1 601.7	1 549.0	1 643.3
2010	1 741.4	1 726.7	1 752.3	1 707.2	1 634.4	1 552.3	1 561.3	1 438.5	1 419.3	1 778.0	1 426.1	1 413.8	1 589.9	1 623.6	1 664.0	1 647.2

[1]Unified Germany from 1991 onward; data for previous years relate to the former West Germany.
. . . = Not available.

Table 10-11.   Percent Change in Average Annual Hours Worked Per Employed Person, 16 Countries, Selected Years, 1979–2010

(Percent.)

Country	1979–2010	1979–1990	1990–1995	1995–2000	2000–2010	2008–2009	2009–2010
United States	-0.2	-0.1	0.4	0.1	-0.6	-1.9	0.5
Canada	-0.2	-0.1	0.1	-0.1	-0.4	-1.8	0.5
Australia	-0.3	-0.3	0.1	-0.1	-0.5	-2.2	-0.2
Japan	-0.6	-0.3	-1.5	-0.6	-0.6	-2.8	0.4
Korea, Republic of	. . .	. . .	-0.5	-0.7	-1.1	-0.2	-1.7
Austria	. . .	. . .	. . .	0.3	-0.5	-2.3	0.0
Belgium	-0.3	-0.3	-1.0	-0.4	0.0	-1.1	0.1
Denmark	-0.2	-0.6	0.0	0.5	-0.2	-0.7	0.1
France	-0.6	-0.8	-0.6	-0.8	-0.3	-1.4	-0.4
Germany[1]	. . .	-1.0	. . .	-0.8	-0.4	-2.5	2.1
Italy	. . .	. . .	-0.1	0.0	-0.5	-1.7	0.3
Netherlands	-0.8	-1.7	-0.2	-0.4	-0.4	-1.3	2.2
Norway	-0.4	-0.5	-0.2	-0.4	-0.3	-1.4	0.8
Spain	-0.3	-0.8	-0.2	0.8	-0.4	0.3	0.7
Sweden	. . .	. . .	0.8	0.0	-0.1	-0.9	1.4
United Kingdom	-0.3	-0.4	-0.3	-0.3	-0.3	-1.3	0.2

[1]Data for Germany for years before 1991 pertain to the former West Germany.
. . . = Not available.

Table 10-12. Real Gross Domestic Product (GDP) Per Capita, 16 Countries, 1960–2010

(2010 U.S. dollars.)

Year	United States	Canada	Australia	Japan	Korea, Republic of	Austria	Belgium	Denmark	France	Germany[1]	Italy	Nether-lands	Norway	Spain	Sweden	United Kingdom
1960	17 368	14 436	14 893	5 938	1 510	11 339	11 441	14 084	11 062	13 003	10 320	13 850	14 960	. . .	13 807	13 610
1961	17 484	14 593	14 417	6 582	1 552	11 876	11 970	14 812	11 470	13 425	11 092	14 063	15 752	. . .	14 523	13 813
1962	18 260	15 326	14 968	7 081	1 540	12 086	12 544	15 511	12 040	13 887	11 701	14 464	16 046	. . .	15 058	13 835
1963	18 786	15 842	15 554	7 627	1 635	12 499	12 993	15 460	12 566	14 141	12 268	14 737	16 528	. . .	15 773	14 340
1964	19 601	16 552	16 254	8 391	1 747	13 165	13 766	16 712	13 234	14 931	12 508	15 792	17 226	10 834	16 723	15 024
1965	20 599	17 291	16 707	8 769	1 801	13 454	14 127	17 378	13 739	15 557	12 808	16 402	17 996	11 389	17 198	15 257
1966	21 691	18 099	16 899	9 586	1 970	14 114	14 476	17 639	14 331	15 848	13 469	16 642	18 525	12 084	17 391	15 467
1967	21 998	18 295	17 742	10 537	2 038	14 430	14 953	18 477	14 912	15 762	14 332	17 327	19 517	12 459	17 840	15 758
1968	22 834	18 894	18 396	11 659	2 217	14 997	15 520	19 383	15 459	16 562	15 174	18 300	19 785	13 148	18 381	16 344
1969	23 312	19 563	19 271	12 902	2 468	15 883	16 504	20 537	16 424	17 630	16 009	19 321	20 504	14 152	19 166	16 608
1970	23 089	19 876	20 125	14 097	2 626	16 955	17 537	20 598	17 284	18 339	16 770	20 257	20 771	14 575	20 222	16 929
1971	23 564	20 093	19 975	14 492	2 843	17 743	18 148	21 107	18 034	18 713	16 995	20 872	21 794	15 052	20 274	17 192
1972	24 553	20 943	20 081	15 495	2 972	18 735	19 031	21 862	18 686	19 400	17 523	21 390	22 766	16 083	20 677	17 766
1973	25 728	22 129	20 684	16 507	3 352	19 542	20 091	22 548	19 763	20 228	18 644	22 373	23 620	17 145	21 458	19 002
1974	25 352	22 628	20 682	16 086	3 604	20 278	20 848	22 260	20 556	20 382	19 542	22 963	24 370	17 947	22 079	18 748
1975	25 054	22 707	20 880	16 377	3 804	20 259	20 479	21 925	20 231	20 279	19 019	22 767	25 454	17 882	22 554	18 635
1976	26 143	23 574	21 436	16 845	4 247	21 223	21 582	23 202	21 034	21 386	20 273	23 586	26 803	18 258	22 712	19 130
1977	27 072	24 106	21 558	17 416	4 676	22 278	21 658	23 584	21 688	22 149	20 704	24 036	27 794	18 518	22 269	19 595
1978	28 282	24 822	21 791	18 169	5 080	22 263	22 229	24 046	22 435	22 842	21 299	24 537	28 756	18 543	22 593	20 233
1979	28 845	25 501	22 388	19 004	5 423	23 518	22 683	24 934	23 109	23 778	22 503	24 861	29 907	18 415	23 410	20 753
1980	28 434	25 719	22 785	19 385	5 238	23 938	23 636	24 810	23 367	24 032	23 227	24 992	31 153	18 555	23 762	20 298
1981	28 867	26 294	23 370	20 048	5 539	23 842	23 570	24 603	23 464	24 113	23 395	24 624	31 527	18 425	23 685	20 042
1982	28 037	25 240	22 983	20 580	5 906	24 289	23 716	25 533	23 888	24 035	23 474	24 208	31 451	18 555	23 953	20 507
1983	29 039	25 670	22 572	21 065	6 529	25 047	23 792	26 232	24 054	24 499	23 740	24 613	32 559	18 794	24 375	21 255
1984	30 854	26 907	23 665	21 863	7 084	25 063	24 379	27 340	24 295	25 292	24 500	25 270	34 381	19 052	25 392	21 791
1985	31 846	27 937	24 654	23 103	7 539	25 667	24 774	28 431	24 565	25 945	25 179	25 805	36 113	19 423	25 908	22 523
1986	32 652	28 331	24 868	23 631	8 378	26 245	25 217	29 800	24 993	26 520	25 897	26 381	37 437	19 994	26 585	23 373
1987	33 397	29 147	25 695	24 484	9 314	26 581	25 776	29 840	25 453	26 887	26 721	26 712	37 926	21 051	27 413	24 388
1988	34 455	30 202	26 424	26 121	10 298	27 305	26 908	29 784	26 489	27 715	27 829	27 452	37 657	22 075	28 017	25 565
1989	35 350	30 440	27 129	27 418	10 885	28 199	27 741	29 942	27 437	28 510	28 750	28 499	37 876	23 095	28 602	26 074
1990	35 612	30 040	27 150	28 848	11 781	29 153	28 526	30 374	28 004	29 444	29 315	29 491	38 474	23 933	28 668	26 204
1991	35 059	29 062	26 580	29 694	12 798	29 827	28 942	30 732	28 156	30 434	29 736	29 967	39 479	24 486	28 156	25 748
1992	35 770	28 969	26 952	29 824	13 396	30 057	29 266	31 190	28 433	30 876	29 954	30 250	40 635	24 632	27 653	25 720
1993	36 315	29 321	27 753	29 780	14 100	29 922	28 871	31 052	28 124	30 408	29 670	30 414	41 520	24 303	26 927	26 233
1994	37 339	30 394	28 740	29 957	15 183	30 467	29 710	32 666	28 651	31 122	30 302	31 129	43 369	24 814	27 836	27 286
1995	37 829	30 925	29 376	30 445	16 373	31 192	30 325	33 508	29 135	31 618	31 158	31 935	44 951	25 439	28 784	28 040
1996	38 788	31 097	30 181	31 175	17 383	31 845	30 692	34 247	29 345	31 841	31 491	32 883	47 004	25 994	29 167	28 780
1997	40 036	32 091	31 157	31 588	18 214	32 485	31 765	35 193	29 882	32 354	32 063	34 111	49 271	26 929	29 969	29 655
1998	41 296	33 129	32 383	30 865	17 050	33 616	32 307	35 829	30 780	33 020	32 503	35 233	50 293	28 033	31 198	30 640
1999	42 797	34 677	33 390	30 766	18 746	34 671	33 375	36 627	31 652	33 660	32 974	36 636	50 962	29 213	32 614	31 592
2000	44 081	36 153	34 101	31 586	20 225	35 851	34 521	37 791	32 596	34 698	34 176	37 810	52 279	30 432	34 038	32 716
2001	44 101	36 404	34 499	31 555	20 874	35 899	34 673	37 924	32 956	35 063	34 776	38 247	53 050	31 188	34 373	33 392
2002	44 465	37 048	35 453	31 582	22 242	36 311	34 990	37 971	33 024	35 003	34 824	38 030	53 558	31 571	35 111	33 974
2003	45 170	37 384	36 203	31 979	22 752	36 439	35 119	38 018	33 088	34 911	34 547	37 979	53 784	32 014	35 789	34 792
2004	46 313	38 173	37 118	32 825	23 714	37 132	36 097	38 794	33 684	35 340	34 733	38 702	55 533	32 527	37 144	35 645
2005	47 296	38 955	37 760	33 457	24 601	37 787	36 514	39 629	34 045	35 622	34 703	39 395	56 667	33 154	38 179	36 182
2006	48 095	39 647	38 220	34 141	25 790	38 945	37 250	40 837	34 645	36 866	35 208	40 659	57 495	33 962	39 597	36 976
2007	48 532	40 084	39 222	34 947	27 018	40 237	38 057	41 306	35 221	37 893	35 469	42 161	58 457	34 545	40 624	37 719
2008	47 923	39 893	39 459	34 556	27 553	40 938	38 138	40 605	34 995	38 334	34 733	42 754	58 153	34 292	40 047	37 441
2009	45 854	38 323	39 137	32 424	27 562	39 222	36 792	38 284	33 853	36 635	32 723	41 033	56 443	32 774	37 594	35 389
2010	46 844	39 104	39 497	33 612	29 184	39 928	37 411	38 778	34 168	38 021	32 997	41 512	55 938	32 625	39 407	35 621

[1]Unified Germany from 1991 onward; data for previous years relate to the former West Germany.
. . . = Not available.

Table 10-13. Real Gross Domestic Product (GDP) Per Employed Person, 16 Countries, 1960–2010

(2010 U.S. dollars.)

Year	United States	Canada	Australia	Japan	Korea, Republic of	Austria	Belgium	Denmark	France	Germany[1]	Italy	Nether-lands	Norway	Spain	Sweden	United Kingdom
1960	45 970	41 576	36 820	11 787	. . .	23 230	29 959	30 250	25 810	27 625	24 758	37 637	35 027	. . .	28 274	29 861
1961	47 023	42 240	36 485	13 002	. . .	24 331	31 217	31 568	27 043	28 507	26 620	38 171	36 672	. . .	29 640	30 208
1962	49 004	43 950	37 675	13 940	. . .	25 031	32 344	32 805	28 906	29 733	28 354	39 031	37 453	. . .	30 736	30 366
1963	50 443	45 233	38 798	15 037	5 894	26 232	33 516	32 556	30 443	30 497	30 450	39 777	38 713	. . .	32 213	31 591
1964	52 218	46 514	39 979	16 503	6 351	27 862	35 343	34 751	32 029	32 500	31 411	42 452	40 539	. . .	33 923	32 879
1965	54 240	47 727	40 601	17 163	6 372	28 852	36 461	35 764	33 458	34 047	33 249	44 325	42 304	. . .	34 977	33 274
1966	56 098	48 905	40 062	18 542	6 966	30 735	37 480	35 993	34 918	35 104	35 823	45 215	43 729	. . .	35 659	33 838
1967	56 184	48 803	41 775	20 207	7 121	32 184	39 104	38 022	36 513	36 175	37 923	47 758	46 190	. . .	37 256	35 079
1968	57 691	50 164	42 997	22 243	7 546	34 071	40 792	39 874	38 229	38 115	40 425	50 489	47 188	. . .	38 207	36 715
1969	58 056	51 082	44 869	24 714	8 383	36 276	42 770	41 652	40 304	40 331	43 201	53 040	48 884	. . .	39 379	37 461
1970	57 841	52 008	45 933	26 966	8 803	38 782	45 455	41 719	42 202	41 833	45 284	55 637	49 067	. . .	41 124	38 402
1971	59 552	52 848	46 610	27 953	9 400	40 322	46 794	43 035	44 217	42 948	46 093	57 695	51 394	35 668	41 593	39 233
1972	60 923	54 095	46 936	30 148	9 595	42 512	49 371	43 950	45 912	44 549	47 918	60 257	53 484	38 104	42 406	40 549
1973	62 396	55 060	47 699	31 850	10 447	43 975	51 828	45 039	48 249	46 121	50 616	63 510	55 484	40 048	43 924	42 794
1974	60 913	54 756	47 924	31 593	10 948	45 122	53 154	45 038	50 028	46 976	52 583	65 064	56 851	42 144	44 447	42 124
1975	61 473	54 744	49 085	32 649	11 480	45 293	53 131	45 082	49 841	47 768	51 444	65 568	58 729	43 229	44 700	42 024
1976	62 725	56 461	50 414	33 672	12 268	47 208	56 393	47 030	51 591	50 342	54 558	68 317	60 121	45 152	45 018	43 388
1977	63 342	57 422	50 446	34 733	13 289	48 976	56 890	48 081	52 957	51 909	55 783	69 368	60 920	46 735	44 210	44 380
1978	64 140	57 928	51 507	36 211	14 002	48 662	58 399	48 823	54 712	52 948	57 400	70 388	62 193	48 622	44 816	45 574
1979	64 344	57 628	52 581	37 808	14 965	51 098	59 105	50 271	56 234	54 100	60 152	70 815	64 009	49 768	45 869	46 324
1980	63 855	57 200	52 678	38 609	14 595	51 540	61 736	50 470	56 902	53 958	61 329	69 645	65 310	51 633	46 137	45 580
1981	64 752	57 529	53 758	39 918	15 295	51 669	62 719	50 856	57 539	54 178	61 897	67 725	65 481	52 831	45 969	46 234
1982	64 015	57 711	53 805	40 931	16 153	53 405	63 920	52 577	58 799	54 384	62 026	67 682	65 543	53 952	46 606	48 197
1983	66 044	58 856	54 535	41 555	17 964	55 350	64 972	53 966	59 563	55 747	62 549	69 958	68 217	55 099	47 341	50 346
1984	68 024	60 753	56 169	43 263	19 839	55 433	66 593	55 391	60 787	56 830	64 571	71 688	71 698	57 365	48 956	50 616
1985	69 439	61 875	57 525	45 755	20 550	56 629	67 376	56 289	61 911	57 349	65 755	72 203	73 499	59 305	49 517	51 795
1986	70 267	61 485	56 555	46 811	22 270	57 770	68 171	57 694	62 972	57 555	67 173	73 086	74 040	59 848	50 621	53 539
1987	70 709	62 301	58 068	48 541	23 704	58 582	69 231	57 603	63 931	57 559	69 160	66 799	73 855	60 280	51 956	54 888
1988	72 049	63 479	58 502	51 413	25 659	59 744	71 127	57 979	66 282	58 855	71 295	67 173	74 137	61 206	52 619	55 812
1989	73 151	63 709	58 565	53 387	26 314	61 237	72 473	58 570	67 894	60 022	73 211	68 740	77 070	61 918	53 304	55 637
1990	73 655	63 395	58 449	55 437	27 926	62 590	73 949	59 846	69 062	61 246	73 542	69 351	79 260	61 907	53 350	55 816
1991	74 172	63 172	59 327	56 138	29 711	63 879	75 051	60 982	69 693	63 029	73 298	69 235	82 539	62 730	53 555	56 530
1992	76 293	64 364	61 204	55 967	30 829	64 715	76 299	62 932	71 216	65 383	74 405	69 008	85 626	64 207	55 374	57 992
1993	77 429	65 558	63 327	55 851	32 397	65 260	76 058	63 872	71 579	65 729	75 779	69 960	87 393	65 400	57 228	59 836
1994	78 839	67 326	64 299	56 270	34 149	66 684	78 842	67 647	72 884	67 546	78 706	71 548	90 571	67 275	60 156	61 905
1995	79 708	68 006	64 017	57 146	36 167	68 503	79 494	68 655	73 692	68 667	81 093	71 688	92 441	67 840	61 535	63 019
1996	81 565	68 492	65 813	58 609	37 950	69 751	80 383	69 743	74 070	69 540	81 516	72 653	95 232	68 496	62 958	64 235
1997	83 376	69 926	67 985	59 114	39 455	70 719	82 837	70 778	75 190	70 861	82 783	73 431	97 508	69 129	65 568	65 194
1998	85 775	71 040	69 855	58 593	39 582	72 529	82 968	71 214	76 424	71 446	83 121	74 154	97 523	69 507	67 164	66 867
1999	88 587	73 102	71 685	59 327	43 067	73 835	84 735	72 343	77 169	71 909	83 433	75 591	98 588	70 259	68 821	68 239
2000	90 001	75 075	72 254	61 405	44 940	75 816	86 123	74 378	77 971	72 852	84 869	76 492	101 221	71 320	70 219	70 096
2001	90 919	75 482	73 293	61 988	45 824	75 665	85 633	74 083	78 214	73 433	84 702	76 047	102 874	71 642	69 636	71 235
2002	92 812	75 836	74 741	63 139	47 779	76 983	86 929	74 334	78 516	73 846	83 656	75 180	104 019	71 996	71 329	72 182
2003	94 234	75 484	75 539	64 241	49 184	77 654	87 590	75 511	79 120	74 390	82 407	75 865	106 169	71 963	73 401	73 519
2004	96 449	76 506	76 911	65 862	50 503	78 538	89 584	77 700	81 053	74 990	83 302	77 711	109 758	71 824	77 017	74 897
2005	97 720	77 731	76 639	66 882	51 814	79 300	89 857	78 745	81 968	75 642	83 368	79 251	111 404	71 531	79 271	75 753
2006	98 503	78 398	76 745	67 948	53 803	81 016	91 184	79 765	83 078	77 710	83 430	80 453	109 957	71 487	81 303	77 181
2007	99 293	78 241	77 767	69 296	55 870	82 548	92 370	78 838	83 788	78 472	83 612	81 607	108 541	71 816	82 139	78 702
2008	99 404	77 480	77 640	68 728	56 805	82 888	91 705	76 668	83 296	78 161	82 282	81 830	105 919	72 737	80 876	78 085
2009	99 624	76 545	78 061	65 364	57 158	80 393	89 505	74 858	81 974	74 482	79 299	78 904	104 581	74 976	78 141	75 509
2010	103 229	77 948	78 047	68 233	59 858	82 064	90 839	77 821	83 050	76 769	80 917	82 403	105 202	76 670	81 678	76 334

[1]Unified Germany from 1991 onward; data for previous years relate to the former West Germany.
. . . = Not available.

Table 10-14. Real Gross Domestic Product (GDP) Per Hour Worked, 16 Countries, 1970–2010

(2010 U.S. dollars.)

Year	United States	Canada	Australia	Japan	Korea, Republic of	Austria	Belgium	Denmark	France	Germany[1]	Italy	Nether-lands	Norway	Spain	Sweden	United Kingdom
1970	30.25	26.97	...	12.33	...	...	24.21	21.94	22.07	21.27	...	26.81	26.74	...	...	...
1971	31.41	27.66	...	12.93	...	...	25.06	23.01	23.13	22.20	...	28.18	28.34	...	...	21.38
1972	32.19	28.48	...	13.90	...	...	26.80	24.24	24.64	23.31	...	29.33	30.04	...	...	21.84
1973	33.00	29.05	...	14.79	...	...	28.57	25.46	26.08	24.50	...	31.14	31.42	...	...	22.94
1974	32.70	29.11	...	14.97	...	...	29.76	25.62	27.49	25.49	...	32.96	32.58	...	...	22.77
1975	33.59	29.36	...	15.69	...	...	29.90	26.70	27.77	26.45	...	33.98	33.99	...	...	23.10
1976	34.40	30.75	...	16.04	...	...	31.68	27.70	28.33	27.68	...	35.49	35.91	...	...	23.95
1977	34.76	31.39	...	16.42	...	...	32.43	28.72	29.67	28.82	...	36.50	37.18	25.44	...	24.36
1978	35.04	31.56	27.99	17.02	...	...	33.60	29.50	31.16	29.71	...	37.70	38.82	26.79	...	25.00
1979	35.19	31.45	28.28	17.74	...	...	34.34	30.52	32.07	30.56	...	38.18	40.51	28.18	...	25.45
1980	35.19	31.66	28.72	18.10	5.19	...	36.29	30.22	32.61	30.82	32.99	38.23	41.34	29.45	30.14	25.46
1981	36.01	31.84	29.16	18.80	5.47	...	37.38	30.96	33.34	31.33	33.19	38.11	41.70	30.60	30.20	26.36
1982	35.84	32.31	29.99	19.32	5.54	...	38.42	31.82	35.52	31.65	33.05	38.56	42.04	31.25	30.33	27.54
1983	36.80	33.00	30.57	19.65	6.22	...	38.91	32.75	36.37	32.69	33.35	40.09	43.92	32.50	30.62	28.86
1984	37.55	33.99	31.09	20.33	6.91	...	39.31	33.73	37.25	33.55	34.61	41.21	46.31	34.55	31.62	28.91
1985	38.23	34.35	31.97	21.68	7.15	...	39.63	34.59	38.72	34.33	35.32	41.94	47.66	36.10	31.90	29.55
1986	39.10	34.19	31.31	22.21	7.92	...	40.58	35.39	39.48	34.85	35.91	42.53	48.13	36.43	32.65	30.63
1987	39.28	34.43	31.87	22.97	8.21	...	41.58	36.11	39.76	35.33	36.60	43.05	48.89	37.79	33.29	31.32
1988	39.71	34.72	32.29	24.30	8.82	...	43.03	36.77	40.97	36.24	37.66	43.84	49.99	38.26	33.72	31.72
1989	40.03	34.96	32.35	25.55	9.26	...	44.08	37.56	42.31	37.50	39.00	44.72	51.02	38.50	33.76	31.55
1990	40.71	35.13	32.61	26.89	9.95	...	44.60	38.72	43.12	38.82	39.40	45.39	52.75	38.49	33.87	31.88
1991	41.19	35.47	33.05	27.86	10.67	...	46.30	39.58	43.76	40.71	39.42	45.90	55.01	39.22	34.29	32.76
1992	42.56	36.17	33.83	28.38	11.26	...	47.75	40.31	44.62	41.75	39.94	45.84	56.70	40.22	35.05	33.74
1993	42.77	36.30	35.26	29.12	11.79	...	48.94	40.90	45.21	42.41	40.68	46.55	58.00	41.20	35.84	34.89
1994	43.16	36.94	35.58	29.48	12.50	...	50.73	43.54	46.28	43.66	42.39	47.35	60.18	42.46	36.79	35.88
1995	43.18	37.52	35.46	29.91	13.21	40.30	50.31	44.41	47.48	44.78	43.63	47.40	62.14	42.61	37.51	36.48
1996	44.25	37.45	37.08	30.65	13.92	40.80	51.73	45.41	47.64	45.82	43.52	47.80	64.23	43.03	38.09	37.20
1997	44.90	38.59	37.74	31.39	14.72	41.20	52.86	45.70	48.61	46.97	44.43	48.65	65.99	43.15	39.55	37.79
1998	45.87	39.39	38.77	31.49	15.15	42.20	52.58	45.54	49.79	47.53	44.22	49.66	66.09	43.07	40.55	38.84
1999	47.16	40.43	39.89	32.19	16.39	43.10	53.60	45.98	50.58	48.21	44.48	50.78	66.90	43.12	41.34	39.83
2000	48.47	41.64	40.16	33.06	17.03	44.10	55.75	46.91	52.37	49.46	45.60	51.70	69.56	43.14	42.76	41.29
2001	49.60	42.09	41.90	33.72	17.44	44.00	54.30	46.66	52.85	50.35	45.96	52.04	71.98	43.45	43.03	41.90
2002	51.16	42.69	42.59	34.63	18.40	44.90	55.02	47.08	54.40	51.09	45.69	52.38	73.56	43.72	44.72	42.90
2003	52.74	42.84	42.85	35.23	19.21	44.90	55.61	47.90	54.93	51.70	45.14	53.10	75.91	44.10	46.41	43.94
2004	53.96	42.98	44.11	36.05	19.89	45.80	57.84	49.20	55.21	52.02	45.62	54.83	77.44	44.40	47.97	44.84
2005	54.77	43.91	43.69	36.88	20.66	46.70	57.41	49.88	56.04	52.75	45.84	55.92	78.44	44.78	49.39	45.27
2006	55.22	44.37	44.43	37.29	21.54	47.90	58.23	50.31	57.66	54.36	45.97	56.91	77.77	45.15	50.84	46.28
2007	55.89	44.47	45.77	38.16	22.75	49.20	59.21	50.23	57.86	54.89	46.03	57.80	76.49	45.92	50.97	47.13
2008	56.31	44.32	44.37	38.29	23.68	49.50	58.48	48.83	56.89	54.80	45.64	57.85	74.47	46.21	50.02	46.90
2009	57.51	44.58	45.61	37.47	23.88	49.20	57.74	48.01	56.77	53.58	44.74	56.54	74.54	47.48	48.79	45.95
2010	59.28	45.14	45.72	38.94	25.45	50.21	58.52	49.84	57.73	54.09	45.51	57.78	74.41	48.22	50.31	46.34

[1]Unified Germany from 1991 onward; data for previous years relate to the former West Germany.
... = Not available.

Table 10-15. Real Gross Domestic Product (GDP) Per Capita and Per Employed Person, Average Annual Percent Change, 16 Countries, Selected Years, 1979–2010

(Percent.)

Category and country	1979–2010	1979–1990	1990–1995	1995–2000	2000–2010	2008–2009	2009–2010
Real GDP Per Capita							
United States	1.6	1.9	1.2	3.1	0.6	-4.3	2.2
Canada	1.4	1.5	0.6	3.2	0.8	-3.9	2.0
Australia	1.8	1.8	1.6	3.0	1.5	-0.8	0.9
Japan	1.9	3.9	1.1	0.7	0.6	-6.2	3.7
Korea, Republic of	5.6	7.3	6.8	4.3	3.7	0.0	5.9
Austria	1.7	2.0	1.4	2.8	1.1	-4.2	1.8
Belgium	1.6	2.1	1.2	2.6	0.8	-3.5	1.7
Denmark	1.4	1.8	2.0	2.4	0.3	-5.7	1.3
France	1.3	1.8	0.8	2.3	0.5	-3.3	0.9
Germany[1]	. . .	2.0	. . .	1.9	0.9	-4.4	3.8
Italy	1.2	2.4	1.2	1.9	-0.4	-5.8	0.8
Netherlands	1.7	1.6	1.6	3.4	0.9	-4.0	1.2
Norway	2.0	2.3	3.2	3.1	0.7	-2.9	-0.9
Spain	1.9	2.4	1.2	3.6	0.7	-4.4	-0.5
Sweden	1.7	1.9	0.1	3.4	1.5	-6.1	4.8
United Kingdom	1.8	2.1	1.4	3.1	0.9	-5.5	0.7
Real GDP Per Employed Person							
United States	1.5	1.2	1.6	2.5	1.4	0.2	3.6
Canada	1.0	0.9	1.4	2.0	0.4	-1.2	1.8
Australia	1.3	1.0	1.8	2.5	0.8	0.5	0.0
Japan	1.9	3.5	0.6	1.4	1.1	-4.9	4.4
Korea, Republic of	4.6	5.8	5.3	4.4	2.9	0.6	4.7
Austria	1.5	1.9	1.8	2.0	0.8	-3.0	2.1
Belgium	1.4	2.1	1.5	1.6	0.5	-2.4	1.5
Denmark	1.4	1.6	2.8	1.6	0.5	-2.4	4.0
France	1.3	1.9	1.3	1.1	0.6	-1.6	1.3
Germany[1]	. . .	1.1	. . .	1.2	0.5	-4.7	3.1
Italy	1.0	1.8	2.0	0.9	-0.5	-3.6	2.0
Netherlands	0.5	-0.2	0.7	1.3	0.7	-3.6	4.4
Norway	1.6	2.0	3.1	1.8	0.4	-1.3	0.6
Spain	1.4	2.0	1.8	1.0	0.7	3.1	2.3
Sweden	1.9	1.4	2.9	2.7	1.5	-3.4	4.5
United Kingdom	1.6	1.7	2.5	2.2	0.9	-3.3	1.1

[1]Data for Germany for years before 1991 pertain to the former West Germany.
. . . = Not available.

Table 10-16. Real Gross Domestic Product (GDP) Per Hour Worked, Average Annual Percent Change, 16 Countries, Selected Years, 1979–2010

(Percent.)

Country	1979–2010	1979–1990	1990–1995	1995–2000	2000–2010	2008–2009	2009–2010
Real GDP Per Capita							
United States	1.7	1.3	1.2	2.3	2.0	2.1	3.1
Canada	1.2	1.0	1.3	2.1	0.8	0.6	1.3
Australia	1.6	1.3	1.7	2.5	1.3	2.8	0.2
Japan	2.6	3.9	2.1	2.0	1.6	-2.1	3.9
Korea, Republic of	. . .	. . .	5.8	5.2	4.1	0.8	6.6
Austria	. . .	. . .	. . .	1.8	1.3	-0.7	2.1
Belgium	1.7	2.4	2.4	2.1	0.5	-1.3	1.3
Denmark	1.6	2.2	2.8	1.1	0.6	-1.7	3.8
France	1.9	2.7	1.9	2.0	1.0	-0.2	1.7
Germany[1]	. . .	2.2	. . .	2.0	0.9	-2.2	1.0
Italy	. . .	. . .	2.1	0.9	0.0	-2.0	1.7
Netherlands	1.3	1.6	0.9	1.8	1.1	-2.3	2.2
Norway	2.0	2.4	3.3	2.3	0.7	0.1	-0.2
Spain	1.7	2.9	2.1	0.2	1.1	2.7	1.6
Sweden	. . .	. . .	2.1	2.7	1.6	-2.5	3.1
United Kingdom	2.0	2.1	2.7	2.5	1.2	-2.0	0.9

[1]Data for Germany for years before 1991 pertain to the former West Germany.
. . . = Not available.

Chapter Eleven

CONSUMER EXPENDITURES

CONSUMER EXPENDITURES

HIGHLIGHTS

The principal objective of the Consumer Expenditure (CE) Survey is to collect information about the buying habits of American households. The survey breaks down expenditures for different demographic categories, such as income, age, family size, and geographic location. These data are used in a variety of government, business, and academic research projects and provide important weights for the periodic revisions of the Consumer Price Index (CPI).

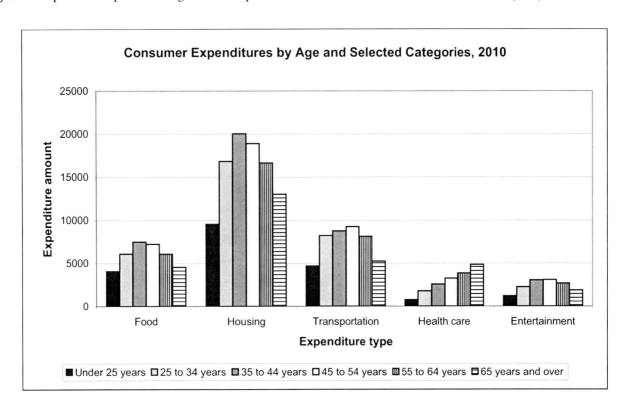

Consumer Expenditures by Age and Selected Categories, 2010

Consumer expenditures averaged $48,109 for all consumer units in 2010. As shown in the figure above, they varied significantly by age. Average health care expenditures increased for every age group shown, ranging from $775 for those under 25 years of age to $4,922 for those 65 to 74 years of age. Expenditures for food, housing, and transportation increased for the younger age groups but then began to gradually decline. (See Table 11-10.)

OTHER HIGHLIGHTS

- Average annual consumer expenditures also varied substantially by occupation. They ranged from $36,111 for retired persons to $67,312 for managers and professional workers in 2010. (See Table 11-6.)

- In 2010, average annual expenditures declined for the second consecutive year after increasing every year from 2000 through 2008. (See Table 11-1.)

- While expenditures declined for most categories between 2009 and 2010, they increased slightly for health care (1.0 percent), education (0.6 percent), and transportation (0.2 percent) (See Table 11-1.)

- As educational attainment increased, so did average annual expenditures. Those with less than a high school diploma had average annual expenditures of $29,753 while those with a master's, professional, or doctoral degree had average annual expenditures of $75,752. (See Table 11-13.)

NOTES AND DEFINITIONS

Purpose, Collection, and Coverage

The buying habits of American consumers change over time because of changes in relative prices, real income, family size and composition, and other determinants of tastes and preferences. The introduction of new products into the marketplace and the emergence of new concepts in retailing also influence consumer buying habits. Data from the Consumer Expenditure Survey (CE), the only national survey that relates family expenditures to demographic characteristics, are of great importance to researchers. The survey data are also used to revise the Consumer Price Index market baskets and item samples.

Until the 1970s, the Bureau of Labor Statistics (BLS) conducted surveys of consumer expenditures approximately once every 10 years. The last such survey was conducted in 1972–1973. In late 1979, in a significant departure from previous methodology, BLS initiated a survey to be conducted on a continuous basis with rotating panels of respondents.

The current CE is similar to its 1972–1973 predecessor in that it consists of two separate components. Each component has its own questionnaire and sample: (1) the Interview Survey, in which an interviewer visits each consumer unit every three months for a twelve-month period; and (2) the Diary Survey, a record-keeping survey completed by other consumer units for two consecutive one-week periods. The Census Bureau, under contract to BLS, collects the data for both components of the survey. Beginning in 1999, the sample was increased from 5,000 to 7,500 households.

In 2003, the survey modified the questions on race and Hispanic origin to comply with the new standards for maintaining, collecting, and presenting federal data on race and ethnicity for federal statistical agencies. Beginning with the data collected in 2003, the CE tables use data collected from the new race and ethnicity questions. A number of new classifications were made with publication of the 2003 data.

Beginning with the publication of the 2004 tables, the CE has been implementing multiple imputations of income data. Prior to 2004, the CE only published income data collected from complete income reporters. The introduction of multiply imputed income data affects the published CE tables in several ways, because income data are now published for all consumer units (instead of for complete reporters only). The most obvious result of this change is seen on the tables showing expenditures categorized by income before taxes, including income by quintile. Starting with the 2004 data, columns describing income, expenditures, and characteristics for "total complete reporting" and "incomplete reporting of income" no longer appear in these tables, and the column entitled "all consumer units" appears

on all income tables. Due to the implementation of income imputation, data for 2004 are not strictly comparable to those of prior years, especially for the income tables. Averages for demographic characteristics and annual expenditures will change due to differences between the incomplete and complete income reporters in these categories. Furthermore, certain expenditures (such as personal insurance and pensions) are computed using income data. As a result of imputation, average annual values for these expenditures may be substantially different in the 2004 CE tables than in tables for previous years. The regular flow of data resulting from this design substantially enhances the usefulness of the survey by providing more timely information on consumption patterns within different kinds of consumer units.

The *Interview Survey* is designed to collect data on the types of expenditures that respondents can be expected to recall after a period of three months or longer. These include relatively large expenditures (such as those for property, travel, automobiles, and major appliances) and expenditures that occur on a regular basis (such as those for rent, utilities, insurance premiums, and clothing). The interview also obtains "global estimates" for food and other selected items. The survey collects data for approximately 95 percent of total expenditures. Each sample household is interviewed once per quarter, for five consecutive quarters.

The *Diary Survey* is designed to collect data on expenditures for frequently purchased items that are more difficult to recall over longer periods of time. Respondents complete a diary of expenses for two consecutive 1-week periods. Expenditures for tobacco, drugs (including nonprescription drugs), and personal care supplies and services are also collected in the Diary Survey.

Participants in both surveys record dollar amounts for goods and services purchased during the reporting period, regardless of whether payment was made at the time of purchase. Excluded from both surveys are business-related expenditures and expenditures for which the family is reimbursed. Information is collected on demographic and family characteristics at the initial interview for each survey.

The tables in this chapter present integrated data from the Diary Survey and the Interview Survey and provide a complete accounting of consumer expenditures and income, which neither survey component is designed to do alone. Data for some expenditure items are only collected in one of the surveys. For example, the Diary Survey does not collect data for expenditures on overnight travel or information on reimbursements, while the Interview Survey records these purchases. Examples of expenditures for which reimbursements are netted out include those for medical care, auto repair, and construction, repairs, alterations, and maintenance of property.

For items unique to one survey or the other, the choice of which survey to use as the source of data is obvious. However, there is considerable overlap in coverage between the two surveys. Integrating the data thus presents the problem of determining the appropriate survey component. When data are available from both survey sources, the more reliable of the two (as determined by statistical methods) is selected. As a result, some items are selected from the Interview Survey and others are selected from the Diary Survey.

Data Included in This Book

Data for single characteristics are for calendar year 2010, and data for two cross-classified characteristics are for an average of calendar years 2009 and 2010. Income values from the survey are derived from "complete income reporters" only. Complete income reporters are defined as consumer units that provide values for at least one of the major sources of their income: wages and salaries, self-employment income, retirement income, dividends and interest, and welfare benefits. Some consumer units are defined as complete income reporters, even though they may not have provided a full accounting of all income from all sources.

Consumer units are classified by quintiles of income before taxes, age of reference person, size of consumer unit, region, composition of consumer unit, number of earners in consumer unit, housing tenure, race, type of area (urban or rural), and occupation.

Concepts and Definitions

A *consumer unit* comprises either (1) all members of a particular household related by blood, marriage, adoption, or other legal arrangements; (2) a person living alone, sharing a household with others, living as a roomer in a private home or lodging house or in permanent living quarters in a hotel or motel, but who is financially independent; or (3) two or more persons living together who pool their income to make joint expenditure decisions. Financial independence is determined by the three major expense categories: housing, food, and other living expenses. To be considered financially independent, at least two of the three major expense categories have to be provided by the respondent.

The terms "family," "household," and "consumer unit" are used interchangeably in descriptions of the CE.

An *earner* is a consumer unit member, 14 years of age or older, who reported having worked at least 1 week during the 12 months prior to the interview date.

The *education of reference person* refers to the number of years of formal education of the reference person, on the basis of the highest grade completed. If enrolled at time of the interview, the interviewer records the grade currently attended. Persons not reporting the extent of their education are classified under no school or not reported.

Housing tenure refers to the family's principal place of residence during the survey. "Owner" includes families living in their own homes, cooperatives or condominium apartments, or townhouses. "Renter" includes families paying rent, as well as families living rent-free in lieu of wages.

The *householder* or *reference person* is the first member of the consumer unit mentioned by the respondent as owner or renter of the premises at the time of the initial interview.

Quintiles of income before taxes refers to the ranking of complete income reporters in ascending order, according to the level of total before-tax income reported by the consumer unit. The ranking is then divided into five equal groups. Incomplete income reporters are not ranked and are shown separately.

Total expenditures include the transaction costs, including excise and sales taxes of goods and services acquired during the interview period. Estimates include expenditures for gifts and contributions and payments for pensions and personal insurance.

Sources of Additional Information

More extensive descriptions and tables can be found in an updated version of Chapter 16 in the *BLS Handbook of Methods* and in an anthology of articles relating to consumer expenditures. These resources can be found on the BLS Web site at <http://www.bls.gov>.

Table 11-1. Consumer Expenditures, Annual Average of All Consumer Units, 2000–2010

(Number, dollar, percent.)

Item	2000	2001	2002	2003	2004	2005	2006	2007	2008	2009	2010
NUMBER OF CONSUMER UNITS (THOUSANDS)	109 367	110 339	112 108	115 356	116 282	117 356	118 843	120 171	120 770	120 847	121 107
CONSUMER UNIT CHARACTERISTICS											
Income Before Taxes	44 649	47 507	49 430	51 128	54 453	58 712	60 533	63 091	63 563	62 857	62 481
Age of Reference Person	48.2	48.1	48.1	48.0	48.5	48.6	48.7	48.8	49.1	49.4	49.4
Average Number in Consumer Unit											
All persons	2.5	2.5	2.5	2.5	2.5	2.5	2.5	2.5	2.5	2.5	2.5
Children under 18 years	0.7	0.7	0.7	0.6	0.6	0.6	0.6	0.6	0.6	0.6	0.6
Persons 65 years and over	0.3	0.3	0.3	0.3	0.3	0.3	0.3	0.3	0.3	0.3	0.3
Earners	1.4	1.4	1.4	1.3	1.3	1.3	1.3	1.3	1.3	1.3	1.3
Vehicles	1.9	1.9	2.0	1.9	1.9	2.0	1.9	1.9	2.0	2.0	1.9
Percent Homeowner	66	66	66	67	68	67	67	67	66	66	66
With mortgage	39	40	41	41	42	43	43	43	42	41	41
Without mortgage	27	26	26	26	25	25	24	23	24	25	25
AVERAGE ANNUAL EXPENDITURES	38 045	39 518	40 677	40 817	43 395	46 409	48 398	49 638	50 486	49 067	48 109
Food	5 158	5 321	5 375	5 340	5 781	5 931	6 111	6 133	6 443	6 372	6 129
Food at home	3 021	3 086	3 099	3 129	3 347	3 297	3 417	3 465	3 744	3 753	3 624
Cereals and bakery products	453	452	450	442	461	445	446	460	507	506	502
Meats, poultry, fish, and eggs	453	452	798	825	880	764	797	777	846	841	784
Dairy products	325	332	328	328	371	378	368	387	430	406	380
Fruits and vegetables	521	522	552	535	561	552	592	600	657	656	679
Other food at home	927	952	970	999	1 075	1 158	1 212	1 241	1 305	1 343	1 278
Food away from home	2 137	2 235	2 276	2 211	2 434	2 634	2 694	2 668	2 698	2 619	2 505
Alcoholic Beverages	372	349	376	391	459	426	497	457	444	435	412
Housing	12 319	13 011	13 283	13 432	13 918	15 167	16 366	16 920	17 109	16 895	16 557
Shelter	7 114	7 602	7 829	7 887	7 998	8 805	9 673	10 023	10 183	10 075	9 812
Owned dwellings	4 602	4 979	5 165	5 263	5 324	5 958	6 516	6 730	6 760	6 543	6 277
Rented dwellings	2 034	2 134	2 160	2 179	2 201	2 345	2 590	2 602	2 724	2 860	2 900
Other lodging	478	489	505	445	473	502	567	691	698	672	635
Utilities, fuels, and public services	2 489	2 767	2 684	2 811	2 927	3 183	3 397	3 477	3 649	3 645	3 660
Household operations	684	676	706	707	753	801	948	984	998	1 011	1 007
Housekeeping supplies	482	509	545	529	594	611	640	639	654	659	612
Household furnishings and equipment	1 549	1 458	1 518	1 497	1 646	1 767	1 708	1 797	1 624	1 506	1 467
Apparel and Services	1 856	1 743	1 749	1 640	1 816	1 886	1 874	1 881	1 801	1 725	1 700
Transportation	7 417	7 633	7 759	7 781	7 801	8 344	8 508	8 758	8 604	7 658	7 677
Vehicle purchases (net outlay)	3 418	3 579	3 665	3 732	3 397	3 544	3 421	3 244	2 755	2 657	2 588
Gasoline and motor oil	1 291	1 279	1 235	1 333	1 598	2 013	2 227	2 384	2 715	1 986	2 132
Other vehicle expenses	2 281	2 375	2 471	2 331	2 365	2 339	2 355	2 592	2 621	2 536	2 464
Public transportation	427	400	389	385	441	448	505	538	513	479	493
Health Care	2 066	2 182	2 350	2 416	2 574	2 664	2 766	2 853	2 976	3 126	3 157
Health insurance	983	1 061	1 168	1 252	1 332	1 361	1 465	1 545	1 653	1 785	1 831
Medical services	568	573	590	591	648	677	670	709	727	736	722
Drugs	416	449	487	467	480	521	514	481	482	486	485
Medical supplies	99	100	105	107	114	105	117	118	114	119	119
Entertainment	1 863	1 953	2 079	2 060	2 218	2 388	2 376	2 698	2 835	2 693	2 504
Personal Care Products and Services	564	465	526	527	581	541	585	588	616	596	582
Reading	146	141	139	127	130	126	117	118	116	110	100
Education	632	648	752	783	905	940	888	945	1 046	1 068	1 074
Tobacco Products and Smoking Supplies	319	308	320	290	288	319	327	323	317	380	362
Miscellaneous	776	750	792	606	690	808	846	808	840	816	849
Cash Contributions	1 192	1 258	1 277	1 370	1 408	1 663	1 869	1 821	1 737	1 723	1 633
Personal Insurance and Pensions	3 365	3 737	3 899	4 055	4 823	5 204	5 270	5 336	5 605	5 471	5 373
Life and other personal insurance	399	410	406	397	390	381	322	309	317	309	318
Pensions and Social Security	2 966	3 326	3 493	3 658	4 433	4 823	4 948	5 027	5 288	5 162	5 054

Table 11-2. Shares of Annual Average Consumer Expenditures and Characteristics of All Consumer Units, 2000–2010

(Number, dollar, percent.)

Item	2000	2001	2002	2003	2004	2005	2006	2007	2008	2009	2010
NUMBER OF CONSUMER UNITS (THOUSANDS)	109 367	110 339	112 108	115 356	116 282	117 356	118 843	120 171	120 770	120 847	121 107
CONSUMER UNIT CHARACTERISTICS											
Income Before Taxes	44 649	47 507	49 430	51 128	54 453	58 712	60 533	63 091	63 563	62 857	62 481
Age of Reference Person	48.2	48.1	48.1	48.4	48.5	48.6	48.7	48.8	49.1	49.4	49.4
Average Number in Consumer Unit											
All persons	2.5	2.5	2.5	2.5	2.5	2.5	2.5	2.5	2.5	2.5	2.5
Children under 18 years	0.7	0.7	0.7	0.6	0.6	0.6	0.6	0.6	0.6	0.6	0.6
Persons 65 years and over	0.3	0.3	0.3	0.3	0.3	0.3	0.3	0.3	0.3	0.3	0.3
Earners	1.4	1.4	1.4	1.3	1.3	1.3	1.3	1.3	1.3	1.3	1.3
Vehicles	1.9	1.9	2.0	1.9	1.9	2.0	1.9	1.9	2.0	2.0	1.9
Percent Homeowner	66	66	66	67	68	67	67	67	66	66	66
With mortgage	39	40	41	41	42	43	43	43	42	41	41
Without mortgage	27	26	26	26	25	25	24	23	24	25	25
AVERAGE ANNUAL EXPENDITURES	38 045	39 518	40 677	40 817	43 395	46 409	48 398	49 638	50 486	49 067	48 109
Food	13.6	13.5	13.2	13.1	13.3	12.8	12.6	12.4	12.8	13.0	12.7
Food at home	7.9	7.8	7.6	7.7	7.7	7.1	7.1	7.0	7.4	7.6	7.5
Cereals and bakery products	1.2	1.1	1.1	1.1	1.1	1.0	0.9	0.9	1.0	1.0	1.0
Meats, poultry, fish, and eggs	2.1	2.1	2.0	2.0	2.0	1.6	1.6	1.6	1.7	1.7	1.6
Dairy products	0.9	0.8	0.8	0.8	0.9	0.8	0.8	0.8	0.9	0.8	0.8
Fruits and vegetables	1.4	1.3	1.4	1.3	1.3	1.2	1.2	1.2	1.3	1.3	1.4
Other food at home	2.4	2.4	2.4	2.4	2.5	2.5	2.5	2.5	2.6	2.7	2.7
Food away from home	5.6	5.7	5.6	5.4	5.6	5.7	5.6	5.4	5.3	5.3	5.2
Alcoholic Beverages	1.0	0.9	0.9	1.0	1.1	0.9	1.0	0.9	0.9	0.9	0.9
Housing	32.4	32.9	32.7	32.9	32.1	32.7	33.8	34.1	33.9	34.4	34.4
Shelter	18.7	19.2	19.2	19.3	18.4	19.0	20.0	20.2	20.2	20.5	20.4
Owned dwellings	12.1	12.6	12.7	12.9	12.3	12.8	13.5	13.6	13.4	13.3	13.0
Rented dwellings	5.3	5.4	5.3	5.3	5.1	5.1	5.4	5.2	5.4	5.8	6.0
Other lodging	1.3	1.2	1.2	1.1	1.1	1.1	1.2	1.4	1.4	1.4	1.3
Utilities, fuels, and public services	6.5	7.0	6.6	6.9	6.7	6.9	7.0	7.0	7.2	7.4	7.6
Household operations	1.8	1.7	1.7	1.7	1.7	1.7	2.0	2.0	2.0	2.1	2.1
Housekeeping supplies	1.3	1.3	1.3	1.3	1.4	1.3	1.3	1.3	1.3	1.3	1.3
Household furnishings and equipment	4.1	3.7	3.7	3.7	3.8	3.8	3.5	3.6	3.2	3.1	3.0
Apparel and Services	4.9	4.4	4.3	4.0	4.2	4.1	3.9	3.8	3.6	3.5	3.5
Transportation	19.5	19.3	19.1	19.1	18.0	18.0	17.6	17.6	17.0	15.6	16.0
Vehicle purchases (net outlay)	9.0	9.1	9.0	9.1	7.8	7.6	7.1	6.5	5.5	5.4	5.4
Gasoline and motor oil	3.4	3.2	3.0	3.3	3.7	4.3	4.6	4.8	5.4	4.0	4.4
Other vehicle expenses	6.0	6.0	6.1	5.7	5.5	5.0	4.9	5.2	5.2	5.2	5.1
Public transportation	1.1	1.0	1.0	0.9	1.0	1.0	1.0	1.1	1.0	1.0	1.0
Health Care	5.4	5.5	5.8	5.9	5.9	5.7	5.7	5.7	5.9	6.4	6.6
Health insurance	2.6	2.7	2.9	3.1	3.1	2.9	3.0	3.1	3.3	3.6	3.8
Medical services	1.5	1.4	1.5	1.4	1.5	1.5	1.4	1.4	1.4	1.5	1.5
Drugs	1.1	1.1	1.2	1.1	1.1	1.1	1.1	1.0	1.0	1.0	1.0
Medical supplies	0.3	0.3	0.3	0.3	0.3	0.2	0.2	0.2	0.2	0.2	0.2
Entertainment	4.9	4.9	5.1	5.0	5.1	5.1	4.9	5.4	5.6	5.5	5.2
Personal Care Products and Services	1.5	1.2	1.3	1.3	1.3	1.2	1.2	1.2	1.2	1.2	1.2
Reading	0.4	0.4	0.3	0.3	0.3	0.3	0.2	0.2	0.2	0.2	0.2
Education	1.7	1.6	1.8	1.9	2.1	2.0	1.8	1.9	2.1	2.2	2.2
Tobacco Products and Smoking Supplies	0.8	0.8	0.8	0.7	0.7	0.7	0.7	0.7	0.6	0.8	0.8
Miscellaneous	2.0	1.9	1.9	1.5	1.6	1.7	1.7	1.6	1.7	1.7	1.8
Cash Contributions	3.1	3.2	3.1	3.4	3.2	3.6	3.9	3.7	3.4	3.5	3.4
Personal Insurance and Pensions	8.8	9.5	9.6	9.9	11.1	11.2	10.9	10.8	11.1	11.2	11.2
Life and other personal insurance	1.0	1.0	1.0	1.0	0.9	0.8	0.7	0.6	0.6	0.6	0.7
Pensions and Social Security	7.8	8.4	8.6	9.0	10.2	10.4	10.2	10.1	10.5	10.5	10.5

Table 11-3. Consumer Expenditures, Averages by Income Before Taxes, 2010

(Number, dollar, percent.)

Item	All consumer units	Less than $5,000	$5,000 to $9,999	$10,000 to $14,999	$15,000 to $19,999	$20,000 to $29,999	$30,000 to $39,999	$40,000 to $49,999	$50,000 to $69,999	$70,000 and over
NUMBER OF CONSUMER UNITS (THOUSANDS)	121 107	4 858	5 280	8 114	8 177	14 729	13 022	11 446	17 368	38 113
CONSUMER UNIT CHARACTERISTICS										
Income Before Taxes	62 481	-1 104	8 082	12 606	17 483	25 001	34 762	44 734	59 253	129 151
Income After Taxes	60 712	-1 269	8 283	12 808	17 715	25 282	34 712	44 496	58 291	123 847
Age of Reference Person	49.4	43.1	47.9	55.1	54.5	52.6	50.3	49.0	48.1	47.4
Average Number in Consumer Unit										
All persons	2.5	1.6	1.7	1.6	2.0	2.2	2.4	2.6	2.8	3.1
Children under 18 years	0.6	0.4	0.4	0.3	0.5	0.5	0.6	0.6	0.7	0.8
Persons 65 years and over	0.3	0.2	0.3	0.4	0.5	0.5	0.4	0.3	0.3	0.2
Earners	1.3	0.5	0.5	0.4	0.6	0.8	1.1	1.3	1.5	1.9
Vehicles	1.9	0.8	0.8	0.9	1.2	1.5	1.7	2.0	2.2	2.7
Percent Distribution										
Male	47	43	40	35	35	42	43	49	50	54
Female	53	57	60	65	65	58	57	51	50	46
Percent Homeowner	66	28	32	43	51	53	62	66	72	86
With mortgage	41	9	9	12	17	21	32	41	50	67
Without mortgage	25	19	23	32	34	32	30	26	23	19
AVERAGE ANNUAL EXPENDITURES	48 109	20 748	18 297	19 909	24 935	29 158	35 556	40 616	47 966	80 708
Food	6 129	3 316	3 073	3 133	3 691	4 008	4 883	5 515	6 304	9 452
Food at home	3 624	2 058	2 169	2 244	2 531	2 797	3 036	3 393	3 690	5 122
Cereals and bakery products	502	289	302	307	354	402	424	446	507	712
Meats, poultry, fish, and eggs	784	433	523	504	589	611	657	769	814	1 069
Dairy products	380	225	225	221	253	296	306	348	388	550
Fruits and vegetables	679	381	382	412	456	531	585	589	663	992
Other food at home	1 278	730	737	800	879	957	1 064	1 241	1 319	1 801
Food away from home	2 505	1 258	904	889	1 160	1 211	1 847	2 122	2 614	4 330
Alcoholic Beverages	412	237	132	128	159	174	304	330	455	728
Housing	16 557	8 629	7 634	8 347	10 047	11 049	12 804	14 351	16 720	25 968
Shelter	9 812	5 554	4 535	4 914	5 746	6 356	7 414	8 449	9 891	15 528
Owned dwellings	6 277	1 998	1 062	1 679	2 267	2 664	3 957	4 836	6 396	11 952
Rented dwellings	2 900	3 322	3 262	3 122	3 349	3 444	3 188	3 321	2 968	2 185
Other lodging	635	234	211	114	130	248	269	293	527	1 391
Utilities, fuels, and public services	3 660	1 832	1 921	2 225	2 777	3 035	3 321	3 530	3 926	4 903
Household operations	1 007	372	284	378	457	487	614	713	928	1 900
Housekeeping supplies	612	296	333	343	365	427	438	546	593	965
Household furnishings and equipment	1 467	576	561	487	702	744	1 016	1 112	1 382	2 671
Apparel and Services	1 700	644	972	606	907	1 139	1 253	1 381	1 554	2 885
Transportation	7 677	2 535	2 314	2 606	3 827	4 882	6 229	7 099	7 782	12 682
Vehicle purchases (net outlay)	2 588	580	451	526	880	1 585	2 141	2 289	2 389	4 668
Gasoline and motor oil	2 132	870	905	979	1 252	1 553	1 879	2 152	2 455	3 055
Other vehicle expenses	2 464	936	812	972	1 511	1 523	1 937	2 371	2 532	3 949
Public transportation	493	148	147	129	184	221	272	287	406	1 010
Health Care	3 157	1 330	955	1 673	2 045	2 659	2 928	2 938	3 405	4 472
Health insurance	1 831	674	631	973	1 209	1 583	1 759	1 791	2 075	2 480
Medical services	722	424	124	231	333	558	589	556	736	1 184
Drugs	485	190	162	413	430	430	468	494	493	615
Medical supplies	119	42	38	55	73	88	112	96	101	193
Entertainment	2 504	1 033	854	981	1 193	1 382	1 703	1 917	2 468	4 438
Personal Care Products and Services	582	237	271	248	336	391	415	484	565	964
Reading	100	59	30	42	53	66	78	78	94	167
Education	1 074	950	873	474	382	395	449	478	642	2 247
Tobacco Products and Smoking Supplies	362	320	334	314	344	375	402	432	412	323
Miscellaneous	849	435	221	428	380	428	570	860	1 062	1 329
Cash Contributions	1 633	674	352	512	792	850	1 202	1 419	1 607	2 878
Personal Insurance and Pensions	5 373	349	281	417	780	1 361	2 336	3 335	4 896	12 175
Life and other personal insurance	318	90	53	83	133	125	200	203	292	635
Pensions and Social Security	5 054	259	227	333	647	1 236	2 137	3 132	4 604	11 540

Table 11-4. Consumer Expenditures, Averages by Higher Income Before Taxes, 2010

(Number, dollar, percent.)

Item	All consumer units	Less than $70,000	$70,000 to $79,000	$80,000 to $99,999	$100,000 and over	$100,000 to $119,000	$120,000 to $149,999	$150,000 and over
NUMBER OF CONSUMER UNITS (THOUSANDS)	121 107	82 994	7 250	10 098	20 766	6 749	5 865	8 151
CONSUMER UNIT CHARACTERISTICS								
Income Before Taxes	62 481	31 865	74 602	89 140	167 651	108 503	132 750	241 739
Income After Taxes	60 712	31 718	72 800	86 772	159 697	104 459	127 524	228 585
Age of Reference Person	49.4	50.4	47.1	46.4	47.9	47.0	47.9	48.8
Average Number in Consumer Unit								
All persons	2.5	2.3	2.9	3.0	3.2	3.1	3.2	3.2
Children under 18 years	0.6	0.6	0.7	0.8	0.8	0.8	0.8	0.9
Persons 65 years and over	0.3	0.4	0.2	0.2	0.2	0.2	0.2	0.2
Earners	1.3	1.0	1.7	1.9	2.0	2.0	2.0	2.1
Vehicles	1.9	1.6	2.5	2.6	2.8	2.7	2.8	2.9
Percent Distribution								
Male	47	43	52	53	54	54	51	57
Female	53	57	48	47	46	46	49	43
Percent Homeowner	66	56	79	84	90	88	89	91
With mortgage	41	29	56	64	72	69	73	75
Without mortgage	25	28	22	19	17	19	17	17
AVERAGE ANNUAL EXPENDITURES	48 109	33 269	57 024	62 966	97 737	74 797	89 614	. . .
Food	6 129	4 661	6 979	7 819	11 161	9 372	10 463	13 317
Food at home	3 624	2 967	3 867	4 540	5 868	5 170	5 650	6 688
Cereals and bakery products	502	410	570	638	800	714	759	911
Meats, poultry, fish, and eggs	784	660	824	921	1 232	1 086	1 203	1 391
Dairy products	380	306	413	482	632	559	584	739
Fruits and vegetables	679	543	707	839	1 171	1 031	1 088	1 366
Other food at home	1 278	1 048	1 353	1 660	2 032	1 779	2 016	2 282
Food away from home	2 505	1 695	3 112	3 279	5 293	4 202	4 814	6 628
Alcoholic Beverages	412	273	444	530	929	645	799	1 288
Housing	16 557	12 254	18 589	20 962	30 999	23 326	27 723	39 787
Shelter	9 812	7 187	10 604	12 475	18 732	13 794	16 320	24 557
Owned dwellings	6 277	3 671	7 391	9 375	14 798	10 909	13 085	19 253
Rented dwellings	2 900	3 228	2 691	2 303	1 951	1 873	1 789	2 132
Other lodging	635	288	522	797	1 983	1 013	1 447	3 171
Utilities, fuels, and public services	3 660	3 089	4 164	4 543	5 336	4 777	5 125	5 952
Household operations	1 007	597	1 146	1 369	2 421	1 546	2 153	3 338
Housekeeping supplies	612	457	816	780	1 113	850	1 153	1 334
Household furnishings and equipment	1 467	924	1 860	1 795	3 396	2 358	2 973	4 607
Apparel and Services	1 700	1 174	1 836	1 913	3 750	2 439	4 334	4 514
Transportation	7 677	5 390	10 706	10 392	14 493	12 557	14 967	15 808
Vehicle purchases (net outlay)	2 588	1 634	4 222	3 717	5 285	4 799	5 806	5 313
Gasoline and motor oil	2 132	1 708	2 686	2 899	3 260	3 248	3 231	3 291
Other vehicle expenses	2 464	1 793	3 309	3 228	4 532	3 508	4 896	5 169
Public transportation	493	255	489	549	1 416	1 003	1 034	2 035
Health Care	3 157	2 555	3 785	4 003	4 942	4 550	4 491	5 594
Health insurance	1 831	1 532	2 183	2 300	2 671	2 400	2 471	3 041
Medical services	722	510	880	1 002	1 378	1 289	1 194	1 583
Drugs	485	427	560	549	669	679	620	697
Medical supplies	119	85	162	153	224	183	206	272
Entertainment	2 504	1 628	2 978	3 118	5 600	4 327	5 093	7 032
Personal Care Products and Services	582	410	622	780	1 176	956	1 139	1 395
Reading	100	69	107	121	210	153	179	280
Education	1 074	537	740	1 036	3 363	1 450	2 638	5 473
Tobacco Products and Smoking Supplies	362	380	406	395	259	294	251	236
Miscellaneous	849	629	1 069	1 090	1 539	922	1 122	2 376
Cash Contributions	1 633	1 061	1 905	2 220	3 538	2 404	2 629	5 132
Personal Insurance and Pensions	5 373	2 249	6 859	8 586	15 777	11 402	13 786	20 832
Life and other personal insurance	318	172	376	424	829	535	612	1 228
Pensions and Social Security	5 054	2 076	6 483	8 163	14 948	10 867	13 174	19 603

Table 11-5. Consumer Expenditures, Averages by Quintiles of Income Before Taxes, 2010

(Number, dollar, percent.)

Item	All consumer units	Lowest 20 percent	Second 20 percent	Third 20 percent	Fourth 20 percent	Highest 20 percent
NUMBER OF CONSUMER UNITS (THOUSANDS)	121 107	24 210	24 277	24 175	24 215	24 231
CONSUMER UNIT CHARACTERISTICS						
Income Before Taxes	62 481	9 906	26 777	45 552	72 794	157 369
Income After Taxes	60 712	10 034	26 966	45 189	71 220	150 144
Age of Reference Person	49.4	51.0	51.7	49.3	47.3	47.8
Average Number in Consumer Unit						
All persons	2.5	1.7	2.3	2.6	2.9	3.2
Children under 18 years	0.6	0.4	0.6	0.6	0.7	0.8
Persons 65 years and over	0.3	0.4	0.5	0.4	0.2	0.2
Earners	1.3	0.5	0.9	1.3	1.7	2.0
Vehicles	1.9	0.9	1.5	2.0	2.4	2.8
Percent Distribution						
Male	47	37	41	49	52	54
Female	53	63	59	51	48	46
Percent Homeowner	66	40	54	67	78	89
With mortgage	41	12	23	41	57	71
Without mortgage	25	28	31	27	21	18
AVERAGE ANNUAL EXPENDITURES	48 109	20 953	30 285	41 212	55 212	92 870
Food	6 129	3 309	4 214	5 596	6 843	10 676
Food at home	3 624	2 270	2 816	3 433	3 917	5 683
Cereals and bakery products	502	315	400	465	552	775
Meats, poultry, fish, and eggs	784	519	608	762	854	1 179
Dairy products	380	230	291	355	414	611
Fruits and vegetables	679	410	539	615	711	1 122
Other food at home	1 278	796	977	1 236	1 385	1 996
Food away from home	2 505	1 039	1 398	2 164	2 926	4 993
Alcoholic Beverages	412	153	211	359	466	869
Housing	16 557	8 667	11 369	14 508	18 625	29 615
Shelter	9 812	5 167	6 586	8 496	10 912	17 897
Owned dwellings	6 277	1 739	2 929	4 960	7 663	14 096
Rented dwellings	2 900	3 262	3 421	3 184	2 657	1 974
Other lodging	635	167	236	353	592	1 827
Utilities, fuels, and public services	3 660	2 216	3 053	3 603	4 185	5 242
Household operations	1 007	373	513	733	1 147	2 270
Housekeeping supplies	612	343	423	525	713	1 054
Household furnishings and equipment	1 467	568	794	1 151	1 668	3 152
Apparel and Services	1 700	774	1 154	1 372	1 737	3 461
Transportation	7 677	2 868	5 002	7 160	9 432	13 924
Vehicle purchases (net outlay)	2 588	627	1 583	2 320	3 373	5 040
Gasoline and motor oil	2 132	1 009	1 598	2 180	2 634	3 240
Other vehicle expenses	2 464	1 082	1 585	2 347	2 967	4 337
Public transportation	493	150	235	313	457	1 307
Health Care	3 157	1 524	2 649	3 068	3 715	4 827
Health insurance	1 831	886	1 578	1 863	2 201	2 624
Medical services	722	264	537	631	845	1 335
Drugs	485	321	437	476	538	653
Medical supplies	119	54	96	98	132	215
Entertainment	2 504	1 018	1 450	1 984	2 792	5 277
Personal Care Products and Services	582	277	386	488	642	1 117
Reading	100	45	66	84	107	197
Education	1 074	635	408	510	813	3 005
Tobacco Products and Smoking Supplies	362	323	375	421	420	272
Miscellaneous	849	356	461	797	1 169	1 461
Cash Contributions	1 633	559	981	1 392	1 927	3 307
Personal Insurance and Pensions	5 373	446	1 560	3 473	6 523	14 861
Life and other personal insurance	318	89	148	215	364	775
Pensions and Social Security	5 054	357	1 412	3 258	6 159	14 086

Table 11-6. Consumer Expenditures, Averages by Occupation of Reference Person, 2010

(Number, dollar, percent.)

Item	Self-employed workers	Wage and salary earners						Retired	All others, including those not reporting
		Total wage and salary earners	Managers and professional workers	Technical sales and clerical workers	Service workers	Construction workers and mechanics	Operators, fabricators, and laborers		
NUMBER OF CONSUMER UNITS (THOUSANDS)	5 339	76 067	30 200	20 308	13 520	3 843	8 197	21 457	18 244
CONSUMER UNIT CHARACTERISTICS									
Income Before Taxes	78 480	74 147	102 752	61 926	50 097	56 039	47 197	35 779	40 563
Income After Taxes	75 689	71 703	98 472	60 351	49 211	54 654	46 296	35 477	40 181
Age of Reference Person	48.7	43.6	44.6	42.2	43.2	42.4	44.3	73.8	45.4
Average Number in Consumer Unit									
All persons	2.9	2.6	2.6	2.6	2.7	2.7	2.8	1.7	2.9
Children under 18 years	0.8	0.7	0.7	0.7	0.7	0.7	0.8	0.1	0.9
Persons 65 years and over	0.2	0.1	0.1	0.1	0.1	0.1	0.1	1.2	0.2
Earners	1.8	1.7	1.7	1.7	1.7	1.7	1.7	0.2	0.6
Vehicles	2.2	2.0	2.2	2.0	1.8	2.2	2.0	1.7	1.6
Percent Distribution									
Male	61	51	48	42	46	89	72	44	30
Female	39	49	52	58	54	11	28	56	70
Percent Homeowner	71	64	75	60	51	58	58	82	51
With mortgage	47	48	60	44	36	43	41	20	31
Without mortgage	24	16	16	15	16	15	18	62	20
AVERAGE ANNUAL EXPENDITURES	59 005	53 218	67 312	47 921	41 517	45 062	37 676	36 111	37 998
Food	6 912	6 658	7 862	6 175	5 732	6 206	5 210	4 608	5 618
Food at home	4 078	3 718	4 173	3 439	3 438	3 822	3 167	3 043	3 797
Cereals and bakery products	532	514	578	472	466	550	451	425	531
Meats, poultry, fish, and eggs	898	789	842	719	803	856	711	672	862
Dairy products	440	390	442	359	361	394	322	321	395
Fruits and vegetables	806	695	794	625	676	668	557	595	680
Other food at home	1 402	1 330	1 517	1 264	1 132	1 355	1 126	1 029	1 328
Food away from home	2 834	2 940	3 689	2 736	2 293	2 384	2 043	1 565	1 821
Alcoholic Beverages	557	488	625	476	338	474	275	279	235
Housing	19 092	18 044	22 613	16 294	14 647	14 943	12 631	12 898	13 933
Shelter	11 615	10 932	13 897	9 717	8 733	8 970	7 572	6 859	8 085
Owned dwellings	7 953	7 081	9 873	5 889	4 700	5 393	4 464	4 703	4 286
Rented dwellings	2 984	3 166	2 861	3 342	3 739	3 258	2 868	1 503	3 406
Other lodging	678	685	1 162	485	294	320	240	652	393
Utilities, fuels, and public services ..	4 105	3 775	4 203	3 606	3 398	3 518	3 359	3 390	3 367
Household operations	1 189	1 138	1 680	973	683	750	488	777	677
Housekeeping supplies	714	613	727	597	553	475	407	621	566
Household furnishings and equipment ...	1 470	1 585	2 106	1 402	1 279	1 229	804	1 251	1 238
Apparel and Services	2 192	1 821	2 249	1 569	1 711	1 365	1 292	978	1 901
Transportation	8 812	8 745	10 283	8 486	7 042	7 736	7 007	5 513	5 489
Vehicle purchases (net outlay)	2 612	3 014	3 559	3 123	2 221	2 148	2 445	1 785	1 753
Gasoline and motor oil	2 372	2 402	2 570	2 316	2 158	2 649	2 288	1 404	1 793
Other vehicle expenses	3 245	2 764	3 324	2 606	2 247	2 601	2 026	1 948	1 641
Public transportation	583	565	830	441	417	338	248	376	302
Health Care	3 529	2 882	3 678	2 549	2 290	2 251	2 045	4 676	2 408
Health insurance	1 940	1 628	2 063	1 441	1 313	1 247	1 187	2 979	1 293
Medical services	977	741	973	635	557	629	505	756	528
Drugs	437	400	489	381	342	298	268	786	499
Medical supplies	175	112	154	93	77	76	84	155	88
Entertainment	3 526	2 727	3 534	2 548	1 802	2 722	1 733	1 936	1 972
Personal Care Products and Services ..	625	631	833	575	492	485	335	517	449
Reading	131	98	144	84	55	52	53	133	58
Education	1 027	1 333	1 933	983	1 031	1 090	602	218	1 020
Tobacco Products and Smoking Supplies	365	361	244	405	385	649	507	226	526
Miscellaneous	1 307	882	1 197	706	641	764	618	880	541
Cash Contributions	1 872	1 640	2 248	1 357	1 029	1 564	1 144	2 119	963
Personal Insurance and Pensions	9 059	6 907	9 869	5 713	4 321	4 761	4 225	1 131	2 884
Life and other personal insurance	496	340	501	287	212	171	174	290	206
Pensions and Social Security	8 562	6 567	9 368	5 426	4 109	4 590	4 051	841	2 678

Table 11-7. Consumer Expenditures, Averages by Number of Earners, 2010

(Number, dollar, percent.)

Item	All consumer units	Single consumer		Consumer units of two or more persons			
		No earner	One earner	No earner	One earner	Two earners	Three or more earners
NUMBER OF CONSUMER UNITS (THOUSANDS)	121 107	14 378	21 101	12 095	26 231	37 747	9 555
CONSUMER UNIT CHARACTERISTICS							
Income Before Taxes	62 481	17 654	43 422	32 544	57 207	92 421	106 121
Income After Taxes	60 712	17 570	41 600	32 652	56 184	89 086	103 694
Age of Reference Person	49.4	67.0	43.0	63.2	47.5	44.0	46.6
Average Number in Consumer Unit							
All persons	2.5	1.0	1.0	2.4	3.1	3.1	4.5
Children under 18 years	0.6	X	X	0.4	1.1	0.8	1.1
Persons 65 years and over	0.3	0.6	0.1	1.2	0.3	0.1	0.1
Earners	1.3	X	1.0	X	1.0	2.0	3.3
Vehicles	1.9	0.9	1.2	1.7	1.9	2.4	3.1
Percent Distribution							
Male	47	37	53	46	42	50	50
Female	53	63	47	54	58	50	50
Percent Homeowner	66	59	45	72	65	75	79
With mortgage	41	13	31	19	41	58	63
Without mortgage	25	46	14	53	24	17	16
AVERAGE ANNUAL EXPENDITURES	48 109	21 859	34 099	37 785	49 122	63 071	70 354
Food	6 129	2 745	3 922	5 282	6 502	7 784	9 927
Food at home	3 624	1 849	1 896	3 654	4 114	4 370	5 881
Cereals and bakery products	502	271	248	498	584	598	819
Meats, poultry, fish, and eggs	784	388	378	856	902	912	1 379
Dairy products	380	196	191	372	434	465	618
Fruits and vegetables	679	366	364	671	748	829	1 107
Other food at home	1 278	629	715	1 257	1 447	1 566	1 957
Food away from home	2 505	896	2 026	1 628	2 387	3 414	4 046
Alcoholic Beverages	412	143	442	303	331	569	541
Housing	16 557	9 334	12 509	12 916	17 498	20 891	21 321
Shelter	9 812	5 674	8 318	6 568	10 198	12 357	12 330
Owned dwellings	6 277	2 887	3 879	3 943	6 390	8 925	8 862
Rented dwellings	2 900	2 577	3 968	1 966	3 144	2 611	2 677
Other lodging	635	210	470	659	665	821	791
Utilities, fuels, and public services	3 660	2 317	2 340	3 564	3 983	4 321	5 217
Household operations	1 007	485	541	770	1 093	1 494	962
Housekeeping supplies	612	316	371	689	680	735	820
Household furnishings and equipment	1 467	542	940	1 324	1 543	1 985	1 992
Apparel and Services	1 700	440	1 048	1 777	1 872	2 181	2 594
Transportation	7 677	2 516	5 027	5 840	7 923	10 363	12 442
Vehicle purchases (net outlay)	2 588	584	1 344	1 894	2 865	3 678	4 170
Gasoline and motor oil	2 132	730	1 460	1 549	2 240	2 818	3 462
Other vehicle expenses	2 464	1 029	1 811	1 993	2 354	3 218	4 087
Public transportation	493	174	412	404	464	649	723
Health Care	3 157	2 630	1 617	4 736	3 305	3 520	3 514
Health insurance	1 831	1 589	894	3 003	1 938	1 957	1 983
Medical services	722	473	408	731	732	960	810
Drugs	485	476	247	852	521	463	553
Medical supplies	119	92	67	150	114	140	168
Entertainment	2 504	1 065	1 696	2 104	2 556	3 376	3 416
Personal Care Products and Services	582	299	401	522	608	730	839
Reading	100	77	83	118	91	115	111
Education	1 074	350	770	330	915	1 495	2 555
Tobacco Products and Smoking Supplies	362	242	285	341	425	380	494
Miscellaneous	849	708	783	802	798	959	977
Cash Contributions	1 633	1 117	1 327	2 194	1 549	1 772	2 059
Personal Insurance and Pensions	5 373	193	4 190	521	4 748	8 934	9 564
Life and other personal insurance	318	141	145	291	321	437	525
Pensions and Social Security	5 054	352	4 045	¹3 229	4 427	8 497	9 040

¹Data are likely to have large sampling errors.
X = Not applicable.

Table 11-8. Consumer Expenditures, Averages by Size of Consumer Unit, 2010

(Number, dollar, percent.)

Item	All consumer units	One person	Two or more persons	Two persons	Three persons	Four persons	Five or more persons
NUMBER OF CONSUMER UNITS (THOUSANDS)	121 107	35 479	85 629	38 658	17 906	16 479	12 585
CONSUMER UNIT CHARACTERISTICS							
Income Before Taxes	62 481	32 979	74 705	67 707	74 377	87 864	79 437
Income After Taxes	60 712	31 862	72 666	65 455	72 377	85 719	78 132
Age of Reference Person	49.4	52.7	48.1	54.1	45.2	42.2	41.4
Average Number in Consumer Unit							
All persons	2.5	1.0	3.1	2.0	3.0	4.0	5.7
Children under 18 years	0.6	X	0.9	0.1	0.7	1.5	2.7
Persons 65 years and over	0.3	0.3	0.3	0.5	0.2	0.1	0.1
Earners	1.3	0.6	1.6	1.2	1.7	1.9	2.1
Vehicles	1.9	1.1	2.3	2.1	2.3	2.4	2.4
Percent Distribution							
Male	47	46	47	49	44	46	44
Female	53	54	53	51	56	54	56
Percent Homeowner	66	50	72	75	68	72	67
With mortgage	41	23	48	40	48	60	54
Without mortgage	25	27	24	35	20	12	13
AVERAGE ANNUAL EXPENDITURES	48 109	29 149	55 929	50 967	56 413	63 268	61 086
Food	6 129	3 450	7 220	5 958	7 297	8 778	9 083
Food at home	3 624	1 877	4 335	3 480	4 431	5 219	5 746
Cereals and bakery products	502	257	601	464	602	756	833
Meats, poultry, fish, and eggs	784	382	948	762	985	1 105	1 276
Dairy products	380	193	457	366	450	561	618
Fruits and vegetables	679	365	807	659	810	968	1 063
Other food at home	1 278	681	1 521	1 229	1 585	1 830	1 955
Food away from home	2 505	1 573	2 885	2 478	2 866	3 559	3 338
Alcoholic Beverages	412	322	449	545	388	441	248
Housing	16 557	11 223	18 763	16 876	18 794	21 684	20 702
Shelter	9 812	7 246	10 875	9 859	10 709	12 541	12 050
Owned dwellings	6 277	3 477	7 437	6 765	7 004	8 895	8 212
Rented dwellings	2 900	3 404	2 690	2 232	2 998	2 929	3 349
Other lodging	635	365	747	863	707	717	489
Utilities, fuels, and public services	3 660	2 331	4 211	3 764	4 229	4 671	4 955
Household operations	1 007	518	1 210	881	1 398	1 742	1 254
Housekeeping supplies	612	349	719	687	660	829	762
Household furnishings and equipment	1 467	779	1 749	1 686	1 799	1 901	1 681
Apparel and Services	1 700	804	2 066	1 704	2 089	2 515	2 588
Transportation	7 677	4 011	9 194	8 439	9 523	9 897	10 133
Vehicle purchases (net outlay)	2 588	1 036	3 232	2 965	3 508	3 262	3 616
Gasoline and motor oil	2 132	1 164	2 533	2 190	2 504	2 926	3 115
Other vehicle expenses	2 464	1 495	2 863	2 694	2 986	3 067	2 944
Public transportation	493	316	566	589	525	641	457
Health Care	3 157	2 027	3 625	4 108	3 346	3 286	2 977
Health insurance	1 831	1 176	2 102	2 421	1 902	1 925	1 636
Medical services	722	435	841	885	802	793	825
Drugs	485	340	545	660	511	424	397
Medical supplies	119	77	136	141	132	143	119
Entertainment	2 504	1 441	2 943	2 707	2 810	3 396	3 276
Personal Care Products and Services	582	360	673	612	727	769	669
Reading	100	81	108	128	100	98	68
Education	1 074	600	1 271	827	1 536	1 833	1 524
Tobacco Products and Smoking Supplies	362	268	401	368	437	393	462
Miscellaneous	849	752	889	866	920	960	821
Cash Contributions	1 633	1 242	1 795	2 046	1 687	1 487	1 584
Personal Insurance and Pensions	5 373	2 570	6 534	5 784	6 758	7 732	6 950
Life and other personal insurance	318	143	391	380	413	402	376
Pensions and Social Security	5 054	2 427	6 143	5 404	6 345	7 330	6 574

X = Not applicable.

Table 11-9. Consumer Expenditures, Averages by Composition of Consumer Unit, 2010

(Number, dollar, percent.)

Item	Husband and wife consumer units							One parent, at least one child under 18 years	Single person and other consumer units
	Total	Husband and wife only	Husband and wife with children				Other husband and wife consumer units		
			Total	Oldest child under 6 years	Oldest child 6 to 17 years	Oldest child 18 years or over			
NUMBER OF CONSUMER UNITS (THOUSANDS)	59 739	25 723	28 172	5 185	14 242	8 745	5 844	7 141	54 227
CONSUMER UNIT CHARACTERISTICS									
Income Before Taxes	85 296	76 543	93 627	87 439	94 807	95 374	83 666	34 652	41 012
Income After Taxes	82 670	73 835	91 024	85 151	92 147	92 678	81 288	35 214	39 880
Age of Reference Person	50.0	58.0	42.8	32.2	40.9	52.0	49.4	37.5	50.4
Average Number in Consumer Unit									
All persons	3.2	2.0	4.0	3.5	4.2	4.0	5.0	2.9	1.7
Children under 18 years	0.9	X	1.6	1.5	2.2	0.7	1.4	1.8	0.2
Persons 65 years and over	0.4	0.7	0.1	(^{1})	(^{1})	0.2	0.6	(^{1})	0.3
Earners	1.6	1.2	1.9	1.6	1.7	2.4	2.1	0.9	0.9
Vehicles	2.5	2.4	2.6	2.0	2.5	3.1	2.7	1.2	1.3
Percent Distribution									
Male	53	55	53	50	53	54	47	16	43
Female	47	45	47	50	47	46	53	84	57
Percent Homeowner	81	85	78	66	78	86	76	40	52
With mortgage	54	44	64	59	67	62	54	31	27
Without mortgage	27	42	14	7	11	24	22	9	25
AVERAGE ANNUAL EXPENDITURES	61 762	56 035	67 383	61 756	69 536	67 057	60 146	36 933	34 471
Food	7 816	6 494	8 876	7 056	9 386	9 054	8 759	5 227	4 352
Food at home	4 670	3 813	5 314	4 311	5 476	5 587	5 514	3 287	2 493
Cereals and bakery products	648	505	759	564	811	781	776	451	343
Meats, poultry, fish, and eggs	1 005	833	1 119	799	1 144	1 247	1 255	725	545
Dairy products	500	401	579	486	604	590	569	318	254
Fruits and vegetables	881	734	978	839	993	1 027	1 098	565	468
Other food at home	1 636	1 340	1 879	1 623	1 925	1 941	1 816	1 230	. . .
Food away from home	3 147	2 681	3 562	2 745	3 910	3 467	3 245	1 939	1 859
Alcoholic Beverages	472	561	424	440	421	420	283	167	376
Housing	20 303	18 028	22 492	24 219	23 095	20 460	19 748	14 224	12 726
Shelter	11 721	10 368	13 067	14 177	13 608	11 526	11 191	8 263	7 912
Owned dwellings	8 756	7 859	9 788	10 029	10 206	8 963	7 733	3 638	3 894
Rented dwellings	2 037	1 425	2 402	3 478	2 491	1 618	2 969	4 422	3 649
Other lodging	928	1 084	877	670	912	944	489	202	369
Utilities, fuels, and public services	4 437	3 988	4 709	3 799	4 778	5 136	5 099	3 342	2 846
Household operations	1 358	934	1 799	3 737	1 643	903	1 096	1 184	598
Housekeeping supplies	797	774	830	656	883	839	739	443	424
Household furnishings and equipment	1 991	1 964	2 088	1 851	2 182	2 057	1 624	991	946
Apparel and Services	2 075	1 650	2 438	2 169	2 672	2 214	2 249	2 012	1 241
Transportation	10 123	9 226	10 984	9 357	11 184	11 569	9 936	6 428	5 142
Vehicle purchases (net outlay)	3 574	3 229	3 970	3 761	4 237	3 658	3 184	2 275	1 544
Gasoline and motor oil	2 752	2 347	3 057	2 451	3 079	3 381	3 064	1 716	1 504
Other vehicle expenses	3 148	2 966	3 301	2 639	3 139	3 905	3 225	2 160	1 745
Public transportation	649	685	655	506	729	624	462	278	348
Health Care	4 280	5 028	3 742	3 124	3 631	4 289	3 577	1 513	2 135
Health insurance	2 478	2 976	2 085	1 777	1 999	2 408	2 181	783	1 255
Medical services	1 007	1 086	1 004	937	1 020	1 017	669	456	444
Drugs	636	800	494	303	447	682	601	216	353
Medical supplies	159	166	160	108	164	182	126	58	83
Entertainment	3 321	2 998	3 627	2 869	4 175	3 186	3 269	1 709	1 704
Personal Care Products and Services	729	665	794	636	819	840	708	525	426
Reading	126	153	112	78	117	123	73	42	79
Education	1 468	803	2 099	652	2 030	3 068	1 359	372	733
Tobacco Products and Smoking Supplies	356	312	334	245	307	429	651	303	377
Miscellaneous	985	968	996	1 132	931	1 025	1 017	610	730
Cash Contributions	2 097	2 535	1 763	1 214	1 843	1 958	1 780	894	1 220
Personal Insurance and Pensions	7 611	6 614	8 703	8 564	8 925	8 422	6 739	2 908	3 231
Life and other personal insurance	495	494	529	468	521	577	332	130	148
Pensions and Social Security	7 116	6 119	8 174	8 096	8 404	7 844	6 406	2 778	3 083

^{1}Value less than or equal to 0.05.
X = Not applicable.

Table 11-10. Consumer Expenditures, Averages by Age of Reference Person, 2010

(Number, dollar, percent.)

Item	All consumer units	Under 25 years	25 to 34 years	35 to 44 years	45 to 54 years	55 to 64 years	65 years and over	65 to 74 years	75 years and over
NUMBER OF CONSUMER UNITS (THOUSANDS)	121 107	8 034	20 166	21 912	25 054	21 359	24 582	13 031	11 551
CONSUMER UNIT CHARACTERISTICS									
Income Before Taxes	62 481	26 881	59 613	76 128	79 589	68 906	41 286	49 711	31 782
Income After Taxes	60 712	26 777	58 558	74 136	76 266	66 611	40 626	48 595	31 638
Age of Reference Person	49.4	21.5	29.7	39.6	49.5	59.2	74.9	69.1	81.4
Average Number in Consumer Unit									
All persons	2.5	2.0	2.9	3.3	2.8	2.2	1.7	1.9	1.6
Children under 18 years	0.6	0.5	1.1	1.3	0.6	0.2	0.1	0.1	(1)
Persons 65 years and over	0.3	(1)	(1)	(1)	0.1	0.1	1.4	1.4	1.3
Earners	1.3	1.2	1.5	1.6	1.6	1.3	0.5	0.7	0.2
Vehicles	1.9	1.1	1.7	2.0	2.3	2.2	1.6	1.9	1.3
Percent Distribution									
Male	47	45	46	47	48	48	44	47	41
Female	53	55	54	53	52	52	56	53	59
Percent Homeowner	66	14	45	65	73	80	81	82	80
With mortgage	41	9	39	56	55	45	21	29	13
Without mortgage	25	5	6	9	18	35	59	53	67
AVERAGE ANNUAL EXPENDITURES	48 109	27 483	46 617	55 946	57 788	50 900	36 802	41 434	31 529
Food	6 129	4 073	6 091	7 483	7 230	6 068	4 558	5 148	3 873
Food at home	3 624	2 197	3 338	4 255	4 369	3 681	2 950	3 213	2 643
Cereals and bakery products	502	312	441	607	600	507	416	442	385
Meats, poultry, fish, and eggs	784	447	713	896	966	792	660	688	627
Dairy products	380	218	353	458	453	378	316	351	274
Fruits and vegetables	679	395	614	787	819	692	577	620	525
Other food at home	1 278	826	1 217	1 508	1 532	1 312	982	1 111	831
Food away from home	2 505	1 876	2 753	3 227	2 861	2 387	1 608	1 935	1 230
Alcoholic Beverages	412	406	473	497	414	402	295	392	184
Housing	16 557	9 553	16 845	20 041	18 900	16 673	13 015	14 420	11 421
Shelter	9 812	6 166	10 451	12 139	11 517	9 397	7 027	7 850	6 098
Owned dwellings	6 277	1 123	5 126	8 149	8 163	6 777	4 881	5 809	3 834
Rented dwellings	2 900	4 813	4 989	3 475	2 493	1 689	1 514	1 275	1 783
Other lodging	635	231	336	515	861	931	632	766	481
Utilities, fuels, and public services	3 660	1 818	3 228	4 077	4 213	3 979	3 402	3 644	3 130
Household operations	1 007	416	1 244	1 414	935	882	827	868	779
Housekeeping supplies	612	279	465	663	650	717	664	761	552
Household furnishings and equipment	1 467	874	1 458	1 748	1 585	1 698	1 095	1 297	862
Apparel and Services	1 700	1 559	2 087	2 040	1 966	1 571	964	1 186	708
Transportation	7 677	4 692	8 231	8 763	9 255	8 111	5 242	6 086	4 288
Vehicle purchases (net outlay)	2 588	1 591	3 415	2 905	3 041	2 584	1 495	1 638	1 335
Gasoline and motor oil	2 132	1 493	2 208	2 537	2 575	2 215	1 396	1 766	980
Other vehicle expenses	2 464	1 333	2 174	2 776	3 023	2 763	1 959	2 199	1 686
Public transportation	493	275	434	545	616	548	391	483	288
Health Care	3 157	775	1 800	2 583	3 261	3 859	4 843	4 922	4 754
Health insurance	1 831	405	1 086	1 453	1 747	2 110	3 085	3 133	3 031
Medical services	722	236	443	681	879	943	795	849	735
Drugs	485	102	200	340	497	665	805	797	814
Medical supplies	119	32	71	109	137	142	158	144	173
Entertainment	2 504	1 221	2 251	3 058	3 088	2 683	1 891	2 341	1 374
Personal Care Products and Services	582	347	517	682	673	599	517	571	455
Reading	100	39	61	80	104	126	141	147	135
Education	1 074	1 906	839	963	2 094	917	193	240	140
Tobacco Products and Smoking Supplies	362	283	362	358	449	450	227	298	147
Miscellaneous	849	277	668	922	938	1 146	772	761	787
Cash Contributions	1 633	314	1 074	1 532	1 747	1 893	2 272	2 276	2 267
Personal Insurance and Pensions	5 373	2 036	5 318	6 944	7 668	6 403	1 872	2 648	996
Life and other personal insurance	318	22	167	280	441	471	314	386	233
Pensions and Social Security	5 054	2 013	5 151	6 664	7 227	5 932	1 557	2 261	763

1Value less than or equal to 0.05.

Table 11-11. Consumer Expenditures, Averages by Race of Reference Person, 2010

(Number, dollar, percent.)

| Item | All consumer units | White, Asian, and other races | | | Black |
		Total	White and other races	Asian	
NUMBER OF CONSUMER UNITS (THOUSANDS)	121 107	106 287	101 137	5 151	14 820
CONSUMER UNIT CHARACTERISTICS					
Income Before Taxes	62 481	64 817	63 773	85 316	45 727
Income After Taxes	60 712	62 858	61 963	80 443	45 321
Age of Reference Person	49.4	49.8	50.0	44.2	47.1
Average Number in Consumer Unit					
All persons	2.5	2.5	2.5	2.7	2.6
Children under 18 years	0.6	0.6	0.6	0.6	0.8
Persons 65 years and over	0.3	0.3	0.3	0.3	0.2
Earners	1.3	1.3	1.3	1.4	1.1
Vehicles	1.9	2.0	2.0	1.6	1.3
Percent Distribution					
Male	47	48	48	53	35
Female	53	52	52	47	65
Percent Homeowner	66	68	69	55	46
With mortgage	41	42	42	39	31
Without mortgage	25	26	27	17	15
AVERAGE ANNUAL EXPENDITURES	48 109	49 815	49 395	58 376	35 863
Food	6 129	6 314	6 253	7 656	4 796
Food at home	3 624	3 700	3 689	3 953	3 075
Cereals and bakery products	502	513	511	563	419
Meats, poultry, fish, and eggs	784	780	776	891	813
Dairy products	380	398	400	350	255
Fruits and vegetables	679	694	683	958	572
Other food at home	1 278	1 314	1 320	1 190	1 016
Food away from home	2 505	2 613	2 564	3 703	1 721
Alcoholic Beverages	412	441	446	322	203
Housing	16 557	16 899	16 712	20 549	14 102
Shelter	9 812	10 046	9 851	13 875	8 132
Owned dwellings	6 277	6 646	6 572	8 099	3 630
Rented dwellings	2 900	2 716	2 604	4 922	4 216
Other lodging	635	684	675	853	286
Utilities, fuels, and public services	3 660	3 647	3 666	3 285	3 749
Household operations	1 007	1 050	1 037	1 298	704
Housekeeping supplies	612	634	638	542	449
Household furnishings and equipment	1 467	1 522	1 520	1 549	1 068
Apparel and Services	1 700	1 737	1 663	3 414	1 429
Transportation	7 677	7 950	7 915	8 673	5 724
Vehicle purchases (net outlay)	2 588	2 727	2 734	2 599	1 591
Gasoline and motor oil	2 132	2 182	2 186	2 098	1 775
Other vehicle expenses	2 464	2 525	2 509	2 885	2 025
Public transportation	493	515	486	1 092	333
Health Care	3 157	3 355	3 397	2 525	1 734
Health insurance	1 831	1 925	1 937	1 685	1 156
Medical services	722	790	804	499	239
Drugs	485	515	528	254	272
Medical supplies	119	126	128	86	66
Entertainment	2 504	2 665	2 687	2 192	1 352
Personal Care Products and Services	582	590	590	593	525
Reading	100	108	109	89	41
Education	1 074	1 163	1 077	2 854	441
Tobacco Products and Smoking Supplies	362	380	392	146	231
Miscellaneous	849	891	907	546	549
Cash Contributions	1 633	1 675	1 700	1 178	1 334
Personal Insurance and Pensions	5 373	5 647	5 546	7 640	3 401
Life and other personal insurance	318	333	333	333	212
Pensions and Social Security	5 054	5 315	5 213	7 306	3 189

Table 11-12. Consumer Expenditures, Averages by Hispanic Origin of Reference Person, 2010

(Number, dollar, percent.)

Item	All consumer units	Hispanic[1]	Not Hispanic		
			Total	White, Asian, and other races	Black
NUMBER OF CONSUMER UNITS (THOUSANDS)	121 107	14 754	106 353	91 816	14 537
CONSUMER UNIT CHARACTERISTICS					
Income Before Taxes	62 481	49 845	64 234	67 283	44 980
Income After Taxes	60 712	49 399	62 282	65 082	44 592
Age of Reference Person	49.4	43.9	50.2	50.7	47.0
Average Number in Consumer Unit					
All persons	2.5	3.3	2.4	2.4	2.6
Children under 18 years	0.6	1.1	0.6	0.5	0.8
Persons 65 years and over	0.3	0.2	0.3	0.4	0.2
Earners	1.3	1.5	1.2	1.3	1.1
Vehicles	1.9	1.6	2.0	2.1	1.3
Percent Distribution					
Male	47	47	47	48	35
Female	53	53	53	52	65
Percent Homeowner	66	48	68	72	46
With mortgage	41	32	42	44	31
Without mortgage	25	16	26	28	15
AVERAGE ANNUAL EXPENDITURES	48 109	41 456	49 032	51 167	35 547
Food	6 129	6 486	6 080	6 287	4 778
Food at home	3 624	4 012	3 572	3 651	3 068
Cereals and bakery products	502	519	499	512	419
Meats, poultry, fish, and eggs	784	964	760	752	808
Dairy products	380	421	375	394	254
Fruits and vegetables	679	820	660	675	570
Other food at home	1 278	1 287	1 277	1 318	1 016
Food away from home	2 505	2 474	2 509	2 635	1 711
Alcoholic Beverages	412	260	433	470	195
Housing	16 557	15 432	16 713	17 153	13 933
Shelter	9 812	9 518	9 852	10 145	8 007
Owned dwellings	6 277	4 676	6 499	6 959	3 594
Rented dwellings	2 900	4 526	2 674	2 436	4 178
Other lodging	635	317	679	750	235
Utilities, fuels, and public services	3 660	3 471	3 686	3 676	3 753
Household operations	1 007	673	1 054	1 110	699
Housekeeping supplies	612	549	620	648	447
Household furnishings and equipment	1 467	1 222	1 500	1 575	1 028
Apparel and Services	1 700	1 998	1 659	1 696	1 429
Transportation	7 677	6 629	7 822	8 161	5 685
Vehicle purchases (net outlay)	2 588	1 907	2 683	2 865	1 532
Gasoline and motor oil	2 132	2 185	2 125	2 180	1 778
Other vehicle expenses	2 464	2 134	2 509	2 583	2 045
Public transportation	493	402	505	533	329
Health Care	3 157	1 842	3 339	3 595	1 726
Health insurance	1 831	971	1 950	2 076	1 154
Medical services	722	519	750	832	235
Drugs	485	284	513	551	272
Medical supplies	119	68	126	136	65
Entertainment	2 504	1 644	2 623	2 828	1 325
Personal Care Products and Services	582	565	585	595	521
Reading	100	37	108	119	40
Education	1 074	803	1 112	1 221	426
Tobacco Products and Smoking Supplies	362	165	389	414	235
Miscellaneous	849	507	896	950	551
Cash Contributions	1 633	1 074	1 711	1 771	1 333
Personal Insurance and Pensions	5 373	4 014	5 561	5 908	3 369
Life and other personal insurance	318	149	342	362	212
Pensions and Social Security	5 054	3 865	5 219	5 546	3 158

[1]May be of any race.

Table 11-13. Consumer Expenditures, Averages by Education of Reference Person, 2010

(Number, dollar, percent.)

Item	All consumer units	Less than a college graduate					College graduate or more		
		Total	Less than a high school graduate	High school graduate	High school graduate with some college	Associate's degree	Total	Bachelor's degree	Master's, professional, or doctoral degree
NUMBER OF CONSUMER UNITS (THOUSANDS)	121 107	85 128	17 303	30 921	25 460	11 443	35 980	22 877	13 103
CONSUMER UNIT CHARACTERISTICS									
Income Before Taxes	62 481	47 858	33 317	47 029	52 113	62 618	97 080	88 003	112 927
Income After Taxes	60 712	47 148	33 288	46 507	51 066	61 120	92 805	84 625	107 086
Age of Reference Person	49.4	50.0	53.9	51.7	46.5	47.7	48.0	46.9	49.8
Average Number in Consumer Unit									
All persons	2.5	2.5	2.8	2.5	2.4	2.5	2.4	2.5	2.4
Children under 18 years	0.6	0.6	0.8	0.6	0.6	0.6	0.6	0.6	0.6
Persons 65 years and over	0.3	0.3	0.5	0.4	0.3	0.2	0.3	0.2	0.3
Earners	1.3	1.2	1.1	1.2	1.2	1.4	1.4	1.4	1.4
Vehicles	1.9	1.8	1.5	1.8	1.9	2.2	2.1	2.1	2.1
Percent Distribution									
Male	47	45	44	44	47	43	51	51	52
Female	53	55	56	56	53	57	49	49	48
Percent Homeowner	66	61	54	64	59	70	76	73	81
With mortgage	41	35	23	34	39	48	54	53	56
Without mortgage	25	26	31	30	20	22	22	20	24
AVERAGE ANNUAL EXPENDITURES	48 109	39 632	29 753	37 969	43 144	50 967	68 189	63 907	75 752
Food	6 129	5 396	4 842	5 138	5 617	6 348	7 871	7 594	8 398
Food at home	3 624	3 368	3 342	3 291	3 308	3 739	4 233	4 055	4 583
Cereals and bakery products	502	465	467	452	455	519	589	570	625
Meats, poultry, fish, and eggs	784	763	795	754	744	782	836	811	887
Dairy products	380	349	337	339	351	388	454	429	505
Fruits and vegetables	679	607	626	582	597	673	851	793	966
Other food at home	1 278	1 184	1 117	1 164	1 161	1 377	1 503	1 452	1 600
Food away from home	2 505	2 028	1 500	1 847	2 309	2 609	3 638	3 539	3 815
Alcoholic Beverages	412	293	141	271	361	411	694	722	638
Housing	16 557	13 659	10 647	13 378	14 635	16 750	23 419	21 968	25 977
Shelter	9 812	7 841	6 057	7 618	8 560	9 542	14 475	13 673	15 875
Owned dwellings	6 277	4 596	2 828	4 534	5 125	6 264	10 254	9 345	11 840
Rented dwellings	2 900	2 896	3 089	2 760	2 961	2 823	2 908	3 114	2 549
Other lodging	635	349	140	323	474	455	1 312	1 214	1 485
Utilities, fuels, and public services	3 660	3 462	3 098	3 525	3 431	3 915	4 127	3 990	4 367
Household operations	1 007	687	329	642	832	1 026	1 765	1 459	2 301
Housekeeping supplies	612	536	460	505	556	676	792	778	819
Household furnishings and equipment	1 467	1 132	704	1 088	1 256	1 591	2 260	2 069	2 616
Apparel and Services	1 700	1 455	1 323	1 279	1 386	2 250	2 282	2 262	2 310
Transportation	7 677	6 756	4 894	6 455	7 388	8 960	9 859	9 525	10 470
Vehicle purchases (net outlay)	2 588	2 260	1 364	2 185	2 508	3 270	3 364	3 400	3 302
Gasoline and motor oil	2 132	2 041	1 647	1 988	2 155	2 526	2 349	2 358	2 333
Other vehicle expenses	2 464	2 163	1 676	2 031	2 391	2 727	3 178	2 932	3 633
Public transportation	493	292	207	251	334	437	968	834	1 203
Health Care	3 157	2 772	2 129	2 820	2 938	3 238	4 069	3 824	4 497
Health insurance	1 831	1 631	1 252	1 733	1 685	1 811	2 302	2 194	2 492
Medical services	722	585	403	533	672	805	1 048	976	1 173
Drugs	485	457	409	454	474	495	552	499	647
Medical supplies	119	99	66	100	107	127	166	156	186
Entertainment	2 504	2 011	1 174	1 864	2 425	2 710	3 673	3 366	4 226
Personal Care Products and Services	582	478	352	433	520	683	829	786	907
Reading	100	70	35	67	90	90	169	143	213
Education	1 074	579	205	347	912	1 020	2 247	1 986	2 705
Tobacco Products and Smoking Supplies	362	438	440	503	381	386	183	219	119
Miscellaneous	849	639	452	616	731	778	1 346	1 319	1 376
Cash Contributions	1 633	1 250	882	1 128	1 471	1 644	2 540	2 243	3 058
Personal Insurance and Pensions	5 373	3 836	2 236	3 669	4 289	5 700	9 007	7 948	10 857
Life and other personal insurance	318	231	136	228	249	340	525	408	729
Pensions and Social Security	5 054	3 606	2 100	3 441	4 041	5 359	8 482	7 540	10 127

Table 11-14. Consumer Expenditures, Averages by Housing Tenure and Type of Area, 2010

(Number, dollar, percent.)

| Item | All consumer units | Housing tenure | | | | Type of area | | | |
| | | Homeowner | | | Renter | Urban | | | Rural |
		Total	Homeowner with mortgage	Homeowner without mortgage		Total	Central city	Other urban	
NUMBER OF CONSUMER UNITS (THOUSANDS)	121 107	79 451	49 278	30 173	41 656	110 689	35 249	75 440	10 418
CONSUMER UNIT CHARACTERISTICS									
Income Before Taxes	62 481	75 653	88 962	53 917	37 359	63 887	57 510	66 866	47 548
Income After Taxes	60 712	73 249	86 056	52 334	36 800	62 066	55 700	65 040	46 331
Age of Reference Person	49.4	53.6	47.8	63.0	41.5	49.0	46.2	50.4	53.5
Average Number in Consumer Unit									
All persons	2.5	2.6	2.9	2.1	2.3	2.5	2.4	2.6	2.5
Children under 18 years	0.6	0.6	0.8	0.3	0.7	0.6	0.6	0.6	0.6
Persons 65 years and over	0.3	0.4	0.2	0.8	0.2	0.3	0.2	0.3	0.4
Earners	1.3	1.4	1.6	0.9	1.1	1.3	1.3	1.3	1.1
Vehicles	1.9	2.3	2.5	2.1	1.1	1.9	1.4	2.0	2.5
Percent Distribution									
Male	47	48	49	45	45	47	46	47	46
Female	53	52	51	55	55	53	54	53	54
Percent Homeowner	66	100	100	100	X	64	50	71	81
With mortgage	41	62	100	X	X	41	32	45	37
Without mortgage	25	38	X	100	X	23	17	26	43
AVERAGE ANNUAL EXPENDITURES	48 109	55 780	63 235	43 179	33 460	48 948	44 438	51 043	39 144
Food	6 129	6 820	7 350	5 715	4 802	6 211	5 847	6 376	5 222
Food at home	3 624	4 000	4 215	3 531	2 902	3 641	3 424	3 739	3 435
Cereals and bakery products	502	559	585	502	391	504	471	518	481
Meats, poultry, fish, and eggs	784	851	885	775	657	789	776	794	737
Dairy products	380	427	450	375	292	381	347	396	378
Fruits and vegetables	679	748	792	652	547	688	653	704	583
Other food at home	1 278	1 415	1 502	1 228	1 015	1 280	1 177	1 326	1 257
Food away from home	2 505	2 820	3 135	2 184	1 900	2 570	2 423	2 637	1 786
Alcoholic Beverages	412	451	519	305	338	420	414	423	320
Housing	16 557	18 503	22 278	12 294	12 843	17 017	15 966	17 504	11 670
Shelter	9 812	10 400	13 557	5 243	8 691	10 213	10 057	10 286	5 549
Owned dwellings	6 277	9 469	12 624	4 316	190	6 464	5 087	7 108	4 290
Rented dwellings	2 900	58	47	76	8 319	3 094	4 356	2 504	835
Other lodging	635	873	886	852	182	655	614	674	424
Utilities, fuels, and public services	3 660	4 314	4 572	3 891	2 413	3 670	3 266	3 859	3 552
Household operations	1 007	1 230	1 421	921	582	1 048	934	1 101	575
Housekeeping supplies	612	741	762	697	362	607	501	655	661
Household furnishings and equipment	1 467	1 817	1 966	1 543	796	1 479	1 208	1 604	1 334
Apparel and Services	1 700	1 781	2 007	1 321	1 544	1 745	1 925	1 664	1 203
Transportation	7 677	9 056	10 047	7 450	5 046	7 701	6 702	8 166	7 430
Vehicle purchases (net outlay)	2 588	3 097	3 490	2 456	1 618	2 599	2 197	2 787	2 476
Gasoline and motor oil	2 132	2 458	2 764	1 958	1 511	2 104	1 701	2 293	2 429
Other vehicle expenses	2 464	2 933	3 150	2 591	1 567	2 480	2 192	2 612	2 297
Public transportation	493	567	643	444	350	517	612	474	228
Health Care	3 157	4 016	3 734	4 478	1 518	3 126	2 383	3 473	3 483
Health insurance	1 831	2 314	2 071	2 710	909	1 816	1 376	2 021	1 990
Medical services	722	937	980	868	312	722	560	798	724
Drugs	485	616	533	754	236	470	357	523	646
Medical supplies	119	149	151	146	61	119	91	132	124
Entertainment	2 504	3 088	3 423	2 513	1 390	2 541	2 140	2 726	2 114
Personal Care Products and Services	582	678	733	572	399	601	561	619	381
Reading	100	124	122	129	52	101	97	103	81
Education	1 074	1 197	1 368	912	840	1 129	1 073	1 155	499
Tobacco Products and Smoking Supplies	362	341	345	335	402	337	296	356	632
Miscellaneous	849	1 045	1 100	973	473	849	695	920	849
Cash Contributions	1 633	2 015	1 899	2 205	905	1 656	1 364	1 793	1 389
Personal Insurance and Pensions	5 373	6 665	8 312	3 975	2 907	5 514	4 975	5 766	3 871
Life and other personal insurance	318	432	505	315	100	320	252	352	297
Pensions and Social Security	5 054	6 233	7 807	3 661	2 807	5 194	4 723	5 414	3 574

X = Not applicable.

Table 11-15. Consumer Expenditures, Averages by Population Size of Area of Residence, 2010

(Number, dollar, percent.)

Item	All consumer units	Outside urban area	Urban consumer units						
			Total	Less than 100,000	100,000 to 249,999	250,000 to 999,999	1,000,000 to 2,499,999	2,500,000 to 4,999,999	5,000,000 and over
NUMBER OF CONSUMER UNITS (THOUSANDS)	121 107	24 708	96 399	17 745	9 492	20 137	15 788	17 050	16 187
CONSUMER UNIT CHARACTERISTICS									
Income Before Taxes	62 481	56 814	63 934	48 931	55 739	59 858	66 377	77 156	73 949
Income After Taxes	60 712	55 185	62 129	48 030	54 744	58 436	64 266	73 901	72 025
Age of Reference Person	49.4	53.3	48.4	49.1	48.5	48.0	48.8	47.1	49.2
Average Number in Consumer Unit									
All persons	2.5	2.5	2.5	2.4	2.5	2.4	2.5	2.6	2.7
Children under 18 years	0.6	0.6	0.6	0.6	0.6	0.6	0.6	0.7	0.6
Persons 65 years and over	0.3	0.4	0.3	0.3	0.3	0.3	0.3	0.3	0.3
Earners	1.3	1.2	1.3	1.1	1.3	1.3	1.3	1.4	1.4
Vehicles	1.9	2.6	1.7	1.8	1.8	1.8	1.8	1.7	1.4
Percent Distribution									
Male	47	47	47	44	43	47	50	48	46
Female	53	53	53	56	57	53	50	52	54
Percent Homeowner	66	83	61	61	63	64	62	61	57
With mortgage	41	43	40	34	42	42	43	43	37
Without mortgage	25	40	21	27	21	22	19	17	20
AVERAGE ANNUAL EXPENDITURES	48 109	44 885	48 937	38 930	41 776	48 593	51 305	55 990	54 834
Food	6 129	5 723	6 234	5 163	5 272	6 669	6 433	6 665	6 804
Food at home	3 624	3 566	3 639	3 167	3 155	3 980	3 756	3 769	3 788
Cereals and bakery products	502	508	500	422	438	555	529	513	516
Meats, poultry, fish, and eggs	784	761	790	659	633	889	786	835	870
Dairy products	380	393	377	330	358	414	383	381	387
Fruits and vegetables	679	599	700	570	556	735	718	764	801
Other food at home	1 278	1 306	1 271	1 186	1 171	1 388	1 340	1 275	1 215
Food away from home	2 505	2 157	2 595	1 996	2 117	2 688	2 676	2 896	3 017
Alcoholic Beverages	412	352	427	307	310	417	504	512	473
Housing	16 557	13 952	17 224	12 720	14 657	15 954	18 085	20 207	21 277
Shelter	9 812	7 154	10 493	6 902	8 604	9 146	11 082	12 678	14 336
Owned dwellings	6 277	5 614	6 447	4 233	5 553	5 868	6 965	7 722	8 273
Rented dwellings	2 900	997	3 387	2 150	2 563	2 700	3 432	4 145	5 239
Other lodging	635	543	659	519	488	579	685	811	824
Utilities, fuels, and public services	3 660	3 799	3 624	3 317	3 436	3 570	3 662	3 910	3 802
Household operations	1 007	786	1 064	713	910	1 005	1 154	1 397	1 173
Housekeeping supplies	612	720	583	520	497	615	605	644	581
Household furnishings and equipment	1 467	1 493	1 460	1 268	1 211	1 616	1 581	1 578	1 385
Apparel and Services	1 700	1 317	1 799	1 256	1 324	1 806	1 753	1 958	2 535
Transportation	7 677	8 180	7 548	6 763	6 771	7 543	8 124	8 286	7 541
Vehicle purchases (net outlay)	2 588	2 829	2 527	2 625	2 318	2 539	3 015	2 659	1 911
Gasoline and motor oil	2 132	2 586	2 016	1 922	1 891	2 029	2 079	2 228	1 891
Other vehicle expenses	2 464	2 489	2 458	1 919	2 168	2 547	2 501	2 723	2 793
Public transportation	493	277	548	297	394	428	529	676	946
Health Care	3 157	3 756	3 003	2 808	2 994	3 212	3 091	3 130	2 745
Health insurance	1 831	2 200	1 736	1 613	1 842	1 813	1 752	1 827	1 599
Medical services	722	792	704	622	628	777	739	753	663
Drugs	485	628	448	456	430	514	463	429	377
Medical supplies	119	135	115	116	95	108	137	120	107
Entertainment	2 504	2 623	2 474	1 973	2 162	2 606	2 663	2 766	2 553
Personal Care Products and Services	582	455	615	478	516	642	630	748	636
Reading	100	94	101	82	83	117	100	116	98
Education	1 074	774	1 151	641	672	1 146	1 142	1 436	1 709
Tobacco Products and Smoking Supplies	362	528	319	355	391	345	331	290	226
Miscellaneous	849	871	843	732	568	925	1 070	856	792
Cash Contributions	1 633	1 606	1 640	1 477	1 514	1 835	1 694	1 880	1 347
Personal Insurance and Pensions	5 373	4 652	5 557	4 175	4 542	5 376	5 687	7 142	6 097
Life and other personal insurance	318	344	311	256	254	314	376	315	336
Pensions and Social Security	5 054	4 308	5 246	3 919	4 288	5 062	5 311	6 827	5 761

Table 11-16. Consumer Expenditures, Averages by Region of Residence, 2010

(Number, dollar, percent.)

Item	All consumer units	Region[1] Northeast	Region[1] South	Region[1] Midwest	Region[1] West
NUMBER OF CONSUMER UNITS (THOUSANDS)	121 107	22 227	26 997	44 449	27 434
CONSUMER UNIT CHARACTERISTICS					
Income Before Taxes	62 481	68 409	58 417	58 824	67 603
Income After Taxes	60 712	66 168	56 918	57 329	65 507
Age of Reference Person	49.4	50.5	49.0	49.8	48.3
Average Number in Consumer Unit					
All persons	2.5	2.5	2.5	2.5	2.6
Children under 18 years	0.6	0.6	0.6	0.6	0.7
Persons 65 years and over	0.3	0.4	0.3	0.3	0.3
Earners	1.3	1.3	1.3	1.2	1.3
Vehicles	1.9	1.6	2.1	1.9	2.0
Percent Distribution					
Male	47	43	47	45	51
Female	53	57	53	55	49
Percent Homeowner	66	63	69	68	60
With mortgage	41	38	43	40	42
Without mortgage	25	26	26	28	18
AVERAGE ANNUAL EXPENDITURES	48 109	52 802	45 278	44 217	53 429
Food	6 129	6 755	5 738	5 645	6 804
Food at home	3 624	3 910	3 577	3 335	3 914
Cereals and bakery products	502	558	501	454	535
Meats, poultry, fish, and eggs	784	860	717	763	826
Dairy products	380	432	386	341	397
Fruits and vegetables	679	753	669	589	779
Other food at home	1 278	1 307	1 303	1 188	1 377
Food away from home	2 505	2 845	2 161	2 310	2 891
Alcoholic Beverages	412	528	380	325	492
Housing	16 557	19 034	14 762	14 890	19 019
Shelter	9 812	11 772	8 514	8 123	12 237
Owned dwellings	6 277	7 429	5 903	5 229	7 412
Rented dwellings	2 900	3 636	1 947	2 353	4 127
Other lodging	635	708	664	542	699
Utilities, fuels, and public services	3 660	3 985	3 415	3 847	3 334
Household operations	1 007	1 093	859	940	1 192
Housekeeping supplies	612	619	634	586	624
Household furnishings and equipment	1 467	1 566	1 340	1 393	1 632
Apparel and Services	1 700	2 084	1 474	1 506	1 932
Transportation	7 677	7 754	7 222	7 590	8 206
Vehicle purchases (net outlay)	2 588	2 353	2 403	2 719	2 749
Gasoline and motor oil	2 132	1 903	2 108	2 229	2 186
Other vehicle expenses	2 464	2 785	2 285	2 315	2 623
Public transportation	493	713	426	327	648
Health Care	3 157	3 125	3 265	3 041	3 265
Health insurance	1 831	1 930	1 888	1 798	1 746
Medical services	722	630	726	660	893
Drugs	485	447	512	491	481
Medical supplies	119	117	138	93	145
Entertainment	2 504	2 688	2 548	2 347	2 568
Personal Care Products and Services	582	602	518	566	655
Reading	100	124	101	80	111
Education	1 074	1 618	1 153	697	1 167
Tobacco Products and Smoking Supplies	362	380	381	401	266
Miscellaneous	849	910	773	716	1 090
Cash Contributions	1 633	1 444	1 589	1 633	1 830
Personal Insurance and Pensions	5 373	5 756	5 371	4 780	6 023
Life and other personal insurance	318	350	384	286	279
Pensions and Social Security	5 054	5 406	4 987	4 494	5 744

[1]The states that comprise the Census regions are: Northeast—Connecticut, Maine, Massachusetts, New Hampshire, New Jersey, New York, Pennsylvania, Rhode Island, and Vermont; South—Alabama, Arkansas, Delaware, District of Columbia, Florida, Georgia, Kentucky, Louisiana, Maryland, Mississippi, North Carolina, Oklahoma, South Carolina, Tennessee, Texas, Virginia, and West Virginia; Midwest—Illinois, Indiana, Iowa, Kansas, Michigan, Minnesota, Missouri, Nebraska, North Dakota, Ohio, South Dakota, and Wisconsin; and West—Alaska, Arizona, California, Colorado, Hawaii, Idaho, Montana, Nevada, New Mexico, Oregon, Utah, Washington, and Wyoming.

Table 11-17. Consumer Expenditures, Averages for Single Men by Income Before Taxes, 2009–2010

(Number, dollar, percent.)

Item	All single men	Complete reporting of income						
		Less than $5,000	$5,000 to $9,999	$10,000 to $14,999	$15,000 to $19,999	$20,000 to $29,999	$30,000 to $39,999	$40,000 and over
NUMBER OF CONSUMER UNITS (THOUSANDS)	16 270	1 530	1 458	1 921	1 543	2 399	1 953	5 465
CONSUMER UNIT CHARACTERISTICS								
Income Before Taxes	36 919	-352	7 846	12 484	17 379	24 589	34 480	75 501
Income After Taxes	35 413	-280	7 854	12 480	17 090	24 285	33 400	71 596
Age of Reference Person	47.6	38.0	43.0	52.9	53.8	50.1	47.6	46.9
Average Number in Consumer Unit								
All persons	1.0	1.0	1.0	1.0	1.0	1.0	1.0	1.0
Persons 65 years and over	0.2	0.1	0.2	0.3	0.4	0.3	0.2	0.1
Earners	0.7	0.4	0.5	0.4	0.5	0.7	0.8	0.9
Vehicles	1.3	0.7	0.9	1.0	1.2	1.3	1.4	1.6
Percent Homeowner	44	19	22	34	41	42	50	60
With mortgage	23	5	5	9	12	14	28	43
Without mortgage	21	14	17	25	29	28	22	17
AVERAGE ANNUAL EXPENDITURES	30 190	16 567	15 087	19 167	21 029	24 340	30 291	46 652
Food	3 751	2 808	2 662	2 720	2 898	2 928	3 264	5 263
Food at home	1 775	1 452	1 692	1 601	1 701	1 595	1 552	2 100
Cereals and bakery products	235	208	229	198	237	218	213	269
Meats, poultry, fish, and eggs	392	339	465	375	390	339	297	455
Dairy products	185	161	164	153	172	168	170	220
Fruits and vegetables	308	264	250	281	297	258	262	379
Other food at home	656	481	584	595	606	613	610	777
Food away from home	1 976	1 356	970	1 119	1 197	1 333	1 712	3 163
Alcoholic Beverages	486	305	269	240	206	347	411	807
Housing	11 077	6 077	5 894	7 735	8 508	9 497	11 167	16 386
Shelter	7 379	4 214	4 015	4 909	5 246	5 935	7 530	11 214
Owned dwellings	3 203	749	592	1 353	1 711	1 936	3 220	6 210
Rented dwellings	3 776	3 302	3 299	3 444	3 386	3 756	4 089	4 161
Other lodging	400	163	[1]125	112	148	242	222	843
Utilities, fuels, and public services	2 181	1 123	1 230	1 722	2 061	2 286	2 484	2 771
Household operations	463	160	179	225	529	484	366	714
Housekeeping supplies	254	204	117	227	221	223	157	359
Household furnishings and equipment	800	377	352	652	451	570	629	1 328
Apparel and Services	817	514	409	1 271	420	558	658	1 128
Transportation	4 593	2 302	2 130	2 465	3 142	4 338	5 555	6 761
Vehicle purchases (net outlay)	1 461	2 481	734	[1]731	714	1 454	2 132	2 159
Gasoline and motor oil	1 311	749	795	841	968	1 267	1 525	1 811
Other vehicle expenses	1 514	971	502	770	1 296	1 396	1 697	2 190
Public transportation	308	101	99	122	165	220	200	601
Health Care	1 605	780	576	1 332	1 594	1 722	1 793	2 084
Health insurance	916	327	363	816	949	984	1 095	1 160
Medical services	387	309	103	214	268	409	356	581
Drugs	244	114	86	268	326	279	259	263
Medical supplies	59	[1]230	[1]224	34	51	51	82	81
Entertainment	1 522	948	835	970	1 203	1 174	1 456	2 310
Personal Care Products and Services	185	120	92	112	147	156	157	282
Reading	75	64	36	45	65	60	79	109
Education	666	1 463	1 157	485	401	393	813	516
Tobacco Products and Smoking Supplies	358	314	277	388	461	420	381	318
Miscellaneous	700	257	180	401	345	415	597	1 306
Cash Contributions	1 336	342	292	572	813	861	1 358	2 509
Personal Insurance and Pensions	3 017	272	278	430	828	1 470	2 604	6 872
Life and other personal insurance	113	[1]287	36	68	76	71	73	201
Pensions and Social Security	2 904	185	243	362	751	1 399	2 531	6 671

[1]Data are likely to have large sampling errors.

Table 11-18. Consumer Expenditures, Averages for Single Women by Income Before Taxes, 2009–2010

(Number, dollar, percent.)

Item	All single women	Complete reporting of income						
		Less than $5,000	$5,000 to $9,999	$10,000 to $14,999	$15,000 to $19,999	$20,000 to $29,999	$30,000 to $39,999	$40,000 and over
NUMBER OF CONSUMER UNITS (THOUSANDS)	18 855	1 643	2 046	3 218	2 455	2 995	2 137	4 361
CONSUMER UNIT CHARACTERISTICS								
Income Before Taxes	29 396	2 102	8 133	12 555	17 317	24 473	34 384	69 814
Income After Taxes	28 358	2 150	8 180	12 507	17 075	24 193	33 443	66 112
Age of Reference Person	57.6	46.3	56.9	65.5	65.4	60.4	54.7	51.5
Average Number in Consumer Unit								
All persons	1.0	1.0	1.0	1.0	1.0	1.0	1.0	1.0
Persons 65 years and over	0.4	0.3	0.4	0.6	0.6	0.5	0.3	0.2
Earners	0.5	0.4	0.3	0.2	0.3	0.5	0.7	0.9
Vehicles	0.9	0.6	0.6	0.7	0.9	1.0	1.1	1.2
Percent Homeowner	55	26	34	49	60	59	64	71
With mortgage	23	8	9	8	15	22	32	47
Without mortgage	32	19	25	40	44	37	32	25
AVERAGE ANNUAL EXPENDITURES	28 489	16 610	15 411	17 692	22 081	25 757	32 198	50 290
Food	3 208	2 446	2 290	2 600	2 443	2 872	3 308	4 848
Food at home	2 031	1 438	1 678	1 944	1 740	1 958	1 993	2 636
Cereals and bakery products	274	209	247	254	247	279	277	325
Meats, poultry, fish, and eggs	397	301	328	389	353	374	386	504
Dairy products	219	148	214	200	191	214	213	275
Fruits and vegetables	401	290	319	331	360	399	392	544
Other food at home	741	490	570	771	589	692	725	987
Food away from home	1 177	1 008	612	656	703	915	1 315	2 213
Alcoholic Beverages	215	110	96	85	77	148	329	451
Housing	11 497	7 412	6 991	7 828	9 760	10 787	12 913	18 569
Shelter	7 251	4 938	4 309	4 782	5 722	6 603	8 064	12 232
Owned dwellings	3 729	1 823	1 222	1 743	2 780	3 311	4 383	7 591
Rented dwellings	3 184	2 933	2 984	2 955	2 772	3 097	3 283	3 784
Other lodging	338	182	103	85	170	194	397	857
Utilities, fuels, and public services	2 430	1 406	1 729	2 008	2 442	2 621	2 781	3 144
Household operations	593	445	184	364	532	524	679	1 048
Housekeeping supplies	424	185	326	312	354	411	375	684
Household furnishings and equipment	799	438	443	363	709	628	1 014	1 461
Apparel and Services	948	574	525	420	668	848	861	1 883
Transportation	3 665	1 597	1 810	1 814	2 755	3 234	4 683	6 917
Vehicle purchases (net outlay)	1 043	[1]3 343	[1]3 343	3 213	[1]802	779	[1]1 528	2 326
Gasoline and motor oil	906	589	544	611	719	932	1 174	1 371
Other vehicle expenses	1 405	520	814	856	1 026	1 346	1 637	2 490
Public transportation	311	146	109	134	208	178	343	731
Health Care	2 372	1 195	1 120	2 008	2 730	2 665	2 815	3 038
Health insurance	1 393	686	725	1 274	1 712	1 590	1 589	1 651
Medical services	486	256	152	307	413	522	599	821
Drugs	409	187	205	372	515	461	529	451
Medical supplies	84	67	38	55	90	92	98	114
Entertainment	1 434	751	790	833	1 011	1 379	1 720	2 534
Personal Care Products and Services	494	256	293	303	349	423	516	924
Reading	92	36	33	54	77	96	119	159
Education	443	933	444	308	255	412	380	515
Tobacco Products and Smoking Supplies	176	218	196	186	161	229	147	129
Miscellaneous	625	346	203	425	358	454	539	1 365
Cash Contributions	1 185	470	398	492	908	954	1 546	2 474
Personal Insurance and Pensions	2 136	266	222	335	529	1 255	2 323	6 484
Life and other personal insurance	146	52	68	108	130	103	160	277
Pensions and Social Security	1 990	215	154	226	398	1 152	2 162	6 207

[1]Data are likely to have large sampling errors.

Table 11-19. Consumer Expenditures, Averages for Age Groups by Income Before Taxes: Reference Person Under 25 Years of Age, 2009–2010

(Number, dollar, percent.)

Item	Total	Complete reporting of income						
		Less than $5,000	$5,000 to $9,999	$10,000 to $14,999	$15,000 to $19,999	$20,000 to $29,999	$30,000 to $39,999	$40,000 and over
NUMBER OF CONSUMER UNITS (THOUSANDS)	7 955	1 482	1 157	880	833	1 115	768	1 720
CONSUMER UNIT CHARACTERISTICS								
Income Before Taxes	26 294	2 656	7 564	12 223	17 485	24 787	34 326	68 128
Income After Taxes	26 156	2 753	7 685	12 466	17 661	25 328	34 295	66 778
Age of Reference Person	21.4	20.4	20.9	21.3	21.6	21.8	22.0	22.2
Average Number in Consumer Unit								
All persons	2.0	1.2	1.5	1.6	2.0	2.3	2.4	3.0
Children under 18 years	0.4	0.2	0.3	0.4	0.5	0.6	0.5	0.5
Persons 65 years and over	(1)	(2)	(1)	(1)	(1)	(1)	(1)	(1)
Earners	1.3	0.7	0.8	0.9	1.1	1.3	1.5	2.2
Vehicles	1.1	0.5	0.6	0.8	1.0	1.2	1.6	2.0
Percent Distribution								
Male	46	48	48	46	45	41	41	48
Female	54	52	52	54	55	59	59	52
Percent Homeowner	14	2	2	5	11	10	22	37
With mortgage	9	1	1	3	4	6	15	28
Without mortgage	5	1	1	2	7	4	8	9
AVERAGE ANNUAL EXPENDITURES	27 796	12 970	15 008	18 809	22 624	27 042	35 373	50 545
Food	4 127	2 580	2 453	3 044	3 245	3 750	4 284	6 483
Food at home	2 324	1 188	1 431	1 800	2 129	2 252	2 555	3 440
Cereals and bakery products	309	183	185	248	339	303	322	432
Meats, poultry, fish, and eggs	509	253	275	370	448	503	538	794
Dairy products	250	131	151	150	251	243	287	374
Fruits and vegetables	397	178	252	295	350	390	432	603
Other food at home	859	443	568	737	740	814	977	1 237
Food away from home	1 803	1 392	1 022	1 244	1 116	1 497	1 729	3 043
Alcoholic Beverages	375	172	170	197	175	471	319	685
Housing	9 643	4 127	5 696	7 199	8 992	10 008	12 216	16 989
Shelter	6 235	2 936	3 897	4 802	5 489	6 378	7 850	10 934
Owned dwellings	1 183	2108	291	260	425	709	1 434	3 880
Rented dwellings	4 848	2 608	3 617	4 354	4 947	5 547	6 183	6 765
Other lodging	203	220	188	2188	2117	2122	234	289
Utilities, fuels, and public services	1 820	611	930	1 247	1 857	2 061	2 512	3 270
Household operations	393	95	187	288	412	443	480	762
Housekeeping supplies	294	118	129	198	173	286	348	508
Household furnishings and equipment	901	366	554	664	1 061	840	1 026	1 514
Apparel and Services	1 476	675	584	721	970	1 715	1 459	2 689
Transportation	5 009	1 397	2 179	3 103	4 180	4 881	8 854	9 429
Vehicle purchases (net outlay)	1 951	2402	2709	21016	1 390	1 518	5 001	3 793
Gasoline and motor oil	1 488	664	869	1 078	1 433	1 581	2 038	2 547
Other vehicle expenses	1 315	239	460	853	1 177	1 486	1 518	2 598
Public transportation	254	91	141	157	181	296	297	491
Health Care	726	141	200	282	560	543	1 206	1 777
Health insurance	394	60	92	100	254	293	713	1 025
Medical services	202	43	59	70	157	148	383	477
Drugs	100	24	36	77	110	66	83	226
Medical supplies	31	213	213	234	239	36	228	49
Entertainment	1 227	547	702	849	1 017	1 195	1 561	2 202
Personal Care Products and Services	354	156	185	208	257	379	469	598
Reading	41	21	31	43	48	38	42	60
Education	1 908	2 790	1 982	1 918	1 427	1 405	1 237	1 956
Tobacco Products and Smoking Supplies	306	123	213	251	223	455	427	448
Miscellaneous	260	48	91	185	135	222	302	619
Cash Contributions	331	67	132	171	192	255	423	852
Personal Insurance and Pensions	2 012	127	389	637	1 204	1 727	2 574	5 758
Life and other personal insurance	27	21	21	215	217	29	45	80
Pensions and Social Security	1 985	126	388	622	1 187	1 718	2 529	5 679

1Value less than or equal to 0.5.
2Data are likely to have large sampling errors.

Table 11-20. Consumer Expenditures, Averages for Age Groups by Income Before Taxes: Reference Person 25 to 34 Years of Age, 2009–2010

(Number, dollar, percent.)

Item	Total	Complete reporting of income								
		Less than $5,000	$5,000 to $9,999	$10,000 to $14,999	$15,000 to $19,999	$20,000 to $29,999	$30,000 to $39,999	$40,000 to $49,999	$50,000 to $69,999	$70,000 and over
NUMBER OF CONSUMER UNITS (THOUSANDS)	20 105	605	641	969	1 069	2 582	2 494	2 272	3 391	6 082
CONSUMER UNIT CHARACTERISTICS										
Income Before Taxes	59 281	1 247	7 787	12 830	17 596	25 275	34 618	44 658	58 985	115 379
Income After Taxes	57 901	1 760	8 566	13 509	18 428	26 017	34 887	44 608	57 991	110 578
Age of Reference Person	29.7	29.4	29.3	29.0	29.3	29.4	29.4	29.5	29.6	30.2
Average Number in Consumer Unit										
All persons	2.9	2.3	2.6	2.6	2.8	2.7	2.8	2.8	2.9	3.1
Children under 18 years	1.1	1.1	1.3	1.2	1.2	1.2	1.1	1.1	1.0	1.0
Persons 65 years and over	(1)	(1)	(2)	(1)	(1)	(1)	(1)	(1)	(1)	(1)
Earners	1.5	0.5	0.7	0.9	1.1	1.2	1.3	1.5	1.7	1.9
Vehicles	1.7	0.8	0.9	1.0	1.1	1.3	1.5	1.7	1.9	2.2
Percent Distribution										
Male	47	42	38	32	37	45	46	49	50	52
Female	53	58	62	68	63	55	54	51	50	48
Percent Homeowner	46	18	13	21	20	24	35	43	53	70
With mortgage	39	9	9	12	10	16	27	36	46	66
Without mortgage	7	9	4	9	10	7	8	7	7	4
AVERAGE ANNUAL EXPENDITURES	46 556	23 684	23 276	23 756	24 368	29 755	35 787	39 293	46 889	73 176
Food	6 130	4 535	4 125	4 156	4 195	4 473	4 806	5 437	6 396	8 627
Food at home	3 408	3 041	2 730	2 945	2 890	2 866	2 759	3 055	3 516	4 310
Cereals and bakery products	457	426	347	361	356	398	360	408	487	578
Meats, poultry, fish, and eggs	735	689	823	651	745	655	610	664	732	867
Dairy products	364	320	282	324	295	319	276	332	359	475
Fruits and vegetables	603	518	417	547	428	491	507	520	606	802
Other food at home	1 249	1 088	861	1 062	1 067	1 003	1 006	1 131	1 332	1 588
Food away from home	2 722	1 494	1 395	1 211	1 305	1 607	2 047	2 383	2 880	4 317
Alcoholic Beverages	477	182	203	147	117	225	336	373	545	829
Housing	17 051	9 710	9 525	10 313	10 269	11 553	13 149	14 972	16 924	25 654
Shelter	10 653	6 296	5 774	6 311	6 329	7 126	8 128	9 449	10 595	16 066
Owned dwellings	5 353	1 143	640	1 444	914	1 599	2 694	3 878	5 266	10 954
Rented dwellings	4 933	5 076	5 035	4 837	5 373	5 409	5 313	5 393	4 994	4 283
Other lodging	367	[2]77	[2]100	[2]30	[2]42	118	122	178	335	829
Utilities, fuels, and public services	3 239	2 075	2 233	2 282	2 462	2 624	2 973	3 250	3 424	4 012
Household operations	1 237	563	490	492	460	651	772	888	1 063	2 306
Housekeeping supplies	486	235	296	443	409	380	333	397	486	702
Household furnishings and equipment	1 437	541	732	785	610	772	942	988	1 356	2 569
Apparel and Services	1 978	935	1 742	1 137	953	1 445	1 467	1 556	1 748	3 210
Transportation	7 952	3 670	3 361	3 581	3 913	5 535	7 061	6 575	7 705	12 338
Vehicle purchases (net outlay)	3 118	[2]1 594	[2]1 216	[2]981	999	2 185	2 900	2 053	2 672	5 315
Gasoline and motor oil	2 140	1 040	1 147	1 289	1 470	1 646	1 883	2 206	2 400	2 752
Other vehicle expenses	2 234	889	787	1 108	1 244	1 494	2 037	2 031	2 204	3 384
Public transportation	461	147	211	202	199	210	241	285	429	887
Health Care	1 803	766	516	561	643	967	1 403	1 564	2 128	2 871
Health insurance	1 085	291	300	293	378	474	890	978	1 359	1 723
Medical services	454	282	114	144	137	298	276	365	491	764
Drugs	198	103	69	92	103	152	161	178	214	288
Medical supplies	66	[2]89	[2]32	[2]31	26	41	76	43	64	97
Entertainment	2 378	1 049	987	1 172	1 063	1 424	1 767	2 022	2 562	3 784
Personal Care Products and Services	536	206	299	343	280	376	373	453	496	867
Reading	65	26	27	34	24	40	52	52	65	106
Education	824	1 329	1 066	859	567	664	1 031	417	698	993
Tobacco Products and Smoking Supplies	365	362	381	332	395	378	419	421	407	291
Miscellaneous	649	105	284	169	275	301	441	638	772	1 052
Cash Contributions	1 038	531	402	261	516	512	647	936	1 125	1 743
Personal Insurance and Pensions	5 311	278	359	690	1 157	1 861	2 837	3 876	5 318	10 810
Life and other personal insurance	161	[2]88	[2]15	[2]20	30	48	80	140	137	333
Pensions and Social Security	5 149	190	344	670	1 127	1 813	2 757	3 736	5 181	10 477

[1]Value less than or equal to 0.05.
[2]Data are likely to have large sampling errors.

Table 11-21. Consumer Expenditures, Averages for Age Groups by Income Before Taxes: Reference Person 35 to 44 Years of Age, 2009–2010

(Number, dollar, percent.)

Item	Total	Complete reporting of income								
		Less than $5,000	$5,000 to $9,999	$10,000 to $14,999	$15,000 to $19,999	$20,000 to $29,999	$30,000 to $39,999	$40,000 to $49,999	$50,000 to $69,999	$70,000 and over
NUMBER OF CONSUMER UNITS (THOUSANDS)	22 055	516	526	793	944	1 978	2 139	2 104	3 603	9 453
CONSUMER UNIT CHARACTERISTICS										
Income Before Taxes	76 569	-2 977	7 953	12 721	17 592	24 825	34 583	44 612	59 368	129 965
Income After Taxes	74 520	-2 455	8 379	13 217	18 382	25 806	34 783	44 341	58 706	125 074
Age of Reference Person	39.6	39.6	39.3	39.5	39.3	39.5	39.5	39.8	39.6	39.7
Average Number in Consumer Unit										
All persons	3.3	2.5	2.4	2.5	2.8	3.1	3.1	3.2	3.4	3.6
Children under 18 years	1.3	1.0	1.1	1.1	1.2	1.3	1.3	1.3	1.3	1.4
Persons 65 years and over	(1)	(2)	(1)	(1)	(1)	(1)	(1)	(1)	(1)	(1)
Earners	1.6	0.6	0.6	0.7	1.0	1.2	1.4	1.5	1.7	1.9
Vehicles	2.1	0.9	1.0	1.0	1.2	1.4	1.7	1.9	2.1	2.6
Percent Distribution										
Male	48	35	43	36	36	39	43	47	50	53
Female	52	65	57	64	64	61	57	53	50	47
Percent Homeowner	65	34	30	27	33	38	51	58	69	84
With mortgage	56	19	12	15	19	26	43	48	58	77
Without mortgage	9	15	18	12	14	13	9	9	10	7
AVERAGE ANNUAL EXPENDITURES	56 640	26 690	21 395	24 344	27 009	29 741	36 037	42 244	48 890	82 708
Food	7 627	4 886	4 200	4 196	4 588	4 957	5 434	6 268	7 023	10 326
Food at home	4 355	3 057	2 921	3 068	3 029	3 497	3 520	3 898	4 154	5 364
Cereals and bakery products	618	436	388	378	434	491	467	513	623	777
Meats, poultry, fish, and eggs	941	706	672	816	758	811	849	925	898	1 073
Dairy products	477	396	326	289	302	349	370	365	467	614
Fruits and vegetables	762	544	481	509	521	596	636	693	725	940
Other food at home	1 556	975	1 054	1 075	1 014	1 249	1 196	1 403	1 441	1 961
Food away from home	3 273	1 829	1 279	1 128	1 559	1 460	1 915	2 370	2 869	4 962
Alcoholic Beverages	498	453	210	257	160	165	298	379	420	754
Housing	20 379	12 347	8 685	10 011	11 240	11 965	13 996	15 495	17 805	28 584
Shelter	12 448	7 516	4 870	6 081	6 753	7 247	8 839	9 470	10 793	17 440
Owned dwellings	8 493	3 591	1 325	1 552	1 958	2 570	4 330	5 048	7 018	13 904
Rented dwellings	3 401	3 779	3 493	4 433	4 709	4 590	4 380	4 220	3 496	2 469
Other lodging	554	2146	252	296	287	87	129	202	280	1 066
Utilities, fuels, and public services	4 085	2 713	2 456	2 526	2 916	3 151	3 377	3 728	4 114	4 922
Household operations	1 395	509	342	308	675	450	565	730	965	2 363
Housekeeping supplies	681	574	328	361	302	395	427	488	610	981
Household furnishings and equipment	1 769	1 034	689	735	593	722	789	1 079	1 322	2 878
Apparel and Services	2 199	1 094	1 770	2 412	1 326	1 409	1 432	1 795	1 527	3 056
Transportation	8 561	2 781	2 975	2 826	4 293	4 424	5 646	6 473	7 934	12 348
Vehicle purchases (net outlay)	2 833	2549	2688	2548	2786	1 369	1 289	1 762	2 403	4 531
Gasoline and motor oil	2 447	1 142	1 069	1 227	1 435	1 744	2 008	2 197	2 515	3 075
Other vehicle expenses	2 734	964	1 109	958	1 705	1 088	2 094	2 252	2 686	3 809
Public transportation	547	126	109	93	366	224	256	262	330	933
Health Care	2 551	1 081	696	916	1 097	1 284	1 863	1 895	2 455	3 625
Health insurance	1 445	522	396	363	546	599	1 114	1 136	1 447	2 053
Medical services	665	402	160	302	229	412	423	394	600	975
Drugs	337	124	114	218	261	215	254	291	320	443
Medical supplies	104	232	226	232	261	57	72	73	88	155
Entertainment	3 192	1 756	822	1 094	1 166	1 386	1 769	2 075	2 624	4 986
Personal Care Products and Services	683	336	371	285	402	414	394	475	551	1 012
Reading	82	27	15	30	30	41	30	48	65	134
Education	949	305	2179	291	291	287	442	492	583	1 646
Tobacco Products and Smoking Supplies	387	442	425	568	439	479	420	433	388	325
Miscellaneous	942	315	318	426	362	505	493	1 289	843	1 262
Cash Contributions	1 557	642	448	421	561	586	990	1 284	1 262	2 368
Personal Insurance and Pensions	7 033	226	282	613	1 056	1 839	2 830	3 845	5 411	12 281
Life and other personal insurance	275	245	221	248	273	70	130	129	209	475
Pensions and Social Security	6 758	181	260	564	983	1 769	2 700	3 715	5 202	11 806

[1]Value less than or equal to 0.05.

Table 11-22. Consumer Expenditures, Averages for Age Groups by Income Before Taxes: Reference Person 45 to 54 Years of Age, 2009–2010

(Number, dollar, percent.)

Item	Total	Complete reporting of income								
		Less than $5,000	$5,000 to $9,999	$10,000 to $14,999	$15,000 to $19,999	$20,000 to $29,999	$30,000 to $39,999	$40,000 to $49,999	$50,000 to $69,999	$70,000 and over
NUMBER OF CONSUMER UNITS (THOUSANDS)	25 247	651	764	955	1 006	2 170	2 343	2 247	4 041	11 070
CONSUMER UNIT CHARACTERISTICS										
Income Before Taxes	80 288	-11 450	8 130	12 404	17 621	24 909	34 765	44 966	59 327	137 522
Income After Taxes	76 868	-12 940	8 421	12 629	17 691	25 060	34 221	44 160	57 878	130 543
Age of Reference Person	49.5	50.0	49.6	49.9	49.6	49.4	49.3	49.5	49.4	49.5
Average Number in Consumer Unit										
All persons	2.8	2.0	1.7	1.8	2.3	2.4	2.5	2.5	2.8	3.2
Children under 18 years	0.6	0.4	0.4	0.2	0.5	0.5	0.6	0.5	0.6	0.8
Persons 65 years and over	(^{1})	(^{1})	(^{1})	(^{1})	(^{1})	0.1	0.1	0	0.1	(^{1})
Earners	1.7	0.5	0.5	0.6	0.9	1.2	1.3	1.5	1.7	2.1
Vehicles	2.3	1.2	0.8	1.1	1.3	1.5	1.8	2.1	2.4	3.0
Percent Distribution										
Male	49	53	41	40	38	41	41	50	45	55
Female	51	47	59	60	62	59	59	50	55	45
Percent Homeowner	73	42	32	41	45	51	61	69	76	90
With mortgage	55	24	19	18	23	33	42	50	58	72
Without mortgage	19	18	14	24	22	18	19	19	18	19
AVERAGE ANNUAL EXPENDITURES	58 243	26 735	17 696	21 835	24 583	29 691	36 339	40 155	47 601	87 124
Food	7 336	3 755	2 859	3 597	3 750	4 740	4 980	5 359	6 316	10 384
Food at home	4 357	2 564	2 184	2 595	2 790	3 402	3 064	3 371	3 749	5 839
Cereals and bakery products	593	377	313	372	346	467	416	464	500	795
Meats, poultry, fish, and eggs	972	569	512	603	690	770	730	819	866	1 255
Dairy products	459	284	236	272	289	345	313	359	394	619
Fruits and vegetables	785	489	371	452	449	608	519	538	663	1 087
Other food at home	1 548	845	752	896	1 016	1 212	1 087	1 190	1 325	2 083
Food away from home	2 979	1 191	674	1 001	960	1 338	1 916	1 989	2 567	4 545
Alcoholic Beverages	457	258	223	206	115	180	342	260	388	693
Housing	18 951	11 761	8 271	9 175	10 134	11 702	13 069	14 536	16 524	26 239
Shelter	11 436	8 138	4 990	5 609	5 598	6 919	7 544	8 700	9 986	15 901
Owned dwellings	8 128	4 848	1 554	2 101	1 995	3 234	4 267	5 409	6 780	12 672
Rented dwellings	2 430	2 994	3 191	3 436	3 501	3 518	3 111	2 975	2 716	1 589
Other lodging	878	^{2}296	^{2}245	^{2}71	^{2}102	168	165	316	490	1 641
Utilities, fuels, and public services	4 245	2 663	2 378	2 530	3 008	3 313	3 514	3 669	4 114	5 228
Household operations	950	432	232	248	318	346	436	572	656	1 559
Housekeeping supplies	676	231	331	357	435	477	421	425	567	969
Household furnishings and equipment	1 645	296	340	432	775	647	1 154	1 170	1 201	2 581
Apparel and Services	1 927	576	1 100	442	1 010	1 352	1 554	1 244	1 409	2 835
Transportation	9 330	3 552	1 921	2 981	3 996	4 442	6 240	6 895	7 870	13 875
Vehicle purchases (net outlay)	3 138	^{2}3 812	^{2}3 319	^{2}3 711	1 165	838	2 049	2 029	2 042	5 164
Gasoline and motor oil	2 486	1 077	820	1 188	1 361	1 764	1 904	2 137	2 530	3 217
Other vehicle expenses	3 110	1 413	678	937	1 316	1 647	2 057	2 479	2 939	4 448
Public transportation	597	249	104	145	155	191	230	250	359	1 046
Health Care	3 217	1 421	650	1 877	1 429	1 747	2 329	2 522	3 035	4 462
Health insurance	1 717	638	423	746	661	895	1 289	1 389	1 743	2 359
Medical services	870	501	82	558	379	448	550	639	724	1 268
Drugs	491	252	128	542	359	351	398	402	428	628
Medical supplies	138	^{2}30	^{2}18	^{2}31	30	52	92	92	139	208
Entertainment	3 130	1 768	823	953	1 225	1 383	1 650	1 917	2 255	4 972
Personal Care Products and Services	670	242	178	182	259	369	411	489	576	999
Reading	112	91	23	22	40	37	57	72	80	179
Education	2 074	^{2}643	^{2}400	208	137	242	542	570	823	4 059
Tobacco Products and Smoking Supplies	481	531	424	626	492	591	557	535	562	391
Miscellaneous	994	439	294	444	290	356	788	766	876	1 449
Cash Contributions	1 902	761	262	589	539	775	895	976	1 421	3 118
Personal Insurance and Pensions	7 661	937	268	535	1 166	1 776	2 925	4 015	5 469	13 468
Life and other personal insurance	434	^{2}227	67	79	171	125	203	208	278	739
Pensions and Social Security	7 227	709	201	456	995	1 652	2 722	3 807	5 191	12 728

^{1}Value less than or equal to 0.05.
^{2}Data are likely to have large sampling errors.

Table 11-23. Consumer Expenditures, Averages for Age Groups by Income Before Taxes: Reference Person 55 to 64 Years of Age, 2009–2010

(Number, dollar, percent.)

Item	Total	Complete reporting of income								
		Less than $5,000	$5,000 to $9,999	$10,000 to $14,999	$15,000 to $19,999	$20,000 to $29,999	$30,000 to $39,999	$40,000 to $49,999	$50,000 to $69,999	$70,000 and over
NUMBER OF CONSUMER UNITS (THOUSANDS)	21 045	749	759	1 168	1 143	2 280	2 082	2 165	3 056	7 643
CONSUMER UNIT CHARACTERISTICS										
Income Before Taxes	69 745	467	8 246	12 693	17 477	25 044	34 899	44 523	59 299	133 327
Income After Taxes	67 091	533	8 273	12 591	17 449	24 866	34 199	43 510	57 197	127 402
Age of Reference Person	59.2	59.2	59.7	59.4	59.7	59.5	59.4	59.4	59.2	58.8
Average Number in Consumer Unit										
All persons	2.1	1.4	1.5	1.5	1.7	1.8	2.0	2.0	2.2	2.5
Children under 18 years	0.2	[1]1.1	[1]1.1	[1]1.1	0.2	0.1	0.1	0.1	0.2	0.2
Persons 65 years and over	0.1	([2])	([2])	([2])	0.1	0.1	0.1	0.1	0.1	0.1
Earners	1.3	0.3	0.4	0.5	0.6	0.8	1.1	1.2	1.5	1.9
Vehicles	2.2	1.2	0.9	1.1	1.4	1.7	1.9	2.2	2.6	2.9
Percent Distribution										
Male	48	46	38	41	41	42	42	46	53	54
Female	52	54	62	59	59	58	58	54	47	46
Percent Homeowner	80	50	41	51	65	72	77	85	86	94
With mortgage	46	21	14	16	29	29	39	45	53	63
Without mortgage	34	29	27	34	37	43	38	39	33	31
AVERAGE ANNUAL EXPENDITURES	51 670	25 973	17 752	21 447	25 043	29 104	33 554	40 552	49 889	81 773
Food	6 184	3 676	3 064	3 492	3 358	3 841	4 288	4 969	5 932	9 285
Food at home	3 679	2 330	2 275	2 488	2 283	2 677	2 800	3 212	3 479	5 127
Cereals and bakery products	486	311	278	303	315	363	396	415	452	677
Meats, poultry, fish, and eggs	820	491	508	645	537	589	663	753	770	1 112
Dairy products	382	218	248	272	228	261	262	341	358	545
Fruits and vegetables	678	433	424	431	415	527	492	567	620	963
Other food at home	1 313	877	818	837	788	938	987	1 136	1 279	1 831
Food away from home	2 505	1 346	789	1 005	1 075	1 164	1 488	1 757	2 452	4 158
Alcoholic Beverages	421	257	233	183	124	167	163	259	408	742
Housing	16 830	10 464	7 685	8 951	10 211	10 944	12 209	13 595	16 382	24 703
Shelter	9 570	6 235	4 391	5 352	5 836	6 061	6 667	7 618	9 303	14 113
Owned dwellings	6 960	2 912	1 525	1 982	3 251	3 638	4 494	5 773	7 209	11 112
Rented dwellings	1 630	2 942	2 644	3 169	2 285	2 099	1 888	1 488	1 327	1 019
Other lodging	980	381	[1]222	201	299	324	285	357	767	1 982
Utilities, fuels, and public services	3 938	2 369	2 228	2 347	2 911	3 270	3 429	3 542	4 117	5 037
Household operations	876	381	238	397	370	462	526	606	781	1 471
Housekeeping supplies	770	474	354	344	412	419	503	692	649	1 226
Household furnishings and equipment	1 675	1 004	474	511	682	732	1 085	1 138	1 533	2 856
Apparel and Services	1 581	717	476	619	663	772	938	1 152	1 353	2 712
Transportation	8 215	3 440	2 053	2 673	4 012	4 593	5 990	7 978	9 131	12 144
Vehicle purchases (net outlay)	2 667	[1]1 052	[1]222	[1]480	[1]778	1 447	1 718	3 141	3 265	3 933
Gasoline and motor oil	2 146	1 067	796	1 011	1 306	1 521	1 774	2 081	2 310	2 924
Other vehicle expenses	2 861	1 075	935	1 046	1 751	1 420	2 324	2 486	3 105	4 240
Public transportation	542	246	100	136	177	205	174	271	450	1 047
Health Care	3 877	2 082	1 259	1 756	2 105	2 877	2 964	3 469	4 049	5 500
Health insurance	2 064	1 232	767	963	1 063	1 628	1 662	1 937	2 177	2 824
Medical services	998	399	185	347	482	618	700	703	1 054	1 569
Drugs	672	368	275	386	512	556	531	706	677	874
Medical supplies	143	84	132	60	49	75	72	123	141	233
Entertainment	2 793	1 518	935	1 048	1 261	1 682	1 808	1 986	2 835	4 415
Personal Care Products and Services	607	333	242	237	263	350	407	439	510	1 005
Reading	136	78	31	45	58	76	82	90	138	223
Education	959	[1]152	[1]265	[1]126	182	189	205	504	487	2 105
Tobacco Products and Smoking Supplies	430	465	431	405	620	524	462	398	456	365
Miscellaneous	1 050	948	239	871	473	607	607	761	1 584	1 338
Cash Contributions	1 991	859	492	516	804	755	935	1 428	1 501	3 664
Personal Insurance and Pensions	6 595	986	349	523	908	1 727	2 495	3 523	5 123	13 572
Life and other personal insurance	459	140	97	126	142	165	255	309	446	815
Pensions and Social Security	6 136	846	252	398	766	1 561	2 240	3 215	4 677	12 757

[1]Data are likely to have large sampling errors.
[2]Value less than or equal to 0.05.

Table 11-24. Consumer Expenditures, Averages for Age Groups by Income Before Taxes: Reference Person 65 Years of Age and Over, 2009–2010

(Number, dollar, percent.)

Item	Complete reporting of income									
	Total	Less than $5,000	$5,000 to $9,999	$10,000 to $14,999	$15,000 to $19,999	$20,000 to $29,999	$30,000 to $39,999	$40,000 to $49,999	$50,000 to $69,999	$70,000 and over
NUMBER OF CONSUMER UNITS (THOUSANDS)	24 570	801	1 395	3 155	2 928	4 751	3 213	2 098	2 935	3 294
CONSUMER UNIT CHARACTERISTICS										
Income Before Taxes	40 574	-6 090	8 454	12 634	17 418	24 818	34 923	44 989	58 729	122 107
Income After Taxes	39 841	-6 607	8 317	12 648	17 347	24 649	34 751	44 476	57 903	118 343
Age of Reference Person	74.9	75.3	76.6	77.8	76.8	75.6	74.6	74.0	72.9	71.6
Average Number in Consumer Unit										
All persons	1.7	1.3	1.2	1.2	1.4	1.7	1.8	2.0	2.1	2.4
Children under 18 years	0.1	(1)	(1)	(1)	(1)	0.1	0.1	0.1	0.1	0.1
Persons 65 years and over	1.4	1.2	1.1	1.1	1.2	1.4	1.5	1.5	1.5	1.5
Earners	0.5	0.1	0.1	0.1	0.1	0.3	0.4	0.6	0.8	1.3
Vehicles	1.6	0.9	0.8	0.9	1.1	1.6	1.7	2.0	2.2	2.6
Percent Distribution										
Male	43	37	25	28	33	42	43	54	57	61
Female	57	63	75	72	67	58	57	46	43	39
Percent Homeowner	80	57	59	63	73	80	89	88	91	95
With mortgage	22	8	12	10	14	18	20	24	31	44
Without mortgage	58	49	47	53	59	62	68	64	60	51
AVERAGE ANNUAL EXPENDITURES	37 178	24 030	17 486	18 751	23 577	29 211	36 724	38 392	49 855	76 169
Food	4 728	3 054	2 598	2 913	2 980	3 781	4 751	5 106	6 128	8 249
Food at home	3 084	2 354	2 121	2 241	2 149	2 678	3 025	3 329	3 908	4 608
Cereals and bakery products	427	337	325	297	304	411	439	466	517	581
Meats, poultry, fish, and eggs	690	495	476	473	466	563	658	711	970	1 073
Dairy products	331	254	262	217	227	294	315	379	419	485
Fruits and vegetables	597	496	402	386	442	515	600	601	750	928
Other food at home	1 040	772	655	868	711	894	1 013	1 171	1 254	1 541
Food away from home	1 643	700	477	672	830	1 103	1 726	1 777	2 220	3 640
Alcoholic Beverages	294	2174	31	58	124	172	332	269	439	734
Housing	13 105	10 251	7 802	7 953	9 755	11 018	12 504	13 098	16 280	24 361
Shelter	7 100	6 130	4 542	4 517	5 245	5 791	6 532	6 898	8 720	13 668
Owned dwellings	4 860	3 024	2 067	2 261	3 038	3 730	4 882	4 928	6 394	10 794
Rented dwellings	1 627	2 979	2 414	2 160	2 031	1 676	1 149	1 410	1 355	874
Other lodging	613	127	261	96	176	385	500	559	971	2 001
Utilities, fuels, and public services	3 342	2 469	2 130	2 299	2 808	3 187	3 473	3 598	3 947	4 934
Household operations	851	843	295	397	624	659	744	747	1 058	1 989
Housekeeping supplies	673	369	399	375	411	600	640	742	869	1 143
Household furnishings and equipment	1 138	440	435	364	667	780	1 116	1 113	1 685	2 626
Apparel and Services	1 016	483	465	449	605	690	858	937	1 443	2 324
Transportation	5 325	2 721	2 017	2 063	2 978	4 231	5 681	5 747	7 903	11 155
Vehicle purchases (net outlay)	1 678	2581	2362	2385	758	1 165	1 720	1 970	2 560	4 288
Gasoline and motor oil	1 319	781	599	614	818	1 173	1 415	1 588	1 905	2 296
Other vehicle expenses	1 963	1 175	930	936	1 228	1 704	2 202	1 846	2 920	3 511
Public transportation	365	183	126	128	173	189	345	342	518	1 060
Health Care	4 845	3 405	2 151	2 642	3 483	4 771	5 164	5 751	6 420	7 434
Health insurance	3 056	1 856	1 497	1 794	2 280	3 089	3 367	3 630	4 007	4 343
Medical services	808	963	279	300	451	735	721	878	1 158	1 630
Drugs	816	454	305	484	613	795	910	1 069	1 038	1 168
Medical supplies	164	131	69	64	139	151	167	173	216	292
Entertainment	1 976	895	858	893	1 113	1 445	2 158	1 865	2 608	4 399
Personal Care Products and Services	524	337	270	272	356	390	500	564	747	1 007
Reading	143	66	48	60	88	113	160	160	189	305
Education	177	2175	237	285	33	81	123	104	407	478
Tobacco Products and Smoking Supplies	217	176	122	122	181	242	225	219	273	298
Miscellaneous	718	578	235	358	379	477	814	590	782	1 770
Cash Contributions	2 249	1 463	632	659	1 189	1 195	2 369	2 323	3 521	5 809
Personal Insurance and Pensions	1 864	253	221	225	314	606	1 084	1 659	2 716	7 845
Life and other personal insurance	317	194	157	146	177	194	291	301	423	822
Pensions and Social Security	1 547	259	64	79	137	412	792	1 358	2 293	7 024

1Value less than or equal to 0.05.
2Data are likely to have large sampling errors.

Chapter Twelve

AMERICAN TIME USE SURVEY

AMERICAN TIME USE SURVEY

HIGHLIGHTS

This chapter presents data from the American Time Use Survey (ATUS). The survey was introduced in the sixth edition of the *Handbook of U.S. Labor Statistics*. Its purpose is to collect data on the activities people do during the day and the amount of time they spend on each one.

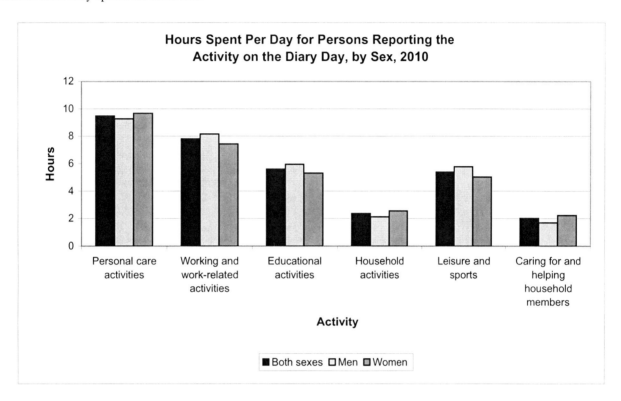

On days that they worked, men worked 41 minutes more than women. This difference partly reflects women's greater likelihood of working part-time. However, even among full-time workers, men worked longer (8.2 hours compared with 7.8 hours). Meanwhile, women spent more time on household activities and caring for and helping household members. On an average day, 20.0 percent of men did housework compared with 48.5 percent of women. (See Table 12-1.)

OTHER HIGHLIGHTS

• Nearly 82 percent of employed persons worked on an average weekday while only 35.4 percent of employed persons worked on an average Saturday, Sunday, or holiday. (See Table 12-3.)

• Transportation and material moving workers had the longest average workday (8.34 hours), followed by production workers (8.25 hours) and construction and extraction workers (8.14 hours). Farming, fishing, and forestry workers had the shortest day on average (5.83 hours). (See Table 12-4.)

• Multiple jobholders were nearly twice as likely to work at home than single job holders (38.9 percent compared to 21.8 percent). (See Table 12-5.)

• The more education a person attained, the greater the likelihood they worked at home in 2010. Over 36 percent of those with a Bachelor's degree reported working at home on an average day compared with 16.6 percent of those with a high school diploma and 10.4 percent of those with less than a high school diploma. (See Table 12-5.)

NOTES AND DEFINITIONS

Survey Methodology

While the Bureau of Labor Statistics (BLS) has long produced statistics about the labor market, including information about employment, hours, and earnings, the American Time Use Survey (ATUS) marks the first time that a federal statistical agency has produced estimates on how Americans spend another critical resource—their time. Data collection for the ATUS began in January 2003. Sample cases for the survey are selected monthly, and interviews are conducted continuously throughout the year. In 2010, approximately 13,200 individuals were interviewed.

ATUS sample households are chosen from the households that have completed their eighth (final) interview for the Current Population Survey (CPS), the nation's monthly household labor force survey. (See Chapter 1 of this *Handbook* for a description of the CPS.) ATUS sample households are selected to ensure that estimates will be representative of the nation.

An individual age 15 years or older is randomly chosen from each sample household. This "designated person" takes part in a one-time telephone interview about his or her activities on the previous day (the "diary day").

All ATUS interviews are conducted using Computer Assisted Telephone Interviewing. Procedures are in place to collect information from the small number of households that did not provide a telephone number during the CPS interview.

Concepts and Definitions

Average day. The average day measure reflects an average distribution across all persons in the reference population and all days of the week. Average day measures for the entire population provide a mechanism for seeing the overall distribution of time allocation for society as a whole. The ATUS collects data about daily activities from all segments of the population age 15 and over, including persons who are employed and not employed. Many activities are not typically done on a daily basis, and some activities are only done by a subset of the population.

Average hours per day. The average number of hours spent in a 24-hour day (between 4 a.m. on the diary day and 4 a.m. on the interview day) doing a specified activity.

Average hours per day, population. The average number of hours per day spent on a particular activity is computed using all responses from the sample population, including those from respondents who did not do the particular activity on their diary day. These estimates reflect the total num-ber of respondents engaged in an activity and the total amount of time they spent on the activity.

Average hours per day, persons reporting the activity on the diary day. The average number of hours per day spent on a particular activity is computed using responses only from those engaged in the particular activity on the diary day.

Diary day. The diary day is the day about which the designated person reports. For example, the diary day of a designated person interviewed on Tuesday would be Monday.

Earnings

Usual weekly earnings. Data represent the earnings of full-time wage and salary workers before taxes and other deductions and include any overtime pay, commissions, or tips usually received (at the main job in the case of multiple jobholders). Usual weekly earnings are only updated in ATUS for about a third of employed respondents—if the respondent changed jobs or employment status or if the CPS weekly earnings value was imputed. This means that the earnings information could be out of date because the CPS interview was done 2 to 5 months prior to the ATUS interview. Respondents are asked to identify the easiest way for them to report earnings (hourly, weekly, biweekly, twice monthly, annually, or other) and how much they usually earn in the reported time period. Earnings reported on a basis other than weekly are converted to a weekly equivalent. The term "usual" is as perceived by the respondent. If the respondent asks for a definition of usual, interviewers are instructed to define the term as more than half the weeks worked during the past 4 or 5 months.

Weekly earnings ranges. The ranges used represent approximately 25 percent of full-time wage and salary workers. For example, 25 percent of full-time wage and salary workers with one job only had weekly earnings of $500 or less. These dollar values vary from year to year.

Employment Status

Employed. All persons who, at any time during the seven days prior to the interview: (1) did any work at all as paid employees, worked in their own business professions, or on their own farms, or usually worked 15 hours or more as unpaid workers in family-operated enterprises; and (2) all those who were not working but had jobs or businesses from which they were temporarily absent due to illness, bad weather, vacation, childcare problems, labor-management disputes, maternity or paternity leave, job training, or other family or personal reasons, whether or not they were paid for the time off or were seeking other jobs.

Employed full time. Full-time workers are those who usually work 35 hours or more per week at all jobs combined.

Employed part time. Part-time workers are those who usually work fewer than 35 hours per week at all jobs combined.

Not employed. Persons are not employed if they do not meet the conditions for employment. Not employed workers include those classified as unemployed as well as those classified as not in the labor force (using CPS definitions).

The numbers of employed and not employed persons in this report do not correspond to published totals from the CPS. While the information on employment from the ATUS is useful for assessing work in the context of other daily activities, the employment data are not intended for analysis of current employment trends. Compared to the CPS and other estimates of employment, the ATUS estimates are based on a much smaller sample and are only available with a substantial lag.

Household children. Household children are children under 18 years of age who reside in the household of the ATUS respondent. The children may be related to the respondent (such as their own children, grandchildren, nieces, nephews, brothers, or sisters) or not related (such as foster children or children of roommates). For secondary childcare calculations, respondents are asked about care of household children under 13 years of age.

Primary activity. A primary activity is the main activity of a respondent at a specified time.

Secondary activities. A secondary (or simultaneous) activity is an activity done at the same time as a primary activity. With the exception of the care of children under age 13, information on secondary activities is not systematically collected in the ATUS.

Major Activity Category Definitions

Personal care activities. Personal care activities include sleeping, bathing, dressing, health-related self-care, and personal or private activities. Receiving unpaid personal care from others (for example, "my sister put polish on my nails") is also captured in this category.

Eating and drinking. All time spent eating or drinking (except when identified by the respondent as part of a work or volunteer activity), whether alone, with others, at home, at a place of purchase, in transit, or somewhere else, is classified in this category.

Household activities. Household activities are those done by respondents to maintain their households. These include housework, cooking, yard care, pet care, vehicle maintenance and repair, and home maintenance, repair, decoration, and renovation. Food preparation is always classified as a household activity. Household management and organizational activities—such as filling out paperwork, balancing a checkbook, or planning a party—are also included in this category.

Purchasing goods and services. This category includes the purchase of consumer goods as well as the purchase or use of professional and personal care services, household services, and government services. Most purchases and rentals of consumer goods, regardless of mode or place of purchase or rental (in person, via telephone, over the Internet, at home, or in a store), are classified in this category. Time spent obtaining, receiving, and purchasing professional and personal care services provided by someone else is also classified in this category, which also includes time spent arranging for and purchasing household services provided by someone else.

Caring for and helping household members. Time spent doing activities to care for or help any child (under age 18) or adult in the household, regardless of relationship to the respondent or the physical or mental health status of the person being helped, is classified here. Caring for and helping activities for household children and adults are coded separately in subcategories.

Caring for and helping non-household members. Time spent caring for and helping any child or adult who is not part of the respondent's household, regardless of the relationship to the respondent or the physical or mental health status of the person being helped, is classified in this category.

Working and work-related activities. This category includes time spent working, doing activities as part of one's job, engaging in income-generating activities (not as part of one's job), and job search activities. "Working" includes hours spent doing the specific tasks required of one's main or other job, regardless of location or time of day. Travel time related to working and work-related activities includes time spent commuting to and from one's job, as well as time spent traveling for work-related activities, generating income, and job searching.

Educational activities. Educational activities include taking classes (including Internet and other distance-learning courses), doing research and homework, and taking care of administrative tasks, such as registering for classes or obtaining a school ID. For high school students, before- and after-school extracurricular activities (except sports) also are classified as educational activities.

Organizational, civic, and religious activities. This category captures time spent volunteering for or through an organization, performing civic obligations, and participating in religious and spiritual activities.

Leisure and sports. The leisure and sports category includes sports, exercise, and recreation; socializing and communicating; and other leisure activities, such as watching television, reading or attending entertainment events.

Telephone calls, mail, and email. This category captures telephone communication and handling household or personal mail and email. Telephone and Internet purchases are classified in purchasing goods and services.

Other activities, not elsewhere classified. This residual category includes security procedures related to traveling, traveling not associated with a specific activity category, ambiguous activities that could not be coded, or missing activities that were considered too private to report.

Sources of Additional Information

Additional information, including expanded definitions and estimation methodology, is available from BLS news release USDL 11-0919, "American Time Use Survey—2010 Results"; the June 2005 edition of the *Monthly Labor Review;* and the *ATUS User's Guide,* June 2008. All of these resources are available on the BLS Web site at <http://www.bls.gov/tus/>.

Table 12-1. Average Hours Per Day Spent in Primary Activities[1] for the Total Population and for Persons Reporting the Activity on the Diary Day, by Activity Category and Sex, 2009 and 2010 Annual Averages

(Hours, percent.)

Activity	Hours per day, total population			Percent of population reporting the activity on the diary day			Hours per day for persons reporting the activity on the diary day		
	Both sexes	Men	Women	Both sexes	Men	Women	Both sexes	Men	Women
2009									
All Activities[2]	24.00	24.00	24.00	X	X	X	X	X	X
Personal care activities	9.45	9.25	9.63	100.0	100.0	100.0	9.45	9.26	9.63
Sleeping	8.67	8.62	8.73	99.9	99.8	100.0	8.68	8.63	8.73
Eating and drinking	1.22	1.26	1.19	96.4	96.1	96.8	1.27	1.31	1.23
Household activities	1.80	1.33	2.24	76.1	66.6	85.0	2.36	2.00	2.63
Housework	0.60	0.26	0.92	36.3	20.2	51.3	1.65	1.27	1.79
Food preparation and cleanup	0.54	0.29	0.77	54.6	39.9	68.3	0.99	0.73	1.13
Lawn and garden care	0.20	0.28	0.12	9.4	11.5	7.4	2.11	2.42	1.67
Household management	0.13	0.11	0.16	19.1	16.4	21.6	0.70	0.67	0.72
Purchasing goods and services	0.76	0.64	0.88	44.4	39.2	49.2	1.71	1.62	1.78
Consumer goods purchases	0.38	0.30	0.46	40.2	35.8	44.4	0.94	0.83	1.03
Professional and personal care services	0.09	0.06	0.11	8.6	6.4	10.7	0.99	0.98	1.00
Caring for and helping household members	0.54	0.37	0.70	25.2	20.2	29.9	2.13	1.81	2.34
Caring for and helping household children	0.43	0.28	0.57	21.6	16.4	26.5	1.98	1.71	2.14
Caring for and helping non-household members	0.21	0.19	0.22	13.4	11.4	15.2	1.55	1.69	1.46
Caring for and helping non-household adults	0.07	0.08	0.06	8.7	7.8	9.6	0.82	1.02	0.67
Working and work-related activities	3.53	4.26	2.85	45.4	51.9	39.2	7.78	8.20	7.26
Working	3.18	3.81	2.58	42.7	48.4	37.3	7.44	7.86	6.93
Educational activities	0.46	0.43	0.50	8.2	7.4	8.9	5.68	5.84	5.56
Attending class	0.26	0.26	0.27	5.2	5.1	5.3	5.03	5.01	5.05
Homework and research	0.16	0.14	0.18	5.6	4.9	6.3	2.82	2.84	2.81
Organizational, civic, and religious activities	0.34	0.32	0.36	14.5	12.6	16.4	2.32	2.53	2.17
Religious and spiritual activities	0.15	0.12	0.17	9.0	7.0	10.8	1.62	1.78	1.53
Volunteering (organizational and civic activities)	0.15	0.15	0.15	7.2	7.1	7.2	2.11	2.17	2.07
Leisure and sports	5.25	5.59	4.93	96.1	95.9	96.2	5.46	5.83	5.13
Socializing and communicating	0.70	0.63	0.76	39.2	34.6	43.4	1.78	1.81	1.76
Watching television	2.82	3.10	2.56	81.8	82.7	81.0	3.45	3.75	3.17
Participating in sports, exercise, and recreation	0.31	0.41	0.21	18.2	20.9	15.7	1.69	1.96	1.36
Telephone calls, mail, and e-mail	0.20	0.14	0.25	25.7	19.6	31.4	0.77	0.71	0.80
Other activities n.e.c.	0.24	0.23	0.26	15.7	13.6	17.8	1.55	1.69	1.44
2010									
All Activities[2]	24.00	24.00	24.00	X	X	X	X	X	X
Personal care activities	9.47	9.25	9.67	99.9	99.9	100.0	9.48	9.26	9.68
Sleeping	8.67	8.56	8.76	99.9	99.9	99.9	8.68	8.58	8.77
Eating and drinking	1.25	1.29	1.21	95.9	96.1	95.7	1.30	1.34	1.26
Household activities	1.79	1.42	2.14	75.5	66.8	83.7	2.38	2.13	2.56
Housework	0.57	0.26	0.87	34.7	20.0	48.5	1.65	1.30	1.79
Food preparation and cleanup	0.56	0.32	0.79	54.8	41.3	67.5	1.02	0.77	1.16
Lawn and garden care	0.21	0.31	0.12	9.9	12.3	7.6	2.14	2.51	1.57
Household management	0.12	0.10	0.15	17.7	14.0	21.3	0.70	0.71	0.69
Purchasing goods and services	0.75	0.62	0.86	43.9	40.2	47.4	1.70	1.55	1.81
Consumer goods purchases	0.37	0.30	0.44	39.8	36.6	42.9	0.94	0.83	1.03
Professional and personal care services	0.08	0.06	0.10	8.1	6.2	9.8	0.99	0.97	1.00
Caring for and helping household members	0.51	0.33	0.67	25.0	19.6	30.1	2.03	1.70	2.24
Caring for and helping household children	0.40	0.26	0.54	21.3	16.3	26.0	1.90	1.57	2.09
Caring for and helping non-household members	0.21	0.19	0.23	12.3	11.3	13.3	1.72	1.73	1.72
Caring for and helping non-household adults	0.08	0.08	0.08	8.0	7.7	8.3	1.01	1.08	0.95
Working and work-related activities	3.50	4.09	2.94	44.7	50.1	39.6	7.82	8.15	7.44
Working	3.14	3.65	2.66	42.0	46.8	37.4	7.48	7.79	7.11
Educational activities	0.47	0.47	0.48	8.4	7.8	9.0	5.61	5.96	5.32
Attending class	0.28	0.30	0.26	5.6	5.8	5.5	4.92	5.20	4.65
Homework and research	0.16	0.13	0.18	5.9	5.3	6.5	2.68	2.53	2.80
Organizational, civic, and religious activities	0.35	0.30	0.40	14.8	11.9	17.6	2.34	2.49	2.25
Religious and spiritual activities	0.16	0.13	0.18	9.2	7.3	11.0	1.69	1.84	1.59
Volunteering (organizational and civic activities)	0.15	0.13	0.18	7.0	5.7	8.2	2.19	2.23	2.16
Leisure and sports	5.18	5.57	4.82	95.8	96.1	95.4	5.41	5.79	5.05
Socializing and communicating	0.70	0.68	0.73	37.0	34.4	39.5	1.90	1.97	1.85
Watching television	2.73	2.94	2.53	79.4	80.4	78.4	3.44	3.66	3.22
Participating in sports, exercise, and recreation	0.31	0.42	0.20	18.5	21.5	15.6	1.66	1.93	1.30
Telephone calls, mail, and e-mail	0.18	0.13	0.21	23.0	18.0	27.8	0.76	0.75	0.77
Other activities n.e.c.	0.35	0.33	0.36	18.8	18.1	19.6	1.84	1.84	1.85

Note: Data refer to respondents age 15 years and over, unless otherwise specified.

n.e.c. = Not elsewhere classified.

[1]A primary activity is designated by a respondent as his or her main activity. Other activities done simultaneously are not included.
[2]All major activity categories include related travel time.
X = Not applicable.

Table 12-2. Average Hours Per Day Spent in Primary Activities[1] for the Total Population, by Age, Sex, Race, Hispanic Origin, and Educational Attainment, 2010 Annual Averages

(Hours.)

Characteristic	Hours per day spent in primary activities[2]											
	Personal care activities	Eating and drinking	Household activities	Purchasing goods and services	Caring for and helping household members	Caring for and helping non-household members	Working and work-related activities	Educational activities	Organizational, civic, and religious activities	Leisure activities	Telephone calls, mail, and e-mail	Other activities n.e.c.
Both Sexes, 15 Years and Over	9.47	1.25	1.79	0.75	0.51	0.21	3.50	0.47	0.35	5.18	0.18	0.35
15 to 19 years	10.34	1.00	0.77	0.51	0.14	0.18	1.00	3.40	0.27	5.69	0.28	0.42
20 to 24 years	9.79	1.16	1.26	0.65	0.56	0.20	3.38	0.95	0.21	5.34	0.13	0.37
25 to 34 years	9.38	1.24	1.44	0.70	1.01	0.17	4.70	0.26	0.27	4.40	0.13	0.30
35 to 44 years	9.13	1.19	1.93	0.79	1.07	0.15	4.67	0.14	0.31	4.17	0.12	0.33
45 to 54 years	9.02	1.22	2.02	0.74	0.38	0.27	4.71	0.10	0.37	4.66	0.16	0.36
55 to 64 years	9.37	1.30	2.07	0.84	0.12	0.27	3.84	0.06	0.38	5.24	0.20	0.29
65 to 74 years	9.67	1.42	2.41	0.94	0.11	0.31	1.15	0.00	0.52	6.85	0.23	0.37
75 years and over	10.11	1.52	2.29	0.74	0.04	0.12	0.23	0.00	0.56	7.69	0.27	0.41
Men, 15 Years and Over	9.25	1.29	1.42	0.62	0.33	0.19	4.09	0.47	0.30	5.57	0.13	0.33
15 to 19 years	10.25	0.93	0.69	0.45	0.07	0.17	1.00	3.13	0.28	6.29	0.28	0.46
20 to 24 years	9.64	1.22	1.01	0.56	0.13	0.20	3.47	1.21	0.15	5.99	0.11	0.32
25 to 34 years	8.98	1.29	1.08	0.61	0.58	0.18	5.56	0.26	0.24	4.80	0.12	0.29
35 to 44 years	8.92	1.25	1.47	0.70	0.79	0.18	5.50	0.07	0.29	4.51	0.08	0.24
45 to 54 years	8.80	1.27	1.64	0.55	0.29	0.21	5.38	0.03	0.35	4.97	0.09	0.41
55 to 64 years	9.21	1.38	1.68	0.68	0.11	0.22	4.35	0.06	0.30	5.58	0.15	0.28
65 to 74 years	9.63	1.45	2.04	0.74	0.10	0.26	1.48	*	0.43	7.37	0.11	0.35
75 years and over	9.87	1.59	1.85	0.72	0.03	0.14	0.33	0.00	0.38	8.41	0.26	0.43
Women, 15 Years and Over	9.67	1.21	2.14	0.86	0.67	0.23	2.94	0.48	0.40	4.82	0.21	0.36
15 to 19 years	10.43	1.08	0.86	0.57	0.22	0.18	1.00	3.67	0.26	5.08	0.27	0.39
20 to 24 years	9.95	1.11	1.51	0.74	0.98	0.20	3.28	0.70	0.27	4.69	0.15	0.43
25 to 34 years	9.78	1.19	1.80	0.80	1.43	0.16	3.83	0.27	0.29	3.99	0.14	0.32
35 to 44 years	9.33	1.12	2.38	0.87	1.35	0.13	3.85	0.21	0.34	3.85	0.15	0.42
45 to 54 years	9.23	1.17	2.40	0.92	0.46	0.34	4.06	0.16	0.38	4.35	0.22	0.32
55 to 64 years	9.52	1.22	2.43	1.00	0.13	0.31	3.38	0.05	0.46	4.93	0.25	0.31
65 to 74 years	9.71	1.39	2.72	1.10	0.12	0.35	0.87	0.00	0.60	6.41	0.33	0.38
75 years and over	10.28	1.48	2.59	0.75	0.05	0.11	0.17	0.00	0.68	7.20	0.28	0.40
White, 15 Years and Over	9.39	1.29	1.86	0.76	0.51	0.21	3.55	0.45	0.33	5.14	0.16	0.35
Men	9.20	1.32	1.47	0.62	0.33	0.19	4.15	0.46	0.27	5.53	0.12	0.33
Women	9.59	1.25	2.24	0.89	0.67	0.23	2.97	0.44	0.39	4.77	0.21	0.36
Black, 15 Years and Over	9.95	0.93	1.38	0.72	0.46	0.23	3.05	0.56	0.51	5.61	0.25	0.33
Men	9.58	0.98	1.12	0.64	0.26	0.19	3.65	0.40	0.55	6.09	0.22	0.32
Women	10.26	0.88	1.60	0.79	0.63	0.27	2.57	0.69	0.49	5.21	0.28	0.34
Hispanic,[3] 15 Years and Over	9.74	1.23	1.77	0.73	0.71	0.21	3.36	0.59	0.27	4.89	0.12	0.37
Men	9.54	1.29	1.12	0.65	0.44	0.21	4.03	0.55	0.24	5.47	0.10	0.36
Women	9.96	1.17	2.46	0.81	0.99	0.20	2.66	0.64	0.31	4.28	0.14	0.38
Marital Status and Sex												
Married, spouse present	9.23	1.34	2.12	0.81	0.72	0.21	3.83	0.08	0.40	4.76	0.14	0.36
Men	9.06	1.38	1.63	0.66	0.52	0.18	4.57	0.05	0.35	5.16	0.10	0.34
Women	9.40	1.30	2.61	0.96	0.93	0.24	3.09	0.11	0.45	4.36	0.19	0.37
Other marital statuses	9.73	1.15	1.44	0.68	0.27	0.21	3.13	0.90	0.30	5.64	0.21	0.34
Men	9.49	1.18	1.18	0.58	0.11	0.21	3.51	0.96	0.24	6.04	0.18	0.32
Women	9.95	1.12	1.67	0.76	0.41	0.22	2.80	0.85	0.34	5.28	0.24	0.35
Educational Attainment, 25 Years and Over												
Less than a high school diploma	9.92	1.13	2.15	0.63	0.50	0.26	2.40	0.04	0.38	6.08	0.10	0.41
High school graduate, no college[4]	9.49	1.22	2.12	0.77	0.41	0.24	3.40	0.05	0.32	5.53	0.14	0.30
Some college or associate degree	9.30	1.24	1.90	0.83	0.56	0.21	3.79	0.21	0.39	5.02	0.21	0.34
Bachelor's degree and higher[5]	9.03	1.42	1.77	0.80	0.67	0.19	4.63	0.13	0.40	4.41	0.19	0.35

Note: Data refer to persons age 15 years and over, unless otherwise specified

n.e.c. = Not elsewhere classified.

[1]A primary activity is designated by a respondent as his or her main activity. Other activities done simultaneously are not included.
[2]All major activity categories include related travel time.
[3]May be of any race.
[4]Includes persons with a high school diploma or equivalent.
[5]Includes persons with bachelor's, master's, professional, and doctoral degrees.
* = Figure does not meet standards of reliability or quality.

Table 12-3. Average Hours Worked Per Day by Employed Persons on Weekdays and Weekends, by Selected Characteristics, 2010 Annual Averages

(Number, percent.)

Characteristic	Total employed (thousands)	Worked on an average day			Worked on an average weekday			Worked on an average Saturday, Sunday, or holiday[1]		
		Number (thousands)	Percent	Hours per day[2]	Number[3] (thousands)	Percent	Hours per day[2]	Number[4] (thousands)	Percent	Hours per day[2]
Both Sexes[5]	147 746	100 837	68.2	7.50	120 718	81.7	7.86	52 356	35.4	5.48
Full-time worker	113 036	81 985	72.5	8.00	99 587	88.1	8.39	39 318	34.8	5.59
Part-time worker	34 701	18 851	54.3	5.37	21 178	61.0	5.43	13 060	37.6	5.16
Men[5]	77 569	54 551	70.3	7.82	64 585	83.3	8.19	29 583	38.1	5.80
Full-time worker	64 043	47 201	73.7	8.17	57 004	89.0	8.56	23 156	36.2	5.86
Part-time worker	13 526	7 351	54.3	5.53	7 667	56.7	5.51	6 506	48.1	5.59
Women[5]	70 178	46 285	66.0	7.14	56 118	80.0	7.49	22 835	32.5	5.08
Full-time worker	48 993	34 785	71.0	7.75	42 579	86.9	8.16	16 178	33.0	5.21
Part-time worker	21 175	11 501	54.3	5.27	13 530	63.9	5.38	6 664	31.5	4.76
Multiple Job Holding Status										
Single job holder	134 253	90 351	67.3	7.51	108 641	80.9	7.85	45 357	33.8	5.47
Multiple job holder	13 484	10 486	77.8	7.48	12 099	89.7	7.97	6 867	50.9	5.58
Educational Attainment, 25 Years and Over										
Less than a high school diploma	10 054	6 639	66.0	7.74	8 120	80.8	7.82	3 211	31.9	7.29
High school graduate, no college[6]	36 218	24 311	67.1	7.75	29 059	80.2	8.01	12 805	35.4	6.33
Some college or associate degree	31 814	21 792	68.5	7.64	26 646	83.8	7.88	10 157	31.9	6.15
Bachelor's degree or higher[7]	49 407	36 323	73.5	7.40	43 699	88.4	8.01	18 304	37.0	3.86

Note: Data refer to persons age 15 years and over, unless otherwise specified.

[1]Holidays are New Year's Day, Easter, Memorial Day, Labor Day, Thanksgiving Day, and Christmas Day. In 2010, data were not collected for the Fourth of July.
[2]Includes work at main and other job(s) and excludes travel related to work.
[3]Number was derived by multiplying the "total employed" by the percentage of employed persons who worked on an average weekday.
[4]Number was derived by multiplying the "total employed" by the percentage of employed persons who worked on an average Saturday, Sunday, or holiday.
[5]Includes workers whose hours vary.
[6]Includes persons with a high school diploma or equivalent.
[7]Includes persons with bachelor's, master's, professional, and doctoral degrees.

Table 12-4. Average Hours Worked Per Day at Main Job Only by Employed Persons on Weekdays and Weekend Days, by Selected Characteristics, 2010 Annual Averages

(Number, percent.)

Characteristic	Total employed (thousands)	Worked on an average day			Worked on an average weekday			Worked on an average Saturday, Sunday, or holiday[1]		
		Number (thousands)	Percent	Hours per day[2]	Number[3] (thousands)	Percent	Hours per day[2]	Number[4] (thousands)	Percent	Hours per day[2]
Class of Worker										
Wage and salary workers	135 964	92 042	67.7	7.50	111 068	81.7	7.84	45 820	33.7	5.50
Self-employed workers[5]	11 654	7 483	64.2	6.63	8 628	74.0	7.00	4 572	39.2	4.86
Occupation										
Management, business, and financial operations	23 670	17 817	75.3	7.70	21 814	92.2	8.41	8 563	36.2	3.52
Professional and related	35 408	24 365	68.8	7.13	29 445	83.2	7.58	11 357	32.1	4.17
Services	24 517	15 059	61.4	7.03	16 727	68.2	7.10	11 062	45.1	6.75
Sales and related	14 964	10 732	71.7	7.16	11 624	77.7	7.44	8 313	55.6	6.07
Office and administrative support	17 835	11 145	62.5	7.23	14 174	79.5	7.44	3 577	20.1	5.25
Farming, fishing, and forestry	*	*	*	5.83	*	*	6.10	*	*	*
Construction and extraction	7 256	4 502	62.0	8.14	5 814	80.1	8.16	1 063	14.6	7.93
Installation, maintenance, and repair	5 380	3 930	73.1	7.93	4 963	92.3	8.13	1 678	31.2	6.70
Production	9 060	6 313	69.7	8.25	7 952	87.8	8.44	2 230	24.6	6.59
Transportation and material moving	8 651	5 185	59.9	8.34	6 638	76.7	8.51	2 335	27.0	7.42
Earnings of Full-Time Wage and Salary Earners[6]										
$0 to $540	23 302	16 138	69.3	7.84	19 115	82.0	7.96	8 878	38.1	7.21
$541 to $810	22 864	15 793	69.1	8.09	19 895	87.0	8.34	6 274	27.4	6.24
$811 to $1,230	22 405	16 294	72.7	8.01	19 927	88.9	8.45	6 973	31.1	4.75
$1,231 and higher	22 905	16 887	73.7	8.11	20 980	91.6	8.69	6 978	30.5	3.85

Note: Data refer to persons age 15 years and over, unless otherwise specified.

[1]Holidays are New Year's Day, Easter, Memorial Day, Labor Day, Thanksgiving Day, and Christmas Day. In 2010, data were not collected for the Fourth of July.
[2]Includes work at main job only and excludes travel related to work.
[3]Number was derived by multiplying the "total employed" by the percentage of employed persons who worked on an average weekday.
[4]Number was derived by multiplying the "total employed" by the percentage of employed persons who worked on an average Saturday, Sunday, or holiday.
[5]Includes self-employed workers whose businesses are unincorporated. Self-employed workers whose businesses are incorporated are classified as wage and salary workers.
[6]These values are based on usual weekly earnings. Each earnings range represents approximately 25 percent of full-time wage and salary workers who held only one job.
* = Figure does not meet standards for reliability or quality.

Table 12-5. Average Hours Worked Per Day at All Jobs by Employed Persons at Workplaces or at Home, by Selected Characteristics, 2010 Annual Averages

(Number, percent.)

Characteristic	Total employed (thousands)	Employed persons who reported working on an average day[1]								
		Number (thousands)	Percent	Average hours of work	Location of work[2]					
					Persons who reported working at their workplaces on an average day			Persons who reported working at home on an average day[3]		
					Number (thousands)	Percent	Average hours of work at workplace	Number (thousands)	Percent	Average hours of work at home
Full- and Part-Time Status and Sex										
Both sexes[4]	147 746	100 837	68.2	7.50	83 512	82.8	7.76	23 805	23.6	2.96
Full-time worker	113 036	81 985	72.5	8.00	69 147	84.3	8.17	18 943	23.1	3.10
Part-time worker	34 701	18 851	54.3	5.37	14 365	76.2	5.80	4 862	25.8	2.41
Men[4]	77 569	54 551	70.3	7.82	46 072	84.5	7.96	12 476	22.9	2.91
Full-time worker	64 043	47 201	73.7	8.17	40 324	85.4	8.28	10 647	22.6	2.98
Part-time worker	13 526	7 351	54.3	5.53	5 748	78.2	5.74	1 829	24.9	2.47
Women[4]	70 178	46 285	66.0	7.14	37 439	80.9	7.52	11 329	24.5	3.02
Full-time worker	48 993	34 785	71.0	7.75	28 823	82.9	8.02	8 296	23.8	3.25
Part-time worker	21 175	11 501	54.3	5.27	8 617	74.9	5.84	3 033	26.4	2.37
Multiple Job Holding Status										
Single job holder	134 253	90 351	67.3	7.51	75 312	83.4	7.78	19 725	21.8	2.97
Multiple job holder	13 484	10 486	77.8	7.48	8 200	78.2	7.60	4 081	38.9	2.93
Educational Attainment, 25 Years and Over										
Less than a high school diploma	10 054	6 639	66.0	7.74	6 090	91.7	7.84	688	10.4	2.64
High school graduate, no college[5]	36 218	24 311	67.1	7.75	20 892	85.9	7.89	4 039	16.6	3.82
Some college or associate degree	31 814	21 792	68.5	7.64	18 299	84.0	7.93	4 965	22.8	2.99
Bachelor's degree or higher[6]	49 407	36 323	73.5	7.40	27 412	75.5	7.84	13 118	36.1	2.67

Note: Data refer to persons age 15 years and over, unless otherwise specified.

[1]Includes work at main and other job(s) and excludes travel related to work.
[2]Respondents may have worked at more than one location.
[3]"Working at home" includes any time the respondent reported doing activities that were identified as "part of one's job"; this category is not restricted to persons whose usual workplace is their home.
[4]Includes workers whose hours vary.
[5]Includes persons with a high school diploma or equivalent.
[6]Includes persons with bachelor's, master's, professional, and doctoral degrees.

Table 12-6. Average Hours Worked Per Day at Main Job Only by Employed Persons at Workplaces or at Home, by Selected Characteristics, 2010 Annual Averages

(Number, percent.)

Characteristic	Total employed (thousands)	Employed persons who reported working on an average day[1]			Location of work[2]					
		Number (thousands)	Percent	Hours of work	Persons who reported working at their workplaces on an average day			Persons who reported working at home on an average day[3]		
					Number (thousands)	Percent	Hours of work at workplace	Number (thousands)	Percent	Hours of work at home
Class of Worker										
Wage and salary worker	135 964	92 042	67.7	7.50	78 978	85.8	7.75	17 449	19.0	2.68
Self-employed worker[4]	11 654	7 483	64.2	6.63	3 609	48.2	7.24	4 807	64.2	3.91
Occupation										
Management, business, and financial operations	23 670	17 817	75.3	7.70	13 721	77.0	8.15	5 870	32.9	3.32
Professional and related	35 408	24 365	68.8	7.13	18 378	75.4	7.77	8 028	32.9	2.58
Services	24 517	15 059	61.4	7.03	12 997	86.3	7.18	2 255	15.0	3.09
Sales and related	14 964	10 732	71.7	7.16	8 560	79.8	7.34	2 857	26.6	3.22
Office and administrative support	17 835	11 145	62.5	7.23	10 196	91.5	7.41	1 177	10.6	3.04
Farming, fishing, and forestry	*	*	*	5.83	*	*	6.16	*	*	*
Construction and extraction	7 256	4 502	62.0	8.14	4 098	91.0	8.13	520	11.6	*
Installation, maintenance, and repair	5 380	3 930	73.1	7.93	3 586	91.2	8.01	498	12.7	2.09
Production	9 060	6 313	69.7	8.25	6 058	96.0	8.27	401	6.3	3.24
Transportation and material moving	8 651	5 185	59.9	8.34	4 602	88.7	8.11	535	10.3	3.48
Earnings of Full-Time Wage and Salary Earners[5]										
$0 to $480	23 302	16 138	69.3	7.84	15 118	93.7	7.96	1 081	6.7	3.09
$481 to $730	22 864	15 793	69.1	8.09	14 572	92.3	8.14	1 860	11.8	2.45
$731 to $1,150	22 405	16 294	72.7	8.01	13 926	85.5	8.25	2 684	16.5	2.38
$1,151 and higher	22 905	16 887	73.7	8.11	13 640	80.8	8.50	5 289	31.3	2.62

Note: Data refer to persons age 15 years and over, unless otherwise specified.

[1]Includes work at main job only and excludes travel related to work.
[2]Respondents may have worked at more than one location.
[3]"Working at home" includes any time the respondent reported doing activities that were identified as "part of one's job"; this category is not restricted to persons whose usual workplace is their home.
[4]Includes self-employed workers whose businesses are unincorporated. Self-employed workers whose businesses are incorporated are classified as wage and salaryworkers.
[5]These values are based on usual weekly earnings. Each earnings range covers approximately 25 percent of full-time wage and salary workers.
* = Figure does not meet standards for reliability or quality.

Table 12-7. Average Hours Per Day Spent by Persons Age 18 Years and Over Caring for Household Children Under 18 Years, by Sex of Respondent, Age of Youngest Household Child, and Day, 2006–2010 Combined Annual Averages

(Number.)

Activity	Hours per day caring for household children								
	Total			Weekdays			Weekends and holidays[1]		
	Both sexes	Men	Women	Both sexes	Men	Women	Both sexes	Men	Women
Persons in Households with Children Under 18 Years									
Caring for household children as a primary activity	1.33	0.87	1.72	1.41	0.85	1.89	1.13	0.91	1.32
Physical care	0.45	0.24	0.62	0.47	0.24	0.67	0.39	0.23	0.52
Education-related activities	0.10	0.06	0.13	0.12	0.07	0.17	0.03	0.02	0.04
Reading to/with children	0.04	0.02	0.05	0.04	0.02	0.05	0.03	0.02	0.04
Talking to/with children	0.05	0.03	0.07	0.06	0.03	0.08	0.03	0.02	0.04
Playing/doing hobbies with children	0.28	0.25	0.31	0.27	0.22	0.30	0.33	0.33	0.32
Looking after children	0.07	0.06	0.09	0.07	0.04	0.09	0.09	0.09	0.10
Attending children's events	0.06	0.05	0.07	0.05	0.03	0.06	0.08	0.07	0.08
Travel related to care of household children	0.17	0.11	0.22	0.20	0.12	0.27	0.09	0.07	0.10
Other childcare activities	0.11	0.06	0.16	0.13	0.06	0.19	0.06	0.04	0.08
Persons in Households with Youngest Child 6 to 17 Years									
Caring for household children as a primary activity	0.78	0.52	1.01	0.86	0.53	1.15	0.58	0.48	0.67
Physical care	0.15	0.08	0.21	0.18	0.09	0.25	0.10	0.06	0.13
Education-related activities	0.11	0.07	0.15	0.14	0.08	0.20	0.04	0.03	0.05
Reading to/with children	0.02	0.01	0.02	0.02	0.01	0.02	0.01	0.01	0.02
Talking to/with children	0.06	0.03	0.09	0.07	0.04	0.10	0.04	0.03	0.06
Playing/doing hobbies with children	0.07	0.08	0.06	0.06	0.07	0.05	0.09	0.10	0.07
Looking after children	0.04	0.03	0.06	0.04	0.02	0.05	0.06	0.05	0.07
Attending children's events	0.07	0.06	0.09	0.06	0.05	0.08	0.10	0.09	0.12
Travel related to care of household children	0.16	0.10	0.20	0.18	0.12	0.25	0.09	0.08	0.10
Other childcare activities	0.09	0.05	0.13	0.11	0.05	0.15	0.05	0.04	0.07
Persons in Households with Youngest Child Under 6 Years									
Caring for household children as a primary activity	1.98	1.30	2.53	2.07	1.25	2.74	1.77	1.42	2.06
Physical care	0.79	0.43	1.09	0.82	0.43	1.15	0.73	0.44	0.96
Education-related activities	0.08	0.05	0.10	0.10	0.06	0.14	0.02	0.01	0.03
Reading to/with children	0.06	0.04	0.08	0.06	0.04	0.08	0.05	0.04	0.07
Talking to/with children	0.03	0.02	0.04	0.04	0.02	0.05	0.02	0.01	0.02
Playing/doing hobbies with children	0.54	0.47	0.60	0.51	0.41	0.60	0.61	0.62	0.60
Looking after children	0.11	0.09	0.13	0.10	0.07	0.13	0.13	0.13	0.14
Attending children's events	0.04	0.03	0.05	0.03	0.02	0.05	0.05	0.05	0.05
Travel related to care of household children	0.19	0.12	0.24	0.23	0.14	0.31	0.09	0.07	0.10
Other childcare activities	0.14	0.06	0.19	0.16	0.07	0.24	0.07	0.05	0.09

Note: Universe includes respondents age 18 years and over living in households with children under 18 years of age, whether or not they provided childcare.

[1]Holidays are New Year's Day, Easter, Memorial Day, the Fourth of July, Labor Day, Thanksgiving Day, and Christmas Day. Data were not collected for New Year's Day in 2007, Christmas Day, 2008, and the Fourth of July 2010.

Table 12-8. Average Hours Per Day Spent in Primary Activities[1] by the Total Population Age 18 Years and Over, by Activity Category, Employment Status, Presence and Age of Household Children, and Sex, 2010 Annual Averages

(Number.)

Activity	Hours spent per day in primary activities								
	Household with children under 6 years			Household with children 6 to 17 years			Household with no children under 18 years		
	Both sexes	Men	Women	Both sexes	Men	Women	Both sexes	Men	Women
TOTAL									
All Activities[2]	24.00	24.00	24.00	24.00	24.00	24.00	24.00	24.00	24.00
Personal care activities	9.22	8.89	9.49	9.29	9.05	9.50	9.53	9.32	9.73
Sleeping	8.56	8.32	8.76	8.52	8.37	8.64	8.68	8.61	8.75
Eating and drinking	1.14	1.20	1.08	1.20	1.27	1.14	1.31	1.34	1.28
Household activities	1.83	1.30	2.28	1.94	1.43	2.40	1.85	1.54	2.15
Housework	0.67	0.31	0.97	0.67	0.26	1.04	0.55	0.26	0.84
Food preparation and cleanup	0.71	0.35	1.02	0.63	0.35	0.88	0.53	0.32	0.74
Lawn and garden care	0.11	0.19	0.05	0.18	0.29	0.09	0.26	0.37	0.16
Household management	0.10	0.11	0.10	0.12	0.09	0.15	0.13	0.11	0.16
Purchasing goods and services	0.79	0.66	0.89	0.73	0.55	0.89	0.76	0.65	0.87
Consumer goods purchases	0.41	0.32	0.48	0.39	0.27	0.49	0.37	0.31	0.42
Professional and personal care services	0.07	0.05	0.08	0.06	0.05	0.07	0.09	0.07	0.12
Caring for and helping household members	1.97	1.35	2.50	0.80	0.55	1.03	0.05	0.04	0.06
Caring for and helping household children	1.74	1.17	2.22	0.61	0.41	0.79	X	X	X
Caring for and helping non-household members	0.13	0.12	0.14	0.17	0.15	0.19	0.25	0.23	0.28
Caring for and helping non-household adults	0.06	0.04	0.07	0.09	0.09	0.08	0.09	0.10	0.08
Working and work-related activities	4.01	5.35	2.89	4.11	4.98	3.33	3.44	3.83	3.06
Working	3.60	4.78	2.62	3.71	4.48	3.02	3.08	3.41	2.76
Educational activities	0.15	0.12	0.17	0.32	0.26	0.37	0.26	0.29	0.23
Attending class	0.06	*	0.06	0.16	0.15	0.17	0.11	0.15	0.08
Homework and research	0.07	0.05	0.09	0.13	0.09	0.16	0.13	0.13	0.13
Organizational, civic, and religious activities	0.27	0.28	0.27	0.39	0.39	0.40	0.36	0.27	0.45
Religious and spiritual activities	0.13	0.14	0.13	0.16	0.16	0.16	0.16	0.13	0.20
Volunteering (organizational and civic activities)	0.10	0.10	0.10	0.18	0.17	0.19	0.16	0.11	0.20
Leisure and sports	4.04	4.38	3.75	4.49	4.87	4.15	5.68	6.02	5.34
Socializing and communicating	0.75	0.70	0.79	0.67	0.67	0.67	0.70	0.68	0.72
Watching television	2.14	2.39	1.94	2.33	2.52	2.15	3.07	3.27	2.87
Participating in sports, exercise, and recreation	0.24	0.34	0.14	0.29	0.41	0.18	0.29	0.38	0.20
Telephone calls, mail, and e-mail	0.09	0.06	0.12	0.14	0.11	0.16	0.20	0.14	0.25
Other activities n.e.c.	0.36	0.29	0.42	0.41	0.38	0.44	0.32	0.32	0.31
EMPLOYED									
All Activities[2]	24.00	24.00	24.00	24.00	24.00	24.00	24.00	24.00	24.00
Personal care activities	9.01	8.83	9.23	9.00	8.76	9.24	9.15	8.97	9.34
Sleeping	8.32	8.25	8.41	8.21	8.06	8.36	8.30	8.25	8.36
Eating and drinking	1.15	1.22	1.08	1.22	1.30	1.15	1.32	1.36	1.26
Household activities	1.42	1.12	1.77	1.71	1.29	2.14	1.46	1.26	1.68
Housework	0.47	0.24	0.75	0.52	0.19	0.87	0.41	0.22	0.62
Food preparation and cleanup	0.52	0.31	0.78	0.55	0.31	0.80	0.40	0.27	0.54
Lawn and garden care	0.10	0.16	0.03	0.17	0.26	0.08	0.20	0.27	0.12
Household management	0.11	0.12	0.09	0.11	0.10	0.13	0.12	0.10	0.14
Purchasing goods and services	0.70	0.60	0.81	0.71	0.58	0.86	0.70	0.60	0.82
Consumer goods purchases	0.36	0.28	0.45	0.38	0.28	0.48	0.35	0.30	0.41
Professional and personal care services	0.06	0.05	0.06	0.05	0.05	0.05	0.06	0.05	0.07
Caring for and helping household members	1.64	1.26	2.08	0.72	0.56	0.89	0.04	0.03	0.05
Caring for and helping household children	1.43	1.12	1.79	0.53	0.41	0.66	X	X	X
Caring for and helping non-household members	0.10	0.08	0.11	0.14	0.12	0.16	0.21	0.18	0.24
Caring for and helping non-household adults	0.03	0.03	0.04	0.06	0.06	0.06	0.08	0.07	0.09
Working and work-related activities	5.65	6.37	4.80	5.67	6.35	4.96	5.70	5.98	5.39
Working	5.16	5.77	4.45	5.19	5.78	4.57	5.21	5.45	4.95
Educational activities	0.09	0.05	0.13	0.19	0.16	0.22	0.20	0.20	0.20
Attending class	0.02	0.00	0.04	0.09	0.11	0.08	0.09	0.12	0.07
Homework and research	0.05	0.03	0.08	0.08	0.04	0.12	0.09	0.07	0.12
Organizational, civic, and religious activities	0.21	0.24	0.18	0.36	0.37	0.35	0.27	0.23	0.33
Religious and spiritual activities	0.10	0.11	0.09	0.16	0.18	0.14	0.13	0.11	0.15
Volunteering (organizational and civic activities)	0.08	0.10	0.06	0.16	0.14	0.17	0.12	0.09	0.14
Leisure and sports	3.65	3.91	3.34	3.80	4.07	3.52	4.54	4.81	4.24
Socializing and communicating	0.67	0.62	0.72	0.58	0.57	0.58	0.65	0.61	0.70
Watching television	1.91	2.13	1.66	1.97	2.11	1.83	2.32	2.50	2.12
Participating in sports, exercise, and recreation	0.22	0.28	0.15	0.26	0.36	0.16	0.27	0.33	0.21
Telephone calls, mail, and e-mail	0.08	0.05	0.11	0.11	0.10	0.13	0.15	0.11	0.19
Other activities n.e.c.	0.31	0.27	0.35	0.37	0.35	0.38	0.27	0.28	0.25

n.e.c. = Not elsewhere classified.

[1] A primary activity is designated by a respondent as his or her main activity. Other activities done simultaneously are not included.
[2] All major activity categories include related travel time.
X = Not applicable.
* = Figure does not meet standards for reliability or quality.

Table 12-8. Average Hours Per Day Spent in Primary Activities[1] by the Total Population Age 18 Years and Over, by Activity Category, Employment Status, Presence and Age of Household Children, and Sex, 2010 Annual Averages—*Continued*

(Number.)

Activity	Hours spent per day in primary activities								
	Household with children under 6 years			Household with children 6 to 17 years			Household with no children under 18 years		
	Both sexes	Men	Women	Both sexes	Men	Women	Both sexes	Men	Women
NOT EMPLOYED									
All Activities[2]	24.00	24.00	24.00	24.00	24.00	24.00	24.00	24.00	24.00
Personal care activities	9.69	9.16	9.87	10.02	10.04	10.00	10.07	9.91	10.21
Sleeping	9.11	8.65	9.27	9.28	9.44	9.18	9.22	9.21	9.23
Eating and drinking	1.10	1.13	1.09	1.16	1.19	1.14	1.31	1.31	1.31
Household activities	2.79	2.17	3.00	2.52	1.87	2.91	2.41	2.01	2.74
Housework	1.12	0.61	1.29	1.04	0.48	1.37	0.75	0.32	1.11
Food preparation and cleanup	1.16	0.54	1.37	0.82	0.48	1.03	0.72	0.42	0.98
Lawn and garden care	0.13	0.34	0.06	0.20	0.37	0.11	0.36	0.53	0.21
Household management	0.10	0.06	0.11	0.14	0.06	0.18	0.16	0.12	0.19
Purchasing goods and services	1.00	1.00	1.00	0.79	0.49	0.97	0.84	0.74	0.93
Consumer goods purchases	0.52	0.50	0.53	0.43	0.27	0.52	0.38	0.33	0.43
Professional and personal care services	0.11	0.08	0.12	0.07	*	0.09	0.14	0.10	0.17
Caring for and helping household members	2.75	1.75	3.10	1.01	0.53	1.30	0.06	0.05	0.07
Caring for and helping household children	2.48	1.43	2.84	0.81	0.40	1.05	X	X	X
Caring for and helping non-household members	0.21	*	0.18	0.25	*	0.24	0.32	0.31	0.32
Caring for and helping non-household adults	0.10	0.08	0.11	0.14	*	0.12	0.11	0.14	0.08
Working and work-related activities	0.22	*	0.16	0.27	0.38	0.21	0.19	0.26	0.14
Working	0.00	*	*	0.07	*	*	0.02	0.00	0.01
Educational activities	0.29	*	0.22	0.64	0.61	0.66	0.35	0.45	0.26
Attending class	0.13	*	0.08	0.32	*	0.34	0.14	0.20	0.09
Homework and research	0.12	*	0.11	0.24	0.26	0.23	0.18	0.23	0.15
Organizational, civic, and religious activities	0.40	0.43	0.39	0.46	*	0.47	0.48	0.34	0.60
Religious and spiritual activities	0.21	*	0.18	0.17	0.11	0.20	0.22	0.16	0.26
Volunteering (organizational and civic activities)	0.14	*	0.16	0.24	*	0.23	0.22	0.14	0.28
Leisure and sports	4.92	6.63	4.33	6.17	7.58	5.34	7.31	8.03	6.71
Socializing and communicating	0.93	1.08	0.88	0.90	0.99	0.84	0.76	0.79	0.73
Watching television	2.67	3.66	2.34	3.20	3.91	2.78	4.15	4.56	3.80
Participating in sports, exercise, and recreation	0.27	*	0.14	0.35	0.58	0.21	0.31	0.45	0.18
Telephone calls, mail, and e-mail	0.13	0.10	0.14	0.19	0.13	0.22	0.26	0.20	0.32
Other activities n.e.c.	0.50	0.42	0.52	0.52	0.47	0.54	0.39	0.40	0.39

n.e.c. = Not elsewhere classified.

[1]A primary activity is designated by a respondent as his or her main activity. Other activities done simultaneously are not included.
[2]All major activity categories include related travel time.
X = Not applicable.
* = Figure does not meet standards for reliability or quality.

Table 12-9. Average Hours Per Day Spent in Leisure and Sports Activities for the Total Population, by Selected Characteristics, 2010 Annual Averages

(Number.)

Characteristic	Total, all leisure and sports activities			Participating in sports, exercise, and recreation		Socializing and communicating		Watching TV	
	Total, all days	Weekdays	Weekends and holidays[1]	Weekdays	Weekends and holidays[1]	Weekdays	Weekends and holidays[1]	Weekdays	Weekends and holidays[1]
Sex									
Men	5.57	4.99	6.96	0.39	0.49	0.54	1.02	2.68	3.56
Women	4.82	4.37	5.88	0.19	0.22	0.56	1.12	2.36	2.91
Age									
Total, 15 years and over	5.18	4.67	6.40	0.29	0.35	0.55	1.07	2.52	3.23
15 to 19 years	5.69	5.27	6.67	0.67	0.77	0.74	1.09	2.23	2.49
20 to 24 years	5.34	4.66	6.97	0.25	0.37	0.71	1.46	2.09	2.85
25 to 34 years	4.40	3.74	5.98	0.26	0.37	0.59	1.28	1.91	2.84
35 to 44 years	4.17	3.61	5.55	0.26	0.33	0.45	0.99	1.96	2.87
45 to 54 years	4.66	4.10	5.97	0.21	0.30	0.54	0.97	2.37	3.26
55 to 64 years	5.24	4.69	6.58	0.23	0.31	0.45	0.92	2.75	3.71
65 to 74 years	6.85	6.66	7.34	0.31	0.27	0.59	0.98	3.77	4.00
75 years and over	7.69	7.59	7.90	0.27	0.14	0.47	0.94	4.50	4.26
Race and Hispanic Origin									
White	5.14	4.62	6.39	0.30	0.36	0.53	1.09	2.45	3.19
Black	5.61	5.19	6.61	0.21	0.21	0.63	1.01	3.18	3.71
Hispanic[2]	4.89	4.40	6.05	0.23	0.27	0.56	1.29	2.50	3.12
Employment Status									
Employed	4.22	3.59	5.78	0.24	0.35	0.48	1.05	1.88	2.86
Full-time workers	3.99	3.26	5.77	0.23	0.36	0.41	1.05	1.74	2.86
Part-time workers	4.97	4.63	5.81	0.27	0.32	0.70	1.07	2.32	2.82
Not employed	6.68	6.40	7.35	0.36	0.36	0.67	1.09	3.54	3.79
Earnings of Full-Time Wage and Salary Earners[3]									
$0 to $480	4.24	3.70	5.57	0.19	0.25	0.43	1.06	2.02	2.80
$481 to $730	4.21	3.47	5.92	0.19	0.32	0.46	1.06	1.94	3.15
$731 to $1,150	4.03	3.24	6.08	0.26	0.40	0.44	1.07	1.70	2.99
$1,151 and higher	3.81	3.00	5.78	0.28	0.43	0.33	0.98	1.56	2.68
Presence and Age of Children									
No household children under 18 years	5.67	5.17	6.88	0.29	0.35	0.56	1.02	2.82	3.56
Household children under 18 years	4.40	3.87	5.65	0.29	0.35	0.54	1.14	2.03	2.71
Children 13 to 17 years, none younger	4.83	4.39	5.99	0.43	0.36	0.61	0.99	2.16	3.09
Children 6 to 12 years, none younger	4.49	4.02	5.58	0.27	0.40	0.52	1.02	2.03	2.61
Youngest child under 6 years	4.08	3.46	5.51	0.22	0.31	0.51	1.32	1.97	2.59
Marital Status and Sex									
Married, spouse present	4.76	4.24	6.00	0.25	0.33	0.50	1.05	2.35	3.12
Men	5.16	4.62	6.49	0.32	0.43	0.47	0.97	2.68	3.56
Women	4.36	3.85	5.52	0.18	0.23	0.53	1.14	2.01	2.69
Other marital status	5.64	5.14	6.85	0.33	0.38	0.61	1.09	2.70	3.35
Men	6.04	5.43	7.52	0.47	0.56	0.62	1.07	2.68	3.57
Women	5.28	4.88	6.26	0.21	0.22	0.60	1.10	2.71	3.15
Educational Attainment, 25 Years and Over									
Less than a high school diploma	6.08	5.77	6.83	0.19	0.20	0.55	1.13	3.82	4.12
High school graduate, no college[4]	5.53	5.07	6.63	0.20	0.28	0.53	0.98	3.01	3.76
Some college or associate degree	5.02	4.49	6.28	0.26	0.29	0.50	0.98	2.48	3.43
Bachelor's degree or higher[5]	4.41	3.81	5.84	0.32	0.38	0.50	1.06	1.82	2.60

Note: Data refer to respondents age 15 years and over, unless otherwise specified.

[1]Holidays are New Year's Day, Easter, Memorial Day, Labor Day, Thanksgiving Day, and Christmas Day. In 2010, data were not collected for the Fourth of July.
[2]May be of any race.
[3]These values are based on usual weekly earnings. Each earnings range covers approximately 25 percent of full-time wage and salary workers.
[4]Includes persons with a high school diploma or equivalent.
[5]Includes persons with bachelor's, master's, professional, and doctoral degrees.

Table 12-9. Average Hours Per Day Spent in Leisure and Sports Activities for the Total Population, by Selected Characteristics, 2010 Annual Averages—*Continued*

(Number.)

Characteristic	Reading		Relaxing/thinking		Playing games and computer use for leisure		Other leisure and sports activities, including travel[6]	
	Weekdays	Weekends and holidays[1]	Weekdays	Weekends and holidays[1]	Weekdays	Weekends and holidays[1]	Weekdays	Weekends and holidays[1]
Sex								
Men	0.24	0.29	0.27	0.33	0.45	0.54	0.43	0.74
Women	0.33	0.38	0.29	0.28	0.33	0.38	0.29	0.57
Age								
Total, 15 years and over	0.29	0.34	0.28	0.31	0.39	0.46	0.36	0.65
15 to 19 years	0.12	0.10	0.11	0.21	0.85	1.10	0.55	0.92
20 to 24 years	*	0.16	0.28	0.26	0.65	0.88	0.50	0.99
25 to 34 years	0.13	0.15	0.18	0.21	0.37	0.41	0.30	0.71
35 to 44 years	0.16	0.19	0.24	0.17	0.29	0.36	0.26	0.64
45 to 54 years	0.24	0.27	0.25	0.32	0.19	0.29	0.30	0.55
55 to 64 years	0.35	0.43	0.26	0.31	0.29	0.35	0.36	0.54
65 to 74 years	0.62	0.72	0.55	0.49	0.38	0.31	0.44	0.56
75 years and over	0.85	1.14	0.64	0.70	0.49	0.30	0.36	0.41
Race and Hispanic Origin								
White	0.31	0.37	0.27	0.28	0.41	0.45	0.36	0.66
Black	0.17	0.18	0.40	0.47	0.27	0.46	0.32	0.58
Hispanic[2]	0.15	0.11	0.33	0.30	0.29	0.33	0.33	0.65
Employment Status								
Employed	0.20	0.25	0.19	0.24	0.29	0.38	0.32	0.66
Full-time workers	0.17	0.23	0.19	0.25	0.24	0.37	0.28	0.65
Part-time workers	0.27	0.31	0.20	0.21	0.42	0.40	0.44	0.68
Not employed	0.43	0.47	0.43	0.41	0.55	0.58	0.41	0.65
Earnings of Full-Time Wage and Salary Earners[3]								
$0 to $480	0.16	0.14	0.23	0.29	0.40	0.43	0.27	0.60
$481 to $730	0.11	0.23	0.22	0.23	0.21	0.41	0.33	0.52
$731 to $1,150	0.18	0.21	0.16	0.31	0.22	0.42	0.29	0.68
$1,151 and higher	0.23	0.36	0.14	0.17	0.19	0.32	0.27	0.84
Presence and Age of Children								
No household children under 18 years	0.37	0.45	0.30	0.36	0.44	0.49	0.39	0.65
Household children under 18 years	0.15	0.16	0.26	0.21	0.30	0.41	0.30	0.65
Children 13 to 17 years, none younger	0.17	0.21	0.29	0.18	0.39	0.52	0.34	0.64
Children 6 to 12 years, none younger	0.18	0.19	0.29	0.28	0.37	0.42	0.36	0.67
Youngest child under 6 years	0.12	0.12	0.22	0.19	0.20	0.35	0.23	0.64
Marital Status and Sex								
Married, spouse present	0.30	0.35	0.28	0.28	0.26	0.29	0.29	0.57
Men	0.27	0.33	0.28	0.33	0.25	0.27	0.35	0.61
Women	0.33	0.38	0.28	0.24	0.27	0.31	0.24	0.53
Other marital status	0.27	0.32	0.29	0.33	0.52	0.64	0.42	0.74
Men	0.19	0.25	0.27	0.33	0.68	0.85	0.52	0.89
Women	0.34	0.39	0.31	0.33	0.38	0.46	0.34	0.62
Educational Attainment, 25 Years and Over								
Less than a high school diploma	0.17	0.16	0.64	0.66	0.18	0.13	0.23	0.43
High school graduate, no college[4]	0.30	0.34	0.33	0.37	0.34	0.38	0.37	0.53
Some college or associate degree	0.31	0.38	0.26	0.25	0.35	0.35	0.32	0.60
Bachelor's degree or higher[5]	0.39	0.52	0.17	0.20	0.31	0.38	0.31	0.70

Note: Data refer to respondents age 15 years and over, unless otherwise specified.

[1]Holidays are New Year's Day, Easter, Memorial Day, Labor Day, Thanksgiving Day, and Christmas Day. In 2010, data were not collected for the Fourth of July.
[2]May be of any race.
[3]These values are based on usual weekly earnings. Each earnings range covers approximately 25 percent of full-time wage and salary workers.
[4]Includes persons with a high school diploma or equivalent.
[5]Includes persons with bachelor's, master's, professional, and doctoral degrees.
[6]Includes other leisure and sports activities, not elsewhere classified, and travel related to leisure and sports activities.
* = Figure does not meet standards for reliability or quality.

Chapter Thirteen

INCOME IN THE UNITED STATES (CENSUS BUREAU)

INCOME IN THE UNITED STATES (CENSUS BUREAU)

HIGHLIGHTS

This chapter presents data on income and earnings in the United States collected by the Census Bureau. Income, as distinguished from earnings, includes income from pensions, investments, and other sources and is measured as real income in 2010 dollars.

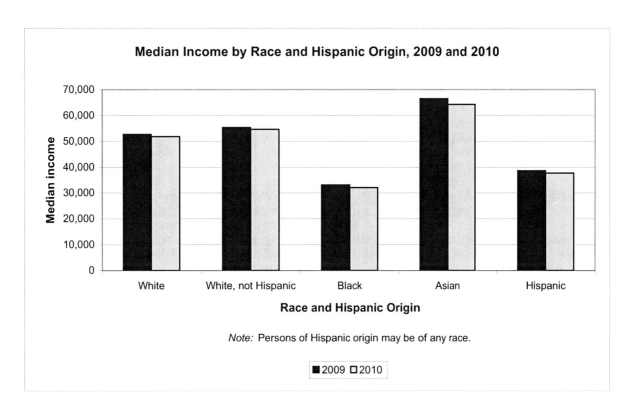

Median Income by Race and Hispanic Origin, 2009 and 2010

Note: Persons of Hispanic origin may be of any race.

■ 2009 □ 2010

In 2010, median income declined for all races. While Asians continued to have the highest median income at $64,308, they also experienced the largest decline as their median income fell 3.4 percent from 2009 to 2010. (See Table 13-1.)

OTHER HIGHLIGHTS

- Median income also varied significantly by type of household. In 2010, a male househoulder with no wife present had a median income of $49,718. However, a female householder with no husband present only had a median income of $32,031. Nonfamily female households had the lowest median income at $25,456. (See Table 13-1.)

- Every region in the country experienced a decline in median income in 2010. The West suffered the greatest decline at -2.9 percent, followed by the Midwest (-2.5 percent), the South (-1.9 percent) and the Northeast (-1.2 percent). (See Table 13-1.)

- The two-year average median household income in 2009–2010 was $50,022—the lowest it has been since 1996–1997. It ranged from a high of $66,187 in Connecticut to a low of $36,821 in Mississippi. (See Table 13-5.)

- Median family income was also the lowest in Mississippi in 2010 at $45,484. Maryland had the highest median family income at $83,137 followed by New Jersey ($82,427) and Connecticut ($81,246). Nationally, median family income was $60,609. (See Table 13-6.)

NOTES AND DEFINITIONS

Collection and Coverage

The data in tables 13-1 through 13-5 are from the Annual Social and Economic Supplement (ASEC) to the 2011 Current Population Survey (CPS). The CPS ASEC provides timely estimates of household income and individual earnings, as well as the distribution of that income. The population represented (the population universe) is the civilian noninstitutionalized population living in the United States. Members of the Armed Forces living off post or with their families on post are included if at least one civilian adult lives in the household. Most of the data from the CPS ASEC were collected in March (with some data collected in February and April), and the data were controlled to independent population estimates for March 2011. The estimates in these tables are based on responses from a sample of the population and may differ from actual values because of sampling variability or other factors. As a result, apparent differences between the estimates for two or more groups may not be statistically significant. All comparative statements have undergone statistical testing and are significant at the 90 percent confidence level unless otherwise noted.

For tables 13-6 and 13-7, the data are from the American Community Survey (ACS). The ACS is an annual survey that covers the same type of information that had been collected every 10 years from the decennial census long form questionnaire. The ACS eliminated the need for a separate long form in the 2010 Census. The CPS ASEC and ACS surveys differ in the length and detail of its questionnaire, the number of households interviewed, the methodology used to collect and process the data, and, consequently, in the income and poverty estimates produced.

The sample size of the ACS is much larger (approximately 3 million) compared to the sample size of the CPS ASEC (100,000). Although it is smaller, the CPS ASEC is a high quality source of information due to its detailed questionnaire and experienced interviewing staff. Another notable difference between the two surveys is that the ACS is mandatory whereas the CPS ASEC is voluntary. More information on the differences between the two surveys is available on the Census Bureau Web site at <http://www.census.gov/hhes/www/income/definitions.html>.

Concepts and Definitions

The *Gini index of income inequality* (also known as the Gini ratio, Gini coefficient, or index of income concentration) is a statistical measure that summarizes the dispersion of income across an entire income distribution. Values range from 0 to 1. A Gini value of 1 indicates "perfect" inequality; that is, one household has all the income and the rest have none. A value of zero indicates "perfect" equality, a situation in which all households have equal income.

Equivalence-adjusted income inequality is another way to measure income inequality. Equivalence adjusted income takes into consideration the number of people living in the household and how these people share resources and take advantage of economies of scale. For example, the household-income-based distribution treats income of $30,000 for a single-person household and a family household similarly, while the equivalence-adjusted income of $30,000 for a single-person household would be more than twice the equivalence-adjusted income of $30,000 for a family household with two adults and two children. The equivalence adjustment used here is based on a three-parameter scale that reflects:

1. On average, children consume less than adults.
2. As family size increases, expenses do not increase at the same rate
3. The increase in expenses is larger for a first child of a single-parent family than the first child of a two-adult family.

Additional Information

Additional information is available in the Census publication "Income, Poverty, and Health Insurance Coverage in the United States: 2010," on the Census Bureau Web site at <http://www.census.gov/hhes/www/income/income.html>.

Table 13-1. Income and Earnings Summary Measures, by Selected Characteristics, 2009 and 2010

(Numbers in thousands, dollars, percent; income in 2010 dollars.)

Characteristic	2009			2010			Percent change in real median income (2010 less 2009)	
		Median income (dollars)			Median income (dollars)			
	Number	Estimate	90 percent confidence interval[1] (+/-)	Number	Estimate	90 percent confidence interval[1] (+/-)	Estimate	90 percent confidence interval[1] (+/-)
ALL HOUSEHOLDS	117 538	50 599	560	118 682	49 445	534	-2.3	1.10
Type of Households								
Family households	78 833	62 276	468	78 613	61 544	438	-1.2	0.80
Married-couple	58 410	73 016	597	58 036	72 751	796	-0.4	1.10
Female householder, no husband present	14 843	33 135	760	15 019	32 031	605	-3.3	2.60
Male householder, no wife present	5 580	48 878	1 512	5 559	49 718	1 544	1.7	4.00
Nonfamily households	38 705	30 947	445	40 069	29 730	576	-3.9	2.00
Female householder	20 442	25 686	576	21 234	25 456	615	-0.9	2.70
Male householder	18 263	37 215	662	18 835	35 627	772	-4.3	2.40
Race[2] and Hispanic Origin of Householder								
White	95 489	52 717	412	96 144	51 846	415	-1.7	0.80
White, not Hispanic	83 158	55 360	767	83 471	54 620	725	-1.3	1.40
Black	14 730	33 122	923	15 065	32 068	814	-3.2	2.90
Asian	4 687	66 550	2 271	4 747	64 308	2 585	-3.4	4.50
Hispanic[3]	13 298	38 667	1 029	13 665	37 759	985	-2.3	3.30
Age of Householder								
Under 65 years	92 268	56 742	528	93 320	55 276	533	-2.6	0.90
15 to 24 years	6 233	31 240	1 036	6 140	28 322	1 421	-9.3	5.20
25 to 34 years	19 257	51 028	799	19 572	50 059	806	-1.9	1.80
35 to 44 years	21 519	62 091	723	21 250	61 644	825	-0.7	1.50
45 to 54 years	24 871	65 295	1 315	24 530	62 485	1 127	-4.3	2.20
55 to 64 years	20 387	57 914	1 155	21 828	56 575	1 100	-2.3	2.30
65 years and older	25 270	31 872	613	25 362	31 408	564	-1.5	2.30
Nativity of Householder								
Native born	102 039	51 337	426	102 647	50 288	425	-2.0	0.80
Foreign born	15 499	44 648	1 331	16 036	43 750	1 714	-2.0	4.20
Naturalized citizen	7 834	52 833	982	8 277	52 642	1 469	-0.4	3.10
Not a citizen	7 666	36 685	993	7 758	36 401	902	-0.8	3.20
Disability Status of Householder								
Households with householder aged 18 to 64	92 061	56 784	530	93 132	55 337	528	-2.5	0.90
With disability	8 419	27 920	1 081	8 827	25 550	1 149	-8.5	4.70
Without disability	83 157	59 988	749	83 888	58 736	716	-2.1	1.30
Region								
Northeast	21 479	53 949	1 431	21 597	53 283	1 772	-1.2	3.20
Midwest	26 390	49 684	999	26 669	48 445	882	-2.5	2.10
South	43 611	46 368	831	44 161	45 492	861	-1.9	1.70
West	26 058	54 722	1 370	26 254	53 142	1 301	-2.9	2.30
Residence								
Inside metropolitan statistical areas	98 379	52 373	426	99 266	51 244	425	-2.2	0.80
Inside principal cities	38 850	45 592	1 039	394 724	4 049	1 216	-3.4	2.40
Outside principal cities	59 529	57 516	760	59 793	56 140	684	-2.4	1.20
Outside metropolitan statistical areas[4]	19 159	40 798	849	19 417	40 287	986	-1.3	2.00
Earnings of Year-Round Full-Time Workers								
Men with earnings	56 053	47 905	351	56 412	47 715	735	-0.4	1.50
Women with earnings	43 217	36 877	229	42 834	36 931	241	0.1	0.80
Disability Status								
Workers without disability, age 15 and older								
Men with earnings	53 610	48 053	365	54 085	48 031	814	0.0	1.60
Women with earnings	41 735	36 993	230	41 539	37 028	237	0.1	0.80
Workers with disability, age 15 and older								
Men with earnings	1 727	42 276	1 175	1 648	41 506	1 028	-1.8	4.00
Women with earnings	1 412	32 504	963	1 213	31 851	972	-2.0	3.90

[1] A 90-percent confidence interval is a measure of an estimate's variability. The larger the confidence interval in relation to the size of the estimate, the less reliable the estimate.
[2] Federal surveys now give respondents the option of reporting more than one race. Therefore, there are two basic ways of defining a race group. A group such as Asian may be defined as those who reported Asian and no other race (the race-alone or single-race concept) or as those who reported Asian regardless of whether they also reported another race (the race-alone-or-in-combination concept). This table shows data using the race-alone concept. The use of the single-race population does not imply that it is the preferred method of presenting or analyzing data; the Census Bureau uses a variety of approaches. Information on people who reported more than one race, such as White and American Indian and Alaska Native or Asian and Black or African American, is available from Census 2010 through American FactFinder. About 2.9 percent of respondents reported more than one race in Census 2010.
[3] May be of any race.
[4] The "outside metropolitan statistical areas" category includes both micropolitan statistical areas and territory outside of metropolitan and micropolitan statistical areas.

Table 13-2. Households, by Total Money Income, Race, and Hispanic Origin of Householder, 1967–2010

(Numbers in thousands, percent, dollars; income in 2010 CPI-U-RS adjusted dollars.)

Race and Hispanic origin of householder and year	Number	Percent distribution										Median income (dollars)		Mean income (dollars)	
		Total	Under $15,000	$15,000 to $24,999	$25,000 to $34,999	$35,000 to $49,999	$50,000 to $74,999	$75,000 to $99,999	$100,000 to $149,999	$150,000 to $199,000	$200,000 and over	Value	Standard error	Value	Standard error
All Races															
1967[1]	60 813	100.0	17.5	11.9	13.5	19.9	22.3	8.6	4.6	0.9	0.8	40 770	148	45 599	148
1968	62 214	100.0	15.9	12.1	12.4	20.0	23.1	9.8	4.9	1.0	0.7	42 527	154	48 112	154
1969	63 401	100.0	15.7	11.4	11.8	18.9	23.6	10.7	5.9	1.2	0.8	44 108	163	50 180	158
1970	64 778	100.0	15.8	11.6	11.8	18.5	23.2	11.0	6.1	1.3	0.8	43 766	160	50 115	160
1971[2]	66 676	100.0	16.1	12.3	11.8	18.4	22.7	10.6	6.1	1.2	0.8	43 340	168	49 845	158
1972[3]	68 251	100.0	15.4	11.8	11.6	17.2	22.9	11.5	7.1	1.6	1.0	45 196	172	52 602	163
1973	69 859	100.0	14.7	12.1	10.8	17.1	22.8	12.0	7.7	1.6	1.2	46 109	175	53 324	162
1974[4,5]	71 163	100.0	14.6	12.3	11.8	18.0	21.9	11.8	7.2	1.5	1.0	44 649	171	52 213	163
1975[5]	72 867	100.0	15.4	12.9	12.1	17.3	22.3	11.2	6.5	1.5	0.8	43 479	177	50 771	158
1976[6]	74 142	100.0	15.0	12.7	12.2	16.4	22.5	11.7	7.1	1.5	0.9	44 201	164	51 992	160
1977	76 030	100.0	14.9	12.9	11.8	16.5	21.6	12.2	7.4	1.6	1.1	44 481	167	52 766	161
1978	77 330	100.0	14.4	12.7	11.5	16.0	21.8	12.3	8.2	2.0	1.1	46 202	187	54 379	209
1979[7]	80 776	100.0	14.6	11.9	12.1	15.4	22.1	12.4	8.3	2.0	1.2	46 074	218	54 731	207
1980	82 368	100.0	15.0	12.4	12.0	16.1	21.6	12.0	8.2	1.8	1.0	44 616	229	53 064	194
1981	83 527	100.0	15.5	12.8	12.6	15.8	21.0	11.4	8.2	1.7	1.1	43 876	230	52 417	191
1982	83 918	100.0	15.7	12.8	12.2	16.4	20.6	11.3	8.0	2.0	1.2	43 758	197	52 735	195
1983	85 407	100.0	15.6	12.9	11.9	16.3	20.3	11.4	8.2	2.1	1.3	43 453	198	52 849	198
1984[8]	86 789	100.0	15.1	12.6	11.8	16.0	20.1	11.9	8.9	2.3	1.4	44 802	204	54 894	202
1985[9]	88 458	100.0	15.1	12.0	11.7	15.7	20.3	12.0	9.3	2.4	1.5	45 640	247	56 167	222
1986	89 479	100.0	14.7	11.7	11.3	15.2	20.1	12.5	9.8	2.8	1.8	47 256	245	58 382	237
1987[10]	91 124	100.0	14.5	11.5	11.0	15.2	19.9	12.5	10.4	2.9	2.0	47 848	226	59 505	244
1988	92 830	100.0	14.2	11.6	10.8	15.2	20.0	12.5	10.5	3.1	2.1	48 216	236	60 245	269
1989	93 347	100.0	13.4	11.5	11.2	14.8	20.0	12.5	10.9	3.2	2.4	49 076	270	62 003	270
1990	94 312	100.0	13.8	11.7	11.0	15.5	20.1	12.3	10.3	3.1	2.2	48 423	247	60 487	256
1991	95 669	100.0	14.3	12.1	11.2	15.6	19.4	12.1	10.2	3.1	2.0	47 032	226	59 203	244
1992[11]	96 426	100.0	14.5	12.6	10.8	15.5	19.1	12.4	10.0	2.9	2.1	46 646	221	59 137	248
1993[12]	97 107	100.0	14.8	12.2	11.2	15.5	18.5	12.0	10.3	3.2	2.4	46 419	217	61 556	333
1994[13]	98 990	100.0	14.3	12.5	11.2	15.0	18.7	11.9	10.5	3.3	2.7	46 937	214	62 750	338
1995[14]	99 627	100.0	13.4	12.1	10.9	15.2	19.1	12.3	10.9	3.3	2.8	48 408	280	63 838	349
1996	101 018	100.0	13.3	12.2	11.1	14.6	18.6	12.6	11.1	3.7	2.9	49 112	248	65 207	365
1997	102 528	100.0	13.0	11.6	10.9	14.4	18.8	12.3	11.7	3.9	3.3	50 123	232	67 307	377
1998	103 874	100.0	12.4	11.2	10.6	14.3	18.7	12.6	12.5	4.1	3.6	51 944	307	69 270	374
1999[15]	106 434	100.0	11.6	11.3	10.6	14.2	18.2	12.8	12.8	4.4	4.1	53 252	249	71 626	372
2000[16]	108 209	100.0	11.5	10.9	10.6	14.2	18.4	13.0	12.6	4.8	4.0	53 164	167	72 339	285
2001	109 297	100.0	12.2	11.2	10.4	14.5	17.9	12.6	12.5	4.5	4.0	52 005	159	71 685	286
2002	111 278	100.0	12.6	11.3	10.3	14.6	17.7	12.7	12.5	4.3	3.8	51 398	168	70 114	263
2003	112 000	100.0	12.8	11.6	10.2	14.4	17.6	12.2	12.7	4.5	3.9	51 353	223	70 023	256
2004[17]	113 343	100.0	12.9	11.4	11.2	13.9	17.7	12.5	12.1	4.6	3.8	51 174	226	69 795	263
2005	114 384	100.0	12.7	11.5	10.7	13.7	18.4	12.0	12.4	4.5	4.2	51 739	173	70 746	267
2006	116 011	100.0	12.2	11.2	11.0	14.1	17.7	12.1	12.7	4.9	4.2	52 124	224	71 988	278
2007	116 783	100.0	12.5	11.0	10.7	13.7	18.0	12.2	13.0	4.8	4.1	52 823	147	71 095	248
2008	117 181	100.0	12.9	11.7	10.8	14.0	17.8	12.0	12.3	4.6	3.9	50 939	139	69 290	245
2009[18]	117 538	100.0	12.9	11.8	11.0	14.1	18.0	11.7	12.1	4.6	4.0	50 599	217	69 098	247
2010	118 682	100.0	13.7	12.0	10.9	13.9	17.7	11.4	12.1	4.5	3.9	49 445	209	67 530	234
White[19]															
1967[1]	54 188	100.0	16.0	11.2	13.1	20.5	23.4	9.1	4.9	1.0	0.9	42 516	154	47 265	160
1968	55 394	100.0	14.6	11.3	12.1	20.5	24.2	10.4	5.3	1.0	0.7	44 279	165	49 842	165
1969	56 248	100.0	14.3	10.6	11.4	19.1	24.7	11.5	6.3	1.3	0.9	46 032	168	52 042	174
1970	57 575	100.0	14.4	11.0	11.4	18.7	24.2	11.6	6.5	1.4	0.9	45 585	175	51 868	170
1971[2]	59 463	100.0	14.7	11.6	11.5	18.8	23.6	11.2	6.5	1.2	0.9	45 332	173	51 650	168
1972[3]	60 618	100.0	13.9	11.1	11.2	17.4	23.8	12.1	7.7	1.7	1.1	47 415	182	54 648	177
1973	61 965	100.0	13.3	11.4	10.4	17.1	23.7	12.8	8.3	1.8	1.4	48 324	184	55 386	175
1974[4,5]	62 984	100.0	13.1	11.7	11.5	18.2	22.8	12.3	7.8	1.6	1.1	46 694	175	54 147	175
1975[5]	64 392	100.0	13.8	12.4	11.9	17.5	23.1	11.9	6.9	1.6	0.9	45 469	166	52 647	173
1976[6]	65 353	100.0	13.5	12.1	12.0	16.5	23.3	12.3	7.6	1.7	1.0	46 302	192	53 992	174
1977	66 934	100.0	13.4	12.2	11.6	16.7	22.4	13.0	7.9	1.8	1.2	46 775	197	54 827	177
1978	68 028	100.0	12.8	12.2	11.3	16.1	22.6	12.9	8.7	2.2	1.3	48 030	212	56 394	227
1979[7]	70 766	100.0	12.9	11.4	11.9	15.5	22.9	13.1	8.9	2.2	1.3	48 307	230	56 889	227

[1]Implementation of a new Curent Population Survey (CPS) Annual Social and Economic Supplements (ASEC) processing system.
[2]Introduction of 1970 census sample design and population controls.
[3]Full implementation of 1970 census-based sample design.
[4]Implementation of a new CPS ASEC processing system. Questionnaire expanded to ask 11 income questions.
[5]Some of these estimates were derived using Pareto interpolation and may differ from published data that were derived using linear interpolation.
[6]First-year medians were derived using both Pareto and linear interpolation. Before this year, all medians were derived using linear interpolation.
[7]Implementation of 1980 census population controls. Questionnaire expanded to show 27 possible values from a list of 51 possible sources of income.
[8]Implementation of Hispanic population weighting controls and introduction of 1980 census-based sample design.
[9]Recording of amounts for earnings from longest job increased to $299,999. Full implementation of 1980 census-based sample design.
[10]Implementation of a new CPS ASEC processing system.
[11]Implementation of 1990 census population controls.
[12]Data collection method changed from paper and pencil to computer-assisted interviewing. In addition, the 1994 ASEC was revised to allow for the coding of different income amounts on selected questionnaire items. Limits either increased or decreased in the following categories: earnings limits increased to $999,999, Social Security limits increased to $49,999, Supplemental Security Income and public assistance limits increased to $24,999, veterans' benefits limits increased to $99,999, and child support and alimony limits decreased to $49,999.
[13]Introduction of 1990 census sample design.
[14]Full implementation of 1990 census-based sample design and metropolitan definitions, 7,000 household sample reduction, and revised editing of responses on race.
[15]Implementation of the 2000 census-based population controls.
[16]Implementation of a 28,000 household sample expansion.
[17]Data revised to reflect a correction to the weights in the 2005 ASEC.
[18]Median income is calculated using $2,500 intervals. Beginning with 2009 income data, the Census Bureau expanded the upper income intervals used to calculate medians to $250,000 or more.
[19]For 2001 and earlier years, the CPS allowed respondents to report only one race group.

Table 13-2. Households, by Total Money Income, Race, and Hispanic Origin of Householder, 1967–2010
—Continued

(Numbers in thousands, percent, dollars; income in 2010 CPI-U-RS adjusted dollars.)

Race and Hispanic origin of householder and year	Number	Percent distribution											Median income (dollars)		Mean income (dollars)	
		Total	Under $15,000	$15,000 to $24,999	$25,000 to $34,999	$35,000 to $49,999	$50,000 to $74,999	$75,000 to $99,999	$100,000 to $149,999	$150,000 to $199,000	$200,000 and over	Value	Standard error	Value	Standard error
White[19]—Continued															
1980	71 872	100.0	13.2	11.8	11.8	16.3	22.4	12.7	8.7	1.9	1.2	47 070	242	55 205	212
1981	72 845	100.0	13.6	12.2	12.5	16.1	21.9	12.0	8.8	1.8	1.2	46 358	214	54 613	207
1982	73 182	100.0	13.8	12.2	12.1	16.6	21.3	11.9	8.6	2.2	1.3	45 811	208	54 909	215
1983	74 376	100.0	13.5	12.4	11.8	16.7	21.1	12.0	8.8	2.3	1.4	45 569	206	55 042	214
1984[8]	75 328	100.0	13.2	12.0	11.7	16.2	20.9	12.5	9.5	2.5	1.6	47 264	238	57 158	222
1985[9]	76 576	100.0	13.3	11.5	11.5	15.9	21.0	12.6	9.9	2.6	1.7	48 132	257	58 473	245
1986	77 284	100.0	12.9	11.2	11.2	15.3	20.9	13.1	10.5	3.0	2.0	49 681	241	60 813	260
1987[10]	78 519	100.0	12.4	11.0	10.9	15.3	20.8	13.3	11.0	3.1	2.1	50 413	253	62 048	268
1988	79 734	100.0	12.2	11.0	10.7	15.4	20.9	13.1	11.1	3.3	2.2	50 972	301	62 814	296
1989	80 163	100.0	11.5	11.0	11.1	15.0	20.6	13.2	11.5	3.5	2.6	51 622	251	64 585	299
1990	80 968	100.0	11.8	11.3	10.9	15.8	20.7	13.0	10.9	3.3	2.4	50 506	231	62 927	281
1991	81 675	100.0	12.2	11.7	11.2	15.7	20.0	12.8	10.9	3.3	2.2	49 285	239	61 703	269
1992[11]	81 795	100.0	12.4	12.2	10.7	15.7	19.7	13.1	10.7	3.1	2.4	49 041	238	61 808	276
1993[12]	82 387	100.0	12.7	11.7	11.0	15.6	19.3	12.7	10.9	3.4	2.7	48 974	285	64 315	371
1994[13]	83 737	100.0	12.4	11.9	11.2	15.1	19.2	12.5	11.2	3.5	3.0	49 504	278	65 515	381
1995[14]	84 511	100.0	11.7	11.7	10.7	15.3	19.6	12.9	11.5	3.6	3.0	50 809	266	66 383	385
1996	85 059	100.0	11.5	11.8	11.0	14.7	19.1	13.1	11.7	4.0	3.1	51 422	266	67 796	401
1997	86 106	100.0	11.4	11.3	10.7	14.4	19.2	12.8	12.4	4.2	3.6	52 787	335	70 300	428
1998	87 212	100.0	10.7	10.8	10.4	14.3	19.2	13.2	13.1	4.3	4.0	54 652	274	72 412	426
1999[15]	88 893	100.0	10.1	10.9	10.4	14.2	18.6	13.4	13.5	4.5	4.4	55 384	280	74 228	420
2000[16]	90 030	100.0	10.3	10.5	10.3	14.2	18.5	13.5	13.3	5.0	4.3	55 603	246	75 022	322
2001	90 682	100.0	10.8	11.0	10.1	14.5	18.2	13.2	13.2	4.7	4.4	54 824	257	74 523	320
White Alone[20]															
2002	91 645	100.0	11.1	10.9	10.1	14.4	18.2	13.3	13.2	4.6	4.1	54 642	222	72 919	297
2003	91 962	100.0	11.2	11.2	10.2	14.4	18.0	12.6	13.4	4.8	4.3	54 095	212	73 011	293
2004[17]	92 880	100.0	11.3	11.1	11.0	13.8	18.0	12.9	12.9	4.9	4.1	53 857	211	72 615	299
2005	93 588	100.0	11.1	11.0	10.6	13.8	18.7	12.6	13.0	4.8	4.5	54 227	237	73 669	305
2006	94 705	100.0	10.7	10.8	10.7	14.1	18.1	12.6	13.4	5.1	4.5	54 797	159	74 732	311
2007	95 112	100.0	10.9	10.8	10.5	13.7	18.3	12.7	13.6	5.1	4.5	54 802	162	73 957	282
2008	95 297	100.0	11.3	11.4	10.6	13.8	18.3	12.6	13.0	4.9	4.2	52 974	154	72 092	277
2009[18]	95 489	100.0	11.2	11.4	10.7	14.1	18.5	12.2	12.8	4.9	4.2	52 717	157	71 709	276
2010	96 144	100.0	11.8	11.6	10.7	13.9	18.2	12.1	12.7	4.8	4.2	51 846	163	70 572	269
White, Not Hispanic[19]															
1972[3]	58 005	100.0	13.7	10.8	10.9	17.2	24.1	12.4	7.9	1.8	1.2	48 091	228	55 282	247
1973	59 236	100.0	13.2	11.2	10.2	17.0	23.8	13.0	8.5	1.8	1.4	48 749	228	56 004	237
1974[4,5]	60 164	100.0	12.9	11.4	11.3	18.1	22.9	12.6	8.0	1.6	1.1	47 093	231	54 757	239
1975[5]	61 533	100.0	13.5	12.1	11.7	17.4	23.3	12.2	7.1	1.6	0.9	45 812	243	53 292	258
1976[6]	62 365	100.0	13.1	11.8	11.8	16.4	23.5	12.6	7.9	1.7	1.1	47 246	275	54 685	244
1977	63 721	100.0	13.1	12.0	11.3	16.5	22.6	13.3	8.1	1.9	1.2	47 702	269	55 506	262
1978	64 836	100.0	12.5	12.0	11.1	16.0	22.8	13.2	8.9	2.2	1.3	48 935	258	57 059	245
1979[7]	67 203	100.0	12.6	11.2	11.7	15.4	23.0	13.3	9.1	2.2	1.4	48 987	271	57 546	252
1980	68 106	100.0	12.8	11.5	11.7	16.2	22.7	12.9	9.0	2.0	1.2	47 904	108	55 930	252
1981	68 996	100.0	13.3	12.0	12.3	16.0	22.1	12.2	9.1	1.9	1.2	47 027	239	55 301	230
1982	69 214	100.0	13.4	11.9	11.9	16.6	21.5	12.1	8.8	2.3	1.4	46 579	234	55 716	239
1983	69 648	100.0	13.0	12.2	11.6	16.6	21.4	12.2	9.1	2.4	1.5	46 740	235	56 488	241
1984[8]	70 586	100.0	12.7	11.7	11.5	16.2	21.2	12.7	9.8	2.6	1.6	48 246	268	58 152	260
1985[9]	71 540	100.0	12.7	11.1	11.4	15.8	21.2	12.9	10.3	2.8	1.8	49 215	251	59 611	271
1986	72 067	100.0	12.4	10.8	11.0	15.3	21.1	13.5	10.8	3.2	2.1	50 811	262	62 020	285
1987[10]	73 120	100.0	11.8	10.7	10.7	15.2	21.0	13.6	11.5	3.2	2.2	51 799	288	63 262	294
1988	74 067	100.0	11.5	10.7	10.6	15.3	21.1	13.4	11.6	3.5	2.3	52 376	308	64 097	301
1989	74 495	100.0	11.0	10.8	10.8	14.9	20.9	13.5	11.9	3.6	2.7	52 733	258	65 879	323
1990	75 035	100.0	11.2	10.9	10.7	15.6	20.9	13.4	11.3	3.5	2.5	51 661	241	64 321	291
1991	75 625	100.0	11.6	11.4	11.0	15.7	20.2	13.1	11.3	3.4	2.3	50 462	248	63 027	281
1992[11]	75 107	100.0	11.7	11.8	10.5	15.6	20.0	13.5	11.2	3.3	2.5	50 687	314	63 378	292
1993[12]	75 697	100.0	12.0	11.4	10.7	15.4	19.7	13.1	11.4	3.6	2.8	50 776	297	66 010	394
1994[13]	77 004	100.0	11.6	11.6	10.9	15.1	19.4	12.8	11.7	3.7	3.1	51 101	271	67 184	399

[3]Full implementation of 1970 census–based sample design.
[4]Implementation of a new CPS ASEC processing system. Questionnaire expanded to ask 11 income questions.
[5]Some of these estimates were derived using Pareto interpolation and may differ from published data that were derived using linear interpolation.
[6]First-year medians were derived using both Pareto and linear interpolation. Before this year, all medians were derived using linear interpolation.
[7]Implementation of 1980 census population controls. Questionnaire expanded to show 27 possible values from a list of 51 possible sources of income.
[8]Implementation of Hispanic population weighting controls and introduction of 1980 census–based sample design.
[9]Recording of amounts for earnings from longest job increased to $299,999. Full implementation of 1980 census–based sample design.
[10]Implementation of a new CPS ASEC processing system.
[11]Implementation of 1990 census population controls.
[12]Data collection method changed from paper and pencil to computer-assisted interviewing. In addition, the 1994 ASEC was revised to allow for the coding of different income amounts on selected questionnaire items. Limits either increased or decreased in the following categories: earnings limits increased to $999,999, Social Security limits increased to $49,999, Supplemental Security Income and public assistance limits increased to $24,999, veterans' benefits limits increased to $99,999, and child support and alimony limits decreased to $49,999.
[13]Introduction of 1990 census sample design.
[14]Full implementation of 1990 census–based sample design and metropolitan definitions, 7,000 household sample reduction, and revised editing of responses on race.
[15]Implementation of the 2000 census–based population controls.
[16]Implementation of a 28,000 household sample expansion.
[17]Data revised to reflect a correction to the weights in the 2005 ASEC.
[18]Median income is calculated using $2,500 intervals. Beginning with 2009 income data, the Census Bureau expanded the upper income intervals used to calculate medians to $250,000 or more.
[19]For 2001 and earlier years, the CPS allowed respondents to report only one race group.
[20]Beginning with the 2003 CPS, respondents were allowed to choose one or more races. White alone refers to people who reported White and did not report any other race category. The use of this single-race population does not imply that it is the preferred method of presenting or analyzing the data; the Census Bureau uses a variety of approaches. Information on people who reported more than one race, such as White and American Indian and Alaska Native or Asian and Black or African American, is available from Census 2010 through American FactFinder. About 2.9 percent of respondents reported more than one race in Census 2010.

Table 13-2. Households, by Total Money Income, Race, and Hispanic Origin of Householder, 1967–2010 —Continued

(Numbers in thousands, percent, dollars; income in 2010 CPI-U-RS adjusted dollars.)

Race and Hispanic origin of householder and year	Number	Percent distribution											Median income (dollars)		Mean income (dollars)	
		Total	Under $15,000	$15,000 to $24,999	$25,000 to $34,999	$35,000 to $49,999	$50,000 to $74,999	$75,000 to $99,999	$100,000 to $149,999	$150,000 to $199,000	$200,000 and over	Value	Standard error	Value	Standard error
White, Not Hispanic[19]—Continued															
1995[14]	76 932	100.0	10.7	11.2	10.4	15.2	20.1	13.3	12.1	3.8	3.2	52 815	276	68 548	411
1996	77 240	100.0	10.8	11.2	10.6	14.6	19.4	13.6	12.3	4.2	3.3	53 672	368	69 846	. . .
1997	77 936	100.0	10.5	10.9	10.3	14.3	19.3	13.3	13.1	4.4	3.9	54 961	287	72 553	. . .
1998	78 577	100.0	9.9	10.3	10.0	13.9	19.5	13.6	13.8	4.6	4.2	56 692	326	74 731	457
1999[15]	79 819	100.0	9.6	10.4	10.0	13.8	18.7	13.7	14.2	4.8	4.8	57 781	365	76 662	454
2000[16]	80 527	100.0	10.0	10.0	10.0	13.8	18.5	13.8	13.9	5.4	4.6	57 764	232	77 305	347
2001	80 818	100.0	10.3	10.5	9.7	14.1	18.3	13.5	13.8	5.0	4.8	57 026	236	76 902	349
White Alone, Not Hispanic[20]															
2002	81 166	100.0	10.7	10.4	9.7	14.0	18.2	13.8	14.0	4.9	4.4	56 841	223	75 281	320
2003	81 148	100.0	10.6	10.6	9.8	13.9	18.1	13.0	14.2	5.2	4.6	56 639	274	75 737	321
2004[17]	81 628	100.0	10.8	10.6	10.5	13.4	18.0	13.4	13.6	5.2	4.5	56 456	259	75 327	328
2005	82 003	100.0	10.5	10.4	10.2	13.4	18.7	13.0	13.8	5.1	4.9	56 718	192	76 619	338
2006	82 675	100.0	10.1	10.2	10.3	13.7	18.2	13.0	14.1	5.5	5.0	56 690	203	77 584	343
2007	82 765	100.0	10.3	10.3	9.9	13.4	18.2	13.0	14.5	5.5	4.9	57 752	260	76 955	310
2008	82 884	100.0	10.5	10.9	10.0	13.4	18.5	13.1	13.7	5.2	4.7	56 232	228	75 039	307
2009[18]	83 158	100.0	10.4	10.8	10.2	14.0	18.6	12.6	13.5	5.3	4.6	55 360	284	74 449	304
2010	83 471	100.0	11.1	11.1	10.2	13.6	18.3	12.4	13.5	5.1	4.6	54 620	277	73 439	297
Black[19]															
1967[1]	5 728	100.0	31.8	19.2	16.8	14.7	12.0	3.2	1.8	0.3	0.2	24 686	411	29 663	331
1968	5 870	100.0	28.7	19.9	15.6	16.4	13.2	4.3	1.6	0.3	. . .	26 110	379	31 800	335
1969	6 053	100.0	27.7	18.6	15.6	17.4	14.0	4.5	2.0	0.2	0.1	27 824	410	33 124	352
1970	6 180	100.0	28.2	17.0	15.7	16.2	14.7	5.5	2.3	0.2	0.2	27 746	381	33 879	366
1971[2]	6 578	100.0	29.4	18.3	14.6	16.2	14.0	5.1	2.0	0.2	0.1	26 778	398	33 182	341
1972[3]	6 809	100.0	28.7	17.7	14.7	15.4	14.9	5.8	2.2	0.3	0.3	27 676	415	34 961	373
1973	7 040	100.0	26.9	17.8	13.7	16.7	16.0	5.2	2.9	0.5	0.2	28 445	443	35 323	351
1974[4,5]	7 263	100.0	27.6	17.9	14.6	16.6	14.2	6.6	2.1	0.2	0.1	27 769	335	34 536	307
1975[5]	7 489	100.0	29.6	17.4	13.3	16.2	15.5	5.4	2.3	0.4	. . .	27 296	402	34 072	302
1976[6]	7 776	100.0	28.1	18.2	13.8	15.0	16.0	5.8	2.6	0.3	0.1	27 532	341	35 177	314
1977	7 977	100.0	27.4	19.4	13.8	15.2	14.6	6.0	3.1	0.4	0.2	27 602	370	35 366	315
1978	8 066	100.0	28.2	17.0	12.9	15.6	14.9	7.2	3.6	0.5	0.1	28 864	610	36 887	482
1979[7]	8 586	100.0	28.5	16.9	14.1	14.0	15.5	7.0	3.5	0.3	0.2	28 362	518	36 392	448
1980	8 847	100.0	29.6	17.4	13.8	14.2	14.5	6.7	3.2	0.4	0.1	27 117	511	35 194	433
1981	8 961	100.0	31.2	17.4	13.8	13.8	14.2	6.1	3.2	0.2	0.1	26 014	437	34 173	414
1982	8 916	100.0	31.0	17.6	13.2	14.3	15.0	5.7	2.6	0.4	0.2	25 963	417	34 161	427
1983	9 236	100.0	31.7	16.7	13.4	14.2	14.1	6.0	3.5	0.4	0.1	25 859	485	34 394	424
1984[8]	9 480	100.0	30.3	17.4	13.0	14.5	13.3	6.8	3.9	0.7	0.1	26 925	518	35 910	442
1985[9]	9 797	100.0	29.3	15.8	13.7	14.1	14.9	7.1	4.0	0.8	0.2	28 636	557	37 363	485
1986	9 922	100.0	29.7	15.8	12.5	14.4	14.7	7.2	4.6	0.8	0.4	28 623	562	38 401	522
1987[10]	10 192	100.0	30.2	15.2	12.5	15.0	13.9	7.1	4.5	1.0	0.6	28 774	551	38 852	534
1988	10 561	100.0	29.6	15.8	11.7	14.4	13.8	7.8	5.1	1.3	0.5	29 057	606	39 807	581
1989	10 486	100.0	27.8	15.0	12.8	14.0	15.8	7.1	5.9	1.1	0.4	30 701	625	40 738	553
1990	10 671	100.0	28.8	14.8	12.4	14.0	15.7	7.6	5.1	1.1	0.5	30 202	689	40 128	542
1991	11 083	100.0	30.0	15.0	11.7	14.4	15.3	7.2	4.8	1.1	0.3	29 361	617	39 097	511
1992[11]	11 269	100.0	30.0	16.1	11.7	14.3	14.6	7.2	4.4	1.0	0.5	28 556	583	38 750	525
1993[12]	11 281	100.0	29.7	15.3	12.6	14.8	13.9	7.1	5.0	1.2	0.6	29 023	574	40 458	672
1994[13]	11 655	100.0	27.3	16.1	12.1	13.7	15.0	8.0	5.6	1.4	0.9	30 590	569	42 566	611
1995[14]	11 577	100.0	25.8	15.4	12.7	14.8	15.9	7.8	5.8	1.0	0.8	31 811	543	43 186	739
1996	12 109	100.0	25.3	16.0	12.0	14.5	15.3	8.9	5.8	1.3	0.8	32 493	639	44 917	877
1997	12 474	100.0	24.2	14.5	13.2	14.6	16.5	8.8	6.0	1.4	0.8	33 930	584	44 648	641
1998	12 579	100.0	24.1	15.1	12.7	14.6	15.3	8.5	6.8	2.0	0.9	33 865	530	45 604	609
1999[15]	12 838	100.0	21.5	14.5	12.4	14.4	16.1	9.3	7.8	2.9	1.1	36 521	680	50 329	722
2000[16]	13 174	100.0	20.1	14.3	13.1	15.2	17.6	9.0	7.4	2.0	1.2	37 562	498	49 604	503
2001	13 315	100.0	21.9	14.2	12.9	15.1	16.4	9.3	7.2	1.8	1.1	36 293	427	48 335	510

[1]Implementation of a new Curent Population Survey (CPS) Annual Social and Economic Supplements (ASEC) processing system.
[2]Introduction of 1970 census sample design and population controls.
[3]Full implementation of 1970 census–based sample design.
[4]Implementation of a new CPS ASEC processing system. Questionnaire expanded to ask 11 income questions.
[5]Some of these estimates were derived using Pareto interpolation and may differ from published data that were derived using linear interpolation.
[6]First-year medians were derived using both Pareto and linear interpolation. Before this year, all medians were derived using linear interpolation.
[7]Implementation of 1980 census population controls. Questionnaire expanded to show 27 possible values from a list of 51 possible sources of income.
[8]Implementation of Hispanic population weighting controls and introduction of 1980 census–based sample design.
[9]Recording of amounts for earnings from longest job increased to $299,999. Full implementation of 1980 census–based sample design.
[10]Implementation of a new CPS ASEC processing system.
[11]Implementation of 1990 census population controls.
[12]Data collection method changed from paper and pencil to computer-assisted interviewing. In addition, the 1994 ASEC was revised to allow for the coding of different income amounts on selected questionnaire items. Limits either increased or decreased in the following categories: earnings limits increased to $999,999, Social Security limits increased to $49,999, Supplemental Security Income and public assistance limits increased to $24,999, veterans' benefits limits increased to $99,999, and child support and alimony limits decreased to $49,999.
[13]Introduction of 1990 census sample design.
[14]Full implementation of 1990 census–based sample design and metropolitan definitions, 7,000 household sample reduction, and revised editing of responses on race.
[15]Implementation of the 2000 census–based population controls.
[16]Implementation of a 28,000 household sample expansion.
[17]Data revised to reflect a correction to the weights in the 2005 ASEC.
[18]Median income is calculated using $2,500 intervals. Beginning with 2009 income data, the Census Bureau expanded the upper income intervals used to calculate medians to $250,000 or more.
[19]For 2001 and earlier years, the CPS allowed respondents to report only one race group.
[20]Beginning with the 2003 CPS, respondents were allowed to choose one or more races. White alone refers to people who reported White and did not report any other race category. The use of this single-race population does not imply that it is the preferred method of presenting or analyzing the data; the Census Bureau uses a variety of approaches. Information on people who reported more than one race, such as White and American Indian and Alaska Native or Asian and Black or African American, is available from Census 2010 through American FactFinder. About 2.9 percent of respondents reported more than one race in Census 2010.
. . . = Not available.

Table 13-2. Households, by Total Money Income, Race, and Hispanic Origin of Householder, 1967–2010 —Continued

(Numbers in thousands, percent, dollars; income in 2010 CPI-U-RS adjusted dollars.)

Race and Hispanic origin of householder and year	Number	Percent distribution										Median income (dollars)		Mean income (dollars)	
		Total	Under $15,000	$15,000 to $24,999	$25,000 to $34,999	$35,000 to $49,999	$50,000 to $74,999	$75,000 to $99,999	$100,000 to $149,999	$150,000 to $199,000	$200,000 and over	Value	Standard error	Value	Standard error
Black Alone[21]															
2002	13 465	100.0	22.9	14.7	12.2	16.2	14.7	8.9	7.0	2.0	1.4	35 178	474	48 492	560
2003	13 629	100.0	23.1	15.0	11.9	15.4	15.6	8.5	7.4	1.9	1.2	35 144	458	47 575	510
2004[17]	13 809	100.0	23.8	14.3	13.2	15.1	15.2	8.9	6.5	1.8	1.3	34 738	361	46 902	508
2005	14 002	100.0	23.4	15.7	12.0	14.1	16.4	8.2	6.9	2.1	1.2	34 464	336	47 415	515
2006	14 354	100.0	22.9	14.8	13.3	14.5	15.4	8.5	7.1	2.0	1.5	34 571	261	48 800	603
2007	14 551	100.0	23.1	13.5	13.0	14.2	16.4	8.8	7.6	2.0	1.3	35 665	499	49 035	547
2008	14 595	100.0	22.9	14.4	13.3	15.6	15.5	8.2	7.0	2.2	1.1	34 651	447	47 122	504
2009[18]	14 730	100.0	23.3	15.3	13.4	14.5	15.2	8.8	6.5	1.8	1.3	33 122	401	46 806	534
2010	15 065	100.0	25.8	14.7	12.7	14.6	15.2	7.6	6.5	1.8	1.1	32 068	330	44 780	462
Black Alone or in Combination															
2002	13 778	100.0	22.8	14.7	12.2	16.2	14.8	8.9	7.1	2.0	1.5	35 361	465	48 883	570
2003	13 969	100.0	23.0	15.0	12.0	15.3	15.6	8.6	7.4	1.9	1.3	35 196	442	47 794	506
2004[17]	14 151	100.0	23.6	14.2	13.1	15.1	15.3	9.0	6.6	1.8	1.2	34 900	320	47 048	500
2005	14 399	100.0	23.3	15.7	11.9	14.1	16.4	8.3	6.9	2.1	1.2	34 571	329	47 720	519
2006	14 709	100.0	22.7	14.7	13.2	14.6	15.5	8.5	7.2	2.1	1.5	34 747	257	49 196	603
2007	14 976	100.0	23.1	13.5	12.9	14.4	16.3	8.8	7.6	2.1	1.3	35 849	489	49 246	538
2008	15 056	100.0	22.7	14.4	13.3	15.6	15.5	8.2	7.0	2.2	1.1	34 779	445	47 269	494
2009[18]	15 212	100.0	23.2	15.3	13.4	14.4	15.2	8.8	6.4	1.9	1.3	33 291	425	47 044	525
2010	15 613	100.0	25.6	14.8	12.8	14.5	15.0	7.7	6.5	1.9	1.2	32 106	317	45 242	469
Asian and Pacific Islander[19]															
1987[10]	. . .	100.0	11.7	11.9	8.9	11.3	18.9	12.5	16.3	5.4	3.0	59 167	2 200	. . .	. . .
1988	1 913	100.0	10.3	11.5	8.2	12.9	20.3	11.9	16.1	5.6	3.2	57 145	2 348	71 445	2 134
1989	1 988	100.0	10.2	8.3	8.8	13.4	19.5	15.7	14.7	4.6	4.8	61 293	1 657	76 196	2 217
1990	1 958	100.0	10.6	9.1	8.3	12.2	20.2	14.1	16.0	5.7	3.8	62 180	1 842	75 056	2 125
1991	2 094	100.0	11.4	8.8	10.2	14.6	17.8	13.7	14.4	5.5	3.7	56 904	1 836	72 249	2 129
1992[11]	2 262	100.0	11.6	10.3	8.6	13.0	20.5	12.2	15.2	5.0	3.5	57 555	1 661	71 333	1 961
1993[12]	2 233	100.0	14.3	9.3	9.5	13.5	15.3	14.0	15.8	4.9	3.4	56 978	2 802	74 655	3 006
1994[13]	2 040	100.0	11.7	10.3	8.0	13.8	18.0	13.6	14.6	5.4	4.7	58 893	2 232	76 467	2 725
1995[14]	2 777	100.0	12.4	9.8	7.2	13.7	20.0	13.3	13.8	5.1	4.6	57 696	1 448	78 456	3 165
1996	2 998	100.0	12.1	8.9	8.4	12.2	19.1	12.7	16.5	6.2	3.9	59 883	2 146	78 247	2 806
1997	3 125	100.0	11.4	8.4	7.9	12.9	18.6	13.9	16.3	6.2	4.5	61 289	1 704	79 766	2 472
1998	3 308	100.0	10.6	8.5	8.5	13.5	17.3	13.5	17.4	5.7	4.9	62 299	1 734	80 428	2 323
1999[15]	3 742	100.0	11.0	6.8	7.6	13.3	16.7	13.5	15.0	8.1	7.9	66 683	2 350	88 179	2 235
2000[16]	3 963	100.0	9.0	7.1	7.9	11.5	17.1	15.0	16.5	9.0	6.9	70 595	1 204	92 169	1 913
2001	4 071	100.0	10.3	7.6	8.5	12.6	17.5	12.6	16.4	7.8	6.6	66 054	1 576	90 098	2 127
Asian Alone[22]															
2002	3 917	100.0	10.0	8.6	7.9	13.6	17.5	13.0	16.0	7.0	6.3	63 781	1 116	84 894	1 656
2003	4 040	100.0	12.9	9.3	5.2	11.9	16.6	13.7	16.4	8.0	5.9	66 030	1 297	82 952	1 469
2004[17]	4 123	100.0	9.9	8.3	8.2	10.9	18.2	13.3	16.4	8.3	6.5	66 376	1 411	88 323	1 708
2005	4 273	100.0	11.1	7.8	7.2	9.8	18.8	12.5	17.5	7.1	8.2	68 233	795	89 455	1 578
2006	4 454	100.0	9.9	7.2	8.3	11.3	16.3	13.7	16.5	9.3	7.5	69 466	1 810	95 479	2 055
2007	4 494	100.0	10.0	7.9	7.7	11.0	16.9	13.3	18.1	8.1	7.1	69 511	1 456	89 402	1 577
2008	4 573	100.0	11.7	8.7	7.5	11.5	15.7	12.3	17.8	7.9	6.9	66 467	1 404	87 275	1 522
2009[18]	4 687	100.0	11.6	7.8	8.1	11.1	16.7	11.8	17.0	7.9	7.9	66 550	1 288	92 310	1 875
2010	4 747	100.0	10.8	9.7	7.4	10.6	18.0	11.3	16.9	8.0	7.3	64 308	1 208	84 828	1 336
Asian Alone or in Combination															
2002	4 079	100.0	10.2	8.5	7.9	13.6	17.7	13.1	16.0	6.9	6.2	63 367	959	84 202	1 601
2003	4 235	100.0	12.9	9.3	5.4	11.8	16.8	13.8	16.3	7.9	5.7	65 512	1 461	82 287	1 415
2004[17]	4 346	100.0	9.9	8.2	8.2	11.1	18.3	13.4	16.3	8.3	6.2	66 313	1 337	87 877	1 659
2005	4 500	100.0	11.0	7.8	7.2	10.1	18.6	12.6	17.6	7.1	8.0	68 181	814	89 344	1 559
2006	4 664	100.0	9.8	7.1	8.2	11.6	16.5	13.8	16.6	9.2	7.3	69 101	1 749	94 652	1 981
2007	4 715	100.0	10.1	7.9	7.7	11.2	16.9	13.4	17.8	8.1	7.0	69 273	1 457	88 921	1 521
2008	4 805	100.0	11.5	8.7	7.6	11.7	15.7	12.5	17.7	7.8	6.9	66 396	1 431	87 415	1 506
2009[18]	4 940	100.0	11.7	7.8	8.2	11.4	16.4	11.9	16.8	7.9	7.9	66 147	1 459	91 598	1 799
2010	5 040	100.0	10.6	9.7	7.6	11.1	18.0	11.4	16.7	7.8	7.1	63 726	1 165	84 078	1 281

[10]Implementation of a new CPS ASEC processing system.
[11]Implementation of 1990 census population controls.
[12]Data collection method changed from paper and pencil to computer-assisted interviewing. In addition, the 1994 ASEC was revised to allow for the coding of different income amounts on selected questionnaire items. Limits either increased or decreased in the following categories: earnings limits increased to $999,999, Social Security limits increased to $49,999, Supplemental Security Income and public assistance limits increased to $24,999, veterans' benefits limits increased to $99,999, and child support and alimony limits decreased to $49,999.
[13]Introduction of 1990 census sample design.
[14]Full implementation of 1990 census–based sample design and metropolitan definitions, 7,000 household sample reduction, and revised editing of responses on race.
[15]Implementation of the 2000 census–based population controls.
[16]Implementation of a 28,000 household sample expansion.
[17]Data revised to reflect a correction to the weights in the 2005 ASEC.
[18]Median income is calculated using $2,500 intervals. Beginning with 2009 income data, the Census Bureau expanded the upper income intervals used to calculate medians to $250,000 or more.
[19]For 2001 and earlier years, the CPS allowed respondents to report only one race group.
[21]Black alone refers to persons who reported Black and did not report any other race category.
[22]Asian alone refers to persons who reported Asian and did not report any other race category.
. . . = Not available.

Table 13-2. Households, by Total Money Income, Race, and Hispanic Origin of Householder, 1967–2010
—Continued

(Numbers in thousands, percent, dollars; income in 2010 CPI-U-RS adjusted dollars.)

Race and Hispanic origin of householder and year	Number	Percent distribution										Median income (dollars)		Mean income (dollars)	
		Total	Under $15,000	$15,000 to $24,999	$25,000 to $34,999	$35,000 to $49,999	$50,000 to $74,999	$75,000 to $99,999	$100,000 to $149,999	$150,000 to $199,000	$200,000 and over	Value	Standard error	Value	Standard error
Hispanic[23]															
1972[23]	2 655	100.0	16.5	17.5	16.3	21.6	18.0	6.2	3.0	0.4	0.5	35 781	699	41 127	699
1973	2 722	100.0	15.7	16.6	16.8	18.9	21.2	7.0	3.2	0.4	0.2	35 722	811	41 503	675
1974[4,5]	2 897	100.0	16.9	18.1	14.6	20.0	19.5	6.7	3.3	0.5	0.4	35 513	778	41 140	670
1975[5]	2 948	100.0	20.1	17.9	15.3	19.0	18.6	6.0	2.4	0.5	0.3	32 665	722	38 778	689
1976[6]	3 081	100.0	20.5	17.3	15.6	17.6	18.7	7.0	2.8	0.4	0.2	33 341	711	39 400	641
1977	3 304	100.0	18.2	16.5	15.8	19.2	18.7	6.9	3.7	0.6	0.3	34 894	613	41 180	636
1978	3 291	100.0	17.6	16.1	14.9	18.7	19.7	7.9	4.0	0.8	0.2	36 200	877	42 761	865
1979[7]	3 684	100.0	17.6	15.1	15.7	17.5	19.5	8.3	4.9	1.0	0.5	36 504	1 052	44 167	887
1980	3 906	100.0	19.3	16.7	14.9	17.6	17.9	8.4	4.1	0.8	0.5	34 391	932	42 006	836
1981	3 980	100.0	19.3	16.2	15.2	17.2	18.4	8.3	4.3	0.8	0.3	35 194	964	42 263	807
1982	4 085	100.0	21.7	17.2	14.5	17.1	16.7	7.7	3.7	0.8	0.5	32 927	870	40 637	824
1983	4 326	100.0	22.7	16.2	13.9	18.3	16.2	7.4	4.3	0.8	0.2	33 094	838	40 299	774
1984[8]	4 883	100.0	21.8	15.7	14.0	16.6	17.3	8.7	4.5	1.0	0.4	33 963	851	42 232	823
1985[9]	5 213	100.0	21.3	17.0	13.7	16.3	17.3	7.8	5.4	0.9	0.3	33 750	788	42 171	686
1986	5 418	100.0	20.4	16.5	13.9	15.9	17.6	8.3	6.0	1.1	0.4	34 833	907	43 983	723
1987[10]	5 642	100.0	21.0	15.6	13.3	16.8	16.9	8.8	5.3	1.3	1.0	35 501	771	45 507	843
1988	5 910	100.0	20.5	15.3	12.9	17.0	17.7	8.8	5.4	1.5	0.8	36 056	914	46 034	976
1989	5 933	100.0	19.1	14.3	14.2	16.1	17.7	9.8	6.2	1.5	1.0	37 217	722	47 524	817
1990	6 220	100.0	19.3	16.4	12.9	17.3	18.5	7.8	5.7	1.3	0.8	36 111	741	45 236	746
1991	6 379	100.0	20.0	16.3	13.4	16.6	17.7	8.2	5.5	1.7	0.7	35 425	737	45 075	721
1992[11]	7 153	100.0	20.4	17.0	13.1	17.3	16.7	8.3	5.3	1.2	0.7	34 406	711	43 884	690
1993[12]	7 362	100.0	21.3	16.0	14.0	17.7	15.2	8.2	5.5	1.1	1.0	34 005	683	45 008	946
1994[13]	7 735	100.0	21.7	16.2	13.6	15.8	16.3	8.0	5.9	1.5	1.0	34 073	633	45 945	1 146
1995[14]	7 939	100.0	21.9	16.8	14.3	16.6	14.9	8.3	5.1	1.2	0.8	32 475	707	44 324	994
1996	8 225	100.0	19.4	17.5	14.7	15.5	16.3	8.2	5.7	1.6	1.1	34 464	668	47 054	1 089
1997	8 590	100.0	19.7	15.3	13.7	16.1	17.9	7.9	6.3	1.7	1.4	36 067	643	48 603	981
1998	9 060	100.0	18.0	15.0	13.8	17.3	16.9	9.0	6.9	1.9	1.4	37 844	729	51 136	1 087
1999[15]	9 579	100.0	14.8	15.4	13.6	17.2	17.8	10.2	7.7	2.1	1.4	40 232	585	52 852	938
2000[16]	10 034	100.0	13.6	14.6	13.2	17.2	19.2	10.7	7.8	2.1	1.7	41 994	605	55 681	801
2001	10 499	100.0	14.7	14.8	12.9	17.4	17.8	10.7	7.9	2.4	1.5	41 337	525	54 659	691
2002	11 339	100.0	14.8	14.9	13.7	17.3	18.0	9.7	7.8	2.2	1.6	40 120	584	54 401	727
2003	11 693	100.0	15.3	15.3	13.5	17.8	17.1	9.6	7.5	2.1	1.7	39 118	544	52 716	583
2004[17]	12 178	100.0	15.3	15.1	14.7	16.2	17.9	9.5	7.5	2.2	1.6	39 559	554	52 955	648
2005	12 519	100.0	15.3	15.1	13.9	16.1	18.8	9.3	7.4	2.3	1.6	40 170	399	52 646	529
2006	12 973	100.0	15.0	14.6	13.4	17.1	17.6	9.9	8.2	2.7	1.6	40 856	546	54 691	627
2007	13 339	100.0	15.3	14.0	14.4	16.1	18.5	10.2	7.8	2.2	1.5	40 673	547	53 449	563
2008	13 425	100.0	16.6	14.6	14.3	16.5	16.9	9.1	7.8	2.6	1.5	38 393	492	52 224	541
2009[18]	13 298	100.0	16.3	15.2	14.3	15.4	17.4	9.4	7.9	2.3	1.8	38 667	510	53 091	582
2010	13 665	100.0	17.4	14.8	13.8	15.7	17.2	9.6	7.7	2.3	1.5	37 759	474	51 540	556

[3]Full implementation of 1970 census–based sample design.
[4]Implementation of a new CPS ASEC processing system. Questionnaire expanded to ask 11 income questions.
[5]Some of these estimates were derived using Pareto interpolation and may differ from published data that were derived using linear interpolation.
[6]First-year medians were derived using both Pareto and linear interpolation. Before this year, all medians were derived using linear interpolation.
[7]Implementation of 1980 census population controls. Questionnaire expanded to show 27 possible values from a list of 51 possible sources of income.
[8]Implementation of Hispanic population weighting controls and introduction of 1980 census–based sample design.
[9]Recording of amounts for earnings from longest job increased to $299,999. Full implementation of 1980 census–based sample design.
[10]Implementation of a new CPS ASEC processing system.
[11]Implementation of 1990 census population controls.
[12]Data collection method changed from paper and pencil to computer-assisted interviewing. In addition, the 1994 ASEC was revised to allow for the coding of different income amounts on selected questionnaire items. Limits either increased or decreased in the following categories: earnings limits increased to $999,999, Social Security limits increased to $49,999, Supplemental Security Income and public assistance limits increased to $24,999, veterans' benefits limits increased to $99,999, and child support and alimony limits decreased to $49,999.
[13]Introduction of 1990 census sample design.
[14]Full implementation of 1990 census–based sample design and metropolitan definitions, 7,000 household sample reduction, and revised editing of responses on race.
[15]Implementation of the 2000 census–based population controls.
[16]Implementation of a 28,000 household sample expansion.
[17]Data revised to reflect a correction to the weights in the 2005 ASEC.
[18]Median income is calculated using $2,500 intervals. Beginning with 2009 income data, the Census Bureau expanded the upper income intervals used to calculate medians to $250,000 or more.
[23]Because Hispanics may be of any race, data in this report for Hispanics overlap with data for racial groups. Hispanic origin was reported by 13.2 percent of White householders who reported only one race, 3.1 percent of Black householders who reported only one race, and 1.9 percent of Asian householders who reported only one race. Data users should exercise caution when interpreting aggregate results for the Hispanic population and for race groups, because these populations consist of many distinct groups that differ in socioeconomic characteristics, culture, and recentness of immigration. Data were first collected for Hispanics in 1972.

Table 13-3. Change in Real Median Household Income and Earnings and Number of Workers by Work Experience During First Calendar Year After a Recesssion, 1970–2010

(Percent, number.)

Recessions[1]	First calendar year after the recession ended	Change in first calendar year after the recession ended				
		Median household income (percentage change)	Median earnings of full-time, year-round workers with earnings (percentage change)		Change in number of workers with earnings (thousands)	
			Male	Female	All workers	Full-time year-round workers
December 1969 to November 1970	1971	-1.0	0.4	0.7	1 277	1 213
November 1973 to March 1975	1976	1.7	-0.3	2.1	2 821	1 538
January 1980 to July 1980	1981[2]	-1.7	-0.6	-2.1	995	362
July 1981 to November 1982	1983	-0.7	-0.4	2.5	1 696	2 887
July 1990 to March 1991	1992	-0.8	0.1	1.4	1 692	1 468
March 2001 to November 2001	2002	-1.2	1.4	1.7	470	286
December 2007 to June 2009	2010	-2.3	-0.4	0.1	-1 608	-24

[1]Business cycle peaks and troughs used to delineate the beginning and end of recessions are determined by the National Bureau of Economic Research, a private research organization.
[2]While 1981 was the first calendar year after the recession that ended in July 1980, the economy entered another recession in July 1981.

Table 13-4. Income Distribution Measures Using Money Income and Equivalence-Adjusted Income, 2009 and 2010

(Percent distribution.)

Measure	2009				2010				Percent change (2009–2010)			
	Money income		Equivalence-adjusted income		Money income		Equivalence-adjusted income		Money income		Equivalence-adjusted income	
	Estimate	90 percent confidence interval[1] (+/-)	Estimate	90 percent confidence interval[1] (+/-)	Estimate	90 percent confidence interval[1] (+/-)	Estimate	90 percent confidence interval[1] (+/-)	Estimate	90 percent confidence interval[1] (+/-)	Estimate	90 percent confidence interval[1] (+/-)
Shares of Aggregate Income by Percentile												
Lowest quintile	3.4	0.05	3.4	0.06	3.3	0.04	3.3	0.06	-3.9	1.72	-2.2	2.05
Second quintile	8.6	0.08	9.2	0.08	8.5	0.08	9.2	0.08	-1.5	1.23	-0.8	1.13
Middle quintile	14.6	0.11	15.0	0.11	14.6	0.10	15.1	0.10	0.2	0.96	0.5	0.92
Fourth quintile	23.2	0.15	22.9	0.15	23.4	0.14	23.2	0.14	1.1	0.88	1.1	0.85
Highest quintile	50.3	0.32	49.4	0.34	50.2	0.30	49.3	0.29	-0.1	0.85	-0.4	0.84
Top 5 percent	21.7	0.40	21.7	0.41	21.3	0.38	21.0	0.35	-2.0	2.51	-3.1	2.39
Summary Measures												
Gini index of income inequality	0.468	0.003	0.458	0.004	0.469	0.003	0.457	0.003	0.30	0.94	-0.20	0.93

[1]A 90-percent confidence interval is a measure of an estimate's variability. The larger the confidence interval in relation to the size of the estimate, the less reliable the estimate.

Table 13-5. Two-Year-Average[1] Median Household Income by State, 2000 to 2010

(Income in 2010 CPI-U-RS adjusted dollars.)

State	2000–2001	2001–2002	2002–2003	2003–2004	2004–2005	2005–2006	2006–2007	2007–2008	2008–2009	2009–2010
UNITED STATES	52 585	51 702	51 376	51 264	51 457	51 932	52 474	51 881	50 769	50 022
Alabama	44 076	44 437	44 870	43 223	41 886	41 266	42 715	44 714	42 840	40 808
Alaska	68 778	67 302	62 706	62 506	62 990	61 716	63 626	65 520	63 710	60 410
Arizona	51 481	50 374	48 479	49 707	50 572	50 493	50 052	48 579	47 001	46 887
Arkansas	39 329	40 155	38 595	39 160	40 662	40 507	41 486	41 493	38 614	37 856
California	58 740	57 848	57 968	57 631	57 310	58 812	59 215	58 172	57 398	55 760
Colorado	60 956	59 682	58 867	58 970	57 541	58 287	62 262	63 004	59 284	58 648
Connecticut	64 611	65 201	64 932	64 381	63 539	65 480	67 466	66 474	65 711	66 187
Delaware	62 427	60 630	59 143	56 787	56 342	56 964	57 055	54 374	52 159	54 122
District of Columbia	51 446	49 026	50 375	51 777	50 203	51 337	52 912	54 848	55 156	54 773
Florida	47 025	45 469	46 142	46 495	47 401	48 704	48 775	46 790	45 905	45 314
Georgia	52 743	52 237	51 175	48 809	49 300	52 326	52 255	48 981	45 434	44 082
Hawaii	61 843	57 876	59 389	63 184	65 734	65 970	66 358	64 811	59 434	57 538
Idaho	47 358	46 402	47 971	50 717	50 270	49 656	50 847	49 870	47 785	47 282
Illinois	57 592	54 312	52 646	53 358	53 620	53 343	53 923	54 571	53 835	52 252
Indiana	50 734	49 738	50 021	49 577	48 128	48 249	49 501	48 504	46 073	45 679
Iowa	51 181	50 107	49 405	49 573	51 010	51 988	51 737	51 103	51 168	50 368
Kansas	51 495	51 328	52 045	49 920	47 170	48 099	50 129	49 740	46 969	45 842
Kentucky	46 626	45 945	44 171	42 446	41 046	41 843	42 093	41 578	42 519	42 302
Louisiana	39 965	41 127	40 469	40 886	41 819	40 523	41 451	41 754	43 123	42 813
Maine	46 136	44 877	44 331	45 852	48 381	49 206	49 860	49 095	48 056	48 210
Maryland	67 486	67 144	65 191	63 966	66 748	68 217	68 932	66 766	64 882	64 636
Massachusetts	61 773	62 387	60 415	60 226	61 304	61 198	60 656	61 280	60 718	60 843
Michigan	56 550	53 623	52 571	51 075	50 038	51 954	52 261	51 167	48 586	46 597
Minnesota	66 783	65 539	64 411	63 691	62 655	60 668	60 919	58 336	56 318	54 785
Mississippi	40 285	37 286	38 113	39 458	38 417	37 138	38 381	38 054	36 282	36 821
Missouri	54 004	51 377	51 861	50 259	48 324	48 108	48 292	47 499	48 097	47 879
Montana	40 532	40 892	41 327	39 815	40 434	43 062	45 178	44 675	42 274	41 286
Nebraska	53 284	52 788	51 999	51 336	52 032	52 793	51 887	51 540	50 892	51 571
Nevada	56 925	55 201	54 026	54 026	54 165	55 190	56 692	56 141	53 860	51 904
New Hampshire	63 847	65 131	66 461	65 728	64 612	65 328	69 037	69 037	66 102	65 949
New Jersey	63 788	64 946	66 288	65 122	67 288	72 186	68 613	64 880	65 989	64 693
New Mexico	42 613	41 883	42 295	43 642	44 582	43 392	44 965	44 639	43 448	44 680
New York	51 726	51 363	50 793	51 131	52 113	52 418	51 807	51 284	51 072	50 436
North Carolina	47 756	45 626	44 225	45 320	46 708	45 003	44 397	44 615	43 036	43 176
North Dakota	44 828	43 977	45 889	46 589	46 197	45 755	47 014	49 949	50 580	51 141
Ohio	52 927	51 596	51 662	50 645	49 533	49 502	50 633	49 579	47 082	46 365
Oklahoma	42 458	44 020	43 374	44 144	43 885	42 022	43 722	46 070	46 665	45 018
Oregon	52 319	50 746	50 012	48 340	48 319	50 122	51 875	52 604	51 145	50 218
Pennsylvania	53 485	52 538	51 201	50 904	51 311	52 067	51 679	51 494	50 510	48 714
Rhode Island	54 868	53 859	52 206	54 168	55 299	56 688	57 558	55 460	53 201	52 200
South Carolina	47 021	46 150	45 722	45 139	44 796	43 886	44 667	44 591	42 234	41 744
South Dakota	47 519	47 378	46 377	47 151	47 821	48 659	48 968	50 532	49 418	46 126
Tennessee	43 619	44 474	44 681	44 215	43 979	44 008	43 662	41 762	40 695	39 936
Texas	49 602	49 490	47 607	47 170	47 023	46 547	47 630	47 753	47 669	47 862
Utah	59 254	58 155	58 211	58 568	59 969	60 146	57 682	59 809	61 393	58 122
Vermont	50 185	51 176	51 699	52 959	55 630	56 420	53 023	50 591	52 265	54 562
Virginia	60 794	61 012	62 548	61 988	58 506	59 874	61 990	62 490	62 135	60 932
Washington	53 085	53 544	55 540	56 973	57 094	57 871	60 126	59 211	59 368	58 821
West Virginia	36 891	36 063	37 211	38 681	39 613	41 125	42 904	41 368	39 817	41 999
Wisconsin	56 466	55 739	55 242	53 820	51 328	52 883	54 910	52 885	51 966	51 303
Wyoming	49 545	48 553	49 320	51 425	51 172	50 407	51 064	52 635	53 674	52 848

[1]The 2-year-average median is the sum of two inflation-adjusted single-year medians divided by 2.

Table 13-6. Median Family Income in the Past Twelve Months, by the Number of Earners and State, 2010

(Income in 2010 inflation-adjusted dollars.)

State	Total	No earners	1 earner	2 earners	3 or more earners
UNITED STATES	60 609	29 310	42 931	79 506	96 656
Alabama	50 429	25 546	38 321	70 962	89 002
Alaska	76 962	30 420	52 611	95 313	124 696
Arizona	55 353	33 414	41 385	74 737	90 988
Arkansas	47 049	26 281	34 203	65 935	82 736
California	65 481	28 022	47 683	86 667	96 642
Colorado	67 800	33 813	47 361	85 092	96 876
Connecticut	81 246	35 801	56 773	100 308	118 038
Delaware	68 746	39 272	48 049	86 197	105 715
District of Columbia	77 514	12 378	50 552	134 133	112 184
Florida	53 093	32 926	40 766	71 943	87 367
Georgia	55 209	25 038	39 694	75 344	90 090
Hawaii	76 134	39 546	51 099	86 532	117 128
Idaho	52 342	33 077	39 120	64 579	78 882
Illinois	65 417	30 733	45 545	83 603	101 241
Indiana	55 368	29 914	39 987	72 633	90 057
Iowa	60 917	33 535	40 650	73 170	87 363
Kansas	61 013	34 039	41 611	74 437	92 043
Kentucky	50 392	24 360	38 356	71 034	90 591
Louisiana	52 456	22 373	37 931	75 201	95 423
Maine	58 197	28 557	40 532	73 585	87 747
Maryland	83 137	34 892	57 455	103 693	119 752
Massachusetts	78 653	28 270	53 496	100 101	116 444
Michigan	56 101	31 826	43 677	75 845	92 116
Minnesota	69 625	35 468	46 161	83 448	98 037
Mississippi	45 484	20 918	33 126	67 065	84 318
Missouri	56 214	30 329	38 895	72 120	92 211
Montana	54 507	31 767	38 369	68 984	90 689
Nebraska	60 812	32 595	39 192	71 987	86 168
Nevada	60 192	31 681	43 146	75 893	90 128
New Hampshire	74 634	33 836	51 550	87 089	111 543
New Jersey	82 427	31 505	60 322	104 786	122 575
New Mexico	51 020	27 643	37 246	72 193	91 053
New York	65 897	26 972	45 931	89 558	110 484
North Carolina	52 920	26 772	37 892	72 035	85 057
North Dakota	65 207	30 284	42 953	74 895	91 074
Ohio	56 518	29 014	40 471	75 852	91 537
Oklahoma	51 958	27 665	37 466	67 290	85 484
Oregon	56 661	33 137	42 877	73 372	87 693
Pennsylvania	61 890	29 304	45 092	80 104	99 420
Rhode Island	67 814	28 042	46 335	86 739	105 339
South Carolina	51 704	26 813	37 660	72 139	83 181
South Dakota	59 987	30 365	36 799	69 616	88 375
Tennessee	51 083	25 406	37 967	69 198	87 033
Texas	56 575	25 813	39 673	75 510	86 415
Utah	61 618	35 830	48 176	68 320	95 025
Vermont	62 575	27 963	43 544	74 287	95 090
Virginia	72 476	32 975	50 605	91 286	109 784
Washington	67 328	36 322	51 671	84 639	99 671
West Virginia	48 927	26 118	40 887	70 922	84 557
Wisconsin	62 088	32 140	41 880	76 777	93 510
Wyoming	65 841	34 421	48 832	80 030	97 376

Table 13-7. Median Family Income in the Past Twelve Months, by Size of Family and State, 2010

(Income in 2010 inflation-adjusted dollars.)

State	Total	2-person families	3-person families	4-person families	5-person families	6-person families	7-or-more-person families
UNITED STATES	60 609	54 274	61 711	72 767	67 060	62 887	63 159
Alabama	50 429	46 025	51 182	61 593	56 517	47 374	46 269
Alaska	76 962	70 811	77 200	88 003	81 698	80 382	93 021
Arizona	55 353	53 781	56 508	61 267	55 782	50 973	51 906
Arkansas	47 049	44 048	47 035	56 275	50 461	47 790	48 141
California	65 481	61 539	66 050	74 806	63 106	62 912	67 786
Colorado	67 800	62 431	69 252	79 905	72 320	68 055	61 710
Connecticut	81 246	70 342	80 263	99 440	99 625	88 056	100 955
Delaware	68 746	59 927	71 259	79 829	80 044	60 951	89 842
District of Columbia	77 514	78 313	69 174	115 995	83 263	53 108	68 559
Florida	53 093	49 729	52 840	62 742	59 974	59 323	56 289
Georgia	55 209	50 712	55 711	64 223	57 776	54 260	58 476
Hawaii	76 134	62 432	75 900	82 726	90 418	94 001	130 868
Idaho	52 342	49 242	52 077	61 301	57 154	58 940	54 867
Illinois	65 417	57 964	66 758	79 074	74 256	68 737	65 937
Indiana	55 368	49 669	57 696	67 296	61 079	59 511	61 180
Iowa	60 917	55 217	62 251	72 234	67 805	65 337	55 020
Kansas	61 013	55 801	62 850	72 665	66 844	63 224	57 002
Kentucky	50 392	44 696	51 859	62 583	55 642	60 828	49 428
Louisiana	52 456	46 169	54 638	65 778	59 731	58 042	50 375
Maine	58 197	51 738	60 195	74 738	70 872	62 873	62 251
Maryland	83 137	73 947	84 151	100 928	91 749	87 954	88 140
Massachusetts	78 653	64 174	80 337	99 067	101 176	100 171	93 845
Michigan	56 101	50 079	58 467	70 237	66 312	58 706	49 962
Minnesota	69 625	61 170	71 784	84 251	82 016	73 769	67 733
Mississippi	45 484	41 601	45 536	54 765	47 144	41 687	48 282
Missouri	56 214	50 603	58 355	67 255	64 472	62 419	58 164
Montana	54 507	49 743	56 308	68 313	59 017	65 356	67 154
Nebraska	60 812	55 519	64 700	71 247	68 167	66 156	55 737
Nevada	60 192	55 573	60 855	65 179	62 097	72 635	77 055
New Hampshire	74 634	61 679	79 349	91 750	92 662	82 450	86 677
New Jersey	82 427	67 503	84 896	101 957	101 670	98 687	83 979
New Mexico	51 020	49 515	51 782	54 640	48 380	54 386	51 859
New York	65 897	56 113	66 953	81 212	79 123	71 167	75 294
North Carolina	52 920	48 710	54 310	65 036	55 884	52 699	47 297
North Dakota	65 207	58 742	67 244	79 336	67 272	76 845	72 873
Ohio	56 518	50 253	58 376	70 599	67 293	62 732	54 470
Oklahoma	51 958	48 313	53 332	60 395	57 247	52 397	52 154
Oregon	56 661	52 316	57 429	66 616	62 897	60 461	57 870
Pennsylvania	61 890	53 091	66 487	76 682	75 916	70 037	69 572
Rhode Island	67 814	59 624	66 800	86 267	81 765	70 530	68 559
South Carolina	51 704	47 853	50 824	62 912	59 407	51 411	50 935
South Dakota	59 987	55 026	61 612	69 006	71 118	62 724	50 825
Tennessee	51 083	47 234	51 642	60 909	59 276	49 648	55 438
Texas	56 575	53 950	57 825	63 859	56 537	50 823	52 581
Utah	61 618	55 555	59 626	64 780	70 337	70 524	75 852
Vermont	62 575	55 110	69 736	77 296	65 153	76 250	61 956
Virginia	72 476	64 288	71 644	87 498	86 298	82 529	82 030
Washington	67 328	61 919	69 195	80 404	72 746	61 435	65 524
West Virginia	48 927	44 018	50 987	61 691	51 955	59 414	54 180
Wisconsin	62 088	55 671	64 724	76 117	72 836	64 818	52 427
Wyoming	65 841	62 072	67 059	73 362	63 825	67 004	72 518

Chapter Fourteen

OCCUPATIONAL SAFETY AND HEALTH

OCCUPATIONAL SAFETY AND HEALTH

HIGHLIGHTS

This chapter includes data on work-related illnesses and injuries and fatal work injuries from the Injuries, Illnesses, and Fatalities (IIF) program. Data are classified by industry and selected worker characteristics.

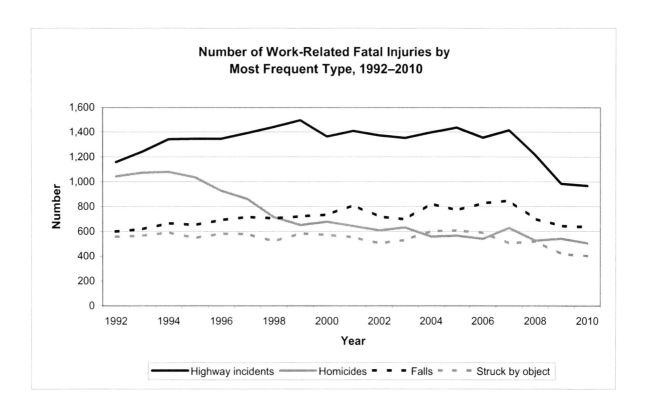

In 2010, there were a preliminary total of 4,547 fatal work injuries, a slight decline from 4,551 fatal work injuries in 2009. The rate of fatal work injuries for U.S. workers was 3.5 per 100,000 full-time workers. Although the number of fatal transportation incidents declined in 2010, they still accounted for nearly 40 percent of all workplace fatalities. (See Tables 14-9.)

OTHER HIGHLIGHTS

- While work-related fatalities from highway incidents, falls, and homicides declined in 2010, the number of fatalities resulting from fires more than doubled from 2009 to 2010. (See Table 14-9.)

- The rate of nonfatal occupational injuries and illnesses continued to decline in 2010 to 3.5 cases per 100 equivalent full-time workers, down from 3.6 cases in 2009, 3.9 cases in 2008, and 4.2 cases in 2007. The incidence rates of nonfatal occupational injuries per 100 full-time workers ranged from 0.3 in securities and commodity contracts to 8.3 in nursing and residential care facilities. (See Table 14-1.)

- Manufacturing was the only industry in the private sector that experienced an increase in the incidence rate of nonfatal injuries and illnesses in 2010—increasing to 4.4 percent from 4.3 percent. (See Table 14-1.)

- There were 933,200 nonfatal occupational injuries requiring days away from work in 2010. Nearly 28 percent of these cases required an employee to be away from work for 31 days or more while another 6.4 percent required an employee to be away from 21 to 30 days. (See Tables 14-6 and 14-7.)

NOTES AND DEFINITIONS

Collection and Coverage

The Injuries, Illnesses, and Fatalities (IIF) program at the Bureau of Labor Statistics (BLS) provides annual reports on the number of workplace injuries, illnesses, and fatalities. BLS has reported annually on the number of work-related injuries, illnesses, and fatalities since 1972 after the Occupational Safety and Health Act of 1970 was passed.

Nonfatal Occupational Injuries and Illnesses

The Survey of Occupational Injuries and Illnesses is a federal-state program in which employer's reports are collected annually from over 230,000 private industry establishments and processed by state agencies cooperating with the BLS. Summary information on the number of injuries and illnesses is copied by these employers directly from their recordkeeping logs to the survey questionnaire. The questionnaire also asks for the number of employee hours worked (needed in the calculation of incidence rates) as well as its average employment (needed to verify the unit's employment-size class).

Occupational injury and illness data for coal, metal, and nonmetal mining and for railroad activities were provided by the Department of Labor's Mine Safety and Health Administration and the Department of Transportation's Federal Railroad Administration. The survey excludes all work-related fatalities as well as nonfatal work injuries and illnesses to the self employed; to workers on farms with 10 or fewer employees; to private household workers; and, nationally, to federal, state, and local government workers.

Injuries and illnesses logged by employers conform with definitions and recordkeeping guidelines set by the Occupational Safety and Health Administration, U.S. Department of Labor. Under those guidelines, nonfatal cases are recordable if they are occupational illnesses or if they are occupational injuries which involve lost worktime, medical treatment other than first aid, restriction of work or motion, loss of consciousness, or transfer to another job. Employers keep counts of injuries separate from illnesses and also identify for each whether a case involved any days away from work or days of restricted work activity, or both, beyond the day of injury or onset of illness.

Occupational injuries, such as sprains, cuts, and fractures, account for the vast majority of all cases that employers log and report to the BLS survey. Occupational illnesses are new cases recognized, diagnosed, and reported during the year. Overwhelmingly, those reported are easier to directly relate to workplace activity (e.g., contact dermatitis or carpal tunnel syndrome) than are long-term latent illnesses, such as cancers. The latter illnesses are believed to be under recorded and, thus, understated in the BLS survey.

Concepts and Definitions

Days away from work are cases that involve days away from work, days of restricted work activity, or both.

The data are presented in the form of *incidence rates*, defined as the number of injuries and illnesses or cases of days away from work per 100 full-time employees. The formula is $(N/EH) \times 200,000$, where N = number of injuries and illnesses or days away from work, EH = total hours worked by all employees during the calendar year, and 200,000 represents the base for 100 full-time equivalent workers (working 40 hours per week, 50 weeks per year).

Median days away from work is a measure used to summarize the varying lengths of absences from work among the cases with days away from work. The median is the point at which half of the cases involved more days away from work and half involved less days away from work.

Occupational illness is an abnormal condition or disorder (other than one resulting from an occupational injury) caused by exposure to environmental factors associated with employment. It includes acute and chronic illnesses and diseases that may have been caused by inhalation, absorption, ingestion, or direct contact. Long-term latent illnesses can be difficult to relate to the workplace and are believed to be understated in this survey.

Occupational injury is any injury—such as a cut, fracture, sprain, or amputation—that results from a work accident or from exposure to an incident in the work environment.

Fatal Occupational Injuries

The Bureau of Labor Statistics (BLS) Census of Fatal Occupational Injuries (CFOI) produces comprehensive, accurate, and timely counts of fatal work injuries. CFOI is a federal-state cooperative program that has been implemented in all 50 states and the District of Columbia since 1992. To compile counts that are as complete as possible, the census uses multiple sources to identify, verify, and profile fatal worker injuries. Information about each workplace fatality—occupation and other worker characteristics, equipment involved, and circumstances of the event—is obtained by cross referencing the source records, such as death certificates, workers' compensation reports, and federal and state agency administrative reports. To ensure that fatalities are work-related, cases are substantiated with two or more independent source documents, or a source document and a follow-up questionnaire.

Data compiled by the CFOI program are issued annually for the preceding calendar year. These data are used by safety and health policy analysts and researchers to help prevent fatal work injuries by:

- informing workers of life threatening hazards associated with various jobs;
- promoting safer work practices through enhanced job safety training;
- assessing and improving workplace safety standards; and
- identifying new areas of safety research

The National Safety Council has adopted the Census of Fatal Occupational Injuries figure, beginning with the 1992 data year, as the authoritative count for work related deaths in the United States.

Sources of Additional Information

For more extensive definitions and description of collection methods see Chapter 9 in the *BLS Handbook of Methods* and BLS news release USDL 11-1162, "Nonfatal Occupational Injuries and Illnesses Requiring Days Away from Work," USDL 11-1502, "Workplace Injuries and Illnesses–2010," and USDL 11-1247 "National Census of Fatal Occupational Injuries in 2010," available on the BLS Web site at <http://www.bls.gov/iif/>.

Table 14-1.   Incidence Rates[1] of Nonfatal Occupational Injuries and Illnesses, by Selected Industries and Case Types, 2010

(Number, rate per 100 full-time workers.)

Industry[2]	NAICS code[3]	2010 average annual employment (thousands)[4]	Total recordable cases	Cases with days away from work, job transfer, or restriction			Other recordable cases
				Total	Cases with days away from work[5]	Cases with job transfer or restriction	
PRIVATE INDUSTRY[6]		106 444	3.5	1.8	1.1	0.8	1.7
Goods-Producing[6]		18 728	4.2	2.3	1.2	1.1	1.9
Natural resources and mining[6,7]		1 580	3.7	2.2	1.4	0.8	1.5
Agriculture, forestry, fishing and hunting[6]	11	968	4.8	2.7	1.7	1.1	2.0
Crop production[6,8]	111	416	4.6	2.7	1.6	1.1	1.9
Animal production[6,8]	112	159	5.2	2.8	2.0	0.9	2.4
Forestry and logging	113	56	3.6	2.0	1.8	0.2	1.7
Support activities for agriculture and forestry	115	329	4.9	2.9	1.6	1.3	2.0
Mining[7]	21	612	2.3	1.4	1.0	0.4	0.9
Oil and gas extraction	211	148	1.2	0.7	0.5	0.2	0.5
Mining (except oil and gas)[9]	212	202	3.1	2.0	1.5	0.5	1.1
Support activities for mining	213	262	2.2	1.4	0.9	0.5	0.9
Construction	23	5 702	4.0	2.1	1.5	0.6	1.9
Construction of buildings	236	1 282	3.5	1.7	1.2	0.5	1.8
Heavy and civil engineering construction	237	828	3.8	2.2	1.3	0.9	1.7
Specialty trade contractors	238	3 592	4.3	2.3	1.7	0.6	2.0
Manufacturing	31-33	11 447	4.4	2.4	1.1	1.3	2.0
Food manufacturing	311	1 442	5.8	3.7	1.4	2.3	2.0
Beverage and tobacco product manufacturing	312	185	6.4	4.4	1.9	2.6	2.0
Textile mills	313	119	3.3	1.7	0.7	1.0	1.5
Textile product mills[8]	314	120	3.1	1.9	0.9	1.0	1.2
Apparel manufacturing[8]	315	160	3.0	1.5	0.7	0.8	1.5
Leather and allied product manufacturing	316	27	5.0	2.6	0.9	1.7	2.4
Wood product manufacturing	321	344	6.2	3.4	1.9	1.5	2.8
Paper manufacturing	322	391	3.4	2.0	1.0	1.0	1.4
Printing and related support activities	323	494	3.2	1.8	1.0	0.8	1.4
Petroleum and coal products manufacturing	324	110	1.5	0.9	0.6	0.3	0.6
Chemical manufacturing	325	789	2.4	1.5	0.7	0.8	1.0
Plastics and rubber products manufacturing[8]	326	615	5.1	3.0	1.3	1.7	2.2
Nonmetallic mineral product manufacturing	327	376	6.0	3.5	1.8	1.7	2.5
Primary metal manufacturing	331	351	6.3	3.4	1.6	1.8	2.9
Fabricated metal product manufacturing	332	1 261	5.5	2.7	1.4	1.3	2.8
Machinery manufacturing[8]	333	979	4.4	2.1	1.0	1.1	2.3
Computer and electronic product manufacturing	334	1 093	1.5	0.8	0.4	0.4	0.8
Electrical equipment, appliance, and component manufacturing	335	356	3.3	1.8	0.7	1.0	1.5
Transportation equipment manufacturing[8]	336	1 303	5.5	3.0	1.2	1.7	2.5
Furniture and related product manufacturing[8]	337	364	5.2	2.8	1.3	1.5	2.4
Miscellaneous manufacturing	339	568	3.0	1.6	0.8	0.8	1.5
Service-Providing		87 717	3.4	1.7	1.0	0.7	1.6
Trade, transportation, and utilities[10]		24 504	4.1	2.4	1.4	1.1	1.7
Wholesale trade		5 488	3.4	2.1	1.1	1.0	1.3
Merchant wholesalers, durable goods	423	2 730	3.1	1.7	0.9	0.8	1.4
Merchant wholesalers, nondurable goods	424	1 940	4.5	3.0	1.5	1.5	1.5
Wholesale electronic markets and agents and brokers	425	818	2.0	1.0	0.7	0.3	*
Retail trade	44-45	14 522	4.1	2.2	1.2	1.0	1.9
Motor vehicle and parts dealers	441	1 621	3.8	1.8	1.2	0.5	2.1
Furniture and home furnishings stores	442	441	4.2	2.4	1.5	1.0	1.7
Electronics and appliance stores	443	501	1.6	0.7	0.4	0.3	0.9
Building material and garden equipment and supplies dealers	444	1 151	5.1	3.0	1.4	1.6	2.2
Food and beverage stores	445	2 830	5.1	2.9	1.5	1.4	2.3
Health and personal care stores	446	985	2.8	1.1	0.7	0.4	1.7
Gasoline stations	447	825	2.9	1.5	1.1	0.4	1.4
Clothing and clothing accessories stores	448	1 370	2.7	0.8	0.6	0.2	1.9
Sporting goods, hobby, book, and music stores	451	609	3.2	1.3	0.7	0.6	2.0
General merchandise stores	452	2 993	5.0	3.2	1.4	1.8	1.8
Miscellaneous store retailers	453	782	3.1	1.6	0.9	0.7	1.5
Nonstore retailers	454	415	3.5	2.2	1.3	0.9	1.2

Note: Components may not sum to totals because of rounding.

[1] The incidence rates represent the number of injuries and illnesses per 100 full-time workers and were calculated as: (N/EH) x 200,000 (where N = number of injuries and illnesses; EH = total hours worked by all employees during the calendar year; 200,000 = base for 100 equivalent full-time workers working 40 hours per week, 50 weeks per year).
[2] Totals include data for industries not shown separately.
[3] North American Industry Classification System—United States, 2007.
[4] Employment is expressed as an average annual value and is derived primarily from the Bureau of Labor Statistics's (BLS) Quarterly Census of Employment and Wages (QCEW) program.
[5] Days away from work cases include those that result in days away from work with or without job transfer or restriction.
[6] Excludes farms with fewer than 11 employees.
[7] Data for mining include establishments not governed by the Department of Labor's Mine Safety and Health Administration (MSHA) rules and reporting, such as those in oil and gas extraction and related support activities. Data for mining operators in coal, metal, and nonmetal mining are provided to BLS by MSHA. Independent mining contractors are excluded from the coal, metal, and nonmetal mining industries. These data do not reflect the changes the Occupational Safety and Health Administration (OSHA) made to its record-keeping requirements effective January 1, 2002; thus, estimates for these industries are not comparable to estimates in other industries.
[8] Industry scope changed in 2009.
[9] Data for mining operators in this industry are provided to BLS by MSHA. Independent mining contractors are excluded. These data do not reflect the changes OSHA made to its record-keeping requirements effective January 1, 2002; thus, estimates for these industries are not comparable to estimates in other industries.
[10] Data for employers in rail transportation are provided to BLS by the Department of Transportation's Federal Railroad Administration (FRA).
* = Figure does not meet standards of reliability or quality.

Table 14-1. Incidence Rates[1] of Nonfatal Occupational Injuries and Illnesses, by Selected Industries and Case Types, 2010—*Continued*

(Number, rate per 100 full-time workers.)

Industry[2]	NAICS code[3]	2010 average annual employment (thousands)[4]	Total recordable cases	Cases with days away from work, job transfer, or restriction			Other recordable cases
				Total	Cases with days away from work[5]	Cases with job transfer or restriction	
Service-Providing—*Continued*							
Transportation and warehousing[10]	48-49	3 937	5.2	3.6	2.3	1.3	1.6
Air transportation	481	453	8.1	6.3	4.6	1.7	1.7
Rail transportation[10]	482	*	2.0	1.4	1.3	0.1	0.6
Water transportation	483	61	3.2	1.6	1.3	0.3	1.6
Truck transportation	484	1 240	5.0	3.3	2.4	0.9	1.6
Transit and ground passenger transportation	485	420	5.3	3.4	2.5	0.9	1.9
Pipeline transportation	486	42	2.5	1.1	0.9	0.2	1.4
Scenic and sightseeing transportation	487	26	4.0	2.6	1.6	0.9	1.4
Support activities for transportation	488	540	3.8	2.6	1.6	1.1	1.2
Couriers and messengers	492	520	7.2	4.6	2.6	2.0	2.6
Warehousing and storage	493	632	5.9	4.1	1.8	2.4	1.8
Utilities	22	557	3.1	1.7	1.0	0.7	1.3
Information	51	2 726	1.8	1.1	0.8	0.3	0.8
Publishing industries (except Internet)	511	767	1.2	0.7	0.4	0.2	0.6
Motion picture and sound recording industries	512	361	2.3	0.8	0.5	0.2	1.6
Broadcasting (except Internet)	515	295	2.8	1.4	0.9	0.5	*
Telecommunications[8]	517	923	2.2	1.6	1.2	0.4	0.7
Other information services[8]	519	139	0.7	0.4	0.4	([11])	0.3
Financial activities		7 508	1.3	0.6	0.4	0.2	0.7
Finance and insurance		5 543	0.8	0.3	0.2	0.1	0.5
Monetary authorities–central bank		21	1.5	0.5	0.3	0.2	1.0
Credit intermediation and related activities	522	2 555	0.9	0.3	0.2	0.1	0.6
Securities, commodity contracts, and other financial investments and related activities	523	807	0.3	0.1	0.1	([11])	0.2
Insurance carriers and related activities	524	2 073	0.8	0.3	0.2	0.1	0.5
Funds, trusts, and other financial vehicles	525	88	1.2	0.4	0.3	*	0.8
Real estate and rental and leasing	53	1 966	2.9	1.6	1.0	0.6	1.2
Real estate	531	1 418	2.7	1.5	1.0	0.5	1.2
Rental and leasing services	532	522	3.3	2.1	1.1	1.0	1.2
Lessors of nonfinancial intangible assets (except copyrighted works)	533	26	1.0	0.2	0.1	0.1	*
Professional and business services		16 645	1.7	0.9	0.6	0.3	0.8
Professional, scientific, and technical services[8]		7 526	1.0	0.4	0.3	0.2	0.6
Management of companies and enterprises		1 888	1.5	0.7	0.4	0.3	0.8
Administrative and support and waste management and remediation services	56	7 231	2.8	1.6	1.1	0.5	1.2
Administrative and support services[8]	561	6 877	2.7	1.5	1.1	0.4	1.2
Waste management and remediation services	562	354	4.5	3.0	1.9	1.1	1.5
Education and health services		18 597	4.8	2.2	1.3	0.9	2.6
Educational services		2 465	2.2	0.9	0.6	0.2	1.3
Health care and social assistance		16 132	5.2	2.4	1.4	1.0	2.8
Ambulatory health care services	621	5 951	2.8	1.0	0.7	0.3	1.7
Hospitals	622	4 616	7.0	2.8	1.6	1.2	4.2
Nursing and residential care facilities	623	3 110	8.3	4.9	2.5	2.5	3.3
Social assistance	624	2 456	3.5	1.8	1.3	0.5	1.7
Leisure and hospitality		13 232	3.9	1.7	1.1	0.6	2.2
Arts, entertainment, and recreation		2 050	4.8	2.3	1.3	1.0	2.5
Performing arts, spectator sports, and related industries		405	6.7	2.8	1.6	1.3	*
Museums, historical sites, and similar institutions	712	127	4.7	2.4	1.4	1.0	2.3
Amusement, gambling, and recreation industries	713	1 518	4.3	2.1	1.2	0.9	2.2
Accommodation and food services	72	11 183	3.7	1.5	1.0	0.5	2.2
Accommodation	721	1 789	5.3	2.8	1.6	1.2	2.6
Food services and drinking places	722	9 394	3.3	1.3	0.9	0.4	2.1
Other services	*	4 505	2.7	1.3	0.9	0.4	1.4
Other services, except public administration	81	4 505	2.7	1.3	0.9	0.4	1.4
Repair and maintenance		1 149	3.3	1.7	1.3	0.4	1.6
Personal and laundry services	812	1 285	2.3	1.3	0.8	0.5	1.0
Religious, grantmaking, civic, professional, and similar organizations	813	1 324	2.6	0.9	0.7	0.3	1.6

Note: Components may not sum to totals because of rounding.

[1]The incidence rates represent the number of injuries and illnesses per 100 full-time workers and were calculated as: (N/EH) x 200,000 (where N = number of injuries and illnesses; EH = total hours worked by all employees during the calendar year; 200,000 = base for 100 equivalent full-time workers working 40 hours per week, 50 weeks per year).
[2]Totals include data for industries not shown separately.
[3]North American Industry Classification System—United States, 2007.
[4]Employment is expressed as an average annual value and is derived primarily from the Bureau of Labor Statistics's (BLS) Quarterly Census of Employment and Wages (QCEW) program.
[5]Days away from work cases include those that result in days away from work with or without job transfer or restriction.
[8]Industry scope changed in 2009.
[10]Data for employers in rail transportation are provided to BLS by the Department of Transportation's Federal Railroad Administration (FRA).
[11]Data too small to be displayed.
* = Figure does not meet standards of reliability or quality.

Table 14-2. Incidence Rates[1] of Nonfatal Occupational Injuries and Illnesses, by Major Industry Sector, Employment Size, and Ownership, 2010

(Rate per 100 full-time workers.)

Industry sector	All establishments	Establishment employment size (workers)				
		1 to 10	11 to 49	50 to 249	250 to 999	1,000 or more
PRIVATE INDUSTRY[2]	3.5	1.6	3.2	4.4	3.8	4.0
Goods-Producing[2]	4.2	2.9	4.6	5.0	3.8	3.5
Natural resources and mining[2,3]	3.7	1.7	3.7	4.3	3.6	2.8
Construction	4.0	3.4	4.6	4.6	2.6	1.2
Manufacturing	4.4	2.1	4.8	5.2	4.0	3.6
Service-Providing	3.4	1.4	2.9	4.3	3.8	4.1
Trade, transportation, and utilities[4]	4.1	1.9	3.7	5.0	4.9	4.5
Information	1.8	*	1.8	2.5	1.7	1.1
Financial activities	1.3	1.3	1.3	1.7	1.2	0.7
Professional and business services	1.7	1.0	2.0	2.1	1.5	1.0
Education and health services	4.8	1.1	2.9	6.0	6.0	5.9
Leisure and hospitality	3.9	1.2	3.1	4.8	6.3	5.5
Other services, except public administration	2.7	1.8	3.0	4.0	3.2	2.5

[1]The incidence rates represent the number of injuries and illnesses per 100 full-time workers and were calculated as: (N/EH) x 200,000 (where N = number of injuries and illnesses; EH = total hours worked by all employees during the calendar year; 200,000 = base for 100 equivalent full-time workers working 40 hours per week, 50 weeks per year).
[2]Excludes farms with fewer than 11 employees.
[3]Data for mining include establishments not goverened by the Mine and Safety and Health Administration rules and reporting such as those in oil and gas extraction and related support activities.
[4]Data for employers in railroad transportation are provided to the Bureau of Labor Statistics (BLS) by the Federal Reserve Administration, U.S. Department of Transportation.
* = Figure does not meet standards of reliability or quality.

Table 14-3. Number of Cases and Incidence Rate[1] of Nonfatal Occupational Injuries and Illnesses for Industries with 100,000 or More Cases, 2010

(Number, rate per 100 full-time workers.)

Industry sector	NAICS Code	2010 Annual average employment (thousands)	Total cases (thousands)	Incidence rate
ALL INDUSTRIES INCLUDING STATE AND LOCAL GOVERNMENT		124 868.5	3 883.6	3.8
Elementary and secondary schools (local government)	6 111	7 236.1	249.9	5.1
General medical and surgical hospitals (private industry)	6 221	4 317.3	241.7	7.0
Food services and drinking places (private industry)	722	9 394.0	194.3	3.3
Specialty trade contractors (private industry)	238	3 591.8	132.7	4.3
Ambulatory health care services (private industry)	621	5 950.8	130.4	2.8
Administrative and support services (private industry)	561	6 877.4	111.2	2.7
Nursing care facilities (private industry)	6 231	1 651.1	110.9	8.6
General merchandise stores (private industry)	452	2 992.6	109.3	5.0
Grocery stores (private industry)	4 451	2 478.3	100.0	5.4

[1]The incidence rates represent the number of injuries and illnesses per 100 full-time workers and were calculated as: (N/EH) x 200,000 (where N = number of injuries and illnesses; EH = total hours worked by all employees during the calendar year; 200,000 = base for 100 equivalent full-time workers working 40 hours per week, 50 weeks per year).

Table 14-4. Incidence Rates[1] of Nonfatal Occupational Injuries and Illnesses, by Major Industry Sector, Category of Illness, and Ownership, 2010

(Rate per 100 full-time workers.)

Industry sector	Total cases	Skin diseases or disorders	Respiratory conditions	Poisonings	Hearing loss	All other illnesses
PRIVATE INDUSTRY[2]	18.1	2.9	1.5	0.3	2.2	11.3
Goods-Producing[2]	31.8	3.8	1.3	0.5	8.4	17.8
Natural resources and mining[2,3]	20.2	5.1	1.1	0.9	2.3	10.9
Construction	12.3	1.8	1.1	0.9	0.2	8.3
Manufacturing	41.9	4.5	1.5	0.2	12.9	22.9
Service-Providing	14.6	2.6	1.5	0.2	0.5	9.7
Trade, transportation, and utilities[4]	12.6	1.8	1.1	0.3	1.3	8.1
Information	11.8	2.2	0.6	0.1	0.9	7.9
Financial activities	8.5	0.7	1.7	*	*	6.0
Professional and business services	9.6	2.7	0.8	0.1	0.3	5.8
Education and health services	28.2	4.6	3.2	0.3	0.1	19.9
Leisure and hospitality	12.0	3.2	1.2	0.4	0.2	7.0
Other services, except public administration	*	1.9	0.7	*	0.2	*

[1]The incidence rates represent the number of injuries and illnesses per 100 full-time workers and were calculated as: (N/EH) x 200,000 (where N = number of injuries and illnesses; EH = total hours worked by all employees during the calendar year; 200,000 = base for 100 equivalent full-time workers working 40 hours per week, 50 weeks per year).
[2]Excludes farms with fewer than 11 employees.
[3]Data for mining include establishments not governened by the Mine and Safety and Health Administration rules and reporting such as those in oil and gas extraction and related support activities.
[4]Data for employers in railroad transportation are provided to the Bureau of Labor Statistics (BLS) by the Federal Reserve Administration, U.S. Department of Transportation.
* = Figure does not meet standards of reliability or quality.

Table 14-5. Number of Cases[1] of Nonfatal Occupational Injuries and Illnesses, by Major Industry Sector, Category of Illness, and Ownership, 2010

(Rate per 100 full-time workers.)

Industry sector	Total cases	Skin diseases or disorders	Respiratory conditions	Poisonings	Hearing loss	All other illnesses
PRIVATE INDUSTRY[1]	157.2	24.9	12.8	2.4	18.8	98.3
Goods-Producing[1]	57.0	6.7	2.4	0.8	15.1	31.9
Natural resources and mining[1,2]	3.1	0.8	0.2	0.1	0.3	1.6
Construction	6.2	0.9	0.5	0.5	0.1	4.2
Manufacturing	47.7	5.1	1.7	0.2	14.7	26.1
Service-Providing	100.2	18.1	10.4	1.6	3.7	66.5
Trade, transportation, and utilities[3]	26.1	3.8	2.2	0.6	2.7	16.9
Information	2.9	0.6	0.2	(4)	0.2	2.0
Financial activities	5.8	0.5	1.2	*	*	4.1
Professional and business services	12.6	3.5	1.0	0.2	0.4	7.6
Education and health services	40.3	6.6	4.6	0.4	0.1	28.5
Leisure and hospitality	10.0	2.7	1.0	0.3	0.1	5.8
Other services, except public administration	*	0.6	0.2	*	0.1	*

[1]Excludes farms with fewer than 11 employees.
[2]Data for mining include establishments not governened by the Mine and Safety and Health Administration rules and reporting such as those in oil and gas extraction and related support activities.
[3]Data for employers in railroad transportation are provided to the Bureau of Labor Statistics (BLS) by the Federal Reserve Administration, U.S. Department of Transportation.
[4]Data too small to be displayed.
* = Figure does not meet standards of reliability or quality.

Table 14-6. Number of Nonfatal Occupational Injuries and Illnesses Involving Days Away from Work,[1] by Selected Worker Characteristics and Private Industry, 2010

(Number.)

Characteristic	Total private[2,3,4]	Goods-producing			
		All goods-producing	Natural resources and mining[2,3]	Construction	Manufacturing
TOTAL CASES	933 200	223 020	20 930	74 950	127 140
Sex					
Men	563 850	190 640	17 820	72 800	100 020
Women	365 610	32 280	3 050	2 140	27 090
Age[4]					
16 to 19 years	22 140	3 780	740	1 110	1 920
20 to 24 years	87 370	17 060	2 510	5 320	9 230
25 to 34 years	201 710	50 700	5 210	20 380	25 110
35 to 44 years	208 520	53 230	4 720	18 550	29 960
35 to 44 years	239 100	60 770	4 420	20 560	35 790
55 to 64 years	132 900	30 210	2 590	7 160	20 450
65 years and over	27 680	4 240	320	1 170	2 740
Length of Service with Employer					
Less than 3 months	85 970	27 490	4 270	10 930	12 290
3 to 11 months	152 270	33 320	3 530	12 320	17 470
1 to 5 years	353 780	75 000	7 340	27 860	39 800
More than 5 years	326 270	85 040	5 310	23 280	56 450
Race and Hispanic Origin					
White only	391 850	113 180	5 280	43 070	64 840
Black only	73 140	13 420	380	2 710	10 330
Hispanic only[5]	122 970	42 580	7 970	13 380	21 230
Asian only	11 850	2 640	50	180	2 410
Native Hawaiian or Pacific Islander only	2 900	570	60	200	300
American Indian or Alaskan Native only	4 630	1 280	70	680	520
American Indian or Alaskan Native only	740	370	*	280	60
Multiple races	820	290	*	250	40
Not reported	324 320	48 700	7 080	14 210	27 400

Characteristic	Service-providing							
	All service-providing	Trade, transportation, and utilities	Information	Financial activities	Professional and business services	Education and health services	Leisure and hospitality	Other services
TOTAL CASES	710 170	284 630	19 330	27 480	75 890	186 830	88 740	27 260
Sex								
Men	373 210	197 500	14 220	14 280	47 640	36 970	43 640	18 960
Women	333 320	83 680	5 110	13 200	28 240	149 740	45 040	8 300
Age[4]								
16 to 19 years	18 360	7 130	290	180	710	2 170	7 260	630
20 to 24 years	70 310	26 890	700	1 250	7 460	15 270	15 260	3 480
25 to 34 years	151 020	55 460	4 270	5 120	17 090	41 710	21 060	6 300
35 to 44 years	155 300	64 730	5 720	6 480	16 590	41 000	15 870	4 900
35 to 44 years	178 320	73 960	5 110	8 460	19 060	47 670	16 290	7 770
55 to 64 years	102 690	42 110	2 710	4 390	10 580	30 490	9 290	3 110
65 years and over	23 440	10 900	300	850	2 180	5 890	2 480	850
Length of Service with Employer								
Less than 3 months	58 480	21 890	780	1 600	8 130	11 670	12 120	2 300
3 to 11 months	118 940	43 210	1 250	4 950	14 570	30 390	19 030	5 540
1 to 5 years	278 790	106 600	6 400	10 580	31 410	78 580	35 030	10 190
More than 5 years	241 220	105 570	10 650	9 840	21 160	63 890	21 290	8 810
Race and Hispanic Origin								
White only	278 670	107 960	4 660	11 040	30 000	79 190	30 670	15 150
Black only	59 720	16 060	860	1 900	5 230	26 300	6 750	2 630
Hispanic only[5]	80 390	27 770	830	3 880	13 040	15 200	16 440	3 230
Asian only	9 210	2 290	90	210	950	3 310	2 010	350
Native Hawaiian or Pacific Islander only	2 340	860	*	60	150	830	400	40
American Indian or Alaskan Native only	3 350	1 250	40	120	170	1 100	650	*
American Indian or Alaskan Native only	370	120	*	*	40	60	130	*
Multiple races	530	120	*	*	30	200	150	*
Not reported	275 620	128 210	12 840	10 270	26 290	60 630	31 550	5 830

Note: Components may not sum to totals because of rounding.

[1]Days away from work cases include those that result in days away from work with or without restricted work activity.
[2]Excludes farms with fewer than 11 employees.
[3]Data for mining include establishments not governed by the Department of Labor's Mine Safety and Health Administration (MSHA) rules and reporting, such as those in oil and gas extraction and related support activities. Data for mining operators in coal, metal, and nonmetal mining are provided to the Bureau of Labor Statistics (BLS) by MSHA. Independent mining contractors are excluded from the coal, metal, and nonmetal mining industries. These data do not reflect the changes the Occupational Safety and Health Administration (OSHA) made to its record-keeping requirements effective January 1, 2002; thus, estimates for these industries are not comparable to estimates in other industries.
[4]Data for employers in rail transportation are provided to BLS by the Federal Railroad Administration, U.S. Department of Transportation.
[5]May be of any race.
* = Figure does not meet standards of reliability or quality.

Table 14-7. Percent Distribution of Nonfatal Occupational Injuries and Illnesses Involving Days Away from Work[1] by Selected Occupation and Number of Days Away from Work, Private Industry, 2010

(Number, percent.)

Occupation	Percent of days away from work cases involving:								Median days away from work
	Total	1 day	2 days	3 to 5 days	6 to 10 days	11 to 20 days	21 to 30 days	31 days or more	
TOTAL CASES	100.0	14.4	10.9	17.9	11.8	11.2	6.4	27.5	8
Sex									
Men	100.0	13.9	10.0	17.6	11.6	11.4	6.9	28.6	9
Women	100.0	15.2	12.3	18.4	12.0	10.7	5.8	25.6	7
Age									
16 to 19 years	100.0	20.3	17.8	22.9	10.5	11.6	4.2	12.7	4
20 to 24 years	100.0	19.3	14.2	21.6	13.1	10.3	5.2	16.2	5
25 to 34 years	100.0	16.3	12.4	19.1	12.0	11.1	5.9	23.1	6
35 to 44 years	100.0	13.4	10.7	18.1	11.3	11.3	6.3	28.9	8
45 to 54 years	100.0	12.7	9.5	16.8	11.7	11.2	6.4	31.6	10
55 to 64 years	100.0	11.1	8.8	15.4	11.5	11.5	8.2	33.6	13
65 years and over	100.0	12.0	7.2	12.5	12.0	12.3	9.3	34.7	15
Length of Service with Employer									
Less than 3 months	100.0	15.5	13.0	20.5	11.7	11.5	5.6	22.1	6
3 to 11 months	100.0	15.5	12.6	18.9	11.8	10.1	6.5	24.6	7
1 to 5 years	100.0	15.7	11.1	18.6	11.6	10.8	5.9	26.3	7
More than 5 years	100.0	12.0	9.4	16.0	12.0	12.0	7.2	31.4	11
Race and Hispanic Origin									
White only	100.0	16.3	11.4	18.3	11.1	11.1	6.6	25.3	7
Black only	100.0	15.5	12.0	20.1	11.3	10.1	5.6	25.5	6
Hispanic only[2]	100.0	14.4	11.0	18.9	12.0	10.9	6.3	26.4	7
Asian only	100.0	16.5	10.6	19.7	13.2	11.2	4.9	23.9	7
Native Hawaiian or Pacific Islander only	100.0	12.1	20.3	18.6	11.0	11.4	5.9	20.3	5
American Indian or Alaskan Native only	100.0	18.1	11.0	21.6	11.9	9.7	4.5	23.3	5
Hispanic[2] and other race	100.0	4.1	4.1	12.2	18.9	4.1	*	55.4	55
Multiple races	100.0	12.2	6.1	11.0	41.5	8.5	3.7	18.3	7
Not reported	100.0	11.7	10.0	16.4	12.5	11.6	6.6	31.2	10

[1]Days away from work cases include those that result in days away from work with or without restricted work activity.
[2]May be of any race.
* = Figure does not meet standards of reliability or quality.

Table 14-8. Fatal Occupational Injuries, by Selected Worker Characteristics and Selected Event or Exposure, 2010

(Number, percent.)

Characteristic	Fatalities		Selected event or exposure[1] (percent of total for characteristic category)			
	Number	Percent	Highway[2]	Homicides	Falls	Struck by object
TOTAL	4 547	100	21	11	14	9
Employee Status						
Wage and salary workers[3]	3 548	78	24	10	14	8
Self-employed[4]	999	22	11	14	14	13
Sex						
Men	4 192	92	21	10	14	9
Women	355	8	27	26	13	2
Age[5]						
Under 16 years	16	(6)	19	. . .	. . .	. . .
16 to 17 years	19	(6)	21	. . .	. . .	. . .
18 to 19 years	53	1	15	11	6	8
20 to 24 years	240	5	19	12	9	10
25 to 34 years	756	17	24	12	9	8
35 to 44 years	849	19	19	13	11	9
45 to 54 years	1 124	25	22	11	16	7
55 to 64 years	921	20	22	11	18	9
65 years and over	565	12	20	7	18	12
Race and Hispanic Origin						
White	3 279	72	22	8	14	10
Black	384	8	27	26	9	5
Hispanic[7]	682	15	15	13	18	9
American Indian or Alaskan Native	31	1	23	. . .	16	. . .
Asian	136	3	15	43	8	2
Native Hawaiian or Pacific Islander	5	(6)	. . .	. . .	. . .	. . .
Multiple races	7	(6)	. . .	43	43	. . .
Other or not reported	23	1	17	13	13	. . .

Note: Totals for 2010 are preliminary. Totals for major categories may include subcategories not shown separately. Components may not sum to totals because of rounding.

[1]The figure shown is the percentage of the total fatalities for that demographic group.
[2]"Highway" includes deaths to vehicle occupants resulting from traffic incidents that occur on the public roadway, shoulder, or surrounding area. It excludes incidents occurring entirely off the roadway, such as in parking lots or on farms; incidents involving trains; and deaths of pedestrians or other non-passengers.
[3]May include volunteers and other workers receiving compensation.
[4]Includes self-employed workers, owners of unincorporated businesses and farms, paid and unpaid family workers, and members of partnerships; may also include owners of incorporated businesses.
[5]There were eight fatalities for which there was insufficient information to determine the age of the decedent.
[6]Less than or equal to 0.5 percent.
[7]May be of any race.
. . . = Not available.

Table 14-9. Fatal Occupational Injuries, by Occupation and Selected Event or Exposure, Preliminary 2010

(Number, percent.)

Occupation[1]	Fatalities		Selected event or exposure (percent of total for characteristic category)[2]			
	Number	Percent	Highway[3]	Homicide	Falls	Struck by object
TOTAL	4 547	100	21	11	14	9
Management	533	12	14	10	9	12
Top executives	29	1	21	10	...	...
Operations specialties managers	34	1	18	9	21	12
Other management	463	10	12	10	9	13
Business and financial operations	25	1	28	...	16	...
Computer and mathematical	11	(4)	...	...	...	...
Architecture and engineering	51	1	25	...	12	...
Engineers	32	(4)	31	...	12	...
Life, physical, and social science	28	(4)	11	...	...	...
Community and social services	24	1	58	12	12	...
Legal	9	(4)	...	...	...	...
Education, training, and library	30	(4)	17	33	23	...
Arts, design, entertainment, sports, and media	53	1	19	6	17	...
Entertainers and performers, sports and related workers	36	1	19	...	11	...
Health care practitioners and technical	65	1	15	11	6	...
Health diagnosing and treating practitioners	41	1	15	10	7	...
Health technologists and technicians	24	1	17	12	...	...
Health care support	17	(4)	24	29	...	...
Protective service	258	6	31	37	3	2
Fire fighting and prevention workers	27	1	33	...	11	...
Law enforcement workers	145	3	41	37	...	2
Other protective service workers	63	1	11	56	...	...
Food preparation and serving related	60	1	7	40	18	...
Supervisors, food preparation and serving workers	21	(4)	...	24	...	...
Building and grounds cleaning and maintenance	226	5	8	5	25	16
Building cleaning and pest control workers	45	1	9	20	24	...
Grounds maintenance workers	141	3	10	...	21	21
Personal care and service	65	1	11	25	6	...
Sales and related	274	6	16	48	9	4
Supervisors, sales workers	140	3	10	48	8	7
Retail sales workers	86	2	7	62	10	...
Sales representatives, services	9	(4)	67	...	...	...
Sales representatives, wholesale and manufacturing	17	(4)	76	...	...	...
Office and administrative support	68	1	31	16	15	4
Material recording, scheduling, dispatching, and distributing workers	29	1	28	17	10	10
Farming, fishing, and forestry	260	6	11	1	6	20
Agricultural workers	156	3	12	...	10	6
Fishing and hunting workers	30	1	...	...	...	...
Forest, conservation, and logging workers	60	1	12	...	...	67
Construction and extraction	760	17	9	1	33	9
Supervisors, construction and extraction workers	110	2	18	...	25	14
Construction trades workers	530	12	7	1	40	7
Extraction workers	91	2	10	...	10	20
Installation, maintenance, and repair	351	8	11	6	17	17
Vehicle and mobile equipment mechanics, installers, and repairers	121	3	13	10	5	32
Other installation, maintenance, and repair	190	4	8	3	23	9
Production	222	5	7	8	14	13
Supervisors, production workers	35	1	9	14	17	...
Metal workers and plastic workers	68	1	7	...	12	24
Transportation and material moving	1 115	25	45	7	6	5
Air transportation workers	78	2	...	...	...	...
Motor vehicle operators	767	17	62	7	5	4
Water transportation workers	19	(4)	...	...	...	...
Material moving workers	200	4	6	6	15	11
Military	42	1	...	...	...	7

Note: Totals for 2010 are preliminary. Totals for major categories may include subcategories not shown separately. Components may not sum to totals because of rounding. There were three fatalities for which there was insufficient information to determine a specific occupation classification.

[1]Based on the 2000 Standard Occupational Classification (SOC) system.
[2]The figure shown is the percentage of total fatalities for that occupation group.
[3]"Highway" includes deaths to vehicle occupants resulting from traffic incidents that occur on the public roadway, shoulder, or surrounding area. It excludes incidents occurring entirely off the roadway, such as in parking lots or on farms; incidents involving trains; and deaths of pedestrians or other non-passengers.
[4]Less than or equal to 0.5 percent.
. . . = Not available.

INDEX

CPSIA information can be obtained at www.ICGtesting.com
Printed in the USA
BVOW050137220512

290638BV00003B/14/P